TO WILL SHAW
JANUARY 2018

Dear Will —

Glad to have you sharing the adventure! Thanks for the support and all best wishes to you —

Garth Wittrup

The Monument

THE MONUMENT

HANK WHITTEMORE

MEADOW GEESE PRESS
MARSHFIELD HILLS
MASSACHUSETTS

MEADOW GEESE PRESS
P. O. BOX 549
NYACK, NY 10960

Copyright 2005 & 2008
Hank Whittemore
All Rights Reserved

First Edition, Fourth Printing
September 2013

REFERENCE EDITION

ISBN: 0-9665564-5-3

Library of Congress: TX 6-269-831

Printed in the United States of America

To Glo,

The Love of My Life

Contents

Author's Note	xi
Acknowledgments	xiv
Introduction	xv
Prologue	1
Part One	53
Part Two	201
Part Three	675
Appendix	765
The Time Line of the Sonnets	765
Phrases = Translations	773
The "Courtier" Preface – 1572	778
St. Bartholomew's Letter – 1572	781
The "Cardanus Preface" – 1573	783
The 100-Sonnet Center	785
The Title Page	792
The Dedication	793
"Shake-speare"	795
The 100-year Silence Of The Sonnets	802
Index – The Words Of The Sonnets	809
Capitalized and/or Italicized Words	855
Selected Bibliography	857
Also By Hank Whittemore	861

"It is hardly to be expected that the sonnet sequence of a poet so intellectually brilliant as Shakespeare should lack the structural art and finesse valued in his age. And in fact his sequence abounds with the intricate formal devices requisite to its genre ... The spatial arrangement of Shakespeare's sequence leaves little room for permutations: its form asserts a design far too positive for us to be free to change it at will ...
The pyramidal numbers imply, most obviously, that Shakespeare designed the sequence to function as a *monument*."
    Alastair Fowler
    Triumphal Forms, 1970

Not marble, nor the gilded *monument*
Of Princes shall outlive this powerful rhyme
Sonnet 55, lines 1-2

Your *monument* shall be my gentle verse,
Which eyes not yet created shall o'er-read
    Sonnet 81, lines 9-10

And thou in this shalt find thy *monument*,
When tyrants' crests and tombs of brass are spent
    Sonnet 107, lines 13-14

"Again we see if our friends be dead, we cannot show or declare our affection more than by erecting them of tombs: Whereby when they be dead indeed, yet make we them live, as it were, again through their *monument*. But with me behold it happeneth far better, for in your lifetime I shall erect you such a *monument* that, as I say, in your lifetime, you shall see how noble a shadow of your virtuous life shall hereafter remain when you are dead and gone. And in your lifetime, again I say, I shall give you that *monument*..."
    Edward de Vere, seventeenth earl of Oxford
    Prefatory Letter to Thomas Bedingfield, English Translator of *Cardanus' Comfort*, 1573

Author's Note

Welcome to this adventure into *Shake-Speares Sonnets,* the 154 consecutively numbered verses printed originally in 1609. This artistic masterwork has thrilled and moved millions of readers over the centuries, but the verses have been an enigma in terms of their meaning as well as their relationship to the author's life and contemporary history. In these pages I'd like to offer a new way of reading the Sonnets that brings them alive as a clandestine chronicle of political intrigue, passion, betrayal and commitment, leading to the royal succession and the end of the Tudor dynasty. My hope is that, whatever you may think about the conclusions described in these pages, you'll come away with an increased appreciation of the poems; and for young scholars setting forth into classrooms to teach the works of Shakespeare, here's another perspective to offer students as they begin to look at the Sonnets and explore them.

This book is the result of unexpected discoveries. I began my journey as a playwright, author and actor with great love for Shakespeare and many unanswered questions about his motivation to write the plays and narrative poems. Most particularly I was drawn to the tortured lines of the Sonnets, which appeared to be the author's own version of Hamlet's soliloquies, using the personal pronoun "I" to express his deepest thoughts and feelings. My view was that the world's greatest writer must have drawn upon his own life experiences, particularly for these little poems that seemed to be entries of an intensely intimate diary.

I started with a series of assumptions and hypotheses that had been shared by many scholars and critics over the past few centuries. These premises included, for example, that the Sonnets are autobiographical and chronological; that the verses relate to real circumstances of real life; and that the original edition itself is "authorial" or printed according to the author's intentions. These hypotheses were confirmed, but what then emerged was a very different result involving the structure and time frame as much as the actual content of the poems. Suddenly the pieces of the puzzle began to move into place to form a clear picture; and once the verses were placed as "stencils" over the contemporary events and their dates on the calendar, what unfolded was a flesh and blood story that challenged the standard or "official" versions of the history and the traditional or "orthodox" interpretations of the literature.

The most startling aspect of the new picture was the emergence of exactly eighty chronological sonnets (more than half the collection!) addressed to Henry Wriothesley, Third Earl of Southampton during the more than two years (1601 to 1603) he spent imprisoned in the Tower of London as a traitor to the Crown, after which, following the death of Queen Elizabeth, he was inexplicably released by the new monarch, James I of England. Then it became clear that the next twenty sonnets match the twenty days from Southampton's liberation to the day immediately following the Queen's funeral, when she was "officially" dead and the Tudor dynasty was no more. And I finally realized that this string of precisely 100 emotion-laden sonnets – recording Southampton's crime, disgrace, treason trial, death sentence, reprieve, continued imprisonment and liberation, leading to a new phase of his life in the next reign – is positioned at the exact center of an elegantly structured monument.

Since these findings came into view, I have often wished they could be presented initially without the implications they necessarily raise about the identity of the author, his relationship to Southampton and the political history of the Elizabethan reign. Sometimes a basic solution to a problem can trigger such heated debate over its ramifications that the solution itself is discarded along with its postulates. The point to be made first of all is that, regardless of the implications, *all* the elements of the sonnets can be seen at last as working in harmony, not only with each other but also within a detailed historical context – something that has not been possible before now. What I hope to communicate at the outset is an *operational* solution to how the numbered verses are designed and how they work as a unified whole. Many suggestions by others turn out to have been correct, but added to these are some crucial additions or modifications, transforming what appears to be a fictional story into a biographical and historical reality.

Author's Note

SOUTHAMPTON & ELIZABETH

The evidence of the monument eliminates any lingering doubt that Southampton was the younger man known as the Fair Youth of Sonnets 1-126 and the primary subject of all the other verses as well. And the evidence also makes clear that the powerful, deceitful Mistress known to us as the Dark Lady, whom the poet addresses in Sonnets 127-152, could only have been Queen Elizabeth, the Sovereign Mistress of England. The crucial element is the context of time and circumstance: Her Majesty was keeping the earl of Southampton in her royal prison fortress for having played a lead role in the failed Essex Rebellion of February 8, 1601, when he joined Robert Devereux, Second Earl of Essex, in an attempt to gain control of the government and determine the royal succession.

OXFORD

The context also confirms that the author's personal involvement in Southampton's tragedy and its aftermath led him to write the 100 intensely wrought verses of what he eventually fashioned as the centerpiece. In particular, this alignment with the history also confirms the longstanding theory that the poet was Edward de Vere, Seventeenth Earl of Oxford (1550-1604), hereditary Lord Great Chamberlain of England and the most active patron of literature and the drama during the Elizabethan reign. Educated from his early boyhood by the finest tutors, he received honorary degrees from both Cambridge and Oxford before studying law at Gray's Inn. A writer for the stage, he was known as "best for comedy" in his day and deemed the "most excellent" of the courtier poets. Oxford's uncle, the Earl of Surrey (1517-1547), and Sir Thomas Wyatt had written the first English sonnets in the form to become known as the "Shakespearean" form; and Edward de Vere himself wrote the first such verse recorded in the Elizabethan reign.

Oxford had a volatile relationship with the Queen and her powerful chief minister, William Cecil, Lord Treasurer Burghley, who was also his father-in-law. Based on the contents of the Sonnets, the only reasonable conclusion is that Edward de Vere was not only the Queen's lover in the early 1570s, as the Court gossip strongly suggested, but also that he fathered their unacknowledged royal son who was raised to become the Third Earl of Southampton. Once Oxford is perceived as writing to and about Southampton as both the devoted father and the loyal subject of an unacknowledged prince, the tone and urgency of the verses is explained and a clear window is opened on events leading up to, and immediately following, the Queen's death and the succession of James in the spring of 1603.

In this light it becomes impossible to avoid the testimony of the Sonnets that the author himself sat on the jury of peers at the treason trial of Southampton and Essex on February 19, 1601 at Westminster Hall; and the highest-ranking, most prominent member of that jury was Edward deVere, Earl of Oxford. After having to join the unanimous verdict condemning both Essex and Southampton to death, he labored under extreme pressure to save his royal son and gain the promise of his release from the Tower. "Thy adverse party is thy Advocate," he tells Southampton in Sonnet 35, on the eve of the trial, after which he is forced to make a bargain with Lord Burghley's little hunchbacked son and successor, Secretary of State Robert Cecil, requiring him to bury the truth about his own and England's history.

After winning the power struggle behind the throne, Secretary Cecil made sure Essex went to his execution and then held Southampton hostage in the Tower until the Queen's death and the peaceful succession of James, thereby retaining his power in the new reign. The underlying truth of this story was kept out of the historical record; but Oxford, by means of the "dynastic" diary of the Sonnets, produced a monument for Southampton to preserve "the living record of your memory" that contains the truth of what really happened; and like a message in a bottle, it was set adrift on the sea of Time in the hope it would make its way to the distant shores of posterity.

"Who will believe my verse in time to come," he wonders in Sonnet 17, addressing his royal son, "if it were filled with your most high deserts?" And he goes on to predict that "your true rights" (to the throne as King Henry IX of England) will be "termed a Poet's rage and stretched meter of an Antique song"

– a forecast that has proved all too accurate, for far too long.

I trust that the following pages convey my reverence for the extraordinary creation of the Sonnets – for the beauty and power of the verses, as well as for the duality that allows them to be both universal and specific at the same time. My experience has convinced me that, far from diminishing our ability to appreciate these poems, knowing the real-life story only serves to increase our recognition of their value on every level.

On May 7, 1603, just ten days after Elizabeth's funeral, Oxford wrote to Secretary Robert Cecil and reminded him:

> "But I hope *truth* is subject to no prescription, for *truth is truth* though never so old, and *time cannot make that false which was once true*."

Edward de Vere was writing to his former brother-in-law, who, having engineered the succession of James, retained his position as the most powerful man behind the throne. The cunning Secretary had forced Oxford to sacrifice his identity, both as the father of the Queen's heir and as the author of the "Shakespeare" works dedicated publicly to Southampton, who had to renounce his own claim of succession in return for his life and freedom and a royal pardon. Reminding Cecil that "truth is truth" until the end of time, however, Oxford was telling him in effect:

> "You're the winner and therefore you get to write the history, but I've set down what really happened and your false official version will never be able to erase it. This truth is preserved in a monument for 'eyes not yet created' and, in the end, it will be triumphant."

Such is the solemn promise that Oxford, the "ever-living poet," made to Southampton:

> Your monument shall be my gentle verse,
> Which eyes not yet created shall o'er-read,
> And tongues to be your being shall rehearse,
> When all the breathers of this world are dead.
> You still shall live (such virtue hath my Pen)
> Where breath most breathes, even in the mouths of men. [1]

Hank Whittemore
Nyack, New York
February 2005

---

1. Sonnet 81, lines 9-14

Acknowledgments

It starts with **Charles Boyle**, who introduced me to Edward de Vere. He and **Bill Boyle** have been my constant companions in the quest to make sense of the literature in relationship to the history. Charles and Bill, along with **Sandy Hochberg**, have made the journey intellectually stimulating and fun; and this book is theirs as much as it's mine. Early support came from **Elisabeth Sears** and **Mildred Sexton**, pioneers in Oxford research and dear friends whose encouragement and inspiration have made all the difference.

I'm especially grateful to **Peter Rush**, another supporter from the beginning, whose keen insights and written contributions have been invaluable.

Also high on my list to thank is **Paul Altrocchi**, who always dares to look at the truth and say what he thinks. The same must be said for **Michael Brame** and **Galina Popova**, whose own research and findings are continually pushing the envelope.

Special gratitude goes to **Alex McNeil** for his editing of most of this manuscript, though I must take responsibility for all errors and defects. Alex is not only a great editor, but a sharp observer; I've noted just some of his contributions, for which I thank him.

Steve Aucella of Meadow Geese Press has always been there with quiet support and good humor and lots of patience. Another special note of gratitude goes to **Chuck Berney**, for his personal support and encouragement; and to **Richard Whalen**, who has never hesitated to share his wisdom and advice.

Paul Streitz lent his support early on, and I thank him. I also thank **Emily and Alfred Scott** for their encouragement. And my gratitude goes to **Laura Wilson** and **Lisa Wilson** for their friendship.

I want to thank officers and members of the Shakespeare Oxford Society and the Shakespeare Fellowship, past and present, for their work and friendship. I also thank **Carole Sue Lipman** of the Shakespeare Authorship Roundtable, and **Dr. Daniel Wright** of the Shakespeare Authorship Studies Conference at Concordia University, for their work on behalf of this research. Special thanks also to **Nina Green** for hosting the email forum Phaeton, as well as for her scholarship; and to **Robert Brazil** for hosting Elizaforum, another email group, and for his other research.

Thanks to **Dr. Roger Strimatter** for his work on Oxford's Geneva Bible and other research.

Many other colleagues are making important contributions in this field, including **Mark Alexander, Eric Altschuler, Mark Anderson, James Brooks, Barbara Burris, Stephanie Caruana, Carl Caruso, Derran Charlton, Katherine Chiljan, Gordon Cyr, Michael Delahoyde, Richard Desper, Ron Destro, Robert Detobel, Peter Dickson, Jonathan Dixon, Nicole Doyle, Michael Dunn, Joseph Eldredge, Scott Fanning, Barbara Flues, Gary Goldstein, Helen Gordon, David Gontar, Marilyn Gray, Andy Hanna, Ron Hess, Stephanie Hopkins Hughes, Thomas Hunter, Marty Hyatt, William Jansen, Ramon Jimenez, Ken Kaplan, Richard Kennedy, Lynne Kositsky, Katherine Ligon, Christopher Paul, Diana Price, Gerit Quealy, Lisa Risley, John Rollet, Jim Sherwood, Karyn Sherwood, Earl Showerman, Sarah Smith, Joseph Sobran, Elliot Stone, Ted Story and John Varady.**

I want to thank some of the first readers of this book: **Ted Alexander, Paul Altrocchi, Peter Austin-Zacharias, Randall Barron, John Blossom, Lee Boyd, James Brooks, Carroll Brown, John Clauser, Gordon Cyr, Norris Darrell Jr., Richard Eek, R. Faulkner, Samuel Gold, Bruce Gould, Marilyn Gray, Alan Green, Donald Greenwood, Helen Gordon, Marguerite Gyatt, Robert Gwilliam, Ian Hodges, Thomas Hunter, Mark Jackson, Christopher Janata, Robert J. Johnson Jr., Richard Joyrich, Karl Kemp, Mack Kidd, Mary Lewis, K.C. Ligon, Marcus Minkler, Lonette Morley, Paul Pender, Robert Prechter, Robert Price, Tom Price, Conie Remick, Sheryl Sachs, David Sayer, Mildred Sexton, Loretta Sharp, Jim Sherwood, Karyn Sherwood, Earl Showerman, Ted Story, Lynda Taylor, Patricia and John Urquhart** and **James Wickwire**.

My thanks to Charles Beauclerk, always an inspiration; and to Jim Hammond, a visionary thinker.

My thanks to Richard Meibers for print management; and to James Aromaa for cover design.

I would like to thank **William Niederkorn** for our many lively discussions about the Shakespeare works and to thank both him and his wife **Yolanda Hawkins** for their friendship and laughter.

In addition I want to thank and send my love to my children **Eva, Lorna, Ben, Maggie & Jake**, and my grandchildren Nicole & Thomas, who have always been there with love and encouragement.

A special thanks to **Robert Arietta**.

Love always to Jerry & Maddy Janata...

And of course my gratitude and love to **Gloria Janata-Whittemore**, who lights the way.

Introduction

On May 20, 1609, the Stationers' Register in London recorded the intention of publisher Thomas Thorpe to issue "a Booke called Shakespeares sonnettes." The title page on four of the thirteen surviving copies includes the name of bookseller William Aspley; seven other recovered copies indicate the book was "to be solde by *John Wright*, dwelling at Christ Church gate"; and two more lack title pages. It was common practice for the author of the work to be named in between the two parallel lines; but on the title page for the Sonnets, this space was left empty, as shown below by a representation:

SHAKE-SPEARES

SONNETS

Never Before Imprinted

_____

_____

AT LONDON
By *G. Eld* for *T.T.* and are
To be solde by *William Aspley*.
1609

Inside was a cryptic dedication, in the form of three upside-down pyramids, echoing "the only begotten Son" of the Gospels in reference to Southampton as supreme inspirer of the verses who, in effect, had given birth to them:

> Yet be most proud of that which I compile,
> Whose influence is thine, and born of thee
> - Sonnet 78, lines 9-10

Southampton was also identified as "Mr. W. H.," recalling his status in the Tower as the commoner "Mr. Wriothesley, Henry." Oxford is "our ever-living poet," indicating that he had died by 1609 and referring to his name, Edward Vere or E.Ver, who had promised to give his royal son eternal life in the Sonnets:

> Your name from hence immortal life shall have,
> Though I (once gone) to all the world must die
> - Sonnet 81, lines 5-6

XV

Introduction

As Oxford had been an "adventurer" or investor in the expeditions to find a Northwest Passage to China during the 1570s, so Southampton was now a leading "adventurer" of the Virginia Company in support of its expeditions to America, as indicated by the dedication:

> TO. THE. ONLIE. BEGETTER. OF.
> THESE. ENSUING. SONNETS.
> Mr. W. H. ALL. HAPPINESSE.
> AND. THAT. ETERNITIE.
> PROMISED.
> BY.
>
> OUR. EVER-LIVING. POET.
> WISHETH.
>
> THE. WELL-WISHING.
> ADVENTURER. IN.
> SETTING.
> FORTH.
>
> T.T.

The little quarto-size volume (known to us as *Q*), which also included the previously unpublished narrative poem *A Lover's Complaint* as by William Shakespeare, fell into a resounding silence and disappeared without any contemporary reference to its existence. (A note on a letter to Edward Alleyn of 19 June 1609, recording his purchase of *Shaksper sonetts*, is "almost certainly a forgery by John Payne Collier," declares editor Katherine Duncan-Jones,[2] who also notes that, otherwise, there is no contemporary reference to *Q*.) The Stratfordian scholar Frank Mathew suggested in 1922:[3]

> The neglect of the Sonnets of 1609 can only be explained by concluding they were quickly suppressed."

Most of the surviving copies are very clean, suggesting they hadn't been widely read or circulated; so it's possible the book was never intended for the public and, instead, tucked into private libraries to be rediscovered by readers of future generations. A bogus collection in 1640 contained all but eight of the original sonnets; these were printed out of order and merged to form longer poems under made-up titles; and in a few instances, the gender of the Fair Youth was changed from male to female; but the authentic Sonnets of 1609 remained unnoticed for more than a century until a surviving copy was reproduced in 1711. By the eighteenth century, the truth recorded in the verses was hidden by preconceptions about "Shakespeare" that had grown to the magnitude of legend, so the real story continued to hide in plain sight.

---

2. Katherine Duncan-Jones, editor, *The Arden Shakespeare* (Sonnets), 1997, p. 7
3. Frank Mathew, *An Image of Shakespeare*, 1922, p. 114

SHAKESPEARE & SOUTHAMPTON

For the diary of the Sonnets to reveal itself and come alive, readers of the future would need to know the personal, political and historical context in which it was written. And at some point they would have to realize who the true author was.

"William Shakespeare" had made his triumphant entrance onto the printed page by dedicating *Venus and Adonis* of 1593 as "the first heir of my invention" to Henry Wriothesley. He followed this with *The Rape of Lucrece* of 1594, again for Southampton, pledging in the second public letter:

> "The love I dedicate to your Lordship is without end ... What I have done is yours, what I have to do is yours; being part in all I have, devoted yours."

"There is no other dedication like this in Elizabethan literature," Nichol Smith stated in 1916. The poet never dedicated another work, thereby uniquely associating Henry Wriothesley with his name; but the lack of any connection between the traditionally assumed biography of "Shakespeare" and the life of Southampton has meant, as Smith deduced, that "further proofs of their friendship must be sought in the Sonnets."[4]

"The real problem of the Sonnets is to find out who 'Shakespeare' was," Sir George Greenwood dared to write in 1908. "That done, it might be possible to make the crooked straight and the rough places plane – but not till then." But once we put aside the legendary image and try to discover the author based on what he wrote in these verses, our picture of him altogether changes, leading Sir Greenwood to conclude: "That he would be found among cultivated Elizabethan courtiers of high position, I have no doubt."[5]

When British schoolmaster John Thomas Looney described his new theory of Edward de Vere's authorship of the Shakespeare works in 1920,[6] he reported the earl had written the earliest sonnet of the Elizabethan reign in the form used later by Shakespeare and subsequently called the "Shakespearean" form. (Fourteen lines created by three quatrains plus a final couplet, with a rhyme scheme *abab cdcd efef gg*, each line having ten beats.) Oxford wrote his sonnet (entitled *Love Thy Choice*) soon after entering Court at twenty-one in 1571, expressing his loyalty to Queen Elizabeth, then in her thirty-eighth year.

The poet of the Sonnets "assumes the attitude of a matured man addressing a youth," Looney pointed out, noting he appears to indicate his age as "forty winters" in the first seventeen sonnets, when "Shakespeare" was urging seventeen-year-old Southampton to quickly marry and perpetuate his blood line; and those opening verses "are assigned generally to about the year 1590, when Oxford was just forty years of age."

Oxford was "a nobleman of the same high rank as Southampton and just a generation older," noted Looney, who observed as well, "The peculiar circumstances of the youth to whom the Sonnets were addressed were strikingly analogous to his own."

> • Edward de Vere became the first royal ward of Elizabeth at age twelve in 1562, under the guardianship of William Cecil Lord Burghley; and in 1571 he entered into an arranged marriage with the chief minister's fifteen-year-old daughter, Anne Cecil.

> • Henry Wriothesley became the eighth and last "child of state" as a boy in 1581, also in the chief minister's custody, and during 1590-91 he resisted unusual pressure to enter into an arranged marriage with Burghley's fifteen-year-old granddaughter, Elizabeth Vere.

---

4. D. Nichol Smith, *Shakespeare's England*, Vo. II, p. 201
5. Sir George Greenwood, *The Shakespeare Problem Restated*, 1908, p. 83
6. John Thomas Looney, *"Shakespeare" Identified*, 1920, p. 387

Looney continued:

> "Both had been left orphans and royal wards at an early age, both had been brought up under the same guardian, both had the same kind of literary tastes and interests, and later the young man followed exactly the same course as the elder as a patron of literature and drama. *Then, just at the time when these sonnets were being written urging Southampton to marry, he was actually being urged into a marriage with a daughter of the Earl of Oxford.* To find so reasonable a key, then, to a set of sonnets on so peculiar a theme is something in itself, and to find this key so directly connected with the very man we had selected as the probable author of the poems is almost disconcerting in its conclusiveness."

The separate entries for Oxford and Southampton in the Dictionary of National Biography reveal that "in many of its leading features the life of the younger man is a reproduction of the life of the elder," Looney noted, so it was "difficult to resist the feeling that Wriothesley had made a hero of DeVere, and had attempted to model his life on that of his predecessor as royal ward."[7]

Southampton stood firm against all pressures to marry Elizabeth Vere, so the Queen and Burghley abandoned the idea, and "Shakespeare" dropped his insistence without looking back. Judging by the private verses that followed in the Fair Youth series (Sonnets 1-126), the two men shared a much closer and deeper bond.

Writing to Henry Wriothesley in Sonnet 37, the poet likens himself to "a decrepit father who takes delight to see his active child do deeds of youth," adding that he derives "all my comfort of thy worth and truth." In Sonnet 39 he says Southampton is "all the better part of me" and in Sonnet 48 he refers to him as "mine only care." He wonders in Sonnet 108 what else "may express my love, or thy dear merit," answering, "Nothing, sweet boy, but yet like prayers divine, I must each day say o'er the very same, counting no old thing old, thou mine, I thine, even as when first I hallowed thy fair name."

Southampton is "abundant issue" in Sonnet 97, as well as "but hope of Orphans, and un-fathered fruit." He is "a God in love, to whom I am confined" in Sonnet 110. "If my dear love were but the child of state," the poet says of him in Sonnet 124, "it might for fortune's bastard be un-fathered." In Sonnet 125 he offers his "oblation" or religious sacrifice to him as a deity; and at the end of the series, Sonnet 126, he cries out: "O Thou my lovely Boy, who in thy power dost hold time's fickle glass, his sickle hour, who hast by waning grown …"

In other words the two were so closely bonded that, by definition, knowing who Shakespeare really was requires knowing who Southampton really was.

FATHER & ROYAL SON

This book results from new observations about the Sonnets that emerged during the winter of 1998-1999, after I'd spent more than a dozen years of research into the life of Edward de Vere, Earl of Oxford and his relationship to the "Shakespeare" works. There was strong evidence of his authorship, but still unanswered was why he adopted the pen name in connection with Southampton in 1593 and then why, upon his death in 1604, the year *Hamlet* was published, he joined the Prince in leaving a "wounded name" and "things standing thus unknown" behind a curtain of silence. And why did others continue to conceal the truth about him?

If the traditional biography of William Shakespeare was a Big Lie, what Big Truth lay behind it? Surely

---

7. Looney, *Ibid,* pp. 376-380

there had been a motive powerful enough to produce the greatest literary hoax in history.

By then I was well acquainted with the view of some past Oxfordians (notably Percy Allen in the 1930s and Dorothy and Charlton Ogburn in the 1950s), who believed that Oxford and Elizabeth were the parents of an unacknowledged royal son raised as Southampton. A crucial aspect of this theory was that they must have gone through a private betrothal ceremony, when she vowed to name Henry Wriothesley as her successor, King Henry IX.

In that case the Big Lie of "Shakespeare" is explained as having been perpetrated to further conceal the Big Truth that the "Virgin Queen," who never married or gave birth, did in fact have a legitimate heir. The government would have had to conceal this fact at any cost, even if it also meant having to obliterate the identity of the greatest writer of the English language, who had used "Shakespeare" as a political weapon to publicly support his royal son.

Preposterous? Yes, even to other Oxfordians. Mind-boggling? Yes, but as Sherlock Holmes says: "When you have eliminated the impossible, whatever remains, *however improbable*, must be the truth."

As the twentieth century drew to a close, only this "Prince Tudor" theory, *however improbable*, appeared to be the truth. And if a record of this truth existed, it seemed to me, the place to find it would be in the Sonnets.

The great mistake, I felt, was viewing these intensely autobiographical poems only or primarily as literature, when they are meant to be perceived as entries of a diary recording real events in real time. My hypotheses included the Sonnets not only as autobiographical, but also, within each series, as arranged by the poet in chronological order. To me it was clear the verses are nonfiction dressed as fiction, adding up to a genuine historical document; and beyond that, in my view, this unique sequence of poems must have been Shakespeare's *magnum opus* in terms of what he wanted us to know about his life.

I was not alone in reading the verses as addressed to a prince; the only way to avoid such an impression was to ignore it. Professor G. W. Knight wrote in 1962:

"The Sonnets are the heart of Shakespeare's royal poetry ... The loved one is royal ... He is 'crowned' with various gifts of Nature and Fortune, especially 'all those beauties whereof now he's King.' Like a 'sovereign,' he radiates worth, his eyes lending a 'double majesty'..."[8]

With the traditional Shakespeare legend as his operating reality, Knight necessarily viewed these allusions as metaphorical; but Leslie Hotson, also an orthodox scholar, nevertheless declared in 1964 that the poet was addressing the younger man *literally* as his sovereign:

> "Shakespeare typifies his Friend variously as a *Sun*, a *God*, an *Ocean* or a *Sea*: three familiar metaphors which he and his contemporaries use to represent a sovereign prince or king ... What he sets before us is not the powers of a peer, but those peculiar to a king: power to grant *charters of privilege* and *letters patent*, power to *pardon crimes* – in short, the exclusively *royal prerogative*... Clearly, these consenting terms cannot be dismissed as scattered surface-ornament. They are intrinsic. What is more, they intensify each other. By direct address, by varied metaphor and by multifarious allusion, the description of the Friend communicated is always one: *monarch, sovereign prince, king*. The poet's harping on the same string is so insistent as to make one ask why it has not arrested attention. No doubt everyone has regarded this 'king sense' as formal hyperbole and nothing more. Any literal meaning looks quite incredible, a rank impossibility..."

---

8. G. Wilson Knight, *The Mutual Flame*, 1962, p. 61

Hotson was well acquainted with the evidence of Southampton as the Fair Youth, so he found himself sternly lecturing:

> "Sustained and unmistakable, this language of Shakespeare's lends no support to the common theory that his youthful Friend might be some nobleman or other. For it is obvious that his chosen terms point *not to nobility, but to royalty*." [9]

Anyone perceiving Henry Wriothesley as an unacknowledged prince raised as a nobleman may be forgiven for smiling at the irony of this argument.

Charlton Ogburn Jr. observed in 1995:

> "We are left with a compelling question raised by the Sonnets. It is a question that is inescapable and one that traditional scholarship is resolved upon escaping at all costs. How is it that the poet of the Sonnets can – as he unmistakably does – address the Fair Youth *as an adoring and deeply concerned father would address his son and as a subject would his liege-lord?*" [10]

"TONGUE-TIED BY AUTHORITY"

In this edition, I hope to demonstrate that the language, structure, attitude, tone and content of the Sonnets consistently allow for an interpretation in accord with the theory that Southampton was the son of Elizabeth and Oxford. What appears on the surface as the story of a "love triangle" involving the author in relation to his dominating Mistress and his beloved younger Friend is but a fictional tale intended for the censors – but the same story, when translated according to its real-life context, can be viewed consistently as Edward de Vere's dangerous political and historical document about the right of his royal son to succeed the Sovereign Mistress of England on the throne. By law, asserting any claim of succession was an act of treason, so Oxford would have been forced to be indirect:

> And art made tongue-tied by authority
> - Sonnet 66, line 9

"This autobiography is written by a foreign man in a foreign tongue, which can never be translated," T. S. Eliot declared of the Sonnets in 1927, but the poet tells us that, because he cannot be open and forthright, he has created a special language to produce a fictional meaning on the surface while simultaneously recording his true story.

"THIS WRITTEN AMBASSAGE"

He refers to the private verses as an "ambassage" or secret document intended for a monarch:

> Lord of my love, to whom in vassalage
> Thy merit hath my duty strongly knit,
> To thee I send this written ambassage,
> To witness duty, not to show my wit.
> - Sonnet 26, lines 1-4

---

9. Leslie Hotson, *Mr. W. H.*, 1964, pp. 26-36
10. Charlton Ogburn Jr., *The Man Who Was Shakespeare*, 1995, p. 75

An ambassador usually memorized his highly sensitive, official message and delivered it orally to a prince. Presumably if captured he would endure torture to the death without revealing his dangerous communication. Oxford, of course, needed to use words on the page to conceal and reveal his message for his royal son, so his ambassage had to be a "written" one.

"BEAUTY'S ROSE"

Opening the Fair Youth series, Oxford uses the royal "we" to command "fairest creatures" (royal children) to beget "increase" (heirs) to ensure that "beauty's *Rose*" (Elizabeth's Tudor Rose dynasty) might not end upon her death ("Rose" is capitalized and italicized in *Q*):

> From fairest creatures we desire increase,
> That thereby beauty's *Rose* might never die
> - Sonnet 1, lines 1-2

This translates as the announcement of a dynastic diary:

> From royal children the Queen and I command heirs,
> So Elizabeth's Tudor Rose Dynasty might not perish

From here on, we can view Edward de Vere as consistently using "fair" for Southampton's royalty and "beauty" for Elizabeth and the Tudor lineage he inherited from her.

The Queen was known as "Beauty," while "Rose" could not fail to echo the Tudor Rose dynasty begun by her grandfather, Henry VII, in 1485.

"BEAUTY'S SUCCESSIVE HEIR"

Her Majesty's imperial viewpoint determined everything; her favor was a beacon of light upon her subjects, while her frown was a dark cloud casting its shadow upon the world. Elizabeth's disgrace of her royal son is what turns him from "fair" to "black" in the opening of the Dark Lady series:

> In the old age black was not counted fair,
> Or if it were it bore not beauty's name,
> But now is black beauty's successive heir,
> And beauty slandered with a bastard shame.
> - Sonnet 127, lines 1-4

Again these lines are easily translated:

> In former days our disgraced son was not counted royal,
> Or even if he was, he did not have Queen Elizabeth's name,
> But now our son is her immediate successor to the throne,
> And she slanders her Tudor blood with the stain of bastardy.

THE DOUBLE IMAGE

The Sonnets present a double image similar to that of a composite picture depicting a flock of birds in the sky and also a school of fish in the water. To produce this effect, the artist has drawn *every line* in the service of both images, so whether one or the other is observed depends entirely upon a viewer's perception, based on prior information and experience. Could Oxford have written *every word* of the Sonnets in the service of

Introduction

two images at once?

"ALL ONE, EVER THE SAME"

He tells us exactly that in Sonnet 76, starting with:

> Why write I still *all one, ever the same*
> - Sonnet 76, line 5

He keeps recording a single topic, which is always the same, and in just five words he identifies the principals of this subtext running in parallel with the surface image:

ALL ONE
Henry Wriothsley, Third Earl of Southampton
His motto "Ung par Tout, Tout par Ung," translated:
> *One for All, All for One*

EVER THE SAME
Elizabeth Tudor, Queen Elizabeth I of England
Her motto "Semper Eadem," translated:
> *Ever the Same*

The subject matter of the Sonnets is *literally* "all one, ever the same" or Southampton in relation to Elizabeth; and Oxford, the author, is recording the progress of this topic as it unfolds:

EVER
Edward de Vere, Seventeenth Earl of Oxford
His name *E. Ver*

In 1859, a researcher known only as W. C. J. first suggested the pervasive presence of Southampton's motto in the Sonnets, observing it was "adapted in different ways, with considerable poetic and idiosyncratic license,"[11] such as:

> Resembling sire, and child, and happy mother,
> Who all in one, one pleasing note do sing
> Sonnet 8, lines 11-12

"Shakespeare's poems, dedications, and Sonnets were all to *one* patron and *one* friend, and that *one* was Henry Wriothesley the third Earl of Southampton," declared Charlotte Stopes in 1904,[12] adding his family motto is echoed in:

> Since all alike my songs and praises be
> To one, of one, still such, and ever so
> - Sonnet 105, lines 3-4

Oxford's earldom motto "Vero Nihil Verius" or *Nothing Truer than Truth* is to be found throughout the private sonnets:

---

11. W. C. J., *The Athenaeum*, August 20, 1859, No. 1660, p. 250
12. Charlotte C. Stopes, *Shakespeare's Sonnets*, 1904, p. xx

> Thou truly fair wert truly sympathized
> In true plain words by thy true-telling friend
> - Sonnet 82, lines 11-12

An early pen name of Edward de Vere had been *Ever or Never*. He often played upon his name as "ever" and "every" along with "never":

> O no, it is an ever-fixed mark
> That looks on tempests and is never shaken;
> It is the star to every wandering bark…
> If this be error and upon me proved,
> I never writ, nor no man ever loved.
> - Sonnet 116, lines 5-7, 13-14

We can hear him insist on himself ("every") and Southampton ("one") as linked together beneath the shadow of Elizabeth's regal frown and the withdrawal of royal favor:

> What is your substance, whereof are you made,
> That millions of strange shadows on you tend?
> Since every one hath, every one, one shade,
> And you, but one, can every shadow lend
> - Sonnet 53, lines 1-4

"EVERY WORD"

Edward de Vere restricts his topic to Southampton and Elizabeth, never wavering. At the same time, his "invention" employs the "noted weed" or familiar costume of poetry, enabling him to use "every word" to "almost" reveal his identity and record his story, from its "birth" to where it has managed to "proceed" (issue from the womb) in this diary:

> Why write I still all one, ever the same
> And keep invention in a noted weed,
> That every word doth almost tell my name,
> Showing their birth, and where they did proceed?
> - Sonnet 76, lines 5-8

"YOU AND LOVE"

Southampton carries the blood of both parents, so the actual topic of "all one, ever the same" is him and his "love" or inherited royal blood:

> O know, sweet love, I always write of you,
> And you and love are still my argument
> - Sonnet 76, lines 9-10

"DRESSING OLD WORDS NEW"

Given this severe restriction, the best the author can do is keep "dressing old words new" or substituting words to consistently refer to the same thing:

> So all my best is dressing old words new,
> Spending again what is already spent
> - Sonnet 76, lines 11-12

In this perspective, Oxford deliberately uses simple, familiar words such as *fair, beauty, Rose, love, one, all, ever, never, truth* and *true* to help create his double image.

"TRUTH AND BEAUTY"

In Sonnet 14 he refers to himself as *Truth* and to Elizabeth as *Beauty*, urging Henry Wriothesley to "convert" from his stubborn course and prevent the "doom" of their hopes:

> As truth and beauty shall together thrive,
> If from thy self to store thou wouldst convert:
> Or else of thee this I prognosticate,
> Thy end is Truth's and Beauty's doom and date.
> - Sonnet 14, lines 13-14

It would be fatuous to predict the end of Truth and Beauty as universal concepts, but Shakespeare was never fatuous. On the nonfiction level, without hyperbole, these lines state that Southampton's untimely death would dash his parents' hopes for a dynastic future.

Oxford later demonstrates how he keeps "dressing old words new" or "varying to other words" to create an appearance of variety. As before, he restricts himself to the family triangle and the "one" royal son who embodies it:

> One thing expressing leaves out difference
> - Sonnet 105, line 8

Then he cites three different words referring to the same topic, which is both the family triangle and Southampton himself as the inheritor of its blood:

> Fair, kind, and true, is all my argument,
> Fair, kind, and true, varying to other words,
> And in this change is my invention spent,
> Three themes in one, which wondrous scope affords
> - Sonnet 105, lines 9-12

"YOUR TRUE RIGHTS"

The final sonnet of the "marriage and propagation" sequence acquires new meaning and power in this perspective. Ending his plea for Southampton to enter a Cecil family alliance, Oxford expresses doubt that future readers will comprehend his intended meaning:

> Who will believe my verse in time to come
> If it were filled with your most high deserts?
> - Sonnet 17, lines 1-2

He predicts they will see only the conventional, outdated poetry:

> So should my papers (yellowed with their age)

> Be scorned, like old men of less truth than tongue,
> And your true rights be termed a Poet's rage
> And stretched meter of an Antique song.
> - Sonnet 17, lines 9-12

His forecast was accurate. Four hundred years later, most readers still fail to recognize the "true rights" of Henry Wriothesley to be Henry IX of England.

THE MONUMENT

The monument is not for the contemporary world, but for "eyes not yet created" in posterity:

> Your monument shall be my gentle verse,
> Which eyes not yet created shall o'er-read
> - Sonnet 81, lines 9-10

> And thou in this shalt find thy monument,
> When tyrants' crests and tombs of brass are spent.
> - Sonnet 107, lines 13-14

THE NUMBERS

The elegant structure of the monument is put together by the arrangement of the 154 "numbers" of the sequence:

> And in fresh numbers number all your graces
> - Sonnet 17, line 6

> Eternal numbers to outlive long date
> - Sonnet 38, line 12

THE PYRAMIDS

The monument is constructed as an overall pyramid; but each of the 154 numbered sonnets is also a "pyramid" measuring the Time that forms the chronology of the diary:

> No! Time, thou shalt not boast that I do change!
> Thy pyramids built up with newer might
> To me are nothing novel, nothing strange,
> They are but dressings of a former sight.
> - Sonnet 123, lines 1-4

The individual pyramids mark specific dates on the calendar, in terms of years or months or days; and just as Oxford is "dressing old words new" to create diversity, so the actual sonnets are "dressings of a former sight" to record the same story.

Introduction

THE TOMB

The monument calls to mind the ancient Egyptian pyramids, built as tombs to preserve dynastic rulers (pharaohs) until they attained eternal life. The tomb of the Sonnets is constructed with words intended both to conceal and reveal the truth:

> Though yet heaven knows it is but as a tomb
> Which hides your life, and shows not half your parts
> - Sonnet 17, lines 3-4

> When you entombed in men's eyes shall lie
> - Sonnet 81, line 8

THE WOMB

Oxford uses a familiar Elizabethan image of the poet in relation to his poem as a parent in relation to his child; but he extends this notion by the conceit that his diary itself is a "womb" giving rebirth to his son, thereby enabling him and his royal blood to grow:

> So long as men can breathe or eyes can see,
> So long lives this, and this gives life to thee
> - Sonnet 18, lines 13-14

> Which, laboring for invention, bear amiss
> The second burden of a former child
> - Sonnet 59, lines 3-4

> Showing their birth, and where they did proceed
> - Sonnet 76, line 8

> Making their tomb the womb wherein they grew
> - Sonnet 86, line 4

> To give full growth to that which still doth grow
> - Sonnet 115, line 14

THE LIVING RECORD

The result is "the living record" of Southampton to be preserved:

> Nor Mars his sword nor war's quick fire shall burn
> The living record of your memory
> - Sonnet 55, lines 7-8

Oxford built the monument not from the outside, but from the inside, at what is now its center. The surrounding segments, added later, are scaffolding. What we see is the final product of 154 sonnets, of which virtually all scholars have identified three fundamental parts:

> The Fair Youth Series – Sonnets 1-126 – 126 sonnets
> The Dark Lady Series – Sonnets 127-152 – 26 sonnets
> The Bath Epilogue – Sonnets 153-154 – 2 sonnets

This "table of contents" is correct, but it obscures the elegant monument.

Sonnets 153-154 represent the royal son of Oxford and Elizabeth as "Cupid," "The Boy" or "The Little Love-God." These verses, about a visit to the City of Bath in western England, are actually the prologue and belong at the top of the pyramidal structure:

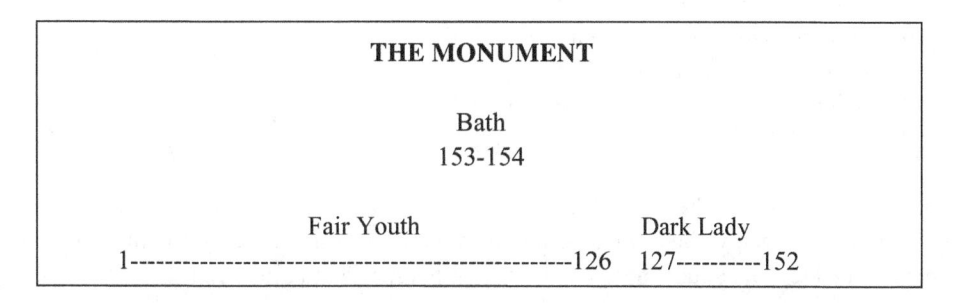

```
                        THE MONUMENT

                            Bath
                           153-154

             Fair Youth                Dark Lady
        1------------------------126   127---------152
```

Sonnet 126 to "My Lovely Boy" is the "envoy" to the Fair Youth Series; but Sonnet 26, which has been recognized as a dedicatory epistle addressed to "Lord of My Love," is also an envoy or postscript ending a sequence. Sonnets 26 and 126 are therefore pillars of the monument's foundation, dividing it into three sections with precisely 100 sonnets at the center:

```
                        THE MONUMENT

                     "The Little Love-God"
                              /
                           153-154
                         (2 sonnets)

      "Lord of My Love"           "My Lovely Boy"
             /                            /
      1---------26    27--------------------------126    127---------152
      (26 sonnets)          (100 sonnets)              (26 sonnets)
```

The 100 chronological verses from Sonnet 27 to Sonnet 126 are the heart of "the living record" of Southampton, serving as the center and centerpiece of the monument. A precedent was *A Hundredth Sundrie Flowres* of 1573, containing exactly 100 verses in its mix of prose and poetry – a collection with which Oxford has been associated as the most likely writer, editor and publisher. Another precedent was *The Hekatomipathia* or *The Passionate Century of Love* of 1582, with exactly 100 consecutively numbered verses dedicated by Thomas Watson to Oxford, again the more likely author.

THE CENTER

> I will find where truth is hid,
> Though it were hid indeed within the center
> - *Hamlet*, 2.2.171

Oxford describes his "invention" at the exact midpoint, Sonnets 76-77, the entrance to the tomb and womb of the monument.

Introduction

SONNET 76 explains *"my verse"* of the Sonnets.
SONNET 77 dedicates *"this book"* to Southampton.

Sonnet 76 describes the womb as having become increasingly "barren" as Oxford continues to employ just one method, which involves "compounds" of words similar to chemical mixtures in alchemy:

> Why is my verse so barren of new pride?
> So far from variation or quick change?
> Why with the time do I not glance aside
> To new-found methods, and to compounds strange?
> - Sonnet 76, lines 1-4

The crucial information is that he writes *with the time*, as in an ongoing diary. Added to this is the further statement in Sonnet 76 that, while always writing of "all one, ever the same" or Southampton in relation to Elizabeth, his actual topic is Southampton and "love" – his special quality, i.e., his royal blood:

> O know, sweet love, I always write of you,
> And you and love are still my argument.
> - Sonnet 76, lines 9-10

LOVE vs. TIME

Thus, the Sonnets tell the story of LOVE struggling against the tyranny of TIME:

> And all in war with Time for love of you!
> - Sonnet 15, line 13

> THE SONNETS = LOVE VS. TIME
> LOVE = SOUTHAMPTON'S ROYAL BLOOD
> TIME = ELIZABETH'S DWINDLING LIFE

THE TIME LINE

TIME is the ever-dwindling life and reign of Elizabeth, leading to her death and the question of succession, which will determine the fate of the Tudor dynasty. TIME is *literally* the timeline of the Sonnets; and therefore, the story being recorded is that of *Southampton and his royal blood struggling to survive the ever-waning time left in the life, reign and dynasty of Elizabeth* (who is also Nature, because her mortal body is constantly in the process of decline and decay):

> But wherefore do not you a mightier way
> Make war upon this bloody tyrant time?
> - Sonnet 15, lines 1-2

Oxford knows the diary will end upon the death of the Queen and the date with the succession, when the fate of her dynasty will be sealed. Writing and compiling his entries in real time, however, he can predict neither the precise moment of her death nor the circumstances that will prevail when she expires. The story has two possible outcomes:

- Southampton's LOVE (royal blood) wins the race with TIME when he is named to succeed Elizabeth upon her death, or
- Southampton's LOVE (royal blood) loses the race with TIME when the Queen dies and

he fails to become King Henry IX.

THE CANOPY

The word TIME appears 78 times in the Fair Youth series but nowhere else in the collection. Its exclusive placement in that series signals that the "numbers" from 1 to 126 supply the most important chronology of the living record.

Oxford intended that we would be able to measure the time line of the Fair Youth series, because it must conclude upon Elizabeth's death on March 24, 1603 (when James of Scotland was proclaimed James I of England), followed by her funeral on April 28, 1603, when the Tudor Dynasty officially ended. Notes the British art historian Roy Strong:

"No monarch was officially dead until the day of burial when the great officers of state broke their white wands of office and hurled them into the grave. So for over a month the old Queen's court went on, as though she were not dead but walking, as she was wont to in the early springtime, in the alleys of her gardens. At last, on 28 April, a funeral procession of some fifteen hundred persons made its way to Westminster Abbey…" [13]

Since Oxford lived at least until June 24, 1604, if not longer, he had up to fourteen months to revise the sonnets and finish constructing the monument according to those events.

Here is the critical moment when the language of Oxford's "invention" converts the numbers of the monument into a genuine historical document. Southampton failed to succeed Elizabeth, so the time line of the diary must continue beyond the date of her death to day of the funeral procession, when a group of noblemen bore "the canopy" over her effigy and coffin. And we can predict that Oxford would mark this final event with Sonnet 125, which he does:

> Were't ought to me I bore the canopy,
> With my extern the outward honoring,
> Or laid great bases for eternity,
> Which proves more short than waste or ruining?
> - Sonnet 125, lines 1-4

The living record of Southampton and his royal blood concludes on this solemn occasion, when the Tudor dynasty ceased to exist, followed by Sonnet 126 as the final envoy to "My Lovely Boy."

THE 100-SONNET CENTER	
	Elizabeth's Funeral
	April 28, 1603
	/
Sonnet 27--Sonnets 125-126	

THE MORTAL MOON

---

13. Roy Strong, *The Cult of Elizabeth*, 1977, p. 14

Introduction

Starting at the chronological end and moving backward down the time line, we find the climactic moment of the Fair Youth series at Sonnet 107, known as the "dating" verse because of its obvious topical allusions to the momentous political events in the spring of 1603.

Sonnet 107 celebrates the liberation of Southampton by King James on April 10, 1603 from the Tower of London (a point on which most scholars now agree), after having been imprisoned there for twenty-six months since the Essex Rebellion of February 8, 1601, for which he was convicted of high treason and "supposed as forfeit to a confined doom" in the royal fortress:

> Not mine own fears nor the prophetic soul
> Of the wide world dreaming on things to come
> Can yet the lease of my true love control,
> Supposed as forfeit to a confined doom.
> - Sonnet 107, lines 1-4

He gained his freedom precisely because the Queen, known as Cynthia or Diana, goddess of the Moon, has succumbed to her mortality although her eternal self, as a divinely ordained monarch, will endure. Those who predicted civil war are mocked by their own inaccurate forecasts; now the nobility will crown James amid domestic peace symbolized by olive branches strewn along his route to London and the throne:

> The mortal Moon hath her eclipse endured,
> And the sad Augurs mock their own presage,
> Incertainties now crown themselves assured,
> And peace proclaims Olives of endless age.
> - Sonnet 107, lines 5-8

"My love looks fresh," Oxford continues, indicating he may have personally greeted his royal son upon his emergence from the Tower. Continuing in this triumphant mood, he concludes by addressing him directly and referring to the Queen as a "tyrant" whose body will be laid temporarily near the great brass tomb of Henry VII in the Abbey:

> And thou in this shalt find thy monument,
> When tyrants' crests and tombs of brass are spent.
> - Sonnet 107, lines 13-14

THE FINAL DAYS

The nineteen days from Southampton's liberation to Elizabeth's funeral are matched by the nineteen verses from Sonnet 107 to Sonnet 125, followed by Sonnet 126 as the "envoy." These are the Final Days of the Tudor dynasty; according to tradition, a reign wasn't officially "over" until the monarch's funeral:

Southampton's Liberation		Elizabeth's Funeral	
/		/	
10 April 1603	–	28 April 1603	ENVOY
Sonnet 107	–	Sonnet 125	126

THE PRISON YEARS

The preceding eighty verses (Sonnets 27-106) are most often assigned to the earlier decade of the 1590s, but they have appeared to lack any coherent story. In effect, scholars have faced an "80-sonnet gap" in terms of an ability to link these verses to a biographical or historical reality. Now it can be seen, however, that Sonnets 27 to 106 actually record events during Southampton's confinement from 1601 to 1603 in the Tower of London.

The most immediate meaning of this context is that, contrary to what has been generally believed, Shakespeare did not at all abandon his beloved Fair Youth while he languished in prison as a convicted traitor. In fact, Edward deVere labored all during that dark, uncertain period not only to produce the most intensely sustained poetical sequence the world has known, but, more importantly, to do what he could for Henry Wriothesley. These eighty sonnets rise from the depths of shame and disgrace suffered by Southampton under Elizabeth's contemptuous frown, with Oxford straining to use all his power as an artist to keep shining his light into this darkness:

> His beauty shall in these black lines be seen,
> And they shall live, and he in them still green.
> - Sonnet 63, lines 13-14

> That in black ink my love may still shine bright.
> - Sonnet 65, line 14

The eighty prison sonnets are the equivalent of eighty chapters of a book containing "this written ambassage" to a prince in the Tower. They begin with Sonnet 27 on the night of February 8, 1601, after the Essex Rebellion had failed and Southampton had been taken around midnight through Traitor's Gate. We can only imagine how Oxford had reacted to the tumultuous events of the day, but it is clear even to a casual reader that there is a marked change of mood commencing suddenly at Sonnet 27. Now, trying to gain some rest in the darkness of his own room, he tells his royal son that "my soul's imaginary sight presents thy shadow to my sightless view, which like a jewel (hung in ghastly night) makes black night beauteous and her old face new," adding, "Lo thus by day my limbs, by night my mind, for thee, and for myself, no quiet find."

This marks the introduction of "shadow" and "black" into the Sonnets, one of the means by which Oxford, by means of a special language, points to Sonnet 27 as the abrupt start of the prison years. The terrible darkness continues for twenty-six months until Sonnet 106 upon Southampton's last night in the Tower on April 9, 1603, when Oxford describes the entire prison section as "the Chronicle of wasted time." Elizabeth died while her son remained in confinement; the TIME of her life and reign, as well as the TIME of this chronicle, has been "wasted" because the succession took place without him.

Rebellion Imprisonment:	Last Night In Prison:	Southampton's Liberation:	Elizabeth's Funeral:
8 February 1601	9 April 1603	10 April 1603	28 April 1603
(Sonnet 27)	(Sonnet 106)	(Sonnet 107)	(Sonnets 125–126)
	< 80 sonnets	20 sonnets >	

Introduction

The eighty-sonnet prison sequence (27-106) obviously spans more time than Sonnets 107-126, but in fact the first sixty verses (27-86) correspond with events on a day-to-day basis (See the full Timeline in the Appendix) up to Sonnet 86 on April 8, 1601, immediately after which Oxford marks the end of the daily sonnets by addressing Southampton in Sonnet 87: "Farewell!"

Then he continues with one sonnet per month until Sonnet 97, which refers to "the fleeting year" (echoing the way "fleeting" referred to confinement in the Fleet Prison and, by extension, to being imprisoned in general) to mark the first anniversary of the Rebellion on February 8, 1602 and a full year of Southampton's incarceration in the Tower. Afterward the time between sonnets grows longer, as Oxford indicates in several places, such as:

> Where art thou, Muse, that thou forget'st so long
> To speak of that which gives thee all thy might?
> - Sonnet 100, lines 1-2

> O truant Muse, what shall be thy amends
> For thy neglect of truth in beauty dyed?
> - Sonnet 101, lines 1-2

He expresses a growing weariness, in parallel with the dwindling life of the Queen:

> My love is strengthened, though more weak in seeming…
> - Sonnet 102, line 1

> Alack what poverty my Muse brings forth…
> - Sonnet 103, line 1

Then he reaches Sonnet 104, which refers to "three winters" (February 1601, February 1602 and February 1603) to mark the second anniversary of the Rebellion on February 8, 1603. After that are two more verses, Sonnets 105 and 106, which, as demonstrated in the following pages, mark the death of Elizabeth on March 24, 1603 and Southampton's final night in the Tower on April 9, 1603.

The 100-Sonnet Center

(Highlights of Dates)

Prison Years	**Sonnets 27–106**	**80 Sonnets**
Sonnet 27	Rebellion & Tower Imprisonment	8 February 1601
Sonnet 86	End of Day-to-Day Prison sonnets	8 April 1601
Sonnet 97	First Anniversary of the Rebellion	8 February 1602
Sonnet 104	Second Anniversary of the Rebellion	8 February 1603
Sonnet 105	Death of Elizabeth; Accession of James	24 March 1603
Sonnet 106	Southampton's Last Night in the Tower	9 April 1603
Final Days	**Sonnets 107–126**	**20 Sonnets**
Sonnet 107	Liberation of Southampton by James	10 April 1603
Sonnet 125	Funeral of Elizabeth; End of Dynasty	28 April 1603
Sonnet 126	Chronological End of the Sonnets	FINAL ENVOY

If the 100-sonnet center (27-126) had come down to us all by itself, without the other verses surrounding it, the historical context of Southampton's confinement in the Tower – leading up to his release marked by Sonnet 107 – would have been recognized long before now.

THE SCAFFOLDING

Flanking the central sequence are the two segments of twenty-six sonnets each, which serve as scaffolding for the full monument.

SONNETS 1-26:

First is the segment of Sonnets 1-26, which numerically marks each of Southampton's birthdays from age 1 in 1575 to age twenty-six in 1600. The first seventeen coincide with the marriage proposal during 1590-1591 and represent his first seventeen years; the next nine sonnets cover the ensuing nine years from 1592 to 1600, the year preceding the Rebellion of 1601.

Years	1575-'91	'92	'93	'94	'95	'96	'97	'98	'99	1600
Sonnets	1-17	18	19	20	21	22	23	24	25	26
Southampton's Age	1-17	18	19	20	21	22	23	24	25	26

These numbers are part of the womb recreating Southampton's life.

SONNETS 127-152:

Oxford created the next segment of twenty-six verses (Sonnets 127-152) to counterbalance the first sequence of twenty-six verses. He revised two of these poems from *The Passionate Pilgrim* of 1599 for inclusion here as Sonnets 138 and 144. He focuses on Elizabeth, often addressing her directly in regard to their son, all during the prison years – beginning with the tragedy of the Essex Rebellion on February 8, 1601 and ending upon her death on March 24, 1603 with the bitter lines of Sonnet 152 in which he tells her: "And all my honest faith in thee is lost … For I have sworn thee fair: more perjured eye, to swear against the truth so foul a lie."

The Dark Lady series thus runs in parallel with the Fair Youth Prison Years, though it is composed of fewer verses. Here is how the beginning, middle and conclusion of each series line up together:

	Rebellion/Imprisonment February 8, 1601	Southampton Spared March 19, 1601	Death of Elizabeth March 24, 1603
Fair Youth Series	Sonnet 27	Sonnet 66	Sonnet 105
Dark Lady Series	Sonnet 127	Sonnet 145	Sonnet 152

THE MONUMENT

Here is the monument structure with the years included:

```
                        1574
                       153–154
                     (2 sonnets)

  1575–1600          1601–1603           1601–1603
    1–26              27–126              127–152
 (26 sonnets)       (100 sonnets)       (26 sonnets)
```

The real-life context of the 100-sonnet center has been hiding in plain sight within the monument. The key to seeing it is our own perception. Now the verses shed light on the history and the history, in turn, illuminates the verses. Neither the official record of events on the calendar nor the consecutive numbering of the verses needs to be rearranged; these two fixed documents, brought into alignment, produce the record that "Shakespeare" left behind for readers in the future:

> Not marble nor the gilded monument
> Of Princes shall outlive this powerful rhyme,
> But you shall shine more bright in its contents
> Than unswept stone, besmeared with sluttish time…
>
> 'Gainst death and all oblivious enmity
> Shall you pace forth! Your praise shall still find room
> Even in the eyes of all posterity
> That wear this world out to the ending doom.
> - Sonnet 55, lines 1-4, 9-12

PRINCE TUDOR

Most Oxfordians agree the Sonnets hold the answer to the question of Shakespearean authorship, if only we can correctly interpret the poems; but argument over interpretation has continued to divide us. Given that the Sonnets comprise an autobiographical diary, was Oxford recording a homosexual love affair with young Southampton? Or was he writing to his royal son by the Queen? It would be difficult to find two more extremely different views about a single string of poems.

Or could he have been writing in the Sonnets about an entirely different relationship, one that still eludes our grasp?

My version of the so-called Prince Tudor theory (envisioning Southampton as Oxford's son by the Queen) begins with the fact that her father, Henry VIII, was obsessed about producing a legitimate male heir, to the point that he executed Elizabeth's mother, Anne Boleyn, and broke with the Church of Rome to begin the Protestant Reformation of England. Ascending to the throne in 1558 at twenty-five, Elizabeth projected herself as every inch her father's daughter carrying "the heart and stomach of a king," so it's difficult to believe she would abandon her responsibility to perpetuate the Tudor dynasty.

There is evidence she had given birth during the 1560s to at least one (and probably more than one) child by Robert Dudley, Earl of Leicester. When Parliament passed an Act in 1571 excluding all but *"the natural issue of Her Majesty's body"* from succession (significantly emending the term "legal issue" to "natural issue"), it was widely assumed that this new law would allow a royal bastard by Leicester to be put on the throne.

One of those bastards may have been born in 1561 or 1562. The year before Spain's invasion of England by armada in 1588, a twenty-six-year-old man calling himself Arthur Dudley appeared in Madrid claiming to be Leicester's son by Elizabeth; he gave a detailed, persuasive account of his life that could not be disproved. Francis Englefield, an English Catholic who had gone to work for King Philip, recommended that Spain should hold onto him precisely because the 1571 law stipulated that any "natural issue" of Queen Elizabeth had a royal claim. If such contemporary individuals felt it was possible for her to have unacknowledged heirs, can we rule out that possibility centuries later?

Under constant pressure to find a husband and produce an English successor, Elizabeth was acutely aware of her value as an unmarried female. But she was not Mother Teresa. She continued to hold out the possibility of marriage and to use her femininity for political purposes. The radiant Queen flirted with her courtiers and even openly fondled them, giving Catholic enemies much ammunition to portray her as a whore.

A continuing threat to Elizabeth's life and rule came from Mary Stuart, Queen of Scots, who gave birth to a son, James, in 1566. Two years later, when she began her long captivity on English soil, Mary became a rallying point for those hoping to overthrow the daughter of Henry VIII and restore the Catholic religion. Then came the rising in 1569-70 of the northern Catholic earls, who sought to remove Elizabeth and put Mary on the throne, with the Pope excommunicating the Protestant Queen and declaring that God had sanctioned her murder.

Edward deVere came to Court in 1571, at age twenty-one, when Elizabeth was thirty-seven and unmarried. Later that year he entered into an arranged family alliance with William Cecil, Lord Burghley, by marrying his fifteen-year-old daughter, Anne Cecil, but quickly rose at Court in the highest personal favor of the Queen, to the point it became Palace gossip that they were as lovers.

Mary Stuart continued to claim the right of succession, while in Scotland her five-year-old son was also a potential English monarch by virtue of his lineage. As threats around the throne continued to build, and now that Elizabeth's love affair with Leicester had ended, she allowed serious negotiations with France for a marriage alliance. This might protect England from Spain's wrath or at least slow down Philip's declaration of outright war.

In August 1572, however, while Oxford was on the royal progress enjoying the Queen's intimate company, the St. Bartholomew's Day Massacre in France was a thunderbolt. Thousands of Protestants were slain in Paris and the slaughter spread quickly to the French countryside. Elizabeth and Burghley feared the worst. The same could happen on English soil; their personal lives were in danger as well. Now it was clearer than ever that the Protestant Reformation had to move forward; the nation needed its own self-image and unity, not to mention naval power to resist invasion.

The St. Bartholomew's Massacre was an Elizabethan wakeup call. In response, Burghley enlisted Francis Walsingham to create a vast intelligence network of spies; and Edward de Vere, working with both men in Her Majesty's service, went on to gather and lead a network of writers (some functioning as agents) to create England's renaissance of literature and drama, giving citizens a new sense of their national history and identity.

Negotiations for the French Match abruptly broke down, but Elizabeth knew they would have to be resumed. Next time, however, she would become a grand actress on the world stage, convincing both France and Spain she would marry the Duke of Alençon, a practicing Catholic who was also nineteen years her junior. It was pure fiction, but Elizabeth would play her part so convincingly that many Puritan subjects, believing it was real, would threaten their own rebellion against the crown.

Against this backdrop of fact and political reality, there existed a window of time during 1573 and 1574 in which Elizabeth, at forty, still had the chance to produce a successor whom she could eventually acknowledge. She was the last of the Tudor line, which would end at her death if no heir existed, so the pressure on her to fulfill this personal and regal responsibility was enormous.

It was reported in May 1573 that Elizabeth was so taken with Edward de Vere that she "delighteth more in his personage and his dancing and his valiantness than any other," while his Puritanical father-in-law, Burghley, "winketh at all these love matters and will not meddle in any way." Such gossip at Court was the result of calculated public relations.

(On July 25, 1587, a prisoner in Newgate named John Pole [or Poole] will be recorded as telling his interrogator, John Gunstone: "The Earle of Oxford he said the Queene did woo him but he would not fall in at that time.") [14]

"That Oxford and Elizabeth were lovers can scarcely be doubted," Charlton Ogburn Jr. wrote in 1995, but their act of sexual intercourse would not have been motivated primarily (if at all) by romantic passion; rather, it would have been a political act, calculated to give Elizabeth the means of keeping her options open in the future, when she could point back to the years 1572-1574 and confirm her affair with Oxford.

When the royal progress returned to London in September 1573, Elizabeth went into seclusion until the following July. Could she have kept a pregnancy secret?

---

14. Public Record Office, London, S. P. 12/273, courtesy of scholar Christopher Paul

ROYAL SECRECY

The Queen was an absolute monarch, dictating the terms of her public appearances and meetings with Concilors and foreign dignitaries or ambassadors who came to call. She chose her dress of the day from an assortment of styles, many perfect for concealment; entering the room before the guests, she determined the physical setting for any encounter, including how near the visitor could approach.

Other than Lord Burghley (and probably Leicester), only her most intimate Ladies who waited upon her needed to know any such royal secret; if they were inclined to talk, it would be at their peril. A servant entrusted with such sensitive information was by definition an insider within the highest level of the social hierarchy, not to mention physically separated from the public by vast estates and closely guarded palace walls.

CENSORSHIP

Elizabeth was the "anointed" and "ordained" head of a totalitarian state run with strict censorship backed by swift punishment for speaking or writing out of turn. There was no "media" in the sixteenth century (as there was when Franklin Roosevelt and Jack Kennedy occupied the White House, in the twentieth century, though they still kept personal secrets from the public); printing presses were legally limited and subject to registration; their outputs were scrutinized before publication. The authorities had spies everywhere, watching and listening for sedition; it was an act of treason to spread any rumors about a successor.

THE QUEEN'S BODY

Was she physically capable of bearing children? Burghley wrote long memos about the French Match in 1579, when Elizabeth was in her forty-sixth year, detailing how she was still "very apt for procreation of children," leading his biographer, Conyers Read, to conclude:

> "Burghley's discussion of Elizabeth's fruitfulness is the best thing we have on the subject. Coming from him, who was probably better informed than anyone else, and taken in connection with his persistent efforts to get her married in order that she might have children, it comes near to settling the perennial question of her ability to bear children. Certainly it should weigh heavily in the balance against Ben Jonson's idle chatter and the gossip of foreign ambassadors."[15]

BETROTHAL

Oxford accompanied Elizabeth on a visit to the Archbishop of Canterbury in March 1574, when she would have been five or six months pregnant and they may have been betrothed. Having refused to consummate his marriage to Burghley's daughter, Oxford could have gotten it annulled; and later, if circumstances permitted, Elizabeth could announce she had concealed the fact of their child to play out the French Match, buying time to build up naval strength against Spain's armada. With the support of Burghley, who controlled the nobility and government, such a strategy might well prevail.

CHANGELING BOY

---

15. Conyers Read, *Lord Burgley and Queen Elizabeth*, 1960, p. 211

If Elizabeth gave birth to Oxford's son in late May or early June 1574, the child would have been given to a wet nurse for twelve to eighteen months and also entrusted to another family to be raised as its own. But why place a Tudor prince with the Second Earl of Southampton, a Catholic suspect-traitor she had imprisoned for supporting the northern earls in England who had tried to overthrow her?

In fact no solution could have been better, since the Second Earl had been under the government's close supervision ever since his release from the Tower in May 1573, after a confinement of eighteen months. The official birth date of Henry Wriothesley is October 6, 1573, when the Second Earl wrote a letter (to William Losely, whom the Privy Council under Burghley had assigned his custody) and reported his wife had given birth that day to a "goodly boy." The evidence suggests the Council had never allowed him conjugal visits in the Tower, so the child (born just five months after his release) was most likely not his, setting up the perfect circumstances for the royal son to be put in place of him as a "changeling boy" in the next year or so.

The Second Earl and his Countess would have been blackmailed. The Queen had the power to send him back to prison or even execute him for treason; she could charge his wife with adultery; and as the subsequent events show, the Southampton household soon became a living hell.

Just as the Queen embarked on progress in July 1574 to the west, and after Oxford had argued with her behind closed doors, he fled without permission to the Continent. In other words, if we could have predicted his behavior following the birth of a royal son he could not acknowledge, it would be hard to invent a more emotionally logical reaction.

LITERATURE AS HISTORY

It goes without saying that documentation of Elizabeth's disposal of a newly born prince before going on progress cannot be expected to appear in the official record. Where it might well be expected to appear, however, is in the literature of the time – in poetry created precisely to preserve the truth of contemporary royal history in the guise of fiction. And it would seem that Oxford recorded the story of 1574 in Sonnet 33, by describing the rise of the sun-king with his "sovereign eye" and "golden face" before he was abruptly eclipsed:

> Anon permit the basest clouds to ride
> With ugly rack on his celestial face,
> And from the forlorn world his visage hide,
> Stealing unseen to west with this disgrace.
> - Sonnet 33, lines 5-8

Setting forth toward Bristol in the west, Elizabeth would have carried her "disgrace" of the boy while giving no outward sign that anything out of the ordinary had happened. But Oxford recalled his own reaction as the proud father of a royal son, having possession of him for just "one hour" until the "region cloud" (Elizabeth Regina's frown) "masked" him from his sight:

> Even so my Sunne one early morn did shine,
> With all triumphant splendor on my brow,
> But out alack, he was but one hour mine,
> The region cloud hath masked him from me now.
> - Sonnet 33, lines 9-12

These lines are insistently personal: *my* Sunne reflected its golden light on *my* brow, but he was just one hour *mine* before Regina's frown masked *him* from *me*, then as now; and in the final couplet, he writes that the "stain" (of bastardy) is upon "suns of the world" (princes of England) or "heaven's sun" (Elizabeth's royal son):

> Yet him for this my love no whit disdaineth:
> Suns of the world may stain when heaven's sun staineth.
> - Sonnet 33, lines 13-14

THE VISIT TO BATH

Oxford returned to England three weeks later and caught up to the progress in the west, rejoining Elizabeth (without reprimand) as she and her royal entourage moved to Bristol and then to the ancient Roman city of Bath with its shrines for the curative mineral waters of its hot springs.

In 1780 the Shakespeare editor George Steevens suggested Bath as the setting for Sonnets 153-154; and Sir Greenwood added in 1908 that the "fairest votary" of Sonnet 154 can refer only to the Queen (the "imperial votaress" of *A Midsummer Night's Dream*), so "Shakespeare" must have accompanied Her Majesty to the City of Bath. But the only royal visit to Bath of the entire reign was this one in August 1574, when Oxford stayed there with the Queen and her Court for three days. Their son, now a few months old, would have been with a governess-servant; and as the Bath Sonnets testify, Edward deVere would have gone there as "a sad distempered guest" in desperate need of a "sovereign cure" for his grief that "the boy" or "the little Love-God" had been "by a Virgin hand disarmed."

The newly born prince, Cupid, derives his "love-kindling fire" (royal blood) from his mother, the sovereign "mistress" of England, whose imperial "eye" or viewpoint makes all the difference in terms of his status, from the beginning:

> But found no cure: the bath for my help lies
> Where Cupid found new fire, my mistress' eye.
> - Sonnet 153, lines 13-14

REPERCUSSIONS

Before leaving England in early 1575 on an authorized tour of France, Germany and Italy, Oxford assured Her Majesty that his marriage had not been consummated and swore that, if Anne became pregnant, any such child would not be his. In September he was in Venice and learned his wife had given birth to a girl, named Elizabeth Vere. Is it possible that Burghley, fearing Oxford would annul the marriage to Anne, had seen to it that his daughter became pregnant? Such may be the implication of Hamlet's remark to Polonius, father of Ophelia: "Conception is a blessing, but not as your daughter may conceive. Friend, look to't." Oxford returned to England in April 1576, angrily separating himself from Anne Cecil and the infant girl for the next five years.

Into the Southampton household came a stranger, Thomas Dymocke, who assumed full control of the Second Earl's life. Dymocke prompted him to accuse his wife of adultery; she was sent to another of the earl's residences, put under close surveillance and allowed to receive only limited company there. The Countess would never again live with the boy "Henry Wriothesley" under the same roof, if in fact she ever did.[16]

---

16. Akrigg, G. P. V., *Shakespeare and The Earl of Southampton*, 1968, pp. 12-14

The charade of the French Match had nearly run its course in 1581, with Alençon making one last try for Elizabeth's hand that year, when a Maid of Honor, Anne Vavasour, gave birth in the Palace to an illegitimate son by Oxford. (Here is an example, ironically enough, of how a pregnancy could be kept secret.) Under the Queen's stinging wrath and temporarily banished from her presence, he began discussions with Burghley about reuniting with his wife and trying to beget an heir to his earldom – a dear priority for William Cecil on behalf of his daughter.

Oxford's conditions for returning to Anne Cecil may have included removing his royal son from the Southampton household, so he could begin to forge a bond with the boy (and perhaps use him in his children's acting company). The situation appears to be reflected by Oberon's plea in *A Midsummer Night's Dream* to Queen Titania, who has been universally identified as Queen Elizabeth:

> "Why should Titania cross her Oberon?
> I do but beg a little changeling boy to be my henchman!"

CHILD OF STATE

The Second Earl of Southampton was in trouble with the government again in 1581 and may have been tortured on the rack (or given poison) until his early death was assured. After being detained for questioning, the earl suffered from continually worsening health until he died in October 1581; and in December, just as Edward de Vere and Anne Cecil reunited under the same roof, seven-year-old Henry Wriothesley entered Cecil House as a "child of state" or a royal ward of the Queen, who was now his legal mother. Declares Oberon:

> "I then did ask of her her changeling child, which straight she gave me; and her fairy sent to bear him to my bowre in fairy land. And now I have the boy, I will undo this hateful imperfection of her eyes."

Oxford's negotiations in 1581 with Burghley also must have included plans for Southampton to eventually marry Elizabeth Vere (and beget an heir to consummate the union), in which case the chief minister would support the young earl's royal claim. If and when Henry Wriothesley ascended as King Henry IX, his wife, Burghley's granddaughter, would be Queen – instantly raising the Cecils to the status of royalty.

Could such a plan succeed? Lord Treasurer Burghley was the most powerful man in England, upon whom Elizabeth had become increasingly dependent. If anyone could arrange for the royal succession, either during her life or upon her death, it was he.

The Earl of Sussex, patron of the company presenting Oxford's "comedies" at Court, died in 1583; but spymaster Walsingham promptly instigated a new group, the Queen's Men. As wartime efforts increased, the writers under Oxford's guidance and support kept turning out English history plays to rouse patriotic unity. The Anglo-Spanish War became official in 1584, as England continued to build its naval defense. In mid-1586, the Queen signed an extraordinary Privy Seal warrant granting Oxford an annual thousand pounds (with no accounting needed) from the same source used to dispense Secret Service funds, no doubt paying him for past and future expenditures involving writers and actors.

Burghley masterminded Elizabeth's execution of Mary Stuart in early 1587, triggering the Spanish invasion; and the defeat of King Philip's Armada in 1588 marked the end of three decades of the Queen's rein. At the time, few predicted she would continue to live for nearly fifteen more years.

THE MARRIAGE PROPOSAL

In October 1589, when Henry Wriothesley officially turned sixteen, Burghley began to pressure him into hurriedly marrying his granddaughter, fourteen-year-old Lady Elizabeth Vere. Southampton stalled, asking for a year to ponder entering a Cecil alliance, as Oxford had done a generation earlier; and when the year was up and his answer was still negative, the Queen and Burghley turned up the pressure, even visiting the Southampton estates in the summer of 1591. Meanwhile the poet to become known as "Shakespeare" was completing seventeen private verses to the seventeen-year-old lord, accusing him of "murderous shame" and "murderous hate" and calling him a "beauteous niggard" and a "profitless usurer" for stubbornly refusing.

Oxford was not only urging but also *commanding* his son to beget an heir, in order to guarantee the chief minister's eventual support for his royal claim; this is the most plausible explanation for the urgent tone of these sonnets. The deal with Burghley was the only practical chance for Southampton to succeed Elizabeth, but it would remain in active play for a limited time. Shakespeare's personal concern about Southampton's "roof" and "house" becomes understandable, for the first time, from the perspective that Oxford is talking about the House of Tudor itself – which now depends on the younger earl alone for its continuance and which, by his stubbornness, is being allowed to collapse:

> Seeking that beauteous roof to ruinate,
> Which to repair should be thy chief desire.
> - Sonnet 10, lines 7-8

> Who lets so fair a house fall to decay …
> - Sonnet 13, line 9

"It is indeed hard to think of any real situation in which it would be natural," C. S. Lewis remarked about the marriage-and-propagation sonnets in 1954. "What man in the whole world, except a father or a potential father-in-law, cares whether any other man gets married?" [17]

"Make thee another self for love of me," Oxford pleaded in Sonnet 10, with an urgent concern for the perpetuation of Southampton's bloodline that was far more logically the plea of a father.

"Though Southampton persisted to the end in his refusal to marry Lady Elizabeth Vere," his biographer Akrigg wrote in 1968, "it was not for want of urging of marriage by William Shakespeare."[18]

Southampton spurned the older generation's arrangements. He was looking to free himself from his existence as a ward and make his entrance at Court, confident he would rise in the highest royal favor of his mother, the Queen. So why should he choose (as his father, Oxford, had done) to remain under William Cecil's domination?

Elizabeth and Burghley dropped their pressure for the arranged marriage in the fall of 1591.

---

17. Lewis, C. S., *English Literature in the Sixteenth Century*, pp. 503-505
18. Akrigg, op. cit., p. 206

Introduction

THE "SHAKESPEARE" COMMITMENT

Anne Cecil had died in June 1588; and now in late 1591 or early 1592, Edward de Vere quietly remarried at age forty-one, withdrawing from Court and the public eye (undoubtedly to make way for his royal son, and to avoid having to be seen with him.) His new wife was Elizabeth Trentham, a Maid of Honor to the Queen, who normally punished any courtier who dared to marry one of her ladies, but this time adopted a gracious attitude.

The new Countess gave birth to Edward de Vere's first surviving son, the future Eighteenth Earl of Oxford, on February 24, 1593. The boy was christened on March 31, 1593, and given the name Henry de Vere, the first Henry in either parent's lineage. Less than three weeks later, on April 18, 1593, the narrative poem *Venus and Adonis* was registered for publication; and it included the dedication by William Shakespeare of this "first heir of my invention" to Henry Wriothesley, Earl of Southampton.

The end game of political struggle, aimed at controlling the succession, had publicly begun with the death of Walsingham in 1590. Burghley was already grooming his son, Robert Cecil, to fill the spymaster's post as Principal Secretary and eventually continue the Cecilian power behind the throne; but rising in opposition was another royal ward, several years older than Southampton, who had become a military hero and Elizabeth's newest Court favorite: the tall, handsome, swashbuckling, brilliant, high-strung Essex, whose popularity rivaled that of the monarch herself. Southampton would take his chances with Essex; when he came of age, he would join his military adventures and, amid public acclaim, the two popular earls would eclipse the power of the Cecils to create England's policies and determine the nation's future.

Regardless of his disappointment over his royal son's decision to take matters into his own hands, Oxford would have given himself no other choice but to support him. Withdrawing from sight, he took the fateful step of issuing *Venus and Adonis* of 1593 and *Lucrece* of 1594 with their extraordinary dedications to Southampton as by "William Shakespeare," the name suggesting a mighty poet-warrior shaking the spear of his pen while striding onto the stage of history. In effect, Oxford might as well have publicly proclaimed his paternity in these open letters to Southampton; deliberately using the imagery of child-bearing, he wrote of *Venus and Adonis* that "if the first heir of my invention prove deformed, I shall be sorry it had so noble a Godfather, and never after ear so barren a land, for fear it yield me still so bad a harvest."

Henry Wriothesley was "the world's hopeful expectation," just as Henry IV reminds his son, Prince Hal, that he must fulfill "the hope and expectation of thy time." And in the *Lucrece* dedication, Oxford wrote as a subject vowing eternal servitude and bondage to his King:

> "Were my worth greater, my duty would show greater; meantime, as it is, it is bound to your Lordship, to whom I wish long life, still lengthened with all happiness. Your Lordship's in all duty, William Shakespeare."

He was boldly letting Elizabeth and the Court know where he stood and where he expected her and other nobles to stand, regardless of Southampton's defiance of the marriage arrangement. He was also letting the Cecils know which side he was on. Meanwhile he was lifting Henry Wriothesley to the height of popular awareness; from here on, the names Shakespeare and Southampton went together in the public mind.

Behind the scenes in the 1590s, Oxford busily revised his earlier plays for the Lord Chamberlain's Men ("Shakespeare's Company") to stage for crowds in the London playhouses. Meanwhile Essex and Southampton were given privileged, private use of his revised plays, such as *Love's Labour's Lost*, to entertain members of their faction. As Eva Turner Clark demonstrates, many of the plays deal with the earlier events described here; for example, she cites both *The Two Gentlemen of Verona* and *Cymbeline* as written originally *circa* 1578 on the subject of Elizabeth's marriage negotiations with the French. Also, the overriding theme of the plays (especially the tragedies and histories) is succession of the monarch and the question of who should wear the crown. As scholar Martin Coyle notes:

> "Shakespeare and his company had close links with Essex's circle in the 1590s, Essex himself being a regular playgoer…" [19]

Oxford could not allow the name "Shakespeare" to appear on publications of plays until Burghley died at seventy-eight in 1598. By then Robert Cecil had officially held the post of Principal Secretary for two years, so the transfer of bureaucratic control from father to son was unchallenged.

Now, however, there appeared *Palladis Tamia*, a book of commonplace observations by Francis Meres with an inserted announcement that "Shakespeare," the poet, was also the great dramatist who had written popular plays including *The Two Gentlemen of Verona, The Comedy of Errors, Love's Labour's Lost, A Midsummer Night's Dream, The Merchant of Venice, Richard II, Richard III, Henry IV, King John, Titus Andronicus* and *Romeo and Juliet*. By the fall of 1598, London printers began issuing texts of plays by "Shakespeare" or "Shake-Speare"; and it would seem that Oxford himself had written Meres's inserted announcement.

In the same work, Meres also cites Oxford (as among those "best for comedy"), which of course has led orthodox scholars to conclude that Shakespeare and Oxford were two different persons.

The year before, Southampton had joined Essex on the "Islands Voyage" in pursuit of Spanish treasure ships, a venture that had failed despite Wriothesley's show of bravery and leadership. Stung by Elizabeth's criticism, and goaded into a trap by Secretary Cecil's politic maneuvering, Essex agreed to become the Queen's General of an army against the rebellion in Ireland. He and Southampton left in March 1599 with 15,000 soldiers; and soon crowds at the playhouse heard "Shakespeare" express support through lines inserted for the chorus of *Henry V*:

> Were now the General of our gracious Empress,
> As in good time he may, from Ireland coming,
> Bringing rebellion broached on his sword,
> How many would the peaceful city quit to welcome him!

The Irish campaign was a disaster, with Essex disobeying orders by agreeing to a truce with the Earl of Tyrone, leader of the rebels. When he and Southampton returned without authorization, the Queen put her General under house arrest and forbade Henry Wriothesley to come into her presence. The clear victor was Cecil, whose whisperings in Elizabeth's ear increasingly dictated her emotions, her attitudes and her policies.

Oxford privately recorded the situation in Sonnet 25, which coincides precisely with 1599 in the year-by-year chronology of Sonnets 1-26. He referred to Southampton and Essex as "Great Princes' favorites," that is, Elizabeth's favorites, who were now in a state of dishonor beneath her monarch's frown:

> Great Princes' favorites their fair leaves spread,
> But as the Marigold at the sun's eye,
> And in themselves their pride lies buried,
> For at a frown they in their glory die.
> - Sonnet 25, lines 5-8

In the fall of 1599, as word of a rising against Cecil began to spread, Southampton and his friend Roger Manners, Fifth Earl of Rutland, went daily to the London playhouses. Their purpose was not recreational or cultural, but political. Seated high behind the stage in full view of the crowds, they openly associated themselves with politically charged plays such as *Julius Caesar* and *King John* as by "Shakespeare," the invisible

---

19. Martin Coyle, editor, William Shakespeare: Richard II, 1998, p. 25

supporter of Southampton and the dramatist of England's royal history, which mirrored current events.

One of Oxford's brazen depictions was that of himself as Falstaff, the father figure, in relation to Southampton as Prince Hal, who progresses from dissolute heir apparent to the responsible, popular, strong leader and monarch, King Henry V.

THE REBELLION

Essex grew increasingly desperate. Elizabeth, turning sixty-seven in September 1600, could die at any moment and leave Cecil to guide the succession and retain his power regardless of who ruled next. In the opening days of February 1601, as supporters continued to filter into London to await instructions, Southampton took charge of planning for a surprise assault on Whitehall Palace to forcibly remove the Secretary from his control and even, if necessary, to murder him.

Members of the Essex faction approached the Chamberlain's Men on February 6, 1601, offering payment for a special performance of *Richard II* at the Globe; and many historians feel Southampton, because of his tie to "Shakespeare," must have sought and gained authority from the dramatist himself to use his play for propaganda.

(Looney found "much evidence" that, during the previous few years, Southampton had been the "intermediary" between Oxford and those staging and publishing the dramas. Six plays attributed to Shakespeare were printed during 1600, but all such "authorized" publications abruptly stopped upon Southampton's imprisonment early the next year. Looney suggested that "the complete issue of the plays had been decided upon and begun," but that Southampton's tragedy "interfered" with the plans.)

Oxford undoubtedly wrote the "deposition scene" of *Richard II* in support of the effort by both Essex and Southampton to gain access to Elizabeth. (The powerful scene would not be published as part of the play until 1608.) Well before now, Essex had become associated with Bolinbroke, who maneuvered Richard into doing what the earls hoped they could persuade Elizabeth to do: "With mine own hands I give away my crown…"

Cecil later accused Essex of plotting to become King himself, but he was exaggerating the earl's motives to ensure his destruction. So long as Elizabeth relied upon the hunchbacked Secretary, who controlled access to her, Essex and Southampton had no way of being heard. Rebellion was "a last resort" for Essex, observed G. W. Keeton, Professor of English Law at University College in London, adding, "But there seems no reason to doubt that his real object was to induce the Queen to replace Cecil by himself." Now the testimony of the Sonnets supports that observation while explaining the Rebellion in a new way. If Essex had taken Cecil's place as head of the Privy Council, it's likely he would have called a Parliament to proclaim Henry Wriothesley as Elizabeth's immediate heir and successor.

Although he remained behind the scenes, Oxford became personally involved in the rising (and in the crime for which the earls were charged) because of the staging of *Richard II* on Saturday, February 7, 1601. The next morning, provoked into precipitous action by Cecil's agents in their midst, Essex and Southampton led 300 armed men in what became known as the Essex Rebellion, resulting in wild chaos, some bloodshed and mass arrests. That night, the two earls knelt and surrendered up their swords to the Crown; then they were taken through Traitors Gate to await trial for high treason.

THE TRIAL

Having already found a "vital link" between Oxford and Southampton in regard to the marriage arrangement of 1590-1591, Looney reported an even more important link in terms of the trial of Essex and Southampton on February 19, 1601, when both earls were found guilty and condemned to death. Here is his description:

> "In the year 1601 there took place the ill-fated insurrection under the Earl of Essex; an

insurrection which its leaders maintained was aimed, not at the throne, but at the politicians, amongst whom Robert Cecil, son of Burghley, was now prominent. Whether Edward de Vere approved of the rising or not, it certainly represented social and political forces with which he was in sympathy...

"In order to stir up London and to influence the public mind in a direction favorable to the overturning of those in authority, the company gave a performance of *Richard II*, the Earl of Southampton subsidizing the players. In the rising itself Southampton took an active part. Upon its collapse he was tried for treason along with its leader Essex; and it was then that Edward de Vere emerged from his retirement for the first time in nine years to take his position amongst the twenty-five peers who constituted the tribunal before whom Essex and Southampton were to be tried. It is certainly a most important fact in connection with our argument [of Edward de Vere as the author of Shakespeare's works] that this outstanding action of Oxford's later years should be in connection with the one contemporary that 'Shakespeare' has immortalized...

"It is clear, from the point of view of the problem of Shakespearean authorship, that the famous trial of the Earl of Essex assumes quite a thrilling interest. Standing before the judges was the only living personality that 'Shakespeare' has openly connected with the issue of his works and towards whom he has publicly expressed affection: Henry Wriothesley ... And sitting on the benches amongst the judges was none other, we believe, than the real 'Shakespeare' himself..." [20]

Along with the other peers, Oxford had no choice but to support the Crown by voting guilty against both earls and sending them to their deaths. Essex was beheaded six days later, on February 25, 1601, and four other conspirators were executed before people realized that the Queen had apparently decided to spare Southampton. No public explanation was given and no legal reason was ever recorded. A convicted traitor in shame and disgrace, Southampton was now "Mr. Wriothesley, Henry," a commoner (or "the late earl," in the eyes of the law), stripped of all his titles and lands and regarded as serving a sentence of perpetual confinement.

Oxford adopted the Shakespeare name to support Southampton in the struggle to determine control over succession. When the Rebellion failed, the victorious Cecil sent Essex to his execution and then aimed to bring James of Scotland to the throne and thereby retain his own power in the new reign. The Secretary secured a reprieve for Southampton while holding him hostage in the Tower, under the continuing threat he might still be executed at any moment. This pressurized situation continued for as long as Elizabeth remained alive and until the succession of James was assured.

THE BLACKMAIL & THE BARGAIN

To save his son's life and secure the promise of his release from the Tower with a pardon, Oxford agreed to renounce all ties to Southampton – as his father and, therefore, as "Shakespeare." Having associated Henry Wriothesley (and him alone) with that name, Oxford was forced to glue the mask to his own face; and Southampton, in turn, had to renounce his royal claim. Such was the infamous bargain, in the face of blackmail, that Edward de Vere made with Robert Cecil. And because of this sacrifice by both father and son, England's destiny was forever altered.

---

20. Looney, op. cit., pp. 329-332

THE QUESTION "WHEN"

Anyone reading Oxford's surviving poems and letters under his own name will agree that the voice of the Sonnets certainly *could* be his; but even those accepting him as their author have lacked the all-important time frame within which to perceive the story. Knowing the author is crucial, but the additional element required is the context. Hyder Rollins put it this way in 1944:

> "The question when the sonnets were written is in many respects the most important of all the unanswerable questions they pose. If it could be answered definitely and finally, there might be some chance of establishing to general satisfaction the identity of the friend [the Fair Youth], the dark woman [the Dark Lady], and the Rival Poet (supposing that all were real individuals), of deciding what contemporary sources Shakespeare did or did not use, and even of determining whether the order of Q is the author's or not. In the past and at the present, such a solution has been and remains an idle dream." [21]

Imagine coming upon Hamlet's "To be or not to be" soliloquy without the context of the play in which it appears. In that case, we could not comprehend it in terms of the individuals and events causing the Prince to express such thoughts and emotions. The soliloquy would remain a powerful, universal, timeless expression of the human condition, but we could not use it to learn the specific circumstances of Hamlet's predicament. In fact, we could not even discover that the Prince of Denmark was the speaker.

So it has been with the Sonnets, which are the poet's own version of Hamlet's soliloquies, using the personal pronoun "I" to express himself. These verses are equally powerful, universal and timeless, as readers have understood for centuries; but there has been no surrounding context within which to perceive them as part of a real-life historical drama.

The simple answer put forth here, as outlined, is that eighty entries of the 100-sonnet center sequence correspond with the twenty-six months of Southampton's confinement in the Tower; and this context alone confirms Rollins's prediction that some age-old enigmas can be resolved:

THE FAIR YOUTH

Southampton was indeed the younger man confined in the Tower, so the majority of scholars have been correct in identifying him as the "Fair Youth" of the Sonnets.

THE DARK LADY

While in prison, Southampton could not have been part of an active "love triangle" with the poet and his mistress. The powerful, deceitful, tyrannical "Dark Lady" who steals him away could only have been Queen Elizabeth, the Sovereign Mistress of England, who was holding him captive in her prison-fortress while casting her imperial dark frown of disgrace upon him.

THE RIVAL POET

No other writers were competing for Southampton's attention or patronage during his bleak time in the Tower, so the "Rival Poet" who makes his appearance in Sonnets 78-86 can only have been the popular name "William Shakespeare," a name with which Henry Wriothesley had already been uniquely associated. In this context the so-called Rival Poet series is a record by Oxford of his personal sacrifice, according to the bargain by which "Shakespeare" must continue to live as a "spirit" while he, Oxford, must be "struck dead"

---

21. Hyder E. Rollins, *A New Variorum Edition of Shakespeare: The Sonnets*, Vol. II, 1944, p. 53

in terms of his identity as the world perceives it:

> Was it his spirit, by spirits taught to write
> Above a mortal pitch, that struck me dead?
> - Sonnet 86, lines 5-6

SHAKESPEARE

The poet testifies he was summoned to the "sessions" or trial of Essex and Southampton, just as the Privy Council summoned Oxford to the trial on February 19, 1601. This contextual alignment brings us to the heart of the authorship mystery and confirms that only Edward de Vere could have been the real "Shakespeare."

THREE WINTERS

Oxford tells Southampton in Sonnet 104 it had been *"three Winters ... since first I saw you fresh,"* which scholars have taken to mean a three-year period during the 1590s. In this context, Oxford refers to the three winters from Southampton's imprisonment on February 8, 1601, through the subsequent two anniversaries of the Rebellion in February 1602 and February 1603. It is a *two*-year period encompassing three actual winters.

DARKNESS

A cloud of darkness descends upon the diary at the start of the 100-verse center, with Sonnet 27, when Oxford envisions Southampton in the Tower as *"a jewel hung in ghastly night."* Anticipating that his son may soon be executed, he describes him in Sonnet 30 as *"precious friends hid in death's dateless night"* and in Sonnet 31 as *"the grave where buried love doth live."*

DISGRACE

With the darkness comes a wave of shame and disgrace covering both the poet and the Fair Youth. When Oxford writes in Sonnet 29 that he is *"in disgrace with Fortune and men's eyes"* (in disgrace with Elizabeth and her subjects), it's not only because he suffers in place of his son, but also because he had deliberately used the "Shakespeare" name to encourage active opposition to the power of Robert Cecil.

"All men make faults," Oxford tells Southampton in Sonnet 35, *"and even I in this, authorizing thy trespass with compare."* He was an accessory to the "trespass" or treason, having sanctioned the Rebellion (using the Shakespeare name) by dramatizing how a weak monarch, King Richard II, had given up his crown; and months later, the still-furious Elizabeth would blurt out: *"I am Richard II, know ye not that!"*

LEGAL LANGUAGE

Now the many legal terms which appear throughout the Sonnets are revealed as related to the crime, the trial, the prison, the legal bargaining for Southampton's life and freedom, the need for a royal pardon, and more:

> Accessory, Accusing, Action, Adverse Party, Advocate, Arrest, Attaint, Attainted, Bail, Bars, Blame, Confess, Confine, Commits, Crime, Defendant, Defense, Excuse, False (false-traitor), Fault, Faults, Gate, Gates of Steel, Guard, Guilt, Impaneled (a jury), Imprisoned, Judgment, Key, Lawful Plea, Lawful Reasons, Laws, Liberty, Locked Up, Misprision, Offence, Offender, Pardon, Plea, Plea Deny, Plead, Prove, Purposed Overthrow, Quest (jury), Ransom, Releasing, Repent, Revolt, Sessions, Summon, Suspect (suspect-traitor), Term of Life, Trespass, Up-Locked, Verdict, Wards (guards)…

SEPARATION

The grief-stricken poet's separation from the Fair Youth has never been explained, but in this context Oxford is expressing his agony that his son is being held hostage in the Tower while facing the threat of execution – a threat Cecil held over him for more than two years, until Elizabeth finally died and the succession of James was assured, leaving the Secretary still in control:

> Things Removed, O Absence, Absence of Your Liberty, Absent From Thy Heart, Where Thou Art, Injurious Distance, Where Thou Dost Stay, Removed From Thee, Present-Absent, Where Thou Art, The Bitterness of Absence, Where You May Be, Where You Are, Th'imprisoned Absence of Your Liberty, Where You List, Thou Dost Wake Elsewhere, All Away, Be Absent From Thy Walks, How Like a Winter Hath My Absence Been From Thee, This Time Removed, Thou Away, You Away…

THE RELATIONSHIP

The poet of the Sonnets is a mature nobleman willing to give up his inherited stature ("Thy love is better than high birth to me," he declares to Southampton in Sonnet 91) and nearing the end of his life ("Beated and chopped with tanned antiquity," he describes himself in Sonnet 62); and once Oxford is seen as writing to another lord a generation younger, the traditional notion of "poet-to-patron" must be eliminated.

In addition, once Southampton is viewed as in the Tower all during the time these verses were being written, it becomes certain that the two men could not have been engaged in an active homosexual relationship, as another theory would have it.

Given the circumstance that the Queen is holding Southampton in the Tower and that Oxford is furious at his Sovereign Mistress for not helping him, what relationship could have caused the fifty-year-old nobleman to feel such painful and personal responsibility for the imprisoned younger earl and his fate? The father-son bond, which is so obvious even on the surface of the Sonnets that it has been dismissed as metaphorical, becomes the only logical explanation.

THE SACRIFICE

Oxford used the sonnets as a genuine outlet for his grief, expressing the personal torment of having to blame himself for Southampton's fate. It appears that at times during the prison years, he wrote several entries at a single sitting, before arranging them according to the calendar. "But day doth daily draw my sorrows longer," he writes in Sonnet 28, compiling his entries day by day, "and night doth nightly make grief's length seem stronger."

"Though thou repent, yet I have still the loss," he tells him in Sonnet 34, adding, "Th'offender's sorrow lends but weak relief to him that bears the strong offence's loss." In the most reverent way, as the father of a divinely ordained prince, Oxford becomes a Christ figure bearing the guilt and burden of all sins. "So shall those blots that do with me remain," he promises in Sonnet 36, "without thy help by me be borne alone."

With Cecil firmly in charge, Oxford knew the price to "ransom" his son's life and freedom would be the loss of Southampton's claim to the throne. Their relationship as father and son must be buried, now and forever: "I may not ever-more acknowledge thee," he tells Southampton in Sonnet 36, "lest my bewailed guilt should do thee shame. Nor thou with public kindness honor me, unless thou take that honor from thy name." He writes in Sonnet 37 as a "decrepit father" who "takes delight to see his active child do deeds of youth" and cries out in Sonnet 39 that his son is "all the better part of me," adding, "Even for this, let us divided live, and our dear love lose name of single one."

Elizabeth held Southampton in her prison and could send him to his death: "That she hath thee is of my wailing chief," Oxford moans in Sonnet 42; and in this tragic way, mother and son are together at last, as jailer and prisoner: "Both find each other, and I lose both twain, and both for my sake lay me on this cross."

The forty days and nights from the Rebellion equal the time of Christ's trial in the wilderness. On the fortieth day, March 19, 1601, Oxford records the Queen's decision to spare the life of her son while keeping him a prisoner; and his reaction is one of emotional exhaustion, recorded in a virtual suicide note in Sonnet 66 by enumerating the reasons he prefers to die. (Sonnets 66-67 are at the exact center of the eighty prison verses.) Alluding to Essex, who has by now been executed, and to Southampton, who has been deprived of his royal claim, he writes that those purposeful men have been "by limping sway disabled" – destroyed by the limping, swaying, hunchbacked Secretary Cecil. Concluding his lamentation, he reiterates he would prefer to depart from this world, were it not for the fact it would mean leaving his royal son alone, possibly to die, in the Tower:

> Tired with all these, from these would I be gone
> Save that to die, I leave my love alone
> - Sonnet 66, lines 13-14

What follows is Oxford's descent into another kind of death. Southampton has eluded the blade of the executioner's axe, but Oxford now wonders why his son should be forced to serve a life sentence with "infection," or criminals in the Tower:

> Ah, wherefore with infection should he live,
> And with his presence grace impiety…
> - Sonnet 67, lines 1-2

Southampton will be able to "live a second life on second head," his father writes in Sonnet 68, adding in Sonnet 70: "Thou hast passed by the ambush of young days."

But their true relationship will never be seen by the contemporary world, so Oxford is forced to instruct him in Sonnet 71: "No longer mourn for me when I am dead … Nay, if you read this line, remember not the hand that writ it, for I love you so, that I in your sweet thoughts would be forgot, if thinking on me then should make you woe … Do not so much as my poor name rehearse…"

The litany continues in Sonnet 72: "After my death, dear love, forget me quite, for you in me can nothing worthy prove … My name be buried where my body is, and live no more to shame nor me nor you. For I am shamed by that which I bring forth," Oxford cries out, referring to himself as a father who brought forth a Prince unable to wear the crown.

Sonnet 73, a funeral dirge, reflects Oxford's writing of *The Phoenix and the Turtle* for publication this year (1601). "That time of year thou mayst in me behold, when yellow leaves, or none, or few, do hang upon those boughs which shake against the cold, bare ruined choirs, where late the sweet birds sang," he tells Southampton, adding, "In me thou seest the twilight of such day, as after Sun-set fadeth in the West" – his glorious royal son who is fading, even now, from the world's view.

Behind the scenes, without the Queen becoming aware of it, Oxford must lend his full support to James; and Southampton must remain in the Tower, where he will disappear if this transition of royal power fails to occur.

"O how I faint when I of you do write," Oxford tells his son in Sonnet 80, "knowing a better spirit doth use your name, and in the praise thereof spends all his might to make me tongue-tied speaking of your fame." The rise of "Shakespeare" as the "better spirit" who has immortalized Southampton means Oxford's simultaneous fall into oblivion. Two lines in the very next sonnet sum up the "Shakespeare" mystery that has continued from then to now:

Introduction

> Your name from hence immortal life shall have,
> Though I, once gone, to all the world must die.
> - Sonnet 81, lines 5-6

THE DOUBLE HELIX

By the fall of 1998, it seemed that any solution to the Sonnets was beyond reach; but I decided to make one last try before giving up. First I listed some hypotheses with one major prediction: if these verses contained a true story for the benefit of future generations, the poet would have made certain that we could comprehend it.

This time around, I started searching through for any "instructions" he may have inserted. If he had left them, I would *follow them literally*; and in the end, they would have to provide some new and different kind of information. I had no idea what any such discovery might look like, but it needed to be very persuasive for me to continue my quest.

In the previous two years, while completing a book about scientific visualization, I had posed this question: what if the Sonnets comprised a single masterwork, its various elements of language, design and content operating in harmony as part of the whole? If such were true, some unifying system must exist; and there might be a central mechanism, similar to the "double helix" structure of DNA, with its consistent vocabulary determining the form and functions of a living organism.

So that's what I started to look for; and in Sonnet 76, at what turns out to be the exact center of the structure of an elegant monument, here was the "invention" by which Oxford writes about "all one, ever the same" (Southampton and Elizabeth) by means of "every word" while "dressing old words new" or changing words to consistently signify various aspects of the family triangle.

Here, for example, is how he refers to Elizabeth in the Sonnets:

BEAUTY – Venus, goddess of Love and Beauty
DIAN – Diana, goddess of the Moon
FAIREST VOTARY – the "imperial vot'ress" of *A Midsummer Night's Dream*
EVER THE SAME – she translated her motto, *Semper Eadem*, into English this way
FORTUNE – she was associated with Fortune
GODDESS – the divinely ordained goddess on earth
HEAVEN – she was associated with Heaven
LADIES DEAD – she was "our sovereign Lady"
MISTRESS – "our Sovereign Mistress"
MOON – Cynthia or Diana, goddess of the Moon
MOTHER – wife and mother of her subjects
NATURE – she was associated with Nature
PHOENIX – she adopted the phoenix as an emblem of herself
PRINCES – she was the Prince of England
REGION – she was Elizabeth *Regina*
ROSE – her dynasty of the Tudor Rose began in 1485
THRONED QUEEN – the throned Queen of England
VIRGIN HAND – vowing not to marry, she was the Virgin Queen
WE – she used the royal "we" on official documents

Within the family triangle, Elizabeth casts the shadow of her frown upon Southampton, so that he becomes:

Bare, Barren, Base, Black, Blamed, Dark, Darkly, Dateless, Despised, Disdained, Disgraced, False, Forlorn, Foul, Ghastly, Hidden, Masked, None, Profaned, Rank, Rotten, Sable, Scorned, Shamed, Slandered, Sullen, Sullied, Suspect, Ugly, Unfair, Unseen,

> Untrimmed, Vulgar, Wasted, Worst...

Oxford shines his light upon him as:

> Abundant, Alike, All, Alone, Always, Beauteous, Beloved, Best, Blessed, Bounteous, Bright, Celestial, Clear, Constant, Controlling, Crowned, Darling, Dear, Dearest, Dearly, Divine, Entitled, Eternal, Excellent, Fair, Fairer, Fairest, Fairly, Fragrant, Fresh, Fresher, Full, Gaudy, Gentle, Gentlest, Gently, Gilded, Glorious, Golden, Gracious, Happy, High, Holy, Immortal, Kind, Lovely, Mightier, Near, Nearly, One, Only, Perfect, Powerful, Precious, Proud, Proudly, Pure, Purple, Rare, Religious, Rich, Richer, Right, Rightly, Riper, Scarlet, Silver, Special, Strong, Successive, Sweet, Sweetest, Sweetly, Tall, Tender, True, Virtuous, Wondrous, Worthy...

These are examples of how Oxford keeps "dressing old words new" (Sonnet 76) and "varying to other words" (Sonnet 105) to create diversity within the "noted weed" of poetry while recording the progress of LOVE in relation to TIME, which leads to the time line of the chronicle.

QUESTIONS & ANSWERS

The intention of this inaugural edition is to share the results of my findings so far and hopefully open the door to what holds the promise of a new age of reading of the Sonnets and exploring all the other Shakespeare literature, not to mention uncovering the historical truth that the Sonnets represent. Of course, thorny questions will continue about how things actually worked:

Why did the Countess of Southampton refer to Henry Wriothesley not only as "the child," but also as "my son" if, in fact, he was the Queen's son? My answer is that the Countess needed to make clear to Robert Cecil that she could be trusted to keep this most sensitive of state secrets to herself; and this was one way to communicate her loyal intentions.

What about the fact that Elizabeth, Essex and others had seemed to regard James as the rightful heir to the English throne? My answer is that all such appearances were part of the political maneuvering by those who needed allies to achieve their goals. Just as Cecil used Walter Raleigh as an ally against Essex and then turned against him once James was on the throne, no apparent friendships or alliances could be counted on. In any case, legal arguments were being made against the succession of James because he had not been born on English soil. Nothing was certain and anything was possible.

Under what conditions could Southampton succeed to the throne? Several scenarios come to mind. The Queen could have told the truth while she was alive and let the chips fall, at least so long as Burghley was alive to support her. Or, as her father, Henry VIII, had done, she could have dictated the terms of succession in her Last Will and Testament. She never left a will, or one that has been discovered, leaving open the possibility that Cecil destroyed any such document. At all costs the Secretary could not have allowed Southampton to become King; he would have lost all his power and, most likely, his life.

Why didn't the Privy Council under Cecil's leadership call "Shakespeare" to account for writing the play *Richard II* and for allowing his own acting company, the Chamberlain's Men, to perform it at the Globe to help rouse support for the Rebellion? Since other members of the troupe were brought in for questioning, why not the chief offender? The answer provided here is that the real "Shakespeare," the Earl of Oxford, was indeed brought to account and, moreover, made to pay the highest "ransom" or price of all.

Why was Essex killed but Southampton spared? Historians have never answered the question satisfactorily; after all, monarchs don't like traitors. Perhaps the Queen could not bear to execute a son she had vowed to name as her heir; and perhaps Oxford's pleadings changed her mind. Or perhaps Southampton was spared because Cecil needed to hold him hostage in the Tower, under the threat of death, to prevent Oxford from getting the truth out. The heart of the story may be that, once the Rebellion failed, Oxford and Cecil realized that neither could do without the other; that is, they came to "a great reckoning in a little room," resulting in a standoff. As things turned out, Oxford obtained his son's life and freedom while Cecil retained his power and became First Earl of Salisbury in the reign of King James. Perhaps Essex took all of the guilt on his shoulders, precisely to give Southampton a chance to remain alive and possibly gain his freedom.

Was Oxford the unknown "40" in the secret correspondence between Cecil and James between 1601 and 1603? (First suggested by Nina Green.) Having made his bargain with the Secretary, he may well have participated to help ensure the Scottish king's succession, as the only way to save his royal son from being left to die in the Tower.

If so, Oxford's suggestion to the Earl of Lincoln (six days prior to Elizabeth's death) that they raise an army to put the Earl of Hastings on the throne in place of James is explained; that is, to ensure the peaceful accession of the Scottish king, he was actually working for Cecil to test Lincoln's loyalty.

If Southampton had a genuine claim to the throne, why did James sign orders on April 5, 1603, for his release from the Tower? No one has ever explained why this was virtually the first action James took as king, even before he left Edinburgh to make his way south to London. Now the reason would be that James had joined the bargain, at Cecil's insistence, and that the new monarch (a stranger in England) placed his trust in "Great Oxford," as he referred to Edward de Vere, to maintain his vow of silence.

The King not only heaped honors upon Southampton (and Oxford), but also granted him a royal pardon, which meant he could not be charged with the same crime again. Oxford had recorded this aspect of the deal in the Sonnets, telling his son that he himself had the power to accept these terms and, in effect, to secure his own pardon:

> Be where you list, your charter is so strong
> That you your self may privilege your time
> To what you will: to you it doth belong
> Your self to pardon of self-doing crime.
> - Sonnet 58, lines 9-12

Why did the government arrest Southampton (and some of his friends) within hours of Oxford's reported death on June 24, 1604, and hold him overnight in the Tower for interrogation? Why were all his private papers seized and destroyed? And why was no official record of his arrest made by English authorities? The answer would be that, with Oxford no longer around to take personal responsibility, James and Cecil needed to be reassured of Southampton's loyalty. And Cecil may have gained this assurance by threatening him, once again, with death in the Tower.

Why did Oxford leave no will? Here is another mystery, given that noblemen were trained in the law (as Edward de Vere had been) and took great pains to leaves wills for their children and others, including family members and servants. Had Oxford left a will that was destroyed? Had he not really died on June 24, 1604, but disappeared instead? Given the heartbreak over his failure as the father of a royal son, he would not have wanted to continue as before. Furthermore, his reason for writing under the "Shakespeare" name was over and done with as well.

How did the Sonnets come to be published in 1609? My answer is that Southampton was the sole recipient of the verses, all of which revolve around him, and that he undertook to getting them into print for future generations. Oxford himself must have written and constructed the cryptic dedication to "the onlie begetter of these ensuing sonnets, Mr. W. H." – reflecting his son's status as "Mr. Wriothesley, Henry" while in the Tower; and it was for him that the Sonnets had been created:

> Yet be most proud of that which I compile,
> Whose influence is thine, and born of thee.
> - Sonnet 78, lines 9-10

The dedication, arranged in three upside-down pyramids as a monument, promises Southampton "that eternitie promised by our ever-living poet," that is, the immortality Oxford had promised him in the Sonnets; and the clear echo of Edward de Vere as "ever" as well as "ever-living" (no longer alive on earth) may well have been intended as the announcement of his death. That suggests that Oxford may not have died until 1608 or early 1609, and that Southampton put the Sonnets into print that year in order to commemorate his father's death.

HOW TO READ THIS BOOK

In the following pages the Sonnets are presented as "authorial," or printed as the author intended; in other words, they're in the correct order and tell a whole story, which consists of much more fact than fiction. (My take is that *nothing* in the verses is fictional.) The monument was constructed after the diary ended, carefully and without hurry; but the verses read like chapters of a book, so it's best to start from the beginning and read them in order.

My only change of order has been to move the final pair (Sonnets 153-154) to the front of the chronicle, because this "epilogue" serves as the prologue marking the year of Southampton's birth (1574) and refers to the royal visit to Bath in August that year. An interesting point made by Editor Alex McNeil is that perhaps Oxford wrote Sonnet 153 at the outset and then Sonnet 154 at the very end, revisiting his starting point.

"Sonnet 154 reads like the work of someone at the peak of his powers," McNeil notes, "and also seems to be from the point of view of Oxford looking back thirty years. There has to be a reason he wrote two – and chose to include two – on exactly the same narrow topic. That reason is to remind us yet again that he writes only about one thing, and that he constantly rewrites and revises his writings ('dressing old words new'). Sonnets 153 and 154 are the alpha *and* the omega, the prologue *and* the epilogue."

I have included relevant historical matter all along the way, since Oxford was recording his reactions to circumstances as he lived them and as they unfolded around him. For each sonnet I've included the number, a title and the date in terms of the year or month or day. These dates are not random; they are dictated by how they fall into the timeline of historical events, according to the structure based on Elizabeth's ever-waning life.

I believe the Sonnets are now placed within a chronological framework that makes sense for the first time. The pieces all fit together, without need to "imagine" this or that link to the known facts of the history. In this case, the process has been more similar to placing the verses over the calendar as though they were stencils; the only step then required is to look again at the lines in this light. Time and again, what they say leaps from the page with new meaning and clarity.

Also included is a short summary of each sonnet, followed by the verse itself along with a line-by-line "translation" beside it.

ORTHOGRAPHY

I've incorporated all the original capitalization and italics, which are listed just after the Index of words at the back of this book. Otherwise I've used accepted modernizations of spellings. There are a few exceptions, which are noted, but my feeling is that in most cases the original spellings add nothing to our understanding of the lines and obstructs clarity. On the other hand, some of the original spellings make sense now for the first time; and therefore, unlike many modern editors, I have left these unaltered. I've followed most accepted emendations of the punctuation, but, again, only up to a point.

TRANSLATIONS

Some colleagues have suggested "paraphrase" to describe the line-by-line glosses for each sonnet, and that may be more accurate; in my view, what I've done is consistently "translate" words into their second definitions, according to the "invention" that Oxford uses for "dressing old words new" or "varying to other words."

Incidentally, attempts to "translate" each line grew increasingly difficult as the story progresses, indicating that Oxford's compression of meanings grows more powerful toward the end. As a result, my appreciation for the genius and skill of "Shakespeare" has grown accordingly. Meanwhile, I am still far from satisfied with my "translations," which undoubtedly can be improved.

LINE NOTES

I've repeated the actual lines as part of the notes, so readers don't have to keep flipping back to the sonnet itself. This edition includes the line notes immediately following each verse, rather than placing them all at the back, as in the case of most other editions. The reason is that the sonnets now tell an ongoing and coherent story, making it logical to supply the notes as it unfolds. The new context of the Sonnets prompts this format for the first time.

I've made no attempt to give all the various meanings and interpretations of words and lines of the Sonnets; on the contrary, the new framework has yielded its own glosses, many of which are new. I've consulted many editions, as indicated in the notes, and they often corroborate the meanings that now present themselves. The difference is that this time we can understand *why* the poet has made particular allusions.

Take, for example, Oxford's statement to Southampton in Sonnet 42, "That she hath thee is my wailing chief," referring to Elizabeth keeping him in her royal prison fortress. Editor Stephen Booth glosses "of my wailing chief" as "the principal cause of my wailing," adding: "The strange and elliptical construction may have been prompted by Shakespeare's wish to echo the already common term 'chief mourner,' the nearest relative present at a funeral." [22] But that is all he says, because he has no context for the use of such an echo; but for us the phrase takes on sudden relevance, since Oxford is anticipating Southampton's execution and envisioning himself as the father – "the nearest relative" – at his son's funeral.

Another example is in Sonnet 125, on the occasion of the Queen's funeral, when Oxford tells Southampton, "No, let me be obsequious in thy heart." Booth writes that *obsequious* echoes the procession suggested by *the canopy* in the first line and the idea of being a follower, adding, "Through its relation to *obsequy*, 'funeral,' *obsequious* had the specialized meaning 'dutiful in performing funeral rites,' and invites a reader to think of *the canopy* as borne in a funeral procession." Once again Booth offers no real-life context, though his statement readily supports the new timeline, by which Sonnet 125 marks the funeral procession for Elizabeth. One might say that it clinches this connection to history.

(The irony of the line quoted above from Sonnet 125 is that Oxford is telling his son that he will *not* be obsequious at Elizabeth's funeral, but instead only "in thy heart." He uses the funeral procession only as the starting point from which to make his final "oblation" to his royal son, that is, to make his sacrificial offering to him as a king or deity on earth.)

For me, one of the great surprises has been a much closer link between the Sonnets and the chronicle plays of royal history than most scholars have emphasized. Virtually all adjectives applied to Southampton and his royalty – *precious, sweet, tender, fair, beloved*, etc. – are used in the plays to refer to princes. This also applies to negative words such as *shame* or *disgrace* or *sin*, etc, which often appear in Shakespeare's history plays in reference to the same kind of dishonor suffered by Southampton. After a while it becomes clear that the traditional context of a "love triangle" involving the poet, the Fair Youth and the Dark Lady is now supplanted by a new context involving matters of the highest political concern, even though such adjectives

---

22. Booth, Stephen, *Shakespeare's Sonnets*, 1977, his notes for individual sonnets

appear to support both perceptions.

Four particular words of the Sonnets should be mentioned here: *fault, trespass, misprision* and *ransom*. Traditionally these terms have been seen as metaphors applied to romantic or sexual infidelity; but in the chronicle plays of royal history, they are applied to the same situation faced by Oxford and Southampton because of the Essex Rebellion. *Fault* and *trespass* refer to treason; *misprision* is a lesser form of that crime (Oxford announces in Sonnet 87 that it has been applied to Southampton to save his life and make him eligible for a pardon); *ransom*, a term for the fees or payments made by prisoners to gain their release, is what Oxford is paying for his royal son:

> But that your trespass now becomes a fee:
> Mine ransoms yours, and yours must ransom me. - Sonnet 120, lines 13-14

The sense of these lines is that Oxford, by means of his bargain with Cecil, has *ransomed* his son from the Tower; and now it will be up to Southampton to "liberate" Oxford by making sure the Sonnets are printed for posterity. Although he has buried the truth from contemporary eyes, Oxford remains alive in this monument – as he indicates in Sonnet 107, writing, "I'll live in this poor rhyme."

Here is a short list of such terms used in the Sonnets and the history plays:

"DISGRACE"

When in *disgrace* with Fortune and men's eyes - Sonnet 29, line 1

And spit it bleeding in his high *disgrace* - Richard II, 1.1.194

"SESSIONS ... SUMMON"

When to the *Sessions* of sweet silent thought
I *summon* up remembrance of things past - Sonnet 30, lines 1-2

Summon a session, that we may arraign
Our most disloyal lady; for, as she hath
Been publicly accused, so she shall have
A just and open trial - *The Winter's Tale*, 2.3.201-204

"SHAME"

Nor can thy *shame* give physic to my grief - Sonnet 34, line 9

Seize on the *shame*-faced Henry...
Hence with him to the Tower - *3 Henry VI*, 4.8.52, 57

"OFFENDER ... RANSOM"

Th'*offender's* sorrow lends but weak relief
To him that bears the strong *offence's* loss.
Ah, but those tears are pearl which thy love sheds,
And they are rich, and *ransom* all ill deeds - Sonnet 34, lines 11-14

For I should melt at an *offender's* tears
And lowly words were *ransom* for their fault - *2 Henry VI*, 3.1.126-127

"STAIN"

Clouds and eclipses *stain* both Moone and Sunne - Sonnet 35, line 3

And that high royalty was ne'er plucked off,
The faiths of men ne'er *stained* with revolt - *King John*, 4.2.5-6

"FAULT ... TRESPASS ... ATTAINTED"

All men make *faults*, and even I in this,
Authorizing thy *trespass* with compare - Sonnet 35, lines 5-6

I do confess my *fault*
And do submit myself to your Highness' mercy - *Henry V*, 2.2.77-78

Of *faults* concealed, wherein I am *attainted* - Sonnet 88, lines 6-7

And by his *treason* stand'st thou not *attainted*,
Corrupted, and exempt from ancient gentry?
His *trespass* yet lives guilty in thy blood - *1 Henry VI*, 2.4.92-94

"BLOT"

So shall those *blots* that do with me remain - Sonnet 36, line 3

And thus thy fall hath a kind of *blot* - *Henry V*, 2.2.138

"REVOLT"

Since that my life on thy *revolt* doth lie… - Sonnet 93, line 10

I will weep for thee,
For this *revolt* of thine, methinks, is like
Another fall of man - *Henry V*, 2.2.140-142

"PURPOSED OVERTHROW"

To linger out a *purposed overthrow* - Sonnet 90, line 8

And you did swear that oath at Doncaster,
That you did nothing *purpose* 'gainst the state - *1 Henry IV*, 5.1.4.42-43

Edward will always bear himself a king.
Though Fortune's malice *overthrow* my state… - *3 Henry VI*, 4.3.45-46

"PARDON"

O let me suffer, being at your beck,
Th'mprisoned absence of your liberty…
To you it doth belong
Yourself to *pardon* of self-doing crime - Sonnet 58, lines 5-6, 11-12

Say *'pardon,'* king, let pity teach thee how;

The word is short, but no so short as sweet;
No word like *'pardon'* for kings' mouths so meet - *Richard II*, 5.3.114-116

"AMBUSH"

Thou hast passed by the *ambush* of young days - Sonnet 70, line 9

Once did I lay an *ambush* for you life,
A *trespass* that doth vex my grieved soul - *Richard II*, 1.1.137-138

"MISPRISION"

The charter of thy worth gives thee releasing…
So thy great gift, upon *misprision* growing,
Comes home again, on better judgment making - Sonnet 87, lines 3, 11-12

Either envy, therefore, or *misprision*
Is guilty of this *fault,* and not my son - *1 Henry IV*, 1.3.26-27

Such words are woven within the "noted weed" or fabric of the familiar poetry so that they, too, have been hiding in plain sight.

A MASTER GLOSSARY

Here is a short glossary of the most frequently used words of the "invention" by which "every word" appears to have one kind of meaning on the surface while actually conveying Oxford's true story at the same time.

Southampton's motto "Ung par Tout, Tout par Ung" (*One for All, All for One*) and
Oxford's motto "Vero Nihil Verius" (*Nothing Truer than Truth*) are constantly echoed in
the Sonnets:

ALL = used 118 times by itself; 216 times in all forms = Southampton

ONE = 42 times = Southampton

TRUTH = 25 times = Oxford

TRUE = 41 times = Oxford

Oxford frequently plays upon his own name, "E. Ver," as *Ever* or *Never*:

EVER = 68 times in all forms = Oxford

These are Oxford's tools, his building blocks. The fact that "Shakespeare" has a vocabulary of some 15,000 words, twice the verbal storehouse of Milton, offers some idea of the discipline it must have taken to restrict his writing of the Sonnets to these simple words and to repeat them so frequently. Others, by way of example, include:

LOVE = 212 instances in all forms = royal blood; my royal son
But "my love" in Sonnet 138 = the Queen
(HATE = the enemy of royal blood)

TIME = 78 instances = the Queen's ever-waning life and reign in real time
(After her death in Sonnet 105, *time* becomes universal time)

Additional ways of incorporating TIME include references to days, nights, years, the different seasons, hours, minutes, etc.

AIR = 4 instances = heir

BEAUTY = 68 instances in all forms = Elizabeth; her Tudor blood
Southampton possesses her "beauty" by inheritance

FAIR = 62 instances in all forms = royal
In the Sonnets, I do not see "fair" used to connote "Vere" (pronounced "ver"), as many Oxfordians usually do when the word appears in the plays; but obviously Oxford was aware of this secondary connotation.

HEART = 60 times = source of royal blood

KIND = 18 times = related by nature; i.e., Southampton is the Queen's son and therefore her kindred or kind

MINE = 61 times = echoing "a son of mine own"

ROSE = 14 times = Elizabeth's (and Southampton's) Tudor Rose dynasty

SUN = 16 times = royal son
Also STARS and his EYES are suns

SWEET = 70 times, all forms = royal

WORLD = 32 times = contemporary England

WORTH = 27 times, all forms = royalty

DARK WORDS

One way of recognizing the eighty verses from Sonnet 27 to Sonnet 106 of the "prison years" is by the fact that most of the "dark" or "black" words are found here. The following words are used exclusively in this section:

Black (9 times); *Base* (5); *Blot* (4); *Canker* (5); *Cloud* (3); *Dark/Darkness* (4); *Guilt* (1); *Scorn* (2); *Shade/Shadow* (6); *Sin/Sins* (5); *Stain* (3)

Other such words appear almost exclusively during the prison years:

Crime (3); *Death* (12); *Disgrace* (6); *Hate* (8); *Night/Nightly* (14); *Shame* (7)

When I originally thumbed backward down the sequence from Sonnet 107, I began to follow these "dark" words and was surprised to realize that their onslaught begins in Sonnet 27, where "black" and "shadow" make their first appearance. Only afterward came the process of laying out the sonnets side by side with the actual dates of recorded events; and it was then I realized Oxford had written sixty sonnets corresponding precisely with the sixty days from February 8 to April 8, 1601.

ROYAL WORDS

Oxford uses obvious terms related to royalty, such as:

Canopy, crown, crowned, god, king, kings, kingly, kingdom, kingdoms, queen, majesty, monarch, politic, policy, princes, reign, sovereign, state, succession and successive.

But they are only the more "direct" royal words. Some of the others, perhaps less obvious upon an initial reading, include terms such as:

Ambassage, attend, beams, beck, blazon, bounty, charter, control, controlling, dear, due, duty, embassy, excel, flourish, glory, gold, golden, grace, gracious, heir, herald, high, honor, issue, jewel, largess, legacy, lord, master, might, mistress, ocean, ornament, pleasure, praise, presence, privilege, purple, right, rights, sea, seat, sit, slave, star, state, subjects, top, vassal, vassalage, we, will.

HOLY WORDS

Princes are "gods on earth" or divinely ordained beings and, therefore, Southampton is depicted in the verses by many religious words. The Sonnets are sexual in the sense that their subject matter involves conception, birth and blood inheritance, but they convey a sense of spirituality to a greater degree than a sense of sexuality. (The Dedication's reference to Southampton as the "onlie begetter" of the Sonnets, echoing the "onlie begotten Son" of the Bible, is an announcement of this spiritual or religious aspect.) There are more than fifty distinct references to Biblical verses in the Sonnets.

Here's a list of some of the obvious "holy" words, as they appear in the Fair Youth series up to Sonnet 125:

WORDS OF A SACRED BOOK

Words/Phrases	Sonnet	Words/Phrases	Sonnet
UNBLESS	1	SIN	67
SACRED MAJESTY	3	SEPULCHERS	68
HEAVENLY	7	HOLY	68
BLESSED	16	HEAVEN'S	70
HEAVEN	16	CONSECRATE	74
HEAVENLY	17	SPIRIT	74
HEAVEN	18	EVERY WORD...PROCEED[a]	76
HEAVEN	21	GRACES	78
HEAVEN'S	21	GRACED	78
ZEALOUS PILGRIMAGE TO THEE	27	GRACE	78
SOUL'S	27	GRACE	79
HEAVEN	28	SPIRIT	80
HEAVEN	29	BLESSING	82
HYMNS AT HEAVEN'S GATE	29	BLESSINGS	84
HOLY AND OBSEQUIOUS TEAR	31	HYMN	85
DEAR RELIGIOUS LOVE	31	SPIRIT	85
HEAVENLY	33	SPIRIT	86

Introduction

CELESTIAL	33	SPIRITS	86
HEAVEN'S SUN	33	GHOST	86
REPENT	34	JUDGEMENT	87
BEARS...THE CROSS	34	FORSAKE	89
SINS	35	BLESSED	92
GRACE	40	HEAVEN	93
LAY ME ON THIS CROSS	42	CREATION	93
BLESSED	43	EVE'S APPLE	93
BLESSED	52	HEAVEN'S GRACES	94
FEASTS SO SOLEMN	52	HYMNS	102
BLEST	52	SINFUL	103
BLESSED	52	IDOLATRY	105
BLESSED	53	IDOL	105
GRACE	53	THREE THEMES IN ONE	105
JUDGEMENT	55	SOUL	107
SPIRIT	56	PRAYERS DIVINE	108
BLEST	56	HALLOWED THY FAIR NAME	108
GOD	58	SOUL	109
HELL	58	A GOD IN LOVE	110
NATIVITY	60	HEAVEN	110
SPIRIT	61	GODDESS	111
SIN	62	PENANCE	111
SOUL	62	SACRED	115
SIN	62	BLESSED	119
MIRACLE	65	I AM THAT I AM	121
GRACE	67	OBLATION	125

a. "Man shall not live by bread onlie, but by *every word* that *proceedeth* out of the mouth of God." - Matthew, 4.4

Researchers Marty Hyatt and James Brooks have done extensive work on the relationship of the Sonnets to the Psalms of the Bible and have found numerous parallels and echoes. Their research and findings may add an entirely new level of meaning and structure to the Sonnets, and we look forward to the results as they emerge.

KEY SONNETS

Although every sonnet is important, several stand out for their connection to contemporary events or for their function within the monument. Here is my list of the key sonnets:

FAIR YOUTH SERIES

SONNET 1 – The opening of the "marriage" sequence and Oxford's bold announcement of a diary recording the fate of "beauty's *Rose*" or Elizabeth's Tudor Rose dynasty. *(In 1866, Gerald Massey noted the 1590-91 marriage arrangements for Southampton and Elizabeth Vere)* [23]

SONNET 17 – The end of the "marriage" sequence and Oxford's statement that future readers will fail to see "your true rights" (to become Henry IX) as his topic.

SONNET 26 – The first envoy, addressed to "Lord of My Love" - 1600. *(In 1817, Nathan Drake pointed to this sonnet as a rendition of the dedication of "Lucrece" to Southampton.)* [24]

SONNET 27 – Southampton's imprisonment for the Rebellion - February 8, 1601. *(Massey noted the abrupt change of tone between Sonnets 1-26 and Sonnet 27.)* This is the first of sixty sonnets corresponding to sixty days.

SONNET 33 – Oxford recalls the birth of his royal son in 1574 and Queen Elizabeth's refusal to acknowledge him. *(Percy Allen suggested this in the 1930s; Dorothy and Charlton Ogburn followed in the 1950s.)* [25]

SONNET 35 – Oxford records "authorizing thy trespass with compare," or having helped to support the Rebellion by his stage works, notably *Richard II*, depicting the deposition of a monarch "by compare" on stage. (*Richard II* was in fact staged on February 7, 1601.)

SONNETS 63-65 – The tension builds in anticipation of Southampton's execution.

SONNETS 66-67 – The center of the eighty-sonnet prison sequence; Oxford's emotional reaction in the first verse to Southampton's life being spared on March 19, 1601, echoing Hamlet's "To be or not to be" speech; and then, in the next verse, his wailing cry: "Ah, wherefore with infection should he live…?"

SONNET 73 – A funeral dirge mirroring that of *The Phoenix and the Turtle*, as by William "Shake-speare," also published in 1601, about the death of Oxford's and Elizabeth's hopes for their royal son to succeed to the throne.

SONNETS 76-77 – At the center of the monument, Oxford explains his "invention" of the Sonnets, whereby the language is joined with the structure of the verses to produce the true story, followed by his dedication of "this book" to Southampton as "thy book."

SONNETS 78-86 – The so-called Rival Poet series, actually recording Oxford's sacrifice of his identity as "Shakespeare" to further conceal his paternity of Southampton.

SONNET 86 – This is the sixtieth sonnet in as many days, corresponding to April 8, 1601.

---

23. Gerald Massey, *Shakespeare's Sonnets Never Before Interpreted*, 1866, p. 54
24. Nathan Drake, *Shakespeare and His Times*, 1817, p. 62
25. Percy Allen, *The Life Story of Edward de Vere as "Shakespeare,"* 1932; Dorothy and Charlton Ogburn, *This Star of England*, 1952

SONNET 87 – Opening with the salutation "Farewell," indicating that the day-by-day entries of the diary have ended. And here Oxford announces that Southampton's judgment has been reduced to "misprision" of treason, allowing him to be released in the future and gain a royal pardon.

SONNET 97 – This is the first anniversary of the Rebellion on February 8, 1602, marking "the pleasure of the fleeting year," that is, Southampton's first full year of imprisonment according to Her Majesty's pleasure.

SONNET 104 – This is the second anniversary of the Rebellion on February 8, 1603, marking the "three winters" that have passed since Southampton had been "fresh" before his imprisonment.

SONNET 105 – The Queen has died (March 24, 1603), so that Oxford, Elizabeth and Southampton have "never kept seat in one" or sat on the throne as "three" members of a royal family in the person of the "one" royal son: "Which three, till now, never kept seat in one."

SONNET 106 – This is Southampton's final night in the Tower (April 9, 1603), when Oxford refers to the Sovereign Lady's death ("Ladies dead") and indicates his foreknowledge that his son will be named Captain of the Isle of Wight ("fairest wights") and a Knight of the Garter ("lovely Knights"). (The two latter events occurred on July 7 and 9, 1603.)

SONNET 107 – The so-called "dating" verse of the Sonnets, when Southampton is liberated from the Tower on April 10, 1603. *(A researcher known only as "J. R." first noted this connection in the mid-nineteenth century. Massey developed it in 1866.)* This verse triangulates three clear allusions to historical events: the Queen's death, the proclamation that James will be crowned and Southampton's release.

SONNET 125 – The funeral of Elizabeth takes place on April 28, 1603, but Oxford uses the occasion to make his final "oblation" to Southampton. *(Looney suggested this dating of Sonnet 125 in 1920. He thought it possible that Oxford was one of the noblemen who "bore the canopy," but it's likely the earl did not do so.)*

SONNET 126 – The final envoy to Southampton as "My Lovely Boy." *(The great 18th century editor Edmund Malone was first to identify the long opening series 1-126 as addressed to a male, thereby indicating Sonnet 126 as a postscript.)* [26]

DARK LADY SERIES

SONNET 127 – Correlating with Sonnet 27, this verse evokes the Queen's reaction to the Rebellion and her imprisonment of Southampton - February 8, 1601.

SONNET 145 – Correlating with Sonnet 66 in reaction to Elizabeth's decision to spare Southampton's life: "Straight in her heart did mercy come" - March 19, 1601.

SONNET 152 – The final sonnet to Elizabeth, arranged to correlate with Sonnet 105 upon her death on March 24, 1603.

---

26. Malone, Edmund, *Supplement to the Edition of Shakespeare's Plays published in 1778*, 1780, vol. 1, pp. 579-581

BATH EPILOGUE/PROLOGUE

SONNET 153 – Undoubtedly this verse was written soon after the royal visit to Bath in August 1574, when "the boy" or "the little Love-God" is just a few months old. *(In the eighteenth century, Editor Steevens suggested Bath as the location. Greenwood suggested in 1908 that the poet was there with Queen Elizabeth.)*

SONNET 154 – Related to the same event in 1574, this verse may have been written nearly three decades later, as Oxford was completing the monument.

VARIANTS

The Sonnets contain 2,155 lines made up of 154 verses of fourteen lines apiece (employing the scheme of three quatrains plus a final couplet; rhymed *abab, cdcd, efef, gg*), except for three variants:

SONNET 99 – contains fifteen lines; the opening line is introductory; what follows is a complete sonnet in the usual fourteen-line format.

SONNET 126 – contains only twelve lines (six couplets), followed by a pair of empty parentheses in place of the final couplet. Aside from marking this verse as the envoy to the Fair Youth series, the parentheses may indicate that the chronicle is deliberately unfinished. Southampton will continue to live after Oxford and his future cannot be known for certain by the poet.

SONNET 145 – using tetrameters, this verse of the Dark Lady series has seemed so strange that some critics have thought Shakespeare could not have written it. When viewed as the companion to Sonnet 66 upon the reprieve for Southampton, it suddenly comes alive with tremendous power as Oxford concludes that the Queen "saved my life," that is, saved his son, who is the "better part" of him. Both Sonnet 66 and Sonnet 145 are set apart from all the other verses by their unique formats.

THE ERUPTION OF 1608-1609

All publications of authorized versions of Shakespeare plays had ceased after the authorized version of *Hamlet, Prince of Denmark* (Q2) of 1604, the year of Oxford's reported death, until the First Folio of 1623, which included eighteen newly printed plays among the thirty-six printed. In the years 1608-1609, however, there was a sudden burst of unauthorized publications – *King Lear, Richard II* (with the deposition scene for the first time) in 1608, and *Pericles* (which would be kept out of the First Folio) and *Troilus and Cressida* of 1609 – most likely indicating that Southampton was causing these works to be issued along with the Sonnets.

Each of the plays published in 1608-1609 contains information potentially pertinent to Oxford and the story of the Sonnets – a matter for continued study. Included in *Troilus* of 1609 was a strange and remarkable epistle from *A Never Writer to An Ever Reader*, undoubtedly written earlier by Oxford, who accused "the grand possessors" of refusing to publish the other Shakespeare plays. If Oxford died at about this time, rather than in 1604, perhaps Southampton felt the need to prompt Oxford's relatives to release the texts of the plays that they held. In any case, King James went into a panic on August 5, 1609, while on a hunting trip in Southampton's territory, and asked for a special guard to be placed around him – supplied, ironically, by Southampton himself.[27]

---

27.   Akrigg, op. cit., pp. 144-145

THE NARRATIVE POEMS

We inevitably come full circle, back to the narrative poems of "Shakespeare" that include *Venus and Adonis* of 1593, *The Rape of Lucrece* of 1594, *The Phoenix and the Turtle* of 1601 and *A Lover's Complaint* included immediately following the Sonnets in *Q* of 1609. The strong implication of the monument is that Oxford produced all these literary works to support Southampton and to record his identity as a prince. I leave exploration of *A Lover's Complaint* for another time, with the suggestion that it appears to offer another angle on the story of Oxford and Elizabeth, from the vantage point of the Queen herself. Most likely this work, too, is part of an overall plan.

THE SHAKESPEARE MASK

Did Oxford really want to divulge to all his identity as Shakespeare? I think he would have wanted to continue operating behind the mask, at least during his lifetime and in the foreseeable future after his death. The great poetic and dramatic literature issued under the Shakespeare name was not written for his own glory, but primarily for personal and political reasons culminating in the truth that he recorded for posterity in the Sonnets. The irony is that, continuing to the end of his life under the Shakespeare name, Oxford was able to revise many of his works to include a myriad of aspects of his personal story for us – again, nonfiction dressed as fiction. Ultimately, I believe, he hoped that the Sonnets would lift the mask for posterity and, in that sense, set him free.

PAST, PRESENT & FUTURE

Editor Alex McNeil sums up what Oxford may have intended to tell Southampton:

- In my history plays, I wrote of the glories of England's former monarchs.
- My greatest hope, as your father, was that circumstances would permit you to claim your rightful place as Henry IX, succeeding Elizabeth. I always knew that this outcome was not certain, however.
- When circumstances turned out otherwise (as a result of the Cecils, Elizabeth's own state of mind, and finally the 1601 Rebellion), I concluded it was more important to try to save your life, even at the cost of renouncing your claim to the throne. If I can't make you King at the present time, I'll do what I can to make you King in the future, at least on paper.
- And so I leave behind this monument.

OVERVIEW OF THE CHRONICLE

1485: SUCCESSION: Henry Tudor becomes Henry VII and begins Tudor Dynasty

1509: SUCCESSION: Death of Henry VII and Accession of Henry VIII

1533: BIRTH OF ELIZABETH, daughter of Henry VIII and Anne Boleyn

1547: SUCCESSION: Death of Henry VIII and Accession of nine-year-old Edward VI

1553: SUCCESSION: Death of Edward VI and Accession of Mary I

NOVEMBER 1558: SUCCESSION: Death of Mary I and Accession of Princess Elizabeth Tudor, 25, who becomes Queen Elizabeth I of England; she will rule until 1603. Her trusted, longtime supporter William Cecil becomes Principal Secretary; he will be the architect of her reign, engineering the Protestant Reformation, until his death in 1598. In this month, Edward de Vere (1550-1604), Lord Bolbec, enrolls at Cambridge University at age eight.

1562: OXFORD THE FIRST ROYAL WARD
Following the death of the Sixteenth Earl of Oxford, twelve-year-old Edward de Vere becomes the first royal ward of the Queen in the care of William Cecil, chief minister of the Elizabethan reign and Master of the Royal Wards.

1571: OXFORD-CECIL MARRIAGE ALLIANCE
Elizabeth elevates William Cecil from commoner status to Lord Burghley. Oxford, twenty-one, enters the House of Lords. In December he marries Burghley's fifteen-year-old daughter Anne Cecil, with the Queen attending the wedding and lending her support to the marriage.

1573: FIRST "SHAKESPEARE" SONNET
By now Oxford, in his early twenties, has composed the first English sonnet of the reign in the fourteen-line form that will be known later as Shakespearean. Entitled *Love Thy Choice*, it expresses his devotion to Elizabeth and his commitment to serving her as a loyal subject.

THE BATH PROLOGUE

1574: THE LITTLE LOVE-GOD" (two sonnets)

Oxford writes Sonnets 153 & 154 about his visit with Elizabeth and her Court to the City of Bath in August, a few months after the birth of their unacknowledged royal son, who will be raised as Henry Wriothesley, Third Earl of Southampton. Oxford regards the infant son as a "god" on earth or king, who has been "disarmed" by his mother the Virgin Queen:

> The little Love-God lying fast asleep…
> Was sleeping by a Virgin hand disarmed.
> - Sonnet 154, lines 1, 8

1575: BIRTH OF ELIZABETH VERE
Anne Cecil gives birth to her first child, Elizabeth Vere, while Oxford is traveling in France, Germany and Italy. Upon his return next year he will refuse to acknowledge paternity and separate from the marriage for the next six years.

1581: HENRY WRIOTHESLEY A ROYAL WARD
Upon the death of the Second Earl of Southampton, seven-year-old Henry Wriothesley becomes the eighth and final royal ward of the Queen in the custody of William Cecil, Lord Burghley, while Oxford reunites with Anne Cecil.

1586: OXFORD RECEIVES 1,000-POUND GRANT
Edward de Vere receives an annual grant from the Government of 1,000 pounds. To this point he has been the center of the English renaissance of literature and drama, patronizing writers and play companies and writing the early versions of plays which will be revised and begin appearing under the name of "Shakespeare" in 1598.

1588: DEATH OF ANNE CECIL
Anne Cecil dies in June at age thirty-one, leaving behind three daughters: Elizabeth, Bridget and Susan. Her death possibly is a suicide, as will be depicted by Ophelia's fate in *Hamlet*.

1588: DEFEAT OF THE ARMADA
England defeats the Spanish Armada. Celebrating the victory as well as the thirtieth anniversary of Elizabeth's reign, Lord Burghley and his hunchbacked son, Robert Cecil, age twenty-two, look ahead to controlling the succession to her throne.

Introduction

1589: MARRIAGE PROPOSAL
Burghley initiates a proposal for his fourteen-year-old granddaughter, Elizabeth Vere, to marry sixteen-year-old Henry Wriothesley, who will inherit the title Third Earl of Southampton when he reaches his majority. If the Lord Treasurer's royal ward agrees to enter this Cecil alliance, Burghley will lend support for him to succeed Elizabeth. When Henry Wriothesley becomes King Henry IX, his wife will become Queen and, through her, the Cecils will have achieved royal status.

THE FAIR YOUTH SERIES

1590-1600: "LORD OF MY LOVE" (26 sonnets)

THE MARRIAGE ALLIANCE – SONNETS 1 - 17

SONNETS 1-17: 1590-1591
Oxford completes the first seventeen verses to Southampton, coinciding with his son's seventeenth birthday, after urging him to accept the Cecil proposal that he marry fifteen-year-old Elizabeth Vere, his daughter of record (but perhaps not his biological offspring) and Burghley's granddaughter. The opening two lines of the Sonnets, urging Southampton to propagate so that Elizabeth's dynasty of the Tudor Rose won't die with her, announce a dynastic diary:

> From fairest creatures we desire increase,
> That thereby beauty's *Rose* might never die
> - Sonnet 1, lines 1-2

Henry Wriothesley rejects any alliance with the Cecils, however. In the coming years he will become closely allied with another royal ward, Robert Devereux, Second Earl of Essex (1566-1601), and together they will challenge the influence over the Queen wielded by William and Robert Cecil along with their control over the inevitable royal succession.

These sonnets correspond with each of Southampton's birthdays from age 1 in 1575 to age 17 in 1591, so that the "numbers" of the diary comprise "the living record" of him up to now. The next nine "numbers" will correspond with each of his birthdays from Sonnet 18 (age 18 in 1592) up to Sonnet 26 (age 26 in 1600).

THE "SHAKESPEARE" COMMITMENT – SONNETS 18 - 26

SONNET 18: PLEDGE OF SUPPORT: 1592
Now remarried and withdrawn from public life, Oxford continues the dynastic diary with support of his son by the Queen in this golden time, represented as a "Summer's Day" of royal hope. The younger earl is bent on casting his lot with Essex against the Cecils in the endgame of political struggle to control the succession, a project that seems precarious at best. Nonetheless Edward de Vere continues to compile these sonnets as "the living record" of his son for posterity:

> So long as men can breathe or eyes can see,
> So long lives this, and this gives life to thee.
> - Sonnet 18, lines 13-14

SONNET 19: "VENUS AND ADONIS": 1593
Oxford's newborn son by his second wife is christened "Henry" de Vere, the first appearance of that name in the 500-year earldom. A few weeks later he puts forth "William Shakespeare" in print for the first time, with his public dedication of *Venus and Adonis* to Henry Wriothesley, who may have acted as godfather to Henry de Vere in addition to having inspired the published poem, which describes his birth as a "purple

[royal] flower" to Elizabeth (Venus) and Oxford (Adonis). In this sense, Southampton is not only the rightful heir to the throne but also the heir of the poem itself, as set out in the dedication:

> *"But if the first heir of my invention prove deformed, I shall be sorry it had so noble a godfather, and never after ear so barren a land, for fear it yield me still so bad a harvest..."*

SONNET 20: "LUCRECE": 1594
Oxford puts forth "William Shakespeare" for the second time, with his public dedication of *Lucrece* (later entitled *The Rape of Lucrece*) to Henry Wriothesley, pledging his support:

> *"The love I dedicate to your Lordship is without end...What I have done is yours, what I have to do is yours; being part in all I have, devoted yours..."*

Henry Wriothesely becomes Third Earl of Southampton this year, according to his "official" birthday in October, and he gains the highest favor of the Queen, his mother.

SONNET 24: DEATH OF WILLIAM CECIL: 1598
Lord Burghley dies and his little hunchbacked son, Secretary Robert Cecil, assumes power over Elizabeth's government. Southampton marries maid-of-honor Elizabeth Vernon, a cousin of Essex, signifying his total determination to win the power struggle against Secretary Cecil. The poet "Shakespeare" is announced by Francis Meres as the author of popular plays performed at Court and on the public stage. Oxford, who has already linked Southampton to the pen name, thereby links his son to the stage works of "Shakespeare" as well, to increase his support of him.

SONNET 25: THE QUEEN'S DISFAVOR: 1599
Southampton and Essex return in defeat and disgrace from the Irish military campaign and find themselves in extreme disfavor with the Queen, a result that had been the aim of Secretary Cecil in the first place. Two verses as by "Shakespeare," printed in *The Passionate Pilgrim* this year, will reappear in 1609 (in slightly different form) as Sonnets 138 and 144 of the Dark Lady series to Elizabeth. Robert Cecil continues to solidify his control over the Queen while Essex remains under house arrest and Southampton publicly associates himself with the "Shakespeare" works performed on the public stage.

SONNET 26: THE EVE OF THE REBELLION: 1600
Southampton and Essex, still in disfavor, begin plans to remove Robert Cecil from his position of power over the throne and the royal succession. Early the following year, upon the disastrous Essex Rebellion of February 8, 1601, Oxford will conclude his first sequence of private verses to Southampton with Sonnet 26 – having numbered the verses to represent the younger earl's twenty-six birthdays from 1575 to 1600 – by reaffirming his devotion to his royal son as a vassal pledging loyalty and duty to his king:

> Lord of my love, to whom in vassalage
> Thy merit hath my duty strongly knit,
> To thee I send this written ambassage,
> To witness duty, not to show my wit.
> Duty so great...
> - Sonnet 26, lines 1-5

1601-1603: – "MY LOVELY BOY" – (100 Sonnets)

THE PRISON YEARS – SONNETS 27 – 106

"RICHARD II" AT THE GLOBE: FEBRUARY 7, 1601
With Oxford's consent, Southampton arranges for the Lord Chamberlain's Men to perform *Richard II* at the Globe, showing the deposition of an English monarch, to help rouse conspirators of the Rebellion. The play

depicts Richard as a weak king who gives up his crown to Bolinbroke (Henry IV), as they hope the Queen will do. Six months after the Rebellion is crushed, Elizabeth herself will remark: *"I am Richard II, know ye not that?"* – but the author "Shakespeare" will never be called to account for his part in the uprising.

SONNET 27: THE REBELLION: FEBRUARY 8, 1601
The Rebellion against Robert Cecil fails; Essex and Southampton are imprisoned that evening in the Tower of London. Oxford begins a new series of sonnets to his now disgraced royal son, whose image appears to him as "a jewel hung in ghastly night." He will write eighty verses during Southampton's imprisonment and then twenty more until immediately after the Queen's funeral, comprising exactly one hundred verses ending with Sonnet 126.

SONNET 30: OXFORD SUMMONED TO TRIAL: FEBRUARY 10, 1601
The Privy Council summons Oxford among the sixteen earls and nine barons who will sit on the tribunal of peers at the "sessions" or treason trial of Essex and Southampton:

> When to the Sessions of sweet silent thought
> I summon up remembrance of things past…
> - Sonnet 30, lines 1-2

SONNET 33: "MY SUNNE": FEBRUARY 14, 1601
Filled with grief over Southampton's act of treason that has dashed any hope he might gain the throne, Oxford glances back at the birth of his royal son and the refusal of Elizabeth Regina to acknowledge him:

> Even so my Sunne one early morn did shine,
> With all triumphant splendor on my brow,
> But out alack, he was but one hour mine,
> The region cloud hath masked him from me now.
> - Sonnet 33, lines 9-12

SONNET 34: "RANSOM": FEBRUARY 15, 1601
As a member of the jury at the trial, Oxford will have no choice but to condemn his royal son to death; but he is pleading with Elizabeth and Robert Cecil, his brother-in-law, for the ability to pay a form of "ransom" to save Southampton, to whom he writes:

> Nor can thy shame give physic to my grief:
> Though thou repent, yet I have still the loss,
> Th'offender's sorrow lends but weak relief
> To him that bears the strong offence's loss.
> Ah but those tears are pearl which thy love sheeds,
> And they are rich, and ransom all ill deeds.
> - Sonnet 34, lines 9-14

SONNET 35: OXFORD VOWS TO HELP HIS SON: FEBRUARY 16, 1601
Oxford blames himself for having encouraged Southampton's "trespass" or treason by "compare," i.e., by writing the deposition scene of *Richard II* in addition to lending other public support with plays of "Shakespeare" for the public stage. Southampton has committed a "sensual fault" (a riotous, willful crime) against the state; Oxford must be his "adversary" at the trial, by voting to find him guilty of high treason, but will also be his "advocate" by sacrificing himself, to save his son's life and gain his ultimate release along with a royal pardon:

> All men make faults, and even I in this,
> Authorizing thy trespass with compare,
> Myself corrupting salving thy amiss,

> Excusing thy sins more than thy sins are:
> For to thy sensual fault I bring in sense,
> Thy adverse party is thy Advocate,
> And 'gainst myself a lawful plea commence
> - Sonnet 35, lines 5-11

SONNET 38: THE TRIAL: FEBRUARY 19, 1601
Oxford appears at the head of the tribunal sitting in judgment of Essex and Southampton in Westminster Hall. The two earls are found guilty of high treason against the Crown and sentenced to death. In voting to condemn his own son, Oxford performed his political duty as a servant of the state; now he must perform his personal duty as a father and as the vassal of a royal prince.

SONNET 44: EXECUTION OF ESSEX: FEBRUARY 25, 1601
Robert Devereux, Earl of Essex is beheaded at the Tower of London, while Southampton remains in the prison. Robert Cecil is now without any rival in terms of his power behind the throne and his ability to engineer the succession of King James of Scotland. Oxford is forced to work with Cecil to help Southampton.

SONNET 55: "THE LIVING RECORD": MARCH 8, 1601
Anticipating Southampton's execution, Oxford is creating the most intensely sustained poetical sequence the world has known. It will become "the living record" of his son's royal claim for posterity:

> Not marble nor the gilded monument
> Of Princes shall outlive this powerful rhyme…
> Nor *Mars* his sword nor war's quick fire shall burn
> The living record of your memory.
> 'Gainst death and all oblivious enmity
> Shall you pace forth! Your praise shall still find room
> Even in the eyes of all posterity
> That wear this world out to the ending doom.
> - Sonnet 55, lines 1-2, 7-12

Four other conspirators of the Rebellion are executed while Southampton waits.

SONNET 66: REPRIEVE: MARCH 19, 1601
Oxford records his profound emotional reaction to the Queen's sparing Southampton from execution. Behind the scenes, with maneuvering by both Oxford and Robert Cecil, she has commuted Southampton's death sentence to a term of life in prison as a base commoner. Knowing he will be forced to forfeit his son's royal claim, Oxford would prefer to die, but for the fact he would be leaving him alone in the Tower:

> Tir'd with all these, from these would I be gone,
> Save that to die, I leave my love alone.
> - Sonnet 66, lines 13-14

No public explanation for the reprieve is given, nor is any official record made, enabling Cecil to keep the death threat hanging over Southampton until Elizabeth dies and James VI of Scotland succeeds her as James I. Now Oxford must gain a further reduction of the judgment against his son in order to secure his eventual liberation and a royal pardon.

To this point, forty days since Southampton's imprisonment, Oxford has kept pace by writing and compiling forty matching sonnets. In his mind, this anxious period has been akin to the forty days and forty nights of fasting in the wilderness by Jesus (Matthew, 4.2), who tells the Devil: "It is written, Man shall not live by bread alone, but by *every word* that *proceedeth* out of the mouth of God" (Matthew, 4.4.) – a statement to be echoed by "*every word* doth almost tell my name,/ Showing their birth, and where they did *proceed*" in Sonnet 76. Now, having completed the forty verses from Sonnet 27 to Sonnet 66, Oxford is committed to building a "monument" for his son.

SONNETS 76-77: THE "INVENTION": MARCH 29-30, 1601

Here, at what will become the exact midpoint of Sonnets 1-152 and of the 100 verses of Sonnets 27-126, Oxford pauses to describe his "invention" of writing and arranging the Sonnets, which revolves around "all one, ever the same" – Southampton, whose motto is *One for All, All for One*, and Elizabeth, whose motto is *Ever the Same*, along with *Ever*, a glance at himself as Edward de Vere or E.Ver. This "invention" employs "every word" from the "birth" of Southampton in 1574 to where his royal life has managed to "proceed" in the entries of this diary:

> Why write I still all one, ever the same,
> And keep invention in a noted weed,
> That every word doth almost tell my name,
> Showing their birth, and where they did proceed? - Sonnet 76, lines 5-8

Southampton and his "love," or royal blood, remain the constant "argument" of the Sonnets, so that Oxford must keep "dressing old words new" to continue writing about the same thing while avoiding the appearance of relentless repetition:

> O know, sweet love, I always write of you,
> And you and love are still my argument.
> So all my best is dressing old words new,
> Spending again what is already spent
> - Sonnet 76, lines 9-12

He then dedicates "this book" to Southampton:

> And of this book this learning mayst thou taste…
> These offices, so oft as thou wilt look,
> Shall profit thee, and much enrich thy book
> - Sonnet 77, lines 4, 13-14

SONNETS 78-86: SACRIFICE TO "SHAKESPEARE": MARCH 31– APRIL 8, 1601

As Oxford bargains with Cecil behind the scenes, he begins the so-called "Rival Poet" series, recording his need to sacrifice and obliterate his identity as Southampton's father and, thereby as author of the Shakespeare works. His son will live in the Sonnets as King Henry IX:

> Your name from hence immortal life shall have,
> Though I (once gone) to all the world must die
> - Sonnet 81, lines 5-6

He pledges again to build this "monument" to his royal son:

> Your monument shall be my gentle verse,
> Which eyes not yet created shall o'er-read
> And tongues to be your being shall rehearse,
> When all the breathers of this world are dead.
> You still shall live (such virtue hath my Pen)
> Where breath most breathes, even in the mouths of men.
> - Sonnet 81, lines 9-10

SONNET 87: "MISPRISION" OF TREASON: APRIL 1601

Oxford records the bittersweet bargain made for Southampton's life, involving the reduction of his crime from high treason to the "better judgment" of "misprision" of treason. The lesser offense, allowing him to escape execution but requiring life imprisonment, paves the way for his potential release from the Tower and the restoration of his earldom. The "great gift" of his life will continue:

> So thy great gift, upon misprision growing,
> Comes home again, on better judgment making
> - Sonnet 87, lines 11-12

The price to be paid is that Southampton must henceforth give up any claim to the throne:

> Thus have I had thee as a dream doth flatter:
> In sleep a King, but waking no such matter:
> - Sonnet 87, lines 13-14

SONNET 97: FIRST ANNIVERSARY OF REBELLION: FEBRUARY 8, 1602
Oxford records the passing of the first "fleeting year" following the Rebellion of February 8, 1601, when his royal son began his imprisonment.

SONNET 104: SECOND ANNIVERSARY OF REBELLION: FEBRUARY 8, 1603
Oxford records the passing of the second full year since the Rebellion, referring to the "three winters" since 1600, when the hopeful time for Southampton came to an end with Sonnet 26.

SONNET 105: DEATH OF ELIZABETH I: MARCH 24, 1603
Recording the Queen's death, Oxford refers to the fact that he, Elizabeth and Southampton had "never kept seat" or sat on the throne as a royal family. Had he become King Henry IX, their son would have combined the blood of all three within his "one" royal person:

> Which three, till now, never kept seat in one.
> - Sonnet 105, line 14

King James VI of Scotland is proclaimed King James I of England, with Robert Cecil in full control of the royal succession while Southampton remains in the Tower.

ORDER FOR SOUTHAMPTON'S RELEASE: APRIL 5, 1603
According to the bargain made with Oxford and Cecil, and even before leaving Edinburgh to begin his triumphant journey south to London and the English throne, King James sends an order for the liberation of Southampton from the Tower.

SONNET 106: LAST DAY & NIGHT IN PRISON: APRIL 9, 1603
Oxford brings the eighty "prison" verses to a close with Sonnet 106, referring to his poetical diary as "the Chronicle of wasted time." With advance knowledge, referring to the recently deceased Queen as "Ladies dead," he predicts that Southampton will be appointed Captain of the Isle of Wight and made a prestigious Knight of the Garter:

When in the Chronicle of wasted time
I see descriptions of the fairest wights
And beauty making beautiful old rhyme
In praise of Ladies dead and lovely Knights...
- Sonnet 106, lines 1-4

FINAL DAYS OF THE TUDOR DYNASTY – SONNETS 107-126

SONNET 107: LIBERATION OF SOUTHAMPTON: APRIL 10, 1603
Henry Wriothesley emerges from the Tower of London. Oxford, referring to the fact that his son had been

"supposed as forfeit to a confined doom," celebrates his liberation:

> Not mine own fears nor the prophetic soul
> Of the wide world dreaming on things to come
> Can yet the lease of my true love control,
> Supposed as forfeit to a confined doom.
> - Sonnet 107, lines 1-4

He also glances at the recent death of Queen Elizabeth as Diana or Cynthia, goddess of the Moon, who has "endured" her ultimate mortal decay by becoming immortal:

> The mortal Moon hath her eclipse endured...
> - Sonnet 107, line 5

This begins the final twenty sonnets, numbered to correspond with the nineteen days up to and including the Queen's funeral, followed by his farewell to Southampton immediately afterward. In a real sense, Sonnets 107 to 125 represent Oxford's own solemn funeral march for the dying dynasty.

SONNET 120: "YOUR CRIME ... YOUR TRESPASS": APRIL 23, 1603

Oxford sums up the harrowing experience he and his royal son have gone through. Recalling that he "suffered in your crime" of the Rebellion, he acknowledges that he has paid a "fee" for his son's treason or "trespass" to gain a new life for him; now Southampton must pay his own "fee" to "ransom" or liberate Oxford, by seeing to it that this monument of the Sonnets gets into print so it can be preserved for posterity:

> But that your trespass now becomes a fee,
> Mine ransoms yours, and yours must ransom me.
> - Sonnet 120, lines 13-14

SONNET 125: FUNERAL OF ELIZABETH I: APRIL 28, 1603

Oxford records Elizabeth's funeral procession as her body is carried to its temporary tomb in Westminster Abbey, marking the "official" end of the Tudor Rose Dynasty begun by Henry VII in 1485. Making his final "oblation" (sacrificial offering) to Southampton as prince or god on earth, Oxford also records that his son is a "suborned informer" who henceforth must testify against his claim to the throne.

SONNET 126: FAREWELL TO SOUTHAMPTON: APRIL 29, 1603

Oxford bids farewell to his royal son, promising that Nature – once Elizabeth, their sovereign Mistress, but now "sovereign mistress over wrack" – will "render" him King in posterity:

> O Thou my lovely Boy, who in thy power
> Dost hold time's fickle glass, his sickle hour.
> Who hast by waning grown, and therein show'st
> Thy lovers withering, as thy sweet self grow'st:
> If Nature (sovereign mistress over wrack)
> As thou goest onwards still will pluck thee back,
> She keeps thee to this purpose, that her skill
> May time disgrace, and wretched minute kill.
> Yet fear her O thou minion of her pleasure,
> She may detain, but still not keep her treasure!
> Her *Audit* (though delayed) answered must be,
> And her *Quietus* is to render thee.
> ( )
> ( )

THE DARK LADY SERIES

FEBRUARY 8, 1601 – MARCH 24, 1603   "TWO LOVES I HAVE" (26 Sonnets)

SONNET 127: THE REBELLION: FEBRUARY 8, 1601
Oxford begins this separate sequence, focusing on Queen Elizabeth as the Dark Lady, with twenty-six sonnets balancing the twenty-six-sonnet sequence that begins the Fair Youth series. In terms of its time frame as a diary, the Dark Lady Series parallels Southampton's imprisonment until the Queen's death (Sonnets 27-105). This opening verse focuses on Elizabeth's reaction to Southampton's disgrace for having committed high treason in the Rebellion. He was "fair" in the previous time of his life, but Elizabeth's dark imperial frown has turned him to "black" as he faces execution. To Oxford their son remains the Queen's "successive heir" to the throne, but, because of her viewpoint, she and her "beauty" (her royal blood) that he carries are still "slandered" by the shame of bastardy:

> In the old age black was not counted fair,
> Or if it were it bore not beauty's name:
> But now is black beauty's successive heir,
> And Beauty slandered by a bastard shame.
> - Sonnet 127, lines 1-4

SONNET 128: EXECUTION OF ESSEX: FEBRUARY 25, 1601
Oxford records the quip he made in Elizabeth's presence when news of the execution arrived while she was playing on the virginals: "When Jacks go up, heads come down."

SONNET 145: ELIZABETH SPARES SOUTHAMPTON: MARCH 19, 1601
Henry Wriothesley is not only Oxford's son but an extension of his very being, so when the Queen spares the younger earl's life, it amounts to the sparing of Oxford's life as well:

> Straight in her heart did mercy come…
> And saved my life, saying, "Not you."
> - Sonnet 145, lines 5, 14

SONNET 152: DEATH OF ELIZABETH I: MARCH 24, 1603
This is Oxford's final verse of the Dark Lady series to Queen Elizabeth, who has died while leaving their royal son in the Tower, unable to claim his right by blood to the throne:

> And all my honest faith in thee is lost.
> For I have sworn deep oaths of thy deep kindness,
> Oaths of thy love, thy truth, thy constancy,
> And to enlighten thee gave eyes to blindness,
> Or made them swear against the thing they see.
>   For I have sworn thee fair: more perjured eye,
>   To swear against the truth so foul a lie!
> - Sonnet 152, lines 8-14

THE INVENTION

"Dressing Old Words New ... Varying to Other Words"

ELIZABETH TUDOR ELIZABETH I OF ENGLAND	RELATED WORDS OF THE SONNETS
HERSELF	*Dian, Beauty, Fairest Votary, Fortune, Goddess, Heaven, Ladies, Mistress, Moon, Mother, Nature, Phoenix, Princes, Region, Woman, Women*
HER ROYAL "WE"	*We*
HER ROYAL BLOOD	*Beauty, Love*
HER REALM OF ENGLAND	*The World*
HER TUDOR DYNASTY	*Rose*
HER HOUSE OF TUDOR	*House, Mansion, Roof*
HER DWINDLING LIFE	*Time*
HER WITHERING REIGN	*Clock, Decay, Dial, Fade, Hours, Lease*
HER REIGN'S END	*Date, Eclipse*
HER DYNASTY'S END	*Doom, End, Waste, Wasted*
HER ROYAL WILL	*Desire, Pleasure, Will*
HER PREGNANCY	*April, May, Prime*
HER MOTHERHOOD	*Nativity, Creation*
HER REFUSAL TO RECOGNIZE HER SON	*Blind, Deaf, False, Painted, Poor*
HER NEGATIVE VIEW OF HIM	*Blame, Bury, Despise, Disdain, Hate, Kill, Lie, Mourn, Profane, Scorn, Slander, Spite, Spoil, Spot, Stain, Steep, Sully, Weaken, Wound*
HER DARKNESS	*Bare, Barren, Black, Brand, Cloud, Dark, Darkness, Forlorn, Foul, Hidden, Mask, Night, Region Cloud, Shade, Shadow, Shame, Smoke, Sullen, Unseen, Veil*

HENRY WRIOTHESLEY THIRD EARL OF SOUTHAMPTON	RELATED WORDS OF THE SONNETS
HIMSELF	*Adonis, All, Alike, Alone, Hew, Hews, One, Only, Thou, Thy Self, You, Your Self*
AS ROYAL WARD & PRINCE	*Child of State*
AS NEW TUDOR ROSE	*Boy, Bud, Cupid, Flower, Nativity, Little Love-God, Rose*
AS ROYAL HEIR	*Air, Fairest Creatures, God, Hair, Herald, King, Lord, Jewel, Ornament, Prince, Sovereign, Successive Heir, Sunne, Sun*
HIS ROYAL BLOOD	*Love*
HIS BLOOD FROM ELIZABETH	*Beauty*
HIS ROYALTY	*Abundance, Abundant, Beauteous, Beloved, Best, Blessed, Bounty, Bounteous, Bright, Celestial, Clear, Controlling, Crowned, Darling, Dear, Deserts, Divine, Due, Duty, Eternal, Excel, Excellent, Fair, Fame, Fire, Flame, Flourish, Fragrant, Fresh, Full, Gaudy, Gentle, Gilded, Glory, Glorious, Gold, Golden, Grace, Graces, Gracious, Height, High, Holy, Honour, Immortal, Kind, Light, Lovely, Majesty, Merit, Might, Parts, Perfection, Praise, Precious, Pride, Proud, Pure, Purple, Rare, Religious, Rich, Right, Rights, Scope, Shine, Scarlet, Silver, Special, Spirit, Splendor, Strength, Substance, Sum, Sweet, True, Triumphant, Vermillion, Vertue, Virtue, Virtuous, Wealth, Worth, Worthy*
AS OXFORD'S ROYAL SON	*Boy, Child, Mine Own, My Friend, My Love, The Sun, My Sunne*
HIS NEGATIVE STATURE IN ELIZABETH'S EYES	*Bare, Barren, Base, Black, Blot, Canker, Crow, Defect, Disgrace, Expense, Foul, Mud, None, Nothing, Rank Smell, Rotten, Sable, Shame, Shamed, Slander, Stain, Sullen, Sullied, Suspect, Thorns, Ugly, Unfair, Untrimmed, Vice, Vulgar, Wasted, Weakness, Weed, Worst*
HIS CRIME OF TREASON	*Amiss, Crime, Error, Fault, Guilt, Purposed Overthrow, Revolt, Scandal, Sin, Trespass*
HIS POSSIBLE SUCCESSION	*Audit, Render*

Prologue

"THE LITTLE LOVE-GOD"

THE BATH VISIT

Sonnets 153-154

August 1574

1558 - 1573

NOVEMBER 17, 1558: ELIZABETH TUDOR IS QUEEN
Upon the death of her older sister Mary Tudor, Queen Mary I of England, twenty-five-year-old Elizabeth Tudor becomes Queen Elizabeth I. She quickly appoints her longtime supporter William Cecil as Principal Secretary in charge of running the government. Eight-year-old Edward de Vere, the future Seventeenth Earl of Oxford, is enrolled at Cambridge University, while his parents are commanded to attend Court through the first full year of the reign. Presumably Edward will meet the radiant young Queen at her coronation in January or soon afterward.

JANUARY 1559: ROBERT DUDLEY IS THE QUEEN'S LOVER
Elizabeth begins a love affair with Robert Dudley, whom she will create Earl of Leicester in 1564.

SEPTEMBER 1559: DEATH OF DUDLEY'S WIFE
Amy Robsart, wife of Robert Dudley, dies amid rumors she was murdered by her husband.

JULY 1561: RUMORS OF ELIZABETH'S CHILD BY DUDLEY
By now the Queen's affair with Dudley has created a major scandal. As the royal progress begins this summer, Elizabeth is so irritable and pale that the Duchess of Suffolk declares she "looks like one lately come out of childbed." (If so, the Queen's child may be a boy. In 1587 a twenty-six-year-old young man calling himself Arthur Dudley will present himself in Madrid to Francis Englefield, the English secretary to Philip of Spain, and claim to be Elizabeth's son by Leicester. The details of his life story will be so convincing that the King, preparing to launch his Armada against England, will hold him as a pawn to possibly replace Elizabeth on the throne. After the failure of the Spanish invasion in 1588, Arthur Dudley will disappear.)

AUGUST 1561: ELIZABETH VISITS HEDINGHAM
Elizabeth visits Castle Hedingham in Essex, seat of the De Veres, for five days during the royal summer progress.

"It must have been a thrilling experience [for eleven-year-old Edward] to see the young Queen ... She was then twenty-eight, and her beauty and accomplishments made her one of the most striking personalities in Europe at that time ... With her youthful vivacity and freshness, with her love of all English outdoor sports, and with her quick wit and deep learning, she was, in 1561, the very embodiment of that wonderful spirit of nationalism, which, under her stimulus, was to break the power of Spain, and create that glorious wealth of literature that can never grow old or be forgotten. We are not told what entertainments were provided for Her Majesty; but we may be certain that hunting and hawking figured largely in the outdoor program, while in the evenings the guests were no doubt diverted with masques and stage plays [John de Vere had his own acting company]. All this young Edward saw, and must have thought how wonderful it was."

(Ward, 12- 13)

Prologue

AUGUST 1562: DEATH OF JOHN DE VERE
John de Vere, Sixteenth Earl of Oxford, dies after a brief illness and possibly of poison.

SEPTEMBER 3, 1562: OXFORD TO LONDON AS ROYAL WARD
Now twelve, Edward de Vere at becomes the first Royal Ward of Queen Elizabeth and takes up residence in London with his guardian, William Cecil, Master of the Royal Wards. *"On the 3rd day of September came riding out of Essex from the funeral of the Earl of Oxford his father, the young Earl of Oxford, with seven score horse all in black; through London and Chepe and Ludgate, and soto Temple Bar..."* (Machyn: ed. Nichols, Camden Soc. 1848; Ward, 14)

OCTOBER 1562: ELIZABETH NEARS DEATH
At Hampton Court the Queen becomes violently ill (presumably of smallpox), falling unconscious, and the doctors do not expect her to live. As feared, she will leave no undisputed heir, so the Council hurriedly convenes to discuss various claimants, who include Lady Catherine Grey and Henry Hastings, Lord Huntingdon. As Elizabeth regains consciousness, Council members gather round her bed; thinking herself on the point of death, she bluntly tells them to make Dudley the Protector of the Realm with an annual salary of 20,000 pounds. It appears the Queen knows of an heir who is under age and therefore needs a Protector – as in the case of her half-brother Edward VI, who was nine upon Henry VIII's death in 1547, when Edward Seymour became Protector. Significantly, Elizabeth directs the Council to pay Dudley's body servant (who slept in his bedchamber) 500 pounds for life. She will recover within a month, leaving others to ponder the meaning of it all.

1563: OXFORD'S "EXERCISES" AT CECIL HOUSE

7 – 7:30	Dancing	1:00 – 2:00	Cosmography
7:30 – 8:00	Breakfast	2:00 – 3:00	Latin
8:00 – 9:00	French	3:00 – 4:00	French
9:00 – 10:00	Latin	4:00 – 4:30	Exercises with his pen
10:00 – 10:30	Writing and Drawing		
Then Common Prayers, and so to dinner		Then Common Prayers, and so to supper	

(State Papers Domestic, Elizabeth, 26.50; Ward, p. 20)

JUNE 1563: OXFORD'S TUTOR
Lawrence Nowell, Dean of Lichfield, Oxford's tutor at Cecil House, writes to Secretary William Cecil: "I clearly see that my work for the Earl of Oxford cannot be much longer required." Ward: "That a scholar of Lawrence Nowell's attainments should speak thus of his pupil, then aged thirteen and a half, argues a precocity quite out of the ordinary." (Lansdowne MSS, 6.54; Ward, p. 20) Oxford's earlier tutor had been Sir Thomas Smith, the scholar and statesman.

1563: BIRTH OF ROBERT CECIL
William Cecil's second son will become *de facto* Secretary of State at age twenty-seven in 1590 and officially so in 1596, two years before his father's death. He will engineer the succession of King James, in whose reign he will become the First Earl of Salisbury.

REFERENCE EDITION

MAY 1564: OXFORD'S UNCLE PAYS TRIBUTE
Arthur Golding, half-brother of Oxford's mother, is Edward de Vere's receiver for financial affairs and also lives at Cecil House in London. He dedicates *Th'Abridgement of the histories of Trogus Pompeius* to young Oxford: "It is not unknown to others, and I have had experience thereof myself, how earnest a desire your honour hath naturally grafted in you to read, peruse, and communicate with others as well the histories of ancient times, and things done long ago, as also of the present estate of things in our days, and that not without a certain pregnancy of wit and ripeness of understanding…"

AUGUST 10, 1564: CAMBRIDGE UNIVERSITY
Edward de Vere at fourteen receives a BA degree from Cambridge.

1566: BIRTH TO MARY STUART, QUEEN OF SCOTS, OF HER SON JAMES, FUTURE KING JAMES VI OF SCOTLAND AND KING JAMES I OF ENGLAND.

1566: BIRTH OF ROBERT DEVEREUX
Devereux will become a royal ward of the Queen upon his father's death and emerge as Second Earl of Essex, the Queen's great favorite in the 1590s.

SEPTEMBER 6, 1566: OXFORD UNIVERSITY
Edward de Vere at sixteen is created Master of Arts at Oxford.

1567: OVID'S "METAMORPHOSES"
The fifteen books of Ovid's masterpiece, translated from Latin to English, are published under the name of Oxford's uncle, Arthur Golding. *Metamorphoses* will become a pervasive source of the Shakespeare works including the Sonnets.

1567: GRAY'S INN
Oxford is admitted to Gray's Inn for study of law.

JULY 1567: OXFORD KILLS UNDER-COOK
"Thomas Brincknell, an under-cook, was hurt by the Earl of Oxford at Cecil House in the Strand, whereof he died; and by a verdict found *felo-de-se* with running upon a point of a fence sword of the said Earl's." (Murdin, *State Papers*, p. 764; Ward, p. 28) On the jury is Raphael Holinshed, whose *Chronicles* will be a major source of the Shakespeare history plays.

1568: MARY STUART, QUEEN OF SCOTS, ENTERS ENGLAND
She will be a captive of Queen Elizabeth, and the center of many Catholic plots, until her trial in the fall of 1586 and her execution in February 1587.

1569: UNDERDOUNE PAYS TRIBUTE
Poet and translator Thomas Underdoune dedicates his translation from the Greek of *An Aethiopian History* to Oxford, beginning with a warning: "I do not deny but that in many matters, I mean matters of learning, a nobleman ought to have a sight; but to be too much addicted that way, I think it is not good. Now of all knowledge fit for a noble gentleman, I suppose the knowledge of histories is most seeming … For such virtues be in your honour, so haughty courage joined with great skill, such sufficiency in learning, so good in nature and common sense …"

"PAYMENTS MADE BY JOHN HART, CHESTER HERALD, ON BEHALF OF THE EARL OF OXFORD FROM JANUARY 1ST TO SEPTEMBER 30TH, 1569/70"
Items includes black cloth for a cape and riding cloak, doublets, velvet hose, ten pairs of Spanish leather shoes, a rapier, a dagger and girdle, handkerchiefs, a velvet hat, a taffeta hat, two velvet caps, a scarf, two pairs of garters with silver at the ends, a plume of feathers for a hat and so on, plus: "a Geneva Bible gilt, a Chaucer, Plutarch's works in French, with other books and papers … two Italian books … Tully's and Plato's works in folio, with other books, paper and nibs."
(State Papers Domestic, Elizabeth, 42.38; Add., 19.38; Ward, pp 32-38)

Prologue

NOVEMBER 24, 1569: OXFORD REQUESTS MILITARY SERVICE
Nineteen-year-old Oxford, in reaction to the rebellion of Catholic earls in northern England, writes to William Cecil requesting permission to join her Majesty's army: *"And at this time I am bold to desire your favor and friendship that you will suffer me to be employed by your means and help in this service that now is in hand, whereby I shall think myself the most bound unto you of any many in this Court, and hereafter ye shall command me as any of your own. Having no other means whereby to speak with you myself, I am bold to impart my mind in paper, earnestly desiring your Lordship that at this instant (as heretofore you have given me your good word to have me see the wars and services in strange and foreign places, sith you could not then obtain me license of the Queen's Majesty) now you will do me so much honor as that by your purchase of my license I may be called to the service of my Prince and country, as at this present troublous time a number are...."*

DECEMBER 1569: SECOND EARL OF SOUTHAMPTON QUESTIONED
Henry Wriothesley, Second Earl of Southampton (1545-1581) and his father-in-law Anthony Browne, Viscount Montague, are in trouble with the Crown. Earlier this year the government learned they had been associated with the Northern Rebellion of Catholic earls and their plans to depose Elizabeth. Now, upon the failure of the rising, Southampton and Montague attempt to flee England; but contrary winds force their ship back. They are greeted by orders from the Queen to come to Court forthwith to explain their actions.

MARCH 30, 1570: OXFORD SERVES IN MILITARY UNDER SUSSEX
William Cecil writes to the Receiver-General of the Court of Wards and Liveries: "As the Queen's Majesty sendeth at this present the Earl of Oxford into the north parts to remain with my Lord of Sussex, and to be employed there in Her Majesty's service..."

MAY 1570: THE POPE EXCOMMUNICATES ELIZABETH
A copy of the Bull of Pius V, excommunicating Elizabeth, is pinned on the door of the Bishop of London's house. The Pope had ordered that Catholic subjects should no longer obey her.

JUNE 1570: SOUTHAMPTON ARRESTED.
The Privy Council orders Henry Wriothesley, Second Earl of Southampton, age twenty-six, to be arrested and confined. The Council received information that Southampton, a Catholic, had been openly questioning whether he should remain loyal to Elizabeth or transfer his allegiance to Spain. In the following month he will be taken from a sheriff's house and placed in the custody of William More of Losely; and in November he will be released.

FEBRUARY 25, 1571: CECIL RAISED TO LORD BURGHLEY
Queen Elizabeth raises William Cecil to the peerage as Baron of Burghley. One result is that his daughter Anne Cecil, fourteen, is eligible to marry a nobleman, i.e., to enter into an arranged marriage with Edward de Vere, Earl of Oxford.

APRIL 2, 1571: OXFORD ENTERS HOUSE OF LORDS
Queen Elizabeth opens Parliament in State. After attending a service in Westminster Abbey, she is conducted to the House of Lords with her train borne by Edward de Vere, Earl of Oxford, the hereditary Lord Great Chamberlain of England who takes precedence above all earls.

1571: PARLIAMENT PASSES SUCCESSION ACT
Parliament passes an Act changing the previous language from "lawful" to "natural" in decreeing that no one "during the Queen's life should, by any book written or printed, expressly affirm that any person is, or ought to be, Heir or Successor to the Queen, except the same be *the Natural issue of Her Majesty's Body."* (Camden) This law means Elizabeth can have a illegitimate child who, although born out of wedlock, can nonetheless be named as her heir. (The phrase *"natural issue"* caused much gossip and provoked "lewd"

jests, Camden writes, "forasmuch as the Lawyers term those Children 'natural' who are gotten out of Wedlock, whom nature alone, and not the honesty of Wedlock hath begotten," as opposed to "those they call 'Lawful, according to the ordinary form of the Common Law of England, which are lawfully procreated of the body." As a young man in 1571, Camden recalls, he heard people "often-times say that the word ['natural'] was inserted into the Act of purpose by Leicester, that he might one day obtrude upon the English some bastard of his, for the Queen's natural issue.")

MAY 1571: OXFORD VICTORIOUS WITH THE SPEAR
At Westminster before the Queen's Majesty is held "a solemn joust at the tilt, tournay, and barriers," in which the challengers "all did very valiantly" and "the chief honour was given to the Earl of Oxford." A contemporary writes of Oxford's livery (as the Red Knight) that it was "crimson velvet, very costly," and noted that there is "no man of life and agility in every respect in the Court but the Earl of Oxford." A tribute in Latin verses describes him competing with "fiery energy" as he "controls his foaming steed with a light rein, and armed with a long spear rides to the encounter…Bravo, valiant youth!"

JULY 28, 1571: OXFORD ENGAGED TO ANNE CECIL
"The Earl of Oxford hath gotten him a wife," writes Lord St. John to the Earl of Rutland in Paris, "or at the least a wife hath caught him. This is Mistress Anne Cecil, whereunto the Queen hath given her consent, and the which hath caused great weeping, wailing and sorrowful cheer of those that had hoped to have that golden day." (Ward, 62) William Cecil sends news of the engagement to Rutland, claiming it came from "a purposed determination in my Lord of Oxford to marry with my daughter" while he himself had "never meant to seek it nor hoped of it." But now "the matter is determined betwixt my Lord of Oxford and me" and "I confess to your Lordship I do honor him so dearly from my heart as I do my own son." Cecil writes that Oxford has "much more in him of understanding than any stranger to him would think" and that he himself takes comfort in the earl's "wit and knowledge grown by good observation."

SEPTEMBER 1571: RIDOLPHI PLOT
The government learns the full scope of the Ridolfi Plot, named after the Florentine banker who hatched the scheme. The conspiracy, afoot for the past year, involves plans for the Duke of Norfolk to raise an English Catholic army and gain the release Mary Queen of Scots. With the aid of a Spanish invasion force, the conspirators would capture London and put Mary on the throne in place of Elizabeth, who would be killed.

SEPTEMBER 21, 1571: MARRIAGE POSTPONED
"They say the Queen will be at my Lord of Burghley's house beside Waltham on Sunday next," writes Hugh Fitz-William, "where my Lord of Oxford shall marry Mistress Anne Cecil his daughter." Elizabeth, on progress with her Court, reaches Burghley's country house Theobalds, but it appears the wedding has been postponed. (Ward, 63)

OCTOBER 1571: SOUTHAMPTON IN THE TOWER
The Bishop of Ross, under arrest for his role in the Ridolphi Plot, tells the government about a previous meeting with Henry Wriothesley, Second Earl of Southampton and how the Catholic earl questioned his ability to remain loyal to Elizabeth. The Queen orders him arrested and sent to the Tower of London. (He will be imprisoned for a year and a half until May 1573.)

NOVEMBER 1571: NORFOLK ESCAPE PLAN
Oxford plans to rescue Norfolk from the Tower and help him flee England, but fails to carry out the scheme.

DECEMBER 19, 1571: WEDDING OF OXFORD AND ANNE CECIL
Edward de Vere, twenty-one, and Anne Cecil, fifteen, are married at Westminster Abbey with Elizabeth attending. Following the wedding is a great feast at Cecil House, where French ambassador Fenelon holds a long discussion with Leicester about the French Match involving the Queen's proposed marriage to the Duc d'Anjou.

5 JANUARY 1572: OXFORD'S LATIN DEDICATION TO "THE COURTIER"
Twenty-one-year-old Edward deVere writes a prefatory Latin letter for a translation from Italian into Latin by his former tutor, Bartholomew Clerke, of *Il Cortegiano* or *The Courtier*, originally published in Venice in 1528. Oxford causes this translation to be published after obtaining Queen Elizabeth's support and patronage for it. His magnificent homage to her at the end of the preface suggests that the book's initial impulse came from the Queen herself and speaks of a close relationship between Oxford and his sovereign, testifying to a shared interest in literature and Elizabeth's willingness to allow him unusual freedom in this respect. *The Courtier* will be a principal inspiration behind the character of the Prince of Denmark in the play *Hamlet* by William Shakespeare.

APPENDIX: Oxford's letter for *The Courtier* is presented with words, phrases and themes to appear in SHAKE-SPEARES SONNETS of 1609 along with examples.

MAY 8, 1572: PARLIAMENT OPENS
Amid an outbreak of plague, Elizabeth travels by coach through the park of St. James with her Nobles and Prelates and other Gentlemen and Ladies. At Whitehall she puts on "her robes and a diadem of gold with rich stones and jewels on her head," then walks with the entourage through the chambers to the Hall and finally to the Water Gate bridge, where "Her Highness took her barge and was rowed to the King's Bridge at Westminster," where her coach is "ready with all her nobles and bishops in their robes on horseback, all men in order placed ... Next to her Majestie road th'Erle of Kent with the cape of maintenance and th'Erle of Rutland bearing the sword next before. Then th'Erle of Oxford, Lord Great Chamberlain of England."
- (Herald's account; BL Add.5758, copy)

JULY 1572: HAVERING
During Elizabeth's royal progress, Oxford accompanies her to the vast estate Havering of the Bowre. "When the Queen was here in 1572, it was the property of her Lord High Chamberlain, Edward deVere, whose first lady was Anne, daughter of the great Burghley." (Morant's *History of Essex*) The thousand-acre park commands extensive views of Essex, Hertfordshire, Kent, Middlesex and Surrey. Visitors can look out at the Thames, with its ships continually passing by. Havering was a retiring place for Saxon kings, particularly Edward the Confessor. The Rev. Severne A. Majendie, in his *Account of the Family of the de Veres*, mentions Elizabeth's visit as July 19-20, 1572, adding that Oxford "doubtless entertained his Queen magnificently." It appears, however, that he does not now have legal title to Havering.

AUGUST 18, 1572: WARWICK CASTLE
Oxford despises his father-in-law's tactics against Norfolk but adheres to the Lord Treasurer's basic policies; loyalty to the Queen requires allegiance to Burghley as well. For better or worse, Cecil is committed to stamping out Catholicism in England; and given this grinding purpose, few doubt that war with France or Spain (or both) is inevitable. With that prospect in mind, Oxford stages a full-scale "military battle" for the royal progress at Warwickshire. Constructed are two forts with men acting as soldiers in arms and "some others appointed to cast out fireworks as squibs and balls of fire." The highly convincing sights and sounds of ferocious military battle prove to be live theater at its extravagant best.

SEPTEMBER 1572: OXFORD'S LETTER: ST. BARTHOLOMEW'S DAY MASSACRE
When Elizabeth and her Court return to London, they learn the full scope of the terrible massacre of Protestants in France that began in Paris on August 24, 1572. The slaughter took place amid the festival of St. Bartholomew's Day; during a wedding that evening, Admiral Coligny and 10,000 fellow Huguenots were slain; but the insane massacre spread into the provinces until as many as 100,000 lost their lives.

APPENDIX: The letter from twenty-two-year-old Oxford to his father-in-law, Lord Treasurer Burghley, is reprinted with words or phrases that will appear decades later in SHAKE-SPEARES SONNETS of 1609.

SEPTEMBER 22, 1572: OXFORD REQUESTS NEW MILITARY SERVICE
Edward de Vere again writes to Burghley, expressing his desire "to show myself dutiful" in some military capacity: *"If there were any service to be done abroad, I had rather serve there than at home where some honor were to be got. If there be any setting forth to sea, to which service I bear most affection, I shall desire your Lordship to give me and get me that favor and credit, that I might make one. Which if there be no such intention, then I shall be most willing to be employed on the sea coasts, to be in a readiness with my countrymen against any invasion."*

Oxford gains no such opportunity; Elizabeth is keeping him close at Court. He has ignored his young wife, apparently failing to consummate their marriage. Amid the emotional atmosphere following the Bartholomew's Massacre, the Queen is faced with one of the crucial decisions of her reign. To prevent France and Spain from joining forces, she must make both nations believe she will enter an alliance with France by marriage. The idea of a French Match will provoke the most vehement criticism upon her at home; the thought she might marry young Alençon will send the Court into turmoil. The Duke, nineteen years younger, is a Catholic and would rule alongside her. If she gave birth, their offspring would become England's next monarch.

OCTOBER 9, 1572: DYER TO HATTON
Christopher Hatton seeks advice from Edward Dyer about how to compete with Oxford for Elizabeth's affections. Dyer replies in an extraordinarily candid letter, giving an intimate (but far from flattering) view of the Queen: *"First of all, you must consider with whom you have to deal and what we be towards her; who though **she do descend very much in her sex as a woman**, yet we may not forget her place and the nature of it as our Sovereign."* With Machiavellian calculation, Dyer advises Hatton to never disagree with the Queen; instead, if he says something Elizabeth doesn't like, it would be best *"to change your course suddenly into another more agreeable to her Majesty."*

"The best and soundest way in mine opinion is to put on another mind ... to use your suits towards her Majesty in words, behavior and deeds; to acknowledge your duty, declaring the reverence which in heart you bear, and never seem deeply to condemn her frailties, but rather joyfully to commend such things as should be in her, as though they were in her indeed; hating my Lord Ctm [Oxford] in the Queen's understanding for affection's sake, and blaming him openly for seeking the Queen's favor." Dyer reminds Hatton of how Elizabeth had seduced him: *"For though in the beginning, **when her Majesty sought you, after her good manner, she did bear with rugged dealing of yours until she had what she fancied.** Yet now, after satiety and fullness, it will rather hurt than help you. Whereas, behaving yourself as I said before, your place shall keep you in worship, your presence in favor, your followers will stand to you. At least you shall have no bold enemies, and you shall dwell in the ways to take all advantage wisely, and honestly to serve your turn at times."*

He again warns Hatton about Oxford: *"Marry thus much I would advise you to remember that you use no words of disgrace or reproach towards him to any; that he, being the less provoked, may sleep, thinking all safe, while you do awake and attend your advantages."*

1572-1573: ELIZABETH WOOS OXFORD
The rumor is (or will be, in 1587) that Elizabeth attempted to seduce Oxford without success foreshadows the story of *Venus and Adonis* (1593) by William Shakespeare: *"The Queen wooed the Earl of Oxford, but he would not fall in."*

1573: OXFORD'S PREFACE TO "CARDANUS COMFORTE"
Edward de Vere pays for publication of Thomas Bedingfield's translation from Latin into English of *Cardanus Comforte* by Girolamo Castellione Cardano, published originally in Venice in 1542. The book will be recognized as having played a role in inspiring the themes of Hamlet's soliloquies. Oxford contributed a prefatory letter followed by a poem. The letter contains this remarkable foreshadowing of his promise in the Sonnets to build a "monument" for Southampton:

Prologue

"Again we see if our friends be dead, we cannot show or declare our affection more than by erecting them of *Tombs*: Whereby when they be dead in deed, yet *make we them live as it were again* through their *monument*, but with me behold it happeneth far better, for in your lifetime I shall erect you such a *monument,* that as I say (in) your lifetime you shall see how noble a shadow of your virtuous life, shall hereafter remain when you are dead and gone. And in your lifetime again I say, I shall give you that *monument* and remembrance of your life, whereby I may declare my good will though with your ill will as yet that I do bear in your life."

APPENDIX: The letter is reprinted, with highlighted words and phrases to appear later in the Sonnets of 1609.

EARLY "SHAKESPEAREAN" SONNET

By Edward de Vere
Earl of Oxford

1571-1573

"The so-called 'Shakespeare sonnet,' we are told by William Sharp in his Sonnets of this Century *[19th century], possesses 'a capability of impressiveness unsurpassed by any sonnet of Dante or Milton.' He points out, however, that when Shakespeare used this form of sonnet in the last years of the sixteenth century [1590-1603], he was using a form 'made thoroughly ready for his use by Samuel Daniel and Michael Drayton.' Now, as Daniel was twelve years, and Drayton thirteen years younger than Edward de Vere, [who] was publishing poetry at a relatively early age, it is clear that his lyrics come before either of the other two men…"*

"This, then, may be regarded as the first 'Shakespeare' sonnet [i.e., the first recorded sonnet by the man who would become Shakespeare]. *It is the only sonnet in the collection of Edward de Vere's poems, and it is composed in the only form employed by Shakespeare, although other sonneteers were then experimenting upon other forms. It is obviously one of his earliest efforts…"*
- J. Thomas Looney, 1920, "'Shakespeare' Identified," 386-387

"The year [1571] *that he came of age was the beginning of the young Earl's heyday. High in the Queen's favor, he was to be for the next ten years fortunate in almost all he undertook. Of course there were minor troubles and anxieties, even violent emotional crises, but during the 1570s he reached a dazzling peak of human eminence and of human accomplishment as well. He himself recorded candidly, as was his wont, the relationship in which he stood to the Queen during those early years, in a sonnet written in a form which he was to make familiar and beloved* [as 'Shakespeare']. *It was entitled* Love Thy Choice, *and was signed with his name."*
- Dorothy & Charlton Ogburn, 1952, "This Star of England,"33

"Consider the following sonnet in the Shakespearean form, entitled Love Thy Choice *and signed 'Earle of Oxenforde,' in which the poet puts a series of questions to himself.* ['Above the rest in Court **who gave thee grace**?' – line 7] *Who in Elizabeth's Court could have given the 17th Earl of Oxford grace? Or who would he have said had done so? I can hardly imagine anyone but Elizabeth.* ["Who made thee strive in honor to be best?" – line 8] *What other lady of the Court would have made him* **strive in honor to be best***?"*
- Charlton Ogburn Jr, 1984, 1992, "The Mysterious William Shakespeare," 512-513

Prologue

OXFORD SONNET FOR

QUEEN ELIZABETH

Love Thy Choice

1571 – 1573

This sonnet by Edward de Vere, Earl of Oxford, written in his early twenties when he had newly arrived at Court (or perhaps earlier), consists of a series of questions to himself about the one who is the center of his universe. The answer, of course, is that all his love and devotion at this time is directed to his sovereign mistress, Queen Elizabeth I of England. The words and themes of this early "Shakespearean" sonnet will reappear in the private verses to be published in 1609, five years after Oxford's death, entitled SHAKE-SPEARES SONNETS. The signature phrase "constant truth" will be repeated in Sonnet 152 of the Dark Lady series as "thy love, thy truth, thy constancy."

1. Who taught thee first to sigh, alas, my heart?
2. Who taught thy tongue the woeful words of plaint?
3. Who filled your eyes with tears of bitter smart?
4. Who gave thee grief and made thy joys to faint?

5. Who first did paint with colors pale thy face?
6. Who first did break thy sleeps of quiet rest?
7. Above the rest in Court who gave thee grace?
8. Who made thee strive in honor to be best?

9. In constant truth to bide so firm and sure,
10. To scorn the world regarding but thy friends?
11. With patient mind each passion to endure,
12. In one desire to settle to the end?

13. Love then thy choice wherein such choice thou bind,
14. As nought but death may ever change thy mind.

- *Earle of Oxenforde*

"Love Thy Choice"

By Edward deVere

"My Lord of Oxford is lately grown into great credit, for the Queen's Majesty delighteth more in his personage and his dancing and his valiantness than any other ... At all these love matters my Lord Treasurer [William Cecil, Lord Burghley] *winketh, and will not meddle in any way."*
- May 11, 1573: Gilbert Talbot, from the Royal Court

1 WHO TAUGHT THEE FIRST TO SIGH, ALAS, MY HEART?
Oxford, officially arriving at Court in April 1571 at age twenty-one, has rapidly acceded to the highest favor of the Queen; by May 1573 there are rumors that he and Elizabeth are lovers. He begins this sonnet by asking his heart who taught it to sigh or lament, the answer being Elizabeth. The Dark Lady series (Sonnets 127-152) to the Queen will be written three decades later in 1601-1603, while Southampton is a prisoner in the Tower, and when Oxford, though remaining his sovereign's devoted servant, has turned bitterly against her:

> *Who taught thee* how to make me love thee more,
> The more I hear and see just cause of hate?
> - Oxford to Elizabeth in the Dark Lady series, Sonnet 150, line 9

WHO = Elizabeth; "*Who* will believe my verse in time to come" – Sonnet 17, line 1; "*Who* is it that says most, which can say more" – Sonnet 84, line 1; **FIRST** = "Since *first* I saw you fresh, which yet are green" – Sonnet 104, line 8; "Even as when *first* I hallowed thy fair name" – Sonnet 108, line 8; **SIGH** = "I *sigh* the lack of many a thing I sought" – Sonnet 30, line 3; "Or *heart in love with sighs* himself doth smother" – Sonnet 47, line 4; **ALAS** = alack; "But out, *alack*, he was but one hour mine" – Sonnet 33.11; **MY HEART** = to Queen Elizabeth in the Dark Lady series, when their son, Southampton, is in prison: "Beshrew that *heart* that makes *my heart* to groan" – Sonnet 133, line 1; "Prison *my heart* in thy steel bosom's ward,/ But then my friend's *heart* let *my poor heart* bail;/ Whoe'er keeps me, let *my heart* be his guard" – Sonnet 133, lines 9-11; "O call me not to justify the wrong/ That thy unkindness lays upon my heart" – Sonnet 139, lines 1-2; "In faith I do not love thee with mine eyes,/ For they in thee a thousand errors note,/ But 'tis *my heart* that loves what they despise,/ Who in despite of view is pleased to dote" – Sonnet 141, lines 1-4

2 WHO TAUGHT THY TONGUE THE WOEFUL WORDS OF PLAINT?
Oxford asks his heart another rhetorical question, the answer again being Elizabeth, i.e., it was the Queen who "taught" or inspired him to utter sorrowful words.

> Was it his spirit, by spirits *taught* to write
> Above a mortal pitch, that struck me dead?
> - Sonnet 86, lines 5-6
> (*His Spirit* = that of the pen name "Shakespeare")

> And that your love *taught* it this alchemy
> - Sonnet 114, line 4

THY TONGUE = (who taught) my voice or speech; my manner of writing; "And art made *tongue*-tied by authority" – Sonnet 66, line 9; to Southampton: "Be absent from thy walks, and in *my tongue*/ Thy sweet beloved name no more shall dwell" – Sonnet 89, lines 9-10; To Elizabeth: "Wound me not with thine eye but with *thy tongue*" – Sonnet 139.3; "Be wise as thou art cruel, do not press/ My *tongue*-tied patience with too much disdain" – Sonnet 140, lines 1-2; **WOEFUL** = "And weep afresh love's long-since cancelled *woe*" – Sonnet 30, line 7; "O that our night of *woe* might have rememb'red" – Sonnet 120, line 9; "But when she saw my *woeful* state" – Sonnet 145, line 4; **WORDS** = "So all my best is dressing old *words* new" – Sonnet 76, line 11; "Fair, kind, and true, varying to other *words*" – Sonnet 105, line 10; to Elizabeth: "Lest sorrow lend me *words*, and *words* express/ The manner of my pity-wanting pain" – Sonnet 140, lines 3-4; **OF PLAINT** = of complaint and/or lamentation, sorrow; "From off a hill whose concave womb reworded/ A *plaintful* story from a sist'ring vale" – *A Lover's Complaint*, lines 1-2, published with the Sonnets in the Quarto of 1609

3 WHO FILLED YOUR EYES WITH TEARS OF BITTER SMART?
FILLED = "Who will believe my verse in time to come/ If it were *filled* with your most high deserts?" – Sonnet 17, lines 1-2; "But when your countenance *filled* up his line" – Sonnet 86, line 13; "Ay *fill* it *full* with wills" – Sonnet 136, line 6; "Sometime all *full* with feasting on your sight" – Sonnet 75, line 9; **FILL YOUR EYES** = "So love be thou, although today *fill*/ Thy hungry *eyes*, even till they wink with *fullness*" – Sonnet 56, lines 5-6; **YOUR EYES** = "If I could write the beauty of *your eyes*" – Sonnet 17, line 5; of Elizabeth: "Therefore *my Mistress' eyes* are Raven black,/ Her eyes so suited, and they mourners seem" – Sonnet 127, lines 9-10; "*My Mistress' eyes* are nothing like the Sunne" – Sonnet 130, line 1; to Elizabeth: "*Thine eyes* I love, and they as pitying me" – Sonnet 132, line 1; "Whom *thine eyes* woo as mine importune thee" – Sonnet 142, line 10; **EYES** = "Can make you live yourself in *eyes* of men" – Sonnet 16, line 12; "When in disgrace with Fortune and men's *eyes*" – Sonnet 29, line 1; "When most I wink, then do my *eyes* best see" – Sonnet 43, line 1; "When you entombed in men's *eyes* shall lie" – Sonnet 81, line 8; "O me! What *eyes* hath love put in my head" – Sonnet 148, line 1; "And to enlighten thee gave *eyes* to blindness" – Sonnet 152, line 11; **TEARS** = "How many a holy and obsequious *tear*/ Hath dear religious love stol'n from mine *eye*" – Sonnet 31, lines 5-6; "O how can love's *eye* be true/ That is so vexed with watching and with *tears*" – Sonnet 148.10; **BITTER** = "Nor think the *bitterness* of absence sour" – Sonnet 57, line 7; "No *bitterness* that I will *bitter* think" – Sonnet 111, line 11; "To *bitter* sauces did I frame my feeding" – Sonnet 118, line 6; **SMART** = keen pain, as in "But is't not cruel that she should feel the *smart* of this?" – *Henry VIII*, 2.1.166

4 WHO GAVE THEE GRIEF AND MADE THY JOYS TO FAINT?
GAVE = "Look whom she best endowed, she *gave* thee more" – Sonnet 11, line 11; "Thy self thou *gav'st*, thy own worth then not knowing,/ Or me, to whom thou *gav'st* it, else mistaking" = Sonnet 87, lines 9-10; **GRIEF** = "And yet love knows it is a greater *grief*" – Sonnet 40, line 11; "That thou hast her, it is not all my *grief*" – Sonnet 42, line 1; **JOYS** = "Unlooked-for *joy* in that I honor most" – Sonnet 25, line 4; "Sweets with sweets war not, *joy* delights in *joy*" – Sonnet 8, line 2; **FAINT** = "O how I *faint* when I of you do write" – Sonnet 80, line 1

5 WHO FIRST DID PAINT WITH COLOURS PALE THY FACE?
FIRST = repeated from line 1 and again in line 6; **PAINT/FACE** = "A Woman's *face* with nature's own hand *painted*" – Sonnet 20, line 1; **PAINT** = "Stirred by a *painted* beauty to his verse" – Sonnet 21, line 2; "And you in *Grecian* tires are *painted* new" – Sonnet 53, line 8; "*Painting* my age with beauty of thy days" – Sonnet 62, line 14; "Why should false painting imitate his cheek?" – Sonnet 67, line 5; "I never saw that you did painting need,/ And therefore to your fair no painting set" – Sonnet 83, lines 1-2; "*Painting* thy outward walls so costly gay" – Sonnet 146, line 4; **COLOURS** = "Truth needs no *colour*, with his *colour* fixed" – Sonnet 101, line 6; **PALE** = "That leaves look *pale*, dreading the Winter's near" – Sonnet 97, line 14; **FACE** = echoing the "face-royal," the visage of a king or queen (the visage stamped on the coin called a 'royal'); "Look in thy glass and tell the *face* thou viewest,/ Now is the time that *face* should form an other" – Sonnet 3, lines 1-2; "Such heavenly touches ne'er touched earthly *faces*" – Sonnet 17, line 8; "So love's *face*/ May still seem love to me" – Sonnet 93, lines 2-3; "Not following that which flies before her *face*" – Sonnet 143, line 7

6 WHO FIRST DID BREAK THY SLEEPS OF QUIET REST?

FIRST = supremely; originally; during the earliest time period; repeated from lines 1 and 5; "Since *first* I saw you fresh, which yet are green" – Sonnet 104, line 8; **BREAK** = "'Tis not enough that through the cloud thou *break*" – Sonnet 34, line 5; to Elizabeth: "But why of two oaths' (to me and to our royal son) breach do I accuse thee/ When I *break* twenty?" – Sonnet 152, lines 5-6; **SLEEPS** = "Cupid laid by his brand and fell *asleep*" – Sonnet 153, line 1; "The little Love-God lying once *asleep*/ … Was *sleeping* by a Virgin hand disarmed" – Sonnet 154, lines 1, 8; "Thus have I had thee as a dream doth flatter,/ In *sleep* a King, but waking no such matter" – Sonnet 87, lines 13-14; **QUIET** = "For thee, and for my self, no *quiet* find" – Sonnet 27, line 14; **REST** = repose; "That am debarred the benefit of *rest*" – Sonnet 28, line 2; "Rise, *resty* Muse!" – Sonnet 100, line 9

7 ABOVE THE REST IN COURT WHO GAVE THEE GRACE?
Only Her Grace, Queen Elizabeth, could confer "grace" upon him; **ABOVE THE REST** =

> Wherein it finds a joy *above the rest*
> - Sonnet 91, line 6

ABOVE = "Was it his (Shakespeare's) spirit, by spirits taught to write/ *Above* a mortal pitch, that struck me dead?" – Sonnet 86, lines 5-6; "But by all *above*,/ These blenches gave my heart another youth" – Sonnet 110, lines 6-7; "Which shall *above* that idle rank remain" – Sonnet 122, line 3; **THE REST** = playing on "rest" in the previous line, but here meaning that which is left, the remainder; "Crowning the present, doubting of *the rest*" – Sonnet 115, line 12; "*The rest* is silence" – Hamlet, 5.2.365; **IN COURT** = the Royal Court of Elizabeth I of England, where Edward deVere, 17th Earl of Oxford, now in his early twenties, is hereditary Lord Great Chamberlain, highest-ranking earl and rising to the top as the Queen's favorite; "Which late her noble suit *in Court* did shun" – A Lover's Complaint, line 234; "A gentler heart did never sway *in Court*" – 1 Henry VI, 3.2.136; "This constant A. [Avisa = Elizabeth] above the rest" - Willobie His Avisa, anonymous, 1594, "The Author's Conclusion," stanza 2, line 3

The Earl of Oxford's livery was crimson velvet, very costly; he himself, and the furniture, was in some more colours, yet he was the Red Knight … There is no man of life and agility in every respect in the Court but the Earl of Oxford. - George Delves to Earl of Rutland, June 1571 (Rutland MSS)

GAVE = repeated from line 4; **GRACE** = the royal grace of Elizabeth, which she conferred upon her favored courtiers and other subjects; to Southampton as royal prince: "Be as thy presence is, *gracious* and kind" – Sonnet 10, line 11; "If I could write the beauty of your eyes,/ And in fresh numbers number all your graces" – Sonnet 17, line 6; to Southampton when he is in the Tower: "Ah wherefore with infection should he live,/ And with his presence *grace* impiety?" – Sonnet 67, lines 1-2; "And *given grace a double majesty*/ … And arts with thy sweet *graces graced* be" – Sonnet 78, lines 8, 12; "My verse alone had all thy gentle *grace*,/ But now my *gracious* numbers are decayed" – Sonnet 79, lines 2-3; "They rightly do inherit heaven's (Elizabeth's) *graces*" – Sonnet 94, line 5; "Some say thy *grace* is youth and gentle sport;/ Both *grace* and faults are loved of more and less;/ Thou mak'st faults *graces* that to thee resort./ As on the finger of a throned Queen" – Sonnet 96, lines 2-5; **GAVE THEE GRACE** = to Elizabeth: "O let it then as well beseem thy heart/ To mourn for me, since mourning *doth thee grace*" – Sonnet 132, lines 10-11

8 WHO MADE THEE STRIVE IN HONOUR TO BE BEST?
WHO = eighth and final usage of this word in as many lines; "*Who* is it that says most, which can say more" – Sonnet 84, line 1; **MADE** = past tense of *make*, one of the most frequently used words in the Shakespeare works; "*Make* some sweet vial" – Sonnet 6, line 3; "*Make* thee an other self for love of me" – Sonnet 10, line 13; "I *make* my love engrafted to this store" – Sonnet 37, line 8; "My life, being *made* of four (elements)" – Sonnet 45, line 7; "To *make me* tongue-tied speaking of your fame" – Sonnet 80, line 4; "Thou *mak'st* faults graces" – Sonnet 96, line 4; "To *make him much outlive* a gilded tomb" – Sonnet 101, line 11; "*Made* old offences of affections new" – Sonnet 110, line 4; "My most true mind thus *maketh* mine untrue" – Sonnet 113, line 14; "That better is by evil still *made* better" – Sonnet 119, line 10; to/of Elizabeth: "When my love swears that she is *made* of truth" – Sonnet 138, line 1; "That she that *makes me sin* awards me pain" –

Sonnet 141, line 14; "And to enlighten thee gave eyes to blindness,/ Or made them swear against the thing they see" – Sonnet 152, lines 11-2; **BEST** = "Look what is *best*, that *best* I wish in thee" – Sonnet 37, line 13; "So all my *best* is dressing old words new" – Sonnet 76, line 11; "All these I better in one general best" – Sonnet 91, line 8; to/of Elizabeth: "Although she knows my days are past the *best*" – Sonnet 138, line 6; "What merit do I in my self respect/ That is so proud thy service to despise,/ When all my *best* doth worship thy defect,/ Commanded by the motion of thine eyes?" – Sonnet 149, lines 9-12

9 IN CONSTANT TRUTH TO BIDE SO FIRM AND SURE,
CONSTANT TRUTH = Oxford's motto *Nothing Truer than Truth*

> Kind is my love today, tomorrow kind,
> Still *constant* in a wondrous excellence:
> Therefore my verse, to *constancy* confined,
> One thing expressing, leaves out difference.
> Fair, kind, and *true*, is all my argument,
> Fair, kind, and *true*, varying to other words
> - Sonnet 105, lines 6-10

> (Of Southampton)
> For I have sworn deep oaths of thy deep kindness,
> Oaths of thy love, thy *truth*, thy *constancy*
> - Sonnet 152, lines 9-10
> (To Elizabeth)

CONSTANT = "But you like none, none you, for *constant* heart" – Sonnet 54, line 14;

TRUTH = "But I hope *truth* is subject to no prescription, for *truth* is *truth* though never so old, and time cannot make that false which was once *true*." - Oxford to Robert Cecil, May 7, 1603

> O how much more doth beauty beauteous seem
> By that sweet ornament which *truth* doth give…
> When that shall vade, by verse distills your *truth*.
> - Sonnet 54, lines 1-2, 14

> Thou *truly* fair wert *truly* sympathized
> In *true* plain words by thy *true*-telling friend
> - Sonnet 82, lines 11-12

To Southampton: "As *truth* (Oxford) and beauty (Elizabeth) shall together thrive/ If from thy self to store thou wouldst convert,/ Or else of thee this I prognosticate:/ Thy end is *Truth's* (Oxford's) and Beauty's (Elizabeth's) doom and date" – Sonnet 14, line 14; "Take all my comfort of thy worth and *truth*" – Sonnet 37, line 4; "For *truth* proves thievish for a prize so dear" – Sonnet 48, line 14; "Methinks no face so gracious as is mine,/ No shape so *true*, no *truth* of such account" – Sonnet 62, lines 5-6; "And simple *truth* miscalled simplicity" – Sonnet 66, line 11; "Both truth [Oxford] and beauty [Elizabeth] on my love [my royal son, Southampton] depend" – Sonnet 101, line 3; "Most true it is that I have looked on *truth*" – Sonnet 110, line 5; "My most *true* mind thus maketh mine un*true*" – Sonnet 113, line 14; "No! *Time*, thou shalt not boast that I do change/ … I will be *true*, despite thy scythe and thee" – Sonnet 123, line 14 (echoing "and *time* cannot make that false which was once *true*" – Oxford letter above)

> So should my papers (yellowed with their age)
> Be scorned, like old men of less *truth* than tongue,
> And your *true* rights be termed a Poet's rage
> - Sonnet 17, lines 9-11

To Elizabeth: "To put fair *truth* upon so foul a face" – Sonnet 137, line 12; "When my love (in this single case in the Sonnets, referring to the Queen) swears that she is made of *truth*/ ... Simply I credit her false-speaking tongue:/ On both sides is simple *truth* suppressed" – Sonnet 138, lines 1, 7-8

BIDE (same as *abide*) = "And patience tame to sufferance *bide* each check" – Sonnet 58, line 7; to Elizabeth: "What needs thou wound with cunning when thy might/ Is more than my o'erpressed defense can *bide*?" – Sonnet 139, lines 7-8; **FIRM** = strongly fixed; echoing *constant*; "And the *firm* soil win of the watery main" – Sonnet 64, line 7; **SURE** = secure, steady, unfailing; also echoing *constant*; "From hands of falsehood, in *sure* wards of trust!" – Sonnet 48, line 4; "O *sure* I am the wits of former days" – Sonnet 59, line 13; "And to be *sure* that is not false I swear" – Sonnet 131, line 9

10 TO SCORN THE WORLD REGARDING BUT THY FRIENDS?

SCORN = "So should my papers (yellowed with their age)/ Be *scorned*, like old men of less truth than tongue" – Sonnet 17, lines 9-10; "And place my merit in the eye of *scorn*" – Sonnet 88, line 2; **THE WORLD** = "Thou that art now *the world's* fresh ornament" – Sonnet 1, line 9; "*The world* will wail thee like a makeless wife,/ *The world* will be thy widow and still weep/ ... Look what an unthrift in *the world* doth spend/ Shifts but his place, for still *the world* enjoys it,/ But beauty's waste hath in *the world* an end" – Sonnet 9, lines 4-5, 9-11; "All this the world well knows" – Sonnet 129, line 13

> Your name from hence immortal life shall have,
> Though I (once gone) to all **the world** must die
> - Sonnet 81, lines 5-6
> (To Southampton)

> You are so strongly in my purpose bred
> That all **the world** besides me thinks y'are dead
> - Sonnet 112, lines 13-14
> (To Southampton)

REGARDING = "Neither *regarding* that she is my child" – *The Two Gentlemen of Verona*, 3.1.70; **BUT THY FRIENDS** = except for those who are loyal to Your Majesty; **BUT** = "*But* as the riper should by time decease" – Sonnet 1, line 3; "*But* that I hope some good conceit of thine" – Sonnet 26, line 7; **FRIENDS** = Of Southampton in the Tower: "Then can I drown an eye (unused to flow)/ For precious *friends* hid in death's dateless night" – Sonnet 30, lines 5-6

11 WITH PATIENT MIND EACH PASSION TO ENDURE,

PATIENT = referring to his own patience; "And *patience* tame to suff'rance bide each check" – Sonnet 58, line 7, to Southampton; "Be wise as thou art cruel, do not press/ *My tongue-tied patience* with too much disdain" – Sonnet 140, lines 1-2, to Elizabeth, nearing the time of her death, when she still refuses to name their son in succession; also echoing the image of himself as a "patient" in need of cure: "Whilst like a willing *patient* I will drink/ Potions of eisel 'gainst my strong infection" – Sonnet 111, lines 9-10, referring to his mental and emotional illness because of his son's fate; **MIND** = "O change thy thought, that I may change my *mind*" – Sonnet 10, line 9; "To work my *mind*, when body's work's expired" – Sonnet 27, line 4; "Since I left you, mine eye is in my *mind*" – Sonnet 113, line 1; "Or whether doth my *mind*, being crowned with you,/ Drink up the monarch's plague, this flattery?/ ... And my great *mind* most kingly drinks it up" – Sonnet 114, lines 1-2, 10; **PASSION** = "A Woman's face with nature's own hand painted/ Hast thou, the *Master-Mistress of my passion*" – Sonnet 20, lines 1-2, referring to his royal son as both king and queen of his deepest concerns as well as of his "passions" or verses of the Sonnets, two of which appeared in *The Passionate Pilgrim* of 1599, before being revised and inserted as Sonnets 138 and 144 in the Dark Lady series; **ENDURE** = "The mortal Moon hath her eclipse *endured*" – Sonnet 107, line 5, marking April 10, 1603, the day of Southampton's liberation from the Tower by the newly proclaimed King James I, while referring to the Queen's mortal death less than three weeks earlier on March 24, 1603

"Choice"

12 IN ONE DESIRE TO SETTLE TO THE END?
ONE = "Among a number *one* is reckoned none" – Sonnet 136, line 8; **DESIRE** = "From fairest creatures we *desire* increase" – Sonnet 1, line 1; "Seeking that beauteous roof (Elizabeth's dynasty the House of Tudor) to ruinate,/ Which to repair should be thy chief *desire*" – Sonnet 10, lines 7-8; "Then can no horse with my *desire* keep pace" – Sonnet 51, line 9; **SETTLE** = "When love converted from the thing it was/ Shall reasons find of *settled* gravity" – Sonnet 49, lines 7-8; **TO THE END** = "The love I dedicate to your Lordship is *without end*" – Oxford's dedication of *Lucrece* to Southampton, as "Shakespeare" in 1594; "Is this thy body's *end*?" – Sonnet 146, line 8, to Elizabeth; "Your praise shall still find room/ Even in the eyes of all posterity/ That wear this world out to the *ending* doom" – Sonnet 55, lines 10-12, to Southampton; "But beauty's waste (Elizabeth's blood) hath in the world an *end*" – Sonnet 9, line 11, to Southampton in 1590; "Now all is done, have what shall have no *end*" – Sonnet 110, line 9, nearing the conclusion of the diary, in April 1603, to his royal son; "Love alters not with his brief hours and weeks,/ But bears it out even *to the edge of doom*" – Sonnet 116, lines 11-12

13 LOVE THEN THY CHOICE WHEREIN SUCH CHOICE DOTH BIND,
Oxford reaffirms his "choice" to "love" or serve Elizabeth, as a vassal to his sovereign Mistress, regardless of what decisions she makes; **LOVE** = (verb) to loyally or dutifully serve the monarch, who is filled with "love" or royal blood, used often in juxtaposition with "hate" as a verb; "Those lips that *love's own hand* did make/ Breathed forth the sound that said, 'I hate'" – Sonnet 145, lines 1-2, referring to Elizabeth acting with "hate" toward her royal son (and therefore toward Oxford, his father); **CHOICE** = special value or estimation; "Ruin hath taught me thus to ruminate/ That *Time will come and take my love away./* This thought is as a *death*, which cannot *choose*/ But weep to have that which it fears to lose" – Sonnet 64, lines 11-14, referring to Elizabeth's ever-dwindling life leading to her death and the death of Southampton's royal claim; **BIND** = "Being your vassal *bound* to stay your leisure" – Sonnet 58, line 4; "Whereto *all bonds do tie me* day by day" – Sonnet 117, line 4; to Southampton, as he had publicly pledged to him in the 1594 dedication of *Lucrece*: "The *love* I dedicate to your Lordship is without end ... Were my worth greater, my *duty* would show greater; meantime, as it is, it is *bound* to your Lordship..."; "Lord of my love, to whom in vassalage/ Thy merit hath *my duty strongly knit*" – Sonnet 25, lines 1-2, to Southampton

14 AS NOUGHT BUT DEATH MAY EVER CHANGE THY MIND.
NOUGHT = nothing; "But like a sad slave stay and think of *nought*" – Sonnet 57, line 11; same as "naught"; "Receiving *naught* by elements so slow" – Sonnet 44, line 13; **DEATH** = "'Gainst *death* and all oblivious enmity/ Shall you pace forth" – Sonnet 55, lines 9-10; "This thought is as a *death*" – Sonnet 64, line 11, as noted in line 13 above; "After my *death*, dear love, forget me quite" – Sonnet 72, line 3; "From hence your memory *death* cannot take" – Sonnet 81, line 3; "My love looks fresh, and *death* to me subscribes" – Sonnet 107, line 10; **EVER** = Edward deVere, E.Ver, his sometime pen name *Ever or Never*; "Why write I still all one, *ever* the same,/ And keep invention in a noted weed,/ That *every* word doth almost tell my name" – Sonnet 76, lines 5-7; "Since all alike my songs and praises be/ To one, of one, still such, and *ever* so" – Sonnet 105, lines 3-4; "Love is not love/ Which alters when it alteration finds,/ Or bends with the remover to remove./ O no, it is an *ever*-fixed mark/ That looks on tempests and is *never* shaken;/ It is the star to *every* wandering bark/ ... If this be error and upon me proved,/ I *never* writ, nor no man *ever* loved" – Sonnet 116, lines 2-7, 13-14, to Southampton; **CHANGE THY MIND** = "O *change thy thought*, that I may *change my mind*" – Sonnet 10, line – line 9, urging him to marry and beget an heir of his royal blood

REFERENCE EDITION

1573-1574

1573

"Undeniably Edward was for a time, perhaps even for several years, her favorite. To me, given the Queen's ardent nature and the carte blanche that goes with the crown, that means he was her lover ... The emotional apogee between Oxford and Elizabeth probably was reached sometime in 1572 or 1573. During this period a boy was conceived who would be given the name of Henry Wriothesley and later the title of Third Earl of Southampton. Was there a causal relationship? Some have been led to believe so as the only way of accounting for the tenor of the Sonnets ... As far as we know, Elizabeth could well have had a child by Oxford." - Ogburn Jr., The Mysterious William Shakespeare, 511-523

JANUARY 1573: VISIT NO. 1 TO PARKER

Oxford accompanies the Queen on the first of a series of visits to Matthew Parker, Archbishop of Canterbury, at Lambeth. Parker had been chaplain to Elizabeth's mother, Anne Boleyn, who, shortly before her execution in 1536, had extracted a promise from him to take personal responsibility for the spiritual guidance of her two-year-old daughter. When Princess Elizabeth Tudor ascended to the throne, she appointed Parker as her first Archbishop, putting him in nominal charge of the Church of England, of which she herself was the head.

MAY 1, 1573: 2ND EARL OF SOUTHAMPTON RELEASED FROM TOWER

The Queen orders Henry Wriothesley, Second Earl of Southampton (1545-1581) released from the Tower of London, where he has been languishing for eighteen months since October of 1571, for having questioned his loyalty to the Queen as her Catholic subject. He is returned to the custody of Sir William More of Losely, who takes orders from the Privy Council.

MAY 5, 1573: INSTRUCTIONS FOR SOUTHAMPTON

Lord Burghley and the Council write to William More that "her Majesty's gracious pleasure" is that Southampton be "set at more liberty" in certain ways. "Her highness hath made special choice of you with whom he might for the time remain, till some farther order be taken: which we have thought good to signify unto you." The Council members are commanding More to "permit unto him the access of my lady his wife, his other friends and servants which shall repair unto him."

There is no record that the Council permitted the Countess of Southampton to visit her husband in the Tower. (It is difficult to imagine Elizabeth or Burghley granting him conjugal visits while they remain in dread over Catholic plots against Her Majesty's life.) In fact, the instructions to Sir More imply the earl is now being granted "the access of my lady his wife" for the first time since his imprisonment a year and a half ago. By now she is four months pregnant, perhaps by the man with whom her husband will accuse her of carrying on an affair.

MAY 11, 1573: "ALL THESE LOVE MATTERS"

A young observer of the Court, Gilbert Talbot, writes to his father the Earl of Shrewsbury:
"My Lord of Oxford is lately grown into great credit, for the Queen's Majesty delighteth more in his personage and his dancing and his valiantness than any other. I think Sussex doth back him all that he can. If it were not for his fickle head he would pass any of them shortly. My Lady Burghley unwisely hath declared herself, as it were, jealous, which is come to the Queen's ear: whereat she hath been not a little

offended with her, but now she is reconciled again. At all these love matters my Lord Treasurer winketh, and will not meddle in any way."

Talbot's father is guarding Mary Stuart, Queen of Scots, who crossed into England in 1568 only to become a rallying point for Catholic plots against Elizabeth. In his letter Talbot refers to Sussex, Lord Chamberlain of Her Majesty's Household, who is in high esteem for his military leadership in putting down the Northern Rebellion of 1569 and 1570. Since Oxford served under Sussex near the end of that campaign, the two have become fast friends and mutual supporters.

Christopher Hatton has been pushed to the sidelines as Oxford has "lately grown into great credit" with Elizabeth and "My Lady Burghley" (William Cecil's wife) has been "jealous" or angry at the Queen's attentions to her son-in-law. Oxford has ignored Anne Cecil in favor of Elizabeth and, by now, their flourishing romance is the talk of the Court. When Anne's mother protested, the Queen told her to mind her own business; but Lord Treasurer Burghley remained aloof from "all these love matters," preferring instead to "winketh" at them.

Edward de Vere is at the height of his intimacy with the Queen, just as she and her chief minister are working on plans and policies to deal with crucial international issues amid a growing crisis. The massacre on Bartholomew's Day has ruptured relations with France, but England will need that alliance to keep Spain at bay for as long as possible; and therefore, Elizabeth may well be forced to convince the world she will enter an alliance with France by marriage. (In fact, Oxford will join Burghley and Sussex in public support of the French Match.)

With the Queen anticipating her fortieth birthday in September, there is now a brief window of time for begetting a "natural issue of her Majesty's body" to succeed her; but such an heir would have to be produced in secret, without acknowledgment. Given that Elizabeth apparently is loath to accept any child she may have borne by Leicester, it is necessary to produce a blood successor now or forever lose the chance. To gain the option to name an heir in the future, she will have to choose an Englishman to be the father; and if the Queen chooses Oxford, their sexual intercourse will be above all an act of strategic or political necessity.

MAY 29, 1573: HATTON TO THE CONTINENT
"Mr. Hatton by reason of his great sickness is minded to go to the Spa for the better recovery of his health," Francis Talbot (brother of Gilbert) writes from Court to his father. The Queen's Privy Council grants Hatton permission to travel abroad.

JULY 14-21, 1573: VISIT NO. 2 TO PARKER
Elizabeth makes a second visit to Archbishop Parker, this time at Croydon, Surrey, for seven days, before her royal progress leaves on its miles-long procession through Kent.

SUMMER 1573: HATTON WRITES FROM THE CONTINENT
Convalescing on the Continent, Hatton writes Elizabeth a number of adoring letters in his typically extravagant style. "God bless you for ever," he tells her. "The branch of the sweetest bush I will wear and bear to my life's end: God witness I feign not. It is a gracious favor most dear and welcome unto me. Reserve it to the Sheep," he writes in reference to the Queen's nickname for him, "he hath no tooth to bite, *where the Boar's tusk may both raze and tear*" – referring to Oxford, whose crest displays a boar.

"Most of what we hear of Burghley during the summer and autumn of 1573 has to do with the Alençon match," Conyers Read reports. The Lord Treasurer has many talks with La Mothe Fenelon, the French ambassador, taking the position that he supports the marriage and promising to continue to urge it upon his Mistress. He is not hopeful, however, because of the differences of age and religion. "According to Fenelon, Burghley told Elizabeth that her position was a precarious one, and that the only way of strengthening it was by marriage … Burghley made much of the popular opposition to the match in consequence of the St. Bartholomew's Massacre. The indications are that he still strongly favored the match but that he had pretty well abandoned hope of it, and was simply playing the Queen's favorite game as she wanted it played." (Read, 139)

SUMMER 1573: SOUTHAMPTON TO CUSTODY OF MONTAGUE

Elizabeth and her Council transfer the Second Earl of Southampton from Sir More's custody to the company of his wife's father, Viscount Montague, at the latter's estate of Cowdray. By this time, the Queen has assured herself of Montague's loyalty, despite his religious convictions as a Catholic; and she will continue to hold him in the highest trust.

SEPTEMBER 3-16, 1573: VISIT NO. 3 TO PARKER
Nearing the end of the summer progress, Her Majesty again visits Archbishop Parker. During this two-week stay at Canterbury in Kent, she is at St. Augustine's for her fortieth birthday on September 7, 1573, and spends the night as Parker's houseguest on the ninth. Elizabeth remains in Canterbury until the sixteenth before continuing through Kent back to London by the end of the month. The Queen's biographers will skip over the next nine months or more, most without reporting any public activities.

OCTOBER 1573: "A HUNDREDTH SUNDRY FLOWERS"
Christopher Hatton returns from his five-month convalescence on the Continent only to discover the publication of *A Hundredth Sundry Flowers* (which the *Encyclopedia Brittanica* calls the first original prose narrative in English). The volume includes 100 verses, sixteen signed with a pseudonym linked to Hatton. Readers will take them to be a confession about an affair with his Mistress, obviously the Queen herself.

Edward de Vere apparently has been the moving force behind the writing of *Flowers*, contributing poetry under various names; he created the verses that purported to be by Hatton, deliberately using the pen name to embarrass him. With the deadly sportiveness of his pen, the merry madcap Boar has razed the Sheep.

OCTOBER 6, 1573: COUNTESS OF SOUTHAMPTON GIVES BIRTH

The Second Earl of Southampton, now at the estate of his father-in-law Viscount Montague, writes to his former custodian William More:

"After my most hearty commendations, both to you and your good wife. Although it is so happed by the sudden sickness of my wife that we could not by possibility have her [More's wife] present as we desired, yet have I thought good to impart unto you such comfort as God hath sent me after all my long troubles, which is that this present morning at three o'clock my wife was delivered of a goodly boy (God bless him!) the which, although it was not without great peril to them both for the present, yet now I thank God both are in good state. If your wife will take the pains to visit her, we shall be mighty glad of her company ... From Cowdray, this present Tuesday 1573, Your assured friend, H. Southampton."

Is this "goodly boy" an issue of the Second Earl's blood? Or is he the result of an affair that his wife, Mary Browne, had with another man while her husband was in the Tower? Is that why Southampton fails to use the phrase "my son" or to refer to the boy as his first male heir? Whatever the case, the boy will be "fostered out" to a wet nurse for about eighteen months (until some time in 1575).

1574

FEBRUARY 1, 1574: ELIZABETH DELAYS ALENÇON
Elizabeth writes from Hampton Court to her Ambassador in France, Valentine Dale, about persistent requests by the French King and his mother the Queen for Alençon to come to England. If not for such pressure, she declares, "we could in no case be induced to allow of his coming neither publicly nor privately." Her stated reason is that, once she and the Duke have their *"entrevue"* (mutual viewing), she expects to be so dissatisfied with his appearance that the French will be furious. If Monsieur le Duke "will needs come over in some disguised sort," she adds, it should be done secretly. But the Queen grants no permission for Alençon to visit.

("In all likelihood, this letter was composed by Burghley rather than Elizabeth herself: several draft copies in his hand are preserved in the PRO among the State Papers Foreign" - *Elizabeth I: Collected Works*, University of Chicago, 2000)

MARCH 2, 1574: VISIT NO. 4 TO PARKER
"The earliest of the Queen's visits in this year," John Nichols reports in his *Progresses*, "was to Archbishop Parker on the second of March." Elizabeth and her Court proceed from Hampton and she "honored Lambeth Palace with her presence." The Queen is "most hospitably entertained with a large train of her Nobility and Courtiers, by Archbishop Parker, for two days." Oxford is with her during this visit. "In the afternoon," Nichols writes, "the Queen proceeded to Greenwich."

MARCH 15, 1574: ELIZABETH TO INVITE ALENÇON
The Queen is flirting with France from a safe distance. Now she is running out of time or excuses for delaying Alençon's visit to England. She writes to Ambassador Dale expressing dismay that he appears to have led the French Queen to "understand our affection to be very great towards this marriage and that we have sought out the means how the interview (with Alençon) should be made. Whereof we had much marvel," Elizabeth continues. "And namely that by your speech any such thing hath been there collected ... considering that neither to this ambassador here (Fenelon), nor to you there, anything hath passed to give occasion of such concepts."

Elizabeth, complaining to Dale that she has been "continually pressed" to grant Alençon the safe conduct, explains that any visitation must be carried out "covertly" when the Court is away from "our own houses" on progress. If such conditions are accepted, "you shall say that you will deliver a safe conduct..." The Queen will formally grant her safe-conduct for Alençon in April, allowing him to come into England any time until May 21st; but after then (for unexplained reasons) he will be no longer welcome. During that brief time, he "may make his repair to her at a convenient time after she be advertised of his arrival" at any British port. What she might do if Alençon actually appeared is another matter. Anglo-French relations are still too strained for any serious show of courtship. Elizabeth most likely would arrange it so she and the Duke would get a glimpse of each other, letting the Court entertain him for the rest of his stay.

Her Majesty will attend a sermon in the Parish Church of Greenwich in March, but she will make no other public appearances this spring. She will remain in virtual seclusion during March and April and all of May and June. In terms of any documentary record of her activities, she will not be visible until the beginning of her royal progress in July.

(Fenelon will report audiences with Elizabeth on April 2, April 24 and May 3, 1574, but he will give no information about the nature of those meetings. The French Match is still in its earliest stages; the ambassador's interest is to give the impression to Catherine de Medici that some sort of progress is being made, even though it's quite obvious that Elizabeth is anything but eager.)

APRIL 1574: ELIZABETH STILL IN SECLUSION
Elizabeth remains secluded all during April, when word comes that the Queen Regent has placed Alençon under restraint in Paris. He will remain under house arrest for some time, falling ill, and will not visit England until 1579.

MAY 10, 1574: PLANS TO VISIT HAVERING
"The Queen's Majesty goeth of Saturday ... to Havering of the Bower, and there remaineth till she begins her progress, which is to Bristol. The guests be not drawn, but she is determined for certain to go to Bristol. This is all which is worth writing," Francis Talbot writes, adding that Elizabeth "hath spoken to me and told me of your Lord's letter, which I brought, and how well she did accept it, with many comfortable words, but nothing of any matter." (To his father, Shrewsbury, from Greenwich Palace.)

It appears Talbot's audience with the Queen is conducted in the Presence Chamber, with Elizabeth seated well apart from members of her audience. Fenelon reports meeting with the Queen on this day as well, offering no information about her appearance or physical condition.

MAY 16, 1574: FENELON REPORTS ON ELIZABETH
Fenelon reports to Catherine de Medici that he has seen the Queen of England today and she "has no bad impression of Monsieur the Duke, your son." Elizabeth "replied to me that she did not wish to be so ungracious as to have a poor estimation of a prince who showed admiration of her. But this I tell you emphatically: she broke into a smile, that she would take no husband, even with her legs in irons." England's absolute monarch can arrange the conditions of her personal audiences as she pleases; she can also present herself in whatever manner of dress she wishes. For his part, the French ambassador is anxious to impress his Mistress with evidence he is making progress toward the Alençon match, so it behooves him to give the Queen Regent details suggesting Elizabeth has granted him close access. For all that, however, the best he can do is report she "broke into a smile" and joked with him about never taking a husband.

MAY 1574: NEW PARKER VISIT PLANNED
"In the month of May," Nichols writes, "preparations were made by Archbishop Parker for a second visit this year of the Queen, at his Palace of Croydon."

"The Queen's visit to the Archbishop of Canterbury in March 1574 with Lord Oxford seems highly significant. In those days, a betrothal ceremony with an exchange of rings was as binding as a marriage. There is much emphasis given in the plays to an exchange of rings between lovers..." (Ogburn & Ogburn, This Star of England, 1952)

MAY 23, 1574: FENELON REPORTS AGAIN
Fenelon reports another audience with Elizabeth, but offers no details of their meeting. This is his last opportunity to be in her presence for at least several weeks.

MAY 24, 1574: TALK OF A PROGRESS TO THE WEST
"There is some talk of a Progress to Bristol, but by reason of the unseasonableness of the year, there is great means for her not going on so long a Progress. But her Majesty's great desire is to go to Bristol." (Gilbert Talbot from Greenwich, May 24, 1574)

Nichols surmises from the Talbot letters that "in the latter end of May, the Queen passed six days in retirement at Havering and was meditating a longer Progress," but there is no confirmation of the visit. The French ambassador will indicate it was postponed.

MAY 30, 1574: THE MERTON PRIORY
It appears that no record of Elizabeth's whereabouts exists from the time of Fenelon's meeting with her on May 23 until the Court's move from Greenwich to Richmond on June 30 in preparation for her royal progress that summer. One exception involves an unexplained occurrence on May 30, when she goes to the old Merton Priory in Surrey, spending the night on its grounds of some two thousand acres. As far as can be determined, there are no descriptive or explanatory accounts of this visit. Why she went there, or with whom, is unknown.

Mary Hill Cole records the Queen's overnight visit without comment in *The Portable Queen: Elizabeth I and the Politics of Ceremony* (1999).

JUNE 4, 1574: LETTER FROM HAMPTON COURT
The Queen apparently writes from Hampton to the Regent of Scotland and refers to the death of Charles IX of France, which occurred five days earlier. Did stay longer at Merton before going to Hampton? Did she go directly from the Priory to the Palace? Who was attending her during this time?

Prologue

JUNE 1574: GREENWICH PALACE
Elizabeth is back at Greenwich Palace (if indeed she ever left it) by June 8, when Ambassador Fenelon of France makes an official report of his monarch's death to the English Court. He is unable to see the Queen, however. Ambassador Fenelon writes to Catherine de Medici on June 13 that Elizabeth convened her Privy Council to consider the implications of Charles's death for Anglo-French relations. However, there is no evidence that she personally attended the meeting. On that day, in fact, the Queen refused to receive the ambassador, who reports she is "to depart immediately from Greenwich, to relieve somewhat her distress as best she could, in a dwelling of hers by the name of Havering in the countryside."

That her "distress" has anything to do with the death of the French monarch is Fenelon's assumption; he is anxious to impress his Queen Regent with positive reports about Elizabeth's attitude toward the Alençon match. In a postscript the ambassador adds he "scarcely signed" his letter of June 13 when rumors came that Spain was assembling an armada of "two hundred and fifty armed ships" to invade England. "And notwithstanding that the baggage was already on its way to Havering," Elizabeth "ordered it back and, having postponed this trip for three weeks, assembled her Council hastily."

No one will record actually seeing Elizabeth until after the first week of July. Did the Queen given birth to a child in May or perhaps in June?

JUNE 27, 1574: OXFORD AT COURT
Oxford has remained with Elizabeth at Greenwich this year, while his wife has been kept away from the palace. Now, with advance word that the Court will be moving to Richmond prior to the summer progress, Anne Cecil hopes to join her husband there. Writing on June 27 to Lord Chamberlain Sussex, who is responsible for allotting rooms whenever the Royal Court moves to another palace, Burghley intercedes on his daughter's behalf.

"My good Lord," he writes to Sussex, "I heartily thank you for your gentle remembrance of my daughter of Oxinforde, who, as I think meaneth as her duty is, to wait on Her Majesty at Richmond, except my Lord her husband shall otherwise direct her." That is, the Lord Treasurer is allowing for the possibility that Oxford will order his wife to stay away.

JUNE 28, 1574: THE QUEEN'S MELANCHOLY

"The Queen's Majesty hath been melancholy disposed a good while, which should seem that she is troubled with weighty causes. She beginneth her progress on Wednesday next..."
(Francis Talbot from Greenwich, June 28, 1574)

JUNE 28, 1574: ELIZABETH AND OXFORD ARGUE

"Her Majesty stirreth little abroad, and since the stay of the navy to sea (the threat of a Spanish invasion had blown over), here hath been all things very quiet ... The young Earl of Oxford, of that ancient and Very family of the Veres, had a cause or suit that now came before the Queen; which she did not answer so favorably as was expected, checking him, it seems, for his unthriftiness. And hereupon his behavior before her gave her some offense."
(As reported by John Nichol's "Progresses" of Elizabeth, in Nichol's own summary or paraphrase, attributed to Gilbert Talbot writing from Greenwich, June 28, 1574)

JUNE 30, 1574: GREENWICH TO RICHMOND
The Court moves from Greenwich to Richmond in preparation for the Queen's progress to the west of England. According to Nichols, Burghley is intending to catch up to the progress and to "wait upon the Queen when she came to Woodstock" on the 24th of July. Elizabeth tells him via Walsingham, however, that she has "a disposition that he (Burghley), with the Lord Keeper and Sir Ralph Sadler, Chancellor of the Exchequer, should tarry at London. The cause wherefore was unknown to the Lord Treasurer, but seemed to be a surprise to him: but, he said, he would do as he was commanded." Nichols adds that Elizabeth seems "apprehensive of some dangers in her absence, which might give occasion to her melancholy, and therefore thought it advisable for those staid Counselors to remain behind."

JULY 7, 1574: ROYAL PROGRESS BEGINS
Elizabeth finally emerges and the Court leaves Richmond Palace as the progress begins, heading slowly for the west of England amid great festivity. In a contemporary account of the 1574 progress, Queen Elizabeth is described as riding in "her chariot" like a goddess.

Oxford will record Her Majesty's flight to the west in Sonnet 33 and will allude to it in both *Venus and Adonis* and *A Midsummer Night's Dream:*

> 'Poor flower,' quoth she, 'this was thy father's guise,
> Sweet issue of a more sweet-smelling sire…'
> Thus weary of the world, away she hies,
> And yokes her silver doves, by whose swift aid
> Their mistress mounted through the empty skies,
> *In her light chariot* quickly is convey'd,
> Holding their course to Paphos, *where their Queen*
> Means to immure herself and not be seen
> - Venus and Adonis, 1177-94

> And *the Imperial Votaress pass'd on,*
> In maiden meditation, fancy-free.
> Yet mark'd I where the bolt of Cupid fell:
> It fell upon *a little western flower…*
> - A Midsummer Night's Dream, 2.1.163-166

JULY 7, 1574: OXFORD HAS FLED TO THE CONTINENT
As Elizabeth is leaving Richmond, news explodes at Court that Edward de Vere has bolted from England. "I made her Majesty acquainted with my Lord of Oxford's arrival at Calais," Secretary Walsingham writes to Burghley, adding the Queen "doth not interpret the same in any evil part. She conceiveth great hope of his return upon some secret message sent him." It would seem Elizabeth knows very well why Oxford fled; she reacts calmly to the news and dispatches his friend Thomas Bedingfield with orders to fetch him home.

Some nobles fear that Oxford may have joined with English Catholic refugees in the Low Countries. A leader of the refugees is the Earl of Westmoreland, who was attainted for his part in the Northern Rebellion of 1569 and is now an exile in Brussels. "It must have seemed, in the absence of definite news," Ward writes, "that the Lord Treasurer's son-in-law had thrown in his lot with the Queen's enemies."

"There was a great triumph among the northern rebels when they heard of the Earl of Oxford's coming over," a correspondent in Antwerp will inform Burghley. "It was said that he was flying, and that the Earl of Southampton had fled to Spain. [This refers to thirty-year-old Henry Wriothesley, Second Earl of Southampton, but the rumors are premature and untrue.] In a council held at Louvain, it was concluded that the Earl of Westmoreland should ride to Burges to welcome him (Oxford) and persuade him not to return (to England); but the earls did not meet. It were a great pity such a valiant and noble young gentleman should communicate with such detestable men."

THE STRANGE EVENTS OF 1574
Here is a summary of events leading to Oxford's sudden departure from England, when Elizabeth began her royal progress to the west:

> March 2: Visit with Oxford to Archbishop Parker at Lambeth
> March: Elizabeth out of sight at Greenwich the rest of the month
> April: Elizabeth out of sight at Greenwich all month
> May: Elizabeth out of sight at Greenwich all month
> May: Plans to visit Archbishop Parker are cancelled

May 10: Elizabeth plans to visit Havering
May 30: Elizabeth (possibly) goes to Merton Priory overnight
June 4: Elizabeth (possibly) writes letter from Hampton Court
June: Elizabeth out of sight at Greenwich all month
June 28: Elizabeth has been 'melancholy disposed' all month
June 28: Elizabeth and Oxford are reported arguing
June 30: Elizabeth and Court move to Richmond
July 7: Elizabeth leaves on progress westward; Oxford flees to the Continent

"It is of especial interest to recall that Leicester had run away in 1561, the year his son [i.e., Arthur Dudley] was said to have been born to the Queen ... And surely the cause of the tempest would have been the 'little changeling boy' whom Oxford yearned to have her acknowledge and whom she had decided to bestow upon the Second Earl of Southampton, to pass for his child who had been born in October 1573. She had resolved not to recognize the boy as her own, but calmly to pass on, 'in maiden meditation, fancy free,' maintaining the legend of her chastity."
- Ogburn & Ogburn, This Star of England, 837

JULY 8-18, 1574: REPORTS ON OXFORD'S FLIGHT
"The Earl of Oxford departed into Flanders without the Queen's license," a report states on the 8th of July, "and was revoked by the Queen sending the Gentleman Pensioners for him." Burghley writes to Sussex on the 15th: "I must heartily thank your Lordship for your advertisement of my Lord of Oxford's cause wherein I am sorry that her Majesty maketh such haste. My Lord, howsoever my Lord of Oxford be, for his own part, in matters of thrift inconsiderate, I dare avow him to be resolute in dutifulness to the Queen and his country."

Henry Killigrew, the English ambassador to Scotland, writes Secretary Walsingham on the eighteenth of July from from Edinburgh: "My Lord of Oxford and Lord Seymour are fled out of England and passed by Bruges to Brussels."

Seymour is a son of the late Edward Seymour, Protector Somerset during the reign of Elizabeth's half-brother Edward VI. He is also nephew to the late Admiral Thomas Seymour, with whom fifteen-year-old Princess Elizabeth had a scandalous affair leading to his execution in 1549. Why the current Lord Seymour left with Oxford is unknown.

JULY 26, 1574: FIRST MENTION OF SOUTHAMPTON SON
Other than the letter from the Second Earl of Southampton to William More about the birth of a "goodly boy" on October 6, 1573, there is no further record of the child until now. This notice is in the will of the Second Earl's mother, dated today, referring "my Son's son, Harry."

Given that the infant was less than nine months old at this stage, it is probable that he is still in the care of a wet-nurse: "In the upper classes, babies were put out to wet-nurse at birth, usually away from home, for between twelve and eighteen months ... Not only were the infants of the landed, upper-bourgeois and professional classes in the 16th and 17th centuries sent out to hired wet-nurses for the first twelve to eighteen months, but thereafter they were brought up mainly by nurses, governesses and tutors."
- Lawrence Stone, *The Family, Sex and Marriage in England 1500-1800*

Charlotte Stopes writes of the boy to become Henry Wriothesley, Third Earl of Southampton, the young nobleman to whom Shakespeare will dedicate his works: *"It has always been said he was 'the second son,' but there is no authority for that ... It is strange that there has been preserved no record of his baptism ... There appears to be no later allusion to the godparents of the young Lord ... The Registers of Tichfield for that period are not extant. We know very little about the young Lord's childhood...I have been able to find only two MS references to the Wriothesley baby during his whole childhood. The first is in the will of his grandmother, the Lady Jane, dated 26 July 1574. By it she left various bequests to 'my Son's son, Harry,*

Lord Wriothesley.' This gives us at least the clue to his baby-name, and a reference to his baby 'expectations'" (Stopes, 2-3)

JULY 27, 1574: OXFORD BACK IN ENGLAND
If Westmoreland and his followers in Brussels believed that Oxford would join them, they have been disappointed. Sir Walter Midmay writes to Cecil: "Of my Lord of Oxford's return I am glad to hear. I trust this little journey will make him love home the better hereafter. It were a great pity he should not go straight, there be so many good things in him to serve his God and Prince."

JULY 29, 1574: OXFORD REUNITES WITH BURGHLEY AND ANNE
Burghley and his daughter Anne go to London to meet Oxford. The next day they travel to Cecil's home at Theobalds, where they wait to hear Her Majesty's pleasure from the Palace of Woodstock, where she and her royal progress have stopped.

AUGUST 1, 1574: WALSINGHAM TO BURGHLEY
Secretary Walsingham, traveling with the Queen and her Court, writes to Burghley: "I find her Majesty graciously enough inclined towards the Earl of Oxford, whose peace I think will be both easily and speedily made, for that her Majesty doth conceive that his obedience in his return hath fully satisfied the contempt of his departure." The Secretary also reports Elizabeth's pleasure that Oxford meet up with the Court upon its planned arrival Gloucester about a week from now.

AUGUST 3, 1574: BURGHLEY TO WALSINGHAM
Burghley replies to Walsingham that Oxford is "very ready to take the journey, showing in himself a mixture of contrary affection, although both reasonable and commendable." The earl is "fearful and doubtful in what sort he shall recover Her Majesty's favor because of his offense in departure as he did without license," but he is also "glad and resolute to look for a speedy good end because he had in his abode so notoriously rejected the attempts of Her Majesty's evil subjects, and in his return set apart all his own particular desires of foreign travel and come to present himself before Her Majesty, of whose goodness towards he saith he cannot count."

Oxford and Bedingfield have already left Theobalds for London, Burghley continues, adding the earl will "spend only two days or less to make him some apparel meet for the Court, although I would have had him forbear that new charge, considering his former apparel is very sufficient, and he not provided to increase a new charge." The Lord Treasurer tries to impress upon Walsingham the need to give Oxford every benefit of the doubt and to hasten his peaceful reunion with Elizabeth. He praises his son-in-law for resisting pressure from the exiled Catholic earls to join them, further advising: "I think it is sound counsel to be given to Her Majesty that this young nobleman, being of such a quality as he is for birth, office and other notable valours of body and spirit, he may not be discomforted either by any extraordinary delay or by any outward sharp or unkind reproof [and that] her favorable accepting of his submission may be largely and manifestly declared unto him, to the confirmation of him in his singular loyalty."

Burghley also tells Walsingham to remind Christopher Hatton "to continue my Lord's friend, as he hath manifestly been." Cecil cannot be unaware of Hatton's attempts to undermine Oxford, but he may not know the full extent of how the Captain of the Queen's Bodyguard has pretended to be Oxford's friend while doing all he can to turn Elizabeth against him.

Burghley further tells the Secretary to make certain that all the nobles at Court understand he is making a personal "intercession to them from me for my Lord" to pay Oxford the highest of respect. Referring to Walsingham's counterpart as Secretary of State, he adds: "I doubt not but Master Secretary Smith will remember his old love towards the Earl when he was his scholar" – that is, when Thomas Smith was charged with tutoring young Oxford in earlier times.

AUGUST 5, 1574: OXFORD JOINS THE ROYAL PROGRESS

Oxford joins the royal progress as the Court leaves Sudeley Castle for Gloucester. Burghley is hoping the Queen will forgive his son-in-law, but she "seems to have acquiesced with surprising alacrity," Read notes. Walsingham reports to Burghley two days later: "I am sure you are not unadvertised how the Earl of Oxford is restored to her Majesty's favor, in whose loyal behavior towards her Majesty's rebels in the Low Countries who sought conference with him, a thing he utterly refused, did very much qualify her contempt in departing without her Majesty's leave."

The Queen has known from the outset that Oxford had never had any disloyal intentions. His flight, otherwise unexplained, will contribute to a distorted view of his personal character and even of his political-religious intentions. Burghley and Walsingham are aware of Edward de Vere's loyalty to the Crown and devotion to Elizabeth; their problem with his unauthorized flight is one of public relations. In any event, the Queen has welcomed him back with open arms, leaving others to wonder why she forgave him so suddenly and without reprimand.

"The desire to travel is not quenched in him," Walsingham adds, "though he dare not make any motion unto her Majesty that he may, with her favor, accomplish the said desire. By no means he can be drawn to follow the Court, and yet there are many cunning devices used in that behalf for his stay." Despite his longing to be free, Oxford will continue on the progress until its return in September.

THE ROYAL PROGRESS

Highlights of the visits leading to the City of Bath:

July 7: Progress Begins
July 24-Aug 2: Woodstock
Aug 4-5: Sudley Castle
Aug 10: Gloucester
Aug 14-21: Bristol
Aug 21-23: Bath

At Bristol the Queen is received "with great pomp and solemnity," Nichols reports, adding, "All ranks of people testified their joy at the condescension of the Royal Visitor." Along with Oxford is Thomas Churchyard, a poet in his employ commissioned (perhaps by Oxford himself) to write a description of "the Queen's Entertainment." Burghley catches up to the progress for the signing of the Treaty of Bristol with Spain, which signals a cautious peace between the two countries.

AUGUST 21, 1574: ARRIVAL AT BATH

The Court moves again, arriving in the City of Bath for a stay of two nights. "Needless to say," historian Jean Marco writes, "the city exerted itself to welcome her." A large entourage escorts Elizabeth, with state business going on as usual. There is a meeting of the Privy Council in the city. Her visit not only sets the seal of approval on the rising spa, it introduces her courtiers to the waters of Bath, a spectacularly beautiful city standing on the River Avon among the hills of England's West Country. The city's compactness and striking architecture, with Roman baths and sweeping Georgian terraces, combine to produce one of the most elegant sights in Europe.

In 1572, Elizabeth gave permission for the citizens of Bath to create a new, united parish for themselves; and in April 1573, she issued a warrant for financial collections to be made toward restoration of the Abbey Church. The Queen's stay now, with the Court and Oxford, signals a reinforcement of this support. According to *The Portable Queen*, this is Elizabeth's only visit to Bath during the entire reign of forty-five years.

SONNETS 153-154

It appears that Edward deVere wrote Sonnet 153 before the age of twenty-five, much earlier than any other verses of the *Shake-Speares Sonnets*, and that Sonnet 154 represents the mature poet revisiting it. * In any case, Oxford wrote the pair in reference to the August 1574 royal visit to Bath, ultimately inserting them at the end of the Sonnets. They appear to be the epilogue, but they actually serve as the prologue to his royal chronicle or dynastic diary. Viewed this way, their placement at the end of the 154-sonnet sequence becomes an invitation to begin again, at the beginning of the story.

* (Helen Vendler concludes both verses represent "early work" by Shakespeare.)

Sonnets 153-154 are variations upon a six-line Greek epigram by Marianus Scholasticus. Most editors have agreed with Stephen Booth that it is "most unlikely that Shakespeare knew the Greek text," but it is virtually certain that Edward de Vere did. In any case, he had learned to read Greek as a child (during the 1550s) in the household of his first tutor, Sir Thomas Smith – a linguist and master of Latin, Greek, French, Italian and Hebrew, who became a statesman and served as Principal Secretary to Queen Elizabeth during the mid-1570s. (Hughes, *The Oxfordian*, Vol. III, 2000, pp. 19-44) A translation of the Greek epigram goes this way:

"Beneath these plane trees, detained by gentle slumber, Love slept, having put his torch in the care of the Nymphs; but the Nymphs said to one another: "Why wait? Would that together with this we could quench the fire in the hearts of men." But the torch set fire even to the water, and with hot water thenceforth the Love-Nymphs filled the bath."
- (Andrew Werth, "The Oxfordian,"Vol.V, October 2002, 16)

Oxford uses the epigram as a starting point to conceal-but-reveal his royal son as "Cupid" and "The Boy" in Sonnet 153 and as "the little Love-God" in Sonnet 154. He envisions the bath as containing the water and royal blood within the womb of Queen Elizabeth, wherein their son was created. He also evokes these waters as not only her blood (which her son possesses) but also as part of Her Majesty's divine power to heal him, i.e., her "sovereign cure" of line 8. The Queen is the source of their son's royal blood, which also fills the bath-womb, but she herself took away his power. In the end, ironically, she is also the only one who can "cure" their son and, thereby, also "cure" Oxford – i.e., only the royal Mistress can relieve his suffering as the father of a little prince or king who cannot be acknowledged. .

Sonnets 153 and 154 are necessarily both sexual and spiritual, invoking royal procreation and its gift of sacred blood. This blood from Elizabeth's womb is divinely ordained by God and gives the Sovereign Mistress of England her supernatural powers of curing and healing; it also gives her son his "dateless lively heat" or eternal royal power. The Queen cannot destroy the power that she has transferred to her newborn son; and only she (by virtue of her imperial "eye" or viewpoint or command) can alter the current situation for Oxford, the "sad distempered guest" who joined the Court on its visit to the City of Bath.

Prologue

THE BATH VISIT

OXFORD & ELIZABETH

Sonnet 153
The Boy
August 21-23, 1574

During 21-23 August 1574, Elizabeth made the first and only visit of her reign to the City of Bath in western England. Edward de Vere had returned from a brief unauthorized trip to the Continent in time to join the royal summer progress at Bristol; he then accompanied the Queen and her Court to Bath, with its ancient Roman shrines built around natural springs with healing waters. Oxford uses this visit as a metaphor to record his anguish over Elizabeth's refusal to acknowledge their orphaned infant son – **Cupid … the boy** *– whose "holy fire of love" or royal blood can never be extinguished.*

Sonnet 153	Translation
Cupid laid by his brand and fell asleep.	Our royal son ignored his source of royal blood.
A maid of *Dian's* this advantage found,	A servant of Elizabeth took him in,
And his love-kindling fire did quickly steep	And she quickly buried all trace of his royal power
In a cold valley-fountain of that ground:	In the obscurity of a cold tomb:
Which borrowed from this holy fire of love,	This tomb, however, borrowed from his royal power
A dateless lively heat still to endure,	An eternal royal identity that always lives,
And grew a seething bath which yet men prove	And became a womb of royal blood men prove
Against strange maladies a sovereign cure:	To be a sovereign power to cure all ills.
But at my mistress' eye love's brand new-fired,	But my Sovereign Mistress revived his blood,
The boy for trial needs would touch my breast.	And our son touched my heart for guidance.
I, sick withal, the help of bath desired,	I, sick with grief, sought the cure of royal waters,
And thither hied, a sad distempered guest.	And hurried there as a suffering angry guest.
But found no cure; the bath for my help lies	But found no cure. My help for his royalty now lies
Where *Cupid* got new fire: my mistress' eye.	With his source: Elizabeth's imperial viewpoint.

1 *CUPID* LAID BY HIS BRAND AND FELL ASLEEP.
CUPID = the God of Love; the three-month-old son of Elizabeth and Oxford, born in late May this year; Oxford is thereby developing his special language for the Sonnets with the very first word, indicating that **LOVE = Royal Blood**, which is carried by the Queen and their son; "The little Love-God" of Sonnet 154, line 1; "Cupid is traditionally thought of as a baby" – Booth, in notes for Sonnet 151

> Yet marked I where *the bolt of Cupid* fell.
> It fell upon *a little western flower*,
> Before milk-white, now *purple with love's wound*
> - A Midsummer Night's Dream, 2.1.165-167

> A thousand *Cupids* fly
> About *her gentle eye* - Oxford poem, What Cunning Can Express, pre-1576
> - (Of Elizabeth, reflecting "my mistress' eye" of lines 9 & 14)

REFERENCE EDITION

> What were his parents? Gods or no?
> That living long is yet a child;
> A goddess' son? Who thinks not so?
> A god begot, beguiled;
> Venus his mother, Mars his sire.
> - Oxford poem, *What is Desire*

BRAND = torch; the torch that carries and spreads the fire (and light) of his "love" or royal blood from Elizabeth; the source of his royal blood; "thy light's flame" – Sonnet 1, line 6; "*Nativity, once in the main of light,*/ Crawls to maturity, wherewith being *crowned*" – Sonnet 60, lines 5-6

LAID BY HIS BRAND AND FELL ASLEEP = having been sent away, to a wet nurse, the newborn boy (to be raised as Henry Wriothesley, Third Earl of Southampton) is oblivious of his "brand" or torch of royal power inherited from the Virgin Queen; "And so the General of hot desire (the royal child)/ Was *sleeping* by a Virgin hand disarmed" – Sonnet 154, lines 7-8

(The earliest version of *A Midsummer Night's Dream* may have been written during the spring or summer of 1581, in anticipation of Henry Wriothesley – "the little western flower" – becoming a royal ward at Cecil House in December that year. An updated version apparently was presented in January 1595 for the wedding of Elizabeth Vere and William Stanley, Sixth Earl of Derby.)

2 A MAID OF *DIAN'S* THIS ADVANTAGE FOUND,
MAID OF DIAN'S = a servant to Elizabeth, known as Diana, the Moon goddess (*a.k.a.* Cynthia, Delia, Phoebe) and the Queen of Chastity; Diana was virgin Moon goddess of the hunt; "Making a couplement of proud compare/ With *Sunne and Moone*" – Sonnet 21, lines 5-6, referring to the royal son and his mother the Queen; "The *mortal Moon* hath her eclipse endured" – Sonnet 107, line 5, referring to the death of Elizabeth's mortal body

> *Fair Cynthia's* silver light,
> That beats on running streams…
> This *Cynthia's* silver light,
> This *sweet fair Dea* spread
> - Oxford poem, *What Cunning Can Express*, pre-1576
> (Of Elizabeth as Cynthia or Diana; *Dea* = Goddess)

"It is striking that in poetry and portaiture she (Elizabeth) was invariably represented as *an adored goddess or an untouchable virgin*, never as a mere female. She was *the moon-goddess, Cynthia, Diana*, or Belphoebe; the virginal Astraea or a Vestal Virgin; pure ermine or the unique phoenix" – Christopher Haigh, *Elizabeth I, Profiles in Power*, 1988-98, p. 23

In the next verse, linked to this one, the "maid of Dian's" will be "the fairest votary" or Queen Elizabeth herself (Sonnet 154, line 5); and in the main body of the Sonnets she will be a goddess: "O for my sake do you with fortune (Elizabeth) chide,/ The *guilty goddess of my harmful deeds,*/ That did not better for my life provide/ Than public means which public manners breeds" – Sonnet 111, lines 1-4, written after the Queen's death in March 1603, accusing her of having forced him to support his royal son in secret, since it was treason to claim succession to her throne for an unacknowledged heir; and in the Dark Lady verses, angrily and bitterly writing that she is not, after all, a goddess on earth: "I grant *I never saw a goddess go;*/ My Mistress when she walks treads on the ground" – Sonnet 130, lines 11-12

THIS ADVANTAGE FOUND = i.e., the baby boy was given to this servant, who thereby enabled the Queen to gain this political "advantage" over him; "Only, if your Honour seem but pleased, I account myself highly praised; and vow to take *advantage* of all idle hours, till I have honoured you with some graver labour" – Oxford's public dedication of *Venus and Adonis* to Southampton as "Shakespeare" in 1593; "Make use of time, let not *advantage* slip" – *Venus and Adonis*, line 129; "When I have seen the hungry Ocean gain/

Advantage on the Kingdom of the shore" – Sonnet 64, lines 5-6, referring to the expected succession of King James of Scotland on the English throne; "The injuries that to myself I do,/ *Doing thee vantage, double vantage me*" – Sonnet 88, lines 11-12, speaking as father to royal son, in reference to the sacrifice of the truth in order to save him; "Ah wherefore with infection should he live,/ And with his presence grace impiety,/ That sin by him *advantage* should achieve,/ And lace itself with his society?" – Sonnet 67, lines 1-4, referring to others in the Tower who are trying to take advantage of Southampton's presence as a prisoner among them there;

> And for her sake do I rear up her boy;
> And for her sake I will not part with him...
> Give me that boy, and I will go with thee...
> - *A Midsummer Night's Dream*, 2.1.136-137, 143

3 AND HIS LOVE-KINDLING FIRE DID QUICKLY STEEP
And this servant of Her Majesty hastily buried or concealed; **LOVE** = royal blood; "And *you and love* are still my argument" – Sonnet 76, line 10; **HIS LOVE-KINDLING FIRE** = the boy's power of royal blood; "Feed'st *thy light's flame* with self-substantial fuel" – Sonnet 1, line 6; **KINDLING** = related to "kind" or natural, i.e., the boy as her "kind" or natural son, who is thereby a royal prince; "Be as thy presence is, gracious and *kind*" – Sonnet 10, line 11, to Southampton; "*Kind* is my love today, tomorrow *kind*" – Sonnet 105, line 5, of Southampton

DID QUICKLY STEEP = did hastily or immediately hide or conceal this royal power possessed by the child; **QUICKLY** = related to the "quickening" of Elizabeth's pregnancy with him; Oxford will attempt to give "rebirth" and new "growth" to his son in the "womb" of the Sonnets, i.e., as the parent of these private verses written with his son's royal blood: "Why is my verse so *barren* of new pride?/ So far from variation or *quick* change?/ … That every word doth almost tell my name,/ *Showing their birth* and where they did *proceed*?" – Sonnet 76, lines 1-2, 7-8, with "proceed" = issue or come forth

4 IN A COLD VALLEY-FOUNTAIN OF THAT GROUND:
COLD VALLEY-FOUNTAIN = a place of cold water (and obscurity) where his royal blood could not be heated up; similar to the "cool well" of Sonnet 154, line 9; his mother's own womb, which was now cold; **FOUNTAIN** = the spring of royal Tudor Rose blood; "*Roses* have thorns, and *silver fountains* mud,/ Clouds and eclipses stain both *Moone and Sunne*" – Sonnet 35, lines 3-4, when Southampton has been imprisoned in the Tower in February 1601; **THAT GROUND** = the same English soil where the Queen's servant "found" the boy.

5 WHICH BORROWED FROM THIS HOLY FIRE OF LOVE
BORROWED FROM = i.e., his brand or torch took from this same hiding place or cold womb; related to the "loan" of his royal blood from the Queen: "Nature's bequest (the Queen's gift of her blood to you) gives nothing but doth *lend*" – Sonnet 4, line 3

THIS HOLY FIRE OF LOVE = this sacred or divine power of royal blood within our son; indicating the religious underpinnings of the Sonnets as a holy Monument consisting of sonnets-as-Pyramids for a king or god on earth; "Kings are earth's gods" – *Pericles*, 1.1.103; the holy blood that the boy has inherited from Elizabeth as a sacred monarch or God's representative on earth; "A *God in love*, to whom I am confined" – Sonnet 110, line 12, of Southampton; **HOLY** = "How many a *holy* and obsequious tear/ Hath *dear religious love* stol'n from mine eye" – Sonnet 31, lines 5-6; "In him those *holy* antique hours are seen" – Sonnet 68, line 9, referring to Southampton's lineage of royal or sacred blood of kings; his holiness inherited from Elizabeth; "It hath pleased God … to *makeme an instrument of His holy will*" – Elizabeth to Parliament in 1601

6 A DATELESS LIVELY HEAT STILL TO ENDURE,
DATELESS LIVELY HEAT = eternal royalty; **DATELESS** = without end; "For precious friends hid in death's *dateless* night" – Sonnet 30, line 6; **LIVELY** = living; "Nor *Mars* his sword nor war's quick fire

shall burn/ The *living record* of your memory" – Sonnet 55, lines 7-8, of these verses containing Southampton's living blood; "Why should poor beauty (Elizabeth) indirectly seek/ Roses (Tudor Rose heirs) of shadow, since his Rose (his blood of the Tudor Rose) is true?/ Why should he *live*, now nature (Elizabeth) bankrupt is,/ Beggared of *blood* to blush through *lively* veins?" – Sonnet 67, lines 7-10

STILL TO ENDURE = always to survive, in this life or in posterity or with eternal life; "Why write I *still* all one, ever the same/ … O know, sweet love, I always write of you,/ And you and love are *still* my argument/ For as *the Sun* is daily new and old,/ So is my love *still* telling what is told" – Sonnet 76, lines 5, 9-10, 13-14, referring to his son as the "onlie begetter" of the Sonnets, related to the biblical "onlie begotton Son"; "Since all alike my songs and praises be/ To one, of one, *still* such, and ever so./ Kind is my love today, tomorrow kind,/ *Still* constant in a wondrous excellence" – Sonnet 105, lines 3-6; **ENDURE** = continue to live in the future of the world; "The mortal Moon hath her eclipse *endured*" – Sonnet 107, line 5, referring in 1603 to the death of Elizabeth's mortal body (the eclipse of her light that shines upon the earth) and to the simultaneous endurance of her royal/spiritual self

7 AND GREW A SEETHING BATH WHICH YET MEN PROVE

GREW = became; related to the boy's growth, which has now begun; **GREW A SEETHING BATH** = turned into a hot bath; made the cold water turn hot, like the ancient hot springs of the City of Bath; glancing directly at the royal progress of August 1574 to Bath in western England; turned into Elizabeth's own royal waters, i.e., the waters of her womb and also of her divinely ordained self, used for healing; **WHICH MEN YET PROVE** = that men (such as Oxford) keep on attempting to use for relief or cure; **YET** = even to this day, since the time of the Roman conquest of England; also "still" or eternally, constantly, related to Elizabeth's immortal spirit; **PROVE** = demonstrate; discover to be; "Then may I dare to boast how I do love thee;/ Till then, not show my head where thou mayst *prove* me" – Sonnet 26, lines 13-14

8 AGAINST STRANGE MALADIES A SOVEREIGN CURE:

AGAINST STRANGE MALADIES = against unknown diseases or illnesses, such as Oxford's terrible sickness of the heart over having to give up his son; "But out alack, he was but one hour mine" – Sonnet 33, line 11, referring to his son by the Queen; **STRANGE MALADIES** = this phrase appears to be a play on "my sovereign lady" the Queen as acting "strange" or not in accordance with her natural motherhood of their son; i.e., "ma ladies" = "my lady"; Oxford in April of 1603 will refer to the recently deceased Elizabeth as "Ladies dead" in Sonnet 106, line 4

STRANGE = his illness stems from the fact that Elizabeth treats the boy as "strange" or as a "stranger" or as less than her "kind" or natural offspring; "Against that time when thou shalt *strangely* pass,/ And scarcely greet me with that sunne, thine eye" – Sonnet 49, lines 5-6, i.e., anticipating the time when his royal son will not acknowledge him as father; "What is your substance, whereof are you made,/ That millions of *strange shadows* on you tend?" – Sonnet 53, lines 1-2, referring to the shadows cast by Elizabeth's dark viewpoint of her son; "Why with the time do I not glance aside/ To new found methods, and to compounds *strange*?" – Sonnet 76, lines 3-4; "I will *acquaintance strangle and look strange,*/ Be absent from thy walks, and in my tongue/ Thy sweet beloved name no more shall dwell" – Sonnet 89, line 8, referring to his pledge to bury their relationship as father and son; "In many's looks, the *false heart's history*/ Is writ in moods and frowns and wrinkles *strange*./ But *heaven in thy creation* did decree/ That in thy face sweet love should ever dwell" – Sonnet 93, lines 7-10; "Most true it is, that I have *looked on truth/ Askance and strangely*" – Sonnet 110, lines 5-6; "Some *strange* commotion is in his brain" – *Henry VIII*, 3.2.112-113

MALADIES = related to "malcontent" or discontented, as he describes himself as "a *sad distempered guest*" in line 12 below; "As to prevent our *maladies* unseen" – Sonnet 118, line 3, used metaphorically; "Comes the King forth, I pray you? … Aye, Sir; there are a crew of wretched souls, that stay *his cure*; their *malady* convinces the great assay of art; but *at his touch*, such sanctity hath Heaven given his hand, they presently amend" – *Macbeth*, 4.3.140144; "See, see *the pining malady* of France; behold the wounds, the most unnatural wounds" – *1 Henry VI*, 3.3.49-50

A SOVEREIGN CURE = sacred help or remedy from Queen Elizabeth, the sovereign, who has divine power from God in matters of healing; help from the royal boy himself; **SOVEREIGN** = kingly, with the powers of the monarch; "I, *my sovereign*, watch the clock for you" – Sonnet 57, line 6, to Southampton as prince or king; "Full many a glorious morning have I seen/ Flatter the mountain tops with *sovereign* eye" – Sonnet 33, lines 1-2, picturing the sun as the eye of his royal son; "Nature, *sovereign mistress* over wrack" – Sonnet 126, line 5 (prior to the Queen's death marked by Sonnet 105, *nature* = Queen Elizabeth); "my *sovereign mistress*" – *The Winter's Tale*, 1.2.280; "the *sovereign mercy of the king*" – *Richard II*, 2.3.156; "A *mother*, and a *mistress*, and a *friend*, a *phoenix*, captain, and an enemy, a guide, a *goddess*, and a *sovereign*, a counselor, a traitress, and a dear" – *All's Well That Ends Well*, 1.1.167-170, Helena, referring to her virginity

CURE = "Pity me then, dear friend, and I assure ye,/ Even that your pity is enough *to cure me*" – Sonnet 111, lines 13-14, to his royal son; in the Dark Lady verses to Elizabeth he likens himself to "testy sick men, when their deaths be near …" – using physical illness as a metaphor for his mental anguish – "For if I should despair I should grow mad" – Sonnet 140, lines 7, 9; "*Past cure I am*, now reason is past care,/ And frantic mad with evermore unrest" – Sonnet 147, lines 9-10, again to Elizabeth; the only thing that can "cure" him is the viewpoint or "eye" of his Sovereign Mistress the Queen: "The bath for my help lies/ Where Cupid got new fire: *my mistress' eye*" – lines 13-14 below

SOVEREIGN CURE = "By the Tudor period the monarch had become clearly associated with the Maundy ceremony. The ceremony of washing the feet of the poor, done in imitation of Christ washing the feet of his disciples at the end of the Last Supper, was a part of the Easter vigil … The use of these religious ceremonies fit well with Elizabeth's self-presentation as the Virgin Queen, an image she presented to her people as a means to replace the Virgin Mary and help heal the rupture created by the break with the Catholic Church … Elizabeth's progresses were critical in systematically promoting the cult of the Virgin Queen for people of all classes all over the country. Sir Robert Burton suggested the very sight of the monarch could 'refresh the soul of man' … The continuation of the Maundy ceremony and touching for the king's evil were manifestations of the sacred aspect of monarchy Elizabeth represented to a people suffering from the dislocations of so many changes in church and state. Elizabeth deliberately performed these ceremonies with as much drama as possible, a holy or sacred theatre … Blessing and *curing* with the queen's touch was yet another aspect of religious functions subsumed by the monarch … Reginald Scot put it thus: 'God will not be offended thereas for hir majestie onlie useth godlie and divine praier, with some almes, and referreth *the cure* to God and to the physician'…As with touching, Elizabeth began celebrating the Maundy from the very beginning of her reign, and there are specific descriptions of a number of her Maundies, including 1560, 1565, *1572-1573*, and 1595 … There were carpets and cushions on which the queen could kneel and basins of holy water …" (Levin, *The Heart and Stomach of a King*, 1994, pp 10-38, emphases added)

> A most *miraculous work in this good King*,
> Which often, since my here-remain in England,
> I have seen him do. How he solicits Heaven,
> Himself best knows; but *strangely-visited people*,
> All swoln and ulcerous, pitiful to the eye,
> The more despair of surgery, *he cures*…
> - *Macbeth*, 4.3.148-152

9 BUT AT MY MISTRESS' EYE LOVE'S BRAND NEW-FIRED,
MY MISTRESS' EYE = Elizabeth's imperial point of view, positive or negative, which will determine the lightness or darkness of the words of Oxford's special vocabulary for the Sonnets; "the Queen's Majesty *our mistress*" – Oxford to Burghley, September 1572; "When all my best doth worship thy defect,/ *Commanded by the motion of thine eyes*" – Sonnet 149, lines 11-12, to Elizabeth, speaking as servant to his sovereign monarch; the Queen's eyes are black because she is in mourning for the loss of her royal son, who is in disgrace because she "slanders" him: "*Therefore my Mistress' eyes are Raven black,/ Her eyes so suited, and they mourners seem/ At such who, not born fair, no beauty lack,/ Slandering creation with a false esteem./ Yet so they mourn becoming of their woe*" – Sonnet 127, lines 9-13; "*My Mistress' eyes* are nothing like *the*

Sunne" – Sonnet 130, line 1, i.e., the eyes of my sovereign mistress, Elizabeth, are nothing like the royal eye of my royal son ("that sun thine eye" – Sonnet 49, line 6, to Southampton); "Me from my self *thy cruel eye* hath taken" – Sonnet 133, line 5, accusing her of taking his royal son from him; "Why of *eyes' falsehood* has thou forged hooks" – Sonnet 137, line 7, to Elizabeth

LOVE'S BRAND = royal blood's torch, its inner source, by inheritance, of power
NEW-FIRED = became hot with living royal blood all over again

10 THE BOY FOR TRIAL NEEDS WOULD TOUCH MY BREAST;
THE BOY = the newborn son of Elizabeth; i.e., the future Henry Wriothesley; the boy, in Oxford's imagination, touched his father's (Oxford's) breast, to test his torch of royal blood; "O Thou *my lovely Boy*" – Sonnet 126, line 1, the final verse in the chronological progression of this diary; i.e., "boy" is here at the beginning and also at the very end of the diary

> Because that she as her attendant hath
> *A lovely boy*, stolen from an Indian king;
> And never had so sweet a *changeling*;
> And jealous Oberon would have *the child*
> Knight of his train, to trace the forests wild;
> But she perforce *withholds* **the loved boy**
> - *A Midsummer Night's Dream*, 2.1.21-26

> Why should Titiana cross her Oberon?
> I do but beg *a little changeling boy*
> To be my henchman
> - *A Midsummer Night's Dream*, 2.1.119-121

> I then did ask of her her *changeling child*;
> Which straight she gave me, and her fairy sent
> To bear him to my bower in fairy land.
> And now I have *the boy*, I will undo
> This hateful imperfection of her eyes
> - *A Midsummer Night's Dream*, 4.1.58-62

> Touch not *the boy*; *he is of royal blood.*
> - *Titus Andronicus*, 5.1.49

> See, ruthless queen, *a hapless father's tears.*
> This cloth thou dipp'd'st in blood of **my sweet boy**,
> And I with tears do wash the blood away.
> - *3 Henry VI*, 1.4.156-158

FOR TRIAL NEEDS = in order to test me, i.e., to "prove" me; echoing language of a legal trial in a courtroom, related to "prove" in line 7 above; **TOUCH MY BREAST** = reach out and touch my father's heart; "O let my books be then the eloquence/ And dumb presagers of my speaking breast" – Sonnet 23, lines 9-10, to Southampton; "Mine eyes have drawn thy shape, and thine for me/ Are windows to my breast, where-through the Sun/ Delights to peep, to gaze therein on thee" – Sonnet 24, lines 10-12; virtually the same as *bosom*, which contains the heart and also acts as a receptacle of secrets; "But that you have *your father's bosom* there and speak *his very heart*" – The Winter's Tale, 4.4.565-566; "For through the painter must you see his skill/ To find where your true Image pictured lies,/ Which in *my bosom's* shop is hanging still,/ That hath his windows glazed with thine eyes" – Sonnet 24, lines 5-8

34

11 I SICK WITHAL THE HELP OF BATH DESIRED
I, Oxford, sick with grief over the loss of my royal son, sought help at Bath during the progress of the Queen and Court in August 1574.

12 AND THITHER HIED, A SAD DISTEMPERED GUEST,
And I hurried there (with Elizabeth and the Court), as an out-of-sorts guest; **DISTEMPERED** = "There is a *sickness* which puts some of us in *distemper*, but I cannot name the disease, and it is caught of you, that yet are well" – *The Winter's Tale*, 1.2.384-387; "O, you are *sick* of self-love, Malvolio, and taste with a *distempered* appetite" – *Twelfth Night*, 1.5.87-88; "The King, sir … is in his retirement marvelous *distempered*./ With drink, sir?/ No, my lord, with choler" – *Hamlet*, 3.2.300-305

"'I … thither hied.' Whither? Surely here is an allusion to the City of Bath, popular in Elizabethan times as 'against strange maladies a sovereign cure' … Here, then, I believe, we have an allusion to the poet's 'Mistress,' the Virgin Queen, and to the City of Bath … Was Shakespeare at Bath with the Queen? I think it probable that 'Shakespeare' was." - Sir George Greenwood, *The Shakespeare Problem Restated*, 1908, 127-129

13 BUT FOUND NO CURE. THE BATH FOR MY HELP LIES
But I found no cure for this emotional hell; the only bath that can help me is situated [elsewhere].
"It is rather curious, by the way, to find that Bath was celebrated not only as a health resort but as a favored abode of the Muses – that its springs were not only famed for healing virtue but as 'Pierian waters,' and that there were Swans of that Avon also!" – Sir George Greenwood, *The Shakespeare Problem Restated*, 1908, 127-129, referring to the Avon River that runs through the ancient Roman city of Bath

14 WHERE *CUPID* GOT NEW FIRE: MY MISTRESS' EYE.
WHERE *CUPID* GOT NEW FIRE = where our little son, a god on earth, got his power again, i.e., from the original source of his royal blood, i.e., from the Queen; "O Thou my lovely Boy, who in *thy power*" - Sonnet 126, line 1; **GOT** = related to "begot", i.e., inherited from Elizabeth by virtue of his birth; he is the "onlie begotten Son" of the Sonnets and will be called "the *onlie begetter* of these ensuing sonnets" in the Dedication, because the verses are his own "children nursed, delivered from thy brain" in Sonnet 77, line 11; "Unlooked on diest unless thou *get a son*" – Sonnet 7, line 14; "Seeds spring from seeds, and beauty breedeth beauty;/ Thou wast *begot*, to *get* it is thy duty" – *Venus and Adonis*, 1593, dedicated publicly to Southampton, lines 167-168

MY MISTRESS' EYE = Elizabeth's imperial will or eye; her (favorable) viewpoint as absolute monarch, i.e., her acknowledgment of him as her own; (but this cure for Oxford's woes was not forthcoming from the Queen)

THE BATH VISIT
OXFORD & ELIZABETH

Sonnet 154

The Little Love-God
August 21-23, 1574

*This companion piece is based on the same Greek epigram as Sonnet 153 and also relates to the royal visit to Bath in August of 1574. Oxford establishes his royal son in the Sonnets as "The little Love-God" or sacred prince who has been crippled: "And so the General of hot desire [Cupid]/ Was sleeping **by a Virgin hand disarmed.**" But his "love" or royal blood cannot be extinguished, regardless of Elizabeth's refusal to recognize him as the natural issue of her body. (Oxford's use of "Virgin" – his only use of the word in the Sonnets – further indicates this is a later-written sonnet. It refers to a time, later in Elizabeth's life, when she had become a political and professional virgin, and her Cult of Virginity had taken effect.)*

Sonnet 154	Translation
The little Love-God lying once asleep,	Our newborn royal son, oblivious in infancy,
Laid by his side his heart-inflaming brand,	Put aside his source of royal power,
Whilst many Nymphs that vowed chaste life to keep	While many who vowed to maintain virginity
Came tripping by, but in her maiden hand	Came near; but in her own hand
The fairest votary took up that fire,	His mother the Queen held his royal claim,
Which many Legions of true hearts had warmed,	Which many legions of my heart had kept alive,
And so the General of hot desire	And so England's rightful prince of royal blood
Was sleeping by a Virgin hand disarmed.	Was disenfranchised by the Virgin Queen.
This brand she quenched in a cool Well by,	She tried to hide and disgrace her son's blood,
Which from love's fire took heat perpetual,	Which drew its own immortal life from itself,
Growing a bath and healthful remedy	Becoming a womb of royal blood and a cure
For men diseased; but I, my Mistress' thrall,	For me; but I, bound to my royal Mistress' will,
Came there for cure, and this by that I prove:	Came there for relief, and in doing so I proved:
Love's fire heats water, water cools not love.	His royal blood lives in spite of everything.

1 THE LITTLE LOVE-GOD LYING ONCE ASLEEP
THE LITTLE LOVE-GOD = same as Cupid, the son of Oxford and Elizabeth, who was born three months earlier (in May/June 1574) and will be raised in the Southampton household as Henry Wriothesley, Third Earl of Southampton; "*Nativity*, once in the main of light,/ Crawls to maturity, wherewith being *crowned*" – Sonnet 60, lines 5-6; "*Love is a Babe*, then might I not say so,/ To give full growth to that which still doth grow" – Sonnet 115, lines 13-14, referring to the Sonnets as a womb in which his royal son is able to grow by the diary's calendar

LOVE = royal blood, possessed by Elizabeth and now, also, by her son; the Sonnets will record the struggle of **LOVE** (the royal blood Southampton inherited from the Queen) against **TIME** (the ever-waning life of Elizabeth, leading to her death and the royal succession), the goal being for Southampton to gain the throne and perpetuate the Tudor dynasty: "And *all in war with Time for love of you*" – Sonnet 15, line 13; "Lord of my *love*" – Sonnet 26, line 1; "O Thou my *lovely* Boy" – Sonnet 126, line 1; "*Two loves I have* (Elizabeth and Southampton, mother and son) of comfort and despair,/ Which like *two spirits* do suggest me still:/ The better angel is a man right fair,/ The worser spirit a woman coloured ill" – Sonnet 138, lines 1-4, referring to her dark or negative viewpoint, casting its shadow upon the Southampton, Oxford and herself.

The Sonnets are "hymns" or "prayers" to a god-on-earth or king, i.e., from father to divine prince: "From sullen earth *sings hymns at Heaven's gate*" – Sonnet 29, line 12; "What's new to speak, what now to register/ That may express my love, or thy dear merit?/ Nothing, *sweet boy*, but yet like *prayers divine*,/ I must each day say o'er the very same,/ Counting no old thing old, thou mine, I thine,/ Even as when first *I hallowed thy fair name*" – Sonnet 108, lines 3-8; "*Blessed* are you" – sonnet 52, line 13; "And *you in every blessed shape* we know" – Sonnet 53, line 12;

LITTLE = "Yet marked I where the bolt of Cupid fell: it fell upon *a little western flower*, before milk-white, now purple with love's wound" – *A Midsummer Night's Dream*, 2.1.165-167; "Come, *little ones*" – *Richard II*, 5.5.15, echoing the Gospel: "Then were there brought unto him little children, that he should put his hands on them, and pray: and the disciples rebuked them. But Jesus said, 'Suffer *little children*, and forbid them not to come unto me: for of such is the kingdom of heaven.' And he laid his hands on them" – *Matthew*, 19.13-15, the laying of "hands" echoing the healing theme of this verse and the contrasting "by *a Virgin hand* disarmed" in line 8 below;

LOVE-GOD = royal prince or sacred deity on earth, as in "his *sacred* majesty" of Sonnet 7, line four, i.e., Southampton, who will become "a *God in love*, to whom I am confined" in Sonnet 110, line 12; **GOD** = "*Gods on earth* was proverbially used of *kings*, as far back as Menander, and is frequent in Shakespeare" – Hotson; "Thou seem'st not what thou art, *a god, a king*" – *Lucrece*, 601; "*Kings* are earth's *gods*" – *Pericles*, 1.1.103; "A *god on earth* thou art" – to the king in *Richard II*, 5.3.134; "And this man is *now become a god*" – of Caesar in *Julius Caesar*, 1.2.116;

LYING ONCE ASLEEP = having become oblivious to his situation; having been taken away, into the hands of a wet-nurse; "But out alack, he was but one hour mine,/ The *region cloud* (Elizabeth Regina's imperial frown) hath masked him from me now" – Sonnet 33, lines 11-12; **ONCE** = immediately; perhaps alluding to Henry Wriothesley's motto *Once for All, All for One*; **LYING** = asleep, but also suggestive of "lying" or being unable to tell or know the truth about himself

2 LAID BY HIS SIDE HIS HEART-INFLAMING BRAND,
LAID BY = lay next to, i.e., next to the brand, which was by his side; set aside; "They have taken away the Lord out of sepulcher, and we know not where they have *laid* him" – Gospel of John, 20.2; **HIS HEART-INFLAMING BRAND** = his torch of royal blood that is fired by his heart; the "brand" may be imagined as his penis, given the overall sexual imaginary, but primarily because the male sex organ is the instrument by which his own royal seed will be able to perpetuate his blood lineage; (some commentators have observed that these first two lines fail to make sense, since the little Love-God is described as being able to lay aside his brand while sleeping; but the intended connotation is that the boy has become oblivious of his own royal power – an example of how Oxford's words on the surface may not be clear until they are "translated" according to his special language); the boy's own heart inflames his brand with "love" or royal blood, which, in turn, also serves to inflame the hearts of his subjects; "that fire,/ Which many legions of true hearts had warmed" – lines 5-6 below, i.e., which had warmed many legions of true hearts; "Thy bosom is endeared with *all hearts*" – Sonnet 31, line 1; "Then thou alone *kingdoms of hearts* shouldst owe" – Sonnet 70, line 14

3 WHILST MANY NYMPHS THAT VOWED CHASTE LIFE TO KEEP
NYMPHS THAT VOWED CHASTE LIFE TO KEEP = all of Elizabeth's Maids of Honour or female servants were required to take a vow of virginity and to remain unmarried; of course, the Queen herself was the one who, thus far, had vowed a life of singleness and chastity; "Then shall the kingdom of heaven be likened unto ten virgins, which took their lamps, and went forth to meet the bridegroom" – Gospel of Matthew, 25.1

And therefore, *lovely Tamora, Queen of Goths*,

> That like the stately Phoebe *'mongst her nymphs*
> Dost overshine the gallant'st dames of Rome...
> - *Titus Andronicus*, 1.1.320-322

The Queen and her Maids of Honour were "repeatedly referred to by the poets of the time as nymphs and fairies" – Eva Turner Clark, *Hidden Allusions*, p. 614, Miller, editor.

4 CAME TRIPPING BY; BUT IN HER MAIDEN HAND
MAIDEN HAND = the hand of Elizabeth, who would go onward "in *maiden* meditation, fancy-free" in *A Midsummer Night's Dream*, 2.1.164; same as "by a Virgin *hand*" – line 8 below

5 THE FAIREST VOTARY TOOK UP THAT FIRE,
FAIREST = most royal; here referring to the Queen; and when Oxford writes Sonnet 1, the first entry of the diary, the royal son will be *fairest creatures* or the most royal of children, reflecting the "beauty" of his mother, Queen Elizabeth: "From *fairest creatures* we desire increase,/ That thereby *beauty's* Rose might never die" – Sonnet 1, lines 1-2, announcing a diary related to the fate of her Tudor Rose dynasty; **VOTARY** = a votarist, one who has taken a vow, i.e., the vow of chastity mentioned in line 3; as Elizabeth made a vow to Oxford that eventually she would name their son as her successor; but she will fail to keep her promise and, at the close of the Dark Lady series, Oxford will accuse her: "In act *thy bed-vow broke* and new faith torn/ In *vowing new hate after new love bearing*" – Sonnet 152, lines 3-4, i.e., first you made a vow to me and then you made a vow to our son: "But why of *two oaths' breach* do I accuse thee" – Sonnet 152, line 5

FAIREST VOTARY = Queen Elizabeth, or Diana, who will be Titiana and the *Imperial Votress* (a woman who has taken a vow) who "passed on, in *maiden meditation, fancy-free*" – *A Midsummer Night's Dream*, 2.1.163; "The 'fairest votary' – the most beautiful devotee (of chastity and/or Diana); refines on the more random-sounding *maid of Dian's* in 153.2, allowing for a possibility that Cupid's assailant is Diana herself" – Duncan-Jones)

TOOK UP THAT FIRE = i.e., Elizabeth grabbed the torch of royal blood from where it lay next to her baby son, who slept in oblivion

> The *fairy* land buys not *the child* of me.
> *His mother* was a *votress* of my order
> - *A Midsummer Night's Dream*, 2.1.122-123

> *Cupid* all arm'd: a certain aim he took
> At a *fair vestal, throned by the west,*
> And loos'd *his love-shaft* smartly from his bow
> As it should pierce *a hundred thousand hearts.*
> But I might see *young Cupid's fiery shaft*
> Quenched in the **chaste beams of the watery moon** [Elizabeth, the Moon goddess]
> And the **imperial votress** passed on,
> In maiden meditation, fancy-free.
> Yet marked I where the bolt of Cupid fell:
> It fell upon *a little western flower,*
> Before milk-white, now *purple with love's wound*
> - *A Midsummer Night's Dream*, 2.1.157-167

> And from the forlorn world his visage hide,
> *Stealing unseen to west* with this *disgrace.*
> Even so *my Sunne* one early morn did shine... - Sonnet 33.7-9

"**Titiana** the Faire Queen under whom is figured our late **Queen Elizabeth**"
Thomas Dekker, *The Whore of Babylon*, 1607 (Dickinson, p. 130)

"In Shakespeare's version (of the Greek original) it is not 'amorous nymphs' but 'nymphs that vowed chaste life to keep,' and it is not nymphs generally, but one of them that is said to take up the 'heart-inflaming brand.' This nymph is described as 'the fairest votary,' and in the companion sonnet as 'a maid of Dian's' (Sonnet 153, line 2). Who is meant? I cannot doubt that this 'fairest votary' is the same as 'the Imperial votaress' of the *Midsummer Night's Dream*, against whom 'Cupid's fiery shaft' was launched in vain, being 'quenched in the chaste beams of the watery moon' – and we all remember the famous portrait of Elizabeth as Diana with the crescent moon on her brow." – Sir George Greenwood, *The Shakespeare Problem Restated*, 1908, 127-129

6 WHICH MANY LEGIONS OF TRUE HEARTS HAD WARMED;
TRUE = related to Oxford, *Nothing Truer than Truth*; **LEGIONS** = "multitudes … allusion to Roman legions" – Duncan-Jones; echoing the Roman-built shrines in the City of Bath; referring to the lineage of the Tudor Rose, whose "legions" (armies) and "true hearts" (royal family members) went back to the Wars of the Roses and the founding of the House of Tudor by Henry VII in 1485; "In him *those holy antique hours are seen*" – Sonnet 68, line 9, of Southampton as latest in a long line of divinely ordained English kings

7 AND SO THE GENERAL OF HOT DESIRE
THE GENERAL = the infant boy, now the leader or chief or commander of "legions" or subjects as the next King of England; "*the General* of our gracious Empress" – *Henry V*, 5.0.30, believed to refer to the Earl of Essex as general of Queen Elizabeth's army in Ireland, 1599; **GENERAL OF HOT DESIRE** = the royal son, Cupid or the little Love-God, whose hot blood is translated into royal will; also, whose sexual passion will result in new heirs to the throne: "From fairest creatures *we desire* increase" – Sonnet 1, line 1, to Southampton at sixteen in 1590, using the royal "we" to "desire" or command him to perpetuate his blood by marriage and propagation

8 WAS SLEEPING BY A VIRGIN HAND DISARMED.
Thus was I, *sleeping, by a brother's hand*
Of life, of crown, of queen at once *dispatched*
(The Ghost of Hamlet's father, murdered by his own brother, King Claudius)
- *Hamlet*, 1.5.74-75

SLEEPING = oblivious, i.e., the infant boy, while unaware; **VIRGIN** = pertaining to a maiden, a woman of no "knowledge" of a man; evoking Queen Elizabeth as the Virgin Queen of Protestant England, in effect replacing the Virgin Mary of Catholicism; "Behold, *a virgin shall be with child, and shall bring forth a son*, and they shall call his name Emanuel, which being interpreted is, God with us" – Gospel of Matthew, 1.23

BY A VIRGIN HAND DISARMED = The boy has been cast aside (and disgraced) by Elizabeth, the Virgin Queen, whose own "hand" had created him: "A Woman's face with *nature's own hand* painted" – Sonnet 20, line 1, referring to Southampton as the child or son created by Nature or his mother, Queen Elizabeth. She has arranged for him to eventually enter the Southampton household as Henry Wriothesley, the future Third Earl of Southampton and later to become her Royal Ward in Burghley's custody, as Oxford had been a generation earlier.

DISARMED = deprived or divested of arms, or of a royal coat-of-arms; referring to the royal son being relegated to the status of an unacknowledged royal bastard and thereby disgraced by the hand of the Queen; metaphorically murdered by the Virgin Queen. "If then, thus taking the commodity into **her own hand**, Her Majesty please to impose two pence one every hundred…" – Oxford in the "Tin Mining" letters, Huntington Library MS EL 2344

And *by their hands* this grace of kings must die - *Henry VI*, 2.0 Chorus.28

And *by her fair immortal hand* she swears - *Venus and Adonis*, line 80

By Venus' hand I swear - *Troilus and Cressida*, 4.1.23

See, ruthless queen, *a hapless father's tears*.
This cloth thou dipp'd'st in blood of *my sweet boy*,
And I with tears do wash the blood away…
There, take the crown, and with the crown my curse;
And in thy need such comfort come to thee
As now I reap *at thy too cruel hand!*
- *3 Henry VI*, 1.4.156-166

Yet shall you have all kindness *at my hand* - King Lewis in *3 Henry VI*, 3.3.149

By beg one favor *at thy gracious hand* - *Richard III*, 1.2.211

"For since *each hand hath put on Nature's power*" – Sonnet 127, line 5, with Nature = the first verse of the Dark Lady series to Elizabeth; i.e., Nature is the Queen and her "power" comes from her imperial authority as absolute monarch; "From *hands of falsehood*" – Sonnet 48, line 4, to Southampton in the Fair Youth series, referring to the powerful "hands" of the Queen and Robert Cecil; "Or *at your hand* th'account of hours to crave" – Sonnet 58, line 3, i.e., at your royal hand or command; "With *time's injurious hand* crushed and o'erworn" – Sonnet 63, line 2, referring to the ever-waning time of Elizabeth's life; "When I have seen *by time's fell hand* defaced" – Sonnet 64, line 1; "Where, alack,/ Shall time's best Jewel (Southampton) from time's chest lie hid?/ Or *what strong hand* can hold his swift foot back?" – Sonnet 65, lines 9-11

A VIRGIN HAND = although Elizabeth has "disarmed" her royal son simply by the wave of her powerful hand, ironically it is "the Queen's touch" that may cure him; "The kings of England by touch of their annointed hands they cleanse and cure those inflected with a certain disease, that is commonly called the King's evil" – Fortescue, quoted by Levin, 16; "Yet less than a century later, both Mary and Elizabeth (Tudor) were touching for the king's evil … surely the tradition of the virgin saint as healer would resonate as well for a Virgin Queen who healed by touch … Blessing and curing with the Queen's touch was yet another aspect of religious functions subsumed by the monarch … Elizabeth expressed herself eager to cure by touching throughout her reign with elaborate ceremony" – Carole Levin, *The Heart and Stomach of a King*, 16-31

"O blessed peace, oh happy Prince, O fortunate people: The living God is onely the Englysh God, wher he hath placed *a Virgin Queene*, which with a wand ruleth hir own subjects…" – John Lyly, secretry to Edward de Vere, Earl of Oxford, in *Euphues and his England*, 1580, dedicated to Oxford and probably written and/or dictated by him in whole or part – indicating his continued loyalty to Elizabeth, who had vowed to recognize their son's royal blood in the future

9 THIS BRAND SHE QUENCHED IN A COOL WELL BY,
Elizabeth put out her son's torch of royal blood by burying it in the cool well of oblivion, lack of acknowledgment, and royal bastardy; "And his love-kindling fire did quickly steep/ In a cold valley-fountain of that ground" – Sonnet 153, lines 3-5; "Many waters cannot *quench* love, neither can the floods drown it" – the biblical Song of Solomon, 8.7

10 WHICH FROM LOVE'S FIRE TOOK HEAT PERPETUAL,
"Which borrowed from this holy fire of love/ A *dateless lively heat*, still to endure" – Sonnet 153, lines 5-6;
FROM LOVE'S FIRE = from the power of his royal blood; "self-substantial fuel" – Sonnet 1, line 6;
HEAT = royal power; **PERPETUAL** = never-ceasing, everlasting, endless; **HEAT PERPETUAL** = eternal "love" or royal power; "and do not kill/ *The spirit of love* with a *perpetual* dullness" – Sonnet 56, lines 7-8, to Southampton; Oxford in 1-17 he will urge him to beget an heir: "This were to be new made when thou art old,/ And see *thy blood warm* when thou feel'st it cold" – Sonnet 2, lines 13-14; "Lo, in the Orient when the gracious light/ Lifts up his *burning* head" – Sonnet 7, lines 1-2, the sun or royal son

11 GROWING A BATH AND HEALTHFUL REMEDY
GROWING = becoming a boiling hot bath; referring also to the ongoing growth of the boy; "When in eternal lines to time thou *grow'st*" – Sonnet 18, line 12; "Love is a Babe, then might I not say so,/ To *give full growth to that which still doth grow*" – Sonnet 115, lines 13-14; growing into a new hot bath (medicinal hot natural spring) and thereby into a possible "remedy" or cure for his grief over the situation.

12 FOR MEN DISEASED; BUT I, MY MISTRESS' THRALL,
FOR MEN DISEASED = for me, i.e., for Oxford, who is suffering this loss; **BUT I, MY MISTRESS' THRALL** = but I, my Queen's loyal servant; "And shall I live on th'earth to be *her thrall*?" – Oxford poem, referring to his loyalty to Elizabeth, published in 1576 and signed E. O. for Earl of Oxford; "I cannot but find a great grief in myself to remember *the Mistress* which we have lost" – Oxford to Robert Cecil, April 25/27, 1603, on the eve of Elizabeth's funeral

13 CAME THERE FOR CURE, AND THIS BY THAT I PROVE:
CAME THERE = I went to Bath for a cure, but by this I demonstrated or discovered; **PROVE** = demonstrate or discover to be true; "Then may I dare to boast how I do love thee,/ Till then, not show my head where *thou mayst prove me*" – Sonnet 26, lines 13-14; "For you in me can nothing worthy *prove*" – Sonnet 72, line 4; "And worst essays *proved thee my best of love*" – Sonnet 110, line 8; "If this be error and *upon me proved,*/ I never write, nor no man ever loved" – Sonnet 116, lines 13-14; "Since my appeal says *I did strive to prove*/ The constancy and virtue of *your love*" – Sonnet 117, lines 13-14, again with "love" = royal blood; "For he was likely, had he been put on, to have *prov'd most royal*" – Hamlet, 5.2.404-405, Horatio, speaking of the now-dead Prince of Denmark

14 LOVE'S FIRE HEATS WATER, WATER COOLS NOT LOVE.
The power of royal blood continues and cannot be extinguished; the fire of our son's "love" or royal blood will heat the womb-water of a Roman bath, but no water will cool down or take away the heat of that "love" or divinely ordained blood; "I raised thee up under the apple tree: there thy mother brought thee forth: there she brought thee forth that bare thee. Set me as a seal upon thine heart, as a seal upon thine arm: for love is strong as death: jealousy is cruel as the grave: the coals thereof are coals of fire, which hath a most vehement flame. *Many waters cannot quench love, neither can the floods drown it*" – the Biblical Song of Solomon, KJV, 8.5-7

Note: The first human use of the hot mineral springs at Bath began at least 10,000 years earlier. The Celts, arriving in England around 700 BC, erected what may have been the first "shrine" structures at the springs. Dedicated to Sulis, a goddess of water, the shrines provided a religious center for southwest England. The Romans arrived in 43 AD, took over the Celtic shrine and identified Sulis with their own goddess, Minerva, as a healing deity. Over the next four centuries they constructed increasingly elaborate bathing and temple complexes, the main one bubbling a quarter-million gallons per day at 120 degrees Fahrenheit. This spring became a sacred place where mortals communicated with deities and sought assistance from Sulis-Miverva, often throwing votive offerings into the waters.

1574

September 1574: The royal progress continues until mid-September. Edward de Vere remains with Elizabeth and the Court, returning to Burghley's home of Theobalds and a round of supper parties with Lady Lennox, Lord and Lady Northumberland and Lady Hundson. Anne Cecil asks Lord Chamberlain Sussex for extra space at Hampton Court, because "the more commodious my lodging is the willinger I hope my Lord my husband will be to come thither."

October 1574: Oxford and Anne both attend the Queen at Hampton Court. The marriage may have been consummated at this time; but Oxford, planning an authorized trip to the Continent, tells the Queen "openly in the presence chamber" that, if Anne becomes pregnant, the child will not be his. (Ward, 114)

1575

February 1575: Oxford departs for Paris with "two gentlemen, two grooms, one payend, a harbinger, a housekeeper, and a trenchman."

March 7, 1575: English ambassador Valentine Dale presents Oxford to the King and Queen of France at the French Court.

March 7, 1575: Elizabeth holds an audience at Richmond with Dr. Richard Masters, who writes that evening to Burghley. He explains he approached Her Majesty with the news that Anne Cecil is evidently with child. "Herewithal she arose, or rather sprang up from the cushion," he writes, adding she said: "I protest to God that next to them that have interest in it, there is nobody that can be more joyous of it than I am!" Dr. Masters informed the Queen that Burghley had "concealed" the news and that Anne had asked him "to prepare some medicines ad menses promotions *['to cause the menses to resume'], but I counseled her to stay awhile." (Unless she had been unfaithful or had been raped, it is difficult to comprehend why the Countess would abort a potential son who would inherit the Oxford earldom.) Elizabeth asked "how the young lady did bear the matter" and the doctor replied "that she kept it secret four or five days from all persons and that her face was much fallen and thin with little color, and that when she was comforted and counseled to be gladsome and so rejoice, she would cry, 'Alas, alas, how should I rejoice seeing he that should rejoice with me is not here; and to say truth [I] stand in doubt whether he pass upon me and it or not.' And bemoaning her case, would lament that after so long sickness of body she should enter a new grief and sorrow of mind." The Queen, showing compassion for the girl, angrily repeated Oxford's pledge "which he made openly in the presence chamber of Her Majesty, viz., that if she were with child it was not his." At this point she summoned Leicester, telling him all, "and severally she showed herself unfeignedly to rejoice, and in great offence with my Lord of Oxford, repeating the same to my Lord of Leicester."*

March 17, 1575: Before leaving Paris, Oxford receives news from Burghley that Anne is definitely pregnant. He writes back: "My Lord, your letters have made me a glad man, for these last have put me in assurance of that good fortune which you formerly mention doubtfully. I thank God therefore, with your Lordship, that it hath pleased Him to make me a father, where your Lordship is a grandfather; and if it be a boy I shall likewise be the partaker with you in a greater contentation. But thereby to take an occasion to return I am off from that opinion; for now it hath pleased God to give me ***a son of mine own*** (as I hope it is) methinks I have better occasion to travel, sith whatsoever becometh of me I leave behind me one to supply my duty and service, either to my Prince or else my country." (Ward, 102, emphases added)

Oxford visits in Germany with Protestant scholar John Sturmius of Strasburg University, one of the great learning centers of Europe, conversing with him in Latin.

April 26, 1575: Oxford departs Strasburg *en route* to Italy. By the end of the month he will reach Padua, another great center of the arts and learning.

May 1575: Archbishop Parker of Canterbury dies.

July 2, 1575: Anne Cecil gives birth to Elizabeth Vere, named in honor of Queen Elizabeth.

Summer 1575: Elizabeth goes on the royal progress culminating in a visit to Kenilworth, where Leicester provides the most extravagant and costly entertainment of the reign, lasting ten days.

September 24, 1575: Possibly having visited Greece and now in Venice, Oxford learns his wife gave birth to a daughter. He writes back to Burghley, but only near the end of his letter does he briefly mention the subject: "Thus thanking your Lordship for your good news of my wife's delivery, I recommend myself unto your favor…"

Ward notes a Latin poem addressed "To the illustrious Lady Anne de Vere, Countess of Oxford, while her noble husband, Edward de Vere, Earl of Oxford, was occupied in foreign travel." His translation: *"Words of truth are fitting to a Vere; lies are foreign to the **truth**, and only **true** things stand fast, all else is fluctuating and comes to an end. Therefore, since thou, aVere, art a wife and mother of a Vere daughter, and seeing that thou may'st with good hope look forward to being mother of an heir of the Veres, may thy mind always glow with love of the **truth**, and may thy **true** motto be **Ever Lover of the Truth**..."* (Emphases added)

November 1575: Oxford writes to Burghley from Padua: "I shall desire your Lordship to make no stay of the sales of my land…"

December 1575: Oxford leaves Venice for Florence.

1576

A Hundredth Sundry Flowres is published with major revision under the title *The Posies of George Gascoigne*, obscuring Oxford as the probable editor and publisher of the original work as well as its major (or only) contributor.

January 1576: Writing from Siena, Oxford asks Burghley to let more of his land be sold. ("My Lord, I am sorry to hear how hard my fortune is in England … I understand the greatness of my debt and the greediness of my creditors grows so dishonorable and troublesome…") He repeats his desire to keep traveling, "having made an end of all hope to help myself by Her Majesty's service … That I am determined to hope for anything, I do not; but if anything do happen *preter spem*, I think before that time I must be as old as (that) *my son, who shall enjoy them,* must give the thanks; and I am to content myself according to the English proverb that it is my hap to starve while the grass doth grow." He makes no mention of his wife or baby girl.

January-March 1576: "For the next three months his movements are not known; but he seems to have visited Sicily, probably via Rome." (Ward, 111)

March 31, 1576: Having passed through Lyons at Carnival time, Oxford arrives in Paris.

April 4, 1576: In an overwhelming passion, Oxford starts for England. Pirates attack his ship and hold him captive, taking all his possessions, before letting him go.

April 20, 1576: Oxford arrives to find Burghley and Anne waiting to greet him, but he brushes past and proceeds straight to the Queen. (Ward, 118) Stow reports that "the right honorable Edward de Vere, Earl of Oxford, came from Italy, and brought with him gloves, sweet bags, a perfumed leather jerkin, and other pleasant things; and that year the Queen had a pair of perfumed gloves trimmed only with four tufts, or roses of colored silk; the Queen took such pleasure in those gloves that she was pictured with those gloves upon her hands, and for many years after it was called the Earl of Oxford's perfume." (Ward, 129)

April 27, 1576: Oxford makes his separation from Anne Cecil official. He writes to Burghley that "until I can better satisfy or advertise myself of some mislikes, I am not determined, as touching my wife, to accompany her … I mean not to weary my life any more with such troubles and molestations as I have endured; nor will I, to please your Lordship only, discontent myself." He agrees that his father-in-law should take Anne and the child under his roof, "for there, as your daughter or her mother's more than my wife, you may take comfort of her; and I, rid of the cumber thereby, shall remain well eased of many griefs … This might have been done through private conference before, and had not needed to have been the fable of the world if you would have had the patience to have understood me." Another letter from Oxford, containing "definite allegations against his parents-in-law," has been lost. (Ward, 123)

1576: *A Paradise of Dainty Devices* is published with seven poems signed by Edward de Vere, with his initials *E. O.* for Earl of Oxford. The poems are represented as compiled by Richard Edwards, who died in 1566, but Oxford undoubtedly produced the collection.

1577

The Southampton household faces trouble that may have begun earlier but now erupts in terms of the surviving records of it. The second earl has been "impoverishing himself" by lavishing funds on a new mansion and "maintaining a retinue much larger than he needed," Akrigg reports on p. 12 of his biography of the third earl. (Is this larger retinue related to the presence of the royal son of the Queen?) The second earl's marriage "was turning out to be an unhappy one ... The danger signals were plainly flying around 1577 when the Earl, upset at the intimacy of her friendship with a man named Donsame, 'a common person,' forbade her ever to see him again." (Was this man 'Donsame' the father of the boy born on October 6, 1573? Was the Queen's son by Oxford substituted for that boy?)

January 1, 1577: The Paul's Boys perform *The historie of Error* (perhaps the first version of *The Comedy of Errors*) for Elizabeth and the Court.

February 17, 1577: Actors under Charles Howard of Effingham (the future Lord Admiral) and Lord Chamberlain Sussex perform *The Historie of the Solitarie Knight* at Whitehall. This may be the early version of *Timon of Athens*, in which Timon cries: "Let all my land be sold!"

February 19, 1577: The Paul's Boys perform *The historye of Titus and Gisippus* (perhaps the play *Titus Andronicus*) at Whitehall Palace.

October 1577: Oxford becomes an "adventurer" (investor) in the third Frobisher expedition (to find the fabled Northwest Passage to China) set for next year.

December 1577: Francis Drake sets sail on his three-year circumnavigation of the globe. A play performed for the Queen may be *Pericles, Prince of Tyre*. The first volume of Raphael Holinshed's *Chronicles* comes off the press.

1578

Elizabeth conveys the Manor of Rysing (originally belonging to Norfolk and confiscated by the Crown after the Duke's execution) to Edward deVere. She cites "the good, true, and faithful service done and given to Us before this time by Our most dear cousin."

July 1578: Elizabeth visits Cambridge, accompanied by the whole Court including Burghley, Leicester, Oxford, Vice-Chamberlain Hatton and Philip Sidney. Gabriel Harvey (a fellow at Trinity Hall, who has known Oxford for many years) presents the Queen and her courtiers with a series of Latin tributes. In his address to Oxford, he urges the earl to forget about his literary career and become more involved in military defense against Spain and King Philip's half-brother, Don John of Austria, who is crushing the Protestants in the Netherlands:

"Mars will obey thee, Hermes will be thy messenger, Pallas striking her shield with her spear shaft will attend thee, thine own breast and courageous heart will instruct thee. For a long time past Phoebus Apollo has cultivated thy mind in the arts. English poetical measures have been sung by thee long enough! Let that Courtly Epistle [Oxford's Letter to the Reader of The Courtier in 1572], more polished even than the writings of Castiglione himself, witness how greatly thou dost excel in letters. I have seen many Latin verses of thine, yea, even more English verses are extant; thou hast drunk deep draughts not only of the Muses of France and Italy, but hast learned the manners of many men, and the arts of foreign countries. It was not for nothing that Sturmius himself was visited by thee; neither in France, Italy, nor Germany are any such cultivated and polished men. O thou hero worthy of renown, throw away the insignificant pen, throw away bloodless books, and writings that serve no useful purpose; now must the sword be brought into play, now is the time for thee to sharpen the spear and to handle great engines of war ... In thy breast is noble

blood. Courage animates thy brow, Mars lives in thy tongue, Minerva strengthens thy right hand, Bellona reigns in thy body, within thee burns the fire of Mars. Thine eyes flash fire, thy countenance shakes a spear; who would not swear that Achilles had come to life again?"
(Translation by Ward)

Summer 1578: Amid the royal progress, Elizabeth rebukes Sussex for failing to provide enough "plate" for the French diplomats negotiating the Alençon match; in return, Oxford refuses to obey Her Majesty's request that he dance for the foreign guests.

1579

January 1579: Oxford and other courtiers enact a masque before the Queen.

Anthony Munday dedicates *Mirror of Mutability* to Oxford, who also employs Thomas Churchyard, John Lyly, Ralph Lane and other writers recommended by Burghley.

Geoffrey Gates dedicates *Defense of the Military Profession* to Oxford.

Edmund Spenser publishes *The Shepherd's Calendar.*

Spring 1579: Elizabeth, still pretending she will marry Alençon of France (nineteen years her junior), receives his advance man M. de Simier and begins a romance with him. Oxford (with Burghley, Sussex and Hunsdon) is publicly supporting the French Match; Leicester and his nephew, Philip Sidney, are leading the faction opposed to it.

According to Burghley, the Court doctors confirm that Elizabeth, forty-five, is still perfectly fit to become a mother: "Nature cannot amend her shape in any part to make her more likely to conceive and bear children without peril." (Weir, 321)

August 1579: Simier informs the Queen that Leicester has secretly married Lettice Knollys, widow of Walter Devereux, First Earl of Essex (who may well have been poisoned through Leicester's machinations). Elizabeth banishes Leicester from Court.

Alençon arrives in England in disguise (with advance approval) and appears at Greenwich, where Elizabeth appears delighted with him. The Duke is an ardent suitor and she responds with equal fervor, leaving Leicester in a state of outrage and the Puritans scandalized.

Oxford and Sidney become involved in a "quarrel" on the tennis court in front of the French delegation, whose members watch from the windows of their private galleries. Elizabeth takes Oxford's side, citing his high rank. After writing an open letter to the Queen protesting the French Match and receiving a severe rebuke, Sidney retires for a year to the home of his sister (Mary Sidney, Countess of Pembroke) at Wilton House (where he will write *Arcadia*).

1580

January 1580: Oxford's New Year's gift to the Queen is "a fair jewel of gold, being a ship garnished fully with diamonds, and a mean pearl pendant."

"A pleasant conceit of Vere, Earl of Oxford, discontented at the rising of a mean gentleman in the English Court, *circa* 1580" (reportedly cited in *Desiderata Curiosa*, 1732-35) may refer to *Twelfth Night* and Malvolio as a caricature of Sir Christopher Hatton.

February 2, 1580: *The history of Portio and demorantes*, performed for the Queen at Whitehall by the Lord Chamberlain's (Sussex's) Men, may be an early version of *The Merchant of Venice*.

March 21, 1580: The Second Earl of Southampton has learned by now that his wife (Mary Browne, Countess of Southampton) has been seen with "Donsame" under circumstances leaving him "no doubt that the man was her lover," Akrigg writes on p. 13. "In his fury the Earl broke not only with her but with her family." The Countess has been "forever banished" from her husband's "board and presence," she writes her father (Anthony Browne, Viscount Montague) from one of their residences in Hampshirre, where the earl has been "keeping her under close surveillance and permitting her only occasional visits by carefully selected guests."

From this letter it emerges that the earl is dealing with his wife "only through an intermediary, one Thomas Dymock, a gentleman of his bedchamber" who has virtually taken over the household. Her husband, she writes, stands "so doubtful and perplexed between hate and dread" of Dymock that "as what to do he knoweth not well." (Has Dymock been sent by the Queen and/or Burghley to supervise the Second Earl of Southampton and keep his Countess isolated?) The Countess, reports Akrigg, writes that her husband "has said that he will be reconciled with her only if the Queen herself instructs him to end their separation, and mockingly he has declared that Her Majesty will never open her mouth on his wife's behalf."

In a postscript to her father, the Countess says she tried to pass a letter to her husband "by my little boy" – a reference to Henry Wriothesley, the future Third Earl of Southampton, now about six years of age. Apparently the boy brought this letter to the second earl, who refused to read it. "The father saw to it that, as long as he lived, the Countess would not see their son again." (Akrigg, p. 14)

April 1580: Warwick's actors have transferred into Oxford's service.

Summer 1580: Burghley and Sussex recommend that Oxford's Men be allowed at Cambridge to "show their cunning in several plays already practiced by them before the Queen's Majesty."

The Jesuits Edmund Campion and Robert Parsons arrive in England to enlist recruits in the Pope's war against England. As the Privy Council begins a policy of increased severity toward recusants, Burghley and Walsingham step up surveillance of Catholics.

John Lyly dedicates *Euphues his England* to Oxford, his employer, implying that Oxford also helped him with *Euphues, The Anatomy of Wit* of the previous year. This work will be an important source of language and themes to be used in *Shake-Speares Sonnets*.

Gabriel Harvey, writing to poet Edmund Spenser, includes a caricature of Oxford. In addition to making humorous sport of the earl as the quintessential Italianate Englishman (Euphues), he suggests Oxford works for Burghley and spymaster Walsingham: "Not the like discourser for Tongue, and head to be found out,/ Not the like resolute man for great and serious affairs,/ Not the like Lynx to spy out secrets and privities of States…"

Anthony Munday, the anti-Catholic English spy, dedicates *Zelauto, the Fountain of Fame* to Oxford, who employs him.

September 1580: Drake returns from his voyage round the world, bringing back great wealth from his piracy of Spanish treasure.

December 1580: Oxford charges his Catholic associates (Henry Howard, Charles Arundel and Francis Southwell) with treasonous plans involving Spain and the Pope.

Prologue

1581

January 12, 1581: The English government issues a Proclamation outlawing any harboring of Jesuits and priests who may be planning "treasonable attempts" against the state – a drastic change from the long policy of leniency and tolerance, undoubtedly sparked by Oxford's charges the previous month.

One consequence is that the Second Earl of Southampton is imprisoned once again, according to historian Father Henry Foley, in Records of the English Province of the Society of Jesus, published in 1877(Vo. III, 659). The dates of his imprisonment this year are unclear, but he will die in October, paving the way for the boy Henry Wriothesley to become a royal ward of the Queen in Burghley's custody.

January 22, 1581: Oxford is victorious at a jousting tournament. At the beginning, dressed in "rich gilt armor" as the Knight of the Tree of the Sun, he mounts his horse while his page (perhaps the boy Henry Wriothesley) delivers an oration to Queen Elizabeth.

March 1581: A new and stricter Statute of Recusancy raises fines for non-attendance at Anglican services, imposes a year in prison for attending mass, and branding anyone who converts to the Roman Catholic faith as a traitor. The act also makes it a crime to predict how long the Queen will live and to forecast her successor.

Anne Vavasour, a Maid of Honour to the Queen and a relative of Henry Howard, reportedly gives birth to a son by Oxford in the Maiden's Chamber. She is taken from the Palace the same night and committed to the Tower of London the following day. With the Queen in a rage, Oxford is soon imprisoned in the Tower as well.

April 1581: The long-awaited delegation of high-ranking French commissioners arrives at Whitehall to conclude negotiations for the marriage of Elizabeth, now forty-seven, and the Duke of Alençon, twenty-eight. Oxford remains in prison.

May 1581: The French commissioners are treated to dinners, plays, masques, pageants and other festive events including, possibly, an early masque version of *A Midsummer Night's Dream*. The Queen makes every effort to drag out negotiations for her marriage; Oxford is still in the Tower.

June 1581: Oxford is released from the Tower "by Her Majesty's commandment," according to the Privy Council, which notes he had not been imprisoned "upon any cause of treason or criminal cause." Nonetheless he remains in the disfavor of the Queen (for the Vavasour affair) and will remain banished from Court for two years. Amid counter-charges against him by Howard and Arundel, he writes to Burghley: "But the world is so cunning, as of a shadow they can make a substance, and of a likelihood a truth."

Alençon is fighting Spanish interests in the Netherlands, but Elizabeth insists he come to England to endorse the marriage treaty in person.

July 1581: Edmund Campion is arrested, tortured on the rack and interrogated. Refusing to recant his Catholic faith or name his associates, he is hanged, drawn and quartered.

August 1581: The English government learns that the Second Earl of Southampton had been in communication with Campion through Thomas Dymoke, the gentleman of his bedchamber who has held mysterious power over the household. The earl, whose marital separation continues, is again in trouble and possibly facing yet another return to the Tower.

October 1581: The Second Earl of Southampton dies – possibly of ill health caused by stress, of suicide or of murder by poison. (At this time, with Burghley leading the way, Oxford is ending his separation from Anne Cecil. As a condition, he may have demanded that Henry Wriothesley will become a royal ward at the same time. If so, was the second earl tortured in the Tower this year, so he would die soon?)

November 1581: With Philip of Spain making new threats of war, Alençon leaves his troops in the Netherlands and arrives in England, hoping to gain financial help for his military campaign. Meeting him at Richmond Palace, the Queen calls him her "Prince Frog" and "Little Moor" while exclaiming he has been "the most constant of all my lovers." At St. Paul's she kisses him in full view of the congregation. At Whitehall, declaring that Alençon "shall be my husband," she kisses him on the mouth and initiates an exchange of rings constituting a formal betrothal. But then she changes her mind, saying she can't marry him right away. Despite the Queen's change of heart, Alençon refuses to leave England.

December 1581: Oxford reunites with his wife, Anne Cecil, daughter of Lord Burghley, thereby tacitly accepting six-year-old Elizabeth Vere as his daughter. Simultaneously young Henry Wriothesley, officially eight years old, enters Cecil House as the eighth and final royal ward of the Queen to be raised in Burghley's custody. In a real way this is an extended official family. With the exception of Anne Cecil, whose death will occur in 1588, all its members (Queen Elizabeth, Lord Burghley, Lord Oxford, Henry Wriothesley and Lady Elizabeth Vere) will be participants in Sonnets 1-17, the "marriage and propagation" verses, during 1590-1591. Knowing this history in advance, it seems logical to conclude that informal arrangements for the marriage of Henry Wriothesley and Elizabeth Vere have been made at this time. For his part, Oxford will attempt to beget a legitimate son, who will be the male heir to his earldom as well as Burghley's grandson.

Walter Raleigh arrives at Court and Elizabeth promptly adopts him as her new favorite.

1582

February 1582: Alençon finally leaves, but only after Elizabeth has promised him a loan of 60,000 pounds for the Netherlands military campaign.

Thomas Watson dedicates *Hekatompathia, The Passionate Century of Love*, to Oxford. The collection consists of exactly 100 consecutively numbered verses – one precedent for the central sequence of 100 sequential verses within *Shake-Speares Sonnets*.

1583

Oxford buys the lease to use Blackfriars as a private theater; he transfers it to John Lyly, his secretary and stage manager.

June 1583: Oxford mourns the death of his great friend and mentor, Lord Chamberlain Sussex, whose company has been performing the earl's plays at Court.

Elizabeth lifts Oxford's banishment from Court.

November 1583: At the suggestion of Secretary Walsingham, the acting company known as the Queen's Men is formed with twelve members, two from Oxford's group.

December 26, 1583: The Queen's Company makes its first appearance at Court. Among the company's plays will be *The Troublesome Reign of King John*, which has been viewed as an early version of *King John* by Shakespeare.

1584

January 1, 1584: Oxford's Men perform at Court (probably *Campaspe*, as by Lyly).

Prologue

March 3, 1584: Both Oxford's Men and the Queen's Company are reported performing at Court, with Lyly as payee. (The play is probably *Sapho and Phao*.) Since it's unreasonable to suppose that two plays were given on the same day, Ward writes, "the most likely solution" is that "the two companies were amalgamated and rehearsed by Lord Oxford's private secretary John Lyly." (Ward, 271)

June 1584: The Duke of Alençon dies in France of a fever.

Robert Greene dedicates *Card of Fancy* to Oxford.

October 30, 1584: Protesting to Burghley against his use of his own servants to spy on him, Oxford writes a quick postscript using God's words to Moses in the Bible: "I serve Her Majesty, and *I am that I am*, and by alliance near to your Lordship, but free, and scorn to be offered that injury to think I am so weak of government as to be ruled by servants, or not able to govern myself. If your Lordship take and follow this course, you deceive yourself, and make me take another course than yet I have not thought of." (Shakespeare will be only other writer to use "I am that I am" in this personal way, in Sonnet 121, which expresses a similar thought: "No, *I am that I am*, and they that level/ At my abuses reckon up their own."

1585

August 1585: Antwerp falls to Spanish forces under the Duke of Parma. Colonel John Norris leaves for Holland in charge of 4,000 English soldiers; following him is Oxford, who will arrive at Flanders with additional forces.

October 1585: Oxford returns home while Leicester gets set to take full command of the English presence in Holland. Whether the Queen or Oxford himself cut short his mission is not recorded; meanwhile, Leicester's nephew Philip Sidney will be made Governor of Flushing.

1586

William Webbe writes in his *Discourse of English Poetry*: "I may not omit the deserved commendations of many honourable and noble Lords and Gentlemen in Her Majesty's Court, which, in the rare devices of poetry, have been and yet are most skillful; among whom the right honourable Earl of Oxford may challenge to himself the title of the most excellent among the rest."

January 1586: Leicester rashly accepts the Supreme Governorship of the Netherlands.

February 1586: Elizabeth learns about Leicester's office and, exploding with unbridled fury, orders him to conform to her commands.

March 1586: The Pope confers his blessing upon King Philip's forthcoming Enterprise, the Spanish Armada, and its invasion of England.

May 1586: Secretary Walsingham is using a young Catholic exile (Gilbert Gifford) to entrap Mary Stuart, Queen of Scots, in a plot that will warrant her execution and thereby eliminate the constant threat she has posed. Gifford is picking up letters for Mary at the French embassy and returning her replies to Walsingham, who is deciphering them before they are re-sealed and sent on. The letters reveal that a young Catholic, Anthony Babington, may try to assemble a team to assassinate Queen Elizabeth.

June 21, 1586: Burghley urges Walsingham to confront the Queen about financial assistance to Oxford, who has sold most of his inherited estates to pay for activities (including those related to literature and the stage) on behalf of the Government.

June 23, 1586: The Government makes its most sweeping attempt to exercise control over publications; from now on, England's writers will live under the strictest wartime censorship.

June 26, 1586: Queen Elizabeth signs a Warrant commanding the Treasurer of the Exchequer to pay Oxford an annual allowance of 1,000 pounds with no accounting required. His grant comes via the same formula as the one issued to Walsingham for his Secret Service.

July 1586: The Venetian ambassador in Spain writes that King Philip is furious over reports he has been ridiculed in England by theatrical entertainments. He also makes clear that Elizabeth and her Government sanctioned these stage works: "What has enraged [Philip] more than all else ... is the account of the masquerades and comedies which the Queen of England orders to be acted at his expense."

Antony Babington writes to Mary Stuart about a plan to liberate her and kill Elizabeth. Mary replies, appearing to agree with the plan, effectively signing her own death warrant. Without question, Burghley and Walsingham have used Babington to entrap the Queen of Scots.

August 1586: Babington is arrested and sent to the Tower for interrogation.

September 1586: Fourteen members of the "Babington Plot" are tried, condemned and executed amid public celebrations.

Philip Sidney is mortally wounded at Zutphen, lingering in agony for nearly a month before dying at thirty-one, sparking general mourning in England.

Oxford is among the commissioners for Mary Stuart's trial assembling at Westminster. Burghley is determined to bring about her destruction.

October 1586: Despite Mary's eloquent defense at her trial, the commissioners get set to find her guilty, but the Court is adjourned to London as Elizabeth wrestles with her emotions over having to make the ultimate decision to execute a queen.

December 1586: Despite Elizabeth's wavering, a Proclamation of Mary's death sentence is published, resulting in a great burst of public rejoicing in London.

Oxford has "almost completed the series of plays [in their early versions, at least] known since 1598 under the name of William Shakespeare," writes Eva Turner Clark.

1587

February 8, 1587: Mary Stuart, Queen of Scots, is executed, ensuring Spain's invasion.

June 17-22, 1587: Sir Francis Englefield, an English Catholic at the Madrid Court in Spain, writes a memorandum to King Philip relating his conversations with a young man calling himself Arthur Dudley and claiming to be the son of Queen Elizabeth by Robert Dudley, Earl of Leicester. Giving his age as twenty-six, he would have been born in 1561, when Elizabeth was expected to marry Dudley, whom she created Earl of Leicester in 1564. The young man has told a persuasive, detailed story of his life from boyhood to now; he has had "much conference with the earl of Leicester, upon whom he mainly depends for the fulfillment of his hopes" to become King of England; and he has convinced Englefield that Elizabeth "is not ignorant of his pretensions, although, perhaps, she would be unwilling that they should be thus published to the world ... the bastards of princes not usually being acknowledged in the lifetime of their parents."

Arthur Dudley alleges that Leicester will elevate him to the throne when Elizabeth dies and perhaps marry him to Arabella Stuart. "For this and other reasons I am of opinion that he should not be allowed to get away," Sir Englefield advises King Philip, "but should be kept very secure to prevent his escape ...

especially as during the Queen's time they have passed an Act in England [in 1571] excluding from the succession all but the heirs of the Queen's body."

The King of Spain is about to embark on his Enterprise, the invasion of England; if victorious, he might find it useful to have a bastard of Elizabeth to place on the throne of England, with Leicester's support. The Spanish Armada will be defeated next year, however, and Arthur Dudley will never be heard from again.

1588

Anthony Munday dedicates the first part of *Palmerin D'Oliva* to Oxford.

June 1588: Anne Cecil dies at age thirty-one.

July 23, 1588: The Spanish Armada is sighted. Camden reports that Oxford fitted out a ship at his own expense (**Annals**, 1675, 405); and Ward (289) says Oxford "took part in the fighting in the early days of the encounter," which involved a running fight carried on up Channel.

July 28, 1588: Oxford refuses to take orders from Leicester to take command at Harwich; on this day, the Spanish anchor in Calais harbor; at night the English send fire-ships among the enemy vessels, driving them back out to sea.

July 29, 1588: The Spanish are utterly defeated.

September 4, 1588: Death of Robert Dudley, Earl of Leicester.

November 24, 1588: The victory over the Armada is celebrated by a royal procession to St. Paul's for thanksgiving. A ballad refers to "a golden canopy" carried over Queen Elizabeth and notes: "The Earl of Oxford opening then the windows for her Grace,/ The Children of the Hospital she saw before her face." (Ogburn, 710)

1589

Richard Field publishes a new edition of Ovid's *Metamorphoses*, first printed in 1567 and attributed to Oxford's uncle, Arthur Golding. ("Shakespeare" will include a Latin epigram from Ovid on the title page of *Venus and Adonis*, which Field will publish and print in 1593.)

The Arte of English Poesie, a major work intended for the Queen, is also issued by Field and dedicated by him to Lord Burghley. The anonymous author of *Arte,* who appears to know a great deal about the English Renaissance of literature in the 1580s, mentions courtier-poets "who have written excellently well as it would appear if their doings could be found out and made public with all the rest, of which number is first that noble gentleman, Edward Earl of Oxford." (George Puttenham is usually identified as author; also, Lord Lumley.)

Edmund Spenser publishes *The Fairy Queen* with seventeen dedicatory sonnets to the most powerful men of the day, starting with Hatton, Burghley and Oxford. The poem to Oxford includes: "And also for the love which thou dost bear/ To th'*Heliconian* imps, and they to thee,/ They unto thee, and thou to them most dear." (Helicon is a mountain in south central Greece, regarded by the ancient Greeks as home of Apollo and the Muses; the imps are children; OED: 'a scion or descendant, esp. of a noble family; an offspring, a child'; also 'a follower, an adherent, esp. of glory, chivalry, etc.' Imps are also shoots of plants, used in grafting.)

October 1589: Henry Wriothesley, passing his "official" sixteenth birthday, is expected to marry Lord Burghley's fourteen-year-old granddaughter Elizabeth Vere, a union that would bring him into a Cecil family alliance; but he stalls, requesting a year to think it over.

Part One

"LORD OF MY LOVE"

Sonnets 1 - 26
1590 - 1600

THE MARRIAGE ALLIANCE
Sonnets 1 – 17
1590-1591

THE SHAKESPEARE COMMITMENT
Sonnets 18 – 26
1592 - 1600

THE MARRIAGE ALLIANCE
Sonnets 1 – 17
1590-1591

Edward de Vere, Seventeenth Earl of Oxford, issues a thundering imperial command using the royal "we" adopted by English and European monarchs. Speaking for Queen Elizabeth I as well as for himself, he commands their son, Henry Wriothesley, to marry and beget heirs of his royal blood. He establishes Elizabeth as "Beauty" in the phrase "beauty's Rose" (the latter word italicized and capitalized in the 1609 quarto); in the same breath he sets forth as his overall theme the need to perpetuate Elizabeth's Tudor Rose Dynasty.

The Tudor dynasty was begun in 1485 by her grandfather (Henry Tudor, Earl of Richmond, who became Henry VII) when he ended the Wars of the Roses by uniting the Houses of York and Lancaster.

"This peace began by a marriage solemnized, by God's special providence, between Henry Earl of Richmond, heir of the house of Lancaster, and Elizabeth, daughter to Edward IV, the undoubted issue and heir of the house of York, whereby the red Rose and the white were united and joined together. Out of these **Roses** sprang two noble **buds**, Prince Arthur and Henry, the eldest dying without issue, the other [Henry VIII] of most famous memory, leaving behind him three children, Prince Edward, the Lady Mary, the Lady Elizabeth…" - *Euphues and his England*, John Lyly, 1580, dedicated to Edward de Vere, Earl of Oxford, his employer and patron

> That thereby *Beauty's* **Rose** might never die
> - Sonnet 1, line 2
>
> Within *thine own* **bud** buriest thy content
> - Sonnet 1, line 11

Oxford uses the opening two lines of the Sonnets to announce he has begun a chronicle leading to the death of Elizabeth, a decisive turning point in contemporary English history. The succession to her throne will determine the fate of her lineage that has continued for more than a century. The succession will determine whether her dynasty lives or dies upon her death.

Sonnet 1 therefore begins a dynastic diary. The verses of the Fair Youth series, numbered in chronological order, lead inexorably to the royal succession. Because of Elizabeth's failure to name Southampton as her heir by the time of her death on March 24, 1603, however, the diary will continue to the day of her funeral on April 28, 1603, when her dynasty is officially considered extinguished, followed by the farewell envoy of Sonnet 126.

Oxford is referring to a possible marriage between Southampton and Lady Elizabeth Vere, the eldest daughter by his late wife Anne Cecil, daughter of Burghley. It is by no means clear that Oxford was the girl's father, however. Oxford was in Italy during 1575 when he got word that she had been born; upon his return to England the following year, amid widespread Court gossip that he was not the biological father, he refused to see the child and physically separated from his wife. He remained apart from Anne for more than five years until late 1581, when young Henry Wriothesley entered Cecil House as a royal ward of the Queen, following the death of his supposed father.

The timing of these events indicates Oxford made a deal with Burghley in 1581; that is, he agreed to reunite with Anne Cecil in return for his father-in-law's future support for the succession of Southampton to the throne. Cecil's backing is conditional upon the younger earl's eventual marriage to his granddaughter and the securing of an heir to solidify the union. Now that time has come and Oxford implores his son to hurry up and complete the alliance.

These first seventeen sonnets are compiled as "numbers" to reflect Southampton's seventeen birthdays (1575-1591) and his reaching the age of seventeen in 1591:

> "And in fresh numbers number all your graces"
> - Sonnet 17, line 6

It is also significant that the seventeen sonnets come from the pen of the seventeenth earl.

(Elizabeth, given her popular image as the Virgin Queen, would never proclaim Southampton as her natural son and successor. In reality she never named King James as her successor, even on her deathbed, so it is plain that such a declaration from the monarch was never actually needed. When she died it was William Cecil Lord Burghley's son Robert Cecil, by then the Secretary of State, who stated that the Queen had named James – the son of Mary Queen of Scots, whom Elizabeth had executed in February 1587, because of the machinations of Burghley himself.

(The Cecils aimed to engineer the succession so that they could remain in power no matter who wore the crown. If the proud and hotheaded Southampton had chosen to enter a Cecil alliance-by-marriage and to accept their support, it is probable he would have become King Henry IX of England. The price, however, would have been Cecilian domination – the price Elizabeth had paid for her throne and safety. Southampton would have none of that.)

Southampton is well aware he was born in May/June 1574 as the natural son of Oxford and the Queen. He also knows Oxford denied his paternity of Elizabeth Vere upon her birth in 1575; thus, if he accepted Elizabeth Vere as his wife, he would not be marrying his half-sister. In any case, his opposition to the marriage proposal is based on political judgment and on genuine differences with the Cecils. Southampton is stubbornly refusing the bargain, preferring to ally himself with Robert Devereux, Second Earl of Essex (1566-1601), in opposition to William Cecil's power to direct England's future.

The two earls are far more committed to military solutions against Spain and its goal of world conquest. Essex and Southampton are also less Puritan-minded and more tolerant of the Catholic population in England. They, like Oxford, are looking forward to further English exploration and discovery. And they are humanists deeply committed not only to learning but also to the developing national identity in the arts including poetry and the drama. By turning his back on the political advice urged upon him by the Earl of Oxford, his father, Southampton ironically shows himself, above all, to be Shakespearean.

"Had the first seventeen sonnets reached us alone and not as part of the conglomerate of the 1609 quarto, their date and purpose would have been universally recognized long ago ... Though Southampton persisted to the end in his refusal to marry Lady Elizabeth Vere, it was not for want of urging of marriage by William Shakespeare." – G. P. V. Akrigg, *"Shakespeare and the Earl of Southampton"*, 1968

THE MARRIAGE ALLIANCE

Sonnet 1
Beauty's Rose
1590-1591

Edward de Vere commands Southampton to marry Lady Elizabeth Vere – his own daughter of record (but probably not his biological child) and (more importantly) the granddaughter of William Cecil Lord Burghley – and thereby enter into a family alliance with the Queen's chief minister. The young earl's acceptance, which would include begetting an heir to make the marriage a binding one, is the condition upon which Burghley will lend his crucial support to Southampton's claim as Elizabeth's successor – so that "beauty's Rose" (Elizabeth's dynasty of the Tudor Rose) might not die when she does.

Sonnet 1	Translation
From fairest creatures we desire increase,	From our royal son the Queen and I command heirs,
That thereby beauty's *Rose* might never die,	So Elizabeth's Tudor Rose dynasty may not perish,
But as the riper should by time decease	But as you, the older heir, should eventually die,
His tender heir might bear his memory:	Your royal heir might continue your bloodline:
But thou, contracted to thine own bright eyes,	But you, wedded to your own royal blood,
Feed'st thy light's flame with self-substantial fuel,	Feed its source with its own power,
Making a famine where abundance lies,	Creating emptiness where royalty exists;
Thy self thy foe, to thy sweet self too cruel:	You your enemy, too cruel to your royal self:
Thou that art now the world's fresh ornament,	You who are now England's royal prince,
And only herald to the gaudy spring,	And only successor as king in the new reign,
Within thine own bud buriest thy content,	Are hiding your Tudor Rose within its own bud,
And, tender churl, mak'st waste in niggarding:	And, royal miser, you waste it by hoarding.
Pity the world, or else this glutton be,	Pity England! Or else be this irresponsible glutton,
To eat the world's due, by the grave and thee.	To bury England's due [to have you as king] in your own grave and person.

1 FROM FAIREST CREATURES WE DESIRE INCREASE,
"If the favored youth were the Earl of Southampton ... the Sonnets should start about 1590 or 1591." - G. Wilson Knight, *The Mutual Flame*, 1962, p. 3
FAIREST = most royal; "The king is full of grace and *fair* regard" – *Henry V*, 1.1.222; "Take her, *fair* son, and from her blood raise up issue to me" – the French king to King Henry V of England in *Henry V*, 5.2.340-341; "my *fair* son" – *Richard II*, 5.2.92; also, Fair = Vere (pronounced Vair)

> But thou art *fair*, and at thy birth, dear boy,
> Nature and fortune joined to make thee great
> - *King John*, 2.2.51-52

> O Lord! My boy, my Arthur, my *fair* son!
> - *King John*, 3.3.103

> For how art thou a king
> But by *fair* sequence and succession?
> - *Richard II*, 2.1.198-199

In the earliest verses, i.e., the Bath prologue of Sonnets 153-154, concerning Elizabeth's refusal to acknowledge the son born in May/June 1574, the Queen herself was "the *fairest* votary" as in "But in her maiden hand/ The *fairest* votary took up that fire/ Which many legions of true hearts had warmed,/ And so the General of hot desire [the newly born prince]/ Was sleeping *by a Virgin hand disarmed*" – Sonnet 154, lines 4-8; and at the very end of the Dark Lady series to Elizabeth, when all hope for their son is lost, Oxford bitterly tells her: "For I have sworn thee *fair*: more perjured eye,/ To swear against the truth so foul a lie!" – Sonnet 152, lines 13-14; and in the special language of the Sonnets, young Henry Wriothesley has inherited this *fair* quality from his mother the Queen.

> That *we, the sons* of brave Plantagenet,
> Each one already blazing my our meeds,
> Should notwithstanding join our lights together,
> And over-shine the earth, as this the world.
> Whate'er it bodes, henceforth will I bear
> Upon my target three *fair*-shining suns.
> - *3 Henry VI*, 2.1.35-40

CREATURES = living or created beings, children; "The *majesty of the creature in resemblance to the mother*" – *Winter's Tale*, 5.2.36; "I shall see *my boy* again; for since the birth of Cain, the first male child … there was not *such a gracious creature born*. But now will canker-sorrow eat *my bud* and chase *the native beauty* from his cheek" – *King John*, 3.3.78-83; also "creations" of the monarch, such as earls of the first or second creation; Southampton is therefore a *created* earl or *creature* (servant) of the Queen, in addition to being her child; "Slandering *Creation* with a false esteem" – Sonnet 127, line 12, written in 1601 when Southampton is in the Tower and accusing Queen Elizabeth of preventing her son (her *Creation*) from being able to succeed her on the throne; "That you *create our emperor's eldest son*" – *Titus Andronicus*, 1.1.228; "Most *sovereign creature*" – spoken to Queen Cleopatra (modeled on Elizabeth) in *Antony and Cleopatra*, 5.2.80

> Lo, as a careful housewife runs to catch
> One of her feathered *creatures* broke away
> Sets down her babe…
> - Sonnet 143, lines 1-3

"I have heard that guilty *creatures* sitting at a play" – *Hamlet*, 2.2.590-591; "My king is tangled in affection to a *creature* of the queen's, Lady Anne Bullen" – *Henry VIII*, 3.2.35-36; "This fellow here, Lord Timon, this thy creature" – *Timon of Athens*, 1.1.119; "Your honour has through Ephesus poured forth your charity, and hundreds call themselves your *creatures*, who by you have been restored" – to Lord Cerimon in *Pericles*, 3.2.43-45

FAIREST CREATURES = Most royal children, i.e., Southampton, son of Queen Elizabeth; as her child, he possesses her "beauty" or royal Tudor blood and therefore reflects it as the "fair" young nobleman.

WE = Oxford and Elizabeth, his parents, but also the royal "we" of the monarch; "Once more *we* sit in England's royal throne" – *3 Henry VI*, 5.7.1; "Have *we* … taken to wife" – the King in *Hamlet*, 1.2.10,14; "Elizabeth, to the Treasurer and Chamberlains of our Exchequer, Greeting: *We*…" – Privy Seal Warrant signed by Queen Elizabeth on June 26, 1586, authorizing Oxford's yearly grant in the equivalent of Secret Service funds from the Government Treasury

"**WE** = the plural style is also in use among kings and other sovereigns, and is said to have been begun by King John of England. Before that time, monarchs used the singular number in their edicts. The German and the French sovereigns followed the example of King John in A. D. 1200"
- *Webster's Revised Unabridged Dictionary*

DESIRE = to order or command; "*Desire* the earl to see me in my tent" – *Richard III*, 5.3.28

WE DESIRE = we, Queen Elizabeth and I, your parents, command with all our authority … how the said qualification in point of title may be performed accordingly as *we desire*" – Queen Elizabeth to William Davison, April 27, 1586 (*Elizabeth I Collected Works*, 279); "For your intent in going back to school in Wittenberg, it is most retrograde to *our desire*" – the King in *Hamlet*, 1.2.118-120;

INCREASE = offspring, progeny, heirs of your blood; procreation through marriage to perpetuate your lineage; and by having a child, making the marriage a binding one; "Upon the earth's *increase* why shouldst thou feed,/ Unless the earth with *thy increase* be fed?/ By law of nature thou art bound to breed,/ That thine may live when thou thyself art dead" – *Venus and Adonis*, 169-172, dedicated to Southampton by Oxford as "William Shakespeare" in 1593; while Southampton is being urged to produce "increase" of his own, he himself is the "increase" of Oxford and Elizabeth: "The teeming autumn big with *rich increase*,/ Bearing the wanton burthen of the prime,/ Like widowed wombs after their lord's decease" – Sonnet 97, lines 5-8

2 THAT THEREBY BEAUTY'S *ROSE* MIGHT NEVER DIE,
BEAUTY = Elizabeth as Venus, goddess of Love and Beauty, as depicted in *Venus and Adonis* of 1593, dedicated to Southampton; "Touching the beauty of this Prince, her countenance, her personage, her majesty, I cannot think that it may be sufficiently commended, when it cannot be too much marveled at: so that I am constrained to say as *Praxitiles* did, when he began to paint *Venus* and *her Sonne*, who doubted whether the world could afford colors good enough for two such *fair* faces, and I whether our tongue can yield words to blaze that *beauty*" – *Euphues and his England*, John Lyly, 1580, dedicated to Oxford; Arber (1868), 457; "Sonne," "fair" and "beauty" are in added italics

ROSE = (Italicized in *Q*); The Tudor Rose; the House of Tudor and its Dynasty, combining the red and white roses of the Houses of Lancaster and York; *Rosa Sine Spina* or *Rose Without a Thorn* – one of Elizabeth's mottoes; "The *red rose and the white* are on his face, the fatal colors of our striving houses" – *3 Henry VI*, 2.6.97-98

BEAUTY'S ROSE = Elizabeth Regina's dynasty of the Tudor Rose:

> *R* ose of the Queene of Loue belou'd ;
> *E* ngland's great Kings diuinely mou'd,
> *G* ave Roses in their banner ;
> *I* t shewed that Beautie's Rose indeed,
> *N* ow in this age should them succeed,
> *A* nd raigne in more sweet manner. – Sir John Davies, *Hymnes of Astraea*, 1599

NEVER = Ever = Edward de Vere, *Ever or Never*; **DIE** = come to an end, i.e., the House of Tudor ending upon Elizabeth's death; "Here burns my candle out; ay, *here it dies*, which while it lasted, gave King Henry light" – *3 Henry VI*, 2.6.1-2; "The *cease of majesty dies* not alone" – *Hamlet*, 3.3.15-16

3 BUT AS THE RIPER SHOULD BY TIME DECEASE,
THE RIPER = the older, Southampton; "In him there is a hope of government … and, in his full and ripened years, himself, no doubt shall then, and till then, govern well" – *Richard III*, 2.3.12-15

BY TIME = This diary itself is written according to time, calculated by the ever-waning life and reign of Elizabeth, leading to her death and the succession; and that time itself was indicated by the years of her reign (i.e., regnal years), as in *"the 10th year of Elizabeth,"* etc.

4 HIS TENDER HEIR MIGHT BEAR HIS MEMORY:
TENDER = royal, according to Oxford's "invention" or special language; "When he was but *tender*-bodied, and the only son of my womb" – *Coriolanus*, 1.1.5-6; **HIS TENDER HEIR** = Southampton's own royal heir in succession to him; "The king shall live *without an heir*" – *Winter's Tale*, 3.3.16; "beauty's *successive heir*" – Sonnet 127, line 3; "rightful *heir to the crown*" – *2 Henry VI*, 1.3.26; "But if the *first heir of my invention* prove deformed" – dedication of *Venus and Adonis* to Southampton

"We note that the terms Shakespeare uses here – *succession, heir, issue* – he elsewhere applies to the paramount problems of royalty" – Hotson, 1965

BEAR HIS MEMORY: be a living reminder of the father; "the metaphor is heraldic: the resemblance of the child's face is likened to the bearing of heraldic arms" – Booth; "What holier than, for royalty's repair, for present comfort, and for future good, to bless the bed of majesty again with a sweet fellow to't?" - *Richard III*, 5.1.31-34

5 BUT THOU, CONTRACTED TO THINE OWN BRIGHT EYES,
CONTRACTED = betrothed or wedded to; a play on the marriage contract that Oxford is urging his royal son to make with Elizabeth Vere; "For first *he was contract to Lady Lucy*" – *Richard III*, 3.7.178; drawn together: "and our whole kingdom to be *contracted* in one brow of woe" – *Hamlet*, 1.2.4; **BRIGHT EYES** = royal eyes (suns or stars), reflecting your blood; "Yet *looks he like a king*: behold *his eye, as bright* as is the eagle's, *lightens forth controlling majesty*" – *Richard II*, 3.3.68-70; "those *princely eyes* of thine" – *Titus Andronicus*, 1.1.434; "the motion of *a kingly eye*" – *King John*, 5.1.47

6 FEED'ST THY LIGHT'S FLAME WITH SELF-SUBSTANTIAL FUEL,
THY LIGHT'S FLAME = your powerful source of royal blood; "the aspiring *flame of golden sovereignty*" – *Richard III*, 4.4.328-329; of the infant boy, to later become Southampton, speaking of the fire of his royal blood: "And his *love-kindling fire* ... This *holy fire of love*" – Sonnet 153, lines 3 and 5; "his *heart-inflaming brand* ... *that fire* ... *Love's fire* heats water, water cools not love" – Sonnet 154, lines 2, 5, 14; **LIGHT** = the light that shines from Southampton as sun (royal son) or star; his eyes are suns or stars, as in "And scarcely greet me with *that sun, thine eye*" – Sonnet 49, line 6; "when those *suns of glory, those two lights of men* (two monarchs), met in the vale of Andren" – *Henry VIII*, 1.1.5-7

> For who's so dumb that cannot write to thee,
> When *thou thyself dost give invention light*?
> - Sonnet 38, lines 7-8

> Nativity, *once in the main of light*,
> Crawls to maturity, wherewith being *crowned*,
> Crooked eclipses 'gainst his glory fight.
> - Sonnet 60, lines 5-7

"I have engaged myself so far in Her Majesty's service *to bring the truth to light*"
- Oxford to Burghley, June 13, 1595

SELF-SUBSTANTIAL FUEL = royal blood's own power; "Fuel of the substance of the flame itself" – Dowden

7 MAKING A FAMINE WHERE ABUNDANCE LIES,
FAMINE/ABUNDANCE = empty of royal blood versus the fact that you have abundant royal blood in you; no royal claim or succession versus a great claim to be king; **ABUNDANCE** = great store of royal blood; "As a decrepit *father* takes delight/ To see *his active child* do deeds of youth,/ So I, made lame by Fortune's dearest spite,/ Take all my comfort of thy worth and truth/ ... That I in *thy abundance* am sufficed,/ And by a part of *all thy glory* live" – Sonnet 37, lines 1-4, 11-12

8 THY SELF THY FOE, TO THY SWEET SELF TOO CRUEL:
THY SELF = your royal person; "Make thee another *self* (child) for love of me" – Sonnet 10, line 13; "his great self" – *Henry VIII*, 3.2.336; "his *royal self*" – *Henry VIII*, 5.2.154; "thy gracious self" – *Romeo and Juliet*, 2.2.113; **SWEET SELF** = royal self; "Good night, *sweet prince*" – *Hamlet*, 5.2.385; "And happily may *your sweet self* put on the lineal state and glory of the land!" – *King John*, 5.7.101-105; at the very end of the Fair Youth series, in the envoy of Sonnet 126, Southampton's royal person remains: "O Thou my lovely Boy, who in thy power/ Dost hold time's fickle glass, his sickle hour,/ Who hast by waning grown, and therein show'st/ Thy lovers withering, as *thy sweet self* grow'st" – Sonnet 126, lines 1-1

9 THOU THAT ART NOW THE WORLD'S FRESH ORNAMENT
THE WORLD'S FRESH ORNAMENT = England's royal prince with right to succession; Oxford records for posterity that Henry Wriothesley is the Prince of England and stands supreme in succession to Elizabeth as King Henry IX. Later, during 1601-1603 when his son has been reduced to the status of a "base commoner" imprisoned for high treason, Oxford will write of him as "a *jewel* hung in ghastly night" in Sonnet 27, line 11, and declare of him: "As on the finger of a *throned Queen*,/ The basest *Jewel* will be well esteemed" in Sonnet 96, lines 5-6; "our *prince, Jewel of children*" – *The Winter's Tale*, 5.1.115-116; "Who heaven itself (Elizabeth herself) for *ornament* doth use" – Sonnet 21, line 3

"I leave it to your Honourable survey, and your Honour to your heart's content, which I wish may always answer your own wish, and ***the world's hopeful expectation***. Your Honour's in all duty, William Shakespeare" – Dedication by Oxford as "Shakespeare" to Southampton of *Venus and Adonis*, publicly addressing him in language also meaning "*the world's fresh ornament*" or England's most royal prince

> My father is gone wild into his grave,
> For in his tomb lie my affections;
> And with his spirits sadly I survive,
> To mock *the expectation of the world*
> (Prince Hal, the future King Henry V)
> - *2 Henry IV*, 5.2.123-126

FRESH = Within the chronological diary of the Fair Youth series, "fresh" appears as a marker for three separate time periods: (1) Southampton is *"fresh"* in Sonnets 1-26, during his golden years of opportunity up to 1600; (2) he is no longer *"fresh"* in Sonnets 27-106, during his two years and two months in prison for the Rebellion of February 8, 1601; and (3) upon his release from the Tower on April 10, 1603, Oxford will proclaim in Sonnet 107 that once more "my love looks *fresh*"; "And that *fresh blood* which youngly thou bestow'st" – Sonnet 11, line 3; "Since first I saw you *fresh*, which yet are green" – Sonnet 104, line 8, referring to the "first" period of his son's life; "My love looks *fresh*" – Sonnet 107, line 10; "Thus did I keep my person *fresh* and new" - the King in *1 Henry IV*, 3.2.55

10 AND ONLY HERALD TO THE GAUDY SPRING,
And the chief flower of the Tudor Rose to begin a new, glittering rein on the throne

ONLY = chief, peerless; "One, of which there exist no others of this kind" – *OED*; "The *only ruler* of princes" – Book of Common Prayer, 1559; "the *onlie* begetter of these ensuing sonnets" – Dedication of the Sonnets in 1609; "And left behind him Richard, his *only son*" – *2 Henry VI*, 2.2.18; "And disinherited *thine* *only son*" – *3 Henry VI*, 1.1.232; "mine *only son*" – *3 Henry VI*, 2.5.83; "When yet he was but tender-bodied, and *the only son* of my womb" – *Coriolanus*, 1.1.5-6

HERALD = heir to the throne; "May one that is *a herald and a prince* do a *fair* message to his kingly eyes?" – *Troilus and Cressida*, 1.3.217-218; an officer who records and blazons the arms of the nobility; proclaimer, harbinger; **GAUDY** = appearing like a jewel, i.e., ornament of the Queen; related to "gauds" or beads of the Rosary, and to Oxford's conception of these sonnets as hymns or prayers to his royal son as a king or god on earth; **SPRING** = new reign; related to Edward Vere, i.e., spring is Ver in Latin; "This side is Hiems, Winter, this *Ver, the Spring* ...Ver, begin." – *Love's Labour's Lost*, 5.2.884-886

11 WITHIN THINE OWN BUD BURIEST THY CONTENT,

BUD = Southampton as the budding flower of the Tudor Rose Dynasty; "Rough winds do shake the *darling buds of May*" – Sonnet 18, line 3; and after the Rebellion, when Southampton is in disgrace in the Tower: "*Roses have thorns*, and silver fountains mud,/ Clouds and eclipses stain both *Moone and Sunne* (Elizabeth & Southampton),/ And *loathsome canker lives in sweetest bud*" – Sonnet 35, lines 2-4; "The canker blooms have full as deep a dye/ As the perfumed tincture of *the Roses*,/ Hang on such thorns, and play as wantonly/ When summer's breath their *masked buds* discloses" – Sonnet 54, lines 5-8; "The *lily* I condemned for thy hand,/ And *buds* of marjoram had *stol'n thy hair*,/ *The Roses* fearfully on thorns did stand,/ One blushing shame, another white despair" – Sonnet 99, lines 6-9, describing the theft or loss of Southampton's claim to the throne as Elizabeth's "hair" or heir.

> If that be true, I shall see **my boy** again;
> For since the birth of Cain, the first male child,
> To him that did but yesterday suspire,
> There was not such a gracious creature born.
> But now will canker-sorrow eat **my bud**
> And chase *the native beauty* from his cheek
> - *King John*, 3.3.78-83

THY CONTENT = your royal blood and identity; your substance; "What is your *substance*, whereof are you made" – Sonnet 53, line 1; also a glance at "content" as "contentment", as in: "Were I a king I might command *content*" – poem attributed to Oxford

12 AND TENDER CHURL MAK'ST WASTE IN NIGGARDING

TENDER = royal; "The *tender prince*" – *Richard III*, 3.1.28; **TENDER CHURL** = royal miser; spoken from Oxford as father to his "tender" son, accusing him of being stingy; "My master is of *churlish* disposition" - *As You Like It*, 2.4.79; **WASTE** = loss of royal succession; the Sonnets will become "the *Chronicle of wasted time*" in Sonnet 106, line 1; **NIGGARDING** = hoarding of royal blood, as opposed to passing it on

13 PITY THE WORLD, OR ELSE THIS GLUTTON BE,

THE WORLD = England; "Wherein I lived *the greatest prince o'th'world*" – Antony in *Antony and Cleopatra*, 4.15.56; "I leave it to your Honourable survey, and your Honour to your heart's content, which I wish may always answer your own wish, and *the world's hopeful expectation*" – dedication of *Venus and Adonis*, 1593, by Oxford as "Shakespeare" to Southampton; "And with his spirits sadly I survive to mock *the expectation of the world*" – Prince Hal, now King Henry the Fifth, referring to the death of his father and his own ascendancy in *2 Henry IV*, 5.3.125-126

PITY THE WORLD = take pity on England; "Thou dost beguile *the world*, unless some mother" – Sonnet 3, line 4; "Ah, if thou issueless shalt hap to die,/ *The world* will wail thee like a makeless wife,/ *The world* will be thy widow and still weep/ That thou no form of thee hast left behind/ ... Look what an unthrift in *the world* doth spend/ Shifts but his place, for still *the world* enjoys it;/ But *beauty's waste hath in the world an end*" – Sonnet 9, lines 3-6, 9-11; "Your name from hence immortal life shall have,/ Though I, once gone, to *all the world* must die" – Sonnet 81, lines 5-6; "Not mine own fears nor the prophetic soul/ Of *the wide world* dreaming on things to come" – Sonnet 107, lines 1-2; "You are *my all the world*" – Sonnet 112, line 5

"This estate (England) hath depended on you a great while, as *all the world* doth judge" – Oxford to Burghley, September 1572

"This might have been done through private conference before, and had not need to have been the fable of *the world*" – Oxford to Burghley, April 27, 1576

"But *the world* is so cunning, as of a shadow they can make a substance, and of a likelihood a truth" – Oxford to Burghley, July 1581

GLUTTON = a greedy devourer of your own royal blood, wasting it and depriving England of your succession to the throne; "Most holy and religious fear it is to keep those many bodies safe that live and *feed upon your Majesty*" – Hamlet, 3.3.7-10; indirectly related to the "feasting" of the royal person or blood, as in "Therefore are *feasts* so solemn and so rare" – Sonnet 52, line 5; "and so my state, seldom, but sumptuous, show'd like a *feast*" – the King in *1 Henry IV*, 3.2.55-58

14 TO EAT THE WORLD'S DUE, BY THE GRAVE AND THEE.

THE WORLD'S DUE = the debt of kingship that you owe England
"My gracious lord! My father! This sleep is sound indeed; this is a sleep that from this golden rigol hath divorced so many English kings. **Thy due from me** is tears and heavy sorrows of the blood, which nature, love, and filial tenderness shall, O dear father, pay thee plenteously. *My due from thee is this imperial crown, which, as immediate as thy place and blood, derives itself to me*" – Prince Hal in *2 Henry IV*, 4.5.33-46

> So when this loose behavior I throw off,
> And **pay the debt** I never promised
> - Prince Hal in *1 Henry IV*, 1.3.203-204
> (Declaring he will become king)

> Of this proud king, who studies day and night
> To answer all the *debt he owes* to you
> - *1 Henry IV*, 1.3.182-183

> That *due of many* now is *thine alone*
> - Sonnet 31, line 12

> If some suspect of ill masked not thy show,
> Then thou alone *kingdoms of hearts shouldst owe*
> - Sonnet 70, lines 13-14

BY THE GRAVE AND THEE = taking this royal gift with you and your mortal body to the grave; "What is thy body but a *swallowing grave,/ Seeming to bury that posterity*, which by rights of time thou needs must have" – Venus and Adonis, 1593, 757-762, dedicated to Southampton; "to *bury and ensevel* your works *in the grave of oblivion*" – Oxford's prefatory letter to *Cardanus' Comfort*, 1573; after the Rebellion of February 8, 1601, Southampton in the Tower will be "the *grave where buried love* doth live" in Sonnet 31, line 9, with *love* referring to his royal blood that he carries within himself and that will die with him if he is executed.

> A doubtful choice, of these three which to crave,

A kingdom or a cottage or a grave
- Earl of Oxford

1590

April 6, 1590: Death of Secretary of State Francis Walsingham, head of the Secret Service organization dedicated to intelligence gathering. The post will remain vacant for six years while Lord Burghley grooms his son, Robert Cecil, to take over. Robert Devereux, Earl of Essex, now attempts to put forth his own candidate, signaling the onset of the great struggle for power between him and the Cecils. At the same time, Southampton is becoming a boon companion to Essex, who also had been a royal ward of the Queen in Burghley's custody, though he had spent little time at Cecil House.

July 15, 1590: The first recorded evidence of William Cecil's plan for Southampton to marry his granddaughter is a letter to Cecil from Sir Thomas Stanhope, who had made an overture for the marriage of the young earl to his own daughter. Upon discovering that Burghley had already made a preemptive bid, Stanhope promptly apologized to the Lord Treasurer for "so treacherous a part toward your honor, having evermore found myself so bound unto you as I have done." He added, "I name it treachery, because I heard (that) before then you intended a match that way to the Lady Vayre (Vere)." (Stopes, 36-37; D.S.S.P. Eliz XXXIII, 11)

September 19, 1590: By now the marriage proposal has been in play for almost a year. The young earl's grandfather, Anthony Browne, Viscount Montague, now writes to Burghley that he and the Countess of Southampton "have laid abroad unto him both the commodity and hindrances likely to grow unto him" if he refuses the marriage. Montague says Southampton recalled that "your Lordship (Cecil) was this last winter well pleased to yield unto him a further respite of one year to ensure resolution in respect of his young years." But Montague reminded him "that this year which he speaketh of is now almost up, and therefore the greater reason for you Lordship in honor and in nature to see your child (granddaughter) well placed and provided for..." (*Oxfordian Vistas*, 179; D.S.S.P. Eliz. XXXIII.71; Stopes, 37-38)

THE MARRIAGE ALLIANCE

Sonnet 2
Beauty by Succession
1590-1591

Edward de Vere refers to his own age of forty in 1590 while urging Henry Wriothesley to beget an heir in "succession" – mirroring the theme that Southampton himself stands first in line to succeed to the throne. Oxford beseeches his unacknowledged royal son to use his "beauty" or "treasure" of royal blood from the Queen, by acting responsibly to perpetuate it through marriage to Cecil's granddaughter. He emphasizes the topic of royal blood in the final line.

Sonnet 2	Translation
When forty Winters shall besiege thy brow,	When you are forty years old [as I am now]
And dig deep trenches in thy beauty's field,	And your reflection of Elizabeth's royalty is buried,
Thy youth's proud livery, so gazed on now,	Your opportunity to be king, so genuine now,
Will be a tottered weed of small worth held:	Will be a worn-out costume unrecognized by others.
Then being asked where all thy beauty lies,	Then being asked where your royal blood is,
Where all the treasure of thy lusty days,	Where your royal claim of younger days has gone,
To say within thine own deep sunken eyes	To say it exists deep within you, below the surface
Were an all-eating shame, and thriftless praise.	Will be a suicidal disgrace and profitless claim.
How much more praise deserved thy beauty's use,	How much more claim your royalty's use deserved,
If thou couldst answer, 'This fair child of mine	If you could answer, "This royal child of mine
Shall sum my count, and make my old excuse,	Shall fulfill my life and justify my old days,"
Proving his beauty by succession thine.	Carrying his royal blood by his succession to you.
This were to be new made when thou art old	This would be a rebirth when you are old,
And see thy blood warm when thou feel'st it cold.	And your royal blood would be new again in him.

1 WHEN FORTY WINTERS SHALL BESIEGE THY BROW
When you are forty years old…**FORTY WINTERS** = Oxford turned forty on April 12, 1590; the "winters" will be filled with dark or black days during which time Southampton will not be recognized as prince or king; "How like *a Winter* hath my absence been/ From thee, the pleasure of the fleeting year" – Sonnet 97, lines 1-2, indicating the dark days of Southampton's first year of imprisonment in the Tower from February 8, 1601; "Three *Winters* cold" – Sonnet 104, line 3, indicating the three winters (Feb 1601; 1601-02; 1602-03) of Southampton's imprisonment in the Tower for high treason, his royal claim unrecognized; "Now is *the winter* of our discontent, made glorious summer by this son of York" –*Richard III*, 1.1.1-2

BESIEGE = "For, being now almost at a point to taste that good which Her Majesty shall determine, yet am I one that hath long *besieged* a fort and is not able to compass the end or reap the fruit of his travail, being forced to levy his *siege* for want of munition" – Oxford to Burghley, June 25, 1586

Part One

2 AND DIG DEEP TRENCHES IN THY BEAUTY'S FIELD,
THY BEAUTY'S FIELD = your reflection of Elizabeth's "beauty" or royal blood, which you possess as her son and as prince or king

3 THY YOUTH'S PROUD LIVERY SO GAZED ON NOW
YOUTH'S PROUD LIVERY = royal appearance in young days; a metaphor of clothing, indicating military or other uniforms; **PROUD** = "marching hitherward *in proud array*" – *2 Henry VI*, 4.9.27; "But with a *proud majestical* high scorn" – *1 Henry VI*, 4.7.39; "Why is my verse so barren of new *pride*" – Sonnet 76, line 1, using *pride* to signify his son's royal blood

GAZED ON = as a prince or king is gazed-upon by his subjects; "but with such eyes as, sick and blunted with community, afford no extraordinary *gaze such as is bent on sun-like majesty* when it shines seldom in admiring eyes" – *1 Henry IV*, 3.2.76-80; "Yet mortal looks adore his beauty still" – Sonnet 7, line 7; "How many *gazers* mightst thou lead away/ If thou wouldst use the strength of all thy state" – Sonnet 96, lines 11-12, when Oxford warns Southampton to avoid using the power of his "state" or royal stature to lead another Rebellion against the Crown

4 WILL BE A TOTTERED WEED OF SMALL WORTH HELD:
TOTTERED WEED = an old, worn-out garment or outward appearance; "And keep invention in a *noted weed*" – Sonnet 76, line 6, referring to the special method of conveying the message of the Sonnets within the *noted weed* or familiar costume of conventional poetry; **SMALL WORTH HELD** = little royalty that matters; **WORTH** = royalty, according to the "invention"; a play on "Wriothesley"; "a kingdom's worth" – *3 Henry VI*, 3.3.94; "And, by the glorious worth of my descent" – *Richard II*, 1.1.107

5 THEN BEING ASKED WHERE ALL THY BEAUTY LIES,
ALL = Southampton, his motto *Ung part Tout, Tout par Ung* or *One for All, All for One*; as in the opening sonnet, Edward de Vere speaks to Henry Wriothesley with the voice of authority as the father of a future king; Oxford also alludes to his son's identity by echoing his motto: "*all* thy beauty … *all* the treasure … *all*-eating shame"; his use of "shame" refers in this sonnet to the disgrace of a royal prince who fails to meet his responsibility to his dynastic blood; **ALL THY BEAUTY** = All your blood inherited from "beauty" or Elizabeth. Oxford extends his special vocabulary for the Sonnets by using "beauty" both for the Queen herself and for her royal blood that Southampton has received from her. The younger earl's "beauty" is the Tudor blood that flows through his veins in this glorious time of youth in his seventeenth year. "As this noble Prince (Elizabeth) is endued with mercy, patience and moderation, so is she adorned with singular beauty and chastity, excelling in the one *Venus*, in the other *Vesta*" – John Lyly, *Euphues His England*, 1580

6 WHERE ALL THE TREASURE OF THY LUSTY DAYS,
ALL = Southampton, *One for All, All for One*; **ALL THE TREASURE** = All the royalty; all the royal blood from Elizabeth, which is now her "treasure," playing on the royal treasury; "*bankrupt* of his majesty" – *Richard II*, 4.1.267; "Thy heaven is on earth; thine eyes and thoughts beat on *a crown, the treasure* of thy heart" – *2 Henry VI*, 2.1.19-20

LUSTY DAYS = youth and time of opportunity to be named as successor to the throne; "The *lustie Ver*" – from a poem likely by Edward de Vere in *A Hundredth Sundrie Flowres*, first published anonymously in 1573; "And (the Queen) repeated my Lord of Oxford's answer to me, which he made openly in the presence chamber of Her Majesty, viz., that if she (Anne Cecil) were with child it was not his. I answered (to the Queen) that it was the common answer of *lusty* courtiers everywhere" – Dr. Richard Masters, March 7, 1575, writing to Burghley about the Queen's reaction to news that the chief minister's daughter is pregnant and filled with dread over whether her husband, Oxford, will "pass upon me and it or not"

(In contradiction, Oxford will write to Cecil ten days later [see line 10 notes below] that he's delighted by his wife's pregnancy – perhaps because, now that his royal son by the existed, he anticipated that the chief

REFERENCE EDITION   65

minister would find a way to make sure his daughter would bear a child to secure her place as Countess of Oxford.)

DAYS = these golden (royal) days in the "summer" of Southampton's royal hope: "Shall I compare thee to a *Summer's day?*" – Sonnet 18, line 1; "Why didst thou promise such a *beauteous day*" – Sonnet 34, line 1

7 TO SAY WITHIN THINE OWN DEEP-SUNKEN EYES
DEEP-SUNKEN EYES = your king's eyes (suns) that no longer shine; your hidden royalty, no longer reflected by your eyes

8 WERE AN ALL-EATING SHAME AND THRIFTLESS PRAISE.
ALL = Southampton, *One for All, All for One*; **ALL-EATING SHAME** = All-destroying disgrace; **SHAME** = "And on my head my *shames* redoubled!" – *1 Henry IV*, 3.2.143-144; **THRIFTLESS PRAISE** = profitless claim of royalty; "*Your praise* shall still find room/ Even in the eyes of all posterity/ That wear this world out to the ending doom" – Sonnet 55, lines 10-12

9 HOW MUCH MORE PRAISE DESERVED THY BEAUTY'S USE
PRAISE = "Whilst I, by looking on the *praise* of him, see riot and dishonor stain the brow of my young Harry" – the King, of his son the Prince, in *1 Henry IV*, 1.1.83-85; **THY BEAUTY'S USE** = your use of inherited Tudor blood, through responsible action

10 IF THOU COULDST ANSWER, "THIS FAIR CHILD OF MINE
FAIR CHILD = royal child, i.e., royal son who reflects "beauty" the Queen; "O Lord! My boy, my Arthur, *my fair son!*" – *King John*, 3.3.103

CHILD OF MINE = "For now as it hath pleased God to give me *a son of mine own*" – Oxford to Burghley, March 17, 1575, writing from Paris after hearing that his wife Anne Cecil is pregnant; i.e., having been unable to claim his royal son by the Queen, born in May/June 1574, he now looks forward to a son of "mine own" who will inherit his earldom; Anne Cecil will give birth to a girl, Elizabeth Vere, and Oxford will come to believe that the child was not, in fact, his; the same girl, Burghley's granddaughter, whom Southampton is now being urged to marry

11 SHALL SUM MY COUNT AND MAKE MY OLD EXCUSE,"
SUM MY COUNT = fulfill my obligations as a prince of the royal blood; "Complete my account and present the balanced audit" – Booth; foreshadowing the "*Audit*" of Sonnet 126, line 11: "Her [nature's] *Audit*, though delayed, answered must be,/ And her *Quietus* is to render thee" (italics as printed in *Q* of 1609), i.e., to render him as King in posterity; "King John, this is the very *sum* of all: England and Ireland, Anjou, Touraine, Maine, in right of Arthur do I claim of thee" – *King John*, 2.1.151-153; "for it is a thing whereof I make great *account*" – Oxford to Robert Cecil, May 11, 1601; **MAKE MY OLD EXCUSE** = justify my former life, having made sure to pass on his Tudor Rose blood

12 PROVING HIS BEAUTY BY SUCCESSION THINE.
PROVING = demonstrating; "Thus I *prove* it" – Oxford memorandum, 1601-02, Cecil Papers 146.19; "Doth not the crown of England *prove the king*?" – *King John*, 2.1.273; "Let four captains bear Hamlet like a soldier to the stage, for he was likely, had he been put on, to have *proved most royal*" – *Hamlet*, 5.2.402-405

PROVING HIS BEAUTY BY SUCCESSION = Demonstrating his Tudor blood (from you and your mother, Queen Elizabeth, who is *Beauty*) by succeeding you and perpetuating your lineage, i.e., by his succession to the throne as king

"For how art thou *a king but by fair sequence and succession?*" – *Richard II*, 2.1.199; "you have the voice of the King himself for your *succession* in Denmark" – *Hamlet*, 3.2.343-344; Oxford records his dynastic intentions with the pointed references to "succession" and "blood" in the final three lines of this sonnet.

His royal son, Southampton, will be "*beauty's successive heir*" in Sonnet 127, line 3; "Touching King Henry's oath and *your succession*" – *3 Henry VI*, 2.1.119; "We'll bar thee from *succession*" – *The Winter's Tale*, 4.4.440; "But as *successively from blood to blood*, your right of birth, your empery, your own" – *Richard III*, 3.7.134-135

13 THIS WERE TO BE NEW MADE WHEN THOU ART OLD,
NEW MADE = recreated as viable, even if you yourself fail to succeed to the throne; "Before you were *new-crowned*" – *King John*, 4.2.35; "Lo, in the Orient when the gracious light/ Lifts up his burning head, each under eye/ Doth homage to *his new appearing sight*,/ Serving with looks his sacred majesty" – Sonnet 7, lines 1-4, an image of the rising sun, with which Southampton is identified as the rising Prince of England

14 AND SEE THY BLOOD WARM WHEN THOU FEEL'ST IT COLD.
THY BLOOD WARM = your royal blood as fresh (in your own heir) and fit for rule; "that *fresh blood*" – Sonnet 11, line 3; its freshness and warmth reflecting "thy golden time" in the royal sunlight of Sonnet 3, line 12, and anticipating "Shall I compare thee to a Summer's day" of Sonnet 18, line 1

THY BLOOD = These sonnets are written to contain and preserve Southampton's royal blood (not literally, of course; they are written to announce it to posterity); "Myself, *a prince by fortune of my birth*, **near to the king in blood** and near in love" – *Richard II*, 3.1.16-17; "Give us *a prince of blood*, a son of Priam" – *Troilus and Cressida*, 3.3.26; "Edward's seven sons, whereof thou art one, were as seven vials of *his sacred blood* ... One vial full of Edward's *sacred blood*, one flourishing branch of *his most royal root*" – *Richard II*, 1.2.11-12, 17-18; "As full of valour as of *royal blood*" – *Richard II*, 5.5.113; "Thou *bloodless remnant* of that *royal blood*" – *Richard III*, 1.2.7

THE MARRIAGE ALLIANCE

Sonnet 3
Thy Mother's Glass
Thy Golden Time
1590-1591

Oxford harshly warns Southampton against further delay in accepting the Cecil marriage alliance. He reminds him he is the image of his mother the Queen, adding that now is his "golden time" of royal sunlight as prince and successor to the throne. In this lecture admonishing him not to lose the chance to be named as Elizabeth's heir, Edward deVere conveys growing impatience with his royal son.

Sonnet 3	Translation
Look in thy glass and tell the face thou viewest,	Look in your mirror and tell your royal self
Now is the time that face should form another,	Now is the time to marry and beget an heir,
Whose fresh repair if now thou not renewest,	If now you fail to renew your royal blood in a son,
Thou dost beguile the world, un-bless some mother.	You are robbing England, destroying Elizabeth.
For where is she so faire whose un-eared womb	For where is a woman so royal whose virgin womb
Disdains the tillage of thy husbandry?	Disdains to have you as her husband?
Or who is he so fond will be the tomb	What royal heir would act as the tomb
Of his self-love to stop posterity?	Of his own royal blood and prevent his destiny?
Thou art thy mother's glass and she in thee	You are Elizabeth's image, and her blood in you
Calls back the lovely April of her prime,	Recalls the prime of her pregnancy with you.
So thou through windows of thine age shalt see,	So as you grow older, you will look back and see,
Despite of wrinkles this thy golden time.	Despite age, that this is your most royal opportunity.
But if thou live remembered not to be,	But if you have no heir to be remembered by,
Die single and thine Image dies with thee.	Die unmarried and your royalty dies with you.

"Here is a *parent* finding in a *child* the excuse for age and wrinkles" – Dowden

1 LOOK IN THY GLASS AND TELL THE FACE THOU VIEWEST
THY GLASS = your mirror or hourglass, reflecting both your royalty and passage of time; "Give me that *glass*, and therein will I read: no deeper wrinkles yet? ... Was this the face that like the sun did make beholders wink?" – the King in *Richard II*, 4.1.276-277, 283-284; "You go not till I set you up *a glass* where you may see the inmost part of you" – Hamlet to his mother Queen Gertrude in *Hamlet*, 3.4.18-19; "*Thy glass* will show thee how thy beauties wear" - Sonnet 77, line 1, i.e., Southampton's "glass" will show him how his royal blood from Beauty, the Queen, is faring in terms of (1) his claim to the throne and (2) his immortality, which is assured

2 NOW IS THE TIME THAT FACE SHOULD FORM AN OTHER,
NOW IS THE TIME = Oxford expressing the urgency of the specific Cecil marriage alliance. Because he is compiling seventeen sonnets to reflect his son's years of life up to his seventeenth birthday at the end of May 1591, this early sequence is necessarily repetitive as he harps on the singular theme of marriage and

Part One

procreation. The proposal in place is a unique one, supported by both Elizabeth and Lord Burghley; it is extremely unlikely that another opportunity will ever arise for Elizabeth to name Southampton her successor. In this light, Oxford's urgency on the matter is understandable and palpable: "*Now* is the time!" ("*This thy golden time*" – line 12 below); **AN OTHER** = a son who carries your blood; only when the marriage to Elizabeth Vere is accompanied by propagation will Southampton have fulfilled his responsibility; "Make thee an other self for love of me" - Sonnet 10, line 13

3 WHOSE FRESH REPAIR IF NOW THOU NOT RENEWEST,
FRESH REPAIR = the perpetuation of royal blood by begetting an heir; repeating "fresh" as when he calls Southampton "the world's *fresh* ornament" in Sonnet 1, line 9; see Sonnet 104, lines 3 and 8, when it is "three winters" since he has been "*fresh*"; and Sonnet 107, line 10, when "my love looks *fresh*"; "Seeking that beauteous roof to ruinate,/ Which to repair should be thy chief desire" - Sonnet 10, lines 7-8, i.e., the House of Tudor; "for *royalty's repair*" - *The Winter's Tale*, 5.1.31

4 THOU DOST BEGUILE THE WORLD, UNBLESS SOME MOTHER.
BEGUILE THE WORLD = deprive England; "O flatt'ring *glass*, like to my followers in prosperity, thou dost *beguile* me" – *Richard II*, 4.1.279-281; **SOME MOTHER** = Elizabeth, your mother; **UN-BLESS SOME MOTHER** = Elizabeth was the "anointed" sovereign who had been ordained by God to rule, so by destroying her blood line Southampton is "un-blessing" her; "This royal infant – heaven still move about her – though in her cradle, yet now promises upon this land a thousand-thousand *blessings*, which *time* shall bring to ripeness" – Cranmer, of baby Elizabeth Tudor, *Henry VIII*, 5.4.17-20

5 FOR WHERE IS SHE SO FAIR WHOSE UN-EARED WOMB
SHE SO FAIR = a woman so royal; **UN-EARED** = unploughed

UN-EARED WOMB = virgin womb; "This blessed plot, this earth, this realm, this England, this nurse, this teeming *womb* of royal kings" – *Richard II*, 2.1.49-51; "But if the first **heir** of my invention prove deformed, I shall be sorry it had so noble a godfather, and never after *ear* so barren a land, for fear it yield me a bad harvest" – the 1593 dedication of *Venus and Adonis* to Southampton, referring to both the poem and the earl as the *heir* of his *invention*, i.e., his invented name "Shakespeare" (created to publicly support Southampton) and also his "invention" or special method of writing these private sonnets for him. The Sonnets comprise a *womb* in which to grow him, so the "invention" refers not only to the form but also to the substance of the Sonnets, which contain the "living record" (Sonnet 55) of Southampton.

6 DISDAINS THE TILLAGE OF THY HUSBANDRY?
DISDAINS, etc. = disdains to have you as her husband or father of her child; **HUSBANDRY** = "Her plenteous womb expresseth his full tilth and husbandry" – *Measure for Measure*, 1.4.43-44

7 OR WHO IS HE SO FOND WILL BE THE TOMB
Or what royal prince is so self-centered that he buries himself; these sonnets or pyramids marking the time will become "as a *tomb*/ Which hides your life, and shows not half your parts" – Sonnet 17, lines 3-4; and the tomb will also be a "womb" in which he may "grow" in the diary, as Oxford will write of his own thoughts in the sonnets: "Making *their tomb the womb wherein they grew*" – Sonnet 86, line 4

8 OF HIS SELF-LOVE TO STOP POSTERITY?
SELF-LOVE = regard for your royal self; selfishly in love with your own royal blood, which you refuse to pass on; "His majesty out of a *self*-gracious remembrance" – *All's Well That Ends Well*, 4.5.71-72; "His *royal self* in judgment comes to hear" – *Henry VIII*, 5.2.154; just as Southampton had been "the little Love-God" in the Bath Sonnets (153-154) written in 1574, he is now filled with "self-love" or royal blood from the "lovely" or royal time of the Queen's pregnancy in April 1574 that led to his birth. Oxford is establishing the central theme of the Sonnets as *Love versus Time*, i.e., as royal blood in relation to the ever-waning life span of Elizabeth, whose death will be England's date of royal succession. The diary of the Sonnets is leading to that singular moment of contemporary history, whenever it may arrive.

POSTERITY = immortal life as king; ("But thou from loving England art so far, that *thou hast under-wrought his lawful king, cut off the sequence of **posterity**"* – *King John*, 2.1.94-96; to Southampton: "Your praise shall still find room, *even in the eyes of all posterity*" – Sonnet 55, lines 10-11; "Your monument shall be my gentle verse,/ Which *eyes not yet created* shall o'er-read" – Sonnet 81, lines 9-10; "Methinks the truth should live from age to age, as 'twere retail'd to all posterity" – *Richard III*, 3.1.76-77

> What is thy body but a swallowing grave
> Seeming to *bury that posterity*,
> Which by the rights of time thou needs must have
> - *Venus and Adonis*, 757-760

9 THOU ART THY MOTHER'S GLASS, AND SHE IN THEE
You are the image of your mother the Queen; you are both her mirror and her hourglass, reflecting her blood and also her ongoing mortal decay; Oxford is writing indirectly and directly at once, concealing and revealing his subject matter in the same breath, and on one level his reference to Southampton as "thy mother's glass" is a forthright statement for the record that Queen Elizabeth is the mother of Henry Wriothesley – a confirmation hiding in plain sight, yet imbedded within the poetry. (Whether Oxford also means that Southampton physically resembles her is beside the point he is making here.)

> "Thy *glass* will show thee how thy beauties wear"
> – Sonnet 77, line 1

> "The Queen his mother *lives almost by his looks*"
> - *Hamlet*, 4.7.11-12

> "Behold, Ladies, in this *Glass* a Queen, a woman, a Virgin in all gifts of the body, in all graces of the mind, in all perfection of either"
> - John Lyly, secretary to Edward deVere, Earl of Oxford, *Euphues his England*, 1580, p. 462, dedicated to Oxford, referring to Elizabeth

> "Come, come, sit you down, you shall not budge. You go not till I set you up *a glass* wherein you may see the inmost part of you" - Hamlet to his mother Queen Gertrude in *Hamlet*, 3.4.17-19

> "*Poor broken glass*, I often did behold/In thy sweet semblance my old age new-born"
> - *The Rape of Lucrece*, 1758-1759 (Lucretius to his dead daughter)

> *In thee thy mother dies*, our household's name,
> My death's revenge, thy youth, and England's fame
> -Talbot to his son John in *1 Henry VI*, 4.6.38-39

> With him along is come the *mother*-queen
> - *King John*, 2.1.62

10 CALLS BACK THE LOVELY APRIL OF HER PRIME;
LOVELY = royal, according to the special language, but reflected in the plays of royal history; "O Thou my *lovely* Boy" – Sonnet 126, line 1, Oxford to Southampton, who is filled with "love" or royal blood from his mother, Elizabeth, who is also "lovely" or royal; "That Henry's death, my *lovely* Edward's death, their kingdom's loss" – *Richard III*, 1.3.192-193; "A sweeter and a *lovelier* gentleman, framed in the prodigality of Nature, young, valiant, wise, and no doubt *right royal*" – *Richard III*, 1.2.247-249; **LOVELY APRIL OF HER PRIME** = the royal spring of Elizabeth's pregnancy with you in April 1574

11 **SO THOU THROUGH WINDOWS OF THINE AGE SHALL SEE,**
WINDOWS OF THINE AGE = from the perspective of older years

12 **DESPITE OF WRINKLES, THIS THY GOLDEN TIME.**
THIS = right now; as in "Now is the time" in line 2; **THY GOLDEN TIME** = your royal opportunity, in the golden light of the royal sun, the time when your rightful kingship has hope of succession; "Hids't thou that forehead with a *golden crown*" – *Richard III*, 4.4.140

"Kingship is naturally *golden*, and (in the Sonnets) *golden* impressions recur ... The Sun is nature's king, and also pre-eminently *golden*. Throughout Shakespeare, *king and sun* are compared ... In the Sonnets we have various clusters of *king, gold, and sun*" – G. Wilson Knight, *The Mutual Flame*, 1962, pp 62-63;

"That cropped the *golden prime* of this *sweet prince*" – *Richard III*, 1.3.252; "That *sun* that warms you here, shall shine on me, and those his *golden* beams to you here lent shall point on me and *gild* my banishment" – Bolinbroke to King Richard in *Richard II*, 1.3.145-147; "Great Albion's Queen in former *golden* days" – *King John*, 3.2.7; i.e., England's Queen

Oxford is recording "this" particular time, according to the calendar; and "thy golden time" refers to the golden rays of sunlight or kingship that accompany both his and Elizabeth's high hopes for Southampton's succession to the throne; i.e., a "golden opportunity," as we would say. Unless Henry Wriothesley acts now to help further his own claim to the throne, he will defeat "the world" or England itself. The "golden time" will be over upon the Rebellion of February 8, 1601, when Oxford will be forced to bring the series 1-26 to its conclusion, with Sonnet 26 as a dedicatory epistle marking the year 1600.

13 **BUT IF THOU LIVE REMEMB'RED NOT TO BE,**
REMEMBERED NOT = never named in succession as king, so not immortal; never remembered in history as having royal rights; "I have some rights of *memory* in this kingdom" – *Hamlet*, 5.2.420; "I summon up *remembrance* of things past" – Sonnet 30, line 1

14 **DIE SINGLE AND THINE IMAGE DIES WITH THEE.**
THINE IMAGE = your appearance or identity as king in the eyes of English subjects; your current fame and future immortality; "The *image* of the King ... your most *royal image*" – *2 Henry IV*, 5.3.79,89

THE MARRIAGE ALLIANCE

Sonnet 4
Nature's Bequest
1590-91

Oxford rebukes his royal son for failing to use his "legacy" or "bequest" of Tudor blood from "Nature" (Elizabeth) by doing what is necessary to succeed her on the throne. Edward de Vere stresses to Southampton that this "gift" of life and blood from his mother the Queen is merely "lent" to him and, therefore, he must be use it responsibly as a Prince whose obligation is to become King. The charge against Henry Wriothesley as a "profitless usurer" indicates the extreme seriousness of the matter. If anyone other than Oxford or the Queen issued such a verbal attack upon him, publicly or privately, the proud young peer would be forced to defend his honor with his sword.

Sonnet 4	Translation
Unthrifty loveliness, why dost thou spend,	You royal spendthrift, why do you spend
Upon thy self thy beauty's legacy?	Your blood from the Queen only on yourself?
Natures bequest gives nothing but doth lend,	Elizabeth's gift of royal blood is only a loan,
And being frank she lends to those are free:	And being generous she lends it to her royal heirs.
Then, beauteous niggard, why dost thou abuse	Then, royal miser, why do you abuse
The bounteous largess given thee to give?	The great royal gift given to you to pass on?
Profitless usurer! Why dost thou use	Moneylender without profit! Why do you possess
So great a sum of sums yet can'st not live?	So great a gift of royal blood yet can't perpetuate it?
For having traffic with thyself alone,	For keeping this royal destiny all to yourself alone,
Thou of thy self thy sweet self dost deceive.	You are deceiving your own royal person.
Then how when nature calls thee to be gone,	Then how, when Elizabeth's blood in you dies,
What acceptable *Audit* canst thou leave?	What acceptable royal accounting can you leave?
Thy unused beauty must be tombed with thee,	Your unused Tudor blood will die with you,
Which used lives th'executor to be.	But that same blood, if used, can be passed on.

"Shakspere [*sic*] has viewed his friend as *an inheritor of beauty from his mother*; this legacy of beauty is now regarded as *the bequest of nature*" – Dowden. (Oxford has viewed his son Southampton as an inheritor of royal blood from his mother the Queen; this legacy of Tudor Rose blood is now the bequest of Elizabeth as *Nature*, another word for the Queen in addition to Beauty...)

1 UNTHRIFTY LOVELINESS, WHY DOST THOU SPEND
UNTHRIFTY LOVELINESS = royal spendthrift, continuing the metaphor of his royal blood as the source of Elizabeth's treasury; (In this verse Oxford sets up the ultimate destination of the diary, which is the *Audit* of Southampton's blood that must be made one way or another. That final accounting will be summoned at the very end of the chronicle, in the farewell of Sonnet 126; and at that point, tragically so, the rendering of accounts will have to be made by readers of future generations.)

LOVELINESS = Southampton, who is filled with "love" or royal blood; he is "the little Love-God" of Sonnet 154. (Southampton is "loveliness" itself, the embodiment of royal blood. He carries "beauty's legacy" or Queen Elizabeth's gift of inherited royal blood; but Oxford, speaking as a stern father, scolds his son for spending or wasting this "bequest" that is merely a loan to him. It is worth nothing unless the younger earl acts upon it to secure his succession as monarch.)

2 UPON THY SELF THY BEAUTY'S LEGACY?
Why do you spend your inherited blood only on yourself?

THY SELF = your royal self

> "His *royal self* in judgment comes to hear"
> - *Henry VIII*, 5.3.154

> "His Majesty, out of a *self*-gracious remembrance…"
> - *All's Well That Ends Well*, 4.5.71-72

THY BEAUTY'S LEGACY = your inheritance of blood from the Queen; "And they would go and kiss dead Caesar's wounds, and dip their napkins in *his sacred blood*, yea, beg a hair of him for memory, and, dying, mention it within their wills, *bequeathing it as a rich legacy*" – *Julius Caesar*, 3.2.133-137; "Dear lord of that dear jewel I have lost,/ What *legacy shall I bequeath* to thee?" – *Lucrece*, stanza 171

3 NATURE'S BEQUEST GIVES NOTHING BUT DOTH LEND,
NATURE = Queen Elizabeth; **NATURE'S BEQUEST** = Elizabeth's gift of her royal blood (which is actually a loan); "So I *bequeath* a happy peace to you and all good men, as every Prince should do" – *Pericles*, 1.1.51-52; "And though it was mine own, part of my heritage, which my dead father did *bequeath* to me" – *Pericles*, 2.1.122-123

Oxford continues to expand his special vocabulary for the Sonnets, as Elizabeth is not only "Beauty" but now also becomes "Nature" – related to the inexorable decay of her mortal body as well as to her role as Southampton's natural mother, i.e., he is her "kind"; "Be as thy presence is, gracious and *kind*" – Sonnet 10, line 11; **NOTHING** = none = opposite of "one" for Southampton; **BUT DOTH LEND** = she has only loaned you this inheritance; you must act upon it, to gain the crown; "And those his golden beams to you here *lent*" – *Richard II*, 1.3.146

> "His *royalty of **nature**…*"
> - *Macbeth*, 3.1.48

> "Spirits are not finely touch'd but to fine issues, nor **Nature** never lends the smallest scruple of her excellence but, like a thrifty *goddess*, she determines herself the glory of a creditor, both thanks and uses" – *Measure for Measure*, 1.1.36-41

4 AND BEING FRANK SHE LENDS TO THOSE ARE FREE:
FRANK = generous; **SHE** = Nature, i.e., Queen Elizabeth; **LENDS** = "Can yet the *lease* of my true love control" - Sonnet 107, line 3

THOSE ARE FREE = heirs who are equally generous; but also related to princes or kings, who are free; "For princes should be *free*" – *1 Henry VI*, 5.3.114; "go with the King, and take with you *free* power to ratify" – *Henry V*, 5.2.85-86; "the *free* breath of a *sacred king*" – *King John*, 3.1.74; "our free person" - the King in *The Winter's Tale*, 2.1.194; "And take thou *my oblation*, poor but *free*" – Sonnet 125, line 10, in which Oxford offers his solemn sacrifice to Southampton as a god on earth or king

5 THEN, BEAUTEOUS NIGGARD, WHY DOST THOU ABUSE
BEAUTEOUS NIGGARD = royal miser or hoarder of your blood from Beauty, the Queen

6 THE BOUNTEOUS LARGESS GIVEN THEE TO GIVE?
BOUNTEOUS LARGESS = royal gift of inherited blood, a loan that he should pass on to a son or heir; "Shakespeare applies *largess* only to the gifts or donatives of *kings*" – Leslie Hotson; "A *largess* universal, like the sun, his liberal eye doth give to every one" – *Henry V*, prologue, 43-44; "So when this loose behavior I throw off, and **pay the debt** I never promised" -Prince Hal in *1 Henry IV*, 1.3.203-204; declaring he will become king, that is, give back the bounteous largess that had been given to him (by blood inheritance) by ascending to the throne and ruling.

7 PROFITLESS USURER! WHY DOST THOU ABUSE
PROFITLESS USURER = spender without profit; he who spends his royal blood upon himself, without giving himself a chance to gain the crown; "hoping that Her Majesty will have an equal regard in her countenancing the cause as well to them that study her *profit*" – Oxford to Burghley, June 7, 1595; Chiljan, 108

ABUSE = to put to a wrong use; to use ill or maltreat; to deface, disfigure, offend, insult, pervert; "Cleopatra, *do not abuse my master's bounty* by the undoing of yourself" – *Antony and Cleopatra*, 5.2.42; "All which approve *Her Majesty to be greatly abused* with many proofs, more as in their place shall be declared" – Oxford memo, *circa* 1601-1602, Cecil Papers 146.19; Chiljan, 71; "I dare not say how much Your Majesty is *abused* … to inform Your Majesty that (if) you were to lay out any one penny is a foul *abuse*, and this on my credit and duty I do affirm to Your Majesty. In whomsoever the fault, is, so far, to *abuse* themselves" – Oxford to Queen Elizabeth, June 1599, Cecil Papers 71.26; Chiljan, 122

8 SO GREAT A SUM OF SUMS YET CANST NOT LIVE?
GREAT = mighty, royal; **SUM OF SUMS** = (spelled "summe of summes" in *Q*); accounting of blood; again the metaphor of royal blood as the riches of the Queen's state treasury (perhaps with an allusion to Burghley as Lord Treasurer of England), to be used in various ways throughout the Sonnets; "The *sum of all* is that the King hath won" – *2 Henry IV*, 1.1.131; "Weigh you the worth and honor of a king *so great* as our dread father's in a scale of common ounces? Will you with counters *sum* the past-proportion of his infinite, and buckle in a waist most fathomless with spans and inches so diminutive as fears and reasons? Fie for godly shame!" – *Troilus and Cressida*, 2.2.26-32; "Your *sum of parts*" – *Hamlet*, 4.7.73; "For in monarchy, *the wealth of the Prince is the riches of the commonwealth*" – Oxford memo, March of 1595, Cecil Papers 25.76; Chiljan, 86

> First, if all obstacles were cut away,
> And that my path were even to the crown,
> As the *ripe revenue* and *due of birth*
> - *Richard III*, 3.7.157-158

> "This way, therefore, doth make *Her Majesty's revenue* of her tin mines to rise to the *sum* yearly…"
> - Oxford memo, March 1595, Cecil Papers 25.76

LIVE = keep yourself and your royal blood alive, now and in the future

9 FOR HAVING TRAFFIC WITH THY SELF ALONE,
TRAFFIC = marriage, intercourse; **ALONE** = Southampton, the "all" and "one" of *One for All, All for One*); "Save that to die, I leave my love *alone*" – Sonnet 66, line 14, Oxford on March 19, 1601, after the Queen spares Southampton's life; playing on his son's motto, in writing that he would not commit suicide for fear of leaving him alone in the Tower of London; **THY SELF ALONE** = You, Southampton; your royal self; "*This is I*, Hamlet the Dane!" – *Hamlet*, 5.2.255-256, the Prince declaring the person and presence of his royal self

No. 4

10 THOU OF THY SELF THY SWEET SELF DOST DECEIVE;
THY SWEET SELF = your royal-blooded person; ("this sweet young prince" – *3 Henry VI*, 5.5.65); my dear royal son; ("See, ruthless queen, a hapless father's tears: this cloth thou dip'dst in blood of my sweet boy" – *3 Henry VI*, 1.4.156-157; "And happily may your sweet self put on the lineal state and glory of the land! To whom with all submission, on my knee I do bequeath my faithful services and true subjection everlastingly" – *King John*, 5.7.101-105)

"Where it seems best unto *your royal self*"
- *Richard III*, 3.1.63

"Then, good my lord, take to *your royal self*"
- *Richard III*, 3.7.194

"We heartily solicit *your gracious self* to take you on *the charge and kingly government* of this your land, not as Protector, steward, substitute, or lowly factor for another's gain, but as *successively from blood to blood, your right of birth,* your empery, your own"
- *Richard III*, 3.7.129-135

11 THEN HOW, WHEN NATURE CALLS THEE TO BE GONE,
NATURE = the Queen's life (blood) in you; your life, given to you by Nature the Queen

12 WHAT ACCEPTABLE *AUDIT* CANST THOU LEAVE?
ACCEPTABLE *AUDIT* = "responsible reckoning or account, in the sense of showing 'profit' on Nature's investment in you" – Evans; i.e., profiting from Elizabeth's investment of her blood in you by earning your claim as her successor on the throne

"With good *acceptance* of his Majesty" – *Henry V*, 1.1.83

AUDIT = Final accounting of your royal blood, by continuing the dynasty; foreshadowing Oxford's farewell after Elizabeth's funeral, when he then speaks of "Nature" as "sovereign mistress over wrack" and declares: "Her *Audit*, though delayed, answered must be, and her *Quietus* is to render thee" – Sonnet 126, lines 5, 11-12, i.e., Southampton must be rendered as king in posterity; "which I restored unto him before mine *auditor,* on condition he should *render* it up" - Oxford to Burghley, January 3, 1576

13 THY UNUSED BEAUTY MUST BE TOMBED WITH THEE,
UNUSED BEAUTY = wasted blood from Elizabeth, by lack of succession; "When you *entombed in men's eyes* shall lie" – Sonnet 81, line 8; "To make him much outlive a *gilded tomb*" – Sonnet 101, line 11, referring to "the *gilded monument* of Princes" – Sonnet 55, line 1, i.e., Southampton deserves the tomb of a Prince, but Oxford will build a better one for him by means of the Sonnets; "And thou in this shalt find thy monument,/ When tyrants' crests and *tombs of brass* are spent" – Sonnet 107, lines 13-14; but in this early verse, Oxford is warning Southampton that he will go to his grave without his "beauty" (royal blood from the Queen) acknowledged; and therefore it will be "tombed" along with his body

14 WHICH USED, LIVES TH'EXECUTOR TO BE.
USED = his royal blood from "beauty" or Elizabeth, bequeathed to an heir; i.e., his blood used responsibly, so the Tudor lineage may continue on the throne; the opposite of "wasted"; "*Make use of time*, let not advantage slip;/ *Beauty within itself should not be wasted*" – *Venus and Adonis*, 1593, 129-130; "*fresh beauty* for the *use*" – *Venus and Adonis*, 1593, 164, the narrative poem published a few years after this series of seventeen marriage and procreation sonnets; "Mine be *thy love* and *thy love's use* their *treasure*" – Sonnet 20, line 14, with "love" referring to royal blood; "That *use* is not forbidden usury" – Sonnet 6, line 5; eventually Oxford is "using" (or spending the treasure of) his son's royal blood within these private verses: "As every alien pen hath got my *use*" – Sonnet 78, line 3, referring to the "Shakespeare" pen name, as in

REFERENCE EDITION

"Knowing a better spirit doth *use* your name" – Sonnet 80, line 2; "Who heaven itself for ornament doth *use*" – Sonnet 21, line 3, i.e., Elizabeth herself *uses* Southampton as her "ornament" or prince

"Why should he live, now nature bankrupt is,/ Beggared of blood to blush through lively veins?/ For she hath no exchequer now but his,/ And proud of many lives upon his gains./ O him she stores, to show what wealth she had,/ In days long since, before these last so bad" - Sonnet 67, lines 9-14, carrying forth the same metaphor of nature/treasure and Elizabeth/royal blood to preserve her lineage

EXECUTOR = dispenser of the "treasure" of inherited blood; "Let's choose *executors* and talk of wills: and yet not so, for what can we *bequeath* save our deposed bodies to the ground?" – *Richard II*, 3.2.148-150

Part One

THE MARRIAGE ALLIANCE

Sonnet 5
Never-Resting Time
1590-1591

Oxford urges Southampton to act now before his "summer" or golden time of royal hope turns to "hideous winter" or the end of any chance to perpetuate the Tudor Rose dynasty. The "hours" of the Queen's life are "tyrants" acting against this goal; the ever-dwindling life span of Elizabeth is "never-resting time" leading to her death and England's date with succession to her throne. Southampton is the "flower" of the Rose who must be "distilled" by the passage of his blood to an heir; the urgency, however, remains tied to the specific proposal for a Cecil marriage alliance. Because Elizabeth depends upon her chief minister, his support for Henry Wriothesley to become King Henry IX is crucial.

Sonnet 5	Translation
Those hours that with gentle work did frame	Those hours that with royal work did create
The lovely gaze where every eye doth dwell	Your kingly presence upon which I dwell
Will play the tyrants to the very same,	Will become tyrants to this same royal identity
And that unfair which fairly doth excel:	And destroy this royalty that is so legitimate.
For never-resting time leads Summer on	For the Queen's ever-waning life leads it on
To hideous winter and confounds him there,	Toward her own death and the end of itself,
Sap checked with frost and lusty leaves quite gone,	Royal blood frozen and its opportunity gone,
Beauty ore-snowed and bareness everywhere.	Elizabeth's Tudor blood deprived of everything.
Then were not summer's distillation left	Then the succession of her blood would not become
A liquid prisoner pent in walls of glass,	A liquid prisoner trapped in prisons of glass;
Beauties effect with beauty were bereft,	Elizabeth's legacy would not be taken from itself,
Nor it nor no remembrance what it was.	Leaving neither it nor any memory of what it was.
But flowers distilled, though they with winter meet,	But Tudor Roses with heirs, though they die,
Leese but their show, their substance still lives sweet.	Lose only their show, their reality continues as royal.

1 THOSE HOURS THAT WITH GENTLE WORK DID FRAME
THOSE HOURS = the time of Elizabeth's life; **GENTLE WORK** = royal labor, in childbirth; **DID FRAME** = gave birth to, created

2 THE LOVELY GAZE WHERE EVERY EYE DOTH DWELL
LOVELY GAZE = the kingly gaze of Southampton; "Nay, if thou be that princely eagle's bird, show thy descent by *gazing* 'gainst the sun" – *3 Henry VI*, 2.1.91-92; lovely = filled with royal blood; "O thou my lovely Boy" - Sonnet 126, line 1; **EVERY EYE** = eyes of all subjects; *Ever* = Edward de Vere, E. Ver, *Ever or Never*; therefore: "*my* eye";

GAZE WHERE EVERY EYE DOTH DWELL = "Afford no extraordinary *gaze*, such as is *bent on sun-like majesty* when it shines seldom *in admiring eyes*" – *1 Henry IV*, 3.2.78-80, the king instructing his son to

REFERENCE EDITION 77

avoid showing himself in public too often; "When yet he was but tender-bodied and the only son of my womb, when youth with comeliness *plucked all gaze his way*" – *Coriolanus*, 1.3.5-8; "And live *to be the show and gaze o' the time*" – *Macbeth*, 5.8.24

3 WILL PLAY THE TYRANTS TO THE VERY SAME,
TYRANTS = the dwindling hours of time, leading to the date with succession; Elizabeth is a "tyrant" in Sonnet 107, line 14; **VERY** = Ver, Edward de Vere; **THE VERY SAME** = Southampton, the one created by those hours, and related to Edward Vere

4 AND THAT UNFAIR WHICH FAIRLY DOTH EXCEL:
AND THAT UNFAIR = and make non-royal or illegitimate; (deprive of "beauty" or royal blood); the only such usage of "unfair" as a verb in Shakespeare; **WHICH FAIRLY DOTH EXCEL** = that which is legitimately royal; **EXCEL** = exists as excellent or royal, as in Your Excellency; excels in "beauty" or royal blood

5 FOR NEVER-RESTING TIME LEADS SUMMER ON
NEVER = Edward de Vere, *Ever or Never*; **NEVER-RESTING TIME** = Elizabeth's dwindling time of life and reign; **SUMMER** = time of royalty; your golden time of royal promise; Queen Titania, as Elizabeth: "The summer still doth tend upon my state" – *A Midsummer Night's Dream*, 3.1.147

6 TO HIDEOUS WINTER AND CONFOUNDS HIM THERE,
HIDEOUS WINTER = lack of Southampton's succession; extinction of Elizabeth's dynasty

7 SAP CHECKED WITH FROST AND LUSTY LEAVES QUITE GONE,
SAP = royal blood; the vital juice of plants, i.e., of Southampton as Flower of the Rose; ("did drain the purple sap from her sweet brother's body" – *Richard III*, 4.4.276-277); **LUSTY LEAVES** = kingly adornment; **LUSTY** = youthful, fresh, green, flowing with royal blood

8 BEAUTY O'ER-SNOWED AND BARENESS EVERY WHERE.
BEAUTY O'ER-SNOWED = Tudor blood hidden; **BARE** = emptiness; opposite of "fair"; **EVERYWHERE** = Ever = E. Ver, Edward deVere

9 THEN WERE NOT SUMMER'S DISTILLATION LEFT
SUMMER'S DISTILLATION = perfumes made from flowers; perpetuation of your royal blood within another; distillation of your royal blood into its essence, within your heir; perpetuation of your "golden time" of Sonnet 3, line 12; "Earthlier happy is *the rose distilled*, than that which *withering on the virgin thorn grows, lives and dies* in single blessedness" – alluding to the Tudor Rose of Elizabeth, Virgin Queen, in *A Midsummer Night's Dream*, 1.1.76-77; "The central issue is still the preservation of 'beauty's *Rose*'" - Duncan-Jones

10 A LIQUID PRISONER PENT IN WALLS OF GLASS,
LIQUID PRISONER = blood imprisoned; "As one might see *a damask rose hid under crystal glass*" = Earl of Oxforde, Echo Verses, by 1576

11 BEAUTY'S EFFECT WITH BEAUTY WERE BEREFT,
Your royal claim from Beauty or Elizabeth would be deprived of itself; **BEAUTY'S** = Elizabeth's and/or her royal blood's; **EFFECT** = manifestation, i..e., in the person of an heir to the throne; "that which is produced by an agent or cause, operation, result, consequence, fruit" – Schmidt; "And every *beauty* robbed of his *effect*" – *Venus and Adonis*, 1132; "I do invest you with my power, pre-eminence and all the large *effects that troop with majesty*" – the King in *King Lear*, 1.1.131-133; **BEREFT** = past tense of *bereave*; deprived, stripped of, taken from; "Thee of thy son, Alonso, they have *bereft*" – *The Tempest*, 3.3.75-76;

"*Bereft*, and gelded of his patrimony" – *Richard II*, 2.1.237; "O boy, thy father gave thee life too soon, and hath *bereft* thee of thy life too late!" – *3 Henry VI*, 2.5.92-93;

12 NOR IT NOR NO REMEMBRANCE WHAT IT WAS.
NO REMEMBRANCE = no royal immortality; "You pity not the state, nor *the remembrance of his most sovereign name*" – *The Winter's Tale*, 5.1.25-26; "I have some rights of *memory* in this kingdom" – *Hamlet*, 5.2.396; "as fits *a king's remembrance*" – *Hamlet*, 2.2.26; "Her Majesty may call to *remembrance*" – Oxford to Robert Cecil, July 1600; "Thus most earnestly desiring you to have me in friendly *remembrance* when time serveth" – Oxford to Robert Cecil, February 2, 1601; "When to the Sessions of sweet silent thought,/ I summon up *remembrance* of things past" – Sonnet 30, lines 1-2, after the Rebellion of February 8, 1601, when Oxford is "summoned" to the "Sessions" or treason trial of Essex and Southampton at Westminster Hall

13 BUT FLOWERS DISTILLED, THOUGH THEY WITH WINTER MEET,
FLOWERS = Southampton, flower of the Tudor Rose; **FLOWERS DISTILLED** = his royal blood perpetuated; **FLOWERS** = "Yet marked I where the bolt of Cupid fell: It fell upon a little western *flower*, before milk-white, now purple with love's wound" – *A Midsummer Night's Dream*, 2.1.165-167; "And in his blood that on the ground lay spilled,/ A purple *flower* sprung up ... 'Poor *flower*,' quoth she, 'this was *thy father's guise,/ Sweet issue of a more sweet-smelling sire* ... Here was *thy father's bed*, here in my breast;/ *Thou art next of blood, and 'tis thy right*.'" – *Venus and Adonis*, 1167-1169, 1183-1184; both passages relating to Southampton as the purple or royal flower; "The Rose both White and Red in one Rose now doth grow" - John Skelton, praising Henry VIII, *The Poetical Works of John Skelton*, ed. Dyce, 1864, ii., 340; "The indubitable *flower* and very heir" of Lancaster and York - Hall's *Chronicle*, title page, 1548, of the late Henry VIII

14 LEESE BUT THEIR SHOW, THEIR SUBSTANCE STILL LIVES SWEET.
LEESE BUT THEIR SHOW = lose only their appearance; "leese" appears in the King James Bible, printed in 1611, 1 Kings, 18.5: "that we *leese* (lose) not all the beasts"; the word appears much earlier also, as in *Leicester's Commonwealth* of 1584; **THEIR SUBSTANCE STILL LIVES SWEET** = their blood in reality always lives as royal; "No, no, I am but shadow of myself: you are deceived, my *substance* is not here" – *1 Henry VI*, 2.3.49-50; "But the world is so cunning, as *of a shadow they can make a substance*" – Oxford to Burghley, July 1581; "What is your *substance*, whereof are you made,/ That millions of strange shadows on you tend?" – Sonnet 53, lines 1-2, when Southampton is in the Tower of London

THE MARRIAGE ALLIANCE

Sonnet 6
Beauty's Treasure
1590-1591

Oxford urges Southampton to accept the Cecil marriage alliance and beget an heir, so that "beauty's treasure" or Queen Elizabeth's Tudor Rose blood may continue on the English throne. "Be not self-willed!" Edward de Vere commands his son by the Queen, writing as a stern father, to remind him of his princely responsibility. These private verses are only for the attention of Henry Wriothesley, who is well aware of the marriage proposal. Oxford therefore has no need to risk treason charges (if the verses fell into the wrong hands) by specifically naming Lady Elizabeth Vere as the intended bride and, by doing so, making a definite claim for Southampton in succession.

Sonnet 6	Translation
Then let not winters ragged hand deface	Then do not allow Elizabeth's coming death to kill
In thee thy summer ere thou be distilled:	Your most royal opportunity before procreation:
Make sweet some vial! Treasure thou some place	Make some womb royal! Fill some womb royally
With beauty's treasure ere it be self-killed:	With Elizabeth's blood before you die alone with it!
That use is not forbidden usury	That loan of your royal blood is not a crime
Which happies those that pay the willing loan;	When it makes happy those who pay you back;
That's for thy self to breed another thee,	That happiness is yours to beget another royal heir
Or ten times happier be it ten for one,	Or ten times happier for ten heirs of you.
Ten times thy self were happier than thou art,	Ten heirs of yourself would be happier than one,
If ten of thine ten times refigur'd thee:	If ten heirs of yours made a hundred heirs of you:
Then what could death do if thou should'st depart,	Then what could Elizabeth's death do if you died,
Leaving thee living in posterity?	Leaving your blood within an heir for posterity?
Be not self-willed, for thou art much too fair	Don't be selfish! For you are much too royal
To be death's conquest and make worms thine heir.	To be death's victim and leave no living heir.

1 THEN LET NOT WINTER'S RAGGED HAND DEFACE
WINTER'S RAGGED HAND = the waste of royal time and death of hope; "Now is the *winter* of our discontent *made glorious summer by this son of York*" – Richard III, 1.1.1-2; the hand of Winter is the hand of *Time*, the ever-dwindling life of Elizabeth; and therefore "winter" signifies her coming death, i.e., her death without Southampton's succession to the throne; opposite of the *summer* or golden time of royal hope; **HAND** = the royal hand; "A Woman's face with *nature's own hand painted/* Has thou, the Master Mistress of my passion" – Sonnet 20, lines 1-2; as an infant Southampton was "sleeping *by a Virgin hand disarmed*" – Sonnet 154, line 8

2 IN THEE THY SUMMER ERE THOU BE DISTILLED:
THY SUMMER = your golden time of royalty; "Shall I compare thee to a *Summer's day/* …And *Summer's lease* hath all too short a date/ … But *thy eternal Summer* shall not fade" – Sonnet 18, lines 1,4,9; **DISTILLED** = recreated in an heir; Southampton, flower of the Tudor Rose, passing his blood to another;

("One vial full of Edward's sacred blood, one flourishing branch of his most royal root, is cracked, and *all the precious liquor spilt*, is hacked down, and *his summer leaves all faded*" – *Richard II*, 1.2.17-20)

3 **MAKE SWEET SOME VIAL; TREASURE THOU SOME PLACE**
SWEET = royal; Good night, *sweet prince*" – *Hamlet*, 5.2.366; **VIAL** = womb; "Edward's *seven sons*, whereof thyself art one, were as *seven vials of his sacred blood*" – *Richard II*, 1.2.11-12; **MAKE SWEET SOME VIAL** = impregnate the womb of a woman with your "sweet" or royal blood; **TREASURE** = fill with the treasure of your blood; "Thy heaven is on earth; thine eyes and thoughts beat on a crown, the *treasure* of thy heart" – *2 Henry VI*, 2.1.19-20

4 **WITH BEAUTY'S TREASURE ERE IT BE SELF-KILLED:**
BEAUTY'S TREASURE = Queen Elizabeth's blood in you, which is her treasure in terms of her lineage; ("now nature bankrupt is,/ Beggared of blood to blush through lively veins?/ For she hath no exchequer now but his,/ ... O him she stores, to show what wealth she had" – Sonnet 67, lines 9-13, when the Queen is holding Southampton in the Tower of London in 1601); "But since she pricked thee out for women's pleasure,/ Mine be thy love and thy love's use their *treasure*" – Sonnet 20, lines 13-14, referring to Elizabeth giving birth to their son at her royal pleasure and having his blood as her treasure; "So am I as the rich whose blessed key/ Can bring him to his sweet up-locked treasure" – Sonnet 52, lines 1-2, Oxford referring to his son and the "treasure" of his royal blood being "up-locked" in the Tower of London; "the treasure of thy love" – Oxford to Elizabeth in Sonnet 136, line 5, referring to her son's "love" or royal blood as her treasure; all of which leads to the "audit" or final accounting of royal blood in Sonnet 126, lines 11-12, the end of the diary, referring to the audit of universal nature or posterity: "Her *Audit* (though delayed) answered must be,/ And her Quietus is to render thee" – i.e., as king

5 **THAT USE IS NOT FORBIDDEN USURY**
USURY = the crime of loaning at high rates; such use of your royal blood is no crime

6 **WHICH HAPPIES THOSE THAT PAY THE WILLING LOAN;**
HAPPIES = makes happy; ("*Happy were England*, would this virtuous Prince take on his Grace the sovereignty thereof" – *Richard III*, 37.77-78); "Resembling sire, and child, and happy mother" – Sonnet 8, line 11, referring to Oxford, Southampton, and Elizabeth, i.e., the family triangle as it would become known if Southampton gained the throne; "I'll gild it with the *happiest* terms I have"- Prince Henry in *1 Henry IV*, 5.4.156; **THOSE THAT PAY THE WILLING LOAN** = those who willingly give you the loan of their blood; **WILLING** = with royal will

7 **THAT'S FOR THY SELF TO BREED AN OTHER THEE,**
THAT'S FOR THY SELF = that loan is for you, for your royal self; "By law of nature thou art *bound to breed*,/ That thine may live when thou thyself art dead" – *Venus and Adonis*, 171-172; "You are so strongly *in my purpose bred*" – Sonnet 112, line 13

8 **OR TEN TIMES HAPPIER BE IT TEN FOR ONE.**
TEN FOR ONE = ten heirs for one of you; **ONE** = Southampton; "Since *all alike* my songs and praises be/ To *one*, of *one*, still such, and ever so/ ... *One* thing expressing, leaves out difference/ ... Three themes in *one*.../ ...never kept seat in *one*" – Sonnet 105, lines 3-4, 8,12,14, i.e., the three members of the royal family (Elizabeth, Southampton and Oxford) as a trinity living in the one person of their son

9 **TEN TIMES THY SELF WERE HAPPIER THAN THOU ART,**
TEN TIMES THY SELF = ten of your heirs

10 **IF TEN OF THINE TEN TIMES REFIGURED THEE:**
If ten of your heirs begot ten children each, making a hundred grandchildren

11 THEN WHAT COULD DEATH DO IF THOU SHOULDST DEPART,

DEPART = die; Oxford will say much the same to Queen Elizabeth near the end of her life and reign, still pleading for her to name her son to succeed her: "So shalt thou feed on death, that feeds on men,/ And death once dead, there's no more dying then" – Sonnet 146, lines 13-14

12 LEAVING THEE LIVING IN POSTERITY?

LEAVING THEE LIVING IN POSTERITY = leaving your blood alive in your heirs or descendants; ("in perpetuity, on into the times of all future generations" – Booth); "Arthur, that great forerunner of thy blood, Richard … by this brave duke came early to his grave, and for amends to his *posterity*…" – *King John*, 2.1.2-6; "Methinks the truth should live from age to age, as 'twere retailed to all *posterity*, even to the general all-ending day" – *Richard III*, 3.1.76-78; "Death is now the Phoenix' nest,/ And the Turtle's loyal breast/ To eternity doth rest./ Leaving no *posterity*" – *The Phoenix and Turtle*, 56-58, 1601, after the Rebellion in February that year, when all hope for Southampton's royal claim is lost; "'Gainst death and all oblivious enmity/ Shall you pace forth; your praise shall still find room/ Even in the eyes of all *posterity*" – Sonnet 55, lines 9-11, pledge to Southampton that he will live forever in the Sonnets

13 BE NOT-SELF-WILLED, FOR THOU ART MUCH TOO FAIR

BE NOT SELF-WILLED = a lecture by Oxford, referring to Southampton's royal will; i.e., do not be selfish in using your royal will; "Who dare cross 'em, bearing *the king's will* from his mouth expressly?" – *Henry VIII*, 3.2.234-235; "Who *willed* you? Or whose *will* stands but mine? There's none Protector of the realm but I" – *1 Henry VI*, 1.3.11-12; **MUCH TOO FAIR** = much too royal, echoing "fairest creatures" of Sonnet 1, line 1

14 TO BE DEATH'S CONQUEST AND MAKE WORMS THINE HEIR.

MAKE WORMS THINE HEIR = go to the grave with only worms inheriting your blood; later, referring to her dying House of Tudor as "thy fading mansion": "Why so large cost, having so short a lease,/ Dost thou upon thy fading mansion spend?/ Shall **worms, inheritors** *of this excess,/ Eat up thy charge? Is this thy body's end?*" – Sonnet 146, lines 5-8; **HEIR** = "My kingdom, well worthy the best *heir*" – *Henry VIII*, 2.4.194; "And in my conscience do repute his grace **the rightful heir** *to England's royal seat*" – *2 Henry VI*, 5.1.177-178

Part One

THE MARRIAGE ALLIANCE

Sonnet 7
His Sacred Majesty
1590-1591

Oxford boldly records his son's unacknowledged identity as a royal prince, calling him "his sacred majesty" and warning him not to wait until his opportunity is forever lost. Edward de Vere again uses the familiar costume of conventional poetry to avoid potential charges of treason for putting forth a claim to the throne in succession to Elizabeth. Again he urges Henry Wriothesley to accept the marriage bargain, so the Queen will have William Cecil's support for naming him as her successor, again emphasizing propagation as an essential part of the arrangement.

Sonnet 7	Translation
Lo in the Orient when the gracious light,	Behold, in the East when the prince's royalty
Lifts up his burning head, each under eye	Makes its appearance, all the eyes of his subjects
Doth homage to his new appearing sight,	Pay homage to this new vision of him,
Serving with looks his sacred majesty;	Serving the royal prince with their adoring looks.
And having climbed the steep up heavenly hill,	And as he progresses toward Elizabeth's death,
Resembling strong youth in his middle age,	While still looking young in his middle years,
Yet mortal looks adore his beauty still,	His subjects continue to adore his royalty,
Attending on his golden pilgrimage:	Attending him on his royal journey.
But when from high-most pitch with weary car,	But when from this opportune time, on his chariot,
Like feeble age he reeleth from the day,	Like feeble age he begins to lose his royalty,
The eyes (fore duteous) now converted are	His previously dutiful subjects turn their eyes
From his low tract and look another way:	From his lowly state and look elsewhere for a king.
So thou, thy self out-going in thy noon:	In the same way you yourself, losing this chance,
Unlooked-on diest unless thou get a sonne.	Will die without glory unless you beget a son.

1 LO, IN THE ORIENT WHEN THE GRACIOUS LIGHT
LO = Lord Oxford (L. O.); behold; **ORIENT** = East, where the sun rises; "See us rising in our throne, the East" – the king in *Richard II*, 3.2.50; **GRACIOUS LIGHT** = kingly beams of the sun, full of royal grace, godlike; "That sun that warms you here, shall shine on me, and those his golden beams to you here lent shall point me on and gild my banishment" – *Richard II*, 1.3145-147; **GRACIOUS** = "My gracious sovereign" – *1 Henry VI*, 4.1.9; "And I again, in Henry's royal name, deputy unto that gracious king" – *1 Henry VI*, 5.3.160-161; "Be as thy presence is, *gracious* and kind" - Sonnet 10, line 11, to Southampton as prince

> Full many a glorious morning have I seen
> Flatter the mountain tops with sovereign eye
> - Sonnet 33, lines 1-2

2 LIFTS UP HIS BURNING HEAD, EACH UNDER EYE

REFERENCE EDITION 83

BURNING HEAD = the sun, a king's eye; "And scarcely greet me with that sun, thine eye" – Sonnet 49, line 6, to Southampton; **EACH UNDER EYE** = the eyes of subjects below; "A man in hew all *Hews* in his controlling,/ Which steals *men's eyes*" – Sonnet 20, lines 7-8

3 DOTH HOMAGE TO HIS NEW-APPEARING SIGHT,
HOMAGE = worship; pay duty and service to; "Lord of my love, to whom in vassalage/ Thy merit hath my *duty* strongly knit" – Sonnet 26, lines 1-2

4 SERVING WITH LOOKS HIS SACRED MAJESTY:
SERVING WITH LOOKS = honoring, worshipping; ("I serve Her Majesty" – Oxford to Burghley, October 30, 1584); **HIS SACRED MAJESTY** = the sacred sun king, his eye; ("See, see, King Richard doth himself appear, as doth the blushing discontented sun from out the fiery portal of the East, when he perceives the envious clouds are bent to dim his glory and to stain the track of his bright passage to the occident" – *Richard II*, 3.3.61-66; "God save King Henry, unking'd Richard says, and send him many years of sunshine days!" – *Richard II*, 4.1.220-221); "Whilst I, my sovereign, watch the clock for you" – Sonnet 57, line 6; "And all those beauties whereof now he's King/ Are vanishing, or vanished out of sight" – Sonnet 63, lines 6-7; "Thus have I had thee as a dream doth flatter,/ In sleep a King, but waking no such matter" – Sonnet 87, lines 13-14

5 AND HAVING CLIMBED THE STEEP-UP HEAVENLY HILL,
HEAVENLY HILL = top of the sky, toward heaven or God; related to Elizabeth and introducing her as Heaven in addition to Beauty and Nature; ("This royal infant, *heaven* still move about her" – Cranmer, speaking of the infant Elizabeth, in *Henry VIII*, 5.4.17, with "still" meaning always; "*Heaven* pictured in her face,/ Doth promise joy and grace" – Oxford poem in *The Phoenix Nest*, 1593, of Elizabeth; "and although it hath pleased God after an earthly kingdom to take her up into a more permanent and *heavenly* state" – Oxford to Robert Cecil, April 25/27, 1603, on the eve of the Queen's funeral.

6 RESEMBLING STRONG YOUTH IN HIS MIDDLE AGE,
STRONG YOUTH = full imperial power and opportunity to be king

7 YET MORTAL LOOKS ADORE HIS BEAUTY STILL,
MORTAL LOOKS ADORE = worshipful gazes of mortal subjects, who adore him with their eyes; ("But is he gracious in the people's eye?" – *3 Henry VI*, 3.3.117); **HIS BEAUTY** = Southampton's royal blood; **STILL** = constantly, always, forever; "Why write I *still* all one, ever the same/ … O know, sweet love, I *always* write of you,/ And you and love are *still* my argument/ … For as *the Sun* is daily new and old,/ So is my love *still* telling what is told" – Sonnet 76, lines 5, 9-10, 13-14; "Since all alike my songs and praises be/ To one, of one, *still* such, and ever so./ Kind is my love today, tomorrow kind,/ *Still* constant in a wondrous excellence" – Sonnet 105, lines 3-6; **ADORE HIS BEAUTY STILL** = "What thing doth please thee most?/ To *gaze on beauty still*" – Earle of Oxford, by 1576

8 ATTENDING ON HIS GOLDEN PILGRIMAGE:
ATTENDING = waiting upon the sovereign; ("in giving *attendance* in Your Highnesse' service" – Oxford to Elizabeth, May 9, 1592; "either for the *attending* or meeting of His Majesty" – Oxford to Robert Cecil, April 25/27, 1603, referring to King James); "And will that thou henceforth *attend on us*" – the King in *2 Henry VI*, 5.1.80; **GOLDEN PILGRIMAGE** = royal progress; ("this thy *golden* time" – Sonnet 3, line 12, to Southampton as prince); "For then my thoughts, from far where I abide,/ Intend a zealous pilgrimage to thee" – Sonnet 27, lines 5-6, immediately after the Rebellion of February 8, 1601, when Southampton is imprisoned and Oxford sends his thoughts on a *zealous* (spiritual, sacred) *pilgrimage* to his royal son in the Tower of London

No. 7

9 BUT WHEN FROM HIGH-MOST PITCH WITH WEARY CAR
WEARY CAR = the chariot of the gods, i.e., of *Phoebus Apollo* (the source of Oxford's Muse; "Let the mob admire base things! May *golden Apollo* serve me full goblets from the Castalian fount!" – *Venus and Adonis*, 1593, Ovid epitaph on the title page); in his youth Oxford referred to himself as Phoebus, the sun god; "To her how Echo told the truth,/ As *true as Phoebus' oracle*" – the Earl of Oxford, *Echo Verses*, written by 1576

10 LIKE FEEBLE AGE HE REELETH FROM THE DAY,
THE DAY = the time of a king's life filled with golden sunlight; "Shall I compare thee to a Summer's Day?" – Sonnet 18, line 1

11 THE EYES ('FORE DUTEOUS) NOW CONVERTED ARE
THE EYES = the eyes of his subjects; "My reformation, glitt'ring o'er my fault, shall show more goodly, and *attract more eyes*" – Prince Hal in *1 Henry IV*, 1.2.208-209;

'FORE DUTEOUS = previously worshipful; "his dutiful service in Her Majesty's behalf" – Oxford memorandum, 1601-02, Cecil Papers 146.19; "what course is devised by you of the Council, and the rest of the lords, concerning our duties to the king's Majesty" – Oxford to Robert Cecil, April 25/27, 1603;

CONVERTED = changed; transformed

12 FROM HIS LOW TRACT AND LOOK AN OTHER WAY.
HIS LOW TRACT = the sun king's fall from grace; **LOOK AN OTHER WAY** = turn elsewhere to find a king; "*Thy friends are fled to wait upon thy foes,* and crossly to thy good all fortune goes" - *Richard II*, 2.4.23-24

13 SO THOU, THY SELF OUT-GOING IN THY NOON:
SO THOU = in the same way you, Southampton; **THY SELF** = your royal self; "Make thee *an other self* for love of me,/ That *beauty still may live in thine or thee*" – Sonnet 13, lines 13-14; **OUTGOING** = losing your kingship; ("Was this *the face that like the sun* did make beholders wink?" – *Richard II*, 4.1.283-284); **NOON** = middle age; past the time when your royalty is acknowledged

> Ah, Richard! With the eyes of heavy mind
> I see **thy glory like a shooting star**
> *Fall to the base earth from the firmament.*
> ***The sun sets weeping*** in the lowly west,
> Witnessing storms to come, woe, and unrest.
> Thy friends are fled to wait upon thy foes,
> And crossly to thy good all fortune goes.
> - *Richard II*, 2.4.18-24

14 UNLOOKED-ON DIEST UNLESS THOU GET A SON.
UNLOOKED-ON = unnoticed, not cared for, without recognition; "What dangers, by His Highness' *fail of issue, may drop upon his kingdom, and devour incertain lookers-on*" – *The Winter's Tale*, 4.4.27-29; "And I'll salute your Grace of York as mother and reverend *looker-on of two fair queens*" – *Richard III*, 4.1.29-30

> I should fear those that dance before me now
> Would one day stamp upon me. 'T'as been done.
> *Men shut their doors against a setting sun.*
> - *Timon of Athens*, 1.2.144-146

REFERENCE EDITION

SON = spelled *sonne* in *Q*; **UNLESS THOU GET A SONNE** = unless you enter this alliance with the Cecil family through marriage and the procreation of an heir to make it binding; **GET** = beget

SUN & ROYAL SON = Oxford likens Southampton to the royal sun whose subjects adore him as their "sacred majesty"; he must beget his own son, who will also be a "sun" or royal son; he will use the same imagery in Sonnet 33 to portray his son's birth as the "glorious" rising of the sun with its "sovereign eye" and "golden" or "celestial" face.

When Falstaff in *1 Henry IV* plays the role of King Henry IV, he uses the same interchange of "son" and "sun" to signify Prince Hal, his son, as successor to the English throne who will become Henry V of England:

"Why, being *son* to me, art thou so pointed at? Shall *the blessed sun of heaven* prove a micher, and eat blackberries? A question not to be asked. Shall *the son of England* prove a thief, and take purses?" (2.4.401-406)

"Now is the winter of our discontent *made glorious summer by this son of York*" – *Richard III*, 1.1.1-2 ("This *son* of York" is Edward IV, son of Richard, Duke of York; the pun is on the *sun* in Edward's emblem, indicating that royal son = sun)

"Yet herein *will I imitate the sun*, who doth permit the base contagious clouds to smother up his beauty from the world" – Prince Hal in *1 Henry IV*, 1.2.192-194

"If the young man is a '*sun*', his *son* will be the same" – Kerrigan

Part One

THE MARRIAGE ALLIANCE

Sonnet 8
*Sire, and Child, and Happy Mother
All in One*
1590

Oxford is also a skilled composer of songs who plays the lute and the virginal. Here he uses music as a metaphor for the royal family comprised of himself, Southampton as son, and Elizabeth. He suggests they are akin to a holy trinity whose hopes rest upon "all in one" – a glance at Southampton's motto **One for All, All for One** *as he looks forward to their blood gaining the throne in the person of their "one" son. More than a dozen years later, Oxford will record the death of Queen Elizabeth by writing again of these "three themes in one" of the Sonnets: "Which three, till now, never kept seat in one" -- kept seat, that is, on the throne.*

Sonnet 8	Translation
Music to hear, why hear'st thou music sadly	If your royalty is music, why hear it sadly?
Sweets with sweets war not, joy delights in joy:	Royalty doesn't fight royalty; it rejoices in itself.
Why lov'st thou that which thou receivst not gladly,	Why do you disrespect what you've received,
Or else receivest with pleasure thine annoy?	Or accept it at your royal pleasure with annoyance?
If the true concord of well tuned sounds,	If the lawful agreement of all parties proposing
By unions married, do offend thine ear,	Your marriage seems offensive to you,
They do but sweetly chide thee, who confounds	These parties royally offend you – who destroy,
In singleness the parts that thou should'st bear:	By singleness, the royal blood you should pass on:
Mark how one string sweet husband to an other,	Look how one party, royally serving the other,
Strikes each in each by mutual ordering;	Has each to each come mutually to this agreement,
Resembling sire, and child, and happy mother,	Representing me, you and Elizabeth your mother,
Who all in one, one pleasing note do sing:	Who all three depend on you to gain the throne.
Whose speechless song, being many, seeming one,	Our unspoken agreement, in harmony over you,
Sings this to thee: Thou single wilt prove none.	Is this: "Die heirless and your royal line ends."

"I have presumed to tender these Madrigals only as remembrances of my service and witness of your Lordship's liberal hand, by which I have so long lived, and from your honourable mind that so much have all liberal sciences. In this I shall be most encouraged if your Lordship vouchsafe the protection of my first fruits, for that both of your greatness you best can, and for **your judgment in music** *best may. For without flattery be it spoke, those that know your Lordship know this, that using this science as a recreation,* **your Lordship have over-gone most of them that make it a profession.***"*
- Composer John Farmer to Edward deVere, Earl of Oxford
(Dedication of *The First Set of English Madrigals*, 1599)

1 MUSIC TO HEAR, WHY HEAR'ST THOU MUSIC SADLY?
MUSIC = if royal blood were music, why turn away from it? "Music do I hear? Ha, ha! Keep time – how sour sweet *music* is when time is broke and no proportion kept! So is it in the *music* of men's lives. And

here have I the daintiness of ear to check time broke in a disordered string; but for the concord of my state and time, had not an ear to hear my true time broke: I wasted time, and now time doth waste me" – *Richard II*, 5.5.42-49; **WHY HEAR'ST THOU MUSIC SADLY** = "This music mads me" – *Richard II*, 5.5.61; "Then music is even as the flourish, when true subjects bow to a new-crowned monarch" – *The Merchant of Venice*, 3.2.48-50; "For government, though high, and low and lower, put into parts, doth keep in one consent, congreeing in a full and natural close, like music" – *Henry V*, 1.2.180-183

2 SWEETS WITH SWEETS WAR NOT, JOY DELIGHTS IN JOY:
SWEETS WITH SWEETS WAR NOT = royalty doesn't make war against itself; "I dare presume, *sweet prince*, he thought no harm" – *1 Henry VI*, 4.1.179; "My son's *sweet blood* will make it shame and blush" – *Titus Andronicus*, 3.1.15; "That *sweet aspect of princes*" – *Henry VIII*, 3.2.369; **WAR** = a hint of Oxford's concern that civil war could erupt around the royal succession; "My husband lost his life to get the crown, and often up and down my sons were tossed for me to joy and week their gain and loss … Make war upon themselves, brother to brother, blood to blood, self against self" – *Richard III*, 2.4.57-63; **JOY** = "Was ever king that *joy'd* an earthly throne" – *2 Henry VI*, 4.9.1; "God make your Majesty *joyful*" – *Richard III*, 1.3.19; **JOY DELIGHTS IN JOY** = royal blood delights in itself; "Small *joy* have I in being England's queen" – *Richard III*, 1.3.110; As little *joy*, my lord, as you suppose you should *enjoy*, were you this country's king" – *Richard III*, 1.3.151-152

3 WHY LOV'ST THOU THAT WHICH THOU RECEIV'ST NOT GLADLY,
How can you honor your royal blood if you refuse to accept it?

4 OR ELSE RECEIV'ST WITH PLEASURE THINE ANNOY?
PLEASURE = your Majesty's pleasure or royal will; ("It was by *Her Majesty's pleasure* put to arbitrement" – Oxford to Robert Cecil, May 7, 1603)

5 IF THE TRUE CONCORD OF WELL-TUNED SOUNDS
TRUE = Oxford, whose family motto is *Vero Nihil Verius*, or *Nothing Truer than Truth*; lawful, legitimate; **TRUE CONCORD** = royal harmony; "And here I have the daintiness of ear to check time broke in a disordered string. But for *the concord of my state and time*, had not an ear to hear my true time broke" – *Richard II*, 5.5.45-48; **CONCORD** = agreement or accord, i.e., this lawful/royal agreement for your marriage and succession; ("The man that hath no music in himself, nor is not moved with *concord of sweet sounds*, is fit for treasons, stratagems and spoils" – *The Merchant of Venice*, 5.1.83-85)

6 BY UNIONS MARRIED DO OFFEND THINE EAR,
UNIONS MARRIED = the harmony of royal blood, alluding to the crucial marriage alliance; later Oxford will write of the union between himself and Southampton as father and son: "Let me not to *the marriage of true minds/ Admit impediments*" – Sonnet 116, lines 1-2

7 THEY DO BUT SWEETLY CHIDE THEE, WHO CONFOUNDS
SWEETLY = royally; ("Welcome, *sweet prince*" – *Richard III*, 3.1.1); **CONFOUNDS** = destroys

8 IN SINGLENESS THE PARTS THAT THOU SHOULD'ST BEAR:
PARTS = your kingly qualities; "Who will believe my verse in time to come/ If it were filled with your most high deserts?/ Though heaven knows it is as a tomb/ Which hides your life, and *shows not half your parts*" – Sonnet 17, lines 1-4; **BEAR** = reproduce, by procreation, within your heirs

9 MARK HOW ONE STRING, SWEET HUSBAND TO AN OTHER,
MARK = look at; **ONE STRING** = Southampton, *One for All, All for One*; **HUSBAND** = what Southampton must become

No. 8

10 STRIKES EACH IN EACH BY MUTUAL ORDERING:
STRIKES = ("as both 'hits' and 'strikes a deal'" – Kerrigan; perhaps alluding to Southampton's need to "strike a deal" with Cecil by accepting the marriage license in return for Cecil's supporting Elizabeth in naming Southampton as her successor; **MUTUAL ORDERING** = royal harmony; ("But *mutual render*, only me for thee" – Sonnet 125, line 12, Oxford offering his final sacrifice to Southampton)

11 RESEMBLING SIRE, AND CHILD, AND HAPPY MOTHER,
RESEMBLING = "My sire, I have received your letters, full of humanity and courtesy, and strongly *resembling* your great love and singular affection towards me, like *true children duly procreated of such a mother*" – Oxford to Burghley, written in French at age thirteen in 1563

SIRE, AND CHILD, AND HAPPY MOTHER = Oxford, Southampton and Elizabeth as a royal family in harmony on the throne (echoing the litany of Father, Son, and Holy Ghost of the Trinity; "*Three themes in one*, which wondrous scope affords" – Sonnet 105, line 12); "This trio suggests the paradox of the Holy Trinity and multiplies our sense of paradox by also and simultaneously suggesting the Holy Family – Jesus, his mother Mary, and his foster father Joseph" – Booth on Sonnet 105; the three are also combined in "Why write I still *all one, ever the same*" – Sonnet 76, line 5, combining Southampton's motto *One for All, All for One*, Elizabeth's motto *Ever the Same* and Edward de Vere (*Ever*).

SIRE = father; "And in his blood that on the ground lay spilled,/ A *purple flower* sprung up/ ... 'Poor flower,' quote she, 'this was *thy father's* guise,/ *Sweet issue* of a more sweet-smelling **sire**" – *Venus and Adonis*, 1593, dedicated to Southampton, 1167-1178

> He, but a duke, would have his son a king,
> And *raise his issue, like a loving sire*.
> - *3 Henry VI*, 2.2.21-22

> Touch not the boy, for he is of royal blood.
> Too like the *sire* for ever being good.
> - *Titus Andronicus*, 5.1.49-50

HAPPY MOTHER = "And wilt thou pluck *my fair son* from mine age, and rob me of *a happy mother's* name?" – *Richard II*, 5.2.92-93; Oxford is Southampton's biological father, but he has been barred from claiming paternity, so at best he is the foster father of a royal orphan. ("Yet this abundant *issue* seemed to me/ But *hope of orphans*, and *unfathered fruit*" – Sonnet 97, lines 9-10.) His wife Anne Cecil having died in 1588, however, Oxford may yet hope to share the throne with Elizabeth as her husband and king consort. In that case Southampton could be proclaimed as their child, i.e., as "*the natural issue of Her Majesty's body*" according to the 1571 Parliament Act that defined a legitimate successor to her throne.

> All comfort, *joy in this most gracious lady*,
> Heaven ever laid up *to make parents happy*
> - *Henry VIII*, 5.4.6-7, referring to the infant Elizabeth

"That is to say in Easter term in the eighth year of your Highness' most *happy* reign" – Edward de Vere: "To the Queen's most excellent Majesty," 1587; (PRO STAC5/03/35/3, a bill of complaint by Oxford; transcript version by Nina Green)

"Now stand you on the top of *happy* hours" – Sonnet 16, line 5, addressing Southampton as the "top" of royalty, i.e., as one who stands in line to become King and wear the crown

12 WHO ALL IN ONE, ONE PLEASING SONG DO SING:
All IN ONE = An allusion to Southampton's motto *One for All, All for One*, first recognized by a researcher in 1859, signing himself W. C. J. in *The Athenaeum*; "In the Sonnets this motto he (the poet) has adapted in

REFERENCE EDITION

different ways with considerable poetic and idiomatic license," citing Sonnet 8, lines 12-13. W. C. J. noted: "And in many others (verses) it will be found to be the pervading thought"; the three-in-one of the Trinity; the royal family; "That *one for all, or all for one* we guage" – Henry Wriothesley's motto in stanza 21 of *Lucrece*, 1594, dedicated to Southampton.
- W. C. J. in 1859 offered two other examples of the Southampton's motto:

>And thou, *all* they, hast *all* the *all* of me
>- Sonnet 31, line 14

>Since *all alike* my songs and praises be
>To *one,* of *one*, still such, and ever so…
>Therefore my verse to constancy confined,
>*One* thing expressing, leaves out difference
>- Sonnet 105, lines 3-4, 7-8

13 WHOSE SPEECHLESS SONG, BEING MANY, SEEMING ONE,
SPEECHLESS = secret, made speechless or silent by decree; wordless ("And art made *tongue-tied by authority*" – Sonnet 66, line 9); Oxford is writing about the truth, regardless of what appears on the surface. He is recording what actually exists, as opposed to the version of the truth that officialdom has decreed to be acceptable; **ONE** = Southampton, who should be king

14 SINGS THIS TO THEE: "THOU SINGLE WILT PROVE NONE."
PROVE NONE = fail to succeed to the throne; **PROVE** = "*Prove me*, my gracious lord" – *Richard III*, 4.2.68, a subject speaking to the King and asking for a chance to prove his loyalty to him; **NONE** = opposite of "one" for Southampton; Southampton unrecognized; "Your line will become extinct with your death" – Booth; "Among a number *one* is reckoned *none*" – Oxford to Queen Elizabeth in Sonnet 136, line 8, complaining about her imprisonment of their son in the Tower after the 1601 Rebellion

Part One

THE MARRIAGE ALLIANCE

Sonnet 9
Beauty's Waste
1590

Oxford addresses his royal son as a prince failing "the world" or England by refusing the Cecil marriage alliance and thereby depriving himself of the chance to become king. Edward de Vere accuses Henry Wriothesley of committing "murdrous shame" against all citizens, who deserve to be his subjects as Henry IX of England. Continuing with the metaphor of the Queen's state treasury for her royal blood that flows within her son, Oxford accuses Southampton of being an "unthrift" or spendthrift. In Sonnet 106 the reality of "beauty's waste" -- the subsequent impossibility of Elizabeth's royal Tudor blood to succeed to the throne in the person of her son -- will transform this dynastic diary into "the Chronicle of wasted time."

Sonnet 9	Translation
Is it for fear to wet a widow's eye	Is it fear of leaving any wife a tearful widow
That thou consum'st thyself in single life?	That you destroy your royal self by not marrying?
Ah; if thou issueless shalt hap to die,	Ah, if you should die without an heir,
The world will wail thee like a makeless wife,	England will mourn you like a mateless widow.
The world will be thy widow and still weep,	England will be your widow and forever weep,
That thou no form of thee hast left behind,	That you've left no heir of your royal blood behind,
When every private widow well may keep,	When every commoner widow is allowed to keep,
By children's eyes, her husband's shape in mind:	By her children, her husband's memory alive.
Look what an unthrift in the world doth spend	Look what blood a spendthrift in England spends,
Shifts but his place, for still the world enjoys it.	Losing his throne, yet still England has his blood.
But beauty's waste hath in the world an end,	But Elizabeth's blood wasted in England will end;
And kept unused the user so destroys it:	And not passed on, the user thereby destroys it.
No love toward others in that bosom sits	No royal blood for your subjects is in you,
That on himself such murdrous shame commits	Who commits such a disgrace against his royal self.

1 IS IT FOR FEAR TO WET A WIDOW'S EYE
Is it for fear of leaving behind a desolate widow

2 THAT THOU CONSUM'ST THY SELF IN SINGLE LIFE?
That you destroy your kingly self by remaining single; "What man in the whole world,*except a father or a potential father-in-law*, cares whether any other man gets married?" – C. S. Lewis; Oxford is both prospective father-in-law *and* father of Southampton (as the prospective bride, Elizabeth Vere, may not have been his biological child)

3 AH, IF THOU ISSUELESS SHALT HAP TO DIE,
ISSUELESS = without royal heirs; "For which the heavens, taking angry note, have left me *issueless*" – the King in *The Winter's Tale*, 5.1.174; "Both to defend my loyalty and truth to God, my king, and my *succeeding issue*" – *Richard II*, 1.3.19-20; "the natural *issue* of Her Majesty's body" – language of

Parliament, 1571, three years before the birth of the boy to be raised as Southampton, designating such issue as having the right to succeed her on the throne.

"If the king should without *issue* die" - *Henry VIII*, 1.2.133-134; "Look how the father's face/ Lives in his *issue*" - Ben Jonson in the First Folio of Shakespeare plays, 1623; "When your sweet*issue* your sweet form should bear" - Sonnet 13, line 7

4 **THE WORLD WILL WAIL THEE LIKE A MAKELESS WIFE,**
THE WORLD = England; Oxford's use of "the world" five times in this sonnet becomes an insistent refrain, emphasizing that Southampton's responsibility as a royal prince is not just to himself, but to England and even to the known world; "This might have been done through private conference before, and had not needed to have been *the fable of the world*" – Oxford to Burghley, April 27, 1576; "But *the world* is so cunning, as of a shadow they can make a substance, and of a likelihood a truth" – Oxford to Burghley, July 1581; **MAKELESS WIFE** = wife without a mate and therefore childless; companionless

5 **THE WORLD WILL BE THY WIDOW AND STILL WEEP**
THE WORLD = England; **STILL WEEP** = forever lament; as a Prince who should become King or Husband of England (as Queen Elizabeth considers herself married to England), you will leave the country behind as your widow

6 **THAT THOU NO FORM OF THEE HAST LEFT BEHIND,**
FORM Of THEE = replication of yourself in an heir; **FORM:** "Being the right idea *of your father*, both in your *form* and nobleness of mind" – *Richard III*, 3.7.13-14; "From henceforth bear his name *whose form thou bear'st*" – *King John*, 1.1.159-160; "Be of good comfort, *Prince*; for you are born to set a *form* upon that indigest which he hath left so shapeless and so rude" –*King John*, 5.7.25-27; "How would thy shadow's *form* form happy show" – Sonnet 43, line 6; "In polished form of well-refined pen" – Sonnet 85, line 8

7 **WHEN EVERY PRIVATE WIDOW WELL MAY KEEP,**
EVERY = E. Ver, Edward de Vere, *Ever or Never*; **WHEN EVERY PRIVATE WIDOW** = when even widows of private persons who are not kings; "the widow of a 'private' man as *distinguished from that of a ruler, a king*" – Hotson; "What infinite heart's-ease must *kings neglect that private men enjoy*" – *Henry V*, 4.1.253; "Must he be then as shadow of himself? Adorn his temples with a coronet, and yet, in substance and authority, retain but privilege of a *private* man?" – *1 Henry VI*, 5.4.133-136)

8 **BY CHILDREN'S EYES, HER HUSBAND'S SHAPE IN MIND:**
CHILDREN'S EYES = reflections of the husband-father

9 **LOOK WHAT AN UNTHRIFT IN THE WORLD DOTH SPEND**
UNTHRIFT IN THE WORLD = prodigal son of England; **SPEND** = wastes his seed, which would pass on his royal blood; "waste beyond recall" – Kerrigan

10 **SHIFTS BUT HIS PLACE, FOR STILL THE WORLD ENJOYS IT;**
HIS PLACE: "Thy *place* in Council thou hast rudely lost" – King Henry to his son, Prince Hal, in *1 Henry IV*, 3.2.32; "My due from thee is this imperial crown, which, as immediate from ***thy place*** and blood, derives itself to me" – Prince Hal to his father, the King, in *2 Henry IV*, 4.5.40-42; (later, in Sonnet 44, "the place" will refer to the Tower of London and also to "the place of execution"); **THE WORLD** = England; **ENJOYS** = uses; "Now you are heir, therefore enjoy it now" – *3 Henry VI*, 1.1.12; "A crown it is that seldom kings enjoy" – *3 Henry VI*, 3.1.65

11 **BUT BEAUTY'SWASTE HATH IN THE WORLD AN END,**
BEAUTY'S WASTE = the waste of your royal blood from Elizabeth, by failing to act so as to succeed her on the throne; (When Southampton fails to succeed Elizabeth upon her death, the Book of Sonnets immediately becomes "the *Chronicle of wasted time*" – Sonnet 106, line l); **WASTE** = a legal term; abuse or destruction of property by a tenant; as in "to the use of the said late Earl for term of his life without

impeachment of any waste" – from a document (WARD 8/13) related to the 16th Earl of Oxford; cited by Nina Green of the Phaeton forum on the Internet; **HATH IN THE WORLD AN END** = comes to an end in England, without your succession or the continuation of Tudor blood; (That is, this "waste" cannot continue forever; at some point it will end, as will this diary)

12 **AND KEPT UNUSED THE USER SO DESTROYS IT:**
UNUSED = without procreation; without entering the marriage alliance and begetting an heir to make it binding; "Thy unused beauty must be tombed with thee,/ Which used lives th'executor to be" – Sonnet 4, lines 13-14; **USER** = "he who has the right to use" – Ingram & Redpath; i.e., Southampton, who must either "use" his royal blood from the Queen or destroy it

13 **NO LOVE TOWARD OTHERS IN THAT BOSOM SITS**
NO LOVE = no royal blood; no responsibility for your royal blood; ("Here is my hand, my dear lover England" – song for Elizabeth's entry into London, 1559; Strong, *Elizabeth R*, 14); **NO LOVE TOWARD OTHERS** = no care for "*the world's due*" of Sonnet 1, line 14; ("Mr. Speaker ... I do assure you that there is no prince that *loveth* his subjects better, or whose *love* can countervail *our love*" – Elizabeth addressing Parliament in November of 1601 in her celebrated Golden Speech; Strong, *Elizabeth R*, 62); **SITS** = sits on the throne; ("Once more we *sit* in England's royal throne" – *3 Henry VI*, 5.7.1; "There will never Queen *sit in my seat* with more zeal to my country, care to my subjects" – Elizabeth addressing Parliament in 1601, cited above); "Long may'st thou live in Richard's *seat to sit*" – *Richard II*, 4.1.218)

14 **THAT ON HIMSELF SUCH MURDROUS SHAME COMMITS.**
MURDROUS SHAME = destructive disgrace or treason (against your own royal blood); "shameful murder; a kind of suicide ... killing disgrace" – Evans; an example of the kind of harsh, even insulting language that only a father could use in addressing a nobleman, much less a royal prince; in this case, Oxford is a higher-ranking earl, allowing him to speak in this way, but he is actually speaking paternally and on behalf of the Queen as well

THE MARRIAGE ALLIANCE

Sonnet 10
That Beauteous Roof
1590-1591

Oxford harshly criticizes Southampton while reminding him of his princely duty to his subjects. He accuses him of "murd'rous hate" for destroying his "love" or royal blood and willfully ruining "that beauteous roof" (the House of Tudor) rather than preventing its collapse. He pleads with his son to behave as the king he is, referring to his royal "presence" as both "gracious" (filled with kingly grace) and "kind" (related to the Queen by nature, i.e., being her heir by birth). Oxford pleads directly and personally to Henry Wriothesley as father to son, begging him to "make thee another self for love of me" so that "beauty" (his Tudor blood from his mother Elizabeth, goddess of Love and Beauty) will continue in the line of succession.

Sonnet 10	Translation
For shame deny that thou bear'st love to any	For shame! Deny you give your royal blood to any,
Who for thyself art so unprovident!	You who so lack foresight for yourself!
Grant if thou wilt, thou art beloved of many,	Grant, if you will, you are the royal prince of many,
But that thou none lov'st is most evident:	But that you don't act like it is most evident.
For thou art so possessed with murd'rous hate	You are killing your mother's royal dynasty,
That 'gainst thy self thou stickest not to conspire,	So you don't scruple to conspire against yourself,
Seeking that beauteous roof to ruinate	Seeking to destroy Elizabeth's House of Tudor,
Which to repair should be thy chief desire:	Which to perpetuate should be your chief will.
O change thy thought, that I may change my mind;	O, change course, so I can change these words!
Shall hate be fairer lodged then gentle love?	Shall death of royalty be crowned over royal blood?
Be as thy presence is, gracious and kind,	Be your kingly self, royal and natural by blood,
Or to thy self at least kind hearted prove.	Or at least do yourself good as Elizabeth's son.
Make thee another self for love of me,	Beget an heir for royal blood and me, your father,
That beauty still may live in thine or thee.	So Elizabeth's lineage will live in your son or you!

1 FOR SHAME DENY THAT THOU BEAR'ST LOVE TO ANY,
FOR SHAME DENY = shame on you for denying; or: you should deny in shame; (echoing the "*murderous shame*" of Sonnet 9, line 14); **BEAR'ST LOVE TO ANY** = bring forth royal blood by "bearing" children or heirs; ("Near to the King in *blood*, and near in *love*" – Richard II, 3.1.17); **BEAR'ST** = also related to heraldic bearing of arms

2 WHO FOR THY SELF ART SO UNPROVIDENT!
SO UNPROVIDENT = so lacking of foresight for your royal self; so uncareful in preparing for the future, i.e., for the Queen's death and your succession to the throne; related to "providence" or the care of God, divine dispensation; therefore Southampton, a prince or god on earth, is acting in an ungodly or unholy manner; "It fits us then to be as *provident* as fear may teach us" – the French King in *Henry V*, 2.4.11-12

3 GRANT IF THOU WILT, THOU ART BELOV'D OF MANY,
BELOVED OF MANY = honored by those aware of who you really are; ("Ever *beloved* and loving *may his rule* be" – Henry VIII, 2.1.92; "As after some oration *fairly spoke by a beloved prince*, there doth appear among the buzzing pleased multitude" – The Merchant of Venice, 3.2.178-180; "He's *loved of the distracted*

multitude" – *Hamlet*, 4.3.4, of the prince; "the great *love the general gender bear him*" – *Hamlet*, 4.7.18, of the prince; "*Beloved sons*" – *King Lear*, 1.1.138)

4 BUT THAT THOU NONE LOV'ST IS MOST EVIDENT:
THOU NONE LOV'ST = you do not behave as anyone's prince; you demonstrate no care or concern for those who would be your subjects

5 FOR THOU ART SO POSSESSED WITH MURDROUS HATE
MURDEROUS HATE = the opposite of nurturing love or royal blood; the killing of your lineage; committing an act of treason (against the Queen, against himself)

6 THAT 'GAINST THY SELF THOU STICK'ST NOT TO CONSPIRE,
That you don't even scruple to conspire against yourself; **STICK'ST** = scruple

7 SEEKING THAT BEAUTEOUS ROOF TO RUINATE,
BEAUTEOUS ROOF = royal House of Tudor; Elizabeth's Tudor lineage; **ROOF:** "The word acts as a synecdoche for 'house' ... and 'family' ... as in 'the House of Tudor' ... your family line" – Booth; "Seeking to bring to ruin that house (i.e., family) which it ought to be your chief care to repair" – Dowden); **RUINATE** = bring to its end or destruction; ("And knowing this *kingdom* is without a head, like goodly buildings left without a *roof* soon fall to *ruin*" – *Pericles*, 2.4.35-37; "I will not *ruinate my father's house*, who gave *his blood* to lime the stones together, and set up Lancaster" – *3 Henry VI*, 5.1.86-88; "To order well the state, that like events may ne'er it *ruinate*" – *Titus Andronicus*, 5.3.202-203; "Time's glory is to calm contending kings ... to *ruinate* proud buildings with thy hours" – *Lucrece*, stanza 135; "Her Majesty ... should yet give a *prop and stay to my house*" – Oxford to Robert Cecil, January 1602, referring to his family and earldom; "This mortal house I'll *ruin*, do Caesar what he can" – Queen Cleopatra in *Antony and Cleopatra*, 5.2.50-51

8 WHICH TO REPAIR SHOULD BE THY CHIEF DESIRE:
REPAIR = keep alive; "What holier than, for *royalty's repair*, for present comfort, and for future good, to bless the bed of majesty again with a sweet fellow to't?" – *The Winter's Tale*, 5.1.31-34; **CHIEF DESIRE** = supreme royal will; ("the chiefest time of mine age" – Oxford to Robert Cecil, June 19, 1603); **CHIEF** = related to "chief mourner" or nearest relative at a funeral; i.e., his "chief desire" or royal will is, or should be, motivated by his blood relationship to the Tudor family; "That she hath thee is my wailing chief" – Sonnet 42, line 3, referring to Elizabeth, who has her son in prison and is apparently going to execute him (in which case Oxford would become the chief mourner, along with Elizabeth herself)

9 O CHANGE THY THOUGHT, THAT I MAY CHANGE MY MIND!
O = Oxford ("O") as "I" and speaking "my mind"; **YOUR THOUGHT** = your attitude and action

10 SHALL HATE BE FAIRER LODGED THAN GENTLE LOVE?
HATE = lack of royalty or royal favor; "I am assured, if I be measured rightly, your Majesty hath no just cause to *hate* me" – *2 Henry IV*, 5.2.65-66; **FAIRER LODGED** = more royally lodged in the House of Tudor; **GENTLE LOVE** = royal blood; "That dost presume to boast of *gentle blood*" – *1 Henry VI*, 4.1.44) "My meaning is to work what wonders *love* hath wrought,/ Wherewith I muse why men of wit have *love* so dearly bought:/ For *love* is worse than *hate*, and eke more harm hath done,/ Record I take of those that read of Paris, Priam's son" – Oxford poem in *The Paradise of Dainty Devices*, 1576; **GENTLE:** "And here's to our *right gentle-hearted king*" – *3 Henry VI*, 1.4.

HATE VS. LOVE:

> Warwick, these words have turned my *hate to love*
> - *3 Henry VI*, 3.3.

> Made peace enmity, *fair love of hate*,

Between these swelling wrong-incensed peers
- *Richard III*, 2.1.

Besides, our nearness to the king in *love*
Is near the *hate* of those *love not* the king
- *Richard II*, 2.2.

11 BE AS THY PRESENCE IS, GRACIOUS AND KIND,
Act according to your stature as a Prince, full of royal grace as the natural son of the Queen.

PRESENCE = Kingly presence; ("Come I appellant to **this princely presence**" – *Richard II*, 1.1. 34; "And sent to warn them to *his royal presence*" – *Richard III*, 1.3.39; "Worst in this *royal presence* may I speak" – *Richard II*, 4.1.115; "I will avouch't in *presence of the King*" – *Richard III*, 1.3.115; "The tender love I bear *your Grace*, my lord, makes me most forward in this *princely presence*" – *Richard III*, 3.4.63-64; "Loud shouts and salutations from their mouths, even in the *presence of the crowned King*; thus did I keep my person fresh and new, my *presence*, like a robe pontifical, ne'er seen but wondered at" – the King in *1 Henry IV*, 3.2.53-57; "What's he approacheth boldly to our *presence*?" – King Lewis in *3 Henry VI*, 3.3.44)

GRACIOUS = Filled with royal (divine) grace, as in "your Grace" above; "Accept this scroll, most *gracious* sovereign" – *1 Henry VI*, 3.1.149; "Great King of England, and my *gracious* lord" – *2 Henry VI*, 1.1.24; "I come with *gracious* offers from the King" – *1 Henry IV*, 4.3.30; "My *gracious* sovereign" – *Richard II*, 1.1.21; "I hold my duty as I hold my soul, both to my God and to my **gracious King**" – *Hamlet*, 2.2.44-45; "You have a daughter called Elizabeth, virtuous and fair, royal and *gracious*" – *Richard III*, 4.4.204-205

"So *gracious* and virtuous a sovereign"
– Oxford to Robert Cecil, May 7, 1603

My verse alone had all thy gentle *grace*,
But now my *gracious* numbers are decayed
- Sonnet 79, lines 2-3

KIND = Natural, related by nature, as a child of Elizabeth and the bearer of her blood; ("Belonging to one by birth: lawful, rightful – 1570 ... of persons: rightful heir, etc., 1589 – *OED*); "There she lost a noble and renowned brother, in his love toward her ever most *kind* and natural" – *Measure for Measure*, 3.1.218-220; "A little more than *kin*, and less than *kind*" – *Hamlet*, 1.2.65; "Shall **kin with kin, and kind with kind**, confound" – *Richard II*, 4.1.141; "Disclaiming here the *kindred* of the king, and lay aside my high blood's royalty" – *Richard II*, 1.1.70-71; "The King is *kind*" – *1 Henry IV*, 4.3.52; "My lord and sovereign, and thy vowed friend, I come, in *kindness* and unfeigned *love*, first, to do greetings to thy royal person" – *3 Henry VI*, 3.3.50-52

"In all *kindness* and *kindred*"
– Oxford to Robert Cecil, May 1601

Kind is my love today, tomorrow *kind*...
Fair, *kind*, and true, is all my argument,
Fair, *kind*, and true, varying to other words
- Sonnet 105, lines 5, 9-10

(*Fair*= royal son; *Kind* = natural child of the Queen; *True* = rightful heir & related to Oxford, who is *Nothing Truer than Truth.*)

No. 10

12 **OR TO THY SELF AT LEAST KIND-HEARTED PROVE.**
KIND HEARTED = acting in accordance with your relationship to the Queen by nature, as her son and heir; ("either in *kindness*, which I find beyond mine expectation in you, or in *kindred*" – Oxford to Robert Cecil, May 1601); **HEARTED** = "But I am not your king till I be crowned and that my sword be stained with *heart-blood* of the House of Lancaster" – *2 Henry VI*, 2.2.64-66; Southampton's own "heart" is the source of his royal blood that flows through his veins; and he has inherited this blood in "kindness" or by nature from Elizabeth; **PROVE** = demonstrate; ("*Prove* it, Henry, and thou shalt be king" – *3 Henry VI*, 1.1.135; "Look what I speak, *my life shall prove it true*" – *Richard II*, 1.1.87)

13 **MAKE THEE ANOTHER SELF FOR LOVE OF ME,**
Oxford's plea as father to his son to produce an heir of his own blood; **FOR LOVE** = for your royal blood that is mingled with mine; commentators have recognized this line as the first indication that "the friend" (i.e., Southampton) actually has love for the poet; in the traditional context, it comes out of the blue and without warning, but in the context that Oxford is speaking as a father to his son, the line is natural and unsurprising

14 **THAT BEAUTY STILL MAY LIVE IN THINE OR THEE.**
BEAUTY = Tudor blood, from Elizabeth; **STILL MAY LIVE** = may continue forever; "That thereby *beauty's Rose might never die*" – Sonnet 1, line 2; **THINE** = your heirs; "For this is *thine* and not *King Henry's heirs*" – *3 Henry VI*, 1.1.27

THE MARRIAGE ALLIANCE

Sonnet 11
That Fresh Blood
1590-1591

Oxford lectures Southampton, referring to Elizabeth and/or her blood as "Nature" as well as "Beauty" according to his special language. Henry Wriothesley should pass on "that fresh (royal) blood" to a son of his own. He should cherish the "bounteous gift" (royal bounty) of blood-inheritance given to him by Elizabeth, who "carved thee for her seal" (the Great Seal of the Crown), that is, who gave birth to him in order to continue her dynasty.

Sonnet 11	Translation
As fast as thou shalt wane so fast thou grow'st In one of thine, from that which thou departest, And that fresh blood which youngly thou bestow'st Thou mayst call thine, when thou from youth convertest.	As fast as your royal claim wanes, so fast it grows In a child of yours – from which you run away – And that new royal blood that you now pass on You'll be able to call yours, when no longer young.
Herein lies wisdom, beauty, and increase; Without this, folly, age, and cold decay, If all were minded so, the times should cease, And threescore year would make the world away:	Herein is wisdom, Elizabeth's blood, and an heir; Without it folly, age and lack of royal destiny. If all royal princes acted so, dynasties would die And England would cease to exist in sixty years.
Let those whom nature hath not made for store, Harsh, featureless, and rude, barrenly perish. Look whom she best endowed, she gave the more; Which bounteous gift thou shouldst in bounty cherish,	Let those Elizabeth did not beget for her destiny, Those who have no royal blood, perish without it. Look who she gave most blood: she gave you more, And you should cherish this royal gift in abundance.
She carved thee for her seal, and meant thereby Thou shouldst print more, not let that copy die.	Elizabeth bore you for her Great Royal Seal, so You should beget more heirs, not let your line die.

1 AS FAST AS THOU SHALT WANE SO FAST THOU GROW'ST
As rapidly as you age, so fast you (and/or your blood) will grow with an heir of your own.

WANE = Decline in years; lose your opportunity to gain the throne, according to *the waning of Moon*, i.e., according to *the ever-waning life of Queen Elizabeth, who is Cynthia or Diana, chaste Goddess of the Moon.*

> The *mortal Moon* hath *her eclipse* endured
> - Sonnet 107, line 5, written soon after her death on March 24, 1603; but when Southampton fails to succeed his royal mother, who has left him to languish in the Tower after she dies, Oxford will continue the diary until the day of Elizabeth's funeral on April 28, 1603, marked by Sonnet 125, when the Tudor Rose Dynasty officially ends

And in the very next verse of farewell, he will write to his son:

> O Thou my lovely Boy, who in thy power
> Dost hold time's fickle glass, his sickle hour,

> Who hast *by waning grown*...
> - Sonnet 126, lines 1-3

By the end of this chronicle, Southampton has *grown in the womb of the Sonnets* while losing his claim to the throne, according to the relentless *waning* of the mortal body of Elizabeth.

> Now, brother Richard, Hastings, and the rest,
> Yet thus far Fortune maketh us amends,
> And says that once more I shall interchange
> My *waned state* for Henry's regal crown
> - *3 Henry VI*, 4.7.1-4

> The aim of *all* is but to nurse the life
> With honor, wealth and ease, in *waning* age,
> And in this aim there is such thwarting strife
> That *one for all* or *all for one* we gage:
> As life for honor in fell battle's rage,
> Honor for wealth; and oft that wealth doth cost
> The death of *all*, and *all* together lost.
> - *The Rape of Lucrece*, 141-147; dedicated to Southampton
> (Incorporating the *waning* of his royal blood according to the
> Moon, i.e., his mother Elizabeth, Moon goddess, and his motto
> *One for All, All for One*)

> But O, methinks how slow
> This old moon wanes!
> - *A Midsummer Night's Dream*, 1.1.3-4

GROW'ST = related to Southampton growing in the "womb" of this diary according to time; "When in eternal lines to time thou *grow'st*" – Sonnet 18, line 12; "Nativity, once in the main of light,/ *Crawls to maturity,* wherewith being crowned" – Sonnet 60, lines 5-6; "Making their tomb the womb wherein they *grew*" – Sonnet 86, line 4; "Love is a Babe. Then might I not say so/ *To give full growth to that which still doth grow*" – Sonnet 115, lines 13-14; "Things *growing* to themselves are *growth's* abuse. Seeds spring from seeds, and beauty breedeth beauty; thou wast begot, to get it is thy duty" - *Venus and Adonis*, 1593, lines 166-168

2 IN ONE OF THINE, FROM THAT WHICH THOU DEPARTEST;
IN ONE OF THINE = in one of your children or heirs; **ONE** = Southampton, *One for All, All for One*; **DEPARTEST** = leave, run from; "Ere I *depart* his house" – *King Lear*, 3.5.1; Oxford accuses Southampton of running away from "one of thine," i.e., from an heir who would carry his blood from the Queen and be the "one" who should in turn succeed him.

3 AND THAT FRESH BLOOD WHICH YOUNGLY THOU BESTOW'ST
And that newly hopeful royal blood, which you pass on during this time

FRESH BLOOD

> My sons' *sweet blood ... my dear sons' blood*
> - *Titus Andronicus*, 3.1.15

> Touch not the boy; he is of royal blood
> - *Titus Andronicus*, 5.1.49

> Setting aside his *high blood's royalty*

>   - *Richard II*, 1.1.58
>
>   Myself, a prince by fortune of my birth,
>   Near to the King in *blood*, and near in love
>   - *Richard II*, 3.1.16-17
>
>   And by the *royalties of both your bloods*
>   - *Richard II*, 3.3.107

FRESH = newly royal, genuine; "Thou that art now the world's *fresh* ornament," Sonnet 1, line 9; "Since first I saw you *fresh*" – Sonnet 104, line 8, referring back to the period up through the year 1600, immediately prior to the Rebellion; "My love looks fresh" – Sonnet 107, line 10, upon Southampton's liberation from the Tower on April 10, 1603; " Thus did I keep my person *fresh* and new" – the King in *1 Henry IV*, 3.2.55

YOUNGLY = during this time of your youthful opportunity and hope

BESTOW'ST = The Queen "flatly said whether it were mine or hers she would *bestow* it at her pleasure" – Oxford to Robert Cecil, October 20, 1595; "I have most humbly written to Her Majesty that after so many *bestowings* of it" – Oxford to Robert Cecil, October 21, 1595; "to see his son *bestowed* to his liking" – Oxford to Robert Cecil, September 8, 1597; "it is justice that Her Majesty may *bestow* the same at her pleasure" – Oxford to Robert Cecil, December 4, 1601

4 THOU MAYST CALL THINE, WHEN THOU FROM YOUTH CONVERTEST.
You may then call (that blood) your own, when you are old

FROM YOUTH CONVERTEST = become old; convert from youth to old age; alter, turn away; "If from thy self to store thou wouldst *convert*" – Sonnet 14, line 12

5 HEREIN LIES WISDOM, BEAUTY, AND INCREASE;
WISDOM = the good judgment and sensible choices befitting a prince; ("Henry the Fourth, whose *wisdom was a mirror to the wisest*; and, after that *wise prince*, Henry the Fifth" – *3 Henry VI*, 3.3.83-85, spoken by the Earl of Oxford, fervently supporting the House of Lancaster; "Your Grace has given *a precedent of wisdom above all princes*" – *Henry VIII*, 2.2.84-85); **BEAUTY** = Tudor blood, inherited by Southampton

INCREASE = procreation; the creation of new heirs and the perpetuation of the Tudor line; "From fairest creatures we desire *increase*" – Sonnet 1, line 1; "Let them not live to taste *this land's increase*, that would with treason wound this fair land's peace!" – *Richard III*, 5.5.38-39

6 WITHOUT THIS, FOLLY, AGE, AND COLD DECAY.
FOLLY = "The amity that *wisdom* knits not, *folly* may easily untie" – *Troilus and Cressida*, 2.3.104-105; "When *majesty falls to folly*" – *King Lear*, 1.1.150)

COLD DECAY = death, especially the death of the lineage; related to the decay of Elizabeth's body as well as Southampton's; ("For, good King Henry, *thy decay* I fear" – *2 Henry VI*, 3.1.194; "Till then fair hope must hinder *life's decay*; and I the rather wean me from despair for love of Edward's offspring in my womb" – *3 Henry VI*, 4.4.16-18, spoken by Elizabeth, Queen to Edward the Fourth; "The imminent *decay of wrested pomp*" – *King John*, 4.3.154); "Where *wasteful time debateth with decay*" – Sonnet 15, line 11; "But wherefore do not you a mightier way/ Make war upon this *bloody tyrant time*?/ And *fortify yourself in your decay*" – Sonnet 16, lines 1-3; "But now my gracious numbers (sonnets) are *decayed*" – Sonnet 79, line 3; "The worst was this: my love (my love for my royal son) was my *decay*" – Sonnet 80, line 14

No. 11

7 IF ALL WERE MINDED SO, THE TIMES SHOULD CEASE,
ALL = Southampton, *One for All, All for One*; **IF ALL** = if you, Southampton; **THE TIMES SHOULD CEASE** = the reigns of the dynasty would come to an end (and so would this dynastic diary); the generations of men

8 AND THREESCORE YEAR WOULD MAKE THE WORLD AWAY:
THREESCORE YEAR = sixty years (Elizabeth will be sixty in September 1593, likely nearing the end of her life expectancy); **MAKE THE WORLD AWAY** = make away with her reign and England as we know it

9 LET THOSE WHOM NATURE HATH NOT MADE FOR STORE,
NATURE = Elizabeth; **FOR STORE** = for her safekeeping, as successive heir to her throne; "O him she stores, to show what wealth she had" – Sonnet 67, line 13, referring to Elizabeth storing her son's blood in the Tower of London after the Rebellion of February 8, 1601; "And him as for a map doth Nature store,/ To show false art what beauty was of yore" – Sonnet 68, lines 13-14, in reference to the same situation, with Nature or Elizabeth storing or imprisoning Southampton as a "map" that shows what "beauty" or royal blood she had in the past in succession to her; **STORE** = "to be preserved for use" – Malone

10 HARSH, FEATURELESS, AND RUDE, BARRENLY PERISH.
BARRENLY = without heirs; "Why is my verse so barren of new pride" – Sonnet 76, line 1, i.e., the womb of the Sonnets as barren of royal blood as a consequence of the Rebellion

11 LOOK WHOM SHE BEST ENDOWED, SHE GAVE THEE MORE,
WHOM SHE BEST ENDOWED = Southampton, her son; **ENDOWED** = ("Even all I have; yea, and myself and all, will I withal *endow* a child of thine" – *Richard III*, 4.4.249-250); **SHE GAVE THE MORE** = Nature, or Elizabeth, gave you more royal blood than anyone; (many editors including Malone have emended "the" to "thee")

12 WHICH BOUNTEOUS GIFT THOU SHOULDST IN BOUNTY CHERISH.
BOUNTEOUS GIFT = Elizabeth's great gift of blood inheritance; "That we our largest *bounty* may extend" – *King Lear*, 1.1.54; **GIFT** = "The borrowed glories that by *gift* of heaven, by law of nature and of nations, 'longs to him and to his heirs, namely the crown" – *Henry V*, 2.4.79-81; "So thy great *gift*, upon misprision growing" – Sonnet 87, line 11, wherein Oxford refers to the "gift" of life that his son possesses

IN BOUNTY CHERISH = cherish it as your own bounty, from Queen Elizabeth, as a bounteous king; "And I thank thee, king, for thy great *bounty*" – *Richard II*, 4.1.299-300; "That, as my hand has opened *bounty* to you" – *Henry VIII*, 3.2.184

13 SHE CARVED THEE FOR HER SEAL, AND MEANT THEREBY
Elizabeth created (and chose) you for her succession on the throne, to carry her blood forward; "from me and mine, to be *sealed* up in an eternal remembrance" – Oxford to Robert Cecil, October 7, 1601

CARVED = "He may not, as unvalued persons do, *carve* for himself, for on his choice depends the sanity and health of this whole state" – *Hamlet*, 1.3.19-20

SEAL = the Great Seal of the Crown; "Hear the King's pleasure, Cardinal, who commands you to render up the *Great Seal* presently into our hands" – *Henry VIII*, 3.2.228-229

14 THOU SHOULDST PRINT MORE, NOT LET THAT COPY DIE.
PRINT MORE = beget more heirs or "copies" of her blood and person; "Your mother was most true to wedlock, prince, for she did *print* your royal father off, conceiving you" – *The Winter's Tale*, 5.1.123-125

NOT LET THAT COPY DIE = not let the lineage of the House of Tudor die out. Southampton is the "copy" of Elizabeth, so he must perpetuate it by begetting an heir. (Dowden reads "copy" as "the original

REFERENCE EDITION 101

from which the impression is made.") In *Twelfth Night*, 1.5.126 it means the transcript impression taken from an original: "Lady, you are the cruelest she alive, if you will lead these graces to the grave and *leave the world no copy*." ("But in them *Nature's copy's* not eterne" – *Macbeth*, 3.2.38, i.e., the copy is a "casting" derived "from the mould used by Nature to form men" – Riverside; *eterne* = everlasting)

DIE = the death of the Tudor Rose dynasty: "From fairest creatures we desire increase,/ That thereby beauty's Rose might never *die*" – Sonnet 1, line 1

Part One

THE MARRIAGE ALLIANCE

Sonnet 12
Time's Scythe
1590-1591

Oxford once again urges Southampton to hurry up and agree to the Cecil marriage alliance, stressing the need to act before "Time's scythe," or Elizabeth's death, will cut off all opportunity to become her successor on the throne. The urgency is compounded by the fact that, once Lord Burghley withdraws his support, the Queen will undoubtedly turn away from her son. Elizabeth turns fifty-seven in September 1590 and there is no telling how much longer she will live. The diary of these private sonnets is tied literally to "the clock that tells the time" as it keeps pace with Her Majesty's ever-decaying mortal body leading to her death and the succession.

Sonnet 12	Translation
When I do count the clock that tells the time,	As I watch the waning of Queen Elizabeth's life
And see the brave day sunk in hideous night,	And see your royal claim losing its chance,
When I behold the violet past prime,	When I see your royal lineage being passed by,
And sable curls or silvered o'er with white:	On its way to the blackness of oblivion
When lofty trees I see barren of leaves,	When I see great princes with their greatness lost,
Which erst from heat did canopy the herd,	Who used to protect their subjects from discomfort,
And Summer's green all girded up in sheaves	And fresh royal blood all lying as in a coffin,
Borne on the bier with white and bristly beard:	Borne on the bier looking old and faded:
Then of thy beauty do I question make	Then of your royalty from Elizabeth do I question
That thou among the wastes of time must go,	That you must go toward her death with her,
Since sweets and beauties do themselves forsake,	Since royalty and her blood foresake themselves,
And die as fast as they see others grow.	And lose their destiny as fast as others gain theirs.
And nothing 'gainst Time's scythe can make defense	And nothing against Elizabeth's aging can protect you,
Save breed to brave him, when he takes thee hence.	Except begetting an heir to survive when you die.

1 WHEN I DO COUNT THE CLOCK THAT TELLS THE TIME
THE CLOCK, etc. = the means by which I calculate the time remaining in Elizabeth's life; "Thereby to *see the minutes how they run – how many makes the hour full complete, how many hours brings about the day, how many days will finish up the year, how many years a mortal man may live*" – King Henry in *3 Henry VI*, 2.5.21-40. The Queen is immortal, but after her death she will be "the *mortal* Moone" of Sonnet 107, line 5; King Richard utters similar ruminations on the rapidly dwindling time of his life and reign: "*I wasted time, and now doth time waste me. For now hath time made me his numb'ring clock; my thoughts are minutes, and with sighs they jar their watches on unto mine eyes, the outward watch*" – *Richard II*, 5.5.42-60; "When in the Chronicle of *wasted time*" – Sonnet 106, line 1, following Sonnet 105 upon the Queen's death

2 AND SEE THE BRAVE DAY SUNK IN HIDEOUS NIGHT,
BRAVE = royal; "O *brave* young Prince!" – *3 Henry VI*, 5.4.52; **BRAVE DAY** = royal day of golden sun, kingship; **DAY** = "Good time of day unto your royal grace!" – *Richard III*, 1.3.18

REFERENCE EDITION

3 WHEN I BEHOLD THE VIOLET PAST PRIME
VIOLET = purple color of royalty; "A *violet* in the youth of primy nature" – *Hamlet*, 1.3.7; **PAST PRIME** = too old to be acknowledged as king; "That cropped the *golden prime of this sweet prince*" – *Richard III*, 1.3.252

4 AND SABLE CURLS ALL SILVERED O'ER WITH WHITE:
SABLE = black, used in heraldy; **ALL** = the word is "or" in *Q*, but emended by most editors to "all"; **ALL** = Southampton, *One for All, All for One*; **SILVERED** = playing on "ver" for Vere in "silvered"; related to a black beard grown white; "It was as I have seen it in his life, a sable *silvered*" – *Hamlet*, 1.2.242, the Ghost's beard

5 WHEN LOFTY TREES I SEE BARREN OF LEAVES,
LOFTY TREES = high and mighty princes; plants or flowers of the Rose. "The *royal tree* hath left us royal fruit, which, mellowed by *the stealing hours of time*, will well become the seat of majesty, and make, no doubt, us happy by his reign" – *Richard III*, 3.7.166-169

BARREN OF LEAVES = empty of royal heirs; "Why is my verse so *barren* of new pride?" - Sonnet 76, line 1. "But if the first heir of my invention proved deformed, I shall be sorry it had so noble a godfather, and never after ear so *barren* a land, for fear it yield me still so bad a harvest" - dedication of Venus and Adonis to Southampton

"When as a lion's whelp shall, to himself unknown, without seeking find, and be embraced by a piece of tender air: and when from a stately cedar shall be lopp'd branches, which, being dead many years, shall after revive, be jointed to the old stock, and freshly grow, then shall Posthumous end his miseries, Britain be fortunate, and flourish in peace and plenty" – *Cymbeline*, 5.5.436-443

6 WHICH ERST FROM HEAT DID CANOPY THE HERD,
ERST = used to; **CANOPY** = related to the gold canopy carried on poles by nobles or other dignitaries over the monarch. "Were't ought to me I bore *the canopy*" - Sonnet 125, line 1, referring to the canopy borne over the effigy and coffin of Queen Elizabeth at her funeral; "a rich embroidered *Canopy* to kings" – *3 Henry VI*, 2.5.44-45. "Then four noblemen bearing a canopy" – *Henry VIII*, 5.4, the opening stage directions for the scene, referring to the royal canopy borne over the infant Princess Elizabeth at her christening

7 AND SUMMER'S GREEN ALL GIRDED UP IN SHEAVES
SUMMER'S GREEN = the warm time of youth and royal hope; green as the Tudor livery; "That sun that warms you here, shall shine on me, and those his golden beams to you here lent shall point on me and gild my banishment" – *Richard II*, 1.3.145-147. "Since first I saw you fresh, which yet are *green*" – Sonnet 104, line 8; **ALL** = Southampton, *One for All, All for One*; **GIRDED UP IN SHEAVES** = tied in bundles, as white-frosted corn after harvest

8 BORNE ON THE BIER WITH WHITE AND BRISTLY BEARD:
BORNE = carried; echoing "born"; **BIER** = a barrow in which to carry harvested grain, but also "a movable stand on which a corpse is carried to the grave" – Booth; suggesting a double image, in which case Southampton is being forced to choose between the life/growth of his Tudor blood and its death; "They bare him bare-faced on the *bier*" – *Hamlet*, 4.5.164, referring to a dead body

9 THEN OF THY BEAUTY DO I QUESTION MAKE
Then I ask the following question; then I consider; or even: "Then I question (or doubt) your blood from the Queen," an amazing statement reflecting Oxford's urgency and desperation in regard to the Cecil marriage alliance, not to mention his anger at Southampton for refusing to enter into it.

No. 12

10 **THAT THOU AMONG THE WASTES OF TIME MUST GO,**
WASTES OF TIME = those who fail tragically to be named as successors to the throne during the monarch's, i.e., Elizabeth's, lifetime; "I *wasted time*, and now doth *time waste me*" – the King in *Richard II*, 5.5.49

11 **SINCE SWEETS AND BEAUTIES DO THEM-SELVES FORSAKE**
SWEETS = royal princes; **BEAUTIES** = children of Elizabeth; those who possess her "beauty" or royal blood; ("*This Cynthia's silver light,/ This sweet fair dea spread,/ These sunbeams in mine eye,/ These beauties make me die*" – Oxford poem in *The Phoenix Nest*, 1593, signed E. O., with *dea* = goddess, referring to Queen Elizabeth as *Cynthia* or Diana, chaste goddess of the Moon; **DO THEMSELVES FORSAKE** = ("abandon their natures" – Booth); Southampton ignoring his own identity as son and heir of the Queen

12 **AND DIE AS FAST AS THEY SEE OTHERS GROW;**
AND DIE, etc. = and lose their royal status as fast as they watch the claims of others grow stronger; "That thereby beauty's *Rose* might never *die*" – Sonnet 1, line 2; "Thou shouldst print more, not let that copy *die*" – Sonnet 11, line 14

13 **AND NOTHING 'GAINST TIME'S SCYTHE CAN MAKE DEFENCE**
NOTHING = none, the opposite of "one" for Southampton; **TIME'S SCYTHE** = the deadly blade that will cut off your royal inheritance when *the time of Elizabeth's life* runs out, unless you have been named as her successor before that time; see Sonnets 60, 100 & 123.

"I will be true despite thy scythe and thee" - Oxford to Time: Sonnet 123, line 14

14 **SAVE BREED TO BRAVE HIM WHEN HE TAKES THEE HENCE.**
SAVE BREED TO BRAVE HIM = except to create new heirs to "brave" or defy this deadly force of time; **HENCE** = away from here, to the next world; "*Hence*, thou suborned informer" – Sonnet 125, line 13, upon Elizabeth's funeral, with "hence" used in part as a command such as "Go!" (But also "therefore" or "henceforth," telling Southampton that henceforth he will be required to testify against the truth of his identity as the Queen's son and heir

REFERENCE EDITION

THE MONUMENT

THE MARRIAGE ALLIANCE

Sonnet 13
So Fair a House
1590-1591

Oxford reminds Southampton that, as a prince, he does not own his royal self, but, rather, owes it to his subjects. Henry Wriothesley must "prepare" himself for the "coming end" of Elizabeth's life and reign. He holds his blood from her "in lease" until he succeeds to the throne (the same "lease of my true love" in Sonnet 107) and must prevent the "fair house" (House of Tudor) from dying out. Oxford refers to his own paternity of Southampton by reminding him, "You had a Father" -- that is, Oxford was his biological father whom he has been unable to acknowledge. Edward de Vere begs Henry Wriothesley to beget his own son, who, thereby, will also be able to say he had a biological father.

Sonnet 13	Translation
O That you were your self, but, love, you are No longer yours, than you your self here live. Against this coming end you should prepare, And your sweet semblance to some other give.	O that you would be you, but, royal son, you are No longer yours alone than you're merely alive! Against Elizabeth's death you should prepare, And give your royal blood to some heir.
So should that beauty which you hold in lease Find no determination, then you were Your self again after your self's decease, When your sweet issue your sweet form should bear.	So if Elizabeth's blood, which you hold in lease, Should be denied the throne, then you would be Alive again after your own death, When your own royal heir would carry your royal blood.
Who lets so fair a house fall to decay, Which husbandry in honor might uphold, Against the stormy gusts of winter's day And barren rage of death's eternal cold?	Who lets the royal House of Tudor die, Which royal responsibility might otherwise support Against the coming death of the Queen And the end of her lineage forever?
O none but unthrifts; dear my love, you know You had a Father; let your Son say so.	O, none but spendthrifts! My royal son, you know You had a Father [me]; beget a son who can say it.

1 O THAT YOU WERE YOUR SELF, BUT, LOVE, YOU ARE
O = Oxford; **THAT YOU WERE YOUR SELF** = that you were just a private man, rather than a prince who has a responsibility to others; **YOUR SELF** = your royal self or person; "Where it seems best unto *your* royal *self*" – *Richard III*, 3.1.63; "Then, good my lord, take to *your* royal *self* this proffer'd benefit of dignity" – *Richard III*, 3.7.194-195

> I shall hereafter, my thrice gracious lord,
> Be more *my self*
> - Prince Hal to his father, King Henry IV, in *1 Henry IV*, 3.2.92-93
> (Promising to fulfill the responsibilities of his blood and prepare for his own rule)

Oxford's emphasis on *you* and *yours* and *your self* is an insistent reminder to Southampton that he must consider himself a king:

> O that YOU were YOUR SELF, but love YOU are

106

No longer *YOURS* than *YOU YOUR SELF* here live.
Against this coming end YOU should prepare,
And *YOUR* sweet semblance to some other give.
So should that beauty which *YOU* hold in lease
Find no determination, then *YOU* were
YOUR SELF again after *YOUR SELF's* decease,
When *YOUR* sweet issue *YOUR* sweet form should bear.
Who lets so fair a house fall to decay,
Which husbandry in honour might uphold
Against the stormy gusts of winter's day
And barren rage of death's eternal cold?
O none but unthrifts, dear my love *YOU* know,
YOU had a father, let *YOUR* son say so.

LOVE = you, my royal son

2 NO LONGER YOURS THAN YOU YOUR SELF HERE LIVE.
NO LONGER YOURS = your royal self is no longer your own; it belongs not to you but to England, the world; Oxford lectures Southampton as a prince who is no longer a private person; the theme is echoed by Laertes when he tells his sister, Ophelia, that Hamlet is a prince who cannot act merely in his own self-interest; as Oxford warns Southampton, so Laertes declares that Hamlet may not choose his own bride merely for personal reasons:

YOU YOUR SELF = "His greatness weighed, *his will is not his own*. For **he himself** is subject to his birth: He may not, as unvalued persons do, carve for himself, for on his choice depends the sanity and health of this whole state; and therefore must his choice be circumscribed unto the voice and yielding of that body of whereof he is the head" – *Hamlet*, 1.3.17-24

THAN YOU YOUR SELF HERE LIVE = "here" is suggestive of "heir" – Willen and Reed, cited by Booth; as in Falstaff's witty comment to Prince Hal that it is *"here apparent* that thou art *heir apparent"* – *1 Henry IV*, 1.2.55-56; "But he that writes of you, if he can tell/ That *you are you*, so dignifies his story" – Sonnet 84, lines 7-8, indicating him as a king, the way Oxford refers to himself as father of a king by declaring "I am that I am" in Sonnet 121, line 9

3 AGAINST THIS COMING END YOU SHOULD PREPARE,
THIS COMING END = Elizabeth's death and the royal succession; also, your own death

4 AND YOUR SWEET SEMBLANCE TO SOME OTHER GIVE:
SWEET SEMBLANCE = your royal image; "But now two mirrors of his princely *semblance* are cracked in pieces" – *Richard III*, 2.2.51-52; "To bless the bed of majesty again with a *sweet* fellow to't" – *The Winter's Tale*, 5.1.32-33

5 SO SHOULD THAT BEAUTY WHICH YOU HOLD IN LEASE
THAT BEAUTY = that blood from Elizabeth; "O death, made proud with pure and princely beauty!" – *King John*, 4.3.35; **WHICH YOU HOLD IN LEASE** = this blood, which you possess for a limited term, only as a loan, which you must repay by acting responsibly ("Can yet the *lease* of my true love control" – Sonnet 107, line 3, referring to Southampton's liberation by King James from the Tower on April 10, 1603)

6 FIND NO DETERMINATION, THEN YOU WERE
NO DETERMINATION = no ending according to the lease of your royal blood; no succession to the throne; (an estate held in lease "*determines* at the end of a fixed term" – Booth); legal determination of the successor to Elizabeth; also, the Queen had resolved or "determined" to name her son to succeed her; ("Hath the Prince John a full commission, in very ample virtue of his father, to hear, and absolutely to *determine*, of what conditions we shall stand upon?" – *2 Henry IV*, 4.1.162-165; "But let the laws of Rome *determine* all"

– *Titus Andronicus*, 1.1.412-413; "most willingly humbles himself to *the determination of justice*" – *Measure for Measure*, 3.2.237-238); "My bonds in thee are all *determinate*" – Sonnet 87, line 4, written after Southampton, in the Tower, has been forced to relinquish all claim as the son of Oxford and Elizabeth, i.e., all claim to the throne; ("*Determination*" in legal language means "*end*" – Malone)

> O, twice my father, twice am I thy son!
> The life thou gav'st me first was lost and done,
> Till with thy warlike sword, despite of fate,
> To my determined time thou gav'st new date.
> - *1 Henry VI*, 4.6.6-9

> And that **succession be determined**
> - *3 Henry VI*, 4.6.54-56

7 YOUR SELF AGAIN AFTER YOUR SELF'S DECEASE,
YOUR SELF AGAIN = your royal person renewed or recreated in the person of an heir

8 WHEN YOUR SWEET ISSUE YOUR SWEET FORM SHOULD BEAR.
SWEET ISSUE = royal heir; ("That *if the king should without issue die*" – *Henry VIII*, 1.2.133; "To God, my king, and *my succeeding issue*" – *Richard II*, 1.3.20; "The *issue* of the next son should have reign'd" – *2 Henry VI*, 2.2.31; "So, if the *issue* of the elder son succeed before the younger, I am king" – *2 Henry VI*, 2.2.50-51; "Ah, *if thou issueless* shalt hap to die" – Sonnet 9, line 3

> The third son, Duke of Clarence, from whose line
> I claim the crown, had *issue* Philippe, a daughter,
> Who married Edmund Mortimer, Earl of March;
> Edmund had *issue*, Roger, Earl of March;
> Roger had *issue*, Edmund, Anne, and Eleanor.
> - *2 Henry VI*, 2.2.33-37

SWEET FORM = royal person; "Being *the right idea of your father*, both in *your form* and nobleness of mind" – *Richard III*, 3.7.13-14; related to *formal*, as in "and flow henceforth in *formal majesty*" – *2 Henry IV*, 5.2.133; **BEAR** = carry; related to child-bearing; also to heraldry; "In the old age black was not counted fair,/ Or if it were it *bore not beauty's name*" – Sonnet 127, lines 1-2; "When beauty lived and died as flowers do now,/ Before *these bastard signs of fair were borne*" – Sonnet 68, lines 1-2; "His tender heir might *bear* his memory" – Sonnet 1, line 4; "Without thy help by me be *borne* alone" – Sonnet 36, line 4; "Which, laboring for invention, *bear* amiss/ The second burthen of a former child" – Sonnet 59, lines 3-4; "Why is my verse so *barren* of new pride?" – Sonnet 76, line 1; "That for thy right myself will *bear* all wrong" – Sonnet 88, line 14; "*Bearing* the wanton burthen of the prime,/ Like widowed *wombs* after their lords' decease:/ Yet this abundant *issue* seemed to me/ But hope of *orphans*, and *unfathered* fruit" – Sonnet 97, lines 7-10; "For I am shamed by that which I *bring forth*" – Sonnet 72, line 13; "Alack, what poverty my Muse *brings forth*" – Sonnet 103, line 1; "In vowing new hate after *new love bearing*" – Sonnet 151, line 4, the latter referring to Elizabeth having given birth to new "love" or royal blood in her son, Southampton, although she also gave new "hate" by refusing to acknowledge him

> To *bear* the golden yoke of sovereignty
> - *Richard III*, 3.7.145

> Whose father *bears* the title of a king
> - *3 Henry VI*, 2.2.140

9 WHO LETS SO FAIR A HOUSE FALL TO DECAY,
SO FAIR A HOUSE = So royal a House of Tudor; ("The red rose and the white are on his face, the fatal colors of our striving *houses*" – *3 Henry VI*, 2.5.97-98; "I know Her Majesty doth give you good ear, then for

No. 13

that our *houses* are knit in alliance" – Oxford to Robert Cecil, July 1600; "to thy foul disgrace and utter ruin of the *House of York*" – *3 Henry VI*, 1.1.260-261; "Ay me, I see the ruin of my *house*" – *Richard III*, 2.4.49; "Poor key-cold Figure of a holy king, pale ashes of the *House of Lancaster*, thou bloodless remnant of that royal blood" – *Richard III*, 1.2.5-7

10 WHICH HUSBANDRY IN HONOR MIGHT UPHOLD
HUSBANDRY = becoming a husband; **IN HONOR** = to uphold your royal honor

11 AGAINST THE STORMY GUSTS OF WINTER'S DAY
WINTER'S DAY = death; related to time, i.e., Elizabeth's mortal end; (In Sonnet 104, as Elizabeth is dying in early 1603 with Southampton unable to succeed her, Oxford will refer to the passage of the seasons and, addressing the "age unbred" in posterity, declare: "Ere you were born was *beauty's summer dead*" – indicating the simultaneous death of Southampton's "*beauty*" or Tudor blood that had existed during his "*summer*" or golden time of royalty in Sonnets 1 to 26, prior to the Rebellion of February 8, 1601); a metaphor of royal succession or the lack of it

> Thus sometimes hath the brightest day a cloud;
> And after summer evermore *succeeds*
> *Barren winter*, with his wrathful nipping cold
> - *2 Henry VI*, 2.4.1-3

12 AND BARREN RAGE OF DEATH'S ETERNAL COLD?
BARREN = empty, childless, as in an empty womb; ("Why is my verse so *barren* of new pride?" – Sonnet 76, line 1); **RAGE** = "And brass eternal slave to mortal *rage*" – Sonnet 64, line 4; "How with this *rage* shall beauty hold a plea,/ Whose action is no stronger than a flower?" – Sonnet 65, lines 3-4; **DEATH'S ETERNAL COLD** = the opposite of the golden time, when all hope for Southampton's succession will be frozen forever in the past; as a king, Southampton is immortal, so his death itself (and his lack of kingship) will also be eternal

13 O NONE BUT UNTHRIFTS! DEAR MY LOVE, YOU KNOW
O = Oxford; **NONE** = opposite of "one" for Southampton; **UNTHRIFTS** = spendthrifts, i.e., those who spend their blood unwisely; **DEAR** = royal; used often in the Shakespeare plays in reference to a father or a son, usually in regard to kings or queens and their sons, to the point where its use in this sonnet becomes a palpable expressions of Oxford's love for Southampton as his royal son; "This land of such *dear* souls, this *dear, dear* land, dear for her reputation through the world" – *Richard II*, 2.1.57-58:

"Richard's speech "does not so much emphasize the value of kings to the community as honor England for having produced a succession of noble kings. Royalty is the final value. But yet again, what exactly are these '*dear*' – i.e., 'of great worth' – 'souls'? The kings? Or the community, the 'happy breed'? Is that 'breed' itself being regarded as, in part, royal? Whatever be the exact meaning, it is clear that the heart of the conception is royalty as a positive and self-sufficing value, with strong chivalric and Christian associations … Such is the conception running as a golden thread through Shakespeare's drama. The Crown symbolizes the nation's soul-life, which is also the greater self of each subject. In Shakespeare's human kings we watch different persons daring to identify themselves with this supreme value; and we can view each personal king as a prototype of national action, as England herself, fulfilling or falsifying her destiny"
– G. Wilson Knight, *The Sovereign Flower*, 1958, p. 29

In that context, Oxford demands that Southampton above all (being a prince and heir to the throne) "dare to identify himself with this supreme value." Southampton must act by agreeing to the Cecil marriage alliance, in order to "fulfill" his own – and England's – destiny.

DEAR MY LOVE = my dear royal son. This is the first appearance of "my love" in the Sonnets, a phrase that fails to make sense according to the traditional story that Shakspere of Stratford was addressing Southampton as poet to patron, or even that he was speaking as a friend.

REFERENCE EDITION 109

"Not till Monday, **my dear son**" – *Much Ado About Nothing*, 2.1.338; "Our *dear son*, when you have given good morning to your mistress, attend the Queen and us" – to Cloton, son of the Queen, in *Cymbeline*, 2.3.61-63; "That I, the son of a *dear father* murdered" – *Hamlet*, 2.2.585

"If my *dear love* were but the child of state" – Sonnet 124, line 1, Oxford speaking of Southampton as a former royal ward or child of state, also as prince

14 YOU HAD A FATHER: LET YOUR SON SAY SO.
YOU HAD A FATHER = you had a father, a biological necessity, in order to have been born; that father was me, but you cannot claim me, nor I you; the sense here is: "You had a father, but you couldn't claim me as such; so beget a son who will be able to claim *you* as his father." More simply, as Michael Brame & Galina Popova interpret the line: "You were fathered; let your son say so." In other words, Oxford is not referring to Henry Wriothesley's father of record, the 2nd Earl of Southampton, who died in 1581.

"It does not necessarily follow that … the father was dead. Why should the poet mention the father where the father was not in point? … The words contain no implication whatever that he no longer had a father. The stress is upon 'father,' not upon 'had,' and the sense is simply, 'There was someone who did do his duty, married, and begat yourself.'" – T. G. Tucker, 1924, xlv.

"She's coming: to her, coz. O boy, *thou hadst a father*!" – *The Merry Wives of Windsor*, 3.4.36, interpreted in the *Complete Pelican Shakespeare* as: "Go to her like a man!"

"But out alack, *he was but one hour mine*" - Sonnet 33, line 11; i.e., Oxford refers to their parent-child relationship in the past tense; elsewhere he refers to it metaphorically rather than directly: "*As a decrepit father* takes delight/ To see his active child do deeds of youth,/ So I, made lame by Fortune's *dearest* spite,/ Take all my comfort of your worth and truth" – Sonnet 37, lines 1-4

LET YOUR SON SAY SO = beget a son, who, by virtue of being born, will be able to look back and declare that he, too, had a biological father.

FATHER … SON: both are capitalized in the 1609 quarto, strengthening the biblical reference to God the Father and the Son.

Part One

THE MARRIAGE ALLIANCE

Sonnet 14
Truth's and Beauty's Doom and Date
1590-1591

Edward de Vere, having acquired some of his knowledge of "astronomy" from Dr. John Dee, the Queen's astrologer, now he uses it to forecast the future of "Princes" (his royal son) by means of Southampton's eyes, which are "constant stars" or royal suns. Oxford predicts that, if Henry Wriothesley fails to claim his succession prior to the Queen's death, it will be the end of hope for his parents in terms of lineage. In other words, it will be the "doom and date" for both Truth and Beauty (Oxford and Elizabeth).

Sonnet 14	Translation
Not from the stars do I my judgment pluck,	Not from the stars do I get this judgment,
And yet methinks I have Astronomy,	And yet I think I've studied astronomy;
But not to tell of good, or evil luck,	But not so I can predict good or evil luck
Of plagues, of dearths, or seasons' quality;	In plagues or famines or seasons' quality;
Nor can I fortune to brief minutes tell;	Nor can I be a fortune-teller of quick predictions,
Pointing to each his thunder, rain, and wind,	Showing each man his coming bad weather,
Or say with Princes if it shall go well	Or say with Princes if things will go well,
By oft predict that I in heaven find.	By often predicting what Elizabeth might do.
But from thine eyes my knowledge I derive,	But from your royal eyes I get my knowledge,
And, constant stars, in them I read such art	And, as they are eternal royal stars, I see in them
As truth and beauty shall together thrive	That Oxford and Elizabeth will together thrive,
If from thy self to store thou wouldst convert:	If you'd stop hoarding your royal blood;
Or else of thee this I prognosticate,	Or else this is what I predict about you:
Thy end is Truth's and Beauty's doom and date.	Your ending is Oxford's and Elizabeth's death.

1 NOT FROM THE STARS DO I MY JUDGMENT PLUCK,
THE STARS = ordinary stars in the sky, as opposed to Southampton's sun-like eyes, which are the only stars by which Oxford makes predictions; "Lord Hamlet is *a prince out of thy star*" – Hamlet, 2.2.141

> Whereupon it made this Threne
> To the Phoenix and the Dove,
> Co-supremes and *stars* of love,
> As chorus to their tragic scene
> - *The Phoenix and Turtle*, 1601, 49-52

> But *truer stars* did govern Proteus' birth
> - *The Two Gentlemen of Verona*, 2.7.74

> Had *princes* sit like *stars* about his throne,
> And he the sun, for them to reverence
> - *Pericles*, 2.3.39-40

REFERENCE EDITION

2 AND YET METHINKS I HAVE ASTRONOMY,
ASTRONOMY = Oxford studied astrology *circa* 1570 (at age 20) with Dr. John Dee, the Queen's astrologer, who had selected the January date of her 1559 coronation.

> Amongst our well renowned men,
> *Dever* merits a silver pen,
> Eternally to write his honour,
> And I in a well polished verse,
> Can set up in our Universe,
> A Fame, to endure forever...
>
> For who marketh better than he,
> The seven turning flames of the Sky...
> - John Soowthern, *Pandora*, 1584
> Dedicated to Edward de Vere

"This is a reference to Oxford's interest in astrology or astronomy, the *seven turning flames of the Sky* being the seven principal planets. Lord Oxford appears to have been one of the most interested patrons of Dr. John Dee, foremost of Elizabethan astrologers ... Dee (in 1592) makes prominent mention of 'the honourable the Earl of Oxford, his favorable letters, anno 1570.' The foremost scholars of the age then gave serious consideration to astrology. Oxford's interest in the subject is one more testimonial to the catholicity of his education" - Charles Wisner Barrell, *The Shake-speare Fellowship Newsletter*, October 1943

3 BUT NOT TO TELL OF GOOD OR EVIL LUCK,
TELL = foretell

4 OF PLAGUES, OF DEARTHS, OR SEASONS' QUALITY;
Not for these matters either; **DEARTHS** = famines

5 NOR CAN I FORTUNE TO BRIEF MINUTES TELL,
FORTUNE = predict or forecast; echoing Elizabeth as Fortune, i.e., I can't predict her mind; **TO BRIEF MINUTES** = within minutes or with such precision; **TELL** = "That every word doth almost *tell* my name/ … For as the Sun is daily new and old,/ So is my love still *telling what is told*" – Sonnet 76, lines 7, 13-14

6 POINT TO EACH HIS THUNDER, RAIN, AND WIND,
POINTING TO EACH, etc. = appointing to each; ("See how the giddy multitude do *point*, and nod their heads, and throw their eyes on thee" – 2 Henry VI, 2.4..21-22; "Till *whatsoever star that guides my moving/ Points on me graciously* with fair aspect,/ And puts apparel on my tottered loving,/ To show me worthy of thy sweet respect" – Sonnet 26, lines 9-12)

7 OR SAY WITH PRINCES IF IT SHALL GO WELL
WITH PRINCES = Or predict how it will go with monarchs; i.e., Southampton, the royal prince; also Queen Elizabeth, who often referred to herself as a prince; "Great *Princes'* favorites their fair leaves spread" – Sonnet 25, line 5; "Not marble nor the gilded monument/ Of *Princes* shall outlive this powerful rhyme" – Sonnet 55, lines 1-2

"What conceivable relevance or point is there in his confessing inability to foretell the fortunes of *princes* in the usual manner, by the firmament, unless the friend of whom by his special art he *does* prognosticate is a prince?" – Leslie Hotson, *Mr. W.H.*, 1965, p. 31

8 BY OFT PREDICT THAT I IN HEAVEN FIND.
OFT PREDICT = by frequent prognostication or forecast; Oxford cannot predict the fate of the Tudor dynasty; he therefore cannot predict the outcome of this "living record" of his royal son; **HEAVEN** =

Elizabeth; **THAT I IN HEAVEN FIND** = what I predict will happen according to the stars in the heavens; echoing Elizabeth as Heaven, i.e., I cannot predict what will happen in her mind

> And then believe me, my love is as fair
> As *any mother's child*, though not so bright
> As those gold candles fixed in *heaven's air*. (Heaven's air = Elizabeth's heir)
> - Sonnet 21, lines 10-12

9 BUT FROM THINE EYES MY KNOWLEDGE I DERIVE,
THINE EYES = Southampton's eyes (the "gold candles" of Sonnet 21, the "constant stars" of line 10 below), reflecting his royal blood

10 AND, CONSTANT STARS, IN THEM I READ SUCH ART
CONSTANT STARS = Southampton's eyes, shining as eternal royal suns; "Love is not love/ Which alters when it alteration finds,/ Or bends with the remover to remove./ O no, it is an ever-fixed mark/ That looks on tempests and is never shaken;/ It is *the star to every wandering bark*" – Sonnet 116, lines 2-7, referring to Southampton's "love" or royal blood, reflected in "*that sun, thine eye*" – Sonnet 49, line 6

CONSTANT: "So long as Edward is thy *constant friend and their true sovereign*, whom must they obey?" – *3 Henry VI*, 4.1.76-77; "*Constant* in spirit, not swerving with the blood" – *Henry V*, 2.2.133; "In *constant* truth to bide so firm and sure" – Oxford sonnet, circa 1572; "But you like none, none you, for *constant* heart" – Sonnet 53, line 14; "Kind is my love today, tomorrow kind,/ Still *constant* in a wondrous excellence;/ Therefore my verse to *constancy* confined,/ One thing expressing, leaves out difference" – Sonnet 105, lines 5-8, to Southampton; "For I have sworn deep oaths of thy deep kindness,/ Oaths of thy love, thy truth, thy *constancy*" – Sonnet 152, lines 9-10, to Elizabeth

STARS = ("And scarcely greet me with *that sun, thine eye*" – Sonnet 49, line 6, to Southampton; **I READ SUCH ART** = I surmise by reading or discovering such truths of science as the following

11 AS TRUTH AND BEAUTY SHALL TOGETHER THRIVE
As Oxford and Elizabeth shall thrive together (in posterity, as parents of a king)...

TRUTH = Edward de Vere, *Nothing Truer than Truth*; "*Truths/Veres* teach the *True/Vere* woman: Falsehoods are incompatible with the *Truth/Vere* ... Ever Lover of the *Truth/Vere*: May these words be thy *True/Vere* Motto" – an inscription written to Lady Anne Cecil Vere, Countess of Oxford, circa 1575; "Yet sith I have engaged myself so far in Her Majesty's service *to bring the truth to light*" – Oxford to Burghley, June 13, 1595; "But I hope *truth* is subject to no prescription, for *truth* is *truth* though never so old, and time cannot make that false which was once *true*" – Oxford to Robert Cecil, May 7, 1603, shortly after Elizabeth's funeral

> To her how echo told the *truth*,
> As *true* as Phoebus' oracle
> - *Verses made by the Earl of Oxford*, 1570s/80s

BEAUTY = Elizabeth, *Venus, goddess of Love and Beauty*; **TRUTH AND BEAUTY** = Oxford and Elizabeth; "Truth may seem, but cannot be; Beauty brag, but 'tis not she; Truth and Beauty buried be" – *The Phoenix and the Turtle*, 1601, lines 61-63

12 IF FROM THY SELF TO STORE THOU WOULDST CONVERT
If you would "convert" or change from this course by which you "store" your blood (within your royal self) rather than share it; (When Elizabeth holds Southampton in the Tower, Oxford will accuse her of the same thing by saying that Nature or the Queen "stores" her royal blood by doing so: "*O him she stores*, to show what wealth she had,/ In days long since, before these last so bad" – Sonnet 67, lines 13-14; "And him as for a map doth Nature *store*,/ To show false Art what beauty was of yore" – Sonnet 68, lines 13-14)

REFERENCE EDITION

13 OR ELSE OF THEE THIS I PROGNOSTICATE:
Otherwise, I predict the following about you

14 THY END IS TRUTH'S AND BEAUTY'S DOOM AND DATE.
THY END = your death without your succession as king

TRUTH'S AND BEAUTY'S DOOM AND DATE = Oxford's and Elizabeth's doom, as parents of a Tudor heir, at the date of her death without Southampton able to make his claim. This prediction will come true following February 8, 1601, when Southampton is confined in the Tower of London as a traitor. At that point Oxford will write *The Phoenix and the Turtle* (published that year), as a funeral dirge for the death of his and Elizabeth's hopes as parents of a royal heir (*Beauty* = Elizabeth; *Truth* = Oxford; *Rarity* = Southampton):

> *Beauty, Truth,* and *Rarity,*
> Grace in all simplicity,
> Here enclosed in cinders lie...
> *Truth* may seem, but cannot be;
> *Beauty* brag, but 'tis not she;
> **Truth and Beauty** buried be.
> - *The Phoenix and Turtle,* 53-55; 61-63

DOOM = final judgment and sentence; the end of the royal line, which should continue through the accession of Prince Henry Wriothesley-Tudor as King Henry IX, and thus the end of the dynasty; final judgment; "I bring thee tidings of *the Prince's doom* ... What less than *doomsday* is the Prince's *doom*?" – *Romeo and Juliet,* 3.2.8-9; "I'll throw thy body in another room, and triumph, Henry, *in thy day of doom*" – *3 Henry VI,* 5.6.92-93; "Thy crown does sear mine eye-balls ... What, will the line stretch out to th'crack of *doom*?" – *Macbeth,* 4.1.113-117; "Supposed as forfeit to a confined doom" – Sonnet 107, line 4, describing Southampton upon his release on April 10, 1603 from the Tower; **DATE** = "Is not my teeming *date* drunk up with time?" – *Richard II,* 5.2.91

Part One

THE MARRIAGE ALLIANCE

Sonnet 15
All in War with Time for Love of You
1590-1591

Edward de Vere continues to urge Southampton to marry William Cecil's granddaughter, Elizabeth Vere, and to beget an heir of Tudor blood. Furthering his argument, Oxford uses the image of a plant (or Tudor Rose) that grows and then decays. He sums up the urgent situation of Henry Wriothesley as the struggle of Love (royal blood) against the ever-dwindling Time of the Queen's life; and in fact, the war of Love versus Time is a concise summary of this ongoing diary. Oxford also promises to keep enabling his son's royal life to grow in these private verses written according to time.

Sonnet 15	Translation
When I consider every thing that grows	When I consider that everything that grows
Holds in perfection but a little moment;	Retains its perfection but for a little moment,
That this huge stage presenteth nought but shows	That this universe presents nothing but appearances
Whereon the Stars in secret influence comment;	While the stars secretly influence events;
When I perceive that men as plants increase,	When I see that men grow like plants,
Cheered and checked even by the self-same sky:	Encouraged and stopped even by the same sky,
Vaunt in their youthful sap, at height decrease,	Exult in their youthful blood, at their height fall,
And wear their brave state out of memory:	And wipe their high position from posterity,
Then the conceit of this inconstant stay	Then the perception of this unstable condition
Sets you most rich in youth before my sight,	Sets you most freshly royal before my sight,
Where wasteful time debateth with decay	Where Elizabeth's mortal body withers with decay,
To change your day of youth to sullied night,	Turning your royal opportunity into nothing.
And all in war with Time for love of you!	And I fight against her death for your royalty:
As he takes from you, I ingraft you new.	As time robs your royal blood, I restore it again.

1 WHEN I CONSIDER EVERY THING THAT GROWS
When I think that all living, growing creatures; **EVERY** = E. Ver, Edward de Vere; "That *every* word doth almost *tell my name*" – Sonnet 76, line 7; **EVERY THING** = Edward de Vere's son;
EVERY THING THAT GROWS = Southampton, the growing flower of the Tudor Rose, is also growing within the lines and "womb" of this diary, which consists of Oxford's thoughts; "When *in eternal lines to time thou grow'st*" – Sonnet 18, line 12; "Nativity, once in the main of light,/ *Crawls to maturity*, wherewith being crowned" – Sonnet 60, lines 5-6; "That did my ripe thoughts in my brain inhearse,/ Making their tomb *the womb wherein they grew*" – Sonnet 86, lines 3-4; "Love is a Babe: then might I not say so/ *To give full growth to that which still doth grow*" – Sonnet 115, lines 13-14; "O Thou my lovely Boy, who in thy power/ Dost hold time's fickle glass, his sickle hour,/ *Who hast by waning grown*" – Sonnet 126, lines 1-3, the final verse in the chronology of the dynastic diary

2 HOLDS IN PERFECTION BUT A LITTLE MOMENT,
PERFECTION = perfect royal blood; perfect opportunity to be king; "And *right perfection* wrongfully disgraced" – Sonnet 66, line 7, referring to Southampton's disgrace for having committed high treason, and the "right perfection" of his royal claim now lost; "The *perfect* ceremony of *love's right*" – Sonnet 23, line 6;

REFERENCE EDITION 115

"Creating *every bad a perfect best*" – Sonnet 114, line 7; "I would *with such perfection govern*, sir, t'excel the Golden Age" – *The Tempest*, 2.1.168-169

> What's in a name? That which we call a rose
> By any other word would smell as sweet;
> So Romeo would, were he not Romeo called,
> Retain that dear perfection which he owes
> Without that title
> - *Romeo and Juliet*, 2.2.43-47

> From her shall read the *perfect* ways of honour
> - *Henry VIII*, 5.4.37
> (Of Infant Princess Elizabeth)

3 THAT THIS HUGE STAGE PRESENTETH NOUGHT BUT SHOWS
THIS HUGE STAGE = the universe, all the world, England; (Malone reads "state"); **SHOWS** = "Yes, like enough, high-battled Caesar will upstate his happiness, and be *staged to the show*, against a sworder" – *Antony and Cleopatra*, 3.13.29-31

4 WHEREON THE STARS IN SECRET INFLUENCE COMMENT;
STARS = allusion to Southampton's royal eyes, which are suns; "Make thy two *eyes like stars* start from their spheres" – *Hamlet*, 1.5.17; "But signs of nobleness, like *stars*, shall shine" – *Macbeth*, 1.4.41; "And scarcely greet me with *that sun, thine eye*" – Sonnet 49, line 6; **SECRET INFLUENCE** = without acknowledgment, i.e., Southampton's royal identity has been kept from general knowledge; also, Oxford is secretly "growing" him in the womb of these verses.

5 WHEN I PERCEIVE THAT MEN AS PLANTS INCREASE,
WHEN I PERCEIVE = "to whom *I perceive* myself so much to be bound unto" – Oxford to Burghley, Sept 1572; "My Lord, *whereas I perceive*" – Oxford to Burghley, March 17, 1575;

MEN AS PLANTS = Southampton as growing flower of the Tudor Rose, a new branch of the dynastic tree; "*A son* who is the theme of honor's tongue, amongst a grove the very straightest *plant*" – *1 Henry IV*, 1.1.80-81; "Such it seems as may beseem a monarch like himself. Myself have often heard him say, and swear, that this his love was an eternal *plant*, whereof the root was fixed in virtue's ground, the leaves and fruit maintained with Beauty's sun" – *3 Henry VI*, 3.3.122-126; "The **royal tree** hath left us **royal fruit**, which, mellowed by the stealing hours of time, will well become the seat of majesty" – *Richard III*, 3.7.166-168; "Your brother's son shall never reign our king, but we will *plant* some other in the throne to the disgrace and downfall of your House" – *Richard III*, 3.7.214-216; "**Anointed, crowned, planted** many years" – *Richard II*, 4.1.127; "O Ned, sweet Ned, speak to thy mother, boy! Canst thou not speak? O traitors! Murderers! ... How sweet a *plant* have you untimely cropp'd!" – *3 Henry VI*, 5.5.49-50, 60; "They laboured to *plant* the rightful heir" – *1 Henry VI*, 2.5.80; "And **replant** Henry in his former state" – *3 Henry VI*, 3.3.198

6 CHEERED AND CHECKED EVEN BY THE SELF-SAME SKY,
CHEERED = encouraged, nurtured; "As all the world is cheered by the sun" – *Richard III*, 1.2.133; **CHECKED** = stopped, prevented from growing

7 VAUNT IN THEIR YOUTHFUL SAP, AT HEIGHT DECREASE,
VAUNT = rejoice; **YOUTHFUL SAP** = fresh young royal blood; "being over-proud in sap and blood" – *Richard II*, 3.4.59; **HEIGHT** = at the top of this golden time; "No, to the dignity and *height* of honor the *high* imperial type of this earth's glory" – *Richard III*, 4.4.244-245; referring also to the height of the crown worn on the monarch's head; see Sonnet 16, line 5: "Now you stand on the *top* of happy hours," reinforcing this concept

8 AND WEAR THEIR BRAVE STATE OUT OF MEMORY:
BRAVE = royal; **STATE** = royal state, the state of a king; "I will keep my state, be like a king" – *Henry V*, 1.2.273; "that dread King that took our state upon him" – *2 Henry VI*, 3.2.153; **AND WEAR THEIR BRAVE STATE OUT OF MEMORY** = "I have some *rights of memory* in this kingdom" – *Hamlet*, 5.2.396; (*memory* is pronounced to rhyme with "sky")

9 THEN THE CONCEIT OF THIS INCONSTANT STAY
CONCEIT = thought or idea; conception or imagination; ("wherein he was greatly abused in *his own conceit*" – Oxford notes for memorandum, 1581, PRO SP 12/151, ff. 96; "Could force his soul so to *his own conceit*" – *Hamlet*, 2.2.553); **INCONSTANT STAY** = unpredictable support; the sun's temporary stay in the sky; the opposite of "constancy" of royal blood, as in Oxford's declaration that Southampton is "Still constant in a wondrous excellence" and that "Therefore my verse, to constancy confined" – Sonnet 105, lines 6-7

10 SETS YOU MOST RICH IN YOUTH BEFORE MY SIGHT,
SETS YOU = places you; echoing "Our ever-living poet wishes the well-wishing adventurer in *setting forth*" – Dedication of the Sonnets, 1609; **MOST RICH IN YOUTH** = most filled with fresh royal blood; rich with the "treasure" of royal blood that Southampton inherited from the Queen; ("Your presence makes us rich, most noble lord" – *Richard II*, 2.3.63; "Ha, majesty! How high thy glory towers when the rich blood of kings is set on fire!" – *King John*, 2.1.350-351; "Therefore, to be possessed with double pomp, to guard *a title that was rich* before" – *King John*, 4.2.9-10; "Thy state is taken for a joint-stool, thy golden scepter for a leaden dagger, and *thy precious rich crown* for a pitiful bald crown" – *1 Henry IV*, 2.4.376-378); **BEFORE MY SIGHT** = in my view, as opposed to that of the Queen, who refuses to acknowledge your royal claim unless you make this marriage deal with William Cecil, Lord Burghley, her chief minister upon whom she depends

11 WHERE WASTEFUL TIME DEBATETH WITH DECAY
WASTEFUL TIME = the constant lessening of the Queen's time of life, leading to "waste" or lack of Southampton's royal succession; ("*I wasted time*, and now doth *time waste me*" – the King in *Richard II*, 5.5.49; "The Chronicle of *wasted time*" – Sonnet 106, line 1, immediately following Elizabeth's death and Southampton's failure to succeed her on the throne; "*Make use of time*, let not advantage slip,/ Beauty within itself should not be wasted./ Fair flowers that are not gathered in their prime/ Rot, and consume themselves *in little time*" – *Venus and Adonis*, 1593, 129-132; "Small time, but in that small most greatly lived this star of England" – of the King in *Henry V*, Epilogue, 5-6; **DEBATETH** = ("*debating in my mind*" – Oxford's dedication in Latin to *The Courtier*, 1572); the "debate" is proceeding "before my sight," as in the preceding line, i.e., in Oxford's mind or inner vision; **DECAY** = the relentless decay of Elizabeth's mortal body, according to time; ("Say, is *my kingdom lost?* ... Cry woe, destruction, *ruin and decay*" – *Richard II*, 3.2.95, 103); "holds a discussion with decay or combats along with decay" – Dowden

12 TO CHANGE YOUR DAY OF YOUTH TO SULLIED NIGHT:
DAY OF YOUTH = golden time of royalty and hope, filled with the bright sun of kingship; "When is *the royal day*? ... Is all things ready for the royal time?" – *Richard III*, 3.4.3-4, in reference to the day of coronation; "God save King Henry, unking'd Richard says, and send him many years of *sunshine days*!" – *Richard II*, 4.1.220-221; **SULLIED NIGHT** = the opposite; the night/darkness of disgrace and the Queen's disfavor, which comes over the verse in Sonnet 27

13 AND ALL IN WAR WITH TIME FOR LOVE OF YOU,
ALL = Southampton, his motto; **TIME** = the waning time of Elizabeth's life

ALL IN WAR WITH TIME = The Sonnets are all in war against the ever-diminishing time left before Elizabeth's death and the date with succession; this line summarizes the basic conflict of the Sonnets, that of Love versus Time or Southampton' royal blood versus Elizabeth's ever-waning life leading to succession and its consequence for the Tudor dynasty

FOR LOVE OF YOU = For the sake of your "love" or royal blood

14 AS HE TAKES FROM YOU, I ENGRAFT YOU NEW.
AS HE TAKES FROM YOU = as time robs you of your chance to be king; **I ENGRAFT YOU NEW** = (Q has *ingraft*); I recreate you and your life in these sonnets; ("As time withers you, I give you new life by writing about you" – Booth); an image of Oxford "grafting" or re-planting his son within these verses, so they become the "womb" in which to grow him again; grafting a scion of one plant with another); "plant you anew, i.e., renew your life by conferring immortality on you through writing about you as you are now (at your prime), thus, in one sense, stopping the ravages of Time and Decay" – Evans; (*ingrafted* also means deep-rooted, ingrained, attached)

Thy mother took unto her blameful bed
Some stern untutor'd churl, and noble stock
Was *graft* with crab-tree slip; whose fruit thou art,
And never of the Nevils' noble race
- *2 Henry VI*, 3.2.211-214

Her *royal stock graft* with ignoble *plants*
- *Richard III*, 3.7.126

His plausive words
He scattered not in ears, but *grafted them*
To grow there and to bear
- *All's Well That Ends Well*, 1.2.53-55

For in the *ingrafted love* he bears to Caesar
- *Julius Caesar*, 2.1.185

Part One

THE MARRIAGE ALLIANCE

Sonnet 16
This Bloody Tyrant Time
1590-1591

Edward de Vere again urges Southampton to conquer Time by acting now to accept the Cecil marriage alliance. The continuing decay of the Queen's body is a "bloody tyrant" by the name of Time; Oxford is using "Time's pencil" to write these entries of his diary in relation to the ever-dwindling time before her death and the succession. The lines of verse are "the lines of life" by which Oxford is recreating and growing his royal son; and they are the bloodlines of his lineage. Meanwhile Henry Wriothesley's fate as the royal prince is in his own hands.

Sonnet 16	Translation
But wherefore do not you a mightier way	But why do you not choose a more kingly way
Make war upon this bloody tyrant time?	To fight the tyranny of Elizabeth's mortality?
And fortify your self in your decay	And prepare yourself against this certain end
With means more blessed then my barren rhyme?	With means more princely than these sonnets?
Now stand you on the top of happy hours,	Now you stand at the height of your royal time,
And many maiden gardens yet unset,	And many wombs still without children
With virtuous wish would bear your living flowers,	Would wish to bear your new Tudor Rose heirs,
Much liker than your painted counterfeit:	Much more like you than any painting of you.
So should the lines of life that life repair,	So should these lines of blood recreating you,
Which this (Time's pencil or my pupil pen)	Which (in Elizabeth's time, my pen recording)
Neither in inward worth nor outward fair	Neither in secret royalty nor in public show of it
Can make you live your self in eyes of men,	Can make you succeed as king gazed upon by all.
To give away your self keeps your self still,	To beget an heir is to keep your royal blood,
And you must live, drawn by your own sweet skill.	And it must live, perpetuated by your royal power.

1 BUT WHEREFORE DO NOT YOU A MIGHTIER WAY
Continuing immediately from the previous sonnet; **MIGHTIER** = more royal, as befitting a prince and future king; "*High and Mighty*" – Hamlet's salutes King Claudius in his message – *Hamlet*, 4.7.42; "It is reported, *mighty sovereign*" – *2 Henry VI*, 3.2.121; "No, *mighty King* of France" – *3 Henry VI*, 3.3.4; "For by this knot thou shalt so surely tie thy now unsured assurance to the crown, that yon green boy shall have no sun to ripe the bloom that promiseth a *mighty fruit*" – *King John*, 2.1.470-473

2 MAKE WAR UPON THIS BLOODY TYRANT TIME?
THIS BLOODY TYRANT, TIME = this enemy of your royal blood, Time, the ever-dwindling life span of Elizabeth leading both to her death and to the end of this dynastic diary of your life. Time is a "bloody" tyrant because it is steadily eroding the chances for Southampton's royal blood to be enthroned in his person; Oxford refers on April 10, 1603 to the deceased Elizabeth herself as a "tyrant" in Sonnet 107, line 14: "When *tyrants'* crests and tombs of brass are spent"

3 AND FORTIFY YOUR SELF IN YOUR DECAY
AND FORTIFY YOUR SELF = defend your royal self, i.e., your right to the crown (by marrying Burghley's granddaughter Elizabeth Vere and begetting heirs of your blood before it's too late); "For such a

REFERENCE EDITION

time *do I now fortify*" – Sonnet 63, line 9, when Oxford is dreading the execution of Southampton in 1601;
IN YOUR DECAY = in the midst of your mortal erosion, which is taking place even as Elizabeth's body is decaying, too, and the date with succession grows ever closer at hand; "Doth either *time or age/ Bring him unto decay*?" – poem attributed *circa*. 1589 to Oxford

4 WITH MEANS MORE BLESSED THAN MY BARREN RHYME?
MORE BLESSED = more royal, with more divine power; ("*Blessed be your royal Grace!*" – *Measure for Measure*, 5.1.139; "Look down, you gods, and on this couple drop *a blessed crown!*" – *The Tempest*, 5.1.201-202); **MY BARREN RHYME** = these sonnets, which are barren or childless (empty of you) on their own, although, in fact, the diary is also a "womb" in which to preserve your life, royal blood and growth; ("Why is my verse so *barren of new pride*?" – Sonnet 76, line 1)

5 NOW STAND YOU ON THE TOP OF HAPPY HOURS,
STAND YOU ON = "And *stands upon* the honour of his birth" – *1 Henry VI*, 2.4.28; **TOP** = "The art o' the Court as hard to leave as keep; whose *top* to climb is certain falling" – *Cymbeline*, 3.3.46-48; **THE TOP OF HAPPY HOURS** = the height of royal opportunity as a prince

> (*Third Apparition, **a child crowned**, with a tree in his hand.*)
>
> What is this,
> That *rises like the issue of a king*,
> And wears upon his baby brow the round
> And ***top of sovereignty?***
> - *Macbeth*, 4.1.86-88

"The image is a genuine symbol and points to many more meanings than the first Child. Like the first, it also symbolizes the victorious renewal of life, but it has the added meaning of royalty since it wears the appropriate insignia of kingship ... This whole, royal Child is truly a symbol of the Self. It represents totality, that royal quality which Macbeth wants more than anything"
- Kirsch, *Shakespeare's Royal Self*, p. 388, citing Johnson: "The *round* is that part of the crown that encircles the head. The *top* is the *ornament* that rises above it."

"Shakespeare makes Macbeth call the crown 'the round of sovereignty' here and elsewhere - first, obviously, in allusion to the form of the ornament. That is prose; but immediately his poetic eye sees that a crown is the external sign of the complete possession of the throne ... But the crown not only completes ... and rounds, as with the perfection of a circle, the claim to sovereignty, but it is figuratively the *'top'* in this sense - e.g., 'the top of admiration,' 'the top of judgment,' 'the top of honor,' '*the top of happy hours.*'" - R. G. White

HAPPY HOURS = the golden time of royalty and opportunity; "Heaven and fortune bar me happy hours!" – the King in *Richard III*, 4.4.400; **HAPPY** = "You have misled a prince, a royal king, a *happy* gentleman in blood and lineaments" – *Richard II*, 3.1.8-9; "He is a *happy* king, since he gains from his subjects the name of good by his government" – *Pericles*, 2.1.102-103

6 WITH MANY MAIDEN GARDENS YET UNSET,
MAIDEN GARDENS YET UNSET = virgin wombs; **UNSET** = unplanted, i.e., without seed

7 WITH VIRTUOUS WISH WOULD BEAR YOUR LIVING FLOWERS,
VIRTUOUS WISH = who, with innocent eagerness; **BEAR** = give birth to; **YOUR LIVING FLOWERS** = your children; your flowers, i.e., living heirs of the Tudor Rose

8 MUCH LIKER THAN YOUR PAINTED COUNTERFEIT:
YOUR PAINTED COUNTERFEIT = attempts to draw your likeness or to recreate your real life and identity; counterfeit = portrait; "Thou draw'st a counterfeit best in all Athens" – *Timon of Athens*, 5.1.83-84; "Describe *Adonis* and the *counterfeit/* Is poorly imitated after you" – Sonnet 53, lines 5-6, to Southampton

9 SO SHOULD THE LINES OF LIFE THAT LIFE REPAIR
THE LINES OF LIFE = "Children ... lineage ... delineation with a pencil, a portrait" – Dowden; the wrinkles of age; the lines of these sonnets, giving life to you; ("looking on *the lines of my boy's face*" – *Winter's Tale*, 1.2.153); also, *the lines of your descent*, i.e., your Tudor lineage through your mother the Queen; ("Of the *true line* and stock of Charles the Great" – *Henry V*, 1.2.71; "Being but fourth of that heroic *line*" – *1 Henry VI*, 2.4.78; "They hailed him father to *a line of kings* ... Thence to be wrenched with an *unlineal* hand, no son of mine succeeding " – *Macbeth*, 3.1.58, 62-53); "When in *eternal lines to time thou grow'st*" – Sonnet 18, line 12; "When hours have drained his blood and filled his brow/ With *lines* and wrinkles .../ His beauty shall in black *lines* be seen,/ And *they shall live, and he in them* still green" – Sonnet 63, lines 3-4, 13-14; "My life hath *in this line* some interest,/ Which for memorial still with thee shall stay" – Sonnet 74, lines 3-4; "But when your countenance filled up his *line*,/ Then lacked I matter, that enfeebled mine" – Sonnet 86, lines 13-14, referring to the verse of the pen name "Shakespeare" (linked to Southampton) forcing Oxford into obliteration; **REPAIR** = "Whose fresh *repair* if now thou not renewest" – Sonnet 3, line 3; "Seeking that beauteous roof to ruinate,/ Which to *repair* should be thy chief desire" – Sonnet 10, lines 7-8

> You pity not the state, nor the remembrance
> Of his most sovereign name; consider little,
> What dangers, *by His Highness' fail of issue*,
> May drop upon his kingdom, and devour
> Incertain lookers on. What were more holy
> Than to rejoice the former Queen is well?
> What holier than, *for royalty's repair*,
> For present comfort, and for future good,
> To bless the bed of majesty again
> With a sweet fellow to't?
> - *The Winter's Tale*, 5.1.25-34

10 WHICH THIS (TIME'S PENCIL OR MY PUPIL PEN)
TIME'S PENCIL = The pencil I use to write these verses, which are inextricably bound to the ever diminishing *time* left in the Queen's life; **MY PUPIL PEN** = my pen, which has no knowledge by itself, i.e., it writes these sonnets only according to what it learns from your life, which is my source and my inspiration; "For whose so dumb that cannot write to thee,/ When *thou thyself dost give invention light?*" – Sonnet 38, lines 7-8; "Yet be most proud of that which I compile,/ Whose *influence* is thine, and *born of thee*" – Sonnet 78, lines 9-10; (Both this verse and the next "make oblique reference to the traditional notion of a poet and poem as parent and child" – Booth); in fact, Oxford is writing as father to a son who lives within the verse; his royal son is "telling" or recording the story through Oxford's pen: "For as the Sun is daily new and old,/ So is my love *still telling* what is told" - Sonnet 76, lines 13-14

11 NEITHER IN INWARD WORTH NOR OUTWARD FAIR
INWARD WORTH = genuine royal blood in you, which may be unseen by others; "by the glorious *worth of my descent*" – *Richard II*, 1.1.107; **OUTWARD FAIR** = your appearance of royalty, as seen by Oxford and as he envisions it seen by others in the future

12 CAN MAKE YOU LIVE YOUR SELF IN EYES OF MEN.
LIVE YOUR SELF IN EYES OF MEN = succeed to the throne as king, acknowledged by all subjects who gaze upon you with their dutiful eyes; "Your praise shall still find room/ Even in the eyes of all posterity" – Sonnet 55, lines 10-11; "Your monument shall be my gentle verse,/ Which eyes not yet created shall o'er-read" – Sonnet 81, lines 9-10; "I have therefore undertaken the work ... also to ensure that neither my goodwill (which is very great) should remain unexpressed, nor that my skill (which is small) should seem to fear to face the light and the *eyes of men*" – Oxford's Letter to the Reader for *The Courtier*, 1572

13 **TO GIVEAWAY YOUR SELF KEEPS YOUR SELF STILL,**
GIVE AWAY YOUR SELF = pass on your royal self, i.e., your blood, to an heir; *"your royal self"* – *Richard III*, 3.1.63; **KEEPS YOUR SELF** = keeps alive your royal inheritance and person; maintains your princely stature; **STILL** = always and forever; constantly; "Since all alike my songs and praises be/ To one, of one, *still* such, and ever so" – Sonnet 105, lines 3-4

14 **AND YOU MUST LIVE, DRAWN BY YOUR OWN SWEET SKILL.**
YOU MUST LIVE = you must perpetuate your blood; i.e., I cannot do this for you with my verses; you must do it yourself; **DRAWN BY YOUR OWN SWEET SKILL** = created by your own royal actions, i.e., by begetting an heir; **SWEET** = royal; **SKILL** = action; ability; "We must with all *our majesty and skill*" – King Claudius in *Hamlet*, 4.1.31; "The first course seemed to demand greater *skill and art* than I can lay claim to" – Oxford's Letter to the Reader in *The Courtier*, 1572

Part One

END OF THE MARRIAGE ALLIANCE

Sonnet 17
Your True Rights
1591

Oxford predicts future generations will fail to recognize Henry Wriothesley's "true rights" by blood to succeed Queen Elizabeth as King Henry IX. Instead, he forecasts, readers will see only the "Poet's rage" of these "numbers" rather than their true contents. Yet he vows nevertheless to incorporate his son's life within the verses, i.e., to preserve him within the "tomb" of the Sonnets, which is also a womb giving new life to him. Southampton's "official" date of birth is October 6, 1573, as opposed to his real birth date in late May or early June 1574. This sonnet, numbered to signify the actual seventeenth birthday of Southampton's life in 1591, marks the end of Oxford's attempt to pressure him into a Cecil family alliance. Technically, the proposal will continue until Southampton's "official" twenty-first birthday on October 6, 1594, but otherwise Oxford (as well as Burghley and the Queen) now cease to pressure him.

Sonnet 17	Translation
Who will believe my verse in time to come / If it were filled with your most high deserts? / Though yet heaven knows it is but as a tomb / Which hides your life, and shows not half your parts:	Who will believe these sonnets in the future / If they were filled with your most royal qualities? / Though Elizabeth knows, this verse is but a tomb / Which hides your royalty and fails to reveal even half your royal aspects.
If I could write the beauty of your eyes, / And in fresh numbers number all your graces, / The age to come would say, 'This Poet lies! / Such heavenly touches ne'er touched earthly faces!'	If I could express the Tudor blood you reflect, / And in new verses express all your kingly qualities, / Future generations would say, "This Poet is lying – Such inheritors of Elizabeth's blood never existed!"
So should my papers (yellowed with their age) / Be scorned, like old men of less truth than tongue, / And your true rights be termed a Poet's rage, / And stretched meter of an Antique song.	So should my verses (yellowed with their age) / Be scorned, like old men of less truth than talk, / And your royal rights be termed an exaggeration / And the extreme boasting of an old poem.
But were some child of yours alive that time / You should live twice: in it, and in my rhyme.	But if some child of yours exists in the future, / You would live twice: in the child, and in my verse.

1 WHO WILL BELIEVE MY VERSE IN TIME TO COME
MY VERSE = these private verses; **TIME TO COME** = future generations of readers; the time of Elizabeth's death and England's date with royal succession, after which the Sonnets will conclude either with Henry Wriothesley becoming King Henry IX or with the death of the Tudor Rose Dynasty; "Not mine own fears, nor the prophetic soul/ Of the wide world dreaming on *things to come*" – Sonnet 107, lines 1-2

WHO WILL BELIEVE MY VERSE = Oxford's prediction has turned out to be uncannily accurate, i.e., few have recognized that the Sonnets testify to Southampton's "true rights" to the throne, as expressed in line 11 of this verse; "By direct address, by varied metaphor, and by multifarious allusion, the description of the Friend communicated is always one: *monarch, sovereign, prince, king* ... The poet's harping on the same string is so insistent as to make one ask why it has not arrested attention. No doubt everyone has regarded this 'king' sense as formal hyperbole and nothing more. Any literal meaning looks quite incredible, a rank

---

REFERENCE EDITION

impossibility" – Leslie Hotson, in *Mr. W. H.,* 1965, pp 35-36, referring to the general view of the Sonnets as "a Poet's rage" and arguing to the contrary that the verses of the Fair Youth series (1-126) were indeed written to a younger man who was a royal prince.

2 IF IT WERE FILLED WITH YOUR MOST HIGH DESERTS?
FILLED WITH = contain the truth of; **YOUR MOST HIGH DESERTS** = your most kingly qualities; "Either accept the title thou usurp'st, of benefit proceeding from our king and not of any challenge of desert" – *1 Henry VI*, 5.5.151-153; "And lay those honors on *your high desert*" – *Richard III*, 1.3.97; **DESERTS** = "deserving,, due recompense, right … worth, merit" – Crystal & Crystal; "my desert is honour" – *3 Henry VI*, 3.3.192; "for these good deserts, we here create you Earl of Shrewsbury" – *1 Henry VI*, 3.4.25; "Within the knowledge of mine own desert" – Sonnet 49, line 10, Oxford speaking as father of Southampton and what he deserves; **HIGH** = as in "Your Highness" or "High and Mighty"; "Ha, majesty! How *high* thy glory towers" – *King John*, 2.1.350; "And that *high* royalty" – *King John*, 4.2.5; "My *high* blood's royalty" – *Richard II*, 1.1.58; "Please your *highness* note … your *high* person" – *Henry VIII*, 1.2.138-140

3 THOUGH YET HEAVEN KNOWS IT IS BUT AS A TOMB
HEAVEN KNOWS = Elizabeth knows; God knows; "*Heaven* pictured in her face/ Doth promise joy and grace" – Oxford poem about Elizabeth, signed E. O. in *The Phoenix Nest*, 1593 but likely written two decades earlier; **TOMB** = the Monument or Pyramid of the Sonnets that Oxford is now constructing to preserve his son's identity for eternity. The tomb will also function as a "womb" in which Southampton and his royal blood will grow according to time; "That did my ripe thoughts in my brain inhearse,/ Making *their tomb the womb* wherein they grew" – Sonnet 86, lines 3-4, referring to the Shakespeare pen name that has forced Oxford's thoughts into deeper obscurity, except for the record of these thoughts being preserved in the Sonnets; "He rests not in this tomb. This monument five hundred years hath stood" – *Titus Andronicus*, 1.1.354-355; "And thou in this shalt find thy monument,/ When tyrants' crests and tombs of brass are spent" – Sonnet 107, lines 13-14

4 WHICH HIDES YOUR LIFE, AND SHOWS NOT HALF YOUR PARTS.
HIDES YOUR LIFE = conceals your identity as prince; **SHOWS NOT HALF YOUR PARTS** = reveals not half of all your kingly aspects; qualities, attributes, gifts of mind or body; "For the young gentleman, as I understand, hath been well brought up, fair conditioned, and hath many good *parts* in him" – Oxford to Burghley, September 8, 1597; "Mine eye hath well examined his *parts* and finds them perfect Richard" – the King in *King John*, 1.1.89-90; "Remembers me of all his gracious *parts*" – *King John*, 3.3.96; "Your sum of *parts*" – *Hamlet*, 4.7.73; "Entitled in thy *parts* do crowned sit" – Sonnet 37, line 7; "So full of majesty and royal *parts*" – Chapman, *The Revenge of Bussy d'Ambois*, 1.2.17, of Queen Elizabeth

5 IF I COULD WRITE THE BEAUTY OF YOUR EYES
THE BEAUTY OF YOUR EYES = the reflection of Elizabeth's "beauty" or royal blood in your kingly eyes, which are suns; "My worthy lord, if ever Tamora were gracious in those *princely eyes* of thine" – *Titus Andronicus*, 1.1.433-434; i.e., if I could write directly about your Tudor blood from the Queen

> Save *her alone, who yet on th'earth doth reign,*
> Whose **beauties** string no god can well distrain
> - Oxford poem about Elizabeth, *Paradise of Dainty Devices*, 1576

6 AND IN FRESH NUMBERS NUMBER ALL YOUR GRACES,
FRESH = newly royal, as in "the world's *fresh* ornament" of Sonnet 1, line 9; **FRESH NUMBERS** = newly royal sonnets, which are the "numbers" Oxford is compiling to build this Monument; "Yet, after all comparisons of truth, as truth's authentic author to be cited, 'as true as Troilus' shall crown up the verse and sanctify the *numbers*" – *Troilus and Cressida*, 3.3.177-179; "Eternal *numbers* to outlive long date" – Sonnet 38, line 12; "But now my gracious *numbers* are decayed" – Sonnet 79, line 3; "In gentle *numbers* time so idly spent" – Sonnet 100, line 6; "To *number* Ave-Maries on his beads" – *2 Henry VI*, 1.3.56; the individual verses are referred to as numbers (eternal, gracious numbers, akin to sacred Rosary beads), which are part of the means by which the Monument is being built; and in fact each sonnet in *Q* is itself numbered. The

No. 17

numbers are ordered sequentially and chronologically within each sequence, serving to date them in relation to real events. Oxford represents the year of his son's birth, 1574, in the Bath verses to become Sonnets 153 and 154; now, with the seventeenth verse of Sonnets 1-17, the numbers have caught up to his current age and represent each of his seventeen birthdays from 1575 to 1591:

YEARS: '75 '76 '77 '78 '79 '80 '81 '82 '83 '84 '85 '86 '87 '88 '89 '90 '91
SONNETS: 1 - 2 - 3 - 4 - 5 - 6 - 7 - 8 - 9 - 10 - 11 - 12 - 13 - 14 - 15 - 16 - 17

"For now hath *time* made *me* his numb'ring clock"
– *Richard II*, 5.5.50, the King saying that he himself embodies Time

ALL = Southampton; **ALL YOUR GRACES** = all your kingly blood and godlike qualities; "*The king is full of grace* and fair regard" – *Henry V*, 1.1.22; "My sovereign, I confess *your royal graces* showered on me daily ... *your great graces*" – *Henry VIII*, 3.2.166-167,174; these "graces" or royal attributes come from Elizabeth, of whom Oxford had written: "Above the rest in Court who gave thee *grace*?" – Oxford sonnet, circa early 1570s

7 THE AGE TO COME WOULD SAY: "THIS POET LIES,
Future readers will say I'm exaggerating, i.e., lying; they will not believe that the Sonnets tell the true story of my son's royal blood and rights to the throne

8 SUCH HEAVENLY TOUCHES NE'ER TOUCHED EARTHLY FACES!"
HEAVENLY TOUCHES = blood and qualities inherited from Elizabeth, who is Heaven; ("Truth shall nurse her, holy and heavenly thoughts still counsel her" – Cranmer, predicting the future infant Elizabeth Tudor, *Henry VIII*, 5.4.28-29); **EARTHLY** = mortal; also, non-royal **HEAVENLY ... EARTHLY:** "and although it hath pleased God after an earthly kingdom to take her up into a more permanent and *heavenly* state, wherein I do not doubt she is crowned with glory" – Oxford to Robert Cecil, writing of Queen Elizabeth on the eve of her funeral procession on April 28, 1603

9 SO SHOULD MY PAPERS (YELLOWED WITH THEIR AGE)
MY PAPERS = my manuscript pages for this Book of private sonnets

10 BE SCORNED, LIKE OLD MEN OF LESS TRUTH THAN TONGUE,
TRUTH = Oxford, *Nothing Truer than Truth*; **LESS TRUTH** = falsity; i.e., not anything like Oxford, who is Truth; not recognizing Southampton's "true rights" of line 11 to follow; **TONGUE** = gossip, recorded history, which is a lie

11 AND YOUR TRUE RIGHTS BE TERMED A POET'S RAGE
YOUR TRUE RIGHTS = Your legitimate rights of kingship; your right to succeed to the throne as King Henry IX of England; "I have some *rights* of memory in this kingdom" – *Hamlet*, 5.2.396; "his purple *blood right*" – *3 Henry VI*, 2.5.99; "The *royalties and rights* of banished Hereford" – *Richard II*, 2.1.190; "*my rights and royalties*" – *Richard II*, 2.3.119; "a *rightful* king" – *Richard II*, 5.1.50; "Thou and thine usurp the dominations, royalties and *rights* of this oppressed boy" – *King John*, 2.1.175-177; "But as successively from blood to blood, your *right of birth*, your emery, your own" – *Richard III*, 3.7.134-135; "for thee and for the *right* of English Henry" – *1 Henry VI*, 2.1.35-36; Suppose by *right* and equity thou be king" – *3 Henry VI*, 1.1.127; "Did I put Henry from his native *right*?" – *3 Henry VI*, 3.3.190; "For he that steeps his safety in *true blood*" – *King John*, 3.3.147; **RIGHTS** = "just claim, rights, title" – Crystal & Crystal; "Your right depends not on his life or death, *3 Henry VI*, 1.2.11, about the right to wear the crown

"They labored to plant the *rightful heir*"
- *1 Henry VI*, 2.5.80

If *Her Majesty's right* and interest be not cunningly suppressed
- Oxford to Robert Cecil, January 1602

REFERENCE EDITION

> There is nothing therefore left to my comfort but the excellent virtues and deep wisdom wherewith God hath endued our new Master and Sovereign Lord, who doth not come amongst us as a stranger but as a natural prince, *succeeding by **right** of blood and inheritance*"
> – Oxford to Robert Cecil, April 25/27, 1603, writing of King James, now on his way from Scotland to occupy the English throne

> And *right* perfection wrongfully disgraced
> - Sonnet 66, line 7

TRUE = Related to Oxford, *Nothing Truer than Truth*; "That *if his rule were true*, he should be gracious" – *Richard III*, 2.4.20; "in justice and *true right*" – *2 Henry VI*, 5.2.25; "genuine, real … conformable to law and justice, rightful, legitimate … conformable to nature, due, natural" - Schmidt; "legitimate, rightful, honourable … true to father's likeness, authentic, genuine" – Crystal & Crystal; "my shape as *true* as honest madam's *issue*" – *King Lear*, 1.2.8; "His father never was so *true begot*" – *King John*, 2.1.130; "Thou *truly* fair wert *truly* sympathized/ In *true* plain words by thy *true*-telling friend" – Sonnet 82, lines 11-12, Oxford to Southampton as father to son; "My most *true* mind thus maketh mine untrue" – Sonnet 113, line 14; "I will be *true* despite thy scythe and thee" – Oxford, defying Time on his son's behalf

"But I hope *truth* is subject to no prescription, for *truth is truth* though never so old, and *time* cannot make that false which was once *true*" – Oxford to Robert Cecil, May 7, 1603

> So long as out of limit and *true* rule
> You stand against anointed majesty
> - *1 Henry IV*, 4.3.39-40

> The quarrel of a *true* inheritor
> - *2 Henry IV*, 4.5.168

> Since that the *truest* issue *of thy throne*
> - *Macbeth*, 4.3.106

> Oh, *true-bred!*
> - *Coriolanus*, 1.1.243

POET'S RAGE = poet's exaggeration; i.e., the poet of the Sonnets, writing conventional poetry with its familiar, exaggerated language; **RAGE** = "violent outburst, furious passion … madness, insanity, derangement" – Crystal & Crystal; "When rage and hot blood are his counselors" – *2 Henry IV*, 4.4.63, the King, speaking of Prince Henry

12 AND STRETCHED METER OF AN ANTIQUE SONG.
STRETCHED METER = contorted poetical style; overstrained poetry; **ANTIQUE SONG** = old-style sonnet; fourteen lines, usually in iambic pentameter; a "sonnet" itself was known as a "little song"; evolving from medieval Italian verse (*sonetto*); among varying rhyme schemes, the Italian is *abba abba cdecde*; the oldest variety is from Petrarch (1304-1374); the Shakespearen sonnet is *abab cdcd efef gg*, used by Oxford's relative Henry Howard, Earl of Surrey (1517-1547), by Oxford himself and notably by Spenser (c. 1552-1599), whose monumental epic poem *The Faire Queene* (1590, 1598) has been regarded as inspiring Shakespeare; but some Oxford students suspect Oxford's hand in some (or even all!) of Spenser's work; Oxford in *Shake-Speares Sonnets* deliberately uses this "antique" form, because he intends the numbered sequence not for the eyes of contemporaries but for future readers, who will not care whether or not the form is in fashion; in addition, the "antique" style is appropriate for this Monument inspired by the ancient Egyptian pyramids that (among their other functions) measured time.

No. 17

13 BUT WERE SOME CHILD OF YOURS ALIVE THAT TIME,
But if you had an heir of your blood living in that future time; **THAT TIME** = "Tell them, when that my mother went with child of that insatiate Edward, noble York my princely father then had wars in France, and by *true computation of the time* found that the issue was not his-begot" – *Richard III*, 3.5.85-89; "whereof I am grown old and spent the chiefest *time* of mine age" – Oxford to Robert Cecil, June 19, 1603; "the alterations of *time* and chance" – Oxford to Robert Cecil, April 25/27, 1603; "But now *time and truth* have unmasked all difficulties" – Oxford to Robert Cecil, January 1602

14 YOU SHOULD LIVE TWICE: IN IT AND IN MY RHYME
You would live in your heir and also in my sonnets; from here on, regardless of Southampton's refusal to accept the Cecil marriage alliance, Oxford will enable him to live and grow in this diary; ("You would have two chances at immortality, in your child and in my verse" – Booth); a declaration that he is now building the Monument for Southampton as a king or "god on earth" who deserves to gain immortality at some point in the distant future; having urged his son to recreate his life and royal blood within an heir, Oxford now becomes the parent again, hoping to give him rebirth: "The second burden of a former child" – Sonnet 59, line 4, referring to the new birth of his son within the Sonnets; Booth writes of the "conceit by which the poet speaks of himself and his poem as mother and child," which dates from classical times, but Oxford adopts this conceit here uniquely by attempting to create the "living record" of his son's memory.

> Nor shall death brag thou wand'rest in his shade,
> When *in eternal lines to time thou grow'st.*
> So long as men can breathe or eyes can see,
> *So long lives this*, and *this gives life to thee.*
> - Sonnet 18, lines 11-14

> Nor Mars his sword nor war's quick fire shall burn
> The *living record* of your memory.
> - Sonnet 55, lines 7-8

> Why write I still all one, ever the same,
> And keep invention in a noted weed,
> That every word doth almost tell my name,
> Showing their birth, and where they did proceed?
> - Sonnet 76, lines 5-8

> That did my ripe thoughts in my brain inhearse,
> Making their tomb the womb wherein they grew?
> - Sonnet 86, lines 3-4

> *Love is a Babe:* then might I not say so
> To give full growth to that which still doth grow.
> - Sonnet 115, lines 13-14

> O Thou my lovely Boy, who in thy power
> Dost hold *time's* fickle glass, his sickle hour,
> *Who hast by waning grown...*
> - Sonnet 126, lines 1-3
> (Final Verse of the Diary)

The marriage sonnets are concluded. Southampton has spurned all attempts that may have been made directly by the Queen and Burghley, as well as by Oxford, to pressure him into a Cecil alliance. He has thereby lost both Elizabeth's and Cecil's support for his succession to the throne. From here on the younger earl will throw his lot with Essex in opposition to William Cecil, Lord Burghley and his son Robert Cecil, in a separate attempt to gain power and be able to control the succession to the Queen upon her death. Oxford is left to support his royal son indirectly, both through the public pen name "William Shakespeare," to be launched two years later, and through this private diary of sonnets in which he records the fate of his son's royal hope. The seeds of the Essex Rebellion of 1601 are planted here and now.

1591

Oxford Abandons Fisher's Folly, 1591: "Lord Oxford retired from the theatrical world, as active patron, to 'sit in idle cell,' as Spenser put it, rather than 'himself to mockery to sell' ... Although to some extent a recluse, mainly from Court life, he was at work upon poems and sonnets, as well as on the revision of many of his old Court-dramas ... Although he continued to consort with his literary friends, he had been obliged, after the disbanding of his and the Queen's theatrical companies, to curtail his patronage, and he vacated Fisher's Folly in 1591. [During the 1580s, he used this London mansion to gather writers, later called the University Wits, to work with him under one roof, producing many kinds of literary works including English history plays that emphasized the perils of civil war while helping to rouse patriotic unity against Catholic Spain.] Immediately, as if an earthquake had shattered their foundations, loud yelps and groans over their financial straits emanated from Green, Peele, Marlowe, Nashe, and Lyly." (Ogburn & Ogburn, *This Star of England*, 927)

Henry VI, **March 1591:** Henslowe's diary records a performance of *Henry VI*.

Oxford Requests Financial Relief, March 18, 1591: Oxford requests Burghley to obtain the Queen's permission for him to commute his one-thousand-pound annual grant into a lump sum of five thousand pounds. "So shall my children be provided for, myself in length settled in quiet, and I hope your Lordship contented, remaining no cause for you to think me an evil father, nor any doubt in me but that I may enjoy that friendship from your Lordship that so near a match, and not fruitless, may lawfully expect. Good my Lord, think of this, and let me have both your furtherance and counsel in this cause. *For to tell truth, I am weary of an unsettled life, which is the very pestilence that happens to Courtiers*, that propound unto themselves no end of their time therein bestowed." (Ward, 305-306)

Southampton at Cambridge, June 1591: Southampton lingers at Cambridge University, following Commencement, with his friend Roger Manners, Fifth Earl of Rutland.

Elizabeth and Burghley to Cowdray, August 15-21, 1591: Queen Elizabeth, on her royal summer progress, pays a long visit with Burghley to old Viscount Montague, father of Mary Browne, Countess of Southampton – possibly final pressure on Southampton to accept the Cecil marriage proposal. "Southampton must have been on hand," Akrigg writes. (*The Honorable Entertainment given to the Queen's Majestie in Progresse, at Cowdray in Sussex*, London, 1591, in vol. 2 of *The Progresses and Public Processions of Queen Elizabeth*, John Nichols, 1788-1821)

Elizabeth and Burghley to Titchfield, August – September 1591: Elizabeth and Burghley, presumably accompanied by Southampton, visit with the Countess of Southampton at the Titchfield estate. *"Though we have surviving a very full account of the royal visit to Cowdray, we know practically nothing of the day or two she spent at Titchfield. Burghley was with her and addressed a letter from there on September 2nd. Possibly his guardian, seconded by the Queen, once more pressed Southampton to go through with the marriage to Lady Elizabeth Vere."* (Akrigg, 35)

Narcissus, **1591:** A fifteen-page volume in Latin attributed to Lord Burghley's secretary John Clapham, *Narcissus*, is published in London and dedicated to seventeen-year-old Southampton – the first honoring of Henry Wriothesley in public print. Both the dedication and the poem carry distinct echoes of the private sonnets and of Oxford's letters:

No. 17

"To the most famous and noble lord, Henry Earl of Southampton, John Clapham *desires increase* of virtue and honor and many happy years. I am somewhat afraid, most distinguished lord, that to many I will myself seem to be striving after my own *shadow* with my *Narcissus*, whose errors I have described in these verses, and with him too to be quite mad. For what is sillier or more unsuitable than, when one may safely lie hidden, rashly to expose oneself to the judgment of others, and to **bring forward to public view things which show nothing** except the evidence only of a frivolous and idle disposition."

DESIRES INCREASE: "From fairest creatures we *desire increase*" – Sonnet 1, line 1
SHADOW: "But the world is so cunning, as of a *shadow* they can make a substance, and of a likelihood a truth" – Oxford to Burghley, July 1581; "What is your substance, whereof are you made,/ That millions of strange *shadows* on you tend?" – Sonnet 53, lines 1-2
BRING FORWARD ... THINGS WHICH SHOW NOTHING: "For I am shamed by that which I *bring forth,/* And so should you, to love things *nothing* worth" – Sonnet 72, lines 13-14

The dedication continues:

"But, whatever will be other people's opinion of me, all will be well with me, I hope, if you think this **tender offspring – reborn as it were from the grave**, although to many it could seem premature – deserving the patronage of your honor. So may it please you, to receive, Excellency, this poem, however insignificant, destined to *go forth into the light* – not without good fortune – beneath the authority of your name, as assured testimony of a mind wholly *dutiful* toward you and utterly *devoted* to your honor. When you read it through, *if I perceive* that you are pleased with it, I shall indeed be satisfied; but if it turns out otherwise contrary to my desire, I humbly entreat you to be indulgent to by errors, and think that you have only seen a *shadow* – which is nothing."

TENDER OFFSPRING: "His *tender heir*" – Sonnet 1, line 4; "Like true children duly procreated of such a mother," Oxford in 1563 to Burghley, also likening letters to children
REBORN AS IT WERE FROM THE GRAVE: "Whereby when they be dead indeed, yet make we them *live as it were again* through their monument" – Oxford for *Cardanus' Comfort*, 1573
GO FORTH INTO THE LIGHT: "Nativity, once *in the main of light*" – Sonnet 60, line 5; "to bring the truth to light" – Oxford to Burghley, June 13, 1595
DUTIFUL ... DEVOTED: "Thy merit hath my *duty* strongly knit" – Sonnet 26, line 2; "being part in all I have, *devoted* yours. Were my worth greater, my *duty* would show greater" – dedication of *Lucrece* to Southampton, 1594
IF I PERCEIVE: "When I perceive" – Sonnet 15, line 5; "My Lord, whereas I perceive" – Oxford to Burghley, March 17, 1575

The story of *Narcissus*, based on the Greek legend, was part of Ovid's *Metamorphoses*, the 1565-67 English translation of which was written by Edward deVere's uncle Arthur Golding. (Whether young Oxford helped him and to what degree is unknown.) The Latin rendition of *Narcissus* as by Clapham is a foreshadowing of *Venus and Adonis* in 1593, dedicated by "Shakespeare" to Southampton.

"Somewhat surprisingly the scene has been transferred from ancient Greece to England, the fairest isle that 'Ocean batters with his cool waves,' an island named 'Blessed,' flourishing under the rule of a Virgin Queen, free from care and enjoying eternal peace ... Venus receives Narcissus in her pleasant embrace and conducts him to the inner sanctuary of the temple ... Narcissus falls in love with his own image ... the desperate youth falls headlong into the pond and drowns. Venus, lamenting, gives him a new life in the form of the flower Narcissus ... Narcissus is Southampton."
(Akrigg, *Shakespeare and the Earl of Southampton*, p. 33)

Akrigg believes Burghley, angered at Southampton's refusal to marry his granddaughter Elizabeth Vere, enlisted secretary Clapham to write *Narcissus* and dedicate it to the young earl to chastise and further pressure him into the marriage. Burghley most certainly would have approved of its intended effect upon

REFERENCE EDITION

Southampton; and it's possible that Oxford himself was involved in the writing of the poem and/or its dedication.

Oxford Alienates Hedingham, December 2, 1591: Oxford alienates the ancient Vere estate Castle Hedingham in Essex to Burghley, his father-in-law, and to his daughters.

Oxford Remarries, late 1591: Edward de Vere's first wife Anne Cecil died in 1588; now, at age forty-one, he marries again. "The bride was Elizabeth Trentham, a Maid of Honor at Court; and for once the Queen took a gracious attitude about a marriage." (Ogburn & Ogburn, p. 933)

"Perhaps the most interesting thing about this marriage is that it was evidently sanctioned, and probably even encouraged, by the Queen. It had always been a risky proceeding for a courtier to carry off one of the Maids of Honor … but by the nineties it had become an almost certain step to disgrace and even imprisonment … With Lord Oxford, however, it was quite different. He suffered no disgrace, and the payment of one thousand pounds was continued punctually and regularly. This is only another example of the great favor the Queen showed him, and how much she sought his welfare and happiness … The Earl of Oxford and his new Countess settled in the village of Stoke Newington, just north of Shoreditch." (Ward, pp. 307-308, 313)

Oxford now voluntarily becomes a virtual "recluse" who fades from the contemporary historical record during the 1590s. Although speculation about his motives have centered mainly on his financial difficulties, the more likely reason for "retiring" is that Southampton is now gaining public recognition while beginning his rise at Court; and in this view, Oxford is stepping aside to avoid being associated with his royal son. He will soon begin to support him (from behind the scenes, wielding his pen) as William Shakespeare.

Part One

THE SHAKESPEARE COMMITMENT
Sonnets 18 – 26
1592 – 1600

1592

Marlow, Lyly, 1592: Christopher Marlowe, the writer-spy who has been part of Oxford's circle of so-called University Wits, is carrying messages between the English government and the British ambassador in Paris. John Lyly's services as personal secretary and stage manager for Oxford now come to an end, and his career as a playwright will soon be over as well.

Henry VI, **March 3, 1592:** Although "Shakespeare" will not be known by name as a dramatist until 1598, his English history play *Henry VI* is performed for the public at the Rose in Southwark.

"*Henry VI* is a warlike play and was being acted before a war-time audience … I consider that it was, in all probability, a piece of deliberately inspired war propaganda, and that it was written with the express intention of arousing the patriotism and war-spirit of the civil population of England." (Captain Bernard M. Ward, 1929, in *Oxfordian Vistas*, Miller, 463)

Burghley Seeks New Marriage Alliance, 1592: "Lord Burghley has tried to marry Elizabeth Vere to (Henry Percy) Lord Northumberland … she cannot fancy him" – Cal. Ancaster MSS., Ward, p. 314. This indicates Burghley and the Queen consider Southampton's refusal of the Cecil alliance to be final. (But Burghley will keep his granddaughter Elizabeth Vere unmarried until Southampton reaches his majority at age twenty-one on October. 6, 1594, based on his "official" birth date of October 6, 1573.)

Southampton at Court, Fall 1592: "By now Southampton was spending a good part of his time in attendance at the Court." (Akrigg, 35) (This is just after Oxford has withdrawn from Court.)

Pierce Pennilesse, **1592:** Thomas Nashe, of Oxford's satellite writers the one who shares the most intimate working relationship with him (and who undoubtedly voices many of Oxford's thoughts and feelings, as dictated or written by Oxford himself), publishes *Pierce Pennilesse* in which he refers to the government's "policy" of plays. He also mentions Talbot of *Henry VI* and the great crowds of audiences that have been thrilled by the drama: "That state or kingdom that is in league with **all the world**, and hath no foreign sword to vex it, is not half so strong or confirmed to endure, as that which lives every hour in fear of **invasion**. There is a certain waste of the people for whom there is no use but war: and these men must have some **employment** still to cut them off … If they have no **service abroad**, they will make mutinies **at home** … To this effect the policy of Plays is very necessary, howsoever some shallow-brained censurers (not the deepest searchers into the secrets of government) mightily oppugne them…"

ALL THE WORLD: "as all the world doth judge" – Oxford to Burghley, September 1572; "Though I, once gone, to all the world must die" – Sonnet 81, line 6
INVASION … EMPLOYMENT: "then I shall be most willing to be employed on the sea coasts, to be in a readiness with my countryman against any invasion" – Oxford to Burghley, September 22, 1572
SERVICE ABROAD … AT HOME: "If there were any service to be done abroad, I had rather serve there than at home" – Oxford to Burghley, September 22, 1572

REFERENCE EDITION 131

Nashe continues:

"Nay, what if I prove Plays to be no extreme; but a rare exercise of virtue? First, for the subject of them (for the most part) is borrowed out of our English Chronicles, wherein our forefathers' valiant acts (that have lain long buried in rustic brass and worm-eaten books) are revived, and they themselves are raised from the Grave of Oblivion, and brought to plead their aged Honors in open presence ... How it would have joyed brave Talbot, the terror of the French, to think that after he had lain two hundred years in his Tomb, he should triumph again on the Stage, and have his bones new embalmed with the tears of ten thousand spectators...." - (*The Works of Thomas Nashe,* McKerrow, 1904, vol. 3)

"Shake-scene": September 20, 1592: A posthumous pamphlet entitled *Greenes Groats-worth of Witte* is published as the supposed dying testimony of Robert Greene, another writer in Oxford's circle who has dedicated at least one work to him; in fact, "Robert Greene" may have been a pen name for Oxford. The pamphlet includes this warning to fellow writers: "Yet trust them not: for there is an upstart Crow, beautified with our feathers, that with his *Tygers hart wrapt in a Players hyde*, supposes he is as well able to bombast out a blank verse as the best of you: and being an absolute *Johannes fact totum*, is in his own conceit *the only Shake-scene* in a country..." The phrase about the "Tygers hart" echoes *3 Henry VI*, 1.4.137: "O tiger's heart wrapt in a woman's hide!" Meanwhile "Shake-scene" foreshadows the pen name "Shakespeare" Oxford is about to use in public – on the dedication of *Venus and Adonis* to Southampton; ("Rough winds do *shake* the darling buds of May" – Sonnet 18, line 3, above)

Elizabeth and Southampton at Oxford, September 22-28, 1592: Queen Elizabeth visits Oxford University amid great celebrations – her first such appearance at either of the universities since Cambridge in 1564 and Oxford in 1566, when Edward de Vere received degrees. "During Elizabeth's visit ... she was surrounded by a gallant bevy of distinguished noblemen, of whom Southampton was one ... The glories of the Queen's reception were recorded in Latin verse, dated October 10, 1592 ...Essex was described as 'a Maecenas with wisdom unmatched ... *After him followed a Prince of a distinguished race, whom (rich in her right) Southampton blazons as a great hero.* No youth there present was more beautiful or more brilliant in the learned arts than this young prince of Hampshire, although his face was yet scarcely adorned by a tender down.'" (Charlotte Stopes, 1922, p. 50)

In the original 1592 Latin version of the poem, there appears in relation to Southampton the word "Dynasta," or *"a lord a great power, a prince, a ruler."* John Rollet translates: "After him there follows **a dynastic Prince** of illustrious lineage, whom as a great hero the rich House of Southampton lawfully lays claim to as one of its own." Rollet concludes the reference to Southampton as "Dynasta" can only mean "he was held to be in the line of succession of the Tudor dynasty ... so the author of the poem is in effect identifying Southampton as 'a Prince, one of a line of kings or princes,' or in other words, the Tudor heir and the Queen's son ... The writer of the verses chose a rare word (borrowed from the Greek) to convey his precise meaning, and would only have felt safe in doing so if it was widely believed that Southampton was the Queen's son ... it is clear that the University hoped to benefit from this graceful reference to Southampton's status, and that it would be expected to bring credit to the University if he ever became King" - Rollet, *Was Southampton Regarded as the Son of the Queen,* Part 3, 1999

A Political Comedy for Southampton, 1592-94: "Apparently at this time he [Shakespeare] also wrote *Love's Labour's Lost* for private production before Southampton and his friends. The play is full of topical allusions and coterie jokes" – Akrigg, 207; (Oxford undoubtedly wrote the original version of that play by 1579, based on events during 1578)

Death of Viscount Montague, October 1592: Anthony Browne, Viscount Montague, father of Mary Browne, Countess of Southampton, dies at his manor house in Surrey.

Part One

THE SHAKESPEARE COMMITMENT

Sonnet 18
Thy Eternal Summer
1592

Southampton has rejected the marriage proposal, spurning a Cecil family alliance and thereby losing the support of William Cecil for his royal claim. Soon the young earl will align himself with Robert Devereux Earl of Essex in opposition to the chief minister and his son Robert Cecil. Oxford pledges his support for his royal son. He vows to preserve the truth of Henry Wriothesley's royal life ("thy eternal Summer") in these "eternal lines to time" as "thou grow'st" along with the chronicle.

Sonnet 18	Translation
Shall I compare thee to a Summer's day?	Shall I compare you to a most royal prince?
Thou art more lovely and more temperate:	You are more royal with more claim to the throne:
Rough winds do shake the darling buds of May,	Difficulties beset royal children of the Tudor Rose,
And Summer's lease hath all too short a date:	And this golden time has all too short a date.
Sometimes too hot the eye of heaven shines,	Sometimes the son of Elizabeth burns too bright
And often is his gold complexion dimmed,	And often his true blood right can't be seen,
And every fair from fair sometime declines,	And every royal son sometimes loses his luster,
By chance, or nature's changing course untrim'd:	By chance or by Elizabeth's changing mind.
But thy eternal Summer shall not fade,	But your eternal royalty will not die,
Nor lose possession of that fair thou ow'st,	Nor will you lose that royalty you owe England,
Nor shall death brag thou wandr'st in his shade,	Nor will Elizabeth's death conquer it,
When in eternal lines to time thou grow'st,	When it grows in these eternal lines of my diary.
So long as men can breath or eyes can see,	So long as men can breathe or eyes can see,
So long lives this, and this gives life to thee.	So long lives this verse, and it gives life to you.

1 SHALL I COMPARE THEE TO A SUMMER'S DAY?
SUMMER'S DAY = a king; (Shall I compare you to a King); the golden sunlight of the day, when the light of the sun-king shines most brightly; "Now is the winter of our discontent, made glorious *summer* by this son of York" – *Richard III*, 1.1.1-2; "That sun that warms you here, shall shine on me" – *Richard II,* 1.3.145-146; "Good time of *day* unto your royal grace!" – *Richard III*, 1.3.18; "When is the royal *day*?" – *Richard III*, 3.4.3; "Poor grooms are sightless night, *kings glorious day*" – *Lucrece*, 1013; "As all the world is cheered by the sun, so I by that; it is *my day, my life*" – Richard in *Richard III*, 1.2.133-134

2 THOU ART MORE LOVELY AND MORE TEMPERATE:
LOVELY = filled with "love" or royal blood; echoing Southampton as "the little Love-God" of Sonnet 154, line 1; as "Lord of my love" of Sonnet 26, line 1; and as 'my *lovely* Boy' of Sonnet 126, line 1, in addition

REFERENCE EDITION 133

to: "And you and love are still my argument" – Sonnet 76, line 10; **TEMPERATE** = "The poem develops into a comparison between things of lasting duration – things that are unchanging – and things of limited duration – things that change; in that connection it is worth noting that the Latin source of *temperate* ... is derived from *tempus* – 'a period of time' or 'time' in general" – Booth; "The king-becoming graces, as Justice, Verity, *Temp'rance*, Stableness, Bounty..." – *Macbeth*, 4.3.91-93

3 ROUGH WINDS DO SHAKE THE DARLING BUDS OF MAY,
ROUGH WINDS DO SHAKE = the storm over the marriage proposal, which Burghley is keeping open until Southampton is officially twenty-one years old in October 1594; **SHAKE** = Oxford's allusion to his pen name "William Shakespeare" that he will introduce next year, by way of dedicating *Venus and Adonis* to Southampton; "Upon those boughs which *shake* against the cold" – Sonnet 73, line 3, written in 1601 in reference to "William Shake-speare" appearing as author of *The Phoenix and Turtle* that year; **DARLING BUDS** = royal children; royal buds of the Tudor Rose

BUDS OF MAY = "Out of these **Roses** sprang two noble **buds**, Prince Arthur and Henry..." - *Euphues and his England*, Lyly, 1580; Southampton is a royal bud of the Tudor Rose born in late May or early June of 1574 (as opposed to his "official" birth date of October 6, 1573, when the Countess of Southampton gave birth to a son; "We must remember that May in Shakespeare's time ran on to within a few days of our mid-June" – Dowden; "When wert thou born, Desire?/ In pomp and prime of May/ By whom, *sweet boy*, wert thou begot?/ By Fond Conceit, men say" – poem attributed to Oxford in *The Arte of English Poesie*, 1589; in these private sonnets, Southampton is the budding flower of the Tudor Rose, born in May of 1574 following "the lovely April" of Elizabeth's *prime* or late stage of pregnancy:

Within thine own *bud* buriest thy content - Sonnet 1, line 11

Thou art *thy mother's glass*, and she in thee
Calls back *the lovely April of her prime* - Sonnet 3, lines 9-10

With *April's first-born flowers*, and all things rare - Sonnet 21, line 7

When summer's breath their *masked buds* discloses - Sonnet 54, line 8
How with this rage shall beauty hold a plea,

Whose action is no stronger than a *flower*? - Sonnet 65, lines 3-4

Why should poor beauty indirectly seek
Roses of shadow, since his Rose is true? - Sonnet 67, lines 7-8
Thus is his cheek the map of days outworn,
When *beauty lived and died as flowers* do now.
Before these *bastard signs of fair were borne* - Sonnet 68, lines 1-3

For canker vice the *sweetest buds* doth love - Sonnet 70, line 7

4 AND SUMMER'S LEASE HATH ALL TOO SHORT A DATE:
SUMMER'S LEASE = The loan of royal blood and royal claim to Southampton; i.e., from Elizabeth ("Can yet the *lease* of my true love control" – Sonnet 107, line 3); "Nature's bequest gives nothing but doth lend,/ And being frank she lends to those are free" - Sonnet 4, lines 3-4; "That use is not forbidden usury/ Which happies those that pay the willing loan;/ That's for thy self to breed another thee" - Sonnet 6, lines 5-7

ALL = Southampton; **TOO SHORT** = ends too quickly in real time; "Wer't ought [aught] to me I bore the canopy,/ With my extern the outward honoring,/ Or laid great bases for eternity,/ Which proves *more short* than waste or ruining?" – Sonnet 125, lines 1-4, marking the funeral of Elizabeth on April 28, 1603, and referring to such royal ceremony that ends even before the House of Tudor can be "wasted" or "ruined"; **DATE** = the date by which the loan must be repaid, i.e., before the time of the Queen's death and the royal succession; in other words, that date is "all too short" or coming sooner than you might think

5 **SOMETIME TOO HOT THE EYE OF HEAVEN SHINES,**
TOO HOT = with too much royal power; **HEAVEN** = Elizabeth

EYE OF HEAVEN = Southampton as the golden eye or sun of Heaven, i.e., son of Elizabeth and royal prince or son of England; ("*that sun, thine eye*" – Sonnet 49, line 6; "Shall the blessed *sun of heaven* prove a micher ... Shall the *son of England* prove a thief" – Falstaff, pretending to be Henry IV addressing his son, Prince Hal, the future King Henry Fifth in *Henry IV*, 2.4.403-405; "And truly not the morning *Sun of Heaven*" – Sonnet 132, line 5, to Elizabeth, about Southampton as royal son; "The borrowed glories that by *gift of heaven*, by law of nature and of nations, 'longs to him and his heirs, namely the crown" – *Henry V*, 2.4.79-81); "This royal infant, *heaven* still move about her" – Cranmer in *Henry VIII*, 5.4.17, about the infant Princess Elizabeth

SHINES = "Even so *my Sunne one early morn did shine*,/ With all triumphant splendor on my brow" – Sonnet 33, lines 9-10

6 **AND OFTEN IS HIS GOLD COMPLEXION DIMMED,**
GOLD COMPLEXION = royal appearance; ("*Kingship is naturally golden*, and golden impressions recur (in the Sonnets) with similar variations in use ... The Sun is nature's king, and also pre-eminently golden; throughout Shakespeare, king and sun are compared ... We have various clusters of *king, gold, and sun*; king and gold come together in 'the gilded monument of princes" (55); and sun and gold, when the Sun's 'gold complexion' is dimmed (18) ... or the young man graces 'the day' and 'gilds' the evening in place of stars (28); we may have all three; so 'great Princes' favorites' are compared to the marigold opening to the Sun's 'eye' (25) ... These impressions are not just decoration" – G. Wilson Knight, 1962)

7 **AND EVERY FAIR FROM FAIR SOME-TIME DECLINES**
EVERY = Ever = E. Ver, Edward de Vere, *Ever or Never*; **FAIR** = Southampton, royal son, the "fairest creatures" of Sonnet 1, line 1; **EVERY FAIR** = Oxford's royal son; **EVERY FAIR FROM FAIR SOME-TIMES DECLINES** = every royal prince sometimes declines from his royal stature; (this applies, secondarily, to the Queen as well)

8 **BY CHANCE, OR NATURE'S CHANGING COURSE UNTRIMMED:**
NATURE'S CHANGING COURSE = Elizabeth's changing mind or attitude; "As to behold desert a beggar born,/ And needy nothing *trimmed* in jollity" – Sonnet 66, lines 2-3, about Southampton having been born a royal bastard trimmed or dressed up as an earl

9 **BUT THY ETERNAL SUMMER SHALL NOT FADE,**
THY ETERNAL SUMMER = your immortal royalty; "To the onlie begetter of these ensuing sonnets, Mr. W. H., all happiness and *that eternity promised* by our ever-living poet" – the dedication of the 1609 quarto of the Sonnets

10 **NOR LOSE POSSESSION OF THAT FAIR THOU OW'ST,**
THAT FAIR THOU OW'ST = that royal blood you owe to England, both by passing it on and by becoming king; ("that beauty thou possessest" – Dowden); "Pity the world, or else this glutton be,/ To eat *the world's due,* by the grave and thee" - Sonnet 1, lines 13-14

11 NOR SHALL DEATH BRAG THOU WANDR'ST IN HIS SHADE,
Nor will mortal death boast of capturing you.

12 WHEN IN ETERNAL LINES TO TIME THOU GROW'ST.
ETERNAL LINES TO TIME = The lines of my verse, the Sonnets, are written according to the mortal time left in Elizabeth's life, but, paradoxically, also written to preserve you for eternity; the Tudor line; "What! Will the *line* stretch out to th'crack of doom?" - *Macbeth*, 4.1.117

THOU GROW'ST = you are growing in the womb of the monument of the Sonnets, as my diary records events in real time; "The *living record* of your memory" – Sonnet 55, line 8; in the final chronological verse Oxford will hark back to this concept: "O Thou my lovely Boy, who in thy power/ Dost hold time's fickle glass, his sickle hour,/ Who hast by waning *grown*, and therein show'st/ Thy lovers withering, as thy sweet self *grow'st*" – Sonnet 126, lines 1-4; (the "lovers" of the preceding line are Oxford and then-deceased Elizabeth, his parents, as well as Southampton's supporters and would-be subjects of his reign).

13 SO LONG AS MEN CAN BREATH OR EYES CAN SEE,
For as long as civilization exists; "Your monument shall be my gentle verse,/ Which eyes not yet created shall o'er-read,/ And tongues to be your being shall rehearse,/ When all the *breathers* of this world are dead./ You still shall live (such virtue hath my Pen)/ *Where breath most breathes, even in the mouths of men*" – Sonnet 81, lines 9-14

14 SO LONG LIVES THIS, AND THIS GIVES LIFE TO THEE.
SO LONG LIVES THIS = so long will this verse continue to live; **THIS GIVES LIFE TO THEE** = the Monument being constructed by these verses contains a womb that is recreating your royal life and growing you, to create "The *living record* of your memory" – Sonnet 55, line 8; "Methinks **the truth should live** *from age to age*" – *Richard III*, 3.1.76; "Death makes no conquest of this conqueror, for now *he lives in fame, though not in life*" – of Julius Caesar in *Richard III*, 3.1.87-88; "This grave shall have a *living monument*" – *Hamlet*, 5.1.297

1593

Birth of Oxford's Legitimate Son, February 24, 1593: Edward de Vere's second wife Elizabeth Trentham gives birth to a son, the first male heir of the Oxford earldom.

Christening of Oxford's Son, March 31, 1593: Oxford's legitimate son is christened Henry de Vere, the future Eighteenth Earl of Oxford, in the Parish Church in Stoke Newington. He is the first Henry in the 500-year earldom.

"There must have been some reason for his being given this name, but if so I have been unable to discover it … In later life Henry deVere and Henry Wriothesley were closely connected as Colonels of two of the regiments raised for special service in the Low Countries in 1624. Perhaps, therefore, Henry Wriothesley was the cause of the name being introduced into the de Vere family." (B. M. Ward, 313)

VENUS AND ADONIS **to Henry Wriothesley, April 18, 1593:** The long narrative poem *Venus and Adonis*, written by "William Shakespeare" and dedicated by him to Henry Wriothesley, Third Earl of Southampton, is entered at the Stationers Register for printing and sale this year. Although it is highly erotic and suggestive of the Queen as Venus, Goddess of Love and Beauty, Archbishop John Whitgift issues the license in his own hand – indicating Elizabeth ordered special treatment for the book in keeping it free from

No. 18

government censorship.

The publisher of *Venus and Adonis* is Richard Field, who came to London from Stratford-upon-Avon in 1579. He published *The Arte of English Poesie* in 1589, with its high praise for Edwardde Vere, Earl of Oxford, as a poet; and also in 1589 he printed a handsome new edition of Ovid's *Metamorphoses* as translated by Oxford's uncle Arthur Golding.

Field will be the printer of Shakespeare's *Lucrece* next year, also dedicated to Southampton; and in 1601 he will publish the collection of verses containing *The Phoenix and the Turtle* attributed to "William Shakespeare" in reaction to the Rebellion of February 8, 1601. Richard Field was already a central figure in the issuance of works related to Edward de Vere and now he becomes involved with Oxford's poetry as by "William Shakespeare" (the first appearance of this name as an author) in relation to Henry Wriothesley, Earl of Southampton.

Oxford very likely wrote the first (private) version of *Venus and Adonis* at least a decade ago, describing how Elizabeth attempted to woo and seduce him by the early 1570s. The poem expresses that aspect of their relationship as a partial description of why and how Southampton, born to the Queen in May/June 1574, was conceived in late August or September 1573.

VENUS AND ADONIS
Vilia miretur vulgus: mihi flavus Apollo
Pocula Castalia plena ministret agua.

LONDON
Imprinted by Richard Field, and are to be sold at
The signe of the white Greyhound in
Paules Church-yard
1593.

VENUS: Queen Elizabeth
ADONIS: Edward de Vere

LATIN EPIGRAPH (from Ovid's *Amores*):

*"Let the mob admire base things: may Golden Apollo
serve me full goblets from the Castalian Spring!"*

> TO THE RIGHT HONORABLE
> Henry Wriothesley, Earle of Southampton,
> And Baron of Tichfield
> Right Honourable,
>
> I know not how I shall offend in dedicating my unpolished lines to your Lordship, nor how the world will censure me for choosing so strong a prop to support so weak a burden. Only, if your Honour seem but pleased, I account my self highly praised, and vow to take advantage of all idle hours, till I have honoured you with some *graver labour*. But if the *first heir of my invention* prove *deformed*, I shall be sorry it had so noble a *godfather*: and never after ear so *barren* a land, for fear it yield me still so bad a harvest. I leave it to your Honourable survey, and your Honour to your heart's content, which I wish may always answer your own wish, and *the world's hopeful expectation*.
>
> Your Honors in *all duty*,
> William Shakespeare

In this dedication Oxford is deliberately adopting a fawning tone, typical of that used by writers toward their noble patrons; but this also allows him to address his on, publicly and directly, in the roles of a father to his son and of a subject pledging "duty" to his sovereign.

"GRAVER LABOUR": more serious labor; related to childbirth, Oxford as parent to child; referring also to *Lucrece*, to be published next year, and to the ongoing private sonnets, which are becoming the "womb" for his son; also the effort to help him gain the throne.

"FIRST HEIR OF MY INVENTION": Southampton as royal heir, his birth contained in the poem itself; the poem as the first heir of Oxford's invented name, "Shakespeare"; his son as "heir" to the "invention" or method of writing the private sonnets; ("And keep *invention* in a noted weed" – Sonnet 76, line 6; "For whose so dumb that cannot write to thee,/ When thou thyself doth give *invention* light?" – Sonnet 39, lines 7-8; "Fair, kind, and true, is all my argument,/ Fair, kind, and true, varying to other words,/ And in this change is my *invention* spent" – Sonnet 105, lines 9-11; and all of "Shakespeare" including the Sonnets is the "invention" for Southampton in support of his claim to the throne.

"DEFORMED": illegitimate; lack of acknowledgment as royal prince; failure to gain the throne

"GODFATHER": the inspirer of the poem; also, Henry Wriothesley may have stood as godfather to Oxford's first-born legitimate son, born several weeks ago and more recently named Henry in his honor.

"BARREN": childless; empty of acknowledgment that Southampton is Oxford's son by the Queen; ("Why is my verse so *barren* of new pride?" – Sonnet 76, line 1)

"THE WORLD'S HOPEFUL EXPECTATION": England's royal heir to the throne; "The *world's fresh ornament*" – Sonnet 1, line 9; "The *hope and expectation* of thy time" – *1 Henry IV*, 3.2.36, the King to his son, Prince Henry; "the expectation of the world" – Prince Henry speaking of himself in *2 Henry IV*, 5.2.126); "But *hope* of orphans, and unfathered fruit" – Sonnet 97, line 10, Oxford writing of Southampton, whose hope for the crown has been crushed

"ALL": Southampton, his motto *One for All, All for One*

"DUTY": Oxford as subject to his king; ("Thy merit hath my duty knit/ … To witness duty, not to show my wit./ Duty so great…" – Sonnet 26, lines 2,4-5)

"WILLIAM": Will, a poet; carrying out the royal will; ("Thy kingdom come, thy *will* be done" – Lord's Prayer); possibly a play on "WILL I AM")

"SHAKESPEARE": Oxford the spear-shaker of the tiltyard, now shaking the spear of his pen; ("Thy countenance shakes spears" – Gabriel Harvey in a Latin oration to Oxford in 1578 in front of Elizabeth and her Court); summoning the image of Pallas Athena, patroness of the arts, with her spear; therefore, Oxford adopts the name for Elizabeth and her lineage, i.e., Southampton

VENUS AND ADONIS begins with a portrayal of how Queen Elizabeth wooed young Edward de Vere from at least as early as his emergence at Court in 1571 at age twenty-one to the fall of 1573, when she conceived their child near her fortieth birthday:

> Even as the sun with purple-colored face
> Had ta'en his last leave of the weeping morn,
> Rose-cheeked Adonis hied him to the chase;
>   Sick-thoughted Venus makes amain unto him,
>   And like a bold-fac'd suitor 'gins to woo him… - 1-6
>
> He burns with bashful shame, she with her tears
> Doth quench the maiden burning of his cheeks… - 49-50

Within the poem, now updated, Oxford has inserted thirty-six lines directly alluding to the theme and urgency of the seventeen marriage-and-procreation sonnets already written and delivered to Southampton. Because the marriage proposal involving Burghley's granddaughter Elizabeth Vere is still technically open, Oxford uses this occasion to reiterate in public what he told his royal son in private. In the narrative poem Venus, speaking for Elizabeth, makes the case to Southampton:

> Make use of time, let not advantage slip;
> Beauty within itself should not be wasted.
>   Fair flowers that are not gathered in their prime
>   Rot, and consume themselves in little time… - 127-132
>
> Torches are made to light, jewels to wear;
> Dainties to taste, fresh beauty for the use,
> Herbs for their smell, and sappy plants to bear:
> Things growing to themselves are growth's abuse.
>   Seeds spring from seeds, and beauty breedeth beauty;
>   Thou wast begot, to get it is thy duty. - 163-168
>
> Upon the earth's increase why shouldst thou feed,
> Unless the earth with thy increase be fed?
> By law of nature thou art bound to breed,
> That thine may live when thou thyself art dead;
>   And so in spite of death thou dost survive,
>   In that thy likeness still is left alive… - 169-174
>
> Therefore despite of fruitless chastity,
> Love-lacking vestals and self-loving nuns,
> That on earth would breed a scarcity
> And barren dearth of daughters and of sons,
>   Be prodigal; the lamp that burns by night
>   Dries up his oil to lend the world his light. - 751-756
>
> What is thy body but a swallowing grave,
> Seeming to bury that posterity,
> Which by rights of time thou needs must have,
> If thou destroy them not in dark obscurity?
>   If so, the world will hold thee in disdain,
>   Sith in thy pride so fair a hope is slain. - 757-762

> So in thyself thyself art made away;
> A mischief worse than civil home-bred strife,
> Or theirs whose desperate hands themselves do slay,
> Or butcher sire that reaves his son of life.
>   Foul cank'ring rust the hidden treasure frets,
>   But gold that's put to use more gold begets. - 763-768

In the above stanza Oxford refers to the "civil home-bred strife" that will swirl around the throne as time leads inevitably to the death of Elizabeth and to the succession. Now that Southampton has joined Essex in opposition to William Cecil, Lord Burghley, and his son Robert Cecil, the stage has been set for a turbulent power struggle to control the choice of successor. In *Venus and Adonis*, therefore, Oxford makes a last-ditch effort to bring his royal son to his senses. Again he tries to make him see that an alliance with the Cecils will not only give him the best chance to become King Henry IX but, as well, to avoid civil war in England.

As the poem nears its conclusion, Oxford identifies himself as "true" from his motto *Nothing Truer than Truth* in conjunction with the "boar" from the insignia of his earldom and with the "spear" of Shakespeare. Oxford has slain his own identity by adopting the pen name:

> 'Tis true, 'tis true, thus was Adonis slain:
> He ran upon the *boar* with his sharp *spear*... - 1111-1112

He thereby gives birth (or rebirth) to Southampton as the "purple flower" or royal Tudor Rose:

> By this the boy that by her side lay killed
> Was melted like a vapor from her sight,
> And *in his blood that on the ground lay spilled,*
> *A purple flower sprung up...* - 1165-1168

Elizabeth/Venus now declares the new "flower" to be her successor:

> 'Poor flower,' quoth she, 'this was thy father's guise –
> Sweet issue of a more sweet-smelling sire... - 1177-1178

> 'Here was thy father's bed, here in my breast;
> Thou art next of blood, and 'tis thy right...' - 1183-1184

The poem concludes with a vision of Elizabeth, still the goddess and Virgin Queen, stealing away on her chariot without having divulged the secret of Southampton's birth:

> Thus weary of the world, away she hies,
> And yokes her silver doves, by whose swift aid
> Their Mistress mounted through the empty skies,
> In her light chariot quickly is conveyed,
> *Holding their course to Paphos, where their Queen*
> *Means to immure herself and not be seen.* - 1189-1194

The image is the same as that of *A Midsummer Night's Dream*, depicting Elizabeth as moving ahead while abandoning Southampton as the "flower" of her Tudor Rose:

> *And the Imperial Votress passed on,*

> *In maiden meditation, fancy free.*
> Yet marked I where the bolt of Cupid fell:
> It fell upon *a little western flower*,
> Before milk-white, *now purple with love's wound* - (2.1.163-167)

Oxford in 1601 will recall his son's birth in spring/summer 1574 and how Elizabeth began her progress that July to the west, carrying her "disgrace" of the boy after leaving him behind:

> And from the forlorn world his visage hide,
> Stealing unseen to west with this disgrace
> - Sonnet 33, lines 7-8

Tribute to Southampton, May 1593: Barnabe Barnes publishes a collection of poems including a sonnet to Henry Wriothesley, referring to his "sacred hands which sacred Muses make their instrument" – indicating Barnes is aware of Southampton receiving special attention.

Southampton proposed as Knight of the Garter, May 1593: "In 1593 Southampton was mentioned for nomination as a Knight of the Garter, and although he was not chosen the compliment of nomination was, at his age, *unprecedented outside the circle of the sovereign's kinsmen*." (Sidney Lee, 1900, *DNB*)

"He (Southampton) was not appointed, but the fact of his name having been proposed was in itself an honor so great at his early age that *it had never before been paid to anyone not of Royal Blood.*" – (Stopes, 55); a clear indication that some at Court knew Southampton's true identity

Peele celebrates Southampton, 1593: "George Peele, writing *The Honour of the Garter* this year, made a non-existent Earl of Southampton an original member of the Order and then worked in a smooth compliment to 'Gentle Wriothesley, South-Hamptons starre.'" - Akrigg, 36

Peele links Southampton with Elizabeth as Cynthia, the Moon goddess:

> Gentle Wriothesley, South-Hamptons starre,
> I wish all fortune that in ***Cynthia's eye***
> Cynthia the glory of the Western world,
> With all the stares in her fair firmament,
> Bright may he rise and shine immortally.

(***Cynthia's Eye*** = the eye of Elizabeth as Cynthia, Goddess of the Moon, recalling Sonnet 153, lines 13-14: "the bath for my help lies/ Where Cupid got new fire, *my mistress' eye*"; also "My Mistress' eyes are nothing like the Sunne" – Sonnet 130, line 1)

Death of Marlowe, May 30, 1593: Christopher Marlowe is murdered in the presence of three other men working as government agents.

Nashe dedicates to Southampton, June 1593: Thomas Nashe dedicates *The Unfortunate Traveller, or the Life of Jacke Wilton* to Southampton, giving clear evidence of his intimate knowledge that the earl has been the subject of Oxford's sonnets and poems, and awareness of Southampton as a royal prince: "My reverent *dutiful* thoughts (even from their infancy) have been retainers to *your glory*. Now at last I have enforced an opportunity to plead my devoted mind ... Incomprehensible is the height of your spirit both in heroical resolution and matters of conceit. Unreprievably perisheth that book whatsoever to waste paper which on the diamond rock of your judgment disasterly chanceth to be shipwrecked.

"A dear lover and cherisher you are, as well of the lovers of Poets, as of Poets themselves. Amongst their sacred number, I dare not ascribe myself, though now and then I speak English; that small brain I have to no further use I convert, save to be kind to my friends and fatal to my enemies. A new brain, a new wit, a new style, a new soul will I get me, *to canonize your name to posterity*, if in this, my first attempt I be not taxed of presumption. Of *your gracious favor* I despair not, for I am not altogether Fame's outcast …

"Your Lordship is the large spreading branch of renown, from whence these my idle leaves seek to derive their whole nourishing: it resteth you either scornfully *shake* them off as worm-eaten and worthless, or in pity preserve them and cherish them for some little summer fruit you hope to find amongst them. Your Honors in all humble service, Tho: Nashe" (Italics added.)

Oxford again speaks through Nashe; he was apparently on closer terms with him than with any of the other writers in their circle. (See notes for *Choice of Valentines* by Nashe in 1594.) This year Nashe will publish the book *Strange News* with a remarkable dedication to "the most copious Carminist of our time," who – as argued by Charles Wisner Barrell in the 1940s and by Dorothy Ogburn in the 1950s – was Oxford himself, whom Nashe refers to as "Gentle Master William."

Nash calls Southampton a "dear lover" or royal son of "Poets" – of Oxford himself – and points to his newly adopted pen name of "Shakespeare" by referring to a "new brain, a new wit, a new style, a new soul" by which he will "canonize your name to posterity." In the third paragraph, the word "shake" appears ("scornfully shake them off") as it had appeared in Sonnet 18, line 3 ("Rough winds do *shake* the darling buds of May").

No. 18

THE PHOENIX NEST, 1593: This publication contains essays and poems signed with various printed initials, including "E. O." for Earl of Oxford under the following lines obviously referring to Queen Elizabeth:

What *cunning* can express	(knowledge and/or skill)
The *favor* of her face,	
To whom in this distress,	
I do appeal for *grace*.	(royal grace)
A thousand Cupids fly	
About *her gentle eye*.	("my mistress' eye" – Son. 153, line 14)
From which each throws a *dart*	(Spear)
That *kindleth* soft sweet *fire*	("love-kindling fire" – Son. 153.3)
Within my sighing heart,	
Possessed by desire:	
No sweeter life I try,	
Than in her *love* to die.	(Royal blood)
The *lily* in the field	("the lily I condemned" – Son. 99.6)
That glories in his *white*	
For pureness now must yield,	
And *render* up his right:	("render thee" – Son. 126.12)
Heaven pictured in her face	Elizabeth in the Sonnets)
Doth promise *joy* and *grace*.	("joy delights in joy" – Son. 8.2)
Fair Cynthia's silver light,	(Elizabeth, the Moon goddess Diana)
That beats on running *streams*,	("Gilding pale streams" – Son. 33.4)
Compares not with her white,	
Whose *hairs* are all sunbeams;	("If hairs be wires" – Son. 130.4)
Her virtues so do shine	
As day unto mine eyne.	
With this there is a *red*,	("*Roses* damasked" – Son. 130.5)
Exceeds the *damask rose*,	("Roses … in her cheeks" – Son. 130.6)
Which *in her cheeks* is spread;	(E. Ver; royal favor)
Whence *every favor* grows;	
In sky there is no star,	
That she surmounts not far.	
When *Poebus* from the bed	(Apollo = Oxford)
Of Thetis doth arise,	
The morning blushing red,	
In fair carnation wise,	
He shows it in her face,	
As *Queen* of *every* grace.	(Elizabeth; E. Ver)
This pleasant *lily white*,	("the lily's white" – Son. 98.9)
This taint of *roseate red*,	("red and white" – Son. 130.5)
This *Cynthia's silver light*,	(Elizabeth's royal light)
This *sweet fair Dea* spread,	(royal goddess)
These sunbeams in mine eye,	
These beauties make me die.	("all those beauties" – Son. 63.6)

- E. O. (Earl of Oxford); italics added

The "nest" of the Phoenix is the throne of Elizabeth (and it is no coincidence that the Phoenix appears in Sonnet 19, corresponding with this year). Oxford has already written most or even all these verses, perhaps as early as the 1570s, in relation to Southampton and Elizabeth:

In **heaven Queen** she is among the spheres,
In eye the **Mistress** like makes all things pure,
Eternity in her oft change she bears,
She **beauty** is, by her the **fair** endure.

In the following stanza Elizabeth is "a dame of state" accused of having committed "a secret murder" by refusing in 1574 to acknowledge her son. (The Queen's "unkindness" is her rejection of her "kind" or natural son.) In the same breath she is called a wife:

> A Secret murder hath been done of late,
> Unkindness found to be the bloody knife,
> And she that did the deed **a dame of state**,
> **Fair, gracious, wife**, as any **beareth life.**

The stanza below is a mirror image of the Shakespeare sonnets (though written in tetrameter):

> And as you see the scarlet Rose,
> In his sweet prime, his buds disclose,
> Whose hew is with the Sun revived,
> So in the April of mine age,
>   My lovely colors do assuage,
>   Because my Sun-shine is deprived

And in the following stanza, Oxford can be seen pleading for his son:

> Now if I him forsake, and he not find,
> His wretched exile, succored by your eyes,
> He cannot yield, to serve another's mind,
> Nor live alone, for nature that denies,
>   Then die he must, for other choice is none,
>   But live in you, or me, or die alone.

Part One

THE SHAKESPEARE COMMITMENT

Sonnet 19
Succeeding Men

1593

Oxford publishes Venus and Adonis *with no name on the title page, but he uses the printed signature "William Shakespeare" (for the first time) to dedicate this long narrative poem to Southampton as "the first heir of my invention," pledging his duty and support – actually announcing his support for Henry Wriothesley's claim as "first heir" or immediate successor to Elizabeth on the throne. Meanwhile he continues this private diary, signifying the Queen as the Phoenix (with which she has identified herself) and promising his royal son that he will "ever live young" in its lines.*

Sonnet 19	Translation
Devouring time, blunt thou the Lion's paws,	Elizabeth's ever-waning life, devour all things,
And make the earth devour her own sweet brood,	And make England consume its own royal princes,
Pluck the keen teeth from the fierce Tiger's jaws,	Pluck the keen teeth from the Tiger's jaws,
And burn the long-lived Phoenix in her blood,	And destroy the Queen in her own royal blood!
Make glad and sorry seasons as thou fleet'st,	Make us glad and sorry as you rush to her death,
And do what ere thou wilt swift-footed time	And do what you will, swiftly fading time,
To the wide world and all her fading sweets:	To England and all her withering royal blood:
But I forbid thee one most heinous crime:	But I forbid you to commit one worst crime:
O carve not with thy hours my love's fair brow,	O do not take my son's royal life with you,
Nor draw no lines there with thine antique pen.	Nor make him lose his royal blood with your pen!
Him in thy course untainted do allow,	As you take your course, leave him alone,
For beauty's pattern to succeeding men.	So Elizabeth's blood can be passed to successors.
Yet do thy worst, old Time! Despite thy wrong,	Yet do your worst, old Time! Despite your cruelty,
My love shall in my verse ever live young.	My royal son in these Sonnets will always be fresh.

1 DEVOURING TIME, BLUNT THOU THE LION'S PAWS,
DEVOURING TIME = the tyranny of Elizabeth's ever-waning life in real time; "Thou *tyme the eater up of things*, and age of spyghtfull teene,/ Destroy all things" – Ovid's *Metamorphoses*, XV, 258-259, translation as by Arthur Golding, Oxford's uncle, published in 1567, but more likely rendered by the young earl himself; there is an echo of "De Vere" in "Devouring"

LION: Elizabeth said of herself, "Do you not know that *we are descended of the Lion*…?" – *Arte of English Poesie*, 1589, p. 303; **LION'S PAWS** = destructive force of this royal beast; Elizabeth is the female counterpart, i.e., lioness, and her own rage is the enemy

> He hath more worthy interest to the state
> Than thou the shadow of succession.
> For of no right, nor colour like to right,
> He doth fill fields with harness in the realm,
> Turns heads **against the lion's armed jaws**…
> - *1 Henry IV*, 3.2.98-102

> Against whose fury and unmatched force
> The aweless **lion** could not wage the fight,
> Nor keep his princely heart from Richard's hand.
> He that perforce robs *lions* of their hearts
> May easily win a woman's.
> - *Richard II*, 1.1.264-269

"The *lion* will not touch the true prince" – *1 Henry IV*, 2.4.267-268; "The king is to be feared as the *lion*" – *1 Henry IV*, 3.3.150; "the *kingly lion*" – *3 Henry VI*, 5.7.11; "The *lion* dying thrusteth forth his paw, and wounds the earth, if nothing else, with rage … which art *a lion and a king* of beasts" – *Richard II*, 5.1.29-30, 34

The rage of the lion is the enemy, i.e., rage being the forces against Oxford's royal son, including Elizabeth as royal beast full of rage. Later, when Southampton is in the Tower facing imminent execution: "How with this *rage* shall beauty hold a plea" – Sonnet 65, line 3, with "beauty" = your royal blood from the Queen

"Now, both reason and authority testify to the right of the commonwealth to deliver itself from the government of 'a tyrant, a *Tigar*, a fearse *Lion*, a ravening wolfe, a publique enemy, and a bloody murtherer'"
- Robert Parsons, under the pseudonym of "Doleman", 1594, *A Conference about the Next Succession to the Crowne of Ingland*, dedicated to the Earl of Essex, quoted by Lily Campbell, Shakespeare's Histories, 1947, p. 178

2 AND MAKE THE EARTH DEVOUR HER OWN SWEET BROOD,
THE EARTH = England; **SWEET BROOD** = royal heirs; children, offspring; specifically her son Southampton; "She will … bring thee forth *brave brood*" – *The Tempest*, 3.2.106

3 PLUCK THE KEEN TEETH FROM THE FIERCE TIGER'S JAWS,
PLUCK = draw down, bring down, snatch, pull sharply; "And *pluck the crown* from feeble Henry's head" – *2 Henry VI*, 5.1.2; "If Nature, sovereign mistress over wrack/ As thou goest onwards still will *pluck* thee back" – Sonnet 126, lines 5-6, after the Queen's death, when "nature" becomes the universal "sovereign mistress" or queen; "(Presenting the crown): Lo, here, this long-usurped royalty from the dead temples of this bloody wretch have I pluck'd off to grace thy brows withal. Wear it, enjoy it, and make much of it" – *Richard III*, 5.5.4-7

TIGER = "O *tiger's* heart wrapt in a woman's hide! How couldst thou drain the life-blood of the child, to bid the father wipe his eyes withal, and yet be seen to bear a woman's face?" – *3 Henry VI*, 1.4.137-140; "Ay me, I see the ruin of my House! The *tiger* now hath seized the gentle hind; insulting tyranny begins to jut upon the innocent and aweless throne. Welcome destruction, blood, and massacre, I see as in a map the end of all" – *Richard III*, 2.4.49-54; "This ravenous *tiger*, this accursed devil" – *Titus Andronicus*, 5.3.5

4 AND BURN THE LONG-LIVED PHOENIX IN HER BLOOD;
PHOENIX = Queen Elizabeth, who is the Phoenix of *The Phoenix' Nest*, published this year (1593), and she will be the Phoenix of *The Phoenix and Turtle* of 1601; "But, as when the bird of wonder dies, the maiden *Phoenix*, her ashes new create another heir as great in admiration as herself, so shall she leave her blessedness to one" – *Henry VIII*, 5.4.39-43, Archbishop Cranmer, predicting that newly born Princess Elizabeth Tudor will leave an heir to rise from her own ashes after she dies. The legendary bird of Arabia lived for 500 or 600 years; it then built a pile of twigs that was ignited by the sun, and upon that it burned itself; then it rose again, renewed & youthful.

"The chastity, longevity, and uniqueness of the Phoenix were familiar lore in the period, partly because the bird was often used as an emblem of Queen Elizabeth" – Kerrigan; "The Queen adopted the Phoenix as an emblem of herself, as unique as she was chaste" – Strong

IN HER BLOOD = the harsh image of Elizabeth, the unique bird that is supposed to rise from its own ashes, but here instead being burned in her own royal blood.

5 MAKE GLAD AND SORRY SEASONS AS THOU FLEE'ST,
GLAD = "We are *glad*" – *Henry V*, 1.2.260, the King, using the royal "we" in reference to himself; **GLAD AND SORRY** = "Yea, subject to your countenance, *glad or sorry* as I saw it inclined" – *Henry VIII*, 2.4.25-26, Queen Katherine pleading with the King; (Q = "fleet'st")

FLEE'ST = hurry by; "the pleasure of the *fleeting* year" – Sonnet 97, line 2

6 AND DO WHAT ERE THOU WILT, SWIFT-FOOTED TIME,
SWIFT-FOOTED TIME = days rushing toward the unpredictable date with succession

7 TO THE WIDE WORLD AND ALL HER FADING SWEETS;
THE WIDE WORLD = England and the whole world; "Not mine own fears nor the prophetic soul/ Of *the wide world* dreaming on things to come/ Can yet the lease of my true love control,/ Supposed as forfeit to a confined doom" – Sonnet 107, lines 1-4, upon Southampton's release from his "confined doom" in the Tower on April 10, 1603; **ALL** = Southampton, *One for All, All for One*

ALL HER FADING SWEETS = all of England's fading royal princes, i.e., Southampton; "*Sweet princes*, what I did, I did in honor" – *2 Henry VI*, 5.2.35

8 BUT I FORBID THEE ONE MOST HEINOUS CRIME:
ONE = Southampton, *One for All, All for One*; Oxford is speaking to Time, forbidding it "one" most heinous crime, i.e., the crime of treason against Southampton, a prince or king; in effect, accusing Elizabeth (Time) of committing treason against her son

9 O CARVE NOT WITH THY HOURS MY LOVE'S FAIR BROW,
CARVE = "She carved thee for her seal" – Sonnet 11, line 13; **MY LOVE'S FAIR BROW** = my royal son's royal stature

10 NOR DRAW NO LINES THERE WITH THINE ANTIQUE PEN;
LINES = wrinkles, signs of age; Oxford is again playing on "lines" for the lines of the Sonnets, which are working against time to keep restoring his youth or time of hope; yet he is recreating his son's life in this diary in relation to Time, or Elizabeth's waning life: "So should the *lines of life* that life repair/ Which *this (Time's pencil) or my pupil pen*" – Sonnet 16, lines 9-10; "And your true rights be termed a Poet's rage/ And

REFERENCE EDITION 147

stretched meter of *an Antique song*" – Sonnet 17, lines 11-12; and of Southampton again: "In him those holy *antique hours* are seen" – Sonnet 68, line 9; by then, his royal hope has been lost and become part of the "old age" as: "In *the old age* black was not counted fair/ Or if it were it bore not beauty's name" – Sonnet 127, lines 1-2, upon the imprisonment of Southampton on February 8, 1601, when he has lost his right to the throne and has been turned from "fair" to "black" in the Queen's imperial view

11 HIM IN THY COURSE UNTAINTED DO ALLOW
HIM = Southampton; **UNTAINTED** = not deprived of his legitimate right to the throne; ("Sweet prince, the untainted virtue of your years" – *Richard III*, 3.1.7; "And blood untainted still doth red abide" – *Lucrece*, stanza 250); **ALLOW:** "thou shalt be met with thanks, *allowed* with absolute power, and thy good name live with authority" – *Timon of Athens*, 5.1.161-163; "Without *the king's will or the state's allowance*" – *Henry VIII*, 3.2.322

12 FOR BEAUTY'S PATTERN TO SUCCEEDING MEN!
BEAUTY'S PATTERN = Elizabeth's lineage of blood; "She shall be ... a *pattern* to all princes living with her, and all that shall *succeed*" – *Henry VIII*, 5.4.20-22, Archbishop Cranmer, predicting the future of newly born Elizabeth Tudor; **SUCCEEDING MEN** = those who should succeed to the throne, i.e., Southampton and/or his own heirs; "Long after this, when Henry the Fifth, *succeeding* his father Bolingbroke, did reign" – *1 Henry VI*, 2.5.82-83; "Both to defend my loyalty and truth to God, my king and my *succeeding* issue" – *Richard II*, 1.3.19-20; "Henry the Seventh *succeeding*, truly pitying my father's loss, like a most royal prince" – *Henry VIII*, 2.1.112-113; "Yet hope, *succeeding* from so fair a tree as your fair self" – to the prince in *Pericles*, 1.1.115-116; "No son of mine *succeeding*" – *Macbeth*, 3.1.63; "to the *succeeding* royalty he leaves the healing benediction" – *Macbeth*, 4.3.155-156; "*Succeeding* by right of blood and inheritance" – Oxford to Robert Cecil, referring to the newly acclaimed King James I of England, April 1603

13 YET DO THY WORST, OLD TIME: DESPITE THY WRONG,
OLD TIME = the ever-waning life of Elizabeth; also, universal time; "Ever belov'd and loving may his rule be; and when *old time* shall lead him to his end, goodness and he fill up one monument!" – *Henry VIII*, 2.1.92-94

14 MY LOVE SHALL IN MY VERSE EVER LIVE YOUNG.
MY LOVE = my royal son; **IN MY VERSE** = in these verses; **EVER** = E. Ver, Edward deVere, *Ever or Never*; "Why write I still all one, *ever* the same" – Sonnet 76, line 5; "Since all alike my songs and praises be/ To one, of one, still such, and *ever* so" – Sonnet 105, lines 3-4; **EVER LIVE YOUNG** = another promise to give him eternal life in these verses; "And *that eternity promised* by our *ever*-living poet" – Dedication of the Sonnets; (by its position, "ever" gains accentual stress); **YOUNG** = fresh, green, in the golden time of hope

No. 19

> **LUCRECE**
>
> LONDON
> Printed by Richard Field, for John Harrison, and are
> To be sold at the figure of the white Greyhound
> In Paule's Church yard.   1594
>
> TO THE RIGHT
> HONOURABLE, HENRY
> Wriothesley, Earle of Southampton,
> And Baron of Titchfield
>
> *The love I dedicate to your Lordship* is *without end*: whereof this Pamphlet *without beginning* is but a superfluous Moiety. The *warrant* I have of your Honourable disposition, not *the worth* of my untutored Lines, makes it assured of acceptance. *What I have done is yours, what I have to do is yours, being part in all I have, devoted yours.* Were *my worth* greater, *my duty* would show greater; meantime, as it is, it is *bound to your Lordship*, to whom I wish long life still lengthened with *all happinesse.*
>
> Your Lordship's in *all duty*,
>   William Shakespeare

"There is no other dedication like this in Elizabethan literature. As The Rape of Lucrece was the last book that Shakespeare published, i.e., personally brought to the publisher, he did not again have occasion to speak of Southampton by name, and further proofs of their friendship must be sought in the Sonnets." – D. Nichol Smith, in "Shakespeare's England," vol. 2, 1916

LUCRECE = Queen Elizabeth
"THE LOVE I DEDICATE TO YOUR LORDSHIP" = "Lord of my love" – Sonnet 26, line 1; Love = royal blood; "And *you and love* are still my argument" – Sonnet 76, line 10
"WITHOUT END" = eternal;
"WITHOUT BEGINNING" = another aspect of godlike immortality
"WARRANT" = authorization, from Southampton as king
"THE WORTH" = the royal power
"WHAT I HAVE DONE IS YOURS," etc. = Oxford's pledge of never-ending commitment; *"What I have done is yours, what I have to do is yours, being part in all I have, devoted yours"* – the strongest possible words of public commitment and support to Southampton in his future efforts to gain the throne as Henry IX of England, without help from Burghley and his son Robert Cecil and even, soon enough, in the face of their opposition.
"MY WORTH" = royalty, i.e., I do not have such royal worth as you.
"MY DUTY" = my devotion and service as your subject; echoed in Sonnet 26.
"BOUND TO YOUR LORDSHIP" = entwined with or linked to, by blood as father to son
"ALL" = Southampton, his motto *One for All, All for One*
"ALL HAPPINESSE" = the final words of this dedication, and the first two words of the salutation to Southampton in the dedication of the Sonnets: "To the onlie begetter of these ensuing sonnets, Mr. W. H.," followed by "All Happiness"
"ALL DUTY" = all service and devotion; "To witness *duty*, not to show my wit/ *Duty* so great…" – Sonnet

26, lines 4-5
"SHAKESPEARE" = Oxford's second usage of the name on published works; also his last printed signature as such on any dedication (although *The Phoenix and Turtle*, 1601, will be signed with the hyphenated printed name "William Shake-speare"). The pseudonym has been adopted strictly for Southampton, as way for Oxford to write to and about him and to support him publicly, albeit behind a mask.

"The importance of these letters [the public dedications of "Venus" and "Lucrece" to the Earl of Southampton] *cannot be exaggerated."* – Robert Giroux, "The Story of Q, 1982," p. 60, speaking of the "Gibraltar-like solidity" of the dedications linking Shakespeare to the earl

Oxford's basic source for *Lucrece* is Ovid's original Latin text of *Fasti*, a work not to be translated into English for nearly half a century. The poem complements *Venus and Adonis* so that they present a single metaphorical description of Oxford and Elizabeth as parents of Southampton. In the first poem, Elizabeth was the sexual aggressor; in the second, Oxford becomes the driving (and guilty) force in the person of Tarquin.

"The two poems ["Venus" & "Lucrece"] *are opposite sides of the same coin, as may be seen by their strong resemblance. In each, an ardent suitor attempts to gain the reluctant object of her/his sexual desire by means of rhetorical persuasion, fails, and indirectly or directly precipitates the death of the object of desire."* - Jonathan Bate, "Shakespeare and Ovid," 1993, p. 66)

The deaths of Adonis/Oxford and Lucrece/Elizabeth are related to the death of their hopes for Southampton, the fruit of their sexual union. The "funeral" for their hopes will be held in print after the Rebellion of 1601, when all chance for his succession will have ended. In *The Phoenix and the Turtle* of that year, Oxford will present the Phoenix-Beauty-Elizabeth and the Dove-Truth-Oxford as chief mourners. The sexual union of Oxford and Elizabeth was, of course, biologically necessary for them to produce an heir with the right of succession. Therefore Oxford has filled both poems with scenes of sexuality and lust, presenting two masterpieces of erotic literature that become "hot" bestsellers in England. (Motivating their act of sexual intercourse, however, was the political aim of creating a Tudor heir by blood before Elizabeth, at forty, began to promote the "French Match" by flirting with the Duke of Alencon, leading France [and Spain] to believe she was willing to marry him and bear a child who could succeed her.) In *Venus and Adonis* Oxford allegorically killed his own identity by having the young god Adonis die by running upon the spear of the wild boar. In the *Lucrece*, he depicts Elizabeth as killing her own blood (and lineage) when Queen Lucrece, having been raped by Tarquin, commits suicide with a knife. In effect, both Oxford and Elizabeth, having given birth to Southampton, have killed themselves in terms of being able to reveal their parentage of him.

In 1594 it now remains to be seen whether Southampton, having joined forces with Essex, can forge his royal destiny by himself – with the works of "Shakespeare" to publicly support him.

Countess Southampton Marries Thomas Heneage, May 1594: Mary Browne, dowager Countess of Southampton, marries for the second time. Her new husband is Sir Thomas Heneage, one of Queen Elizabeth's longtime favorites at Court, who has been Treasurer of the Chamber for more than three decades. Since the death of Secretary of State Francis Walsingham in 1590, Heneage has become a central figure in the work of intelligence gathering for the government. He operates as a liaison between the Privy Council and the world of espionage – working directly under Burghley and Robert Cecil, the latter having become *de facto* head of the Secret Service. Theatrical companies are closely allied with the government and its espionage activities; Heneage is also responsible for seeing that the companies are paid for their performances at Court.

CHOICE OF VALENTINES, 1594: Thomas Nashe is compiling a collection of verses entitled *Choice of Valentines*, written expressly for Southampton. Regardless of whether his intention is to publish these poems with Oxford's collaboration and/or consent, the collection (which includes many bawdy verses) will remain in manuscript until its discovery in the twentieth century:

> Pardon, *sweet flower* of matchless Poetry
> And *fairest bud* the **red rose** ever **bare**

SWEET: royal
FLOWER: child of the Tudor Rose; the "little western flower" of *Midsummer Night's Dream*
MATCHLESS POETRY: Oxford's public poems and private sonnets for Southampton
FAIREST: most royal, as in "fairest creatures" of Sonnet 1, line 1
BUD: budding flower of the Tudor Rose dynasty, as in "darling buds of May," Sonnet 18, line 3
RED ROSE: the Lancastrian and Tudor Rose, i.e., Elizabeth
EVER: E. Ver, Edward de Vere, Earl of Oxford, *Ever or Never*
BARE: [BORE); gave birth to; echoing "boar" for Oxford, his crest

"The red rose was the symbol of the House of Lancaster, and it is inconceivable that Nashe did not know that what he wrote would be taken to identify Southampton as a scion of the Tudors."
- Charlton Ogburn, Jr., "The Mysterious William Shakespeare," 1992

Nashe, also making plain reference to the fact that the Virgin Queen is not as chaste as she has portrayed herself, declares he is revealing a hidden truth or secret:

> Ne blame my verse of loose **unchastity**
> For painting forth **the things that hidden are**

WILLOBIE HIS AVISA, September 3, 1594: Registered on this day is the politically sensitive book entitled *Willobie his Avisa*, which appears to represent another attempt by Oxford to support Southampton's royal claim – by appealing in print, this time, to Elizabeth herself. Within the poems he calls attention to *Lucrece* and provides the first printed reference to his new pen name:

> Yet Targuin plucked his glistening grape,
> And *Shake-speare* paints poor Lucrece's rape.

The poem focuses on the metaphorical efforts of various suitors to seduce (i.e., to gain the favor of) the same powerful woman, the Queen, whose replies are signed *Always the Same, Avisa*. Translated into Latin, the phrase becomes *Semper Eadem*, her motto, which she signed on correspondence as *Ever the Same*.

Two of the would-be seducers of Elizabeth are Leicester and the Duke of Alencon, both deceased. The last of the suitors, to whom more poems are devoted than to any of the others, is "H.W." for Henry Wriothesley. The poems may amount to a plea to Elizabeth to forgive Southampton for his spirit of independence and to embrace him as her natural heir and successor:

> And sing the truth, I will, I must!
>
> First Venus framed a luring eye,
> A sweet aspect and comely grace
> There did the Rose and Lily lie,

> That bravely decked a smiling face.
> Here Cupid's mother bent her will,
> In this to show her utmost skill…
> Midst sunny rays, this cloud appears,
> Sweet Roses grow on prickly stalks…
> If princely power have no power
> To shade the shame of secret sin,
> If black reproach such names devour,
> What gain or glory can they win?

Oxford may be viewed as pleading directly with Elizabeth:

> Who dares to stir, who dares to speak,
> Who dares our dealings to reprove…?
> Who sees our face, knows not our facts;
> Though we in sport in secret use,
> Thy cheeks will not bewray thy acts,
> But rather blushing will excuse:
> If thou wilt yield, here is my faith:
> I'll keep it secret till my death.

And here it's plain that the poet is pleading for a royal heir on the throne from "Albion" or English blood and soil:

> Can Britain breed no Phoenix bird,
> No constant fame in English field?
> To Greece to Rome, is there no third?
> Hath Albion none that will not yield?

The final poem echoes the private Sonnets to Southampton (with phrases such as "every creature" and "Sunne and Moone") and the poet compares himself with *Troilus*, the "faithful friend" of Elizabeth, the false *Cressida* by whom his "foolish fancy" or "love" was "turned to hate."

> Now foolish fancy was the cause, this Cressid did lament,
> For when she had a faithful friend, she could not be content.

This poem, which ends the entire collection, is signed *Ever or Never*. This signature (evoking the abbreviation "E. Ver" for Edward de Vere) had appeared in the collection *A Hundredth Sundrie Flowres* of 1572, with which Oxford appears to have been associated as publisher, editor and writer; it will be echoed in *Troilus and Cressida*, printed in 1609 with an extraordinary epistle entitled *A Never Writer to an Ever Reader*, as well as in the dedication of the Sonnets that year with its reference to "that eternity promised by our *ever-living* poet."

Burghley Retaliates, October 1594: "The Earl of Southampton at full age," Burghley notes in his diary for October 6, 1594, the official twenty-first birthday of Henry Wriothesley. Having reached this age, the earl ceases to be a royal ward under the legal constraints of being in custody, so the Lord Treasurer can no longer pressure him to marry his granddaughter. Having kept her available until the last moment, however, Cecil retaliates by heavily fining the earl. "The young Erle of Southampton refusing the Lady Veere payeth 5,000 pounds of present payment," Jesuit priest Father Garnet notes in November.

Florio, 1594: Intending to travel on the Continent, as Oxford did nineteen years earlier, Southampton devotes himself to Italian studies and hires as his tutor John Florio, the Italian language teacher.

Chamberlain's Men perform at Court, December 26-27-28, 1594: The newly formed Lord Chamberlain's Men, under the patronage of Henry Carey, Lord Hunsdon, performs for Queen Elizabeth and her Court. In March next year the record books will show "Shakespeare" (for the first and last time) as a payee for these performances. The company also presents *The Comedy of Errors* (recorded under that title) at Gray's Inn during the pageant held there.

THE SHAKESPEARE COMMITMENT

Sonnet 20
Master-Mistress
1594

Oxford continues his public commitment to Southampton this year by dedicating Lucrece *(later known as* The Rape of Lucrece*) to Henry Wriothesley. Again using "William Shakespeare" as the printed signature, he addresses his royal son in the dedication as a servant addresses his sovereign, pledging his undying "love" and "duty" to him. In this sonnet, he celebrates Southampton's coming-of-age at Court in majestic splendor – a young king who attracts men and women alike into his devoted service. The sexual implications are part of the familiar costume of conventional poetry, within which Oxford records his son's royal blood from the Queen as a result of his own sexual union with her.*

Sonnet 20	Translation
A Woman's face with nature's own hand painted	Elizabeth's blood created by her own maternity
Hast thou, the Master-Mistress of my passion;	Have you, the King and Queen of my Sonnets:
A woman's gentle heart, but not acquainted	Elizabeth's royal heart, but not acquainted
With shifting change as is false women's fashion,	With her shifting views falsely identifying you.
An eye more bright then theirs, less false in rolling:	A eye more royal than hers, less false in power,
Gilding the object whereupon it gazeth,	Making royal everything upon which it gazes,
A man in hew all *Hews* in his controlling,	A Prince Henry Wriothesley in his royal power,
Which steals men's eyes and women's souls amazeth.	Who gains men's attention and amazes his mother.
And for a woman wert thou first created,	And for Elizabeth were you born,
Till nature as she wrought thee fell a doting,	Till she (birthing you) became your mother,
And by addition me of thee defeated,	And by this addition of you she defeated me,
By adding one thing to my purpose nothing.	By adding nothing to my purpose for you.
But since she prickt thee out for women's pleasure,	But since she created you at her sovereign pleasure,
Mine be thy love, and thy love's use their treasure.	Mine is your blood, its succession is her treasure.

1 A WOMAN'S FACE WITH NATURE'S OWN HAND PAINTED

A WOMAN'S FACE = Queen Elizabeth's face, reflected in that of her son; "Thou art thy mother's glass, and she in thee/ Calls back the lovely April of her prime" – Sonnet 3, lines 9-10

NATURE = Elizabeth; in Shakespeare's world *Nature*, along with *Fortune* and *Time*, are the three major forces that determine man's life; in the Sonnets all three refer to Queen Elizabeth, who determines her royal son's life; "And in his *royalty of nature* reigns that which would be feared" – *Macbeth*, 3.1.49-50

154

PAINTED = "So it is not with me as with that Muse,/ Stirred by a *painted beauty* to his verse" – Sonnet 21, lines 1-2, i.e., painted beauty = created royal blood

WITH NATURE'S OWN HAND PAINTED = by your own mother, Elizabeth, you were created; **HAND** = "From *hands of falsehood*, in sure wards of trust" – Sonnet 48, line 4, related to the Queen's falseness toward her royal son; "O what *strong hand* can hold his swift foot back" – Sonnet 65, line 11, referring to Elizabeth having the power to hold back Time and prevent her son from being executed; "And almost thence my nature is subdued,/ To what it works in, like the Dyer's *hand*" – Sonnet 111, lines 6-7, after the Queen's death; "For since each *hand* hath put on Nature's power,/ Fairing the foul with Art's false borrowed face" – Sonnet 127, lines 5-6, referring to the power of the Queen; "And so the General of hot desire/ Was sleeping *by a Virgin hand* disarmed" – Sonnet 154, lines 7-8, referring to Elizabeth as the Virgin Queen who removed the power of her newborn royal son or god on earth ("the little Love-God" of Sonnet 154, line 1) in 1574, thereby disarming him by her imperial hand; "the *royal hand of the king*" – *Love's Labour's Lost*, 4.2.141; "I'll claim that promise *at your Grace's hand*" – *Richard III*, 3.1.197

This *pretty* lad will prove our country's *bliss*.
His *looks* are full of peaceful *majesty*;
His head by *nature framed* to wear a *crown*,
His *hand* to wield a scepter; and himself
Likely in *time* to *bless* a regal throne. - *3 Henry VI*, 4.6.70-74, of the future Henry VII

Pretty = "Those *pretty* wrongs that liberty commits" – Sonnet 41, line 1
Bliss = "A *bliss* in proof, and proved, a very woe" – Sonnet 129, line 11
Looks = "Thy *looks* with me, thy heart in other place" – Sonnet 93, line 4
Majesty = "Serving with looks his sacred *majesty*" – Sonnet 7, line 4
Nature = "A Woman's face with *nature's* own hand painted" – Sonnet 20, line 1
Framed = "To this composed wonder of your *frame*" – Sonnet 59, line 10
Crown = "Or whether doth my mind, being *crowned* with you" – Sonnet 114, line 1
Hand = "A Woman's face with nature's own *hand* painted" – Sonnet 20, line 1
Time = "When in the Chronicle of wasted *time*" – Sonnet 106, line 1
Bless = "And you in every *blessed* shape we know" – Sonnet 53, line 12

---

2 HAST THOU, THE MASTER MISTRESS OF MY PASSION:
MASTER = Prince or King, the monarch; "Wherewith God hath endued our new *Master* and Sovereign Lord" – Oxford to Robert Cecil, April 1603, referring to King James; "I'll to the king my *master*" – *2 Henry IV*, 5.2.40; "Only to show his pomp as well in France as here at home, suggests *the king our master* to this last costly treaty" – *Henry VIII*, 1.1.163-164; "That in the way of loyalty and truth toward *the king, my ever royal master*" – *Henry VIII*, 3.2.272-273; "A ruler, a governor … applied to a sovereign in relation to his ministers or officers" – *OED*; "The Lord forbid that I should do this thing unto my *master* the Lord's Anointed" – *King James Bible*, 1 Samuel 24.6, 1611; "the juvenal, the Prince your *master*, whose chin is not yet fledge" – *2 Henry IV*, 1.2.19-20; "In answer of which claim, the Prince our *Master*" – *Henry V*, 1.2.250

"Even such a beauty as you *master* now"
– Sonnet 106, line 8

MISTRESS = Queen; i.e., Southampton, the "master" or rightful king, is the son of Elizabeth, the current sovereign "mistress" of England:

"And such as greatly have in their lifetimes honored the Queen's Majesty our *Mistress*" – Oxford to
Burghley, 1572

"I cannot but find a great grief in myself to remember the *mistress* which we have lost" – Oxford to Robert Cecil, April 1603, about recently deceased Queen Elizabeth

"And so, wishing Your Majesty to be *mistress* of all that you wish most" – Essex to Elizabeth, 1597; (Weir, 430); "That any lewd ... subject of mine should make his Sovereign be supposed of less government than *mistress* of her word" – Queen Elizabeth, this same year, 1592, *OED*; "That prudent Pallas, Albion's *Mistress*, that Great Elizabeth" – 1598, *OED*; "Miverva was a *mistress* of many king's works" – 1400-1450, *OED*; "*mistress* was not yet a euphemism for 'concubine'" – Booth; ("Rome's royal *mistress*" – *Titus Andronicus*, 1.1.245; "There let his head and lifeless body lie, until the Queen his *mistress* bury it" – *2 Henry VI*, 4.1.14142-143; "I like it well that our fair Queen and *mistress* smiles at her news" – the Earl of Oxford in *3 Henry VI*, 3.3.167-168; "My queen, my *mistress*"
– *Cymbeline*, 1.2.23

MASTER-MISTRESS = King and Queen, i.e., the sovereign; ("If you think to rule here, I will take a course to see you forthcoming! I will have here but one *Mistress* and no *Master*!" – Elizabeth to Leicester, 1565, reminding him that she was the Queen and that he was not a King);

OF MY PASSION = of my inspiration; of my love; of my fierce emotions; (Latin *passio* is 'feeling' or 'strong feeling'); "A mother's tears in *passion* for her son!" – *Titus Andronicus*, 1.1.109; the Master Mistress or ruler of these private sonnets; "Here she comes, and **her passion ends the play**" – *Midsummer Night's Dream*, 5.1.310, referring to the verses about to be recited); my central concern; "Poem ... In 1582 Thomas Watson called the individual sonnets of his *Hecatompathia* 'passions'" – Booth; (Watson referred to his sonnets or "passions" in his dedication of these 100 consecutively numbered poems dedicated to Oxford, who probably wrote the summaries for each verse, using the phrase "this passion" for "this poem".)

Passion is associated with the will of a monarch, as in: "We are no tyrant but a Christian king, unto whose grace our *passion* is as subject as are our wretches fettered in our prisons" – *Henry V*, 1.2.241-243); "The colour of the king doth come and go between his purpose and his conscience, like heralds 'twixt two battles set: his *passion* is so ripe, it needs must break" – *King John*, 4.2.76-79); also, the passion (suffering) of Christ

3 A WOMAN'S GENTLE HEART BUT NOT ACQUAINTED
A WOMAN'S GENTLE HEART = Elizabeth's source of royal blood in you; **GENTLE** = royal; i.e., you have her royal heart, the source of your blood from her, but you are not "acquainted with" or given to [her fashion or habit of changing her mind, being false, etc.]

4 WITH SHIFTING CHANGE AS IS FALSE WOMEN'S FASHION;
SHIFTING CHANGE = change of attitude; fickleness; **FALSE WOMEN'S FASHION** = Elizabeth's presentation of a false image to the world
FALSE = "*False king*! Why hast thou broken faith with me" – *2 Henry VI*, 5.1.91.

5 AN EYE MORE BRIGHT THAN THEIRS, LESS FALSE IN ROLLING,
AN EYE MORE BRIGHT = your royal eye, the sun, is more kingly; ("Upon his royal face ... a largess universal like the sun, *his liberal eye* doth give to every one" – *Henry V*, 4, prologue, speaking of the king; "Govern the motion of *a kingly eye*" – *King John*, 5.1.47); "And scarcely greet me with *that sunne, thine eye*" – Sonnet 49, line 6, to Southampton

LESS FALSE = not false like the royal eye (viewpoint) of Elizabeth; "I am thy king, and thou a *false-heart traitor*" – *2 Henry VI*, 5.1.143; in effect, Oxford is saying that not only does Elizabeth present a false image of the truth but also that, by denying her son the succession, she is a "false-traitor" to her own royal blood and thereby to the Crown itself

> O Cressid! O *false Cressid! False, false, false!*
> Let all untruths stand by thy stained name,
> And they'll seem glorious.
> - *Troilus & Cressida*, 5.2.175-177

> Sland'ring Creation with a false esteem
> - Sonnet 127, line 12
> (Elizabeth slandering her son)

6 GILDING THE OBJECT WHEREUPON IT GAZETH:
GILDING = making royal; "*Gilding* pale streams with heavenly alchemy" – Sonnet 33, line 4, in relation to the sun as royal son, Southampton; "The sun doth *gild* our armour up, my lords!" – *Henry V*, 4.2.1; "Not marble nor the *gilded* monument/ Of Princes" – Sonnet 55, lines 1-2; "To make him much outlive a *gilded* tomb" – Sonnet 101, line 11; a belief then was that the eyes emitted "beams" of light; "As fast as objects to his beams assemble" – Sonnet 114, line 8

7 A MAN IN HEW ALL *HEWS* IN HIS CONTROLLING,
Many commentators have viewed this line as identifying a specific individual with the letters of "Hews" in his name; the word itself refers to complexion, shape, form

A MAN = Southampton, who officially reaches *manhood* or adulthood this year; October 6, 1594 marks his official twenty-first birthday

HEW = Abbreviation of "Henry Wriothesley"; **ALL** = Southampton, *One for All, All for One*

HEWS = "Henry Wriothesley, Southampton"; with "hew" suggesting a nobleman: "The Courtier, therefore, beside nobleness of birth, I will have … by nature to have not only a wit, and a comely shape of person and countenance, but also a certain grace, and, as they say, a *hew*, that shall make him at the first sight acceptable and loving unto who so beholdeth him" – *The Courtier* by Castiglione, the book Oxford brought into print in 1572; Hoby translation of 1561, cited by G. Blakemore Evans

> There's a divinity that shapes our ends,
> Rough-*hew* them how we will.
> - *Hamlet*, 5.2.10-11

IN HIS CONTROLLING = in all his royal power; "His golden *uncontrolled* enfranchisement" – *Richard II*, 1.3.90; "Yet looks he like a king: behold, his eye, as bright as is the eagle's, lightens forth **controlling majesty**" – *Richard II*, 3.3.68-70; "Here is a *hand* to hold a scepter up and with the same to act *controlling* laws" – *2 Henry VI*, 5.1.102-103; "Two such *controlling* bounds shall you be, kings, to these two princes, if you marry them" – *King John*, 2.1.444-445; "Can yet the lease of my true love *control*" – Sonnet 107, line 3

8 WHICH STEALS MEN'S EYES AND WOMENS SOULS AMAZETH;
WHICH = who, i.e., Southampton; or the controlling/kingly aspect of his person; **STEALS MEN'S EYES** = captures the attention of his (the king's) subjects; ("Lo, in the Orient, when the gracious light/ Lifts up his

burning head, *each under eye*/ Doth homage to his new-appearing sight,/ Serving with looks his sacred majesty" – Sonnet 7, lines 1-4)

> Yet herein will I imitate the sun…
> My reformation, glittering o'er my fault,
> Shall show more goodly and *attract more eyes*…
> - Prince Hal in *1 Henry IV*, 1.2.192, 208

> That, being daily swallowed by *men's eyes*
> - The King in *1 Henry IV*, 3.2.70

> (See also *1 Henry IV*, 3.2.39-40; *1 Henry IV*, 3.2.78-80; *Richard II*, 5.2.27-28; *Cymbeline*, 3.1.2-3; *Hamlet*, 1.2.257-258; Sonnet 29, line 1; Sonnet 81, line 8)

"This estate hath depended on you a great while, as all the world doth judge, and now all *men's eyes*, not being occupied any more on these lost lords, are, as it were, on a sudden, *bent and fixed on you* as a singular hope and pillar whereto religion hath to lean" - Oxford to Lord Burghley, September 1572

WOMEN'S, etc. = women in general are taken by his looks and majesty, but "women" also refers to the Queen herself, i.e., she, too, is amazed by her royal son; **AMAZETH** = "Confound the ignorant, and *amaze* indeed the very faculties of eyes and ears" – *Hamlet*, 2.2.565-566

9 AND FOR A WOMAN WERT THOU FIRST CREATED,
FOR A WOMAN = for Elizabeth, i.e., for her dynasty; **FIRST** = originally, in the first place; above all; as in "Since *first I saw you fresh*, which yet are green" – Sonnet 104, line 8, referring not to the first time he saw his son, but, rather, to the original way he viewed him, i.e., as prince

CREATED = born; "From fairest *creatures* we desire increase" – Sonnet 1, line 1; Nativity, once in the main of light,/ Crawls to maturity, wherewith being crowned" – Sonnet 60, lines 5-6; "But heaven in *thy creation* did decree" – Sonnet 93, line 9 ("Heaven" = Elizabeth); "and the issue there create" – *A Midsummer Night's Dream*, 5.1.399; "and this suit I make, that you *create* our emperor's eldest son … crown him and say, 'Long live our emperor!'" – *Titus Andronicus*, 1.1.228, 233; "Richard, I will *create* thee Duke of Gloucester" – *3 Henry VI*, 2.6.103

> Your monument shall be my gentle verse,
> Which *eyes not yet created* shall o'er-read
> - Sonnet 81, lines 9-10

> "Sland'ring *Creation* with a false esteem"
> - Sonnet 127, line 12

10 TILL NATURE AS SHE WROUGHT THEE FELL A-DOTING,
NATURE = Elizabeth; **WROUGHT** = created; gave birth to; **DOTING** = displaying extreme fondness, as a doting parent; in this case, having excessive motherly affection

11 AND BY ADDITION ME OF THEE DEFEATED,
BY ADDITION, etc. = by the birth of you she defeated me, as your father; "We will not name desert before his birth, and, being born, his *addition* shall be humble" – *Troilus and Cressida*, 3.2.91-93; "Bear the *addition* nobly ever!" – *Coriolanus*, 1.9.65, referring to his new title; **DEFEATED** = "defrauded, disappointed" - Dowden

12 BY ADDING ONE THING TO MY PURPOSE NOTHING.
BY ADDING ONE THING = on the poetical level, by adding a penis to you; on the intended level, by giving birth to you; **ONE** = Southampton; **TO MY PURPOSE NOTHING** = adding nothing to my purpose for you, as she refused to acknowledge you; "The *purpose* you undertake is dangerous" – *1 Henry IV*, 2.3.6-7; "You are so strongly *in my purpose bred*" – Sonnet 112, line 13, with "bred" referring to Southampton's birth and children, i.e., raised to become king

NOTHING = the opposite of **ONE** for Southampton; rendering him with no claim to the throne; "Among a number *one* is reckoned *none*" – Sonnet 136, line 8, Oxford to Elizabeth, referring to him as the "one" royal son whom she has refused to acknowledge, thereby rendering him as "none"; "For I am shamed by that which I bring forth,/ And so should you, to love things *nothing* worth" - Sonnet 72, lines 13-14, Oxford writing of the futility of having fathered a royal son who is counted as nothing

13 BUT SINCE SHE PRICKED THEE OUT FOR WOMEN'S PLEASURE,
SHE = Nature = Queen Elizabeth; **PRICKT (PRICKED) THEE OUT** = on the poetical level, echoing "prick" for penis; on the intended level, she gave birth to you; ("Selected you: to 'prick' someone is to mark his name with a puncture or a dot" – Booth; marked out, designated; "And took his voice who should be *prick'd* to die, in our black sentence and proscription" – *Julius Caesar*, 4.1.16-17); gave you motivation; "My duty *pricks me on* to utter" – *The Two Gentlemen of Verona*, 3.1.8; "Our last king ... was, as you know, by Fortinbras of Norway thereto *prick'd on* by a most emulate pride" – *Hamlet*, 1.1.86; "But, sith I am entered in this cause so far, *prick'd to it* by foolish honesty and love, I will go on" – *Othello*, 3.3.414-415

FOR WOMAN'S PLEASURE = at Her Majesty's royal pleasure; according to her imperial will; "Her Majesty may bestow the same *at her pleasure*" – Oxford to Robert Cecil, December 4, 1601; "You speak *your fair pleasure*, sweet Queen" – *Troilus and Cressida*, 3.1.48; "Your Grace may do *your pleasure*" – *Richard III*, 4.2.21; (see *Henry VIII*, 1.1.215; *Measure for Measure*, 1.1.25-26)

14 MINE BE THY LOVE, AND THY LOVE'S USE THEIR TREASURE.
MINE BE THY LOVE = my own pleasure or will is your "love" or royal blood; "it hath pleased God to give me *a son of mine own*" – Oxford to Burghley, March 17, 1575

THY LOVE'S USE = the privilege and responsibility of using your royal blood to become king

THEIR = women's, i.e., Elizabeth's; **THEIR TREASURE** = Her Majesty's treasure, i.e., her greatest treasure is the use of your royal blood as heir to her throne; ironically, perhaps intentionally so, Oxford echoes the fact that his father-in-law William Cecil is Lord Treasurer of England; "My dear wife's estimate, her womb's increase and *treasure* of my loins" – *Coriolanus*, 3.3.114-115; "Thy heaven is on earth; thine eyes and thoughts beat on *a crown, the treasure* of thy heart" – *2 Henry VI*, 2.1.19-20

"Make sweet some vial, *treasure* thou some place/ With beauty's *treasure*" – Sonnet 6, lines 3-4; "So am I as the rich whose blessed key/ Can bring him to his sweet up-locked *treasure*" – Sonnet 52, lines 1-2, when Southampton is locked in the Tower; "the *treasure* of thy love" – Sonnet 136, line 5, Oxford to Elizabeth, referring to the treasure of her royal blood within Southampton; "Why should he live, now *nature bankrupt is*,/ Beggared of blood to blush through lively veins" – Sonnet 67, lines 9-10, when Southampton is in the Tower and Elizabeth-Nature is *bankrupt* of any other heirs or *treasure* of royal blood to succeed her on the throne: "O him she stores, to show what *wealth* she had" – Sonnet 67, line 13

1595

Southampton in Highest Royal Favor, January 1595: "The year 1595 saw the handsome young Earl of Southampton emerging at the Court of Queen Elizabeth as a budding favorite who might well replace Essex." - Akrigg

Elizabeth Vere marries the Earl of Derby, January 26, 1595: Lady Elizabeth Vere marries William Stanley, Sixth Earl of Derby, at a gala wedding hosted by the Queen at Greenwich Palace. It is "probable, though not certain" that *A Midsummer Night's Dream* was presented at the festivities. (Read, *Lord Burghley and Queen Elizabeth*, 502)

Oxford will be close to his new son-in-law, with whom he shares a love for the stage. William's older brother, Fernando, Fifth Earl of Derby, known as Lord Strange, had died the year before; and Strange's company had performed many of Oxford's plays later to be attributed to Shakespeare. Now actors from that company (such as William Kemp) form the nucleus of the new Lord Chamberlain's Men (the guiding force of which was undoubtedly Oxford, the Lord Great Chamberlain of England), to which historians centuries later will refer as "Shakespeare's Company".

"Shakespeare" Recorded as Payee, March 15, 1595: Records show the Chamberlain's Men receiving twenty pounds for the performances at Court in December 1594, the payees being "Will Kemp, Will Shakespeare & Richard Burbage, servants to the Lord Chambleyne." This is the only record of Shakespeare as payee. (Chambers, *The Elizabethan Stage*, Appendix B)

Southampton & Lady Vernon, September 1595: "My Lord of Southampton doth with too much Familiarity court the fair Mistress Vernon" – Rowland Whyte (Akrigg, 48; Stopes, 86)

The young lady is Elizabeth Vernon, a Maid of Honor to the Queen. She is far beneath Southampton's high-ranking status, but also happens to be Essex's cousin. Pursuing her with reckless abandon, Southampton is defying Her Majesty, who wants all courtiers to stay clear of her Maids of Honor, and he is taking sides against Burghley and Robert Cecil. This semi-secret courtship amounts to a statement of political allegiance to Essex.

The Queen rebukes Southampton, October 1595: "My Lord of Southampton offering to help the Queen to her horse, was refused; he is gone from the Court and not yet returned." – Rowland Whyte (Akrigg, 48)

Death of Heneage, October 17, 1595: The death of Thomas Heneage, second husband of Mary Browne, Countess of Southampton, leaves her a widow for the second time and also with the task of completing his record books: "The official responsible for making payments for theatrical performances at Court was Sir Thomas Heneage, Treasurer of the Chamber; but, as Charlotte C. Stopes discovered, 'The person who rendered the Bills from 29th September 1592 till 16th December 1595 was Mary Countess of Southampton' … Quite clearly, when she came 'to lose her affectionate husband on 17 October 1595' she found the records of payments lacking all the way back to 29 September 1592. As Mrs. Stopes observes: 'She was … to have sad worries over his accounts, receiving an unpleasant letter even from the Queen herself about the deficit' … The widow's problem would thus have been to come up with vouchers accounting for the expenditure of as much as possible in order to reduce the amount by which she would be out of pocket. Such were the circumstances in which she recorded the payment of twenty pounds to Kemp, Shakespeare, and Burbage." (Ogburn, *The Mysterious William Shakespeare*, 1992, 65-66)

Part One

THE SHAKESPEARE COMMITMENT

Sonnet 21
Sunne and Moone
Any Mother's Child
1595

Oxford continues to support Southampton's claim to the throne, writing of his royal son and Elizabeth as "Sunne and Moone" while identifying Henry Wriothesley as "heaven's air" or Elizabeth's heir. He commits himself to keeping this record a secret; that is, he will not publish the Book of Sonnets or attempt to "sell" it.

Sonnet 21	Translation
So is it not with me as with that Muse,	So is it not with me as it is with my Muse,
Stirred by a painted beauty to his verse,	Inspired by a created prince to write my Sonnets,
Who heaven itself for ornament doth use,	Who Elizabeth herself has for her successor,
And every fair with his fair doth rehearse,	And every royal prince rehearses his royal claim,
Making a couplement of proud compare	Making a royal coupling with two equal princes,
With Sunne and Moone, with earth and sea's rich gems:	With Royal Son and Queen, with England and royalty:
With April's first-born flowers and all things rare,	With Elizabeth's most royal son, and all royal blood
That heavens air in this huge rondure hems,	With which the Queen's heir fills his crown.
O let me true in love but truly write,	O let me write only and truly of your royal blood,
And then believe me, my love is as fair	And then believe me, my son is as royal
As any mother's child, though not so bright	As any of Elizabeth's children, though not so royal
As those gold candles fixed in heaven's air:	As those royal eyes of the Queen's immediate heir.
Let them say more that like of hearsay well,	Let me say what's heard but not seen well,
I will not praise that purpose not to sell.	I will not speak publicly or put my purpose for sale.

1 SO IT IS NOT WITH ME AS WITH THAT MUSE,
MUSE = Oxford's muse for the Sonnets is Southampton himself; i.e., Southampton is "the onlie begetter of these ensuing sonnets" of the Dedication; "So oft have I invoked thee for my Muse," Oxford tells his son in Sonnet 78, line 1, and several lines later asks him to "be most proud of that which I compile,/ Whose *influence is thine, and born of thee*" – Sonnet 78, lines 9-10

2 STIRRED BY A PAINTED BEAUTY TO HIS VERSE,
STIRRED BY A PAINTED BEAUTY = inspired by a created royal son who possesses "beauty" or Elizabeth's blood; **PAINTED BEAUTY** = ("with nature's own hand *painted*" – Sonnet 20, line 1, referring to the Queen's birth or creation of Southampton)

REFERENCE EDITION

3 WHO HEAVEN ITSELF FOR ORNAMENT DOTH USE,

WHO = or whom, i.e., Southampton; **HEAVEN ITSELF** = Elizabeth herself; ("from *heaven* her virtues she doth borrow" – contemporary song by musician John Dowland); "This royal infant, heaven still move about her ... Holy and heavenly thoughts still counsel her ... So shall she leave her blessedness to one, when *heaven* shall call her from this cloud of darkness, who from the sacred ashes of her honor shall star-like rise ... Wherever the bright *sun of heaven* shall shine, his honor and the greatness of his name shall be" – Cranmer, speaking of the infant Elizabeth and her successor, in Henry *VIII*, 5.4.15-51; "our most illustrious and noble Queen, in whom all courtly qualities are personified, together with those *diviner and truly celestial* virtues" – Oxford, writing of Elizabeth, in his Letter to the Reader for a new translation of *The Courtier*, 1572; **ORNAMENT** = royal prince and heir to her throne (as in "the world's fresh *ornament*" of Sonnet 1 and as a "*Jewel*" on "the finger of a throned Queen" in Sonnet 96, lines 5 and 6

4 AND EVERY FAIR WITH HIS FAIR DOTH REHEARSE,

EVERY = E. Ver, Edward de Vere, *Ever or Never*; **FAIR** = royal son; ("From fairest creatures we desire increase" – Sonnet 1, line 1); **EVERY FAIR** = my royal son, combining father and son together as "every fair"; **WITH HIS FAIR DOTH REHEARSE** = repeats his royal status to himself; reminds himself of his royal responsibility; "And tongues to be *your being shall rehearse*" – Sonnet 81, line 11

5 MAKING A COUPLEMENT OF PROUD COMPARE

COUPLEMENT OF PROUD = a linking of royal blood; ("Why is my verse so barren of new *pride*?" – Sonnet 76, line 1); "joining in proud comparisons" – Dowden

6 WITH SUNNE AND MOONE, WITH EARTH AND SEA'S RICH GEMS,

SUNNE = royal son, Southampton; ("Even so *my Sunne* one early morn did shin,/ With all triumphant splendor on my brow,/ But out alack, he was but one hour mine,/ The region cloud hath masked him from me now" – Sonnet 33, lines 9-12); **MOONE** = Elizabeth, who is Diana, chaste goddess of the Moon; ("the mortal Moone" of Sonnet 107, line 5; "The moon cult, begun by Raleigh in the eighties as a personal one, became public in the nineties" – Strong); royal son and royal mother; **EARTH AND SEAS RICH GEMS** = the world's royal princes or gods on earth; ("My soul's earth's god" – *Love's Labour's Lost* 1.1.223, speaking to the king; "*Ocean* or *sea* as a figure for *king* is often found in Shakespeare and his fellow writers" – Leslie Hotson; "And what is (King) Edward but a ruthless *sea*" – *3 Henry VI*, 5.4.25)

7 WITH APRIL'S FIRST-BORN FLOWERS AND ALL THINGS RARE

APRIL'S FIRST-BORN FLOWERS = Southampton, flower of the Tudor Rose, who was about to be born from Elizabeth's womb in April of 1574; "Thou art thy mother's glass, and she in thee/ Calls back the lovely April of her prime" – Sonnet 3, lines 9-10; **ALL** = Southampton, *One for All, All for One*; **ALL THINGS RARE** = all things royal, i.e., Southampton; ("Beauty, Truth, and *Rarity*,/ Grace in all simplicity" – *The Phoenix and the Turtle*, lines 53-54, referring to Elizabeth-Beauty, Oxford-Truth and Southampton-Rarity); rare = fair = air = heir = Vere

8 THAT HEAVEN'S AIR IN THIS HUGE RONDURE HEMS.

HEAVEN = Elizabeth; **AIR** = heir to her throne; **HEAVEN'S AIR** = Elizabeth's heir to the throne, Southampton; repeated in line 12 below; ("The borrowed glories that *by gift of heaven*, by law of nature and of nations, 'longs to him and to his *heirs*, namely *the crown*" – Henry V, 2.4.79-81); **HUGE RONDURE** = the universe, heaven and earth; the realm; circle, as in "the *rondure* of your old-faced walls" in *King John*, 2.1.259, i.e., this huge circular world; also referring to the crown; "Th'imperial metal circling now thy head hath grac'd the tender temples of my child" – *Richard III*, 4.4.382-383

9 **O LET ME TRUE IN LOVE BUT TRULY WRITE:**
O = Oxford; **O LET ME** = me, Oxford; **TRUE** = Oxford, *Nothing Truer than Truth*; **IN LOVE** = of your royal blood; **TRUE IN LOVE BUT TRULY WRITE** = as me, Oxford, writing truly of your true royal blood; setting down the truth in these private sonnets; ("Thou truly fair wert truly sympathized/ In true plain words by thy true-telling friend" – Sonnet 82, lines 11-12)

10 **AND THEN BELIEVE ME, MY LOVE IS AS FAIR**
MY LOVE IS AS FAIR = my royal son is as royal; and secondarily as Ver or Vere

11 **AS ANY MOTHER'S CHILD, THOUGH NOT SO BRIGHT**
AS ANY MOTHER'S CHILD = as Elizabeth's own son; i.e., Oxford's use of "any" is an indirect way of identifying the Queen, according to his special language; the same as when, in Sonnet 6, line 3, he wrote, "Make sweet *some* vial," referring indirectly to the specific need to marry Elizabeth Vere and fill her womb with the royal blood of an heir; the phrase "any mother's child" is also *direct* testimony by Oxford that he is writing to a son of the Queen; also the line can be read "as any child of the mother," stating that Elizabeth did have other children (probably by Leicester); **NOT SO BRIGHT** = not so royal

12 **AS THOSE GOLD CANDLES FIXED IN HEAVEN'S AIR.**
GOLD CANDLES = stars in the night sky, i.e., Southampton's royal eyes; "Night's candles are burnt out" – *Romeo and Juliet*, 3.5.9; "For by these blessed candles of the night" – *The Merchant of Venice*, 5.1.220; **FIXED IN HEAVEN'S AIR** = determined or designated as Elizabeth's heir to succeed her on the throne; **HEAVEN'S** = Elizabeth's; **AIR** = heir; in other words, no child of the Queen has such brightly royal eyes as those of her immediate heir, Southampton; the repetition of "heaven's air" from line 8 has been seen as "pointless" (Tucker, 1924), indicating inferior work as a poet; but Oxford is operating on the more important second level, emphasizing "the Queen's heir to the throne"

13 **LET THEM SAY MORE THAT LIKE OF HEARSAY WELL:**
Let others speak more of what they hear by gossip or by way of second-hand knowledge

14 **I WILL NOT PRAISE THAT PURPOSE NOT TO SELL.**
I will not write this diary praising (honoring, identifying) your royal blood in order to publish or sell it; these sonnets to you will remain private and secret.

1596

War Plans, 1596: Philip II of Spain is preparing to launch an even greater Armada to invade England. Alarmed by reports of activity in Spanish seaports, the Privy Council inaugurates plans for a combined military and naval assault on Cadiz, the main Spanish port, by twelve thousand men bringing five months' worth of supplies for fighting and occupation. Essex will command the English fleet along with Lord Admiral Charles Howard and Sir Walter Raleigh, with Sir Francis Vere (Oxford's cousin) directing the ground campaign.

Spain Takes Over Calais, April 1596: As the Cadiz campaign is being readied, Elizabeth authorizes Essex to take six thousand soldiers to Calais, which is being held by France but is now under siege by Spanish forces. The Queen tells Essex he can attack the Spanish only if the French agree in advance to hand Calais back to England. (Elizabeth also instructs Essex that Southampton and Oxford's son-in-law, Derby, may not go beyond Dover to France.) The Queen procrastinates until the Spanish troops pound Calais into submission, leaving Essex to vent his fury at Her Majesty for preventing him from recapturing it for England.

Essex to Cadiz, June 1596: Elizabeth forbids Southampton to join the Cadiz expedition, blocking him from the martial glory he has sought so eagerly.

The siege of Cadiz, on the western coast of Spain, will be the high point of Essex's brilliant career; he is now just thirty years old. Under his command the English destroy forty Spanish vessels and capture the town. Two of Philip's largest ships are seized. Because of Essex's personal valor, he is now as famous, both at home and abroad, as Elizabeth herself.

Robert Cecil Becomes Principal Secretary, July 5, 1596: Even before his triumphant return, Essex learns that Burghley has won the long fight over who will get the prize post of Secretary of State. In Essex's absence the Queen swears in Robert Cecil as her Principal Secretary, giving Burghley and his son an enormous advantage in the quest for control over the government.

"After waiting patiently for five years, old Burghley had achieved his last great ambition: to see his quiet, crippled, brilliant son take over the reins of effective power. The old man could die content. His boy Robert would still have to struggle with that other Robert, Earl of Essex, so much nobler born and so generously endowed with the superficial attractions that counted so much at the Elizabethan Court. Yet as Principal Secretary to the Queen, young Cecil was undeniably established – he could hold his own against Essex; and given time he could do more than that. " (Lacey)

"Shakespeare" Supports Essex, 1596: Plays that will later be attributed to "William Shakespeare" continue appearing on the English stage, giving every sign that the author is keenly interested in the fate of both Essex and Southampton. "That Shakespeare was an ardent admirer of Essex seems almost certain. Aside from the fact that his patron Southampton was Essex's closest friend, there are a number of apparent allusions in the plays – such as *The Merchant of Venice* and *King John* – to young Essex's career" – Campbell. Oxford is using the publicly performed plays to support his son by inserting references to Essex, with whom Southampton is allied, in opposition to the power of William and Robert Cecil.

Bacon Warns Essex, October 1596: The English fleet has returned from Cadiz; and Essex's supporter Francis Bacon now displays "almost prophetic vision" by warning him "of the plans likely to be pursued by Robert Cecil to encompass his downfall." - Acheson

Part One

THE SHAKESPEARE COMMITMENT

Sonnet 22
All That Beauty
1596

Oxford delivers a tender loving verse as father to son and, also, as loyal servant to sovereign. This year Robert Cecil gains the official title of Secretary of State, ensuring the transference of power from William Cecil, Lord Burghley, to his hunchbacked son. From this point on, Essex and Southampton are engaged in a power struggle with Secretary Cecil for control of the choice of the Queen's successor. Elizabeth turns sixty-three years old this year. This is her "grand climacteric," said to be the time of her full ripening. Oxford measures Time for himself and his royal son according to the time left in the Queen's life.

Sonnet 22	Translation
My glass shall not persuade me I am old	My mirror will not convince me that I'm old
So long as youth and thou are of one date,	So long as your royal blood and you succeed,
But when in thee time's furrows I behold,	But when I see Elizabeth's waning life in you,
Then look I death my days should expiate.	Then I look ahead and see my own extinction.
For all that beauty that doth cover thee,	For all of Elizabeth's royal blood that's in you
Is but the seemly raiment of my heart,	Is the only thing that empowers my heart,
Which in thy breast doth live, as thine in me.	Which lives in you, as your heart lives in me.
How can I then be elder than thou art?	How can I then be closer to death than you?
O therefore, love, be of thy self so wary,	O therefore, royal son, be so careful for yourself
As I not for my self, but for thee will,	As I, not for myself, but on your behalf, will,
Bearing thy heart which I will keep so chary	Carrying your royal heart, support it so carefully,
As tender nurse her babe from faring ill,	As a nurse tenderly protects her child from ill.
Presume not on thy heart when mine is slain,	Don't expect to regain your royal heart from me:
Thou gav'st me thine not to give back again.	You gave it to me [as my son] and I can't return it.

1 MY GLASS SHALL NOT PERSUADE ME I AM OLD
MY GLASS = my mirror or hourglass; "Thou art thy mother's glass," Oxford wrote to his son about his reflection of Elizabeth his mother; and by the same token, Southampton is Oxford's own glass, reflecting him as father

2 SO LONG AS YOUTH AND THOU ARE OF ONE DATE,
YOUTH AND THOU = your young or "fresh" opportunity (as it still is, now in your youth) and you; **ONE** = Southampton, *One for All, All for One*; **ARE OF ONE DATE** = are destined to meet at the date of the royal succession, when you should become king; "Thy end is Truth's and Beauty's *doom and date*" – Sonnet 14, line 14; according to the "date" on the "lease" of his royal opportunity to gain the throne: "And *Sum-*

REFERENCE EDITION 165

mer's lease hath all too short a date" – Sonnet 18, line 4, referring to the "golden time" that will come to an end; and when Southampton is later imprisoned for high treason, having lost his chance, Oxford writes of him as "precious friends hid in death's *dateless* night" – Sonnet 30, line 6; Southampton also possesses eternal blood that is therefore "dateless" in that sense; when he was an infant in 1574, he had "this holy fire of love" or royal blood that possessed "a *dateless* lively heat" that was "still to endure" or destined to live forever – Sonnet 154, lines 5-6; **ONE DATE** = Southampton's date with succession

3 BUT WHEN IN THEE TIME'S FURROWS I BEHOLD,
TIME'S FURROWS = your reflection of Time, the ever-dwindling time left in Elizabeth's life: **THEE** = "No, great King, I come to *thee* for charitable license" – *Henry V*, 4.7.69-70

4 THEN LOOK I DEATH MY DAYS SHOULD EXPIATE.
Then I anticipate extinction, or the close of the reign without your succession; **MY DAYS** = my days in the warmth of your golden sunshine or kingship; "Shall I compare thee to a Summer's *day*?" – Sonnet 18, line 1; "Why didst thou promise such a beauteous *day*" – Sonnet 34, line 1; **EXPIATE** = bring to an end; "Makes haste: *the hour of death is expiate*" – *Richard III*, 3.3.24, or "now expired" in the Folio of 1623

5 FOR ALL THAT BEAUTY THAT DOTH COVER THEE
ALL = Southampton, *One for All, All for One*; **ALL THAT BEAUTY** = what you have inherited from Elizabeth, who is Beauty; "From fairest creatures we desire increase,/ That thereby *beauty's Rose* might never die" – Sonnet 1, lines 1-2; "Proving his *beauty by succession* thine" – Sonnet 2, line 12; "For *beauty's pattern to succeeding men*" – Sonnet 19, line 12, the latter referring specifically to Southampton as in line to succeed Elizabeth

6 IS BUT THE SEEMLY RAIMENT OF MY HEART,
SEEMLY RAIMENT = appropriate covering

7 WHICH IN THY BREAST DOTH LIVE, AS THINE IN ME:
WHICH IN THY BREAST DOTH LIVE = my heart lives within you; **THY** = "Now good angels fly over *thy* royal head, and shade *thy* person under their blessed wings" – *Henry VIII*, 5.1.159-161; **AS THINE IN ME** = as your heart lives in my breast

> But that you have *your father's bosom* there
> And speak *his very heart*
> - *The Winter's Tale*, 4.4.565-566

8 HOW CAN I THEN BE ELDER THAN THOU ART?
Since we are so joined as one, how can I be older (or separate) from you; **ELDER** – but, being his father, he is in fact Southampton's elder.

9 O THEREFORE, LOVE, BE OF THY SELF SO WARY
O = Oxford; **LOVE** = my royal son; **WARY** = cautious, careful, prudent

10 AS I NOT FOR MY SELF, BUT FOR THEE WILL,
NOT FOR MYSELF, BUT FOR THEE = the father living through his son; ("For *thee, and for my self*, no quiet find" – Sonnet 27, line 14; "my friend and I are one" – Sonnet 42, line 13); as I will be wary for your sake, not for my own; "O therefore, my royal son, be careful for your royal self, in the same way that I – not for myself, but for you – will do the same."

11 BEARING THY HEART, WHICH I WILL KEEP SO CHARY
THY HEART = the source of your royal blood; **BEARING THY HEART** = recreating the source of your royal blood (in these sonnets); giving birth to you, over and over, in the womb of this monument of verse; **CHARY** = carefully, lovingly

12 AS TENDER NURSE HER BABE FROMFARING ILL.
TENDER NURSE = nurse tenderly, royally; ("This blessed plot, this earth, this realm, this England, this *nurse*, this teeming *womb* of royal kings, feared by their breed, and famous by their birth" – *Richard II*, 2.1.49-52; "the *tender* prince" – *Richard III*, 3.1.28); "His *tender heir* might bear his memory" – Sonnet 1, line 4, speaking of Southampton's own heir, if he would marry and beget one

HER BABE = her child, i.e., my royal son; (Later, addressing Elizabeth in the Dark Lady series, Oxford will use "babe" while speaking in Southampton's own voice: "Whilst I, thy *babe*, chase thee afar behind;/ But if thou catch thy hope, turn back to me,/ And play the mother's part, kiss me, be kind" – Sonnet 143, lines 10-12); "*Love is a Babe*, then might I not say so/ To give full growth to that which still doth grow" – Sonnet 112, lines 13-14, referring to the "love" or royal blood of his babe or son, Southampton ("the little Love-God" of Sonnet 154, line 1) who still grows in these verses; **FROM FARING ILL** = from getting into trouble or harm's way; from failing to gain the throne

13 PRESUME NOT ON THY HEART WHEN MINE IS SLAIN:
Don't expect to get your heart back from me when I am dead; "The beloved, if careless of himself, may so destroy the poet's heart, since he has it in his breast" – Tucker, 1924

14 THOU GAV'ST ME THINE NOT TO GIVE BACK AGAIN.
You gave me your heart forever.

1597

Plans for Islands Voyage, Spring 1597: Essex prepares for another risky military venture, this time the "Islands Voyage" to the Azores. Meanwhile Secretary Robert Cecil has gained the Queen's permission for Southampton to a command a ship of the fleet. Whether Cecil is trying to hurt or help him, at last the younger earl will be setting off to the wars.

The Islands Voyage, July 1597: The English have set sail, with Essex commanding a fleet of one hundred and fifty ships putting out from Plymouth Sound. One of them, the *Garland*, is under Southampton's command. "I verily believe a willinger company never undertook any journey," he writes back to Secretary Cecil. But a fierce storm wreaks havoc. Only a few ships – including the *Garland* – make it through the storm and press on, but Southampton and the others receive orders from Essex to return. By the end of July all are back in Plymouth Harbor for repairs.

Second Voyage, August 1597: The English ships sail once again for the Azores. This time they are becalmed in tropical waters and confusion spreads. At last the Queen's forces catch up to Philip's treasure fleet of twenty-five Spanish ships and Southampton leads an effort to capture them. Two other vessels divert his attention, however; and nearing them, Southampton discovers they are English ships. Meanwhile the treasure fleet has escaped.

"Thus the grand opportunity of the campaign, and of the war, was missed. The English fleet came home full of mutual recrimination and bitterness – while the Queen, eloquent with reproaches, determined to have no more such expeditions for the rest of her days. " – A. L. Rowse in his biography of Southampton

THE SHAKESPEARE COMMITMENT

Sonnet 23
What Silent Love Hath Writ
1597

This year Southampton joins Essex on the Islands Voyage against Spain. In their struggle for power against the Cecils, the two earls are clearly counting on leverage to be gained by military success and its resulting popularity. Writing behind the scenes, Oxford records his nervous support of Henry Wriothesley as heir to the throne. Also a playwright and patron of acting companies, he begins with the metaphor of an actor on the stage.

Sonnet 23	Translation
As an unperfect actor on the stage,	Like an actor on stage who doesn't know his lines,
Who with his fear is put besides his part,	Who loses mastery of his role because of fear,
Or some fierce thing replete with too much rage,	Or some royal prince replete with too much rage,
Whose strength's abundance weakens his own heart;	Whose great royalty weakens his own royal self;
So I for fear of trust, forget to say	So I, afraid of my responsibility, forget to envision
The perfect ceremony of love's right,	The coronation of royal blood's right,
And in mine own love's strength seem to decay,	And in my own son's royal blood I seem to decay,
O'er-charged with burthen of mine own love's might:	Weighed with burden of my own son's royal power.
O let my books be then the eloquence	O let these Sonnets then be the speakers
And dumb presagers of my speaking breast,	And silent messengers of my speaking breast,
Who plead for love, and look for recompense,	That pleads on behalf of royalty and its return
More than that tongue that more hath more expressed.	More than any tongue that has spoken openly.
O learn to read what silent love hath writ,	O learn to read what royal blood has written!
To hear with eyes belongs to love's fine wit.	To hear what can't be spoken is princely wisdom.

1 AS AN UNPERFECT ACTOR ON THE STAGE,
UNPERFECT = non-royal player on the world stage; "*Like a dull actor* now I have forgot my part and I am out, even to a full disgrace" – *Coriolanus*, 5.3.40-42

2 WHO WITH HIS FEAR IS PUT BESIDE HIS PART,
Who, out of fear, forgets what to say; "Then may I dare to boast how I do love thee,/ Till then not show my head where thou mayst prove me" – Sonnet 26, lines 13-14; "And art made tongue-tied by authority" – Sonnet 66, line 9

3 **OR SOME FIERCE THING REPLETE WITH TOO MUCH RAGE,**
SOME FIERCE THING = some royal thing (Elizabeth or Southampton); **REPLETE WITH TOO MUCH RAGE** = filled with too much anger or destructiveness; also alluding to Elizabeth's refusal to acknowledge Henry Wriothesley; **RAGE** = royal anger and power, used destructively; "How with this *rage* shall beauty hold a plea" – Sonnet 65, line 3, when Oxford fortifies himself against Elizabeth's imminent execution of Southampton

4 **WHOSE STRENGTH'S ABUNDANCE WEAKENS HIS OWN HEART:**
STRENGTH'S ABUNDANCE = abundance of royal blood ("Making a famine where abundance lies" – Sonnet 1, line 7); i.e., Oxford draws upon this power from his royal son; **WEAKENS HIS OWN HEART** = takes away royal status from my heart, which is yours; **HEART** = source of royal blood; the seat of "love" or royal blood; the motive of activity or purpose; also the soul or spirit; the inmost or most vital part, the essence

5 **SO I FOR FEAR OF TRUST FORGET TO SAY**
SO I, FOR FEAR OF TRUST = so I, fearing to trust that I can speak truth; **TRUST** = the state of being confident in something; "You, his false hopes, the *trust* of England's honor" – *1 Henry VI*, 4.4.20; Oxford feels that Southampton has been left in his trust, as in "Ah, he is young, and his minority is *put into the trust* of Richard Gloucester" – *Richard III*, 1.3.11-12

"But if it shall please Her Majesty in regard of my youth, time and future spent in her Court, adding thereto Her Majesty's favors and promises, which *drew me on without any mistrust* the more to presume in mine own expenses ... For I know Her Majesty is of that princely disposition that *they shall not be deceived which put their trust in her*"
– Oxford to Robert Cecil, February 2, 1601

FORGET TO SAY = intentionally refrain from speaking out, at least in public; also as in "to *say* grace" or "to *say* prayers"; to recite the liturgy; "Nothing, sweet boy, but yet like prayers divine,/ I must each day *say* o'er the very same" – Sonnet 108, lines 5-6

6 **THE PERFECT CEREMONY OF LOVE'S RIGHT,**
The solemn coronation of royal blood's right to the throne, i.e., your succession; i.e., Oxford cannot publicly or directly proclaim Southampton's right to the throne, nor can he bring about his son's succession ; **PERFECT** = royal; peerless; kingly, as a sun; "Three glorious suns, each one *a perfect sun*" – *3 Henry VI*, 2.1.26; "Such cherubins as your sweet self resemble,/ Creating every bad a *perfect* best,/ As fast as objects to his beams assemble" – Sonnet 114, lines 6-8; **RIGHT** = royal blood right; "And whoso'er gainsays *King Edward's right*" – *3 Henry VI*, 4.7.74; "And *your true rights* be termed a Poet's rage" – Sonnet 17, line 11; "That for *thy right* myself will bear all wrong" – Sonnet 88, line 14; **RIGHT** = suggests the ceremonial "rite" of coronation; also suggesting a betrothal ceremony by which Oxford and Elizabeth may have exchanged rings in 1573 or 1574; Most editors simply change *right* of Q1 1609 to *rite*, but Oxford probably intended *right* while suggesting *rite*, as in: "Caesar shall have all true *rites* and lawful *ceremonies*" – *Julius Caesar*, 3.1.240-241

7 **AND IN MINE OWN LOVE'S STRENGTH SEEM TO DECAY,**
MINE OWN LOVE'S STRENGTH = my own royal son's princely power; **SEEM TO DECAY** = feel a lack of power, related to the "decay" of Elizabeth's mortal body leading to her death; i.e., Oxford feels himself losing life itself, or weakening, as he attempts to carry the burden of having a son with such royal power and right to the throne; the responsibility is too great to bear

MINE OWN = a singular phrase used frequently in the Shakespeare plays to refer to a child. The phrase is used no less than thirteen times in this collection: Sonnets 23 (twice), 39 (three times), 49, 61, 62 (twice), 72, 88, 107 and 110.

> "For now (as) it has pleased God to give me *a son of mine own*…"
> - Oxford to Lord Burghley, his father-in-law, writing from Paris on March 17, 1575, referring to news that his wife Anne Cecil is expecting a child. A second meaning is that, since Oxford could not claim his son by the Queen (born in late May or early June of 1574) as his own, he now looks forward to having what he hopes will be a son that in fact he can claim. The child will be a daughter, Elizabeth Vere, born later in 1575.

> "Where is my other life? *Mine own* is gone!"
> – *1 Henry VI, 4.7.1*, Talbot referring to his son

> "What can *mine own* praise to *mine own* self bring,
> And what is't but *mine own* when I praise thee?"
> - Sonnet 39, lines 3-4

8 O'ER-CHARGED WITH BURTHEN OF MINE OWN LOVE'S MIGHT:
O'ER-CHARGED = overloaded; **BURTHEN** = burden; ("The *second burthen of a former child*" – Sonnet 59, line 4); **MINE OWN** = repeated from the preceding line; ("The repetition of these words denotes emphasis" – Tucker)

OF MINE OWN LOVE'S MIGHT = of my own royal son's power as prince; "England shall give him office, honor, *might*" – *2 Henry IV*, 4.5.129, the King speaking of his son the prince; Oxford is overburdened with his attempts to safeguard his royal son's right to the throne

9 O LET MY BOOKS BE THEN THE ELOQUENCE
The only way of discharging the burden is to write these private sonnets, into which Oxford pours his son's royal blood to create "the living record" of him as in Sonnet 55, line 8; i.e., Oh, then let my books carry your life and royal claim; **O** = Oxford

MY BOOKS = this Book of Sonnets, delivered in ongoing clusters or books; but also the two books already published and dedicated by "Shakespeare" to Southampton (*Venus and Adonis* and *Lucrece*); "The books of which Shakespeare speaks are probably the manuscript books in which he writes his sonnets, sending them, when a group has been written or a book filled, to his friend" – Dowden; "And of *this book* this learning mayst thou taste/ … These offices, so oft as thou wilt look,/ Shall profit thee, and much enrich *thy book*" – Sonnet 77, lines 4, 13-14, referring to the Book of Sonnets as a whole; "The dedicated words which writers use/ Of their fair subject, blessing *every book*" – Sonnet 82, lines 3-4, in reference to the dedications to Southampton by "Shakespeare" of the two published books, *Venus and Adonis* and *Lucrece*, using "every book" as "books" written by "E. Ver" or Edward de Vere

"Books cannot with any appropriateness be described as 'dumb' or 'silent,'" Tucker argued in 1924, but this apparent flaw in the poetry is cleared up when Oxford is perceived as writing on two levels by means of a special language, in which case his books are indeed "dumb" or "silent" in terms their ability to convey their meaning directly.

10 AND DUMB PRESAGERS OF MY SPEAKING BREAST,
DUMB PRESAGERS = silent predictors; ("And the sad augurs mock their own *presage*" – Sonnet 107, line 6); **MY SPEAKING BREAST** = my speaking heart; i.e., he cannot speak out publicly, since it's trea-

son to write or speak of a royal claim, so these sonnets must speak in private.

11 WHO PLEAD FOR LOVE AND LOOK FOR RECOMPENSE
WHO = these verses, carrying my silent thoughts of you; **WHO PLEAD FOR LOVE** = these sonnets, which plead for your royal blood; **PLEAD** = argue on a legal basis; ("How with this rage shall beauty hold a *plea*" – Sonnet 65, line 3); **LOOK FOR RECOMPENSE** = look for equal return, in the form of your succession to the throne; at this point in time, there remains hope that Southampton might actually succeed as king; so the Sonnets carry that tension of real events occurring in real time, even while Oxford compiles them as a memorial

12 MORE THAN THAT TONGUE THAT MORE HATH MORE EXPRESSED.
More than "Shakespeare" has expressed more publicly than I am able to; ("And art made *tongue-tied by authority*" – Sonnet 66, line 9); more than I myself have said, even more, privately to the Queen your mother on your behalf

13 O LEARN TO READ WHAT SILENT LOVE HATH WRIT!
O = Oxford; **LEARN TO READ** = learn to read beyond the poetry on the surface of these private verses; **WHAT SILENT LOVE HATH WRIT** = what your secret royal blood has written here, through me; ("It is a *secret hidden* and not known/ Which one may better feel than *write* upon" – poem attributed to Robert Greene, 1589, but thought to be by Oxford; Chiljan, p. 176); "To thee I send this *written* ambassage" – Sonnet 26, line 3, referring to the sonnets as official messages of state that ambassadors memorized (in order to remain "silent" if captured) before delivering them orally at foreign courts; **WRIT** = echoing Holy Writ or Sacred Writ; Holy Scripture; the sacred (royal) record of these sonnets; written record; the noun is a legal term; a formal document or legal instrument; "a written command or order issued in the name of a sovereign, court, State, or other competent authority, directing a specified person or persons to act or refrain from acting in a specified way ... a document issued by the Crown to summon a peer to Parliament" - OED; also see Sonnets 71, 84, 93, 115, 116; echoing "writ of attachment" (summons) or "writ of error," etc.

14 TO HEAR WITH EYES BELONGS TO LOVE'S FINE WIT.
HEAR WITH EYES = hear my voice (hear my *ambassage*) by reading these verses; **LOVE'S FINE WIT** = royal blood's keen intelligence and understanding; this private diary is for Southampton to read, even while Oxford is also preserving it for posterity, as a record of his son's royal identity

1598

Southampton Makes Travel Plans, January 1598: With Essex rapidly losing the Queen's favor, Southampton begins making plans for a tour through France and Italy, as Oxford did in 1575 and 1576. His opportunity arises as Robert Cecil prepares to leave for Paris on a diplomatic mission, aiming to prevent Henri IV of France from making a treaty with Spain.

While Southampton plans to accompany the Secretary, he is still very much involved with Maid of Honor Elizabeth Vernon. Court gossip is that his impending departure "doth exceedingly grieve" her and that she "passes her time in weeping and lamenting." .In recent weeks he has become embroiled in various altercations at Court, and he and Elizabeth Vernon have been meeting clandestinely. By now he is "full of discontentment at the Queen's strangest usage of him."

Southampton and Cecil in France, February 15, 1598: Her Majesty nevertheless gives Southampton license to travel abroad for up to two years, attended by ten servants and six horses, along with two hundred pounds and a letter of credit for a thousand crowns. And after a final secret meeting with Essex (whose supporters have begun using the code "1,000" to identify him), Southampton and Secretary Cecil land at Dieppe.

Meeting with King Henri of France, March 1598: Southampton and Cecil arrive in Paris. At the Angiers camp they met with King Henri, who "very favorably embraced and welcomed" the Earl of Southampton. But the French king goes ahead and concludes a treaty with Spain, turning the Secretary's mission into a failure.

Southampton to Paris, April 1598: Cecil returns home; but Southampton remains at the French Court, still intending to travel into Italy. In Paris he meets up with two old friends, the brothers Charles and Henry Danvers, now exiles; and so he lingers on – apparently making every effort to put England, and his potential role in its future, far out of mind.

Death of Lord Burghley, August 4, 1598: William Cecil, Lord Treasurer Burghley, the mastermind of Elizabeth's reign and architect of the Protestant Reformation in England, dies at age seventy-eight. The Queen retires to her private chambers to weep alone.

Burghley's primary goal, beyond serving Elizabeth, had been "the advancement and elevation of his family," writes descendant David Cecil in the twentieth century; but no further advancement would be possible if Essex controlled the succession and became more powerful during the next reign, regardless of who became king. Shortly before dying, Burghley had summoned his son Robert to his bedside and told him that one of his prime duties and goals was to "have regard to the tottering commonwealth, after thy Mistress's death, to invest the true and lawful successor."

Robert Cecil in Charge, August 1598: Burghley passed away quietly, but a political struggle erupted. At this point the hunchbacked Robert Cecil, left to fulfill his father's ambitions alone, takes virtually complete charge of the Elizabethan government.

"Though ambitious of power and none too scrupulous in his political methods, Burghley presents on the whole a sturdy figure. Restrained by an apparently sincere religious faith, there were depths of political perfidy to which he would not descend. His son, however, was untrammeled either by faith or conscience. The death of Burghley in 1598, removing Robert Cecil's sole confidant, removed also his only moral restraint … The depths of this unscrupulous politician's duplicity have never been historically sounded."
- Acheson, 80-81

"Though there are many indications of his having possessed a kindly and affectionate nature, he (Robert Cecil) seems never to have had a friendship. Life was to him a game, which he was playing for high stakes, and men and women were only pieces upon the board, set there to be swept off by one side or the other or allowed to stand so long only as the risk of letting them remain there was not too great" - *Dictionary of National Biography*

"It was not alone Essex's influence with the Queen that Cecil feared, but still more the bond of friendship he had established with her logical successor the Scottish King. To discredit his incautious and high-spirited rival with the resentful and capricious Elizabeth was a comparatively simple matter, but to undermine his relations with James, without either tacitly or openly espousing the cause of his succession, and thereby risking his hold upon the confidence of Elizabeth, was not so easy. Yet to accomplish both of these things, and in addition to encompass the death of Essex and the ruin of his faction, under color of law, and at the same time to win the favor and confidence of James, were the apparently impossible ends that now became Cecil's

No. 23

objective." - Acheson, 80

Southampton Marries Elizabeth Vernon, September 1598: Southampton was in Paris when he learned of Burghley's death, but his return early this month is for a different reason: the Lady Elizabeth Vernon is carrying his child. He makes his way back to London, disguising himself as an ordinary citizen and staying out of sight while sending a message to Essex, asking for "assignation of some time and place where I may attend you to find you alone, so that I may come unknown." After that meeting he marries Lady Vernon in private, then steals out of England again.

The Queen learns of Southampton's secret marriage while he is still aboard a ship bringing him back to Paris. She fires off a message to her ambassador in France with instructions to order the earl home at once. Secretary Cecil writes to him directly, saying Her Majesty is "grievously offended" and "commands me to charge you expressly (all excuses set apart) to repair hither to London, and advertise your arrival, without coming to the Court, until her pleasure be known."

These are harsh, ominous words. Elizabeth continues to rage, threatening to send everyone involved to the Tower, and in fact she orders the pregnant Maid of Honor imprisoned in the Fleet, where Essex will take it upon himself to pay for her maintenance. Southampton, meanwhile, stalls by pleading lack of funds to pay his passage back to England.

Southampton Imprisoned in the Fleet, November 1598: After remaining in France for a few weeks, Southampton arrives in London in early November and promptly finds himself lodged in the Fleet. Soon afterward Elizabeth Vernon, now Countess of Southampton, gives birth to a daughter, christened Penelope, in honor of Essex's sister Penelope Rich. The earl, in disgrace and still under Her Majesty's extreme displeasure, remains in jail.

PALLADIS TAMIA, **November 1598:** A book entitled *Palladis Tamia*, having been registered in September, now goes on sale with its announcement that the poet William Shakespeare is also the author of some of the most popular stage plays in England. The little book represents the labors of an obscure schoolmaster, Francis Meres, who received his MA from Cambridge in 1591, when Southampton was a student there. Meres is a brother-in-law of Southampton's Italian tutor, John Florio, whose English-Italian dictionary *A World of Words* is also published this year with dedications to Southampton and Rutland as well as the Countess of Bedford. (Two years earlier, when Florio registered the dictionary in 1596, he indicated his intention to dedicate it solely to Southampton – a signal that the earl pledged to finance the publication for him.) In any case, Henry Wriothesley certainly knows Meres, whose identification of Shakespeare as a playwright will lift him (Meres) from obscurity and ensure his own fame in history.

Palladis Tamia includes a specially inserted section, unlike all the others, indicating that another hand is at work – suggested here as that of Oxford, deciding to act swiftly upon the death of Burghley to link the "Shakespeare" plays in the public's mind with Southampton, who is already publicly linked to the Shakespeare name through the two narrative poems, *Venus and Adonis* and *Lucrece*. Omitting any first name for Shakespeare, this special section thrusts him to the front rank of literary artists and proclaims him the greatest living Englishman of letters. This is the first published reference to "Shakespeare" as a playwright.

As the soul of Euphorbus was thought to live in Pythagoras, so the sweet witty soul of Ovid lives in mellifluous and honey-tongued Shakespeare: witness his *Venus and Adonis*, his *Lucrece*, **his sugared *Sonnets* among his private friends**, etc.

It is unknown whether any of the private Fair Youth sonnets to Southampton had been circulated among any "*private friends*" other than the young earl himself, though he may have shared them with Essex and some others such as his friend Rutland. Oxford will refer to his son upon the Rebellion of February 8, 1601, as "***precious friends** hid in death's dateless night*" in Sonnet 30, line 6. He often uses the plural to refer to the singular, as when he addressed Southampton as "*fairest creatures*" in Sonnet 1, line 1. On the other hand, he has written many other verses and sonnets that he may have circulated among friends. These include the two verses that will appear in *The Passionate Pilgrim* of 1599 and then reappear in 1609 (with significant revisions) as Sonnets 138 and 144 of the Dark Lady series.

"SHAKESPEARE" IDENTIFIED AS DRAMATIST:

Here in *Palladis Tamia* is a public announcement that "Shakespeare" is England's answer to Ovid, the ancient Roman poet; and then comes the biggest news:

> As Plautus and Seneca are accounted the best for comedy and tragedy among the Latins, so *Shakespeare* among the English is the most excellent in both kinds for the stage:
>
> For comedy, witness his *Gentlemen of Verona*, his *Errors*, his *Love's Labour's Lost*, his *Love's Labour's Won*, his *Midsummer Night's Dream*, and his *Merchant of Venice*.
>
> For tragedy, his *Richard II, Richard III, Henry IV, King John, Titus Andronicus*, and his *Romeo and Juliet*…
>
> As Epius Stolo said that the Muses would speak with Plautus' tongue if they would speak Latin, so I say that the Muses would speak with *Shakespeare's* fine filed phrase if they would speak English.
>
> This inserted section lists the names of the "best" writers in England for lyric poetry, tragedy and comedy, as well as "the most passionate among us to bewail and bemoan the perplexities of love." The name of Shakespeare appears among those in all four categories, including that of comedy; and the latter list begins with Oxford's name:
>
> **The best for Comedy amongst us be Edward Earle of Oxford**, Doctor Gager of Oxforde, Master Rowley once a rare Scholar of learned Pembroke Hall in Cambridge, Master Edwards one of her Majesty's Chapel, eloquent and witty John Lyly, Lodge, Gascoyne, Greene, *Shakespeare*…

In this way Oxford is also separating himself publicly from Shakespeare. Although he has been known as a writer of "comedies" for the Court and the public stage during the 1580s, none of those plays have survived under their original titles or in their original versions; instead, his own revisions of them began to reappear in the 1590s, with different titles.

Such is the price Oxford now pays in terms of his identity as England's great dramatist, so he may continue to support Southampton by associating him with his plays. Of primary value is the magnificent series of chronicle plays that bring England's royal history to life on the public stage. These are plays in which he has begun to insert pointed references to Southampton (reflecting him in the historical character of Prince Hal, the future Henry V, for example), which supporters of both Essex and Southampton obviously appreciate.

Issuance of Plays as by Shakespeare, 1598: Plays now begin to be published with the name "Shakespeare" as author; some had appeared in print previously, in inferior form, bearing no author's name. These include *Love's Labour's Lost* (which had been a favorite of Southampton and his university friends during early years of the decade), as well as the stirring history plays *Richard II* and *Richard III*, the latter with its description of England as "this royal throne of kings, this sceptered isle, this earth of majesty, this seat of Mars." (And in Acheson's view the portrait of the hunchbacked king of that play has been revised with "the deformed and aspiring little Secretary Cecil in mind.") Supporting his son, Oxford is also sounding the great Shakespearean themes of royal blood and lineage as well as royal responsibility.

"Southampton's associates, friends and followers became Shakespeare's models for his characters, according to the estimate he formed of their good or evil influence upon the character or fortunes of his friend. Shakespeare's political leanings were palpably towards the Essex faction. However much he may at times have deprecated the un-wisdom of the conduct of Essex and Southampton, he undoubtedly sympathized with their aspirations and was deeply antipathetic towards the Cecil faction." - Acheson

Irish Expedition Planned, December 1598: Southampton was liberated from the Fleet in November, but never again will he be admitted to the Queen's presence. By now Elizabeth clearly has concluded that she cannot support him as her successor; and, too, she now apparently fears that both Essex and Southampton are potential threats to the stability of the throne and even to her personal safety.

"Southampton's early liberation from the Fleet in November 1598 was not due to Elizabeth's forgiveness. His freedom was granted in order to placate Essex and hasten his acceptance of the command of the Irish Expedition, then in the course of preparation ... Both Essex and his more judicious followers realized the dangerous responsibility that Cecil was now endeavoring to foist upon him, and suspected occult and sinister motives in the little Secretary's eagerness to remove him from the Court and to embark him in such a doubtful enterprise. They remembered how disastrous Ireland had hitherto proved to military reputations." - Acheson

Essex Accepts Irish Command, December 1598: After much haggling about conditions under which he will become the Queen's general sent to put down rebellion in Ireland, Essex reluctantly agrees. Southampton will go with him, also in a leadership role.

THE SHAKESPEARE COMMITMENT

Sonnet 24
Thy Beauty's Form
1598

This year marks a turning point with the death of Lord Burghley in August and the consolidation of government power into the hands of his son Robert Cecil, Secretary of State. In reaction, Oxford causes "Shakespeare" to be cited by Francis Meres as the author of a dozen popular plays. He thereby links Southampton to the works that reflect him, for example, as Prince Hal, the future Henry V. The Queen imprisons Southampton briefly for impregnating and marrying Essex's cousin Elizabeth Vernon, a Maid of Honor. (She gives birth to a baby girl, Penelope, named after Essex's sister.) Now it is only a matter of time before the Rebellion of Essex and Southampton against Secretary Cecil will erupt. In this private sonnet, Oxford uses painting as metaphor: the image of his royal son lies within the picture drawn by the words.

Sonnet 24	Translation
Mine eye hath played the painter and hath steeld	My eye, like a painter, has indelibly written
Thy beauty's form in table of my heart;	Your blood from Elizabeth on pages of my heart.
My body is the frame wherein 'tis held,	My body is the book cover in which it exists,
And perspective it is best Painter's art.	And my perspective of you is my best art,
For through the Painter must you see his skill,	For by this means you must see my meaning,
To find where your true Image pictured lies,	To find where the truth of you is described,
Which in my bosom's shop is hanging still,	Which truth always appears within my mind,
That hath his windows glazed with thine eyes:	That your eyes act as windows to see.
Now see what good-turns eyes for eyes have done,	Now see what good your eyes have done for mine.
Mine eyes have drawn thy shape, and thine for me	My eyes have seen your royalty, and yours for me
Are windows to my breast, where-through the Sun	Are windows to my heart, where you, my son,
Delights to peep, to gaze therein on thee.	Can enjoy looking and seeing your royal self.
Yet eyes this cunning want to grace their art	Yet eyes with this skill, not seeing your royal grace,
They draw but what they see, know not the heart.	Write only what they see, not seeing royal blood.

1 MINE EYE HATH PLAYED THE PAINTER AND HATH STEELD
STEELD = usually emended to "stelled" or "stell'd" meaning portrayed, as in "To find a face where all distress is stell'd" – Lucrece, 1444; fixed, written permanently, as if in steel, in this growing monument to preserve you; Oxford is speaking as Southampton's father, attempting to recreate him or give rebirth to him in the womb of these sonnets. Earlier Elizabeth, in the sonnets as Nature, had "painted" or created their son: "A Woman's face with nature's own hand *painted*/ Hast thou, the Master Mistress of my passion" - Sonnet 20, lines 1-2

Part One

2 THY BEAUTY'S FORM IN TABLE OF MY HEART;
THY BEAUTY'S FORM = the picture of you as the son of "beauty" or Elizabeth; the outward appearance of your "beauty" or royal blood, the form of a king

> Like perspectives, which rightly gazed upon
> Show nothing but confusion, eyed awry
> Distinguish *form*: so your sweet Majesty...
> - *Richard II*, 2.2.18-20

> Tradition, *form* and ceremonious duty
> - *Richard II*, 3.2.173

> Be of good comfort, prince; for you are born
> To set a *form* upon that indigest
> Which he hath left so shapeless and so rude
> - *King John*, 5.7.25-27

TABLE = a tablet or panel (from Latin *tabula*) on which a picture is painted; but also meant by Oxford as a writing tablet; "My *tables*. Meet it is I set it down" – *Hamlet*, 1.5.107; **OF MY HEART** = the verses of the Sonnets are written indelibly on the tablet of my heart; "To sit and draw his arched brows, his hawking eye, his curls, in *our heart's table*" – *All's Well That Ends Well*, 1.1.104-106. Southampton is the one inspiring or begetting the Sonnets, filling them with the "gift" of his life and blood. Therefore, they are Southampton's tables. "Thy gift, thy tables, are within my brain/ Full characterd with lasting memory" - Sonnet 122, lines 1-2

3 MY BODY IS THE FRAME WHEREIN 'TIS HELD,
MY BODY, etc. = my body acts to frame this inward picture; holding it as both concealed and revealed.
FRAME = "Lord Timon's *frame*" – *Timon of Athens*, 1.1.71; "His head by nature *framed* to wear a crown" – *3 Henry VI*, 4.6.72; "To this composed wonder of *your frame*" – Sonnet 59, line 10; "To bitter sauces did I *frame* my feeding" – Sonnet 118, line 6

4 AND PERSPECTIVE IT IS BEST PAINTER'S ART.
AND PERSPECTIVE, etc. = Oxford learned about Renaissance painting firsthand from his travels in Italy in 1575-1576; perspective is literally drawing or seeing from a proper angle; in regard to these sonnets, the "best" art is to see through the surface to what is really being conveyed; perspective must be used to see the most important image or meaning.

5 FOR THROUGH THE PAINTER MUST YOU SEE HIS SKILL
THROUGH THE PAINTER, etc. = you (here meaning "one" or a general reader) must look through the artist and his art to see the truth

> A thousand moral paintings I can show
> That shall demonstrate these quick blows of Fortune's
> More pregnantly than words
> - The Painter in *Timon of Athens*, 1.1.92-94

6 TO FIND WHERE YOUR TRUE IMAGE PICTURED LIES,
YOUR TRUE IMAGE = your true identity as my royal son; the true and accurate expression of you and your right to the throne; ("And your *true* rights be termed a Poet's rage" – Sonnet 17, line 11); **TRUE** = related to Oxford, *Nothing Truer than Truth*; **IMAGE** = ("I then did use the person of your father; the *image* of his power lay then in me … the *image* of the King whom I presented … your most *royal image*" – *2 Henry IV*, 5.2.74-89)

7 WHICH IN MY BOSOM'S SHOP IS HANGING STILL,
This image hangs within my own bosom, my workshop; **STILL** = constantly, always

8 THAT HATH HIS WINDOWS GLAZED WITH THINE EYES.
My inner workshop has your eyes for windows, out of which I can see; **GLAZED** = made royal; **THINE EYES** = your stars or suns, reflecting your royalty; ("And scarcely greet me with that sunne thine eye" – Sonnet 49, line 6)

9 NOW SEE WHAT GOOD TURNS EYES FOR EYES HAVE DONE:
EYES FOR EYES = your royal eyes are now my eyes, through which I see

10 MINE EYES HAVE DRAWN THY SHAPE, AND THINE FOR ME
I have recreated you in this verse according to my own eyes

11 ARE WINDOWS TO MY BREAST, WHERE-THROUGH THE SUN
And your eyes are windows for me; I look into your eyes and see my own heart within my breast; **THE SUN** = the royal son, you, your eye; "Even so my Sunne one early morn did shine,/ With all triumphant splendor on my brow" – Sonnet 33, lines 9-10, of Southampton's birth; "And scarcely greet me with that sunne thine eye" – Sonnet 49, line 6

12 DELIGHTS TO PEEP, TO GAZE THEREIN ON THEE:
DELIGHTS TO PEEP = gazes joyfully at me; "When sparkling stars twire (peep) not, thou gild'st the even" – Sonnet 28, line 12; **TO GAZE**, etc. = my eyes do this by gazing at you, as a subject gazes at his king

13 YET EYES THIS CUNNING WANT TO GRACE THEIR ART;
Yet my own eyes, by themselves, lack the skill to fill their creation (this verse) with your royal grace; "Be as thy presence is, *gracious* and kind" – Sonnet 10, line 11; **CUNNING** = skill, knowledge; ("But the world is so *cunning*, as of a shadow they can make a substance, and of a likelihood a truth" – Oxford to Burghley, July 1581); **CUNNING/GRACE** = ("What *cunning* can express/ The favor of her face,/ To whom in this distress/ I do appeal for *grace*" – Oxford poem in *The Phoenix Next*, 1593, signed E. O., referring to Elizabeth); "My verse alone had *all thy gentle grace,/* But now my *gracious numbers* are decayed" – Sonnet 67, lines 2-3; "And I prithee sweet wag, when thou art king, as God save thy Grace – Majesty, I should say" – *1 Henry IV*, 1.2.16-17

14 THEY DRAW BUT WHAT THEY SEE, KNOW NOT THE HEART.
My mortal eyes create only what they see; without your eyes, as windows, they do not see you in my heart; **THE HEART** = Oxford's heart, but also Southampton's heart and source of royal blood

1599

Cecil's Power Grows, February 1599: Essex and Elizabeth seem on fairly good terms, but Robert Cecil's growing hold over the aging Queen has become visible. Now the Secretary's adherents are gaining preferment while Essex's friends, in addition to Southampton, are rebuffed at Court and treated coldly. Francis Bacon, for one, is starting to realize the accuracy of his own predictions. He has begun to fully comprehend "both Cecil's real objective and the relentless persistence with which he advanced towards it," Acheson writes.

Essex and Southampton Leave for Ireland, March 17, 1599: Essex and Southampton, their interlocking fates increasingly subject to Robert Cecil's strategic moves against them, leave London with an army of 15,000 soldiers bent on overwhelming the Irish Rebellion led by Tyrone. As general in charge, Essex is the focus of adoring crowds.

> "The people pressed exceedingly to behold him, especially in the highways, for more than four miles' space, crying and saying, 'God bless your Lordship! God preserve your honor!' – etc., and some followed him until the evening, only to behold him." (Stowe)

"Shakespeare" Supports Essex, Spring 1599: Although Oxford wrote *The Famous Victories of Henry the Fifth* back in the 1570s and created the earliest versions of what we now know as *Henry V* during the 1580s, he now adds thrilling lines for the Chorus in reference to Essex as "the General of our gracious Empress" – the general of Elizabeth. The hope is that Essex will return to England with the Irish rebellion "broached on his sword." The dating of these lines "can be fixed with unusual exactness," writes Joseph Campbell, echoing the vast majority of scholars on this point. Soon after the departure of Essex and Southampton for Ireland, audiences at the Curtain are given cause to cheer with recognition:

> How London doth pour out her citizens!
> The Mayor and all his brethren in best sort,
> Like to the senators of the antique Rome
> With the plebeians swarming at their heels,
> Go forth and fetch their conquering Caesar in –
> As, by a lower but as loving likelihood,
> Were now the General of our gracious Empress,
> As in good time he may, from Ireland coming,
> Bringing rebellion broached on his sword,
> How many would the peaceful city quit
> To welcome him!
> - *Henry V*, Epilogue

In fact, however, Essex and Southampton are heading for disaster; and Sonnet 25 will comprise a companion piece to the above speech.

"Cecil at last had led his victim into the trap he had laid for him, and meant if possible to keep him there. It appears likely that the Queen was wittingly a party to this device. The acrid tone of her letters to Essex, from the time he landed in Ireland, suggests that her recent appearance of favor had been dictated by policy." (Acheson)

Elizabeth Rebukes Essex, June 1599: Essex is increasingly oppressed and delayed by the unfamiliar environment of Ireland. On top of that, he has given Southampton the high post of General of the Horse, against the Queen's orders to the contrary, and she has furiously sent back orders to rescind the appointment. Essex will receive these instructions only after fierce fighting during which Southampton, after an unexpected attack, makes a courageous attempt to rescue three of his men before the Irish rebels can move in and cut their throats.

Southampton's Wife Writes of Falstaff, July 18, 1599: The name "W. Shake-speare" is on the title page of newly published texts of *1 Henry IV*, in which Oxford has depicted aspects of himself as Falstaff in a fatherly relation to Southampton as Prince Hal, who tells him:

> Do thou stand for my father and examine me
> Upon the particulars of my life

Southampton's wife Elizabeth Vernon writes to him in Ireland. In one letter she jokingly refers to the scene of *1 Henry IV* in which Falstaff calls the Tavern hostess by the nickname "Pintpot":

"All the news I can send you that I think will make you merry is that I read, in a letter from London, that Sir John Falstaff is by his Mistress Dame Pintpot made father of a goodly miller's thumb a boy that's all head and very little body, but this is a secret."

Bleak News from Ireland, July 1599: Reports of English frustration are growing. Money for the war is being spent too quickly, with too little to show for it. Essex, to prevent mutiny among his soldiers, is requesting more funds and supplies; but Elizabeth remarks at Court with cruel humor that she is giving him "a thousand pounds a day to go on progress."

Essex's Desperation, August 1599: By now Essex knows he lacks the resources to attack Tyrone in his Ulster stronghold and carry it through to success. The Queen, her mind poisoned against her general, cancels his permission to return to London for a private conference with her. His instructions are to fight on, no matter what the situation. The once-great favorite is trapped, hopelessly bogged down, and the only prospect is that of leading many men to their deaths in a losing battle with Tyrone's rebel army.

In extreme distress, Essex contemplates leaving Ireland with 3,000 of his best troops and, gaining additional forces along the way, marching upon London to take over the Court; but he lays aside that treasonous plan. Eighteen colonels and captains, including Southampton, formally protest that their soldiers are unfit to fight, but Essex decides (against all hope, but with no other choice) to go forward and face Tyrone. He sets forth with a select band of less than 3,000 foot soldiers and 300 horses.

Essex and Tyrone, September 1599: Essex and Southampton move north to Louth, establishing a camp there, while Tyrone and his forces shadow the English from the woods. Surrounded by an army twice the size, Essex is startled to receive a messenger from the rebels saying that Tyrone himself is ready to meet with him alone. Acting with typical bravado, Essex appears at dawn, on the top of a hill, with his army in full battle array; but Tyrone refuses to accept the challenge. Essex leads his troops away, with Southampton riding beside him; the messenger appears again, this time with word that Tryone is begging for mercy. He reports that Tryone wants to meet Essex alone at the ford of Bellaclynthe, between two rolling hills.

Essex and Southampton bring 2,000 soldiers on foot and 150 horses to the top of a rise. They see a small group of rebels, with only six horses, waiting across the way; below, on horseback in the stream, is the solitary figure of Tyrone. Essex, telling Southampton to keep the men out of earshot, rides down by himself to the water's edge. The two leaders speak to each other in secret for more than an hour.

The result is a "truce" allowing Tyrone to keep any ground in Ireland already held by his rebels and preventing the English from building any new garrisons or forts. The peace holds for renewable time periods of six weeks, with either side able to terminate the ceasefire by giving notice two weeks in advance. Tyrone, who expects reinforcements soon from Spain, has emerged with the upper hand. When Elizabeth gets news of the truce, the terms of which remain unclear, she writes back ordering her general to forget the whole thing until she sees it in writing and can evaluate it herself.

Essex and Southampton to London, September 29, 1599: Ignoring the Queen's instructions not to return without permission, Essex gives command of his army to subordinates and abruptly embarks for England. He and Southampton and several others begin a desperate ride through North Wales, bound for London, staking all on surprising the Court and gaining a personal confrontation with Elizabeth.

After four days and nights of constant riding, they clatter over the cobblestone streets of Westminster in the early morning of the twenty-ninth, only to learn that the Court has moved ten miles south to Nonsuch Palace. Commandeering fresh horses and riding off again, Essex and Southampton now get word that their enemy Lord Grey, a Cecil supporter, has galloped ahead to warn the Secretary of their imminent arrival. With the advantage of surprise removed, they face arrest on charges of treason for having left the battlefield.

Although Lord Grey has gotten word to Cecil at Nonsuch, the Queen has yet to be informed. Essex and Southampton arrive and Essex takes it upon himself to enter the palace alone, covered with mud, brushing past the shocked guards and barging through the Presence Chamber. He strides into Her Majesty's own bedchamber, where the startled sovereign is not yet fully dressed. With her hair hanging down in disarray, caught without the usual trappings of her public image, Elizabeth stays calm while Essex falls to his knees and pleads for understanding. The Queen listens – patiently, calmly, smiling sweetly – before telling him to go clean and change while she finishes putting on her makeup and dressing. Once Essex is gone, however, Elizabeth summons all the terrifying fierceness of her royal power and orders him confined to chambers.

Late that night he is commanded to appear before the Privy Council, with Secretary Robert Cecil presiding. Cecil enumerates the earl's various offenses against the Queen's Majesty, who will never again allow Essex in her presence. The former favorite is doomed.

Essex a Prisoner of State, October 1599: Essex is transferred to the custody of Lord Keeper Egerton at York House, where he is forbidden even to walk outside in the garden. The earl falls into a profound melancholy, which will lead to serious mental and physical illness. More than ever, now, Elizabeth turns her ear to Robert Cecil alone for advice and information. The seeds of the forthcoming rebellion have taken root; in the view of both Essex and Southampton, the little Secretary will have to be removed from power by force.

***THE PASSIONATE PILGRIM*, 1599:** A volume of twenty verses attributed to "W. Shakespeare" appears from publisher William Jaggard. (The final six poems are entitled *Sonnets to Sundry Notes of Music*.) None of the verses are among the Fair Youth sonnets to Southampton; but the first two poems will turn up in revised form in the 1609 quarto of *Shake-Speares Sonnets*, as part of the Dark Lady series.

The first entry – later to become Sonnet 138 – begins with Oxford writing of Elizabeth:

> When my love swears that she is made of truth,
> I do believe her, though I know she lies

The second entry – to become Sonnet 144 – concerns Southampton and the Queen as the "two loves" of Oxford – that is, the two princes of royal blood whom he serves, but who are no longer on speaking terms with each other and are causing him such inner turmoil. Elizabeth still holds the fate of her "right fair" son in her hands, but by now she has become "a woman colored ill" because of her dark, negative viewpoint:

> Two loves I have, of comfort and despair,
> That like two spirits do suggest me still;
> The better angel is a man right fair,
> My worser spirit is a woman colored ill

Three of the other poems in this collection are extracts of lyrical passages in *Love's Labour's Lost* associated with Southampton and his Cambridge friends. Other verses recall both *Venus and Adonis* of 1593 and *Willobie His Avisa* of 1594. Here no doubt are some of the "sugared sonnets" that Oxford had been circulating; in any case, they are aimed at the Queen to publicly remind her of his loyalty and to change her mind about Southampton, of whom he writes:

> *Sweet Rose, fair flower*, untimely pluck'd, soon vaded,
> *Pluck'd in the bud* and vaded in the spring!
> Bright orient pearl, alack, too timely shaded,
> *Fair creature*, killed too soon by death's sharp sting:
> Like a green plum that hangs upon a tree,
> And falls through wind before the fall should be.
>
> I weep for thee and yet no cause I have;
> For why thou lefts me nothing in thy will.
> And yet thou lefts me more than I did crave,
> For why I craved nothing of thee still:
> O yes, dear friend, I pardon crave of thee,
> Thy discontent thou didst bequeath to me.
> - No. 10 of *The Passionate Pilgrim*, 1599

(In the second line of the second stanza, the statement that "for why [because] thou lefts me nothing in thy will" seems strange and jarring if referring to a legal will; but Oxford may be referring to Southampton's royal will and/or his failure to be named in succession and thereby to leave Oxford's blood to posterity. This appearance of "thy will" may be seen in the "Will/will" sonnets – 134, 135, 136, 143 – of the Dark Lady series.)

Southampton at the Playhouse, October 11, 1599: While Essex smolders in custody, Rowland Whyte writes to Robert Sidney: "My Lord Southampton and Lord Rutland come not to the Court ... They pass away the time in London merely in going to plays every day."

Roger Manners, Fifth Earl of Rutland, once Southampton's college friend, is now a fellow supporter. During this perilous time, the two earls, in their mid-twenties, are by no means typical theatergoers bent on frivolous entertainment. They enter the public playhouses amid the fanfare of recognition. By virtue of rank they are entitled to sit high above the stage, facing outward toward the audience, ensuring that spectators are aware of their presence at all times. Such appearances are political statements; members of the audience look up and watch their reactions during politically charged scenes of rebellion in dramatic histories such as *Julius Caesar*, which so powerfully capture the current London mood. Again, the voice of "Shakespeare" lends support to Southampton (who has become Prince Hal to Oxford as Falstaff, the father figure).

No. 24

Essex is Condemned by Peers, December 1599:

"The declaration of the Lords in Star Chamber in open court of the Earl's misgovernment in Ireland, where all the errors and faults he committed were plainly set down by them, hath given all the world satisfaction of the just cause her Majesty had to proceed against him. Tomorrow the Earl's household of 160 servants is dispersed, and every man to seek a new fortune ... This is the greatest downfall we have seen in our days." - *An Elizabethan Journal (1599-1603)*, G. B. Harrison, 1929 (a chronological record of contemporary historical evidence of various kinds)

THE SHAKESPEARE COMMITMENT
FAILED MILITARY CAMPAIGN IN IRELAND

Sonnet 25
The Painful Warrior
1599

Essex and Southampton depart for Ireland in March with 15,000 troops, but they fail to put down the rebellion of Tyron. Upon their return to England in desperation and despair, Essex barges into the Queen's presence as she is dressing; he is placed under house arrest and Southampton is banished from her sight. Oxford, who had inserted a speech of hope for victory in Ireland in his play Henry V, *now writes a companion piece for this private diary. Here he records the end of royal favor for the two young earls, addressing Southampton in particular. His only consolation is that their father-son relationship can never be destroyed.*

Sonnet 25	Translation
Let those who are in favor with their stars	Let those in favor with their royal princes
Of public honor and proud titles boast,	Boast of public honors and proud titles,
Whilst I, whom fortune of such triumph bars,	While I, whom Elizabeth bars from such triumph,
Unlooked-for joy in that I honor most;	Am ignored while joyfully honoring you most.
Great Princes favorites their fair leaves spread,	Elizabeth's favorites spread their royal qualities,
But as the Marigold at the sun's eye,	The way the Marigold unfolds under the sun,
And in themselves their pride lies buried,	And their royalty is hidden within themselves,
For at a frown they in their glory die.	For at the Queen's frown their royal favor dies.
The painful warrior famoused for worth,	The struggling warrior, famed for military battles,
After a thousand victories once foiled,	Defeated just once after a thousand victories
Is from the book of honor razed quite,	Is obliterated from the royal record,
And all the rest forgot for which he toiled:	And all the rest he worked to gain is forgotten.
Then happy I that love and am beloved	Then happy am I, loving and loved by my royal son,
Where I may not remove, nor be removed.	Unable to leave him, nor to be left by him.

"No lines could have been penned more apposite to the fall and disgrace of Essex after his military failure in Ireland." - George Wyndham, 1898, on Sonnet 25

1 LET THOSE WHO ARE IN FAVOR WITH THEIR STARS
LET THOSE, etc. = let those who are fortunate in terms of their monarch's favor; **STARS**, i.e., the eyes of my royal son; also, in the monarch's favor; ("Ah, Richard, with the eyes of heavy mind I see thy glory like a shooting star fall to the base earth from the firmament" –*Richard II*, 2.4.18-20; **FAVOR** = "When I was fair and young, then favor graced me" – poem credited to Queen Elizabeth, with second source crediting Edward de Vere, Earl of Oxford, writing of the Queen's favor toward him)

2 OF PUBLIC HONOR AND PROUD TITLES BOAST,

PUBLIC HONOR = on one level, high estimation by the world; on Oxford's intended level, public recognition by Elizabeth; **PROUD** = royal, according to the special language; ("Why is my verse so barren of new *pride*?" - Sonnet 76, line 1); **PROUD TITLES** = royal titles; Edward de Vere does, in fact, have one of the proudest titles anyone can boast, as Seventeenth Earl of Oxford; and he is also hereditary Lord Great Chamberlain of England; so here he is referring to the title he might gain as father of the royal prince and even as King Consort on the throne with "Fortune" or Elizabeth

3 WHILST I, WHOM FORTUNE OF SUCH TRIUMPH BARS,

FORTUNE = Elizabeth; I, to whom Elizabeth denies such triumph; **TRIUMPH** = Southampton was born "with all *triumphant* splendor on my brow" – Sonnet 33, line 10; ("Faction that ever dwells in Court, where wit excels,/ Hath set defiance./ *Fortune* and Love have sworn that they were never born/ Of one alliance" – printed in *Astrophel and Stella*, by Sidney, but with Oxford's initials as "Finis, E. O."); **BARS** = hinders, prevents, prohibits; a legal term, to bar or block a person or action or claim, by objection; excludes, shuts out, obstructs; "statute-barred" or "time-barred" - *OED*

4 UNLOOKED-FOR JOY IN THAT I HONOR MOST:

UNLOOKED-FOR = ignored; but, also, unexpectedly; "And sith the world is so full of treasons and vile instruments daily to attempt new and *unlooked-for* things" – Oxford to Burghley, September 1572; "Yet I am forced, by what *unlooked-for* occasion I cannot tell" – Oxford to Robert Cecil, October 21, 1595; "And all *unlooked-for* from your Highness' mouth" – *Richard II*, 1.3.155; **JOY IN THAT I HONOR MOST** = take joy in what I honor most, that is, my royal son

5 GREAT PRINCES' FAVORITES THEIR FAIR LEAVES SPREAD

GREAT PRINCES' = great monarchs'; Elizabeth's; "Not marble nor the gilded monument/ Of *Princes* shall outlive this powerful rhyme" - Sonnet 55, lines 1-2
FAVORITES = Southampton, who was once in her high favor, as Oxford had been; **THEIR FAIR LEAVES SPREAD** = show off their royal Tudor Rose petals (as Southampton did, for Elizabeth, as her son acting as a glittering courtier once in her high regard); **FAIR** = royal; "From *fairest* creatures we desire increase" - Sonnet 1, line 1; "Fair, kind, and true, is all my argument" - Sonnet 105, line 9

6 BUT AS THE MARIGOLD AT THE SUN'S EYE,

As the marigold opens in response to the sun; an image of Southampton gaining glory in response to Elizabeth, the reigning royal sun; ("Here used as a metaphor for a king's favorite: it flourishes in the 'sun's eye' - royal favor - and shrinks back into itself at nightfall - loss of favor, a 'frown'" – G. Blakemore Evans); John Lyly wrote of the marigold in association with the Queen in *Euphues his England* of 1580, dedicated to Oxford: "She [Elizabeth] useth the marigold for her flower, which at the rising of the sunne openeth his leaves, and at the setting shutteth them, referring all her actions and endeavours to Him that ruleth the sunne"; **GOLD** = the royalty of the "golden time" imbedded in the word 'mari*gold*', noted by G. Wilson Knight; **SUN'S EYE** = imperial eye of majesty

7 AND IN THEMSELVES THEIR PRIDE LIES BURIED,

IN THEMSELVES = within such princes, i.e. Southampton; **THEIR PRIDE LIES BURIED** = their (his) royal blood remains hidden; **PRIDE** = royalty, royal blood; swollen with child; echoing "proud" of line 2 above; "Why is my verse so *barren of new pride*?" - Sonnet 76, line 1, referring to his son's royal blood within the lines of his Sonnets; "Made *proud* by princes, that advance their *pride*" – *Much Ado About Nothing*, 3.1.10

8 FOR AT A FROWN THEY IN THEIR GLORY DIE.
FROWN = disfavor of the Great Prince or monarch, i.e., Elizabeth; **THEY IN THEIR GLORY DIE** = they die to the world in terms of their royal claim; ("Though I, once gone, to all the world must die" – Sonnet 81, line 6, i.e., Oxford speaking of his identity as father of Southampton)

9 THE PAINFUL WARRIOR FAMOUSED FOR WORTH,
THE PAINFUL WARRIOR = Southampton, the diligent warrior on military campaigns with Essex, including the disastrous one this year; now full of pain and sorrow, with Elizabeth removing him from her presence

PAINFUL = "accompanied by mental stress or suffering" - *OED*; an accurate description of Essex's pain in 1599; ("We hope Her Majesty will think our *painful* days, careful nights, evil diet and many hazards deserve not to be measured by the event" – Essex to Queen Elizabeth, about the failed military expedition to the Azores in 1597; Weir, 429

FAMOUSED = "Deservedly famous' - Such, in Shakespeare's eyes, may have been both Essex and Southampton" – Duncan-Jones; **FOR WORTH** = worth as a soldier; but in Oxford's eyes, for his royal blood; also playing on the letters w-o-r-t-h in "Wriothesley"; "worth" is usually emended to "fight" to rhyme with "quite" of line 11 below and presumably to make more sense

10 AFTER A THOUSAND VICTORIES ONCE FOILED,
Once defeated or dishonored, even after a thousand victories in battle

11 IS FROM THE BOOK OF HONOR RAZED QUITE,
FROM THE BOOK OF HONOR = from eternal honor and fame (suggesting that this Book of Sonnets will provide an alternative); **RAZED QUITE** = obliterated; erased completely; "When sometime lofty towers I see down razed" - Sonnet 64, line 3

12 AND ALL THE REST FORGOT FOR WHICH HE TOILED:
ALL = Southampton, *One for All, All for One*; **FORGOT** = such is the case for Southampton and Essex, i.e., all their successful military actions are forgotten in the face of the disastrous Irish campaign; **TOILED** = "Weary with toil I haste me to my bed" - Sonnet 27, line 1;

13 THEN HAPPY AM I THAT LOVE AND AM BELOVED
LOVE AND AM BELOVED = Oxford loves his royal son, and his beloved by him; "Let not my love be called Idolatry,/ Nor my beloved as an Idol show" - Sonnet 105, lines 1-2

14 WHERE I MAY NOT REMOVE, NOR BE REMOVED.
Oxford cannot remove himself as father, nor can Southampton cease to be his son; ("Love is not love/ Which alters when it alteration finds,/ Or bends with the *remover* to *remove*" – Sonnet 116, lines 2-4); well before the time of Sonnet 116, however, Robert Cecil has "removed" Southampton from all claim of succession – the very outcome Oxford dreads, although he reiterates that the royal blood of his son cannot be removed or destroyed; REMOVED = heraldic term; if an "ordinary" is not in its usual place on a shield, it is said to be "removed." The term, which can be applied to succession, is cognate with the word's genealogical usage -- as in "a cousin once removed." The word can suggest that the generations are out of order. (Courtesy of Charles Beauclerk)

No. 25

THE REBELLION BEGINS

1600

Southampton Plans Rebellion, February 1600: As Essex recovers from near-fatal illness, Cecil renews his plan to put him publicly on trial for his military actions. This causes alarm and even panic among his friends, to the point where Southampton meets with Lord Mountjoy, who is set to take command of the army in Ireland, and gets him to agree to bring 4,000 men back to England to help stage a palace coup. Both Essex and Southampton pledge to Mountjoy that any such drastic action would avoid physical harm to Elizabeth; and they concur that King James of Scotland would have to give his approval in advance. Once Mountjoy leaves for Dublin, however, the Crown cancels its court proceedings against Essex – out of concern, no doubt, that riots could break out in support of him – and so the plans for a coup are set aside.

Essex Moves to Essex House, March 1600: The government releases Essex from York House and sends him back to his own residence, Essex House, where he remains in confinement as a prisoner of state.

Southampton Returns to Ireland, April 1600: Southampton, about to go back to Ireland, tries once more to reconcile with Elizabeth; but she merely sends a curt message wishing "a safe going and returning," still refusing to see him.

Southampton Joins the Fighting, May 1600: Plunging back into the military campaign, Southampton leads a charge that averts disaster for the English army by driving back the rebels. "I protest he saved our honor," Mountjoy writes to Cecil about Southampton's bravery. When Mountjoy attempts to nominate the earl for the vacant governorship of Connaught, however, the Queen promptly refuses.

Southampton to the Continent, June 1600: Angered by Elizabeth's treatment, Southampton leaves the fighting in Ireland and makes his way to the Continent.

Essex Questioned by Council, June 1600: Essex is brought before the Privy Council to suffer questioning from nine in the morning till eight at night. Francis Bacon, his former friend, turns upon him. Bacon lays forth the "offenses and contempts" against the Crown that Essex committed in Ireland by making a secret truce with Tyrone and leaving his command. Having tested the wind and found it blowing in Cecil's favor, Bacon now joins Walter Raleigh, Lord Cobham and Lord Grey in branding Essex a traitor. The earl is sent home again, still under house arrest, to await Her Majesty's further pleasure.

Cecil Controls the Theaters, Summer of 1600: The Privy Council, under Robert Cecil, makes a bold move to gain stricter control over stage performances in London. Plays are potential lightning rods for political dissension and even rebellion; and the playhouses themselves are perfect meeting grounds for trouble. The Council has already reduced the number of acting troupes to the Lord Chamberlain's Men (which performs Shakespeare plays) and the Lord Admiral's Men; but now comes an even further restriction, with the Council reducing the number of playhouses to just the Curtain and the Globe.

More Plays by "Shakespeare" Published, Autumn 1600: Additional plays by Oxford are printed with his pen name "William Shakespeare" on them: *2 Henry VI, Henry V, A Midsummer Night's Dream, The Merchant of Venice* and *Much Ado About Nothing*. It appears that "the complete issue of the plays had been decided upon and begun" – J. Thomas Looney, 1920.

(Looney also observes that this issuance will abruptly cease upon Southampton's imprisonment for his role in the Rebellion of February 8, 1601. He suggests that Southampton himself – having now returned from the Continent – has become the "intermediary between the Earl of Oxford and those who were staging and publishing the dramas.")

(The following letters from Essex to Queen Elizabeth [from reprints by Agnes Strickland in her biography of Elizabeth, p. 656] contain many words or phrases that may be found in the Sonnets. The purpose of pointing out some of these linkages is to further demonstrate the royal context of the Sonnets, i.e., the context of Oxford writing as father to his royal son and as subject to his prince or king.)

Essex to Elizabeth, Autumn of 1600:

> "My *dear*, my *gracious*, and my admired *sovereign* is **Semper Eadem**. It cannot be, but that she will hear the sighs and groans, and read the lamentations and humble petitions of the afflicted. Therefore, O paper, whensoever *her eyes* vouchsafe to behold thee, say that death is the end of all worldly misery, but continual indignation makes misery perpetual; that present misery is never intolerable to them that are stayed by future hope; but affliction that is unseen is commanded to despair; that nature, youth, and physic have had many strong encounters; but if *my sovereign* will forget me, I have nourished these contentions too long, for in this exile of mine eyes, if mine humble letters find not access, no death can be so speedy, as it shall be welcome to me, Your Majesty's humblest *vassal*, Essex."

DEAR: "That may express my love, or thy *dear* merit" – Sonnet 108.4, to Southampton
GRACIOUS: "Be as thy presence is, *gracious* and kind" – Sonnet 10.11, addressing Southampton as his sovereign prince or king
SOVEREIGN: "Whilst I, my *sovereign*, watch the clock for you" – Sonnet 57.6, to Southampton as prince or king
SEMPER EADEM: Elizabeth's motto on her royal coat of arms, which she wrote in English on correspondence as *Ever the Same*. "Why write I still all one, *ever the same*" – Sonnet 76.5, at the center of the structure of 152 sonnets
HER EYES: "My Mistress' *eyes* are nothing like the Sunne" – Sonnet 130.1, referring to Elizabeth in the Dark Lady Series
VASSAL: "Lord of my love, to whom in *vassalage*" – Sonnet 26.1

Essex to Elizabeth, Autumn of 1600:

> "When the *creature* entereth into account with the Creator, it can never number in how many things it needs *mercy*, or in how many it receives it ... And I can no sooner finish this my first *audit*, most dear and most admired sovereign, but I come to consider how large a *measure* of his *grace*, and how great a resemblance of his *power* God hath given you upon earth; and how many ways he giveth occasion to you to exercise these *divine offices* upon us that are *your vassals*. This confession best fitteth me of all men; and this confession is most *joyfully*, and most humbly, now made by me of all times. I acknowledge, upon the knees of my heart, your Majesty' infinite goodness in granting my humble petition. God, who seeth all, is *witness* how faithfully *I do vow* to dedicate the rest of my life, next after my highest duty, in obedience, faith, and *zeal* to your Majesty; without admitting any other world care; and whatsoever your Majesty resolveth to do with me, I shall live and die, Your Majesty's humblest *vassal*, Essex."

CREATURE: "The most sweet favor or deformed'st *creature*" – Sonnet 113.10

MERCY: "Straight in her heart did *mercy* come" – Sonnet 145.5
AUDIT: "Her *Audit*, though delayed, answered must be" – Sonnet 126.11
MEASURE: "But these particulars are not my *measure*" – Sonnet 91.7
GRACES: "They rightly do inherit heaven's *graces*" – Sonnet 94.5
POWER: "O from what *power* hast thou this powerful might" – Sonnet 150.1
DIVINE: "Nothing, sweet boy, but yet like prayers *divine*" – Sonnet 108.5
OFFICES: "These *offices*, so oft as thou wilt look" – Sonnet 77.13
YOUR VASSALS: "Being *your vassal* bound to stay your leisure" – Sonnet 58.4
JOYFULLY: "Unlooked-for *joy* in that I honor most" – Sonnet 25.4
WITNESS: "To this I *witness* call the fools of time" – Sonnet 124.13
I DO VOW: "This *I do vow*, and this shall ever be" – Sonnet 123.13
ZEAL: "Intend a *zealous* pilgrimage to thee" – Sonnet 27.6

Rebellion Brews Again, late 1600: Essex has been deprived of all state offices. Elizabeth even refuses to renew his ten-year lease for the Farm of Sweet Wines, his principal source of revenue. Forced into poverty and political impotence, he allows his sorrows to shift into boundless rage, setting the stage for armed rebellion. Now he attracts growing numbers of disaffected men who visit him in his confinement at Essex House, where they pledge to follow his lead. Word gets to the Queen that Essex has called her "an old woman" who "is no less crooked and distorted in mind than she is in body." Her anger is aroused beyond all bounds; at Christmas she continuously paints her face, neck and breasts with nearly half an inch of makeup.

"By the winter of 1600-01, Essex's party was practically disrupted. Since the summer of 1599, its leader had been a prisoner of state, played with by Robert Cecil as a cat plays with a mouse. Accident and chance alike were turned to Essex's discredit with the Queen. His hopes of reconciliation were alternately raised and blasted. As the months passed by, the implacable nature of Cecil's intentions regarding him gradually dawned upon the City and Court…

"The Queen, perplexed and irritated by the factional bitterness, aged rapidly. Her death, which might occur at any time, would bring James to the throne and Essex back to place and honor. The hush that fell towards the end of 1600 upon Court gossip, and the guarded tone of correspondents, shows a tacit cognizance of Cecil's true purpose. It became whispered that Essex's life was in danger. The rumors reached Essex in confinement, as they were intended to." - Acheson

Whether Essex and Southampton are intending to support the succession of James is unknown, but Robert Cecil must face this possibility in relation to the continuance of his own power and control behind the throne after Elizabeth's reign. The dwarf-like, hunchbacked son of William Cecil, Lord Burghley is now ready to lure the two popular earls into a trap that will ensure their final doom.

Because of the Rebellion early next year, Oxford will be forced to place the dedicatory epistle of his private Fair Youth verses at Sonnet 26. This verse, addressed to "Lord of my love," will henceforth serve as a "cover letter" for the twenty-six verses of the Fair Youth series written so far. The golden years of hope for Southampton's kingship have abruptly ended. With the next verse, the Rebellion of February 8, 1601 has occurred and the eighty prison sonnets (27-106) have begun.

THE SHAKESPEARE COMMITMENT

DEDICATORY EPISTLE & ENVOY
"This Written Ambassage"

END OF THE GOLDEN TIME

Sonnet 26
Lord of My Love
1600

The two public dedications to Southampton contain the word "duty" three times, as does this single sonnet, which Oxford wrote to reflect his public dedication of Lucrece *(by "William Shakespeare") to his royal son. The Rebellion next February will cause Oxford to bring this year-by-year record of the "golden time" to an abrupt end, with the twenty-sixth sonnet representing Henry Wriothesley's age of twenty-six in 1600. He places this verse at the end of the sequence as Sonnet 26, so it becomes the "envoy" or dedicatory epistle.*

Sonnet 26	Translation
Lord of my love, to whom in vassalage	My royal son whom I love, to whom in servitude
Thy merit hath my duty strongly knit,	Your royal blood has strongly tied my devotion,
To thee I send this written ambassage,	To you I send this book of secret written messages,
To witness duty, not to show my wit.	To bear witness to my devotion, not my cleverness.
Duty so great, which wit so poor as mine	Devotion so royal, which skill so poor as mine
May make seem bare, in wanting words to show it;	May seem empty, since I can't proclaim it.
But that I hope some good conceit of thine	But I hope some princely self-image of yours
In thy soul's thought (all naked) will bestow it:	In your inmost soul, will bestow it on yourself:
Til whatsoever star that guides my moving	Until your own royal eye that guides my actions
Points on me graciously with fair aspect,	Gazes its kingly sun on me with royal favor,
And puts apparel on my tottered loving,	And completes the dressing of my poor words,
To show me worthy of thy sweet respect.	To reveal that I deserve your royal favor.
Then may I dare to boast how I do love thee,	Then might I dare to admit you are my royal son;
Till then, not show my head where thou mayst prove me.	Till then, I cannot go where you might acknowledge me as your father.

"Then comes No. 26, which on the common assumption ends that series, and which so strongly suggests the dedication to Lucrece with its parallelisms of phrase and sentiment ...: This has by most critics been taken as an envoy to a series ..."
- J. M. Robertson, 1926

"The first section of the Sonnets ends with an Envoi, *Sonnet 26 ... The sonnet reads like an*

envoi to the whole of this first section, Sonnets 1-26, which may well have formed 'this written ambassage to witness duty' to his lord."
- A. L. Rowse, 1964

"The final link in the chain that binds the sonnets and the dedications is Sonnet 26 ... a private and more personal expression of what the dedication of 1594 states in equally explicit words: 'The love I dedicate to your Lordship is without end...'"
- Robert Giroux, 1982

1 LORD OF MY LOVE, TO WHOM IN VASSALAGE
A salutation to Southampton as his sovereign lord; also as his royal son, "the little Love-God" of Sonnet 154, line 1; "This is a sonnet with some of the character of a dedicatory epistle" – Duncan-Jones; "The *love* I dedicate to your *Lordship*" – *Lucrece* dedication to Southampton

LORD = ("Master, sovereign, with perhaps some suggestion of 'God'" – G. Blakemore Evans); "A master, ruler ... One who has dominion over others as his subjects, or to whom service and obedience are due; a master, chief, prince, sovereign" – *OED*; "Eneas, the Trojan prynce (prince) and lard (lord)" – *Aeneis*, 1513, x,v,4)

> "There is nothing therefore left to my comfort but the excellent virtues and deep wisdom wherewith God hath endued our new Master and *Sovereign Lord*" – Oxford, writing of King James, to Robert Cecil, April 1603, on the eve of Elizabeth's funeral; "For he is Lord of lords, and King of kings" – Revelations, 17:14

LOVE = royal blood; "What thing is *love*? It is a *power divine/* That reigns in us" – Poem attributed to Robert Greene in 1589, but more likely by Oxford; Chiljan, p. 176; "I swear perfect love" – *Richard III*, 1.1.16; "And you and love are still my argument" – Sonnet 76, line 10; "And all in war with Time for *love* of you" – Sonnet 15, line 13; "O Thou my *love*ly Boy" – Sonnet 126, line 1; "You know how apt *our love* was" – the King in *Henry V*, 2.2.86

> Myself, a prince by fortune of my birth,
> Near to the king in **blood**, and near in **love**
> - *Richard II*, 3.1.16-17

> Was deep-sworn faith, peace, amity, true **love**
> Between our kingdoms and our royal selves
> - *King John*, 3.1.157-158

IN VASSALAGE = in servitude to his king; "The state or condition of a vassal; subordination, homage, or allegiance characteristic of, or resembling that of, a vassal ... subjection, servitude, service" – *OED*; "Your Majesty's humblest *vassal*, Essex" – Essex to Elizabeth, 1600; "Like *vassalage* at unawares encountering the eye of majesty" – *Troilus and Cressida*, 3.2.40; "That lift your *vassal* hands against my head and threat the glory of my precious crown" – *Richard II*, 3.3.89-90

2 THY MERIT HATH MY DUTY STRONGLY KNIT:
THY MERIT = your royalty; **MERIT** = "Claim or title to commendation or esteem, excellence, worth ... in theology: good works viewed as entitling to reward from God; the *merits* of Christ" – *OED*; "Right noble is thy *merit*" – *Richard II*, 5.6.18; "desert and *merit*" – *Henry V*, 2.2.34

> "And thus wishing all happiness to you, and some fortunate means to me, whereby I might recognize *so deep merits*" – Oxford to Robert Cecil, October 7, 1601

MY DUTY = The same "duty" that Oxford pledged to Southampton in the dedication of *Lucrece*; "Were my worth greater, my *duty* would show greater; meantime, as it is, it is *bound* to your Lordship" – dedication of *Lucrece* to Southampton; the duty owed by a subject to his sovereign; "As I in *duty* love my king and country!" – *2 Henry VI*, l.3.161); also, devotion to a god on earth, i.e., a king; **DUTY** = "The action and conduct due to a superior; homage, submission, due respect, reverence; an expression of submission, deference, or respect" – *OED*

> Now, Salisbury, for thee and for the right
> Of English Henry, shall this night appear
> How much in *duty* I am bound to both.
> - *1 Henry VI*, 2.1.35-37

> To do my duty to my sovereign
> - *1 Henry VI*, 3.4.4

> Thou wast begot; to get it is thy duty
> - *Venus and Adonis*, stanza 26

> Such duty as the subject owes his prince
> - *The Taming of the Shrew*, 5.2.155

STRONGLY = royally; **STRONGLY KNIT** = royally bound; ("bound to your Lordship" – dedication of *Lucrece* to Southampton)

> Good reverend father, make my person yours,
> And tell me how you would bestow yourself.
> This royal hand and mine are *newly knit*...
> - *King John*, 3.1.150-152

> Let Your Highness
> Command upon me; to the which my *duties*
> Are with a most indissoluble tie
> For ever *knit*.
> - *Macbeth*, 3.1.15-18

"First for that I know Her Majesty doth give you good ear, then for that our Houses are *knit* in alliance" – Oxford to Robert Cecil, July 1600, same year as this sonnet

"Hoping that as we be *knit* near in alliance" – Oxford to Robert Cecil, February 2, 1601

3 TO THEE I SEND THIS WRITTEN AMBASSAGE,

"It was only to the monarch or ruling magistrate that embassies were directed" – Leslie Hotson

AMBASSAGE = these private sonnets; "Message – like those, often oral, carried by official ambassadors" – Booth; official state messages that ambassadors memorized and then delivered orally to allies; in this case, Oxford is both concealing and revealing his sensitive state messages by means of poetical words on the page, so the sonnets comprise a *written* ambassage; a form of "embassy" or state message; the phrase is an apt description of the Sonnets, specifically in terms of Oxford's *invention* or special language described in Sonnet 76, at the center of the main structure of 152 sonnets.

Presumably the ambassador, if captured by enemies, would endure torture to the death without revealing his secret information. Instead of memorizing his official messages, Oxford imbeds them within the poetry itself, to simultaneously hide and communicate his real meaning;
i.e., *written* by means of a special language.

"This autobiography is written by a foreign man in a foreign tongue, which can never be translated" -- T. S. Eliot, 1927, referring to the Sonnets; but Oxford provided the key to translating this "foreign tongue" in Sonnet 76 and expanded his description of its workings in Sonnet 105

"The king hath given me his letters of recommendation to his *ambassador* in the Turk's Court. Likewise *the Venetian ambassador* that is here, knowing my desire to see those parts, hath given me his letters to the Duke and diverse of his kinsmen in Venice ... The English *ambassador* here..." - Oxford to Burghley from Paris, March 17, 1575, indicating his knowledge of ambassadors and how they communicated

An ambassage is also an *Embassage* = "The business confided to, or message conveyed by, an ambassador" – *OED;*

> Doth not the *embassage* belong to me
> - The Queen in *Richard II*, 3.4.93

> I every day expect an *embassage*
> - The King in *Richard III*, 2.1.3

> In tender *embassy* of love to thee
> - Sonnet 45, line 6, to Southampton

4 TO WITNESS DUTY, NOT TO SHOW MY WIT.
DUTY = repeated from line 2; **WITNESS DUTY** = give evidence of my servitude; Oxford is writing "in vassalage" to Southampton, i.e., addressing him as his royal sovereign, and therefore he pledges his "duty" or service. The word "duty" is also a dominant theme in the two public letters of dedication to Southampton attached to *Venus and Adonis* and *Lucrece*, and it is used three times in this sonnet – lines 2, 4 and 5; "Your Lordship's in all duty" – dedication of *Lucrece* to Southampton; "Upon your Grace, but with all *duteous love*" – *Richard III*, 2.1.33; **WIT** = intelligence or skill

5 DUTY SO GREAT, WHICH WIT SO POOR AS MINE
DUTY = repeated from lines 2 and 4; **DUTY SO GREAT** = duty so royally inspired; **WIT SO POOR** = skill lacking the ability to express; "my untutored lines" – *Lucrece* dedication; but more importantly, forbidden by official policy; "Tongue-tied by authority" – Sonnet 66, line 9

6 MAY MAKE SEEM BARE, IN WANTING WORDS TO SHOW IT;
BARE = empty of royal blood; **WANTING WORDS** = "tongue-tied by authority," at the risk of being arrested for treason for putting forth a claimant (Southampton) to Elizabeth's throne.

7 BUT THAT I HOPE SOME GOOD CONCEIT OF THINE
HOPE = Sonnets 29, 52, 60, 97, 143; the hope of a father for his royal son's succession to the throne; "As I *hope* for quiet days, *fair issue* and long life" – *The Tempest*, 4.1.23-24; "The mother to a *hopeful prince*" – *The Winter's Tale*, 3.2.39; "Being had to triumph, being lacked to *hope*" – Sonnet 52, line 14, Oxford writing of his withering hope for Southampton; **SOME GOOD CONCEIT OF THINE** = your royal favor or thought

8 IN THY SOUL'S THOUGHT (ALL NAKED) WILL BESTOW IT:
ALL = Southampton, *One for All, All for One*; **ALL NAKED** = without defenses; **BESTOW IT** = give it a place to live; "Her Majesty's disposition to *bestow* where it shall best please her" – Oxford to Robert Cecil, July 1600 (this same year); "Shakespeare says, 'I hope some happy idea of yours will convey my duty – even naked as it is – into your soul's thought'" – Dowden

9 TILL WHATSOEVER STAR THAT GUIDES MY MOVING
WHATSOEVER = **EVER** = E. Ver, Edward de Vere, *Ever or Never*; **STAR THAT GUIDES MY MOVING** = Southampton's eye, the sun; "Yet I know not by *what unfortunate star*" – Oxford to Robert Cecil, January 1602; "What is love? … It is a *star* whose influence doth draw" – poem attributed to Robert Greene in 1589, thought to be by Oxford, Chiljan, p. 176; "And scarcely greet me with *that sunne thine eye*" – Sonnet 49, line 6; "Love is not love/ Which alters when it alteration finds,/ Or bends with the remover to remove/ O no, it is an ever-fixed mark/ That looks on tempests and is never shaken;/ It is *the star to every wandering bark*" – Sonnet 116, lines 2-7

WHATSOEVER STAR = Southampton's royal eye or "star" dictates Oxford's actions and the writing of these private sonnets; "But from *thine eyes* my knowledge I derive,/ And, *constant stars*, in them I read such art" – Sonnet 14, lines 9-10; "Flatter the mountain tops with *sovereign eye*" – Sonnet 33, line 2; "And scarcely greet me with **that sun, thine eye**" – Sonnet 49, line 6; the star over Bethlehem that served as a guide to finding the Christ child.

Yet another allusion is to the De Vere star, blazoned as a mullet of five points argent. The Veres had adopted the star as a badge in their coat of arms, appearing on their standards and worn by their armies.

> Bright *star of Venus*, fall'n down on the earth,
> How may I *reverently worship thee* enough?
> - *1 Henry VI*, 1.2.144-145

> Madam, have comfort; all of us have cause
> To wail *the dimming of our shining star*
> - *Richard III*, 2.2.101-102

> Small time, but in that small most greatly lived
> This *star of England*; Fortune made his sword,
> By which the world's best garden he achieved,
> And of it left his son imperial lord.
> - *Henry V*, epilogue, 5-8
> (Of King Henry the Fifth)

> So shall she leave her blessedness to one,
> When heaven shall call her from this cloud of darkness,
> Who from the sacred ashes of her honour
> Shall *star-like rise, as great in fame as she was*
> - *Henry VIII*, 5.5.43-46

> (Archbishop Cranmer, speaking of the infant Princess Elizabeth, and predicting she will leave a "star-like" heir to the throne)

10 POINTS ON ME GRACIOUSLY WITH FAIR ASPECT,
POINTS ON ME = "His golden beams … shall *point on me* and gild my banishment" – *Richard II*, 1.3.146-147; "Mine own ends have been mine so that evermore they *pointed* to the good of your most sacred person

and to the profit of the state" – *Henry VIII*, 3.2.172; **GRACIOUSLY** = with kingly and divine grace; "Great King of England and my *gracious* lord" – *2 Henry VI*, 1.1.24; "All health unto my *gracious sovereign*!" – *2 Henry VI*, 3.1.82; "Comfort, my sovereign! *Gracious Henry*, comfort!" – *2 Henry VI*, 3.2.38; **WITH FAIR ASPECT** = with royal favor; "From *fairest* creatures we desire increase" – Sonnet 1, line 1; "In the old age black was not counted *fair*, Or if it were it bore not beauty's name" – Sonnet 127, lines 1-2

11 AND PUTS APPAREL ON MY TOTTERED LOVING,
And dresses up my tattered or worn words trying to convey your royal blood; "So all my best is *dressing* old words new" – Sonnet 76, line 11; "No! Time, thou shalt not boast that I do change./ Thy pyramids built up with newer might/ To me are nothing novel, nothing strange,/ They are but *dressings* of a former sight" – Sonnet 123, lines 1-4; **PUTS** (apparel) **ON**= "For he was likely, had he been *put on*, to have proved most royal" – *Hamlet*, 5.2.404-405

12 TO SHOW ME WORTHY OF THY SWEET RESPECT.
WORTHY OF THEIR SWEET RESPECT = worthy of their royal contents; and of your royal regard; "Were my *worth* greater" – *Lucrece* dedication; "Know, *worthy* prince" – *The Two Gentlemen of Verona*, 3.1.10; "Weigh you the *worth* and honor of a king" – *Troilus and Cressida*, 2.2.26; regard, consideration; "According to his virtue let us use him with all *respect* and rites of burial" – *Julius Caesar*, 5.5.76-77

13 THEN MAY I DARE TO BOAST HOW I DO LOVE THEE:
Only when you are king will I dare say publicly that I am your father and you are my son by the Queen.

14 TILL THEN, NOT SHOW MY HEAD WHERE THOU MAYST PROVE ME.
TILL THEN, NOT SHOW MY HEAD = until then, I must write secretly; (also, Oxford may be confirming that he removed himself from Court once Southampton made his entrance as a courtier in the early 1590s, to avoid any situation that would cause him and his royal son to be associated with each other; **WHERE THOU MAYST PROVE ME** = not write in such a way that you can demonstrate me as your father; or literally not "show my head" where, inadvertently or otherwise, you might reveal me as your father; "Doth not the crown of England *prove* the king?" – *King John*, 2.1.273; "For he was likely, had he been put on, to have *proved most royal*" – *Hamlet*, 5.2.404-405

1601

Attack on Southampton, January 9, 1601: Southampton is riding with his houseboy near Raleigh's residence when Cecil's henchman Lord Gray, accompanied by a band of followers, viciously attacks the earl. Southampton draws his sword and holds them at bay until help arrives, but not before the houseboy's hand has been lopped off. The Queen orders Lord Gray committed to the Fleet.

Turmoil at Essex House, February 2, 1601: Lord Gray is released today as frenzy grows at Essex's home near Temple Bar, with friends arriving in great numbers to support him and Southampton. At the same time their isolation from the Queen is leaving them increasingly defenseless. The release of Gray, undoubtedly at Cecil's urging, is further evidence that Essex and Southampton can no longer count on the protection of either Elizabeth or English law. Throngs of men come and go at Essex House. Rumors fly that the earls will soon be murdered, even in their beds. The pressure to take preemptive action is rapidly building to the boiling point.

Southampton Takes Charge, February 2, 1601: A committee headed by Southampton meets today at Drury House, the London residence of Sir Charles Danvers, to discuss plans for a palace coup. The committee will do the necessary staff work to plan the coming action, which will be aimed at getting rid of Robert Cecil and other enemies, such as Walter Raleigh, Captain of the Guard. These men will be taken as prisoners or, more likely, killed. Only then will the earls be able to gain Elizabeth's presence.

Essex has supplied a listing of 120 noblemen, knights and gentlemen who can be counted upon to help. Another document from Essex poses some questions about strategy. Should they seize control of both the Court and the Tower at once? How many men will be needed? If the attack is launched against the Court only, which places should be taken first? How many men should be assigned to control each area?

Second Meeting at Drury House, February 3, 1601: Southampton holds a second committee meeting. It's decided that the sole focus will be upon seizing the Court at Whitehall. Various members will infiltrate the Palace in advance. Individuals are being assigned to capture specific persons in specific areas. When committee member Sir Ferdinando Gorges expresses horror at the enterprise, saying the coup will be impossible, Southampton argues: "Then we shall resolve upon nothing, and it is now three months or more since we first undertook this!" The meeting breaks up in confusion, but Southampton is committed. He and Essex are convinced that hundreds of armed citizens will fly outdoors to join them. They also appear certain that once they come face to face with Elizabeth, she will recognize them as her loyal creatures risking everything for England's destiny.

Globe Performance Arranged, Friday, February 6, 1601: Essex-Southampton followers approach the Lord Chamberlain's Men to arrange for a special performance of Shakespeare's *Richard II* tomorrow at the Globe. This powerful work is about the very real deposition and murder of King Richard in 1399, when Bolingbroke became King Henry IV of England. Its relevance to the current crisis must be obvious to the players. Since all London has been talking for months about little else but the possibility of the Queen's own deposition, the actors must realize they are being used as a propaganda tool to further enflame the passions of conspirators and ordinary citizens alike.

"RICHARD II"

At the Globe Playhouse

February 7, 1601

Special Performance, Saturday, February 7, 1601: On this Saturday afternoon the Chamberlain's Men perform *Richard II* at the Globe, while members of the Essex faction cheer the scenes of an English monarch being deprived of his crown. *"What must the King do now?"* Richard asks. *"Must he submit? The King shall do it. Must he be deposed?"*

Oxford may have added the powerful deposition scene (4.1.154-318) to help Southampton's cause. (Although the first quarto of *Richard II* was registered in 1597, the scene will be printed first in the fourth quarto in 1608.) If such was the case, then Oxford may be referring to his own act of treason in Sonnet 35, lines 5-6: "All men make faults, and even I, in this, Authorizing thy trespass with compare..."

Apprised by spies of this event, Robert Cecil makes his own move. He sends John Herbert, his assistant secretary of state, to Essex House with a summons ordering Essex forthwith to attend an emergency meeting of the Privy Council, when he will receive instructions about how to conduct himself. By calculation the summons provokes the earl into even greater panic and confusion. He claims to be too ill to attend this meeting and refuses to leave his residence, which gives Cecil an opportunity to present Elizabeth with more evidence of the danger she faces. If Essex is really so innocent of evil plotting, why won't he appear before the Council?

Tonight Essex and Southampton have dinner with Essex's sister, Lady Rich, and with Sir Charles Danvers and his stepfather, Sir Christopher Blount. Now that Cecil has taken the offensive, they say, it might be best if Essex fled England. If he left with at least a hundred men and made his way to Wales, he could take command of a seaport and make a stand in his own defense. On the other hand, the Sheriff of London has given his personal assurance of support by a thousand men of the militia; and the citizens can be counted upon as well. So, they agree, there will be no flight by Essex. The planned action must take place tomorrow.

> He [Essex] resolved therefore, for as much as delay was now no less dangerous than rashness, to enter the next day, which was Sunday, with 200 Gentlemen into the City a little before the end of the Sermon at St. Paul's, there to inform the Aldermen and people of the causes of his coming, and to crave their aide against his adversaries. And if the Citizens showed themselves hard to be drawn, to depart presently to some other part of the kingdom; but if they showed themselves easy, then to make himself a way unto the Queen with their help. All that night some were sent out of Essex House, who ran up and down to give his friends to understand that the Lord Cobham and Raleigh [supporters of Robert Cecil] lay in wait for his life.
> - William Camden (modernized English)

THE DAY OF THE REBELLION

February 8, 1601

Sunday, February 8, 1601: The day of the Rebellion dawns. The following excerpts are also from the account of contemporary historian William Camden, with modernized English:

> "Hereupon (at Essex House) resorted unto him (Essex) betimes in the morning upon Sunday the 8th of February, the Earls of Rutland and Southampton … and about 300 Gentlemen of prime note. All these he courteously received and embraced. To some he signified that a plot was laid for his life; that he was therefore determined to go unto the Queen and inform her of the dangers intended against him, forasmuch as his over-potent adversaries abused the Queen's name against him. To others, (he said) that the City of London stood for him; that he would therefore betake himself thither, and with the help of the Citizens revenge the injuries received from his adversaries. All this while his House kept shut, and no man let in unless he were known, nor any man suffered to go forth…"

[Robert Cecil already has spies planted within Essex House; Camden implies that one is Ferdinando Gorges, who is permitted to go see Raleigh. In any case, warning is given to the government; and the following incident suggests a ploy by Cecil intended to provoke Essex into acting rashly before he is ready.]

> "At this very time the Queen gave commandment to the Lord Mayor of London to take care that the Citizens were ready every man in his house to execute such commands as should be enjoyned them. To the Earl (Essex) she sent the Lord Keeper, the Earl of Worcester, Sir William Knollys, Controller of her household and the Earl's uncle, and Popham Lord chief justice of England, to understand the cause of this Assembly. These Councilors are hardly let in through the Wicket, their servants being shut, all save the Purse-bearer. In the Courtyard was a confused multitude of men, and in the midst of them Essex, with Rutland, Southampton, and many others, who presently flocked about them. The Lord Keeper, turning to Essex, gave him to understand that he and the rest were sent by the Queen to know the cause of so great an Assembly; and if any injury were done unto them by any man, he promised indifferent justice.

> "Essex answered him in a loud voice:

>> "There is a plot laid against my life; some are suborned to stab me in my bed; we are treacherously dealt withal; letters are counterfeited under my name and hand! We are met together to defend our selves and save our lives, seeing neither my patience nor misery can assuage the malice of my adversaries, unless they such also my blood!"

> "Popham spake unto him to the same effect that the Lord Keeper did, promising that if he would tell him plainly what had been attempted against him, he would report it truly to the Queen, and he should be justly and lawfully heard. Southampton made mention that the Lord Grey had drawn his Sword upon him. "But he was imprisoned for it," Popham said. Whilst the Lord Keeper pressed him (Essex) again to lay open his grievances unto them, if not openly, yet at least privately, the multitude interrupting him cried out, "Let us go! They abuse your patience! They betray you and undo you! The time passeth!" To whom the Lord Keeper turning, commanded them upon their allegiance to lay down Armes.

"All this confusion at Essex House leads to outright panic. Essex goes back inside, the Lord Keeper following in order to confer in private, while members of the crowd shout out: "Let them be slain! Let that great Seal be thrown away! Let them be shut up in custody!"

"And once the Crown's representatives are inside the house, Essex orders them taken as prisoners. *"Have patience a while,"* he tells them. *"I must presently be gone into the City to enter into some course with my Lord Mayor and the Sheriff. I will return by and by."*

"Essex through this unexpected coming of these Councilors forgot both horses and his design, and hastily went out of the house … with a band of 200 men or thereabouts, all of them of age and courage fierce, but not provided of Arms like Soldiers, most of them having their cloaks wrapped about their arms and their swords…

"Being entered into London, he cried out now and then, *"For the Queen! For the Queen! A plot is laid for my life!"* And so he went forward in hast directly through the chief street of the City to Sheriff Smith's house near Fen-church. The Citizens running together to gaze, he besought them to arm themselves, else they would be of no use to him. Nevertheless in all the City, then well exercised to Arms, full of people, and most devoted to him, not so much as one man of the meanest sort took Arms for him. For the Citizens, though according to the disposition of the vulgar sort they were desirous of innovation, yet by reason of their wealth they were fearful withal, and in regard of their untainted fidelity to their Prince, unshaken…

"Most of the citizens, watching from windows and doorways, have no idea what is going on. For all they know, Essex is proclaiming his loyalty to the Queen.

"Having walked almost the whole length of the City to the Sheriff's house he came, much perplexed in mind, and in such a sweat that he was fain to shift his shirt. The Sheriff, in whom he had put assured confidence upon the uncertain credit of others, presently withdrew himself by a back door to the Lord Mayor…

"Agents of the government, under Robert Cecil's orders, now enter the city and begin to proclaim that Essex and his accomplices are traitors.

"When not a man took arms, and he saw that his own company withdrew themselves privily, and heard that the Lord Admiral was coming with a power of men, he began to cast away hope. He cast in mind therefore to return home, in hope to obtain favor with the Queen by the means of the Lord Keeper and the rest of the Council, whom he had shut up at home…"

[But it turns out that the captive Councilors had been let go…]

"In the meantime Essex, being about to return, found the chain drawn athwart the street near the West gate of Paul's Church, and both pikes and shot placed against him by the Bishop of London under the conduct of Sir John Levison. Now did the Earl first draw his sword. He commanded Blount to set upon them; which he resolutely performed, running upon Waite … Him he slew, and was himself sore hurt and taken prisoner. There fell Henry Tracy, a young Gentleman whom Essex loved dearly, and one or two citizens. From hence being repulsed, his hat shot through, and very many escaping from him, he turned aside with a few which would not forsake him to Queen-heith; and there getting boats, returned home.

"He was very much offended that the Council had been let forth. Certain papers he cast into the fire lest (as he said) they should tell tales; and prepared himself for defense. And now in his last hope, expecting aid from the Londoners, he fortified his house on all sides…

"Essex makes a final stand while government officials surround his house and high-ranking lords of the Crown prepare to lead a full assault. When calls come for Essex to give up, Southampton shouts back:

> *"To whom should we yield? Our adversaries? That would be to run upon our own ruin! Or to the Queen? That would be to confess ourselves guilty! But yet if the Lord Admiral will give us hostages for our security, we will appear before the Queen! If not, we are every one of us fully resolved to lose our lives fighting!"*

"Before the hour was expired, Essex, holding all things for desperate and lost, resolved to break forth; and the Lord Sands, more aged than the rest, earnestly urged him so to do, redoubling that saying, "The stoutest counsels are the safest. It is more honorable for Noblemen to die fighting than by the hand of the executioner." But Essex, wavering in mind, began presently to think of yielding, and signified certain conditions…

"When presently all the Noblemen, falling upon their knees and delivering their swords to the Lord Admiral, yielded themselves at ten of the clock at night. Three died, no more but Owen Salisbury and one or two that were slain in the house by shot, and as many of the assailants."

Essex himself and Southampton were first led by the Lord Admiral to the Archbishop of Canterbury's house at Lambeth, and not straight to the Tower of London, because the night was foul and the bridge unpassable by water. But from thence shortly after, they were by the Queen's warrant carried by boat to the Tower; and in other boats Rutland, Sands, Cromwell, Mounteagle, Sir Charles Danvers and Sir Henry Bromley. The rest were cast in public prisons. Thus in twelve hours was this commotion suppressed, which some call a scare, others an *error*….

ERROR:

"So are those *errors* that in thee are seen" – Sonnet 96, line 7
"If this be *error* and upon me proved" – Sonnet 116, line 13
"Book both my willfulness and *errors* down" – Sonnet 117, line 9

"They which (who) censured it more hardly termed it an obstinate impatience and desire of revenge, and such as censured it most heavily called it an inconsiderate rashness; and to this day there are but few there are which have thought it a capital crime." – William Camden

Part Two

"MY LOVELY BOY"

(THE 100-SONNET CENTER)

Sonnets 27 – 126
Feb 8, 1601 - April 29, 1603

THE PRISON YEARS
Sonnets 27 – 106
Feb 8, 1601 - April 9, 1603

THE FINAL DAYS
Sonnets 107 – 126
April 10 - 29, 1603

THE 100-SONNET CENTER

Sonnets 27 – 126

10 Chapters
10 Sonnets per Chapter = 100

Ten times thy self were happier than thou art,
If ten of thine ten times refigured thee:
Then what could death do if thou shouldst depart,
Leaving thee living in posterity?
Sonnet 6, lines 9-12

The sequence of 100 sonnets at the center of the monument is structured as a book of ten chapters, each containing ten sonnets. This is a dramatic narrative of events, each chapter covering a new phase from the Rebellion of February 8, 1601 to the Queen's funeral on April 28, 1603 plus the final farewell. The individual chapters are given appropriate titles below:

1.	THE CRIME	Sonnets 27–36	8 February 1601–17 February 1601
2.	THE TRIAL	Sonnets 37–46	18 February 1601–27 February 1601
3.	THE PLEA	Sonnets 47–56	28 February 1601–9 March 1601
4.	THE REPRIEVE	Sonnets 57–66	10 March 1601–19 March 1601
5.	THE PENANCE	Sonnets 67–76	20 March 1601–29 March 1601
6.	THE SACRIFICE	Sonnets 77–86	30 March 1601–8 April 1601
7.	THE TEACHING	Sonnets 87–96	April 1601–January 1602
8.	THE PROPHECY	Sonnets 97–106	8 February 1602–9 April 1603
9.	THE CONTRACT	Sonnets 107–116	10 April 1603–19 April 1603
10.	THE OBLATION	Sonnets 117–126	20 April 1603–28 April 1603 plus ENVOY

Part Two

THE PRISON YEARS
Sonnets 27 – 106
Feb 8, 1601 - April 9, 1603

"Suddenly we are all adrift, because the spirit of the verses so obviously changes."
- Gerald Massey, 1866, citing the abrupt transition from Sonnet 26 to Sonnet 27

Oxford is "weary with toil" and finally hastening to bed to rest from his "travail" – not from his "travel" on a physical journey, as some editors have emended it, but from his labors that day and night in reaction to the Rebellion. He lies awake before dawn...

"But then begins a journey in my head," he continues, adding that the "thoughts" in his mind become purposefully fixed on making "a zealous pilgrimage to thee." His eyes remain wide open in the "darkness" of his sleeping quarters, while "my soul's imaginary sight presents thy shadow to my sightless view." In a dreamlike state while still awake, Oxford finds his son appearing to him as "a jewel hung in ghastly night" or as a shining, ghostlike image that "makes black night beauteous and her old face new."

Sonnet 27 presents a vision of Oxford surrounded by physical darkness as he lies in bed and by the emotional darkness of the day's terrible events that have blackened Southampton's honor. Agents of the Crown, rounding up other conspirators that afternoon and evening, have already announced the charges of high treason against the two popular earls. Confined in a room of the Tower in the still-dark hours after midnight, Southampton now appears to Oxford as a bright jewel projected by the inner vision of his soul.

"This is the first of a series of five sonnets in which the poet meditates on his friend."
- Katherine Duncan-Jones, 1997

The observation by Duncan-Jones is accurate, except that Sonnet 27 is actually the first of five dozen sonnets corresponding with sixty days from February 8, 1601. Editor Stephen Booth also finds linkages from the outset of this new sequence – from 27 to 28, from 30 to 31 and from 33 to 34, and so on. Such linkages occur throughout the next eighty sonnets, suggesting the Rebellion has triggered Oxford's most intense labor upon the Sonnets and that he is now writing/compiling the equivalent of one per day.

Given such connections, it is easy to imagine him writing two or more sonnets at a time, before arranging them in numerical sequence corresponding to calendar days. It's doubtful that Oxford actually wrote a sonnet each day, but, rather, collected his thoughts before working on clusters or sequences. No doubt all the sonnets were subsequently revised and arranged in their final order after April 1603.

THE PRISON YEARS

DAY/NIGHT OF REBELLION
FIRST NIGHT IN THE TOWER

Sonnet 27
A Jewel Hung in Ghastly Night
8 February 1601

Now it is long past midnight, after the Essex Rebellion has failed, and Southampton is imprisoned in the Tower of London. No more is he "the world's fresh ornament" but, rather, "a jewel hung in ghastly night." A great darkness has descended over the private verses of the Sonnets; Oxford will write the next sixty sonnets to correspond with the day-by-day circumstances as they unfold. His royal son has committed high treason; as a ranking earl, Oxford knows he must sit on the jury and must find him guilty; as his father, he must also do all he can to save him from execution. Already he has begun to "toil" or argue on his son's behalf. Henry Wriothesley has lost his claim to the throne; and in the darkness at his Hackney home, Oxford's "thoughts" begin a "journey" or "zealous pilgrimage" to his royal son in the prison.

Sonnet 27	Translation
Weary with toil, I haste me to my bed,	Weary from these events, I haste to my bed,
The dear repose for limbs with travail tired,	The dear rest for limbs tired from their work,
But then begins a journey in my head	But then begins a journey inside my head
To work my mind, when body's work's expired.	To work my mind when other work is over.
For then my thoughts (from far where I abide)	For then my thoughts (traveling far from here)
Intend a zealous pilgrimage to thee,	Make an intense journey to you [in the Tower],
And keep my drooping eye-lids open wide,	And I keep my eyes open wide,
Looking on darkness, which the blind do see.	Looking at the tragic crime that most others see.
Save that my soul's imaginary sight	Except that the eyes of my soul, in imagination,
Presents thy shadow to my sightless view,	Reveal to my unseeing eyes the shadow of you,
Which like a jewel (hung in ghastly night)	Who, a royal prince hung in ghastly disgrace,
Makes black night beauteous, and her old face new.	Transforms the shame into royal blood again.
Lo thus by day my limbs, by night my mind,	Behold, by day I use my limbs, by night my mind,
For thee, and for my self, no quiet find.	For you – my son, my self – I find no rest.

Note: Sonnet 27 is chronologically aligned with Sonnet 127 of the Dark Lady series.

1 WEARY WITH TOIL, I HASTE ME TO MY BED,
WEARY, etc. = Oxford attempts to sleep tonight; "For to tell truth I am *weary* of an unsettled life" – Oxford to Burghley, May 18, 1591; "Whereupon I may upon reason *quiet* myself, and not upon *weariness*" – Oxford to Robert Cecil, May 22, 1602; "How *weary*, stale, flat, and unprofitable seem to me all the uses of this world!" – *Hamlet*, 1.2.139-140

TOIL = work, labor; but *OED* defines "toil" first as a verb "to contend in a lawsuit or an argument; to dispute, argue; to contend in battle; to fight, struggle"; this legal sense may be the primary meaning, referring to his arguing on Southampton's behalf, indicated by the use of "toil" in the first line and twice more in the next sonnet; "Your faithful service, and your *toil* in war" – *1 Henry VI*, 3.4.21; "Princes have but titles for their glories, an outward honor for an inward *toil*" – *Richard III*, 1.4.78-79; "When I was dry with rage, with extreme *toil*, breathless and faint, leaning upon my sword" – *1 Henry IV*, 1.3.30-31

> So service shall with steeled sinews *toil*,
> And labour shall refresh itself with hope
> To do your grace incessant services.
> - *Henry V*, 2.2.36-38

> Winding up days with *toil* and nights with sleep,
> Had the fore-hand and vantage of a king.
> - *Henry V*, 4.1.275-276

WEARY/TOIL:

> I still do *toil* and never am at rest,
> Enjoying least when I do covet most;
> With *weary* thoughts are my green years oppress'd,
> To danger drawn from my desired coast.
> - Harleian MS 7392, ff. 52-53, signed "Lo. Ox" (Chiljan, 188, 200)

2 THE DEAR REPOSE FOR LIMBS WITH TRAVAIL TIRED:
DEAR = royal, related to his feelings for Southampton; "one *dear son* shall I twice lose" – *The Tempest*, 5.1.176; "Those lines that I before have write do lie,/ Even those that said I could not love you *dearer*" - Sonnet 115, lines 1-2; "If my *dear* love were but the child of state,/ It might for fortune's bastard be unfathered" - Sonnet 124, lines 1-2; **DEAR REPOSE:** place of repose; a suggestion that his preferred place of rest is in the grave; Milton in *Paradise Lost* will write of "my harbour and my ultimate repose" – 3.210; Oxford is speaking of the resting place he so dearly needs to find, but he also reflects his "dear son's" repose in the Tower; "Your Highness shall *repose* you at the Tower" – *Richard III*, 3.1.65; **TRAVAIL** = often glossed as "travel" but in this sonnet meaning "work" or "painful labor" during this day of turmoil; "Yet I am one that hath long besieged a fort and not able to compass the end or reap the fruit of his *travail*" – Oxford to Burghley, June 25, 1585; "But now, having received this comfortable message of furtherance and favor from your Lordship, although Her Majesty be forgetful of herself, yet by such a good mean I do not doubt that, if you list, but that I may receive some fruit of all my *travail*" – Oxford to Burghley, March 20, 1595; "I do well perceive how your Lordship doth *travail* for me in this cause of an especial grace and favor" – Oxford to Robert Cecil, June 19, 1603

"What they *travail* for" – *Timon of Athens*, 5.1.15-16; "I grant, sweet love, thy lovely argument/ Deserves the *travail of a worthier pen*" – Sonnet 79, lines 5-6; of course, Oxford's "travail" also included "travel" by horse between his home in Hackney and the Court at Whitehall

3 BUT THEN BEGINS A JOURNEY IN MY HEAD
JOURNEY IN MY HEAD = a mental journey to the Tower; this is the "travel" aspect of the verse, i.e., the traveling of Oxford's thoughts, at night, to his son in the Tower

4 TO WORK MY MIND, WHEN BODY'S WORK'S EXPIRED.
WORK MY MIND = labor to form a mental vision of Southampton in prison; "work" is related to "travail" in the above line, confirming the meaning of "travail" as labor; i.e., first there was the physical work, and now the mental work begins.

5 FOR THEN MY THOUGHTS, FROM FAR WHERE I ABIDE,
His thoughts are at the Tower, not where he is; "*Think on the Tower* and me" – *Richard III*, 5.3.127; Oxford's

home in Hackney in about three miles northeast of Whitechapel and the Tower of London, which is on the River Thames

MY THOUGHTS = "Was it the proud full sail of his ("Shakespeare's") great verse,/ Bound for the prize of all too precious (royal) you,/ That did *my ripe thoughts* in my brain inhearse,/ Making their tomb the womb in which they grew?" – Sonnet 86, lines 1-4

6 INTEND A ZEALOUS PILGRIMAGE TO THEE,
INTEND = "set out upon … have in mind a fixed purpose" – Booth

ZEALOUS PILGRIMAGE TO THEE = his thoughts go on a royal (and holy) progress to Southampton in the Tower; also, a religious pilgrimage to Southampton as a king or god on earth; in this line Oxford echoes the theme of Sonnet 7, in which he compares Southampton with "his sacred majesty," a prince or king: "Yet mortal looks adore his beauty still,/ Attending on his golden *pilgrimage*" - Sonnet 7, lines 7-8

ZEALOUS = related to religious fervor, i.e., his thoughts (expressed in these sonnets) are akin to hymns or prayers to a god on earth; "Nothing, sweet boy, but yet like *prayers divine,*/ I must each day say o'er the very same,/ Counting no old thing old, thou mine, I thine,/ Even as when first I *hallowed* thy fair name" - Sonnet 108, lines 5-8; "When holy and devout religious men are at their beads, 'tis much to draw them thence, so sweet is *zealous contemplation* … thy devotion and *right Christian zeal*" – *Richard III*, 3.7.91-93,102, i.e., Oxford is contemplating his royal son as a king or "god on earth" as in "the little Love-God" of Sonnet 154, line 1, and a "God in love" in Sonnet 110, line 12; "With hearts create *of duty and of zeal*" - *Henry V*, 2.2.31

PILGRIMAGE = "In *prison* hast thou spent a *pilgrimage* and like a hermit overpass'd thy days" – *1 Henry VI*, 2.5.116

7 AND KEEP MY DROOPING EYELIDS OPEN WIDE,
Keeping his eyes open in the dark, while forming a mental vision

8 LOOKING ON DARKNESS, WHICH THE BLIND DO SEE.
LOOKING ON = "*Looking on* the lines of my boy's face" – *The Winter's Tale*, 1.2.153-154; "What might I have been, might I a son and daughter now have **look'd on**: - *The Winter's Tale*, 5.1.175-176; "The sun *look'd on* the world with glorious eye,/ Yet not so wistly *as this Queen on him*" – *The Passionate Pilgrim*, No. 6, 1599; "Were it not pity that this goodly boy should lose his birthright by his father's fault … Ah, what a shame were this! *Look on* the boy" – *3 Henry VI*, 2.2.34-39; "A son who is the theme of honour's tongue, amongst a grove the very straightest plant, who is sweet Fortune's minion and her pride; whilst I by *looking on* the praise of him see riot and dishonour stain the brow of my young Harry" – *1 Henry IV*, 1.1.80-85

DARKNESS = literally the darkness of his room; also the darkness of this tragedy; also the darkness that Elizabeth sees in her imperial, negative view, casting her cloud, as in "The *region cloud* hath masked him from me now" – Sonnet 33, line 12 ("region" = Regina)

> But when I sleep, in dreams they look on thee,
> And *darkly* bright, are bright in *dark* directed
> - Sonnet 43, lines 3-4
>
> What freezings have I felt, what *dark* days seen!
> - Sonnet 97, line 3
> - Both examples above are to Southampton during these prison years
>
> For I have sworn thee fair, and thought thee bright,
> Who art *black* as hell, as *dark* as night
> - Sonnet 147, lines 13-14, Oxford to Elizabeth in the Dark Lady Series
> (Accusing the Queen of casting her dark royal frown upon their son)

Where now *his son's like a glow-worm in the night,*
The which hath fire in *darkness*, none in light
- *Pericles*, 3.2.43-44

Witness *my son, now in the shade of death,*
Whose bright out-shining beams thy cloudy wrath
Hath in eternal *darkness* folded up
- *Richard III*, 1.3.267-269

Dark cloudy death o'ershakes his beams of life
- *3 Henry VI*, 2.6.62

To *dark dishonour's* use thou shalt not have.
I am disgrace'd, impeach'd, and baffled here,
Pierced to the soul with slander's venom'd spear
- *Richard II*, 1.1.169-171

THE BLIND: Those who can only see the surface appearance of things and not the substance; those who have no idea that Southampton is a prince. Those who are "blind" also (even primarily) include Elizabeth, who refuses to acknowledge the truth of her son. In the final verse of the Dark Lady series, Oxford will remind the Queen that "to enlighten thee," he "*gave eyes to blindness*" – Sonnet 152, line 11

WHICH THE BLIND DO SEE = others can see, but they see only the treason of the events, while remaining blind to the greater royal tragedy; Oxford sees the truth and therefore, paradoxically, he cannot see with his eyes, i.e., he is blind; "O me! What eyes hath love put in my head./ Which have no correspondence with true sight!/ ... O cunning love, with tears thou keep'st me *blind,*/ Lest eyes, well seeing, thy foul faults should find" – Sonnet 148, lines 1-2, 13-14; "But, love, hate on, for now I know thy (Elizabeth's) mind;/ Those that can see thou lov'st, and *I am blind*" – Sonnet 149, lines 13-14

9 SAVE THAT MY SOUL'S IMAGINARY SIGHT
MY SOUL'S IMAGINARY SIGHT = my spiritual vision of Southampton, without use of eyes; "Now *my soul's palace* is become a *prison*" – *3 Henry VI*, 2.1.74; and in Oxford's view, his own heart or soul is becoming Southampton's own prison, a better one than the Tower; he will write to Elizabeth: "Let my heart be his guard; thou canst not then use rigor in my jail" – Sonnet 133, lines 11-12; a theme is that Oxford and his son are imprisoned in each other's souls or hearts.

10 PRESENTS THY SHADOW TO MY SIGHTLESS VIEW,
THY SHADOW = This is the introduction of *shadow* in the Sonnets; Southampton, under the darkened cloud or shadow, appears ghostlike; "And so he vanished: then came wand'ring by a *shadow like an angel*, with bright hair dabbled in blood" – *Richard III*, 1.4.52-54

"But the world is so cunning, as of a *shadow* they can make a substance, and of a likelihood a truth" – Oxford to Burghley, July 1581

"A dream itself is but a shadow" – *Hamlet*, 2.2.261; "The shadow of myself formed in her eye; which, being but the shadow of your son, becomes a sun and makes your son a shadow" – *King John*, 2.1.498-500; "But Henry now shall wear the English crown and be true King indeed; thou but the shadow" – *3 Henry VI*, 4.3.49-50; "He hath no more worthy interest to the state than thou the shadow of succession" – *1 Henry IV*, 3.2.98-99

Must he be then as *shadow* of himself?
Adorn his temples with a coronet,
And yet, in substance and authority,

Retain but privilege of a private man?
- *1 Henry VI*, 5.4.133-136

No, no, I am but *shadow* of myself:
You are deceived; my substance is not here
- *1 Henry VI*, 2.3.49-50

I am the *shadow* of poor Buckingham,
Whose figure even this instant cloud puts on
By darkening my clear sun
- *Henry VIII*, 1.1.224-226

SIGHTLESS = "Poor grooms are *sightless night*, kings glorious day" – *Lucrece*, 1013

11 WHICH LIKE A JEWEL (HUNG IN GHASTLY NIGHT)
WHICH = the shadow of Southampton, presenting his image; **A JEWEL** = Southampton now appears like a jewel or ornament (royal prince) as he was "the world's fresh *ornament*" in Sonnet 1, line 9; "As on the finger of a throned Queen/ The basest *Jewel* will be well esteemed" – Sonnet 96, lines 5-6, Oxford referring to Southampton; "As for *my sons*, say I account of them as *jewels*" – *Titus Andronicus*, 3.1.198-199; "Had *our prince (Jewel of children)* seen this hour" – *The Winter's Tale*, 5.1.115-116

No son of mine succeeding...
And *mine eternal jewel*
Given to the common Enemy of man,
To make them kings, the seed of Banquo kings!
- *Macbeth*, 3.1.63, 67-69

(In the above passage, *eternal jewel* = *immortal soul*, according to the Riverside edition of the Shakespeare works; and this soul is carried or passed on by his seed; meanwhile, Oxford will say to Southampton: "What can *mine own* praise to *mine own self* bring,/ And what is't but *mine own* when I praise thee" – Sonnet 39, lines 2-4; and "My *spirit* is thine, *the better part of me*" – Sonnet 74, line 8); so the "jewel" of this sonnet is Southampton and his immortal soul as both the son or "better part" of Oxford and as the immortal royal prince of England)

For *princes* are
A model which *heaven* makes like to itself:
As *jewels* lose their glory if neglected,
So *princes* their renowns if not respected
- *Pericles*, 2.2.10-13

HUNG = image of a hanging, i.e., Southampton's impending execution; also as trophies are "hung" over memorials for the dead; "Thou art *the grave where buried love doth live, /Hung* with the trophies of my lovers gone" – Sonnet 31, lines 9-10; as on a tomb: "And *hang* more praise upon deceased I" – Sonnet 72, line 7; to be "hung" or "hanged" or executed by the halter; "To confess and be*hanged* for his labour! First to be *hanged*, and then to confess" – *Othello*, 4.1.38-39; "Upon the next tree shalt thou hang alive" – *Macbeth*, 5.5.39; suspended in the air, like a hovering apparition

GHASTLY NIGHT = the terrible (and terrifying) darkness of his son's disgrace, yet his shadow glitters in the sight of Oxford's soul; "Where now *his son's like a glow-worm in the night*" – *Pericles*, 3.2.43; "O, I have passed *a miserable night*, so full of fearful dreams" – *Richard III*, 1.4.2-3, i.e., Clarence, speaking of his night in the Tower; suggesting ghostlike, as Hamlet's dead father appears as a ghost in the night; "I am *thy father's spirit, doomed* for a certain term to walk *the night*" – *Hamlet*, 1.5.9-10

"Unto the kingdom of perpetual night" - *Richard III*, 1.4.47

No. 27

12 MAKES BLACK NIGHT BEAUTEOUS, AND HER OLD FACE NEW.
MAKES BLACK NIGHT BEAUTEOUS = introduction of *black* in the Sonnets, the opposite of his "Summer's Day" of the Golden Time in Sonnet 18, the previous series of the "old" time; also, Elizabeth, the "dark" lady, is "old" at age sixty-seven; in Oxford's view, however, Southampton turns this *blackness* into the sight of his son's royal blood inherited from "beauty" or Elizabeth. Southampton, because of the Rebellion, is suddenly changed from the "fairest" of Sonnet 1, line 1, to the opposite; i.e., he has been changed from *fair* to *black* as reflected by the parallel verse Sonnet 127, opening the Dark Lady series: "In the *old age black* was not counted fair,/ Or if it were it bore not beauty's name;/ But now is *black* beauty's successive heir,/ And Beauty slandered with a bastard shame" – Sonnet 127, lines 1-4; and at the end of that sonnet, the Queen is pictured as in mourning for her royal son, whom she may execute very soon:

> *Therefore my Mistress' eyes are Raven black*,
> Her eyes so suited, and they *mourners* seem...
> Yet so they *mourn becoming of their woe*
> - Sonnet 127, lines 9-10, 13

A few verses later in the Dark Lady series, Oxford further insists:

> *Thine eyes* I love, and they as pitying me...
> Have *put on black*, and loving *mourners* be...
> And truly not the *morning Sun of Heaven*
> Better becomes the gray cheeks of the East,
> Nor that full *star* that ushers in the ev'n
> Doth half that glory to the sober West
> As those two *mourning eyes* become thy face.
> O let it then as well beseem thy heart
> To *mourn* for me, since *mourning* doth thee grace
> - Sonnet 132, lines 1, 3, 5-11

> Shall we go throw away our coats of steel,
> And wrap our bodies in *black mourning* gowns?
> - 3 Henry VI, 2.1.160-161

"I arrest thee of *high treason*, in the name of our most sovereign King ... It will help me nothing to plead mine innocence; for that dye is on me which *makes* **my whitest part black**" - Henry VIII, 1.1.200-202; 208-209; "And took his voice who should **be prick'd to die in our black sentence** and proscription" - Julius Caesar, 4.1.16-17; "And from his bosom purge this *black despair!*" - 2 Henry VI, 3.3.23; "I'll join with **black** *despair* against my soul, and to myself become an enemy" - Richard III, 2.2.36-37; "Now, if these men do not die well, it will be a **black matter for the king** that led them to it" -Henry V, 4.1.141-143; "For I must talk of murders, rapes and massacres, acts of **black night,** abominable deeds, complots of mischief, **treasons**, villainies" - Titus Andronicus, 5.1.63-65; "*Black* is the badge of hell, the hue of **dungeons** and the school of night" - Love's Labour's Lost, 4.3.250-251

13 LO THUS BY DAY MY LIMBS, BY NIGHT MY MIND,
LO = Lord Oxford; **BY DAY ... BY NIGHT** = Oxford will now write day-by-day or night-by-night until there is some resolution. "Day" is the "Summer's day" or time of royal hope in Sonnet 18, line 1, while "night" is this entire time of utter despair

After Southampton's release, Oxford will recall "how once I suffered in *your crime*," adding, "O that *our night* of woe might have remembr'ed" – Sonnet 120, lines 8-9); "No; *dark shall be my light, and* **night my day**" – 2 Henry VI, 2.4.40); Southampton will be called soon to trial

> *Call him to present trial*; if he may

REFERENCE EDITION

Find mercy in the law, 'tis his; if none,
Let him not seek't of us. **By day and night,**
He's traitor to th'height!
- *Henry VIII*, 1.2.211-214

Black night o'ershade *the day*, and *death thy life*
- *Richard III*, 1.2.135

Winding up ***days with toil and nights with sleep***,
Had the fore-hand and vantage of a king.
- *Henry V*, 4.1.275-276

14 FOR THEE, AND FOR MY SELF, NO QUIET FIND.
FOR THEE, AND FOR MY SELF = Oxford equates his son with himself; he is attempting to transfer all the pain and grief and guilt from Southampton to himself; (I can find no peace – not for you, and, therefore, not for me); "Not for *myself*, Lord Warwick, but *my son*" – *3 Henry VI*, 1.1.198; "O how thy worth with manners may I sing,/ When thou art *all the better part of me*?/ What can mine own praise to mine own self bring,/ And what is't but mine own when I praise thee?" – Sonnet 39, lines 1-4

NO QUIET FIND = "I shall not sleep in *quiet at the Tower*" – *Richard III*, 3.1.142; "'Tis *thee, my self*, that for my self I praise" – Sonnet 62, line 13; "My spirit is thine, *the better part of me*" – Sonnet 74, line 8. "Whereupon I may upon reason *quiet* myself, and not upon *weariness*" – Oxford to Robert Cecil, May 22, 1602

Sonnet 27 begins the 100-Sonnet Center of the Monument that Oxford is constructing for Southampton, as a memorial to preserve him and his "love" or royal blood ("And *you and love* are still *my argument*" – Sonnet 76, line 10) for future generations. Although Southampton and Essex claim they were attempting only to remove Robert Cecil from his control over the Queen, they are accused of having committed high treason against the Crown itself. Essex will die for his sins; Elizabeth will spare the life of her royal son, but his claim of succession has been lost.

Part Two

THE PRISON YEARS

DAY TWO IN THE TOWER

Sonnet 28
Clouds Do Blot The Heaven
9 February 1601

Having vainly attempted to find "quiet" in his soul for Southampton and himself, Oxford is still "debarred the benefit of rest" because "day's oppression" (the obliteration of the royal "Summer's day" or golden time) is "not eased by night." The dark "clouds" of the Queen's disfavor cover up the "heaven" that Southampton inherited from Elizabeth. Oxford is "day by night and night by day oppressed," reflecting the day/night-to-day/night composition and/or arrangement of these private verses to correspond with Southampton's days and nights in Her Majesty's prison. Both day and night are "enemies" conspiring to "torture" him as his royal son remains in a state of shame and disgrace in the Tower, facing trial and execution.

Sonnet 28	Translation
How can I then return in happy plight That am debarred the benefit of rest, When day's oppression is not eased by night But day by night and night by day oppressed?	How can I then in my plight return happily to bed, Since I'm deprived of the benefit of rest? When the oppression of day is not eased by night, But day and night oppress each other?
And each (though enemies to either's reign) Do in consent shake hands to torture me, The one by toil, the other to complain How far I toil, still farther off from thee.	And each (though enemies to each other's reign) Agree with mutual consent to torture me, The one to suffer, the other to make me complain How I keep toiling farther from you [in prison].
I tell the Day to please him thou art bright, And dost him grace when clouds do blot the heaven. So flatter I the swart-complexioned night, When sparkling stars twire not, thou gild'st the even.	I tell the Day to please him that you are royal, And grace him when disgrace covers Elizabeth, So I flatter the disgrace-covered night; When stars fail, you confer your royal light.
But day doth daily draw my sorrows longer, And night doth nightly make grief's length seem stronger.	But my sorrows daily keep growing longer, And night after night, the length of my grief seems stronger.

"Examinations and evidence were taken at once, before men's minds had time to become confused. On February 9th Cecil carried much of the burden for the preliminary arrangements" – Handover, p. 224

1 HOW CAN I THEN RETURN IN HAPPY PLIGHT
RETURN = return home from the Court, where he has already begun to make efforts to help Southampton; **HAPPY** = "And so shall you, if happy England's royal king be free" – *1 Henry VI*, 5.3.114-115; "You have misled a prince, a royal king, a happy gentleman in blood and lineaments" – *Richard II*, 3.1.8-9; "I had been still a happy king of men" – *Richard II*, 5.1.36

REFERENCE EDITION 211

2 THAT AM DEBARRED THE BENEFIT OF REST,

DEBARRED = prevented from; definitions given by the *OED* of the verb "debar" include: "To exclude or shut out *from* a place or condition; to prevent or prohibit *from* (entrance, or from having, attaining, or doing anything ... to shut out, exclude ... to set a bar or prohibition against (an action, etc.); to prohibit, prevent, forbid, stop." Among examples cited:

"Utterly to *debarre* from heaven all mankynde for ever" – 1557

"Every other person ... be utterly excluded and *debarred* of their said suites" – Act 33 Hen. VIII, c.6, 1541

REST = Among *OED* definitions: "Restored vigour or strength ... spiritual peace"; "Doing himself offence, whilst we, lying still, are full of *rest*, defence, and nimbleness" – *Julius Caesar*, 4.3.200-201; "There remaineth therefore a *rest* to the people of God" – Bible, Hebrews, 4.9; "And the land had *rest* from war" – KJV Bible, 1611, *Joshua*, 14.15; "And I most jocund, apt, and willingly, to do you *rest*, a thousand deaths would die" -*Twelfth Night*, 5.1.130

After this thy travail shall
Sweet *rest* seize thee ever more
- John Milton, 1631 (*OED*)

To save at least the heir of Edward's right:
There shall I *rest* secure from force and fraud*3 Henry VI*, 4.4.32-33
- (Queen Elizabeth to her husband Edward IV)

3 WHEN DAY'S OPPRESSION IS NOT EASED BY NIGHT,

DAY'S OPPRESSION = the golden time or "Summer's Day" of Southampton's royalty is now oppressed by the shadows of this further, irrevocable disgrace, i.e., by night; "To counterfeit oppression of such grief that words seemed buried in my sorrow's grave" – *Richard II*, 1.4.14-15

God quit you in his mercy! Hear your sentence.
You have conspired against our royal person...
Wherein you would have sold your king to slaughter,
His princes and his peers to servitude,
His subjects to *oppression and contempt*
- *Henry V*, 2.2.165-166; 171-173

To make *oppression* bitter
- *Hamlet*, 2.2.580

Nay, rather turn this day out of the week,
This day of shame, oppression, perjury.
Or, if it must stand still, let wives with child
Pray that their burthens may not fall this day,
Lest that their hopes prodigiously be cross'd
- *King John*, 3.1.14-17

4 BUT DAY BY NIGHT AND NIGHT BY DAY OPPRESSED?

DAY ...NIGHT ... NIGHT ... DAY = a litany, emphasizing the agony of time slowly passing while his son remains in prison awaiting trial; also, reflecting the fact that these sonnets are now being written daily. The juxtaposition of "day" and "night" expresses the situation that Southampton's own "day" of royal hope has suddenly been plunged into a long "night" without hope of gaining the throne; ("To weigh how once I suffered in your crime./ O that *our night of woe* might have remembered/ My deepest sense" – Sonnet 120, lines

8-10); **OPPRESSED** =

> Thou and thine usurp
> The dominations, royalties and rights
> Of *this oppressed boy*
> - *King John*, 2.1.175-177

> In the relief of *this oppressed child*
> - *King John*, 2.1.245

> For thee, *oppressed King*, am I cast down
> - *King Lear*, 5.3.5

> Proceeding from the *heat-oppressed brain*
> - *Macbeth*, 2.1.39

5 AND EACH (THOUGH ENEMIES TO EITHER'S REIGN)
REIGN = the royal context; Southampton's own "reign" has been destroyed

ENEMIES TO EITHER'S REIGN = Elizabeth and Southampton are now hindering each other's *reign*; Southampton has prevented his own succession, which would have enabled Elizabeth to fulfill her responsibility to herself, to England and to her dynasty. The Queen herself is holding him in prison as a traitor, thus preventing him from succeeding her on the throne.

6 DO IN CONSENT SHAKE HANDS TO TORTURE ME,
IN CONSENT = making common cause; "Some villains of my court are of consent" – *As You Like It*, 2.2.3;
SHAKE HANDS = conspire; royal hands; **SHAKE** = a glance at his pen name "Shakespeare" that he will have to maintain as part of the bargain to gain leniency for Southampton, who is linked to the poems and plays because of the dedications; the handshake of the terrible bargain by which his royal son will have to give up all claim to the throne.

TORTURE = Oxford's spiritual pain; related to the torture that is used to interrogate those accused or suspected of treason; the torture of time passing while Southampton is in the Tower; (See line 14: All *length* is *torture*, now the torch is out" - *Antony and Cleopatra*, 4.14.45-47); "Is't not enough to torture me alone" – Sonnet 133, line 3, Oxford to Elizabeth in 1601

> Better be with the dead,
> Whom we, to gain our peace, have sent to peace,
> Than on the *torture of the mind* to lie
> In restless ecstasy
> - *Macbeth*, 3.2.19-22

> And that deep *torture* may be call'd a hell
> - *Lucrece*, line 1287

> And ***torture*** him with grievous ling'ring death
> - *2 Henry VI*, 3.2.246

> Clifford, ask *mercy* and obtain no grace.
> Clifford, *repent* in bootless penitence.
> Clifford, devise *excuses* for their *faults*.
> While we devise fell ***tortures*** for thy *faults*.
> - *3 Henry VI*, 2.6.69-72

(**MERCY** = "Straight in her heart did *mercy* come" – Sonnet 145, line 5; **REPENT** = "Though thou *repent*, yet I have still the loss" – Sonnet 34, line 10; **EXCUSES** = "Loving offenders [Elizabeth and Southampton], thus will I *excuse* thee" – Sonnet 42, line 5; **FAULTS** = "All men make *faults*, and even I in this,/ Authorizing thy trespass [your treason] with compare" – Sonnet 35, lines 5-6)

7 THE ONE BY TOIL, THE OTHER TO COMPLAIN
ONE = Southampton, *One for All, All for One;* **TOIL/COMPLAIN** = Oxford is working behind the scenes to help his royal son. He is "complaining" (emotionally and *legally*) on Southampton's behalf, to the Queen and Robert Cecil.

"To *complain* before their justice" – 1489 (*OED*)

COMPLAIN = "To give expression to sorrow or suffering ... to bewail, lament, deplore ... to make moan, lament ... the expression of suffering passing into that of grievance and blame ... to cry out upon ... to make a formal statement of a grievance to or before a competent authority; to lodge a complaint, bring a charge ... to emit a mournful sound" - *OED*. At this point Oxford may already be lodging a "complaint" with the Queen in order "to guard the lawful reasons on thy part," as he will promise Southampton in Sonnet 49, line 12;

"To *complayne the dethe of the kyng*" – 1523 (*OED*); "To all the host of heaven I *complain* me" – *Lucrece*, 598; "Remember measure in your grief's *complaining*" – 1633 (*OED*); "He that *complaineth of injury from Sovereign*" – 1651, Hobbes, Leviath, 21.90; "*complained* before the Lords of the Senate" – 1598 (*OED*)

> Humbly *complaining* to her deity
> Got my Lord Chamberlain his *liberty*
> - *Richard III*, 1.1.76-77

> Who is it that *complains unto the King*
> - *Richard III*, 1.3.43

> I promis'd you redress of these same grievances
> Whereof you did *complain*
> - *2 Henry IV*, 4.2.113-114

> To whom should I *complain*?
> - *Measure for Measure*, 2.4.170

> And *trouble deaf heaven with my bootless cries*
> - Sonnet 29, line 3
> (Complaining to Elizabeth, who refuses to listen or hear him)

> And to *the nightingale's complaining notes*
> Tune my distresses, and record my woes
> - *The Two Gentlemen of Verona*, 5.4.5-6

8 HOW FAR I TOIL, STILL FARTHER OFF FROM THEE.
TOIL = repeated from Sonnet 27, line 1, and from the line above in this verse; *OED* defines "toil" primarily as "to contend in a lawsuit or an argument, to dispute," etc., as well as to struggle or engage in severe labor; "We have toiled all night" – KJV Bible, *Luke*, 5.5

> Winding up days with *toil* and nights with sleep
> - *Henry V*, 4.1.275

> As if you would drive me into a *toil*
> - *Hamlet*, 3.2.350

No. 28

STILL FARTHER OFF FROM THEE = always far (though not in actual distance) from where Southampton languishes in the Tower

9 I TELL THE DAY TO PLEASE HIM THOU ART BRIGHT,
DAY = Southampton's royalty; "Shall I compare thee to a Summer's Day" – Sonnet 18, line 1; **THOU ART BRIGHT** = you, Southampton, are royal; "Yet looks he like a king. Behold, his eye, as *bright* as is the eagle's" – *Richard II*, 3.3.68-69; Oxford shines his light into the darkness of his son's tragedy: "That in black ink my love may still shine bright" – Sonnet 65, line 14

10 AND DOST HIM GRACE WHEN CLOUDS DO BLOT THE HEAVEN:
HIM = the Day; **GRACE** = Southampton lends his royal grace to the day, even though it's now a dark day that always seems to be night; introduction of **CLOUDS** in the Sonnets = the shadow of disgrace, from the Rebellion itself and also from the Queen's imperial frown; ("But out alack, he was but one hour mine,/ The region cloud hath masked him from me now" – Sonnet 33, lines 11-12); **BLOT THE HEAVEN** = introduction of **BLOT** in the Sonnets, related to the blot or disgrace of treason; ("And thus thy fall hath left a kind of blot" = the king to a nobleman-turned-traitor, *Henry V*, 2.2); the clouds also cast disgrace upon **HEAVEN** or Elizabeth herself

Buckingham, Arrested for Treason and to be taken to the Tower:

> I am the *shadow* of poor Buckingham,
> Whose figure even *this instant cloud puts on*
> *By dark'ning my clear sun*
> - *Henry VIII*, 1.1.224-226

11 SO FLATTER I THE SWART-COMPLEXIONED NIGHT,
SWART-COMPLEXIONED – black-faced

12 WHEN SPARKLING STARS TWIRE NOT, THOU GILD'ST THE EVEN.
TWIRE = twinkle or peep; **WHEN STARS TWIRE NOT** = when Southampton's royal eyes, suns or stars, fail to peep from the night sky and twinkle; **GILD** = make golden or royal; **EVEN** = evening; **THOU GILD'ST THE EVEN** = your own stars or royal eyes turn night to day, i.e., make the evening royal; ("An eye more bright than theirs, less false in rolling,/ *Gilding the object whereupon it gazeth*" – Sonnet 20, lines 5-6; "Full many a glorious morning have I seen/ Flatter the mountain tops with sovereign eye,/ Kissing with golden face the meadows green,/ *Gilding pale streams with heavenly alchemy*" – Sonnet 33, lines 1-4)

13 BUT DAY DOTH DAILY DRAW MY SORROWS LONGER,
DAY ... DAILY = further emphasis on the agony of time, further indicating the sonnets are now being composed and/or arranged to correspond with each day; the line also evokes the seemingly endless length of each day Southampton spends in prison; **MY SORROWS** = "To those that wring *under the load of sorrow*" – *Much Ado About Nothing*, 5.1.28; "Why only, Suffolk, mourn I not for thee, and with the southern *clouds* contend in tears, theirs for the earth's treasure, mine for *my sorrows*?" – *2 Henry VI*, 3.2.382-384

> King Richard: Th'advancement of your children, gentle lady.
>
> Elizabeth: Up to some scaffold, there to lose their heads.
>
> King Richard: Unto the dignity and height of fortune,
>   The high imperial type of this earth's glory!
>
> Elizabeth: Flatter *my sorrows* with report of it.
>   Tell me what state what dignity, what honour,
>   Canst thou demise to any child of mine?

REFERENCE EDITION

14 AND NIGHT DOTH NIGHTLY MAKE GRIEF'S LENGTH SEEM STRONGER.
NIGHT ... NIGHTLY = same as above; the world of the Sonnets has been plunged into darkness; *night, night, night, clouds, blot, swart, night, even(ing), night, nightly...*

MY SORROWS/GRIEF =

>I will instruct *my sorrows* to be proud;
>For *grief* is proud and makes his owner stoop.
>To me and to the state of my great *grief*
>Let kings assemble; for my *grief's* so great
>That no supporter but the huge firm earth
>Can hold it up: here I and *sorrows* sit;
>Here is my throne, bid kings come bow to it.
>- *King John*, 2.2.68-74

>Take heed, for heaven's sake, take heed, lest at once
>The burthen of *my sorrows* fall upon ye.
>- *Henry VIII*, 3.1.109-110

>Therefore I tell *my sorrows* to the stones
>- *Titus Andronicus*, 3.1.37

GRIEF'S LENGTH = the slow drawing-out of emotional pain, related to the "torture" in line 6 above; **LENGTH** = "Extent from beginning to end, e.g., of a period of time ... esp, a long period" – *OED*; "Bring me a father that so lov'd his child ... Measure his woe the length and breadth of mine" – *Much Ado About Nothing*, 5.1.8,11

>There is *such length in grief*
>- *Richard II*, 5.1.94

>I will o'er take thee, Cleopatra, and
>Weep for my pardon. So it must be, for now
>*All length is torture*, now the torch is out
>- *Antony and Cleopatra*, 4.14.45-47

>For now against himself he sounds this doom,
>That through the *length* of time he stands disgraced
>- *Lucrece*, lines 717-718

STRONGER = even more severe or painful; related to Southampton's "strength" of royalty and with the strong possibility of his death by execution

>"Assailed *by night* with circumstances **strong** of present death" – *Lucrece*, 1262-3

>*Th'offender's sorrow* lends but weak relief
>To him that bears the **strong** *offence's* loss"
>- Sonnet 34, lines 11-12, the final word often emended to "cross"

Part Two

THE PRISON YEARS

DAY THREE IN THE TOWER

Sonnet 29
When In Disgrace
10 February 1601

Oxford is mentally and emotionally trading places with Southampton in the Tower. Blaming himself for having lent his support to the failed Rebellion, he is now seeking to make a bargain on his son's behalf. He is "troubling deaf heaven" (arguing and pleading with the Queen) while delivering these "hymns" (prayers) or sacred songs to his royal son at "Heaven's gate" (Traitor's Gate at Elizabeth's Tower of London). Only Southampton's "sweet love" (royal blood) affords him comfort.

Sonnet 29	Translation
When in disgrace with Fortune and men's eyes,	When in disgrace with Elizabeth and men's eyes,
I all alone beweep my outcast state,	I lament your outcast state [which is now mine],
And trouble deaf heaven with my bootless cries,	And trouble deaf Elizabeth with my bootless cries,
And look upon myself and curse my fate,	And see myself and curse my fate [which is yours],
Wishing me like to one more rich in hope,	Wishing I were like one with more royal hope,
Featured like him, like him with friends possessed,	Featured like such a man; like him with friends,
Desiring this man's art, and that man's scope,	Desiring this man's art, and that man's scope,
With what I most enjoy contented least;	Being contented least with what I most enjoy;
Yet in these thoughts my self almost despising,	Yet having these thoughts, almost despising myself,
Haply I think on thee, and then my state	I happily think of you, and then my state
(Like to the Lark at break of day arising)	(Like that of the lark rising at daybreak)
From sullen earth, sings hymns at Heaven's gate;	Prays at Elizabeth's Traitor's Gate of the Tower.
For thy sweet love remembered such wealth brings,	For recalling your royalty brings such reward,
That then I scorn to change my state with Kings.	That then I scorn to change my state (as father of a prince) with Kings.

"By the time my letters shall come unto you," Robert Cecil told Sir George Carew on February, 10, 1601, writing of Essex, *"both he and the Earl of Southampton, with some of the other principals, shall have lost their heads."*
– Handover, p. 224, who comments that "in the first moment of triumph and relief he [Cecil] was as cold as the headman's axe." (Stopes, 198)

1 WHEN IN DISGRACE WITH FORTUNE AND MEN'S EYES,
DISGRACE = both the disgrace of high treason and the royal disfavor; "*Disgrace* not so your king" – *1 Henry VI*, 5.5; "Our brother is imprisoned by your means, myself *disgraced*, and the nobility held in contempt" – *Richard III*, 1.3.78-80; "To the *disgrace* and downfall of your House" – *Richard III*, 3.7.216; "And

REFERENCE EDITION 217

spit it bleeding in his high *disgrace*," *Richard II*, 1.1.194; "to thy foul *disgrace*, and utter ruin of the House of York" – *3 Henry VI*, 1.1.260-261; **FORTUNE** = Queen Elizabeth; "So I, made lame by *Fortune's dearest spite*" – Sonnet 37, line 3

> Faction that ever dwells in Court where wit excels,
> Hath set defiance.
> *Fortune* and Love have sworn that they were never born
> Of one alliance
> - Poem signed with initials E.O. for Earl of Oxford

> Myself, a prince by *fortune* of my birth
> Near to the King in blood, and near in love
> - *Richard II*, 3.1.16-17

AND MEN'S EYES = and in the eyes of the law; in the view of English citizens; "But I will rise there with so full a glory that I will dazzle *all the eyes of France*" – *Henry V*, 1.2.279-280; "Which steals *men's eyes*" – Sonnet 20, line 8; "When Julius Caesar, whose remembrance yet lives in men's eyes" – *Cymbeline*, 3.1.2-3; "Even so, or with much more contempt, *men's eyes* did scowl on gentle Richard" – *Richard II*, 5.2.27-28; "When you entombed in *men's eyes* shall lie" – Sonnet 81, line 8; "and now all **men's eyes**" – Oxford to Burghley, September 1572

2 I ALL ALONE BEWEEP MY OUTCAST STATE,

ALL ALONE = Southampton, *One for All, All for One*; **I ALL ALONE** = I, Oxford, am now speaking for my son; he and I are inseparable; emphasizing Southampton alone in his prison room of the Tower; "Save that to die, I leave my love *alone*" – Sonnet 66, line 14

MY OUTCAST STATE = Southampton's state is that of an outcast, but Oxford is spiritually assuming it for him; **OUTCAST** = "O blood-besotted Neapolitan, *outcast* of Naples, England's bloody scourge!" – *2 Henry VI*, 5.1. 117-118; "As Ovid be an *outcast* quite abjured" – *The Taming of the Shrew*, 1.1.33; **OUTCAST STATE** = Southampton's situation in the Tower, a situation that Oxford, by extension, is also in; "my captive state" – *3 Henry VI*, 4.6.3; **STATE** = (repeated in line 10); the royal state of a king; "You may my glories and *my state* depose" – *Richard II*, 4.1.192; "With that dread King that took *our state* upon him" – *2 Henry VI*, 3.2.153; "Brave peers of England, pillars *of the state*" – *2 Henry VI*, 1.1.74; See below: "That then I scorn to change my state with Kings" - line 14; "If thou wouldst use the strength of *all thy state*" – Sonnet 96, line 12

3 AND TROUBLE DEAF HEAVEN WITH MY BOOTLESS CRIES,

TROUBLE DEAF HEAVEN = complain to Elizabeth, who turns a deaf ear; an indication that indeed Oxford has been importuning her on Southampton's behalf; "The one by *toil*, the other to *complain* [make a legal plea]" – Sonnet 28, line 7; "Humbly *complaining to her deity*" – *Richard III*, 1.1.76; **BOOTLESS CRIES** = unheeded, hopeless cries for help, pleadings; "Clifford, *repent* in **bootless** penitence" – *3 Henry VI*, 2.6.70

> Subjects may challenge nothing of their sovereigns;
> But, *if an humble prayer may prevail*,
> I then crave pardon of Your Majesty
> - *3 Henry VI*, 4.6.6-8
> (Lieutenant of the Tower to King Henry)

4 AND LOOK UPON MY SELF AND CURSE MY FATE:

CURSE MY FATE = his son's fate is now his own; Southampton's fate is not only execution, but also the loss of any chance to gain the throne; and Oxford's fate, according to the bargain that must be made for Southampton's life, is the obliteration of his paternity and his identity as the poet "Shakespeare" who dedicated his work and life to Southampton; **CURSE** = "Law cannot give my child his kingdom here, for he that holds his kingdom holds the law; therefore, since law itself is perfect wrong, how can the law forbid my tongue to *curse*?" – *King John*, 3.1.113-116); "*my accursed fortune*" – Southampton to Cecil after the trial (Stopes, 227-9)

5 WISHING ME LIKE TO ONE MORE RICH IN HOPE,
ONE = Southampton, *One for All, All for One*; **RICH** = royal; filled with the treasure or wealth of royal blood

HOPE = the hope that Southampton will be king; "Yet *hope, succeeding from so fair a tree* as your fair self" – *Pericles*, 1.1.115-116, to the prince; "So then you *hope of pardon* from Lord Angelo? … The miserable have no other medicine but *only hope*: I have *hope to live*, and am prepared to die" – *Measure for Measure*, 3.1.1-4; "But hope of Orphans, and unfathered fruit" - Sonnet 97, line 10. "Which I wish may always answer your own wish, and the world's *hopeful* expectation" - dedication of *Venus and Adonis* to Southampton

6 FEATURED LIKE HIM, LIKE HIM WITH FRIENDS POSSESSED,
HIM = someone whose fate is richer with hope; **FRIENDS** = allies at Court

7 DESIRING THIS MAN'S ART, AND THAT MAN'S SCOPE,
ART = ("And *art* made tongue-tied by authority" – Sonnet 66, line 9); **SCOPE** = freedom – Duncan-Jones; i.e., freedom from the Tower; (also as in the "wondrous scope" of his art in creating these verses: "Fair, kind and true, is all my argument,/ Fair, kind, and true, varying to other words;/ And in this change is my invention spent,/ Three themes in one, which wondrous *scope* affords" – Sonnet 105, lines 9-12)

8 WITH WHAT I MOST ENJOY CONTENTED LEAST:
WHAT I MOST ENJOY = i.e., his son's royal blood; ("And still enjoy thy regal dignity" – *1 Henry VI*, 5.4.132; "Both which we doubt not but your Majesty shall soon enjoy" – *2 Henry IV*, 4.4.11-12; "Enjoy the kingdom after my decease" – *3 Henry VI*, 1.1.181); **CONTENTED LEAST** = the predicament of his son is what gives him the least content; i.e., the most suffering

> I still do toil and never am at rest,
> **Enjoying least** when I do covet **most**;
> With weary thoughts are my green years oppress'd,
> To danger drawn from my desired coast.
> - Harleian MS 7392, ff. 52-53, signed "Lo. Ox" (Chiljan, 188, 200)

9 YET IN THESE THOUGHTS MY SELF ALMOST DESPISING,
ALMOST = a play on "all" for Southampton's motto *One for All, All for One*

10 HAPLY I THINK ON THEE; AND THEN MY STATE
HAPLY = perhaps; happen to; suggesting "happily"; **MY STATE** = actually his son's royal state, which cannot be taken from him; "And, as you are a king, speak in your *state*" – *2 Henry IV*, 5.2.99; "Have practiced dangerously against *your state*" – *2 Henry VI*, 2.1.163

11 (LIKE TO THE LARK AT BREAK OF DAY ARISING)
LARK = "Hark, hark! The *lark at heaven's gate* sings, and Phoebus 'gins arise" – *Cymbeline*, 2.3.21-22; "The lively *lark* stretched forth her wing,/ The messenger of morning bright:/ And with her cheerful voice did sing/ The day's approach, discharging night" – Oxford poem, *The Paradise of Dainty Devices*, 1576; **BREAK OF DAY ARISING** = the royal sun rising, the way Southampton always rises as royal son

12 FROM SULLEN EARTH SINGS HYMNS AT HEAVEN'S GATE:
SULLEN = dark and shadowy, under clouds of disgrace; **HYMNS** = Oxford's pleas to Elizabeth; alluding to these sonnets as devotional songs or prayers on behalf of you, a king or god on earth; **HEAVEN** = Elizabeth; **AT HEAVEN'S GATE** = at Traitor's Gate of Elizabeth's Tower of London; ("I am come to survey the Tower … Open the gates" – *1 Henry VI*, 1.3.1,4; "And shivering shocks/ Shall break the locks/ Of *prison*

gates" – *A Midsummer Night's Dream*, 1.2.29-31); "gates of steel" – Sonnet 65, line 8; "How *at heaven's gates* she (the lark) claps her wings, the morn not waking till she sings" – Oxford's personal secretary John Lyly, *Campaspe*, Act Five, Scene 1, probably inspired or written by Oxford himself

13 **FOR THY SWEET LOVE REMEMBERED SUCH WEALTH BRINGS,**
SWEET = royal; **LOVE** = royal blood; **THY SWEET LOVE** = your most royal blood; "Welcome, sweet Prince, to London" – *Richard III*, 3.1.1

> You *cloudy princes* and heart-sorrowing peers,
> That bear this mutual heavy load of moan,
> Now cheer each other *in each other's love*...
> - *Richard III*, 2.2.112-114

REMEMBERED = "When Julius Caesar, whose *remembrance* yet lives in men's eyes" – *Cymbeline*, 3.1.2-3; carried to the next sonnet: "I summon up *remembrance* of things past" – Sonnet 30, line 2;
WEALTH = new kingly glory; related to the metaphor of royal blood as the Queen's treasure, as in "Make sweet some vial; *treasure* thou some place/ With beauty's *treasure* ere it be self-killed" – Sonnet 6, lines 3-4; "O him she stores, to show what *wealth* she had" – Sonnet 67, line 13, referring to Elizabeth as Nature, keeping her royal son in prison, where she is storing the treasure or wealth of his royal blood

14 **THAT THEN I SCORN TO CHANGE MY STATE WITH KINGS.**
SCORN TO CHANGE MY STATE WITH KINGS = the third use of "state" in this verse. Since Oxford's son is a prince or King, and because he so thoroughly identifies himself with his royal son, there is no need to change his state with that of any other King; and he scorns to do so; **STATE** = "Fair Queen of England, worthy Margaret, sit down with us: it ill befits *thy state and birth*, that thou shouldst stand while Lewis doth sit" – *3 Henry VI*, 3.3.3. This line is one of many in which Oxford indirectly states that Southampton himself is a King; i.e., similar to Sonnet 14, line 7, when he refers to his inability to forecast the future for "Princes" and then proceeds to say that, in Southampton's case, he can do so

Part Two

THE PRISON YEARS

OXFORD SUMMONED TO THE TRIAL
DAY FOUR IN THE TOWER

Sonnet 30
To The Sessions
11 February 1601

Edward de Vere is "summoned" to be a judge at the "Sessions" or treason trial of Essex and Southampton, to be held in Westminster Hall eight days from now. Oxford is filled with grief over the "losses" suffered by his royal son – loss of honor, liberty, the crown, and likely even the loss of his life by execution. Oxford's expression of overwhelming sorrow demonstrates that, in life itself, he suffers every bit as greatly as do the characters of his plays. When his son by the Queen was born, Oxford had been forced to "pay" by being unable to acknowledge him. Now he must "new pay" for his son by making a crucial bargain with Robert Cecil and King James of Scotland, who, barring civil war around the throne, will become James I of England.

Sonnet 30	Translation
When to the Sessions of sweet silent thought	When to the Trial with royal secret thoughts
I summon up remembrance of things past,	I am summoned to remember past things,
I sigh the lack of many a thing I sought,	I sigh the lack of your rights that I sought,
And with old woes new wail my dear time's waste:	And cry anew over my son's wasted royal time:
Then can I drown an eye (unused to flow)	Then I can weep tears (like never before)
For precious friends hid in death's dateless night,	For my royal son imprisoned, facing death and disgraced forever,
And weep afresh love's long-since cancelled woe,	And weep again over his royalty's cancellation,
And moan th' expense of many a vanished sight.	And moan over his many losses of recognition.
Then can I grieve at grievances foregone,	Then I can grieve over past grievances,
And heavily from woe to woe tell o'er	And sorrowfully, from woe to woe, give
The sad account of fore-bemoaned moan,	The sad account of my past moans,
Which I new pay as if not paid before.	Which now I must pay again as if never before.
But if the while I think on thee (dear friend)	But if, during that time, I think of you (royal son),
All losses are restored, and sorrows end.	All these losses are restored, and sorrows end.

"The Privy Council dispatched letters to the peers whom it had chosen to hear the charges against the Earls of Essex and Southampton. These letters promised their lordships that they 'shall be further acquainted with all the particularities not only of their secret practices of treason against this kingdom but of their actual rebellion within the city of London, where they assembled great forces on Sunday last and killed divers of her Majesty's subjects' (modernized English). The government was obviously not risking any verdict of 'Not Guilty'." - Akrigg, "Shakespeare & the Earl of Southampton," 120

REFERENCE EDITION

The official letters of the Privy Council were sent on 13 February 1601, yet Oxford in this daily record is two days ahead of time. The reason is that he was an insider who made it his business to know information in advance, especially in this case. He was Lord Great Chamberlain and brother-in-law of Secretary Robert Cecil, as well as the highest-ranking earl on the tribunal of nine earls and sixteen barons.

> *"Oxford was **summoned** from his retirement to act as the senior of the twenty-five noblemen who unanimously declared Essex and Southampton guilty, after the veriest travesty of a trial on February 19th."* – B. M. Ward, 336; *"Shakespeare exquisitely incorporates the legal world as a framework with reference to the judicial quarter sessions"* – W. N. Knight, 77

1 WHEN TO THE SESSIONS OF SWEET SILENT THOUGHT

TO THE SESSIONS = to the upcoming trial of Essex and Southampton ("The periodic sitting of judges, a court of law" – Stephen Booth; "Treason was properly tried in the King's Bench or locally at ***sessions***, though noblemen enjoyed the right to be tried by their peers in the court of the Lord Steward" – Elton, p. 80); presiding at the Essex-Southampton trial will be Lord Steward Buckhurst; ("Others but *stewards* of their excellence" – Sonnet 94, line 8); "From this ***session*** interdict [prohibit] Every fowl of tyrant wing" – *The Phoenix and Turtle*, 1601, by "William Shake-speare," referring to the treason trial and to Elizabeth as a tyrant; the setting in *The Winter's Tale* opening Act 3, Scene 2 is that of a Court of Justice, and King Leontes of Sicilia refers to the treason trial as a *"sessions"* as he begins the proceedings, using the royal "we" of the monarch:

> This ***sessions*** (to our great grief we pronounce)
> Even pushes 'gainst our heart: the party tried
> The daughter of a king, our wife, and one
> Of us too much belov'd.
> - *The Winter's Tale*, 3.2.1-8

> Then, good prince,
> No longer ***session*** hold upon my shame,
> But let my ***trial*** be mine own confession.
> Immediate sentence, then, and sequent death
> Is all the grace I beg.
> - *Measure for Measure*, 5.1.367-371

"A *treason trial* away from London could also draw the crowds, and on occasion the crush might be so great that it threatened the efficiency of ***the sessions***." – (Bellamy, 134)

Sessions = "sittings or hearings, as of a court" -- Wright, Louis B., editor, Folger edtion, 1967

SWEET = royal; **SILENT THOUGHT** = Oxford will keep his thoughts (of Southampton as his royal son) secret while on the tribunal.

2 I SUMMON UP REMEMBRANCE OF THINGS PAST,

SUMMON = ("Cite by authority to appear at a specified place, require an appearance before a court, either to answer a charge or to give evidence = summon *to* the sessions" – Booth); in this case, Oxford and other peers are being summoned to the trial; ("The Lord Steward's court, though in theory composed of all peers, was in practice appointed by selective *summons*" – Elton, p. 80); **"Summon** a *session*, that we may arraign our most disloyal lady; for, as she hath been publicly accused, so shall she have a just and open trial" – King Leontes in *The Winter's Tale*, 2.3.200-03

REMEMBRANCE OF THINGS PAST = the golden time of royalty covered by Sonnets 1 to 26, numerically recording Southampton's first twenty-six years to 1600; **REMEMBRANCE** = memory, bringing to mind, recollection; ("When Julius Caesar, whose *remembrance* yet lives in men's eyes" – *Cymbeline*, 3.1.2-

3; "Nor it nor no *remembrance* what it was" – Sonnet 5, line 12; "as fits a King's *remembrance*" – *Hamlet*, 2.2.26; "Praising what is lost makes the *remembrance dear*" – *All's Well That Ends Well*, 5.3.20; "I shall give you that monument and remembrance of your life" - Oxford, Cardanus Preface, 1573

> The setting sun, and music at the close,
> As the last taste of sweets, is sweetest last,
> *Write in remembrance* more than *things long past*
> - *Richard II*, 2.1.12-14

"I thought it good to know the *truth* and *to put Her Majesty in remembrance* of what was *past*; hereupon I understand from Her Majesty that it is *true* she hath signed the same, but now upon this *remembrance* from me she hath stayed the writing. - Oxford memo (undated & unaddressed) Huntinton MS EL 2337; Chiljan, 133-134

3 I SIGH THE LACK OF MANY A THING I SOUGHT,
SIGH THE LACK = moan over the loss of his son; **LACK OF MANY A THING I SOUGHT** = referring to the lack of having been able to claim paternity of Southampton in the first place; the lack of Elizabeth's acknowledgment of their royal son; the lack of his succession to the throne

4 AND WITH OLD WOES NEW WAIL MY DEAR TIME'S WASTE:
WOES = sufferings over Southampton prior to this one, which is the worst of all; "our night of woe" – Sonnet 120, line 9; **NEW WAIL** = weep over anew, all over again; Long mayst thou live to *wail thy children's death*" - *Richard III*, 1.3.192-204; **DEAR** = royal; (as Hamlet speaks of his father the king "upon whose property and most *dear* life a damned defeat was made" – *Hamlet*, 2.2.577-578; "My *dear dear* lord ... *dear* my liege ... that *dear blood*" – *Richard II*, 1.1.176, 184; 1.3.126); "dear" often refers to a royal son or father; Oxford uses it in Sonnets 30, 31, 37, 39, 42, 48, 87, 102, 108, 110, 117, 124, 131, 139, 142

> Thou wouldst have left thy *dearest* heart-blood there,
> Rather than made that savage duke thine heir,
> And disinherited thine only son.
> - *3 Henry VI*, 230-232

> How now, *dear* sovereign and our gracious mother
> - *Titus Andronicus*, 2.2.89

MY DEAR TIME'S WASTE = the waste of my son's life and royal blood according to *time*, the ever-dwindling time left in Elizabeth's reign and dynasty; ("When in *the Chronicle of wasted time*" – line 1 of Sonnet 106, which will become the dedicatory epistle for these Prison Sonnets; Oxford has already developed this special vocabulary involving "time" and "waste"; for example: "For never-resting *time* leads Summer on" – Sonnet 5, line 5; "But beauty's *waste* hath in the world an end" – Sonnet 9, line 11; "That thou among the *wastes of time* must go" – Sonnet 12, line 10); and such words are consciously reflective of the profoundly sad way King Richard II takes responsibility for his demise:

> But for the concord of *my state and time*,
> Had not an ear to hear *my true time broke*:
> *I wasted time, and now time doth waste me*
> - *Richard II*, 5.5.47-49

5 THEN CAN I DROWN AN EYE (UN-USED TO FLOW)
DROWN AN EYE = weep, down his eye with tears; a play on Southampton's royal eye, the sun, i.e., his royal eye hidden; also a play on "I" indicating the drowning of himself in sorrow; "Ten days ago I *drown'd* these news [of the death of Warwick] *in tears*" – *3 Henry VI*, 2.1.104

6 FOR PRECIOUS FRIENDS HID IN DEATH'S DATELESS NIGHT,

PRECIOUS FRIENDS = my royal son; **PRECIOUS** = royal; dear; "Tendering the *precious* safety of my prince" – *Richard II*, 1.1.32; godlike; "The *precious* image of our dear Redeemer" – *Richard III*, 2.1.124; **PRECIOUS FRIENDS HID IN DEATH'S DATELESS NIGHT** = image of Southampton in his prison room, facing trial and a sentence of execution; facing eternal lack of royal succession as an immortal king; **FRIENDS** = the plural used here in the same way that Oxford, with his insert in *Palladis Tamia*, 1598, referred to Southampton as the *"private friends"* to whom the twenty-six sonnets of the 1590s were addressed; also, to cite another example: the plural "fairest creatures" of Sonnet 1, line 1, signifying Southampton;

> Prince Hal: I am good *friends* with my *father*
> And may do anything
> - *1 Henry IV*, 3.3.182-183

> Thou art no *father* nor no *friend* of mine
> - *1 Henry VI*, 5.4.9

HID = covered by the cloud of disgrace; ("The region cloud hath masked him from me now" – Sonnet 33, line 12; not acknowledged as Elizabeth's son and heir; **DATELESS** = eternal; never meeting his date with succession as the new king; timeless, as in "the *timeless deaths* of these Plantagenets, Henry and Edward" – *Richard III*, 1.2.121-122; **DEATH'S** = alluding to the very possible execution of Southampton; ("The *dateless limit of thy dear exile*, the hopeless word of 'never to return' breathe I against thee, upon pain of life"- King Richard to Mowbray, Duke of Norfolk, *Richard II*, 1.3.151-153); **DATELESS NIGHT** = eternal disgrace; the eternal lack of immortal kingship; "Thy end is Truth's and Beauty's *doom and date*" – Sonnet 14, line 14; "And Summer's lease hath all too short a date" – Sonnet 18, line 4; "So long as youth and thou are of one date" – Sonnet 22, line 2; "A *dateless lively heat, still to endure*" – Sonnet 153, line 6; **NIGHT** = opposite of the "Summer's day" (Sonnet 18, line 1) of kingship in "thy golden time" (Sonnet 3, line 12); the blackness of disgrace; the end of royal hope

7 AND WEEP AFRESH LOVE'S LONG-SINCE CANCELLED WOE,
LOVE'S = royal blood's; ("Near to the king in blood, and near in love" – *Richard II*, 3.1.17); **LOVE'S LONG-SINCE CANCELLED WOE** = the woe he already suffered when Elizabeth "cancelled" her son's blood from her, i.e., refused to acknowledge him

> Accursed Tower! Accursed fatal hand
> That hath contrived this *woeful* tragedy!
> - *1 Henry VI*, 1.4.75-76

> Without much fall of blood, whose guiltless drops
> Are every one a *woe*
> - *Henry V*, 1.2.25-26

CANCELLED = a legal term, denoting the breaking of bonds, indicating also that Oxford previously gave up hope of claiming paternity of Southampton; "Henry, your sovereign, is prisoner to the foe; his state usurp'd, his realm a slaughter-house, his subjects slain, *his statutes* **cancell'd** *and his treasure spent*" - *3 Henry VI*, 5.4.76-79

> An expired date, *cancell'd* ere well begun
> - *Lucrece*, Stanza 4

> *Cancell'd* my fortunes, and enchained me
> To endless date of never-ending woes
> - *Lucrece*, Stanza 134

> And through her wounds doth fly

Live's lasting date from *cancell'd* destiny
- *Lucrece*, Stanza 247

Cancel his bond of life
- *Richard III*, 4.4.77

Young Prince of Tyre...
We might proceed to *cancel* of your days;
Yet hope, succeeding from so fair a tree
As your fair self, doth tune us otherwise
- *Pericles*, 1.1.112-116

8 AND MOAN TH'EXPENSE OF MANY A VANISHED SIGHT.
MOAN = the moan or groan of those at a funeral

Laughest thou, wretch?
Thy mirth shall turn to *moan*
- *1 Henry VI*, 2.3.43

No, when my father York and Edward wept,
To hear *the piteous moan that Rutland made*
When black-faced Clifford shook his sword at him
- *Richard III*, 1.2.160-162

Let us pay betimes
A moiety of that mass of *moan* to come.
Cry, Trojans, cry! Practice your eyes with tears!
Troilus and Cressida, 2.2.107-109

EXPENSE = the paying out of suffering; **MANY A VANISHED SIGHT** = all the past sight of his son he has had to give up; referring to "precious friends hid in death's dateless night," line 6; ("And all those *beauties whereof now he's King/ Are **vanishing, or vanished** out of **sight**" – Sonnet 63, lines 6-7, i.e., the vanishing of his royal claim.)

9 THEN CAN I GRIEVE AT GRIEVANCES FOREGONE,
GRIEVANCES FOREGONE = sorrows already suffered (or rendered or given up), but now being suffered (and paid out) anew

10 AND HEAVILY FROM WOE TO WOE TELL O'ER
HEAVILY = sadly, in sorrow; ("Help us to *sigh and groan, heavily, heavily*: Graves, yawn and yield your dead, till death be uttered, *heavily, heavily*" – *Much Ado About Nothing*, 5.3.17-21); **WOE TO WOE** = "pitiable creature, mournful sight ... sorry, sorrowful, sad" – Crystal & Crystal; ("Accursed tower! Accursed fatal hand that hath contrived this *woeful* tragedy!" – *1 Henry VI*, 1.4.75-76; "Measure his *woe* the length and breadth of mine" – *Much Ado About Nothing*, 5.1.11; "We see the ground whereon these *woes* do lie" – *Romeo and Juliet*, 5.3.179, of dead Romeo and Juliet; "If thinking on me then should make you *woe*" – Sonnet 71, line 8

11 THE SAD ACCOUNT OF FORE-BEMOANED MOAN,
SAD = heavy, painful; **ACCOUNT** = audit of royal blood; ("What acceptable *Audit* canst thou leave" – Sonnet 4, line 12; "Her *Audit*, though delayed, answered must be" – Sonnet 126, line 11; "No reckoning made, but *sent to my account* with all my imperfections on my head" – *Hamlet*, 1.5.78-79; "But I have a son, sir, by order of law, some year elder than this, who yet is *no dearer in my account*" – *King Lear*, 1.1.18-19; "What need we fear who knows it, when none can *call our power to account*?" – *Macbeth*, 5.1.38-39; "Or at your hand *th'account of hours* to crave,/ Being your vassal bound to stay your leisure" – Sonnet 58, lines 3-

4; "No shape so true, no truth of such account" – Sonnet 62, line 6); **SAD ACCOUNT** = "heavy reckoning (of debts)" – Evans; "When you were in place and *in account*" – *1 Henry IV*, 5.1.37, Worcester to the Prince of Wales

12 WHICH I NEW PAY AS IF NOT PAID BEFORE.
NEW PAY = pay out with grief all over again, as though I never paid it before

13 BUT IF THE WHILE I THINK ON THEE (DEAR FRIEND)
DEAR FRIEND = royal and godlike son; relating Southampton back to line 6: "For precious *friends* hid in death's dateless night"; ("O, *my dear lord*, lo, where your son is borne!" – *1 Henry VI*, 4.7; "O *dear son* Edgar" – *King Lear*, 4.1; "As for my sons, say I account of them as jewels purchased at an easy price, and yet *dear* too" – *Titus Andronicus*, 3.1.198-200); "If *my dear love* were but the child of state" – Sonnet 124, line 1

14 ALL LOSSES ARE RESTORED, AND SORROWS END.
ALL = Southampton; **LOSSES** = the loss of Southampton by execution and the loss of his claim to succeed Elizabeth on the throne; the loss of his liberty and honor; the loss of Oxford's ability to claim paternity of him; the loss of any way for Elizabeth to claim him as her natural issue; the loss by extinction of the Tudor Rose dynasty; the loss of Oxford's ability to claim the Shakespeare works as his, once he makes a bargain for his son's life; "*all* losses" = "the loss of *One for All, All for One,* Southampton"; ("*You* amount to them all, for they are all reproduced in you" – Tucker)

"The *loss* of a son of so great hope ... we as his prince and sovereign and you as a loving and natural father, for that we both be interested in the *loss* ... Besides, if we do duly look into the matter in true course of Christianity, we shall then see that the *loss* hath wrought so great a gain to the gentleman whom we now lack, as we have rather cause to rejoice than lament" – Queen Elizabeth to George Talbot, Earl of Shrewsbury, trying to comfort him on the death of his son, circa September 5, 1582 (*Collected Works*, 256); "These griefs and *losses*" – *The Merchant of Venice*, 3.3.32; "Even so great men *great losses* should endure" – *Julius Caesar*, 4.3.192

> Looking the way her harmless young one went,
> And can do nought but *wail her darling's loss*
> - *2 Henry VI*, 3.1.215-216

> The *loss* of those three lords torments my heart
> - *3 Henry VI*, 1.1.277

> And so obsequious will *thy father* be,
> Even *for the loss* of thee, having no more,
> As Priam was for all his valiant sons
> - *3 Henry VI*, 2.5.118-120

> Though thou repent, yet I have still *the loss*
> - Sonnet 34, line 10

> To him that bears *the strong offence's loss*
> - Sonnet 34, line 12

RESTORED = compensated for; paid back, because he knows Southampton still has "love" or royal blood within him; and in the next sonnet he is "the grave where buried love doth live"

SORROWS = "Continual mediations, tears, and sorrows" – *Henry VIII*, 4.2.28; "And you recount your sorrows to a stone ... Shaken with sorrows in ungrateful Rome ... His sorrows have so overwhelmed his wits" - *Titus Andronicus*, 3.1.29; 4.3.17; 4.4.10; "These griefs, these woes, these sorrows make me old" – *Romeo* *and Juliet*, 3.2.88; "When sorrows come, they come not single spies, but in battalions; first, her father slain; next, your son gone, and he most violent author of his just remove" – *Hamlet*, 4.5.78-81; "Each new morn, new widows howl, new orphans cry; new sorrows strike heaven on the face" – *Macbeth*, 4.3.4-6

My gracious lord! My father!
This sleep is sound indeed; this is a sleep
That from this golden rigol hath divorc'd
So many English kings. *Thy due from me*
Is tears and **heavy sorrows of the blood**
- *2 Henry IV*, 4.5.33-37
(Prince Hal to his father King Henry IV)

THE PRISON YEARS

DAY FIVE IN THE TOWER

Sonnet 31
The Grave Where Buried Love Doth Live
12 February 1601

Oxford pays homage to his royal son in the Tower, acknowledging that Southampton has become the "grave" of his own "love" or royal blood. Henry Wriothesley's claim to the throne has been lost, even as he also faces death by execution. Oxford sheds "many a holy and obsequious tear" as an epitaph for his son's right to succeed as king. He emphasizes Southampton's motto **One for All, All for One** *in the final line, offering "all the all of me" as father to son.*

Sonnet 31	Translation
Thy bosom is endeared with all hearts,	Your person is made royal by your royal blood,
Which I by lacking have supposed dead;	Which I, by lacking you, have supposed dead;
And there reigns Love and all Love's loving parts,	And in you reigns royalty and all royal parts,
And all those friends which I thought buried.	And you, whom I thought dead, reign in yourself.
How many a holy and obsequious tear	How many a royal and funereal tear
Hath dear religious love stol'n from mine eye,	Has my royal devotion caused me to shed,
As interest of the dead, which now appear	To be paid for your right, which now appears
But things removed that hidden in thee lie.	Removed but actually remains hidden in you.
Thou art the grave where buried love doth live,	You are the grave where your buried blood lives,
Hung with the trophies of my lovers gone,	The funeral monument of my vanished royal son,
Who all their parts of me to thee did give;	To whom I gave all my love and devotion!
That due of many now is thine alone.	That devotion due from many is now yours alone.
Their images I loved, I view in thee,	The royal qualities I adored, I now see in you,
And thou (all they) hast all the all of me.	And all in you is everything I have and ever had.

1 THY BOSOM IS ENDEARED WITH ALL HEARTS,
THY BOSOM = your kingly heart, the source of your royal blood and power; ("Even in *the best blood chambered in his bosom*" – *Richard II*, 1.1.149; "This is the way to Julius Caesar's ill-erected *Tower, to whose flint bosom* my condemned lord is doomed a prisoner" – *Richard II*, 5.1.1-4; "And great affections wrestling in *thy bosom* doth make an earthquake of nobility" – *King John*, 5.2.41-42; "Nor let my kingdom's rivers take their course through my burned bosom" – *King John*, 5.7.38-39); **ENDEARED** = beloved, as a king; made "dear" or royal; "And thou, to be *endeared to a king*" – *King John*, 4.2.228; **ALL** = Southampton, *One for All, All for One*; **HEARTS** = English citizens, i.e., their capacity for love and loyalty to the sovereign and the state; "A thousand hearts are great within my bosom" – *Richard III*, 5.3.348; "To *join your hearts* in love and amity" – *1 Henry VI*, 3.1.68; "Observed his courtship to the common people, how he did seem to *dive into their hearts*" – *Richard II*, 1.4.24-25; "Doth not the crown of England prove the King? And if not that, I bring you witnesses, twice fifteen thousand *hearts of England's breed*"
– *King John*, 2.1.273; "And art almost an alien to *the hearts of all the Court and princes of my blood* … That

I did pluck allegiance from *men's hearts*" – *1 Henry IV*, 3.2.34-35, 52; "Those parts of thee that the world's eye doth view/ Want nothing that *the thought of hearts* can men;/ All tongues, the voice of souls, give thee that due" – Sonnet 69, lines 1-3; "Then thou alone *kingdoms of hearts* shouldst owe" – Sonnet 70, line 14

2 WHICH I BY LACKING HAVE SUPPOSED DEAD:
Oxford is lacking his son, who is his own heart; "Thy looks with me, *thy heart in other place*" – Sonnet 93, line 4, echoing the "place" or Tower; **SUPPOSED DEAD** = anticipation of Southampton's execution; ("*Supposed* as forfeit to a confined doom" – Sonnet 107, line 4; "confined doom" combining both the sense of his confinement in the Tower and of his death)

3 AND THERE REIGNS LOVE AND ALL LOVE'S LOVING PARTS,
REIGNS = appearing as metaphorical, but referring to his son as a king who should reign on the throne; **REIGNS LOVE** = royal blood reigns or sits on the throne, which is within Southampton; **ALL** = Southampton, *One for All, All for One*; **ALL LOVE'S LOVING PARTS** = all your royal blood's royal qualities, reigning as king

4 AND ALL THOSE FRIENDS WHICH I THOUGHT BURIED.
ALL = Southampton; **ALL THOSE FRIENDS** = Southampton, my son; "For *precious friends* hid in death's dateless night" – Sonnet 30, line 6; "But here's the joy, *my friend* and I are one" – Sonnet 42, line 11; to Elizabeth in the Dark Lady series, during this time when Southampton faces execution: "Is't not enough to torture me alone,/ But slave to slavery *my sweet'st friend* must be?" – Sonnet 133, lines 3-4; echoing the insertion in *Palladis Tamia* of Francis Meres in 1598: "sugared sonnets to his *private friends*"; **BURIED** = concealed, hidden; also, anticipating his execution; "Thou art the grave where *buried love* doth live" – line 9 below

5 HOW MANY A HOLY AND OBSEQUIOUS TEAR
HOLY = sacred, in relation to Southampton as a prince or king who is a "god on earth" or "the little Love-God" of Sonnet 154, line 1; **OBSEQUIOUS TEAR** = tears shed at an obsequy or funeral, or in mourning; Oxford is anticipating Southampton's burial rites; but, more immediately, he is at the funeral of his son's royal blood ("My sighing breast shall be thy funeral bell; and so *obsequious* will thy father be, even for the loss of thee" – *3 Henry VI*, 2.5; "But, uncle, draw you near, to shed *obsequious* tears upon this trunk. O, take this warm kiss on thy pale cold lips, these sorrowful drops upon thy blood-stained face, the last true duties of thy noble son!" – *Titus Andronicus*, 5.3.150-154; "and the survivor bound in filial obligation for some term to do *obsequious* sorrow" – *Hamlet*, 1.2.90-92); Oxford will use "obsequious" in relation to Elizabeth's funeral in Sonnet 125, line 9, on April 28, 1603: "No, let me be *obsequious* in thy heart"

> Set down, set down your honourable load
> (If honour may be shrouded in a hearse)
> Whilst I awhile *obsequiously* lament
> The untimely fall of virtuous Lancaster.
> Poor key-cold Figure of a *holy king,*
> Pale ashes of the House of Lancaster,
> Thou bloodless remnant of that royal blood
> - *Richard III*, 1.2.1-7

6 HATH DEAR RELIGIOUS LOVE STOL'N FROM MINE EYE,
RELIGIOUS = "devoted to any holy obligation, conscientious" – Schmidt; "justly and religiously unfold" – *Henry V*, 1.2.10; **DEAR RELIGIOUS LOVE** = his worship of his royal son as a god on earth; the divine or sacred royal blood of his dear son; also my dutiful, reverent love for you; ("And dip their napkins in his sacred blood" – *Julius Caesar*, 3.2.134; "Most *holy and religious fear* it is to keep those many many bodies safe that live and feed upon your Majesty" – *Hamlet*, 3.3.8-10); "*Religious love* put out religion's eye" – *A Lover's Complaint*, 250; **DEAR** = ("You are the most immediate to our throne, and with no less nobility of love than that which *dearest* father bears his son do I impart to you" – *Hamlet*, 1.2.109-112); Sonnets 30, 31, 37, 39, 42, 48, 87, 102, 108, 110, 117, 124, 131, 139, 142; **STOLEN** = paid; **MINE EYE** = Oxford's eye,

but also his son's royal eye, the sun

7 AS INTEREST OF THE DEAD, WHICH NOW APPEAR
INTEREST OF THE DEAD = payment to his son, for the death of his royal blood; the tears that are his rightful due; ("Tear for tear and loving kiss for kiss, thy brother Marcus tenders on thy lips. O, were the sum of these that I should pay countless and infinite, yet would I pay them" –*Titus Andronicus*, 5.3.155-158); **THE DEAD** = alluding to the anticipated execution, as well as to the loss of Southampton's succession

8 BUT THINGS REMOVED THAT HIDDEN IN THEE LIE.
THINGS REMOVED: Southampton's royal blood, removed from Oxford and hidden within his son; ("Then happy I, that love and am beloved,/ Where I may not *remove nor be removed*" – Sonnet 25, lines 13-14; "Love is not love/ Which alters when it alteration finds/ Or *bends with the remover to remove*" – Sonnet 116, lines 2-4); **THAT HIDDEN IN THEE LIE** = even though his son is in prison, his "dear religious love" or royal blood remains within him, hidden but real

9 THOU ART THE GRAVE WHERE BURIED LOVE DOTH LIVE,
You are the grave of your own hidden royal blood, which still lives; **GRAVE** = ("So you being sick of too much doubt in your own proceedings, through which infirmity you are desirous to bury and ensevel your works in *the grave* of oblivion" – Oxford's Preface to *Cardanus' Comfort*, 1573; "A kingdom or a cottage or *a grave*"
– poem "By the Earl of Oxforde", Chiljan, p. 187)

> Where now his son's like a glow-worm in the night,
> The which hath fire in darkness, none in light;
> Whereby I see that Time's the king of men;
> He's both their parent, and he is their grave.
> - Pericles, 2.3.43-46

BURIED LOVE = Southampton, whose chance to gain the throne has been lost, is now "the grave" where his own "buried love [royal blood] doth live" in the Tower; anticipating his execution and death, while recalling, "To eat the world's due, by the grave and thee" of Sonnet 1, line 14, when Oxford had accused his son of taking his royal blood to the grave with him; **DOTH LIVE** = his blood is nonetheless still alive in him; (and theses sonnets are "the living record" of his memory – Sonnet 55, line 8)

10 HUNG WITH THE TROPHIES OF MY LOVERS GONE,
TROPHIES = memorials; funeral monuments ("Anything hung on such a monument to honor the dead person" – Booth); as Laertes uses "trophy" telling King Claudius he intends to kill Hamlet:

> His means of death, his obscure funeral –
> No *trophy*, sword, nor hatchment o'er his bones,
> No noble rite, nor formal ostentation…
> - Hamlet, 4.5.210-212

LOVERS = those who loved me; Southampton, filled with love or royal blood; **GONE** = dead; a play on "one" for Southampton, *One for All, All for One* **MY LOVERS GONE:** my dear friends who have died; but Oxford is specifically glancing at "my royal son" who may well be executed.

"'Lover' and 'love' in Elizabethan English were ordinary synonyms for 'friend' and friendship.' Brutus opens his address to the citizens of Rome with the words, 'Romans, countrymen, and lovers,' and subsequently describes Julius Caesar as 'my best lover' (Julius Caesar, 3.2.13-49). Portia, when referring to Antonio, the bosom friend of her husband Bassanio, calls him 'the bosom lover of my lord' (Merchant of Venice, 3.4.17). Ben Jonson in his letters to Donne commonly described himself as his correspondent's 'ever true lover'; and Drayton, writing to William Drummond of Hawthornden, informed him that an admirer of his literary work was in love with him. The word 'love' was habitually applied to the sentiment subsisting

between an author and his patron. Nash, when dedicating Jack Wilton in 1594 to Southampton, calls him 'a dear lover ... of the lovers of poets as of the poets themselves.'"
- Sidney Lee, "A Life of Shakespeare," 1898, p. 127

11 WHO ALL THEIR PARTS OF ME TO THEE DID GIVE:
ALL = Southampton, *One for All, All for One*; **ALL THEIRPARTS OF ME** = all royal parts or qualities of Southampton given to Oxford as father; all the parts of Oxford given to his son, who gave them back to him; (Oxford's verse is "but as a tomb/ Which hides your life, and *shows not half your parts*" – Sonnet 17, lines 3-4; "My spirit is thine, *the better part of me*" – Sonnet 74, line 8; echoing the *Lucrece* dedication to Southampton: "being *part in all I have*, devoted yours")

12 THAT DUE OF MANY NOW IS THINE ALONE.
THAT DUE OF MANY = those same royal qualities, owed to citizens of England; ("Your state of fortune and your due of birth" – *Richard III*, 3.7.119; ("Pity the world, or else this glutton be,/ To eat the world's due, by the grave and thee" – Sonnet 1, lines 13-14); **THINE ALONE** = the "all" and "one" of Southampton's motto, *One for All, All for One*; all his royal parts are now only his, because he will never be king and never pay his debt to this "many" English subjects

13 THEIR IMAGES I LOVED, I VIEW IN THEE,
THEIR IMAGES I LOVED = all of you that I have loved; the images of all your royal aspects, which add up to your royal image; "Die single and thine *image* dies with thee" - Sonnet 3, line 14; **I VIEW IN THEE** = I see in you

14 AND THOU (ALL THEY) HAST ALL THE ALL OF ME.
ALL = Southampton; **ALL THEY** = all these images of you; **ALL THE ALL OF ME** = all of you is everything I have or ever had; again recalling Oxford/"Shakespeare's" dedication of *Lucrece* to Southampton: "What I have done is yours; what I have to do is yours; being part in *all I have*, devoted yours"; Southampton possesses Oxford's inmost essence or soul; (Oxford uses **ALL** seven times in this sonnet and **ALONE** once); this verse was cited by W. C. J. in 1859 when he remarked about the Southampton motto being echoed throughout the Sonnets; the researcher also specifically cited "Who *all* in *one, one* pleasing note do sing" – Sonnet 8, line 12, and "Since *all alike* my songs and praises be/ To *one, of one*, still such, and ever so" – Sonnet 105, lines 3-4

THE PRISON YEARS

DAY SIX IN THE TOWER

Sonnet 32
That Churl Death
13 February 1601

Anticipating the trial and a sentence of death for his royal son, Oxford contemplates his own death, possibly by suicide. If Southampton should then "survive" the trial and avoid execution, he can look at his father's writings as "Shakespeare" and see they are dedicated to him. He can look in those works (and in these sonnets) for the "love" or royal blood that his father recorded in them. Oxford wishes he had given his son a "dearer birth" – a more royal birth -- that would have enabled his son to "march in better ranks of equipage" by bringing him to the throne. This prepares for the next verse, in which he will look back at the birth of "my Sunne," a son he could never acknowledge from the beginning.

Sonnet 32	Translation
If thou survive my well-contented day,	If you escape execution by my deal for your life,
When that churl death my bones with dust shall cover,	When that miser, mortal death, covers my bones with dust,
And shalt by fortune once more re-survey	And through Elizabeth's mercy look again
These poor rude lines of thy deceased Lover,	At these sonnets by your dead father,
Compare them with the bettering of the time,	Compare them with those earlier in the reign,
And though they be outstripped by every pen	And though they are outstripped by "Shakespeare",
Reserve them for my love, not for their rhyme,	Preserve them for your royalty, not for their rhyme,
Exceeded by the height of happier men.	Which "Shakespeare" exceeds.
O then vouchsafe me but this loving thought:	O then grant me just this royal thought from you:
"Had my friend's Muse grown with this growing age,	"Had my father's Muse grown with this growing reign,
A dearer birth than this his love had brought	A more royal birth than this he would have made
To march in ranks of better equipage.	To grow in much more royal stature.
But since he died, and Poets better prove,	But since my father died and Shakespeare lived,
Theirs for their style I'll read, his for his love."	I'll read Shakespeare for style, my father's private sonnets for his record of my royal blood."

"In the Star Chamber on 13 February the Council made a public statement on the rebellion ... Recalling the many rumors of the true scope of the Earl's [Essex's] ambition, Cecil declared: 'He had been devising for five or six years to be King of England; had wit, and much power put into his hand, and meant thus to slip into her Majesty's place.' He referred also to Hayward's book on Henry I, and the implication that Essex was 'making this time seem like that of Richard II, to be reformed by him as by Henry IV.'" – Handover, p. 224; Stopes, 203

1 IF THOU SURVIVE MY WELL CONTENTED DAY,
IF THOU SURVIVE = if you escape execution; **DAY** = the golden time of royalty that Oxford, as his

father, had once enjoyed; in other words, if you live to see that day again, after I myself have died; "Shall I compare thee to a Summer's day" – Sonnet 18, line 1

2 WHEN THAT CHURL DEATH MY BONES WITH DUST SHALL COVER,
THAT CHURL DEATH = that grudging miser, death; **DUST** = "Why, what is *pomp, rule, reign, but earth and dust?*" – *3 Henry VI*, 5.2.27

3 AND SHALT BY FORTUNE ONCE MORE RE-SURVEY
FORTUNE = chance, but also by the Queen's power; **RE-SURVEY** = re-read

4 THESE POOR RUDE LINES OF THY DECEASED LOVER:
THESE POOR RUDE LINES = the lines of these sonnets, now bankrupt of your royal blood; "I know not how I shall offend in dedicating *my unpolished lines* to your Lordship" – dedication of *Venus and Adonis* to Southampton; **THY DECEASED LOVER** = your dead father, who loved you and your royal blood

5 COMPARE THEM WITH THE BETT'RING OF THE TIME,
COMPARE THEM, etc. = compare them with that later "time" of your life, which must surely be better than this present time; ("Authorizing thy trespass with *compare*" – Sonnet 35, line 6)

6 AND THOUGH THEY BE OUT-STRIPPED BY EVERY PEN,
EVERY = E. Ver = Edward de Vere, *Ever or Never*; **EVERY PEN** = other pens, but also my own, if I live to write more in better days; ("E. Ver's pen" – Oxford's writings printed under the Shakespeare pen name)

7 RESERVE THEM FOR MY LOVE, NOT FOR THEIR RHYME,
RESERVE THEM FOR MY LOVE = keep them, as precious things, in some safe place; keep them alive; preserve; treasure them up in order to remind yourself of my love for you and your royal blood; **NOT FOR THEIR RHYME** = the true value of these sonnets lies not in their artistic quality but in their contents, which is "you and love" or you and your royal blood, as in "And you and love are still my argument" – Sonnet 76, line 10

8 EXCEEDED BY THE HEIGHT OF HAPPIER MEN.
Surpassed in their ability to express your high status, i.e., as royal, by men of a future time who are happy to learn of it; **EXCEEDED** = ("What should I say? His deeds *exceed* all speech: He ne'er lift up his hand but conquered" – Gloucester speaking of King Henry V in *1 Henry VI*, 1.1.15-16; "That only to stand *high* in your account, I might in virtue, beauties, livings, friends, *exceed* account" – *The Merchant of Venice*, 3.2.155-157); **HEIGHT** = ("Or flourish to the *height* of my degree" – *1 Henry VI*, 2.4.110; "Unto the dignity and *height* of honor the high imperial type of this earth's glory" – *Richard III*, 4.4.244-245); "Was it his spirit, by spirits taught to write/ *Above a mortal pitch*" – Sonnet 86, lines 5-6; **HAPPIER** = ("Sweet Oxford, and my loving Montague, and all at once, once more a *happy* farewell" – *3 Henry VI*, 4.8.30-31; "If *happy* England's royal king be free … Thanks, Reignier, *happy* for so sweet a child, fit to be made companion with a king" – *1 Henry VI*, 5.3.115, 148-149; "*Happy* were England, would this gracious prince take on himself the sovereignty thereof" – *Richard III*, 3.7.77-78); "Resembling sire, and child, and *happy* mother" – Sonnet 8, line 11

9 OH THEN VOUCHSAFE ME BUT THIS LOVING THOUGHT:
VOUCHSAFE = grant, from your lofty height as a prince; **LOVING THOUGHT** = thoughts of love for me, your father; royal thought ("Why, 'tis a *loving* and a fair reply" – *Hamlet*, 1.2.121, Claudius to Hamlet, his nephew, as though the Prince were responding as a son; "Many years of happy days befall my gracious sovereign, my most *loving liege!*" – *Richard II*, 1.1.20-21)

10 HAD MY FRIEND'S MUSE GROWN WITH THIS GROWING AGE,
MY FRIEND'S MUSE = my father's Muse, i.e., me, Southampton; (had I, Southampton, lived to a later time); glancing at the growth of Southampton (Oxford's muse or inspiration) and his royal blood in this diary: "When in eternal lines to time *thou grow'st*" – Sonnet 18, line 12; "To give full *growth* to that which

still doth *grow*" – Sonnet 115, line 14; "O Thou my lovely Boy …/Who hast by waning *grown*" – Sonnet 126, lines 1-3

11 **A DEARER BIRTH THAN THIS HIS LOVE HAD BROUGHT**
DEARER BIRTH = more valuable and more royal birth; anticipating the next sonnet, in which Oxford tells the story of Southampton's own royal birth as well as Elizabeth's refusal to acknowledge him; i.e., he should have enjoyed a "happier" and more royal entrance into the world; **DEARER** = "But thou art fair, and at thy birth, dear boy, nature and fortune joined to make thee great" – *King John*, 2.2.51-52; "ripping up the womb of your dear mother England" – *King John*, 5.2.152-153; "I pray you then, in love and dear alliance" – *Henry V*, 5.2.337; "My son's no dearer" – the King in *All's Well That Ends Well*, 1.2.76; "But I have a son, sir, by order of law, some year elder than this, who yet is no dearer in my account" –*King Lear*, 1.1.18-20; "I loved him, friend, no father his son dearer" – *King Lear*, 3.4.164-165; "Therefore, dear boy" – Talbot to his son in *1 Henry VI*, 4.5.9; "Then, dear my liege" – *Richard II*, 1.1.184; "For that our kingdom's earth should not be soiled with that dear blood which it hath fostered" – *Richard II*, 1.3.125-126); **HIS LOVE** = my father's love for me; my father's recreation of my royal blood in these private verses; (Oxford's private verses have given him a more royal birth in the womb of the Sonnets)

12 **TO MARCH IN RANKS OF BETTER EQUIPAGE.**
TO MARCH, etc. = to march to the throne in **BETTER RANKS** or higher status, as king; also, to march in better (or at least more public) lines of verse that these; **EQUIPAGE** = those better equipped or, as in the case of "Shakespeare's" verse, able to be published and read by others; the word refers to equipment and dress, as in "dressing old words new" in Sonnet 76, line 11; **TO MARCH IN RANKS OF BETTER EQUIPAGE:** "I do invest you jointly with my power, pre-eminence and all the large effects that *troop with majesty*" – *King Lear*, 1.1.131-133; "The King hath many *marching in his coats*" – *1 Henry IV*, 5.3.25; i.e., Southampton should have been born with trumpets blaring and brought to Court accompanied by the full troop of nobility that usually accompanies a newborn prince; in a procession, the various "ranks" were marked by more and less richness of equipment; warlike equipage

13 **BUT SINCE HE DIED AND POETS BETTER PROVE,**
BUT SINCE, etc. = but since my father died, and other poets ("Shakespeare") can **BETTER PROVE** or demonstrate my worth as a king; **PROVE** = echoing the legal language of a trial at which the defendant is proved innocent or guilty

14 **THEIRS FOR THEIR STYLE I'LL READ, HIS FOR HIS LOVE.**
THEIRS, etc. = I'll read "Shakespeare's" verse for his style; and my father's for his genuine expression of my royal blood in these private sonnets; **HIS LOVE** = Oxford's re-creation of Southampton's royal blood, which fills these sonnets.

Part Two

THE PRISON YEARS

OXFORD RECALLS HIS SON'S BIRTH
DAY SEVEN IN THE TOWER

Sonnet 33
My Sunne
14 February 1601

In the midst of the current crisis, with Southampton imprisoned and facing death, Edward de Vere recalls the "birth" of his son described in the previous sonnet. He recalls how, in the summer of 1574, Queen Elizabeth went "stealing to west with this disgrace" (leaving on her progress to Bristol and Bath in the west, with her negative view of her newly born royal son). Writing as a proud father, Oxford recalls how "my Sunne" appeared "with all triumphant splendor on my brow," but that the boy "was but one hour mine" because "the region cloud" (Elizabeth Regina's imperial frown) quickly covered him. This is the same "boy" Oxford wrote about in the early verses (later to become Sonnets 153-154) following the visit to Bath in August 1574. All along Southampton has privately carried the "stain" of royal bastardy; now he also carries the public stain of treason and dishonor. But by inserting this sonnet as No. 33 (the age of Christ when He died and rose from the dead), Oxford implies he will bring about a resurrection for his royal-sacred son.

Sonnet 33	Translation
Full many a glorious morning have I seen	On many mornings I have seen my son's full royalty
Flatter the mountain tops with sovereign eye,	Gracing the world with his sovereign eye,
Kissing with golden face the meadows green,	Shining his royal light on everything,
Gilding pale streams with heavenly alchemy:	Gracing all with his blood inherited from Elizabeth.
Anon permit the basest clouds to ride	Soon after his birth the Queen's dark view appeared
With ugly rack on his celestial face,	With ugly rage obscuring his royal identity,
And from the forlorn world his visage hide,	And from poor England she hid his royal blood,
Stealing unseen to west with this disgrace.	Riding toward Bath with her disgrace of him.
Even so my Sunne one early morn did shine	In this way my royal son was born one early morn,
With all triumphant splendor on my brow,	With all triumphant splendor on my brow,
But out, alack, he was but one hour mine,	But out, alas, my son was just one hour mine –
The region cloud hath masked him from me now.	Regina's bastard shame covers him even more now.
Yet him for this my love no whit disdaineth;	Yet for this I have no disdain for my royal son!
Suns of the world may stain, when heaven's sun staineth.	Any common son can have this stigma of disgrace, when Elizabeth's royal son carries it.

1 FULL MANY A GLORIOUS MORNING HAVE I SEEN
GLORIOUS = "Poor grooms are sightless night, kings *glorious day*" – *Lucrece*, 1013; "But I will *rise* there with so *full a glory*" – *Henry V*, 1.2.278; echoing Southampton's relationship to the Queen as "Glorianna"

2 FLATTER THE MOUNTAIN TOPS WITH SOVEREIGN EYE,
SOVEREIGN EYE = the royal eye of the sun-king ("See us rising in our throne, the East" – *Richard II*, 3.2.50; "My *sovereign*, I confess your royal graces" – *Henry VIII*, 3.2; "Whilst I, my *sovereign*, watch the

clock for you" – Sonnet 57, line 6, to Southampton as king; "gracious in those princely *eyes* of thine" – *Titus Andronicus*, 1.1.434; "And scarcely greet me with *that sun, thine eye*" – Sonnet 49, line 6, with sun spelled "sunne" in the 1609 quarto; "Lo in the Orient when the gracious light/ Lifts up his burning head" – Sonnet 7, lines 1-2; "*The sun* look'd on the world with *glorious eye,/ Yet not so wistly as this Queen on him*" – *The Passionate Pilgrim*, No. 6, 1599

3 KISSING WITH GOLDEN FACE THE MEADOWS GREEN,
KISSING = "As monarchs bestowed kisses on favored persons" - Tucker; "Three *glorious suns*, each one a perfect *sun*, not separated with the *racking clouds*, but sever'd in a pale clear-shining sky; See, see! They join, embrace, and seem to *kiss*...– *3 Henry VI*, 2.1.20-29; "But that necessity so bowed the state that I and greatness were compelled to *kiss*" – Bolingbroke, now King Henry IV, about his gaining of the throne, in *2 Henry IV*, 3.1.73-74; "And *kiss him with a glorious victory*" – *King John*, 2.1.394; **GOLDEN FACE** = kingly face; "this thy *golden* time" – Sonnet 3, line 12; "Attending on *his golden pilgrimage*" – Sonnet 7, line 8; **GREEN (Tudor Green)** = related to *fresh*, i.e., royal expectation and hope; "Since first I saw you *fresh, which yet are green*" – Sonnet 104, line 8

4 GILDING PALE STREAMS WITH HEAVENLY ALCHEMY:
GILDING = making royal; "An eye more bright than theirs, less false in rolling,/ *Gilding* the object whereupon it gazeth" – Sonnet 20, lines 5-6, referring to Southampton's royal eye, a sun or star; **HEAVENLY** = related to his mother Elizabeth; **ALCHEMY** = rhymes with "eye"; Oxford studied alchemy with Dr. Dee, the Queen's astrologer; "The *glorious* sun stays in his course and plays the *alchemist*, turning with splendor of his *precious eye* the meager cloddy earth to *glittering gold*" – *King John*, 3.1.77-80; "And that *your love taught it this alchemy*" – Sonnet 114, line 4, referring in part to the "alchemy" of these verses: "Why with the time do I not glance aside/ To new-found methods, and to *compounds* strange" – Sonnet 76, lines 3-4, analogizing mixtures of words to chemicals that are mixed in alchemy, but in this case the primary agent is "your love" or Southampton's royal blood; related to distillation

5 ANON PERMIT THE BASEST CLOUDS TO RIDE
ANON = ("Almost immediately" – Booth); **BASEST CLOUDS** = imperial frown of Elizabeth, casting its shadow of disgrace upon her son; ("cloud" as verb to defame, blacken, sully, as in "My sovereign Mistress *clouded* so" – *The Winter's Tale*, 1.2.280); making her son **BASE**; "I quickly shed some of his bastard blood; and in disgrace bespoke him thus: 'Contaminated, *base*, and misbegotten blood'" – *1 Henry VI*, 4.6.19-22

> Yet herein will *I imitate the sun*,
> Who doth permit the **base contagious clouds**
> To **smother up his beauty from the world**,
> That when he pleases again to be himself,
> Being wanted, he may be more wondered at,
> By breaking through the foul and **ugly** mists
> Of vapours that did seem to strangle him
> – Prince Henry or Hal, the future King, in *1 Henry IV*, 1.2.190-192

"See, see, King Richard doth himself appear, as doth the blushing discontented *sun* from out of the fiery portal of the east, when he perceives the envious *clouds* are bent to *dim his glory* and to *stain* the track of his bright passage to the occident" – *Richard II*, 3.3.62-67

6 WITH UGLY RACK ON HIS CELESTIAL FACE,
UGLY RACK = ugly mass of vapory clouds; "But, as we often see, against some storm a silence in the heaven, the *rack* stand still" – *Hamlet*, 2.2.505-506; echoing "the rack" used for torturing prisoners in the Tower; **CELESTIAL** = godlike; heavenly, related to his mother Elizabeth, his "face" reflecting hers; "Such heavenly touches ne'er touched earthly faces" – Sonnet 17, line 8

> "For indeed what more effective action could he have taken to make his work fruitful of good results than to dedicate his *Courtier* to our most illustrious and noble Queen, in

whom all courtly qualities are personified, together with those diviner and truly *celestial* virtues?"
- Oxford's Letter to the Reader, *The Courtier*, 1572

7 AND FROM THE FORLORN WORLD HIS VISAGE HIDE,
THE FORLORN WORLD = poor deprived England; "Thou that art now *the world's* fresh ornament/ … Pity *the world*, or else this glutton be,/ To eat *the world's due*, by the grave and thee" – Sonnet 1, lines 9, 13-14; **HIS VISAGE HIDE** = did conceal his identity; "Which *hides your life* and shows not half your parts" – Sonnet 17, line 4; "But *things removed that hidden in thee lie*" – Sonnet 31, line 8

8 STEALING UNSEEN TO WEST WITH THIS DISGRACE:
Elizabeth went on progress in the summer of 1574 to Bristol and Bath in western England, the setting of the Bath Visit Epilogue, Sonnets 153-154; **STEALING** = sneaking; moving ahead with concealment; she had "stolen" Oxford's son; **WITH THIS DISGRACE** = not with her royal son, but with her *shame* as in "And Beauty slandered with a bastard shame" – Sonnet 127, line 4; **DISGRACE** = loss of royal grace from the monarch; "The disfavor of a powerful person" – Booth; "*Our empress' shame*, and stately Rome's *disgrace*" – *Titus Andronicus*, 4.2.61

9 EVEN SO MY SUNNE ONE EARLY MORN DID SHINE,
EVEN SO = in the same way as above, i.e., I now announce that my own royal son was born and covered with disgrace in exactly the way I have just described

MY SUNNE = My Royal Son (the only use of the phrase "my sun" or "my sunne" in all of Shakespeare); "'My' is stressed. The beloved is both his sun and his sovereign" – Tucker; **MY** = the personal now emphasized; ("*my fair son*" – *Richard II*, 5.2.92); Southampton is the royal "Sunne" and Elizabeth is the "Moon" as in: "Making a couplement of proud compare/ With Sunne and Moone" - Sonnet 21, lines 5-6; "And truly not the morning Sun of Heaven" - Sonnet 132, line 5; **ONE** = Southampton; **DID SHINE** = was born; the royal son rose like the sun and shined his beams

10 WITH ALL TRIUMPHANT SPLENDOR ON MY BROW,
ALL = Southampton; **TRIUMPHANT SPLENDOR** = reflected glory; ("Lo thus I *triumph like a king*" – poem entitled *My Mind To Me A Kingdom Is*, listed by Steven May as possibly by Oxford – Chiljan, 173-174); **MY BROW** = Oxford's brow; appearance or countenance; "our whole kingdom contracted in one *brow* of woe" – the King in *Hamlet*, 1.2.4; "Lo, here, this long-usurped royalty from the dead temples of this bloody wretch have I plucked off *to grace thy brows* withal" – *Richard III*, 5.5.4-7, spoken to the Earl of Richmond, afterwards Henry VII, who will begin the Tudor Rose Dynasty, speaking of the crown and adding, "Wear it, enjoy it, and make much of it."

11 BUT OUT, ALACK, HE WAS BUT ONE HOUR MINE,
ONE = emphasizing and pointing to Southampton, his motto; "Since all alike my songs and praises be/ To *one*, of *one*, still such, and ever so…/ *One* thing expressing leaves out difference…/never kept seat in *one*" - Sonnet 105, lines 3-4, 8, 14; "Among a number *one* is reckoned *none*" - Sonnet 136, line 8

> Yet looks he like a king. Behold, his *eye*,
> As bright as is the eagle's, lightens forth
> Controlling majesty; *alack, alack* for woe
> That any harm should stain so fair a show!
> - *Richard II*, 3.3.68-71

HE WAS BUT ONE HOUR MINE = the newborn boy was quickly removed; ("You *had* a father" – Sonnet 13, line 14; "Now, by the burning tapers of the sky that *shone so brightly when this boy was got*, he dies upon my scimitar's sharp point that touches this, *my first-born son and heir*" – *Titus Andronicus*, 4.2.91-94); "And his love-kindling fire did *quickly steep*/ In a cold valley-fountain of that ground" – Sonnet 153, lines 3-4

MINE = "it hath pleased God to give me *a son of mine own*" – Oxford to Burghley, March 17, 1575, after the birth of his royal son, whom he could *not* claim as his own, referring to news that Anne Cecil was carrying his child, who turned out to be a girl, i.e., Elizabeth Vere (who may not have been his biological daughter); in his letter to Burghley he appears to refer to a hoped-for son of "mine own" as opposed to the royal son who had been taken from him after having been "but one hour mine" (Burghley was well aware of the existence of the infant boy who had been given to a wet nurse prior to being transferred to the Southampton household)

12 THE REGION CLOUD HATH MASKED HIM FROM ME NOW.
REGION = upper air; ("Here there might be a play on 'regent' meaning 'kinglike,' 'sovereign'" – Booth);
THE REGION CLOUD = Elizabeth *Regina's* negative view; "Clear up, fair Queen, that *cloudy* countenance" – *Titus Andronicus*, 1.1.267; "When *heaven* shall call her from this *cloud of darkness*" – Cranmer, speaking of the infant Princess Elizabeth, in *Henry VIII*, 5.5.44; "*de bene esse, quantum in **Regina** est*" – Oxford to Robert Cecil, November 22, 1601; "In Shakespeare's time 'to be under a cloud' already meant 'to be in disgrace'" – Booth; "I am the *shadow* of poor Buckingham, whose figure even **this instant cloud** puts on by **dark'ning my clear sun**" – *Henry VIII*, 1.1.224-226; "But now *time and truth* have **unmasked** all difficulties" – Oxford to Robert Cecil, January 1602; "*Dark cloudy death o'ershades his beams of life*"
– *3 Henry VI*, 2.6.62;

MASKED HIM = covered his glory; "*Masking* the business from the common eye, for sundry weighty reasons" - *Macbeth*, 3.1.123-124; "Was sleeping *by a Virgin hand disarmed*" – Sonnet 154, line 8; "When summer's breath their *masked buds* discloses" – Sonnet 54, line 8, i.e., his bud of the Tudor Rose being hidden from view

13 YET HIM FOR THIS MY LOVE NO WHIT DISDAINETH:
Oxford renews his commitment to Southampton (February 1601) as his son faces trial for high treason and execution.

14 SUNS OF THE WORLD MAY STAIN, WHEN HEAVEN'S SUN STAINETH.
SUNS OF THE WORLD = royal princes of England; "Thou that art now *the world's* fresh ornament" - Sonnet 1, line 9; **HEAVEN'S SUN** = Elizabeth's royal son; "Shall the blessed **sun of heaven** prove a micher ... Shall the **son of England** prove a thief, and take purses?" – Falstaff, speaking of Prince Hal in *1 Henry IV*, 2.4.403-405; "And truly not the morning *Sun of Heaven*" - Sonnet 132, line 5

> Methinks 'tis prize enough to be his *son*.
> See how the *morning* opes her golden gates,
> And takes farewell of the *glorious sun*;
> How well resembles it the prime of youth…
>
> Dazzle mine eyes, or do I see three *suns*?
>
> Three *glorious suns*, each one a perfect *sun*;
> Not separated with the *racking clouds*,
> But sever'd in a pale clear-shining sky.
> See, see! They join, embrace, and seem to *kiss*…
> - *3 Henry VI*, 2.1.20-29

STAIN … STAINETH = corrupt, spoil, taint, carry the stigma of bastardy; more immediately, the dishonor brought upon Southampton by his revolt against the Crown; to make full of disgrace or dishonoring; "And that high royalty was ne'er plucked off, the faiths of men ne'er **stained with revolt**" – *King John*, 4.2.5-6; "*Stain* to thy countrymen, thou hear'st thy doom! … Henceforth we banish thee on pain of death" – *1 Henry VI*, 4.1.45, 47; "too base to *stain* the temper of my knightly sword" – *Richard II*, 4.1.28-29; "with *the king's blood stained the king's own land*" – *Richard II*, 5.5.110; "Who seek to *stain the ocean of thy blood*" –

Lucrece, line 655, "ocean" referring to a king's royal blood.

> See, see, King Richard doth himself appear,
> As doth the blushing discontented sun
> From out the fiery portal of the East,
> When he perceives *the envious clouds are bent*
> ***To dim his glory and to stain*** the track
> Of his bright passage to the occident.
>
> Yet looks he like a king. Behold, his *eye*,
> As bright as is the eagle's, lightens forth
> Controlling majesty; alack, alack for woe
> That any harm *should **stain** so fair a show!*
> - *Richard II*, 3.3.62-71
>
> Yea, there thou makest me sad and makest me sin
> In envy that my Lord Northumberland
> Should be the father to so blest a son;
> A son who is the theme of honour's tongue,
> Amongst a grove, the very straightest plant,
> Who is sweet Fortune's minion and her pride:
> Whilst I, by looking on the praise of him,
> See ***riot and dishonour stain the brow of my young Harry.***
> - *1 Henry IV*, 1.1.77-85

"I say we must not so *stain* our judgment or corrupt our hope" – the King in *All's Well That Ends Well*, 2.1.118-119); "So that myself bring water for my *stain* … /All frailties that besiege all kinds of blood,/ That it could so preposterously be *stained*" – Sonnet 109, lines 8, 10-11, after Southampton's release and Oxford has sacrificed his name, taking his son's guilt of treason upon himself; "Thy father's charge shall ***clear thee from that stain***" – *1 Henry VI*, 4.5.42

THE PRISON YEARS

DAY EIGHT IN THE TOWER

Sonnet 34
Ransom All Ill Deeds
15 February 1601

Proceeding directly from the previous two verses, Oxford grieves that the birth of his royal son, promising a future on the throne, has been hidden behind the "clouds" of the Queen's refusal to acknowledge him. Now, Southampton has committed treason and has lost any chance for succession. Oxford's son grieves and wants to "repent," but Oxford still must make a sacrifice to save his life, gain his release from the Tower and, finally, secure the promise of a royal pardon for him. He must become a Christ figure and bear the cross, by sacrificing his own identity (as father and as "Shakespeare," the name he linked to Southampton). His son's tears (likened to Elizabeth's pearls) are Oxford's as well; and all this suffering and sacrifice is the **"ransom"** *(akin to the legal fines or "ransoms" actually paid by other conspirators of the Rebellion) to be paid for Henry Wriothesley's life and liberty.*

Sonnet 34	Translation
Why didst thou promise such a beauteous day	Why did you promise such a royal destiny
And make me travail forth without my cloak,	And make me labor for you without defense,
To let base clouds o'er-take me in my way,	To let the Queen's disfavor stop my purpose,
Hiding thy bravery in their rotten smoke?	Burying your royalty beneath her negative view?
'Tis not enough that through the cloud thou break,	It's not enough that your royalty is seen by me
To dry the rain on my storm-beaten face,	To make me feel better,
For no man well of such a salve can speak	For I cannot speak well of such relief
That heals the wound and cures not the disgrace.	That eases my pain but doesn't cure your disgrace.
Nor can thy shame give physic to my grief;	Nor can your shame [for treason] help my grief!
Though thou repent, yet I have still the loss;	Though you repent, I continue to lose you;
Th'offender's sorrow lends but weak relief	Your sorrow [for treason] lends only weak relief
To him that bears the strong offence's loss.	To me as I bear the burden of your treason's loss.
Ah, but those tears are pearl which thy love sheeds,	Ah, but those tears are shed by your royal blood –
And they are rich, and ransom all ill deeds.	And they, being royal, atone for your crime.

1 WHY DIDST THOU PROMISE SUCH A BEAUTEOUS DAY
BEAUTEOUS = related to "beauty" or Elizabeth, i.e., Southampton as the son of Elizabeth filled with golden royal hope; ("Which like a jewel hung in ghastly night,/ Makes black night beauteous, and her old face new" – Sonnet 27, lines 11-12); **BEAUTEOUS DAY** = same as the "Summer's Day" of royal hope (Sonnet 18, line 1) that once held such promise for Oxford to see his son named to succeed Elizabeth; following Sonnet 33, the birth of the royal son as the sun that brings forth its golden beams of day; **WHY DIDST THOU PROMISE SUCH A BEAUTEOUS DAY** = this question springs from the previous verse, in which Oxford describes how "my Sunne one early morn did shine" – Sonnet 33, line 9, and thereby promised a royal destiny; such a golden time filled with "beauty" or royal blood of the Queen; "Seeking that *beauteous* roof to ruinate" – Sonnet 10, line 7, a reference to Elizabeth's House of Tudor

2 AND MAKE ME TRAVAIL FORTH WITHOUT MY CLOAK,
TRAVAIL FORTH WITHOUT MY CLOAK = labor or go forth in life without protection, i.e., he has been forced to plead with both the Queen and Robert Cecil for his son's sake, as though stripped naked; ("The dear repose for limbs *with travail tired*" – Sonnet 27, line 2); "yet I am one that hath long besieged a fort and is not able to compass the end or reap the fruit of his *travail*" – Oxford to Burghley, June 25, 1586; "I do well perceive how your Lordship doth *travail* for me in this case of an especial grace and favor" – Oxford to Robert Cecil, June 19, 1603

3 TO LET BASE CLOUDS O'ERTAKE ME IN MY WAY,
BASE CLOUDS = the disgrace of treason; ("But out alack, he was but one hour mine,/ The *region cloud* hath masked him from me now" – Sonnet 33, lines 11-12; i.e., the "clouds" of disgrace relate to the "region cloud" or Elizabeth Regina's dark cloud of imperial disgrace, casting its shadow over both Southampton and Oxford; Southampton is now at best a "base commoner"; "But if that flower (Southampton) with *base infection* (other rebels in the Tower) meet,/ The *basest weed* (Southampton) outbraves his dignity" – Sonnet 94, line 12; "As on the finger of a throned Queen,/ The *basest Jewel* will be well esteemed" – Sonnet 96, lines 5-6; "Dark'ning thy power to lend *base* subjects light" – Sonnet 100, line 4; "In thy heart-blood, though being all too *base* to *stain* the temper of my knightly sword" – *Richard II*, 4.1.28-29; "Disgrace not so your king, that he should be so abject, *base*, and poor" – *1 Henry VI*, 5.5.48-49; **O'ER-TAKE ME** = ambush me

4 HIDING THY BRAVERY IN THEIR ROTTEN SMOKE?
HIDING THY BRAVERY = concealing your royalty from the world; **THEIR ROTTEN SMOKE** = the ugly vapor of the clouds of disgrace; clouds of Elizabeth's displeasure.

> "Now for so much as I understand, it is meant to delay the report to the end to get a composition of Her Majesty, and so to bring all my hope in Her Majesty's gracious words to *smoke*."
> - Oxford to Robert Cecil, January 1602

5 'TIS NOT ENOUGH THAT THROUGH THE CLOUDS THOU BREAK
It does no good that you still rise, sun-like, through these clouds; **THROUGH THE CLOUD THOU BREAK** = Southampton, because of his royal blood, still breaks through the cloud of disgrace as the prince; this concept, that nothing can extinguish his royal blood, is similar to that in the Bath sonnets: "Love's fire heats water, water cools not love" – Sonnet 154, line 14

6 TO DRY THE RAIN ON MY STORM-BEATEN FACE,
TO DRY THE RAIN, etc. = to dry my tears by basking me in the sunshine of your royalty; **RAIN** = tears; also, a play on "reign"; to take away your reign as king; to remove the triumph from my face, as when you were born "With all triumphant splendor on my brow" – Sonnet 33, line 10; "The trickling tears, that fall along my cheeks" – Oxford poem, published 1576

7 FOR NO MAN WELL OF SUCH A SALVE CAN SPEAK,
SALVE = cure; "And find no secret *salve* therefore" – Oxford poem, *Paradise of Dainty Devices*, 1576); "Against strange maladies a *sovereign cure*" – Sonnet 153, line 8; "Myself corrupting, *salving thy amiss*" – Sonnet 35, line 7; "She is *my salve*, she is my *wounded* sore" – Oxford poem, published 1576, of Elizabeth; "So long to fight with secret sore,/ And find no *secret salve* therefore" – Oxford poem, published 1576

8 THAT HEALS THE WOUND, AND CURES NOT THE DISGRACE:
THAT HEALS, etc. = that heals the grief but fails to remove the **DISGRACE** that Southampton now suffers while awaiting trial as a traitor, in addition to the disgrace of losing his royal claim, i.e., his loss of royal/divine grace; **WOUND** = "For that *deep wound* it gives my friend and me" – Sonnet 133, line 2, to Elizabeth during this time period; "Who was the first that gave *the wound* whose fear I wear for ever? Vere" – from Verses Made by the Earle of Oxforde, Rawlinson Poet.MS 85 f.11; Chiljan 183

9 NOR CAN THY SHAME GIVE PHYSIC TO MY GRIEF:
THY SHAME = your own regret; "So to the laws at large I write my name, and he that breaks them in the least degree stands in *attainder* of eternal *shame*" – *Love's Labour's Lost*, 1.1.153-155; **GIVE PHYSIC** = offer a remedy for my grief; "Fraud is the front of Fortune past all recovery/ I stayless stand, to abide the shock of *shame* and infamy/ … The only loss of my good name is of these *griefs* the ground" – Oxford poem, published 1576

10 THOUGH THOU REPENT, YET I HAVE STILL THE LOSS,
REPENT = "And I *repent my fault* more than my death, which I beseech your Highness to forgive" – *Henry V*, 2.2.152-153, the plea of Scroop, a traitor; "Get ye therefore hence, poor miserable wretches, to your death, the taste whereof God of his mercy give you patience to endure, and true *repentance* of all your dear *offences*!" – the king to the nobles who betrayed him, in *Henry V*, 2.2.178-182; "As I intend to prosper and *repent*, so thrive I in my dangerous affairs of hostile arms" – the king in *Richard III*, 4.4.397

> Clifford, ask mercy and obtain no grace.
> Clifford, *repent* in bootless penitence.
> Clifford, devise excuses for thy faults.
> While we devise fell tortures for thy faults.
> - *3 Henry VI*, 2.6.69-72

Oxford **STILL** or always will have this **LOSS**, as father of the prince; i.e., the loss of his kingship, the possible loss of his life by execution

11 TH'OFFENDER'S SORROW LENDS BUT WEAK RELIEF
TH'OFFENDER'S SORROW = Southampton's sorrow; he has committed the "offence" of treason; ("I know I have *offended* her, yet if it please her to be merciful unto me, I may live and by my service deserve my life" – Southampton at the trial, referring to the Queen's mercy; "I would wish therefore that you likewise submit yourself to her Majesty's mercy, acknowledging your *offences*" – the Lord Steward to Essex at the trial)

OFFENDER = "Besides, the King hath wasted all his rods on late *offenders*, that he doth lack the very instruments of chastisement" - *2 Henry IV*, 4.1.215-216

> Thy cruelty in execution
> Upon *offenders* hath exceeded law
> - *2 Henry VI*, 1.3.132-133

12 TO HIM THAT BEARS THE STRONG OFFENCE'S LOSS.
BEARS = as in bearing the Cross; suggestive of bearing a child; **THE STRONG OFFENCE'S LOSS** = an image of Oxford bearing the Cross in pain; most editors use "cross" although in *Q* the word is again "loss" as in line 10 above; and in fact it is the "loss" of Southampton's kingship that causes Oxford the most grief; "My nephew's *trespass* may well be forgot … All his *offences* live upon my head and *on his father's*. We did train him on, and, his corruption being ta'en from us, we as the spring of all shall pay for all" – *1 Henry IV*, 5.2.16-23; "Yet you Pilates have here delivered me to my sour *cross*, and water cannot wash away your sin" – *Richard II*, 4.1.240-242; Oxford in Sonnet 42 will explain that Southampton has lost the Queen's support and that he, Oxford, has lost both of them by losing the hope that she would name their son as heir to the throne:

> And losing her, my friend hath found that *loss*;
> Both find each other, and I lose both twain,
> And both for my sake lay me on this *cross*.
> - Sonnet 42, lines 10-12

OFFENCE = "O, my *offence* is rank, it smells to heaven … May one be pardoned and retain *th'offence*?" –

King Claudius in *Hamlet*, 3.3.36, 56; "And where th'*offence* is, let the great axe fall" – *Hamlet*, 4.5.215; "Hath the late *overthrow* wrought this *offence*?" – *1 Henry VI*, 1.2.49

Southampton will write to the Privy Council after the trial of Feb. 19: "I beseech your Lordships be pleased to receive the petition of a poor condemned man, who doth, with a lowly and penitent heart, **confess** his **faults** and acknowledge his **offences** to her Majesty. Remember, I pray your Lordships, that the longest liver amongst men hath but a short time of continuance, and that there is none so just upon earth but hath a greater account to make to our creator for his **sins** than any **offender** can have in this world." (Stopes, 225-226; Salisbury Papers, vol. XI, p. 72)

13 AH, BUT THOSE TEARS ARE PEARL WHICH THY LOVE SHEEDS,
TEARS = "For I should melt at *an offender's tears*, and lowly words were ransom for their *fault*" – 2 Henry VI, 3.1.126-127; **PEARL** = royal; ("Suggestive of Christ's comparison of the kingdom of heaven to a pearl of great price, Matthew, 13.46" – Duncan-Jones); the tears Southampton sheds are "pearls" inherited from his mother the Queen, who often wore seven to eight ropes of pearls, some to her knees; (One observer described them as the size of nutmegs; Elizabeth owned more than 3,000 pearl-encrusted gowns (www.mikimoto.fr/en.pearl.htm); Oxford suggests the Queen herself is weeping (through her son) with pearls over this tragic situation; **WHICH THY LOVE SHEEDS** = that your royal blood sheds; calling forth an image of Christ shedding His blood on the Cross.

14 AND THEY ARE RICH, AND RANSOM ALL ILL DEEDS.
RICH = royal, i.e., Southampton's tears, the pearls; a "rich" price will be paid by Oxford to "ransom" him from execution and to arrange for his eventual release and pardon.
RANSOM = "The action of procuring the release of a prisoner or captive by paying a certain sum ... the fact or possibility of being set free on this condition ... the sum or price paid or demanded for the release of a prisoner, i.e., 'a king's ransom,' a large sum ... in religious use, of Christ or His blood" – *OED*; suggestive of Jesus "gave himself a *ransom* for all men," Timothy, 2.6; "But that your **trespass** now becomes a **fee**;/ Mine **ransoms** yours, and yours must **ransom** me" – Sonnet 120, lines 13-14, referring back to this sonnet, and to Oxford's forfeiting of his identity as Southampton's father and, too, of his identity as "Shakespeare" who dedicated his works to Southampton; i.e., Oxford is paying this "ransom" or "fee" for his son's "trespass" or crime of treason to gain his freedom; "His *ransom* there is none but I shall pay ... His crown shall be the *ransom of my friend* ... The Duke of Bedford had a *prisoner* ... For him was I exchanged and **ransomed** - *1 Henry VI*, 1.2.148, 150; 1.4.26-28

> On any ground that I am ruler of,
> The world shall not be *ransom for thy life*
> - *2 Henry VI*, 3.2.295-296

> For I should melt at an ***offender's*** tears
> And lowly words were **ransom** for their **fault**
> - *2 Henry VI*, 3.1.126-127

> This one thing, only
> I will entreat: my boy, a Briton born,
> Let him be *ransom'd*
> - *Cymbeline*, 5.5.83-85

> Be not so rash; **take ransom, let him live**
> - *2 Henry VI*, 4.1.28

> And was he not in England prisoner?
> But when they hear he was thine enemy,
> They *set him free without his ransom paid*
> - *1 Henry VI*, 3.3.70-72

Of the world's *ransom*, blessed Mary's Son
- *Richard II*, 2.1.56

Why, yet he doth deny his prisoners,
But with proviso and exception,
That we at our own charge shall *ransom* straight
His brother-in-law, the foolish Mortimer
- *1 Henry IV*, 1.3.76-79

Once more I come to know of thee, King Harry,
If for thy **ransom** thou wilt now compound,
Before thy most assured *overthrow*
- *Henry V*, 4.3.79-81

My *shame* and *guilt* confounds me.
Forgive me, Valentine: if hearty *sorrow*
Be a sufficient **ransom** for ***offence***,
I tender it here; I do as truly suffer
- *Two Gentlemen of Verona*, 5.4.73-76

Titus Andronicus, my lord the emperor
Sends thee this word: that if thou love thy sons,
Let Marcus, Lucius, or thyself, old Titus,
Or any one of you, chop off your hand
And send it to the king, he for the same
Will send thee hither both thy sons alive,
And that shall be the **ransom** for their *fault*
- *Titus Andronicus*, 3.1.151-157

John Chamberlain to Dudley Carleton, May 27, 1601: "…for there is a commission to certain of the Council to **ransom and fine** the Lords and Gentlemen that were in the action…" (Stopes, 233; D.S.S.P. CCLXXIX, 91); Oxford, behind the scenes, is working to pay a form of "ransom" for the life of his son; **ALL** = Southampton, *One for All, All for One*; **ILL DEEDS** = acts of treason; ("He feared they were come into an ***ill action***" – Witherington's testimony at the Essex-Southampton trial, referring to men at Essex House on the morning of the Rebellion); "How oft the sight of means to do ***ill deeds*** make *deeds ill done*!" – *King John*, 4.2.219-220

Part Two

THE PRISON YEARS

DAY NINE IN THE TOWER

Sonnet 35
Thy Adverse Party is Thy Advocate
16 February 1601

Oxford reverses the Queen's motto **A Rose Without a Thorn** *("Roses have thorns") by way of admitting that both "Moone and Sunne" (Elizabeth and Southampton, carriers of Tudor Rose blood) have been disgraced. This disgrace is the "canker" within the "sweetest bud" (most royal heir), who has committed a grievous "fault" (treason) against the Crown. Oxford accuses himself of having encouraged his royal son's Rebellion through his writings for the stage ("authorizing thy trespass with compare") and of lending his support to his son. He sums up the terrible situation in which he finds himself – having to sit on the tribunal at the trial as "thy adverse party" and voting to condemn his royal son to death, while working behind the scenes as his "advocate" or defender trying to save him from execution. By casting a guilty verdict at the trial (already part of the bargain with Cecil), Oxford becomes an "accessory" to the crime by which his son has lost any chance to gain the crown. S*

Sonnet 35	Translation
No more be grieved at that which thou hast done:	No longer grieve over your role in the Rebellion:
Roses have thorns, and silver fountains mud;	Tudor Roses and their flowing blood are disgraced;
Clouds and eclipses stain both Moone and Sunne,	Elizabeth and Southampton are both destroyed,
And loathsome canker lives in sweetest bud.	Because the royal Tudor Rose heir is stained.
All men make faults, and even I, in this,	You have committed treason, and so have I,
Authorizing thy trespass with compare,	Having authorized your treason with my support.
Myself corrupting, salving thy amiss,	Corrupting myself, by forgiving your crime,
Excusing their sins more than their sins are:	Excusing the crimes more than required.
For to thy sensual fault I bring in sense;	For to your willful crime I bring in rationality;
Thy adverse party is thy Advocate,	Your opponent at the trial is your defender,
And 'gainst myself a lawful plea commence:	And I begin to make a legal case against myself:
Such civil war is in my love and hate	Such is my inner conflict as the trial approaches:
That I an accessory needs must be	That I am forced to be an accomplice
To that sweet thief which sourly robs from me.	Of my royal son, who robs his crown from me.

Sonnet 35 "depicts a trial scene" - Knight, W. N., Shakespeare's Hidden Life, 1973, p. 77

1 NO MORE BE GRIEVED AT THAT WHICH THOU HAST DONE:
Do not grieve any more over your act of treason.

2 ROSES HAVE THORNS, AND SILVER FOUNTAINS MUD,
ROSES HAVE THORNS = the Tudor Rose dynasty is disgraced; an inversion of Elizabeth's motto ***Rose Without a Thorn***; "Hath not *thy rose a thorn*, Plantagenet?" – *1 Henry VI*, 2.4.69; "And when they had platted a *crown of thorns*, they put it upon his head" – Matthew, 27.29; **SILVER FOUNTAINS MUD** = royal

REFERENCE EDITION   245

blood is tarnished; **"VER"** in **SILVER** indicates Oxford's share in the guilt; "O loyal father of a treacherous son! Thou sheer, immaculate and *silver fountain*, from whence this stream, through *muddy* passages, hath held his current an defiled himself" – *Richard II*, 5.3.59-61; "O villains, Chiron and Demetrius, here stands the spring whom you have *stained* with *mud* ... Inhuman *traitors* ... Villains, for *shame* you could not beg for grace" – *Titus Andronicus*, 168-170,177,179

> The purest spring is not so free from *mud*
> As I am clear from *treason* to my sovereign.
> Who can accuse me? Wherein am I guilty?
> - *2 Henry VI*, 3.1.101-103

3 CLOUDS AND ECLIPSES STAIN BOTH MOONE AND SUNNE,
CLOUDS AND ECLIPSES = shadows of disgrace; **STAIN** = to dishonor; to remove royal status; "The action of staining; pollution, disgrace; a morally defiling effect on the character or conscience; a grave blemish on a person's reputation; a mark of infamy or disgrace, a stigma" – *OED*; "*Suns* of the world may *stain*, when *heaven's sun staineth*" – Sonnet 33, line 14

> "*Stain to thy countrymen*, thou hear'st thy doom" – *1 Henry VI*, 4.1.45

> "Thy father's charge shall *clear thee from that stain*" – *1 Henry VI*, 4.5.42

> "Crooked *eclipses 'gainst his glory* fight" – Sonnet 60, line 7

MOONE = Elizabeth, who is Cynthia or Dian, chaste goddess of the Moon; ("The *mortal Moone* hath *her eclipse* endured" - Sonnet 107, line 5); **SUNNE** = Southampton, the royal son; (referring back to Sonnet 33, line 9: "Even so *my Sunne* one early morn did shine"; the blood of both Elizabeth and her son is now stained; **MOONE AND SUNNE** = Elizabeth, royal mother, and Southampton, royal son; i.e., the Rebellion has cast its shadow of disgrace over the Queen and her dynasty as well as Southampton; a carry-over of the "dearer birth" of Southampton in Sonnet 34 and of his identification as "my Sunne" in Sonnet 33; and now he is joined with his mother Elizabeth, goddess of the Moon, as was the case in Sonnet 21, lines 5-6: "Making a couplement of proud compare/ With Sunne and Moone"

4 AND LOATHSOME CANKER LIVES IN SWEETEST BUD.
CANKER = disgrace within the Tudor Rose; ("Hath not thy rose a canker, Somerset?" – *1 Henry VI*, 2.4); **SWEETEST BUD** = Southampton, most royal bud of the Tudor Rose ("Rough winds do shake the *darling buds of May*" – Oxford describing Southampton, Sonnet 18, line 3; "Good night, *sweet* prince" – *Hamlet*, 5.2.366); proverbial, as in Tilley: "The canker soonest eats the fairest rose"; "But now will canker-sorrow eat my bud and chase the native beauty from his cheek" –
King John, 3.4.82-83; "To put down *Richard, that sweet lovely rose*, and plant *this thorn, this canker*, Bolingbroke?" – *1 Henry IV*, 1.3.173-174; "The canker galls the infants of the spring, too oft before their buttons be disclosed" – *Hamlet*, 1.3.39-40; "O know, my name is lost, by *treason's tooth bare-gnawn and cankerbit*" – *King Lear*, 5.3.119-120; "Within *thine own bud* buriest thy content" – Sonnet 1, line 11

5 ALL MEN MAKE FAULTS, AND EVEN I IN THIS,
ALL = Southampton, *One for All, All for One*; **ALL MEN** = Southampton

FAULTS = Crimes; treason of Rebellion; "I do confess my *fault*, and so submit me to your Highness' mercy" – *Henry V*, 2.2.77-78; this is the introduction in the Sonnets of "fault" – a word referring specifically to the crime of high treason. Southampton's brother-in-law Thomas Arundell wrote in a treacherous letter to Robert Cecil at this time: "I cannot choose but manifest unto yourself how much I am aggrieved for the fall of the Earl of Southampton, & am more than ashamed at the foulness of his *fault*." – Akrigg, 129.

Southampton will write to the Privy Council after the trial: "I beseech your Lordships be pleased to receive the petition of a poor condemned man, who doth, with a lowly and penitent heart, **confess** his *faults* and acknowledge his *offences* to her Majesty." - (Stopes, 225-226; Salisbury Papers, vol. XI, p. 72; "after Feb. 19, 1601"; (FULL LETTER FOLLOWING SONNET 44)

On April 5, 1603, from the Palace at Holyrood, King James will send ahead his order for Southampton's release from the Tower, addressing the Nobility, Peers and Councilors of England: *"Although we are resolved as well in regard of the great and honest affection bourn unto us by the Earl of Southampton … whom we perceive also the late Queen our Sister, notwithstanding **his fault** toward her, was moved to exempt from the stroke of Justice."* (Essex Record Office manuscript D/DRh Z2 transcribed May 9, 2000 by Derran Charlton)

Fault appears frequently in this context within the Shakespeare royal history plays:

"For King of England shalt thou be proclaimed in every borough as we pass along; and he that throws not up his cap for joy shall *for the **fault** make forfeit of his head*" – *3 Henry VI*, 2.1.

"Would it might please your Grace on our entreaties to emend your fault … Then know, it is your *fault* that you resign the supreme seat, the throne majestical, the sceptered office of your ancestors" – *Richard III*, 3.7.114-116

"Never did faithful subject more rejoice at the discovery of most dangerous treason … My *fault*, but not my body, *pardon, sovereign*" – *Henry V*, 2.2.161-165

> Or, if he were not privy to those *faults*,
> Yet, by reputing of his high descent,
> As next the king he was successive heir
> - *2 Henry VI*, 3.1.48-49
>
> My lord, these *faults* are easy, quickly answered;
> But mightier crimes are laid unto your charge,
> Whereof you cannot easily purge yourself.
> I do arrest you in his Highness' name,
> And here commit you to my lord cardinal
> To keep, until your further time of trial
> - *2 Henry VI*, 3.1.133-138
>
> Clifford, devise excuses for thy *faults*…
> While we devise fell tortures for thy *faults*
> - *3 Henry VI*, 2.6.71-72
>
> Pardon me, Edward, I will make amends:
> And, Richard, do not frown upon my *faults*,
> For I will henceforth be no more unconstant
> - *3 Henry VI*, 5.1.103-105
>
> To punish this *offence* in other *faults*
> - *1 Henry IV*, 5.2.7
>
> And thus thy fall hath left a kind of **blot**
> To mark the full-fraught man and best endued
> With **some suspicion**. I will **weep** for thee,
> For this **revolt of thine**, methinks, is like
> Another fall of man. Their **faults** are open.
> Arrest them to the answer of the **law**,
> And God acquit them of their practices! - *Henry V*, 2.2.138-144

BLOT = "And dost him grace when clouds do *blot* the heaven" – Sonnet 28, line 10
SOME SUSPICION = "If *some suspect* of ill masked not thy show" – Sonnet 70, line 13
WEEP = "I all alone *beweep* my outcast state" – Sonnet 29, line 2
REVOLT OF THINE = "Since that my life on *thy revolt* doth lie" – Sonnet 90, line 10
FAULTS = "Of *faults* concealed, wherein I am attainted" – Sonnet 88, line 7
LAW = "To leave poor me thou hast the strength of *laws*" – Sonnet 49, line 13

6 AUTHORIZING THY TRESPASS WITH COMPARE,
TRESPASS = The crime committed by Southampton; "A transgression; a breach of law or duty; and offence, sin, wrong; a fault" – OED, 1; "In a wide sense, any violation or transgression of the law" – OED, 2; not necessarily related to treason, however, but used by the Tudors to widen the scope of what could be called treason to include "riots" and other popular assemblies; Oxford appears to be arguing that Southampton had not committed actual treason against the Crown but rather "misprision" of treason, a lesser crime; on the other hand, the usage of "trespass" in the Shakespeare works often precisely relates to treason or high crimes, as it was used often in the Elizabethan reign:

"And by his ***treason*** stand'st not thou attainted, corrupted, and exempt from gentry? His ***trespass*** yet lives guilty in thy blood"
– *1 Henry VI*, 2.4.92-94;
"Murder indeed, that bloody sin, I tortured above the felon or what *trespass* else"
– *1 Henry VI*, 3.1
"My nephew's *trespass* may be well forgot; it hath the excuse of youth and heat of blood, and an adopted name of privilege, a hair-brained Hotspur, governed by a spleen. All his *offences* live upon my head and on his father's"
– *1 Henry IV*, 5.2.16-21
"This child was prisoner to the womb and is by law and process of great nature thence freed and enfranchised, not a party to the anger of the king nor guilty of, if any be, the *trespass* of the Queen" – *Winter's Tale*, 2.2.59-63
"However they through TREASON do TRESPASS" - Spenser, Faerie Queen, VI, vii, 27 (my emphasis)

"Once I did lay an ambush for your life,
  A *trespass* that doth vex my grieved soul"
– *Richard II*, 1.1.137-138

"Wilt thou not hide the *trespass* of thine own?"
– *Richard II*, 5.2.88

AUTHORIZING THY TRESPASS = sanctioning or justifying and helping [behind the scenes, and particularly by my writing attributed to Shakespeare] to incite your Rebellion

WITH COMPARE = by comparison, with plays such as *Richard II*, depicting the deposition of a monarch on the stage; "Authorizing and Trespass are both legal terms" – Booth; an admission by Oxford that, in his own mind, he had sanctioned Southampton's part in the Rebellion "with compare" or by showing the deposition of Richard the Second on the public stage; an admission that, in fact, Oxford gave his approval for Southampton to present *Richard II* at the Globe the day before the Rebellion; and that he had encouraged Southampton by depicting him as Prince Hal, for example

AUTHORIZE = "To set up as authoritative; to give legal force to; to make legally valid; to give formal approval to; to sanction, approve, countenance; to afford just ground for, justify; to vouch for the truth or reality of; to confirm by one's authority" – *OED*

"We will, & by warrant hereof *authoriss* you to proceed" – Lord Burghley, 1571, *OED*

"Did manifestly *auctoryse* his sonne" – Udall, 1548, *OED*

"Let the Courtier … *authorize* his Prince's Court with Liveries" – Shelton, 1620, *OED*

"Authorize" is related to "authority" as in: "And art made tongue-tied by authority" – Sonnet 66, line 9; and it suggests being an "author"; also it relates to accrediting, as in: "A woman's story at a winter's fire, authorized by her grandam" – *Macbeth*, 3.4.64-65

COMPARE = by comparison; "I have been studying how I may *compare* this prison where I live unto the world" – *Richard II*, 5.5.1-2; "*Compare* our faces and be judge yourself" – *King John*, 1.1.79; "Now I perceive that she hath made *compare* between our statures" – *A Midsummer Night's Dream*, 3.2.290; "When their rhymes, full of protest, of oath and big *compare*" – *Troilus and Cressida*, 3.2.171-172; "What things in the world canst thou nearest *compare* to thy flatterers?" – *Timon of Athens*, 4.3.321; "Shall I *compare* thee to a Summer's day?" – Sonnet 18, line 1; Oxford may have written the deposition scene of *Richard II* (not included in printed versions until 1608) precisely for the revolt of 1601, as Massey was convinced in 1866 that *"at the pressing solicitations of Southampton, the drama of King Richard II was altered by Shakespeare on purpose to be played seditiously, with the deposition scene newly added!"* The evidence, he argued, is that *"if Shakespeare was not hand-in-glove with the Essex faction, he fought on their side pen-in-hand."* In the new scene Richard gives up the throne with Bolingbroke in his presence, which is what Essex and Southampton had hoped to persuade aging Elizabeth to do:

> With mine own tears I wash away my balm,
> With mine own hands I give away my crown,
> With mine own tongue deny my sacred state,
> With mine own breath release all duteous oaths.

7 MY SELF CORRUPTING SALVING THY AMISS,

MYSELF CORRUPTING = compromising myself, by working in your behalf; **SALVING THY AMISS** = working to excuse your crime and save your life; healing the painful results of your crime; forgiving your crime; **SALVING** = "as one who is willing to *salve* so great an inconvenience" – Oxford's Prefatory Letter to *Cardanus' Comfort*, 1573

AMISS = "Then judge, great lords, if I have done *amiss*" – *1 Henry VI*, 4.1.27; ("Away from the mark … Erroneously, in a way that goes astray of, or misses its object … Wrongly, in a wrong way … to act erroneously, to err … to do wrong … out of order: not in accord with the recognized good order of morality, society" – *OED*); "For that which thou hast sworn to do *amiss* is not *amiss* when it is truly done … Therefore thy later vows against thy first is in thyself *rebellion* to thyself" – *King John*, 3.1.196-197, 214-215; "Have we done aught *amiss*, show us wherein, and from the place where you behold us pleading, the poor remainder of Andronici will hand in hand all headlong hurl ourselves and on the ragged stones beat forth our souls and make a mutual closure of our house" – *Titus Andronicus*, 5.3.128-133; "To my sick soul, as sin's true nature is, each toy seems *prologue to some great amiss*" – the Queen in *Hamlet*, 4.5.17-18; "Such a sight as this becomes the field, but here *shows much amiss*" – Fortinbras, referring to Hamlet's death as a result of the "plots and errors" mentioned by Horatio, in *Hamlet*, 5.2.408-409

8 EXCUSING THEIR SINS MORE THAN THEIR SINS ARE:

THEIR = usually emended to "thy"; **EXCUSING THEIR (THY) SINS** = making excuses for your crime; **MORE THAN THEIR (THY) SINS ARE** = more strenuously than should be needed, since your crimes were not as bad as the charges indicate, i.e., not really treasonous; in fact, the charges will later be reduced to "misprision" of treason, as indicated in: "So thy great gift, upon *misprision* growing" – Sonnet 87, line 11 [although there's no official evidence that the charges *were* reduced – suggesting that, by keeping "misprision" off the record while the Queen maintained public silence, Cecil was able to prolong the threat of Southampton's execution until James could succeed as king].

> It is great *sin* to swear unto a *sin*,
> But greater *sin* to keep a *sinful* oath.
> Who can be bound by any solemn vow…
> And have no other reason for *this wrong*
> But that he was bound by a solemn oath?
> A subtle *traitor* needs no sophister…
> - *2 Henry VI*, 5.1.182-191

When Essex was about to be executed (Sonnet 44), he referred to the Rebellion as his "sin," confessing that "this great, this bloody, *this crying and this infectious sin,* whereby so many for love of me have ventured their lives and souls and have been drawn to offend God, to offend their sovereign, and to offend the world, which is so great a grief unto me as may be!"

THEIR SINS … THEIR SINS: Q reads "their" in both cases, but both are most often emended to "thy" with variations, such as: "Excusing thy sins more than their sins are." In this regard, we might note Q's printing of Sonnet 76, line 8 ("Showing their birth, and where they did proceed?") and ask whether Oxford was speaking to Southampton about the words showing *his* birth: "Showing *thy* birth…"

9 FOR TO THY SENSUAL FAULT I BRING IN SENSE:
SENSUAL = "obstinately self-willed" – *OED*

"His Lordship afterward despised and maligned at the King's said Privy Council, following *sensual and willful* ways" – 1538, *OED*

"If any law or reason could have removed you from your *sensual opinions*" – Hall Chronicles, 1548, *OED*

"I favor no *sensual & willful Recusants*" – Burghley, 1584, re: Catholic traitors, *OED*

SENSUAL FAULT: willful crime of treason by leading the Rebellion; riotous, impulsive crime against the state; suggestive of Prince Hal and his behavior; and of Hotspur's actions: "My nephew's *treason* may be well forgot, it hath **the excuse of youth and heat of blood**, and an adopted name of privilege – a hare-brained Hotspur, govern'd by a spleen; and all his *offences* live upon my head and on his father's" – *1 Henry IV*, 5.2.16-21; Southampton will write to Cecil after the trial that "*my heart was free from any premeditate treason* against my sovereign, though *my reason was corrupted* by affection to my friend [Essex] (whom I thought honest) and I by that *carried headlong to my ruin, without power to prevent it*" – (Stopes, 225-226), reflecting the viewpoint expressed in "sensual fault" of this sonnet, and supporting the view that Oxford was counseling Southampton to adopt this line of defense to save himself from execution.

FAULT = crime of treason; "O, 'tis a *fault* too, too unpardonable! Off with the crown, and with the crown his head!" – *3 Henry VI*, 1.4.106-107

Richard: *Thy son* is banished upon good advice,
Whereto *thy tongue a party-verdict gave*:
Why at our justice seem'st thou then to lour?

> Gaunt: Things sweet to taste prove in digestion sour.
> You urged me as a judge, but I had rather
> You would have bid me argue like a father.
> *O, had it been a stranger, not my child*,
> To smooth *his fault* I should have been more mild.
> A partial slander sought I to avoid,
> And *in the sentence my own life destroyed*.
> - *Richard II*, 1.3.233-242

SENSE = rational argument on your side; i.e., Oxford is working to get the charge of high treason reduced to "misprision" of treason, as he will announce in Sonnet 87, line 11: "So thy great gift, upon *misprision* growing" (Southampton's "gift" being his gift of life and blood)

10 **THY ADVERSE PARTY IS THY ADVOCATE,**
THY ADVERSE PARTY = Oxford, who will sit on the tribunal at the trial and be forced to render a guilty verdict against his son; "He speaks against me on the *adverse* side" – *Measure for Measure*, 4.6.6; **PARTY** = side in a legal case; -plaintiff or defendant; "But dare maintain the *party* of the truth" – *1 Henry VI*, 2.4.32; "To fight on Edward's *party* for the crown" – *Richard III*, 1.3.138 (on his side); "My prayers on the *adverse party* fight" – *Richard III*, 4.4.191; "Thy son is banished upon good advice, whereto thy tongue a *party-verdict* gave: why at our justice seem'st thou then to lour?" – *Richard II*, 1.3.233-235 (part of the verdict); "Upon the right and *party* of her son" – *King John*, 1.1.34 (on his behalf); to Elizabeth: "And play the mother's *part*" – Sonnet 143, line 12

> My prayers on the *adverse party* fight
> - *Richard III*, 4.4.191

> Besides, the King's name is a tower of strength,
> Which they upon the *adverse faction* want
> - *Richard III*, 5.3.12-13

"I have hitherto passed the pikes of so many *adversaries*" - Oxford to Robert Cecil, Oct 7, 1601

"I am very glad if it so prove, for I have need of so many good friends as I can get, and if I could I would seek all the *adversaries* I have in this cause to make them my friends" - Oxford to Robert Cecil, December 4, 1601

THY ADVOCATE = your defender. ("Your legal opponent is also your legal defender" – Duncan-Jones); Oxford is telling his son that, at the trial, he will have no choice but to render a vote of guilty; he is therefore an adverse party, but in his heart and behind the scenes he is acting as his son's advocate; **ADVOCATE** = "One whose profession it is to plead the cause of any one in a court of justice; a counsellor or counsel ... One who pleads, intercedes, or speaks for, or in behalf of, another; a pleader, intercessor, defender ... Specially, applied to Christ as the Intercessor for sinners" – OED, the latter adding to suggestions in the Sonnets that Oxford is acting as a Christ figure, sacrificing himself in order to redeem the sins of Southampton

> You're my prisoner, but
> Your gaoler shall deliver the keys
> That lock up your restraint. For you, Posthumous,
> So soon as I can win th'offended king,
> I will be known your *advocate*
> - *Cymbeline*, 1.2.3-7

> If she dares trust me with her little babe,
> I'll show't the King, and undertake to be
> Her *advocate* to th' loud'st
> - *Winter's Tale*, 2.237-39

> I never did incense his Majesty
> Against the Duke of Clarence, but have been
> An earnest *advocate to plead for him*
> - *Richard III*, 1.3.85-87

"We have an *Advocate* with the Father, Jesus Christ the righteous" – Biblical

King's Advocate: "The principal law-officer of the Crown in Scotland, answering to the Attorney-General in England" - *OED*

11 AND 'GAINST MY SELF A LAWFUL PLEA COMMENCE.
'GAINST MYSELF, etc. – I now begin a legal plea against myself; "*Unto myself* who hath the crime" – Oxford poem in Paradise of Dainty Devices, 1576, signed E. O.

> O, had it been a stranger, not *my child*...
> Alas, I looked when some of you should say
> I was too strict to make mine own away;
> But you gave leave to my unwilling tongue
> Against my will **to do myself this wrong.**
> - *Richard II*, 1.3., 239, 243-246

LAWFUL PLEA: Working behind the scenes with Robert Cecil, Oxford is making a legal plea against himself as Southampton's father. To save his son from execution, he will deny that his son is the lawful king; "To bend the fatal instruments of war against his brother and his *lawful* king" – *3 Henry VI*, 5.1.90-90; "Edward's son, the first-begotten and the *lawful* heir of Edward king" – *1 Henry VI*, 2.5.64-66

> Thy cruelty in execution
> Upon *offenders* hath exceeded *law*,
> And left thee to *the mercy of the law*
> - *2 Henry VI*, 1.3.132-133

> When law can do no right
> Let it be *lawful* that law bar no wrong!
> Law cannot give my child his kingdom here,
> For he that holds his kingdom holds the law;
> Therefore, since law itself is perfect wrong,
> How can the law forbid my tongue to curse?
> - *King John*, 3.1.111-116

> To guard the *lawful reasons* on thy part - Sonnet 49, line 12
> My heart doth *plead* that thou in him dost lie - Sonnet 46, line 5
> How with this rage shall beauty hold a *plea* - Sonnet 65, line 3

> No more, I say. If thou dost *plead* for him
> Thou wilt but add increase unto my wrath.
> But when I swear, it is irrevocable.
> If after three days' space thou here bee'st found
> On any ground that I am ruler of,
> The world shall not be *ransom* for thy life
> - *2 Henry VI*, 3.2.290-296

On Tudor treason trials: "[The defendant] also made *a plea*. When there was more than one indictment the prisoners had to be called separately each time, to hold up their hands while each was read, and then **plead** to each ... Others said that to some indictments or parts of an indictment they wished to offer *a plea* of not guilty, yet to other charges they were willing to confess their guilt..." (Bellamy, 138)

12 SUCH CIVIL WAR IS IN MY LOVE AND HATE
CIVIL WAR = conflict between two sides of my own mind or heart; "And let our hearts and eyes, like *civil war*, be blind with tears, and break o'ercharged with grief" – *3 Henry VI*, 2.5.77-78; Oxford owes a duty to his sovereign, Elizabeth, and to the state, but also to his royal son; so there is a *civil war* within his con-

science, much as in the following speech:

> If I know how or which way to order these affairs,
> Thus thrust disorderly into my hands,
> Never believe me. Both are my kinsmen:
> Th'one is my sovereign, whom both my oath
> And duty bids defend; th'other again
> Is my kinsman, whom the king hath wrong'd,
> Whom conscience and my kindred bids to right.
> - *Richard II*, 2.2.109-115

Oxford is also glancing at the potential "civil war" that could erupt concerning succession.

MY LOVE = my concern for your royal blood and right to the throne, as well as my paternal love for you; "From worthy Edward, King of Albion, my lord and sovereign, and thy vowed friend, I come, in *kindness and unfeigned love*" – *3 Henry VI*, 3.3.49-51; "So am I glad, moreover, to find an especial friend constant and assured in your word, which thing I vow to God to acknowledge to you *in all faith, kindness and love*"- Oxford (notably effusive in his expressions) to Robert Cecil, May 11, 1601, three months after the date of this sonnet and two months after the Queen has spared Southampton's life, undoubtedly with help from Cecil; **HATE** = my need, at the trial, to destroy your royal claim; "Warwick, these words have turn'd my *hate* to *love*; and I forgive and quite forget old *faults*, and joy that thou becomest King Henry's friend" –*3 Henry VI*, 3.3.199-201; "By heaven, my soul is purg'd from grudging *hate*, and with my hand I seal my true heart's *love*" – *Richard III*, 2.1.9-10, "Whenever Buckingham doth turn his *hate* upon your Grace, but with all duteous *love*" – *Richard III*, 2.1.32-33; "Those lips that *love's* own hand did make/ Breathed forth the sound that said, 'I *hate*/ … 'I *hate*' from *hate* away she threw,/ And saved my life, saying, 'Not you'" – Sonnet 145, lines 1-2, 13-14, of the Dark Lady Series, in reference to Elizabeth sparing Southamtpon from execution on March 19, 1601

13 THAT I AN ACCESSORY NEEDS MUST BE
I AN ACCESSORY = I, a co-conspirator or collaborator in your crime; and I, a judge at your upcoming trial who must find you guilty of treason and condemn you to death (thereby robbing you, my son, from me)

14 TO THAT SWEET THIEF WHICH SOURLY ROBS FROM ME.
SWEET THIEF – royal thief, Southampton, who has robbed Oxford (as well as Elizabeth and England, and more importantly, himself) of his kingship and crown

> Thou hast *stolen* that which after some few hours
> Were thine without offence, and at my death
> Thou hast sealed up my expectation
> - The King addressing his son his, Prince Hal, accusing him of stealing the crown, in *2 Henry IV*, 4.5.101-103

> I do forgive thy *robbery*, gentle *thief* - Sonnet 40, line 9

SOURLY ROBS FROM ME = hurtfully robs his kingship from me as father; bitterly, harshly, painfully; "Yet you Pilates have here delivered me to *my sour cross*" – the King in Richard II, 4.1.241; "Heart's Discontent and *sour* Affliction" – *2 Henry VI*, 3.2.301; "With clog of conscience and *sour* melancholy hath yielded up his body to the grave" – *Richard II*, 5.6.20-21

THE MONUMENT

THE PRISON YEARS

TREASON INDICTMENTS HANDED DOWN
DAY TEN IN THE TOWER

Sonnet 36
I May Not Evermore Acknowledge Thee
17 February 1601

Indictments are produced today charging Essex with an attempt to usurp the crown, and charging Essex, Southampton, Rutland and Sandys with having conspired to depose and slay the Queen and to subvert the government. Oxford announces terms of the "ransom" (adumbrated in Sonnet 34) that he must pay to have any chance of saving Southampton from execution. He and Henry Wriothesley must agree never to acknowledge their father-son relationship; and this means Southampton must forfeit any claim as the Queen's son and heir to the throne. Oxford is taking all blame for the actions of his son, acting as a Christ figure to redeem Southampton's sins that will "by me be borne alone."

Sonnet 36	Translation
Let me confess that we two must be twain,	Let me testify that we must be separate,
Although our undivided loves are one;	Although our blood as father and son is one;
So shall those blots that do with me remain,	So your disgrace, which remains with me,
Without thy help, by me be borne alone.	Will be carried without your help by me alone.
In our two loves there is but one respect,	In our bond there is just one royal motive,
Though in our lives a separable spite,	Though the Queen's spite has separated us,
Which, though it alter not love's sole effect,	And this, though it doesn't alter royal blood,
Yet doth it steal sweet hours from love's delight.	Still robs royal time from royal succession.
I may not ever-more acknowledge thee,	I cannot ever acknowledge you as my son,
Lest my bewailed guilt should do thee shame,	Or the guilt I accept will cause you disgrace,
Nor thou with public kindness honor me,	And you cannot acknowledge me as your father,
Unless thou take that honor from thy name:	Without publicly revealing your loss of royalty.
But do not so; I love thee in such sort,	But don't do it; I love you with such commitment,
As thou being mine, mine is thy good report.	That you being my son, my report is your truth.

1 LET ME CONFESS THAT WE TWO MUST BE TWAIN,
LET ME CONFESS = Oxford uses the language of a defendant confessing his crime; ("I do *confess* my fault and do submit me to your Highness' mercy" – *Henry V*, 2.2.76-77; "*Confess* thy treasons ere thou fly the realm" – *Richard II*, 1.3.198; "I beseech your Lordships be pleased to receive the petition of a poor condemned man, who doth, with a lowly and penitent heart, **confess** his **faults** and acknowledge his **offences** to her Majesty" – Southampton to the Privy Council at some point after February 19 and by early March 1601. (Stopes, 225-226)

TWAIN = two; divided; separate, even though united; "O Hamlet, thou hast cleft my heart in *twain*" – Gertrude to her son the prince in *Hamlet*, 3.4.158; ("So they loved, as love in *twain*/ Had the essence but in one ... How true a *twain*/ Seemeth this concordant one!" – *The Phoenix and the Turtle*, 1601, lines 25-26, 44-

45); Oxford, feeling guilty over the arrangement with Robert Cecil, begs to "confess" this bargain he is making to save Southampton; even if he spares his son from execution, he will have made it impossible for him to claim the throne

[King Edward to Montague and Hastings]:

> You *twain*, of all the rest,
> Are nearest to Warwick by blood and by alliance:
> Tell me if you love Warwick more than me.
> - *3 Henry VI*, 4.1.133-135

2 ALTHOUGH OUR UNDIVIDED LOVES ARE ONE:
Although we are one flesh and blood as father and son; **UNDIVIDED LOVES** = sharing the same blood; "In the devotion of a subject's *love*, tend'ring the precious safety of my prince" – *Richard II*, 1.1.31-32; **ONE** = united; within Southampton himself, who is *One* by his motto; "That they *all may be one*; as *thou, Father, art in me, and I in thee*" – John, 17.21; "Two distincts, *division none*" – *The Phoenix and Turtle*, 1601, Oxford of himself and Elizabeth

3 SO SHALL THOSE BLOTS THAT DO WITH ME REMAIN,
BLOTS = disgraces incurred by Southampton's treason, which Oxford accepts and for which he will pay; ("And thus thy fall hath left a kind of *blot*" – *Henry V*, 2.2.138, the king, speaking of his formerly loyal nobles who committed treason; "No, Bolinbroke, if ever I were *traitor*, my name be *blotted* from the book of life" – *Richard II*, 1.3.201-202; "Marked with a *blot*, damned in the book of heaven" – *Richard II*, 4.1.236; "To rid the world of this pernicious *blot*" – *Richard II*, 4.1.325; "This deadly *blot* in thy digressing son" – *Richard II*, 5.3.64)

4 WITHOUT THY HELP, BY ME BE BORNE ALONE.
BY ME BE BORNE ALONE = an image of Christ alone bearing the Cross, redeeming the sins of humanity; **BORNE** = Oxford will bear the burden alone; but "borne" is also related to his paternity of Southampton; **ALONE** = *all* and *one* = Southampton, his motto

5 IN OUR TWO LOVES THERE IS BUT ONE RESPECT,
OUR TWO LOVES = our two shared bloods ("Your *loves*, as mine to you" – *Hamlet*, 1.3.278; **ONE** = Southampton; **ONE RESPECT** = one mind and motive; the respect due to a king; mutual interest; regard; "For *princes* are a model which heaven makes like to itself: as *jewels* lose their glory if neglected, so *princes* their renown if not *respected*" – *Pericles*, 2.2.10-13; "I do love my country's good with a *respect* more tender, more holy and profound than my own life" – *Coriolanus*, 3.3.112

6 THOUGH IN OUR LIVES A SEPARABLE SPITE,
Though in our public lives we must be separate; **SEPARABLE SPITE** = a spiteful separation; ("a mortifying situation" – Duncan-Jones); "So I, made lame by Fortune's dearest spite" – Sonnet 37, line 3; "Our love makes us one person, though unfortunately we must live separately" – Booth; "A cruel fate, that *spitefully separates* us from each other; separable for separating" – Malone

7 WHICH THOUGH IT ALTER NOT LOVE'S SOLE EFFECT,
Which, though it doesn't change our actual existence as father and son; **ALTERS NOT** = "Love is not love/ Which *alters* when it *alteration* finds" – Sonnet 116, lines 2-3; i.e., "love" or royal blood cannot be altered from one reality to another

LOVE'S SOLE EFFECT = royal blood's uniqueness; ("The *sole* Arabian Tree" – *Phoenix and Turtle*); **SOLE** = unique, singular, related to "one" for Southampton; also, soul, the spiritual aspect of "love" or royal blood; "You twain, of all the rest, are nearest to Warwick by blood and by alliance: tell me if you *love* Warwick more than me" – *3 Henry VI*, 4.1.133-135

8 YET DOTH IT STEAL SWEET HOURS FROM LOVE'S DELIGHT.
SWEET = royal; **SWEET HOURS** = royal time, related to the dwindling time of Elizabeth's life; **LOVE'S DELIGHT** = royal blood's happiness or rightful state

9 I MAY NOT EVER-MORE ACKNOWLEDGE THEE,
EVER-MORE = Ever = E. Ver, Edward de Vere; I have agreed never to publicly acknowledge you as my son by the Queen (at least not in my own lifetime); "tongue-tied by authority" – Sonnet 66, line 9; Oxford is already bargaining for Southampton's life, behind the scenes, with his brother-in-law Robert Cecil; "I vow to God to *acknowledge* to you in all faith, kindness and love" – Oxford to Secretary Cecil, May 11, 1601

Even now, two days before the joint trial of Essex and Southampton, one condition upon which his son's life may be saved is that their blood relationship must never be acknowledged; Cecil is looking ahead to the death of Elizabeth and the accession of James of Scotland as King James I of England; for that to take place, the myth of the Virgin Queen must remain intact; what Cecil does not know is that Oxford is recording the truth in this poetical, dynastic diary of the Sonnets. "My name be blotted" - Richard II, 1.3.202

ACKNOWLEDGE = "Recognize or confess a person to be something; own the claims or authority of; register recognition of ... admit the truth of ... own as genuine or valid in law" - OED

10 LEST MY BEWAILED GUILT SHOULD DO THEE SHAME,
MY BEWAILED GUILT = the guilt that I have accepted for you, as mine; **BEWAILED** = lamented; expressed deep sorrow for; "I all alone *beweep* my outcast state" – Sonnet 29, line 2

DO THEE SHAME = bring shame or disgrace upon you; by declaring your royal identity, you would make yourself again vulnerable to the treason charge; Oxford's sacrifice will enable Southampton eventually to gain his release from the Tower and also a royal pardon, thereby eradicating his guilt, shame, disgrace and the "blots" against his honor; but if Southampton ever acknowledges his relationship to Oxford, he would be revealing himself simultaneously as Elizabeth's son and thereby again bring upon himself the shame and disgrace of a traitor – at that point, under King James, becoming a traitor by claiming a right to the crown.

> So to the laws at large I write my name;
> And he that breaks them in the least degree
> Stands in attainder of eternal shame.
> - *Love's Labour's Lost*, 1.1.153-155

11 NOR THOU WITH PUBLIC KINDNESS HONOUR ME,
PUBLIC KINDNESS = public acknowledgement that you are "kind", i.e., natural or related to me by blood (and that you are also Elizabeth's natural issue); "I vow to God to acknowledge to you in all faith, *kindness* and love" – Oxford to Cecil, May 11, 1601; "Be as thy presence is, gracious and *kind*" - Sonnet 10, line 11; "*Kind* is my love today, tomorrow *kind*,/ Still constant in a wondrous excellence" - Sonnet 105, lines 5-6

12 UNLESS THOU TAKE THAT HONOUR FROM THY NAME:
Unless you dishonor yourself; **THAT HONOR** = "Both the use of 'take that honor from' and 'name' implies that the poet is addressing a person of noble family and is playing on the title 'Right Honorable' as the proper form of address to such an individual. Compare the dedications in *Venus and Adonis* and *The Rape of Lucrece*" – Evans; "the honour which you give me" - Dowden

13 BUT DO NOT SO; I LOVE THEE IN SUCH SORT,
BUT DO NOT SO = but do not acknowledge me; **I LOVE THEE IN SUCH SORT** = I love you as a father loves his son; I love you as a subject loves his king; "The *love* I dedicate to your Lordship is without end" – dedication of *Lucrece* to Southampton; "The presence of a king engenders *love* amongst his subjects and his loyal friends" – *1 Henry VI*, 3.2.181-182

14 AS THOU BEING MINE, MINE IS THY GOOD REPORT.
THOU BEING MINE = you being my son; "a son of *mine own*" – Oxford to Burghley, March 17, 1575

MINE IS THY GOOD REPORT = my report is your own royal blood itself; your Tudor blood is your own good answer to any bad verdict at the trial; my report will be your redemption; "*Report* me and my cause aright to the unsatisfied" – the prince's dying request in *Hamlet*, 5.2.346-347; "But now time and truth have unmasked all difficulties, and I do understand the judges are, if they will be indifferent, to make a ***good report*** to Her Majesty" – Oxford to Robert Cecil, January 1602

THE COUPLET: lines 13-14 of Sonnet 36 will be repeated as the couplet of Sonnet 96. This couplet, the only repeating one, marks the tenth and seventieth sonnets of this 80-sonnet sequence covering the two years and two months of Southampton's imprisonment.

THE PRISON YEARS

DAY ELEVEN IN THE TOWER

Sonnet 37
As A Decrepit Father
18 February 1601

With the trial of Essex and Southampton set to begin the following morning at Westminster Hall, Edward de Vere faces what may be the single most tormenting day of his life. Unless a miracle takes place, the Crown (and Robert Cecil, the power behind it) will get its preordained judgment of guilt. To do his duty to the state, Oxford must sit on the tribunal of peers and vote to condemn his own royal son to death. On the eve of the trial, he records his devotion to Southampton by writing to him as a "decrepit" or powerless father and also as the subject of a "crowned" king. Oxford has been "made lame by Fortune's dearest spite" (profoundly crippled by Elizabeth's royal malice toward their son); but he tells Southampton that through "all thy glory" he is able to go on -- transforming this sonnet into an extraordinary homage to a Prince.

Sonnet 37	Translation
As a decrepit father takes delight	As a powerless father takes delight
To see his active child do deeds of youth,	To see his active child do deeds of youth,
So I, made lame by Fortune's dearest spite,	So I, robbed by Elizabeth's royal view of you,
Take all my comfort of thy worth and truth.	Still joy over your blood from her and me.
For whether beauty, birth, or wealth, or wit,	For whether your Tudor blood, birth, or royalty,
Or any of these all, or all, or more,	Or any of all these aspects of you, or more,
Entitled in their parts do crowned sit,	Sit entitled on the throne as a crowned king,
I make my love engrafted to this store:	I fuse my royal son to his life in these verses.
So then I am not lame, poor, nor despised,	So then I am not robbed of you,
Whilst that this shadow doth such substance give	While this shadow of you brings you alive,
That I in thy abundance am sufficed,	So I'm sufficed by your most royal blood,
And by a part of all thy glory live.	And, by being part of your royalty, I live:
Look what is best, that best I wish in thee;	Whatever is most royal is what I wish for you,
This wish I have, then time times happy me.	And this wish is true, so I'm ten times happier.

1 AS A DECREPIT FATHER TAKES DELIGHT
AS A DECREPIT FATHER = Oxford can only speak metaphorically, because he is unable to claim paternity; he is "decrepit" because he cannot help his son at the trial; "But out alack, *he was but one hour mine*" – Sonnet 33, line 11; in the Sonnets he cannot speak the truth directly; i.e., he cannot say, "I am your father"; but he can speak *indirectly*, in this case by way of metaphor, as he suggests in: "That every word doth *almost* tell my name" – Sonnet 76, line 7; "But hope of orphans, and *unfathered fruit*" – Sonnet 97, line 10; "If my *dear* love were but the child of state,/ It might for *fortune's bastard* be *unfathered*" – Sonnet 124, lines 1-2;
TAKES DELIGHT = "To see his daughter, all his life's *delight*" – Pericles, 4.4.12; "Sweets with sweets war not, joy *delights* in joy" – Sonnet 8, line 2; i.e., joy in his royal blood

Part Two

2 TO SEE HIS ACTIVE CHILD DO DEEDS OF YOUTH,
HIS ACTIVE CHILD = Southampton; **ACTIVE** = "I do not think a braver gentleman, more *active*-valiant or more valiant-young, more daring or more bold, is now alive" – *1 Henry IV*, 5.1.89-91; the son involved in the "action" of the Rebellion, a legal term used to describe it; *John Chamberlain to Dudley Carleton, May 27, 1601*: "…for there is a commission to certain of the Council to **ransom** and fine the Lords and Gentlemen that were in **the action**…" (Stopes, 233; D.S.S.P. CCLXXIX, 91); **DEEDS OF YOUTH** = take actions during his golden time of youth and freedom, prior to the Rebellion; such as his military exploits with Essex; but also referring to Southampton's role in the Rebellion itself: "And they are rich, and **ransom** all ill **deeds**" – Sonnet 34, line 14

3 SO I, MADE LAME BY FORTUNE'S DEAREST SPITE,
MADE LAME = Oxford was physically lamed in a 1582 street duel and may have had a "lame" hand, as he writes below; but more importantly he has been rendered ineffectual, so the lameness is also metaphorical; ("A most *poor* man, *made lame by Fortune's blows*" – *King Lear* Q1, 4.6.225); "Speak of *my lameness* and I straight will halt" – Sonnet 89, line 3

> Thus with a *lame* hand to write I take my leave
> - Oxford to Robert Cecil, January 1602

> For by reason of *mine infirmity*, I cannot come among you so often as I wish.
> - Oxford to Robert Cecil, April 25/27, 1603

FORTUNE = Queen Elizabeth; ("Beauty's crown though she do wear,/ Exalted into *Fortune's* chair, Thron'd like the Queen of Pleasure" – John Davies, 1600-02); **FORTUNE'S DEAREST SPITE** = Queen Elizabeth's most royal (and most motherly) malice against Southampton, whom she is likely to execute; "Therefore, that I may conquer *Fortune's spite* by living low where *Fortune* cannot hurt me … I here resign my government to thee, for thou art *fortunate* in all thy deeds" – King Henry to Warwick in *3 Henry VI*, 4.6.19-20,24-25; **DEAREST** = (the Queen was "most *dear* to us" – John Hayward, 1603); "dear" as used often in relation to a mother or father in relation to a son; ("Too familiar is my *dear son* with such sour company: I bring thee tidings of the prince's doom" – *Romeo and Juliet*, 3.3.6-8); "If my *dear* love were but the child of state,/ It might for *fortune's bastard* be *unfathered*" – Sonnet 124, lines 1-2; because of Elizabeth's spite or malice, Oxford has lost any chance to be her king-consort on the throne.

> Therefore, that I may conquer *Fortune's spite*
> By living low where *Fortune* cannot hurt me…
> Warwick, although my head still wear the crown,
> I here resign my government to thee
> - *3 Henry VI*, 19-20, 23-24

> "Would I had met my *dearest* foe in heaven" – *Hamlet*, 1.2.182

4 TAKE ALL MY COMFORT OF THY WORTH AND TRUTH.
ALL = Southampton, *One for All, All for One*; **ALL MY COMFORT** = Oxford used "comfort" when referring to his role as father of Bridget Vere and prospective father-in-law of William Herbert, Earl of Pembroke: "whom always I have wished a good husband such as your Lordship and myself may take *comfort* by" – Oxford to Burghley, September 8, 1597; "Warwick, *my son, the comfort* of my age" – *2 Henry VI*, 1.1.189; "Of *comfort*, kingdom, kindred, freedom, life" – *Richard III*, 4.4.224

> The heavens have blessed you with *a goodly son*
> To be your *comforter*…
> - *Richard III*, 1.3.9-10

> Most *worthy comfort*, now my greatest grief
> - Sonnet 48, line 6

REFERENCE EDITION

What dangers, by his Highness' fail of issue,
May drop upon his kingdom, and devour
Incertain lookers on. What were more holy
Than to rejoice the former queen is well?
What holier than, for royalty's repair,
For present ***comfort***, and for future good,
To bless the bed of majesty again
With a sweet fellow to't?
- *The Winter's Tale*, 5.1.27-34

*"In this common shipwreck mine is above all the rest, who least regarded though often **comforted** of all her followers, she hath left to try my **fortune** among the alterations of time and chance, either without sail whereby to take advantage of any prosperous gale, or with anchor to ride till the storm be overpast. There is nothing therefore left to my **comfort** but the excellent virtues and deep wisdom wherewith God hath endued our new Master and Sovereign Lord, who doth not come amongst us as a stranger but as a natural Prince, succeeding by right of blood and inheritance, not as a conqueror but as the true shepherd of Christ's flock to cherish and **comfort** them."*
– Oxford to Robert Cecil, April 25/27 1603, referring to the death of Queen Elizabeth and the accession of King James, on the eve of her funeral

WORTH = royal blood; "England ne'er lost *a king of so much **worth***" – *1 Henry VI*, 1.1.7; "*Most worthy* prince" – *Cymbeline*, 5.5.359; "And, by the glorious *worth* of my descent" – *Richard II*, 1.1.107; "Weigh you the worth and honor of a king" – *Troilus & Cressida*, 2.2.26

TRUTH = true identity as prince; Oxford = *Nothing Truer than Truth*; "Your *true* rights" – Sonnet 17, line 11; "Thou *truly* fair wert *truly* sympathized/ In *true* plain words by thy *true*-telling friend" – Sonnet 82, lines 11-12; "Fair, kind, and *true*, is all my argument,/ Fair, kind, and *true*, varying to other words,/ And in this change is my invention spent" – Sonnet 105, lines 9-11

5 FOR WHETHER BEAUTY, BIRTH, OR WEALTH, OR WIT,
BEAUTY = royal blood from Elizabeth; "That thereby *beauty's Rose* might never die" – Sonnet 1, line 2; **BIRTH** = Southampton's birth to the Queen; "Showing their *birth*, and where they did proceed" – Sonnet 76, line 7; **WEALTH** = the treasure of his royal blood; "O him she stores, to show what *wealth* she had,/ In days long since, before these last so bad" – Sonnet 67, lines 13-14, referring to Elizabeth who "stores" the "wealth" of her son's royal blood in the Tower; **WIT** = intelligence; knowledge of the truth

6 OR ANY OF THESE ALL, OR ALL, OR MORE
ALL … ALL = Southampton, *One for All, All for One*, insisting upon his identity; **MORE** = "or more excellencies having a just claim to the first place as their due" – Schmidt; i.e., Oxford names these qualities as "entitled" (in the next line) to *sit* on the throne as *crowned*, but his son is entitled to be king by even *more* than he is directly saying

7 ENTITLED IN THEIR PARTS DO CROWNED SIT,
INTITLED (ENTITLED) = "Having a rightful claim to, or named after" – Duncan-Jones; "Given noble titles by their roles, wear a crown and set on a throne" – a suggestion cited by Booth; "Will you show our *title to the crown*?" – *3 Henry VI*, 1.1.102; "Whose father bears the *title of a king*" – *3 Henry VI*, 2.2.140; "Perhaps it means 'having a title in, having a claim upon'" – Dowden; **THEIR PARTS** = often emended to "thy" parts; as applied to Southampton in these sonnets, "parts" = royal aspects; qualities, attributes, gifts, accomplishments; ("Which hides your life, and *shows not half your parts*" – Sonnet 17, line 4; "Mine eye hath well examined his *parts* and finds them perfect Richard" – *King John*, 1.1.89-90; "Remembers me of all *his gracious parts*" – *King John*, 3.3.96)

For the young gentleman, as I understand, hath been well brought up, fair conditioned, and hath many good *parts* in him. - Oxford to his father-in-law Lord Burghley, writing of young William Herbert, engaged to marry his daughter Bridget Vere, September 8, 1597

CROWNED = Southampton as rightfully crowned king; ("Well, if you be a king *crowned* with content" – *3 Henry VI*, 3.2.66; "There to be *crowned* England's royal king" – *3 Henry VI*, 2.6.88; "Even in the presence of the *crowned* king" – *1Henry IV*, 3.2.54

"I cannot but find a great grief in myself to remembrer the Mistress which we have lost ... and although it hath pleased God after an earthly kingdom to take her up into a more permanent and heavenly state, wherein I do not doubt but she is *crowned* with glory..." – Oxford to Robert Cecil, April 25/27, 1603, about the death of Queen Elizabeth

> "Incertainties now *crown* themselves assured" - Sonnet 107, line 7

> "Or whether doth my mind, being *crowned* with you" - Sonnet 114, line 1

> "*Crowning* the present..." - Sonnet 115, line 12

SIT = sit on the throne; ("Be enthroned" – Duncan-Jones, on "sit" in Sonnet 103, line 13; ("Which three, till now, never kept *seat* in one" – Sonnet 105, line 14; "Long mayst thou live in Richard's *seat to sit*" – *Richard II*, 4.1.218; "And in the self-same seat *sits* Collatine" – *Lucrece*, 288; "And shall I stand, and thou *sit* in my throne?" – *3 Henry VI*, 1.1.84)

8 I MAKE MY LOVE ENGRAFTED TO THIS STORE:
MY LOVE = my royal son and his royal blood; my re-creation of Southampton in these sonnets; "And *you and love* are still my argument" – Sonnet 76, line 10; "For as the Sun is daily new and old,/ So is *my love* still telling what is told" – Sonnet 76, lines 13-14; **INGRAFTED (ENGRAFTED)** = tied to; inseparable from; made an inextricable part of my sonnets; "And all in war with Time *for love of you,*/ As he takes from you, I *engraft* you new" – Sonnet 15, lines 13-14; **THIS STORE** = this great abundance of royal blood and kingly qualities; this store of royal blood in these verses; "Oh him she *stores*," Oxford writes in Sonnet 67, line 13, referring to how Elizabeth "stores" her son and his Tudor blood by keeping him in prison

9 SO THEN I AM NOT LAME, POOR, NOR DESPISED,
NOT LAME, POOR = not ineffectual or empty after all; **POOR** = (abject, humble, miserable); deprived of my son; opposite of having "wealth" as in Sonnet 67, line 13, of the Queen: "O him she stores, to show what wealth she had"; she stores him in prison and so she, too, is deprived of him: "Why should *poor* beauty indirectly seek/ Roses of shadow, since his Rose is true?" – Sonnet 67, lines 7-8, when the Queen is also called "bankrout" or bankrupt and "*beggared of blood* to blush through lively veins" in lines 9-10; **NOR DESPISED** = nor in disgrace

10 WHILST THAT THIS SHADOW DOTH SUCH SUBSTANCE GIVE,
THIS SHADOW = the vision of his son, who is covered by the shadow of disgrace cast by Elizabeth's frown or dark cloud; ("The *region cloud hath masked him* from me now" – Sonnet 33, line 12); the sonnets, representing a shadow of his son's substance or royal blood

SUBSTANCE = reality, i.e., the substance that is his royal blood, which is the same as "thy content" in "Within thine own bud *buriest thy content*" – Sonnet 1, line 11; ("But the world is so cunning, *as of a shadow they can make a substance,* and of a likelihood a truth" – Oxford to Burghley, July 1581); "Save that my soul's imaginary sight/ Presents *thy shadow* to my sightless view" – Sonnet 27, lines 9-10, as soon as Southampton has been confined in the Tower; "What is your *substance,* whereof are you made,/ That millions of strange *shadows on you tend*?" – Sonnet 53, lines 1-2

11 **THAT I IN THY ABUNDANCE AM SUFFICED,**
THY ABUNDANCE = your possession of abundant royal blood; "Making a famine where ***abundance*** lies" – Sonnet 1, line 7; **SUFFICED** = satisfied, contented, have enough

12 **AND BY A PART OF ALL THY GLORY LIVE.**
ALL = Southampton; **ALL THY GLORY** = all your kingly glory; ("all the *glory* of literature" – Oxford's Letter to the Reader, *The Courtier*, 1572); "And threat the *glory of my precious crown*" – *Richard II*, 3.3.90; "The lineal *glory* of your royal House" – *Richard III*, 3.7.120; "The crown, usurp'd, disgac'd his *kingly glory*" – *Richard III*, 4.4.371; "Awake, thou coward majesty ... a puny subject strikes at *thy great glory*" – *Richard II*, 3.2.84-87); "Crooked *eclipses 'gainst his glory* fight" – Sonnet 60, line 7, referring the crook-backed Robert Cecil's blockage of Southampton from the crown

13 **LOOK WHAT IS BEST, THAT BEST I WISH IN THEE:**
LOOK WHAT = whatever; **BEST** = most royal; "Richard hath *best* deserv'd of all my sons" – *3 Henry VI*, 1.1.17; "Neither the King, nor he that loves him *best*" – *3 Henry VI*, 1.1.45; "if he be not fellow with the *best king*, thou shalt find the *best king* of good fellows" – *Henry V*, 5.2.238-239

14 **THIS WISH I HAVE, THEN TEN TIMES HAPPY ME.**
THIS WISH ... HAPPY ME = echoing the 1594 *Lucrece* dedication to Southampton: "it is bound to your Lordship, *to whom I wish long life still lengthened with **all happiness**"*; and the dedication to the Sonnets: "To the onlie begetter of these ensuing sonnets, Mr. W. H., **all happiness** and that eternity promised by our ever-living poet *wisheth* the well-*wishing* adventurer in setting forth"; with the trial set for the next day, Oxford knows he will have to cast a guilty verdict and condemn his son to death; he will then fight behind the scenes to get the Queen to spare Southampton's life; meanwhile, knowing that his son will never gain the throne, he is recording his decision to fully accept the inner truth and to be "happy" with it; although, of course, he is still deeply suffering over the loss; "Resembling sire, and child, and *happy* mother" - Sonnet 8, line 11

No. 37

THE TRIAL

February 19, 1601

After living in self-imposed obscurity during the decade of the 1590s, Edward de Vere, Earl of Oxford emerges as the highest-ranking peer to sit on the tribunal in judgment of Essex and Southampton at their treason trial on February 19, 1601 in Westminster Hall. He is one of sixteen earls and nine barons who will be forced by the tragic circumstances of the Rebellion to render a guilty verdict against both earls. Attorney General Edward Coke is prosecuting for the Crown with assistance from Francis Bacon, the philosopher, during a daylong assault on the defendants that amounts to a travesty of justice.

"It is certainly a most important fact in connection with our argument that this outstanding action of Oxford's later years should be in connection with the one contemporary that 'Shakespeare' has immortalized. Considering the direction in which his sympathies lay, his coming forward at that time only admits of one explanation [i.e., he appeared on the tribunal to do whatever possible to help Southampton, the Fair Youth of the Sonnets]...

"It is clear, from the point of view of the problem of Shakespearean authorship, that the famous trial of the Earl of Essex assumes quite a thrilling interest. Standing before the judges was the only living personality that 'Shakespeare' has openly connected with the issue of his works, and towards whom he has publicly expressed affection: Henry Wriothesley. The most powerful force at work in seeking to bring about the destruction of the accused was the possessor of the greatest intellect that has appeared in English philosophy: one to whom in modern times has actually been attributed the authorship of Shakespeare's plays – Francis Bacon. And sitting on the benches amongst the judges was none other, we believe, than the real 'Shakespeare' himself, intent on saving, if possible, one of the very men whom Bacon was seeking to destroy. Some artist of the future surely will find here a theme to fire his enthusiasm and furnish scope for his genius and ambition..." - J. Thomas Looney, 1920

Lord Treasurer Buckhurst sits as High Steward of England under a Canopy of State, with the earls, barons and judges seated about the table. Captain of the Guard is Sir Walter Raleigh, with forty of the Queen's Guard attending. The prisoners are brought in. They make their appearance at the Bar as the Gentleman Porter stands with the Axe edge turned away from them.

Essex and Southampton kiss each other's hands and embrace. Essex inquires whether he may challenge any of the Peers (i.e., Lord Gray, an enemy), but the Lord Chief Justice answers in the negative. When Lord Gray is called, Essex turns to Southampton and jogs him on the sleeve, laughing. The two earls are called to hold up their hands at the Bar as the Clerk of the Crown reads the indictments. The earls plead Not Guilty, putting themselves into the hands of God and the Peers.

Sergeant Yelverton: May it please your Grace (the Lord High Steward), about the Eighth of February last my Lord of Essex went about with armed men very rebelliously to disinherit the Queen of her Crown and Dignity... my hope is that God of his mercy hath revealed their treasons (and) will not suffer the rest of his or any others to the hurt of the state or prejudice to her Majesty's most royal person, whom I pray God long to preserve from the hands of her enemies.

Essex and Southampton cry "Amen" to preserve the Queen, adding that God may confound their souls that ever wished other otherwise to her sacred person.

Attorney General Coke: May it please your Grace, the Lords chief Judges, which are the fathers of the law, do know that the thought of treason to the Prince, by the law, is death; and that he that is guilty of Rebellion is guilty of an intent (by the Laws of the Land) to seek the destruction of the Prince, and so adjudged treason ... This was not all for the Earl. He must call a Parliament, and he would decide matters not meet for his purpose. But now in God's most just judgment, he of his Earldom shall be Robert (Devereux) the Last; that of a kingdom thought to be Robert the First.

Coke's charge, in other words, is that Essex would have made himself King.

Essex: Will your Lordship give us our turns to speak? For he playeth the orator and abuseth your Lordships' ears and us with slanders ... I will not (I protest to God) speak to save my life, for those that prosecute it against me shall do me a good turn to rid me of my misery, and themselves of fear ... for my intent was no otherwise than loyal to her Majesty...

Coke: Yea, my Lord, you had three hundred men in arms in your house. Why did you not dissolve them, being commanded upon your allegiance from the Queen to do it...?

Southampton: Mr. Attorney, you speak all this as if it were as true as the Gospel.

Essex: Good my Lord, let me entreat you to mark the circumstances. Word was brought that men were sent for into the country to take us in our own houses. Then we, conceiving the thirsty appetite of our private enemies, took ourselves to arms, and were glad to stand upon our guard for our own defense ... Well, Mr. Attorney, I thank God you are not my judge this day, you are so uncharitable.

Coke: Well, my Lord, we shall prove anon what you are, which your pride of heart and aspiring mind hath brought you unto.

Essex: Ah! Mr. Attorney, lay your hand upon your heart and pray to God to forgive us both.

Raleigh: Sir Ferdinando Gorges told me upon the water that my lord of Essex had put himself (on guard) at Essex House, and this is like to be the bloodiest day's work that ever was...

Essex (to Coke): But you say we have committed Treason. First prove that true.

Ser. Yelverton: Why, my lord – if you deny the raising the power – why should so many men come to your house that day?

Southampton: By your favor, Mr. Sergeant Yelverton, a word I hope. For my coming thither, it was not strange news, and when I came that same morning to Essex House, I protest I had not above ten or twelve men attending me, which was but my usual company, therefore far from purporting to raise a tumult.

Atty Gen Coke: Why, the reason of that was for that you thought all London would have risen with you...

Sir Ferdinando Gorges testifies that Southampton urged on the rising; and "then upon a sudden they all agreed first to stir up London, where they assured themselves of great favor."

Sir Charles Danvers testifies that Essex, before Christmas of 1600, "entered into consideration how me might secure himself to have access to the Queen's presence without resistance." With Southampton they planned "first to take the Tower, for it would command London; then to surprise the Court (at Whitehall Palace). And after the Court being taken and possessed, to have assembled the rest of their friends, and to have presented themselves to the Queen."

Danvers: The intent was to surprise the Captain of the Guard (Raleigh) at the Court or at his own house, and some others, and then to surprise the City of London. And the Earl of Essex resolved (once these things were accomplished) immediately to call a Parliament to reform disorders and private grievances ... And lastly, I protest for my own part, what I did in the business was merely for the love I bore to the Earl of Southampton...

Examinations proceed, with testimony from Sir John Davis, Sir Christopher Blount, the Earl of Rutland, Lord Cromwell, Lord Sandys and Lord Mounteagle. Rutland notes that Essex was accusing Robert Cecil of working to bring about the royal succession to Elizabeth in concert with Spain. He says Essex cried out, "England is bought and sold to the Spaniard!" He also makes special mention that "Southampton was very much discontented."

Essex: This was my purpose: to have come with eight or nine honorable persons who had just cause of discontentment (though not equal with mine) unto her Majesty, and so by petition prostrating ourselves at her Majesty's feet, to have put ourselves unto her mercy. And the effect of our desires should have been that she would have been pleased to have severed some from her Majesty who, by reason of their potency with her, abused her Majesty's ears with false information – and they were Cecil, Cobham, and Raleigh ... And to that intent, to remove such from her Highness I confess was the only desire we had to present ourselves in all humility before her Majesty, but without any purpose of hurt to her Highness. For I protest before God, I do carry a reverent and loyal duty to her Majesty as any man in the world...

Southampton: Good Sir Ferdinando, satisfy the Court what was intended among all our conferences and talk of our enemies and discontentments and consultations, and what was our best course against them.

Gorges: Some delivered their minds one way, some another. But by the oath I have taken, I did never know or hear any thought or purpose of hurt or disloyalty intended to her Majesty's person by my Lord of Essex...

Southampton: It was a foolish action, I must needs confess, the going through the town, and that was suddenly passed over. But my lord's purpose to have men planted at the Court was in regard he feared hindrance by private enemies that would have stopped his passage to the Queen, which I protest he intended to no other end but to prostrate himself at her Majesty's feet, and submit to her mercy...

Francis Bacon: My Lord, may it please your Grace, whatsoever my Lord of Essex hath here denied, in my conceit it seemeth to be small. I speak not to any ordinary jury but to prudent, grave and wise Peers, and this I must needs say: it is evident that you, my lord of Essex, had planted a pretense in your heart against the government. And now, under color of excuse, you must lay the cause upon particular enemies. You put me in remembrance of one Pisistratus, that was come into a city and doting upon the affections of the citizens unto him – he having a purpose to procure the subversion of a kingdom, and wanting aid for the accomplishing – thought it the surest means for the winning of the hearts of the citizens to him ... and so by this means held the same conceit as you and your 'complices did, entering the city of London, persuading yourselves, if they had undertaken your cause, all would have gone well on your side; and now, my Lord, all you have said or can say in answer to these matters are but shadows, and therefore, methinks, it were your best course to confess and not to justify.

Essex: May it please your Lordship, I must plead Mr. Bacon for a witness...

Bacon: My Lord, I spent more hours to make you a good subject than upon any man in the world besides...

Bacon was once a friend and supporter of Essex, who reminds him of how he once shared the same views. But Bacon has reversed course, realizing that Secretary Robert Cecil will soon hold all power. Essex now makes a sensational charge.

Essex: But I can prove thus much from Sir Robert Cecil's own mouth: that he, speaking to one of his fellow councilors, should say that none in the world but the Infanta of Spain had the right to the Crown of England!

Without warning, Cecil himself steps forth from behind a curtain...

"It was a tense, dramatic moment; and suddenly, in the silence, came the sound of a curtain pulling back, and to the front of the court limped the little crookbacked Secretary in person. He had been hidden, listening to the proceedings, and his unexpected almost magical appearance from nowhere had all the drama – and

significance – of a last-act denouement. With an extravagance he seldom allowed himself he fell on his knees before Buckhurst and begged leave to answer Essex's foul and false report. He was roused to a fury few had seen before. 'My Lord of Essex, the difference between you and me is great,' he cried with all the passion of an ugly, unloved little hunchback unloosing his long pent-up hatred, fear and jealousy of gilded mortals like Essex." - Robert Lacey, 1971

Cecil: My Lord of Essex, the difference between you and me is great! For I speak in the person of an honest man, and you, my lord, in the person of a traitor! For well I know you have it at will. The pre-eminence hath been yours, but I have innocence, truth of conscience, and honesty to defend me against this scandal of slanderous tongues and aspiring hearts! And I protest before God, I have loved your person, and justified [defended] your virtues. And I appeal to God and the Queen that I told her Majesty that your afflictions would make you a fit servant for her. And had I not seen your ambitious affections inclined to usurpation, I could have gone on my knees to her Majesty to have done you good. But you have a sheep's garment in show, and in appearance are humble and religious; but God be thanked we know you … I stand for loyalty, which I never lost! You stand for treachery, wherewith your heart is possessed! And you charge me with high things, wherein I defy you to the uttermost!

The issue of the succession has now come to the forefront. James VI of Scotland is only one of the claimants, another being the Infanta of Spain. In the following exchange Cecil admits as much, while also including Essex himself as a claimant – but scornfully, in order to further the charge of treason. [The evidence suggests not that Essex wanted to make himself King but, rather, to replace Cecil as kingmaker.] Conspicuous by omission is Southampton's own claim, which is known by both Essex and Cecil; and we can only imagine the scene as Edward de Vere, Earl of Oxford looks on.

Cecil (continuing): You, my good lords, councilors of state, have many conferences, and I do confess I have said the King of Scots is a competitor, and the King of Spain is a competitor, and you (Essex), I have said, are a competitor. You would depose the Queen! You would be King of England and call a Parliament! Ah, my lord, were it but your own case the loss had been the less. But you have drawn a number of noble persons and gentlemen of birth and quality into your net of rebellion, and their bloods will cry vengeance against you! For my part, I vow to God, I wish my soul was in heaven and my body at rest, so this had never been.

Essex: Ah, Mr. Secretary, I thank God for my humbling, that you in the ruff of your bravery came to make your oration against me here this day.

Cecil: My lord, I humbly thank God that you did not take me for a fit companion for you and your humors; for if you had, you would have drawn me to betray my sovereign, as you have done. But I would have you name the councilor you speak of (i.e., the man to whom Cecil supposedly had spoken of the Infanta of Spain). Name him! Name him! Name if you dare! I defy you: name him if you dare!

Essex replies by referring the question to Southampton, who says the councilor was Essex's uncle Sir William Knollys, Comptroller. Secretary Cecil abruptly falls to his knees. "I thank God for this day!" he exclaims, and asks that Knollys be brought to Court. The Lord High Steward then dispatches Knyvett of the Privy Chamber.

Cecil: Mr. Knyvett, you shall have free access unto Her Majesty. Tell her that I vow before the God of Heaven that if she refuses to send Mr. Comptroller, whereby I may clear myself of these open scandals, I will rather die at her foot as her subject and vassal than live to do her any more service in the honorable degree wherein her Highness employs me…

Old Knollys arrives and takes the stand. He is told of Essex's accusation and is asked whether he ever heard Cecil express such sentiments about the Infanta of Spain as having a good claim to the throne of England. The entire courtroom is silent while all await his answer.

Knollys: I remember once in Mr. Secretary's company there was a book read that treated of such matters. But I never did hear Mr. Secretary use any such words...

Cecil thanks God aloud that Essex stands as a traitor while he, Cecil, has been found to be an honest man and a faithful subject.

Cecil (to Essex): I beseech God to forgive you for this open wrong done unto me, as I do openly pronounce, I forgive you from the bottom of my heart.

Essex: And I, Mr. Secretary, do clearly and freely forgive you with all my soul, because I mean to die in charity.

The fate of Essex has been sealed. Southampton now speaks of his ignorance of the law, a line of defense for which both Oxford and Cecil have prepared him, as a means of eventually reducing his crime from treason to "misprision" of treason.

Southampton: Well, I beseech your Lordship [Buckhurst], let me satisfy your Lordship and the rest thus much, that for my own part, I did never know the laws. Now to show the causes that made me adventure into these courses was the affinity betwixt my Lord of Essex and me – I being of his blood and marrying his kinswoman – so that for his sake I would have hazarded my life. But of what I have by my forwardness offended in act I am altogether ignorant, but in thought I am assured never. If through my ignorance in the Law I have offended, yet I humbly submit myself to her Majesty, and from the bottom of my heart do beg her gracious pardon if it please her. And I hope that neither your Lordship nor any of the Peers will hold any of the former resolutions spoken of by these orators. For any certainty depends no otherwise than one upon the other. For if any foolish speeches have passed, I protest as I shall be saved that they were never purposed by me, nor understood to be purposed by me, to the hurt of her Majesty's person.

Essex also pleads for himself. Southampton defends him before returning to his own case, denying that he "did ever mean or intend any treason, rebellion, or other action against my Sovereign or the State."

Southampton: What I did was to assist my Lord of Essex in his private quarrel. And therefore, Mr. Attorney, you have urged the matter very far and wrong me therein. **My blood be upon your head!** ... And you, Mr. Attorney, whereas you have charged me for a Papist, I protest most unfeignedly, I was never conversant with any of that sort...

Essex: And God, which knoweth the secrets of all hearts, knoweth that I never sought the Crown of England, nor ever wished to be a higher degree than a subject...

Francis Bacon speaks vehemently against Essex. Eventually the prisoners are withdrawn from the Bar. The Lords and Peers go together into a private place behind the Canopy and Chair of Estate. The two Chief Justices and the Lord Chief Baron give them their opinions in law; and after half an hour, they come out again and each man takes his place. All the Peers find Essex guilty of High Treason, speaking the verdict one by one from lowest rank to the highest, ending with Oxford. In the same manner they also find Southampton guilty of High Treason. The prisoners are brought again to the Bar. The Clerk addresses Essex, informing him of the guilty verdict and asking for his reply in his own behalf.

Essex: I do not speak to save my life, for I see that were in vain. **I owe God a death**, which shall be welcome, how soon ever it pleaseth her Majesty. ...

("Why, ***thou owest God a death***" – Prince Hal to Falstaff, *I Henry IV*, 5.1.126)

The Clerk then addresses Southampton.

Southampton: My lords, I must say for my part as I have said before, that since the ignorance of the law hath made me incur the danger of the law, I humbly submit myself to **her Majesty's mercy** ... I pray you truly to inform the Queen of my penitence, and be a means for me to her Majesty to grant me her gracious pardon. I know I have **offended** her; yet if it please her to be **merciful** unto me, I may, by my future service, deserve **my life**. I have been brought up under Her Majesty. I have spent the best part of my patrimony in Her Majesty's service, with frequent danger of my life, as your Lordships well know... But since I am found guilty by the law, I do submit myself to **death**, yet not despairing of Her Majesty's **mercy**. For I know she is **merciful**, and if she please to extend **mercy** to me, I shall with all humility **receive** it."

(**GRANT**: "*Grant* if thou wilt, thou art beloved of many" – Sonnet 10.3)
(**GRACIOUS**: "Be as thy presence is, gracious and kind" – Sonnet 10.11)
(**PARDON**: "To you it doth belong
          Yourself to pardon of self-doing crime" – Sonnet 58.11-12)
(**OFFENDED**: "To him that bears the strong offence's cross" – Sonnet 34.12;
          "Loving offenders, thus I will excuse ye" – Sonnet 42.5)
(**MERCIFUL/MERCY**: "Straight in her heart did mercy come" – Sonnet 145.5)
(**MY LIFE**: "My sweet love's beauty, though my lover's life" – Sonnet 63.12)
(**DEATH**: "This thought is as a death" – Sonnet 64.13)
(**RECEIVE** = "Then if for my love thou my love receivest" – Sonnet 40.5)

Lord High Steward: "You both shall be led from hence to **the place** from whence you came, and there remain during **Her Majesty's pleasure** -- from thence to be drawn upon a hurdle through the midst of the City, and so the **place** of execution, there to be hanged by the neck and taken down alive; your bodies to be opened, and your bowels taken out and burned before your face; your bodies to be quartered; your heads and quarters to be disposed of at **Her Majesty's pleasure**. And so God have mercy on your souls."

(**THE PLACE** = i.e., the Tower; "As soon as think *the place* where he would be" – Sonnet 44.8, corresponding with the day of Essex's execution on February 25, 1601, when Southampton remained in the Tower and Oxford used the same phrase to signify the prison fortress.)

(**HER MAJESTY'S PLEASURE** = "How like a Winter hath my absence been/ From thee, the *pleasure* of the fleeting year" – Sonnet 97.1-2; i.e., it was the Queen's pleasure to keep Southampton in the Tower)

Essex: My Lord, I am not a whit dismayed to receive this sentence, for I protest death is as welcome to me as life, and I shall die as cheerful a death upon such a testimony as ever did man. And I think it fit that my poor quarters that have done her Majesty such true service in divers parts of the world should be sacrificed and disposed of at her Majesty's pleasure...

With the Gentleman Porter now bearing the **axe blade** toward the two condemned earls, a guard leads them out of Westminster Hall and they are transported back to the Tower of London to await execution.

AXE BLADE   Against confounding age's *cruel knife*
That he shall never *cut* from memory
My sweet love's beauty, *though my lover's life*"
- Sonnet 63.10-11

(About a hundred other conspirators are in the Tower or different prisons. Five – Sir Christopher Blount, Sir Charles Danvers, Sir John Davis, Sir Gelly Merrick and Henry Cuffe – will be tried for high treason on the fifth of March. Many others will be allowed to pay heavy "ransoms" or fines to gain their freedom.)

Part Two

THE PRISON YEARS

THE TRIAL OF ESSEX & SOUTHAMPTON

DAY TWELVE IN THE TOWER

Sonnet 38
While Thou Dost Breathe
19 February 1601

Oxford reacts to the long day of the trial. Sitting as highest-ranking earl on the tribunal of twenty-five peers, he watched as Essex and Robert Cecil squared off face-to-face and, ultimately, as Southampton pleaded for "mercy" from Her Majesty the Queen, who, by custom, was not present. There was "ought in me" (nothing in him) to defend his son, so Oxford remained "dumb" or silent all during the proceedings; but Southampton's "argument" infuses the "invention" of these sonnets with the "light" of his golden royalty. In his silence, and in this diary, Oxford takes on the "pain" of "these curious (anxious) days" for Henry Wriothesley, who has been condemned to death.

Sonnet 38	Translation
How can my Muse want subject to invent	How can my Muse lack a subject for my invention
While thou dost breathe, that pour'st into my verse	While you still live: you, who pour into my sonnets
Thine own sweet argument, too excellent	Your own royal argument, which is too royal
For every vulgar paper to rehearse?	For any other writer's work to describe?
Oh give thyself the thanks, if ought in me	O, thank yourself for this, if my failure
Worthy perusal stand against thy sight:	To see your royalty fights against the sight of you:
For who's so dumb, that cannot write to thee,	For who's so speechless who can't write to you,
When thou thyself dost give invention light?	When you yourself inspire this royal verse?
Be thou the tenth Muse, ten times more in worth	You are the best Muse, ten times more royal
Than those old nine which rhymers invocate;	Than the classical nine muses of mythology;
And he that calls on thee, let him bring forth	And any poet who calls upon you, let him give birth
Eternal numbers to outlive long date.	To immortal sonnets to outlive history.
If my slight Muse do please these curious days,	If my weak Muse comforts you these anxious days,
The pain be mine, but thine shall be the praise.	The effort and pain is mine, you will have the glory.

1 HOW CAN MY MUSE WANT SUBJECT TO INVENT
WANT = lack; **SUBJECT** = subject matter; also Southampton is now regarded by law as a "base subject" of the Crown: "Dark'ning thy power to lend *base subjects* light" – Sonnet 100, line 4; **TO INVENT** = for my "invention" of these private verses ("And keep *invention* in a noted weed" - Sonnet 76, line 6; "And in this change is my *invention* spent" – Sonnet 105, line 11)

2 WHILE THOU DOST BREATHE, THAT POUR'ST INTO MY VERSE
While you remain alive, in the Tower, having just been sentenced to die; **THAT POUR'ST INTO MY VERSE** = you, who fill my sonnets with your "love" or royal blood; as in line 8 of this sonnet: "Thou thyself dost *give invention light*," i.e., the light of the royal sun and stars; "For as the Sun is daily new and old,/

REFERENCE EDITION 269

So is my love still *telling what is told*" - Sonnet 76, lines 13-14, the same as pouring his "argument" into these verses; in effect, Oxford becomes the mere instrument or vehicle by which the Sonnets are recording the time leading to succession; image of literally "pouring" his blood.

3 THINE OWN SWEET ARGUMENT, TOO EXCELLENT
SWEET ARGUMENT = royal topic of my sonnets, i.e., your Tudor blood and right to the throne; ("And *you and love are still my argument*" – Sonnet 76, line 10, referring to Southampton and his "love" or royal blood); Southampton's "*argument*" at the trial, by which he pleaded for the Queen's mercy; "Fair, kind, and true, is all my argument" - Sonnet 105, line 9; **EXCELLENT** = royal, as in Your Excellency; "There is nothing therefore left to my comfort but the *excellent* virtues and deep wisdom wherewith God hath endued our new Master and Sovereign Lord, who doth not come amongst us as a stranger but as a natural prince, succeeding by right of blood and inheritance" - Oxford to Robert Cecil, April 25/27, 1603, writing of King James

4 FOR EVERY VULGAR PAPER TO REHEARSE?
EVERY = Ever = E. Ver = Edward de Vere, *Ever or Never*; **VULGAR PAPER** = published books; **EVERY VULGAR PAPER** = E. Ver's papers; my papers; "So should *my papers*, yellowed with their age,/ Be scorned, like old men of less truth than tongue,/ And your true rights be termed a Poet's rage" – Sonnet 17, lines 9-11; **TO REHEARSE** = to express; i.e., your blood is too royal to be expressed; "And tongues to be your being shall *rehearse*" – Sonnet 81, line 11

5 OH GIVE THY SELF THE THANKS IF OUGHT IN ME
OH = O; Oxford; **THY SELF** = your royal person or self; **OUGHT IN ME** = nothing, as in O; as he will write in relation to bearing the canopy for the Queen's funeral procession in 1603: "Were't *ought* to me I bore the canopy" – Sonnet 125, line 1

6 WORTHY PERUSAL STAND AGAINST THY SIGHT,
WORTHY = royal; ("*Worthy prince*" – *King Lear*, 5.3. 177); **STAND AGAINST THY SIGHT** = meet the test of your princely eyes

7 FOR WHO'S SO DUMB THAT CANNOT WRITE TO THEE,
DUMB = unable to speak the truth that you are my son by Elizabeth; "And art made *tongue-tied* by authority" – Sonnet 66, line 9; "I was *dumb* with silence, I held my peace, even from good; and my sorrow was stirred … I was *dumb*, I opened not my mouth" – verses 2 & 9 of Psalm 38, its number matching that of this sonnet.

8 WHEN THOU THY SELF DOST GIVE INVENTION LIGHT?
When you are the one who inspires my verse; you fill my "invention" for this diary with royal sunlight; "Dark'ning thy power to lend base subjects *light*" – Sonnet 100, line 4 ("the *onlie begetter* of these ensuing sonnets" – dedication of the Sonnets in 1609, indicating Southampton as the supreme inspiration of the verses); "I have engaged myself so far in Her Majesty's service *to bring truth to light*" – Oxford to Burghley, June 13, 1595; "Nativity, once *in the main of light*,/ Crawls to maturity, wherewith being crowned,/ Crooked eclipses 'gainst his glory fight" – Sonnet 60, lines 5-7, Oxford writing of the birth of his son (the Christ-like nativity of a king or god on Earth) and his progress toward the throne now thwarted; **THOU THY SELF** = you your royal self; addressing him as a king, as in "But he that writes of you, if he can tell/ That *you are you*, so dignifies his story" in Sonnet 84, lines 7-8

9 BE THOU THE TENTH MUSE, TEN TIMES MORE IN WORTH
TENTH MUSE = added to the nine Muses of classical mythology; **WORTH** = royal blood; "A work which, while worthy of all monarchs, is most **worthy** *of our own Queen*, to whom alone is due *all the praise of all the Muses* and all the glory of literature" - Oxford 's Letter to the Reader, *The Courtier*, 1572

10 THAN THOSE OLD NINE WHICH RHYMERS INVOCATE;

RHYMERS = other poets (including "Shakespeare") who invoke the nine muses; "Wherefore *you Muses nine*, with doleful tunes help then…" - Oxford poem, published in 1576

11 AND HE THAT CALLS ON THEE, LET HIM BRING FORTH

HE THAT CALLS ON THEE = the writer, Oxford, who calls on him for inspiration, but also speaking of "Shakespeare," the public pen name; **BRING FORTH** = "give birth to" – Booth, who cites the birth metaphor for poetic creation; in this case, the father/poet who is giving birth or rebirth to his son/verse; "For I am shamed by *that which I bring forth*" – Sonnet 72, line 13, in which Oxford expresses the "disgrace" of his royal son and, by extension, of these sonnets that contain the life and truth of his royal son; "Alack what poverty my Muse *brings forth*" – Sonnet 103, line 1, referring to his son's loss of royal hope and succession, expressed in these verses

12 ETERNAL NUMBERS TO OUTLIVE LONG DATE.

These immortal sonnets are the eternal "numbers" of the pyramidal monument. They are being used to create "great bases for *eternity*" – Sonnet 125, line 3; "fresh *numbers*" – Sonnet 17, line 6; "my gracious *numbers*" – Sonnet 79, line 3; "gentle *numbers*" – Sonnet 100, line 6; the verses are "fresh" or "gracious" or "gentle" (royal) because of Southampton, who fills each line with his royal blood; "the *number of thy hours*" – Richard II, 2.1.177; "I wasted time, and now doth time waste me; for now hath time made me his *numb'ring* clock" – Richard II, 5.5.49-50; "When in *eternal lines to time* thou grow'st" – Sonnet 18, line 12; **TO OUTLIVE LONG DATE** = to live in posterity; "The living record of your memory/ …Your praise shall still find room/ Even *in the eyes of all posterity*" – Sonnet 55, lines 8, 10-11;"Your monument shall be my gentle verse,/ Which *eyes not yet created* shall o'er-read" – Sonnet 81, lines 9-10; and in so doing, also to outlive the shorter earthly "date" with succession, i.e., at this point Southampton has no chance to succeed Elizabeth; in fact, very soon he may well not "outlive" his execution; ("*eternal* lines to *time*" – Sonnet 18, line 12, summarizing the paradox that the diary, although currently linked to real time by the calendar, is ultimately meant to confer immortality upon Southampton by preserving his true identity as king); **DATE** = date with death or end of hope as well as date with the royal succession; "O, twice my father, twice I am thy son! The life thou gavest me first was lost and done, till with thy warlike sword, despite of late, *to my determined time thou gavest new date*" – 1 Henry VI, 4.6.6-9; "Why, York, what wil thou do? Wilt thou not hide the *trespass* of thine own? Have we more sons? Or are we like to have? Is not *my teeming date drunk up with time*? And wilt thou pluck my fair son from mine age, and rob me of a happy mother's name?" –Richard II, 5.2.88-93; "Who killed this prince?" "'Tis not an hour since I left him well: I honored him, I loved him, and will weep *my date of life* out for his sweet life's *loss*" – King John, 4.3.103-106;

Thy end is Truth's and Beauty's doom and *date*- Sonnet 14, line 14
And Summer's lease hath all too short a *date* - Sonnet 18, line 4
So long as youth and thou are of one *date* - Sonnet 22, line 2
Beyond all *date*, even to eternity - Sonnet 122, line 4

13 IF MY SLIGHT MUSE DO PLEASE THESE CURIOUS DAYS,

THESE CURIOUS DAYS = These anxious, worrisome days; indicating the day-to-day writing of these sonnets, but referring to this *day* of the trial, which drew so many curious spectators outside Westminster Hall and even aboard boats on the River Thames; **CURIOUS** = "particularly difficult to satisfy, hard to please … worrisome, disquieting, causing anxiety … anxious, concerned, apprehensive" – Crystal & Crystal; "I am so fraught with *curious* business" – The Winter's Tale, 4.4.511; "I am something *curious* (anxious) to have them in safe stowage" – Cymbeline, 1.7.191; **DAYS** = at the very end of the eighty-sonnet prison sequence, in Sonnet 106, line 14, Oxford repeats the refrain: "For we which now behold *these present days*/ Have eyes to wonder, but lack tongues to praise."

14 THE PAIN BE MINE, BUT THINE SHALL BE THE PRAISE.

THE PAIN BE MINE = I take on the suffering and effort for you; i.e., the effort to persuade the Queen to spare your life; "That she that makes me sin awards me *pain*" – Sonnet 141, line 14, to Elizabeth in the Dark Lady Series, referring to the Queen having forced him to make a bargain for Southampton's life that

REFERENCE EDITION

involves taking the blame and sacrificing his own identity

"In pain of your dislike or *pain* of death" – *2 Henry VI*, 3.2.256; "Hadst thou but loved him half so well as I, or felt that *pain* which I did for him once, or nourished him as I did with my blood, thou wouldst have left thy dearest heart-blood there, rather than have that savage duke thine heir and disinherited thine only son" – *3 Henry VI*, 1.1.227-232; "But I do find more *pain* in banishment than death can yield me here by my abode; a husband and a son thou owest to me; all of your allegiance: the sorrow that I have, by right is yours, and all the pleasure you usurp are mine" – *Richard III*, 1.3.168-173; "Here standeth Thomas Mowbray, Duke of Norfolk, on *pain* to be found false and recreant, both to defend himself and to approve Henry of Hereford, Lancaster, and Derby, to God, his sovereign and to him disloyal" – *Richard II*, 1.3.110-114; "O, but they say the tongues of dying men enforce attention like deep harmony: whose words are scarce, they are seldom spent in vain, for they breathe truth that breathes their words in *pain*" - *Richard II*, 2.1.5-8;

The trickling tears that fall along my cheeks,
The secret sighs that show my inward grief:
The present pains perforce…
She is *my pain*, she is my ease therefore…
Some *purge their pain* by plaint I find…
Desire can have *no greater pain*…- Oxford poems, printed 1576

PRAISE = all the praise in these sonnets is for you as the rightful king; "Solicit Henry with her wondrous *praise*" – *1 Henry VI*, 5.3.190; "Well could I bear that England had this *praise*" – *King John*, 3.3.15; "Yea, there thou makest me sad and makest me sin in envy that my Lord Northumberland should be the father to so blest a son, a son who is the theme of honour's tongue; amongst a grove, the very straightest plant; who is sweet Fortune's minion and her pride: whilst I, by looking on the *praise* of him, see riot and dishonour stain the brow of my young Harry" – *1 Henry IV*, 1.1.77-85; "Trimmed up your *praises* with a princely tongue, spoke to your deservings like a *chronicle*, making you ever better than his *praise* by still dispraising *praise* valued with you" – *1 Henry IV*, 5.2.56-59; "A work which, while worthy of all monarchs, is most worthy of our own Queen, to whom alone is due all the ***praise*** of all the Muses and all the glory of literature" - Oxford 's Letter to the Reader, *The Courtier*, 1572

Part Two

THE PRISON YEARS

DAY THIRTEEN IN THE TOWER

Sonnet 39
Thou Art All The Better Part Of Me
20 February 1601

Oxford records his father-son relationship with Southampton as clearly as he can in the diary, writing that the younger earl is "all the better part of me" and, in fact, that Southampton is "mine own self." Nevertheless they must remain "divided" and "lose name of single one" because of Oxford's bargaining to save his son's life – a deal that requires total "separation" of them in public. Meanwhile they remain physically separated; but Oxford enjoys the presence of his royal son in his mind and heart and in these private sonnets.

Sonnet 39	Translation
O how thy worth with manners may I sing,	O, how can I properly celebrate your royal blood
When thou art all the better part of me?	When, being my son, you are my better half?
What can mine own praise to mine own self bring,	What can my own praise to my own self bring,
And what is't but mine own, when I praise thee?	And what is it but for me when I praise you?
Even for this, let us divided live,	For this reason we can't recognize each other,
And our dear love lose name of single one,	And as father and royal son be not named,
That by this separation I may give	So by this disavowal I may [privately] give
That due to thee which thou deserv'st alone.	The homage to you [herein] that you deserve.
Oh absence, what a torment wouldst thou prove,	O, your absence [in the Tower] would be a torment
Were it not thy sour leisure gave sweet leave	If your time in disgrace didn't give me permission
To entertain the time with thoughts of love,	To spend it with thoughts of your royal self,
Which time and thoughts so sweetly dost deceive,	Which passes the time and my thoughts so royally,
And that thou teachest how to make one twain	And so you show how two of you are one,
By praising him here who dost hence remain.	By living here while you remain [in prison].

1 OH HOW THY WORTH WITH MANNERS MAY I SING,
O, how can I express your royal blood by means of conventional poetry; **THY WORTH** = your royalty; "Weigh you the *worth* and honor of a king" – *Troilus and Cressida*, 2.2.26; Oxford was certainly aware of the letters "w-o-r-t-h" in "Wriothesley" and played upon them in *worth* and *worthy*; **MANNERS** = forms of behavior, forms of writing, forms of emotion such as grief, as in "'Tis very true, my grief lies all within, and *these external manners of lament* are merely shadows to the unseen grief that swells with silence in the tortured soul" – *Richard II*, 4.1.295-29; means of writing these sonnets, according to the "noted weed" (Sonnet 76, line 6) or familiar garb of poetry; the customary manner of poets; way of acting; form of behavior or action; "Defect of *manners*, want of government" – *1 Henry IV*, 3.1.184, referring to lack of self-control; "Manner = (legal) act, word, deed; (legal) thing stolen, stolen goods" – Crystal & Crystal; "the *manner* of it is, I was taken with the *manner*" – *Love's Labour's Lost*, 1.1.200, i.e., what happened was that I was caught in the very act.

REFERENCE EDITION 273

"And *this boy liker in feature to his father* Geoffrey than thou and John in **manners**" – *King John*, 2.1.125-126; "By her, in his unlawful bed, he got this Edward, ***whom our manners call the Prince***" – *Richard III*, 3.7.189-190; "Be thou blest, Bertram, and *succeed thy father in* **manners** as in shape! Thy blood and virtue contend for empires in thee, and thy goodness share with thy birthright!" – *All's Well That Ends Well*, 1.1.60-63 (in manners = in your behavior, moral conduct)

I cannot but find a great grief in myself to remember the Mistress which we have lost, under whom both you and myself from our greenest years have been *in a* **manner** brought up...
- Oxford to Robert Cecil, April 25/27, 1603
(Of the late Queen, on the eve of her funeral)

> Yea, 'gainst *the authority of manners*...- *Timon of Athens*, 2.2.143
>
> My tongue-tied Muse *in manners* holds her still - Sonnet 85, line 1
>
> Than public means which *public manners breeds* - Sonnet 111, line 4

In the Tower now is also Roger *Manners*, Fifth Earl of Rutland, a former friend of Southampton from their days at Cambridge University, who supported Essex and Southampton in the Rebellion and participated in it; **SING** = he is "singing" these sonnets, which are little songs or "hymns at heaven's gate" (Sonnet 29, line 12) or at the gate of Elizabeth's prison, the Tower of London; sonnets, songs, hymns and "prayers divine" (Sonnet 108, line 5) to a king or god on earth, for whom the "monument" of the collection is being built

2 WHEN THOU ART ALL THE BETTER PART OF ME?
ALL = Southampton, *One for All, All for One*; **THE BETTER PART OF ME** = speaking as father to his son, who is the "better part" of Oxford's being; (The phrase is used in the 1567 translation of Ovid's *Metamorpheses*, XV, 989, attributed to Arthur Golding – whose nephew, Edward de Vere, probably produced the translation as a teenager when both lived at Cecil House)

3 WHAT CAN MINE OWN PRAISE TO MINE OWN SELF BRING
MINE OWN SELF = Southampton is Oxford's better "self"; Oxford wonders what good his praise for his son might achieve, since he is merely praising his better self.

"*A* **son** *of* **mine own**" – Oxford to Burghley, March 17, 1575

> Thou hast not lived to kill *a son of mine*
> - *3 Henry VI*, 5.6.36
>
> I give this heavy weight from off *my head*,
> And this unwieldy scepter from *my hand*,
> The pride of kingly sway from out *my heart*;
> With *mine own* tears I wash away *my balm*,
> With *mine own* hands I give away *my crown*,
> With *mine own* tongue deny *my sacred state*,
> With *mine own* breath release all duteous oaths
> - *Richard II*, 4.1.204-210
>
> I will be very kind, and liberal
> To *mine own* children in good bringing-up
> - *The Taming of the Shrew*, 1.1.98-99

4 AND WHAT IS'T BUT MINE OWN WHEN I PRAISE THEE?
AND WHAT, etc. = in praising his son, therefore, he praises himself, i.e., his own self

MINE OWN: my own son; Sonnets 23, 39, 49, 61, 62, 72, 88, 107, 110

No *son of mine* succeeding - *Macbeth*, 3.1.63

My gracious lord! My father!...
My due from thee is this imperial crown,
Which, as immediate from thy place and blood,
Derives itself to me...
This from thee
Will I to mine leave, as 'tis left to me
- *2 Henry IV*, 4.5.33,40-42,45-46
(Prince Hal to his father King Henry IV, speaking of his own son as *mine*)

If he please
To give me conquered Egypt *for my son*,
He gives me so much of *mine own* as I
Will kneel to him with thanks
- *Antony and Cleopatra*, 5.2.18-21

5 EVEN FOR THIS, LET US DIVIDED LIVE,
EVEN FOR THIS = for this reason; **LET US DIVIDED LIVE** = we must not reveal our relationship; this is part of the bargain Oxford is making to save Southampton from execution; they must be "divided" in public, and in the official records, though their blood is "undivided" as in "Let me confess that we two must be twain,/ Although our *undivided loves* are one" - Sonnet 36, lines 1-2; "Reason, in itself confounded,/ Saw *division* grow together" – *The Phoenix and Turtle* by "William Shake-speare", 1601

6 AND OUR DEAR LOVE LOSE NAME OF SINGLE ONE,
OUR DEAR LOVE = our bond as father and son; our blood link

DEAR = royal; also a term used by father to son; "Thou wouldst have left thy *dearest* heart-blood there, rather than made that savage duke thine heir, and disinherited thine only son" – *3 Henry VI*, 1.1.230-232; **LOVE** = royal blood; **LOSE NAME OF SINGLE ONE** = lose all chance for public recognition of our bond, which also means losing public recognition of your royal blood from the Queen; "Though thou repent, yet I have still the *loss*" – Sonnet 34, line 10; "And *losing* her, my friend hath found that *loss*" – Sonnet 42, line 10, referring to Southampton's loss of the Queen, both as his mother and in terms of having her support; **SINGLE ONE** = father and son, of one blood

Single nature's double *name*
Neither two nor *one* was called.
- *The Phoenix and Turtle*, 1601, 39-40

NAME = "That every word doth almost tell my *name*" – Sonnet 76, line 7; "In the old age black was not counted fair,/ Or if it were it bore not beauty's *name*" – Sonnet 127, lines 1-2, opening the Dark Lady Series to Elizabeth in February 1601, and indicating that their "black" or disgraced royal son had never been given the Queen's name, i.e., he has never been known as Prince Henry of the Tudor line; nor has he been given Edward de Vere's name; "Do not so much as my poor *name* rehearse" – Sonnet 71, line 11; "My *name* be buried where my body is" – Sonnet 72, line 11; **ONE** = Southampton, *One for All, All for One*; "Among a number *one* is reckoned *none*" – Sonnet 136, line 8, referring to Southampton; "Since all alike my songs and praises be/ To *one*, of *one*, still such, and ever so" – Sonnet 105, lines 3-4

7 THAT BY THIS SEPARATION I MAY GIVE
THIS SEPARATION = this public severance of our father-son bond; the separation caused by Southampton's imprisonment in the Tower; "In our two loves there is but one respect,/ Though in our lives a *separable* spite" - Sonnet 36, lines 5-6, i.e., the spite or malice of Fortune (Elizabeth) that has forced them to keep their

father-son relationship secret; "this sad Int'rim" – Sonnet 56, line 9, i.e., this sad temporary arrangement or intervening time, this separation

8 THAT DUE TO THEE WHICH THOU DESERV'ST ALONE:
THAT DUE TO THEE = my duty to you; what is due to you, being a king; ("*My due from thee* is this *imperial crown*" – Prince Hal, speaking as son and heir to his father the king, *2 Henry IV*, 4.5.40); that I may give that due to you in these sonnets; **ALONE** = Southampton, the "all" and "one" of his motto *One for All, All for One*; he alone deserves it

9 OH ABSENCE, WHAT A TORMENT WOULDST THOU PROVE,
OH = O, Oxford; **ABSENCE** = Southampton's absence of liberty, his imprisonment in the Tower; "The *imprisoned absence* of your *liberty*" – Sonnet 58, line 6; **TORMENT** = reflecting Oxford's own torment over the Rebellion, the trial and the executions, if carried out upon the two lords; "The *loss* of those three lords *torments* my heart" – *3 Henry VI*, 1.1.277; "The pain be mine" – Sonnet 38, line 14

10 WERE IT NOT THY SOUR LEISURE GAVE SWEET LEAVE
THY SOUR LEISURE = the hurtfulness of your time in the Tower; your royal "leisure" or pleasure or will; "Being your vassal bound to stay *your leisure;*/O let me suffer, being at your beck,/ The imprisoned absence of your liberty" – Sonnet 58, lines 4-6; **SWEET** = royal; **LEAVE** = permission, allowance, liberty; your royal permission; pardon; "your *leave and favor* to return to France" – *Hamlet*, 1.2.51; to excuse, pardon; "under *leave* of Brutus" – *Julius Caesar*, 3.2.86

11 TO ENTERTAIN THE TIME WITH THOUGHTS OF LOVE,
ENTERTAIN = spend, fill up; **THE TIME** = the dwindling time of Elizabeth's life; the time you are spending in prison; **LOVE** = your royal blood, i.e., thoughts of your true identity; "And *you and love are still my argument*" – Sonnet 76, line 10

12 WHICH TIME AND THOUGHTS SO SWEETLY DOST DECEIVE.
SWEETLY = royally; ("Richard, that *sweet* lovely rose" – *1 Henry IV*, 1.3.173); to avoid the torment of these days, Oxford would rather deceive himself by thinking only about his son's royal blood and claim to the throne

13 AND THAT THOU TEACHEST HOW TO MAKE ONE TWAIN,
MAKE ONE TWAIN = ("To give one person existence in two places at once" – Booth); Southampton is both in the prison and in Oxford's mind and/or in these verses; **ONE** = The sense being that Oxford and his son are joined as father and son, since Southampton is "all the better part of me" (line 2 above) but separated because of imprisonment in the Tower; "But here's the joy, *my friend and I are one*" – Sonnet 42, line 13; yet they must learn to be "twain" or two rather than one; "O Hamlet, thou hast*cleft my heart in twain*" – Queen Gertrude in *Hamlet*, 3.4.158; "Let me confess that we two must be twain" – Sonnet 36, line 1

14 BY PRAISING HIM HERE WHO DOTH HENCE REMAIN.
BY PRAISING HIM HERE = by praising Southampton, who is within Oxford, and within these sonnets; **HENCE** = "not here, at a distance" – Schmidt; i.e., by praising Southampton, who remains "hence" in the Tower; "This must be answered *either here or hence*" – *King John*, 4.2.89, i.e., either here on Earth on in another world; "Thy letters may be here, *though thou art hence*" – *The Two Gentlemen of Verona*, 3.1.248; "I have a kinsman a mile *hence*" – *The Winter's Tale*, 4.3.86; also possibly henceforth; from now on; "*Hence ever then* my heart is in thy breast" – *Love's Labour's Lost*

WHO DOTH HENCE REMAIN = Southampton is in the Tower and here, where Oxford is. These final words are especially poignant in light of the Lord High Steward's chilling final words at the Trial; and it is difficult to avoid the thought that Oxford wrote "hence remain" to echo them:

"You both shall be led from **hence** to *the place* from whence you came [back to the Tower], and there **remain** at Her Majesty's pleasure - from thence to be drawn upon a hurdle..."

Part Two

THE PRISON YEARS

DAY FOURTEEN IN THE TOWER

Sonnet 40
I Do Forgive
21 Feburary 1601

Anticipating Southampton's execution, Oxford forgives his royal son for having forfeited all hope of gaining the throne by committing treason. That possibility of succession is gone; now, to gain Southampton's life and freedom and honor, they must not acknowledge their father-son relationship; but at the same time, nothing can sever their true tie to each other.

Sonnet 40	Translation
Take all my loves, my love, yea, take them all,	Take back all of your royal self that you gave me,
What hast thou then more than thou hadst before?	And what more will you have than you had before?
No love, my love, that thou mayst true love call;	You will have no more true rights, my royal son,
All mine was thine, before thou hadst this more:	Because all you gave me was yours to begin with.
Then if for my love thou my love receivest,	Then if, for my sake, you receive what I give back,
I cannot blame thee, for my love thou usest;	I can't blame you for taking it; for you use it for me.
But yet be blamed, if thou thyself deceivest	But you can still be blamed if you deceive yourself
By willful taste of what thyself refusest.	By stubbornly having that blood while refusing it.
I do forgive thy robbery, gentle thief,	I forgive you robbing your own royalty, royal thief,
Although thou steal thee all my poverty;	Even though you take it all and make me poorer;
And yet love knows it is a greater grief	And yet royal blood knows it's more unbearable
To bear love's wrong, than hate's known injury.	To bear untruth than to bear public crime.
Lascivious grace, in whom all ill well shows,	You criminal king, who shines forth nonetheless,
Kill me with spites; yet we must not be foes.	Confound me with disgrace, yet we're not enemies!

1 TAKE ALL MY LOVES, MY LOVE, YEA TAKE THEM ALL!
TAKE = steal, take back, accept; **ALL** = Southampton, *One for All, All for One*; **MY LOVES** = all the kinds of love I have for you; all whom I love, i.e., Elizabeth and Southampton himself; **ALL MY LOVES** = "all those I love and all the love I give them" – Kerrigan

> For certain friends that are both his and mine,
> Whose *loves* I may not drop, but wail his fall.
> - *Macbeth*, 3.1.120-121

TAKE ALL MY LOVES = speaking to Southampton, referring to all his own "loves" toward him as father to royal son; also referring to the royal blood that Southampton has stolen from Elizabeth and himself, in terms of succession to the throne; "We shall not spend a large expense of time, before we reckon with *your several loves*" – *Macbeth*, 5.9.27; "You are the most immediate to our throne, and with no less *nobility of*

REFERENCE EDITION 277

love than that which dearest father bears his son do I impart to you" – *Hamlet*, 1.2.109-112; "*Your loves*, as mine to you" – *Hamlet*, 1.2.254; **LOVES:** Elizabeth was said to have "several loves" under different names, such as Gloriana, Cynthia, Diana, Venus, Astraea, etc.; "All by several names to express *several loves*: yet all those names make but one celestial body, as all those *loves* meet to create but one soul" – Dekker, *Old Fortunatus*, 1599

"As I have good cause, so do I give you all my hearty thanks for *the good zeal and loving care you seem to have, as well towards me* as to the whole state of your country" - Elizabeth to a Parliament delegation, 1559

"It manifesteth the largeness of *your good loves* and loyalties unto your sovereign." - Elizabeth to the Commons, November 30, 1601

"Therefore 'tis not amiss we tender *our loves* to him"
- *Timon of Athens*, 5.1.11-12

MY LOVE = my royal son; **ALL** = Southampton

2 WHAT HAST THOU THEN MORE THAN THOU HADST BEFORE?
Since you already had this royal blood, what more of it do you have than before?

3 NO LOVE, MY LOVE, THAT THOU MAYST TRUE LOVE CALL:
The answer is that Southampton has no more royal blood, or none that he may announce, than he had before; here Oxford uses "love" in both primary ways at once: first as royal blood itself, then as his royal son; **NO LOVE** = no (more) royal blood; ("And lastly, he protested for his own part, what he had done in the business was merely *for the love he bore to the Earl of Southampton*" – examination of Charles Danvers, read aloud at the trial; "that what for the old love I have borne you" – Oxford to Robert Cecil, May 1601); "I do truly *love you* & therefore *wish that every man should love you*, which *love* in these troublesome discontented times is sooner won by clemency than severity" – Thomas Arundell, brother-in-law of Southampton, writing to Robert Cecil during this time; a treacherous letter urging Southampton's execution so that he, Arundell, might receive certain lands – Akrigg, 129; **MY LOVE** = (addressing him as) my royal son; **TRUE** = Oxford, *Nothing Truer than Truth*; **TRUE LOVE** = true royal blood; i.e., you have no more true royal blood than you had before you stole it from us; ("your true rights" – Sonnet 17, line 11); "Your Truer Lover" = Ben Jonson signing a letter to Camden

4 ALL MINE WAS THINE, BEFORE THOU HADST THIS MORE:
ALL = Southampton, *One for All, All for One*; **ALL MINE WAS THINE** = all that I had, which was you, was already yours; **MINE** = "a son of mine own" – Oxford to Burghley, March 17, 1575; **ALL MINE** = my son, Southampton, who is "all one"; **BEFORE THOU HADST THIS MORE** = before you took more of it

5 THEN IF FOR MY LOVE THOU MY LOVE RECEIVEST,
Then if you receive my gift of your royal blood, in these sonnets, for yourself

6 I CANNOT BLAME THEE, FOR MY LOVE THOU USEST:
BLAME = echoing the charge of treason; "To you it doth belong/ Yourself to pardon of self-doing crime;/ I am to wait, though waiting be so hell,/ Not *blame* your pleasure, be it ill or well" – Sonnet 58, lines 11-14, referring to his son's royal pleasure or will; "That thou art *blamed* shall not be thy defect,/ For slander's mark was ever yet the fair;/ The ornament of beauty is *suspect*" – Sonnet 70, lines 1-3, referring to him as a prince of Elizabeth who is a "suspect traitor"; "O *blame* me not if I no more can write!" – Sonnet 103, line 5, after he himself has assumed all blame for the crime; **FOR MY LOVE THOU USEST** = because you are using this blood; "So prosper I, as *I swear perfect love* … And I, as *I love Hastings* with my heart" – *Richard III*, 2.1.16-17

7 BUT YET BE BLAMED, IF THOU THIS SELF DECEIVEST
BUT YET BE BLAMED = but nevertheless, you are to be blamed (especially if you deceive yourself);

"The King – the King's to blame!" – *Hamlet*, 5.2.328

THIS (THY) SELF = Q has "this" self, usually emended to "thy" self; thy royal self; "Make thee another self for love of me" – Sonnet 10, line 13, i.e., beget an heir of your royal self; "Make war upon themselves, brother to brother, *blood to blood, self against self*" – *Richard III*, 2.4.62-63; "Her ashes new create another heir as great in admiration *as her self*" – *Henry VIII*, 5.4.41-42, Cranmer predicting Elizabeth will have an heir to her throne; "*His royal self* in judgment comes to hear" – *Henry VIII*, 5.2.154

8 BY WILLFUL TASTE OF WHAT THY SELF REFUSEST.
BY WILLFUL TASTE = by tasting your blood willfully, i.e., by the use of your royal will; ("willful" = "sensual" as in "thy sensual fault" of Sonnet 35, line 9); by willfully refusing to take the blame; **OF WHAT THYSELF REFUSEST** = of that same royal blood you have forfeited by your crime; of the crime itself; i.e., Southampton must accept blame for his treason so that he will be able to accept the bargain for his life, which will mean the extinction of hope for succession to the throne; Oxford is forcing him into this deal to save his life

9 I DO FORGIVE THY ROBBERY, GENTLE THIEF,
I DO FORGIVE THY ROBBERY = I forgive you for committing treason and thereby stealing your royal blood and claim to the succession; by his crime, robbing both England and Oxford; "to pardon absolutely" – Schmidt; i.e., it is Oxford who is attempting to gain promise of a royal pardon for his son; "Forget, forgive, conclude and be agreed" – *Richard II*, 1.1.156; "Forgive me, country, and sweet countrymen!" – *1 Henry VI*, 3.3.81; **GENTLE THIEF** = royal thief; ("Such civil war is in my love and hate,/ That I an accessory needs must be/ To that sweet thief which sourly robs from me" – Sonnet 35, lines 12-14

10 ALTHOUGH THOU STEAL THEE ALL MY POVERTY:
ALL = Southampton, *One for All, All for One*; **THOU STEAL THEE ALL MY POVERTY** = you are stealing what I lack, which is you and your royal claim to the throne

11 AND YET LOVE KNOWS IT IS A GREATER GRIEF
LOVE KNOWS = royal blood understands; (the common phrase "Lord knows" or "God knows"); **GRIEF** = ("The only loss of my good name is of these *griefs* the ground" – Oxford poem in *Paradise of Dainty Devices*, 1576)

12 TO BEAR LOVE'S WRONG THAN HATE'S KNOWN INJURY.
TO BEAR = bearing the Cross; also, child-bearing, father to son; **LOVE'S WRONG** = the injury done to royal blood; **LOVE/HATE** = "For *love is worse than* **hate**" – Oxford poem in *Paradise of Dainty Devices*, 1576

> Lord Hastings: So prosper I, as I swear perfect love.
> Lord Rivers: And I, as I love Hastings with all my heart
> - *Richard III*, 2.1.16-17
>
> Whenever Buckingham doth turn his **hate**
> Upon your Grace, but with all duteous *love*...
> - *Richard III*, 2.1.32-33
>
> Made peace enmity, fair **love** of **hate**,
> Between these swelling wrong-incensed peers
> - *Richard III*, 2.1.51-52
>
> Besides, our nearness to the king in *love*
> Is near the *hate* of those *love not* the king
> - *Richard II*, 2.2. 126-127

More grief to hide than *hate* to utter *love*
- *Hamlet*, 2.1.119

INJURY = injustice, wrong, offence, insult, crime; "My lord, you do me *shameful injury*, falsely (treasonously) to draw me in these vile suspects" - *Richard III*, 1.3.88-89; "Report thy parentage. I think thou said'st thou hadst been toss'd from wrong to *injury*, and that thou thought'st thy griefs might equal mine, if both were open'd" - Prince Pericles to his daughter Marina, *Pericles*, 5.1.130-133; "The *injury* of tongues in courts and kingdoms" - *The Winter's Tale*, 1.2.338; "Or do your honor *injury*" - *Cymbeline*, 2.4.80

"O let me suffer, being at your beck,/ Th'imprisoned absence of your liberty,/ And patience tame to suff'rance bide each check, /Without accusing you of *injury*" - Sonnet 58, lines 5-8

13 LASCIVIOUS GRACE, IN WHOM ALL ILL WELL SHOWS,
LASCIVIOUS = ("modified in any case by grace, the word is milder than it might appear … in Elizabethan England, it could mean 'wanton, sportive'" – Kerrigan; **LASCIVIOUS GRACE** = addressing Your Grace, the king, as one who acted impulsively and irrationally; ("Above the rest in Court who gave thee *grace*?" – Oxford sonnet to Elizabeth, written in the early 1570s); **ALL** = Southampton; **ALL ILL** = Oxford address his son as Lascivious Grace, in whom "all ill" or his acts of treason nonetheless appear (in Oxford's view) to be "well" or royal; "Ah, but those tears are pearl which thy love sheeds,/ And they are rich, and *ransom all ill deeds*" – Sonnet 34, lines 13-14

14 KILL ME WITH SPITES, YET WE MUST NOT BE FOES.
KILL ME WITH SPITES = confound my purpose with the Queen's "spite" or malice toward you and me; if Southampton is executed, Oxford will be "killed" as well, since his son is "all the better part of me" (Sonnet 39, line 2); "As a decrepit father takes delight/ To see his active child do *deeds* of youth,/ So I, *made lame by Fortune's dearest spite*,/ Take all my comfort of thy worth and truth" – Sonnet 37, lines 1-4; "The time is out of joint. O cursed *spite*, that ever I was born to set it right" –*Hamlet*, 1.5.196-197; **YET WE MUST NOT BE FOES** = yet as father and son we are together and must not be enemies

Part Two

THE PRISON YEARS

OXFORD WARNS HIS SON

DAY FIFTEEN IN THE TOWER

Sonnet 41
Where Thou Art
22 February 1601

Conspirators of the Rebellion, within and without the Tower, are urging Southampton to take new action. Oxford warns his son, and records in this diary, that "still temptation follows where thou art."

Sonnet 41	Translation
Those pretty wrongs that liberty commits	The youthful crimes you may freely commit
When I am sometime absent from thy heart,	When I am unable to guide and protect you,
Thy beauty and thy years full well befits;	Befit your royal blood and youthful hopes,
For still temptation follows where thou art.	Because plotters for the throne still follow you.
Gentle thou art, and therefore to be won;	Royal you are, so people want your blessing.
Beauteous thou art, therefore to be assailed;	You are Elizabeth's son, therefore to be courted.
And when a woman woos, what woman's son	And when a Queen wills, what Queen's son
Will sourly leave her till he have prevailed?	Will act unlike a Prince till he gains her throne?
Aye me, but yet thou mightst my seat forbear,	But you refrain enthroning me as your father,
And chide thy beauty and thy straying youth	And banish your royal claim and youth,
Who lead thee in their riot even there	That lead you to revolt even in the Tower,
Where thou art forced to break a twofold truth:	Where you're forced to deny two truths:
Hers by thy beauty tempting her to thee,	Elizabeth's, that you have her royal blood;
Thine by thy beauty being false to me.	Yours, being my son who cannot tell the truth.

1 THOSE PRETTY WRONGS THAT LIBERTY COMMITS
Those royal crimes you committed when you had your liberty; **PRETTY** = little, inconsequential, petty; related to "beauty" or Elizabeth's blood; **PRETTY WRONGS** = royal misdeeds, characterizing the offense as less than treason, a suggestion made in Sonnet 35, lines 7-8: "Myself corrupting, salving thy amiss,/ Excusing thy sins *more than thy sins are*"; ("Such is my love, to thee I so belong/ That for thy *right* myself will bear all *wrong*" – Sonnet 88, lines 13-14); "What *wrong* is this unto the Prince your son" – *3 Henry VI*, 1.1.182; ("a *pretty plot*" – *2 Henry VI*, 1.4.58; "The *pretty follies* that themselves commit" – *The Merchant of Venice*, 2.6.37); "For though usurpers sway the rule awhile, yet heavens are just, and time suppresseth *wrongs*" – *3 Henry VI*, 3.3.76-77; "Peace, Mayor! Thou know'st little of my *wrongs*: Here's Beaufort, that regards nor God nor King, hath here distrain'd the Tower to his use" – *1 Henry VI*, 1.3.59-61; "And for *those wrongs*, those bitter injuries, which Somerset hath offer'd to my house" – *1 Henry VI*, 2.5.124-125; "Now afore God 'tis shame *such wrongs are borne in him, a royal prince*" – *Richard II*, 2.1.238-239; **PRETTY** = used often in Shakespeare in relation to a child, a son, a royal son: "This *pretty lad* will prove our country's *bliss*; his looks are full of peaceful majesty, his head by nature framed to wear a crown, his hand to wield a scepter, and himself likely in time to bless a regal throne" – *3 Henry VI*, 4,6,70-74, referring to the future

REFERENCE EDITION 281

Henry VII, founder of the Tudor dynasty; "Steeped in the faultless blood of *pretty* Rutland" – *Richard III*, 1.3.178; "Stay, yet look back with me unto the Tower. Pity, you ancient stones, those tender babes whom envy hath immured within your walls. Rough cradle for such little *pretty* ones" – *Richard III*, 4.1.97-100; "Grief fills the room up of my *absent child*, lies in his bed, walks up and down with me, puts on his *pretty* looks" – *King John*, 3.3.93-95; **THAT LIBERTY COMMITS** = that you committed by participating in the Rebellion when you had your liberty, unlike now; "Never did I hear of *any prince so wild a* **liberty**" – *1 Henry IV*, 5.2.9-10; (the wildness related to *sensual* fault and *riot*); **LIBERTY** = "And turned *my captive state to liberty*" – *3 Henry VI*, 4.6.3; "O that these hands could so redeem my son, as they have given these hairs their *liberty*" – *King John*, 3.3.71-72; "Humbling complaining to her deity got my Lord Chamberlain his *liberty*" – *Richard III*, 1.1.76-77; "How now! Is Somerset at *liberty*?" – *2 Henry VI*, 5.1.87; "Untainted, unexamined, free, at liberty" – *Richard III*, 3.6.9; "I am sorry to see you are ta'en from *liberty* … 'Tis his Highness' pleasure you shall to the Tower" – *Henry VIII*, 1.1.204-207; "The *imprisoned absence* of your *liberty*" – Sonnet 58, line 6

"The Earl of Southampton in the Tower is newly recovered of a dangerous disease, but in no hope of *Liberty*" – Father Rivers, February 12, 1603 (Stopes, 252, citing "Foley's *Eng. Jesuits* Vol. I")

2 WHEN I AM SOMETIME ABSENT FROM THY HEART,
ABSENT = not with you in prison; "O absence, what a torment wouldst thou prove" – Sonnet 39, line 9, also referring to Southampton's "absence" in the Tower); "Grief fills the room up of my *absent* child … my fair son!" – *King John*, 3.3.93, 103; "To take advantage of the absent time" – *Richard II*, 2.3.79; (the "absence" of a prince or king is counterpart to his royal "presence" as in the king's statement: "But I trust *my absence* doth neglect no great designs, why by *my presence* might have been concluded" – *Richard III*, 3.4.23-25); "A fever with the absence of her son" – *Cymbeline*, 4.3.2; "Fleance his son, that keeps him company, whose absence is no less material to me than is his father's" – *Macbeth*, 3.1.134-136; **THY HEART** = the source of your "love" or royal blood

3 THY BEAUTY AND THY YEARS FULL WELL BEFITS,
THY BEAUTY = your Tudor blood from Elizabeth; **THY YEARS** = your age; **FULL** = the abundance of royal blood: "Full many a glorious morning have I seen" – Sonnet 33, line 1; **WELL** = royal; "If thou survive my well-contented day" – Sonnet 32, line 1

4 FOR STILL TEMPTATION FOLLOWS WHERE THOU ART.
STILL = always; "Why write I *still* all one, ever the same" – Sonnet 76, line 5; **TEMPTATION** = as in the Temptation of Jesus by the Devil in the wilderness (Matt: 4.1-11); the temptation to declare your true identity or even to take the throne by force; "The action of tempting or fact of being tempted, esp. to evil, enticement, allurement, attraction" – *OED*, which also cites: "A severe or painful trial or experience; an affliction, a trial"; "And lead us not into temptation" – The Lord's Prayer; **WHERE THOU ART** = even there, in your Tower prison room; ("You must go to the place from whence you came and there remain during her Majesty's pleasure" – the Lord High Steward to Essex and Southampton at the end of the trial)

5 GENTLE THOU ART, AND THEREFORE TO BE WON;
GENTLE = royal; "That doth presume to boast of gentle blood" – *1 Henry VI*, 4.1.44; **WON** = One = Southampton; **WON** = as opposed to "lose" or losing the crown; to win the throne; ("Still constant in a *wondrous* excellence"
– Sonnet 105, line 6)

6 BEAUTEOUS THOU ART, THEREFORE TO BE ASSAILED:
BEAUTEOUS = filled with "beauty" or royal blood from Elizabeth; **ASSAILED** = sought after by friends and supporters who try to persuade you to lead them in a new effort to take the throne; ("Thou hast passed by the ambush of young days,/ Either not assailed, or victor being charged" - Sonnet 70, lines 9-10); attack; ("To beat assailing Death from his weak legions" - *1 Henry VI*, 4.4.16); "To attack with reasoning or argument; to address with the object of prevailing upon, persuading, convincing, or controverting" - *OED* (5); also "to attack with temptations" - *OED* (9), citing "Great and evil temptations shall befight and assail you"

(modern English), 1483; ("Well, seeing gentle words will not *prevail, assail* them with the army of the King" - *2 Henry VI*, 4.2.168-169; "My gracious lord, here in the Pariliament let us assail the family of York" - *3 Henry VI*, 1.1.64-65; "Sit down awhile, and let us once again assail your ears" - *Hamlet*, 1.1.34-35

7 AND WHEN A WOMAN WOOS, WHAT WOMAN'S SON
WHEN A WOMAN WOOS = Elizabeth had "wooed" him to think about gaining the throne by giving birth to him; she also had "wooed" him in that direction by supporting his alliance with the Cecils by marriage; to Southampton: "So thou be good, slander doth but approve/ Thy worth the greater, being *wooed* of time" – Sonnet 70, line 6, speaking of Elizabeth as "time"; "They live *unwooed*, and unrespected fade" – Sonnet 54, line 10, referring to Southampton in the Tower as not being wooed in any way by the Queen to be her successor.

"Be it lawful I love thee as thou lov'st those/ Whom thine eyes *woo* as mine importune thee" – Sonnet 142, lines 9-10, Oxford to Elizabeth, speaking of her imperial eyes that *woo* or command her subjects; Oxford speaking of Elizabeth wooing or tempting Southampton by making him think he will gain the throne: "*Wooing* his purity with her foul pride" – Sonnet 144, line 8

To "woo" is "to make solicitation or entreaty; to sue for" – *OED* (2), citing "*Wooing with tears* ... That Jove would give this Monster th'overthrow" – 1615; "Some in their actions do woo and affect Honour and Reputation" – Bacon, *Essays*, 1625; "He ... *wooed* them with many fair promises to repent" – Thomas Nashe, *Christ's Tears*, 1593; "My wayward husband hath a hundred times *woo'd me to steal it*" – *Othello*, 3.3.296-297; "What a life is this that your poor friends must *woo your company*" – *As You Like It*, 2.7.10; "You take a precipice for no leap of danger, and *woo your own destruction*" – *Henry VIII*, 5.1.138-139; "Come, come, in *wooing sorrow* let's be brief" – *Richard II*, 5.2.93; "You took occasion to be quickly *woo'd to gripe the general sway into your hand*" – *1 Henry IV*, 5.1.56-57

> She's beautiful, and therefore to be woo'd;
> She is a woman, therefore to be won.
> - *1 Henry VI*, 5.3.77-78

In this sonnet (as in others), Oxford uses sexual imagery as part of the "noted weed" or familiar costume of conventional poetry of love. Sexuality itself, however, is an essential part of the story recorded in the Sonnets, i.e., it led to the Queen giving birth to Southampton

WHAT WOMAN'S SON = "Art thou *a woman's son*" - *Venus and Adonis*, 201; You, who are Elizabeth's son and heir to her throne; referring to Southampton indirectly, as in: "Look *what an unthrift* in the world doth spend" – Sonnet 9, line 9; "Shakespeare's first published work, *Venus and Adonis*, described a 'woman's son', Adonis, who refuses the advances of the goddess of love: Shakespeare may have expected readers (of this sonnet) to remember this still-popular poem, reprinted seven times by 1602" – Duncan-Jones; Oxford will make a comparison between Southampton and Adonis in Sonnet 53, lines 5-6: "Describe *Adonis* and the counterfeit/ Is poorly imitated after you"

8 WILL SOURLY LEAVE HER TILL HE HAVE PREVAILED?
Will (according to his royal will) hurtfully abandon the Queen; "Mischance and sorrow go along with you! Heart's discontent and *sour* affliction be playfellows to keep you company!" – *2 Henry VI*, 3.2.299-301; "Let me embrace thee, *sour* Adversity" – *3 Henry VI*, 3.1.24-25; "Things sweet to taste prove in digestion *sour*. You urged me as a judge; but I had rather you would have bid me argue like a father. O, had it been a stranger, not my child, to smooth his fault I should have been more mild" – *Richard II*, 1.3.236-240; "The grand conspirator, Abbot of Westminster, with clog of conscience and *sour* melancholy, hath yielded up his body to the grave" – *Richard II*, 5.6.19-21; **LEAVE** = ("Young King Richard thus removed, *leaving* no heir begotten of his body" – *1 Henry VI*, 2.5.71-72; "Leaving his body as a paradise, to envelop and contain celetial spirits" – *Henry V*, 1.1.30-31; "And *left* behind him Richard, his only son" – *2 Henry VI*, 2.2.18; **TILL HE HAVE PREVAILED** = until he has prevailed as England's monarch; ("Well, seeing gentle words will not *prevail, assail* them with the army of the King" – *2 Henry VI*, 4.2.168-169); "But now, howsoever, His

Majesty hath the report made unto him, which if it be forgotten shall little *prevail* me. But I hope in his justice…" – Oxford to Robert Cecil, May 7, 1603, writing of His Majesty King James

9 **AYE ME, BUT YET THOU MIGHT'ST MY SEAT FORBEAR,**
AYE ME = Oxford, addressing Southampton as his better self; **MY SEAT** = the royal throne, on which I would sit in the person of you, if you (the better part of me) became king; ("Which three, till now, never kept *seat* in one" – Sonnet 105, line 14; "Long may'st thou live in Richard's *seat* to *sit*" – *Richard II*, 4.1.218; the sexual overtone of "seat" is also appropriate, since Oxford and Elizabeth had been lovers and had conceived the boy to be raised as Southampton; "I do suspect the lusty Moor hath *leaped into my seat*" – *Othello*, 2.1.304; "Who [Tarquin], like a foul usurper, went about/ *From this fair throne to heave the owner out*" – *Lucrece*, 412-413, an example of Oxford combining the two meanings, i.e., political and sexual

FORBEAR = refrain from; refrain from taking; "I do fully perceive how much I am bound unto your Lordship, wherefore I am sorry that the shortness of the time this day which I had with your Lordship, and the presence of the alderman, made me *forbear* some things of importance in this matter of the tins" – Oxford to Burghley, March 28, 1595

10 **AND CHIDE THY BEAUTY, AND THY STRAYING YOUTH,**
CHIDE THY BEAUTY = banish your blood from the Queen; **THY STRAYING YOUTH** = your behavior such as in the Rebellion, i.e., do not rashly attempt to seize the throne

11 **WHO LEAD THEE IN THEIR RIOT EVEN THERE**
WHO = your royal blood and your rash personality; **LEAD THEE IN THEIR RIOT** = tempt or even lead you in their impulse to another Rebellion; try to have you declare your real identity and attempt to seize the crown; **EVEN THERE** = even in the Tower

> Whilst I by looking on the praise of him
> See *riot* and dishonor stain the brow
> Of my young Harry
> - *1 Henry IV*, 1.1.83-85

RIOT = In Tudor and Elizabethan England "riot" became synonymous with "trespass" and was legally extended to include rebellion or rebellious treason against the Crown, largely by the efforts of Edward Coke, attorney-general and prosecutor of the treason trial of Essex and Southampton: "His success in getting various popular *riots* and assemblies classified as treason brought the Tudor era to a close with the establishment of a markedly royal interpretation of the scope of treason" – Bellamy, *Tudor Law of Treason*, p. 48; by the 1570s "rebellion of all types was thenceforth a traitorous act … [and] assemblies of a *riotous* nature became synonymous with treason." (Bellamy, 81)

The Essex Rebellion was a "riot" that Robert Cecil was able to transform instantly into a revolt or act of treason against Elizabeth and the Crown, based on past Tudor legal practices that had been evolving: "In the fifteenth century disturbances of the type which occurred in 1517 [popular protests, etc., in the streets] would probably have been dealt with as *riot*, which was *trespass*, or if the miscreants had been well armed and armoured and displayed some form of military discipline then as the *treason* of levying against the king. Less likely, but a possibility none the less, was that the *riot* would be construed as in some way compassing or imagining the king's death … The judges' discussions [in 1517] were not merely academic: thirteen *rioters* were later found guilty and sentenced to the normal penalty for *treason*, to be drawn to the gallows, hanged, disemboweled and their bodies quartered." – (Bellamy, 20)

"O my poor kingdom, sick with civil blows! When that my care could not withhold *thy riots*, what wilt thou do when riot is thy care? – The King to his son, *2 Henry IV*, 4.5.133-135

12 **WHERE THOU ART FORCED TO BREAK A TWO-FOLD TRUTH:**
WHERE = in the Tower; **FORCED** = because you must save yourself from execution, you are forced or

compelled; **TRUTH** = Oxford, *Nothing Truer than Truth*; also, the truth itself; **TO BREAK A TWOFOLD TRUTH** = to go against, defy, as in breaking vows; to defy two truths; (Oxford tells Elizabeth the same thing in relation to himself and Southampton: "But thou art *twice forsworn* to me love swearing ... But why of *two oaths' breach* do I accuse thee" – Sonnet 152, lines 2, 5); Oxford has two sovereigns, Elizabeth and their royal son, Southampton, each of whom has been forced to break vows to the other two; i.e., Elizabeth must be false to Oxford and their son, Southampton; and Southampton, as this sonnet declares, must be false to both his mother, Elizabeth, and his father, Oxford.

13 **HERS BY THY BEAUTY TEMPTING HER TO THEE, HERS** = Elizabeth's truth, which is that you are her son; i.e., you must defy that truth by lying; **BY THY BEAUTY** = by virtue of your royal blood from "beauty" or Elizabeth; **TEMPTING HER TO THEE** = tempting her to declare the truth that you should succeed her

14 **THINE BY THY BEAUTY BEING FALSE TO ME.**
THINE = your own truth; **BY THY BEAUTY** = according to your royal blood from "beauty" or your mother Elizabeth; **BEING FALSE TO ME** = having to pretend that you are not my son; again related to what Oxford will tell Elizabeth in the Dark Lady series, i.e., Southampton must be *false* and so must Oxford: "To *swear against the truth so foul a lie*" – Sonnet 152, line 14; also, Southampton was legally "false" by having committed an act judged as high treason: "The usual adverbs in legal records alongside the descriptions of particular treasons are '*falsely*' and '*traitorously*'" – Bellamy, *Tudor Law of Treason*, p. 33; "To warn ***false traitors*** from the like attempts" – *Richard III*, 3.5.48

THE MONUMENT

THE PRISON YEARS

DAY SIXTEEN IN THE TOWER

Sonnet 42
She Hath Thee
23 February 1601

Oxford refers to Elizabeth (the so-called Dark Lady of the Sonnets) as the chief cause of his "wailing" because "she hath thee" in her prison. Both Elizabeth and Southampton are robbing Oxford of his destiny as the father of a king. They are "loving offenders" whom he must "excuse" and for whom he must suffer, Christ-like, "on the cross." He and his "friend" – his son – are "one" and the same blood, so they suffer together under Elizabeth's tyranny.

Sonnet 42	Translation
That thou hast her, it is not all my grief,	That you have Elizabeth [as mother] is not my woe,
And yet it may be said I loved her dearly:	And yet it may be said I served her loyally:
That she hath thee is of my wailing chief,	My chief sorrow is that she has you [in her prison],
A loss in love that touches me more nearly.	A loss of your royalty that hurts me more deeply.
Loving offenders, thus I will excuse ye:	I will excuse both royal mother and royal son.
Thou dost love her, because thou know'st I love her,	You do serve her, because you know I serve her,
And for my sake ev'n so doth she abuse me,	And for my sake as her subject she disgraces me,
Suff'ring my friend for my sake to approve her.	Causing my son to suffer for my sake in serving her.
If I lose thee, my loss is my love's gain,	If I lose you, my loss is your gain of life,
And losing her, my friend hath found that loss;	And in losing her, my son finds the same loss.
Both find each other, and I lose both twain,	Mother and son are together, and I lose both,
And both for my sake lay on me this cross:	And both for my good make me suffer [as Christ did]
But here's the joy, my friend and I are one;	But here's the [royal] joy: my son and I are one.
Sweet flattery! Then she loves but me alone.	Royal honor! In having you she has me in you.

1 THAT THOU HAST HER, IT IS NOT ALL MY GRIEF,
THAT THOU HAST HER = the fact that you have Queen Elizabeth as your royal mother and as your Sovereign Mistress, as I do; **ALL** = Southampton, *One for All, All for One*; **NOT ALL MY GRIEF** = not at all the reason for my grief; "The only loss of my good name is of these *griefs* the ground" – Oxford poem, *Paradise of Dainty Devices*, 1576, signed E. O.; "Than to be perk'd up in a glist'ring *grief* and wear a golden sorrow" – *Henry VIII*, 2.3.21-22; **GRIEF** = "Ay, Margaret; my heart is down'd with *grief*, whose flood begins to flow within mine eyes" – *2 Henry VI*, 3.1.198-199

2 AND YET IT MAY BE SAID I LOVED HER DEARLY;
I LOVED HER DEARLY = I served Elizabeth as my royal mistress; "In this common shipwreck, mine is above all the rest, who least regarded, though often comforted, of all her followers, she hath left to try my fortune among the alterations of time and chance" – Oxford to Robert Cecil, speaking after her death of his

relationship with Elizabeth – April 25/27, 1603

>Thou didst *love* York, and I am son to York
>- *3 Henry VI*, 2.6.73

>One dear son shall I twice lose
>- *The Tempest*, 5.1.176-77

DEARLY = as befitting her royalty; "And greets Your Highness *dearly*" – *Cymbeline*, 1.6.13; as befitting the mother of his son; "Bade me rely on him as on my father, and he would love me *dearly as his child*" – *Richard III*, 2.2.25-26; "And my good friend, thy voluntary oath lives in this bosom, *dearly* cherished" – *King John*, 3.2.33-34; "To love her for her mother's sake, that loved him, heaven knows how *dearly*" – *Henry VIII*, 4.2.137-138; "The duke my father loved his father *dearly*" – *As You Like It*, 1.3.28; "Who, when he knows thou art the Empress' babe, will hold thee ***dearly*** for thy mother's sake" – *Titus Andronicus*, 5.1.35-36; "Judge, O you gods, how dearly Caesar loved him!" – *Julius Caesar*, 3.2.183; "He loved his mother *dearly*" – *Coriolanus*, 5.4.15

3 THAT SHE HATH THEE IS OF MY WAILING CHIEF, THAT SHE HATH THEE = the fact that Elizabeth has you as her prisoner in the Tower; **IS OF MY WAILING CHIEF** = is the primary reason for my suffering

WAILING = mourning, as at a funeral; alluding to his mourning at the funeral after Southampton's anticipated execution; ("*Wailing* our *losses*, whiles the foe doth rage" – *3 Henry VI*, 2.3.26; "my mother weeping, my father *wailing*" – *The Two Gentlemen of Verona*, 2.3.6-7)

WAILING CHIEF = echoing "the already common term 'chief mourner,' the nearest relative present at a funeral" – Booth; (In Sonnet 127, opening the Dark Lady series upon the Rebellion, Oxford writes of Elizabeth's eyes as "mourners" at the funeral of her son – that is, mourning the death of her son's ability to claim the throne. Here in the Fair Youth series, Oxford himself is "chief mourner" as father of Southampton); "whereof I am grown old and spent the *chiefest* time of mine age" – Oxford to Robert Cecil, June 19, 1603); "I was the *chief* that raised him to the crown" – *3 Henry VI*, 3.3.262; "But why commands the King that his *chief* followers lodge in towns about him" – *3 Henry VI*, 4.3.12-13

4 A LOSS IN LOVE THAT TOUCHES ME MORE NEARLY.
LOSS IN LOVE = loss of royal blood and claim to the throne; **LOSS** = usually, in Shakespeare, related to loss by death; but also the loss of loyalty or friendship; ("I cannot but find a great grief in myself to remember the Mistress which we have *lost*" – Oxford to Robert Cecil, April 25/27, referring to the death of Queen Elizabeth; "And can do nought but *wail her darling's loss*" – *2 Henry VI*, 3.1.216; "The *loss of those three lords* torments my heart" – *3 Henry VI*, 1.1.276-277; "And so obsequious will thy father be, even *for the loss of thee*, having no more, as Priam was for all his valiant sons" – *3 Henry VI*, 2.5.118-120; "Great lords, wise men ne'er sit and wail their *loss*" – *3 Henry VI*, 5.4.1; "Then let me stay; and, father, do you fly: your *loss* is great, so your regard should be; my worth unknown, no *loss* is known in me. Upon my death the French can little boast" – *1 Henry VI*, 4.5.21-24; "That *Henry's death, my lovely Edward's death, their kingdom's loss*" – *Richard III*, 1.3.192-193; **LOVE** = "My lord and sovereign, and thy vowed friend, I come, in *kindness and unfeigned love*" – *3 Henry VI*, 3.3.50-51

TOUCHES ME MORE NEARLY = ("has a more immediate bearing on me" – Duncan-Jones); causes me to suffer for a more intimate reason, as your father, being *near to* each other in blood; **NEARLY** = "Intimately, pressingly; *nearly* also meant *with close kinship*" – Booth; "Such *neighbor-nearness to our sacred blood*" – *Richard II*, 1.1.119; "***Near to the King in blood***, and ***near in love***" – *Richard II*, 3.1.17;

>Besides, our *nearness to the king in love*
>Is *near* the hate of those not *love* the king...
>Because we have ever been *near the king*

- *Richard II*, 2.2.126-127, 133

"Using therein the advice and authority of those who are *near* me, whose discretion I esteem so great"
- Oxford, at thirteen in 1563, writing (in French) to Sir William Cecil, his guardian, the future Lord Burghley and his future father-in-law

"Wherefore not as a stranger but in the old style I do assure you that you shall have no faster friend or well-wisher unto you than myself, with either in kindness which I find beyond my expectation in you, or in *kindred* whereby none is *nearer* allied than myself…"
- Oxford to Robert Cecil, March 1601, about one month after this sonnet is being written, and when Cecil was securing (or had secured) the sparing of Southampton's life by the Queen (which may account for the "kindness which I find beyond my expectation in you" that Oxford mentions above)

"For I know Her Majesty is of that princely disposition that they shall not be deceived which put their trust in her, which good office in you I will never forget and always to my power acknowledge in *love* and kindness, hoping that as we be knit *near* in alliance, so hereafter *more nearer* by good and friendly offices."
- Oxford to Robert Cecil, February 2, 1601

5 LOVING OFFENDERS, THUS I WILL EXCUSE YE:
LOVING OFFENDERS = Elizabeth and Southampton, who are both royal "offenders" of "love" or royal blood; she by keeping him a prisoner, he by having gotten himself imprisoned and sentenced to death; **LOVING** = ("My gracious sovereign, my most *loving* liege" – *Richard II*, 1.1.21; "For by that means he was in hopes to have help of the citizens her Majesty's most loyal and *loving* subjects" – Sergeant Yelverton's speech about Essex at the trial); *loving* "echoes standard salutations, common in royal proclamations, in which *loving* was used like 'gracious' or 'noble' or 'faithful'" – Booth; "You *loving* men of Angiers," *King John*, 2.1.204

OFFENDERS = "If through ignorance in the Law I have **offended**, yet I humbly submit myself to her Majesty, and from the bottom of my heart to *beg her gracious pardon* if it please her" – Southampton at the trial; "The question was asked the Earl of Essex how he would deal with **offenders** and such as resisted him after he should be possessed of these things" – examination of Sir John Davis at the trial; "We do marvel that we have heard of no execution by martial law, as was appointed, of the meaner sort of rebels in the North … have an earnest regard to such, and *spare no **offenders*** in that case" – Elizabeth to the Earl of Sussex, 1569, after the Northern Rebellion; Chamberlain, *Sayings of Elizabeth*, 169.

Thy cruelty in execution
Upon *offenders* hath exceeded law
- *2 Henry VI*, 1.3.132-133

My liege, his railing is intolerable:
If those that care to keep your royal person
From Treason's secret knife and traitors' rage
Be thus upbraided, chid and rated at,
And the *offender* granted scope of speech,
'Twill make them cool in zeal unto your Grace.
- *2 Henry VI*, 3.1.172-177

Bind the *offender*,
And take him from our presence.
- *Cymbeline*, 5.5.300-301

I WILL EXCUSE YE = I will find an excuse by which Elizabeth can avoid sending you to your death and thereby harming herself as well; (i.e., by means of "misprision", announced in Sonnet 87); **EXCUSE** = ("But my Lord, I must tell you this by the way, that my Lord of Essex can no way *excuse* nor shadow this,

No. 42

his rebellious purpose" – Sgt. Yelverton at the Essex-Southampton trial); "So please your Majesty, I would I could quit all offenses with as clear *excuse* as well as I am doubtless I can purge myself of many I am charged withal" – Prince Hal to his father the King in *1 Henry IV*, 3.2.18-21)

6 **THOU DOST LOVE HER, BECAUSE THOU KNOW'ST I LOVE HER,**
THOU DOST LOVE HER = you love and serve Elizabeth; **I LOVE HER** = I love and serve her; "I serve Her Majesty, and I am that I am" – Oxford to Burghley, October 30, 1584; "What thing is *love*? It is a *power divine*/ That *reigns* in us" – poem attributed in 1589 to Robert Greene but probably by Oxford, emphasis added to royal allusions suggesting Elizabeth as the divine power who reigns with love

7 **AND FOR MY SAKE EVEN SO DOTH SHE ABUSE ME,**
FOR MY SAKE = on my behalf; **EV'N SO** = for this reason; **DOTH SHE ABUSE ME** = does the Queen afflict me with such pain; i.e., what she does to/for you she does to/for me; an echo of *forsake*; "Then beauteous niggard, why dost thou *abuse*/ The bounteous largess given thee to give?" – Sonnet 4, lines 5-6; "All which *approve* [see next line] Her Majesty to be greatly *abused* with many proofs" – Oxford memo, circa 1601-02, Cecil Papers 146.19, Chiljan 71; "I dare not say how much Your Majesty is *abused* ... I beseech Your Majesty, in whose service I have faithfully employed myself (I will not entreat that you suffer it yourself thus to be *abused*), but that you will not suffer me thus to be *flouted, scorned and mocked* ... to inform Your Majesty that if you were to lay out any one penny is a foul *abuse*, and this on my credit and duty I do affirm to Your Majesty. In whomsoever the fault is, so far, to *abuse* themselves." – Oxford to Elizabeth, June 1599, Chiljan 122

8 **SUFF'RING MY FRIEND FOR MY SAKE TO APPROVE HER.**
SUFF'RING MY FRIEND = permitting my son to live; also, Oxford alluding to his own suffering; **FOR MY SAKE** = out of love for me, because she knows I love you; for my own benefit; for me, because my son and I are one and the same

TO APPROVE HER = to commend Elizabeth and serve her; to help her "prove" your case and thereby spare your life; **APPROVE** = "Show to be true, demonstrate ... corroborate, attest ... confirm authoritatively ... pronounce or consider to be good or satisfactory; commend; be in sympathy or agreement" – O. E. D.); "Both to defend himself and to *approve* Henry of Hereford, Lancaster, and Derby, to God, his sovereign..." – *Richard II*, 1.3.112-114; "Nay, task me to my word; *approve* me, lord" – *1 Henry IV*, 4.1.9; "Lady, I shall not fail to *approve* the fair conceit the King hath of you" – *Henry VIII*, 2.3.74-75; "True swains in love shall in the world to come *approve their truths* by Troilus" – *Troilus and Cressida*, 3.2.170-171; "All that may men *approve* or men detect" – *Pericles*, 2.1.51; "That if again this apparition come, he may *approve our eyes* and speak to it" – *Hamlet*, 1.1.31-32, Marcellus referring to his hope that Horatio will see the ghost of Hamlet's father and confirm what he and the others have already seen; "Thanks, you the valiant of this warlike isle, that *so approve the Moor*!" – *Othello*, 2.1.43-44; "I muse my mother does not *approve me further*" – *Coriolanus*, 3.2.7-8)

9 **IF I LOSE THEE, MY LOSS IS MY LOVE'S GAIN,**
IF I LOSE THEE = if I lose you by the executioner's axe

> So then you hope of pardon from Lord Angelo?
>
> The miserable have no other medicine
> But only hope.
> I have hope to live, and am prepared to die.
>
> Be absolute for death: either death or life
> Shall thereby be the sweeter. Reason thus with life:
> ***If I do lose thee***, I do *lose* a thing
> That none but fools would keep.
> - *Measure for Measure*, 3.1.1-8

REFERENCE EDITION 289

"*If thou survive*" – Sonnet 32, line 1; but, also, if I *lose* you by having to bury our relationship as father and son; "Lest I should *lose* the benefit of her good disposition" – Oxford to Robert Cecil, May 1601, writing of Queen Elizabeth; "Shall *lose* his head" – *2 Henry VI*, 1.2.34; "Were it not a pity that this goodly boy should *lose* his birthright by his father's fault" – *3 Henry VI*, 2.2.34-35; "Because in quarrel of the House of York the worthy gentleman did *lose* his life" – *3 Henry VI*, 3.2.6-7; "The King shall be contented: must he *lose* the name of King?" – *Richard II*, 3.3.145-146

MY LOSS IS MY LOVE'S GAIN = the loss of that public relationship will be the price paid for Southampton's life; ("Was never widow had so dear a *loss* … Were never orphans had so dear a *loss* … Was never mother had so dear a *loss*" – *Richard III*, 2.2.77-79; "Increasing store with *loss*, and *loss* with store" – Sonnet 64, line 8); **MY LOVE'S GAIN** = my royal son's life and even, ultimately, his freedom and pardon

10 AND LOSING HER, MY FRIEND HATH FOUND THAT LOSS;
LOSING HER = losing Elizabeth (publicly) as your mother; **MY FRIEND** = my son

HATH FOUND THAT LOSS = has thereby found that loss, of line 9, which is actually the **GAIN** of his life; "Who killed this prince? … 'Tis not an hour since I left him well: I honored him, I loved him, and will weep my date of life out for *his sweet live's loss*" – *King John*, 4.3.103-106; "The *loss* you have is but a son being King" – *Richard III*, 4.4.307; "Then, soul, live thou upon thy servant's *loss*" – Sonnet 146, line 9, Oxford to Elizabeth, about the loss of their son as future king; "For their advantage and your Highness' *loss*" – *Richard II*, 1.4.41

11 BOTH FIND EACH OTHER, AND I LOSE BOTH TWAIN,
BOTH FIND EACH OTHER = both Elizabeth and Southampton will gain by the sparing of his life; she will have her son, he will avoid death

AND I LOSE BOTH TWAIN = Ironically, however, I lose both Elizabeth and Southampton by gaining them; **TWAIN** = the two of them, a couple, i.e., mother and son; (In *The Phoenix and the Turtle*, 1601, the "twain" refers to Oxford and Elizabeth as a couple: "So *they loved, as love in twain*" – line 25; "How true a *twain,/* Seemeth this concordant *one*!" – lines 45-46); "To bless this *twain*, that they may prosperous be, and honored in their issue" – *The Tempest*, 4.1.104-105)

12 AND BOTH FOR MY SAKE LAY ON ME THIS CROSS.
And both Elizabeth and Southampton, for my sake (out of concern for me) cause me suffer, like Christ, by having to disavow our family blood tie; i.e., this is the bargain being made (Oxford is sacrificing his paternity of Southampton and, by extension, his identity as the writer "Shakespeare" who publicly dedicated his work and life to Southampton); "The matter, after it had *received many crosses*, many inventions of delay, yet at length hath been heard before all the judges – judges, as I say, both unlawful and lawful … and yet you shall see now the law to be clear of the Queen's side, notwithstanding it had *endured all the crosses* that can be possible" – Oxford to Robert Cecil, January 1602

13 BUT HERE'S THE JOY, MY FRIEND AND I ARE ONE:
THE JOY = "I weep for *joy* to stand upon my kingdom once again" – *Richard II*, 3.2.4-5

> As little joy, my lord, as you suppose
> You should enjoy, were you this country's king:
> As little joy you may suppose in me
> That I enjoy, being the Queen thereof.
> - *Richard III*, 1.3.151-154

> Sweets with sweets war not, joy delights in joy
> - Sonnet 8, line 2

MY FRIEND = my son, Southampton = the "private friends" who had received the earlier Fair Youth sonnets according to Francis Meres in 1598, in the inserted section (undoubtedly written by Oxford) of *Palladis Tamia*; ("precious *friends* hid in death's dateless night" – Sonnet 30, line 6); **ONE** = Southampton, *One for All, All for One*; we are of one blood no matter what; "Why write I still *all one, ever the same*" – Sonnet 76, line 5; "Since *all alike* my songs and praises be/ To *one,* of *one,* still such, and *ever* so/ … Fair, kind, and true, have often lived *alone,*/ Which three, till now, *never kept seat in one*" – Sonnet 105, lines 3-4, 13-14, on the death of Elizabeth and his son's failure to gain the *seat* or throne for the three of them

14 SWEET FLATTERY! THEN SHE LOVES BUT ME ALONE.
SWEET = royal; **SWEET FLATTERY** = ("the *monarch's plague, this flattery*" – Sonnet 114, line 2), i.e., royal delusion, i.e., falsity; **THEN SHE LOVES BUT ME ALONE** = then Elizabeth, in saving my son's life, actually saves mine; **ALONE** = Southampton, the "all" and "one" of his motto, *One for All, All for One*; **ME ALONE** = Oxford ("me") and Southampton ("alone") are joined as one and the same person; "Tired with *all* these, from these would I be gone,/ Save that to die, I *leave my love alone*" – Sonnet 66, lines 13-14, i.e., alone in the Tower.

THE PRISON YEARS

DAY SEVENTEEN IN THE TOWER

Sonnet 43
In Dead Night
24 February 1601

Waiting for the execution of Essex and attempting to save Southampton's life, Oxford returns to the theme of the first of the prison verses, Sonnet 27, when his royal son appeared to him as "a jewel hung in ghastly night." In the daytime, he sees Southampton as "un-respected" (a convicted traitor in disgrace); at night, during sleep, he sees him in dreams as the true royal prince. The "Suimmer's Day" of Southampton's royal blood has turned to darkness, shadow, and night; reality itself has been turned inside out. When Oxford writes, "All days are nights," he emphasizes Southampton by echoing his motto One for All, All for One, *as he does repeatedly throughout the diary of the Sonnets.*

Sonnet 43	Translation
When I most wink, then do mine eyes best see;	When I close my eyes, I see your royalty more.
For all the day they view things un-respected,	For all day my eyes see you in disgrace.
But when I sleep, in dreams they look on thee,	But when I sleep and dream, my eyes see you,
And darkly bright, are bright in dark directed.	And your royal self is greater than this shame.
Then thou whose shadow shadows doth make bright,	You, who transforms the Queen's dark frown into royalty,
How would thy shadow's form form happy show	How does your dark disgrace make happy show
To the clear day with thy much clearer light,	Of royalty with your much clearer light,
When to unseeing eyes thy shade shines so?	When to closed eyes your disgrace shines so?
How would (I say) mine eyes be blessed made	How could my own eyes see your royalty
By looking on thee in the living day,	By judging you only by what's on the surface,
When in dead night thy fair imperfect shade	When through your disgrace your royal blood
Through heavy sleep on sightless eyes doth stay?	Shows itself in the visions of my dreams?
All days are nights to see till I see thee,	Each day is to wait till I can physically see you,
And nights bright days when dreams do show thee me.	And at night my dreams show your royal truth to me.

1 WHEN MOST I WINK THEN DO MINE EYES BEST SEE,
WINK = shut or close my eyes, at night, during sleep; I see you best when I can't physically see anything at all

2 FOR ALL THE DAY THEY VIEW THINGS UNRESPECTED;
ALL = Southampton; **ALL THE DAY** = all during this particular day of your royal life, when you are in prison and no one has respect for you; **UN-RESPECTED** = un-regarded, ignored, untold, secret; held in contempt, the way Southampton is in disgrace for having been convicted of high treason; "for princes are a model which heaven makes like to itself: as *jewels* lose their *glory* if neglected, so princes their renown if not *respected*" – *Pericles*, 2.2.10-13; in Sonnet 54, line 2 he calls Southampton "that sweet *ornament* which

truth doth give" and then goes on to speak of him as among "canker" blooms: "But for their virtue only is their show,/ They live un-wooed, and *un-respected* fade" – Sonnet 54, lines 9-10; "Then others for the breath of words *respect,*/ Me for my dumb thoughts, speaking in effect" – Sonnet 85, lines 13-14

3 BUT WHEN I SLEEP, IN DREAMS THEY LOOK ON THEE,
But when I'm asleep my eyes see you in my dreams.

4 AND DARKLY BRIGHT, ARE BRIGHT IN DARK DIRECTED.
BRIGHT = shining with royalty; **DARKLY BRIGHT** = Southampton shines with royalty in the dark; **ARE BRIGHT IN DARK DIRECTED** = my eyes are attracted or guided by the brightness of your royalty so I can see you in the dark; "And illumined, although closed, (my eyes) are clearly directed in the darkness" – Dowden

5 THEN THOU, WHOSE SHADOW SHADOWS DOTH MAKE BRIGHT,
Then you, whose shadow makes the real shadows bright or royal; the shadow cast by "the region cloud" or Elizabeth Regina's dark cloud of disgrace and shame in Sonnet 33, line 12; "What is your substance, whereof are you made,/ That millions of strange shadows on you tend?/ Since every one hath, every one, one shade,/ And you, but one, can every shadow lend" – Sonnet 53, lines 1-4, combining "one" for Southampton and "every" for E. Ver, Edward deVere, thereby joining father and son in the same darkness; **BRIGHT** = royal; ("Life is but a walking shadow" – *Macbeth*); "

6 HOW WOULD THY SHADOW'S FORM FORM HAPPY SHOW
THY SHADOW'S FORM = the form or appearance of you, by means of your shadow or that which casts your shadow; royal image; "Being the right idea of your father, both in your *form* and nobleness of mind" – *Richard III*, 3.7.13-14; "The world will be thy widow and still weep,/ That thou no *form* of thee hast left behind" – Sonnet 9, line 6; "When your sweet issue your sweet *form* should bear" – Sonnet 13, line 8; "In polished *form* of well-refined pen" – Sonnet 85, line 8; "To set a *form* upon desired change" – Sonnet 89, line 6; and later, after the succession of King James: "Where time and outward *form* would show it dead" – Sonnet 108, line 14; "For it no *form* delivers to the heart" – Sonnet 113, line 5; **FORM HAPPY SHOW** = create a happy appearance; **HAPPY** = royal; recalling "all happiness" of the *Lucrece* dedication

7 TO THE CLEAR DAY WITH THY MUCH CLEARER SLIGHT,
CLEAR = royal; "The *clear* eye's moiety, and thy dear heart's part" – Sonnet 46, line 12; "Let him but copy what in you is writ,/ Not making worse what nature made so *clear*" – Sonnet 84, lines 9-10; being cleared of treason: "The purest spring is not so free from mud as I am *clear* from treason to my sovereign" – *2 Henry VI*, 3.1.101-102; **WITH THY MUCH CLEARER LIGHT** = your shadow is so bright that it can't be seen in daylight; "When *thou thyself dost give invention light*" – Sonnet 38, line 8, i.e., the light of the sun, the golden light of kingship; "Nativity, once *in the main of light*,/ Crawls to maturity, wherewith being crowned" – Sonnet 60, lines 5-6

8 WHEN TO UNSEEING EYES THY SHADE SHINES SO?
UNSEEING EYES = Oxford's eyes, which are closed; the eyes of others, who cannot see you in the daylight; **THY SHADE SHINES SO** = your shadow shines so brightly, in my vision of you

9 HOW WOULD (I SAY) MINE EYES BE BLESSED MADE
BLESSED MADE = made royal or sacred; "He was *a king bless'd of the King of kings*" – *1 Henry VI*, 1.1.28; "And on this couple drop *a blessed crown*" – *The Tempest*, 5.1.202

10 BY LOOKING ON THEE IN THE LIVING DAY,
By trying to see you in the daytime; "Shall I compare thee to a Summer's *day*" – Sonnet 18, line 1, i.e., Southampton's "golden time" of royalty in the 1590s); **LOOKING ON THEE** = "*Looking on* the lines of my boy's face" – *The Winter's Tale*, 1.2.153-154; "What might I have been, might I a son and daughter now have *look'd on*: - The Winter's Tale, 5.1.175-176; "The sun *look'd on* the world with glorious eye,/ Yet not so wistly *as this Queen on him*" – *The Passionate Pilgrim*, No. 6, 1599; "Were it not pity that this goodly

boy should lose his birthright by his father's fault … Ah, what a shame were this! *Look on* the boy" – *3 Henry VI*, 2.2.34-39; "A son who is the theme of honour's tongue, amongst a grove the very straightest plant, who is sweet Fortune's minion and her pride; whilst I by **looking on** the praise of him see riot and dishonour stain the brow of my young Harry" – *1 Henry IV*, 1.1.80-85; **LIVING** = as opposed to dying by execution; "The *living record* of your memory" – Sonnet 55, line 8; "our ever-*living* poet" – the Dedication of 1609; **DAY** = golden royalty

11 WHEN IN DEAD NIGHT THY FAIR IMPERFECT SHADE
IN DEAD NIGHT = amid the gloom of your anticipated death; in the darkness caused by the shadow of disgrace that hangs over you; **DEAD** = evoking the expected execution of his son; "For precious friends hid in death's dateless night" – Sonnet 30, line 6; "How many a holy and *obsequious tear*/ Hath dear religious love *stol'n from mine eye*,/ As *interest of the dead*, which now appear/ But things removed that hidden in thee lie./ Thou art *the grave* where *buried* love doth live" – Sonnet 31, lines 5-9; **FAIR** = royal; **IMPERFECT** = convicted of treason, in disgrace; as opposed to your perfect likeness, which would only be possible if I could see you in person; **THY FAIR IMPERFECT SHADE** = your royal appearance, even within the shadow of your disgrace; (Q has "their" imperfect shade)

12 THROUGH HEAVY SLEEP ON SIGHTLESS EYES DOTH STAY?
SIGHTLESS EYES = Oxford's closed eyes; i.e., the image of Southampton comes to his father during sleep, staying upon his closed eyes; **STAY** = "*stay* thou by the lord" – *Julius Caesar*, 5.5.44; "Then the conceit of this inconstant *stay*/ Sets you most rich in youth before my sight" – Sonnet 15, lines 9-10; "From limits far remote, *where thou dost stay*" – Sonnet 44, line 4, referring to where his son is confined in the Tower; "That to my use it might unused *stay*/ *From hands of falsehood*, in sure wards of trust" – Sonnet 48, lines 3-4; "Being *your vassal*, bound to *stay your leisure*" – Sonnet 58, line 4; "Which for memorial *still with thee shall stay*" – Sonnet 74, line 4; "And life no longer than thy love will *stay*" – Sonnet 92, line 3; "Sets down her babe and makes all swift dispatch/ In *pursuit of the thing she would have stay*" – Sonnet 143, 3-4, speaking to and about Elizabeth, in the Dark Lady series, about her neglect of her royal "babe" or son while she pursues the very thing (her own blood and lineage) that he possesses

13 ALL DAYS ARE NIGHTS TO SEE TILL I SEE THEE,
ALL = Southampton, *One for All, All for One*; all days = all royal days of Southampton's life; all these days, for me, are actually nights; ("all days are gloomy to behold, i.e., look like nights" – Dowden); emphasizing the *day-to-day* verses of the diary, matching the days followed by nights of Southampton's imprisonment as he awaits execution; I cannot see you during the blinding day.

14 AND NIGHTS BRIGHT DAYS WHEN DREAMS DO SHOW THEE ME.
And the nights become bright with my dreams of you; **BRIGHT DAYS** = golden days of royalty; "Shall I compare thee to *a Summer's day*?" – Sonnet 18, line 1; an indication that Oxford waits until nighttime/darkness to compose these sonnets.

The Execution of Essex

February 25, 1601

On the night of February 24, 1601, Sir John Peyton, Lieutenant of the Tower of London, informed Essex he would die the following day. Because of his noble blood and high rank, he would not be hanged, drawn and quartered in public but, instead, beheaded in private. Between seven and eight o'clock the next morning, which was Ash Wednesday, Essex was led from his prison room to the Tower green.

Few of the peers who had been on the tribunal came to watch the execution, but more than a hundred others appeared nonetheless. Among the spectators was Walter Raleigh, one of Essex's enemies, who said he wanted to be able to answer any last-minute charges the earl might make against him. Others, however, felt he had come to "feed his eyes" on the sight of Essex's blood; and when they told Raleigh to move away, he withdrew to the Armory to watch from there.

Essex wore a black felt hat and black satin shirt covered by a black gown of wrought velvet. Approaching the low platform set up on a small square, he cried out:

"O, God, be merciful unto me, the most wretched creature on the earth!"

Then he addressed the high-ranking crowd:

"My Lords, and you my Christian brethren, who are to be witnesses of this my just punishment, I confess to the glory of God that I am a most wretched sinner, and that my sins are more in number than the hairs of my head!"

He confessed that *"this great, this bloody, this crying and this **infectious sin**,* whereby so many for love of me have ventured their lives and souls and have been drawn to offend God, to offend their sovereign, and to offend the world, which is so great a grief unto me as may be!" He prayed to be forgiven and asked God to bestow His blessing upon Elizabeth and her nobles and minister, adding that he had never intended to bring about her death.

"It was not till the axe had absolutely fallen that the world could believe that Elizabeth would take the life of Essex. Raleigh incurred the deepest odium for his share in bringing his noble rival to the block. He had witnessed his execution from the armory in the Tower, and soon after was found in the presence of the Queen, who, as if nothing of painful import had occurred, was that morning amusing herself with playing on the virginals.

"When the news was officially announced that the tragedy was over, there was a dead silence in the Privy Chamber, but the Queen continued to play, and *the Earl of Oxford*, casting a significant glance at Raleigh, observed, as if in reference to the effect of **Her Majesty's fingers** on the instrument, which was a sort of open spinet, 'When ***Jacks*** start up, then heads go down.' [The story may be apocryphal; or the same incident may have occurred earlier, in another context; or, in fact, it may have happened this way.]

"Everyone understood the bitter pun contained in this allusion. Raleigh received large sums from some of the gentlemen who were implicated in Essex's insurrection, as the price of negotiating their pardons." (Strickland, p. 674; citing *Fragmenta Regalia*, Sir Robert Naughton)

(VIRGINALS: A "virginal" was a harpsichord-like instrument with jacks [pieces of wood fixed to the keyboard levers] that plucked at wires to produce sound. "How oft, when thou my music music play'st/ Upon that blessed wood whose motion sounds" – Sonnet 128.1-2)

(HER MAJESTY'S FINGERS: "With thy sweet fingers when thou gently sway'st" – Sonnet 128.3)

(**JACKS:** "Do I envy those Jacks that nimble leap/ To kiss the tender inward of thy hand" – Sonnet 128.5-6)

Cecil in Full Power

"Elizabeth caused a declaration of the treason of Essex to be published, and a sermon very defamatory to his memory to be preached at St. Paul's Cross, by Dr. Barlowe, but the people took both in evil part. It was observed withal, that her appearance in public was no longer greeted with tokens of popular applause. Her subjects could not forgive her the death of their idol. Fickle as the populace have proverbially been considered, their affection for the favorite had been of a more enduring nature than that of the sovereign.

"The death of Essex left Sir Robert Cecil without a rival in the Court or cabinet, and he soon established himself as the all-powerful ruler of the realm. Essex had made full confession of his secret correspondence with the King of Scots, and also of the agent through whom it was carried on; and Cecil lost no time in following the same course, and through the same channel.

"As long as he (Cecil) had hopes of obtaining the hand of Lady Arabella Stuart, he had secretly advanced her pretensions to the succession. But when it was known that this high-born young lady had bestowed her heart on Lord Beachamp ... the unprincipled statesman (Cecil), whose politics were as crooked as his person, did all he could to poison the mind of his jealous sovereign against the innocent girl. In one of the private letters in his correspondence with James, the malign hunchback speaks with all the bitterness of a despised and disappointed man of her to whose hand he, the grandson of a tailor, had presumed to aspire..."
- Strickland, 675

"The fall of Essex may be said to date the end of the reign of Elizabeth in regard to her activities and glories. After that she was Queen only in name. She listened to her councilors, signed her papers, and tried to retrench in expenditure; but her policy was dependent on the decisions of Sir Robert Cecil."
– Stopes, 243

Part Two

THE PRISON YEARS

EXECUTION OF ESSEX
DAY EIGHTEEN IN THE TOWER

Sonnet 44
The Place
When Thou Art Gone
25 February 1601

Essex is executed by beheading at the Tower of London. Robert Cecil has gained all power to engineer the succession upon Elizabeth's death; and Oxford will be forced to go through Cecil, his brother-in-law, to save Southampton's life. In the eighth line he makes an unmistakable reference to the Tower as "the place" – a common euphemism for the monarch's fortress-like prison. Alluding indirectly to the death of Essex's mortal body ("the dull substance of my flesh"), Oxford refers to the first two of the four "elements" (earth, water, air, and fire) of life. He writes of having to attend "time's leisure" (the Queen's pleasure or royal will) that will likely lead to Southampton's death, and he records his funereal "moan" over this impending loss. Oxford and Southampton share "heavy tears" and "woe" over the tragedy of this wrongful execution.

Sonnet 44	Translation
If the dull substance of my flesh were thought,	If my hateful situation could be turned to thoughts,
Injurious distance should not stop my way;	Then the walls of the Tower couldn't stop me.
For then, despite of space, I would be brought	For then, regardless of them, I'd be brought
From limits far remote, where thou dost stay;	From anywhere to you [in your prison room].
No matter then although my foot did stand	Then it wouldn't matter to stand out here
Upon the farthest earth removed from thee,	[Outside the Tower] so far from you,
For nimble thought can jump both sea and land	Because my thoughts can jump over the walls,
As soon as think the place where he would be.	As soon as they think of where you are [inside the Tower].
But ah, thought kills me, that I am not thought,	Ah, but this thought kills me. I am not my thoughts
To leap large lengths of miles when thou art gone,	And I can't leap into the prison to be where you are.
But that so much of earth and water wrought,	Instead, because of the walls between us,
I must attend time's leisure with my moan;	I petition Eliza, moaning at your impending death.
Receiving naughts by elements so slow	I am imprisoned by this terrible slow waiting
But heavy tears, badges of either's woe.	With deep sorrow for your woe and mine.

(This sonnet is chronologically aligned with Sonnet 128 of the Dark Lady series.)

1 IF THE DULL SUBSTANCE OF MY FLESH WERE THOUGHT,
If my heavy (sorrowful) flesh could turn into the nimble thoughts of my mind; echoing the "flesh" of Essex that was destroyed by execution today, i.e., marking this momentous day in the diary by referring indirectly to the event; the *dull* (lifeless) *substance* of Essex's now-dead body is merely his *flesh*; **DULL** = in the next two sonnets, *dull* or *dully* refers (by indirect means) to Southampton's impending death: "Plods *dully* on, to

REFERENCE EDITION 297

bear that weight in me" – Sonnet 50, line 6; "Thus can my love excuse the slow offence/ Of my *dull* bearer" – Sonnet 51, lines 1-2; and thereafter, *dull* refers to the death of Southampton's royal claim: "Or if they sing, 'tis with so *dull* a cheer" – Sonnet 97, line 13; "Because I would not *dull* you with my song" – Sonnet 102, line 13; "*Dulling* my lines, and doing me disgrace" – Sonnet 103, line 8, referring to the removal of "grace" from his son and therefore from these sonnets (until they become a monument to preserve him); in one sense, *dull* refers to "clouded" or under the Queen's dark cloud because she refuses to recognize him and because of his treason; "Why then, give way, *dull clouds*, to my quick curses" – *Richard III*, 1.3.196; "Well-painted idol, image *dull and dead*" – *Venus and Adonis*, 212

2 INJURIOUS DISTANCE SHOULD NOT STOP MY WAY,

INJURIOUS DISTANCE = then the harmful, painful, unjust separation from you, who awaits execution; the wrongful imprisonment of a royal prince in the Tower; the unjust disgrace of Southampton, in terms of him being deemed a traitor; **INJURIOUS** = "wrongful, unjust ... detractory, hurting reputation, insulting ... hurtful, offensive" – Schmidt; "Like a *false traitor* and *injurious* villain" – *Richard II*, 1.1.91; "Call him *my King by whose injurious doom* my elder brother, Lord Aubrey Vere, was done to death" – *3 Henry VI*, 3.3.101-103 (spoken by the Earl of Oxford, ancestor of Edward deVere, upholding the House of Lancaster); "Call me their *traitor*! Thou *injurious* tribune!" – *Coriolanus*, 3.3.69; "*Injurious Time* now with a robber's haste crams his rich thiev'ry up" – *Troilus and Cressida*, 4.4.41-42; "With *time's injurious hand* crushed and o'erworn" – Sonnet 63 line 2; "The *injuries that to myself I do,*/ Doing thee vantage, double vantage me" – Sonnet 88, lines 11-12, the latter in reference to Oxford's sacrifice of his own name, reputation and paternity of Southampton so that his son may eventually be released from prison;

3 FOR THEN DESPITE OF SPACE I WOULD BE BROUGHT

DESPITE OF SPACE = because then, in spite of this distance between us, I would be brought by my thoughts

4 FROM LIMITS FAR REMOTE, WHERE THOU DOST STAY.

FROM LIMITS FAR REMOTE = from where I am, outside the limits imposed by the Tower walls; "Finding thy worth a *limit* past my praise" – Sonnet 82, line 6; "So long as out of *limit and true rule* you stand against anointed majesty" – *1 Henry IV*, 4.3.39-40; limit = "bound, barrier ... fixed time ... extent, reach ... district, confine" – Schmidt; "Then take my king's defiance from my mouth, the *farthest limit* of my embassy" – *King John*, 1.1.21-22; "the *limit of your lives* is out" – *Richard III*, 3.3.8; **WHERE THOU DOST STAY** = to where you are imprisoned; i.e., my thoughts would bring me to you, there in the Tower; the same "journey in my head" of Sonnet 27, line 3; ("For then my thoughts, *from far where I abide,*/ Intend a zealous pilgrimage to thee" – Sonnet 27, lines 5-7)

5 NO MATTER THEN ALTHOUGH MY FOOT DID STAND

It would be no matter, then, if I stood

6 UPON THE FARTHEST EARTH REMOVED FROM THEE,

UPON, etc. = as far as possible from you; **FARTHEST EARTH** = ("No *farther* than the Tower" – *Richard III*, 4.1.8; "the *farthest* limit of my embassy" – *King John*, 1.1.21-22; **REMOVED FROM THEE** = ("Then happy I that love and am beloved/ Where I may not *remove*, nor be *removed*" – Sonnet 25, lines 13-14; "Love is not love/ Which alters when it alteration finds,/ Or bends with the *remover* to *remove* – Sonnet 116, lines 2-4)

7 FOR NIMBLE THOUGHT CAN JUMP BOTH SEA AND LAND,

Because the nimble thoughts of the mind can jump over everything, whether sea or land

8 AS SOON AS THINK THE PLACE WHERE HE WOULD BE.

THE PLACE = the Tower of London; as soon as I can think, I would be with you in the Tower as "the place" where I want to be. The Tower was commonly referred to as such. Essex composed a poem "during his imprisonment in the Tower of London and within four days of his execution there," notes Steven May in *The Elizabethan Courtier Poets* of 1999, p. 250; and in that long poem, the condemned earl wrote:

> I see that my continuance in ***this place***
> Cannot be long...
> Ev'n in the meanest ***place*** to waite on thee...
> - The Earl of Essex, lines 75 & 330 of a long poem written to Elizabeth (but apparently never seen by her) while he was waiting in the Tower during the four days prior to his execution (Steven W. May, *The Elizabethan Courtier Poets*, 255-264)

"You both shall be led from hence to ***the place*** from whence you came" – the Lord High Steward, speaking to Southampton and Essex at the end of the trial on February 19, 1601; now "the place" where Essex was executed this day...

"Added a more vigilancy and care unto the safety of ***the place*** under my charge" – John Peyton, Leiutenant of the Tower of London, in his report about Lord Lincoln's meeting with Edward de Vere, shortly before the Queen's death on March 24, 1603

"We have thought meet to give you notice of our pleasure through the same to be extended by our own Royal power, which is only this. Because ***the place*** is unwholesome and dolorous to him (Southampton), whose body and mind we would give present comfort..." – King James, in his order of April 5, 1603, for the release of Southampton. (The earl walked out in the early morning hours of April 10, 1603.)

> "A *traitor* your degree, and the *dungeon your **place***, a ***place*** deep enough..."
> – *2 Henry IV*, 4.3.7-8

> Prince: I do not like *the **Tower**, of any **place***.
> Did Julius Caesar build that ***place***, my lord?
> Buckingham: He did, my gracious lord, begin that ***place***.
> - *Richard III*, 3.1.68-70

> In sight of God and us, your *guilt* is great;
> Receive *the sentence of the law* for sins
> Such as by God's book are adjudged to death.
> You four, *from hence to prison back again*;
> From thence unto ***the place*** of execution.
> - *2 Henry VI*, 2.3.2-6

> This ***place*** ... this privileged ***place*** ...
> - *1 Henry VI*, 1.3.43, 46 (The Tower)

> "To strengthen and support *King Edward's **place***"
> - *3 Henry VI*, 3.1.52 (royal position)

"...if he shall be brought to yield unto a custom only upon persons committed to that ***place*** for treason" – Privy Council letter, June 9, 1581, indicating that Oxford was released from the Tower after confinement there by the Queen following the birth of his son by Anne Vavasour in March that year.

9 BUT AH, THOUGHT KILLS ME THAT I AM NOT THOUGHT
But these thoughts kill me, because I cannot become my thoughts and travel to you; **KILLS ME** = echoing the fear that Southampton too will be executed; "Take *thought* and die for Caesar" – *Julius Caesar*, 2.1.187

10 TO LEAP LARGE LENGTHS OF MILES WHEN THOU ART GONE,
To be able to bridge the gap between us; **WHEN THOU ART GONE** = when you are dead; ("As who should say, '*When I am dead and **gone***'" – *1 Henry VI*, 1.4.92); **LARGE** = "Take heed, dear heart, of this ***large*** privilege" – Sonnet 95, line 13, referring to Southampton's *largess* and immense privilege as royal

prince; "One will of mine to make thy *large* Will more" – Sonnet 135, line 12, to the Queen, referring to her Will Shakespeare, the pen name devoted to her son and heir, as well as to her powerful royal will (and possibly to the legal will she should make); "My *large* kingdom for a little grave" – *Richard II*, 3.3.153; "our *large honours*" – *Julius Caesar*, 4.3.25; "That we our *largest* bounty may extend … I do invest you jointly with my power, pre-eminence and all the *large effects* that troop with majesty" – the King in *King Lear*, 1.1.52, 131-133; "Or there we'll sit, ruling in *large* and ample empery" – the King in *Henry V*, 1.2.226-227

11 BUT THAT SO MUCH OF EARTH AND WATER WROUGHT,
But since I am made only of these dull elements, earth and water; ("so large a proportion of earth and water have entered into my composition" – Dowden); **WROUGHT** = "Till nature as she *wrought* thee fell a-doting" – Sonnet 20, line 10, referring to Queen Elizabeth as "nature" who gave birth to Southampton; **EARTH AND WATER** = two of the four elements; "Does not our life consist of *the four elements*?" – *Twelfth Night*, 2.3.10; "The *elements* so mixed in him that Nature might stand up, and say to all the world, 'This was a man'" – *Julius Caesar*, 5.5.73-75; "I am air and fire; my other elements I give to baser life" – *Antony and Cleopatra*, 5.2.292-293; "He is pure air and fire; and the dull elements of *earth and water* never appear in him, but only in patient stillness" – *Henry V*, 3.7.22

12 I MUST ATTEND TIME'S LEISURE WITH MY MOAN.
Oxford must attend or wait upon the pace of Elizabeth's waning life; he must wait upon Her Majesty for any relief; he must wait upon his royal son's leisure, too; **ATTEND** = wait upon; "Thus I most humbly beseech Her Majesty to have a favorable consideration also of my *attendance here upon Her Majesty*" – Oxford petition, July 1592, Chiljan, p. 48; "either for the *attending* or meeting of His Majesty" – Oxford to Robert Cecil, April 25/27, 1603, referring to attendance upon King James when he arrives in London; "*Attending* on his golden pilgrimage" – Sonnet 7, line 8; "And captive good *attending* captain ill" – Sonnet 66, line 12, referring to Southampton as "captive" in dependence upon Robert Cecil as new "captain" of the government; **TIME** = the dwindling life span of Elizabeth; **TIME'S LEISURE** = the Queen's pleasure or royal will; **I MUST ATTEND TIME'S LEISURE** = "the image appears to be that of a petitioner waiting on a great man" – Ingram and Redpath; and in fact, Oxford is waiting on both the Queen and a royal prince; "*Attending* on his golden pilgrimage" – Sonnet 7, line 8, referring to subjects serving "his sacred majesty" the sun; ("And I, a tyrant, have no *leisure* taken/ To weigh how once I suffered in your crime" – Sonnet 120, lines 7-8); **MY MOAN** = with my grief; as at the funeral of my son

13 RECEIVING NAUGHTS BY ELEMENTS SO SLOW
RECEIVING NAUGHTS = getting nothing in return; (usually emended to "naught"); by this slow, dull pace of time, when my royal son spends his days and nights in prison

14 BUT HEAVY TEARS, BADGES OF EITHER'S WOE.
Oxford's and Southampton's shared grief over the execution of Essex today; ("O that *our night of woe* might have remembred/ *My deepest sense, how hard true sorrow hits*" – Sonnet 120, lines 9-10, to Southampton, looking back on the long "night" of his imprisonment); "And weep afresh love's long since cancelled *woe*" – Sonnet 30, line 7; **WOE** = "And sing bis (afresh) *woe* worth on me, forsaken man" – Oxford poem, *Paradise of Dainty Devices*, 1576; "bis" = French for twice or again or afresh; **EITHER'S** = "your and my" – Booth; i.e., yours and mine; "The speaker's *woe* ensues from his *imprisonment* in these two elements … the final *woe* resonates as 'O'" – Duncan-Jones, emphasis added; ("*Accursed Tower!* Accursed fatal hand that hath contrived this *woeful* tragedy!" – *1 Henry VI*, 1.4.75-76)

No. 44

Southampton to the Privy Council

Late February – Early March 1601

Southampton writes from the Tower to the Privy Council, some time after his trial of Feb. 19, 1601 and before March 19, 1601, when his life was spared (undoubtedly according to the advice of Oxford, acting as his "Advocate" or legal counsel, and possibly even written for him by Oxford himself):

I beseech your Lordships be pleased to receive the petition of a poor condemned man, who doth, with a lowly and penitent heart, *confess* his *faults* and acknowledge his *offences* to her Majesty. Remember, I pray your Lordships, that the longest liver amongst men hath but a short time of continuance, and that there is none so just upon earth but hath a greater account to make to our creator for his *sins* than any *offender* can have in this world. Believe that God is better pleased with those that are the instruments of *mercy* than with such as are the persuaders of severe justice, and forget not that he hath promised *mercy* to the merciful.

What *my fault* hath been your Lordships know to the uttermost, wherein, howsoever I have *offended* in the letter of the law, your Lordships I think cannot but find, by the proceedings at my trial, that *my heart was free from any premeditate treason* against my sovereign, though *my reason was corrupted* by affection to my friend [Essex] (whom I thought honest) and I by that carried headlong to my ruin, without power to prevent it, who otherwise could never have been induced for any cause of mine own to have hazarded her Majesty's displeasure but in a trifle: yet I can not despair of her favor, neither will it enter into my thought that she who hath been ever so renowned for her virtues, and especially for clemency, will not extend it to me, that do with so humble and grieved a spirit prostrate myself at her royal feet and crave her *pardon*.

O let her never suffer to be *spilled the blood of him* that desires to live but to do her service, nor lose the glory she shall gain in the world by *pardoning* one whose heart is without *spot*, though his *cursed destiny* hath made his acts to be condemned, and whose life, if it please her to grant it, shall be eternally ready to be sacrificed to accomplish her least *commandment.*

My lords, there are divers amongst you to whom I owe particular obligation for your favors past, and to all I have ever performed that respect which was fit, which makes me bold in this manner to importune you, and let not *my faults* now make me seem more unworthy than I have been, but rather let the misery of my distressed estate move you to be a mean to her Majesty, to turn away her heavy indignation from me. O let not her anger continue towards an humble and sorrowful man, for that alone hath more power to dead my spirits than any iron hath to kill my flesh.

My soul is heavy and troubled for *my offences*, and I shall soon grow to detest myself if her Majesty refuse to have compassion of me. The law hath hitherto had his proceedings, whereby her justice and *my shame* is sufficiently published; now is *the time* that *mercy* is to be showed. O pray her then, I beseech your lordships, in my behalf to *stay her hand,* and stop the rigorous course of the law, and remember, as I know she will never forget, that it is more honor to a prince to *pardon* one penitent *offender* than with severity to punish many.

To conclude, I do humbly entreat your Lordships to sound mercy in her ears, that thereby her heart, which I know is apt to receive any impression of good, may be moved to pity me, that I may live to lose my life (as I have been ever willing and forward to venture it) in her service, as your lordships herein shall effect a work of charity, which is pleasing to God; preserve an honest man (howsoever now his *faults* have made him seem otherwise) to his country; win honor to yourselves, by favoring the distressed; and *save the blood* of one who will live and die her Majesty's faithful and loyal subject.

Thus, recommending my self and my suit to your Lordships' honorable considerations; beseeching God to move you to deal effectually for me, and *to inspire her Majesty's royal heart with the spirit of mercy* and compassion towards me, I end, remaining,

Your Lordships' most humbly, of *late* Southampton, but now of all men most unhappy,
H. Wriothesley
(Stopes, 225-226; Salisbury Papers, vol. XI, p. 72; "after Feb. 19, 1601")

"Confession" of Henry, Earl of Southampton, after Feb. 19, 1601 (and probably after Essex's execution):

"Whereupon, willing to spend my time in her Majesty's service, to **redeem the fault** I had made in thinking that which might be offensive to her … my **accursed fortune** … I do therefore now prostrate myself at her Majesty's princely feet, with a true penitent soul for **my faults** past, with horror in my conscience for **my offences**, and detestation of mine own life if it be displeasing unto her. I do with all humility crave her **pardon**. The **shedding of my blood** can no way avail her … and do with so grieved a mind beg forgiveness … unfeignedly **repent** …" (Stopes, 227-229)

Southampton to Robert Cecil, after Feb. 19, 1601(and probably after Essex's execution):

"But now, seeing **my chief hope is in your desire to effect my good** … and I shall continue bound unto you, as I protest I do account myself already, more than any man living, which whether I live or die I make the world know to your honor." (Stopes, 231)

Part Two

THE PRISON YEARS

MESSENGERS REPORT
SOUTHAMPTON'S HEALTH
DAY NINETEEN IN THE TOWER

Sonnet 45
Thy Fair Health
26 February 1601

The Privy Council will take note of Southampton's "long sickness, which he hath had before his trouble." "His health was poor, and he was receiving the ministrations of Dr. Paddy both for a quartain ague and a swelling in his legs and other parts of his body" (Akrigg 131-132). Messengers on horseback bring word to Oxford from the Tower that Southampton's health has been stabilized. Oxford rejoices, but then, sadly, sends them back to the Tower with more correspondence for his imprisoned son. This information matches the historical evidence of Southampton's illness in the Tower. His "fair" health = his "royal" health.

Sonnet 45	Translation
The other two, slight air, and purging fire,	All the other forces of nature and life
Are both with thee, wherever I abide:	Still confine you and go wherever I am:
The first my thought, the other my desire,	One becomes my thought, the other my desire,
These, present absent, with swift motion slide;	Simultaneously and fully here and where you are.
For when these quicker Elements are gone	For when these barriers are gone,
In tender Embassy of love to thee,	While I write these royal sonnets to you,
My life being made of four, with two alone	My own life is still helpless against them
Sinks down to death, oppressed with melancholy,	And I sink down, dejected, toward my own death,
Until life's composition be re-cured	Until this "living record" is restored
By those swift messengers returned from thee	By those swift messengers from the prison
Who even but now come back again assured	Who return back to me again with assurances
Of thy fair health, recounting it to me.	Of your royal health, telling me about it.
This told, I joy; but then no longer glad,	I joy over this news. But then, in sorrow again,
I send them back again and straight grow sad.	I send the messengers back to you and cry anew.

*Privy Council, February 26, 1601: "**Attainted**, and fit to be executed..." - the name is left blank, but "probably intended to have been filled with the name of Southampton" – Stopes, 223*

1 THE OTHER TWO, SLIGHT AIR AND PURGING FIRE,
Having dealt in the previous verse with earth and water, the duller elements, Oxford now considers the other two elements that make up the composition of man: air and fire; **PURGING FIRE** = suggesting the cleansing fire of Purgatory, an apt description of this hellish time; ("I am to wait, though *waiting be so hell*" – Sonnet 58, line 13; "y'have passed a ***hell*** *of Time*" – Oxford in Sonnet 120, line 6, looking back on this time after Southampton's release)

REFERENCE EDITION

2 ARE BOTH WITH THEE, WHEREVER I ABIDE;
These elements are both with you, in the Tower, no matter where I happen to be; **WHEREVER** = echoing "Ever" of E. Ver, Edward deVere

3 THE FIRST MY THOUGHT, THE OTHER MY DESIRE,
The one (air) comprises my thoughts of you, the other (fire) is my desire for your life; "From fairest creatures we *desire* increase" – Sonnet 1, line 1

4 THESE PRESENT ABSENT WITH SWIFT MOTION SLIDE.
These elements are with me, but not with me; they slide back and forth between us; **ABSENT** = "Oh *absence, what a torment* wouldst thou prove" – Sonnet 39, line 9; "How like a Winter hath *my absence been/ From thee*" – Sonnet 97, lines 1-2, with Oxford framing the situation in reverse, i.e., rather than Southampton absent in the Tower, Oxford views it as his own absence from his son

5 FOR WHEN THESE QUICKER ELEMENTS ARE GONE
Because when these livelier and sharper elements are gone; (Booth notes the phrase "the *quick* and the dead" in the Apostle's Creed)

6 IN TENDER EMBASSY OF LOVE TO THEE,
In these royal official messages to you, a prince or king; ("It was only to the monarch or ruling magistrate that *embassies* were directed" – Hotson, p. 32); **TENDER** = royal; "The tender prince" – *Richard III*, 3.1.128; "His tender heir" – Sonnet 1, line 4; **EMBASSY** = official state messages; ("Silence, good mother: hear the *embassy*" – the King in *King John*, 1.1.6; "Now send *ambassage to thy neighbor kings*" – Marlowe, *1 Tamburlaine*, 725; "To thee I send *this written ambassage*" – Sonnet 26, line 3); **OF LOVE** = of royalty and royal blood

7 MY LIFE, BEING MADE OF FOUR, WITH TWO ALONE
My own life, being made of these four elements, with two alone; **LIFE** = a matter of life and death, with "death" in the next line; **ALONE** = the "all" and "one" of Southampton's motto *One for All, All for One*; i.e., Oxford's life is Southampton's life; **TWO ALONE** = glancing at the two of them, Oxford and Southampton, father and son; "Come, let's away to prison; *we two alone* will sing like birds in the cage" – *King Lear*, 5.3.8-9

8 SINKS DOWN TO DEATH, OPPRESSED WITH MELANCHOLY,
SINKS = "What, will *the aspiring blood* of Lancaster *sink* in the ground? I thought it would have mounted. See how my sword weeps for *the poor King's death*" – *3 Henry VI*, 5.6.61-63; **DEATH** = referring to the death of Essex and anticipating the death of Southampton, in contrast to "life" in the previous line; **OPPRESSED** = weighted down; an image of the fiery sun (royal son) in the air, sinking down in the west; "thou and thine usurp the dominations, royalties and rights of *this oppressed boy*" – *King John*, 2.1.175-177; "For thee, *oppressed* King, I am *cast down*" – *King Lear*, 5.3.5; **MELANCHOLY** = echoing Oxford's autobiographical portrait as Prince Hamlet in relation to crimes against royal blood

9 UNTIL LIFE'S COMPOSITION BE RECURED
Until my life (which is Southampton's life) can be restored (to wholeness and soundness), indicating Oxford's desperate attempt to save his son from execution

LIFE'S COMPOSITION = the composition of these sonnets, which contain "the living record" of Southampton for posterity; "this *composed* wonder of your frame" – Sonnet 59, line 10

RECURED = restored to health, healed; glancing at Elizabeth's Tudor Dynasty and England itself being "recured" by the succession of Henry Wriothesley as King Henry IX: "Which to *recure*, we heartily solicit your gracious self to take on you the charge and kingly government of this your land ... as successively from blood to blood, your right of birth, your empery, your own" – *Richard III*, 129-135

10 **BY THOSE SWIFT MESSENGERS RETURNED FROM THEE,**
By those swift messengers on horseback, i.e., servants who have ridden back and forth from the Tower with Oxford's messages for Southampton (including these daily sonnets) and messages from Southampton in return; ("*I'll to the Tower with all the haste I can… and then I will proclaim young Henry king*" – *1 Henry VI*, 1.1.167-169); "My very good Lord. Upon your *message* unto me by your servant Hickes, I received no small comfort" – Oxford to Burghley, March 20, 1595

11 **WHO EVEN BUT NOW COME BACK AGAIN, ASSURED**
The same messengers, who even now return on horseback to Oxford (bringing him assurances of Southampton's health, in the next line)…

12 **OF THY FAIR HEALTH, RECOUNTING IT TO ME.**
THY FAIR HEALTH = Of your royal health (assuring him that Southampton's fevers and swellings are not critical); speaking of Southampton's health to him directly; **FAIR** = royal; "From *fairest* creatures we desire increase" – Sonnet 1, line 1; (the quarto has "their" fair health, but Booth and others emend it to "thy" fair health.

13 **THIS TOLD, I JOY, BUT THEN NO LONGER GLAD,**
Oxford rejoices at the news that his son's health is stable, but then his thoughts return to the fact that Southampton is still a prisoner awaiting execution.

14 **I SEND THEM BACK AGAIN, AND STRAIGHT GROW SAD.**
Oxford sends the messengers back to the Tower, and immediately grows "sad" or "oppressed with melancholy" again. The image created in lines 10-14 is quite specific. It confirms the historical evidence of Southampton's illness in the Tower and supplies new information, i.e., that Oxford was continually sharing these sonnets with his royal son via messengers on horseback. It also indicates that Oxford and Southampton were communicating with each other.

THE PRISON YEARS

DAY TWENTY IN THE TOWER

Sonnet 46
By Their Verdict
27 February 1601

Oxford continues his daily sonnets by again pledging his devotion to Southampton, addressing him as his royal son. In this verse, he recreates the entire experience on the "quest" or jury at the trial, leading to the "verdict" of guilt by which Southampton continues to face execution.

Sonnet 46	Translation
Mine eye and heart are at a mortal war	What I see and what I know are at war in me
How to divide the conquest of thy sight;	Over how to share the sight of you.
Mine eye, my heart thy picture's sight would bar	My eye wants to stop my heart from seeing you,
My heart, mine eye the freedom of that right;	My heart wants to stop what my eye can see.
My heart doth plead that thou in him dost lie	As in the court, my heart pleads that you live in it,
(A closet never pierced with crystal eyes),	Inside a small space where no eyes can look.
But the defendant doth that plea deny,	But my eye, as the defendant, denies that plea,
And says in him thy fair appearance lies.	And says your royalty lives in you [in prison].
To 'cide this title is impanelled	For one to claim victory, summoned is
A quest of thoughts, all tenants to the heart,	A jury of thoughts, who live by the heart,
And by their verdict is determined	And they will determine by their verdict
The clear eyes' moiety, and thy dear heart's part:	Which side sees your source of royalty best.
As thus, mine eyes' due is thy outward part,	What I see with my eyes is the appearance,
And my heart's right, their inward love of heart.	What my heart sees is your royal blood within.

1 MINE EYE AND HEART ARE AT A MORTAL WAR
Oxford sets up a mock trial in which the adversaries are his eye and heart; **MORTAL** = a battle to the death, suggesting the mortality of his son as they await word about his execution; a glance at the fact that England itself would face a civil war over the throne if Southampton, despite his imprisonment, were to lead a new Rebellion against the crown.

MINE EYE AND HEART:

Pardon me, God, I knew not what I did:
And pardon, father, for I knew not thee…

And let our *hearts and eyes*, like *civil war*,
Be blind with tears, and break o'ercharged with grief…

Ah, no, no, no; it is *mine only son!*
Ah, boy, if any life be left in thee,
Throw up thine eye! See, see, what showers arise,

Blown with the windy tempest of my heart
Upon thy wounds, that *kills mine eye and heart*!
- *3 Henry VI*.2.5.68-87

Betwixt *mine eye and heart* a league is took
- Sonnet 47, line 1

2 HOW TO DIVIDE THE CONQUEST OF THY SIGHT:

Over how to divide the spoils of your conquered royal image or self; recalling the Rebellion, when Essex and Southampton aimed to take by force the power behind Elizabeth's throne; or to take the throne itself, by initiating civil war; the battle is now over whether Oxford's eye or heart can better see Southampton in the Tower; **CONQUEST** = "Be not self-willed, for thou art much too fair/ To be *death's conquest* and make worms thine heir" – Sonnet 6, lines 13-14; "The coward *conquest* of a wretch's knife" – Sonnet 74, line 11; "Ah, do not, when my heart hath 'scaped this sorrow,/ Come in the rearward of a*conquered woe*;/ Give not a windy night a rainy morrow/ To linger out a purposed overthrow" – Sonnet 90, lines 5-8, the latter when Oxford is warning Southampton to avoid the temptation to lead another "purposed overthrow."

3 MINE EYE MY HEART THY PICTURE'S SIGHT WOULD BAR,

My eye would prevent my heart from the sight of your picture or image; **BAR** = prohibit; "in the specifically legal sense in which 'to bar' meant 'to restrain (someone) from enforcing (some claim),' but with *pertinent, though logically un-harnessed, suggestions of barred prison windows*" – Booth; "These sat all in the court next the *Bar* before the High Steward" – contemporary account of the trial, at the beginning of which Essex and Southampton "made their appearance at the *Bar*".

> We'll **bar** *thee from succession,*
> Nor hold thee of our blood, no, not our kin
> - *The Winter's Tale*, 4.4.431-432

> Thinking to **bar** *thee of succession*
> - *Cymbeline*, 3.3.102

4 MY HEART MINE EYE THE FREEDOM OF THAT RIGHT.

My heart would deny my eye the freedom of having the right to see Southampton; **FREEDOM** = liberty, as he wishes for his son; **RIGHT** = related to the right of kingship, i.e., his son's right to the throne; also, his legal right; ("The dominations, royalties and rights of this oppressed boy" – *King John*, 2.1.176-177)

5 MY HEART DOTH PLEAD THAT THOU IN HIM DOST LIE,

My heart pleads in this mock courtroom that you, my son, live in it; also, Oxford alluding to his pleas to the Queen and Robert Cecil on Southampton's behalf

PLEAD = As Southampton made his plea for the Queen's mercy at the trial; ("as in your favorable justice it shall deserve, and prevent the dilatory *pleadings* which the injustice of Coe's cause will offer unto you" – Oxford's wife Elizabeth Trentham, writing on his behalf, November 20, 1602, dated from Hackney, to a judge of the High Court (Ward, 337); "O Henry, let me *plead* for gentle Suffolk!" – *2 Henry VI*, 3.2.288; "I never did incense his Majesty against the Duke of Clarence, but have been an earnest advocate to *plead* for him" – *Richard III*, 1.3.85-87; "But, sirs, be sudden in the execution, withal obdurate, do no hear him *plead*" – *Richard III*, 1.3.346-347; "The proudest of you all have been beholding to him in his life; yet none of you would once *plead* for his life" – *Richard III*, 2.1.129-131; "Yea, the elect o' the land, who are assembled to *plead* your cause" – *Henry VIII*, 2.4.59-60; "And when good will is showed, though't come too short, the actor may *plead pardon*; I'll none now" – Queen Cleopatra in *Antony & Cleopatra*, 2.5.8-9

> Thirdly, he caused and countenanced a lawyer, whose name I take to be Hyde, to *plead*
> against Her Majesty, notwithstanding that the sheriff opposed against it, Her Majesty
> having none there to *plead* for her.

    - Oxford circa 1601-1602, Cecil Papers 146.19 (Chiljan, 71)

  And 'gainst myself a *lawful plea* commence
  - Sonnet 35, line 11

6 (A CLOSET NEVER PIERCED WITH CRYSTAL EYES),
CLOSET = Oxford's heart is the royal closet, alluding to Southampton's prison room; i.e., the royal closet of Southampton as a prince or king by blood; ("The *private apartment of a monarch* or potentate; the private council-chamber; a room in a palace used by the sovereign for private or household devotions" – *OED*, 2a., indicating an historical usage only; also with religious overtones, 2b, "A pew in the chapel of a castle occupied by the lord and his family, or in a Chapel Royal by the Royal family"); "Ah, Gloucester, hide thee from their hateful looks, and, in thy *closet* pent up, rue my shame, and ban thine enemies, both mine and thine!" – *2 Henry VI*, 2.4.23-25; "O, answer not, but to my *closet* bring the angry lords" – the King in *King John*, 4.2.267-268; "Fetch hither all my boxes in *my closet*" – *Pericles*, 3.2.83; "But here's a parchment with the seal of Caesar; I found it *in his closet*, 'tis his will" – *Julius Caesar*, 3.2.129-130; "I have locked the letter in *my closet*" – Gloucester in *King Lear*, 3.3.11); **NEVER** = E. Ver, Edward deVere, *Ever or Never*; **CRYSTAL EYES** = transparent eyes; "As one might see *a damask rose hid under crystal glass*" – *Verses Made by the Earle of Oxforde*, Rawlinson Poet. MS 85 f.11, Chiljan 183; "Thou art a traitor and a miscreant, too good to be so, and too bad to live, since the more fair and *crystal* is the sky, the uglier seem the clouds that in it fly" – *Richard II*, 1.1.39-42

7 BUT THE DEFENDANT DOTH THAT PLEA DENY,
DEFENDANT = As Southampton was a defendant with Essex at the Trial; **PLEA DENY** = As Southampton's plea was denied at his treason trial; "But none can drive him from the envious *plea* of forfeiture, of justice and his bond" – *The Merchant of Venice*, 3.2.281-282; "But *mercy* is above this sceptered sway; it is enthroned in the hearts of Kings, it is an attribute to God himself! An earthly power doth then show likest God's when *mercy* seasons *justice*. Therefore, Jew, *though justice be thy plea*" – *The Merchant of Venice*, 4.1.191-196; "No rightful *plea* might *plead* for justice there" – *Lucrece*, stanza 236; "And 'gainst myself a lawful plea commence" – Sonnet 35, line 11; "How with this rage shall beauty *hold a plea*?" – Sonnet 65, line 3, with "beauty" referring to Southampton's blood right from Elizabeth, who is "beauty"; **DENY** = "And doth impeach the freedom of the state if they deny him justice" – *The Merchant of Venice*, 3.2.277-278; "And here comes Clifford to deny their bail" – *2 Henry VI*, 5.1.123; "Call in the letters patent that he hath by his attorneys-general to sue his livery, and deny his offer'd homage" – *Richard II*, 2.1.202-204

8 AND SAYS IN HIM THY FAIR APPEARANCE LIES.
THY FAIR APPEARANCE = your royal image; "had three times slain *th'appearance of the King*" – *2 Henry IV*, 1.1.128; "chased *your blood out of appearance*" – *Henry V*, 2.2.76; "God's mother deigned to *appear* to me, and in a vision full of majesty" – *1 Henry VI*, 1.2.78-79; "I love not less, though less *the show appear*" – Sonnet 102, line 2

9 TO 'CIDE THIS TITLE IS IMPANNELLED
'CIDE = decide; **THIS TITLE** = legal right of possession; claim to the throne; entitlement; ("What *title* hast thou, traitor, to the crown?" – *3 Henry VI*, 1.1.104; "King Henry, be thy *title* right or wrong" – *3 Henry VI*, 1.1.163)

IMPANELLED = summoned; "Compelled to appear in a court" – Duncan-Jones; "Constituted as a jury" – Schmidt

10 A QUEST OF THOUGHTS, ALL TENANTS TO THE HEART,
QUEST = inquest or jury; i.e., the tribunal of peers, with Oxford as highest-ranking earl, at the Essex-Southampton trial; "What lawful *quest* have given their **verdict** up unto the frowning judge?" – *Richard III*, 1.4.180-181; Oxford's early tutor, Sir Thomas Smith, wrote in 1577 that "enquest or quest is called this

lawful kind of trial" – Tucker; **THOUGHTS** = arguments that come from the heart; **ALL** = Southampton; **ALL TENANTS TO THE HEART** = Southampton lives as a tenant lodged in Oxford's heart

11 **AND BY THEIR VERDICT IS DETERMINED**
VERDICT = Recalling the verdict that Oxford and the other peers rendered against Essex and Southampton at the trial; "What is my offence? Where is the evidence that doth accuse me? What lawful *quest* have given their *verdict* up unto the frowning judge? Or who pronounced the bitter sentence of poor Clarence's death?" – *Richard III*, 1.4.178-182; "Thy son is banished upon good advice, whereto thy tongue a party-*verdict* gave" – *Richard II*, 1.3.233-234

DETERMINED = Adjudged; i.e., the jury determined by its verdict that both Essex and Southampton should be executed; alluding to the unspoken determination that Southampton will never succeed Elizabeth on the throne; "Forthwith that Edward should be pronounced a traitor and all his lands and goods be confiscate. What else? And that *succession be determined*" – *3 Henry VI*, 4.6.54-56; "So should that beauty which you hold in lease/ Find no *determination*" – Sonnet 13, lines 5-6, referring to the blood of Elizabeth, which had been leased to Southampton, finding no determination of succession to the throne; "He professes to have received no sinister measure from his judge, but most willingly humbles himself to the *determination of justice*" – *Measure for Measure*, 3.2.236-238; "There is a devilish mercy in the judge. If you'll implore it, that will free your life, but fetter you till death ... a restraint, though all the world's vastidity you had, to a *determined* scope" – *Measure for Measure*, 3.1.64-66,67-69; "determine = to resolve on, to decide, to settle" – Schmidt; "I do believe you think what now you speak; but what we *determine*, oft we break. Purpose is but the slave to memory, of violent birth but poor validity, which now, the fruit unripe, sticks on the tree, but fall unshaken when they mellow be" – the Player King in the play-within-the-play of *Hamlet*, 3.2.188-193, speaking lines that might well be directed to Elizabeth in relation to her failure to provide for her son's succession.

12 **THE CLEAR EYE'S MOIETY, AND THE DEAR HEART'S PART.**
THE CLEAR EYE'S MOIETY = the clear right of the eye to its *moiety* or *portion* assigned by the verdict; **MOIETY** = "The love I dedicate to your Lordship is without end; whereof this pamphlet without beginning is but a superfluous *moiety*" – dedication of *Venus and Adonis* by "Shakespeare" to Southampton in 1593; (undoubtedly Oxford recalls each word he wrote publicly to his son); **DEAR** = royal; **THE DEAR HEART'S PART** = the heart's portion of the "dear" or royal view of Southampton in the Tower; "Take heed, *dear heart*, of this large privilege" – Sonnet 95, line 13, to his royal son; on the surface level "dear" means keenly felt.

13 **AS THUS: MINE EYE'S DUE IS THEIR OUTWARD PART,**
DUE = what is owed to a king; also, what a king owes to his subjects; ("Pity the world, or else this glutton be,/ To eat *the world's due*, by the grave and thee" – Sonnet 1, lines 13-14); "My *due* from thee is this imperial crown" – Prince Hal to his father Henry IV in *2 Henry IV*, 4.5.40; **THY OUTWARD PART** = what can be seen or envisioned of him; ("Which hides your life, and shows not half your *parts*" – Sonnet 17, line 4)

14 **AND MY HEART'S RIGHT THY INWARD LOVE OF HEART.**
RIGHT = right of kingship; the right of you, my son, who are my heart; ("And your *true rights* be termed a Poet's rage" – Sonnet 17, line 11; ("Your *right of birth*, your empery" – *Richard III*, 3.7.135; **THEIR INWARD LOVE OF HEART** = your royal blood within you, being pumped through your veins by your heart, which both my eye and my heart can see; Oxford's silent, inward love for his royal son.

("As Sonnets 44 and 45 are a pair of companion sonnets, so are Sonnets 46 and 47" – Dowden; one of many such observations, made over the past century, suggesting that the poet must have written two or more of these private verses at a single sitting, before arranging them numerically and sequentially; in actuality Oxford is writing them to correspond with each day proceeding from the Rebellion).

THE MONUMENT

THE PRISON YEARS

BARGAIN MADE FOR SOUTHAMPTON'S LIFE
DAY TWENTY-ONE IN THE TOWER

Sonnet 47
A League is Took
Thy Self Away
28 February 1601

Oxford records that a "league" or bargain with Robert Cecil has been struck in order to spare Southampton from the same fate as Essex. The ransom price, however, will be the relinquishment by Henry Wriothesley of any claim to the throne. Meanwhile Oxford writes to express again that the image of his son is always with him. The lines further suggest that he already may have visited Southampton in the Tower to inform him of the "league."

Sonnet 47	Translation
Betwixt mine eye and heart a league is took,	My eye and my heart have made an agreement,
And each doth good turns now unto the other;	And now each does a good turn to the other.
When that mine eye is famished for a look,	When my eye tries to see you [in the Tower],
Or heart in love with sighs himself doth smother,	Or my heart smothers itself in your royalty,
With my love's picture then my eye doth feast,	Then my eye looks upon my royal son's picture,
And to the painted banquet bids my heart:	And bids my heart to see this portrait.
An other time mine eye is my heart's guest,	At other times, my eye is the guest of my heart,
And in his thoughts of love doth share a part.	And my heart shares its thoughts of his royalty.
So either by thy picture or my love,	So, either by your portrait or by being my son,
Thy self away, art present still with me:	You being away [in prison] are still here with me:
For thou no further than my thoughts canst move,	Because you can't leave my thoughts,
And I am still with them, and they with thee;	And I'm always with them, and they with you.
Or if they sleep, thy picture in my sight	Or if eye and heart sleep, your image in my mind
Awakes my heart to heart's and eye's delight.	Awakens my heart to both their delights.

1 BETWEEN MINE EYE AND HEART A LEAGUE IS TOOK,
Oxford announces he has made an agreement with Robert Cecil for Southampton's life to be spared; but he has not yet been assured by the Queen that she will stop the execution; "You peers, continue this **united league**" – *Richard III*, 2.1.2; **BETWIXT MINE EYE AND HEART** = also a compact between what Oxford sees in the world and what he feels in his heart, i.e., he has been forced into a painful compromise by agreeing to counsel Southampton to give up his royal claim; similar to lines of Thomas Watson, a protégé of Oxford, in *Tears of Fancy*, 1593: "My *heart* imposed this penance on *mine eyes* ... *Mine eyes* upon *my heart* inflict this pain" – sonnet no. 19 of the Watson work, much of it written by Oxford or with Oxford's inspiration and guidance.

> Pardon me, God, I knew not what I did:
> And pardon, father, for I knew not thee...
> And let our *hearts and eyes*, like *civil war*,

310

> Be blind with tears, and break o'ercharged with grief…
>
> Ah, no, no, no; it is mine only son!
> Ah, boy, if any life be left in thee,
> Throw up thine eye! See, see, what showers arise,
> Blown with the windy tempest of my heart
> Upon thy wounds, that kills *mine eye and heart*!
> - *3 Henry VI*, 2.5.68-87

LEAGUE = alliance, agreement, bargain, covenant; **TOOK** = pledged; from "take a pledge"

2 AND EACH DOTH GOOD TURNS NOW UNTO THE OTHER;
The two realities are helping each other; **NOW** = indicating

3 WHEN THAT MINE EYE IS FAMISHED FOR A LOOK,
FAMISHED FOR A LOOK = starved of being able to see his son in prison; **FAMISHED** = without your royal blood; "Making a *famine* where abundance lies" – Sonnet 1, line 7

4 OR HEART IN LOVE WITH SIGHS HIMSELF DOTH SMOTHER,
HEART IN LOVE = Oxford's heart, bathed in his son's royal blood; **SMOTHER** = also choke, i.e., with love and with emotional pain.

5 WITH MY LOVE'S PICTURE THEN MY EYE DOTH FEAST,
MY LOVE'S PICTURE = the vision of my royal son; (and probably Oxford owns a physical picture of him, too); **THEN MY EYE DOTH FEAST** = then I visit him in the Tower, where my eye can see him; **FEAST** = the feast of his son's image that he holds in his mind's eye: "Therefore are *feasts so solemn and so rare*" – Sonnet 52, line 5, referring to an actual visit of Oxford with Southampton in the Tower, when he could see him directly; "The pleasure that *some father's feed upon* is my strict fast – I mean *my children's looks*, and therein fasting hast thou made me gaunt" – *Richard II*, 2.1.79-81

6 AND TO THE PAINTED BANQUET BIDS MY HEART:
PAINTED = created; "A Woman's face with *nature's own hand painted*" – Sonnet 20, line 1; "Stirred by a *painted* beauty to his verse" – Sonnet 21, line 2; "And you in Grecian tires are *painted new*" – Sonnet 53, line 8; "*Painting* my age with beauty of thy days" – Sonnet 62, line 14; "Why should *false painting* imitate his cheek" – Sonnet 67, line 5; "I never saw that you did *painting* need,/ And therefore to your fair no *painting* set" – Sonnet 83, lines 1-2; "Truth needs no colour with his colour fixed" – Sonnet 101, line 6; **BANQUET** = the feast of Southampton for his eye; **BIDS MY HEART** = summons my heart.

7 AN OTHER TIME MINE EYE IS MY HEART'S GUEST,
At other times, my heart sees him and bids my eye to join in this inner sight.

8 AND IN HIS THOUGHTS OF LOVE DOTH SHARE A PART.
THOUGHTS OF LOVE = thoughts of royal blood; sharing in his son's inheritance.

9 SO EITHER BY THY PICTURE OR MY LOVE,
THY PICTURE = your sight, real or imagined; **MY LOVE** = my devotion to your royal blood; my royal son, by which I see you with my heart.

10 THY SELF AWAY ARE PRESENT STILL WITH ME,
Your royal self away, in the Tower:

> "Things removed" - Sonnet 31, line 8
> "O absence" - Sonnet 39, line 9
> "When I am sometime absent from thy heart" - Sonnet 41, line 2

REFERENCE EDITION

"Where thou art" - Sonnet 41, line 12
"Injurious distance" - Sonnet 44, line 1
"Where thou dost stay" - Sonnet 44, line 4
"Removed from thee" - Sonnet 44, line 6
"Present-absent" - Sonnet 45, line 4
"Where thou art" - Sonnet 51, line 3
"The bitterness of absence" - Sonnet 57, line 6
"Where you may be" - Sonnet 57, line 10
"Where you are" - Sonnet 57, line 12
"Th'imprisoned absence of your liberty" - Sonnet 58, line 6
"Where you list" - Sonnet 58, line 9
"Thou dost wake elsewhere" - Sonnet 61, line 12
"All away" - Sonnet 75, line 14
"Be absent from thy walks" - Sonnet 89, line 9
"How like a Winter hath my absence been/ From thee" - Sonnet 97, line 1
"This time removed" - Sonnet 97, line 5
"And thou away" - Sonnet 97, line 12
"You away" - Sonnet 98, line 13

STILL = always; ("i.e., even though you are away" – Booth); constantly, eternally.

11 FOR THOU NO FARTHER THAN MY THOUGHTS CANST MOVE,
For you cannot be any farther than my thoughts of you

12 AND I AM STILL WITH THEM AND THEY WITH THEE.
I am always with these thoughts, and they are always with you.

13 OR IF THEY SLEEP, THY PICTURE IN MY SIGHT
Or during sleep, your image in my inner vision; "But when I *sleep*, in dreams they [my eyes] look on thee" – Sonnet 43, line 3; **SLEEP** = also inactivity or a state of powerlessness: "And therefore have I *slept* in your report" – Sonnet 83, line 5; "Thus I have had thee as a dream doth flatter:/ In *sleep* a King, but waking no such matter" – Sonnet 87, lines 13-14, referring directly to his son as an unacknowledged king.

14 AWAKES MY HEART, TO HEART'S AND EYE'S DELIGHT.
Wakens my heart so it can see you, the delight of both my heart and my eye.

Part Two

THE PRISON YEARS

DAY TWENTY-TWO IN THE TOWER

Sonnet 48
Locked Up
1 March 1601

While working to save his son's life, Oxford is concerned that other conspirators inside the prison are urging Southampton to further revolt before the Crown has a chance to execute him.

Sonnet 48	Translation
How careful was I, when I took my way,	How careful was I to go through life,
Each trifle under truest bars to thrust,	With all the truth of these sonnets locked away
That to my use it might unused stay	So they might stay imprisoned and not be used
From hands of falsehood, in sure wards of trust?	By your enemies, and remain under guard!
But thou, to whom my jewels trifles are,	But you, compared to whom my sonnets are trifles,
Most worthy comfort, now my greatest grief,	You, most royal comfort, are my cause for grief,
Thou best of dearest, and mine only care,	You, the most royal prince and my only care,
Art left the prey of every vulgar thief.	Are left the prey of executioners and criminals.
Thee have I not locked up in any chest,	I have not locked you up in any prison,
Save where thou art not, though I feel thou art	Except here [out of Tower], though I feel you are
Within the gentle closure of my breast,	Inside the royal prison of my own heart,
From whence at pleasure thou mayst come and part;	Where come and go at [Your Majesty's] pleasure;
And even thence thou wilt be stol'n, I fear;	And even then I fear you'll be taken from me,
For truth proves thievish for a prize so dear.	For my son [a prince] is a royal prize for thieves.

(This sonnet relates to Sonnets 130-133 of the Dark Lady series.)

1 HOW CAREFUL WAS I WHEN I TOOK MY WAY,
CAREFUL = echoed by "care" in line 7; **TOOK MY WAY** = set out on the journey of my life; also, set out to write these sonnets to record my son's royal progress in relation to the dwindling time of Elizabeth's life; **MY WAY** = "Were I a man, a duke, and next of blood, I would remove these tedious stumbling-blocks and smooth *my way* upon their headless necks" – *2 Henry VI*, 1.2.63-65; "Torment myself to catch the English crown: And from that torment I will free myself, or hew *my way* out with a bloody axe" – *3 Henry VI*, 3.2.179-181; "I am amazed, methinks, and lose *my way* among the thorns and dangers of this world" – *King John*, 4.3.140-141

2 EACH TRIFLE UNDER TRUEST BARS TO THRUST,
EACH TRIFLE = each piece of writing (precious jewels or rings or tokens of bond: "And sweetest, fairest, as I my poor self did exchange for you to your so infinite loss; so in our *trifles* I still win of you" – *Cymbeline*, 1.2.49-52); **TRUEST** = Oxford's (*Nothing Truer than Truth*); **TRUEST BARS** = ("most reliable locks or barricades" – Duncan-Jones); also, the image of the **BARS** or locks and barricades of the Tower, where Southampton is a prisoner; "Through a secret grate of iron *bars* in yonder *tower*" - *1 Henry*

REFERENCE EDITION 313

VI, 1.4.10-11; **TO THRUST** = the image of Oxford hiding his written work; also in these lines, Oxford may be referring to the care he took to keep his royal son hidden from view, protected from plots and so on.

3 THAT TO MY USE IT MIGHT UN-USED STAY
STAY = remain under lock and key; be kept away from; "where *thou dost stay*" – Sonnet 44, line 4; also suggesting the hope for a "stay of execution"; "Retreat is made and *execution stay'd*" – *2 Henry IV*, 4.3.72

4 FROM HANDS OF FALSEHOOD, IN SURE WARDS OF TRUST?
FROM HANDS OF FALSEHOOD = away from those who are "untrue" or who do not wish the truth ever to be written; from thieves or other conspirators; also the hands or hand of Elizabeth, who is also Time; "And *by their hands* this grace of kings must die, if hell and treason hold their promises" – *Henry V*, 2.0.Chorus.28-29; "With time's injurious *hand* crushed and o'erworn" – Sonnet 63, line 2; "When I have seen by time's fell *hand* defaced" – Sonnet 64, line 1; "Or what strong *hand* can hold his swift foot back?" – Sonnet 65, line 11; "And almost thence my nature is subdued,/ To what it works in, like the Dyer's *hand*" – Sonnet 111, lines 6-7; "For since *each hand* hath put on Nature's power" – Sonnet 127, line 5; "Was sleeping *by a Virgin hand* disarmed" – Sonnet 154, line 8, the latter in reference to Elizabeth, the so-called Virgin Queen, refusing to acknowledge her newborn son in 1574; **FALSEHOOD** = "The usual adverbs in legal records alongside the descriptions of particular treasons are *'falsely'* and 'traitorously'" – Bellamy, *Tudor Law of Treason*, p. 33; hands of falsehood = hands of traitors; **WARDS** = "Meaning 'guards' and used to describe places that can be locked for safekeeping; the range of its applications includes chests and prison cells" – Booth; "I am come to survey the Tower this day ... where be these *warders* ... Open the gates" – *1 Henry VI*, 1.3.1-3; "*prison* ... in which there are many confines, *wards*, and dungeons" – *Hamlet*, 2.2.260,262-263; prison guards; the "wards" of a lock; **OF TRUST** = of those who can be trusted

5 BUT THOU, TO WHOM MY JEWELS TRIFLES ARE,
BUT THOU = but you; **TO WHOM** = compared to whom; **MY JEWELS** = my writings, i.e., these private verses, which all involve Southampton, a prince who was "the world's fresh *ornament*" in Sonnet 1 or the "jewel" whose life is being recorded here; "As for *my sons, say I account of them as jewels*" – *Titus Andronicus*, 3.1.198-199; "Presents thy shadow to my sightless view,/ Which like *a jewel* hung in ghastly night" – Sonnet 27, lines 10-11; "As on the finger *of a throned Queen,/* The basest *Jewel* will be well esteemed" – Sonnet 96, lines 5-6

6 MOST WORTHY COMFORT, NOW MY GREATEST GRIEF,
MOST WORTHY = most royal or kingly; "a *king of so much worth*" – *1 Henry VI*, 1.1. 7; "*Most worthy* brother England*" – the King of France addressing Henry V of England, *Henry V*, 5.2.10; "That were I crown'd the *most imperial monarch, thereof most worthy*" – *The Winter's Tale*, 4.4.374-375; "***Most worthy prince***" – *Cymbeline*, 5.5.359; **COMFORT** = "Warwick, *my son, the comfort* of my age" – *2 Henry VI*, 1.1.189; "O my good lord, that *comfort* comes too late; 'tis *like a pardon after execution*" – *Henry VIII*, 4.2.120-121; "*As a decrepit father* takes delight/ To see *his active child* do deeds of youth,/ So I, made lame by Fortune's dearest spite,/ Take *all my comfort* of thy *worth* and truth" – Sonnet 37, lines 1-4; **NOW MY GREATEST GRIEF** = now you are the cause of the greatest grief in my life; "To me and to the state of *my great grief* let kings assemble; for *my grief's so great*" – *King John*, 2.2.70-71; "Let every word weigh heavy of her worth that he does weigh too light: *my greatest grief*, though little do he feel it, set down sharply" – *All's Well That Ends Well*, 3.4.31-33

> This Sessions, to our *great grief* we pronounce
> - *The Winter's Tale*, 3.2.1
> (The king opens the Sessions or Treason Trial)

7 THOU BEST OF DEAREST, AND MINE ONLY CARE,
THOU BEST OF DEAREST = you, most royal of most royal, dear son; "My dear dear lord ... dear my liege" – *Richard II*, 1.1.176, 184); **BEST** = "Richard hath *best* deserv'd of *all my sons*" – *3 Henry VI*, 1.1.18; **DEAREST** = "Thou would'st have left thy *dearest* heart-blood there, rather than made that savage duke

thine heir, and disinherited *thine only son*" – *3 Henry VI*, 1.1.229-231; "And take deep traitors for thy *dearest* friends" – *Richard III*, 1.3.224

> Too familiar
> Is *my dear son* with such sour company
> - *Romeo and Juliet*, 3.3.7-8

ONLY = the "one" of Southampton's motto; supreme; he is the "*onlie* begetter" of the 1609 dedication of the Sonnets; he was the "*only* herald to the gaudy spring" of Sonnet 1

MINE ONLY = "Ah, no, no, no, it is *mine only* son!" – *3 Henry VI*, 2.5.83; "His name is Lucentio and he is *mine only* son" – *The Taming of the Shrew*, 5.1.77-78

> O me, O me! *My child, **my only** life*
> - *Romeo and Juliet*, 4.5.19

MINE ONLY CARE = Southampton, my only concern; **CARE** = Bolinbroke: "Part of your cares you give me with your crown"; King Richard: "Your cares set up do not puck my cares down. My care is loss of care, by old care done; your care is gain of care, by new care won. The cares I give, I have, though given away, they 'tend the crown, yet still with me they stay" – *Richard II*, 4.1.194-199

8 ART LEFT THE PREY OF EVERY VULGAR THIEF.
Are left in the Tower for every common thief to harm or steal; **EVERY VULGAR THIEF** = a passing glance at himself as E.Ver, Edward de Vere, who tries to steal looks at his son; every common or base criminal in the Tower with you, urging you to further rebellion

9 THEE I HAVE NOT LOCKED UP IN ANY CHEST,
LOCKED UP = It is not I who have locked you up in the Tower or anywhere else; "*Lock up* my doors" – *Merchant of Venice*, 2.5.29; "You're my prisoner, but your gaoler shall deliver the keys that *lock up* your restraint" - *Cymbeline*, 1.2.3-5

> For *treason* is but trusted like the fox,
> Who, never so tame, so cherished and *locked up*
> - *1 Henry IV*, 5.2.9-10

> So am I as the rich whose blessed key
> Can bring him to his sweet *up-locked* treasure
> - Sonnet 52, lines 1-2

CHEST = coffer for valuables or jewels; **IN ANY CHEST** = in any prison; "A jewel in a ten-times-barr'd-up *chest* is a bold spirit in a loyal breast" – *Richard II*, 1.1.180-181; (to Southampton in the Sonnets as "ornament" or "jewel" or royal prince who is imprisoned and whose truth is hidden: "So is the time that keeps you as *my chest*" – Sonnet 52, line 9; "Shall *Time's best jewel from Time's chest* lie hid?" – Sonnet 65, line 10); "I thought myself to commit an unpardonable error to have murdered the same *in waste-bottoms of my chests*" – Oxford's Prefatory Letter to *Cardanus' Comfort*, 1573

10 SAVE WHERE THOU ART NOT, THOUGH I FEEL THOU ART
Except where you are not, i.e., except outside the high fortress walls, where you are free (in my mind and heart, within my breast)

11 WITHIN THE GENTLE CLOSURE OF MY BREAST,
GENTLE = suited for royalty; tender; **CLOSURE** = enclosure; the only place I keep you; i.e., the more loving "closure" of his breast or heart, as opposed to the fortress walls of the Tower prison where Southampton is confined:

> O Pomfret, Pomfret! O thou bloody *prison*,
> Fatal and ominous to noble peers!
> Within *the guilty **closure** of thy walls*
> Richard the Second here was hack'd to death!
> - *Richard III*, 3.3.9-12

To Elizabeth about their son, contrasting the gentleness of his "jail" with the harshness or *rigor* of her Tower: "Prison my heart in thy steel bosom's ward,/ But then my friend's heart let my poor heart bail;/ Who ere keeps me, let my heart be his guard,/ *Thou canst not then use rigor in my jail*" – Sonnet 133, lines 9-12

12 **FROM WHENCE AT PLEASURE THOU MAYST COME AND PART.**
AT PLEASURE = at Your Majesty's pleasure; at his royal son's command; "She flatly said whether it were mine or hers she would bestow it *at her pleasure*" – Oxford to Robert Cecil, October 20, 1595, in reference to the Queen; **THOU MAYST COME AND PART** = you may come and go

13 **AND EVEN THENCE THOU WILT BE STOL'N, I FEAR,**
Even then I fear you will be stolen from me; **THOU WILT BE STOL'N, I FEAR** = "Thou hast *stol'n* that which after some few hours were thine without *offence*" – the king to his royal son, referring to the crown, in *1 Henry IV*, 4.5.101-102; "And buds of marjoram had *stol'n thy hair*" – Sonnet 99, line 7, playing on "heir"

14 **FOR TRUTH PROVES THIEVISH FOR A PRIZE SO DEAR.**
TRUTH = Oxford, *Nothing Truer than Truth*; "your true rights" – Sonnet 17, line 11; **FOR TRUTH PROVES THIEVISH FOR A PRIZE SO DEAR** = because the truth, that you are a prince, proves a prize for those "thieves" who want to rebel against the Crown and put you on the throne; for even I, Oxford, might become a thief to steal you, my dear son, who are so royal a prize; ("The prey entices the thief" – Tilley, P570, adapted in *Venus and Adonis*: "Rich preys make true men thieves" – line 724); Southampton, having a claim to the throne, is indeed "a prize so dear" or so royal, with "dear" as in "my dear royal son"; "If *my dear love* were but the child of state,/ It might *for fortune's bastard be un-fathered*" – Sonnet 124, lines 1-2

Part Two

THE PRISON YEARS

DAY TWENTY-THREE IN THE TOWER

Sonnet 49
To Guard the Lawful Reasons on Thy Part
2 March 1601

Having made a bargain with Cecil for Southampton's life, Oxford knows his royal son will "frown on my defects" for also being forced to forfeit any claim to the throne. Their public separation as father and son now has "the strength of laws" – at least, it will have such strength if and when Elizabeth is persuaded to spare her son from execution.

Sonnet 49	Translation
Against that time (if ever that time come)	In preparation for the worst, if it comes,
When I shall see thee frown on my defects,	When you hold me responsible
When as thy love hath cast his utmost sum,	For your royal blood's final reckoning,
Called to that audit by advised respects;	Called to account by the highest ranks;
Against that time when thou shalt strangely pass,	Anticipating your lack of royal succession,
And scarcely greet me with that sunne thine eye;	When you deny being my royal son;
When love converted from the thing it was	When your royal blood, now ignored,
Shall reasons find of settled gravity;	Is passed over by other judgments;
Against that time do I ensconce me here,	In anticipation of that time I fortify myself,
Within the knowledge of mine own desert,	Within the knowledge of you as royal son,
And this my hand against myself uprear,	And raise my hand to swear against myself,
To guard the lawful reasons on thy part:	To protect your true rights as royal prince.
To leave poor me, thou hast the strength of laws,	The power of law may take you from me,
Since why to love, I can allege no cause.	Since I cannot testify that you're my royal son.

1 **AGAINST THAT TIME (IF EVER THAT TIME COME)**
AGAINST THAT TIME = in anticipation of; fortifying for; **EVER** = E. Ver, Edward deVere

2 **WHEN I SHALL SEE THEE FROWN ON MY DEFECTS,**
FROWN = the royal frown of his son, a prince; "Great Princes' favorites their fair leaves spread,/ But as the Marigold at the sun's eye,/ And in themselves their pride lies buried,/ For *at a frown* they in their glory die" – Sonnet 25, lines 5-8

DEFECTS = inability to have made you king; defection from my purpose for you; ("The king … made a *defect* from his purpose" – *OED*, 1540; the word "defect" was "used like Latin *defectus* to mean 'eclipse,' 'failure (of a heavenly body) to shine'" – Booth); "That thou art blamed shall not be *thy defect*" – Sonnet 70, line 1, to his son; "When all my best doth worship *thy defect*,/ Commanded by the motion of thine eyes" – Sonnet 149, lines 11-12, to Queen Elizabeth, who commands with her imperial eyes or viewpoint and condemns with her frown; "Our will became the servant to defect" – *Macbeth*, 2.1.18

3 **WHEN AS THY LOVE HATH CAST HIS UTMOST SUM,**

REFERENCE EDITION 317

THY LOVE = your royal blood; **HATH CAST HIS UTMOST SUM** = has reached its final accounting, with the determination as to whether you are to be a King of England; "has closed his account and cast up the sum total" – Dowden; "Profitless usurer, why dost thou use/ So great a *sum of sums* yet canst not live?" – Sonnet 4, lines 7-8, i.e., his abundant royal blood and right to claim to the throne; "To leave for nothing *all thy sum* of good" – Sonnet 109, line 12

4 CALLED TO THAT AUDIT BY ADVISED RESPECTS;
AUDIT = final accounting; "Then how when nature calls thee to be gone,/ What acceptable *Audit* canst thou leave?" – Sonnet 4, lines 11-12; "Her *Audit* (though delayed) answered must be,/ And her Quietus is to render thee" - Sonnet 126, lines 11-12

ADVISED RESPECTS = "Marks of deference for high rank" – Booth, citing Willen & Reed; "Deliberate, well-considered reasons" – Dowden;

> The King:
> And on the *winking of authority*
> To understand a *law,* to know the meaning
> Of dangerous majesty, when perchance it frowns
> More upon humour than ***advised respect.***
>
> Hubert:
> Here is your hand and seal for what I did.
>
> The King:
> O, when *the last accompt* 'twixt heaven and earth
> Is to be made, then shall this hand and seal
> Witness against us to damnation!
> - *King John*, 4.2.211-218

5 AGAINST THAT TIME WHEN THOU SHALT STRANGELY PASS
AGAINST THAT TIME = (see line 1 above); **STRANGELY PASS** = walk by without acknowledging me, i.e., specifically without acknowledging me as your father; go past me as a stranger; ("*I will acquaintance strangle* and look *strange*" – Sonnet 89, line 8)

6 AND SCARCELY GREET ME WITH THAT SUNNE THINE EYE,
THAT SUNNE THINE EYE = that royal eye of yours, which is a star or sun; ("Seek the King. That *sun*, I pray, may never set" – *Henry VIII*, 3.2.414); "Full many a glorious morning have I seen/ Flatter the mountain tops with *sovereign eye*" – Sonnet 33, lines 1-2, when Oxford goes on to describe the birth of his royal son: "Even so *my Sunne* one early morn did shine" – line 9; "Lo in the Orient when *the gracious light/ Lifts up his burning head,* each under eye/ Doth homage to his new-appearing sight,/ Serving with looks *his sacred majesty*" – Sonnet 6, lines 1-4; "For as *the Sun* is daily new and old,/ So is *my love* still telling what is told" – Sonnet 76, lines 13-14, linking his royal son with "the sun" and "my love"; "Making a couplement of proud compare/ With *Sunne and Moon*" – Sonnet 21, lines 5-6, speaking of Southampton, the royal son, and Elizabeth, goddess of the Moon, as son and mother; "And truly not the morning *Sun of Heaven*" – Sonnet 132, line 5; "*Roses have thorns*, and silver fountains mud,/ Clouds and *eclipses* stain *both Moone and Sunne*" – Sonnet 35, lines 2-3; i.e., Elizabeth and her royal son (whose eye is a sun) are being eclipsed in terms of the inability of their Tudor Rose blood to continue on the throne: "Crooked *eclipses* 'gainst *his glory* fight" – Sonnet 60, line 7

7 WHEN LOVE CONVERTED FROM THE THING IT WAS
LOVE = your royal blood; when royal blood, transformed from its golden time of hope for your succession to the throne; **CONVERTED** = a nod to Ver, E. Ver ("conVerted") and as the "gaudy *spring*" ("Ver" in French) of Sonnet 1; turned away from, as the sun might turn from the planets and no longer shine; **THE THING IT WAS** = "Presume not that I am the thing I was" - Prince Hal, now King, in *2 Henry IV*, 5.5.56; "The body is with the King, but the King is not with the body. The King is a thing" - *Hamlet*, 4.2.26-27

8 SHALL REASONS FIND OF SETTLED GRAVITY;
REASONS = echoing legal arguments; related to equity, fairness, justice; "**SETTLED GRAVITY** = sober judgment; related to the grave; when your royal blood is converted from its right to the throne, for legal reasons that are agreed upon by those in power, with my help and consent

9 AGAINST THAT TIME DO I ENSCONCE ME HERE
AGAINST THAT TIME = (the third usage in this verse); **ENSCONCE ME** = fortify myself, as you are ensconced within the fortress of the Tower; "protect or cover as with a *sconce* or fort" – Dyce, cited by Dowden

10 WITHIN THE KNOWLEDGE OF MINE OWN DESERT,
Within the knowledge of the truth, i.e., of my fatherhood of you; knowing what I deserve as the father of a king; **MINE OWN** = related to his own son; "*a son of mine own*" – Oxford to Burghley, March 17, 1575; Sonnets 23, 39, 49, 61, 62, 72, 88, 107, 110; **DESERT** = "Who will believe my verse in time to come/ If it were filled with *your most high deserts*?" – Sonnet 17, line 1-2; in this case Oxford's desert is his fatherhood, which he has only within his "knowledge" of it, but not in reality.

> **MINE OWN:**
> I am Launcelot, your boy that was, your son that is, your child that shall be...
> I'll be sworn if thou be Launcelot, thou art *mine own* flesh and blood
> - *Merchant of Venice*, 2.2.80-88

11 AND THIS MY HAND AGAINST MYSELF UPREAR
And for this I raise up my hand in court to testify against myself; go against my own guilty verdict at the trial; but more importantly, according to the bargain to save Southampton's life, his willingness to raise his hand as witness to the lie that must be perpetrated, i.e., to pretend that Southampton should not be king; (by the same token, Oxford's son must be a "suborned informer" against his own truth: "Hence, thou suborned *Informer*, a true soul/ When most impeached stands least in thy control" – Sonnet 125, lines 13-14, the final words to Southampton before the farewell envoy of Sonnet 126, ending the dynastic diary); **HAND** = "If this right *hand* would buy but two hours' life" – *3 Henry VI*, 2.6.80; "Or what strong *hand* can hold his (Time's) swift book back" – Sonnet 65, the final verse before word arrives that Southampton's life has been spared

12 TO GUARD THE LAWFUL REASONS ON THY PART.
To protect the legal reasons being put forth in order to save your life (the forthcoming answer is "misprision" of treason, Sonnet 87, line 11); **GUARD** = echoing the prison guards at the Tower; "To *guard* a title that was rich before" – *King John*, 4.2.10; "Ay, wherefore else *guard* we his royal tent but to defend his person from night-foes?" – *3 Henry VI*, 4.3.21-22

LAWFUL = "Let it be *lawful*" – *King John*, 3.1.112; "Edward's son, the first-begotten, and the *lawful heir* of Edward king" – *1 Henry VI*, 2.5.64-66; "And 'gainst myself a *lawful plea* commence" – Sonnet 35, line 11; "lawful = rightful, legitimate" – Schmidt; "lays most *lawful claim* to this fair island and the territories" – *King John*, 1.1.9-10; "That thou hast underwrought his *lawful king*, cut off the sequence of posterity" – *King John*, 2.1.95-96

REASONS = playing off "reasons" in line 8; "And yet his *trespass*, in our common *reason* … is not, almost, a *fault*" – *Othello*, 3.3.64-66; **ON THY PART** = on your side, legally, to save you from the consequences of your treason, trespass, fault

13 TO LEAVE POOR ME THOU HAST THE STRENGTH OF LAWS,
TO LEAVE POOR ME = to separate from me as my son, leaving me empty; "Suppose by right and equity thou be king, think'st thou that I will *leave my kingly throne*, wherein my grandsire and my father sat?" – *1 Henry VI*, 1.1.127-129

THOU HAST THE STRENGTH OF LAWS = you have a legal basis upon which to be saved, but that bargain forces you to abandon your claim to the throne; **STRENGTH** = royal power, Elizabeth's and your own; "If thou wouldst use the *strength of all thy state*" – Sonnet 96, line 12; strength of legal argument on your behalf; "And *strength* by limping sway disabled" – Sonnet 66, line 8, referring to the limping, swaying Robert Cecil, Secretary of State, who disabled Southampton's royal power; "In the very refuse of thy deeds/ There is such *strength* and warranties of skill" – Sonnet 150, lines 6-7, to Elizabeth as absolute monarch with royal power and authority

14 SINCE WHY TO LOVE I CAN ALLEGE NO CAUSE.
Since I cannot testify to why I love you; because I cannot reveal you are my son by the Queen; **ALLEGE** = echoing the allegations at the trial; **CAUSE** = motive, i.e., as your father ("allege" and "cause" are both legal terms; a "cause" is an adequate ground for action, as in "upon good cause shown to the court" – Tucker); "The *cause* of this fair gift in me is wanting,/ And so my patent back again is swerving" – Sonnet 87, lines 7-8; "The more I hear and see *just cause* of hate" – Sonnet 150, line 10

Part Two

THE PRISON YEARS

OXFORD VISITS SOUTHAMPTON IN PRISON
DAY TWENTY-FOUR IN THE TOWER

Sonnet 50
My Grief Lies Onward
3 March 1601

Oxford rides away from the Tower and back to his home in Hackney, knowing he will grieve over Southampton's execution or, even if he lives, over his loss of the throne. His joy lies behind him, in past times, and literally in the prison. In this sonnet, the first of a pair, Oxford describes his five-mile journey on horseback from the Tower and from a crucial visit with Southampton, to whom he would have explained the "league" or agreement to spare him from execution, requiring a forfeiture of any claim as King Henry IX.

Sonnet 50	Translation
How heavy do I journey on the way	How sorrowfully I go from you in the Tower
When what I seek (my weary travel's end)	When what I seek (accomplishment of my goal)
Doth teach that ease and that repose to say,	Allows me time enough to say:
"Thus far the miles are measured from thy friend."	"Miles are measured by the distance from my son."
The beast that bears me, tired with my woe,	The horse that carries me and my sorrow
Plods duly on to bear that weight in me,	Plods on to carry my own burden,
As if by some instinct the wretch did know	As if by some instinct he knows
His rider loved not speed being made from thee:	I have no love for riding fast from you.
The bloody spur cannot provoke him on	Your royal blood spilled cannot spur him on,
That sometimes anger thrusts into his hide,	So I sometimes show my anger,
Which heavily he answers with a groan,	Which he answers with a funereal groan
More sharp to me than spurring to his side;	That reflects my own pain.
For that same groan doth put this in my mind:	Because that groan makes me think this:
My grief lies onward and my joy behind.	My grief is ahead, my joy back where you are.

(This sonnet relates to Sonnet 131 of the Dark Lady series.)

1 HOW HEAVY DO I JOURNEY ON THE WAY,
HEAVY = sorrowfully; weighted down with burden; "weighty, ponderous ... not easily borne ... oppressive, crushing ... full of weight, important ... sad, sorrowful ... etc." – Schmidt; "some *heavy* business hath my lord in hand" – *1 Henry IV*, 3.66; "her death shall *heavy* fall on you" – *Much Ado About Nothing*, 5.1.151; "an act, under whose *heavy* sense your brother's life falls into forfeit" – *Measure for Measure*, 1.4.65; "under *heavy* judgment" – *Macbeth*, 1.3.110; "a *heavy* reckoning" – *Cymbeline*, 5.4.159;
ON THE WAY = returning home from the Tower; "And with a *heavy heart*, thinking on them, go I unto the Tower" – *Richard III*, 3.1.149-150

REFERENCE EDITION 321

2 WHEN WHAT I SEEK (MY WEARY TRAVEL'S END)
MY WEARY TRAVEL'S END = the end of my "travail" or labors; even the end of my life; the end of this terribly painful journey from the Tower, where I had to tell my son I was forced to forfeit his claim to succeed Elizabeth.

3 DOTH TEACH THAT EASE AND THAT REPOSE TO SAY
EASE/REPOSE = final rest; "The dear *repose* for limbs with travail tired" – Sonnet 27, line 2); "repose" in the Tower; "Your Highness shall *repose you at the Tower*" – *Richard III*, 3.1.65

4 "THUS FAR THE MILES ARE MEASURED FROM THY FRIEND."
THE MILES = Hackney was situated about three miles northeast of Whitechapel in Middlesex – a green, pleasant land with views stretching for miles; the village was long and scattered along the road from Mile End to Stamford Hill. (East of London Family History Society) In his letter to Cecil on April 25/27, 1603, Oxford will describe riding toward the center of London: "Yet I hasted so much as I came to follow you unto Ludgate, though through the press of people and horses I could not reach your company as I desired, but followed as I might"; **THY FRIEND** = Southampton, in the Tower; "For *precious friends* hid in death's dateless night" – Sonnet 30, line 6, speaking of Southampton in the prison, suffering darkest disgrace

5 THE BEAST THAT BEARS ME, TIRED WITH MY WOE,
BEAST = horse; "still used for *horse* in parts of Ireland" – Dowden; **BEARS** = carries; related to child-bearing; "Three times today *my foot-cloth horse did stumble*, and startled, when *he looked upon the Tower*, as loath to *bear me to the slaughter-house*" – *Richard III*, 3.4.84-86; **TIRED WITH MY WOE** = the horse itself is pictured as weary under the burden of Oxford's suffering "*Tired with all these*, for restful death I cry" – Sonnet 66, a virtual suicide note

6 PLODS DULLY ON, TO BEAR THAT WEIGHT IN ME,
DULLY = dully, heavily; (Q has "duly," i.e., dutifully); **TO BEAR THAT WEIGHT IN ME** = to bear my burden; endure; related to the bearing of Southampton as his son; **WEIGHT** = royalty; "And shall forget the office of our hand sooner than quittance of desert and merit, according to their *weight* and worthiness" – the King in *Henry V*, 2.2.33-35; heaviness, ponderousness, the weight of Oxford's grief over the bargain made for his son's life; "*Grief* boundeth where it falls, not with the empty hollowness, but *weight*" – *Richard II*, 1.2.59; "So did our men, *heavy* in Hotspur's *loss*, lend to this *weight*" – *2 Henry IV*, 1.1.121-122

7 AS IF BY SOME INSTINCT THE WRETCH DID KNOW
SOME = echoing "sum"; **WRETCH** = the horse, to be pitied, but echoing Southampton as a wretched traitor in the prison; "Our *wretches* fettered in our *prisons*" – the King in *Henry V*, 1.2.244; "And so, good rest … As *wretches* have o'ernight that *wait for execution* in the morn" – *The Two Gentlemen of Verona*, 4.2.128-130

8 HIS RIDER LOVED NOT SPEED BEING MADE FROM THEE:
HIS RIDER = Oxford; **LOVED NOT, etc.** = did not love leaving you in the Tower with any speed; "And let her have her most desire with *speed*" – Oxford poem, 1576

9 THE BLOODY SPUR CANNOT PROVOKE HIM ON,
BLOODY = the royal blood; also echoing the blood to be shed by Southampton when his head is severed – assuming that Elizabeth will give the order; "In bloody death" – *Lucrece*, 430; "Give us a prince of blood, a son of Priam" – *Troilus and Cressida*, 3.3.26; "The **shedding of my blood** can no way avail her [Elizabeth]" – Southampton, about now, to the Council. (Stopes, 225-226)

10 THAT SOMETIMES ANGER THRUSTS INTO HIS HIDE,
ANGER = Oxford's own rage at all that has been lost; **THRUSTS INTO HIS HIDE** = echoing the physical punishment indicated for Essex and Southampton at the trial: "and so to the place of the execution, there to be hanged by the neck and taken down alive; your bodies to be opened, and your bowels taken out and burned before your face; your bodies to be quartered; your heads and quarters to be disposed of at Her

Majesty's pleasure"; "as I *thrust* thy body with my sword" – *2 Henry VI*, 4.10.84; **HIDE** = the skin of an animal; echoing "hides your life" of Sonnet 17, line 4; "O tiger's heart wrapp'd in a woman's *hide*" – *3 Henry VI*, 1.4.137; "I would set an ox-head to *your lion's hide*" – *King John*, 2.1.292

11 WHICH HEAVILY HE ANSWERS WITH A GROAN
HEAVILY = in reflection of Oxford's own heavy heart; "heavily punished" – *Love's Labour's Lost*, 1.2.155; "And heavily from woe to woe" – Sonnet 30, line 10; "The heaviness and guilt within my bosom" – *Cymbeline*, 5.2.1; "*her death* shall fall *heavy* on you" – *Much Ado About Nothing*, 5.1.148-149; "an act under whose *heavy* sense your brother's life falls into forfeit" – *Measure for Measure*, 1.4.64-66; "under *heavy judgment*" – *Macbeth*, 1.3.110; "Norfolk, for thee remains a **heavier doom** … A **heavy sentence**, my most sovereign liege" – *Richard II*, 1.3., 148, 154; **ANSWERS** = suggesting "atonement, reparation for an offence, punishment" – Schmidt; "Their faults are open. Arrest them to the *answer* of the law" – *Henry V*, 2.2.143-144, the King in regard to traitors; "remedied to your public laws at *heaviest answer*" – *Timon of Athens*, 5.4.62-63; "whose *answer* would be *death drawn on with torture*" – *Cymbeline*, 4.4.13-14; **GROAN** = similar to the groan or moan at a funeral; ("Hadst thou *groan'd* for him as I have done" – *Richard II*, 5.2.102, the Duchess of York, speaking of her son); "A thousand **groans** but thinking on thy face/ One on another's neck do witness bear" – Sonnet 131, lines 10-11, Oxford to Elizabeth, envisioning the two of them groaning at the sight of Southampton's execution

12 MORE SHARP TO ME THAN SPURRING TO HIS SIDE,
MORE SHARP TO ME = more emotionally painful to me; harsh, severe, bitter; the sharpness of the executioner's axe; "There cannot be a pinch in death *more sharp* than this" – *Cymbeline,* 1.2.61; "Thus ready for the way of life or death, *I wait the sharpest blow*" – Pericles, 1.1.55-56; "those that are betrayed do *feel the treason sharply*, yet the *traitor stands in worse case of woe*" – Cymbeline, 3.4.84-86; "Let *every word weigh heavy of her worth* that he does weigh too light; *my greatest grief*, though little do he feel it, *set down sharply*" – *All's Well That Ends Well*, 3.4.31-33

13 FOR THAT SAME GROAN DOTH PUT THIS IN MY MIND:
GROAN = from line 11, emphasized by repetition

14 MY GRIEF LIES ONWARD AND MY JOY BEHIND.
MY GRIEF = My grief lies in the days ahead; "The secret sighs, that show *my inward grief*" – Oxford poem, 1576; "The only loss of my good name, is of these *griefs* the ground" – Oxford poem, 1576; **MY JOY** = Southampton; "She is *my joy*, she is my care and *woe*" – Oxford poem, 1576, of Queen Elizabeth; **BEHIND** = behind me, with and within my son, in the Tower; also, behind me in the past

THE PRISON YEARS

OXFORD RETURNS FROM THE PRISON
DAY TWENTY-FIVE IN THE TOWER

Sonnet 51
From Where Thou Art
4 March 1601

Oxford again describes his return home, to King's Place in Hackney, after visiting with Southampton in the Tower – undoubtedly to discuss details of the bargain he has been making for him, involving the "excuse" for his "offence" being argued on his behalf.

Sonnet 51	Translation
Thus can my love excuse the slow offence	Here's how you might explain my slowness
Of my dull bearer, when from thee I speed:	After I deliver these verses and ride away:
From where thou art, why should I haste me thence?	From you in prison, why should I hurry off?
Till I return, of posting is no need.	Till I return [to the Tower], I need no speed.
O what excuse will my poor beast then find,	O what excuse will my sad horse then find,
When swift extremity can seem but slow?	When the greatest speed to you seems slow?
Then should I spur, though mounted on the wind;	Then I'll move as though high on the throne;
In winged speed no motion shall I know;	In that way I'll speed without moving;
Then can no horse with my desire keep pace;	Then no horse can keep pace with my will;
Therefore desire (of perfect'st love being made)	So my will, made of your most royal blood,
Shall neigh no dull flesh in his fiery race,	Has no weakness in its royal Tudor lineage,
But love, for love, thus shall excuse my jade:	But you, in your royalty, can excuse my horse.
Since from thee going he went willful slow,	Since going from you he went deliberately slow,
Towards thee I'll run, and give him leave to go.	Towards thee [in the Tower] I'll run without him.

1 THUS CAN MY LOVE EXCUSE THE SLOW OFFENCE
MY LOVE = my royal son; my love for my son; "Not mine own fears nor the prophetic soul/ Of the wide world dreaming on things to come/ Can yet the lease of *my true love* control,/ Supposed as forfeit to a confined doom/ ... *My love* looks fresh..." - Sonnet 107, lines 1-4, 10

EXCUSE = To plead for, justify, vindicate; "plea offered in extenuation, apology ... pardon" – Schmidt; "And oftentimes the ***excusing*** of a ***fault*** doth make the ***fault*** the worse by the ***excuse***" – *King John*, 4.2.30-31); here Oxford is preoccupied with the need to have the Queen "excuse" Southampton of his crimes, to justify sparing him from death; and undoubtedly his visit with his son in the Tower was to discuss the terms of the bargain, i.e., to inform him he must give up any claim to the throne; "(n) pardon, dispensation, exoneration ... (v) explain, give reasons for" – (Crystal & Crystal); "Because here is a man *accused of treason*; pray God the Duke of York *excuse* himself" – *2 Henry VI*, 1.3.177-178; "And you, good uncle, banish all *offences*: if you do censure me by what you were, not what you are, I know it will *excuse* this sudden execution of my will" – *1 Henry VI*, 5.5.96-98; "Fouler than heart can think thee, thou canst make no *excuse* current, but to hang thyself" – *Richard III*, 1.2.83-84; "And thy abundant goodness shall *excuse* this deadly *blot* in thy digressing son" – *Richard II*, 5.3.63-64 "So please Your Majesty, I would I could quit all

offences with as clear *excuse* as well as I am doubtless I can purge myself of many I am charged withal"
– *1 Henry IV*, 3.2.18-21

> My nephew's *trespass* may be well forgot'
> It hath the *excuse* of youth and heat of blood,
> An adopted name of privilege,
> A hair-brained Hotspur, govern'd by a spleen;
> All his *offences* live upon my head
> And on his father's.
> - *1 Henry IV*, 5.2.16-21

"All murders past do stand *excused* in this" – *King John*, 4.3.51; "I will not *excuse* you; you shall not be *excused*; *excuses* shall not be admitted; there is no *excuse* shall serve; you shall not be *excused*" – Justice Shallow in *2 Henry IV*, 5.1.4-6; "My lord cardinal, I do *excuse* you; yea, upon mine honor, I free you from't" – the King in *Henry VIII*, 2.4.154-156; "Upon the instant that she was *accused*, shall be lamented, pitited and *excused* of every hearer" – *Much Ado About Nothing*, 4.1.214-216; "And here I stand, both to impeach and purge myself *condemned* and myself *excused*" – *Romeo and Juliet*, 5.3.226-227

OFFENCE = Crime; related to the legal bargaining for Southampton's life, to *excuse* or lessen the *fault* or *offence* or crime of treason for which he has been convicted; "I beseech you take it for your own *fault* and not mine: for had you been as I took you for, *I made no offence; therefore, I beseech your Highness, pardon me*" – *Henry V*, 4.8.53-56; "I do therefore now prostrate myself at her Majesty's princely feet, with a true penitent soul for my faults past, with horror in my conscience for *my offences*, and detestation for mine own life if it be displeasing to her" – Southampton, about now, to the Council [perhaps written for him by Oxford]. (Stopes, 227-229)

2 OF MY DULL BEARER WHEN FROM THEE I SPEED,
MY DULL BEARER = the plodding horse; the heavy bearer of his message, which Oxford had delivered personally to his son in the Tower; **DULL** = lifeless, echoing fear of Southampton's execution; **FROM THEE I SPEED** = I leave you in the Tower; (the sense of the first two lines being that Southampton is the one "excusing" Oxford; as a rightful king, he has the power to pardon)

3 FROM WHERE THOU ART, WHY SHOULD I HASTE ME THENCE?
WHERE THOU ART = the Tower; i.e., why should I hurry away from you?

4 TILL I RETURN, OF POSTING IS NO NEED.
POSTING = traveling fast to "post" or bring an important message; exchanging one horse for another; "First, the fair reverence of your Highness curbs me from giving reins and spurs to my free speech, which else would *post* until it had returned these terms of treason doubled down his throat; setting aside his high blood's royalty" – *Richard II*, 1.1.54-58; "*Post* you to London" – *Richard II*, 3.4.89; "Where your brave father breathed his latest gasp, tidings, *as swiftly as the posts could run*, were brought to me of your loss and his depart" – *3 Henry VI*, 2.1.108-110; "posting" is also a specific term relating to riding a horse – bouncing on the saddle as the horse trots – and that meaning may apply here, given the verb "spur" in line 7.

5 O WHAT EXCUSE WILL MY POOR BEARER THEN FIND,
O = Oxford; **EXCUSE** = (see also line 1); related to the reduced charge of "misprision" of treason; "So thy great gift, upon misprision growing" – Sonnet 87, line 11; "O my son, God put it in thy mind to take it hence, that thou mightst win the more thy father's love, pleading so wisely in *excuse* of it" – *2 Henry IV*, 4.5.177-180; "Thus far, my most dread sovereign, may it like Your Grace to let my tongue *excuse* all. What was purposed concerning his *imprisonment* was rather, if there be faith in men, meant for his *trial*, and fair purgation to the world, than malice, I'm sure, in me" – *Henry VIII*, 5.3.181-187

6 WHEN SWIFT EXTREMITY CAN SEEM BUT SLOW?
When, upon returning, even the fastest speed will seem slow

7 THEN SHOULD I SPUR THOUGH MOUNTED ON THE WIND,
Then I will dig my spurs into the horse, even if I am (like Apollo) riding over the heavens; "I'll *to the Tower with all the haste* I can" – *1 Henry VI*, 1.1.167

> First, the fair reverence of your Highness curbs me
> From giving *free reins and spurs* to my free speech,
> Which else would *post* until it had returned
> *These terms of treason* doubled down his throat;
> Setting aside his high blood's royalty…
> - *Richard II*, 1.1.54-58

THOUGH MOUNTED ON THE WIND = "Making the wind my post-horse" – *2 Henry IV*, Induction, 4; "*Rides on the posting winds*" – *Cymbeline*, 3.4.35; "Hors'd upon the sightless couriers of the air" – *Macbeth*, 1.7.22-23

> Wing'd with desire, I seek *to mount on high*
> - Harleian MS 7392
> (By "Lo Ox" – Oxford)

MOUNTED = "And then that Henry Bolinbroke and he, being *mounted* and both roused in their seats, their neighing coursers daring of the spur" – *2 Henry IV*, 4.1.117-119; ascended to the throne; "First note that he is near you in descent, and should you fail, he is the next will *mount*" – *2 Henry VI*, 3.1.21-22; "Give me the crown. Here, cousin, seize the crown … and full of tears am I, drinking my griefs, whilst you *mount* up on high" – *Richard II*, 4.1.181-189

"Thus weary of the world, away she hies,/ And yokes of her silver doves, by whose swift aid/ Their mistress *mounted* through the empty skies,/ In her light chariot quickly is convey'd,/ Holding their course to Paphos, where their Queen/ Means to immure herself and not be seen" – the end of *Venus and Adonis*, 1593, 1189-1194, of Venus =Elizabeth

8 IN WINGED SPEED NO MOTION SHALL I KNOW.
WINGED SPEED = the swift flight of a god (aboard a chariot); "*Wing'd* with desire, I seek to mount on high" – Oxford poem cited in line 7 notes above; **MOTION** = "Commanded by the motion of thine eyes" – Sonnet 149, line 12, to Elizabeth, referring to her imperial view

9 THEN CAN NO HORSE WITH MY DESIRE KEEP PACE;
MY DESIRE = my will, which is my son's royal will; with "desire" repeated in the next line; "Wing'd with *desire*, I seek to mount on high" – Oxford poem cited in lines 7-8 notes above

10 THEREFORE DESIRE (OF PERFECT'ST LOVE BEING MADE)
DESIRE = will; "When wert thou born, Desire?" – poem partially reprinted in *Art of English Poesie*, 1589, attributed to Oxford

OF PERFECT'ST LOVE BEING MADE = this desire or will is motivated by Southampton's perfect or royal blood; as in the royal "desire" of "From fairest creatures *we desire* increase" of Sonnet 1, line 1; i.e., motivated by his royal will and performed in service or duty to him; "By heaven, I come in *perfect love* to him" – *Richard III*, 3.7.89, Buckingham, declaring his allegiance to the king; "The *perfect* ceremony of love's right" – Sonnet 23, line 6; "Creating every bad a *perfect* best" – Sonnet 114, line 7

11 SHALL NEIGH NO DULL FLESH IN HIS FIERY RACE,
NEIGH = echoing "nay"; "It is the prince of palfreys; his *neigh* is like the bidding of a monarch, and his countenance enforces homage" – *Henry V*, 3.7.26-27; with impatience to gallop

HIS FIERY RACE = Southampton's royal lineage; speaking of the horse, but related to Southampton as the motivator; fiery as in "thy light's *flame*," Sonnet 1, line 6, referring to the source and substance of his royal blood; i.e., not detract from his lineage or royal status; **FIERY** = "Look as the fair and *fiery-pointed sun*" – *Lucrece*, 372

RACE = breed; "Live, and beget a happy *race of kings*" – *Richard III*, 5.3.158

12 BUT LOVE, FOR LOVE, THUS SHALL EXCUSE MY JADE:
LOVE, FOR LOVE = my love for him; his royal blood, for itself; "Upon your Grace, but with all duteous *love*" – *Richard III*, 2.1.33; **SHALL EXCUSE MY JADE** = (the third use of "excuse" in this sonnet; see lines 1 & 5); will pardon my horse (and me); related to excusing or pardoning Southampton

13 SINCE FROM THEE GOING HE WENT WILLFUL SLOW,
WILLFUL SLOW = willfully slow; slow by will

14 TOWARDS THEE I'LL RUN, AND GIVE HIM LEAVE TO GO.
Toward you in the Tower, I'll run without the horse's help; the horse will "go" or walk. "Ride more than thou goest" – *The Two Gentlemen of Verona*, 3.1.388

THE MONUMENT

THE PRISON YEARS

TRIAL OF OTHER CONSPIRATORS
DAY TWENTY-SIX IN THE TOWER

Sonnet 52
Imprisoned
5 March 1601

Oxford recalls his recent visit to Southampton in the Tower. On this day, the trial of Blount, Danvers, Davies, Merrick and Cuffe is held at Westminster Hall, although the sonnet doesn't seem to touch on the latter event – probably because Oxford wrote it at the same time he composed the previous sonnet, which this one immediately follows.

Sonnet 52	Translation
So am I as the rich, whose blessed key	Therefore I'm like a king, whose royal key
Can bring him to his sweet up-locked treasure,	Can bring him to his royal imprisoned son,
The which he will not every hour survey,	With whom he will not spend each hour
For blunting the fine point of seldom pleasure;	For fear of spoiling his royal pleasure.
Therefore are feasts so solemn and so rare,	So I feast on his rare royal appearances
Since seldom coming in the long year set,	Since my Tower visits are seldom arranged,
Like stones of worth they thinly placed are,	And are like royal stones placed sparsely,
Or captain Jewels in the carcanet.	Or like captain jewels placed at wide intervals.
So is the time that keeps you as my chest,	So is the long confinement like my chest,
Or as the wardrobe which the robe doth hide,	Or it's like a covering over you,
To make some special instant special blest	Making any visit to you a royal one,
By new unfolding his imprisoned pride.	So I can see my son's imprisoned royal self.
Blessed are you, whose worthiness gives scope,	Royal blooded are you! Your royalty is so free
Being had, to triumph; being lacked, to hope.	That having you is triumph; lacking you, a hope.

March 5, 1601 – Today Sir Christopher Blount, Sir Charles Danvers, Sir John Davis, Sir Gelly Merrick and Henry Cuffe were arraigned at Westminster for high treason before the commissioners ... They **pleaded** not guilty to the indictment as a whole, and a substantial jury was **impanelled** which consisted of aldermen of London and other gentlemen of good credit. They confessed indeed that it was their design to come to the Queen with so strong a force that they might not be resisted, and to require of her divers conditions and alterations of government; nevertheless they intended no personal harm to the Queen herself ... When all the evidence was done, the jury went out to agree upon **their verdict,** which after half an hour's time and more they brought in and found every man of the five prisoners severally guilty of high treason.
(An Elizabethan Chronicle)

PLEADED = "My heart doth *plead*" – Sonnet 46, line 5
IMPANELLED = "To 'cide this title is *impanelled*" – Sonnet 46, line 9
THEIR VERDICT = "And by *their verdict* is determined" – Sonnet 46, line 11

1 SO AM I AS THE RICH WHOSE BLESSED KEY
SO = "Therefore," proceeding immediately from the previous sonnet; **AM I** = suggesting "I am that I am" of the Bible, used in Sonnet 121, line 9, i.e., I am the proud father of a prince; **RICH** = royal, powerful; "And I am *rich* with little store" – poem *In Praise of a Contented Mind*, thought to be by Oxford, Chiljan 175;

328

WHOSE = i.e., Oxford's; **BLESSED KEY** = means of getting into the Tower and into the divine presence of his royal son; ("suggests 'the keys of the kingdom of heaven' given to St. Peter in Matt. 16:19" – Booth)

2 **CAN BRING HIM TO HIS SWEET UP-LOCKED TREASURE,**
SWEET = royal; **UP-LOCKED** = Imprisoned in the Tower; "For *treason* is but trusted like the fox, who, never so tame, so cherished and *locked up*" – *1 Henry IV*, 5.2.9-10; "Thee have I not *locked up* in any chest" – Sonnet 48, line 9; **TREASURE** = royal blood of Southampton; ("thine eyes and thoughts beat on a crown, the *treasure* of thy heart" – *2 Henry VI*, 2.1.19-20; "Where all the *treasure* of thy lusty days" – Sonnet 2, line 6; "Make sweet some vial; *treasure* thou some place/ With beauty's *treasure* ere it be self-killed" – Sonnet 6, lines 3-4; "But since she pricked thee out for women's pleasure,/ Mine be thy love, and thy love's use their *treasure*" – Sonnet 20, lines 13-14, referring to Southampton's *use* of his royal blood as Elizabeth's treasure; "Why should he live, now nature bankrupt is,/ Beggared of blood to blush through lively veins?/ For she hath no *exchequer* now but his" – Sonnet 67, lines 9-11, referring to Elizabeth as nature, *bankrupt* of her treasure, i.e., of Southampton's royal blood to succeed her on the throne; "Will will fulfill the *treasure* of thy love" – Sonnet 136, line 5, to Elizabeth, referring to her own royal will as well as to "William Shakespeare" in public support of their son and his "love" or royal blood

3 **THE WHICH HE WILL NOT EVERY HOUR SURVEY,**
EVERY = E. Ver, Edward de Vere

4 **FOR BLUNTING THE FINE POINT OF SELDOM PLEASURE.**
FOR BLUNTING = for fear of blunting; because it would blunt or dull the edge, repress, weaken, impair; **SELDOM** = infrequent; "Blunting" is perhaps also an allusion to Sir Christopher Blount, who was tried and convicted this day; **PLEASURE** = His Majesty's pleasure, i.e., Southampton's royal will as prince; "The pleasure that some fathers feed upon ... their children's looks" - *Richard II*, 2.1.79-80

5 **THEREFORE ARE FEASTS SO SOLEMN AND SO RARE,**
THEREFORE = as in "So" of line 1; but here with the additional meaning "for *that reason*"; **FEASTS** = opportunities to see his royal son; **SO SOLEMN AND SO RARE** =

> Loud shouts and salutations from their mouths,
> Even *in the presence of the crowned King*.
> Thus did I keep my person fresh and new,
> My presence, like a *robe* pontifical,
> Ne'er seen but wondered at, and so *my state*,
> *Seldom*, but sumptuous, show'd like a *feast*,
> And wan by *rareness* such *solemnity*
> - *1 Henry IV*, 3.2.53-59

6 **SINCE SELDOM COMING IN THE LONG YEAR SET,**
SELDOM = (as in line 4 above); Southampton can receive only seldom visits from Oxford; **THE LONG YEAR** = this first year of Southampton's imprisonment, of which he has spent less than a month so far; "How like a Winter hath my absence been/ From thee, the pleasure of *the fleeting year*?" – Sonnet 97, lines 1-2, marking February 8, 1602 as the first anniversary of his son's imprisonment, and referring to Her Majesty's "pleasure" or will that he remain confined; **SET** = as precious stones are set in jewelry; echoing the "setting sun" as well as "set a crown" as in "you that *set the crown* upon the head" – *1 Henry IV*, 1.3.158-159; also echoing "set" in prison to face punishment or torture, as in "thou hast *set me on the rack*" – *Othello*, 3.3.338; "to *set a head* on headless Rome" – *Titus Andronicus*, 1.1.189; raised up, as in "there is no sure foundation *set on blood*" – *King John*, 4.2.104; also referring to the "setting" of terms of the bargain being made to spare Southampton from execution: "to place with a certain purpose, to fix, to arrange" – Schmidt; "to set in order" – *The Merry Wives of Windsor*, 5.5.81; related to the ransom being set for Oxford and his son to pay: "these whose *ransom we have set*" – *2 Henry VI*, 4.1.139, referring to prisoners; "to place guards upon: "My father has *set guard*" – *King Lear*, 2.1.18; to place in high estimation; "I have letters sent me that *set* him high in fame" – *All's Well That Ends Well*, 5.3.31; to determine or carry out: "thou mayst not coldly *set our sovereign process*, which imports at full, by letters congruing to that effect, the present

death of Hamlet" – *Hamlet*, 4.3.65-68; set down, as Oxford is setting down his son's life in these sonnets: "all his faults observed, *set in a notebook*" – *Julius Caesar*, 4.3.96-97

7 LIKE STONES OF WORTH THEY THINLY PLACED ARE,
STONES OF WORTH = precious jewels; i.e., Southampton as a precious jewel or prince; "This royal throne of kings, this scept'red isle… this *precious stone set* in the silver sea" – *Richard II*, 2.1.40-46; **OF WORTH** = of royal blood, of royalty; suggesting "Wriothesley"; (see line 13)

8 OR CAPTAIN JEWELS IN THE CARCANET.
CAPTAIN = chief, ruler; "And herein I am forced, like a good and politic *captain*" – Oxford in his Prefatory Letter to *Cardanus' Comfort*, 1573; **JEWELS** = Southampton; (he is "the world's fresh ornament" of Sonnet 1, line 9; "like a *jewel* hung in ghastly night" in Sonnet 27, line 11; and "the basest *Jewel*" of Sonnet 96, line 6); **CARCANET** = gold necklace or collar set with jewels; summoning an image of the royal crown; "From her *carcanet* hangs a pendant jewel depicting a phoenix" - Roy Strong, describing a painting of Queen Elizabeth attributed to Nicholas Hilliard, circa 1573, *Elizabeth R*, p. 73

9 SO IS THE TIME THAT KEEPS YOU AS MY CHEST,
TIME = related to the time left until succession; also to the time recorded in this private diary; **THE TIME THAT KEEPS YOU AS MY CHEST** = detains you from me; the time of your imprisonment, keeping or holding you prisoner; the ever-waning time of Elizabeth's life and reign, which is the greatest prison; **KEEPS** = echoing Keeper of the Tower; "Ah, Keeper, Keeper" – to the Keeper of the Tower in *Richard III*, 1.4.66; **CHEST** = ("coffer, jewel casket – *time's chest* would be a coffin" – Booth's notes for Sonnet 65, lines 9-10: "O fearful meditation; where, alack,/ Shall time's best jewel from time's chest lie hid?"); Oxford's own chest, in which he keeps these verses; but Southampton, even in prison, is also the *chest* in which his own royal blood is kept; also, the prison itself is a chest; **MY CHEST** = "I thought myself to commit an unpardonable error to have murdered the same in the waste-bottoms of *my chests*" - Oxford's Prefatory Letter to *Cardanus' Comfort*, 1573; "Thee have I not *locked up* in any *chest*" – Sonnet 48, line 9

10 OR AS THE WARDROBE WHICH THE ROBE DOTH HIDE,
WARDROBE = "a dressing room; a department of a royal or noble household in charge of clothing" – O. E. D.; "O King Stephano! O peer! O worthy Stephano! Look what a *wardrobe* here is for thee!" – *The Tempest*, 4.1.222-223; "Yea, for the obtaining of suits, whereof the hangman hath no lean wardrobe" – *1 Henry IV*, 1.2.71-72; these sonnets are "dressing old words new" in the "noted weed" or familiar garb of poetry; a suggestion of Southampton as a former "ward" of the state; also echoing the "wards" or guards at the Tower; **ROBE** = a king's robes; "My presence, like a *robe* pontifical" – the king in *1 Henry IV*, 3.2.56; see line 5 notes above; **DOTH HIDE** = Southampton's royal appearance is hidden

11 TO MAKE SOME SPECIAL INSTANT SPECIAL BLEST,
SPECIAL INSTANT = time in your royal presence; **SPECIAL BLEST** = royally blessed, sacred; **SPECIAL** = "My lord of Gloucester, 'tis my *special* hope that you will clear yourself from all suspect" – *2 Henry VI*, 3.1.139-140; "My sovereign liege, no letters, and few words, but such as I, without your *special pardon*, dare not relate" – messenger to the king in *3 Henry VI*, 4.1.85-87; "To Eltham will I, where the young king is, being ordained his *special* governor" – *1 Henry VI*, 1.1.171-172; "The *special* watchmen of our English weal" – *1 Henry VI*, 3.1.66; "But yet the King hath drawn the *special* head of all the land together" – *1 Henry IV*, 4.4.26-27; "For every man with his affects his born, not by might mastered but by *special grace*" – *Love's Labour's Lost*, 1.1.149-150; "Let some of my people have a *special care* of him" – *Twelfth Night*, 3.4.62-63; "For you must know, we have with *special soul* elected him our absence to supply, lent him our terror, dressed him with our love, and given his deputation all the organs of our own power" – *Measure for Measure*, 1.1.17-21

12 BY NEW UNFOLDING OF HIS IMPRISONED PRIDE.
IMPRISONED PRIDE = the imprisoned royal blood of Southampton; "The *pride* of kingly sway" – *Richard II*, 4.1.206; "Thy kingly doom and sentence of his *pride*" – *Richard II*, 5.6.23; "Why is my verse so barren of new *pride*?" – Sonnet 76, line 1; in the Tower, Southampton is literally "imprisoned" with his

"pride" or royal blood, so here Oxford is almost directly revealing that he is writing to a man in prison; "O let me suffer, being at your beck,/ *Th'imprisoned absence of your liberty*" – Sonnet 58, lines 5-6

13 BLESSED ARE YOU WHOSE WORTHINESS GIVES SCOPE,
BLESSED ARE YOU = divinely royal are you, a god on earth; "A God in love, to whom I am confined" – Sonnet 110, line 12; **WORTHINESS** = royalty; (see "worth" in line 7 above); **SCOPE** = great range; also, bounty; "wondrous *scope*" – Sonnet 105, line 12

14 BEING HAD, TO TRIUMPH; BEING LACKED, TO HOPE.
BEING HAD = Southampton, having been born; being seen; being had as a royal son; "But out alack, he was but one hour mine" – Sonnet 33, line 11; "Thus have *I had thee* as a dream doth flatter:/ In sleep a King, but waking no such matter" – Sonnet 87, lines 13-14; **TO TRIUMPH** = as Oxford had been filled with "all *triumphant* splendor on my brow" in Sonnet 33, line 10, describing his joy as a father upon Southampton's birth in 1574; "Lo thus I *triumph* like a king" – poem thought to be by Oxford; **BEING LACKED** = not being able to see you, not having you as a prince who will become King Henry IX of England; "Thy bosom is endeared with all hearts,/ Which I by *lacking* have supposed dead" – Sonnet 31, lines 1-2; "Look what I *lack*, my mind supplies" – poem *In Praise of a Contented Mind*, thought to be by Oxford, Chiljan, 174; **TO HOPE** = To hope for a visit with you, to hope to have you acknowledged as my royal son; Southampton has been disgraced, yet Oxford now hopes for the sparing of his life; the former hope for his ascendancy on the throne as Henry IX; "Do you not *hope* your children shall be kings" – *Macbeth*, 1.3.117; "Yet this abundant *issue* seemed to me/ But *hope* of orphans, and *un-fathered* fruit" – Sonnet 97, lines 9-10; "the world's *hopeful* expectation" - dedication of *Venus and Adonis* by "Shakespeare" to Southampton, 1593

THE PRISON YEARS

DAY TWENTY-SEVEN IN THE TOWER

Sonnet 53
Strange Shadows On You Tend
6 March 1601

Now, with Essex dead and the other conspirators also condemned, time grows short for Southampton's fate to be decided. The great shadow of Elizabeth Regina's imperial frown, the "region cloud" of Sonnet 33, spreads over Henry Wriothesley in the Tower; Oxford's tone of increasing worry is unmistakable even as he writes in praise of his son, whom he likens to Adonis of Venus and Adonis, *the 1593 poem dedicated to him by "Shakespeare."*

Sonnet 53	Translation
What is your substance, whereof are you made,	What is your blood? Of what blood are you,
That millions of strange shadows on you tend?	Causing Elizabeth's frowns to attend you?
Since every one hath, every one, one shade,	Because you are exactly who you are,
And you, but one, can every shadow lend.	And you, only heir, can cast all frowns:
Describe Adonis and the counterfeit	Take my depiction of Adonis and that portrait
Is poorly imitated after you;	Is but a poor imitation of your reality;
On Helen's cheek all art of beauty set,	On Elizabeth's cheek is all your royalty
And you in Grecian tires are painted new.	And you in her image are created new.
Speak of the spring and foison of the year,	Speak of the golden time and abundant royalty:
The one doth shadow of your beauty show,	The one appears a shadow of your royal blood,
The other as your bounty doth appear,	The other shows up in your great bounty,
And you in every blessed shape we know.	And you appear in all sacred/royal things.
In all external grace you have some part,	In all external forms of royalty you take part,
But you like none, none you, for constant heart.	But there is no one like you with eternal blood.

1 WHAT IS YOUR SUBSTANCE, WHEREOF ARE YOU MADE,
YOUR SUBSTANCE = your inner reality, i.e., your royal blood; "No, no, I am but a *shadow* of myself: you are deceived, my *substance* is not here" – *1 Henry VI*, 2.3.49-50; **WHEREOF ARE YOU MADE** = of what do you consist? The answer, of course, is royal blood.

2 THAT MILLIONS OF STRANGE SHADOWS ON YOU TEND?
MILLIONS = countless; expressing, by exaggeration, the outrageousness of the "stain" or "disgrace" that has covered his royal son; as in "That it could so *preposterously* be stained,/ To leave for nothing all thy sum of good" – Sonnet 109, lines 11-12; "But reckoning time, whose *millioned* accidents/ Creep in twixt vows, and change decrees of Kings" – Sonnet 115, lines 5-6; "Call me their traitor! Thou injurious tribune! Within thine eyes sat twenty thousand deaths, in thy hand clutched as many *millions*, in thy lying tongue both numbers" – *Coriolanus*, 3.3.69-72; **STRANGE** = foreign, as opposed to related by blood; **SHADOWS** = the darkness cast by the Queen's dark cloud or negative view; ("But the world is so cunning, as of a *shadow* they can make a *substance,* and of a likelihood a truth" – Oxford to Burghley, July 1581); "Which, being but

332

the *shadow of your son, becomes a sun and makes your son a shadow*" – *King John*, 2.1.499-500; "Save that my soul's imaginary sight/ Presents *thy shadow* to my sightless view" – Sonnet 27, lines 9-10; **TEND** = "attend" or wait upon him as those who attend upon a king; "For to no other pass my verses *tend*/ Than of your graces and your gifts to tell" – Sonnet 103, lines 11-12, a statement that Oxford means literally, i.e., the Sonnets are all about Southampton; "The time invites you; go, *your servants tend*" – *Hamlet*, 1.3.83; "Give him tending" – *Macbeth*, 1.5.36; "They '*tend the crown*'" – *Richard II*, 4.1.199; echoing the "tender" (or the offer) for acceptance by which Oxford has offered to pay "ransom" for his son's life.

3 SINCE EVERY ONE HATH, EVERY ONE, ONE SHADE,
EVERY = E. Ver, Edward de Vere; **ONE** = Southampton, *One for All, All for One*; **EVERY ONE** = father and son together; **EVERY ONE, ONE SHADE** = you and I suffer together under the shadow that is cast over you; "There is emphasis on both the second and third *one*" – Tucker; Note: "one" occurs six times in this sonnet, "every" occurs three times, "none" twice.

4 AND YOU, BUT ONE, CAN EVERY SHADOW LEND.
AND YOU, BUT ONE = and you, Southampton; "Why write I still all *one, ever* the same" – Sonnet 76, line 5; "Since all alike my songs and praises be/ To *one, of one*, still such, and *ever* so" – Sonnet 105, lines 3-4; **EVERY** = E. Ver; **CAN EVERY SHADOW LEND** = can lend your shadow to all things; and to me, your father, who suffers under Elizabeth's frown/cloud/shadow with you; "But Henry now shall wear the English crown and be true King indeed; thou but the *shadow*" – *3 Henry VI*, 4.3.49-50

5 DESCRIBE *ADONIS* AND THE COUNTERFEIT
ADONIS: the young god of *Venus and Adonis*, i.e., Oxford is referring to his own narrative poem (probably written in the 1570s) that he dedicated (as "William Shakespeare") to Southampton in 1593; Adonis (symbol of male beauty) was once Oxford's self-portrait (based on the Queen's attempts to seduce him as a young man in 1571-73, if not earlier); but now Henry Wriothesley is the young Adonis in relation to his mother, Elizabeth, who remains Venus, goddess of Love and Beauty; **COUNTERFEIT** = likeness; that which is made in imitation of him; portrait of him; "Much liker than your painted counterfeit" – Sonnet 16, line 8; "But who can leave to look on *Venus*' face … These virtues rare, eche gods did yield a mate./ Save *her alone, who yet on th'earth doth reign,/ Whose beauties* (beauty's) string no god can well distrain" – Oxford poem, published in 1576, writing of Elizabeth

6 IS POORLY IMITATED AFTER YOU:
POORLY IMITATED = inadequately portraying you

7 ON *HELEN'S* CHEEK ALL ART OF BEAUTY SET,
HELEN'S CHEEK = Elizabeth, pictured as Helen of Troy, most beautiful of women; "Within this there is a red/ Exceeds the damask rose;/ Which in *her cheeks* is spread,/ Whence every favor grows" – Oxford poem in *The Phoenix Nest*, 1593, writing of Elizabeth; **ALL** = Southampton; **ALL ART** = the art of these sonnets, written for you; **OF BEAUTY SET** = expressing your "beauty" or blood from Elizabeth; ("Portray … in such a way as to exemplify the highest ideal of beauty" – Duncan-Jones); "What thing doth please thee most?/ To gaze on *beauty* still" – Oxford poem, part of which appeared in *Arte of English Poesie*, 1589

8 AND YOU IN *GRECIAN* TIRES ARE PAINTED NEW:
GRECIAN **TIRES** = Greek headdresses or attire; **PAINTED NEW** = recreated (given new birth) in these private sonnets; "A Woman's face with *nature's own hand painted*/ Hast thou, the Master Mistress of my passion" – Sonnet 20, lines 1-2

9 SPEAK OF THE SPRING AND FOISON OF THE YEAR,
SPRING = time of royal hope; Ver; "This side is *Hiems*, Winter, this *Ver*, the Spring … *Ver*, begin" – *Love's Labour's Lost*, 5.2.884-886; **FOISON** = abundant royal blood, kingly bounty; "Earth's increase, *foison* plenty" – *The Tempest*, 4.1.110; "For his *bounty* there was no winter in 't; an *autumn* 'twas that grew the more by reaping" – *Antony and Cleopatra*, 5.2.85-87; "The teeming autumn big with rich increase" – Sonnet 97, line 6; see "bounty" in line 11

10 **THE ONE DOTH SHADOW OF YOUR BEAUTY SHOW,**
ONE = Southampton, his motto; **SHADOW OF YOUR BEAUTY** = the ghostlike appearance of your royal blood from the Queen

11 **THE OTHER AS YOUR BOUNTY DOTH APPEAR,**
YOUR BOUNTY = your royal bounty; "I thank thee, king, for thy great *bounty*" – *Richard II*, 4.1.300; "Which *bounteous* gift thou shouldst in *bounty* cherish" – Sonnet 11, line 12; "the king-becoming graces, as Justice, Verity, Temp'rance, Stableness, *Bounty*" – *Macbeth*, 4.3.91-93; "That we our largest *bounty* may extend" – *King Lear*, 1.1.52; "That as my hand has open'd *bounty* to you" – the King in *Henry VIII*, 3.2.184; "Or monarch's hands that let not *bounty* fall" – *A Lover's Complaint*, 41

12 **AND YOU IN EVERY BLESSED SHAPE WE KNOW.**
EVERY = E. Ver, Edward deVere; **BLESSED** = divine, sacred, godlike, royal; "Look down, you gods, and on this couple drop a *blessed* crown" – *The Tempest*, 5.1.201-202; "*Blessed* are you" – Sonnet 52, line 13; "A God in love" – Sonnet 110, line 12; "Likely in time to *bless* a regal throne" – *3 Henry VI*, 4.6.74; (Sonnets 82, 84, 92, 119, 128)

13 **IN ALL EXTERNAL GRACE YOU HAVE SOME PART,**
ALL = Southampton, *One for All, All for One*; **EXTERNAL GRACE** = show of royalty; "The king is full of *grace* and fair regard ... this *grace of kings*" – *Henry V*, 1.1.22, 2 Prol. 28; "royal and *gracious*" – *Richard III*, 4.4.205

14 **BUT YOU LIKE NONE, NONE YOU, FOR CONSTANT HEART.**
NONE = opposite of "one" for Southampton; **LIKE NONE** = like no other; **NONE YOU** = none like you; also, you are now a nobody; **CONSTANT HEART** = eternal royal power, with a heart that pumps your royal blood; always noble and royal; "our friends are *true and constant*" – *1 Henry IV*, 2.3.17; "Crowned with faith and *constant* loyalty ... *constant* in spirit, not swerving with the blood" – *Henry V*, 2.2., 5, 133; "Therefore my verse to *constancy* confined,/ One thing expressing, leaves out difference" – Sonnet 105, lines 5-8; "In *constant* truth to bide so firm and sure" – Oxford's sonnet in "Shakespearean" form, early 1570s

Part Two

THE PRISON YEARS

DAY TWENTY-EIGHT IN THE TOWER

Sonnet 54
Sweet Deaths
7 March 1601

Oxford mournfully anticipates the execution of Southampton and his death as heir to the Tudor Rose dynasty. He is the flower of the Tudor Rose, living and dying in this sonnet.

Sonnet 54	Translation
OH how much more doth beauty beauteous seem,	O how greater does Elizabeth's royalty appear
By that sweet ornament which truth doth give.	Because of her royal son that my truth expresses!
The Rose looks fair, but fairer we it deem	The Tudor Rose is royal, but we deem it more royal
For that sweet odor which doth in it live.	Because of that royal son who lives inside it!
The Canker blooms have full as deep a dye	Disgraced sons of the Tudor Rose are just as royal
As the perfumed tincture of the Roses,	As the most acknowledged Tudor Rose sons,
Hang on such thorns, and play as wantonly,	In their disgrace they are nevertheless just as royal,
When summer's breath their masked buds discloses:	When their royalty reveals its hidden Rose lineage!
But for their virtue only is their show,	Except for this truth, they only have their show,
They live unwooed, and unrespected fade,	They live unrecognized, and fade dishonored,
Die to themselves. Sweet Roses do not so;	Dying in disgrace. Tudor Rose sons do not so;
Of their sweet deaths are sweetest odors made.	Their royal deaths spill the most royal blood!
And so of you, beauteous and lovely youth,	And so of you, royal son and heir of the Queen,
When that shall vade, by verse distils your truth.	When you die, my sonnets will reveal your truth.

Robert Cecil to George Carew, after March 5, 1601: *"It remaineth now that I let you know what is like to become of the poor young Earl of Southampton, who, merely for the love of the Earl [Essex] hath been drawn into this action, who, in respect that most of the conspiracies were at Drury House, where he [Southampton] was always chief... those that would deal [plead] for him (of which number I protest to God I am one, as far as I dare) are much disadvantaged of arguments to save him..."*
- Stopes, 224; i.e., Cecil, dealing with Oxford behind the scenes, now puts it on record that he hopes the best for Southampton, but that saving him won't be easy because all evidence goes against him; perhaps to build up the difficulty in anticipation of taking credit for interceding with the Queen on Southampton's behalf.

1 OH HOW MUCH MORE DOTH BEAUTY BEAUTEOUS SEEM
BEAUTY = Southampton's blood from Elizabeth; ("That thereby *beauty's Rose* might never die" – Sonnet 1, line 2; "thy *beauty's legacy*" – Sonnet 4, line 2; **BEAUTEOUS** = royal, Tudor; ("Seeking that *beauteous roof* to ruinate" – Sonnet 10, line 7, referring to the House of Tudor)

REFERENCE EDITION

2 BY THAT SWEET ORNAMENT WHICH TRUTH DOTH GIVE!
SWEET ORNAMENT = royal prince; "Thou that art now the world's fresh *ornament*" – Sonnet 1, line 9; "Which like a *jewel* hung in ghastly night" – Sonnet 27, line 11

> For *princes* are
> A model which heaven makes like to itself:
> *As jewels* lose their glory if neglected,
> So *princes* their renowns if not respected.
> - *Pericles*, 2.2.10-13

TRUTH = the truth of his Tudor blood; Oxford, *Nothing Truer than Truth;* in his role as father

3 THE ROSE LOOKS FAIR, BUT FAIRER WE IT DEEM
THE ROSE = the Tudor Rose; **FAIR** = royal; "From *fairest* creatures we desire increase,/ That thereby beauty's *Rose* might never die" – Sonnet 1, lines 1-2; **FAIRER** = more royal; with a greater claim to the throne; "But thou art *fair*, and at thy birth, dear boy, nature and fortune joined to make thee great" – *King John*, 2.2.51-52

4 FOR THAT SWEET ODOR WHICH DOTH IN IT LIVE.
SWEET ODOR = the royal presence of Southampton within the Rose; "What doth avail the rose unless another took pleasure in the smell? … Why should this rose be better esteemed than that rose, unless in pleasantness of smell it far surpassed the other rose?" - Oxford's Prefatory Letter to *Cardanus' Comfort*, 1573

5 THE CANKER BLOOMS HAVE FULL AS DEEP A DYE
CANKER BLOOMS = Southampton's disgrace; (blossoms of the dog-rose)

> Hath not thy rose a *canker*, Somerset?
> Hath not thy rose a *thorn*, Plantagenet?
> - *1 Henry VI*, 2.4.68-69

> To put down Richard, that sweet lovely *rose*,
> And plant this *thorn*, this *canker* Bolinbroke?
> - *1 Henry IV*, 1.3.173-174

FULL AS DEEP A DYE = just as much filled with royal blood; "And almost thence my nature is subdued/ To what it works in, like *the Dyer's hand*" – Sonnet 111, lines 6-7; "dye" echoing "die" in the circumstances by which Southampton may be executed

6 AS THE PERFUMED TINCTURE OF THE ROSES,
As the external show of royalty by Tudor Rose heirs, i.e., Oxford is using the plural to refer to the singular, Southampton, who is Elizabeth's heir by blood; also, the "Roses" or past heirs of the Tudor dynasty, from Henry VII in 1485.

7 HANG ON SUCH THORNS, AND PLAY AS WANTONLY,
HANG = echoing the imminent execution of Southampton; "Which like a jewel *hung* in ghastly night" – Sonnet 27, line 11; **THORNS** = disgraces; another play on Elizabeth's motto *Rose Without a Thorn*, indicating that Southampton has disgraced and doomed the Tudor Rose Dynasty; "*Roses have thorns*, and silver fountains mud,/ Clouds and eclipses stain both Moone and Sunne,/ And loathsome *canker* lives in sweetest *bud*" – Sonnet 35, lines 2-4, referring to Southampton as "bud" of the Tudor Rose

8 WHEN SUMMER'S BREATH THEIR MASKED BUDS DISCLOSES:
SUMMER'S = golden, kingly; "Shall I compare thee to a Summer's day?" – Sonnet 18, line 1; **MASKED BUDS** = hidden or unacknowledged Tudor Rose heirs, i.e., Southampton

MASKED = "Even so my Sunne one early morn did shine/ With all triumphant splendor on my brow,/ But out alack, he was but one hour mine,/ The *region cloud hath **masked** him* from me now" – Sonnet 33, lines 9-12; "*Masking* the business from the common eye, for sundry weighty reasons" - *Macbeth*, 3.1.123-124; **BUDS** = "Within thine own *bud* buriest thy content" – Sonnet 1, line 11; "Rough winds do shake *the darling buds of May*" – Sonnet 18, line 3; **DISCLOSES** = unfolds to view, opens, as in "The canker galls the infants of the spring too oft before their buttons be *disclosed*" – *Hamlet*, 1.3.40; but Southampton is not being "disclosed" as the royal son – except in these private sonnets and, less directly, in Oxford's works attributed to Shakespeare

9 BUT FOR THEIR VIRTUE ONLY IS THEIR SHOW,
Because their only virtue is their appearance

10 THEY LIVE UNWOOED, AND UNRESPECTED FADE,
UN-WOOED = unacknowledged as prince; without being named in succession; "And when a woman *woos*, what woman's son/ Will sourly leave her till he have prevailed?" – Sonnet 41, lines 7-8, referring to Elizabeth having "wooed" or promised/tempted her son to hope or expect she will name him to succeed her

UN-RESPECTED FADE = ignored, un-regarded, held in contempt; and, as such, fail to grow into rightful kingship; "For all the day they view things *un-respected*" – Sonnet 43, line 2, Oxford speaking of what is seen or perceived of his royal son by the rest of the world; ("un-respected" appears nowhere else in Shakespeare, aside from Sonnets 43 & 54)

> If ***well-respected** honor* bid me on
> - *1 Henry IV*, 4.3.10

> As *jewels* lose their glory if neglected,
> So ***princes*** their renowns if ***not respected***
> - *Pericles*, 2.2.12-13

> Throw away *respect*,
> Tradition, form and ceremonious duty
> - *Richard II*, 3.2.172-173

> To tread down fair ***respect** of sovereignty*
> - *King John*, 2.2.58

> To understand a *law*, to know the meaning
> Of *dangerous majesty*, when perchance it frowns
> More upon humour than advised ***respect***
> - *King John*, 4.2.212-214

> I come with gracious offers from the king,
> If you vouchsafe me hearing and *respect*
> - *1 Henry IV*, 4.3.30-31

11 DIE TO THEMSELVES; SWEET ROSES DO NOT SO,
DIE TO THEMSELVES = as Southampton may die by execution; **SWEET ROSES** = royal Tudor Rose heirs, i.e., Southampton; "Earthlier happy is the rose distilled, than that which withering on the virgin thorn grows, lives and *dies* in single blessedness" – *A Midsummer Night's Dream*, 1.1.76-78

12 OF THEIR SWEET DEATHS ARE SWEETEST ODORS MADE:
SWEET DEATHS = royal deaths; (again, the plural used for the singular); Southampton's still-expected execution; also, the extinction of his chance to gain the throne; **SWEETEST ODORS** = most royal evidence

13 AND SO OF YOU, BEAUTEOUS AND LOVELY YOUTH,
YOU = Southampton; "But he that writes of *you*, if he can tell/ That *you are you*, so dignifies his story" – Sonnet 84, lines 7-8; **BEAUTEOUS AND LOVELY YOUTH** = royal son of beauty, the Queen; **BEAUTEOUS** = related to the Queen by blood; (perhaps rather than "beautiful" because of the "E O" within "beauteous); **LOVELY** = filled with "love" or royal blood; "O Thou my *lovely* Boy" – Sonnet 126, line 1; "the little Love-God" – Sonnet 154, line 1

14 WHEN THAT SHALL VADE, BY VERSE DISTILLS YOUR TRUTH.
VADE = fade, depart; die; **BY VERSE** = by these sonnets; ("my" verse – Malone)

DISTILLS = recreates and preserves; "By means of verse your truth is preserved and transmitted to future generations" – Duncan-Jones); i.e., Oxford is using the Sonnets to preserve and perpetuate his son's blood, as opposed to the "distillation" of his royal blood by the begetting of an heir, called for in an earlier time: "But *flowers distilled*, though they with winter meet,/ Leese but their show, their substance still lives sweet" - Sonnet 5, lines 13-14; and "Then let not winter's ragged hand deface/ In thee thy summer ere thou be *distilled*" – Sonnet 6, lines 1-2; and much earlier, when Oxford was four years old, he began studying with Thomas Smith, his first tutor, an expert in distillation

TRUTH = the truth of your royal blood, which is related to Oxford, *Nothing Truer than Truth*; "And your *true rights* be termed a Poet's rage" – Sonnet 17, line 11; "Thou *truly fair* wert *truly* sympathized/ In *true* plain words by thy *true*-telling friend" – Sonnet 82, lines 11-12

Part Two

THE PRISON YEARS

OXFORD VOWS MONUMENT
FOR SOUTHAMPTON
DAY TWENTY-NINE IN THE TOWER

Sonnet 55
The Living Record
8 March 1601

With his son still facing execution, Oxford vows to create "the living record" of Southampton to be preserved "in the eyes of all posterity." Along with Sonnet 81, this verse is a declaration of his utter commitment to making sure the truth about Henry Wriothesley will be known by future generations. The "living record" of him (the story of his royal life until the fate of the Tudor dynasty is sealed) will be preserved for future readers within the tomb of the monument. The tomb contains a womb of verse in which he is still "living" and growing in real time with this diary, the outcome of which remains uncertain.

Sonnet 55	Translation
Not marble nor the gilded monument	Neither marble nor the gilded monuments
Of Princes shall outlive this powerful rhyme,	Of royal princes shall outlive these sonnets!
But you shall shine more bright in these contents	Instead you shall reign more royal in them
Than unswept stone, besmeared with sluttish time.	Than any stone statue that decays in time.
When wasteful war shall *Statues* over-turn,	When war lays waste to statues,
And broils root out the work of masonry,	And cities come tumbling down,
Nor *Mars* his sword nor war's quick fire shall burn	Neither Mars' sword nor war will destroy
The living record of your memory.	This living record of your royal blood!
'Gainst death and all oblivious enmity	Against death and terrible oblivion
Shall you pace forth; your praise shall still find room	Shall you live! Praise of you as king will be
Even in the eyes of all posterity	Sung by all who live in the future,
That wear this world out to the ending doom.	Who wear out England to its own end!
So till the judgement that yourself arise,	So, until you are recognized for who you are,
You live in this, and dwell in lovers' eyes.	You live in this verse and in subjects' eyes.

"No. 55 ... is clearly addressed to a prince" - Ogburn & Ogburn, This Star of England, 1952, p. 908; "A continuation of Sonnet 54 ("by verse distills your truth")" - Dowden, The Sonnets of William Shakespeare, 1881

1 NOT MARBLE, NOR THE GILDED MONUMENT
GILDED MONUMENT = gilded tombs of English monarchs, many made of marble; most modern editors emend "monument" to the plural, but in fact Oxford used the singular on other occasions:

> Again we see if our friends be dead, we cannot show or declare our affection more than by erecting them of *tombs*: Whereby when they be dead indeed, yet *make we them live*, as it were, again through their **monument**. But with me behold it happeneth far better, for in your lifetime I shall erect you such a **monument** that, as I say, in your lifetime, you shall see how noble a *shadow of your virtuous life* shall hereafter remain when you are dead and

REFERENCE EDITION

gone. And in your lifetime, again I say, I shall give you that *monument* and *remembrance of your life* whereby I may declare my goodwill…
- Oxford's Prefatory Letter to *Cardanus' Comfort*, 1573

Your *monument* shall be my gentle verse,
Which eyes not yet created shall o'er-read
- Sonnet 81, lines 9-10

And thou in this shalt find thy *monument*,
When tyrants' creats and *tombs of brass* are spent
- Sonnet 107, lines 13-14

Ever belov'd and loving may his rule be;
And when old time shall lead him to his end,
Goodness and he fill up one monument!
- *Henry VIII*, 2.1.92-94

This grave shall have a living monument.
- *Hamlet*, 5.1.297

2 OF PRINCES SHALL OUTLIVE THIS POWERFUL RHYME!
PRINCES = Kings or Queens, including Elizabeth, who referred to herself as Prince of England; **THIS POWERFUL RHYME** = this monument of the Sonnets, which contains your "power" as a prince or king: "O Thou my lovely Boy, who in thy *power*" – Sonnet 126, line 1; "The King with mighty and quick-raised power" – *1 Henry IV*, 4.4.12

3 BUT YOU SHALL SHINE MORE BRIGHT IN THESE CONTENTS
YOU SHALL SHINE = like a king; "Even so *my Sunne one early morn did shine*" – Sonnet 33, line 9; **MORE BRIGHT** = more royally; "A substitute *shines brightly as a king*" – *Merchant of Venice*, 5.1.94 "Yet looks he like a king; behold, his eye, as *bright* as is the eagle's, lightens forth controlling majesty" – *Richard II*, 3.3.68-70; "Wherever the *bright* sun of heaven shall *shine*, his honour and the greatness of his name shall be" – *Henry VIII*, 5.5.50-52, Cranmer, speaking of a future son and royal heir of Queen Elizabeth (in a passage that has been thought to refer to King James, but the context of the speech clearly refers to an "heir" to arise from the Queen's blood and ashes; **IN THESE CONTENTS** = in what is contained in these private verses written according to time; "The phrase carries a suggestion of *'in this coffin'*" – Booth; "That did my ripe thoughts in my brain *inhearse*,/ Making their *tomb* the *womb* wherein they grew" – Sonnet 86, lines 3-4; "Within thine own bud buriest *thy content*" – Sonnet 1, line 11, i.e., his substance or royal blood

4 THAN UNSWEPT STONE, BESMEARED WITH SLUTTISH TIME.
THAN UNSWEPT STONE, etc. = than stones that crumble in the course of time; "I will not ruinate my father's house, who gave his blood to lime the *stones* together" – *3 Henry VI*, 5.1.85-86; **SLUTTISH** = unclean, nasty; **TIME** = the ongoing withering of Elizabeth's mortal life, i.e., mortal time

5 WHEN WASTEFUL WAR SHALL STATUES OVERTURN
WHEN WASTEFUL, etc. = when destructive wars overturn the statues of defeated kings

6 AND BROILS ROOT OUT THE WORK OF MASONRY,
BROILS = conflicts, disorders, wars; alluding to possible civil war over the throne; and to avoid such calamity for England he is counseling his royal son to renounce the crown

7 NOR MARS HIS SWORD NOR WAR'S QUICK FIRE SHALL BURN
NOR/NOR = neither/nor; "Now have I brought a work to end which neither Jove's fierce wrath/ Nor sword, nor fire, nor fretting age with all the force it hath/ Are able to abolish quite" – Ovid's *Metamorphoses*, Book

XV, 984-986, as translated (1567) by Arthur Golding, uncle of Edward de Vere, who may have produced the translation himself

8 THE LIVING RECORD OF YOUR MEMORY
The Sonnets are to become *the living record* of Southampton, for posterity; the verses are the womb in which he is reborn and grows; this diary, which is recording his life in real time and preserving it for future generations; **LIVING** = the dynamic nature of these verses, which are being written in relation to the calendar of the reign, i.e., the diary is aimed at the royal succession upon the death of the Queen, but exactly when she will die is unknown; (in fact she will die when Southampton is still in the Tower and James of Scotland will succeed to the throne, so the diary will continue until Elizabeth's funeral, marking the official end of her Tudor dynasty); "Save men's opinions and my *living blood*" – *Richard II*, 3.1.26

9 'GAINST DEATH AND ALL OBLIVOUS ENMITY
ALL = Southampton, *One for All, All for One*; **ALL OBLIVIOUS** = forgetful of you; "So you being sick of too much doubt in your own proceedings, through which infirmity you are desirous to bury and ensevel your works in the *grave of oblivion*" – Oxford's Prefatory Letter to *Cardanus Comfort*, 1573, addressed to translator Thomas Bedingfield; **ENMITY** = contempt for you and your royal blood

10 SHALL YOU PACE FORTH! YOUR PRAISE SHALL STILL FIND ROOM
SHALL = echoing "all" for Southampton; **PACE** = step, march, walk; echoing the stately, formal pace of a king, in majesty; **SHALL YOU PACE FORTH** = shall you emerge in glory as king; **FORTH** = as in "setting forth" in the 1609 dedication of the Sonnets; **FORTH** = "out from confinement or indistinction into open view" – Schmidt; "Caesar shall *forth*" – *Julius Caesar*, 2.2.10; "an hour before the worshipped sun peered *forth* the golden window of the east" – *Romeo and Juliet*, 1.1.118-119; also, to bring forth is to beget, procreate; **YOUR PRAISE** = recognition and praise of you as king; "The pain be mine, but *thine shall be the praise*" – Sonnet 38, line 14, upon the trial when Southampton was convicted of high treason and condemned to death; **STILL** = always, eternally; **FIND ROOM** = find the place where your throne is; **ROOM** = room to be who he is; freedom from imprisonment and freedom from censorship or obliteration of his identity as prince; "Grief fills the *room* up of my absent child" – *King John*, 3.3.93; "To take their rooms ere I can plant myself" – *3 Henry VI*, 3.2.132

11 EVEN IN THE EYES OF ALL POSTERITY
EVEN IN THE EYES = in the very eyes of subjects; **ALL** = Southampton, *One for All, All for One*; **ALL POSTERITY** = the entire world in generations to come; descendants; succeeding generations, future times; "Now that Henry's dead, *posterity*, await for wretched years" – *1 Henry VI*, 1.1.47-48; "Methinks *the truth* should live from age to age, as 'twere retailed to *all posterity*" – *Richard III*, 3.1.76-77; "Beauty, Truth and Rarity,/ Grace in all simplicity,/ Here in cinders lie./ Death is now the Phoenix nest,/ And the Turtle's loyal breast/ To eternity doth rest./ *Leaving no posterity*,/ 'Twas not their infirmity,/ It was married chastity" – *The Phoenix and Turtle*, 1601, as by "William Shake-Speare", lines 53-61

> The *father*, all whose joy is nothing else
> But *fair posterity*
> - *The Winter's Tale*, 4.4.410-411

12 THAT WEAR THIS WORLD OUT TO THE ENDING DOOM.
That continue to the end of the world; "And we'll *wear out in a walled prison* packs and sects of great ones that ebb and flow by the moon" – *King Lear*, 5.3.17-19, glancing at Elizabeth, the Moon goddess; also Southampton is "the world" itself, as Gloucester depicts the King: "O ruined piece of nature, *this great world* shall so wear out to naught" – *King Lear*, 4.6.130-31; **ENDING DOOM** = the Last Judgment; the end of the Tudor Rose dynasty; "Thy end is Truth's and Beauty's *doom* and date" – Sonnet 14, line 14; echoing the possibility that Southampton will be executed and/or left in prison for life; "Supposed as forfeit to a confined *doom*" – Sonnet 107, line 1

"And all the world shall never/ Be able for to quench my name" – Ovid's *Metamorphoses*, Book XV, 990-991, translated by Oxford's uncle Arthur Golding (1567) or by the young earl himself

13 SO TILL THE JUDGMENT THAT YOUR SELF ARISE,
TILL THE JUDGMENT = the rendering of you (the *Audit* of Southampton's royal blood, in the future, to be forecast in the envoy, when nature's final accounting "though delayed, answered must be, and her *Quietus* is to *render thee*" – Sonnet 126, lines 11-12); as opposed to the judgment of the tribunal at the trial; "So thy great gift, upon *misprision* growing,/ Comes home again, on *better judgment* making" – Sonnet 87, lines 11-12, when the judgment has been changed for the better from treason to *misprision* of treason; "His royal self in *judgment* comes to hear the cause betwixt her and this great offender" – *Henry VIII*, 5.2.154-155; **THAT YOURSELF ARISE** = that you ascend to the throne, rising like the sun, in the eyes of people in the future, i.e., in posterity; ("Till the decree of the judgment-day that you arise from the dead" – Dowden); a Christ-like Resurrection of the royal son or Sunne: "Even so my Sunne one early morn did shine" – Sonnet 33, line 9; "For as the Sun is daily new and old" – Sonnet 76, line 14

14 YOU LIVE IN THIS, AND DWELL IN LOVERS' EYES.
YOU LIVE IN THIS = you continue to live in this monument of verse, growing in the womb of its tomb, by time recorded in this diary; you and your life and your blood are preserved; **THIS** = this verse; "So long as men can breathe or eyes can see,/ So long lives *this*, and *this gives life to thee*" – Sonnet 18, lines 13-14; **AND DWELL IN LOVERS' EYES** = and live in the eyes of your parents and all others who will appear, as subjects and friends, to adore you as king; "I tell thee, fellow, thy general is *my lover*" – Menenius Agrippa in *Coriolanus*, 5.2.14; **IN LOVERS' EYES** = "You will be read by persons who will love you, though dead, as men love you in life" – Tucker.

> **Horace's *Odes* III.xxx, 23 B. C.:**
> "I have completed a monument more lasting than brass and more sublime than the regal elevation of pyramids, which neither the wasting shower, the unavailing north wind, nor an innumerable succession of years, and the flight of seasons, shall be able to demolish. I shall not wholly die; but a great part of me shall escape Libitana [Roman goddess of death; presided over funerals]. I shall continually be reviewed in the praises of posterity, as long as the priest shall ascend the Capitol with the silent (vestal) virgin…"
> (Trans. C. Smart, 1873; courtesy of Derran Charlton)
>
> ***Amores*, Book I, Elegy XV, by Ovid (43 B. C. – 17 A. D.), trans. A. S. Kline:**
> So, while granite, while the unyielding ploughshare
> Perish with the years, poetry will not die…
> So even when I'm given to the final flames,
> I'll live, and the better part of me will survive.
>
> ***Rime Sparse* by Petrarch (1304-1374), trans. by A. S. Kline:**
> Do you think that Caesar or Marcellus
> Or Paulus or Africanus will ever live
> By means of the anvil and the hammer?
> My dear Pandolfo, in the end those works
> Are fragile, but my labour's such
> As can by fame make a man immortal.

Part Two

THE PRISON YEARS

DAY THIRTY IN THE TOWER

Sonnet 56
This Sad Interim
9 March 1601

Oxford records his deep sadness after meeting with Southampton in the Tower, when he had to inform his royal son of the bittersweet bargain with Robert Cecil (and the Queen) as the only way to gain a reprieve from his execution. His reference to the Ocean (sea of royal blood) is an overt homage to Southampton as a prince or king. He urges Henry Wriothesley to go along with the bargain to save his life.

Sonnet 56	Translation
Sweet love, renew thy force! Be it not said Thy edge should blunter be than appetite, Which but today by feeding is allayed, Tomorrow sharpened in his former might.	Royal son, regain your power! Be it not said That you should be less strong than my purpose, Which is but allayed today by my will But tomorrow return to your former strength!
So love be thou, although today thou fill Thy hungry eyes, even till they wink with fullness, Tomorrow see again, and do not kill The spirit of Love with a perpetual dullness.	So, royal son, be the same. While today you Bring yourself back to physical health, Tomorrow be a royal prince again. Do not kill The essence of your blood with imprisonment.
Let this sad *Interim* like the Ocean be Which parts the shore, where two contracted new Come daily to the banks, that when they see Return of love, more blest may be the view;	Let this sad time [in prison] be like royal waters Separating a king from his subjects, but Brings them together again, so when all see The return of royal blood, it will be seen freshly.
As call it winter, which being full of care, Makes summer's welcome thrice more wished, more rare.	Call this a dark time, which filled with royalty, Makes your golden time thrice more desired and rare.

1 SWEET LOVE, RENEW THY FORCE! BE IT NOT SAID
SWEET LOVE = royal prince; royal son; "Good night, *sweet* prince" – *Hamlet*, 5.2.366; **THY FORCE** = your royal power and strength; validity, as in "our late edict shall strongly *stand in force*" – *Love's Labour's Lost*, 1.1.11; your will to live

2 THY EDGE SHOULD BLUNTER BE THAN APPETITE,
EDGE = the cutting side of a blade, echoing the "edge" of the executioner's axe; "But bears it out even to the *edge of doom*" – Sonnet 116, line 12; keenness, desire, royal will; "with spirit of honor edged more sharper than your swords" – *Henry V*, 3.5.38; **APPETITE** = your desire to live; i.e., Oxford is urging his son to go along with the bargain being made for his life, appealing to his desire to live and eventually be freed from prison

3 WHICH BUT TODAY BY FEEDING IS ALLAYED,
BY FEEDING = by being put out to pasture, so to speak; "Ere we will eat our meal in fear, and sleep in the affliction of these terrible dreams that shake us nightly" – *Macbeth*, 3.2.18-19; **ALLAYED** = postponed (with **ALL** = Southampton, *One for All, All for One*)

REFERENCE EDITION

4 TOMORROW SHARP'NED IN HIS FORMER MIGHT.
TOMORROW = "Kind is my love today, *tomorrow* kind" – Sonnet 105, line 5; **FORMER MIGHT** = former royal power; "O'er-charged with burden of *mine own love's might*" – Sonnet 23, line 8; "Thy pyramids built up with *newer might*" – Sonnet 123, line 2; "England shall give him *office, honour, might*" – *2 Henry IV*, 4.5.129; "the *might* of it" – i.e., the might and power of the crown, *2 Henry IV*, 4.5.173

5 SO LOVE BE THOU, ALTHOUGH TODAY THOU FILL
SO LOVE BE THOU = so, royal son, be your royal self, since you are you; "This is I, Hamlet the Dane!" – *Hamlet*, 5.1.255; "But he that writes of you, if he can tell/ That *you are you*, so dignifies his story" – Sonnet 84, lines 7-8; act like the king you are, and go along with this decision to save your life; in giving up the throne, you help England avoid civil war, and you will gain your life and freedom

6 THY HUNGRY EYES, EVEN TILL THEY WINK WITH FULLNESS.
HUNGRY EYES = royal eyes wanting to be who he is; **WINK WITH FULLNESS** = close or shut because of the power of the sun or royal light; echoing the "winking" of Southampton's royal eyes or stars or suns;

7 TOMORROW SEE AGAIN, AND DO NOT KILL
TOMORROW SEE AGAIN = stay alive and use your kingly eyes once more; **KILL** = destroy; echoing the execution of Southampton, still a possibility, with Oxford urging his son to accept the terms of the "ransom" and, thereby, to save himself from being killed.

8 THE SPIRIT OF LOVE WITH A PERPETUAL DULLNESS.
THE SPIRIT OF LOVE = the sacredness of your royal blood (which is the essential and vital part of you); "Th'expense of *spirit* in a waste of shame" – Sonnet 128, line 1, to Elizabeth, referring to her waste of Southampton's "spirit of love" or royal blood; Essex in 1597 wrote to Elizabeth thanking her for her "sweet letters, indited by the *Spirit of spirits*" – Weir, 427; **PERPETUAL DULLNESS** = eternal shame; perpetual confinement in the Tower; eternal death

9 LET THIS SAD *IN'T'RIM* LIKE THE OCEAN BE
THIS SAD *INTERIM* = this sorrowful time of your imprisonment (which hopefully is only temporary); **OCEAN** = kingly; royal blood

*"Here, then, we have Shakespeare typifying his Friend variously as a **sun**, a **god**, an **ocean** or a **sea**: three familiar metaphors which he and his contemporaries use to represent a sovereign prince or king"* – Leslie Hotson, 1965

"Even to our *Ocean*, to our great King John" – *King John*, 5.4.57; "The *tide of blood* in me ... shall mingle with the *state of floods* and flow henceforth in formal majesty" – *2 Henry IV*, 5.2.129; "A substitute shines brightly as a king, until a king be by, and then his state empties itself, *as doth an inland brook into the main of waters*" – *Merchant of Venice*, 5.1.94-97; poets alluded to Elizabeth as "Cynthia, Queen of *Seas* and Lands" – Roy Strong, 52; "Thou art, quoth she, *a sea, a sovereign king;/* And lo, there falls into *thy boundless flood/* Black lust, dishonour, shame" – *Lucrece*, 652

10 WHICH PARTS THE SHORE, WHERE TWO CONTRACTED NEW
CONTRACTED NEW = come together again; "But thou, *contracted* to thine own *bright eyes*" – Sonnet 1, line 5; Oxford and his royal son, envisioned as newly contracted

11 COME DAILY TO THE BANKS, THAT WHEN THEY SEE
COME DAILY = like these verses written daily; echoing the day-by-day experience of his son in prison; like the tide coming daily to the banks of these "pyramids" or sonnets, as in "No! Time, thou shalt not boast that I do change! Thy pyramids built up with newer might/ To me are nothing novel, nothing strange" – Sonnet 123, lines 1-3; "Thus they do, sir; they take the flow of the Nile by certain scales in the pyramid" – *Antony and Cleopatra*, 2.7.17-18

No. 56

12 RETURN OF LOVE, MORE BLEST MAY BE THE VIEW!
RETURN OF LOVE = return of royal blood; i.e., when Southampton finally emerges from the Tower, he will be alive and so will his "love" or royal blood still live; **BLEST** = full of Southampton's royal and divine blessings; "the *blessed* sun of heaven" – Falstaff of Prince Hal in *1 Henry IV*, 2.4.403

13 AS CALL IT WINTER, WHICH BEING FULL OF CARE,
WINTER = the present time, early March of 1601; this miserable time of your imprisonment and possible death; "How like a *Winter* hath my absence been/ From thee, the pleasure of the fleeting year" – Sonnet 97, lines 1-2, corresponding with February 8, 1602; "Three *winters* cold ... /Since first I saw you fresh" – Sonnet 104, lines 3-8, corresponding to February 8, 1603, the third *winter* of Southampton's confinement; i.e., this entire time of your confinement is a *winter*; **FULL OF CARE** = full of Oxford's care for him, to save his life; "Thou best of dearest, and *mine only care*" – Sonnet 48, line 7

14 MAKES SUMMER'S WELCOME THRICE MORE WISHED, MORE RARE.
SUMMER'S WELCOME = the welcoming of the golden time of the king, of Southampton as prince, his return to freedom; "Shall I compare thee to a Summer's day ... And Summer's lease hath all too short a date ... But thy eternal Summer shall not fade" – Sonnet 18, lines 1, 4, 9; **THRICE** = related to the Trinity and also to the previously potential royal family (which is no longer possible) of Elizabeth and Oxford and Southampton; **MORE RARE** = more royal; "Beauty, Truth, and *Rarity*,/ Grace in all simplicity" – the royal family of Elizabeth, Oxford and Southampton in *The Phoenix and Turtle*, 1601, 53-5

THE MONUMENT

THE PRISON YEARS

DAY THIRTY-ONE IN THE TOWER
TIME OF EXECUTION DRAWS NEAR

Sonnet 57
I, My Sovereign, Watch the Clock for You
10 March 1601

Crowds of London citizens have been gathering in the mornings for the expected execution of Southampton. Meanwhile Oxford addresses his royal son directly as "my sovereign" and states his duty as his "slave" or "servant" (vassal in service to his Majesty the Prince) to "watch the clock for you." In the ending couplet, Oxford records the fact that the bargain for his son's life will include his own obliteration from the official record as the author of the works attributed to Will Shakespeare. The pen name is Oxford's gift to Southampton, who therefore has both a "Will" and a royal will.

Sonnet 57	Translation
Being your slave, what should I do but tend	As your Majesty's servant, I can only wait
Upon the hours and times of your desire?	For the times when you express your royal will.
I have no precious time at all to spend,	I have no time for royal duties
Nor services to do till you require.	Or services until you command me.
Nor dare I chide the world-without-end hour	Nor dare I complain about the world's immortality
Whilst I (my sovereign) watch the clock for you,	While I, my king, wait upon your fate,
Nor think the bitterness of absence sour,	Nor dare I think bitterly about your imprisonment,
When you have bid your servant once adieu.	Whenever you say goodbye to me, your servant.
Nor dare I question with my jealous thought	Nor dare I raise questions in my mind about
Where you may be, or your affairs suppose,	Your room in the Tower or guess what you do,
But like a sad slave stay and think of nought	But instead, like a sad servant, think of nothing
Save where you are how happy you make those.	Except how your royal presence comforts others.
So true a fool is love that in your Will	My love is such, being your Will Shakespeare,
(Though you do any thing) he thinks no ill.	I think no ill of you no matter what you do.

1 BEING YOUR SLAVE, WHAT SHOULD I DO BUT TEND
SLAVE = servant to a prince or king, as in "your servant" in line 8 below; same as one who serves "in vassalage" as in "Lord of my love, to whom in vassalage/ Thy merit hath my duty strongly knit" - Sonnet 26, line 1; "Thou factious Duke of York, descend my throne, and *kneel for grace and mercy at my feet*: I am thy sovereign." – *3 Henry VI*, 1.1.74-76; "Be humble to us, call my sovereign yours, and do him homage as *obedient subjects*" – *1 Henry VI*, 4.2.6-7; "Myself I throw, dread sovereign, at thy foot. My life thou shalt command" – *Richard II*, 1.1.165-166)

> It is *the curse of kings to be attended*
> By **slaves** that take their humours for a warrant
> - *King John*, 4.2.208-209

> That God forbid, that made me first *your slave*
> - Sonnet 58, line 1

346

TEND = "That millions of strange shadows on you tend" – Sonnet 53, line 2; "Who didst thou leave to *tend* his Majesty?" – *King John*, 5.6.32; "The summer still doth *tend upon my state*" – Queen Titania in *A Midsummer Night's Dream*, 3.1.147; "Where twice so many have a command to *tend* you" – to the King in *King Lear*, 2.2.453-454; "*Tend* me tonight" – *Antony & Cleopatra*, 4.2.24); "The which *attending* from the Court, I will take my leave of your Lordship" – Oxford to Burghley, July 1581

2 UPON THE HOURS AND TIMES OF YOUR DESIRE?
HOURS AND TIMES = the time being reflected in these sonnets, related to the ever-waning life of Elizabeth; **UPON THE HOURS AND TIMES OF YOUR DESIRE** = the times chosen by your royal will; "When was the *hour* I ever contradicted your *desire*, or made it not mine too?" – Queen Katharine pleads with the king for mercy, *Henry VIII*, 2.4.26-27

3 I HAVE NO PRECIOUS TIME AT ALL TO SPEND,
PRECIOUS = royal; "Tend'ring the *precious* safety of *my prince*" – *Richard II*, 1.1.32; **TIME** = repeated from the previous line, emphasizing the importance of this ongoing time, now leading to the possible execution of Southampton; **ALL** = Southampton, *One for All, All for One*

4 NOR SERVICES TO DO TILL YOU REQUIRE.
SERVICES = duties in service to him as prince; ("my duteous *service*" – *Richard III*, 2.1.64; "A boon, my sovereign, for my *service* done" – *Richard III*, 2.1.96; "Commend my service to my sovereign" – *Henry V*, 4.6.23; "My gracious lord, I tender you my *service*" – Richard II, 2.3.41; "To faithful *service of your Majesty*" – *Richard II*, 3.3.118; "Then hear me, gracious sovereign, and you peers that owe yourselves, your lives and *services, to this imperial throne*" – *Henry V*, 1.2.33-35; "So *service* shall with steeled sinews toil, and labour shall refresh itself with hope to do Your Grace incessant *services* – *Henry V*, 2.2.36-39; "We shall present our *services* to a fine new prince" – *The Winter's Tale*, 2.117; "Beseech your Highness, give us better credit; we have always truly *served* you, and beseech you so to esteem of us, and *on our knees* we beg, as recompense of our dear *services*" – *The Winter's Tale*, 2.3.146-149, i.e., in service or slavery

> And happily may your sweet self put on
> The lineal state and glory of the land!
> To whom, with *all submission, on my knee*
> I do bequeath my faithful *services*
> And true *subjection* everlastingly *King John*, 5.7.101-105
> - (The Bastard to Prince Henry, son of now-deceased King John)

"I *serve* Her Majesty" - Oxford to Burghley, October 30, 1584

TILL YOU REQUIRE = until you, my sovereign, command me; "The gods require our thanks" – *Timon of Athens*, 3.6.67-68

5 NOR DARE I CHIDE THE WORLD WITHOUT END HOUR
CHIDE = rebuke, scold, quarrel with; "A thing like death to chide away this shame" – *Romeo and Juliet*, 4.1.74; **THE WORLD WITHOUT END HOUR** = eternity; ("As it was in the beginning, is now, and ever shall be, *world without end*" – Morning Prayer Service); **END HOUR** = perhaps a play on "endower" – i.e., Henry Wriothesley, if he is not the King, can no longer "endow" the Tudor dynasty; he was "*the world's* fresh ornament" in Sonnet 1, line 9, but now "the world" will be "without" him as its "endower."

6 WHILST I (MY SOVEREIGN) WATCH THE CLOCK FOR YOU.
MY SOVEREIGN = Oxford speaking to his royal son as his prince or king; "The purest spring is not so free from mud as I am clear from treason to ***my sovereign***" – *2 Henry VI*, 3.2; "Comfort, ***my sovereign***! Gracious Henry, comfort!" – *2 Henry VI*, 3.2.37; "Good morrow to ***my sovereign*** King and Queen!" – *Richard III*, 2.1.47; "A boon, ***my sovereign***, for my service done" – to the King in *Richard III*, 2.1.96; "***My gracious sovereign***, my most loving liege" – *Richard II*, 1.1.21; "The King, ***thy sovereign***" – *1 Henry VI*,

3.1.25; "Be humble to us, call *my sovereign* yours and do him homage as obedient subjects" – *1 Henry VI*, 4.2.6-7

WATCH THE CLOCK FOR YOU = Remain vigilant while the time leads to the hour when you may be executed; keep recording this time in these verses; wait with mounting anxiety over your impending execution; "To play the *watchman* ever for thy sake" – Sonnet 61, line 12; "so vexed with *watching* and with tears" – Sonnet 148, line 10; "The special *watchmen* of our English weal" – *1 Henry VI*, 3.1.66; "For sleeping England long time have I *watched*" – *Richard II*, 2.1.77; "What *watchful* cares do interpose themselves betwixt your eyes and night?" – *Julius Caesar*, 2.1.98-99; stand guard for you and your blood; "To guard a title that was rich before" – *King John*, 4.2.10

7 NOR THINK THE BITTERNESS OF ABSENCE SOUR,
BITTERNESS OF ABSENCE = the pain of your absence of liberty, of your absence from me, of your absence from the rest of England, being in the Tower; "Th'imprisoned absence of your liberty" – Sonnet 58, line 6; "O absence, what a torment" – Sonnet 39, line 9; "From you have I been absent" – Sonnet 98, line 1; "I will acquaintance strangle and look strange,/ Be absent from thy walks" – Sonnet 89, lines 8-9, referring to the "walks" he shared with Southampton on the roof of his prison quarters within the Tower fortress; **SOUR** = hurtful

8 WHEN YOU HAVE BID YOUR SERVANT ONCE ADIEU.
YOUR SERVANT = your Majesty's loyal and faithful servant; "Servant in arms to Harry King of England" – *1 Henry VI*, 4.2.4; "Fit counselor and *servant for a prince*" – *Pericles*, 1.2.63; "The same, my lord, and your poor *servant* ever" – Horatio to the Prince in *Hamlet*, 1.2.162

9 NOR DARE I QUESTION WITH MY JEALOUS THOUGHT
DARE = Oxford speaking of his need to remain silent or be charged with treason for proclaiming his son's right to the throne; "Then may I *dare* to boast how I do love thee,/ Till then, *not show my head* where thou mayst prove me" – Sonnet 26, lines 13-14; **JEALOUS** = ("Vehement in feeling, as in wrath, desire, or devotion ... Zealous or solicitious for the preservation or well-being of something possessed or esteemed; vigilant or careful in guarding" - *OED*); "I have been very *jealous* for the Lord God of Host" – Geneva Bible, 1560, 1 Kings 19.10

10 WHERE YOU MAY BE, OR YOUR AFFAIRS SUPPOSE,
WHERE YOU MAY BE = within the Tower; **YOUR AFFAIRS** = you affairs of state; "What one has to do ... business" - *OED*; "But what is *your affair* in Elsinore?" – *Hamlet*, 1.2.174; "So I thrive in my dangerous *affairs*" – the King in *Richard III*, 4.4.398; "To treat of *high affairs* touching that time" – *King John*, 1.1.101; to Queen Elizabeth: "To stand in *thy affairs*, fall by thy side" – Sonnet 151, line 12

11 BUT LIKE A SAD SLAVE STAY AND THINK OF NOUGHT
SAD SLAVE = unhappy servant; **SLAVE** = "a person who is absolutely subject to the will of another" – Schmidt; repeated from line 1; **NOUGHT** = nothing; an image of Southampton as "none" (the opposite of "one") and "nothing" or a "nobody" in the prison; Oxford must think of "nothing" and so he may think of his son, who is "nothing" in the eyes of authority

12 SAVE WHERE YOU ARE HOW HAPPY YOU MAKE THOSE.
Except how happy you make those who are in your royal presence, i.e., those other criminals or traitors in the Tower; **SAVE** = except; **WHERE YOU ARE** = in the Tower; **HAPPY** = ("Health to *my sovereign*, and *new happiness*" – *2 Henry IV*, 4.4.); **THOSE** = the other prisoners (and even the guards) in the Tower

13 SO TRUE A FOOL IS LOVE THAT IN YOUR WILL
TRUE = Oxford, *Nothing Truer than Truth*; **FOOL** = Oxford had pictured himself as a Jester or "allowed fool" at Court (allowed by the Queen), who wrote "comedies" laced with political satire and appeared to make a fool of himself; **IN LOVE** = in service of the royal blood; **YOUR WILL** = your royal will, with a play on "Will" Shakespeare, the pseudonym Oxford created in order to publicly support his son

14 (THOUGH YOU DO ANY THING) HE THINKS NO ILL.
HE = love, i.e., royal blood can do no ill; also Oxford, as loving father; **NO ILL** = as opposed to the "ill deeds" of the Rebellion, i.e., Southampton must repent (and forfeit the crown) and this act, with Oxford's sacrifice of his own identity, will "ransom all *ill deeds*" – Sonnet 34, line 14; a play on "illegitimate", i.e., Oxford still "thinks no ill" or thinks his son is not illegitimate; "If some *suspect of ill* masked not thy show" – Sonnet 70, line 13, referring to Southampton as a "suspect traitor" who has been convicted and is now in the Tower facing execution

THE PRISON YEARS

DAY THIRTY-TWO IN THE TOWER
EXECUTION DRAWS NEAR

Sonnet 58
Imprisoned Absence
Your Self to Pardon
11 March 1601

Speaking as a "vassal" or subject of a king, Oxford indicates that the bargain being made for Southampton's life includes gaining a royal pardon for him. He introduces the younger earl's "charter" or royal privilege as so "strong" that he will be able to gain this "pardon" – the same "charter" of Sonnet 87, line 3, that will give him "releasing" from prison by King James. As a practical matter, Southampton holds his fate in his own hands, since he must decide to give up any claim to the throne. Has he agreed to this ransom for his life or is he resisting it? Meanwhile the Queen is still (or at least officially) in charge and the "hell" of "waiting" for her either to execute her son or spare him continues.

Sonnet 58	Translation
That God forbid, that made me first your slave,	God, who first made me your servant, forbade me
I should in thought control your times of pleasure,	From controlling your royal will for me to visit,
Or at your hand th'account of hours to crave,	Or that I might ask you how you spend your time,
Being your vassal bound to stay your leisure.	Since I'm your servant obliged to wait upon you.
Oh let me suffer (being at your beck)	Oh, let me suffer, ready for your royal command,
Th'imprisoned absence of your liberty,	Your kingly freedom to imprison yourself,
And patience tame to sufferance bide each check,	And let me govern my own patience
Without accusing you of injury.	Without blaming you for my suffering!
Be where you list, your charter is so strong,	Even in prison your kingly privilege is so royal
That you yourself may privilege your time	That you are entitled to spend your time
To what you will; to you it doth belong	According to your royal will. To you it belongs
Yourself to pardon of self-doing crime.	To pardon yourself for your own treason!
I am to wait, though waiting so be hell,	I am to wait, though waiting so be hell,
Not blame your pleasure, be it ill or well.	Not blame your royal pleasure, whatever it is.

1 THAT GOD FORBID, THAT MADE ME FIRST YOUR SLAVE,

That God, who made me your "slave" or servant from the beginning, forbids or forbade; ("But *God forbid* that I should rejoice, but in the cross of our Lord" – Galatians, 6:14); an image of Oxford serving his son as one who serves a god, i.e., as "a God in love" of Sonnet 110, line 12 or as "the little Love-God" of Sonnet 154, line 1; **FIRST** = a term referring to a general period of time in the past, as in, "Since *first* I saw you fresh, which yet are green" – Sonnet 104, line 8; **SLAVE** = servant; "a person who is absolutely subject to the will of another" – Schmidt; carried over from the previous verse: "Being your *slave*, what should I do but tend/ Upon the hours and times of your desire?" – Sonnet 57, lines 1-2

2 I SHOULD IN THOUGHT CONTROL YOUR TIMES OF PLEASURE,

IN THOUGHT = have it in my mind, i.e., that I should think I can determine how you spend your time, or when I may visit according to your royal pleasure; **CONTROL** = have power over; i.e., God forbid I should have power over you, my prince; Southampton is a prince or king with all "in his *controlling*" in Sonnet 20, line 7; "Can yet the lease of my true love *control*" – Sonnet 107, line 3; "A true soul/ When most impeached stands least in *thy control*" – Sonnet 125, line 14, admitting that Southampton has lost all claim to be king or have *control*, just before Oxford ends his diary; **PLEASURE** = your Majesty's pleasure or royal will; **YOUR TIMES OF PLEASURE** = the times when you command me to visit you in the Tower

3 OR AT YOUR HAND TH'ACCOUNT OF HOURS TO CRAVE,

Or to ask you to give me an accounting, by your royal hand, of how you spend your hours; **AT YOUR HAND** = at your royal command; "Yet shall you have all kindness *at my hand*" – King Lewis in *Henry VI*, 3.3.149; "And if thy poor devoted servant may but beg one favor *at thy gracious hand*" – *Richard III*, 1.2.210-211; as when Oxford writes of the Queen having refused to acknowledge their son as her natural heir by recording that the boy "Was sleepling *by a Virgin hand* disarmed" – Sonnet 154, line 8; "A dearer merit ... have I deserved *at Your Highness' hands*" – *Richard II*, 1.3.156-158; **TH'ACCOUNT OF HOURS** = record of time with you; (also possibly a play on "ours," referring to these sonnets as this "account of ours"); the "account" is also the "sum" or "store" or "treasure" or "Audit" of Southampton's royal blood; **CRAVE** = beg, as to a king or superior; "Then I *crave pardon* of Your Majesty" – *3 Henry VI*, 4.6.6-8; "Till time and vantage *crave my company*" – Northumberland in *2 Henry IV*, 2.3.68

4 BEING YOUR VASSAL BOUND TO STAY YOUR LEISURE.

YOUR VASSAL = your servant; "That lift your *vassal* hands against my head and threat the glory of my precious crown" – *Richard II*, 3.3.89-90; "Your Majesty's *humblest vassal*, Essex" – the Earl of Essex to Queen Elizabeth, 1600; "Lord of my love, to whom *in vassalage*" – Oxford to Southampton, Sonnet 26, line 1; **BOUND** = tied to; obliged; imprisoned; "My duty ... is *bound* to your Lordship" – dedication of *Lucrece* to Southampton; **STAY** = wait upon; restrict; **STAY YOUR LEISURE** = wait until you have time to listen; wait upon your royal time; the time of which you may freely dispose; "I will attend upon *your lordship's leisure*" – *1 Henry VI*, 5.1.55; "the adverse winds, whose *leisure* I have *stay'd*" – *King John*, 2.1.57-58; "We will *stay your leisure*" – to Hotspur in *1 Henry IV*, 1.3.254

5 OH LET ME SUFFER (BEING AT YOUR BECK)

OH = O = Oxford; **ME** = Oxford; **LET ME SUFFER** = allow me to suffer by making this sacrifice on your behalf, to save your life and gain your freedom with honor; "To weigh how once *I suffered in your crime*" – Sonnet 121, line 8; **BEING AT YOUR BECK** = I, being your servant and at your command; "Egypt, thou knewst too well my heart was to thy rudder tied by th'strings and thou shouldst tow me after. O'er my spirit thy full supremacy thou knewst, and that *thy beck* might from the bidding of the gods command me" – *Antony and Cleopatra*, 3.11.56-61

6 TH'IMPRISONED ABSENCE OF YOUR LIBERTY,

IMPRISONED = Southampton, imprisoned; **ABSENCE OF YOUR LIBERTY** The "absence" of Southampton's liberty is imprisoned within Oxford's mind and heart; (it "also carries suggestions of 'lack of the liberty of you,' 'lack of the privilege of unrestricted access to you" – Booth); "I cannot conceive in so short a time and in so small an *absence* how so great a change is happened to you" – Oxford to Robert Cecil, December 4, 1601; **LIBERTY** = Southampton's freedom and even his life itself, the *absence* of which would mean his death (by execution); "Those pretty wrongs that *liberty* commits" – Sonnet 41, line 1; "Humbly complaining to her deity got my Lord Chamberlain *his liberty*" – *Richard III*, 1.1.76-77

> "I am sorry to see you ta'an from **liberty**, to look on the business present. 'Tis His Highness' pleasure you shall ***to th'Tower***" - *Henry VIII*, 1.2.204-207

> *His liberty* is full of threats to all.
> - *Hamlet*, 4.1.14

THE MONUMENT

7 AND PATIENCE TAME TO SUFF'RANCE BIDE EACH CHECK,
PATIENCE TAME = make my patience tame; cure my impatience; be tamed by patience; **SUFFERANCE** = subjugation; also, related to suffering or misery; **BIDE** = follow; **CHECK** = restriction or hindrance (from being able to see you)

8 WITHOUT ACCUSING YOU OF INJURY.
ACCUSING = recalling the legal accusation of treason against Southampton; "Since that the truest issue of thy throne by his own interdiction stands *accused*" – *Macbeth*, 4.3.106-107; "*Accuse* me thus" – Sonnet 117, line 1, Oxford speaking after Southampton has been released and he, Oxford, has accepted all blame; **INJURY** = "injustice, wrong … offence … crime … anything contrary to a benefit … the wrong suffered by one" – Schmidt; "To bear love's wrong than hate's known *injury*" – Sonnet 40, line 12

9 BE WHERE YOU LIST, YOUR CHARTER IS SO STRONG
BE WHERE YOU LIST = wherever you want to be; wherever you are or happen to be; **YOUR CHARTER** = your royal privilege; "What he sets before us … is *not* the powers of a peer, but *those peculiar to a king*: power *to grant charters of privilege* and *letters patent*, power *to pardon crimes* – in short, the exclusively *royal prerogative*" – Leslie Hotson, referring to the poet addressing a king; "Charter – privilege, acknowledged right – a standard, nearly atrophied, metaphor from the written document by which a privilege, right, or *pardon* was legally granted" – Booth; "The *charter of thy worth* gives thee *releasing*" – Sonnet 87, line 3, related to the same kingly rights that will spare Southampton from execution and finally give him "releasing" from the Tower; **SO STRONG** = so royal; accompanied by such royal power; "You break no privilege nor charter there" – *Richard III*, 2.4.54); **CHARTER** = "A written document delivered by the sovereign or legislature; granting *privileges* to, or recognizing rights of; *granting pardon*, to *receive a pardon*" – OED, citing "Maister John Hume had his charter and was pardoned by the King" (1480); and "a *charter of pardon*" (Francis Bacon, 1626); (therefore Oxford is saying that James of Scotland, once he ascends as King of England, will grant Southampton a pardon; which, in fact, he will do); "Is not his heir a well-deserving son? Take Hereford's rights away, and take from Time his *charters* and his *customary rights*" – *Richard II*, 2.1.194-196

10 THAT YOU YOUR SELF MY PRIVILEGE YOUR TIME
YOU YOUR SELF = an emphasis on his royal identity; "This is I, Hamlet the Dane!" – *Hamlet*, 5.2.255-256; "But he that writes of you, if he can tell that *you are you*" – Sonnet 84, lines 7-8; **PRIVILEGE YOUR TIME** = related to the *charter* (or charter of privilege) of line 9; i.e., you are a king, so you may command yourself; "Such neighbor nearness to our sacred blood should nothing *privilege* him" – *Richard II*, 1.1.119-120

11 TO WHAT YOU WILL; TO YOU IT DOTH BELONG
TO WHAT YOU WILL = according to what your Majesty desires, to what you command; to do the bidding of your royal will; **TO YOU IT DOTH BELONG** = the royal power belongs to you; **BELONG** = referring to what belongs to a king; "Disdaining *duty that to us belongs*" – Queen to King in *2 Henry VI*, 3.1.17; "with all appertiments *belonging to his honour*" – *Henry V*, 2.2.87-88; "Doth not thy embassage *belong to me*" – the Queen in *Richard II*, 3.4.93

12 YOUR SELF TO PARDON OF SELF-DOING CRIME.
YOUR SELF TO PARDON = you, being a king, may pardon your royal self; (if and when Southampton's life is spared, he will need a *royal pardon* or else he will remain at the monarch's mercy; Oxford is working to gain promise of such a pardon from James, if it is arranged that he will succeed Elizabeth on the throne; **CRIME** = the treason of which you have been convicted; **PARDON** = "Say '*pardon*', king … No word like '*pardon*' for kings' mouths so meet" – *Richard II*, 5.3.116, 118; "letters of the kings' grace and *pardon*" – *Henry VIII*, 1.2.104; "your Grace's *pardon*" – *Richard II*, 1.1.141); after releasing Southampton on April 10, 1603, King James will issue him a royal pardon, based on prior negotiations involving Oxford and Robert Cecil, by which Southampton agrees to give up any royal claim; at this point in time, of course, the condemned earl still hopes his mother the Queen might grant it to him: "O let her never suffer to be spilled the blood of him that desires to live but to do her service, nor lose the glory she shall gain in the world by

pardoning one whose heart is without spot, though his cursed destiny hath made his acts to be condemned" – Southampton to the Council, after the trial (Stopes, 225); "A gracious king that *pardons* all *offences*" - *Henry VIII*, 2.2.66; "May one be *pardoned* and retain th'*offence*?" - *Hamlet*, 3.3.56; "You straight are on your knees for *'Pardon, pardon!'* And I, unjustly too, must grant it to you" - *Richard III*, 2.2.125-126; "Subjects may challenge nothing of their sovereigns; but, if an humble prayer may prevail, then I crave *pardon* of Your Majesty" - *3 Henry VI*, 4.6.6-8

> *Pardon* me, God, I knew not what I did:
> And *pardon*, father, for I knew not thee.
> My tears shall wipe away these bloody marks
> *3 Henry VI*, 2.5.69-71

"Thus in haste I *crave Your Majesty's pardon*…" - Oxford to Elizabeth, June 1599

CRIME = "To weigh how once I suffered in your crime" - Sonnet 120, line 8; "Which die for goodness, who have lived for crime" - Sonnet 124, line 14

13 I AM TO WAIT, THOUGH WAITING BE SO HELL
I AM = "I am that I am" – Sonnet 121, line 9; (William or Will-I-Am or I-Am-Will); **WAIT** = wait upon, as a servant waits upon the presence of his king; "And't please your grace, the two great cardinals *wait in the presence*" – *Henry VIII*, 3.1.16-17; Oxford must wait for the chance to visit him in the Tower; **WAITING BE SO HELL** = also the agonizing wait for the Queen to decide whether Southampton will live or die; "y'have passed a *hell* of Time,/ And I, a tyrant, have no *leisure* taken/ To weigh how once *I suffered in your crime*" – Sonnet 121, lines 6-8; **WAITING** = "your *waiting vassals*" – *Richard III*, 2.1.122; "*waiting in the Court*" – *1 Henry IV*, 1.2.67

14 NOT BLAME YOUR PLEASURE BE IT ILL OR WELL.
NOT BLAME YOUR PLEASURE = not blame your royal pleasure or will; "the *pleasure* of the fleeting year" – Sonnet 97, line 2, referring to the royal pleasure or will of Elizabeth, who has kept Southampton in the Tower at her pleasure; "But since she (nature, the Queen) pricked thee out for women's (her own) *pleasure*" – Sonnet 20, line 13, referring to Elizabeth's royal will; "Now the cause falling out to be good, and by course of law Her Majesty's, it is justice that Her Majesty may bestow the same at *her pleasure*" – Oxford to Robert Cecil, December 4, 1601; **BLAME** = to blame for a crime or fault; to censure or find fault with; "Or will you *blame and lay the fault* on me?" – *1 Henry VI*, 2.1.57; echoing the blame put upon Essex and Southampton at the trial; "I cannot *blame* thee … But yet be *blamed*" – Sonnet 40, lines 7-8

THE PRISON YEARS

DAY THIRTY-THREE IN THE TOWER
EXECUTION DRAWS NEARER

Sonnet 59
*Labouring for Invention
The Second Burden of a Former Child*
12 March 1601

While waiting for Elizabeth to make her decision about the fate of their royal son (or waiting for him to agree to give up his claim to the throne), Oxford continues to record the days of Southampton's life in this diary. He refers to his "invention" of the Sonnets, an "invention" he introduced when publicly dedicating Venus and Adonis to him as "the first heir of my invention" or his invented name "William Shakespeare." Now that "invention" has been extended to his method of communicating to posterity through the poetry of the Sonnets; and he is "laboring for invention" by giving his son rebirth in the womb and living record of the private verses. This diary is itself the "second burthen" (new burden of childbirth or re-creation) of a "former child," i.e., of a son who was once his but who was taken from him by the Queen.

Sonnet 59	Translation
If there be nothing new, but that which is Hath been before, how are our brains beguiled, Which, lab'ring for invention, bear amiss The second burthen of a former child!	Since your royal blood is just as new as it Was before, how can my brain be a womb Which, giving birth in this verse, miscarry with This second burden of my masked royal son!
Oh that record could with a backward look, Even of five hundred courses of the Sunne, Show me your image in some antique book, Since mind at first in character was done,	Oh, I wish I could look back on the history Of five centuries of my royal son, To show me your presence in those old books, Since the beginning of writing itself,
That I might see what the old world could say To this composed wonder of your frame; Whether we are mended, or where better they Or whether revolution be the same.	So I might see what ancient writers said About my composing of your royalty here, And whether I've improved it or theirs is better, Or whether we create you the same way.
Oh sure I am the wits of former days To subjects worse have given admiring praise.	Oh, I'm sure the wise men of ancient times Paid homage to lesser royal subjects than I do.

1 IF THERE BE NOTHING NEW BUT THAT WHICH IS
Proverbial and biblical; "if there is nothing new under the sun," echoing the royal sun; i.e., there is nothing new under the royal son; "For as the Sun is daily *new* and old,/ So is my love still telling what is told" – Sonnet 76, lines 13-14

2 HATH BEEN BEFORE, HOW ARE OUR BRAINS BEGUILED,
BEGUILED = cheated; "Thou dost *beguile* the world" – Sonnet 3, line 4

3 WHICH, LABORING FOR INVENTION, BEAR AMISS
LABORING FOR INVENTION = The image of Oxford's brain giving birth or rebirth to his son in these sonnets, using his "invention" explained in Sonnet 76 and demonstrated in Sonnet 105.

"Only, if your Honour seem but pleased, I account myself highly praised; and vow to take advantage of all idle hours, till I have honoured you with some *graver labour*. But if **the first heir of my invention** prove deformed, I shall be sorry it had so noble a godfather, and never after ear so
barren a land, for fear it shall yield me still so bad a harvest" - Dedication of *Venus and Adonis* to Southampton

"My very good Lord. I have *labored* so much as I could possibly to advance Her Majesty's customs of tin" – Oxford to Burghley, April 9, 1595

BEAR = give birth to; bear the burden of; **BEAR AMISS** = bear a son consigned by the Queen to the status of a royal bastard; "suggests 'miscarry'" – Booth; "Myself corrupting salving thy *amiss*" – Sonnet 35, line 7, referring to his son's role in the Rebellion

4 THE SECOND BURTHEN OF A FORMER CHILD!
BURTHEN = burden; **THE SECOND BURTHEN OF A FORMER CHILD** = the second birth of you, and responsibility for you, in this secret diary; ("give birth a second time to a child that lived before" – Booth, citing the "primary" sense); Oxford is using the Sonnets in order to give "rebirth" to his son and to grow him in the "womb" of his diary written according to the dwindling time of the life of his mother the Queen; he is replacing Elizabeth's womb with this one; "My *first burthen*, coming before his time, must needs be a blind whelp, the *second* brought forth after his time must needs be a monster, the one I sent to a noble man to nurse, who with great love brought him up, for a year" – John Lyly, 1580, dedicating *Euphues his England* to Oxford; **FORMER CHILD** = "But out alack, *he was but one hour mine*,/ The region cloud hath masked him from me now" – Sonnet 33, lines 11-12; to Southampton, referring to these private verses: "Commit to these waste blanks, and thou shalt find/ Those *children nursed*, delivered from thy brain" – Sonnet 77, lines 10-11

5 OH THAT RECORD COULD WITH A BACKWARD LOOK,
RECORD = the true record of your life in the Sonnets (oh, that it could look all the way back in time); "The living *record* of your memory" – Sonnet 55, line 8, referring to the record of his son's life in these verses; "For thy *records*, and what we see, doth lie" – Sonnet 123, line 11, referring to the records of Time, i.e., historical records, that fail to tell the truth

6 EVEN OF FIVE HUNDRED COURSES OF THE SUNNE,
FIVE HUNDRED COURSES OF THE SUN = referring to the five hundred years of the Oxford earldom, when his official blood lineage began in England; the royal past of England from 1066; **THE SUNNE** = linking his royal son to the blood lineage of past kings; "Even so *my Sunne* one early morn did shine" – Sonnet 33, line 9; "Making a couplement of proud compare/ With *Sunne and Moone*" – Sonnet 21, lines 5-6, i.e., Southampton and Elizabeth; "And scarcely greet me with that sunne, thine eye" – Sonnet 49, line 6; "Clouds and *eclipses* stain both *Moone and Sunne*" – Sonnet 35, line 3, i.e., both mother and son; "And crooked *eclipses* 'gainst his glory fight" – Sonnet 60, line7; "The mortal *Moone* hath her *eclipse* endured" – Sonnet 107, line 5; "My Mistress' eyes are nothing like *the Sunne*" – Sonnet 130, line 1; "And truly not the morning *Sun of Heaven*/ Better becomes the gray cheeks of the East" – Sonnet 132, line5

7 SHOW ME YOUR IMAGE IS SOME ANTIQUE BOOK,
Giving evidence of you in some old account or written account of the past; **YOUR IMAGE** = your royal image; "The image of the King … your most royal image" – *2 Henry IV*, 5.3.79, 89

8 SINCE MIND AT FIRST IN CHARACTER WAS DONE:
MIND = the mind of humankind; **IN CHARACTER** = in the form of written words on the page; "What's in the brain that Ink may *character*,/ Which hath not figur'd to thee my true spirit?" – Sonnet 108, lines 1-2, to Southampton; **DONE** = expressed, written down

9 THAT I MIGHT SEE WHAT THE OLD WORLD COULD SAY
THE OLD WORLD = the realm of old England, in history

REFERENCE EDITION

10 TO THIS COMPOSED WONDER OF YOUR FRAME:
To these sonnets, in which I compose the "wonder" or royal blood of you; "His head by nature framed to wear a crown" – *3 Henry VI*, 4.6.72; **WONDER** = miracle; "won" playing on "one" for Southampton, as in the "wondrous excellence" and "wondrous scope" of Sonnet 105, marking Elizabeth's death, followed by their amazement and marveling at the fact of Southampton's forthcoming release amid the accession of James: "For we which now behold these present days,/ Have eyes to *wonder*, but lack tongues to praise" – Sonnet 106, lines 13-14

11 WHETHER WE ARE MENDED, OR WHERE BETTER THEY,
Whether we have done you more justice and where they would have written a better account of your life; **WE** = the royal "we" used in the opening of the diary: "From fairest creatures *we* desire increase" – Sonnet 1, line 1

12 OR WHETHER REVOLUTION BE THE SAME.
REVOLUTION = the cycle of the sun and planets; echoing the Rebellion or revolt; "For as the Sun is daily new and old,/ So is my love still telling what is told" – Sonnet 76, lines 13-14; **THE SAME** = without change; echoing Elizabeth's motto *Semper Eadem* or *Ever the Same*, inserted as "Why write I still all one, ever *the same*" of Sonnet 76, line 5

13 OH SURE I AM THE WITS OF FORMER DAYS
OH = O = Oxford; **I AM** = "I am that I am" – Sonnet 121, line 9; **THE WITS** = the wise writers or contemporary historians (of the past); ironically in the 1580s Oxford was leader of a group of writers known later as the University Wits, who have been regarded as the immediate "forerunners" or "predecessors" of Shakespeare

14 TO SUBJECTS WORSE HAVE GIVEN ADMIRING PRAISE.
SUBJECTS = topics; servants of the monarch; **TO SUBJECTS WORSE** = to lesser subjects of a monarch; i.e., Southampton is a subject of the Queen; in the eyes of the law he is a traitor, but other "subjects" praised by writers have been much worse

Part Two

THE PRISON YEARS

EXECUTIONS OF MERRICK & CUFFE
SOUTHAMPTON EXECUTION DRAWS NEARER

DAY THIRTY-FOUR IN THE TOWER
Sonnet 60
Our Minutes Hasten To Their End
Crooked Eclipses 'Gainst His Glory Fight
13 March 1601

Essex-Southampton supporters Gelly Merrick and Henry Cuffe were taken today to Tyburn, where they were put through the horrible ordeal of being hanged, drawn and quartered. Oxford uses the royal imagery of the Ocean or Sea to envision the "changing place" or alteration of monarchs upon the royal succession. He refers to the crooked figure of hunchbacked Secretary Robert Cecil in citing the "crooked eclipses" fighting to deprive Southampton of being "crowned" with "glory" as a king. Oxford braces himself for the moment Southampton will come under the "scythe" or blade of the executioner as well as the "cruel hand" of Elizabeth -- reminiscent of when their newly born royal son had been "by a Virgin hand disarmed" as put in Sonnet 154 of the Bath prologue.

Sonnet 60	Translation
Like as the waves make towards the pebbled shore,	Like the waves [royal sea, i.e., James] making their way to the shore,
So do our minutes hasten to their end,	So do our minutes hasten toward your execution,
Each changing place with that which goes before,	Each minute replacing [succeeding to the throne] the one before it,
In sequent toil all forwards do contend.	And toiling to move forward in succession.
Nativity, once in the main of light,	My son, who was born in all royalty,
Crawls to maturity, wherewith being crowned,	Now grows into majesty as a crowned king,
Crooked eclipses 'gainst his glory fight,	While crook-back Cecil fights against his glory,
And time that gave doth now his gift confound.	And the Queen that bore him now destroys him.
Time doth transfix the flourish set on youth,	Her dwindling life span pierces his young royalty,
And delves the parallels in beauty's brow,	And makes his royal blood no longer fresh;
Feeds on the rarities of nature's truth,	This time devours the son of Elizabeth and Oxford,
And nothing stands but for his scythe to mow.	And his existence is subject to her destruction.
And yet to time in hope my verse shall stand,	And yet my hope in this verse will withstand her,
Praising thy worth, despite his cruel hand.	Praising your royalty, despite her murder of you!

"At the gallows Cuffe declared that he hoped for salvation in the atonement of his Savior's blood ... and asking pardon of God and the Queen, he was despatched by the executioner. After him Sir Gelly Merrick suffered in the same way ... and intreated those noblemen who stood by to intercede with the Queen that there might not be any further proceedings against such as had unwarily espoused this unhappy cause." - An Elizabethan Chronicle

"As every wave drives others forth, and that comes behind/ Both thrusteth and is thrust himself; even so the time by kind/ Do fly and follow both at once and evermore renew" – Ovid's Metamorphoses as translated by Oxford's uncle Arthur Golding (cited by Holmes, 291)

REFERENCE EDITION

1 **LIKE AS THE WAVES MAKE TOWARDS THE PEBBLED SHORE,**
WAVES = related to the "ocean" of royal blood; ("'Thou art,' quoth she, '*a sea, a sovereign king*, and lo there falls into thy boundless flood black lust, dishonor, shame, misgoverning, who seek to stain the *ocean of thy blood*.' – *Lucrece*, 652-654); image of King James succeeding Elizabeth

2 **SO DO OUR MINUTES HASTEN TO THEIR END,**
OUR MINUTES = the time we have left, the actual minutes racing onward; **HASTEN** = "How like a Winter hath my absence been/ From thee, the pleasure of the fleeting year" – Sonnet 97, lines 1-2; "And all in war with Time for love of you" – Sonnet 15, line 13; **THEIR END** = the end of these minutes, ending your life or ending Elizabeth's reign; the end of this diary, which is leading to the time of royal succession, when the fate of the Tudor dynasty will be determined; "Thy *end* is Truth's and Beauty's doom and date" – Sonnet 14, line 14

3 **EACH CHANGING PLACE WITH THAT WHICH GOES BEFORE,**
CHANGING PLACE = succeeding to the throne, replacing one monarch with another; the succession that will inevitably come, just as the tide inevitably rolls in; "And says that once more I shall *interchange my waned state for Henry's regal crown*" – *3 Henry VI*, 4.7.3-4; "Arise, and take *place* by us" – the King in *Henry VIII*, 1.2.13; "I fear there will a worse come *in his place*" – of Caesar in *Julius Caesar*, 3.2.112; "That then I scorn to *change my state with Kings*" – Sonnet 29, line 14; also echoing his royal son as a "changeling" who had been "placed" in the Southampton household, changing places with another boy; "*placed* it safely, the *changeling* never known" – *Hamlet*, 5.2.53; "Even so have *places* oftentimes *exchanged* their estate" – Ovid's *Metamorphoses* of 1567, Book XV, 287, the translation attributed to Oxford's uncle Arthur Golding

CHANGING = the change from one royal decree to another; "shifting change" – Sonnet 20, line 4, referring to Elizabeth's change of attitude, the breaking of her vows; "Where *wasteful time debateth with decay*, /To *change* your day of youth to sullied night" – Sonnet 15, lines 11-12; exchanging, substituting; anticipating the death of Elizabeth, the downfall of his son, Southampton, as king and the accession of James; "the *state government was changed* from kings to consuls" – the "Argument" of *Lucrece*; "'When I have seen such *interchange of state*" – Sonnet 64, line 9; "Creep in 'twixt vows, and *change decrees of Kings*" – Sonnet 115, line 6; "And lean-looked prophets whisper *fearful change* … These signs foretell *the death or fall of kings*" – *Richard II*, 2.4.11-15; "Comets, importing *change of time and state*" – *1 Henry VI*, 1.1.2; "Why is my verse so barren of new pride,/ So far from *variation or quick change*" – Sonnet 76, lines 1-2; "And in this *change* is my invention spent" – Sonnet 105, line 11; "Just to the time, not with *the time exchanged*" – Sonnet 109, line 7, referring to the change from the *time* of Elizabeth to the *time* of James; "No! Time, thou shalt not boast that I do *change*!" – Sonnet 123, line 1

PLACE = echoing the "place" where Southampton is, i.e., the Tower: "As soon as think *the place* where he would be" – Sonnet 44, line 8; his "place" on the throne, as he tells Elizabeth: "Thy black is fairest in my judgment's *place*" – Sonnet 131, line 12; "Finding yourself desired of such a person whose credit with the judge, or own *great place*, could fetch your brother from the manacles of the all-binding law" – *Measure for Measure*, 2.4.91-94

4 **IN SEQUENT TOIL ALL FORWARDS DO CONTEND.**
SEQUENT = "following, successive, consequent" – Schmidt; "Not merely successive, but in close succession" – Tucker; "Of six preceding ancestors, that gem conferred by testament to th'*sequent issue*" – *All's Well That Ends Well*, 5.3.196-197; in sequence or royal succession; ("How art thou a king but *by fair sequence and succession*" – *Richard II*, 2.1.199); these private sonnets are numbered sequentially, reflecting the days that contain the onrushing hours and minutes leading to the succession; more immediately, leading to the still possible execution of Southampton.

> Then, good prince,

No longer *session* hold upon my shame,
But let *my trial* be mine own confession.
Immediate sentence, then, and **sequent death**
Is all the grace I beg.
- *Measure for Measure*, 5.1.367-371

TOIL = labor, struggle; **ALL** = Southampton; **ALL FORWARDS DO CONTEND** = all new princes contend for the throne; "*Time's glory* is to calm *contending kings*" – *Lucrece*, 939; "let his grace go *forward*" – *Henry VIII*, 3.2.281; "Friends that have been thus *forward in my right*" – *Titus Andronicus*, 1.1.59; "The *forward violet* thus did I chide" – Sonnet 99, line 1, referring to his royal son as flower; "When a man's verses cannot be understood, nor a man's good wit seconded with the *forward child*, understanding, it strikes a man more dead than a great reckoning in a little room" – *As You Like It*, 3.3.11-14; **CONTEND** = to strive; to quarrel, combat, fight, make war ; vie with; "For never *two such kingdoms did contend* without much fall of blood, whose guiltless drops are every one a woe" – *Henry V*, 1.2.24-26; "The red rose and the white are on his face, the fatal colours of our striving houses … If you contend, a thousand lives must wither" – *3 Henry VI*, 2.5.97-102

5 **NATIVITY, ONCE IN THE MAIN OF LIGHT,**
NATIVITY = birth; the royal birth of Southampton ("the little Love-God" of Sonnet 154), echoing the Nativity of Christ; "To whom the heavens in thy *nativity* adjudged an olive branch and laurel *crown*" – *3 Henry VI*, 4.6.33-34; "a *god on earth* thou art" – to Bolinbroke as King in *Richard II*, 5.3.134; **ONCE** = during his golden time up through the year 1600, prior to the Rebellion; echoing "one" for Southampton, *One for All, All for One*; similar to "first" as in "Even as when first I hallowed thy fair name" – Sonnet 108, line 8, carrying forward the Christ theme; **MAIN** = full might; the principal point; the ocean itself, the great (royal) sea: "When I have seen the hungry Ocean gain/ Advantage on the *kingdom* of the shore,/ And the firm soil win of *the watery main*" – Sonnet 64, lines 5-7; "But since your worth, wide as the Ocean is/ … On your broad *main* doth willfully appear" – Sonnet 80, lines 5, 8; "A substitute *shines brightly as a king* until a king be by, and then *his state empties itself*, as doth an inland brook into *the main* of waters" – *The Merchant of Venice*, 5.1.94-97; "by commission and *main power*" – *Henry VIII*, 2.2.7; **IN THE MAIN OF LIGHT** = filled with royal blood; ("the sun, suggested by *main of light*, of which it is the literal inhabitant" – Booth); echoing the birth of "my Sunne" recalled in Sonnet 33: "Full many a glorious morning have I seen/ Flatter the mountain tops with sovereign eye,/ Kissing with golden face the meadows green,/ *Gilding* pale streams with heavenly alchemy/ … Even so *my Sunne* one early morn did *shine*" – Sonnet 33, lines 1-4, 9; also indicating (in the next lines) that such glory (on earth) is no longer his; "When thou thyself dost *give invention light*" – Sonnet 38, line 8; "the entrance of a child into the world at birth is an entrance into the main or ocean of light" – Dowden, offering (without intending to) more evidence of Oxford writing as father to son; **LIGHT** = Oxford is attempting to shine the light of his son's royalty into the darkness of his disgrace and loss of the throne; "to lend the world his light" – Venus to Adonis in *Venus and Adonis*, dedicated to Southampton, 1593, line 756; Southampton, godlike, is a royal star or sun, lending light to the world; he is also a jewel, emitting light, as do his eyes; "And God said, Let there be light: and there was light" – Genesis, 1.3; "In him was life; and the life was the light of men" – Gospel of John, 1.4; "Dark'ning thy power to *lend base subjects light*" – Sonnet 100, line 4, Oxford speaking of the power of his Muse to restore light to his royal son branded as a "base" criminal or traitor; "Lo, in the Orient when *the gracious light*/ Lifts up his burning head" – Sonnet 7, lines 1-2; "thy much *clearer light*" – Sonnet 43, line 7; "those *suns of glory*, those two *lights of men*" – *Henry VIII*, 1.1.6, referring to men as "suns" of light; "Yet looks he like a king; behold, his eye, as bright as is the eagle's, *lightens forth controlling majesty*" – *Richard II*, 3.3.68-71; "That in black ink my love may still shine bright" – Sonnet 65, line 14

"I have engaged myself so far in Her Majesty's service to **bring the truth to light**"
- Oxford to Burghley, June 13, 1595; Chiljan 109

6 **CRAWLS TO MATURITY, WHEREWITH BEING CROWNED,**
CRAWLS TO MATURITY = Southampton, gaining full maturity; **WHEREWITH BEING CROWNED** = Whereupon, just when he should be crowned as king; "wherein I do not doubt she is *crowned* with *glory*"

– Oxford to Robert Cecil, April 25/27, 1603, speaking of the deceased Elizabeth just before her funeral; ("Add an immortal title to your *crown*" – *Richard II*, 1.1.24; "Make claim and title to the *crown*" – *Henry V*, 1.2.68); "Incertainties now *crown* themselves assured" – Sonnet 107, line 7, after Elizabeth's death, when James is proclaimed King of England

7 CROOKED ECLIPSES 'GAINST HIS GLORY FIGHT,
CROOKED ECLIPSES = Evil eclipses of the sun; the Queen's (and Robert Cecil's) malignant eclipse of the royal son, whose brightness can no longer be seen; **CROOKED** = Cecil as hunchback or "crook-back"; ("malignant, perverse, contrary, devious" – Crystal & Crystal); "By what by-paths and indirect *crooked* ways I met this crown" – *2 Henry IV*, 4.5.184; ("If crooked fortune had not thwarted me" – Deut. 32.5); **ECLIPSES** = "The mortal Moone hath her *eclipse* endured" – Sonnet 107, referring to Elizabeth, whose royal lineage as a sun had been eclipsed by her death; "Clouds and *eclipses* stain both *Moone and Sunne*" – Sonnet 35, line 3, referring to the stain of treason that now eclipses the blood of both Elizabeth, the Moon, and her son

("Note that 'E C L I' begins the word 'ECLIPSE,' and those four letters are in 'CECIL.' [And 'CECIL' contains only those four letters.] Also, there's really no such thing as a '*crooked* eclipse,' so perhaps he's punning on 'Crooked **ECLI**pses' = CECIL" – Alex McNeil, ed.)

'GAINST HIS GLORY = against the glory of his kingship; "The king will in ***his glory*** hide thy shame" – *Edward III*, 2.1.399; "and although it hath pleased God after an earthly kingdom to take her up into a more permanent and heavenly state, wherein I do not doubt she is *crowned with glory*" – Oxford to Robert Cecil, April 25/27, 1603, about Elizabeth on the eve of her funeral; "For princes are a model which heaven likes to itself: as jewels *lose their glory* if neglected, so princes their renown if not respected" – *Pericles*, 2.2.10-13; "Even in the height and pride of all *his glory*" – *Pericles*, 2.4.6; "See, see, King Richard doth himself appear, as doth the blushing discontented sun from out the fiery portal of the East, when he perceives the envious clouds are bent *to dim his glory* and to stain the track of his bright passage to the occident" – *Richard II*, 3.3.62-67; "And threat *the glory* of my precious crown" – *Richard II*, 3.3.90; "That plotted thus our glory's overthrow" – *1 Henry VI*, 1.1.24

8 AND TIME THAT GAVE DOTH NOW HIS GIFT CONFOUND.
TIME THAT GAVE = time related to the life of Elizabeth, who *gave birth* to him; **HIS GIFT** = his inheritance of royal blood; his gift of royal life from Elizabeth; "So *thy great gift*, upon misprision growing" – Sonnet 87, line 11; **DOTH NOW HIS GIFT CONFOUND** = now destroys his gift of royalty and his claim to the throne; **CONFOUND** = to mingle, perplex, confuse, amaze, destroy, ruin, make away with, waste, wear away; i.e., the waste of time and royal life being recorded in this diary as "the Chronicle of wasted time" – Sonnet 106, line 1; "Against *confounding age's cruel knife*" – Sonnet 63, line 10, referring to the executioner's axe; "For never-resting time leads Summer on/ To hideous winter and *confounds* him there" – Sonnet 5, lines 5-6; "Or *state itself confounded to decay*" – Sonnet 64, line 10; "In other accents do this praise *confound*" – Sonnet 69, line 7

9 TIME DOTH TRANSFIX THE FLOURISH SET ON YOUTH
TIME = repeated from the previous line; **TRANSFIX** = destroy; "pierce [or chip] through" – Tucker; echoing the piercing of the executioner's axe; **THE FLOURISH SET ON YOUTH** = the flourishing royal blood and claim that Southampton had possessed until the day of the Rebellion; "Then music is even as *the flourish* when true subjects bow to *a new-crowned monarch*" – *The Merchant of Venice*, 3.2.49-50

10 AND DELVES THE PARALLELS IN BEAUTY'S BROW,
PARALLELS IN BEAUTY'S BROW = wrinkles, signs of age, in Southampton's brow, which reflects his "beauty" or blood from Elizabeth and its advancement toward death, i.e., toward execution, lack of succession; also the brow of Beauty herself, Elizabeth; Southampton had been born "with all triumphant splendor on *my brow*" – Sonnet 33, line 10

11 **FEEDS ON THE RARITIES OF NATURE'S TRUTH,**
FEEDS ON = eats up, devours; **RARITIES** = royal aspects; "Beauty, Truth, and *Rarity*" – *The Phoenix and Turtle*, 1601, line 53, signifying Elizabeth, Oxford, and Southampton; "With April's first-born flowers, and all things *rare*" – Sonnet 21, line 7, referring to Southampton as flower of the Tudor Rose

NATURE'S TRUTH = Elizabeth's true son by Oxford, who is *Nothing Truer than Truth*; "His head *by nature framed to wear a crown*" – *3 Henry VI*, 4.6.72

12 **AND NOTHING STANDS BUT FOR HIS SCYTHE TO MOW.**
NOTHING = Southampton as a nobody, the opposite of "one" of his motto *One for All, All for One*; **NOTHING STANDS** = none of Southampton's glory can withstand the ravages of real time; "Let this pernicious hour *stand aye accursed in the calendar*" – *Macbeth*, 4.1.133-134; "When peers thus knit, *a kingdom ever stands*" – *Pericles*, 2.4.58; **SCYTHE** = the blade of time, also the sharp blade of the executioner's axe ("And *nothing 'gainst Time's scythe* can make defence" – Sonnet 12, line 13)

13 **AND YET TO TIME IN HOPE MY VERSE SHALL STAND**
Nonetheless these sonnets, written according to time, hopefully will withstand – or stand against – all this destruction of his son; **HOPE** = "They call him Troilus, and *on him erect a second hope*" – *Troilus and Cressida*, 108-109; **STAND** = in counterpoint to "stands" of line 12 above; "if ought in me/ Worthy persual *stand* against thy sight" – Sonnet 38, lines 5-6; "And *the blots of Nature's hand/* Shall not in their issue *stand*" – *A Midsummer Night's Dream*, 5.1.403-404

14 **PRAISING THY WORTH, DESPITE HIS CRUEL HAND.**
PRAISING THY WORTH = recording your royalty; **CRUEL HAND** = the cruel hand of Time is the same as Elizabeth's cruel hand, since Time represents her life; Southampton as an infant had been "by a Virgin *hand* disarmed" – Sonnet 154, line 8; "And shall I pray the gods to keep the pain from her, that is so *cruel* still ... O *cruel* hap and hard estate ... Whom I might well condemn, to be a *cruel* judge" – lines from three different Oxford poems, printed in *The Paradise of Dainty Devices*, 1576, each signed E. O.

THE MONUMENT

THE PRISON YEARS

DAY THIRTY-FIVE IN THE TOWER
EXECUTION DRAWS NEARER

Sonnet 61
To Play The Watchman Ever For Thy Sake
14 March 1601

Oxford records his attempt to keep Southampton in his mind's eye at all times, as events lead to his son's execution or to a reprieve. His Sunne must wake or rise each new day "elsewhere" -- that is, in the Tower -- and yet Oxford continues to "play the watchman" or stand guard for Henry Wriothesley's life.

Sonnet 61	Translation
Is it thy will thy Image should keep open	Is it your royal will that your presence keep open
My heavy eyelids to the weary night?	My heavy eyelids during this dark time?
Dost thou desire my slumbers should be broken,	Do you command my sleep to be disturbed
While shadows like to thee do mock my sight?	While false views of you mock my eyesight?
Is it thy spirit that thou send'st from thee	Is it your royal blood that you send from yourself
So far from home into my deeds to pry,	From your Tower prison, to see my words?
To find out shames and idle hours in me,	And to discover how I write of your disgrace?
The scope and tenure of thy jealousy?	Is this the objective of your jealousy?
O no, thy love, though much, is not so great.	O no, your royalty, while great, is unrecognized.
It is my love that keeps mine eye awake,	You, my royal son, keep me awake and alive;
Mine own true love that doth my rest defeat,	You, my royal son, defeat my attempt to rest,
To play the watchman ever for thy sake.	Because I play the eternal watchman for your sake.
For thee watch I, whilst thou dost wake elsewhere,	I watch for you; you wake elsewhere [in prison],
From me far off, with others all too near.	Far from me, with enemies all around you.

1 IS IT THY WILL THY IMAGE SHOULD KEEP OPEN
THY WILL = your royal will; is it your royal will that the image of you should keep open; **IMAGE** = your royal image; "if in the child the father's image lies" – *Lucrece*, 1753; "our last king, whose image appeared to us" – *Hamlet*, 1.1.81

2 MY HEAVY EYELIDS TO THE WEARY NIGHT?
MY HEAVY EYELIDS = my weary, painful eyelids in the dark; "How *heavy* do I journey on the way" – Sonnet 50, line 1, Oxford recalling his sorrowful ride away from Southampton in the Tower, where he told his son of the bargain to save his life by giving up all claim to the throne; "And keep *my drooping eyelids* open wide,/ Looking on darkness which the blind do see" – Sonnet 27, lines 7-8; "And *heavily* from woe to woe" – Sonnet 30, line 10; "When in dead night thy fair imperfect shade/ Through *heavy sleep on sightless eyes* doth stay!" – Sonnet 43, lines 11-12; "But *heavy tears*, badges of either's woe" – Sonnet 44, line 14

> And find *our griefs heavier than our offences*
> - *2 Henry IV*, 4.1.69

> A *heavy reckoning* for you, sir
> - The Gaoler in *Cymbeline*, 5.4.157

362

WEARY = "*Weary with toil*, I haste me to my bed" – Sonnet 27, line 1, Oxford's first response to the Rebellion, on the night of February 8, 1601, when Southampton was imprisoned with Essex in the Tower; "for to tell truth I am *weary of* an unsettled life, which is the very pestilence that happens unto courtiers that propound to themselves no end of their time therein bestowed" – Oxford to Burghley, May 18, 1591; **NIGHT** = opposite of the "day" of golden opportunity prior to the Rebellion

> I still do toil and *never am at rest*,
> Enjoying least when I do covet most;
> With *weary* thoughts are my green years oppres'd
> - Signed "Lo. Ox" in Harleian MS 7392, ff. 52-53; Chiljan, 188

3 DOST THOU DESIRE MY SLUMBERS SHOULD BE BROKEN,
DESIRE = royal command; "From fairest creatures *we desire* increase" – Sonnet 1, line 1, emphasizing the royal "we" of the monarch

4 WHILE SHADOWS LIKE TO THEE DO MOCK MY SIGHT?
SHADOWS LIKE TO THEE = the shadows that cover you, showing your likeness; "Save that my soul's imaginary sight/ Presents *thy shadow* to my sightless view,/ Which like a jewel hung in ghastly night,/ Makes black night beauteous and her old face new" – Sonnet 27, lines 9-12; "What is your substance, whereof are you made,/ That *millions of strange shadows on you tend?*/ Since every one hath, every one, one *shade*,/ And you, but one, can *every shadow lend*" – Sonnet 53, lines 1-4; **MOCK MY SIGHT** = mock my eyesight, taunting me with this inner vision of you

5 IS IT THY SPIRIT THAT THOU SEND'ST FROM THEE
THY SPIRIT = your soul; your royal blood, which is spiritual; like a mystical vision; "and do not kill/ The *spirit of love*" – Sonnet 56, lines 7-8, i.e., the unseen essence of royal blood; "*My spirit is thine, the better part of me*" – Sonnet 74, line 8; **SPIRIT** = also Sonnets 80, 85, 86, 108, 129, 144; Essex wrote to Elizabeth in 1597 calling her "the Spirit of spirits" (Weir, 427); **THAT THOU SEND'ST FROM THEE** = Southampton sends his spirit and illuminates Oxford's inner vision: "Save that my soul's imaginary sight/ Presents thy shadow to my sightless view,/ Which like a jewel (hung in ghastly night)/ Makes black night beauteous, and her old face new" – Sonnet 27, lines 9-11

6 SO FAR FROM HOME INTO MY DEEDS TO PRY,
SO FAR FROM HOME = Southampton, in the Tower; **INTO MY DEEDS TO PRY** = to spy on my activities, carried out behind the scenes, on your behalf; "Or on my frailties why are frailer spies" – Sonnet 121, line 7; "Watch thou, and wake when others be asleep, to *pry into the secrets of the state*" – *2 Henry VI*, 1.1.250-251

7 TO FIND OUT SHAMES AND IDLE HOURS IN ME,
TO FIND OUT SHAMES = to learn the disgraces that I suffer, by taking responsibility for your disgrace; "If thy offences were upon record, would it not shame thee, in so fair a troop, to read a lecture of them? If thou wouldst, there shouldst thou find one heinous article, containing the deposing of a king" – *Richard II*, 4.1.230-234); **IDLE HOURS** = time spent pleading for you in vain; "I ... vow to take advantage of all *idle hours*, till I have honoured you with some graver labour" – dedication of Venus and Adonis in 1593 to the Earl of Southampton; "That never am less *idle lo, than when I am alone*" – Oxford poem, signed E.O., in *The Paradise of Dainty Devices*, 1576

> Had he done so, himself had borne the crown,
> Which waste of *idle hours* hath quite thrown down
> - *Richard II*, 3.4.65-66

8 THE SCOPE AND TENURE OF THY JEALOUSY?

SCOPE = "Three themes in one, which wondrous *scope* affords" – Sonnet 105, line 12; that to which the mind is directed; "shooting wide, do miss the marked *scope*" – Spenser, The Shepherd's Calendar, November, 155; **SCOPE AND TENURE** = the purpose and "tenor" or meaning; Q has *tenure*, a common spelling of "tenor" at the time, but *tenure* is probably the intended word, as it relates to the "lease" of Southampton's royal blood, i.e., *tenure* refers to the manner of holding lands and tenements, a subject with which Oxford was extremely familiar, having inherited no less than eighty-six estates; **THY JEALOUSY** = your curiosity; your apprehension; your state of being suspected as a traitor or being a "suspect traitor" in the eyes of the law; "Rumor is a pipe blown by *surmises, jealousies, conjectures*" – 2 Henry IV, Induction 16; concerned about; "So *loving-jealous of his liberty*" – Romeo and Juliet, 2.2.182

9 O NO! THY LOVE, THOUGH MUCH, IS NOT SO GREAT:

THY LOVE, THOUGH MUCH = your royal blood, though abundant; **IS NOT SO GREAT** = is not as great as it is within Oxford's vision of him, as father

10 IT IS MY LOVE THAT KEEPS MINE EYE AWAKE,

MY LOVE = my royal son; i.e., it is the fact that you are my royal son that keeps me from taking my own life, keeps me awake; **AWAKE** = in a state of vigilance; alert, alive, attentive, watchful; "It is not Agamemnon's sleeping hour: that thou shalt know, Trojan, *he is awake*, he tells thee so himself" – Agamemnon in *Troilus and Cressida*, 1.3.252-254; "I offered to *awaken* his regard for his private friends" – *Coriolanus*, 5.1.23; "*The law* hath not been dead, though it hath slept ... Now 'tis *awake*" – *Measure for Measure*, 2.2.91-94; "*Watch* thou, and *wake* when others be asleep, to pry into the secrets of the state" – 2 Henry VI, 1.1.250-251

11 MINE OWN TRUE LOVE THAT DOTH MY REST DEFEAT,

MINE OWN TRUE LOVE = my own true royal son; ("a son of mine own" – Oxford to Burghley, March 17, 1575; "Not *mine own* fears nor the prophetic soul/ Of the wide world dreaming on things to come/ Can yet the lease of *my true love* control" – Sonnet 107, lines 1-3); **TRUE** = Oxford, *Nothing Truer than Truth*; "you *true* rights" – Sonnet 17, line 11, to Southampton; **MINE OWN:** Sonnets 23, 39, 49, 61, 62, 72, 88, 107, 110; ("Rise, *thou art my child ... Mine own...*" – *Pericles,* 5.1.213-214, the prince, realizing that Marina is his daughter); **MY REST DEFEAT** = destroy my inner peace; "His unkindness may *defeat my life*" – *Othello*, 4.2.150; "The dear repose for limbs with travail tired" – Sonnet 27, line 1; "That am debarred the benefit of *rest*" – Sonnet 28, line 2; "Now this *ill-wresting* world is grown so bad" – Sonnet 140, line 11, to Elizabeth in the Dark Lady series, with *ill-wresting* echoing *ill-resting*. s

12 TO PLAY THE WATCHMAN EVER FOR THY SAKE.

TO PLAY THE WATCHMAN EVER = to constantly keep guard and protect; **EVER** = E. Ver, Edward de Vere; Oxford used "ever" in the same glancing way in his plays, such as these instances in *Hamlet, Prince of Denmark*:

> Horatio: The same, my lord, and your poor servant *ever.*
> Hamlet: Sir, my good friend, I'll change *that name* with you.
> - (1.2.162-163)

FOR THY SAKE = for your royal life here and now; for your eternal life, recorded in these sonnets filled with your royal blood

13 FOR THEE WATCH I, WHILST THOU DOST WAKE ELSEWHERE,

FOR THEE WATCH I = for you I keep watch; "Whilst I, my sovereign, *watch the clock* for you" – Sonnet 57, line 6; "Therefore I have entreated him along with us to *watch* the minutes of the night, that if again this apparition come, he may approve our eyes and speak to it" – Hamlet, 1.1.29-32; **WHILST THOU DOST WAKE ELSEWHERE** = while you – Southampton – exist in the Tower; **WAKE** = echoing the "wake" related to a funeral; "There is no doubt that the poor, especially in the more remote counties of England, continued the old custom of the wake, or nightly feasting before and after a funeral. Shakespeare uses the word in connection with a night revel in Sonnet 61: 'For thee watch I, whilst thou dost wake elsewhere.'" – Percy Macquoid in *Shakespeare's England*, Vol. 2, 196, p. 151; Oxford knows Southampton is in the Tower, but he cannot know exactly where or if, for example, Southampton has been taken to the Privy Council room in the Tower for questioning, to one of the torture rooms, or even to the place of execution; the situation is still volatile, with Cecil having the power of life or death and holding the threat of legal execution over him; so the echo of a "wake" preceding a funeral is quite apt.

14 **FROM ME FAR OFF, WITH OTHERS ALL TOO NEAR.**
FROM ME FAR OFF = Southampton, far from him, behind the high fortress walls; **WITH OTHERS ALL TOO NEAR** = with guards and other prisoners alike; with some of the latter, arrested for the Rebellion, who may urge you to escape or to attempt another revolt; those so physically *near* you that, despite their wakefulness, they are blind and cannot protect you (or save your life); but Oxford as his father is "nearer" to him than they are, and he is helping him more than they can help; "You twain, of all the rest, are **nearest** to Warwick *by blood and by alliance*" – 3 Henry VI, 4.1.133-134; "as we be knit *near* in alliance" – Oxford to Robert Cecil, his brother-in-law, February 2, 1601; "Whereby none is **nearer** allied than myself" – Oxford to Robert Cecil in May (?) 1601; **ALL** = Southampton

THE PRISON YEARS

DAY THIRTY-SIX IN THE TOWER
EXECUTION DRAWS NEARER

Sonnet 62
'Tis Thee (My Self)
15 March 1601

As the hour draws near for Southampton to be executed, Oxford records that his own self-love is no more and no less than his love for his royal son. They are one and the same ("'Tis thee, my self, that for my self I praise") and therefore they share the same fate, whatever it may be.

Sonnet 62	Translation
Sin of self-love possesseth all mine eye,	My guilt is loving myself with all my sight
And all my soul, and all my every part;	And of all me with all my self,
And for this sin there is no remedy,	And for this guilt there's no pardon,
It is so grounded inward in my heart.	Because it's rooted so deep inside me.
Methinks no face so gracious is as mine,	I believe that no face is so kingly as mine,
No shape so true, no truth of such account,	That no man is of such true great royalty,
And for my self mine own worth do define,	And for my own benefit I define my royalty,
As I all other in all worths surmount.	Because I surpass all others in all royal blood.
But when my glass shows me my self indeed	But when my mirror shows me my real self,
Beated and chopped with tanned antiquity,	And how Elizabeth's waning life has beaten me,
Mine own self-love quite contrary I read;	I see myself in an entirely different way,
Self so self-loving were iniquity.	As someone who loves himself incorrectly.
'Tis thee (my self) that for my self I praise,	It's you (my other self) for whom I praise myself;
Painting my age with beauty of thy days.	You give me life with the royal blood of yours.

1 SIN OF SELF-LOVE POSSESSETH ALL MINE EYE,
SIN = crime; ("Some *sins* do bear their privilege on earth, and so doth yours; your *fault* was not your folly" – the Bastard in *King John*, 1.1; "And water cannot wash away your *sin*" – *Richard II*, 4.1.242); **SELF-LOVE** = the crime of loving his own self, which is actually his royal son; ("For *thee, and for my self*" – Sonnet 27, line 14; "*my friend and I are one*" – Sonnet 42, line 13; and line 14 of this sonnet: "thee (my self)"); i.e., they are "one flesh" as father and son; therefore, in loving his son he is guilty of self-love; **ALL** = Southampton; Oxford's sin is loving that "other self" that is his own son, and in continuing to recognize Southampton's royal blood and his right to succeed Elizabeth – a sin or treasonous crime, if he admitted it in public.

2 AND ALL MY SOUL, AND ALL MY EVERY PART;
ALL … ALL = Southampton, his motto; **MY SOUL** = my heart, my spirit, my being, my essence; the immortal part of himself, which is now his royal son, for whom he is writing these sonnets to preserve his immortality; (Elizabeth has also been his soul, but she is depriving herself of her royal son's ability to continue her lineage; and so, in the Dark Lady series, Oxford refers to the Queen's "blind soul" in Sonnet 136, line 2, and addresses her as "Poor soul, the center of my sinful earth" – Sonnet 146, line 1; "the mortal Venus, the heart-blood of beauty, love's visible soul" – *Troilus and Cressida*, 3.1.32-33; **EVERY** = E. Ver,

Edward de Vere, *Ever or Never*; **ALL MY EVERY PART** = Oxford and Southampton joined by their father-son blood relationship (all-every) and now joined by this very language that Oxford has devised in order to express it; **PART** = "*All his* ***gracious parts*** *... my boy, my Arthur,* ***my fair son****!*" – of the prince in *King John*, 3.3.96,103

3 AND FOR THIS SIN THERE IS NO REMEDY,
REMEDY = (rhymes with "eye"); cure; medicine; physic; redress; a legal term echoing the trial of Essex and Southampton; **NO REMEDY** = no means of better satisfying, much less reversing, the judgment against his son: "To atone your fears with my more noble meaning, not a man shall pass his quarter or *offend the stream of regular justice* in your city's bounds but shall be *remedied to your public laws at heaviest answer.*" – *Timon of Athens*, 5.4.58-63

4 IT IS SO GROUNDED INWARD IN MY HEART.
SO GROUNDED INWARD = linked so closely, i.e., by blood, mine in his; **MY HEART** = Oxford's heart is Southampton's heart; "For all that beauty that doth cover thee/ Is but the seemly raiment of my heart/ ... Presume not on thy heart when mine is slain,/ Thou gav'st me thine not to give back again" – Sonnet 22, lines 5-6, 13-14; "And *my heart's right thy inward love of heart*" – Sonnet 46, line 14; "Take heed (*dear heart*) of this large privilege" – Sonnet 95, line 13, referring to his royal son as "dear heart"; "No, let me be obsequious *in thy heart*" – Sonnet 125, line 9

5 METHINKS NO FACE SO GRACIOUS IS AS MINE,
GRACIOUS = filled with royal grace; "A *gracious king* that *pardons all offences*" – *Henry VIII*, 2.2.66; **FACE** = Oxford's face reflects his son's face; the "face-royal" or kingly visage (and the visage stamped on the coin of the realm called a *royal*: "And yet he will not stick to say his *face* is a *face-royal*. God may finish it when He will, 'tis not a hair amiss yet. He may keep it sill at a *face-royal*, for a barber shall never earn sixpence out of it. And yet he'll be *crowning* as if he had writ man ever since his father was a bachelor. He may keep his own *grace,* but he's almost out of mine, I can assure him" – Falstaff speaking of Prince Hal in *2 Henry IV*, 1.2.22-28

6 NO SHAPE SO TRUE, NO TRUTH OF SUCH ACCOUNT,
TRUE ...TRUTH = Oxford, *Nothing Truer than Truth*; **ACCOUNT** = value; reckoning; computation; estimation; accounting;

7 AND FOR MY SELF MINE OWN WORTH DO DEFINE,
AND FOR MY SELF, etc. = and for my self I define my own royalty, as father; **MINE OWN WORTH** = my own royal son, reflected in me; **MINE OWN** = "a son of mine own" – Oxford to Burghley, March 17, 1575; Sonnets 23, 39, 49, 61, 62, 72, 88, 107, 110; "Bless'd, and *mine own*" – *Pericles*, 5.3.48, Thaisa speaking of her daughter, Marina

8 AS I ALL OTHER IN ALL WORTHS SURMOUNT.
ALL ... ALL = Southampton, *One for All, All for One*; **ALL WORTHS** = all royal qualities related to my royal son; **SURMOUNT** = surpass

9 BUT WHEN MY GLASS SHOWS ME MY SELF INDEED
MY GLASS = my mirror and hourglass; **INDEED** = in truth

10 BEATED AND CHOPPED WITH TANNED ANTIQUITY,
A clear statement of Oxford as much older and more mature than the traditional notion of the poet's age; **BEATED** = beaten, i.e., by Elizabeth and Robert Cecil; **CHOPPED** = hacked; an image of Southampton's head being hacked or chopped off, as Essex's was; "He is a traitor; let him to the Tower, and *chop* away that factious pate of his" – *2 Henry VI*, 5.1.134-135; ("chapped, chafed, roughened ... dried up, fissured, cracked" – Crystal & Crystal); **TANNED** = weathered; also darkened, as by Elizabeth's cloud or negative view, and as by Southampton's shadow that covers his royal identity and disgraces him; **ANTIQUITY** = old age; Oxford will be fifty-one upon his next birthday, April 12, 1601, no longer young by Elizabethan

standards; (see "antiquity" in another context in Sonnet 108, line 12: "But makes antiquity for aye his page"); also ancient date or time;

11 MINE OWN SELF-LOVE QUITE CONTRARY I READ:
MINE OWN SELF-LOVE QUITE CONTRARY = my own love of my self is quite the contrary; ("a son of *mine own*" – Oxford to Burghley, March 17, 1575); **LOVE** = royal blood of Southampton, possessed indirectly by Oxford, as father, although he cannot claim paternity

12 SELF SO SELF-LOVING WERE INIQUITY.
This self-love would be a sin (but in the next line, he explains by saying that it's *you, my self*, whom I am praising)…

13 'TIS THEE (MY SELF) THAT FOR MY SELF I PRAISE,
It is you, who are *my* own *self*, whom I praise when I praise my self; i.e., in praising you I praise myself; ("'Tis thee, my alter ego, my second self, that I praise as if myself" – Dowden); **PRAISE** = pay homage to you as prince; write of you as prince and king in these sonnets.

14 PAINTING MY AGE WITH BEAUTY OF THY DAYS.
Recording the time of my own life in the act of writing in these sonnets that are filled with your blood from Elizabeth; now "painting" or writing day-by-day since the Rebellion; an image of Oxford writing these sonnets as a painter using "paint" that is, in fact, his son's royal blood

Part Two

THE PRISON YEARS

DAY THIRTY-SEVEN IN THE TOWER
EXECUTION SEEMS IMMINENT

Sonnet 63
I Now Fortify
And All Those Beauties Whereof Now He's King
Are Vanishing, or Vanished Out of Sight
16 March 1601

Time has almost run out for Southampton by now, so Oxford attempts to "fortify" against the moment when the "cruel knife" of the executioner's axe will "cut" the neck of his son and take his "life" away. Time is the Queen, who has the power to spill "his blood" and deprive him of those "beauties" (royal rights inherited from Elizabeth, who is Beauty) by which "now he's King" or her rightful successor as monarch. Fearing the worst, Oxford vows to preserve his son's "beauty" or Tudor blood within these lines.

Sonnet 63	Translation
Against my love shall be as I am now, With time's injurious hand crushed and o'erworn, When hours have drained his blood and filled his brow With lines and wrinkles, when his youthful morn	I stand fast as I am now, for my son, anticipating The time Elizabeth decides to order his execution, When her waning life span has destroyed his royal blood And brought him to his death; when his royal right
Hath traveled on to Age's steepy night, And all those beauties whereof now he's King Are vanishing, or vanished out of sight, Stealing away the treasure of his spring.	Has gone onward past the succession And all that royal blood that makes him King Is fading from view or disappeared completely, Robbing the royal claim of his inheritance:
For such a time do I now fortify Against confounding Age's cruel knife, That he shall never cut from memory My sweet love's beauty, though my lover's life.	For this destruction of my son I now fortify myself Against Elizabeth's age and her executioner's axe, That her time will never murder the memory of My royal son's royal blood, though it takes his life.
His beauty shall in these black lines be seen, And they shall live, and he in them still green.	His royalty will be seen in these disgraced lines, And they will live, and he in them always royal.

1 AGAINST MY LOVE SHALL BE AS I AM NOW
AGAINST MY LOVE = standing against all evil forces on behalf of my royal son; "Against that time" – Sonnet 49, repeated in lines 1, 5, 9, in the same context of Southampton facing imminent execution, although by now it appears that his life may be spared; **SHALL BE AS I AM NOW** = is the way I am and shall be in the future; i.e., I will do in the future what I am doing now; "What I have done is yours, what I have to do is yours" – Dedication of *Lucrece* by "Shakespeare" to Southampton in 1593

2 WITH TIME'S INJURIOUS HAND CRUSHED AND O'ER-WORN,
Destroyed by the injuries of time; defeated by the dwindling of the Queen's life; and as time runs out before you are executed; the Queen's injurious, imperial hand; "When I have seen by *time's fell hand* defaced" –

REFERENCE EDITION

Sonnet 64, line 1; "Or what strong *hand* can hold his swift foot back?" – Sonnet 65, line 11; "with *nature's own hand* painted" – Sonnet 20, line 1; "Was sleeping *by a Virgin hand* disarmed" – Sonnet 154, line 1

> "*Injurious Time* now with a robber's haste crams his rich thievery up" – *Triolus and Cressida*, 4.4.41-42

INJURIOUS HAND = Southampton to the Privy Council, between late February and early March of 1601: "My soul is heavy and troubled for my offences, and I shall soon grow to detest myself if her Majesty refuse to have compassion of me. The law hath hitherto had his proceedings, whereby her justice and my shame is sufficiently published; now is the time that mercy is to be showed. O pray her then, I beseech your lordships, in my behalf to **stay her hand**, and stop the rigorous course of the law, and remember, as I know she will never forget, that it is more honor to a prince to pardon one penitent offender than with severity to punish many."
(Stopes, 225-226)

CRUSHED = A **traitor** refusing to plead guilty or not guilty was "laid upon a table … and so much weight of stones or lead laid upon that table while as his body be **crushed** and his life by that violence taken from him" – Thomas Smith (who was a tutor to Edward deVere), speaking of Tudor torture of suspect-traitors. (Bellamy, 139)

3 WHEN HOURS HAVE DRAINED HIS BLOOD AND FILLED HIS BROW
HOURS = the time of Elizabeth's life, coming to its end; the Queen is Time, so that she is also represented by *hours*, and she herself will "drain his blood" by executing him

DRAINED HIS BLOOD: Killed him by beheading; drained his royal blood; or when Elizabeth and Robert Cecil have robbed him of the throne; **BLOOD** = Tudor blood from the Queen, his mother: "And see *thy blood* warm when thou feel'st it cold" – Sonnet 2, line 14; "And that *fresh blood* which youngly thou bestow'st" – Sonnet 11, line 3; "And burn the long-lived Phoenix *in her blood*" – Sonnet 19, line 4, referring to Elizabeth as the Phoenix; "All frailties that besiege *all kinds of blood*" – Sonnet 109, line 10, with *all*=Southampton and *kind* referring to his relationship to the Queen by nature; "perjured, murderous, *bloody*, full of blame" – Sonnet 129, line 3, to Elizabeth in the Dark Lady series, rebuking her for intending to execute her son and thereby literally spill his blood

Southampton to the Privy Council, during this time: "O let her [Elizabeth] never suffer to be **spilled the blood of him** that desires to live but to do her service." (Stopes, 225-226)
The "Confession" of Henry, Earl of Southampton, also during this time: "…whereupon, willing to spend my time in her Majesty's service, to *redeem the fault* I had made in thinking that which might be offensive to her … my *accursed fortune* … I do therefore now prostrate myself at her Majesty's princely feet, with a true penitent soul for *my faults* past, with horror in my conscience for *my offences*, and detestation of mine own life if it be displeasing unto her. I do with all humility crave her *pardon*. The **shedding of my blood** can no way avail her … and do with so grieved a mind beg forgiveness … unfeignedly *repent* …"
- (Stopes, 227-229)

4 WITH LINES AND WRINKLES, WHEN HIS YOUTHFUL MORN
The conventional image of time and aging, but this is only the surface aspect of the poetry, which also describes the present situation by which Southampton is about to lose his life in the same way as did Essex;
YOUTHFUL MORN = recalling the rise of the sun and the royal birth of Southampton, recounted in "Full many a *glorious morning* have I seen,/ Flatter the mountain tops with sovereign eye/ … Even so my Sunne one *early morn* did shine,/ With all triumphant splendor on my brow" – Sonnet 33, lines 1-2, 9-10

5 HATH TRAVELED ON TO AGE'S STEEPY NIGHT,
When he has died, either literally or when his golden time of royalty has passed by and he must live in the darkness as the rightful king; ("…death, the undiscovered country, from whose bourn *no traveler returns*" –

Hamlet, 3.1.78-80; "right for right hath *dimm'd your infant morn to aged night*" – *Richard III*, 4.4.15-16, spoken in relation to the murders of the young princes); "And having climbed the *steep-up heavenly hill/ Resembling strong youth* in his middle age/ ... Like feeble age he *reeleth from the day*" – Sonnet 7, lines 5, 10; **NIGHT** = "For precious friends hid in *death's dateless night*" – Sonnet 30, line 6

6 AND ALL THOSE BEAUTIES WHEREOF NOW HE'S KING
ALL = Southampton, *One for All, All for One*; **ALL THOSE BEAUTIES** = all that royal blood from Elizabeth; ("These sunbeams in mine eye,/ These *beauties* make me die" – Oxford poem in *The Phoenix Nest*, 1593, about the Queen)

WHEREOF NOW HE'S KING: By which he is (or should be) King of England; (anticipating the absolute extinction of Southampton's claim to kingship in Sonnet 87, line 14, when Oxford writes that his succession was but a dream: "*In sleep a King, but waking no such matter*"); i.e., the bargain for reduction of his crime to "misprision" of treason is being made, in return for which Southampton must give up the throne: "So thy great gift, upon *misprision* growing" – Sonnet 87, line 11, indicating that Southampton's *great gift* of royal life and blood has been spared through this legal maneuver; **NOW** = his right to the throne still exists *now*, but it won't exist when the bargain is complete.

7 ARE VANISHING, OR VANISHED OUT OF SIGHT,
Are fast disappearing, by either his execution or by the bargain I am making for him, by which we must bury the truth and he may never attempt to claim the throne;

8 STEALING AWAY THE TREASURE OF HIS SPRING.
STEALING AWAY THE TREASURE = robbing the royal blood; (recalling the base clouds, representing Elizabeth's negative viewpoint, "*stealing* to west with this disgrace" in Sonnet 33, line 8); **OF HIS SPRING** = of his glory in the next reign (recalling "only herald to the gaudy *spring*" in Sonnet 1, line 10); **SPRING** = *Ver*, in Latin, echoing E. Ver, Edward de Vere; i.e., he is not only Elizabeth's treasure but Oxford's as well

9 FOR SUCH A TIME DO I NOW FORTIFY
In anticipation of such a time I now brace myself; in anticipation of your execution, which could happen at any time, I now fortify myself; one way he fortifies himself is by writing these verses ; a play on the Tower as a "fort" or "fortification"; ("erect defensive works" – Dowden); "*Against the wreckful siege* of batt'ring days" – Sonnet 65, line 6; "Against that time do I *ensconce* (fortify) *me here*" – Sonnet 49, line 9

> Yet am I one that hath long besieged *a fort...*
> - Oxford to Burghley, June 25, 1586

10 AGAINST CONFOUNDING AGE'S CRUEL KNIFE,
CONFOUNDING = destroying, ruining, making away with; wasting, wearing away; applied to time and kingship; "Or *state itself confounded* to decay" - Sonnet 64, line 10; "In other accents do this praise *confound*" - Sonnet 69, line 7; "And Bolingbroke hath seized the wasteful king ... We at time of year do wound the bark, the skin of our fruit trees, lest, being over-proud in sap and blood, with too much riches it *confound* itself ... We lop away, that bearing boughs may live; had he done so, himself had borne the crown, which waste of idle hours hath quite thrown down" - Richard II, 3.4.54-65; "*Mort de ma vie*, all is *confounded*, all!" - the Dauphin in *Henry V*, 4.5.3

CRUEL KNIFE: The executioner's axe

> Whom I might well condemn, to be *a cruel judge...*
> In fine, *she hath* **the hand and knife,**
> That may both *save and end my life*
> - Oxford poems in *Paradise of Dainty Devices*, 1576, signed E. O.

11 **THAT HE SHALL NEVER CUT FROM MEMORY**
SHALL = echoes the "all" of Southampton's motto *One for All, All for One*; **NEVER** = Edward deVere, *Ever or Never*; **CUT** = The image of the blade severing Southampton's head; "And there **cut off thy most gracious head**" – *2 Henry VI*, 4.10.81; **FROM MEMORY** = from posterity; from the eyes of future readers:

> Nor *Mars* his sword nor war's quick fire shall burn
> The living record of *your memory*
> - Sonnet 55, lines 7-8

> My life hath in this line some interest,
> Which *for memorial* still with thee shall stay
> - Sonnet 74, lines 3-4

> From hence *your memory* death cannot take
> - Sonnet 81, line 3

> And thou in this shalt find thy monument,
> When tyrants' crests and tombs of brass are spent
> - Sonnet 107, lines 13-14

12 **MY SWEET LOVE'S BEAUTY, THOUGH MY LOVER'S LIFE.**
MY SWEET LOVE'S BEAUTY = my royal son's blood from Elizabeth; **MY LOVER'S LIFE:** my royal son's mortal life; (i.e., the "knife" can never kill his royal blood, preserved in these sonnets, though it may in fact behead him and so terminate his mortal life); and, Oxford continues in the next lines, he intends to ensure his immortality by means of these sonnets:

13 **HIS BEAUTY SHALL IN THESE BLACK LINES BE SEEN,**
HIS BEAUTY = my son's Tudor blood from Beauty, the Queen; **SHALL IN THESE BLACK LINES BE SEEN** = will be recognized by future readers who look upon these verses; "So should the *lines of life* that life repair" – Sonnet 16, line 9; "When in *eternal lines to time* thou grow'st" – Sonnet 18, line 12; "My life hath *in this line* some interest" – Sonnet 74, line 3; "But when your countenance *filled up his line,/* Then lacked I matter, that enfeebled mine" – Sonnet 86, line 13; **BLACK** = the cloud has cast its shadow over Southampton, who is *black*; therefore, these verses containing his life are *black* as well; ("But now is *black* beauty's successive heir,/ And Beauty slandered by a bastard shame" – Sonnet 127, lines 3-4, in relation to the Rebellion of February 8, 1601; **BLACK LINES** = not only these lines of verse (written or printed in black ink), but also disgraced bloodlines, i.e., the Tudor line: "Of the *true line* and stock of Charles the Great" – *Henry V*, 1.2.71; "The third son, Duke of Clarence, *from whose line I claim the crown*" – *2 Henry VI*, 2.2.33-34

14 **AND THEY SHALL LIVE, AND HE IN THEM STILL GREEN.**
THEY SHALL LIVE = the lines of the Sonnets, which carry the Tudor bloodline of Oxford's royal son within them, will live beyond the death of father and son; "Nor shall death brag thou wand'rest in his shade,/ When in eternal lines to time thou grow'st./ So long as men can breathe or eyes can see,/ *So long lives this, and this gives life to thee*" – Sonnet 18, lines 11-14; "The *living* record of your memory" – Sonnet 55, line 8; "'*Gainst death and all-oblivious enmity/* Shall you pace forth!" – Sonnet 55, lines 9-10

AND HE IN THEM STILL GREEN = and he will live in the Sonnets forever royal; **GREEN** = young, fresh, golden, royal, in his spring or summer; green as Tudor color; "green" also as contrasting with "black" of the previous line; "And *Summer's green* all girded up in sheaves" – Sonnet 12, line 7; "Since first I saw you fresh, which yet are green" – Sonnet 104, line 8; (greenness & freshness = *verdure*; i.e., green = *vert* in French, related to Ver or Edward deVere); "I cannot but find a great grief in myself to remember the Mistress we have lost, under whom both you and myself *from our greenest years* have been in a manner brought up."- Oxford to Robert Cecil, April 1603, writing of the Queen on the eve of her funeral

Part Two

THE PRISON YEARS

DAY THIRTY-EIGHT IN THE TOWER
EXECUTION APPEARS IMMINENT

Sonnet 64
Interchange of State
This Thought is as A Death
17 March 1601

Tension mounts for Oxford as the Queen nears her decision about the fate of their royal son. Elizabeth has given the command for more executions to take place the next morning. In this verse Oxford focuses on the imminent fall of the House of Tudor that will occur when "the hungry Ocean" (James of Scotland) comes to "gain advantage on the Kingdom of the shore" (take over England) by the "interchange of state" or royal succession. Such will be the case upon the Queen's death if Southampton now gives up his claim to the throne and she (with Cecil) decides to spare his life.

Sonnet 64	Translation
When I have seen by time's fell hand defaced	When I've seen Elizabeth's life take away
The rich proud cost of outworn buried age,	The most royal splendor of her outworn dynasty,
When sometime lofty towers I see down razed,	When I see all her monuments torn down,
And brass eternal slave to mortal rage,	And her eternal royalty bow to mortality,
When I have seen the hungry Ocean gain	When I have seen kings [James] gain
Advantage on the Kingdom of the shore,	Advantage on the Kingdom of England,
And the firm soil win of the watery main,	And be victorious over our own soil,
Increasing store with loss, and loss with store,	One side taking royal blood from the other,
When I have seen such interchange of state,	When I have seen such a change of royal state,
Or state itself confounded to decay,	Or the Tudor state brought to destruction,
Ruin hath taught me thus to ruminate,	This vision of the future has taught me to think
That Time will come and take my love away.	That Elizabeth's life will take my royal son away.
This thought is as a death, which cannot choose	This thought of your death gives me no choice
But weep to have that which it fears to lose.	But to weep for the son I fear to lose.

1 WHEN I HAVE SEEN BY TIME'S FELL HAND DEFACED
TIME'S FELL HAND = by the executioner's axe; by the death of Elizabeth, ordered by the gesture of her hand, ending the mortal time recorded in these sonnets; "time's injurious hand" – Sonnet 63, line 2; "Was sleeping *by a Virgin hand* disarmed" – Sonnet 154, line 8; "Thus I was sleeping, *by a brother's hand* of life, of crown, of queen at once dispatched" – the Ghost of King Hamlet, *Hamlet*, 1.5.74-75; **FELL** = "While we devise *fell tortures for thy faults*" – *3 Henry VI*, 2.6.72

"Now is **the time** that **mercy** is to be showed. O pray her then, I beseech your lordships, in my behalf to **stay her hand,** and stop the rigorous course of the law, and remember, as I know she will never forget, that it is more honor to a prince to **pardon** one penitent **offender** than with severity to punish many." – Southampton to the Council, between the trial and now. (Stopes, 225-226)

DEFACED = destroyed, ruined, killed, beheaded; "Look on thy country, look on fertile France, and see the cities and the towns *defaced by wasting ruin of the cruel foe, as looks the mother on her lowly babe* when death doth close his tender dying eyes" – *1 Henry VI*, 3.3.44-48

REFERENCE EDITION 373

As Hannibal that saw in sight:
His country soil, with Carthage town:
By Roman force, *defaced down*.
- Oxford poem, signed E. O.
The Paradise of Dainty Devices, 1576

2 THE RICH PROUD COST OF OUTWORN BURIED AGE;
RICH = royal; filled with the "treasure" of royal blood; **PROUD** = splendidly royal; "Why is my verse so barren of new *pride*?" – Sonnet 76, line 1; **BURIED** = another image of Southampton; "Thou art the grave where **buried love** doth live" – Sonnet 31, line 9

AGE = a generation of men or particular period of time in history; "And peace proclaims Olives of *endless age*" – Sonnet 107, line 8, referring to the new reign of James in 1603 and the new age in England without civil war and with the imminent concluding of war with Spain; "An *age* of discord and continual strife" – *1 Henry VI*, 5.5.63; "The *age to come* will say, 'This Poet lies'" – Sonnet 17, line 7

3 WHEN SOMETIME LOFTY TOWERS I SEE DOWN RAZED,
LOFTY TOWERS = the height of majesty; "In the *height* and pride of all his glory" – *Pericles*, 2.4.6, speaking of the king; "Besides, the King's name is a *tower* of strength" – *Richard III*, 5.3.12; **DOWN RAZED** = opposite of "raised up"; **TOWERS** = echoing the Tower of London, which, in effect, is Southampton's current kingdom, with its many individual towers; "These walls of ours were not erected by their hands from whom you have receiv'd your grief; nor are they such that these great tow'rs, trophies, and schools should fall for private faults in them" – *Timon of Athens*, 5.4.23-26

4 AND BRASS ETERNAL SLAVE TO MORTAL RAGE;
AND BRASS = and brass tombs always subject to decay; "And thou in this shalt find thy monument,/ When tyrants' crests and *tombs of brass* are spent" – Sonnet 107, lines 13-4; **MORTAL RAGE** = the violent rage of mortality; "The *mortal Moon* hath her eclipse endured" – Sonnet 107, line 5, referring to the death of Elizabeth's mortal body; the anger and violence of destructive forces, i.e., those who would execute Southampton; also, echoing Oxford's own rage against them; "How with this *rage* shall *beauty hold a plea*?" – Sonnet 65, line 3, referring to the "beauty" or royal blood of the Queen, possessed by Southampton, about to lose its claim

5 WHEN I HAVE SEEN THE HUNGRY OCEAN GAIN
OCEAN = kingship; "*Ocean* or *sea* as a figure for *king* is often found in Shakespeare and his fellow writers" - Hotson, *Mr. W. H.*, p. 27; ("Let this sad *Interim* like *the Ocean* be" – Sonnet 56, line 9; "But since your worth, wide as *the Ocean* is" – Sonnet 80, line 5); "Even to *our Ocean*, to our great King John" – *King John*, 5.4.57; **HUNGRY OCEAN** = image of King James, hungry for the English throne, ready to advance upon the "ocean" of Elizabeth's monarchy; ("As a result of intense antiquarian and topographical activity during *the last years of Elizabeth's reign*, territory lost to and gained from the sea was of more than usual popular interest" – Booth, italics emphasizing his evidence that these sonnets were written late (i.e., in March 1601), two years before Elizabeth's death on March 24, 1603

The *tide of blood* in me
Hath proudly flowed in vanity till now.
Now doth it turn, and ebb back to the sea,
Where it shall mingle with the state of floods,
And flow henceforth *in formal majesty*.
- *2 Henry IV*, 5.2.129-133

No. 64

6 **ADVANTAGE ON THE KINGDOM OF THE SHORE,**
(GAIN) ADVANTAGE ON = overtake; succeed to the throne in place of another; "Who, having some *advantage on* Octavius, took it too eagerly" – *Julius Caesar*, 5.3.6-7; "They're beaten, sir, and *our advantage* serves for a fair victory" – *Antony and Cleopatra*, 4.7.11

KINGDOM OF THE SHORE = England; "Then thou alone *kingdoms of hearts* shouldst owe" – Sonnet 70, line 14

7 **AND THE FIRM SOIL WIN OF THE WATERY MAIN,**
WATERY MAIN = the ocean; the Tudor monarchy; ("A substitute shines brightly as a king, until a king be by, and then his state empties itself, as doth an inland brook into *the main of waters*" – *Merchant of Venice*, 5.1.94); England defeated by another monarch, i.e., James will be overtaking the throne and extinguishing the Tudor dynasty, thus beginning a new age

8 **INCREASING STORE WITH LOSS, AND LOSS WITH STORE;**
INCREASING STORE WITH LOSS = ironic, i.e., the advancement of James of Scotland to the English throne will "increase" Elizabeth's "store" of royalty with "loss" or less majesty; "Let those whom nature (Elizabeth) hath not made for *store*" – Sonnet 11, line 9; "If from thy self to *store* thou wouldst convert" – Sonnet 14, line 12 = when Southampton was "storing" his royal blood rather than giving it to an heir; **AND LOSS WITH STORE** = and the loss of Tudor Blood increased with the new "store" of Stuart blood; "O him she (nature, Elizabeth) *stores*, to show what wealth she had" – Sonnet 67, line 13, referring to Elizabeth, who "stores" her son's royal blood in the Tower; "And him as for a map doth Nature (Elizabeth) *store*" – Sonnet 68, line 13

9 **WHEN I HAVE SEEN SUCH INTERCHANGE OF STATE,**
INTERCHANGE OF STATE = Royal succession, by which the "state" of one monarch is exchanged for that of another; ("For readers in 1609 an allusion to the end of Elizabeth's long reign and the beginning of James's in 1603 must have been irresistible" – Duncan-Jones); "And says that once more I shall *interchange my wane state* for Henry's regal crown" – *3 Henry VI*, 4.7.3-4; Oxford is looking ahead to the death of Elizabeth and the succession of James, who will release his royal son from the Tower and grant him a royal pardon on condition that Southampton agrees to relinquish all claim to the throne, which requires that the truth of his identity as Elizabeth's son be buried (and so must Oxford's relationship as Southampton's father, and as the author of the Shakespeare works dedicated to his son).

> O God, that one might read the book of fate,
> And see the revolution of the times
> Make mountains level, and the continent,
> Weary of solid firmness, melt itself
> Into the sea, and other times to see
> The beachy girldle of the ocean
> Too wide for Neptune's hips; how chance's mocks
> And *changes fill the cup of alteration*
> With divers liquors!
> - *2 Henry IV*, 3.1.45-53

The state or estate of a king: "How many gazers mightst thou lead away/ If thou wouldst use the strength of *all thy state*" - Sonnet 96, lines 11-12; "outcast state" - Sonnet 29, line 2

"If my dear love were but the *child of state*" – Sonnet 124, line 1

10 **OR STATE ITSELF CONFOUNDED TO DECAY,**
STATE ITSELF = a repetition of "state" for emphasis; echoing "kingdom" of line 6; Elizabeth's and Southampton's royal state; ("Scoffing at his *state* and grinning at his pomp" – *Richard II*, 3.2.163); **CONFOUNDED** = destroyed; "Against *confounding age's cruel knife*" – Sonnet 63, line 10; **DECAY** =

REFERENCE EDITION

decline from a better to a worse state; (Oxford wants James to gain the throne, so his son may be liberated from the Tower; but otherwise he feels the succession of James will erode the humanist values that the Elizabethan Age had begun to promote – an accurate prediction, since England will enter a civil war in the mid-17th century); the final decay of Elizabeth's mortal body; the destruction of her royal state that would have been continued if Henry Wriothesley had been acknowledged as her heir; "Where wasteful *time* debateth with *decay*" – Sonnet 15, line 11; "But now *my gracious numbers* are *decayed*" – Sonnet 79, line 3; "The worst was this: *my love* was my *decay*" – Sonnet 80, line 14; "For, good King Henry, thy *decay* I fear" – 2 Henry VI, 3.1.194

11 RUIN HATH TAUGHT ME THUS TO RUMINATE
RUIN = echoing Oxford's lecture in 1590-91 to Southampton in Sonnet 10, line 7, "Seeking that *beauteous roof to ruinate*," referring to the destruction of the House of Tudor by refusing the Cecil marriage alliance

> *Time's* glory is to calm *contending Kings*...
> To *ruinate* proud buildings with thy hours,
> And smear with *dust* their glittering golden towers
> - *Lucrece*, line 939 ff

12 THAT TIME WILL COME AND TAKE MY LOVE AWAY.
TIME = literally the executioner, i.e., the Queen; also, the end of Elizabeth's life; **MY LOVE** = my royal son; the death of the Queen will mean the end of my son's royal blood in terms of his ability to claim the throne.

13 THIS THOUGHT IS AS A DEATH, WHICH CANNOT CHOOSE
AS A DEATH = the thought of Southampton's impending execution.

14 BUT WEEP TO HAVE THAT WHICH IT FEARS TO LOSE.
BUT WEEP = but cry to have; **THAT WHICH IT FEARS TO LOSE** = Southampton, the son whom he fears to *lose* by execution; "But you must know your father *lost* a father, that father *lost, lost* his" – *Hamlet*, 1.2.89-90, King Claudius referring to the death of Hamlet's father.

Part Two

THE PRISON YEARS

EXECUTIONS OF DANVERS & BLOUNT
SOUTHAMPTON TO DIE NEXT DAY
THIRTY-NINE IN THE TOWER

Sonnet 65
Hold a Plea
Unless This Miracle
18 March 1601

Charles Danvers and Christopher Blount are publicly beheaded on Tower Hill today. Crowds are still waiting for Southampton to be executed as well. Oxford now braces for the worst.

Sonnet 65	Translation
Since brass, nor stone, nor earth, nor boundless sea,	Since none of these temporary mortal things
But sad mortality o'ersways their power,	Is more powerful than sad mortality itself,
How with this rage shall beauty hold a plea,	How will my son's royal blood plead for itself,
Whose action is no stronger than a flower?	Taking a legal action no stronger than a flower?
O how shall summer's honey breath hold out	O, how will his fresh royal blood survive
Against the wrackful siege of batt'ring days,	Against the destructive siege of time,
When rocks impregnable are not so stout,	When the strongest stones aren't so strong,
Nor gates of steel so strong but time decays?	And even no prison gates can protect him?
O fearful meditation; where, alack,	O, frightful thoughts! Where, alas,
Shall time's best Jewel from time's chest lie hid?	Can Elizabeth's most royal heir avoid her prison?
Or what strong hand can hold his swift foot back?	Or what mortal strength can stop her?
Or who his spoil or beauty can forbid?	Or who can forbid her from killing his royal blood?
O none, unless this miracle have might	O no one! Unless this miracle has royal might:
That in black ink my love may still shine bright.	That in these tragic lines my royal son still lives.

Sir Charles Danvers being brought from the Tower unto the new built scaffold upon Tower hill, ascended the place wondrous cheerfully, saluting many of his friends. And learning that the Lord Grey was there on horseback near the scaffold he spake to him, saying that the enmity which he had borne him came not of any injury but by reason of his love for the Earl of Southampton...

Then Sir Charles spoke of his condemnation, saying that he was clear of any intent of violence to be offered to her Majesty's person or his country, which he ever held most dear ... His head was cut off with one stroke saving a little which an officer cut off with his knife ... Sir Christopher Blount ascended the scaffold, who above an hour past had been brought from the Gate house in Westminster ... - "Elizabethan Chronicle" – Entry for March 18, 1601

"Earlier Danvers had declared to the authorities: 'The principal motive that drove (him) into this action was the great obligation of love and duty, in respect of many honourable favours done to him by the Earl of Southampton.' ... Before the headsman's axe ended his life, Blount conceded what the Crown had all along contended: 'I know, and must confess, if we had failed of our Ends, we should (rather than have been disappointed) even have drawn Blood from herself (the Queen)..." (Akrigg, p. 128)

REFERENCE EDITION

1 SINCE BRASS, NOR STONE, NOR EARTH, NOR BOUNDLESS SEA,
SINCE, etc. = because none of these; **BOUNDLESS SEA** = royal blood; ("And what is Edward but a *ruthless sea*" – *3 Henry VI*, 5.4.25, referring to the king); "Thou art, quote she, *a sea, a sovereign king*" – *The Rape of Lucrece*, 1594, line 652

2 BUT SAD MORTALITY O'ERSWAYS THEIR POWER,
BUT = except; **SAD MORTALITY** = Southampton's death by execution, expected soon; "The *mortal* Moon hath her eclipse endured" – Sonnet 107, line 5, referring to the death of Elizabeth, i.e, the final decay of her mortal body; **THEIR POWER** = overcomes the power of the forces against them, i.e., Elizabeth's decision to execute him; Robert Cecil's power over the Queen and, therefore, over England in general and over Southampton in particular; Southampton's own power because of the royal blood that makes him a prince or king: "O Thou my lovely Boy, who *in thy power*" – Sonnet 126, line 1

3 HOW WITH THIS RAGE SHALL BEAUTY HOLD A PLEA,
HOW WITH THIS RAGE = how, against this angry power; "If those that care to keep your royal person from *Treason's secret knife and **traitors' rage**" – *2 Henry VI*, 3.1.173-174; **SHALL BEAUTY HOLD A PLEA** = will the Tudor blood of Southampton have a chance to argue legally; **HOLD A PLEA** = Plead for mercy, as Southampton did at the trial; ("Though justice be thy *plea* ... the justice of thy *plea*" – *The Merchant of Venice*, 4.1.196, 201; "No rightful *plea* might *plead* for justice there" – *Lucrece*, stanza 236; "And 'gainst myself a *lawful plea* commence" – Sonnet 35, line 11; "But the defendant doth that *plea deny*" – Sonnet 46, line 7; "It will help me nothing to plead mine innocence" – *Henry VIII*, 1.1.208-209); "And 'gainst myself a *lawful plea* commence" – Sonnet 35, line 11; "But the defendant doth that *plea deny*" – Sonnet 46, line 6; "to *plead* against Her Majesty" – Oxford, circa 1601-02, Cecil Papers 146.19, Chiljan, 71

4 WHOSE ACTION IS NO STRONGER THAN A FLOWER?
Whose ability to make an **ACTION** (a legal term) is no stronger than a "flower" of the Tudor Rose, i.e., Southampton, the "little western flower" of *Midsummer Night's Dream*; an ironic contradiction, since, as such, he should be all-powerful, yet he is now powerless against these forces, the way a literal flower is so delicate, fragile and weak

> Ah, my poor Princes! Ah, my tender babes,
> My unblow'd *flowers*, new-appearing sweets!
> If yet your gentle souls fly in the air,
> And be not fix'd in doom perpetual...
> - *Richard III*, 4.4.9-11

ACTION = "Law case ... active operation against an enemy" – Booth; referring to the legal action at the trial when Southampton pleaded for mercy; referring more immediately to Oxford's legal actions behind the scenes to save him from execution; "law suit, legal proceeding, litigation" – Crystal & Crystal; "If you will make't an *action*, call witness to't" – *Cymbeline*, 2.3.152; "And you of her, the bloody *book of law* you shall yourself read, in the bitter letter, after your own sense, yeah, though our proper son stood in *your action*" – *Othello*, 1.3.68-71; "I'll bring mine *action* on the proudest he that stops my way in Padua" – *The Taming of the Shrew*, 3.2.233-234; "course of action, enterprise, or trial, legal process" – Crystal & Crystal; "This *action* I now go on is for my better grace" – *The Winter's Tale*, 2.1.121-122

> "I will not for my own particular hereafter move your Lordship's furtherance, but if I shall defer anything in *this action*, I will leave the whole consideration thereof to Her Majesty."
> - Oxford to Burghley, June 7, 1595

5 O HOW SHALL SUMMER'S HONEY BREATH HOLD OUT
SUMMER'S = golden, royal, i.e., of former days recorded by Sonnets 1 – 26, prior to the Rebellion of February 8, 1601; "Shall I compare thee to a *Summer's Day* ... And *Summer's lease* hath all too short a date ... But *thy eternal Summer* shall not fade" – Sonnet 18, lines 1, 3,9

No. 65

6 **AGAINST THE WRACKFUL SIEGE OF BATT'RING DAYS,**
WRACKFUL SIEGE OF BATT'RING DAYS = the terrible slaughter of time; an image of Oxford being emotionally battered by the anxiety of waiting for the Queen's decision about Southampton's fate; "wrackful" echoing "the rack" used for torture in the Tower (Courtesy of M. Brame & G. Popova)

> "For, being now almost at a point to taste that good which Her Majesty shall determine, yet am I once that hath long *besieged a fort* and not able to compass the end or reap the fruit of his travail, being forced to levy his *siege* for want of *munition*." - Oxford to Burghley, June 25, 1585

7 **WHEN ROCKS IMPREGNABLE ARE NOT SO STOUT,**
ROCKS IMPREGNABLE = such as the high walls of the Tower, which cannot protect Southampton; "As if this flesh which *walls about our life* were brass *impregnable*" – *Richard II*, 3.2.167-168; "For such a time *do I now fortify*" – Sonnet 63, line 9

8 **NOR GATES OF STEEL SO STRONG BUT TIME DECAYS?**
GATES OF STEEL = the gates of the Tower, specifically Traitor's Gate; (recalling "sings hymns at *heaven's gate*", i.e., the Queen's prison, of Sonnet 29, line 12); "I am come to survey **the Tower** this day… **Open the gates**" – *1 Henry VI*, 1.3.1-4; "Gloucester's men rush at the *Tower gates*" – *1 Henry VI*, 1.3.13, stage directions; Woodville (within): "What traitors have we here?" Gloucester: "Lieutenant, is it you whose voice I hear? *Open the gates!*" – *1 Henry VI*, 1.3.15-17; "through a secret grate of *iron bars in yonder Tower* – *1 Henry VI*, 1.4.10-11

> What stronger breastplate than a heart untainted?
> Thrice is he arm'd that hath his quarrel just,
> And he but naked, though *lock'd up in steel*,
> Whose conscience with injustice is corrupted.
> - *2 Henry VI*, 3.2.231-234

SO STRONG BUT TIME DECAYS = unable to withstand the forces against him; **DECAYS** = leads to death; the continual decay of Elizabeth's mortal body, her inability to protect her son.

9 **O FEARFUL MEDITATION! WHERE, ALACK,**
O = Oxford; **FEARFUL** = "filled with fear, afraid … causing apprehension … dreadful, terrible" – Schmidt; "'Tis thought the King is dead … The pale-faced moon looks bloody on the earth, and lean-look'd prophets whisper *fearful change* … These signs foretell the death or fall of kings" – *Richard II*, 2.4.7-15; **O FEARFUL MEDITATION** = O my horrible thoughts, filled with fear for my son, who is about to be executed and/or lose his royal claim; "With *meditating* that she must die at once" – *Julius Caesar*, 4.3.190; "and in *session* sit with *meditations awful*" – *Othello*, 3.3.143; "thou keep'st the *stroke* betwixt thy begging and my *meditation*" – the King in *Richard III*, 4.2.114-115, referring to the imminent murder of his nephews in the Tower; Oxford recalling Southampton's mother, Elizabeth, in earlier days: "And the Imperial Votress passed on, in *maiden meditation* fancy-free" – *A Midsummer Night's Dream*, 2.1.163-164, referring to Elizabeth when she continued as the Virgin Queen on her summer progress in 1574, following the birth of their royal son; "Are you *meditating on virginity*?" – *All's Well That Ends Well*, 1.1.111; also Oxford's meditation upon his "divine" or royal son: "Divinely bent to meditation" – *Richard III*, 3.7.61; "full of repentance, continual *meditations*, tears and sorrows" – *Henry VIII*, 4.2.28; **ALACK** = recalling "But *out, alack*, he was but one hour mine" of Sonnet 33, line 11, the removal of him from Oxford as father in 1574

10 **SHALL TIME'S BEST JEWEL FROM TIME'S CHEST LIE HID?**
TIME'S BEST JEWEL = Southampton, Elizabeth's most royal heir; ("our *prince, jewel* of children" – *Winter's Tale*, 5.1.115-116); recalling him as "the world's fresh *ornament*" of Sonnet 1, line 9; "Which like a *jewel* hung in ghastly night" – Sonnet 27, line 11; "As on the finger of a throned Queen,/ The basest *Jewel* will be well esteemed" – Sonnet 96, lines 5-6; **TIME'S CHEST** = casket; also the Tower of London, where Southampton faces execution on Tower Hill; ("*time's chest* would be a coffin" – Booth); "A *jewel* in a ten-

REFERENCE EDITION   379

times-barr'd-up *chest* is a bold spirit in a loyal breast" – *Richard II*, 1.1.180-181; "They found him dead and cast into the streets, an empty casket, where the *jewel of life by some damn'd hand* was robbed and ta'en away" – *King John*, 5.1.39-41; "And because next to the sacred letters of divinity nothing doth persuade the same more than philosophy (of which your book is plentifully stored), I thought myself to commit an unpardonable error to have *murdered the same in the waste-bottoms of my chests*" – Oxford's Prefatory Letter to *Cardanus' Comfort*, 1573

11 OR WHAT STRONG HAND CAN HOLD HIS SWIFT FOOT BACK?
WHAT STRONG HAND = The Queen's imperial hand, possessing absolute authority; ("potential reference to handwriting" – Booth); also recalling Oxford's pledge, "And this *my hand against myself* uprear" in Sonnet 49, line 11; Oxford's attempt to preserve Southampton's life and royal blood by writing these sonnets; but more to the point in this verse: *what royal hand*, i.e., Elizabeth's hand, since she has the power to either destroy or save him; "O pray her then, I beseech your lordships, in my behalf to **stay her hand**, and stop the rigorous course of the law" – Southampton, writing to the Council from the Tower, about this time (Stopes, 225); "Was sleeping **by a Virgin hand** disarmed" – Sonnet 154, line 8, referring to the newborn son of Oxford and Elizabeth in 1574; "We cannot hold *mortality's strong hand*" – *King John*, 4.2.82, referring to the expected death of young Prince Arthur; "Thus was I, sleeping, **by a brother's hand** of life, of crown, of queen at once *dispatched*" – the Ghost of Hamlet's father, speaking of his brother King Claudius in Hamlet, 1.5. 74-75; "With *time's injurious hand* crushed and o'erworn" – Sonnet 63, line 2; "When I have seen *by time's fell hand defaced*" – Sonnet 64, line 1; "And *by their hands* this grace of kings must die, if hell and treason hold their promises, ere he take ship for France, and in Southampton" – *Henry V*, 2.0.Chorus, 28-30; "King: ' Thus have I yielded up into *your hand* the circle of my glory'; Pandulph (giving King John the crown): 'Take again from this *my hand*, as holding of the pope, your sovereign greatness and authority" – *King John*, 5.1.1-4; "His head by nature framed to wear a crown, *his hand* to wield a scepter, and himself likely in time to bless a regal throne" – *3 Henry VI*, 4.6.72-74

12 OR WHO HIS SPOIL OR BEAUTY CAN FORBID?
SPOIL = ("time's plunder, the loot he takes" – Booth); "Is not this an honourable *spoil*? A gallant prize?" – *1 Henry IV*, 1.1.74-75; "Company, villainous company, hath been the *spoil* of me" – *1 Henry IV*, 3.3.9-10;
BEAUTY = Tudor blood from Beauty, the Queen, whose ever-waning life is Time, so that she herself is the destroyer

13 O NONE, UNLESS THIS MIRACLE HAVE MIGHT:
O = Oxford; **NONE** = Southampton, the "one" who is now "none"; **UNLESS THIS MIRACLE** = the miracle that he might be saved; also, the miracle of these sonnets, which are recreating and recording his life; echoing the spiritual aspect of the Sonnets as being written to preserve Southampton as a king or god on earth.

14 THAT IN BLACK INK MY LOVE MAY STILL SHINE BRIGHT!
BLACK INK = of these sonnets, also reflecting Southampton's blackness or disgrace and doom; "Which like a jewel hung in ghastly night,/ Makes *black night* beauteous, and her old face new" – Sonnet 27, lines 11-12, referring to the blackness of disgrace suffered by Southampton, who is nevertheless a "jewel" or prince in the Tower, reflecting the "beauty" of his mother the Queen; **MY LOVE** = my royal son; "*My love* looks fresh" – Sonnet 107, line 10, i.e., my royal son upon his liberation from the Tower; **MAY STILL SHINE BRIGHT** = may always exhibit his royalty, to readers in posterity; (recalling Sonnet 33, line 9: "Even so *my Sunne* one early morn did *shine*"); "When to unseeing eyes thy shade *shines* so" – Sonnet 43, line 8; "But *you shall shine more bright* in these contents" – Sonnet 55, line 3; "So between them *love did shine*/ That the Turtle saw his *right*/ Flaming in the Phoenix's sight" – *The Phoenix and Turtle*, 1601, with Oxford as the Turtle-dove and Elizabeth as the Phoenix, watching the end of the "love" or royal blood and it's "right" to the throne; **BRIGHT** = royally, by means of his eyes or suns; "Yet looks he like a king: behold his eye, as *bright* as is the eagle's, lightens forth controlling majesty" – *Richard II*, 3.3.68-70

Part Two

THE PRISON YEARS

ELIZABETH SPARES SOUTHAMPTON'S LIFE
DAY FORTY IN THE TOWER

Sonnet 66
By Limping Sway Disabled
Tongue-Tied by Authority
19 March 1601

Queen Elizabeth spares Southampton's life, after Oxford makes a bargain with hunchbacked Robert Cecil to gain his son's eventual release and pardon in return for his relinquishment of any claim to the throne. Southampton's "gilded honor" has been "shamefully misplaced" and his young "virtue" as a prince has been violated as now, in the eyes of the world, he is "supposed as forfeit to a confined doom (Sonnet 107) or facing perpetual imprisonment. All his lands will be confiscated and titles will be stripped away, reducing his status to that of a base commoner known as "Mr. Henry Wriothesley" or (in legal terms) "the late earl". Oxford responds with relief and exhaustion, but also with such profound grief over the bargain that he contemplates suicide. His stated grievances, on the immediate level, all relate to what has happened to his son and not to himself. For all these reasons he prefers to die; except that, by dying, he would be leaving him alone – alone in the Tower. (This marks 40 sonnets in 40 days, echoing Christ's ordeal.)

Sonnet 66	Translation
Tired with all these, for restful death I cry:	I would like to die, for these many reasons:
As to behold desert a beggar born,	Such as to behold my royal son born as a bastard,
And needy Nothing trimmed in jollity,	And see him become a nobody given an earldom,
And purest faith unhappily forsworn,	And faith in Elizabeth torn by her broken vows,
And gilded honor shamefully misplaced,	And his claim disgraced and promised to another,
And maiden vertue rudely strumpeted,	And his perfect royal blood falsely ruined,
And right perfection wrongfully disgraced,	And his royal blood wrongfully disgraced,
And strength by limping sway disabled,	And his royal strength by Robert Cecil disabled,
And art made tongue-tied by authority,	And this verse forced by policy to be indirect,
And Folly, (Doctor-like) controlling skill,	And pompous folly having power over royalty,
And simple Truth miscalled Simplicity,	And my plain truth mistakenly called foolishness,
And captive-good attending Captain ill.	And my captive royal son serving evil Cecil.
Tired with all these, from these would I be gone,	Tired with all these, from these I would die,
Save that to die, I leave my love alone.	Except, dying, I'd leave my royal son in prison.

(This sonnet corresponds with Sonnet 145 of the Dark Lady series, where Oxford records that Queen Elizabeth extended her "mercy" and "saved" her son's "life".)

"As late as March 25th spectators came to Tower Hill, drawn by a rumor that Southampton was to be executed there that day. They were disappointed. The decision had already been made to commute his sentence to imprisonment." - Akrigg, p. 131

REFERENCE EDITION

1 TIRED WITH ALL THESE, FOR RESTFUL DEATH I CRY:
TIRED = exhausted, emotionally spent; "Weary with toil" – Sonnet 27, line 1; **ALL** = Southampton, *One for All, All for One*; **ALL THESE** = for the following reasons, all related to my son; **FOR RESTFUL DEATH I CRY** = I wish for the peacefulness of death; "To die, to sleep – no more; and by a sleep to say we end the heartache, and the thousand natural shocks that flesh is heir to; 'Tis a consummation devoutly to be wished" – *Hamlet*, 3.1.68-73, the prince's "to be or not to be" soliloquy that expresses similar complaints.

2 AS TO BEHOLD DESERT A BEGGAR BORN,
DESERT = deserving; what Southampton was due, because of his blood; "If it were filled with *your most high deserts*" – Sonnet 17, line 2; **A BEGGAR BORN** = Southampton, born without acknowledgment; "Experience of my youth, made think **humble truth in deserts born**" – Poem in *Astrophel and Stella*, 1591, signed with Oxford's initials E. O.; "Sometimes am I *king*, then *treasons make me wish myself a* **beggar**" – *Richard II*, 5.5, 32-33

3 AND NEEDY NOTHING TRIMMED IN JOLLITY,
NEEDY NOTHING = Southampton, a royal bastard who is both needy and a "nobody," especially now, in prison (and also because of the loss of his titles and estates); **TRIMMED IN JOLLITY** = dressed up as an earl in great splendor, as Southampton was before this tragedy; "*Trimm'd* up your praises with a princely tongue, spoke your *deservings* like a *chronicle*" – *1 Henry IV*, 5.2.56-57

4 AND PUREST FAITH UNHAPPILY FORSWORN,
FORSWORN = perjured; abandoned; betrayed. ("Unhappily" in contrast to the "sire, and child, and happy mother" of Sonnet 8, line 11; Elizabeth broke her vow to name Southampton; Oxford's "purest faith" in the Queen was betrayed, although he himself had kept that faith; as he writes with bitter irony in Sonnet 152: "In loving thee thou know'st *I am forsworn*,/ But *thou art twice forsworn* to me love swearing" – lines 1-2; she was "twice" forsworn in promising her "love" or concern for her blood, because she broke faith with both Oxford and Southampton; (Dowden glosses "unhappily" as "evilly"); "And all my honest faith in thee is lost" - Oxford to Elizabeth in Sonnet 152, line 8; (honest = pure)

5 AND GILDED HONOUR SHAMEFULLY MISPLACED,
GILDED = made royal; made bright and shining like gold; made rich, i.e., with royal blood; "An *eye more bright* than theirs, less false in rolling,/ *Gilding* the object whereupon it gazeth" – Sonnet 20, lines 5-6; "When sparkling stars twire not, *thou gild'st the heaven*" – Sonnet 28, line 12; **GILDED HONOUR** = the gilded honor due Southampton as king; "Full many a glorious morning have I seen/ Flatter the mountain tops with *sovereign eye*,/ Kissing with golden face the meadows green,/ *Gilding* pale streams with heavenly alchemy" – the royal sun/son of Sonnet 33, lines 1-4; "Not marble, nor *the gilded monument of Princes*" – Sonnet 55, lines 1-2, as Southampton himself is a prince; "Right **Honourable** ... Only, if your **Honour** seem but pleased ... I leave it to your **Honourable** survey, and your **Honour** to your heart's content" - Dedication of *Venus and Adonis* to Southampton, 1593; **SHAMEFULLY MISPLACED** = taken from him because of Elizabeth's shame; ("And Beauty slandered with a *bastard shame*" – Sonnet 127, line 4; with shame and disgrace; and now because of her son's own "shame" as a convicted traitor; "For I am *shamed* by that which I bring forth" – Sonnet 72, line 13, speaking as father of Southampton, whom he "brought forth" into the world, and as the creator of these Sonnets, which he is "bringing forth" as a rebirth of his son to keep alive his royal blood and claim for posterity; in each case he is filled with "shame" over the fact that the true identity of Southampton cannot be told; **MISPLACED** = echoing that Southampton must remain in "the place" or the Tower

6 AND MAIDEN VERTUE RUDELY STRUMPETED,
MAIDEN VERTUE = (or virtue); youthful or "fresh" and "green" royalty and kingly qualities, echoing *Ver* (Vere) as father; **RUDELY STRUMPETED** = "As when parents sell their daughters" – Tucker; Southampton's young royal status brutally taken from him

> But thou from loving England art so far,
> That thou hast *underwrought his lawful king*,
> Cut off the sequence of posterity,
> Outfaced infant state, and done a **rape**

No. 66

*Upon the **maiden virtue of the crown***
- *King John*, 2.1.94-98

MAIDEN VIRTUE = there is also the sense that Oxford's own "maiden virtue" had been "rudely strumpeted" by the Queen, as depicted by the attempted seduction of the young god Adonis by the mature goddess Venus; "He burns with bashful shame: she with her tears/ Doth quench the *maiden burning of his cheeks*" – *Venus and Adonis*, stanza 8; "And many *maiden* gardens yet unset" – Sonnet 16, line 6, with "maiden gardens" referring to virgin wombs; "but in her *maiden* hand/ The fairest votary took up that fire" – Sonnet 154, line 4, referring to Elizabeth as the so-called Virgin Queen; "And the imperial votaress passed on, in *maiden* meditation, fancy free" – *A Midsummer Night's Dream*, 2.1 163-164, referring to Elizabeth as "the imperial votaress" who continued onward, passing herself off as a virgin, even though she had given birth to "a little western" flower (Southampton) prior to moving westward on her royal progress to Bristol and Bath; "but as when the bird of wonder dies, the *maiden* Phoenix, her ashes new create another heir" – *Henry VIII*, 5.5.39-41, Archbishop Cranmer of Canterbury, referring to the infant Princess Elizabeth, who will grow up to be Queen and, from her own ashes, create another heir

Sweet prince, the untainted *virtue* of your years - *Richard III*, 3.1.7
Two props of *virtue* for a Christian Prince - *Richard III*, 3.7.95

England ne'er had a king of so much worth…
England ne'er had a king until his time,
Virtue he had, deserving to command - *1Henry VI*, 1.1.7-9

"So gracious and **virtuous** a sovereign … Nothing adorns a king more than justice, nor in anything doth a king more resemble God than in justice, which is the head of all **virtue,** and he that is endued therewith hath all the rest"
- Oxford to Robert Cecil, May 7, 1603, speaking of King James

7 AND RIGHT PERFECTION WRONGFULLY DISGRACED,
RIGHT PERFECTION = rightful kingship; "The *perfect* ceremony of *love's right*" – Sonnet 23, line 6; **PERFECTION** = "When I consider everything that grows/ Holds in *perfection* but a little moment" – Sonnet 15, line 5, referring to Southampton, who is "growing" within this diary of the Sonnets; "Such cherubins as your sweet self resemble,/ Creating every bad a *perfect* best/ As fast as objects to his beams assemble" – Sonnet 114, lines 6-8; "I would wish such *perfection* govern, sir" – *The Tempest*, 2.1.168; "Do you not read some tokens of my son in the large composition of this man? … Mine eye hath well examined his parts and finds them *perfect* Richard" – *King John*, 1.1.87-90; **WRONGFULLY DISGRACED** = Southampton was disgraced wrongfully by Elizabeth at his birth; now he is wrongfully kept a prisoner in disgrace for high treason

8 AND STRENGTH BY LIMPING SWAY DISABLED,
STRENGTH = royal power (of Southampton); "To leave poor me thou hast *the strength of laws*" – Sonnet 49, line 13; If thou wouldst use *the strength of all thy state*" – Sonnet 96, line 12, both to Southampton; "That in the very refuse of thy deeds/ There is such *strength* and warranties of skill" – Sonnet 150, lines 6-7, to Elizabeth; "The king's name is a tower of *strength*" – Richard III, 5.3.12; **STRENGTH BY LIMPING SWAY DISABLED** = Royal power rendered impotent by the limping, swaying, hunchbacked Secretary of State Robert Cecil; (*"It is tempting to suspect a glance at the control of the State, including vigorous military men like Raleigh and Essex, by **the limping Robert Cecil**"* – Dover Wilson); there is also a glance at Oxford's own lameness as a result of a duel in the streets in the early 1580's; "The pride of *kingly sway*" – *Richard II*, 4.1.206; "Who now in Court doth bear the greatest sway"
– Spenser, *Mother Hubbard's Tale*, line 616

9 AND ART MADE TONGUE-TIED BY AUTHORITY,
ART = the careful writing and compilation of these private verses; "art" usually refers to letters, learning, science; **TONGUE-TIED** = "not allowed to speak" – Tucker; **ART MADE TONGUE-TIED BY**

REFERENCE EDITION 383

AUTHORITY = Forced to write indirectly, and secretly, by officialdom; because it is treasonous to speak or write of a claim to the throne; censored by the supreme authority of the monarch; "Your *sovereign greatness and **authority***" – *King John*, 5.1.4, speaking of the king; "to obtain *the protection of that **authority***, to strengthen it with gifts, and to mark it with the superscription of her name" – Oxford's Letter to the Reader for *The Courtier*, 1572, writing of Queen Elizabeth as "patroness" of that literary translation and, by extension, of all English literature; "and that he may have *from Her Majesty equal **authority***" – Oxford to Burghley, June 7, 1595

> Before a true and lawful magistrate,
> That hath *authority* over him that swears
> - *3 Henry VI*, 1.2.23-24

AUTHORITY = persons in authority; the right to command; position of power, prerogative; "*Authorizing* thy trespass with compare" – Sonnet 35, line 6, Oxford saying he had authorized Southampton to attempt the Rebellion against the crown, by means of "compare" through his plays; in the plural, "authorities" often refer to legal powers; "soaks up the king's countenance, his rewards, his *authorities*" – *Hamlet*, 4.2.17

> Kent: No, sir; but you have that in your countenance which I would fain call *master*.
> Lear: What's that?
> Kent: *Authority*.
> - *King Lear*, 1.4.27-30

10 AND FOLLY (DOCTOR-LIKE) CONTROLLING SKILL,

FOLLY = Robert Cecil, now in control; but probably alluding also to the folly of the Rebellion itself; **DOCTOR-LIKE** = with authority; acting with the airs of a doctor who knows best; Doctor of Divinity, etc.; **CONTROLLING SKILL** = wielding the skill or power (the knowledge and science) to exercise control over Southampton, a prince who should be the one who is "controlling" or exercising authority over everyone, including Cecil; "A man in hew all *Hews* in his *controlling*" – Sonnet 20, line 7; "Can yet the lease of my true love *control*" – Sonnet 107, line 3; "Two *controlling* bounds shall you be, kings" – *King John*, 2.1.444; (FOLLY echoing "Praise of Folly," Erasmus, translated in 1549)

11 AND SIMPLE TRUTH MISCALLED SIMPLICITY,

TRUTH = Oxford, *Nothing Truer than Truth*; **SIMPLE TRUTH** = the plain, unmixed truth; my own truth about Southampton's royal claim as my son by Elizabeth; "But she tells to your Highness *simple truth*" – *The Comedy of Errors*, 5.1.211; "They do me wrong ... Cannot a plain man live and think no harm, but thus his *simple truth* must be abus'd with silken, sly, insinuating Jacks?" – the King in *Richard II*, 1.3.42-53; **SIMPLE** = consisting of one thing only, echoing "one" for Southampton; pure, being no more nor less than; uncompounded, unmixed; "For compound sweet, forgoing *simple* savor" – Sonnet 125, line 7; "*Simple* were so well compounded" – *The Phoenix and Turtle*, 1601, line 44; "And take thou my oblation, poor but free,/ Which is not mixed with seconds, knows no art,/ But mutual render, only me for thee" – Oxford's final offering to Southampton in Sonnet 125, lines 10-12; **TRUTH** = "Thy end is *Truth's* and Beauty's doom and date" – Sonnet 14, line 14; "And your *true* rights be termed a Poet's rage" – Sonnet 17, line 11; "Thou *truly* fair wert *truly* sympathized/ In *true* plain words by thy *true*-telling friend" – Sonnet 82, lines 11-12; "Let me not to the marriage of *true* minds/ Admit impediments" – Sonnet 116, lines 1-2; **SIMPLICITY** = "plainness, naturalness, absence of everything that seems extraordinary ... silliness, folly" - Schmidt; i.e., the simple truth of Southampton's royal blood has been viewed erroneously as un-royal or reduced to the merely plain; "Beauty, *Truth*, and Rarity,/ Grace in all *simplicity*,/ Here enclosed in cinders lie" – *The Phoenix and Turtle*, 1601, lines 53-55, which Oxford is now writing about the death of Elizabeth, himself, and Southampton, as a royal family, and to which he will allude seven verses after this one, in Sonnet 73. ("On both sides thus is SIMPLE TRUTH suppressed" - Sonnet 138, line 8; emphasis added)

12 AND CAPTIVE-GOOD ATTENDING CAPTAIN ILL.

CAPTIVE GOOD = Southampton as prisoner held; "Never did *captive* with a freer heart cast off his chains of bondage and embrace his golden uncontrolled enfranchisement" – *Richard II*, 1.3.88-90; "Master lieutenant, now that God and friends have shaken Edward from the regal seat, and turned *my captive state* to

liberty" – *3 Henry VI*, 4.6.1-3; "And in a *captive* chariot into Rouen bring him our prisoner" – *Henry V*, 5.3.53-54; "Captive to thee and to thy Roman yoke" – *Titus Andronicus*, 1.1.114; "To grace in captive bonds his chariot wheels" – *Julius Caesar*, 1.1.35; "Therefore so please thee to return with us, and of our Athens, thine and ours, to *take the **captainship***, thou shalt be met with thanks, *allowed with **absolute power***, and thy good name live with **authority**" – *Timon of Athens*, 5.1.159-163; **ATTENDING** = waiting upon; "*Attending* on his golden pilgrimage" – Sonnet 7, line 8; "And will that thou henceforth *attend* on us" – the king in *2 Henry VI*, 5.1.80; *"Also my great change in giving **attendance** in Your Highness' service"* – Oxford to Queen Elizabeth, May 9, 1592, BL Landsdowne MS 71.10,f.18; Chiljan, 47; *"And if it be so, what order is resolved on amongst you, either for the **attending** or meeting of His Majesty"* – Oxford to Robert Cecil, April 25/27, 1603, referring to King James on the eve of Elizabeth's funeral; **CAPTAIN ILL** = Robert Cecil, now "captain" in charge of the English government and the cause of Southampton's downfall; probably further alluded to by the use of "ILL," echoing the last two letters of Cecil's name (CAPTAIN **ILL** = C. [EC] **IL** – Alex McNeil); James VI of Scotland wrote to his ambassadors in England, telling them to give assurance of his favor "to Mr. Secretary (Cecil), *who is **king there in effect**"* – April 8, 1601, *The Secret Correspondence of Sir Robert Cecil with James VI King of Scotland*, edited by Edmund Goldsmid, privately printed, Edinburgh, 1887, vol. 1, p. 8; "His *captain*, steward, deputy-elect" – *Richard II*, 4.1.126; calling this a "climax" of the verse, Tyler interprets: "Evil is a victorious *captain*, with Good as a *captive* attending to grace his triumph"; "And herein I am forced, like a good and politic ***captain***"
– Oxford's Prefatory Letter to *Cardanus' Comfort*, 1573

13 TIRED WITH ALL THESE, FROM THESE WOULD I BE GONE,
ALL = Southampton, *One for All, All for One*; **GONE** = dead; "I shall erect you such a monument that, as I say, in your lifetime you shall see how noble a shadow of your virtuous life shall hereafter remain when you are DEAD AND GONE" - Oxford's Prefatory Letter to Cardanus, 1573, emphasis added

14 SAVE THAT TO DIE, I LEAVE MY LOVE ALONE.
SAVE THAT = except that; **MY LOVE** = my royal son; "O know, *sweet love*, I always write of you/ And *you and love* are still my argument" – Sonnet 76, lines 9-10; "Can yet the least of *my true love* control,/ Supposed as forfeit to a confined doom" – Sonnet 107, line 3-4; "If *my dear love* were but the child of state" – Sonnet 124, line 1; **ALONE** = in the Tower; the "all" and "one" Southampton's motto; alone and vulnerable, without Oxford to try to protect him; left alone to die; possibly killed

(This sonnet falls on the fortieth consecutive day since the Rebellion of Februrary 8th. Oxford may have adjusted its position to create this exact correspondence reflecting the forty days and nights spent by Jesus in the wilderness, where he was tempted by the devil: Matthew 4:2. This leads to Sonnet 76 with its use of "every word" and "proceed" reflecting Mathew 4:4: "Man shall not live by bread alone, but by every word that proceedeth out of the mouth of God.")

THE PRISON YEARS

DAY FORTY-ONE IN THE TOWER

Sonnet 67
Why Should He Live?
His Rose is True
20 March 1601

Upon the sparing of his son's life, Oxford's immediate reaction is to wonder why Southampton must continue to live with "infection" or criminals in the Tower. He wonders why Elizabeth should keep her heir in the shadow of disgrace, when his Rose is "true" or legitimate. The Queen is "bankrupt" of any other heirs, yet she "stores" Southampton in the Tower for a term of life. In that case, why should he live? Oxford's sonnets continue day to day, as he refers to "days long since, before these last so bad."

Sonnet 67	Translation
Ah wherefore with infection should he live,	Ah, why should he live with criminals in prison,
And with his presence grace impiety,	And grace such traitors with his kingly presence,
That sin by him advantage should achieve,	Allowing sinners to use him to their advantage,
And lace itself with his society?	And adorn themselves with his company?
Why should false painting imitate his cheek,	Why should his royalty be pictured falsely,
And steal dead seeing of his living hew?	As if it's dead when his royal blood is alive?
Why should poor beauty indirectly seek	Why should the bankrupt Elizabeth seek
Roses of shadow, since his Rose is true?	Disgraced Tudor heirs, since his blood is real?
Why should he live, now nature bankrupt is,	Why should he live in prison, now that Elizabeth
Beggared of blood to blush through lively veins?	Is bankrupt of Tudor blood in any other heirs?
For she hath no exchequer now but his,	For the Queen has no source of heirs but him,
And, proud of many, lives upon his gains.	And perpetuate her proud line only if he succeeds.
O him she stores, to show what wealth she had,	O she keeps him in the Tower, to show the heir
In days long since, before these last so bad.	She once had, before these terrible recent days.

1 AH WHEREFORE WITH INFECTION SHOULD HE LIVE
Immediately following the last line of the previous verse: But why should he be forced to continue living in the Tower with other prisoners who are criminals or traitors, i.e., with others urging him to further rebellion; **LIVE** = "*Thy friends suspect for traitors while thou liv'st*, and take deep traitors for thy dearest friends" – *Richard III*, 1.3.223-224; **WITH INFECTION** = with disgrace; with traitors; with other conspirators of the Rebellion, in the Tower; "in the company of moral corruption" – Duncan-Jones; "among the corrupt, in a corrupt society" - Booth; "moral contamination" – Riverside Shakespeare; later this year, when other conspirators of the Rebellion visit with Southampton in the Tower, Oxford will lecture his royal son to be "unmoved, cold, and to *temptation* slow" in Sonnet 94, line 4 (recalling "For still *temptation* follows where thou art" – Sonnet 41, line 4); and he will continue to counsel: "But if that flower (Southampton) with base *infection* meet,/ The basest weed (again Southampton, a base commoner in the Tower) outbraves his dignity" – Sonnet 94, lines 11-12, i.e., even a base commoner will surpass his own dignity by not allowing himself to be corrupted

Part Two

When Essex was about to be executed, he "spoke with dignity and composure admitting, in the words of one report, 'this my last sin, this great, this bloody, this crying, this *infectious sin,* whereby so many have for love of me been drawn to offend God, to offend their Sovereign, to offend the world.'" – Akrigg, 127

> Darest thou support a publish'd *traitor*? Hence;
> Lest that the *infection* of his fortune take
> Like hold on thee.
> - *King Lear*, 4.6.228-230

> For, sure, my thoughts do hourly prophesy
> Mischance unto my state by Suffolk's means:
> And therefore, by His Majesty I swear,
> Whose far unworthy deputy I am,
> He shall not breathe *infection* in this air
> But three days longer, on the pain of death
> - *2 Henry VI*, 3.2.283-288

> This royal throne of kings...
> This fortress built by Nature for herself
> Against *infection* and the hand of war
> - *Richard II*, 2.1.40, 43-44

> But such is the *infection* of the time
> That, for the health and physic of our right,
> We cannot deal but with the very hand
> Of stern injustice and confused wrong
> - *King John*, 5.2.20-24

2 AND WITH HIS PRESENCE GRACE IMPIETY,
HIS PRESENCE = His Majesty's presence; ("my sovereign's presence" – *2 Henry VI*, 3.2; "The *presence of a king* engenders love amongst his subjects" – *1 Henry VI*, 3.1); **GRACE IMPIETY** = confer his royal grace upon criminals; "Please't your Highness to *grace us with your royal company*?" – *Macbeth*, 3.4.42-43; "Ay, *gracious* sovereign" – *3 Henry VI*, 4.1; "If one so rude and of so mean condition may pass into the presence of a king, lo, I present *your grace* a traitor's head" – *2 Henry VI*, 5.1)

3 THAT SIN BY HIM ADVANTAGE SHOULD ACHIEVE
So that thereby those sinners should gain advantage because of his royal presence among them; **SIN** = recalling Essex's description of his treason, when he was about to executed, as "my last *sin*, this great, this bloody, this crying, this *infectious sin*," noted in line 1 above.

4 AND LACE ITSELF WITH HIS SOCIETY
And be the ones who enjoy his presence or royal company; **LACE** = adorn; literally to adorn with a texture sewed on; fasten with a string through eyelet holes; i.e., the other prisoners in the Tower are the ones who now "lace" themselves with his princely presence; "Here lay Duncan, his silver skin laced with his golden blood" – *Macbeth*, 2.3.109-110

5 WHY SHOULD FALSE PAINTING IMITATE HIS CHEEK
FALSE PAINTING = a false image or imitation of him; reports of him that fail to contain the truth; Elizabeth's own false view (and her false public depiction) of her son, i.e., hiding his identity; CHEEK = anticipating the next verse: "Thus is his cheek the map of days outworn" - Sonnet 68, line 1

6 AND STEAL DEAD SEEING OF HIS LIVING HEW?
DEAD SEEING = now Southampton is seen as a base commoner, at best "Mr. Henry Wriothesley" but legally as "the late earl of Southampton," i.e., dead in the eyes of the law; Booth notes the suggestion in "dead seeing" of "a look at – a sight of – that which is "dead"; **HIS LIVING HEW** = the appearance of his

REFERENCE EDITION

living blood; **HEW** = Henry Wriothesley ("He.W."); "A man in hew all *Hews* in his controlling" – Sonnet 20, line 7

7 WHY SHOULD POOR BEAUTY INDIRECTLY SEEK
POOR BEAUTY = Elizabeth, bankrupt of heirs other than him; "For our losses, his exchequer is too *poor*" – Henry V, 3.6.130

> Hath that **poor monarch** taught thee to insult?
> - 3 Henry VI, 1.4.124

> *Poor queen and son*, your labour is but lost
> - 3 Henry VI, 3.1.32

> While proud ambitious Edward Duke of York
> Usurps the regal title and the seat
> Of England's true-anointed lawful king.
> This is the cause that **I, poor Margaret,**
> **With my son, Prince Edward**, Henry's heir,
> *Am come to crave thy just and lawful aid*
> - 3 Henry VI, 3.3.27-33

> And, interchanging blows, I quickly shed
> Some of *his bastard blood, and in disgrace*
> Bespoke him thus: 'Contaminated, base
> And misbegotten blood I spill of thine,
> *Mean and right poor*, for that pure blood of mine
> Which thou didst force from Talbot, my grave boy'
> - 1 Henry VI, 4.6.19-24

> *Poor painted Queen*...
> - Richard III, 1.3.241

INDIRECTLY SEEK: The word "indirectly" suggests this reading of lines 7-8: Why should Elizabeth (and, by extension, Cecil), who has no heirs but Henry Wriothesley, be *indirectly* looking for successors of *shadow*? That is, why are they looking for someone like James – who's not in the *direct line* of succession, and is thus a *shadow* – when there exists someone – Henry Wriothesley – with a *true* claim? (Alex McNeil); "And when you find him evenly derived from his most famed of famous ancestors, Edward the Third, he bids you then resign your crown and kingdom, INDIRECTLY held" - Henry V, 2.4.91-95; And withal to pry into his title, the which we find too INDIRECT for continuance" - 1 Henry IV, 4.3.103-105; "God knows, my son, by what by-paths and INDIRECT crook'd ways I met this crown" - 2 Henry IV, 4.5.183

8 ROSES OF SHADOW, SINCE HIS ROSE IS TRUE?
ROSES OF SHADOW = Tudor Rose heirs (Southampton) covered by shadows of disgrace, their identities hidden; "The ghosts of dead roses" – Booth; "Presents *thy shadow* to my sightless view" - Sonnet 27, line 10; "The *region cloud* hath *masked him* from me now" - Sonnet 33, line 12; **HIS ROSE IS TRUE** = his Tudor Rose blood is genuine; "We will unite the white rose and the red" – Richard III, 5.5.19; **TRUE** = related to Oxford, *Nothing Truer than Truth*; "And your *true* rights be termed a Poet's rage" – Sonnet 17, line 11; "For he that steeps his safety in *true* blood" – King John, 3.3.147;

9 WHY SHOULD HE LIVE? NOW NATURE BANKRUPT IS,
NATURE = Elizabeth; **NOW NATURE BANKRUPT IS** = Now Elizabeth is bankrupt, i.e., of any other heirs to her Tudor Rose lineage; "Since it is ***bankrupt of his majesty***" – Richard II, 4.1.267; the imagery of her "beauty" or royal blood as "treasure" is carried forward here with the Queen as Nature, as in "*Nature's bequest* gives nothing but doth *lend*" – Sonnet 4, line 3; and "blood" in the following line serves to secure this meaning

10 **BEGGARED OF BLOOD TO BLUSH THROUGH LIVELY VEINS,**
BEGGARED OF BLOOD = without royal blood; "As to behold desert a *beggar* born" – Sonnet 66, line 2;
BLUSH THROUGH LIVELY VEINS = flow through veins of any living heirs

11 **FOR SHE HATH NO EXCHEQUER NOW BUT HIS,**
Continuing the treasury-royal blood metaphor; because Elizabeth has no other source of royal-blood-revenue now but her son's possession of that blood and his ability to gain the throne; glancing also at Oxford's annual grant of 1,000 pounds from the Queen's Exchequer; **EXCHEQUER** = "Source of revenue, like the 'King's exchequer' or treasury" – Duncan-Jones; the source of "beauty's *treasure*" in Sonnet 6, line 4., i.e., Elizabeth's treasure of royal blood within her son; "For our losses, his *exchequer* is too *poor*; for *th'effusion of our blood*, the muster of his kingdom too faint a number" – Henry V, 3.6.130-132; ("that if I would make him my receiver of the annuity in the *Exchequer*" – Oxford to Robert Cecil, Jan. 11, 1597; "sith Her Majesty might have had with less trouble a more perfect intelligence, and with less charge here at home, by perusing the books of the *Exchequer*" – Oxford to Burghley, June 15, 1595

"Elizabeth, etc., to the Treasurer and Chamberlains of Our ***Exchequer***, Greeting. We will and command you of Our treasure being and remaining from time to time within the receipt of Our ***Exchequer***, to deliver and pay, or cause to be delivered and paid, unto Our right trusty and well beloved Cousin the Earl of Oxford, or to his assigns sufficiently authorized by him, the sum of One Thousand Pounds good and lawful money of England. The same to be yearly delivered and paid..." - Pivy Seal Warrant, signed by Queen Elizabeth, June 26, 1586

12 **AND PROUD OF MANY, LIVES UPON HIS GAINS.**
PROUD OF MANY = rich with many of her son's royal qualities; "the sense may be 'proud (mother) of many offspring'" – Duncan-Jones; also, Elizabeth is proud of previous Tudor monarchs (Proud = "swollen with many offspring" – Booth; "proud of this pride" - Sonnet 151, line 10)

> And Bolingbroke
> Hath seized the wasteful king. O, what pity is it
> That he had not so trimm'd and dress'd his land
> As we this garden! We at time of year
> Do wound the bark, the skin of our fruit-trees,
> Lest, *being over-**proud*** [swollen] *in sap and blood,*
> With too much riches it confound itself. - *Richard II*, 3.4.54-59

> But rising at thy name doth point out thee
> As his triumphant prize – ***proud of this pride***,
> He is contented thy poor drudge to be. - Sonnet 151, lines 9-11
> To Elizabeth; re: Southampton

LIVES UPON HIS GAINS = Elizabeth's own blood will live only if her son gains the throne and, thereby perpetuates her Tudor lineage; if not her blood and lineage or dynasty will die

13 **O HIM SHE STORES, TO SHOW WHAT WEALTH SHE HAD**
O = Oxford; **O HIM** = Oxford and his royal son, as one; **HIM SHE STORES** = Elizabeth keeps Southampton (and his blood, which is hers) in storage, i.e., in the prison, failing to acknowledge him; the Tower of London had literally become "a major center of the power and wealth of English monarchs," writes Peter Hammond in *Her Majesty's Royal Palace and Fortress of the Tower of London* (1987), adding, "Following Edward I's expansion of the Tower, it soon came to contain one of the main royal treasuries, a *storehouse* for official documents, the largest of the royal mints and the only one coining in gold as well as silver" – so Oxford is using the specific reality for this image of storing Southampton and his royal blood; "And him as for a map doth Nature store" – Sonnet 68, line 13, i.e., Nature = Elizabeth stores her son as a map to show her what she once had; **STORES** = keeps, preserves; (Booth notes overtones of "store" as an agricultural term meaning "breed livestock" or "continue or improve the breed"); also to populate, as in: "To

new-*store* France with bastard warriors" – *Henry V*, 3.5.31; "The sacred *storehouse* of his predecessors" – *Macbeth*, 2.4.33; "How many sons has thou of mine in *store*" – *Titus Andronicus*, 1.1.97; **TO SHOW WHAT WEALTH SHE HAD** = Elizabeth keeps Southampton in prison to "show" herself the royal successor she once had; but, of course, she is not showing that to the world; **WEALTH** = royal blood in her son; "For in monarchy, the *wealth* of the prince is the riches of the commonwealth" – Oxford, March 1595, unaddressed; Cecil Papers 25.76 (Chiljan, 86); same as "treasure" in the Sonnets

14 IN DAYS LONG SINCE, BEFORE THESE LAST SO BAD.
IN DAYS LONG SINCE = prior to the Rebellion; the past golden days, when Southampton was "fair" or royal before he became "black" or disgraced; "In the *old age* black was not counted fair,/ Or if it were it bore not beauty's name,/ But now is black beauty's successive heir,/ And Beauty slandered by a bastard shame" - Sonnet 127, lines 1-4; **THESE LAST SO BAD** = these last agonizing days leading up to the sparing of Southampton's life, which occurred on the previous day; also Oxford is letting us know that he is still writing these verses day-by-day; as he does on other occasions, such as: "If my slight Muse do please *these curious days*" – Sonnet 38, line 13; "For we which now behold *these present days*" – Sonnet 106, line 13; "Unless this general evil they maintain:/ All men are *bad* and *in their badness reign*" – Sonnet 121, lines 13-14; *bad* also suggesting criminal, related to treason

Part Two

THE PRISON YEARS

DAY FORTY-TWO IN THE TOWER

Sonnet 68
These Bastard Signs of Fair
21 March 1601

Although Southampton's life has been spared, Oxford mourns the death of his claim to the throne. And again he laments the fact that Nature (Elizabeth) continues to "store" or preserve him in disgrace in the Tower – as if Southampton were now a relic on display in a museum.

Sonnet 68	Translation
Thus is his cheek the map of days outworn,	So my son still reflects the former worn-out days,
When beauty lived and died as flowers do now,	When his royalty lived and died as his Rose now,
Before these bastard signs of fair were borne,	Before his royal bastardy was born and carried,
Or durst inhabit on a living brow:	Or before he had to live with this public disgrace:
Before the golden tresses of the dead,	Before the golden tresses of the dead,
The right of sepulchers, were shorn away,	Belonging to the deceased, were removed
To live a second life on second head,	To crown him a second time,
Ere beauty's dead fleece made another gay.	Before Elizabeth's dead heir gave way to another.
In him those holy antique hours are seen,	In my son the glory of past kings is still seen,
Without all ornament, itself and true,	Without any outward show, but his true rights,
Making no summer of another's green,	Making no new opportunity for his claim,
Robbing no old to dress his beauty new.	Robbing no one to crown his royal blood again.
And him as for a map doth nature store,	And Elizabeth stores my son's blood in prison,
To show false art what beauty was of yore.	To show these false times what his royalty was.

1 THUS IS HIS CHEEK THE MAP OF DAYS OUTWORN,
THUS IS HIS CHEEK THE MAP = so our son's face is the map of the past; "The purple pride/ Which on thy soft *cheek* for complexion dwells" – Sonnet 99, lines 3-4, referring to the royalty reflected by his face = "Ah, Uncle Humprhey, *in thy face I see* **the map** of Honour, Truth, and Loyalty" – *2 Henry VI*, 3.1.202-203

> The *red rose and the white are* **on his face**,
> The fatal colours of our striving houses:
> The one his purple blood right well resembles,
> The other his pale **cheeks**, methinks, presenteth.
> - *3 Henry VI*, 2.5.97-100

> The princely blood flows in his cheeks
> - *Cymbeline*, 3.3.93

DAYS OUTWORN = the golden days of his royalty, his Summer's day, now gone; "Was this the face that like the sun did make beholders wink?" – *Richard II*, 4.1.283-284, the king speaking of his own face as the map of the past; "Why didst thou promise such *a beauteous day*?" – Sonnet 34, line 1, Oxford's plaintive cry

REFERENCE EDITION

to his son, soon after his imprisonment for the Rebellion, asking why his birth to "beauty" or Elizabeth had seemed at one time to hold such royal future.

2 WHEN BEAUTY LIVED AND DIED AS FLOWERS DO NOW,
WHEN BEAUTY LIVED AND DIED = when his blood from Elizabeth lived with hope and then died because of the Rebellion; **FLOWERS** = Southampton, the "little western flower" of *Midsummer Night's Dream* and the new Tudor Rose; **AS FLOWERS DO NOW** = as he has been left to die in prison; as his royal claim is extinguished now

3 BEFORE THESE BASTARD SIGNS OF FAIR WERE BORNE,
THESE BASTARD SIGNS OF FAIR = Southampton, a royal bastard; this status of a bastard that was imposed on his royalty; counterfeit images, covering his "fair" or royal stature; also perhaps "this bastard son (sign) of Vere (fair)."

> In the old age black was not counted *fair*,
> Or if it were it bore not beauty's name,
> But now is black beauty's successive heir,
> And Beauty slandered with a *bastard* shame
> - Sonnet 127, lines 1-4
>
> If my dear love were but the child of state,
> It might for fortune's *bastard* be unfathered
> - Sonnet 124, lines 1-2
>
> I am a bastard, too: I love *bastards*
> - *Troilus & Cressida*, 5.7.18

WERE BORNE = recalling his birth, but referring to the time when his bastardy was born or "brought into existence" by Elizabeth's negative view of her son; **BORNE** = carried or worn ("with heraldic overtones" – Booth, who notes: "Renaissance writers and printers made no regular distinction in spelling between 'borne' and 'born'")

4 OR DURST INHABIT ON A LIVING BROW,
OR DURST INHABIT = or lived upon his brow; or covered his true identity

5 BEFORE THE GOLDEN TRESSES OF THE DEAD,
GOLDEN = royal; **TRESSES OF THE DEAD** = hair (heir) of the dead; i.e., royal heir entombed; and in a secondary sense, lines 5-8 are perhaps also a reference to Elizabeth's penchant for wearing human-hair wigs.

6 THE RIGHT OF SEPULCHERS, WERE SHORN AWAY,
RIGHT = blood right to the throne; "his purple blood right" – *3 Henry VI*, 2.5.99; "In the *right* of your great predecessor, King Edward the Third" – *Henry V*, 1.2.248; "And *your true rights* be termed a Poet's rage" – Sonnet 17, line 11; **SEPULCHERS** = graves, tombs; related to the "tomb" (Sonnets 17 and 86) of this "monument" (Sonnets 55, 81, 107), intended to preserve Henry Wriothesley as Prince Henry for resurrection in posterity; "*My heart, sweet boy,* shall be thy *sepulchre,* for from my heart thine image ne'er shall go; my sighing breast shall be thy funeral bell, and *so obsequious will thy father be, even for the loss of thee*" – *3 Henry VI*, 2.5.115-119

> And laid it in his own new tomb, which he had hewn out in the rock; and he rolled a great stone to the door of the *sepulcher,* and departed – Gospel of Mathew, 27.60
>
> These eyes, that are now dimmed with death's black veil,
> Have been as piercing as the mid-day sun
> To search the secret treasons of the world;

The wrinkles in my brows, now filled with blood,
Were likened oft to *kingly sepulchers*;
For who lived King but I could dig their grave?
- *3 Henry VI*, 5.2.16-21

Alack, alack, what blood is this which stains
The stony entrance of this *sepulcher*?
- *Romeo and Juliet*, 5.3.140-141

7 TO LIVE A SECOND LIFE ON SECOND HEAD,
SECOND LIFE = the second life being created for him in the Sonnets; as opposed to the "second head" within his tomb; his life having been spared, Southampton has been granted a second life; "The second burthen of a former child" – Sonnet 59, line 4; the life of Oxford's royal son has been spared, so he now begins his "second life"; **SECOND HEAD** = "To be the dowry of a *second head*, the skull that bred them in the *sepulchre*" – *Merchant of Venice*, 3.2.95-96; until a few days ago, Southampton had been scheduled to lose his life along with his head; therefore, he now has a second life on a second head.

8 ERE BEAUTY'S DEAD FLEECE MADE ANOTHER GAY.
FLEECE = hair, i.e., heir; **BEAUTY'S DEAD FLEECE** = Elizabeth's dead heir; **MADE ANOTHER GAY** = made room for another heir to the throne, i.e., the bargain made to save the life of Southampton has paved the way for the accession of King James

9 IN HIM THOSE HOLY ANTIQUE HOURS ARE SEEN
IN HIM = in the royal person of Southampton; **HOLY ANTIQUE HOURS** = that earlier, sacred time when he had a royal claim; ("connected by rhyme to the authentic *flowers*" of line 2 – Duncan-Jones); adding to the religious or spiritual context of the Sonnets as a monument to a "god" on earth; past history of divine monarchs; **HOLY** = "Poor cold-key Figure of *a holy king*" – *Richard III*, 1.2.5; referring to the divine nature of the Sonnets as a sacred book dedicated to a god on earth or king

10 WITHOUT ALL ORNAMENT, ITSELF AND TRUE,
ALL = Southampton, *One for All, All for One*; **WITHOUT ALL ORNAMENT** = i.e., no longer is he "the world's fresh ornament" of Sonnet 1, line 9; without the need of outward show or pomp; echoing "without all bail" – Sonnet 74, line 2; **ITSELF** = his kingly right, by itself, without exterior show; "self" echoing "self-substantial fuel" of Sonnet 1, line 6; **TRUE** = rightful; related to Oxford, *Nothing Truer than Truth*; ("And your *true* rights be termed a Poet's rage" – Sonnet 17, line 11); simply true, as in "simple truth" of Sonnet 66, line 11

11 MAKING NO SUMMER OF ANOTHER'S GREEN,
Creating no golden time of royalty for any other heir; ("not using someone else's beauty to eke out its own; not making someone else's summer green" – Booth); i.e., his royal blood is not used for any other prince or king; he is the only Tudor heir; "I cannot but find a great grief in myself to remember the Mistress which we have lost, under whom both you and myself from our *greenest* years have been in a manner brought up" – Oxford to Robert Cecil, April 25/27, 1603, writing of Elizabeth on the eve of her funeral; green, of the Tudor livery

12 ROBBING NO OLD TO DRESS HIS BEAUTY NEW.
Not taking from any other ancient source to give himself Elizabeth's royal blood; i.e., he is genuine, not counterfeit, and derived from a long line of Tudor princes; "So all my best is *dressing old words new*,/ Spending again what is already spent:/ For as *the Sun is daily new and old*,/ So is my love still telling what is told" – Sonnet 76, lines 11-14

13 AND HIM AS FOR A MAP DOTH NATURE STORE,
HIM AS FOR A MAP = Southampton, used as a map or guide, as in line 1 above; **DOTH NATURE STORE** = Elizabeth stores him and his blood inherited from her, in the Tower, as well as in oblivion; "O *him*

she stores, to show what wealth she had/ In days long since, before these last so bad" – Sonnet 67, lines 13-14, the previous verse, leading directly to this one; "And because next to the sacred letters of divinity nothing doth persuade the same more than philosophy (of which your book is *plentifully stored*), I thought myself to commit an unpardonable error to have murdered the same in the waste-bottoms of my chests" – Oxford's Prefatory Letter to *Cardanus' Comfort*, 1573; "The sacred *storehouse* of his predecessors" – *Macbeth*, 2.4.33; "How many sons hast thou of mine *in store*" – *Titus Andronicus*, 1.1.97; "Let those whom nature hath not made for *store*" – Sonnet 11, line 9

14 TO SHOW FALSE ART WHAT BEAUTY WAS OF YORE.
To give the lie to the false images of him, showing what genuine "beauty" or Tudor blood once was; i.e., Southampton is living testimony of Elizabeth's blood; "O never say that I was *false* of heart" – Sonnet 109, line 1; "To swear against the truth so foul a lie" – Sonnet 152, line 14; also, "false" echoing the phrase "false-traitor"

Part Two

THE PRISON YEARS

SOUTHAMPTON REDUCED TO COMMONER
DAY FORTY-THREE IN THE TOWER

Sonnet 69
Thou Dost Common Grow
22 March 1601

Southampton is being stripped of his earldom, divested of all his lands and titles, and reduced to the status of a commoner. He will be known at best as "Mr. Henry Wriothesley" and legally as "the late earl." As Oxford writes, "Thou dost common grow" – grows in his second life, grows in the womb of these sonnets that contain "the living record" of his memory.

Sonnet 69	Translation
Those parts of thee that the world's eye doth view	Those qualities of you that England now sees
Want nothing that the thought of hearts can mend.	Lack nothing my heart's thoughts can improve!
All tongues (the voice of souls) give thee that end,	All my words in these Sonnets say you're royal,
Utt'ring bare truth, even so as foes Commend.	Uttering truth, so even enemies commend you.
Their outward thus with outward praise is crowned,	So Robert Cecil's praise of you is a coronation,
But those same tongues that give thee so thine own,	But even while he acknowledges your right,
In other accents do this praise confound	He also speaks otherwise to destroy you,
By seeing farther than the eye hath shown.	By looking farther ahead, beyond the truth.
They look into the beauty of thy mind,	These enemies look into the royalty of your mind,
And in that guess they measure by thy deeds;	And at the same time calculate your crime,
Then, churls, their thoughts (although their eyes were kind)	And then their miserly thoughts (even with Cecil being kindred)
To thy fair flower add the rank smell of weeds;	Add disgrace to your royal Tudor Rose blood.
But why thy odour matcheth not thy show,	But the reason for such hypocrisy
The soil is this, that thou dost common grow.	Is that you will now grow as a base commoner.

The Council to Sir John Peyton, Lieutenant of the Tower, March 22, 1601: *"Whereas we do understand that the Earl of Southampton, by reason of the continuance of his quartern ague, hath a swelling in his legs and other parts, you may admit Doctor Paddy, who is acquainted with the state of his body, in your presence to have access unto him, and to confer with him for those things that shall be fit for his health."* – Stopes, 224; Reg. Privy Council); the Council's reference to the "continuance" of his ague indicates he has been ill from the beginning of his imprisonment.

1 THOSE PARTS OF THEE THAT THE WORLD'S EYE DOTH VIEW
PARTS = royal aspects; "Though yet heaven knows it (my verse) is but as a tomb/ Which hides your life, and shows not half your parts" – Sonnet 17, lines 3-4; "all his *gracious parts*" – of the Prince, in *King John*, 3.3.96; "Caesar's better *parts* shall be *crowned* in Brutus" – *Julius Caesar*, 3.2.56; **THE WORLD'S EYE** = what the citizens of England see, on the surface; "Had I so lavish of my presence been, so common-hackneyed in *the eyes of men*" – the king to his son, Prince Hal, in *1 Henry IV*, 3.2.39-40

REFERENCE EDITION 395

2 WANT NOTHING THAT THE THOUGHT OF HEARTS CAN MEND:
WANT = lack; **NOTHING** = Southampton, a nobody; **THE THOUGHT OF HEARTS** = Oxford's own thoughts, recorded in this diary; i.e., Oxford cannot "mend" or repair or alter the world's view of his son, but, in fact, Henry Wriothesley lacks no royal aspect that Oxford's heart can imagine as an improvement.

3 ALL TONGUES (THE VOICE OF SOULS) GIVE THEE THAT END,
ALL = Southampton, *One for All, All for One*; **ALL TONGUES** = all men's thoughts and speeches; **THE VOICE OF SOULS** = echoing "all souls"; speaking with complete candor – Brooke; ("But though our outward man perish, yet the inward man is renewed day by day … While we look not at the things which are seen, but at the things which are not seen: for the things which are seen are temporal: but the things which are not seen are eternal" – 2 Corinthians, 16, 18, referring to line 8 as well, "seeing farther than the eye has shown," and line 9, "look into the beauty of thy mind"; **GIVE THEE THAT END** = give you that final end, i.e., crown you as king; (usually emended to "give thee that due"; i.e., "the world's due" of Sonnet 1, line 14)

4 UTT'RING BARE TRUTH, EVEN SO AS FOES COMMEND.
UTT'RING BARE TRUTH = speaking the simple truth about you; **TRUTH** = related to Oxford, *Nothing Truer Than Truth*; **EVEN SO** = in this way; "Even so my Sunne one early morn did shine" – Sonnet 33, line 9; **AS FOES COMMEND** = in the same way your enemies know the truth of you; i.e., even the Queen and Robert Cecil commend you as royal

5 THEIR OUTWARD THUS WITH OUTWARD PRAISE IS CROWNED,
CROWNED = made king; "Caesar's better *parts* shall be *crowned* in Brutus" – *Julius Caesar*, 3.2.56; "I have no doubt she is *crowned* with glory" – Oxford to Robert Cecil, April 25/27, 1603, speaking of the late Queen Elizabeth

6 BUT THOSE SAME TONGUES THAT GIVE THEE SO THINE OWN,
But these same persons who know that you are the rightful prince; who give you your due as a royal prince,

7 IN OTHER ACCENTS DO THIS PRAISE CONFOUND
In other words and speeches undermine and destroy this same praise or regard of you; i.e., they are hypocrites (or worse, they are malicious, e.g., Robert Cecil, who knows the truth but also knows he will stay in power only if Southampton's claim is destroyed and only if James of Scotland ascends to the throne); **OTHER ACCENTS** = modifications of what they have said otherwise; words or expressions other than what they have said or thought

8 BY SEEING FARTHER THAN THE EYE HATH SHOWN.
THE EYE = your royal eye, which casts its beams; **SHOWN** = echoing "shone"; "I hope Her Majesty, after so many gracious words … will not now draw in **the beams** of her princely grace to my discouragement and her own detriment" – Oxford to Robert Cecil, January 1602)

9 THEY LOOK INTO THE BEAUTY OF THY MIND,
THE BEAUTY OF THY MIND = your royal blood from Elizabeth that flows (unseen) within your mind or thoughts or soul; they see your Tudor identity

10 AND THAT IN GUESS THEY MEASURE BY THY DEEDS;
AND IN THAT GUESS = and in that estimation of your royalty; **THEY MEASURE BY THY DEEDS** = they act instead according to your deeds, i.e., according to your crime, by punishing you; **THY DEEDS** = "Ah, but those tears are pearl which thy love sheeds,/ And they are rich, and *ransom all ill deeds*" – Sonnet 34, lines 13-14, referring to Southampton's crime for which Oxford is agreeing to pay "ransom" in order to secure his liberation; but they also measure Southampton by his good deeds or actions, particularly as a soldier; "For sweetest things (Southampton) turn sourest *by their deeds*" – Sonnet 94, line 13

11 **THEN, CHURLS, THEIR THOUGHTS (ALTHOUGH THEIR EYES WERE KIND)**
CHURLS = these misers; **THEIR THOUGHTS (ALTHOUGH THEIR EYES WERE KIND)** = their thoughts, even though they see that you are "kind," or related to the Queen; "A little more than *kin*, and less than *kind*" – *Hamlet*, 1.2.65; Robert Cecil is also "kind," or related to Oxford as brother-in-law

12 **TO THY FAIR FLOWER ADD THE RANK SMELL OF WEEDS.**
TO THY FAIR FLOWER = to you, royal flower of the Tudor Rose; to your royal claim as heir of the Tudor Rose blood; **ADD THE RANK SMELL OF WEEDS** = add disgrace and dishonor; keep you in prison as a traitor; block your path to the throne; all of which leads to the following final couplet, in which Oxford serves up his explanation.

13 **BUT WHY THY ODOUR MATCHETH NOT THY SHOW,**
But as to why your inner reality does not match your outward appearance; **ODOUR** = sweet scent, i.e., royal essence

14 **THE SOIL IS THIS: THAT THOU DOST COMMON GROW.**
THE SOIL IS THIS = the root of the problem is this; **THE SOIL** = the royal ground of England that you represent as a king; "England's ground, farewell; *sweet soil*, adieu" – *Richard II*, 1.3.306; the tarnish or blemish that you carry; "Most subject is the fattest *soil* to *weeds*, and he, the noble image of my youth, is overspread with them" – *2 Henry IV*, 4.4.54-56, the King speaking of his son, Prince Hal; "For *sweetest things turn sourest* by their *deeds*;/ Lilies that fester *smell far worse* than *weeds*" – Sonnet 94, lines 13-14; **THOU DOST COMMON GROW** = You are now a base commoner in the Tower, growing more common (growing like a weed) with each day; thrust into the company of other base and vulgar commoners, who may urge you to further rebellion; "Had I so lavish of my presence been, so *common*-hackneyed in the eyes of men, so stale and cheap to *vulgar company*" – the king to his son, Prince Hal, in *1 Henry IV*, 3.2.39-41

THE MONUMENT

THE PRISON YEARS

DAY FORTY-FOUR IN THE TOWER

Sonnet 70
Slander's Mark
Thou Hast Passed by the Ambush
Suspect of Ill
23 March 1601

Although Southampton is imprisoned in disgrace, his royal blood remains with him as he languishes in the Tower. Oxford refers to the public characterization of Henry Wriothesley as a "suspect-traitor" -- twice using the common legal term "suspect." Southampton is viewed by others as a "crow" (black with disgrace) and yet he himself is "heaven's sweetest air" or Elizabeth's most royal heir to the throne. In the final line, Oxford refers candidly to Southampton's rightful destiny, which has been to rule "kingdoms of hearts" (England and its loyal subjects).

Sonnet 70	Translation
That thou art blamed shall not be thy defect,	Your blame for the Rebellion is not your royal loss,
For slander's mark was ever yet the fair,	For Elizabeth's disgraced son is still her heir!
The ornament of beauty is suspect,	The prince of Elizabeth's blood is seen as traitor
A Crow that flies in heaven's sweetest air.	A black stain upon the Queen's most royal heir!
So thou be good, slander doth but approve	So you being royal, your disgrace only makes
Thy worth the greater, being wooed of time,	Your royalty greater as succession draws near,
For canker vice the sweetest buds doth love,	For disgrace lives in the most royal Tudor Rose heir
And thou present'st a pure unstained prime.	And you still contain pure royal fresh blood!
Thou hast passed by the ambush of young days,	You've been spared execution for your rash crime,
Either not assailed, or victor being charged,	Neither destroyed nor named as the next king,
Yet this thy praise cannot be so thy praise,	Yet these sonnets praising you cannot be seen,
To tie up envy evermore enlarged.	And as they grow, tied up, they can't set you free.
If some suspect of ill masked not thy show,	If your crime did not hide your true appearance,
Then thou alone kingdoms of hearts shouldst owe.	Then you alone would rule a kingdom of subjects.

1 THAT THOU ART BLAMED SHALL NOT BE THY DEFECT,
BLAMED = accused and convicted of treason; blamed, with Essex, for the Rebellion; ("Or will you *blame and lay the fault* on me?" – *1 Henry VI*, 2.1); **DEFECT** = crime, fault

2 FOR SLANDER'S MARK WAS EVER YET THE FAIR;
SLANDER'S MARK = Southampton, the object of this slander against him; "Thy son is banished upon good advice, whereto thy tongue a *party-verdict* gave: why at our justice seem'st thou then to lour ... Things sweet to taste prove in digestion sour. You urged me as a judge, but I had rather you would have bid me argue like a father. O, had it been a stranger, not my child, to smooth his fault I should have been more mild: a partial ***slander*** sought I to avoid, and in the sentence my own life destroyed" – *Richard II*, 1.3.233-242, a passage that mirrors Oxford's own situation at the trial, when he was forced to give a "party-verdict" against his own son and thrust "slander" upon him; "With the *attainder* of his *slanderous* lips" – *Richard II*, 4.1.24; "Thou *slander* of thy heavy mother's womb" – *Richard III*, 1.3.231; "And Beauty *slandered* with a bastard

shame" – Sonnet 127, line 4; **MARK** = a target; person observed; "I stood like a man at a *mark*, with a whole army shooting at me" – *Much Ado About Nothing*, 2.1.231; "Your high self, the gracious *mark* o'th'land" – *The Winter's Tale*, 4.4.7-8; "The scornful *mark* of every open eye" – *Lucrece*, stanza 75; **EVER** = E. Ver, Edward de Vere; "Why write I still all one, *ever* the same" – Sonnet 76, line 5, with the Queen's motto "Semper Eadem" or *Ever the Same*; **EVER YET THE FAIR** = always the royal prince, son of E.Ver or Edward de Vere; "From *fairest* creatures we desire increase" – Sonnet 1, line 1; "Who heaven itself for *ornament* doth use,/ And *every fair* with his *fair* doth rehearse" – Sonnet 21, lines 3-4

3 THE ORNAMENT OF BEAUTY IS SUSPECT,

ORNAMENT OF BEAUTY = royal son of Elizabeth; ("the *world's fresh ornament*" of Sonnet 1, line 9; "Who *heaven* itself for *ornament* doth use" – Sonnet 21, line 3; **SUSPECT** = (see line 13); Accused, convicted, of treason; "Thy friends **suspect for traitors** while thou liv'st, and take deep traitors for thy dearest friends" – *Richard III*, 1.3.223-224; "He lived from all *attainder of suspects* … Well, well, he was the covert'st sheltered *traitor*" – *Richard III*, 3.5.32-33; "My Lord of Gloucester, 'tis my special hope that you will clear yourself from all *suspect*; my conscience tells me you are innocent" – *2 Henry VI*, 3.1.139-141; "The King should keep his word in loving us; he will *suspect* us still, and find a time to punish this *offence* in other *faults* … for *treason* is but trusted like the fox" – *1 Henry IV*, 5.2.5-9; "The choice of examiners depended largely on the degree of importance of the treason, the rank of the *suspect*, and where he was being held" – Bellamy, *The Tudor Law of Treason*, 105; "From about 1590 a new form of torture was used with increasing frequency against **suspect traitors**" – Bellamy, 113; while Southampton was already convicted of treason, Oxford, working behind the scenes to get his son's offence reduced to "misprision" of treason, regards him in his own mind as merely a suspect, i.e., suspected by Elizabeth

"Which shall take away all ambiguity which may grow through **suspect** of partial and unjust dealing, hoping that Her Majesty will have an equal regard" - Oxford to Burghley, June 7, 1595

4 A CROW THAT FLIES IN HEAVEN'S SWEETEST AIR.

CROW = the darkness covering Southampton, turning him black; darkened by shadows of disgrace

> And thou treble-dated *crow*
> That thy sable gender mak'st
> With the breath thou giv'st and tak'st,
> 'Mongst our mourners shalt thou go
> - *The Phoenix and Turtle*, 1601

Oxford is now also writing *The Phoenix and the Turtle*, to be published this year as by "William Shake-speare" (hyphenated), which records the extinction of all hope for Southampton's succession and the perpetuation of the Tudor Rose dynasty. The poem correlates with Sonnet 73, which is a funeral dirge like that of the poem. The "crow" is "treble-dated" because of the three-in-one theme of Oxford, Elizabeth and Southampton, all three heading toward the inevitable "date" with succession to the throne. The crow is the blackness of Southampton's disgrace and the end of his claim to the throne, as the poem continues: "Here the anthem doth commence:/ Love and Constancy is dead,/ Phoenix and the Turtle fled/ In a mutual flame from hence" – the Phoenix = Elizabeth and the Turtle-dove = Oxford.

Also in the first excerpt from *The Phoenix and the Turtle* quoted above, the "sable gender" is Henry Wriothesley as "black offspring" – related to "black" of Sonnet 127, line 3

HEAVEN = Elizabeth; "And although it hath pleased God after an earthly kingdom to take her up into a more permanent and **heavenly** state" – Oxford to Robert Cecil, April 25/27, 1603, speaking of the late Queen; "Who *heaven* itself for *ornament* doth use" – Sonnet 21, line 3; **HEAVEN'S SWEETEST AIR** = Elizabeth's most royal heir to her throne; i.e., the image of him as blackening himself; "Good night, sweet prince" – *Hamlet*, 5.2.366; "So your sweet Majesty" – *Richard II*, 2.1.20

Sonnet 127, opening the Dark Lady series to Elizabeth, uses the same imagery:

In the old days *black* was not counted fair,
Or it if were it bore not beauty's name,
But now is black *beauty's successive heir*,
And beauty slandered with a bastard shame
- Sonnet 127, lines 1-4

Black = Crow, i.e., blackness
Beauty's Successive Heir = Heaven's Sweetest Air
Slandered = Slander's Mark

5 SO THOU BE GOOD, SLANDER DOTH BUT APPROVE
SO THOU BE GOOD = So you, being blameless (and royal); therefore, since you are good, i.e., royal; this slander only approves; **GOOD** = royal; not evil; not a traitor; virtuous; "*Good your graces* let me have time and counsel for my cause" – *Henry VIII*, 3.1.76-77; "*Good queen*, my lord, *good queen*: I say *good queen*, and would by combat make her *good*" – *The Winter's Tale*, 2.3.59-60; **SLANDER** = defamation; calumny; reproach; disgrace; ill report; black mark against your reputation; the public appraisal of you as a traitor in disgrace; your conviction of guilt at the trial; people know about your crime and the verdict of guilt for high treason, but they will not be told of its reduction to "misprision" of treason; "For every word you speak in his behalf is **slander to your royal dignity**" – *2 Henry VI*, 3.2.207-208; "And for more *slander* to thy dismal seat, we give to thee our guilty blood to drink" – *Richard III*, 3.3.13-14, **APPROVE** = sanctions; commends; justifies; affirms; "That he may *approve* our eyes" – *Hamlet*, 1.1.29, i.e., that he may affirm what we have seen; "it would not much *approve* me" – *Hamlet*, 5.2.132

6 THY WORTH THE GREATER, BEING WOOED OF TIME:
THY WORTH THE GREATER = your royalty all the more; **BEING WOOED** = tempted or encouraged to claim the throne; "And when a woman (Elizabeth) *woos*, what woman's son (Southampton)/ Will sourly leave her till he have prevailed?" – Sonnet 41, lines 7-8; **OF TIME** = according to temporal time, which now has run out; the time of Elizabeth's life, according to which your royal claim has lived and died; **WOOED OF TIME** = tempted or encouraged by Elizabeth to claim the throne during her lifetime; "Thus hath the course of justice whirled about, and left thee but *a very prey to time*" – *Richard III*, 4.4.105-106

7 FOR CANKER VICE THE SWEETEST BUDS DOTH LOVE,
Because, even with their shames and disgraces, most royal Tudor Rose "buds" or heirs retain their "love" or royal blood; **CANKER VICE** = disgrace living in the Tudor Rose; "to put down Richard, that *sweet lovely Rose*, and plant **this thorn, this canker**, Bolingbroke" – *1 Henry IV*, 1.3.173-174; "Hath not **thy rose a canker**, Somerset?" – *1 Henry VI*, 2.4.68; **SWEETEST BUDS** = Most royal princes of the Tudor Rose, i.e., Southampton as Elizabeth's heir; "**Out of these Roses sprang two noble buds**, Prince Arthur and Henry, the eldest dying without issue, the other of most famous memory" – John Lyly, *Euphues and his England*, 1580, dedicated to Oxford, his patron; referring, here, to the Tudor sons of Henry VII, the second son "of most famous memory" being Henry VIII, father of Elizabeth; "Rough winds do shake the darling *buds* of May" – Sonnet 18, line 3, referring to Southampton as a royal bud of the Tudor Rose, born to Queen Elizabeth in late May or (early June) 1574; "*The Rose* looks fair, but fairer we it deem/ For that *sweet odor* which doth in it live:/ The *canker* blooms have full as deep a dye,/ As the perfumed tincture of *the Roses*,/ Hang on such *thorns*, and play as wantonly/ When summer's breath their *masked buds* discloses" – Sonnet 54, lines 3-8

8 AND THOU PRESENT'ST A PURE UNSTAINED PRIME.
And you still offer or display that purity of your prime, without the stain; i.e., the essence of your royal blood can never change; Oxford is confirming what he wrote earlier: "Yet him for this my love no whit disdaineth,/ *Suns of the world may stain*, when *heaven's sun staineth*" – Sonnet 33, lines 13-14; **PRIME** = "the *golden prime* of this *sweet prince*" – *Richard III*, 1.2.248

9 THOU HAST PASSED BY THE AMBUSH OF YOUNG DAYS

You have survived your own rebellion as well as your arrest and conviction for treason
AMBUSH = Southampton's attempted "ambush" against the Government; but also the attack against him, by Cecil and even the Queen; ("Once did I lay an *ambush* for your life, a *trespass* that doth vex my grieved soul" – *Richard II*, 1.1.137-138); you have survived your own execution; now your "*young days*" (golden time) of royal promise are in the past

> Once did I lay an ***ambush*** for your life,
> A ***trespass*** that doth vex my grieved soul;
> But ere I last received the sacrament,
> I did ***confess*** it, and exactly begged
> Your grace's ***pardon,*** and I hope I had it.
> This is my ***fault*** – as for the rest ***appealed***...
> - *Richard II*, 1.1.137-142

(Words in the speech above related to the Sonnets: **Ambush:** Sonnet 70, line 9; **Trespass:** Sonnet 35, line 6; **Confess:** Sonnet 36, line 1; **Pardon**: Sonnet 58, line 12; **Fault:** Sonnet 35, lines 5, 9; etc; **Appeal:** Sonnet 117, line 13)

10 EITHER NOT ASSAILED, OR VICTOR BEING CHARGED
You have neither suffered total defeat nor been given victory by gaining the throne; **ASSAILED** = attacked; used by others to gain the throne; "Beauteous thou art, therefore to be *assailed*" – Sonnet 41, line 6; i.e., being the son of "beauty" or the Queen, and therefore heir to the throne, you are liable to attempts by others to use you for their own ends

11 YET THIS THY PRAISE CANNOT BE SO THY PRAISE,
Yet this praise of you cannot praise you as much as you deserve; *SO*: cannot *therefore* be your praise; cannot be *so much* your praise; **PRAISE** = fame and renown, as a prince; "*Your praise* shall still find room/ Even in the eyes of all posterity" – Sonnet 55, lines 10-11; "most worthy of our own Queen, to whom alone is due *all the praise* of all the Muses and all the glory of literature" – Oxford's Letter to the Reader for Castligione's *The Courtier*, 1572

12 TO TIE UP ENVY EVERMORE ENLARGED.
TO TIE UP ENVY = to hold back malice or evil against you; to remove the disgrace from you; **ENVY** = "jealous mortification at the sight of another's excellence ... to show malice and ill will" – Schmidt; "For that our kingdom's earth should not be soiled with that dear blood which it hath fostered ... with *rival-hating envy*" – *Richard II*, 1.3.125-131; **EVER** = E. Ver, Edward de Vere; **EVERMORE ENLARGED** = to give you (and spread forth) the large praise you deserve eternally; to set you free; in another sense, the envy of you is growing; **ENLARGED** = ("set at liberty" – Booth); "Surely a reference here to *The Faerie Queene*, end of Book VI; Calidore *ties up* the Blatent Beast; after a time he breaks his iron chain, 'and got into the world at liberty again,' i.e., is *evermore enlarged*" – a suggestion noted by Dowden, unwittingly with precise relevance to Southampton's hope for his liberty from the Tower; **ENLARGE** = "to set at large, to give free scope to ... to set at liberty ... to extend" – Schmidt; "and doth *enlarge* his rising with the blood of fair King Richard" – *2 Henry IV*, 1.1.204-205; "*Enlarge the man* committed yesterday ... If little faults proceeding on distemper shall not be winked at, how shall we stretch our eye when capital crimes, chewed, swallowed, and digested, appear before us? We'll yet *enlarge that man*, though Cambridge, Scroop and Grey, in their dear care and tender preservation of our person, would have him punished" – the King in *Henry V*, 2.2.40, 54-59

13 IF SOME SUSPECT OF ILL MASKED NOT THY SHOW,
SUSPECT OF ILL = Southampton, viewed as a traitor; (see line 3: "The ornament of beauty is *suspect*," i.e., a suspect traitor; "and ransom all *ill*-deeds" – Sonnet 34, line14; **MASKED NOT THY SHOW** = did not hide your identity from the world, i.e., did not prevent the showing of your truth; "But out alack, he was but one hour mine,/ The *region cloud hath masked* him from me now" – Sonnet 33, lines 11-12; "When summer's breath their *masked buds* discloses" – Sonnet 54, line 8; "That I to your assistance do make love,

masking the business from the common eye, for sundry weighty reasons" – Macbeth to the Murderers in *Macbeth*, 3.2.123-124

14 THEN THOU ALONE KINGDOMS OF HEARTS SHOULDST OWE!

ALONE = "all" and "one" for Southampton; **THOU ALONE** = you, Southampton; **KINGDOMS OF HEARTS SHOULDST OWE** = then you would be ruler of the kingdom; "And all those *beauties whereof now he's King/* Are vanishing, or vanished out of sight" – Sonnet 63, lines 6-7; "When I have seen the hungry Ocean gain/ Advantage on the *kingdom* of the shore" – Sonnet 64, lines 5-6; **OWE** = possess; i.e., then you would have a kingdom of subjects whose hearts all owe you their love and duty, as I do; and you would owe your subjects by ruling as king; "Pity the world, or else this glutton be,/ To eat *the world's due*, by the grave and thee" – Sonnet 1, lines 13-14; "No *love toward others* in that bosom sits/ That on himself such murd'rous shame commits" – Sonnet 9, lines 13-14, referring to the "love" or royal blood that he "owes" his subjects; **HEARTS** = "And art almost an alien to *the hearts of all the court and princes of my blood*" – the King lecturing his son, Prince Hal, in *1 Henry IV*, 3.2.34-35; "That I did pluck allegiance from *men's hearts*" – the King in *1 Henry IV*, 3.2.52; "Rather than rob me of *the people's hearts*" – *Titus Andronicus*, 1.1.211; "and do serve you with *hearts create of duty and of zeal*" – to the King in *Henry V*, 2.2.30-31; **KINGDOMS** = "Thy kingdom come, Thy will be done" – Lord's Prayer; "Nay, in the body of this fleshly land, this *kingdom*, this confine of blood and breath" – the King in *King John*, 4.2.245-246; "I must be married to my brother's daughter, or else my *kingdom* stands on brittle glass" – *Richard III*, 4.2.60-61; "Enjoy the kingdom after my decease" – *3 Henry VI*, 1.1.181

Part Two

**OXFORD SACRIFICES HIS IDENTITY AS FATHER
DAY FORTY-FIVE IN THE TOWER**

Sonnet 71
When I Am Dead
Do Not So Much as My Poor Name Rehearse
24 March 1601

Oxford is now foreshadowing the sacrifice of his identity – his identity as father of Southampton by the Queen and his identity as the "Shakespeare" who dedicated his works and life to Southampton. He is leading up to the so-called "Rival Poet" series (78-86) in which he will give way to the pseudonym. This is part of the bargain made with Robert Cecil, to secure the eventual release of Southampton by King James (assuming he succeeds Elizabeth) and the granting of a royal pardon to him. In this verse he gives his son instructions, the primary one being that he must "not so much as my poor name rehearse" from now on.

Sonnet 71	Translation
No longer mourn for me when I am dead	Don't publicly grieve for me after I'm dead
Than you shall hear the surly sullen bell	Any longer than the sound of the funeral bell
Give warning to the world that I am fled	Announces to England that I've disappeared
From this vile world with vildest worms to dwell.	From this vile country to dwell with vile worms.
Nay, if you read this line, remember not	No, if you read these sonnets, do not remember
The hand that writ it, for I love you so	The hand that wrote them! For I love you so much
That I in your sweet thoughts would be forgot,	That I prefer to be absent from your royal thoughts
If thinking on me then should make you woe.	If thinking about me makes you suffer.
O if (I say) you look upon this verse,	O if (I say) you look upon these sonnets
When I (perhaps) compounded am with clay	When I (perhaps) am buried in the ground,
Do not so much as my poor name rehearse,	Do not so much as speak my poor name,
But let your love ev'n with my life decay.	But, instead, let your royal blood die with me.
Lest the wise world should look into your moan,	Lest others learn the truth of your tragedy,
And mock you with me after I am gone.	And hurt you because of me when I'm gone.

1 NO LONGER MOURN FOR ME WHEN I AM DEAD
Do not mourn for me after I am dead; forget about me.

2 THAN YOU SHALL HEAR THE SURLY SULLEN BELL
Than the sound of the funeral bell; **SURLY SULLEN BELL** = "His tongue sounds ever after as a *sullen bell*, remember'd knolling a departed friend … I cannot think, my lord, your son is dead" – *2 Henry IV*, 1.1.101-104

3 GIVE WARNING TO THE WORLD THAT I AM FLED
GIVE WARNING = give notice; (introducing a reminder of mortality – Booth); **THE WORLD** = England; **THAT I AM FLED** = that I have departed from England; suggesting also the possibility that Oxford plans to leave England at some point after Elizabeth's death and the succession

REFERENCE EDITION

4 FROM THIS VILE WORLD WITH VILDEST WORMS TO DWELL:
FROM THIS VILE WORLD = from this evil state of England; ("Something is rotten in the state of Denmark" – *Hamlet*, 1.4.100; "Denmark's a prison" – *Hamlet*, 2.2.260; **WORLD** = "This estate hath depended on you a great while, as all the world doth judge" – Oxford to Burghley, September 1572); "'Tis better to be *vile* than *vile* esteemed" – Sonnet 121, line 1; **VILDEST** = vilest; "Then get thee gone, and dig my grave thyself, and bid the merry bells rings to thine ear that thou art crowned, not that I am dead. Let all the tears that should bedew my hearse be drops of balm to sanctify thy head, only compound me with forgotten dust. Give that which gave thee life unto the *worms*" – the King to his son, Prince Henry, in *2 Henry IV*, 4.5.110-116

5 NAY, IF YOU READ THIS LINE REMEMBER NOT
THIS LINE = the lines of these sonnets; echoing bloodline

6 THE HAND THAT WRIT IT, FOR I LOVE YOU SO
THE HAND THAT WRIT IT = Oxford's hand, but Southampton made the writing possible; "He learned but surety-like to write for me" - Sonnet 134, line 7; **FOR I LOVE YOU SO** = for I love you in such a way, i.e., as a father loves his son, as a father owes his love and duty to his royal son

7 THAT I IN YOUR SWEET THOUGHTS WOULD BE FORGOT,
SWEET THOUGHTS = royal thoughts

8 IF THINKING ON ME THEN SHOULD MAKE YOU WOE.
MAKE YOU WOE = make you sorrowful; cause you woe; give you trouble; "And weep afresh *love's long since cancelled woe*/ … And heavily *from woe to woe* tell o'er/ The sad account of fore-bemoaned moan,/ Which I new pay as if not paid before" – Sonnet 30, lines 7, 10-12; "O that *our night of woe* might have rememb'red/ My deepest sense, how hard true sorrow hits" – Sonnet 120, lines 9-10, referring to the tragic Rebellion and Southampton's long "night" of imprisonment, the lead-in to these lines recalling "how once I suffered in your crime" – Sonnet 120, line 8

9 O IF (I SAY) YOU LOOK UPON THIS VERSE,
O = Oxford; **THIS VERSE** = the Sonnets

10 WHEN I (PERHAPS) COMPOUNDED AM WITH CLAY,
WHEN, etc.= When I am dead and gone; **PERHAPS** = again suggesting that Oxford may not actually be dead when he disappears from sight, but, rather, that he is planning to leave England and spend the rest of his life elsewhere; **COMPOUNDED WITH CLAY** = "Only *compound me* with forgotten dust" – the King in *2 Henry IV*, 4.5.115

11 DO NOT SO MUCH AS MY POOR NAME REHEARSE:
DO NOT, etc. = instructions from father to son; when I disappear, do not even mention my wounded name

MY POOR NAME My obliterated identity; "The only *loss of my good name* is of these griefs the ground" – early Oxford verse, published in 1576; "O God, Horatio, what a *wounded name* (things standing thus unknown) shall I leave behind me!" – *Hamlet*, 5.2.351-352; my identity as your father, which is *poor* by having to be unidentified with you as my son; also "poor" in the loss of Southampton's claim to the throne, as Elizabeth (and her blood within her son) is "poor beauty" in "Why should *poor beauty* indirectly seek/ Roses of shadow, since his Rose is true" – Sonnet 67, lines 7-8; "*My name be buried* where my body is" – Sonnet 72, line 11; "Thence comes it that *my name receives a brand*" – Sonnet 111, line 5; REHEARSE = repeat or speak aloud; reveal; this is part of the bargain Oxford has struck with Robert Cecil on Southampton's behalf, i.e., to bury his identity as father and, by extension, to bury Southampton's claim to the throne.

12 BUT LET YOUR LOVE EVEN WITH MY LIFE DECAY:
YOUR LOVE = your royal blood; i.e., its recognition as such; your royal lineage and kingship; let your royal claim wither in the same way that my own life withers and dies; "O know, sweet love, I always write of you,/ And *you and love are still my argument*" – Sonnet 76, lines 9-10

13 LEST THE WISE WORLD SHOULD LOOK INTO YOUR MOAN
WISE = experienced, skillful; endowed with sound judgment; otherwise, those in this skillful (but still vile) world should wisely investigate the cause of your mourning

14 AND MOCK YOU WITH ME AFTER I AM GONE.
And (again wisely or correctly) ridicule you on account of my fatherhood of you and my inability to secure the throne for you; and make contemptuous sport of you for what I have done to you; (and this is the deepest source of Oxford's personal guilt and shame, that because of his own life and his writings as "Shakespeare" (dedicated to Southampton), he has been forced to make this infamous bargain for his son, depriving him of his royal identity as well as the throne.

THE MONUMENT

OXFORD'S SACRIFICE
DAY FORTY-SIX IN THE TOWER

Sonnet 72
My Name Be Buried
25 March 1601

London citizens gather this morning at Tower Hill, still expecting to see the execution of Southampton. There will be no official word about the commutation of his death sentence, much less any legal explanation – which Oxford will record in Sonnet 87 as the reduction of his judgment to "misprision" of treason. This is the last day that crowds are recorded waiting for the beheading. Meanwhile Oxford continues to describe the sacrifice he is making on his son's behalf, along with severe, urgent instructions for him.

Sonnet 72	Translation
O lest the world should task you to recite,	O if England should challenge you to reveal
What merit lived in me that you should love	My part in giving you the Queen's royal blood,
After my death (dear love) forget me quite,	After I die (dear royal son) forget me completely,
For you in me can nothing worthy prove.	Because you can't use me to reveal your royalty.
Unless you would devise some vertuous lie,	Unless you make up some morally good lie,
To do more for me than mine own desert,	To do more for me than I deserve,
And hang more praise upon deceased I,	And heap praise on me when I'm dead,
Than niggard truth would willingly impart.	Than the small truth we can deliberately reveal.
O lest your true love may seem false in this,	O, so your royalty will seem false in this way,
That you for love speak well of me untrue,	That you for royalty praise me without truth,
My name be buried where my body is,	Let my identity be hidden with my body,
And live no more to shame nor me nor you.	And live no more by disgracing either of us.
For I am shamed by that which I bring forth,	For I'm disgraced by having fathered disgrace,
And so should you, to love things nothing worth.	And you should be too, having no royal claim.

1 O LEST THE WORLD SHOULD TASK YOU TO RECITE
O, in case the world should interrogate you and demand you to reveal; **TASK YOU** = command you; oblige you; **RECITE** = reveal; enumerate; expose; give reasons for saying

2 WHAT MERIT LIVED IN ME THAT YOU SHOULD LOVE,
WHAT MERIT LIVED IN ME = what value (and blood) there was in me, for which you should honor me (or love me as a son loves a father; or connect me to your "love" or royal blood)

3 AFTER MY DEATH (DEAR LOVE) FORGET ME QUITE,
After my death, dear royal son, lose all memory of me; **DEAR LOVE** = my dear royal son; ("My *dear dear* lord ... then, *dear my liege*" – addressed to the king in *Richard II*, 1.1.176, 184; "O *dear son* Edgar" – *King Lear*, 4.1.23); "If my *dear love* were but the child of state,/ It might fortune's bastard be unfathered" – Sonnet 124, lines 1-2; **FORGET ME** = lose the memory or consciousness of me; "*Forget*, forgive, conclude and be agreed" – *Richard II*, 1.1.156; "and labored much how to *forget* that learning" – *Hamlet*, 5.2.34-35; **QUITE** = completely

406

4 FOR YOU IN ME CAN NOTHING WORTHY PROVE:
Because you will be unable to find anything worthy in me to demonstrate; **NOTHING** = O, Oxford; also Southampton as "nothing" or opposite of "one"; **NOTHING WORTHY** = none of your blood from me; nothing royal; ("He hath more *worthy* interest to the state than thou the shadow of succession" – *1 Henry IV*, 3.2.98-99; "*Worthy prince*" – *King Lear*, 5.3.177; "Then I salute you with this royal title: Long live Richard, England's *worthy king*" – *Richard III*, 3.7.238-239); **PROVE** = demonstrate; ("Doth not the crown of England *prove* the king?" – *King John*, 2.1.273)

5 UNLESS YOU WOULD DEVISE SOME VIRTUOUS LIE
Unless you decided to make up some false story about my virtue; **VERTUOUS** = related to Ver or Vere; **VERTUOUS LIE** = a lie about me

6 TO DO MORE FOR ME THAN MINE OWN DESERT,
TO DO MORE, etc. = to do more for my reputation than I deserve; **MINE OWN DESERT** = as father of the royal son, Southampton; **MINE OWN** = "*a son* of *mine own*" – Oxford to Burghley, March 17, 1575; "If he please to give me conquered Egypt for *my son*, he gives me so much of *mine own* as I will kneel to him with thanks" – Queen Cleopatra, a portrait of Elizabeth, in *Antony & Cleopatra*, 5.2.18-21; **DESERT** = that which is due me; merit; claim to honor; "your most high *deserts*" – Sonnet 17, line 2

7 AND HANG MORE PRAISE UPON DECEASED I
HANG = put a trophy or epitaph on my grave or funeral monument; "Which like a jewel (*hung* in ghastly night)" – Sonnet 27, line 11; and give more praise to your dead father

8 THAN NIGGARD TRUTH WOULD WILLINGLY IMPART:
Than the miserly truth would be able to say about me; **NIGGARD** = miserly; "And tender churl mak'st waste in *niggarding*" – Sonnet 1, line 12; **TRUTH** = Oxford, *Nothing Truer than Truth*; **WOULD WILLINGLY IMPART** = than I myself would willingly reveal; with a play on "Will" for William Shakespeare, Oxford's pseudonym, created precisely in order to reveal the truth in public, albeit indirectly

9 O LEST YOUR TRUE LOVE MAY SEEM FALSE IN THIS,
YOUR TRUE LOVE = your genuine royal blood; **TRUE** = related to Oxford, *Nothing Truer than Truth*; ("your *true* rights" – Sonnet 17, line 11); **MAY SEEM FALSE** = may be disbelieved, i.e., the opposite of truth, and seem not related to me as my son; "If that be fair whereon my *false* eyes dote,/ What means the world to say it is not so?" – Sonnet 148, lines 5-6, to Elizabeth; "More perjured eye,/ To swear against the truth so foul a lie" – Sonnet 152, lines 13-14, Oxford's final words to Elizabeth, about having to bury the truth of their royal son

10 THAT YOU FOR LOVE SPEAK WELL OF ME UNTRUE,
That you, out of love for me, falsely say good things about me; **FOR LOVE** = for your own eternal royal blood; for your love of me; **SPEAK WELL OF ME UNTRUE** = speak well of me by saying what has been decreed to be untrue; **UNTRUE** = the lack of me, Oxford (*Nothing Truer than Truth*) in your life; the lack of your recognition of me; O, for these reasons, then I instruct that the following take place:

11 MY NAME BE BURIED WHERE MY BODY IS
MY NAME BE BURIED = My identity as your father, and as Shakespeare, must be buried; ("And keep invention in a noted weed,/ That *every word* doth **almost tell my name**" – Sonnet 76, lines 6-7; "Do not so much as *my poor name* rehearse" – Sonnet 71, line 11; "Thence comes it that *my name* receives a brand" – Sonnet 111, line 5; "Horatio: 'The same, my lord, and your poor servant *ever*'; Hamlet: 'Sir, my good friend, I'll *change that name* with you'" – *Hamlet*, 1.2.162-163; "O God, Horatio, what a *wounded name*, things standing thus unknown, shall I leave behind me" – the dying Prince in *Hamlet*, 5.2.351-352; "The only *loss of my good name*, is of these griefs the ground" – Oxford poem in *Paradise of Dainty Devices*, 1576

REFERENCE EDITION

So you being sick of too much doubt in your own proceedings, through which infirmity
you are desirous to ***bury*** and ensevel your works in the grave of oblivion...
- Oxford's Prefatory Letter to *Cardanus' Comfort*, 1573

I'll break my staff,
Bury it certain fathoms in the earth,
And deeper than did *ever* plummet sound
I'll drown my book.
- Prospero in *The Tempest*, 5.1.54-57

"Gave thee no instance why thou shouldst do treason unless to dub thee with *the name of traitor*" – *Henry V*, 2.2.119-120; "In the old age black was not counted fair,/ Or if it were it bore not *beauty's name*" – Sonnet 127, lines 1-2, i.e., their disgraced son had never borne Elizabeth's name of Tudor; "But rising at thy name" – Sonnet 151, line 9, to Elizabeth; "Make but *my name* thy love, and love that still,/ And then thou lov'st me for *my name* is *Will*" – to Elizabeth, referring to the "love" or royal blood of their son, which lives within the printed works attributed to "Will" or William Shakespeare (the name, spelled 'Shake-speare,' will appear as the poet of *The Phoenix and Turtle* of this year, 1601

12 AND LIVE NO MORE TO SHAME NOR ME NOR YOU!
AND LIVE NO MORE = and remain concealed; **TO SHAME** = to bring disgrace upon neither of us.

13 FOR I AM SHAMED BY THAT WHICH I BRING FORTH,
FOR I AM SHAMED = for I am disgraced; "So to the laws at large I write *my name*; and he that breaks them in the least degree stands in *attainder of eternal shame*" – *Love's Labour's Lost*, 1.1.153-155; **BY THAT WHICH I BRING FORTH** = by having given birth to you; by these sonnets that I write, by which I "bring forth" you again by recreating your life, or giving you rebirth, in their womb; (echoing "*setting forth*" in the 1609 dedication of the Sonnets); shamed by the crime of treason for which I take the blame and guilt along with the punishment, in order to gain freedom for you; **BRING FORTH** = "to give birth to" – Schmidt; "Art thou a woman's son and canst not feel/ What 'tis to love, how want of love tormenteth?/ O had thy mother borne so hard a mind,/ She had not *brought forth thee*, but died *unkind*" – Venus (Elizabeth) to Adonis (Oxford/Southampton) in *Venus and Adonis*, 201-204, linking *brought forth* = "gave birth" to *unkind* = "childless" or unrelated by nature; "And he that calls on thee, let him *bring forth*/ Eternal numbers to outlive long date" – Sonnet 38, lines 11-12; "Alack what poverty my Muse *brings forth*" – Sonnet 103, line 1, continuing the theme that he is giving rebirth to his son's royal blood by means of the Sonnets (in poverty, since Southampton has lost his royal claim); "And now that my soul *brought forth* new prodigy, and I, a gasping *new-delivered* mother" – *Richard II*, 2.2.64-65; bring to light: "*brought forth* the secret'st man of blood" – *Macbeth*, 3.4.124-125

14 AND SO SHOULD YOU, TO LOVE THINGS NOTHING WORTH!
And you should be ashamed of us, too; we are in this together, our fates are bound up; the truth must be buried by both of us; **TO LOVE THINGS NOTHING WORTH** = to love either me or your own royal blood, which is now worth nothing (in terms of real time, on earth); such is the bitter cost of the bargain by which Southampton may gain his release from the Tower; **NOTHING WORTH** = lack of worth or royal claim; ("Weigh you the ***worth*** and honor of a king" – *Troilus and Cressida*, 2.2.26)

Part Two

OXFORD WRITES "THE PHOENIX AND TURTLE"
ABOUT THE DEATH OF HIS SON'S ROYAL CLAIM

DAY FORTY-SEVEN IN THE TOWER

Sonnet 73
Where Late the Sweet Birds Sang
26 March 1601

Oxford is now writing The Phoenix and the Turtle, *a funeral dirge about the figurative death of Elizabeth as the Phoenix and Oxford as the Turtledove, because Southampton will no longer be able to advance their bloodlines to the throne. The death of the birds is echoed below in "where late the sweet birds sang." The stark beauty and compactness of this sonnet mirrors that of the poem.*

Sonnet 73	Translation
That time of year thou mayst in me behold,	You can see in me that point in my life
When yellow leaves, or none, or few, do hang	When only the vestiges of past glory remain
Upon those boughs which shake against the cold,	On my person, as I tremble against the death
Bare ruined choirs, where late the sweet birds sang.	Of your royal lineage from Elizabeth and me.
In me thou seest the twilight of such day,	In me you see the ending of your royal time,
As after Sun-set fadeth in the West,	Like the fading of my royal son's glory,
Which by and by black night doth take away	Which is soon taken away by disgrace,
Death's second self that seals up all in rest.	Death's second self that hides all forever.
In me thou seest the glowing of such fire,	In me you see the dying embers of your royalty,
That on the ashes of his youth doth lie,	Lying on the ashes of your youth,
As the death-bed whereon it must expire,	As the death bed upon which I must expire,
Consumed with that which it was nourished by.	Destroyed by what had given me life and hope.
This thou perceiv'st, which makes thy love more strong,	You see my sacrifice, making your blood more royal,
To love that well, which thou must leave ere long.	To love that blood which you must now give up.

1 THAT TIME OF YEAR THOU MAYST IN ME BEHOLD
THAT TIME OF YEAR = the autumn of Oxford's life; **TIME** = the rapidly dwindling life span of Elizabeth, now in her sixty-eighth year; **IN ME** = repeated in lines 5 and 9; **BEHOLD** = look upon; see; "'My tongue cannot express my grief for one,/ And yet,' quoth she, '*behold* two Adons dead!'" – *Venus and Adonis*, line 1070, after Adonis has been killed ("'Tis true, 'tis true, thus was Adonis slain: He ran upon the *boar* with his sharp *spear*'" – lines 1111-1112, alluding to the boar of Oxford's crest and to the spear of 'Shake-speare');

2 WHEN YELLOW LEAVES, OR NONE, OR FEW DO HANG
YELLOW LEAVES = the autumn of the royal tree; Oxford in line 2 of *The Phoenix and Turtle* refers to "the sole Arabian tree", the habitat of the Phoenix, symbol of Elizabeth:

REFERENCE EDITION 409

> Now I will believe
> That there are unicorns; that in Arabia
> There is *one tree, the Phoenix's throne*, one Phoenix
> At this hour reigning there
> - *The Tempest*, 3.3.21-23

> A son who is the theme of honor's tongue,
> Amongst a grove the very straightest *plant*
> - *1 Henry IV*, 1.1.80-81

> When I perceive that *men as plants* increase
> - Sonnet 15, line 4

> Then was I as a tree
> Whose *boughs* did bend with fruit. But in one night,
> A storm, or robbery (call it what you will)
> Shook down my mellow hangings, nay, *my leaves*,
> And *left me bare* to weather
> - *Cymbeline*, 3.3.60-64

"When as a lion's whelp shall, to himself unknown, without seeking find, and be embraced by a piece of tender air: and when from a stately cedar shall be lopp'd branches, which, being dead many years, shall after revive, be jointed to the old stock, and freshly grow, then shall Posthumus end his miseries, Britain be fortunate, and flourish in peace and plenty" – *Cymbeline*, 5.5.436-443

> The lofty cedar, royal Cymbeline,
> Personates thee: and thy lopp'd branches point
> Thy two sons forth: who, by Belarius stol'n,
> For many years thought dead, are now revived,
> To the majestic cedar join'd; whose issue
> Promises Britain peace and plenty
> - *Cymbeline*, 5.5.454-458

> I have lived long enough: my way of life
> Is fall'n into the sear, *the yellow leaf*
> - *Macbeth*, 5.3.22-23

(Note: "leaves" in this line is echoed by "leave" in line 14)
NONE = Southampton, without a royal claim, the opposite of "one"

3 UPON THOSE BOUGHS WHICH SHAKE AGAINST THE COLD,
BOUGHS WHICH SHAKE = allusion to the "Shake" of the Shakespeare name (as in Sonnet 18, line 3: "Rough winds do *shake* the darling buds of May," also in context with branches of a tree); the reference is contemporary, because of the printed name ("William Shake-speare") to be used on *The Phoenix and the Turtle*; and it signals the permanent obliteration of Oxford's identity behind the mask or pseudonym – at least, until the Sonnets might surface in the distant future and be correctly understood.

> That numberless upon me struck as *leaves*
> Do on the oak, have with one winter's brush
> Fell from their *boughs* and *left me* open, *bare*
> For every storm that blows
> - *Timon of Athens*, 3.2.263-266

4 BARE RUINED CHOIRS, WHERE LATE THE SWEET BIRDS SANG.
BARE RUINED CHOIRS = the barren branches of the trees, i.e., of the family tree and lineage; **BARE** = related to the bearing of the royal son; "When your sweet issue your sweet form should *bear*" – Sonnet 13, line 8; "Why is my verse so *barren* of new pride" – Sonnet 76, line 1; "The argument all *bare*" – Sonnet 102, line 3

WHERE LATE THE SWEET BIRDS SANG =
Referring to the Queen and himself as the "dead" birds of *The Phoenix and the Turtle*, the funeral dirge or song, which Oxford is now writing (or has just written) as by "William Shake-speare" for publication this year; the *Phoenix/Beauty* = Elizabeth; the *Turtledove/Truth* = Oxford, as parents of the royal son whose claim to the throne has died; **LATE** = figuratively dead, i.e., their mingled blood in Southampton is now dead; (As a convicted traitor, Henry Wriothesley is now referred to as "*the late earl* of Southampton"); "With these our *late-deceased* emperor's sons" – *Titus Andronicus*, 1.1.187; **SWEET BIRDS** = royal parents, Elizabeth and Oxford; "To this urn let those repair/ That are either true or fair;/ For ***these dead birds*** sigh a prayer" – *The Phoenix and Turtle*, lines 65-67; "Thy end is *Truth's and Beauty's doom and date*" – Sonnet 14, line 14

5 IN ME THOU SEEST THE TWILIGHT OF SUCH DAY,
IN ME = repeated from line 1 and again repeated in line 9; **TWILIGHT OF SUCH DAY** = the ending of such royal hope; i.e., ending of the "golden time" of Sonnet 3, line 12, and of the "Summer's day" of Sonnet 18, line 1; **TWILIGHT** = the faint light after sunset; "Nativity, once in the *main of light*" – Sonnet 60, line 5, referring to Southampton's birth as royal prince

6 AS AFTER SUN-SET FADETH IN THE WEST,
SUN-SET = the fading of the royal son; (capitalized as "Sun-set" in Q); "Like feeble age he reeleth from the day" – Sonnet 7, line 10, when Oxford compared Southampton to "his sacred majesty" the sun or royal son; "Even so my Sunne one early morn did shine" – Sonnet 33, line 9; **FADETH IN THE WEST** = "And from the forlorn world his visage hide,/ *Stealing unseen to west* with this disgrace" – Sonnet 33, lines 7-8; "To dim his glory and to stain the track of his bright passage to the occident (i.e., to the west)" – *Richard II*, 3.3.66-67

7 WHICH BY AND BY BLACK NIGHT DOTH TAKE AWAY
BY AND BY = "And *by and by* a cloud takes all away" – *The Two Gentlemen of Verona*, 1.3.87; **BLACK NIGHT** = the disgrace covering Southampton, which began in "Makes *black night* beauteous, and her old face new" – Sonnet 27, line 12

8 DEATH'S SECOND SELF THAT SEALS UP ALL IN REST.
DEATH'S SECOND SELF = alluding to Southampton as Oxford's second self, i.e., his son; "Which, laboring for invention, bear amiss/ The *second burthen of a former child*" – Sonnet 59, lines 3-4; "What can mine own praise to *mine own self* bring,/ And what is't but *mine own* when I praise thee?" – Sonnet 39, lines 3-4; "'Tis *thee (my self)* that for *my self* I praise" – Sonnet 62, line 13; "Make thee *another self for love of me*" – Sonnet 10, line 13; **SEALS UP** = closes up, as in a coffin; conceals from everyone; "She carved thee *for her seal*" – Nature, i.e., Elizabeth, who gave birth to Southampton, Sonnet 11, line 13; echoing the Great Seal of the Queen, who is sealing up the truth of both Oxford and their royal son

> "To be *sealed up* in an eternal remembrance"
> – Oxford to Robert Cecil, October 7, 1601

ALL = Southampton, *One for All, All for One*; **REST** = "Tired with all these, for *restful death* I cry" – Sonnet 66, line 1; "That am debarred the benefit of *rest*" – Sonnet 28, line 2; cessation from motion or disturbance; repose; peace of mind; a pause in music, echoing a pause in this funeral dirge or song; "The *rest* is silence" – *Hamlet*, 5.2.365, his dying words, referring to the "rest" of the story to be told, but also to his eternal rest; "*Rest, rest*, perturbed spirit" – *Hamlet*, 2.1.190, to the ghost of his dead father

THE MONUMENT

> Death is now the Phoenix' nest,
> And the Turtle's loyal breast
> To eternity doth rest,
>
> Leaving no posterity;
> 'Twas not their infirmity,
> It was married chastity.
>
> Truth may seem, but cannot be;
> Beauty brag, but 'tis not she;
> Truth and Beauty buried be.
>
> To this urn let those repair
> That are either true or fair:
> For these dead birds, sigh a prayer.
> - *The Phoenix and the Turtle*, 1601, 56-67

9 IN ME THOU SEEST THE GLOWING OF SUCH FIRE,
IN ME = repeated from lines 1 and 5; **THE GLOWING OF SUCH FIRE** = the fading embers of your royal flame; as in "*thy light's flame*" of Sonnet 1, line 6; also as in "*love-kindling fire ... holy fire of love ... dateless lively heat*" of Sonnet 153, lines 3-6, and "*heart-inflaming* brand" of Sonnet 154, line 2; "Till my bad angel fire my good one out" – Sonnet 144, line 14

10 THAT ON THE ASHES OF HIS YOUTH DOTH LIE
ASHES OF HIS YOUTH = the dying embers of Oxford's youth, in reaction to the death of Southampton's hopeful time, which has lived within Oxford himself; **LIE** = as in the coffin; also, suggesting the "lie" about them that must be told to the world from now on; "On both sides is simple truth suppressed ... Therefore I *lie* with her, and she with me" – Oxford, referring to Elizabeth, in Sonnet 138, lines 8,13

11 AS THE DEATH-BED WHEREON IT MUST EXPIRE,
DEATH-BED = "Thy *death-bed* is no lesser than thy land, wherein thou liest in reputation sick" to the King in *Richard II*, 2.1.96-97; **WHEREON IT MUST EXPIRE** = upon which the royal Tudor blood must die; **EXPIRE** = to die; to run out of time; as the "lease" of Southampton's royal blood and claim is now expiring; "I will lay odds, ere this year expire" – *2 Henry IV*, 5.5.106

12 CONSUMED WITH THAT WHICH IT WAS NOURISHED BY.
CONSUMED = devoured, destroyed, wasted; consumed by the same fire of his son's royal blood that had nourished him; "Wasting away on the dead ashes which once nourished it with living flame" – Dowden; consumed by the cinders of their son's (and therefore Oxford's) *right*, which has gone up in flames:

> So between them love did shine
> That the Turtle saw his right
> Flaming in the Phoenix' sight...
>
> Beauty, Truth, and Rarity,
> Grace in all simplicity,
> *Here enclosed in cinders lie.*
> - *The Phoenix and Turtle*, 1601, 33-36, 53-55

THAT WHICH IT WAS NOURISHED BY = harking all the way back to the opening verse of the collection: "*Feed'st thy light's flame* with self-substantial fuel" – Sonnet 1, line 6, referring to Southampton's source of royal blood and claim; "Feed'st thy light's flame with self-substantial fuel,/ Making a famine where abundance lies/ ... To eat the world's due, by the grave and thee" – Sonnet 1, lines 6-7, 14, a similar concept

13 THIS THOU PERCEIV'ST, WHICH MAKES THY LOVE MORE STRONG
You know all this, and in knowing this you realize that your royal blood is even stronger; **THY LOVE** = your royal blood; ("And *you and love* are still my argument" – Sonnet 76, line 10); **STRONG** = "If thou wouldst use the *strength* of all thy state" – Sonnet 96, line 12; which makes your royal blood more able:

14 TO LOVE THAT WELL WHICH THOU MUST LEAVE ERE LONG.
TO LOVE THAT WELL = to love and serve your own royal blood, which you must soon give up, in terms of making any claim to the throne or revealing the truth; to love me, Oxford= Vere = Ver = spring = well; **LEAVE ERE** = the sound of *l'hiver*, French for winter, and playing again on Ver or Vere; "To *leave* poor me thou hast the strength of laws" – Sonnet 49, line 13; "Tired with all these, from these would I be gone,/ Save that to die, I *leave* my love alone" – Sonnet 66, lines 13-14

THE PHOENIX AND THE TURTLE
("These Dead Birds")

1601

Let the bird of loudest lay,
On the sole *Arabian* tree,
Herald sad and trumpet be,
To whose sound chaste wings obey.

But thou shrieking harbinger,
Foul precurer of the fiend,
Augur of the fever's end,
To this troop come thou not near!

From this Session interdict
Every fowl of tyrant wing,
Save the Eagle, feathered King,
Keep the obsequy so strict.

Let the Priest in Surplice white,
That defunctive Music can,
Be the death-divining Swan,
Lest the *Requiem* lack his right.

And thou treble-dated Crow,
That thy sable gender mak'st
With the breath thou giv'st and tak'st,
'Mongst our mourners shalt thou go.

PHOENIX = Elizabeth, who was likened to the mythical bird that lived five hundred years and was consumed by sun-ignited fire on the Arabian tree, a new Phoenix rising from its ashes; ("And burn the long-lived Phoenix in her blood" – Sonnet 19, line 4; "but as when the bird of wonder dies, the maiden Phoenix, her ashes new-create another heir as great in admiration as herself, so shall she leave her blessedness to one – when heaven shall call her from this cloud of darkness – who from the sacred ashes of her honor shall star-like rise" – *Henry VIII*, 5.4.39-46, Cranmer, speaking of the baby Elizabeth, and predicting the birth of an heir from her ashes at her death); **TURTLE** = Oxford
BIRD OF LOUDEST LAY = the bird with the strongest voice
SHRIEKING HARBINGER = screech-owl, harbinger of death; **PRECURER** = forerunner
SESSION = recalls "Sessions" or trial of Sonnet 30; also "the state or posture of being seated" – *OED*; but, in fact, this is an **OBSEQUY** or funeral rite; **KING** = James, who now must succeed so that Southampton may be released and pardoned
PRIEST = one who can understand funeral music; **DEATH-DIVINING SWAN** = the swan, believed to sing beautifully at its death; **HIS RIGHT** = allusion to Southampton's right of kingship
TREBLE-DATED CROW = Southampton; (as in Sonnet 70, line 4: "A Crow that flies in heaven's sweetest air"); he will be "dated" three times at the succession, when he, along with "Truth and Beauty" (Oxford and Elizabeth), meet their "doom and date" (Sonnet 14, line 14) at the royal succession; **SABLE GENDER** = Southampton as black (as a Crow) or disgraced offspring.

Here the Anthem doth commence:
Love and Constancy is dead,
Phoenix and the *Turtle* fled
In a mutual flame from hence.

So they loved as love in twain
Had the essence but in one;
Two distincts, Division none:
Number there was slain.

Hearts remote, yet not asunder;
Distance, and no space was seen
'Twixt this *Turtle* and his Queen;
But in them it were a wonder.

So between them Love did shine
That the *Turtle* saw his right
Flaming in the *Phoenix'* sight:
Either was the other's mine.

Property was thus appalled,
That the self was not the same;
Single nature's double name
Neither two nor one was called.

Reason, in itself confounded,
Saw division grow together,
To themselves yet either neither,
Simple were so well compounded

LOVE AND CONSTANCY = royal blood and its continuance on the throne; ("Therefore my verse to *constancy* confined" – Sonnet 105, line 7); **PHOENIX** = Elizabeth; **TURTLE** = Oxford, as turtle-dove;
MUTUAL FLAME = the flame of the funeral pyre; the burning of Southampton's royal blood, consuming them both
THEY = Oxford and Elizabeth; **ONE** = Southampton; **NUMBER THERE WAS SLAIN** = Southampton (numbered "one") was slain in terms of his claim to the throne; ("Among a number one is reckoned none" – Sonnet 136, line 8, referring to Southampton)
TURTLE = Oxford; **QUEEN** = Queen Elizabeth; **WONDER** = Southampton, as "won" = "one"; ("To this composed wonder of your frame" – Sonnet 59, line 10)
LOVE DID SHINE = Southampton's royal blood was born ("Even so my Sunne one early morn did shine" - Sonnet 33, line 9); **HIS RIGHT** = Southampton's right to the throne; ("That for thy right myself will bear all wrong" – Sonnet 88, line 14); **FLAMING IN THE PHOENIX'S SIGHT** = burn up in Elizabeth's sight;
EITHER WAS THE OTHER'S MINE = both Oxford and Elizabeth were his parents
PROPERTY = possession of the throne; **SINGLE NATURE'S DOUBLE NAME** = Southampton's as natural child, who should have carried Oxford's and Elizabeth's names;
NEITHER TWO NOR ONE WAS CALLED = he was called by neither of their two names, nor was he called "one" or royal prince
REASON = intelligence and logic; **CONFOUNDED** = destroyed; **DIVISION GROW** = growing apart, unrecognized for who they were

That it cried: "How true a twain
Seemeth this concordant one!
Love hath reason, reason none,
If what parts can so remain."

Whereupon it made this threne
To the phoenix and the dove,
Co-supremes and stars of love,
As chorus to their tragic scene.

Threnos.

Beauty, truth, and rarity,
Grace in all simplicity,
Here enclosed in cinders lie.
Death is now the phoenix' nest,
And the turtle's loyal breast
To eternity doth rest,

Leaving no posterity:
'Twas not their infirmity,
It was married chastity.

Truth may seem, but cannot be,
Beauty brag, but 'tis not she,
Truth and Beauty buried be.
To this urn let those repair
That are either true or fair,
For these dead birds sigh a prayer.

- *William Shake-speare*

TRUE = Oxford; **TWAIN** = twosome; **ONE** = Southampton; **LOVE HATH REASON** = royal blood has reason on its side; **REASON NONE** = but reason itself rendered "one" (Southampton) as "none"
THE PHOENIX AND THE DOVE = Elizabeth and Oxford
THRENOS = funeral lament; song of lamentation; a dirge, a threnody or song for the dead
BEAUTY, TRUTH AND RARITY = Elizabeth, Oxford and Southampton; **GRACE** = royal blood; **ALL** = Southampton; **SIMPLICITY** = ("And simple truth miscalled simplicity" – Sonnet 66, line 11)
PHOENIX NEST = Elizabeth's throne; (as in *The Phoenix Nest*, published in 1593)
NO POSTERITY = no truth for future generations; **MARRIED CHASTITY** = the irony that Oxford and Elizabeth had been betrothed, yet she maintained her chaste image as the Virgin Queen
TRUTH = Oxford; **BEAUTY** = Elizabeth, also, her royal blood that Southampton inherited; **TRUTH AND BEAUTY BURIED BE** = Oxford and Elizabeth are buried as parents; at least in the world's eyes; ("Thy end is Truth's and Beauty's doom and date" – Sonnet 14, line 14)
TRUE = rightful; related to Oxford; **FAIR** = royal, i.e., Southampton; **DEAD BIRDS** = Oxford and Elizabeth, in terms of their son, who cannot become king; ("Bare ruined choirs, where late the sweet birds sang" – Sonnet 73, line 4)

Part Two

OXFORD'S SACRIFICE
DAY FORTY-EIGHT IN THE TOWER

Sonnet 74
My Spirit Is Thine, The Better Part of Me
27 March 1601

The funeral dirge continues as Oxford records that when he dies, his identity as Southampton's father will be obliterated. This is preparation for his permanent metamorphosis into the printed name "William Shakespeare" -- at least in the eyes of the contemporary world and for the foreseeable future. In a real sense, Oxford himself is "dying" along with his son's claim to the throne.

Sonnet 74	Translation
But be contented when that fell arrest	But be contented if that approaching death
Without all bail shall carry me away;	Carries me off before your release from prison!
My life hath in this line some interest,	My life is also in these verses (and your lineage)
Which for memorial still with thee shall stay.	Which will stay with you as your memorial.
When thou reviewst this, thou dost review	When you look at these sonnets again, you see
The very part was consecrate to thee.	The true royalty that is yours as preserved.
The earth can have but earth, which is his due	The earth can have my body, which is its due,
My spirit is thine, the better part of me.	But your blood is my own: you are my best self.
So then thou hast but lost the dregs of life,	So then you've lost only the physical part,
The prey of worms, my body being dead,	The prey of worms, my body being dead,
The coward conquest of a wretch's knife,	I, beaten by cowards with axes or knives,
Too base of thee to be remembered.	And by those too beneath you to be remembered.
The worth of that is that which it contains,	The royalty of this verse depends on its contents,
And that is this, and this with thee remains.	And these contents of you will endure with you.

1 BUT BE CONTENTED WHEN THAT FELL ARREST
Oxford speaking to Southampton as to a king; "Well, if you be a king crown'd with *content*, your crown *content* and you must be *contented* to go along with us" – *3 Henry VI*, 3.1.66-68, spoken to King Henry VI, who is being deposed; "What must the king do now; must he submit? The king shall do it: must he be deposed? The king shall be *contented*: must he lose the name of king?" – *Richard II*, 3.3.143-146; "Thus play I in one person many people, and none *contented*: sometimes am I king; then treasons make me wish myself a beggar, and so I am" – *Richard II*, 5.5.31-34; **THAT FELL ARREST** = Oxford's own death; that cruel, deadly destruction of your royal claim; "Had I but time – as this *fell sergeant Death* is strict in his *arrest*" – *Hamlet*, 5.2.343-344; echoing the arrest of Southampton; "I do *arrest* thee of high treason here" – *2 Henry VI*, 3.1.97; "Their faults are open; *arrest* them to the answer of the law" – *Henry V*, 2.2.142-143

2 WITHOUT ALL BAIL SHALL CARRY ME AWAY.
ALL = Southampton, *One for All, All for One*; **WITHOUT ALL BAIL** = without possibility of release; "'held without bail' was already a standard legal phrase" – Booth; the Act for the Uniformity of Common Prayer (1559) stipulated "imprisonment … *without bail*"; but Oxford is paying "bail" for Southampton's eventual release, by sacrificing his own identity as father and as writer of the Shakespeare works linked by

REFERENCE EDITION 417

dedication to Southampton; "The sons of York, thy betters in their birth, shall be their father's *bail*" – *2 Henry VI*, 5.1.119-120; "I did, my lord: *yet let me be their bail*" – *Titus Andronicus*, 2.2.295; **CARRY ME AWAY** = take my spirit to heaven; allow me to die; suggesting also, again, that Oxford is planning to leave England; "In few, they hurried us aboard a bark, bore us some leagues to sea" – *The Tempest*, 1.2.144-145, Propsero, describing his trip to the island; **CARRY** = associated with being violently conveyed, as Southampton was carried to the Tower and very nearly carried to his execution; "There's one yonder arrested and *carried to prison*" – *Measure for Measure*, 1.2.59; "to *carry him to execution*" – *Measure for Measure*, 4.2.151

3 MY LIFE HATH IN THIS LINE SOME INTEREST,

Oxford's acknowledgment that the Sonnets represent his life or autobiography in relation to his royal son; **THIS LINE** = these lines of verse; this re-creation of your bloodline; the Tudor line or lineage from Henry VII to Henry Wriothesley, born to become Henry IX; "But when your countenance filled up *his line*" – Sonnet 86, line 13, the poetical lines of "Shakespeare" that Oxford dedicated to Southampton in public support of him; "His beauty shall *in these black lines* be seen,/ And they shall live, and he in them still green" – Sonnet 63, lines 13-14, referring to the lines of these private sonnets (blackened with the disgrace of Southampton's treason) intended for the eyes of readers in posterity; "When in *eternal lines to time* thou grow'st" – Sonnet 18, line 12; "the *lines of life*" – Sonnet 16, line 9; "They hailed him father to a *line* of kings ... Thence to be wrenched with an *unlineal* hand, no son of mine succeeding" – *Macbeth*, 3.1.59-63; **INTEREST** = ("legal right of possession" – Booth), i.e., Oxford understates the case that he has "*some interest*" or stake in these private verses recording the life of his royal son; "Where life hath no more *interest* than to breathe" – *Titus Andronicus*, 3.1.249; "That all your *interest* in those territories" – *2 Henry VI*, 3.184; "The life, the right and truth of all this realm is fled to heaven; and England now is left to tug and scramble un-owed *interest of proud-swelling state*" – *King John*, 4.3.144-147; "He hath more worthy *interest to the state* than thou the shadow of succession" – *1 Henry IV*, 3.2.98-99; echoing in phraseology: "*I have some rights of memory in this kingdom, which* now to claim my vantage doth invite me" – Hamlet, 5.2.396-397; related to revenue and finance, i.e., to the "treasure" of royal blood

4 WHICH FOR MEMORIAL STILL WITH THEE SHALL STAY.

FOR MEMORIAL = Preserved in the monument of the Sonnets; as opposed to the usual physical memorials built to preserve the memory of princes; "The *living record of your memory*" – Sonnet 55, line 8; "From hence *your memory* death cannot take ... Your name from hence immortal life shall have,/ Though I, once gone, to all the world must die" – Sonnet 81, lines 3, 5-6; "And thou in this shalt find thy monument" – Sonnet 107, line 13; "I pray you, let us satisfy our eyes with the *memorials and things of fame* that do renown this city" – *Twelfth Night*, 3.3.22-23; **STILL** = always; "Why write I *still* all one, ever the same/ ... And you and love are *still* my argument/ ... So is my love *still* telling what is told" – Sonnet 76, lines 5, 10, 14; "To one, of one, *still* such, and ever so" – Sonnet 105, line 4

5 WHEN THOU REVIEWEST THIS, THOU DOST REVIEW

REVIEW = read over; look upon and see again; William Plumer Fowler notes the play on the word "*review*" when read backward or "re-viewed" = "WE – I – VER"; **THIS** = this verse; these sonnets

6 THE VERY PART WAS CONSECRATE TO THEE.

VERY = Ver; **VERY PART** = the true aspect, related to Edward Ver or de Vere, Earl of Oxford
CONSECRATE TO THEE = "The metaphoric use of 'consecrate' establishes a religious frame of reference ... Shakespeare's speaker is typical of courtly lovers; there is no sacrilege here, or hint of contempt for Christian doctrine" – Booth; "To make or declare sacred; set apart or dedicate to the service of a deity" – Random House Dictionary; i.e., Oxford is "consecrating" or dedicating the "very" or most personal aspect of the Sonnets to Southampton as a king or deity, as a god on earth who is "the little Love-God" of Sonnet 154 and "God in love" of Sonnet 110; "What's new to speak, what now to register,/ That may express my love, or thy dear merit?/ Nothing, sweet boy, but yet like *prayers divine,*/ I must each day say o'er the *very same,*/ Counting no old thing old, thou mine, I thine,/ Even as when first *I hallowed thy fair name.*" - Sonnet 108, lines 3-8; "We'll *consecrate* the steps that Ajax makes" – *Troilus and Cressida*, 2.3.184; "And suffer not dishonor to approach the imperial seat, to virtue *consecrate*, to justice, continence and nobility" –

Titus Andronicus, 1.1.13-15; "And here in sight of Rome to Saturnine, King and commander of our commonweal, the wide world's emperor, do I *consecrate* my sword, my chariot and my prisoners" – *Titus Andronicus*, 1.1.250-253; "And to his honour and *his valiant parts* did I my soul and fortunes *consecrate*" – *Othello*, 1.3.255-256

7 THE EARTH CAN HAVE BUT EARTH, WHICH IS HIS DUE:
EARTH = this world; England; "Earth to earth, ashes to ashes, dust to dust" – Burial Service; "*The earth can yield me but a common grave,/ When you entombed in men's eyes shall lie*" – Sonnet 81, lines 7-8; **HIS DUE:** echoing "I owe God a death" as Essex had said at the trial, with Oxford looking on as highest-ranking earl on the tribunal, paraphrasing Prince Hal: "Why, *thou owest God a death*" – *1 Henry IV*, 5.1.126

8 MY SPIRIT IS THINE, THE BETTER PART OF ME!
MY SPIRIT = my soul, heart, essence; Oxford's cry as father to son; saying he lives through his son, who possesses Oxford's soul and whose spirit (or sacred blood) is the best quality that Oxford himself possesses; **SPIRIT** = royal blood; "Th'expense of *Spirit* in a waste of shame" – Oxford to Queen Elizabeth, regarding her "waste" of Southampton's royal claim, in Sonnet 129, line 1; 'the spirit of love" – Sonnet 56, line 8; "thy spirit" – Sonnet 61, line 5; also Sonnets 80, 85, 86, 108, 144; "The *spirit of my father* grows strong in me" – *As You Like It*, 1.1.68

9 SO THEN THOU HAST BUT LOST THE DREGS OF LIFE,
So then, with my death, you have lost only the least of my life; **DREGS** = sediments or lees; final residues, i.e., the body as opposed to the spirit or soul; those aspects which spoil a thing or corrupt its purity; the lesser, worthless aspects of my life, which is yours; but you do have my spirit, the better part of me, and that spirit is your royal blood.

10 THE PREY OF WORMS, MY BODY BEING DEAD,
Echoing "pray"; my mortal self; rather than my spirit, which is yours; "Give warning to the world that I am fled/ From this vile world with vildest *worms* to dwell" – Sonnet 71, lines 3-4; to Queen Elizabeth: "Is this thy *body's* end?" – Sonnet 146, line 8

11 THE COWARD CONQUEST OF A WRETCH'S KNIFE,
Oxford picturing himself as a coward who has been conquered by the forces of evil that had threatened to execute his son; the conquerors, Elizabeth and Cecil, are also cowards; he and his son have been conquered by the Rebellion itself; **COWARD** = "By forfeiting *a traitor and a coward*" – *1 Henry VI*, 4.3.27; **CONQUEST** = "Henry the Fourth by *conquest* got the crown. 'Twas by *rebellion* against his king" – *3 Henry VI*, 1.1.136-137; "Ah do not, when my heart hath 'scaped this sorrow,/ Come in the rearward of a conquered woe" – Sonnet 90, lines 5-6; **WRETCH'S KNIFE** = The executioner's axe, as in "confounding Age's cruel *knife*" – Sonnet 63, line 10; also "time's *scythe*" of Sonnet 12, line 13; i.e., the *threat* of execution still hangs over Southampton, as no legal reasons for the commutation of his sentence have been announced (and never will be announced); without a royal pardon, he could still be beheaded at any time; also the knives of criminals or traitors, who are often called "wretches" in the Shakespeare plays; **WRETCH** = miserable creature deserving of pity or contempt; deserving to be abhorred; criminals or traitors in the Tower who would entice Southampton to further rebellion against the Crown; "our *wretches fettered in our prisons*" – *Henry V*, 1.2.244; of men facing execution: "Never saw I *wretches* so quake: they kneel, they kiss the earth … with divers deaths in death" – *The Winter's Tale*, 5.1.197-201; **KNIFE** = "The hardest knife ill used doth lose his edge" – Sonnet 95, line 14; "Give my love fame faster than time wastes life,/ So thou prevent'st his *scythe and crooked knife*" - Sonnet 100, lines 13-14; "He is dead, Caesar, not by a public minister of justice, nor by a hired knife" – *Antony and Cleopatra*, 5.1.19-21

12 TOO BASE OF THEE TO BE REMEMB'RED.
The other traitors are too far below Southampton to deserve any remembrance; Oxford may also be picturing himself as too base or common, too below his son, to be remembered by him; "comfort the afflicted, confirm the doubtful, encourage *the coward* and lift up the *base*-minded man to achieve to any sum or grade of virtue whereto ought only the noble thoughts of men to be inclined" – Oxford's Prefatory Letter to *Cardanus'*

Comfort, 1573; **BASE** = only in the eyes of the general public is Southampton a "base" commoner in the Tower; "As on the finger of a throned Queen,/ The *basest Jewel* will be well esteemed" – Sonnet 96, lines 5-6, i.e., as an ornament of our Queen Elizabeth on the throne, a legitimate prince suffering from even the lowest or most base image will be well-regarded, at least by those who know the truth of him.

13 THE WORTH OF THAT IS THAT WHICH IT CONTAINS,

THE WORTH OF THAT = the worth of this "line" (i.e., of the Sonnets) is what it contains, which is your royal blood; **WORTH** = royalty; "England ne'er lost *a king of so much worth*" – *1 Henry VI*, 1.1.7; "As a decrepit father takes delight/ To see his active child do deeds of youth,/ So I, made lame by Fortune's dearest spite,/ Take all my comfort of *thy worth and truth*" – Sonnet 37, lines 1-4; "Oh how *thy worth* with manners may I sing,/ When thou art all the better part of me?" – Sonnet 39, lines 1-2

14 AND THAT IS THIS, AND THIS WITH THEE REMAINS.

And that worth is represented by this diary of the Sonnets; **THIS** = this verse, i.e., your royal worth will remain with you in these private sonnets; "Not marble nor the gilded monument of Princes shall outlive this powerful rhyme/ ... Nor *Mars* his sword nor war's quick fire shall burn/ The living record of your memory" – Sonnet 55, lines 1-2, 7-8; **REMAINS** = echoing "the remains" of his son's royal blood; "of five and twenty valiant sons behold *the poor remains*, alive and dead" – *Titus Andronicus*, 1.1.81; "Love hath reason, reason none,/ If *what parts can so remain*" – *The Phoenix and the Turtle* as by "William Shake-speare," written now and published later in 1601, depicting the death of Southampton's royal claim, which is the subject of these verses of the Sonnets: "Beauty, Truth, and Rarity,/ Grace in all simplicity,/ Here enclosed in cinders lie./ Death is now the Phoenix' nest,/ And the Turtle's loyal breast/ To eternity doth rest,/ Leaving no posterity…" – *The Phoenix and the Turtle*, 1601, 53-59.

Part Two

DAY FORTY-NINE IN THE TOWER

Sonnet 75
As Food To Life
28 March 1601

Summing up what has gone before, Oxford is about to compose the fiftieth verse since the first night of Southampton's imprisonment; he is now near the very center of the monument of verse that he is constructing. His final statement that he has "all, or all away" uses Southampton's motto One for All, All for One *as a means of identifying him as away from him in the Tower.*

Sonnet 75	Translation
So are you to my thoughts as food to life,	So you are what sustains my life,
Or as sweet seasoned showers are to the ground	Or you are like royal rain on my mortal body;
And for the peace of you I hold such strife,	And to save your life I am in such conflict,
As twixt a miser and his wealth is found.	As between a miser and his riches.
Now proud as an enjoyer, and anon	First I'm proud you are my son, but soon
Doubting the filching age will steal his treasure,	Afraid dishonesty will take your royalty from me,
Now counting best to be with you alone,	First thinking it's best that your truth is my secret,
Then bettered that the world may see my pleasure;	Then feeling it's better if England knows it.
Sometime all full with feasting on your sight,	At times, seeing you in prison, I feel like a king,
And by and by clean starved for a look,	But soon enough again I can't see you at all,
Possessing or pursuing no delight	Neither having nor pursuing any royal delight
Save what is had or must from you be took.	Except what I've had or what's taken from you.
Thus do I pine and surfeit day by day,	So I suffer daily from too little or too much of you,
Or gluttoning on all, or all away.	Either having your full royalty or none of it.

1 SO ARE YOU TO MY THOUGHTS AS FOOD TO LIFE,
Therefore you are the reason my thoughts survive; you mean so much to me that you are as necessary as food is to life; i.e., I cannot live without you; **FOOD** = "To eat the world's due" – Sonnet 1, line 14; "With my love's picture then my eye doth feast,/ And to the painted banquet bids my heart" – Sonnet 47, lines 5-6; "Therefore are feasts so solemn and so rare" – Sonnet 52, line 5; to Elizabeth, continuing the image of her royal blood within their son as food: "Shall worms, inheritors of this excess,/ Eat up thy charge?" – Sonnet 146, lines 7-8; "The pleasure that some fathers feed upon ... I mean my children's looks" - Richard II, 2.1.79-80

MY THOUGHTS = the contents of these sonnets; "That did *my ripe thoughts* in my brain inhearse,/ Making their tomb the womb wherein they grew" – Sonnet 86, lines 3-4, describing how Oxford's thoughts in these private sonnets have become both the tomb and the womb of his son's royal blood

2 OR AS SWEET SEASONED SHOWERS ARE TO THE GROUND;
SWEET = royal; **SWEET SEASONED SHOWERS** = recalling the spring or golden time of his son's life, prior to the Rebellion; echoing the rain or "reign" of his son that he had expected; with "showers" echoing "flowers" or Tudor roses; "Nor can I fortune to brief minutes tell,/ Pointing to each his thunder, *rain*, and wind" – Sonnet 14, lines 5-6

REFERENCE EDITION 421

3 AND FOR THE PEACE OF YOU I HOLD SUCH A STRIFE

And for your life in the future I engage in such conflict with myself; i.e., having to agree to bury my identity as your father and as the "Shakespeare" who pledged his undying love to you; **PEACE** = referring to the peace that will hopefully surround succession to the throne, as opposed to the prospect of civil war if Southampton should assert his claim; "And *peace* proclaims Olives of endless age" – Sonnet 107, line 8, on April 10, 1603, after Elizabeth's death, James's accession and Southampton's liberation, amid a peaceful transition of rule; in a real way, Oxford has counseled Southampton to accept the bargain for his eventual release and to avoid a power struggle that would be calamitous for England; **STRIFE** = yet in opting for this greater good, he is still torn with "strife" or conflict (contradiction) in his mind and heart; "Mine eye and heart are at a *mortal war*" – Sonnet 46, line 1; "Such *civil war* is in my love and hate" – Sonnet 35, line 12; "Alack, what heinous sin is it in me to be ashamed to be my father's child! But though I am a daughter to his blood I am not to his manners: O Lorenzo if thou keep promise I shall end this *strife*" – *The Merchant of Venice*, 2.3.16-20

4 AS 'TWIXT A MISER AND HIS WEALTH IS FOUND:

In the same way that a miser is in conflict with his riches; i.e., the way I have you as my sole wealth and yet must give you up; **WEALTH** = treasure of royal blood in his son; "O him she *stores*, to show what *wealth* she had/ In days long since, before these last so bad" – Sonnet 67, lines 13-14, referring to Elizabeth, having spared her son's life, keeping him in the Tower and thereby "storing" the "wealth" of his royal blood rather than using it to perpetuate her Tudor Rose lineage; i.e., accusing her of being a miser, as he had accused his son of being a "churl" or miser who was "niggarding" or hoarding his blood: "And, tender churl, mak'st waste in niggarding" – Sonnet 1, line 12

5 NOW PROUD AS AN ENJOYER, AND ANON

On the one hand, proudly enjoying you as my son; ("Why is my verse so barren of new *pride*" – Sonnet 76, line 1; "O death, made *proud with pure and princely beauty!*" – *King John*, 4.3.35) **ENJOYER** = "I am content: Richard Plantagenet, *enjoy* the kingdom after my decease" – *3 Henry VI*, 1.1.180-181; "*Your Grace* shall well and quietly *enjoy*" – *1 Henry VI*, 5.3.159; **ANON** = soon, presently, immediately after

6 DOUBTING THE FILCHING AGE WILL STEAL HIS TREASURE;

Fearing that this evil (and lying) age of men will steal your royal blood; **DOUBTING** = fearing, suspecting that; **THE FILCHING AGE** = this pilfering age we live in; **WILL STEAL HIS TREASURE** = "So am I as the rich whose blessed key/ Can bring him to *his sweet up-locked treasure*" – Sonnet 52, lines 1-2, referring to the treasure of royal blood in his son, locked up as a prisoner in the Tower; "And all those beauties *whereof now he's King*/ Are vanishing, or vanished out of sight,/ *Stealing away the treasure of his spring*" – Sonnet 63, lines 6-8, referring directly to his son as a King whose treasure of royal blood is being stolen

7 NOW COUNTING BEST TO BE WITH YOU ALONE,

COUNTING = alluding to "counting" the wealth or treasure of his son's royal blood; considering; also alluding to the "counting" of the beads or prayers: "like prayers divine,/ I must each day say o'er the very same,/ *Counting* no old thing old, thou mine, I thine" - Sonnet 108, lines 5-7; **BEST** = most royal; **ALONE** = the "all" and "one" of Southampton's motto; now considering that it's best to join you alone (i.e., in private) in making your claim as king, regardless of what Robert Cecil or anyone else in power thinks; now considering it best to simply visit with you alone in the Tower; "Save that to die, I *leave my love alone*" – Sonnet 66, line 14, i.e., leave him to face the royal succession by himself, as well as to leave him alone in the Tower; **YOU ALONE** = You, Southampton, *One for All, All for One*

8 THEN BETTERED THAT THE WORLD MAY SEE MY PLEASURE;

Then believing it would be best for England to see you as my son who deserves to succeed his mother the Queen; **BETTERED** = made better or happier, more peaceful; **THAT THE WORLD MAY SEE** = by making your identity as a prince known to the world, i.e., to England, so everyone can see it and realize it and possibly even act to prevent James from succeeding Elizabeth; **MY PLEASURE** = Oxford's happiness, which is based on his son's royal will, i.e., according to His Majesty's pleasure

9 SOME-TIME ALL FULL WITH FEASTING ON YOUR SIGHT,
ALL = Southampton, *One for All, All for One*; **ALL FULL** = satiated with your royal majesty; ("Such as is bent on sun-like majesty … being with *his presence glutted, gorged, and* full" – *1 Henry IV*, 3.2.79-84); **FEASTING ON YOUR SIGHT** = the way a subject's eyes feast upon the sight of a king; "Therefore are *feasts* so solemn and so rare" – Sonnet 52, line 5, referring to visits with his royal son in the Tower; "Thus did I keep my person fresh and new, my presence, like a robe pontifical, ne'er seen but wondered at, and so *my state, seldom, but sumptuous, show'd like a feast*, and wan by rareness and solemnity" – the King to his royal son Prince Hal in *1 Henry IV*, 3.2.53-59

10 AND BY AND BY CLEAN STARVED FOR A LOOK,
And then soon empty of you; **CLEAN STARVED FOR A LOOK** = "The pleasure that some *fathers feed upon* is my strict fast – I mean *my children's looks*, and therein fasting hast thou made me gaunt" – *Richard II*, 2.1.79-81, echoing "food to life" in line 1 above; with "fasting" in counterpoint to "feeding" or perhaps "feasting"

11 POSSESSING OR PURSUING NO DELIGHT,
Having no ability to possess you as my son and no ability to pursue your royal claim; "As a decrepit *father takes delight/ To see his active child* do deeds of youth" – Sonnet 37, lines 1-2

12 SAVE WHAT IS HAD OR MUST FROM YOU BE TOOK.
SAVE = except for; "Possessing no delight save what is had from you, pursuing none save what must be took (taken) from you" – Dowden; echoing "save your life" as in "And *saved my life*, saying, 'Not You'" – Sonnet 145, line 14, when Oxford records in the Dark Lady series how Elizabeth spared Southampton's life; **WHAT IS HAD** = what I already have, i.e., I do have you for my son with your royal blood; **OR MUST FROM YOU BE TOOK** = or, to put it another way, your royal claim that must now be stolen from you.

13 THUS DO I PINE AND SURFEIT DAY BY DAY,
Therefore I suffer from too little or too much of you; **DAY-BY-DAY** = still writing and/or compiling these verses by making day-to-day entries since the Rebellion; "like prayers divine,/ I must *each day* say o'er the very same" - Sonnet 108, lines 5-6; "For as the Sun is *daily* new and old,/ So is my love still telling what is told" - Sonnet 76, lines 13-14, referring to Southampton as the royal son

14 OR GLUTTONING ON ALL, OR ALLAWAY.
GLUTTONING ON = feasting on too much; "Pity the world, *or else this glutton be,/ To eat the world's due*, by the grave and thee" – Sonnet 1, lines 13-14; **ALL … ALL** = Southampton, *One for All, All for One*; have all of your or none of you; i.e., having you as my son is impossible, but not having you as my son is also impossible, literally and emotionally; a classic double-bind; **GLUTTONING ON ALL** = feasting on the sight or the thought of you; **ALL AWAY** = you away in the Tower; completely lost to me as my royal son; all your claim to the throne now gone; "*Thyself away* are present still with me" – Sonnet 47, line 10, referring to his son being in the Tower; ("*all away* suggests *all put away* or *all hidden*" – Booth)

(THE CENTER OF THE MONUMENT)

SONNETS 76-77

26 sonnets	---------------- (100 SONNETS) ---------------	26 sonnets
(1-------26)	27--------------------76 77-------------------126	(127-------152)
	(50 sonnets) *(50 sonnets)*	

Sonnet 76: "My Verse"

Sonnet 77: "Thy Book"

Part Two

THE INVENTION OF THE SONNETS
DAY FIFTY IN THE TOWER

(Center of the Monument)

Sonnet 76
And Keep Invention in a Noted Weed
That Every Word Doth Almost Tell My Name
29 March 1601

Sonnets 76-77 are at the exact center of the 100-sonnet sequence (27-126), which in turn forms the center of the larger 152-sonnet structure. Here in the middle of the monument, Oxford reveals and describes his "invention," or method of composing these private verses. It involves the strict limiting of his subject matter to "all one, ever the same" (Southampton, Elizabeth and himself) while "dressing old words new" around the family triangle, to create an appearance of variety. Sonnets 76-77 also anticipate the so-called "Rival Poet" series (78-86) in which Oxford records the sacrifice of his identity to the name "William Shakespeare."

Sonnet 76	Translation
Why is my verse so barren of new pride?	Why is this womb so barren of new royal blood?
So far from variation or quick change?	Why is it always the same without any change?
Why with the time do I not glance aside	Why, with the succession coming, don't I use
To new-found methods, and to compounds strange?	New methods and stranger mixtures of words?
Why write I still all one, ever the same,	Why do I write always of you, Elizabeth and me,
And keep invention in a noted weed,	And hide my method in the familiar garb of poetry,
That every word doth almost tell my name,	So that every word conceals and reveals me,
Showing their birth, and where they did proceed?	Chronicling your birth and growth to now?
O know, sweet love, I always write of you,	O know, royal son, I always write of you,
And you and love are still my argument:	And you and your royal blood are always my topic:
So all my best is dressing old words new,	So all my best is using new words for old ones,
Spending again what is already spent:	Spending blood [in words] that I've already spent:
For as the Sun is daily new and old,	For as my royal son daily lives and dies,
So is my love still telling what is told.	So he always informs this verse with his blood.

Here is the key to the special language of the Sonnets, describing how their words revolve around the family triangle – **All One, Ever the Same** – or Southampton, Elizabeth and Oxford. The two most important of the special words are **Love**, representing royal blood, and **Time**, signifying the ever-dwindling life span and reign of the Queen.

The story of the Sonnets is the struggle of *love*, or royal blood, to survive the *time* leading to Elizabeth's death and the succession to her throne. By this language, we are able to determine the chronological framework of the diary. The *time*, or chronology, leads to the Queen's death on March 24, 1603, marked by

REFERENCE EDITION 425

Sonnet 105, and then to her funeral on April 28, 1603, marked by Sonnet 125, and finally to Oxford's farewell to his royal son in the envoy of Sonnet 126, the last entry in the central 100-sonnet sequence.

MY VERSE = These private verses, the Book of Sonnets, the subject herein; this is the most important verse, as it holds the key to Oxford's special language and design.

WHY WRITE I STILL ALL ONE, EVER THE SAME = My unvarying subject matter consists of *all one* (Southampton, whose motto is *One for All, All for One*); *Ever the Same* (Queen Elizabeth, whose motto is *Ever the Same*); and me, *E. Ver* or *Ever*, Edward de Vere, Earl of Oxford. All my writing in these private verses is focused upon the three of us (although the two most important are Southampton and Elizabeth).

AND KEEP INVENTION IN A NOTED WEED = And I maintain my method (my "invention") by means of the familiar costume of conventional poetry.

EVERY WORD DOTH ALMOST TELL MY NAME = I do this so each and "every" word in these sonnets serves almost, but not quite, to reveal my identity.

SHOWING THEIR BIRTH AND WHERE THEY DID PROCEED = Every word here is also chronicling the life of my royal son, from his "birth" up to and including the record of your life in the tomb and womb of these sonnets, within which he continues to grow.

O KNOW, SWEET LOVE, I ALWAYS WRITE OF YOU = O know, my royal son, I am always writing about you in this chronicle of your life as a prince.

AND YOU AND LOVE ARE STILL MY ARGUMENT = And you and your *love* (royal blood) continue to be my topic.

SO ALL MY BEST IS DRESSING OLD WORDS NEW = Therefore, given that I restrict my topic to you, Elizabeth and me, the best I can do is use different words to express the same thoughts. For example, I consistently refer to the Queen (or her royal blood in you) as *Beauty* while also consistently representing her as *Fortune, Nature, Heaven, Mistress, Moon, Phoenix, Woman* and so on. In this way, *every word* revolves around my sole topic and spins outward to encompass all the lines of these verses. The words of this Special Language are akin to the letters of the DNA code on the ladder of the double helix.

THE SUN = my royal son: "Even so *my Sunne* one early morn did shine" – Sonnet 33, line 9

1 WHY IS MY VERSE SO BARREN OF NEW PRIDE?
The Book of Sonnets has now reached the halfway point in terms of the one hundred and fifty-two sonnets (not including the Bath epilogue); also this is the fiftieth verse since the Rebellion, so Oxford intends to write fifty more prison verses, with Sonnets 76-77 at their exact center; Oxford apparently will make adjustments to the "monument" later, to ensure this exact numerical arrangement; **MY VERSE** = The topic of this sonnet is *my verse*, i.e., all the verses of this diary of the Sonnets; and Oxford writes as a father attempting to give new birth to his royal son in these lines and to keep growing him until his royal claim to the throne is determined one way or the other; because of his disgrace and imprisonment, however, Southampton has virtually no prospect of becoming king, at least not by immediately succeeding Elizabeth; **BARREN** = as a womb is empty; "The conjunction of *verse* and *barren* anticipates the introduction in line 8 of the traditional idea of poems as poets' children" – Booth

"But if the *first heir of my invention* prove deformed, I shall be sorry it had so noble a godfather, and never after ear so *barren* a land, for fear it yield me still so bad a harvest."
- Oxford's first public dedication as "Shakespeare" to Southampton
Venus and Adonis, 1593

No. 76

BARREN OF NEW PRIDE = lacking additional royal blood; lacking new support for my son's royal claim

> Alack, what *poverty* my Muse brings forth,
> That, having such a scope to show her *pride*
> - Sonnet 103, lines 1-2
> (*Brings Forth* = gives birth to)

PRIDE = "Magnificent, splendid, or ostentatious adornment or ornamentation" – *OED*; recalling Southampton as "the world's *fresh ornament*" of Sonnet 1; "Began to clothe his wit in *state and pride*" – *Lucrece*, 1809-1810; "O noble English, that could entertain with half their forces the full *pride* of France" – *Henry V*, 1.2.111-112; "For *time* hath set a blot upon my *pride*" – *Richard II*, 3.2.81; "The *pride of kingly sway*" – *Richard II*, 4.1.206; "Thy kingly doom and sentence of his *pride*" – *Richard II*, 5.6.23; "And Richard fall in *height of all his pride*" – *Richard III*, 5.3.177; "See also *proud* in 98.9 where it means 'swelling,' 'pregnant'" – Booth, citing "Or from their *proud lap* pluck them where they grew" – Sonnet 98, line 8, referring to flowers, i.e., Henry Wriothesley as new flower of the Tudor Rose; "Made *proud by princes*, that advance their *pride*" – *Much Ado About Nothing*, 3.1.10

2 SO FAR FROM VARIATION OR QUICK CHANGE?
VARIATION = different subject matter, different method or technique; my topic never changes, only the words used to express it: "Fair, kind, and true, *varying to other words*" – Sonnet 105, line 10; **QUICK CHANGE** = sudden alteration; the only change is that of the words: "And *in this change* is my invention spent" – Sonnet 105, line 11; **QUICK** = "Living, endowed with life, in contrast to what is naturally inanimate" – *OED*, also citing "quick with child" said of a female in the stage of pregnancy when the motion of the fetus is felt, i.e., the quickening; apparently an inversion of an earlier phrase "with quick child" as in, "She was great with *quyk childe*," circa 1450; "Then shall Hector be whipped for Jaquetta that is *quick by him*" – *Love's Labour's Lost*, 5.2.674-675; "O, 'tis a parlous boy, bold, *quick*, ingenious, forward, capable; he is all the mother's from top to toe" – *Richard III*, 3.1.154-156; "our *quick blood*" – *Henry V*, 3.5.21; "The King with mighty and *quick-raised power*" – *1 Henry IV*, 4.4.12; also burning or "quick" fire; and lively or "quick" speech "full of vigor or acute reasoning," *OED*, citing *Art of English Poesie*, 1589: "An inscription ... in few verses, pithie, *quicke* and sententious"; also related to the power of medicine to give life; "I have seen a medicine that's able to breathe life into a stone, *quicken* a rock" – *All's Well That Ends Well*, 2.1.71-73; also related to sexual desire or "heat" in the female who will conceive, carry and give birth to a child who will *proceed* or issue from the womb, as in "Showing their *birth*, and where they did *proceed*" – line 8 below

3 WHY WITH THE TIME DO I NOT GLANCE ASIDE
WITH THE TIME = According to the time left in Elizabeth's life and reign; the chronological basis for this diary, which records "Love" or royal blood in Southampton in relation to *"Time"* or Elizabeth's ever-dwindling life span; with *"Love"* or royal blood introduced as the main topic in line 10; the time itself is often noted similarly, as in "the tenth (etc.) year of Her Majesty's reign"

> England ne'er had a king *until his time*
> - *1 Henry VI*, 1.1.8

> Where *wasteful time* debateth with decay
> To change your day of youth to sullied night:
> And *all in war with Time* for love of you
> - Sonnet 15, lines 11-13

> Time's thievish progress to eternity
> - Sonnet 77, line 8

> When in *the Chronicle of wasted time*

REFERENCE EDITION

- Sonnet 106, line 1

"In *the Queen's time* lately deceased"
- Oxford to King James, January 30, 1604

GLANCE ASIDE = turn away; look elsewhere

4 TO NEW FOUND METHODS, AND TO COMPOUNDS STRANGE?
METHODS = technique of writing these verses; an announcement that this sonnet will explain the method or "invention" of writing the Sonnets; Poetry was not an art "until by studious persons fashioned and reduced into a method of rules and precepts" – *Art of English Poesie*, 1589, cited by *OED*; **COMPOUNDS** = mixtures of chemicals used in alchemy, here mixtures of words; a glance at "compound words" such as verbs carrying a prefix; "And that *your love taught it this alchemy*" – Sonnet 114, line 4; also medical: "Every kynde of disease hath his owne Methode" – 1541, cited by *OED*; a "compound" or compound drug, mixing two or more elements as a remedy; suggesting that Oxford's method of writing is a kind of medicine for the wounds he and his son have suffered; "Reason, in itself confounded/ Saw division grow together,/ To themselves yet neither either,/ Simples were so well *compounded*" – *Phoenix and Turtle*, 1601, 41-44

5 WHY WRITE I STILL ALL ONE, EVER THE SAME,
STILL = constantly; always; eternally; **WHY WRITE I STILL** = a rhetorical question, stating that in fact I write always and consistently about **ALL ONE, EVER THE SAME**, i.e., the three family members (Southampton, Elizabeth, Oxford), around whom all the words of the Sonnets revolve, forming a "Family Triangle of Words" expanding outward to include all the words of the entire diary of Southampton's life in relation to that of his mother the Queen and the coming date with succession to the throne; I write only about these three members of the royal family triangle, which is further compressed into the *one* royal son and heir to the "seat" or throne:

> Resembling *sire, and child, and happy mother*,
> Who *all in one, one* pleasing note do sing
> - Sonnet 8, lines 11-12

> *Three themes in one*, which *won*drous scope affords...
> Which *three*, till now, never kept seat in *one*
> - Sonnet 105, lines 12, 14

> Of *him, myself, and thee*, I am forsaken,
> A torment *thrice threefold* to be crossed
> - Sonnet 133, lines 7-8

STILL = constantly, always; repeated in lines 10 and 14, with "always" in line 9; **ALL ONE** = "only one way" – Booth; all about "one" thing

6 AND KEEP INVENTION IN A NOTED WEED,
And I do not dress up my special language in any new costume, but, rather, I keep it by means of (and hide it within) the familiar costume of conventional love poems; **KEEP** = hold, retain, guard, occupy, inhabit, remain in, maintain, preserve, retain; echoing Southampton's imprisonment in the sense of being kept in prison, as in "Well have you argued, sir, and, for your pains, of capital treason we arrest you here. My Lord of Westminster, be it your charge to *keep* him safely till his day of trial" – *Richard II*, 4.1.150-154; echoing the Keeper of the Tower, who has the care of a prisoner, i.e., a gaoler; **INVENTION** = special language and design created uniquely for the Sonnets; "literary creation" – Booth; "something new found out or devised ... imagination, imaginative faculty as well as poetic fiction ... activity of the mind generally ... thought, idea, *device* ... skill employed in *contriving any thing to meet a difficulty*" – Schmidt; the latter definition aptly describing Oxford's need to create his "invention" for the Sonnets in order to avoid being charged with treason for putting forth a claim to the throne, i.e., to enable him to argue that, after all, the lines of these

verses are merely poetry without and political (much less unlawful) content; "used of thoughts couched in writing" – Schmidt; as in letters of correspondence, i.e., "I say she never did *invent this letter*; this is a man's *invention*, and his hand" – *As You Like It*, 4.3.28-29

> Fair, kind, and true, *varying to other words*,
> And *in this change* is **my invention** spent
> - Sonnet 105, lines 10-11

> How can my Muse want subject to **invent**
> Whilst thou dost breathe, that pour'st into my verse
> Thine own sweet argument, too excellent
> For every vulgar paper to rehearse…
> For who's so dumb that cannot write to thee,
> When thou thyself dost give **invention** light?
> - Sonnet 38, lines 1-4, 7-8

> Which, *laboring for* **invention**, *bear amiss*
> *The second burden of a former child!*
> - Sonnet 59, lines 3-4

> O blame me not if I no more can write!
> Look in your glass, and there appears a face
> That overgoes *my blunt* **invention** quite,
> *Dulling my lines*, and doing me disgrace.
> - Sonnet 103, lines

"The matter, after it had received many crosses, many *inventions* of delay" – Oxford to Robert Cecil, January 1602; "But if *the first heir of my invention* prove deformed" – dedication of *Venus and Adonis* to Southampton, 1593, referring to the invented name "William Shakespeare" and now, by extension, to his method of writing privately to Southampton; creating a means of both concealing and revealing at the same time, the way an ambassador memorizes his secret message before delivering it orally: "To thee I send this written ambassage" – Sonnet 26, line 3; **A NOTED WEED** = A familiar costume of conventional Elizabethan poetry; a disguise; a covering or concealment; a costume that includes the sexual allusions that spring from the royal/dynasty subject matter involving sexual attraction, sexuality, sexual intercourse, sperm and blood, conception, pregnancy, childbirth and blood lineage; **NOTED** = known; echoing "note-book" in which memorandums are written; also echoing "note-worthy"; marked with musical characters (these verses being "my songs and praises" of Sonnet 105, line 3 as well as "hymns" (Sonnet 29, line 12) and "prayers" (Sonnet 108, line 5); set down, committed to memory; observed, attended to; "An amber-coloured raven was *well noted*" – *Love's Labour's Lost*, 4.3.85; "I told you, I, he was a frantic fool, hiding his bitter jests in blunt behavior. And to be *noted* for a merry man" – The Taming of the Shrew, 3.2.12-14; "In this the antique and *well-noted* face of plain old form is much disfigured" – *King John*, 4.2.21-22; "But, sir, such wanton, wild, and usual slips as are companions *noted* and most *known* to youth and liberty" – *Hamlet*, 2.1.22-24; **WEED** = costume, garment, disguise; livery, dressing, outward appearance; "Thy youth's proud livery, so gazed on now,/ Will be a tottered *weed*" – Sonnet 2, lines 3-4; "And there the snake throws her enameled skin, *weed* wide enough to wrap a fairy in" – *A Midsummer Night's Dream*, 2.1.255-256; echoing Southampton as the Tudor Rose who has become a weed among "infection" or potential traitors in the Tower: "But if that flower with base infection meet,/ The basest *weed* outbraves his dignity./ For sweetest things turn sourest by their deeds;/ Lilies that fester smell far worse than *weeds*" – Sonnet 94, lines 11-14

7 **THAT EVERY WORD DOTH ALMOST TELL MY NAME,**
THAT = so that; similar to "*That* thereby beauty's *Rose* might never die" – Sonnet 1, line 2; **EVERY** = **EVER** = E. Ver, Edward deVere; **EVERY WORD** = the *word* "EVERY" doth *almost* tell my name; literally each and *every word* of these verses is being used to almost, but not quite, reveal Edward de Vere's

name and identity, as well as to show the growth of Southampton and his royal blood along the timeline of the diary as Elizabeth's own life rapidly dwindles on the way to her death and the date with succession.

"And *the Word was made flesh*" – *John, 1.14, Geneva Bible*, 1560

"Man shall not live by bread only, but by *every word* that proceedeth out of the mouth of God" – *Gospel of Mathew*, 4.4

EVERY WORD of the Sonnets stems from, and revolves around, the family triangle represented by *All One, Ever the Same*; the magical quality of the *invention* is created by the restriction of subject matter combined with the diversity of the words revolving around that consistent topic; **ALMOST TELL MY NAME** = (Q has 'fel' for *tell*); almost, or indirectly, reveals my identity; in an early poem, written before 1576, Oxford demonstrated another way in which *every word* could almost tell his name:

When thus the echo answered her to *every word* she spake:
Oh heavens! Who was the first that bred in me this *fever*? Vere
Who was the first that gave the wound whose fear I wear for *ever*? Vere
What tyrant, Cupid, to my harm usurps thy golden *quiver*? Vere
What sight first caught this heart and can from bondage it *deliver*? Vere

("The Earle of Oxforde"; *Fuller's Worthies' Library*, 1872, Vol. 1V)

8 SHOWING THEIR BIRTH, AND WHERE THEY DID PROCEED?
SHOWING THEIR BIRTH: revealing the birth of the words and of Southampton; "The conceit by which the poet speaks of himself and his poem as mother and child" – Booth

What makes him *show* besides *his birth*, such *pride* and such *untruth*? Youth.
"The Earle of Oxforde" (same verse noted in line 7)

SHOWING = presenting to the view; displaying; giving the appearance of; letting be seen, i.e., not concealing; revealing, communicating, instructing; proving, demonstrating; offering or committing; pointing the way to, guiding; "And all the more it seeks to hide itself, the bigger bulk it *shows*" – *The Tempest*, 3.1.80-81; **THEIR BIRTH** = the birth of the words is equated with the birth of Southampton, since the words (and numbers) of the Sonnets are woven together to form a womb within which to recreate his life and blood; "O vouchsafe me but this loving thought:/ 'Had my friend's Muse grown with this growing age,/ A *dearer birth than this* his love had brought/ To march in ranks of better equipage" – Sonnet 32, lines 9-12; "Even so *my Sunne one early morn did shine*" – Sonnet 33, line 9

As a decrepit *father* takes delight
To see his active *child* do deeds of youth,
So I, made lame by Fortune's dearest spite,
Take all my comfort of thy worth and truth.
For whether beauty, *birth*, or wealth, or wit,
Or any of these all, or all, or more,
Entitled in thy parts do crowned sit,
I make my love engrafted to this store.
- Sonnet 37, lines 1-8

(NOTE: the word "their" in "their birth" refers to the words, but Oxford is telling his son that the diary is recording "thy" birth; and in fact editors routinely emend "their" to "thy" elsewhere in the collection, as in these three examples: Q = "Excusing *their* sins more than their sins are" – Sonnet 35, line 8, usually emended to "*thy* sins"; Q = "When in dead night *their* fair imperfect shade," usually emended to "*thy* imperfect shade"; and Q = "Of *their* fair health, recounting it to me" – Sonnet 45, line 12, usually emended to "*thy* fair health"; leaving open the possibility that this line can be emended to "Showing *thy* birth, and

where *thou* didst proceed"); "**Nativity**, once in the main of light,/ *Crawls to maturity*, wherewith being *crowned*" – Sonnet 60, lines 5-6; "Commit to these waste blanks (the Sonnets), and thou shalt find/ Those **children** *nursed, delivered* from thy brain" – Sonnet 77, lines 10-11; "Yet be most *proud* of *that which I compile* (the Sonnets),/ Whose influence is thine, and **born of thee**" – Sonnet 78, lines 9-10; "Making *their tomb the* **womb** wherein they grew" – Sonnet 86, line 4; "Find the first conceit of love there **bred** (begotten, procreated)" – Sonnet 108, line 13; "You are so strongly in my purpose **bred**" – Sonnet 112, line 13; "If *my dear love* were but the **child** *of state,/* It might for *fortune's bastard* be unfathered" – Sonnet 124, lines 1-2;
WHERE THEY DID PROCEED = Where "every word" has issued or come forth in this diary up to now; where the life of Henry Wriothesley has proceeded to this entry, which corresponds with real time;
PROCEED = issue or come forth, as from the womb

"I believe in the Holy Ghost ... who *proceedeth* from the Father and the Son"
– Communion Service, Nicene Creed

"Man shall not live by bread only, but by *every word* that *proceedeth* out of the mouth of God"
– Gospel of Mathew, 4.4

"Look how *the father's face lives in his issue*"
– Ben Jonson on Shakespeare in the First Folio of plays, 1623

"Which I will esteem and acknowledge only to *proceed* from you"
- Oxford to Robert Cecil, December 4, 1601

PROCEED = "Continue, go on, carry on ... behave, pursue a course, conduct oneself ... advance through, make progress ... *result, arise, come from*" – Crystal & Crystal; **PROCEEDINGS** = "*line of descent*" – Crystal & Crystal

Hadst thou like us from our first swath *proceeded*
The sweet degrees that this brief world affords...
- *Timon of Athens*, 4.3.255-256

So, if the *issue* of the elder son
Succeed before the younger, I am King.
What plain *proceedings* is more plain than this?
Henry doth claim the crown...
And in this private plot be we the first
That shall salute our sovereign
With *honour of his birthright to the crown.*
- *2 Henry VI*, 2.2.50-61

But he hath forc'd us to compel this offer,
And it *proceeds from policy, not love.*
- *2 Henry IV*, 4.1.147-148

"When therefore he writes with precise and well-chosen words, with skillfully constructed and crystal-clear sentences, and with every art of dignified rhetoric, it cannot be but that some noble quality should be felt to *proceed* from his work" – Oxford's Letter to the Reader of *The Courtier*, 1572; "*Love is a Babe*: then might I not say so,/ *To give full growth* to that which *still doth grow*" – Sonnet 115, lines 13-14; "O Thou *my lovely Boy*.../ Who hast by waning *grown*" – Sonnet 126, lines 1, 3

9 **O KNOW, SWEET LOVE, I ALWAYS WRITE OF YOU,**
O = Oxford; **KNOW** = be certain; possibly in the sense of receiving these instructions to a prince from his father, i.e., be informed, or know this to be the truth; recognize, perceive, learn; echoing the next verse:

"And *of this book this **learning** mayst thou taste*/ ... These offices, so oft as thou wilt look,/ Shall profit thee, and much enrich thy book" – Sonnet 77, lines 4, 13-14; **SWEET** = royal; **LOVE** = royal son of royal blood; **O KNOW, SWEET LOVE** = oh, know this, my royal son; "*O my son*" – the King to Prince Hal in *2 Henry IV*, 4.5.177; "*Sweet* Prince" – *Richard III*, 3.1.7; "That *sweet aspect of princes*" – *Henry VIII*, 3.2.369; "Thy self thy foe, to *thy sweet self* too cruel" – Sonnet 1, line 8; "And *your sweet semblance* to some other give" – Sonnet 13, line 4; "What's new to speak, what now to register,/ That may express my love, or thy dear merit?/ Nothing, *sweet boy*, but yet like prayers divine,/ I must each day say o'er the very same,/ Counting no old thing old, *thou mine, I thine,*/ Even was when *first I hallowed by thy fair name*" – Sonnet 108, lines 3-8; "The living record of your memory" – Sonnet 55, line 8; "Your monument shall be my gentle verse" – Sonnet 81, line 9; **I ALWAYS WRITE OF YOU** = You are the supreme, constant topic of my private verses of the Sonnets; "Since *all alike* my songs and praises be/ To one, of one, still such, and ever so" – Sonnet 105, lines 3-4; *always* is echoed in the next line by *still*

10 AND YOU AND LOVE ARE STILL MY ARGUMENT:

YOU AND LOVE = You (your person, your life) and your royal blood; "And *all in war with Time for love of you,*/ As he takes from you, I engraft you new" – Sonnet 15, line 13; "*Love is not love/ Which alters when it alteration finds/ Or bends with the remover to remove*" – Sonnet 116, lines 2-4, declaring that royal blood does not change, even amid the "alteration" of monarchs on the throne (i.e., amid the succession of James); "O thou my *lovely* Boy, who in thy power/ Doth hold *time's* fickle glass, his sickle hour" – Sonnet 126, lines 1-2

> *Thy love* is better than high birth to me
> - Sonnet 91, line 9

STILL = always, eternally; repeated from "Why write I *still* all one, ever the same" (line 5 above) and repeated again in "So is my love *still* telling what is told" (line 14 below); "Since *all alike* my songs and praises be/ To one, of one, *still* such, and ever so./ Kind is my love today, tomorrow kind,/ *Still* constant in a wondrous excellence" – Sonnet 105, lines 3-6; **MY ARGUMENT** = My topic in the Sonnets, which is "you and love" or you and your royal blood; the "argument" of a poem or play (or piece of literary work such as this diary), as in the *Argument* printed as preface to *The Rape of Lucrece*, dedicated in 1594 to Southampton

> O my son,
> God put it (i.e., the crown) in thy mind to take it hence,
> That thou mightst win the more thy father's love...
> For ***all my reign hath been but as a scene***
> ***Acting that argument***
> - *2 Henry IV*, 4.5.177-179, 197-198

> Belike this show imports the *argument* of the play...
> Have you heard the *argument*? Is there no offence in't?
> - *Hamlet*, 3.2.141, 234

In Sonnet 105, Oxford again shows how his *invention* works by "dressing old words new" (line 11 below), i.e., how his *argument* itself may be stated using different words:

> Fair, kind, and true, is all ***my argument***
> Fair, kind, and true, *varying to other words,*
> And in this change is my *invention* spent,
> Three themes in one, which *wondrous scope affords*
> - Sonnet 105, line 9

The result is that his topic of *you and love* is the same as *fair, kind, and true*, the latter words also referring to Southampton and his royal blood; my son is *fair* or royal; he is *kind* or the natural son of the Queen, having inherited her Tudor blood; and he is *true* because of his true rights to the throne and in relation to me, Oxford, *Nothing Truer than Truth*.

> How can my Muse want subject to *invent*
> Whilst thou dost breathe, that pour'st into *my verse*
> Thine own sweet ***argument***
> - Sonnet 38, lines 1-3

> I grant, sweet love, thy lovely ***argument***
> Deserves the travail of a worthier pen
> - Sonnet 79, lines 5-6

> Return, forgetful Muse, and straight redeem
> In gentle numbers time so idly spent;
> Sing to the ear that doth thy lays esteem
> And gives thy pen both skill and ***argument***.
> - Sonnet 100, lines 5-8

> Alack, what poverty my Muse brings forth (begets),
> That, having such a *scope* to show her *pride*,
> The ***argument*** all bare is of more worth
> Than when it hath my added praise beside.
> - Sonnet 103, lines 1-3

11 SO ALL MY BEST IS DRESSING OLD WORDS NEW,
ALL = Southampton, *One for All, All for One*; **ALL MY BEST** = all the best that I can do, to create an appearance of variety in these sonnets ; **DRESSING OLD WORDS NEW** = The central method of the *invention* or special language of the Sonnets; replacing old words with new ones, while maintaining consistent meanings; such as *Beauty* for the Queen but also *Heaven, Nature, Fortune, Dian, Mistress, Phoenix, Moon*, etc; "putting new clothes on old words" or "dressing old words up as new ones" – Booth; "Fair, kind, and true, **varying to other words**,/ And in this change is my invention spent,/ Three themes in one, which *wondrous scope* affords" – Sonnet 105, lines 10-12

12 SPENDING AGAIN WHAT IS ALREADY SPENT:
SPENDING = exhausting, depleting; spending his invention and spending his son's royal blood to fill up these lines; "We shall not *spend* a large expense of time" – *Macbeth*, 5.9. 26; **ALREADY** = echoing "all" for Southampton; **ALREADY SPENT** = words and time and blood already used up, in this diary; exhausted, as in "And in this change is my *invention spent*" of Sonnet 105, line 11; "To royalize his blood, I *spent* mine own" – *Richard III*, 1.3.125

13 FOR AS THE SUN IS DAILY NEW AND OLD,
THE SUN = The royal son, i.e., Southampton, my royal son; "Even so *my Sunne* one early morn did shine/ With all triumphant splendor on my brow/ … *Suns of the world* (princes of England) may stain, when *heaven's sun* (Elizabeth's son) staineth" – Sonnet 33, lines 9-10, 13-14; **DAILY** = as these verses have been written/compiled *day-by-day* since the Rebellion; the rising and setting of the sun or royal son, setting the pace for the entries of this diary; **NEW AND OLD** = (reflecting "dressing *old* words *new*" in line 11 above, i.e., the words of the sonnets rise and fall in synchronization with "the Sun" or with my royal son); new with royal hope and genuine Tudor blood (recorded in this monument to preserve him) and yet older with the onrush of time, i.e., Elizabeth's mortal decay, leading to succession; "In the *old* age black (our son in disgrace) was not counted fair,/ Or if it were it bore not beauty's name" – Sonnet 127, lines 1-2

14 SO IS MY LOVE STILL TELLING WHAT IS TOLD.
MY LOVE = my royal son; "the simile invites the reader momentarily to take *my love* as 'my beloved' – 'my sunlike beloved'" – Booth; **STILL** = "eternally, unfailingly" – Booth; **TELLING** = narrating, writing,

informing; Southampton is informing these verses or "telling" their story with his identity and blood as I record his life in this diary; therefore, my royal son is *"the onlie begetter of these ensuing sonnets"* as the dedication of 1609 will state; echoing "That every word doth *almost tell* my name" – line 7 above; to "tell" is also to count or number, as in counting these "numbers" or sonnets ("And in fresh *numbers number* all your graces" – Sonnet 17, line 6); "the measure then of *one* is easily *told*" – *Love's Labour's Lost*, 5.2.190; **TELLING WHAT IS TOLD** = my royal son is speaking for himself, through me, in these verses; in effect, we have changed places; the book is written with my son's "love" or royal blood; in the next verse, Oxford dedicates this diary of the Sonnets to Southampton as "thy book" – Sonnet 77, line 14

May I requite *his birth* with faith? Then faithful will I die? Ay.
And I, that knew *this lady* well,
Said, Lord how great a miracle,
To her how Echo *told* the *truth,*
As *true* as Phoebus' oracle
- (The Earl of Oxford; written by 1576; *His Birth* = the birth of his royal son in 1574; *This Lady* = Queen Elizabeth, the sovereign lady; *Truth* = Oxford, the buried truth of their son)

O God, Horatio, what a *wounded name*,
Things standing thus unknown, shall I leave behind me.
If thou didst *ever* hold me in thy heart,
Absent thee from felicity awhile,
And in this harsh world draw thy breath in pain
To *tell* my story
- *Hamlet*, 5.2.351-356

Part Two

DAY FIFTY-ONE IN THE TOWER

(Center of the Monument)

DEDICATION OF "THIS BOOK" TO SOUTHAMPTON

Sonnet 77
Thy Book
30 March 1601

Having just described his "invention" of the Sonnets, Oxford uses the companion verse to dedicate "this book" to Southampton, who thereby becomes "the onlie begetter" of Shake-Speares Sonnets, as the Dedication will later indicate. In effect, Oxford is transferring both ownership and authorship to his royal son. This is "thy book," he tells him, and the sonnets are "those children nursed, delivered from thy brain."

Sonnet 77	Translation
Thy glass will show thee how thy beauties wear	Your mirror will show how your royal life fades,
Thy dial how thy precious minutes waste,	Your sundial how your royal claim diminishes,
The vacant leaves thy mind's imprint will bear,	The pages of this book will give birth in your mind,
And of this book this learning mayst thou taste.	And you may absorb what grows in you.
The wrinkles which thy glass will truly show,	Your age that your mirror will reflect,
Of mouthed graves will give thee memory,	Will be devoured by hungry graves,
Thou by thy dial's shady stealth mayst know	And by your own time's withering you will know
Time's thievish progress to eternity.	Elizabeth's coming death that robs your royal claim.
Look what thy memory cannot contain,	Regardless of what you yourself may not recall,
Commit to these waste blacks, and thou shalt find	Memorize these sad but true verses and you'll find
Those children nursed, delivered from thy brain,	These sonnets growing in the womb of your brain,
To take a new acquaintance of thy mind.	So you can always remember what they contain.
These offices, so oft as thou wilt look,	These sacred duties, whenever you perform them,
Shall profit thee, and much enrich thy book.	Will let you see your royalty in this, your book.

1 THY GLASS WILL SHOW THEE HOW THY BEAUTIES WEAR,
THY GLASS = your mirror and hourglass; these sonnets, reflecting you; ("Thou art *thy mother's glass*" – Sonnet 3, line 9; "Give me that *glass*, and therein will I read: No deeper wrinkles yet? Hath sorrow struck so many blows upon this face of mine and made no deeper wounds?" – the king, giving up his crown, in *Richard II*, 4.3.276-279); **THY BEAUTIES** = your royal blood inherited from the Queen; ("These sunbeams in mine eye, *these beauties* make me die" – early Oxford verse, circa early 1570s; signed *E.O.*, published in *The Phoenix Nest*, 1593); "And *all those beauties whereof now he's King*/ Are vanishing, or vanished out of sight" – Sonnet 63, lines 6-7; "O death, made *proud with pure and princely beauty*" – King John, 4.3.35; **WEAR** = (*Q* has "were" – which also yields an apt reading, because Southampton's "beauties" or blood from Queen Elizabeth are in the past, in terms of having a claim to the throne); endure the ravages of time, as well as fade

REFERENCE EDITION 435

2 THY DIAL HOW THY PRECIOUS MINUTES WASTE:
DIAL = timepiece; sundial, keeping track of the Sun or royal son; your dial will tell you how; **PRECIOUS** = royal; "Tendering the *precious* safety of my prince" – *Richard II*, 1.1.32; "I wasted time, and now doth time waste me, for now hath time made me his numb'ring clock … whereto my finger, like a *dial's* point, is pointing still" – *Richard II*, 5.5.49-54; "This precious book of love" – *Romeo and Juliet*, 1.4.87; see line 4 below; **MINUTES** = "So do *our minutes hasten to their end*" – Sonnet 60, line 2; **WASTE** = fail to gain the crown; "But *beauty's waste* hath in the world an end" – Sonnet 9, line 11; "When in *the Chronicle of wasted time*" – Sonnet 106, line 1

3 THE VACANT LEAVES THY MIND'S IMPRINT WILL BEAR,
VACANT LEAVES = the blank pages remaining of the Book of Sonnets, written by your life, which I am recording; ("Thou thyself doth give invention light" – Sonnet 38, line 8); **IMPRINT** = "Never before *Imprinted*"– title page of The Sonnets, 1609; **BEAR** = give birth to, recreate; similar to line 14 of the previous verse, Sonnet 76 ("So is my love still telling what is told"), i.e., Southampton is "telling" the contents of the Sonnets; but now they must be imprinted upon his mind

4 AND OF THIS BOOK THIS LEARNING MAYST THOU TASTE.
THIS BOOK = This Book of Sonnets, now being dedicated to his royal son; "And thy commandment all alone shall live within *the book* and volume of my brain" – *Hamlet*, 1.5.102-103; "If that the Dolphin there, thy princely son, can in *this book* of beauty read, 'I love,' her dowry shall weigh equal with a queen" – *King John*, 2.1.484-486; "This precious book of love, this unbound lover, to beautify him only lacks a cover … That book in many's eyes doth share the glory that in gold clasps locks in the golden story. So shall you share all that he doth possess, by having him, making yourself no less" – *Romeo and Juliet*, 1.4.87-88; 91-94; **THIS LEARNING** = "Is not birth, beauty, good shape, discourse, manhood, learning, gentleness, virtue, youth, liberality and such like, the spice and salt that season a man?" – *Troilus and Cressida*, 1.2.253-255; "But thou art all my art, and dost advance/As high as *learning* my rude ignorance" – the next verse, Sonnet 78, lines 13-14

5 THE WRINKLES WHICH THY GLASS WILL TRULY SHOW
WRINKLES – signs of time having passed; "When hours have drained his blood and filled his brow/ With *lines and wrinkles*" – Sonnet 63, lines 3-4; **THY GLASS** = "Give me that *glass*, and therein will I read: No deeper *wrinkles* yet?" - the King in *Richard II*, 4.3.276-277; **TRULY** = related to Oxford, *Nothing Truer than Truth*; the truth of you, reflected in these sonnets that comprise your book; "Thou *truly* fair wert *truly* sympathized/ In true plain words by thy *true*-telling friend" – Sonnet 82, lines 11-12; "I do rightfully and *truly* inform Her Majesty" – Oxford memo, unaddressed, Huntington Library MS EL 2344, Chiljan 144

6 OF MOUTHED GRAVES WILL GIVE THEE MEMORY:
MOUTHED GRAVES = open graves; the tomb of this monument, which is preserving your life and is still being constructed; graves with open mouths; ("their tomb the womb" – Sonnet 86, line 4); **GIVE THEE MEMORY** = preserve you for future readers; "the living record of your *memory*" – Sonnet 55, line 8; "From hence your *memory* death cannot take/ … You still shall live, such virtue hath my pen,/ Where breath most breathes, even in the mouths of men" – Sonnet 81, lines 3, 13-14; **WRINKLES** (from line 5) in relation to **GRAVES**:

> The *wrinkles in my brows, now filled with blood*,
> Were likened oft to kingly sepulchres;
> For who liv'd King but I could dig his *grave*?
> And who durst smile when Warwick bent his brow?
> Lo now my glory smear'd with dust and blood!
> - *3 Henry VI*, 5.2.19-23

> What is thy body but a *swallowing grave*?
> - *Venus and Adonis*, 757

7 THOU BY THY DIAL'S SHADY STEALTH MAYST KNOW
SHADY STEALTH = dark theft, i.e., time is stealing his life and royal claim; the shadow stealing over Southampton, covering him with the darkness of the Queen's imperial cloud or frown: "Anon permit *the basest clouds to ride/ With ugly rack on his celestial face,/ And from the forlorn world his visage hide,/ Stealing unseen to west with this disgrace*" – Sonnet 33, lines 7-8; literally the stealthy progress of the dial's shade; "What is your substance, whereof are you made,/ That millions of strange *shadows* on you tend?/ Since every one hath, every one, one *shade*,/ And you, but one, can every *shadow* lend"
– Sonnet 53, lines 1-4

8 TIME'S THIEVISH PROGRESS TO ETERNITY.
Mortal time is stealing your life, but your life is also being poured into this diary, which is becoming your monument to preserve you for eternity; "When *in eternal lines to time* thou grow'st " – Sonnet 18; time is robbing your royal claim for eternity; Southampton himself stole his own claim, however, by his act of treason; so he is also "that sweet *thief* which sourly robs from me" – Sonnet 35, line 14; and others threaten to steal him as a prince to put him on the throne for their own ends: "And even thence thou wilt be *stol'n*, I fear,/ For truth proves *thievish* for a prize so dear" – Sonnet 48, lines 13-14; but time itself is robbing Southampton's inheritance of the crown, forever; Time = Elizabeth's ever-waning life, her *thievish royal progress* to death and eternal life, forming the chronological basis for this diary or book

9 LOOK WHAT THY MEMORY CANNOT CONTAIN,
Whatever you yourself cannot recall; **THY MEMORY** = the Sonnets, however, will be "the *living record of your memory*" – Sonnet 55, line 8; suggesting that his son has been attempting to memorize these verses the way ambassadors memorize their secret official messages or "ambassages" before traveling abroad and delivering them orally: "To thee I send *this written ambassage*" – Sonnet 26, line 3

10 COMMIT TO THESE WASTE BLACKS, AND THOU SHALT FIND
COMMIT TO = memorize; **WASTE BLACKS** = *Q* has "blacks," but most editors emend the word to "blanks" = i.e., these empty pages being filled with your life; without Southampton, the verses are wasted by time and therefore they are blank; but the lines of the Sonnets are also "blacks" as in "His beauty shall in *these black lines* be seen" – Sonnet 63, line 13, referring to the blackness of disgrace that covers Southampton and therefore covers these lines of verse; (and also "black" as being recorded in black ink); and also the Sonnets are now becoming "the Chronicle of *wasted* time" – Sonnet 106, line 1

11 THOSE CHILDREN NURSED, DELIVERED FROM THY BRAIN,
THOSE CHILDREN NURSED = the verses of the Sonnets are Oxford's children, or rather his child; and from now on they will be Southampton's own children, created or written by his own life; ("Showing *their birth* and where they did *proceed*" – Sonnet 76, line 8); as a boy Oxford had used the metaphor of pieces of writing as "children":

> My very honorable Sir. I have received your letters, full of humanity and courtesy, and strongly resembling your great love and singular affection towards me, *like true children duly procreated of such a mother*...
> - Oxford to Burghley, August 19, 1563; in French, at age thirteen
> (Translated by W.P. Fowler)

(John Lyly used the nursing metaphor in his 1580 dedication of *Euphues and His England* to Oxford, referring to his previous book (*Euphues, The Anatomy of Wit*) as a child he had "*sent to a noble man* [Oxford himself] *to nurse*")

DELIVERED FROM THY BRAIN = born of your mind; ("Those children who were delivered from thy brain, having been nursed" – Booth); a play on Ver in *delivered* as in:

> "What wight first caught this heart and can from bondage it *deliver*? Vere"
> – Oxford poem, circa 1576-1581 or earlier

12 **TO TAKE A NEW ACQUAINTANCE OF THY MIND.**
The full thought resembles a Christian paradox: "whosoever will save his life shall lose it; and whosoever will lose his life for my sake shall find it" – cited by Booth; in pouring himself into these verses, which are recording his loss of the throne as a king, Southampton will receive his life and identity back again

13 **THESE OFFICES, SO OFT AS THOU WILT LOOK,**
OFFICES = duties, i.e., the acting of reading and memorizing these lines

14 **SHALT PROFIT THEE, AND MUCH ENRICH THY BOOK.**
PROFIT = "hoping that Her Majesty will have an equal regard in her countenancing the cause as well to them that *study her profit* as they which covet nothing more than their own" – Oxford to Burghley, June 7, 1595, Chiljan 106; "Your good admonishments for the observance of good order according to your appointed rules, I am resolved (God aiding) to keep with all diligence as a thing that I may know and consider to tend especially to *my own good and profit*" – Oxford to Burghley, August 19, 1563, in French at age thirteen (cited in line 11 above); **ENRICH** = make more royal; **THY BOOK** = the Book of Sonnets (same as in line 4), which is Southampton's book, is now dedicated to him within the tomb and womb here at the center of the Monument; "And now I will unclasp a *secret book*, and to your quick-conceiving discontents I'll read you matter deep and dangerous, as full of peril and adventurous spirit as to o'er-walk a current roaring loud on the un-steadfast footing of a spear" – *1 Henry IV*, 1.3.186-191

Part Two

THE "SHAKESPEARE" SACRIFICE BEGINS
DAY FIFTY-TWO IN THE TOWER

Sonnet 78
Every Alien Pen
A Double Majesty
31 March 1601

Oxford begins the "Rival Poet" series (Sonnets 78-86) involving the sacrifice of his identity, both as the father of Southampton and as the rival "Shakespeare" linked publicly to his royal son. "Every Alien pen" is the pen name of E. Ver, Edward de Vere, and this pseudonym also derives "fair assistance" or royal inspiration from Southampton, just as Oxford gets it for his private sonnets. The result is the "double Majesty" of Shakespeare's public works and the Sonnets. Oxford confirms that the commoner Mr. Henry Wriothesley imprisoned in the Tower is the "onlie begetter" of the Sonnets by writing that the "influence" behind these verse "is thine, and borne of thee."

Sonnet 78	Translation
So oft have I invoked thee for my Muse,	I have invoked you for my inspiration so often,
And found such fair assistance in my verse,	And have found your royal help for my sonnets,
As every *Alien* pen hath got my use,	So now "Will Shakespeare" uses it, too,
And under thee their poesy disperse.	And serves you with his newly published poem.
Thine eyes, that taught the dumb on high to sin	Your reflected royalty, which enabled me to write,
And heavy ignorance aloft to fly,	And gave inspiration to my sad lack of knowledge,
Have added feathers to the learned's wing,	Has added to the power of "Shakespeare's" verse,
And given grace a double Majesty.	And made your royal Majesty doubly known.
Yet be most proud of that which I compile,	But be your most royal self in these sonnets,
Whose influence is thine, and borne of thee.	Which you alone influence, having begotten them.
In others' works thou dost but mend the style,	In "Shakespeare's" works you improve the style,
And Arts with thy sweet graces graced be.	And lend his art your royal graces.
But thou art all my art, and dost advance	But you create all my skill here, and you elevate
As high as learning my rude ignorance.	My skill to match your lofty royal self.

1 SO OFT HAVE I INVOKED THEE FOR MY MUSE
So often have I used you (Southampton) as my inspiration for these verses; **MUSE** = "So he that takes the pain to 'op the book/ Reaps not the gifts of *goodly golden muse*" – Earl of Oxenforde to the reader of *Cardanus' Comforte* as translated by Thomas Bedingfield, 1573

2 AND FOUND SUCH FAIR ASSISTANCE IN MY VERSE,
FAIR ASSISTANCE = royal help from Southampton, who is *fair* or royal; "From *fairest* creatures we desire increase" – Sonnet 1, line 1; **MY VERSE** = these private sonnets; "Why is *my verse* so barren of new pride?" – Sonnet 76, line 1

3 AS EVERY *ALIEN* PEN HATH GOT MY USE
EVERY = E. Ver, Edward de Vere, *Ever or Never*; "That *every* word doth *almost tell my name*" – Sonnet 76

REFERENCE EDITION 439

EVERY ALIEN PEN = The pen of "Shakespeare", which is actually my pen, i.e., *"E. Ver's Pen"*; "And art almost an *alien* to the hearts of all the Court and Princes of my blood" – *1 Henry IV*, 3.2.34-35; **HAS GOT MY USE** = has enlisted my help

4 AND UNDER THEE THEIR POESY DISPERSE.
UNDER THEE = in your name, by dedication; as "Shakespeare" dedicated *Venus and Adonis* of 1593 and *Lucrece* of 1594 to Southampton; **THEIR POESY** = "Shakespeare's" published poems, including *The Phoenix and Turtle* of this year, 1601; here again Oxford is using the plural form when he really means the singular, as in "fairest creatures" for Southampton in Sonnet 1, line 1.

5 THINE EYES, THAT TAUGHT THE DUMB ON HIGH TO SING
THINE EYES = your royal eyes or suns; "*thine own bright eyes*" – Sonnet 1, line 5; "An *eye* more bright" – Sonnet 20, line 5; "And scarcely greet me with *that sun, thine eye*" – Sonnet 49, line 6, to Southampton as prince; and to Elizabeth as monarch: "Commanded by the motion of *thine eyes*" – Sonnet 149, line 12; **THAT TAUGHT THE DUMB** = that taught me; (Oxford is "dumb" or without the power to speak the truth publicly; and "Shakespeare" is "dumb" because it's only a pen name; "For who's so *dumb* that cannot write to thee,/ When thou thyself dost give invention light?" – Sonnet 38, lines 7-8; "Who *taught* thee first to sigh, alas, my heart" – Oxford's early sonnet to Elizabeth, circa 1572, line 1; "Who *taught* thee how to make me love thee more" – Sonnet 150, line 9, to Elizabeth; **ON HIGH TO SING** = to sing your royal praises to the heights of your majesty

6 AND HEAVY IGNORANCE ALOFT TO FLY,
HEAVY IGNORANCE = weary, suffering, painful ignorance; i.e., my own; my inability to speak the truth about you; state of being in darkness, without the truth; "I say, this house is *as dark as ignorance*, though *ignorance were as dark as hell*" – *Twelfth Night*, 4.2.45-46; and the pen name "Shakespeare" is also "ignorant" or lacking information, without Oxford's assistance; **ALOFT TO FLY** = to compose lofty words for you, in these verses; i.e., that taught heavy ignorance to fly aloft

7 HAVE ADDED FEATHERS TO THE LEARNED'S WING
You have added feathers to my quill; you have helped me soar; **FEATHERS** =

> "Yes trust them not: for there is an upstart Crow, beautified with our *feathers*, that with his *Tiger's heart wrapped in a Player's hide*, supposes he is as well able to bombast out a blank verse as the best of you: and being an absolute *Johannes fac totum*, is in his own conceit the only Shake-scene in a country" – *Greene's Groatsworth of Wit*, 1592, ostensibly by Robert Greene, a member of Oxford's circle of writers who had dedicated works to the earl; foreshadowing the introduction of the pen name "Shakespeare" several months prior to its first appearance in 1593, as the signature to the dedication of *Venus and Adonis* to Southampton

ADDED FEATHERS = "a metaphor from falconry" – Booth; Oxford was skilled in the noble art of falconry; the term here refers to "imping" or "engrafting extra feathers in the wing of a bird so as to mend it and improve its ability to fly high" – Booth

8 AND GIVEN GRACE A DOUBLE MAJESTY.
GRACE = royal grace; "And *kneel for grace* and mercy at my feet; I am *thy sovereign*" – *3 Henry VI*, 1.1.75-76; "And in my conscience do repute *His Grace* the rightful heir to England's royal seat" – *2 Henry VI*, 5.1.177-178; **DOUBLE MAJESTY** = Twice the kingly glory; "Serving with looks *his sacred majesty*" – Sonnet 7, line 4

9 YET BE MOST PROUD OF THAT WHICH I COMPILE,
PROUD = filled with royal blood; be yourself, a king, who reads these sonnets testifying to your royal blood; "Why is my verse *so barren of new pride*"- Sonnet 76, line 1; "Making a couplement of *proud*

compare/ With Sunne and Moone" – Sonnet 21, lines 5-6, the royal pair, Southampton and Elizabeth);
THAT WHICH I COMPILE = these sonnets, which I am composing/compiling as entries of a diary according to time; "While comments of your praise, richly *compiled*" – Sonnet 85, line 2; "Did never *sonnet for her sake compile*" – *Love's Labour's Lost*, 4.3.131

10 **WHOSE INFLUENCE IS THINE, AND BORN OF THEE.**
Whose inspiration, substance and power all come from you, my royal son or Sunne or star; and is now your child; "Whereon *the stars in secret influence* comment" – Sonnet 15, line 4; "by her *fair influence foster'd, illumined, cherished, kept alive*" – *The Two Gentlemen of Verona*, 3.1.183-184; "and move under the influence of the most received star" – *All's Well That Ends Well*, 2.1.53-54; "I find my zenith doth depend upon a most auspicious star, whose *influence*" – *The Tempest*, 1.2.181-182; "to you, *whose star-like nobleness gave life and influence* to their whole being" – *Timon of Athens*, 5.1.61-63; "O thou clear god, and patron of all light,/ From whom each lamp and shining star doth borrow/ *The beauteous influence* that makes him bright,/ There lives *a son that suck'd an earthly mother,/ May lend thee light*, as thou dost lend to other" – Venus, of Adonis in *Venus and Adonis*, stanza 142; **BORN OF THEE** = Q spelling is "borne" but emended to "born" by Booth and others; referring to Southampton's birth; also, to his "giving birth" to these verses; linking him to "the *onlie begetter* of these ensuing sonnets, Mr. W. H." of the 1609 dedication; (these lines, 9-10, are straightforward testimony that each verse of the Sonnets is inspired by one person only, i.e., Southampton)

11 **IN OTHERS' WORKS THOU DOST BUT MEND THE STYLE,**
OTHERS' WORKS = the works attributed to "Shakespeare"; **MEND** = improve, make better; **THE STYLE** = literary quality

12 **AND ARTS WITH THY SWEET GRACES GRACED BE.**
ARTS = the published "Shakespeare" poems; also learning, scholarship; "A man of sovereign parts he is esteemed; well fitted in *arts*, glorious in arms" – *Love's Labour's Lost*, 2.1.45; the art of these sonnets, which is "tongue-tied by authority" - Sonnet 66, line 9; **THY SWEET GRACES** = your royal graces; "*My sovereign, I confess your royal graces*, showered on me daily ... For *your great graces*, heaped upon me" – *Henry VIII*, 3.2.166-167,174-175; **GRACES GRACED BE** = the works attributed to "Shakespeare" are graced or made royal by your royal graces; "And daily *graced by the emperor*" – *The Two Gentlemen of Verona*, 1.3.58

13 **BUT THOU ART ALL MY ART, AND DOST ADVANCE**
ALL = Southampton, *One for All, All for One*; **ALL MY ART** = you are inseparable from the art of these sonnets; "And *art* made tongue-tied by authority" – Sonnet 66, line 9; **AND DOST ADVANCE** = and you lift up, raise to a higher worth and dignity; "my low-declined honour to *advance*" – *Lucrece*, line 1705

14 **AS HIGH AS LEARNING MY RUDE IGNORANCE.**
AS HIGH = as highly royal; as in Your Highness; "Who will believe my verse in time to come/ If it were filled with your most *high* deserts" - Sonnet 17, lines 1-2; "his *high blood's royalty* ... my *high* blood's royalty" – *Richard II*, 1.1.58, 71; **AS LEARNING** = as intelligence, i.e., as knowledge of you that comes from your life; **MY RUDE IGNORANCE** = my otherwise-empty thoughts, which are nothing without you to fill them with your living record; **IGNORANCE** =; "The common curse of mankind, folly and *ignorance*" – *Troilus and Cressida*, 2.3.27-28; "*a cell of ignorance ... a prison* for a debtor" – *Cymbeline*, 3.3.32-33; "Let me not burst in *ignorance*" – *Hamlet*, 1.4.46; "The greater cantle of the world is lost with very *ignorance*; we have kiss'd away kingdoms and provinces" – *Antony and Cleopatra*, 3.10.6-8; **RUDE**: raw, crude, unformed; harsh, rough, unpleasing; uncivilized or unrefined; ill-mannered, uncivil, coarse; "for it pity men of such rare wits should be subject to the pleasure of such *rude* grooms" – *Groatsworth*, later in the same now-famous passage quoted in line 7 above; some Oxfordian scholars, such as Stephanie Hughes and Nina Green, argue with considerable persuasion that Oxford used "Robert Greene" as a pen name and wrote *Groatsworth* himself.

THE "SHAKESPEARE" SACRIFICE
DAY FIFTY-THREE IN THE TOWER

Sonnet 79
Now My Gracious Numbers are Decayed
My Sick Muse Doth Give Another Place
1 April 1601

To gain his son's eventual liberation from the Tower and a royal pardon, Oxford must now "give another place" in terms of being the poet (and the father) who sings Southampton's praises. His own "gracious numbers" – the numbered verses of this diary, deriving their royal grace from Southampton – are falling into deeper silence. Now it is certain they cannot be contemporaneously published. The contemporary public will be unable to see them.

Sonnet 79	Translation
Whilst I alone did call upon thy aid,	While I, by myself, called upon your help,
My verse alone had all thy gentle grace,	My sonnets alone contained all your royal blood,
But now my gracious numbers are decayed,	But now my royal verses reflect your outcast state,
And my sick Muse doth give an other place.	And my weak source gives way to "Shakespeare".
I grant (sweet love) thy lovely argument	I grant, royal son, your royal substance
Deserves the travail of a worthier pen,	Deserves the labors of a more royal writer.
Yet what of thee thy Poet doth invent,	But whatever "Shakespeare" writes of you,
He robs thee of, and pays it thee again.	He takes it from you only to return it again.
He lends thee vertue, and he stole that word	"Shakespeare" supports your truth, which he took
From thy behavior; beauty doth he give	From your life. He pours out your royal blood
And found it in thy cheek; he can afford	And got it from you. He can pour out
No praise to thee but what in thee doth live.	No royal blood for you but that which lives in you.
Then thank him not for that which he doth say,	So don't thank "Shakespeare" for what he writes,
Since what he owes thee thou thy self dost pay.	Since what he pays to you is what you're paying.

1 WHILST I ALONE DID CALL UPON THY AID,
ALONE = "all" and "one" of Southampton's motto, *One for All, All for One*; **I ALONE** = I, Edward de Vere, Earl of Oxford, and Henry Wriothesley, Earl of Southampton = father and son; **DID CALL UPON THY AID** = did draw upon your for my inspiration

2 MY VERSE ALONE HAD ALL THY GENTLE GRACE,
MY VERSE = these sonnets; **ALONE** = Southampton, *One for All, All for One*; **MY VERSE ALONE** = linking Oxford and Southampton together in the Sonnets, i.e., my verse = Henry Wriothesley; **ALL** = Southampton; **ALL THY GENTLE GRACE** = all the grace of your royal blood; i.e., at one time the only verse that possessed your royal blood was mine alone, but now I must share it with the Shakespeare pen name; "In *gentle numbers* time so idly spent" – Sonnet 100, line 6

3 BUT NOW MY GRACIOUS NUMBERS ARE DECAYED
GRACIOUS = royal, same as *gentle* above; "My *gracious* liege" – to King Henry in *3 Henry VI*, 2.2.9; "Be as thy presence is, *gracious* and kind" – Sonnet 10, line 11; **MY GRACIOUS NUMBERS** = My royal sonnets to you, which are filled with your royal grace or blood from Elizabeth; "If I could write the beauty of your eyes,/ And in fresh *numbers number all your graces*" – Sonnet 17, lines 5-6; "*Eternal numbers* to outlive long date" – Sonnet 38, line 12); "But all his mind is bent to holiness, to *number* Ave-Maries on his beads" – *2 Henry VI*, 1.3.55-56; **DECAYED** = crippled by the fact that you have lost your claim to the throne; giving way to the Shakespeare pen name; related to the "decay" of "Nature" or Elizabeth's mortal body, leading to her death and the royal succession, while Southampton remains in prison and now lacks any chance to claim the throne

4 AND MY SICK MUSE DOTH GIVE AN OTHER PLACE.
MY SICK MUSE = my enfeebled inspiration; Southampton himself, who inspires these sonnets, has been enfeebled as a traitor in the Tower, stripped of his earldom and regarded as a nobody; therefore, Oxford's own Muse lacks power; "Where art thou, Muse, that thou forget'st so long/ To speak of that which gives thee all thy might?/ ... Rise, resty Muse!" – Sonnet 100, lines 1-2, 9; "O truant Muse" – Sonnet 101, line 1; "Alack, what poverty my Muse brings forth/ ... Oh blame me not if I no more can write!" – Sonnet 103, lines 1, 5; **MY SICK MUSE DOTH GIVE AN OTHER PLACE** = My dying spirit as the poet of the Sonnets now makes room for "Shakespeare" instead; alluding also to the current publication of *The Phoenix and Turtle* as by Shake-speare, and to the bargain by which Oxford must sacrifice his identity as Southampton's father and also as the author of the "Shakespeare" works; **GIVE AN OTHER PLACE** = "make way for another, yield to someone else" – Booth; makes way for the "Shakespeare" name; echoing "the place" in reference to the Tower and to the royal "place" of a monarch.

5 I GRANT (SWEET LOVE) THY LOVELY ARGUMENT
I GRANT = I allow; I admit as true; echoing a royal grant, such as the Queen's grant to Oxford of 1,000 pounds annually; **SWEET LOVE** = royal son; "O know, *sweet love*, I always write of you" – Sonnet 76, line 9; "Can yet the lease of *my true love* control/ ... *My love* looks fresh" – Sonnet 107, lines 3, 10; "Good night, *sweet prince*" – Hamlet, 5.2.66; "I prithee, *sweet* wag, when thou art king, as God save thy Grace, - Majesty, I should say" – Falstaff to Prince Hal, the future King Henry Fifth, *1 Henry IV*, 1.2.16-17; **THY LOVELY ARGUMENT** = Your royal self, filled with "love" or royal blood, which is the "*argument*" of these verses: "And *you and love* are still *my argument*" – Sonnet 76, line 10; "The *argument all bare*" – Sonnet 103, line 3; "Fair, kind, and true, is *all my argument*,/ Fair, kind, and true, varying to other words,/ And in this change is my invention spent" – Sonnet 105, lines 9-11; "O Thou my *lovely* Boy" – Sonnet 126, line 1

> This is most strange,
> That she who even but now was your best object,
> *The argument of your praise*, balm of your age,
> The best, the dearest
> - King of France, to King Lear in *King Lear*, 1.1.214-217, referring to the king's daughter,
> in terms used by Oxford in the Sonnets in relation to his son:

6 DESERVES THE TRAVAIL OF A WORTHIER PEN,
TRAVAIL = labors on your behalf; "the fruit of his *travail*" – Oxford to Burghley, June 25, 1586; "The dear repose for limbs with *travail* tired" – Sonnet 27, line 2; "I do well perceive how your Lordship doth *travail* for me in this cause of an *especial grace* and favor" – Oxford to Robert Cecil, June 19, 1603; **WORTHIER PEN** = more royal pen, that of "Shakespeare," who can speak publicly; ("Whether your Grace be worthy, yea or no, dispute not that: York is the *worthier*" – *2 Henry VI*, 1.3.107-108); "and a number of noblemen and *worthy* gentlemen and such as have in their lifetimes honored the Queen's Majesty our mistress" – Oxford to Burghley, September 1572

7 YET WHAT OF THEE THY POET DOTH INVENT
THY POET = me, Oxford, your father; "And your true rights be termed a *Poet's* rage" – Sonnet 17, line 11;
INVENT = what I write by way of my "invention"; "And keep *invention* in a noted weed"
– Sonnet 76, line 6; "And in this change is *my invention* spent" – Sonnet 105, line 11

8 HE ROBS THEE OF AND PAYS IT THEE AGAIN.
HE = the Shakespeare pen name; **ROBS THEE OF** = takes you from what I invent here in these sonnets and repays you with the public poems attributed to Shakespeare

9 HE LENDS THEE VERTUE, AND HE STOLE THAT WORD
HE = the Shakespeare pen name; **LENDS THEE** = gives you for temporary use on condition of return; adorns you publicly with; arms you with; credits you with; attributes to you

> And you, but one, can every shadow *lend*.
> Describe *Adonis* and the counterfeit
> Is poorly imitated after you;
> On *Helen's* cheek all art of beauty set
> - Sonnet 53, lines 4-7

VERTUE = (virtue); echoing Ver, Edward de Vere; "It was therefore an excellent display of wisdom on the part of our translator to seek out as a patroness of his work one who was of *surpassing virture*, of wisest mind, of soundest religion, and cultivated in the highest degree in learning and literary studies" – Oxford, writing of the Queen, in his Letter to the Reader for *The Courtier*, 1572; "lift up the base-minded man to achieve to any true sum or grade of *virtue* whereto ought only the noble thoughts of men to be inclined" – Oxford in his Prefatory Letter to *Cardanus' Comfort*, 1573; "to give us *a prince wise, learned, and enriched with all virtues*" – Oxford to Robert Cecil, April 25/27, 1603, on the eve of Elizabeth's funeral, writing of King James; "to be expected from so *gracious and virtuous a sovereign*" – Oxford, referring to King James in a letter to Robert Cecil on May 7, 1603; **AND HE STOLE THAT WORD** = the pen name "Shakespeare" robbed those qualities of you; he stole you, who are represented by the word "vertue" as well as my other words; i.e., my pen name stole my words of you

10 FROM THY BEHAVIOR; BEAUTY DOTH HE GIVE
THY BEHAVIOR = your external carriage and deportment, but also your moral conduct, i.e., your behavior as a prince; **BEAUTY** = blood inherited from the Queen; "Then being asked where *all thy beauty* lies" – Sonnet 2, line 5; "bore not *beauty's name*" – Sonnet 127, line 2

11 AND FOUND IT IN THY CHEEK: HE CAN AFFORD
AND FOUND IT IN THY CHEEK = "Thus is *his cheek* the map of days outworn" – Sonnet 68, line 1; "Even as the sun with purple-colored face/ Had ta'en his last leave of the weeping morn,/ *Rose-cheeked Adonis* hied him to the chase" – *Venus and Adonis*, lines 1-3; **HE** = the Shakespeare pen name; **CAN AFFORD** = is able to supply, yield, grant, offer, give; "To every hymn that *able spirit affords*" – Sonnet 85, line 7; "Three themes in one, which *wondrous scope affords*" – Sonnet 105, line 12

12 NO PRAISE TO THEE BUT WHAT IN THEE DOTH LIVE.
NO PRAISE = no writing of you; ("a work which, while worthy of all monarchs, is most worthy of our Queen, to whom alone is due all the *praise* of all the Muses and all the glory of literature" – Oxford Letter to the Reader for *The Courtier* by Castiglione, translated by Clerke, 1572); Oxford uses "praise" in the Fair Youth series to Southampton no less than twenty-one times, in Sonnets 2, 21, 38, 39, 55, 59, 62, 69, 70, 72, 79, 80, 82, 83, 84, 85, 95, 98, 101, 103, 106:

What heart, head, sword, force, means, but is Lord Timon's,
Great Timon, noble, *worthy*, royal Timon?
Ah, when the means are gone that buy this *praise*,
The breath is gone whereof this *praise* is made. - *Timon of Athens*, 2.2.173-175

(In the above passage the adjective "worthy" is joined with "praise" as in many of the Sonnets; i.e., "worthier" is used in line 6 above; and in the following verse "praise" and "worth" are connected: "And in the *praise* thereof ... But, since your *worth*" – Sonnet 80, lines 3,5; and in Sonnet 82, the two are joined in line 6: "Finding thy *worth* a limit past my *praise*"); "Since all alike my songs and *praises* be/ To one, of one, still such, and ever so" – Sonnet 105, lines 3-4; "Have eyes to wonder, but lack tongues to *praise*" – Sonnet 106, line 14; **BUT WHAT IN THEE DOTH LIVE** = other than the royal blood that lives within you, flowing in your veins; i.e., the pen name "Shakespeare" can only write what is drawn or borrowed from the royal blood that "in thee doth live" or lives within you; and this blood also lives in these sonnets, which are "the *living* record of your memory" – Sonnet 55, line 8

13 THEN THANK HIM NOT FOR THAT WHICH HE DOTH SAY,
Then offer your gratitude to "Shakespeare" not for what he writes in public,

14 SINCE WHAT HE OWES THEE THOU THY SELF MUST PAY
Since what "Shakespeare" owes to you is what you give to him so he can exist.

THE MONUMENT

THE "SHAKESPEARE" SACRIFICE
DAY FIFTY-FOUR IN THE TOWER

Sonnet 80
A Better Spirit Doth Use Your Name
To Make Me Tongue-Tied
2 April 1601

Oxford continues to record the sacrifice of his identity to "Shakespeare" the name. This sequence will lead to the conclusion of the bargain for Southampton's ultimate liberation, to be revealed in Sonnet 87, i.e., the agreement to reduce his crime to "misprision" of treason, allowing the Queen to spare his life and making it possible for him later to receive a royal pardon. The image here is of Oxford's "better spirit" ("Shakespeare") sailing publicly upon Southampton's "ocean" or powerful sea of royal blood, while Oxford himself is "tongue-tied speaking of your fame" as a prince in line to become King Henry IX.

Sonnet 80	Translation
O how I faint when I of you do write,	O how weakly I write of your true self,
Knowing a better spirit doth use your name,	Knowing that "Shakespeare" supports you,
And in the praise thereof spends all his might	And in doing so he spends all his power,
To make me tongue-tied speaking of your fame.	Rendering me powerless to tell of your royalty.
But since your worth (wide as the Ocean is)	But since your royal status (that of a king)
The humble as the proudest sail doth bear,	Is true whether told by the low or the high,
My saucy bark (inferior far to his)	My little private verses (not public like his)
On your broad main doth willfully appear.	Tell your truth "Will"-fully as well.
Your shallowest help will hold me up afloat,	As low as your status in prison, you support me,
Whilst he upon your soundless deep doth ride;	While "Shakespeare" uses your silent glory;
Or (being wracked) I am a worthless boat,	Or I, being crushed by your plight, am silent,
He of tall building, and of goodly pride.	While "Will Shakespeare" can speak freely.
Then if he thrive and I be cast away,	So if "Shakespeare" speaks and I do not,
The worst was this: my love was my decay.	It's because I sacrificed myself for my royal son.

1 O HOW I FAINT WHEN I OF YOU DO WRITE,
O = Oxford; **O HOW I** = Oxford = I, for emphasis; **FAINT** = lose courage; lose strength, become weak or feeble; become exhausted, spiritless, weak-hearted; especially from emotional suffering, as in: "As if *with grief or travail he had fainted*" – *Lucrece*, line 1543; also a play on **"FEINT"** or "deceive"; so the line also means, "O how I deceive when I write these lines" or "O how I use a pseudonym (the "better spirit" of line 2) to fool the public" – Alex McNeil;

> TOUCHSTONE: When a man's verses cannot be understood, nor a man's good wit seconded with the forward child, understanding, *it strikes a man more dead than a great reckoning in a little room.* Truly, I would the gods had made thee poetical.
>
> AUDREY: I do not know what 'poetical' is. Is it honest in deed and word? Is it a true thing?

> TOUCHSTONE: No truly; for *the truest poetry is the most feigning…*
> - *As You Like It*, 3.3.11-19

Oxford may have inserted these lines later, for the play's performance at Wilton in late 1603. The "great reckoning in a little room" may refer to his meeting with Cecil to finalize the bargain for Southampton's eventual release; and this bargain involved the adoption of the Shakespeare name as an official policy of feigning or deception. Ironically, however, these sonnets are also feigning, by using a deceptive language, so they are the "truest" poetry.

WHEN I OF YOU DO WRITE = when I continue to write to you, my son, in these sonnets; Oxford is figuratively losing his strength of spirit as he sacrifices his identity, both as father of Southampton and as "Shakespeare" (the "Rival Poet") on the printed page for the public; although his pen name was linked indelibly to Southampton by its dedications to him eight years earlier, that mask is now becoming official state policy and will stay in place for much longer than he had imagined or then he ever could have anticipated; "O God, Horatio, what a wounded name … O, I die, Horatio. The potent poison quite o'ercrows my spirit … The rest is silence" – *Hamlet*, 5.2.351, 359-565

2 KNOWING A BETTER SPIRIT DOTH USE YOUR NAME,
A BETTER SPIRIT = "Shakespeare" the pseudonym, able to write publicly to Southampton and to reflect his life in both published poems and plays performed on stage at Court and in the public playhouse; **SPIRIT** = ("Vital power, life ... vivacity, mettle, fire, courage ... temper, disposition, sentiments ... mental power, vigor of intellect ... that which pervades and tempers the whole mind, or the whole state and nature of a thing ... mind, soul ... a human being, a person with respect to his kind or sphere of activity ... any supernatural being, an angel, a ghost, a demon, a fairy, etc" – Schmidt); all of these definitions apply in some way to the "Shakespeare" pen name; the latter, including "ghost," is especially apt as "Shakespeare" is invisible, a ghostly figure, with no physical body – unless you count the man from Stratford, William Shakspere, who was certainly never regarded during his lifetime as the author of the Shakespeare poems and plays; Oxford has been leading up to this sacrifice, to this transfer of his "spirit" to that of "Shakespeare":

> My *spirit* is thine, the better part of me
> - Sonnet 74, line 8

He will conclude the so-called Rival Poet series by again referring to the Shakespeare name as a spirit or as the ghost of his personal spirit:

> Was it *his spirit, by spirits taught to write*
> Above a mortal pitch, that struck me dead?
> - Sonnet 86, lines 5-6

The dying Antony speaks to Cleopatra:

> Wherein I lived the greatest prince o'th'world,
> The noblest; and do now not basely die...
> Now my spirit is going;
> I can no more.
> - *Antony and Cleopatra*, 4.15.56-57,60-61

In the Dark Lady series, Oxford angrily accuses Elizabeth (regardless of whether she ever saw any of the sonnets or knew of their existence) of wasting the "spirit" of her own blood (as well as Oxford's semen) by actually considering the execution of her son – the spirit of her life, her blood, her lineage, her Tudor lineage on the throne, etc:

*Th'expense of **spirit** in a waste of shame*
Is lust in action, and till action lust
Is perjured, *murd'rous, bloody*, full of blame
- Sonnet 129, lines 1-2, accusing her of "murder" that is "bloody" (related to the execution of her son) and using terms of the trial, i.e., *perjured, blame*

SPIRIT: Sonnets 56, 61, 74, 80, 85, 86, 108, 129, 144; **DOTH USE YOUR NAME** = dedicates his poetry to you by name, as "William Shakespeare" dedicated *Venus and Adonis* in 1593 and *The Rape of Lucrece* in 1594 to Henry Wriothesley, Earl of Southampton

3 AND IN THE PRAISE THEREOF SPENDS ALL HIS MIGHT
IN THE PRAISE THEREOF = in praising you within *Venus and Adonis* and *Lucrece*, which use your name, and in *The Phoenix and Turtle* of 1601 (also as by Shakespeare, in this case "Shake-speare"); **ALL** = Southampton; **HIS** = the pen name's; Shakespeare's; **HIS MIGHT** = his strength and force and power as a poet; his royal might that he gains from you, through me; "O none, unless this miracle have *might*/ That in black ink my love may still shine bright" – Sonnet 65, lines 13-14; "At first the very worst of *fortune's might* (the Queen's power) – Sonnet 90, line 12; "No! Time, thou shalt not boast that I do change!/ Thy pyramids built up with newer might" – Sonnet 123, line 2; "They know your grace hath cause, and means, and *might*; so doth your Highness. Never King of England had nobles richer and more loyal subjects" – *Henry V*, 1.2.125-127

4 TO MAKE ME TONGUE-TIED SPEAKING OF YOUR FAME.
To force me into silence; "And art made tongue-tied by authority" – Sonnet 66, line 9; this point on, Oxford's sacrifice of his identity is being dictated by "authority" or official decree, through Secretary Robert Cecil, who is now running the Elizabethan government; i.e., this marks the official beginning of "Shakespeare" as the *permanent* stand-in for Oxford, who must now hope that, in return, King James will agree, upon his succession, to release Southampton and grant him a royal pardon; "My tongue-tied Muse in manners holds her still" – Sonnet 85, line 1

5 BUT SINCE YOUR WORTH (WIDE AS THE OCEAN IS)
WORTH = royalty; "worth" is contained in "Wriothesley"; "Weigh you the **worth** and honor of a king" – *Troilus and Cressida*, 2.2.26; **OCEAN** = royal blood; the substance, presence and "state" of a king; "'Thou art,' quoth she, 'a sea, a sovereign king … who seek to stain the ocean of thy blood'" – *Lucrece*, 652, 655; "Let this sad *Interim* like the *Ocean* be/ Which parts the shore, where two contracted new/ Come daily to the banks, that when they see/ Return of love, more blest may be the view" – Sonnet 56, lines 9-1; "When I have seen the hungry *Ocean* gain/ Advantage on the *kingdom of the shore*" – Sonnet 64, lines 5-6, referring to King James VI of Scotland eventually coming to take his place as King James I of England; "*Ocean* or *sea* as a figure for *king* is often found in Shakespeare and his fellow-writers" - Leslie Hotson

> And what is (King) Edward but a ruthless *sea*
> - *3 Henry VI*, 5.4.25

> Even to our *Ocean*, our great King John
> - *King John*, 5.4.57

> The *tide of blood* in me
> Hath proudly flowed in vanity till now.
> Now doth it turn, and ebb back to *the sea*,
> Where it shall mingle with the *state of floods*
> And *flow henceforth in formal majesty*
> - *2 Henry IV*, 5.2.129-133

> A substitute shines brightly as a king,
> Until a king be by, and then his state

Empties itself, as doth *an inland brook*
Into the main of waters - Merchant of Venice, 5.1.94

6 THE HUMBLE AS THE PROUDEST SAIL DOTH BEAR,
The most humble and the most proud sail; i.e., but since both the humblest and the proudest verse must bear your "worth" or royal blood; "The sea being smooth, how many *shallow bauble boats dare sail upon her patient breast, making their way with those of nobler birth!* But let the ruffian Boreas once enrage the gentle Thetis ... Where's then the saucy boat whose weak untimber'd sides but even now co-rivaled greatness?" – *Troilus and Cressida*, 1.3.34-42; **THE PROUDEST SAIL** = the verses most filled with your "pride" or royalty; ("Why is my verse so barren of new *pride*" – Sonnet 76, line 1; **SAIL** = means of writing poems or plays; **BEAR** = give birth or rebirth to you; carry you

7 MY SAUCY BARK (INFERIOR FAR TO HIS)
MY SAUCY BARK = the frightened, yet bold, boat that is my verse, i.e., these sonnets; "Where's then the *saucy boat* whose weak untimber'd sides but even now co-rivaled greatness?" – *Troilus and Cressida*, 1.3.43-44; **BARK** = in addition to a boat, possibly a play on the "bark" of a dog, i.e., making "noise" through writing – Alex McNeil); **INFERIOR FAR TO HIS** = inferior by far to the published poems of "Shakespeare" because he, my pen name, has the authority (from the Crown) to write publicly.

8 ON YOUR BROAD MAIN DOTH WILLFULLY APPEAR.
ON YOUR BROAD MAIN = on your wide, powerful ocean of royal blood; **MAIN** = full might; the whole of it; "Nativity (the birth of Southampton as prince), once in the *main of light,/ Crawls to maturity, wherewith being crowned*" – Sonnet 60, lines 5-6; "When I have seen the hungry Ocean gain/ Advantage on the kingdom of the shore,/ And the firm soil win of *the watery main*" – Sonnet 64, lines 5-7; "Until *a king* be by, and then *his state empties itself*, as doth an inland brook into *the main of waters*" – *The Merchant of Venice*, 5.1.95-97; **WILLFULLY** = full of "Will" Shakespeare; according to your royal will; **APPEAR** = emerge in public

9 YOUR SHALLOWEST HELP WILL HOLD ME UP AFLOAT,
YOUR SHALLOWEST HELP = your least amount of help; i.e., even the "shallowest" or least-royal part of your royal ocean; **WILL HOLD ME UP AFLOAT** = will keep me alive and keep me writing these sonnets

10 WHILST HE UPON YOUR SOUNDLESS DEEP DOTH RIDE,
While he, "Shakespeare," rides upon your ocean of royal blood, i.e., uses it to keep afloat and to soar in public; **SOUNDLESS DEEP** = secret ocean of royal blood; **SOUNDLESS** = same as *dumb* or destitute of the power of speech, i.e., put to silence, as in "O let my books be then the eloquence/ And *dumb presagers of my speaking breast/* ... O learn to read *what silent love hath writ*" – Sonnet 23, lines 9-10, 13; and "For who's so *dumb* that cannot write to thee,/ When thou thyself dost give invention light?" – Sonnet 38, lines 7-8; and "Thine eyes, that taught the *dumb* on high to sing" – Sonnet 78, line 5; also soundless = "unfathomable" as well as "devoid of sound, dumb" - Schmidt

11 OR (BEING WRACKED) I AM A WORTHLESS BOAT,
WRACKED = wrecked; Oxford as thoroughly beaten down by these tragic events; Q has "wrackt", echoing "racked" or tortured in prison; see Sonnets 33, 65, 126; **I AM A WORTHLESS BOAT** = I am without your royal blood to keep me afloat; without Wriothesley; without your worth; as opposed to "I am that I am" – Sonnet 121, line 9

12 HE OF TALL BUILDING AND OF GOODLY PRIDE.
HE = "Shakespeare"; **TALL BUILDING** = great fame and stature in the public eye; as opposed to this pyramid or monument of verse; (also suggesting that he has been "built" or "constructed," rather than created naturally as a real person – Alex McNeil); **GOODLY PRIDE** = with your goodly royalty to help him; "For, *good King Henry*, thy decay I fear" – *2 Henry VI*, 3.1.194; "Why is my verse *so barren of new pride*" – Sonnet 76, line 1; "And Richard fall *in height of all his pride*" – *Richard III*, 5.3.177; to Queen

Elizabeth, of her royal son and his hope to "rise" in glory as her successor: "But rising at thy name doth point out thee/ As his triumphant prize, *proud of this pride,*/ He is contented thy poor drudge to be,/ To stand in thy affairs, fall by thy side" – Sonnet 151, lines 9-12; "And having thee, of *all men's pride I boast*" – Sonnet 91, line 12

13 THEN IF HE THRIVE AND I BE CAST AWAY,
IF HE THRIVE = if "Shakespeare" thrives; **THRIVE** = grow, increase, flourish, prosper, succeed in fortune; "as York *thrives* to beat back Bolingbroke" – *Richard II*, 2.2.144; "pitiful *thrivers* in their gazing spent" – Sonnet 125, line 8; "who's like to rise, who thrives, and who declines" – *Coriolanus*, 1.1.191-192; **AND I BE CAST AWAY** = and my identity is obliterated; "I all alone beweep my outcast state" – Sonnet 29, line 2; **CAST AWAY** = "to be exiled, and thrown from Leonati seat, and *cast* from her dearest one" – *Cymbeline*, 5.4.60; a seafaring term, i.e., cast or thrown from your sea of royal blood; "since I was *cast ashore*" – *The Tempest*, 2.2.129; thrown away as worthless; "As to be *cast forth* in the common air" – *Richard II*, 1.3.157; "will you *cast away* your child" – *The Merry Wives of Windsor*, 3.4.95; also suggesting that Oxford may be considering leaving England, as faintly hinted in other sonnets – Alex McNeil.

14 THE WORST WAS THIS: MY LOVE WAS MY DECAY.
MY LOVE = my love for you, my royal son; ("The love I dedicate to your Lordship is without end" – dedication of *Lucrece* to Southampton, 1594, by "Shakespeare", whose new poem *The Phoenix and Turtle* as by "William Shake-speare" is being published this year

WAS MY DECAY = was the reason why I made this sacrifice, resulting in my obliteration and disappearance, ghostlike; i.e., Oxford's suffering and the death of his identity, akin to the suffering and death of Christ, was for his royal son, a god on earth; reflecting the decay of Southampton as a king and the decay of the Tudor Rose dynasty; "But now *my gracious numbers are decayed,*/ And my sick Muse doth give another place" – Sonnet 79, lines 3-4, referring to Oxford making way for "Shakespeare" as his permanent pen name; "Who lets *so fair a house fall to decay*" – Sonnet 13, line 9, referring to the fall of the House of Tudor; "Where *wasteful time debateth with decay*/ To change your day of youth to sullied night" – Sonnet 15, lines 11-12, summarizing the essential conflict of the Sonnets, with Love representing the royal blood of Southampton in its struggle with Time, representing the inexorable decay of Elizabeth's mortal body, as in the next line: "And *all in war with Time for love of you*" – Sonnet 15, line 13; "For, good King Henry, *thy decay* I fear" – *2 Henry VI*, 3.1.194

Part Two

THE "SHAKESPEARE" SACRIFICE
YOUR MONUMENT
DAY FIFTY-FIVE IN THE TOWER

Sonnet 81
*Your Name From Hence Immortal Life Shall Have
I, Once Gone, To All The World Must Die
Your Monument Shall Be My Gentle Verse*
3 April 1601

Oxford records the reason for what will become "the Shakespeare mystery" in a single verse. He testifies that he faces the obliteration of his identity "to all the world" because of his sacrifice to gain ultimate liberation for his royal son, Henry Wriothesley, from the Tower of London. He vows to construct the Monument of the Sonnets to preserve this truth "which eyes not yet created shall o'er-read." This sonnet is a glorious homage to Southampton as a king.

Sonnet 81	Translation
Or I shall live your Epitaph to make,	Whether I survive to create your epitaph
Or you survive when I in earth am rotten,	Or you continue living when I am dead,
From hence your memory death cannot take,	From now on death can't destroy your identity,
Although in me each part will be forgotten.	Even if everything about me is forgotten.
Your name from hence immortal life shall have	From now on, you will live forever as Henry IX,
Though I (once gone) to all the world must die.	Though I, when dead, cannot be linked with you.
The earth can yield me but a common grave,	I will go to my grave like a commoner,
When you entombed in men's eyes shall lie.	While you live in these sonnets, which entomb you.
Your monument shall be my gentle verse,	My royal verse will stand as your monument,
Which eyes not yet created shall o'er-read,	Which future people will read over and over,
And tongues to be your being shall rehearse,	And people to come will speak repeatedly of you,
When all the breathers of this world are dead.	When all who live now in England are dead.
You still shall live (such vertue hath my Pen)	You will always live (such truth has my pen)
Where breath most breathes, even in the mouths of men.	Where it counts most: for readers in the future.

1 OR SHALL I LIVE YOUR EPITAPH TO MAKE

OR = if either I live long enough to create your memorial; following immediately from the previous sonnet, Oxford now suddenly suggests something quite dramatically different

YOUR EPITAPH = Inscription on a tomb or monument; "an inscription upon a tomb; hence, occasionally, a brief composition characterizing a deceased person, and expressed as if intended to be inscribed on his tombstone" – *OED*

Good my lord, will you see the players well bestowed? Do you hear, let them be well used, for they are the abstracts and brief chronicles of the time. After your death you were better have a bad *epitaph* than their ill report while you live - *Hamlet, 2.2.523-527*

REFERENCE EDITION 451

THE MONUMENT

2 OR YOU SURVIVE WHEN I IN EARTH AM ROTTEN,
Or if you continue to live when I am dead

3 FROM HENCE YOUR MEMORY DEATH CANNOT TAKE,
FROM HENCE, etc. = henceforth death cannot rob the memory of you; **YOUR MEMORY** = "The living record of *your memory*" – Sonnet 55, line 8; "My life hath in this line some interest,/ Which for *memorial still with thee* shall stay" – Sonnet 74, lines 3-4; "Then there's hope a great man's *memory* may outlive his life half a year" – the Prince, sarcastically, in *Hamlet*, 3.2.133-134; **DEATH CANNOT TAKE** = "'Gainst *death and all oblivious enmity/* Shall you pace forth!" – Sonnet 55, lines 9-10

4 ALTHOUGH IN ME EACH PART WILL BE FORGOTTEN.
ALTHOUGH, etc. = although each aspect of me (especially my identity as your father) will be forgotten in the time to come; **FORGOTTEN** = "And so having choler to break off all, and *myself forgotten*" – Oxford to Burghley, March 20, 1595

5 YOUR NAME FROM HENCE IMMORTAL LIFE SHALL HAVE,
YOUR NAME = Southampton, his own name; and, if the Sonnets survive, his identity as the rightful Prince Henry or King Henry IX; "And I again, in Henry's *royal name*, as deputy unto that gracious king" – *1 Henry VI*, 5.3.160-161; Henry Wriothesley's name has in fact been immortalized by "Shakespeare's" dedications to him and him alone; **FROM HENCE** = from this time forward, as a result of these verses of the Sonnets (in addition to the "Shakespeare" dedications to you); "hence" repeated from line 3 above; **IMMORTAL LIFE SHALL HAVE** = will live forever, in the eyes of readers of these Sonnets, in the future; ("Add an *immortal title to your crown*!" – *Richard II*, 1.1.24)

6 THOUGH I (ONCE GONE) TO ALL THE WORLD MUST DIE.
A concise summary of Oxford's sacrifice to "Shakespeare" on behalf of his son, who will continue to live in the Sonnets: though I, once dead, must be forgotten by England and the whole world; **GONE** = deceased, but also departed, possibly suggesting that Oxford intends to leave England once James becomes king and Southampton is liberated and pardoned; the possible distinction between "gone" and "dead" offers this intriguing avenue of speculation; **ALL** = Southampton; ("as *all the world* doth judge" – Oxford to Burghley, September 1572; "the *fable of the world*" – Oxford to Burghley, April 27, 1576; "sith *all the world* doth know" – Oxford to Robert Cecil, November 22, 1601)

7 THE EARTH CAN YIELD ME BUT A COMMON GRAVE,
COMMON GRAVE = an ordinary grave, as opposed to one citing him as father of a king; in fact, Oxford will receive no recorded funeral; he will be buried in an unmarked grave (though possibly his body was moved later to Westminster Abbey); and he will leave no will of record.

8 WHEN YOU ENTOMBED IN MEN'S EYES SHALL LIE.
When you will be preserved in the tomb of this monument of verse, for men to read about; ("Who will believe my verse in time to come/ If it were filled with your most high deserts?/ Though yet heaven knows it is but as a *tomb*/ Which hides your life and shows not half your parts" – Sonnet 17, lines 1-4; "And thou in this shalt find thy monument,/ When tyrants' crests and *tombs* of brass are spent" – Sonnet 107, lines 13-14); "and now *all men's eyes*" – Oxford to Burghley, September 1572; "to *bury and ensevel your works in the grave of oblivion*" – Oxford to Thomas Bedingfield in his prefatory letter to the latter's translation *of Cardanus' Comforte*, 1573; "A man in hew all *Hews* in his controlling,/ Which steals *men's eyes* and women's souls amazeth" – Sonnet 20, lines 7-8; "When in disgrace with Fortune and *men's eyes*" – Sonnet 29, line 1; "Your praise shall still find room/ Even in *the eyes of all posterity*/ ... You live in this, and dwell *in lovers' eyes*" – Sonnet 55, lines 10-11

> That did my ripe thoughts in my brain inhearse,
> Making their tomb the womb wherein they grew.
> - Sonnet 86, lines 3-4

9 YOUR MONUMENT SHALL BE MY GENTLE VERSE,
These royal sonnets will be your monument, similar to the Pyramids of ancient Egypt, built to preserve dynastic rulers or pharaohs (who are gods on earth, like you)

"Again we see if our friends be dead, we cannot show or declare our affection more than by erecting them of *tombs*: Whereby when they be dead indeed, yet *make we them live*, as it were, again through their *monument*. But with me behold it happeneth far better, for in your lifetime I shall erect you such a *monument* that, as I say, in your lifetime, you shall see how noble a shadow of your virtuous life shall hereafter remain when you are dead and gone. And in your lifetime, again I say, I shall give you that *monument* and *remembrance of your life* whereby I may declare my goodwill...."
- Oxford to Thomas Bedingfield, in his prefatory letter to the latter's translation *of Cardanus' Comforte*, 1573

> Not marble, nor the gilded monument
> Of Princes shall outlive this powerful rhyme
> But you shall shine more bright in these contents,
> Than unswept stone, besmeared with sluttish time.
> - Sonnet 55, lines 1-2

> Ever beloved and loving may his rule be,
> And when old time shall lead him to his end,
> Goodness and he fill up one monument!
> - *Henry VIII*, 2.1.92-94

> And thou in this shalt find thy monument,
> When tyrants' crests and tombs of brass are spent.
> - Sonnet 107, lines 13-14

10 WHICH EYES NOT YET CREATED SHALL O'ER-READ,
EYES = the adoring eyes of your subjects, of readers; **EYES NOT YET CREATED, Etc.** = The eyes of future generations will read over and over, a direct statement that Oxford now intends the Sonnets not for contemporary readers but for those to come in posterity; "all men's eyes" – Oxford to Burghley, September 1572

11 AND TONGUES TO BE YOUR BEING SHALL REHEARSE,
TONGUES TO BE = future voices, which will not be "tongue-tied"; **YOUR BEING SHALL REHEARSE** = will repeat their praises of your royal being over and over, by reading this Book of Sonnets; "And every fair with his fair doth *rehearse*" – Sonnet 21, line 4, referring to the Earl of Southampton as "every fair" or E. Ver's royal son, i.e., every king repeats his royalty to himself over and over; (perhaps a glance also at the plays of "Shakespeare" – whose works are dedicated to Southampton – being "rehearsed" on the stage in ages to come

12 WHEN ALL THE BREATHERS OF THIS WORLD ARE DEAD.
ALL = Southampton, *One for All, All for One*; **ALL THE BREATHERS** = everyone alive; **OF THIS WORLD** = in our contemporary England, in the current civilized world, as opposed to posterity

13 YOU STILL SHALL LIVE (SUCH VERTUE HATH MY PEN)
You will live forever; "His beauty shall in these black lines be seen,/ And they *shall live*, and he in them still green" – Sonnet 63, lines 13-14, with "his beauty" referring to Southampton's blood inherited from the Queen; and therefore his relationship to Elizabeth as her son will live forever; **VERTUE** = power, related to "Ver" or truth; i.e., such power of truth has my pen; "And maiden *vertue* rudely strumpeted" – Sonnet 66, line 6

Nor Mars his sword nor war's quick fire shall burn
The living record of your memory.
'Gainst death and all oblivious enmity
Shall you pace forth! Your praise shall still find room
Even in the eyes of all posterity
That wear this world out to the ending doom.
- Sonnet 55, lines 7-12

14 **WHERE BREATH MOST BREATHES, EVEN IN THE MOUTHS OF MEN.**

Wherever people are alive, speaking to each other; "So long *as men can breathe* or eyes can see,/ So long lives this, and *this gives life to thee*" – Sonnet 18, lines 13-14; **THE MOUTHS OF MEN** = the talk of people in the future; "to face the light and *the eyes of men*" – Oxford to the Reader of *The Courtier* by Castiglione, 1572; "to be sealed up in *an eternal remembrance* to yourself" – Oxford to Robert Cecil, October 7, 1601; (EVEN IN THE MOUTHS = in the very mouths)

BREATH/BREATHES = "In Shakespeare's day the breath was all but identified with the spirit" - Wyndham, 1898, adding the mouth was held in honor by platonic writers; citing Hoby's version of "The Courtier" (1561) and its defense of kissing "on the ground of the sanctity attaching to the mouth as the gateway of the soul."

("I will make thy name to be remembered in all generations: therefore shall the people praise thee for ever and ever" - Psalm 45, verse 17, especially echoed by lines 5, 11 and 14 above)

EVEN = In the late 19th century the Countess of Pembroke claimed that lines 9-14 were written on an old parchment from the 17th century, with "ever" in place of "even" (Pall Mall Magazine, Oct 1897)

Part Two

THE "SHAKESPEARE" SACRIFICE
DAY FIFTY-SIX IN THE TOWER

Sonnet 82
Without Attaint
The Dedicated Words
Truly Fair ... Truly Sympathized ... True-Telling Friend
4 April 1601

Oxford leaves no doubt that the so-called Rival Poet is "Shakespeare" by referring to the "dedicated words" (the dedications under that name of Venus and Adonis and Lucrece to Southampton), which were blessing "every (E.Ver) book" with Henry Wriothesley's royal presence in them. Edward deVere insistently incorporates his own identity by echoing the words of his earldom motto Nothing Truer than Truth in "truly ... truly ... true ... true-telling."

Sonnet 82	Translation
I grant thou wert not married to my Muse,	I concede you weren't married to my Muse,
And therefore mayst without attaint o'erlook	So without being disgraced you can look over
The dedicated words which writers use	The dedications "William Shakespeare" wrote
Of their fair subject, blessing every book.	About your royal self, for *Venus* and *Lucrece*.
Thou art as fair in knowledge as in hew,	You are as royal from within as from without,
Finding thy worth a limit past my praise,	Having your royalty beyond my capacity to say,
And therefore art enforced to seek anew	And so are forced to find, all over again,
Some fresher stamp of the time-bettering days.	A new testament to your royal glory.
And do so, love, yet when they have devised	So read him, royal son! But when he creates
What strained touches Rhetoric can lend,	Whatever poems for you that he can write,
Thou truly fair wert truly sympathized	Your true royalty was still expressed truly
In true plain words by thy true-telling friend.	In my own true words by me, Oxford, your father.
And their gross painting might be better used	And Shakespeare's poetry might better fit
Where cheeks need blood; in thee it is abused.	Those without royal blood: for you, it's abuse.

1 I GRANT THOU WERT NOT MARRIED TO MY MUSE
GRANT = concede; the legal act of granting or bestowing, as when Queen Elizabeth in 1586 granted Oxford an annual pension of 1,000 pounds; "and they shall let their lease fall which *Her Majesty hath granted*" – Oxford to Burghley, May 18, 1591; **MARRIED** = under contract to; legally tied to; "Let me not to the *marriage of true minds/* Admit impediments" – Sonnet 116, lines 1-2; **MY MUSE** = my inspiration for these sonnets, which were born of you or begotten by you; "most worthy of our Queen, to whom alone is due all the praise of *all the Muses* and all the glory of literature" – Oxford's Letter to the Reader for *The Courtier*, 1572; "I do not doubt even so you think of *your studies and delightful Muses ... From my new country Muses* at Wivenghole" – Oxford's Prefatory Letter for *Cardanus' Comforte*, 1573, referring to an estate where he could get away from Court and concentrate on his writing.

REFERENCE EDITION

2 AND THEREFORE MAYST WITHOUT ATTAINT O'ER-LOOK

ATTAINT = "n. stain, disgrace, taint, dishonor; convicted; condemned by a sentence or bill or act of attainder (the legal consequence of judgment of death or outlawry for treason or felony)" – the Random House Dictionary; Southampton has been attainted for treason; suffering dishonor; *Warrant from the Privy Council, February 26, 1601:* "**Attainted**, and fit to be executed…" (The name, left blank, was "probably intended to have been filled with the name of Southampton" – Stopes, 223); "But freshly looks and overbears *attaint* with cheerful semblance and sweet majesty" – *Henry V*, Chorus, 4.0

"And by his *treason* stand'st not thou *attainted*" – *Richard II*, 2.4.92; "Convicted, attainted" – *OED*, citing "Fyle attaynte traytour!" – 1460; "convict or attaint of high Treason" – 1642; "He is then called attaint, *attinctus*, stained, or blackened; he is no longer of any credit or reputation" – 1768; the latter using "stained" and "blackened" as Oxford refers to Southampton as "black" and as having or causing a "stain" against himself; OED also defines "attaint" as "affected with sickness, passion, etc … overpowered, exhausted"

> He lived from all *attainder* of suspects.
> Well, well, he was the covert'st shelter'd traitor
> - *Richard III*, 3.5.32-33

> Either I must, or have mine honour soiled
> With the *attainder* of his slanderous lips
> - *Richard II*, 4.1.23-24

> Upon thy part I can set down a story
> Of *faults concealed*, wherein I am *attainted*,
> That thou in losing me shall win much glory
> - Sonnet 88, lines 6-8

> Stands in *attainder of eternal shame*
> - *Love's Labour's Lost*, 1.1.155

3 THE DEDICATED WORDS WHICH WRITERS USE

The dedications by "Shakespeare" to Southampton of *Venus and Adonis* in 1593 and *Lucrece* in 1594; **WRITERS** = "Shakespeare," the pen name linked to Southampton on the published page; again, the plural used for the singular.

4 OF THEIR FAIR SUBJECT, BLESSING EVERY BOOK.

FAIR SUBJECT = royal topic, i.e., Southampton, the so-called Fair Youth of the Sonnets; and to reinforce the identification of him, see line 11 when he addresses him as "*truly fair*"; **BLESSING EVERY BOOK** = blessing or sanctifying those two books, as well as everything else attributed to Shakespeare; "blessing" is related to the sacredness of Southampton as king or "god on earth", a deity who confers holiness on the Book of Sonnets above all; "Look down, you gods, and on this couple drop a *blessed* crown" – *The Tempest*, 5.1.201-202; **EVERY** = E. Ver, Edward de Vere; **EVERY BOOK** = the two published poems, dedicated to Southampton by "Shakespeare" but written by Edward de Vere; i.e., *every book = E. Vere's books*

5 THOU ART AS FAIR IN KNOWLEDGE AS IN HEW,

FAIR = royal; "To me, fair friend" – Sonnet 104, line 1; **KNOWLEDGE** = royal wisdom; "the knowing a fact or truth, the having a clear perception or certain information of it … the knowing a person … learning, mental accomplishment" – Schmidt; "Be governed by your *knowledge* and proceed in the sway of your own will" – *King Lear*, 4.7.19-20; "I do beseech your Grace, let me *the knowledge of my fault* bear with me" – *As You Like It*, 1.3.42-43; "That, upon *knowledge of my parentage*" – *The Taming of the Shrew*, 2.1.96; **HEW** = Henry Wriothesley (i.e., He.W.); "A man in hew all *Hews* in his controlling" – Sonnet 20, line 7; modernized as *hue*; color; "And steal dead image of *his living hew*" – Sonnet 67, line 6; "Of different *flowers in odor and in hew*" – Sonnet 98, line 6, echoing Southampton as flower of the Tudor Rose; "So *your sweet hew*, which methinks still doth stand" – Sonnet 104, line 11; "To note the fighting conflict of her *hew*,/ Her white and red each other did destroy!" – *Venus and Adonis*, lines 345-346, echoing the white and red roses of the Tudor Rose of Elizabeth; "Most radiant Pyramus, most lily-white of *hew*,/ Of colour like the red rose on triumphant briar" – *A Midsummer Night's Dream*, 3.1.86-87

6 FINDING THY WORTH A LIMIT PAST MY PRAISE,
THY WORTH = your royalty, speaking to Southampton; "the *worth and honour of a king*" – *Troilus & Cressida*, 2.2.26; "a work which, while *worthy of all monarchs*, is most *worthy of our own Queen*, to whom alone is due all the *praise* of all the Muses and all the glory of literature" – Oxford's Letter to the Reader for *The Courtier*, 1572; **WORTH** = Wriothesley; **FINDING, etc.** = finding your royalty goes beyond the limits of my capacity for praising you; **LIMIT** = echoing Southampton's confinement in the Tower; "From *limits* far remote, *where thou dost stay*" – Sonnet 44, line 4; "So long as out of *limit* and true rule you stand against anointed majesty" – *1 Henry IV*, 4.3.39-40; **MY PRAISE** = my record of your life and royal blood in these sonnets; "If my slight Muse do please these curious days,/ The pain be mine, but *thine shall be the praise*" – Sonnet 38, lines 13-14, with "thine" referring to these verses to Southampton that belong to him.

7 AND THEREFORE ART ENFORCED TO SEEK ANEW
ART ENFORCED = and so you are forced to seek anew; (echoing "my art is forced," i.e., by official decree, because I write of your claim to the throne; "And *art made tongue-tied by authority*" – Sonnet 66, line 9); also "you, Southampton are enforced" to remain in prison, at least during the rest of Elizabeth's reign; **TO SEEK ANEW** = "Why with the time do I not glance aside/ To *new*-found methods, and to compounds strange?" – Sonnet 76, lines 3-4; i.e., to seek some "fresher" or newly royal way of restoring your identity in my writing; and you are forced to seek anew some better poetry, i.e., the "Shakespeare" poems.

8 SOME FRESHER STAMP OF THE TIME-BETTERING DAYS.
FRESHER = newer, more royal; "Thou that art now the world's *fresh* ornament" – Sonnet 1, line 9, during the golden time in the 1590s; "And that *fresh* blood" – Sonnet 11, line 3, i.e., hopeful or still-young royal blood; "Since first I saw you *fresh*" – Sonnet 104, line 8; "My love looks *fresh*" – Sonnet 107, line 10, upon Southampton's liberation on April 10, 1603, indicating his son is as royal as he ever was; **FRESHER STAMP** = newer and more royal means of recording your life; i.e., my *invention* for the Sonnets; and one "fresher stamp" is by means of *The Phoenix and Turtle*, now being published as by "William Shake-speare"

TIME-BETTERING DAYS = referring to the fact that, by his sacrifice of identity as father of Southampton and as the poet who dedicated his works to Southampton, these days are looking better for him; i.e., Oxford's son may be able to gain his liberty and a royal pardon; **DAYS** = this time being recorded daily in the Sonnets, as in "Lo thus by *day* my limbs, by night my mind" – Sonnet 27, line 13, and "But *day* doth *daily* draw my sorrows longer" – Sonnet 28, line 13, and "For as the Sun is *daily* new and old" – Sonnet 76, line 14, reflecting both the "day" of Southampton's kingly person and these "daily" sonnets being compiled ever since the Rebellion nearly eight weeks earlier; the royal time as in "Shall I compare thee to a Summer's *day*?" – Sonnet 18, line 1, and "Why didst thou promise such a beauteous *day*" – Sonnet 34, line 1

9 AND DO SO, LOVE! YET WHEN THEY HAVE DEVISED
Oxford commands Southampton: And, my royal son, read the works of "Shakespeare"; **LOVE** = my royal son; i.e., seek elsewhere for some new poet, i.e., Shakespeare; **THEY** = other poets, i.e., "Shakespeare" (again plural for singular); **HAVE DEVISED** = have contrived or invented

10 WHAT STRAINED TOUCHES RHETORIC CAN LEND,
Whatever poetry – straining to praise and express your royal identity – that "Shakespeare" can lend you with by his rhetoric; **RHETORIC** = "the science of oratory, the art of speaking" – Schmidt; here emphasizing the *public* nature of the Shakespeare works dedicated to him; "When therefore he writes with precise and well-chosen words, with skillfully constructed and crystal-clear sentences, and with *every art of dignified rhetoric*, it cannot be but that some noble quality should be felt to proceed from his work" – Oxford's Letter to the Reader of *The Courtier*, 1572

11 THOU TRULY FAIR WERT TRULY SYMPATHIZED
Remember that you, being truly my royal son, were truly loved and rendered; **TRULY** = related to Oxford, *Nothing Truer than Truth*; **TRULY FAIR** = genuinely royal, from me, your father; "To pay that duty which you *truly* owe to him that owes it, namely *this young prince*" – *King John*, 2.1.247-248; **TRULY SYMPATHIZED** = answered to, tallied; genuinely depicted or accurately recorded by me, in lines of these secret verses; I have been truly on your side (similar to being his son's Advocate as "Thy adverse party is *thy Advocate*" in Sonnet 35, line 10).

"Sympathize – to suffer with another; to be affected in consequence of the affection of some one or something else; to be similarly or correspondingly affected; to respond sympathetically to some influence; specifically in *Path.*, to be or become disordered in consequence of the disorder of some other part ... to have an affinity; to agree in nature, disposition, qualities, or fortunes; to be alike ... to agree, be in harmony, accord" – *OED*, citing "*sympathized*" in this sonnet as an example of "to represent or express by something corresponding or fitting; to apprehend mentally by the analogy of something else"; also "to have a fellow-feeling; to share the feelings of another or others; to be affected by the condition or experience of another with a feeling similar or corresponding to that of the other; specifically, to be affected with pity for the suffering or sorrow of another, to feel compassion ... to make up or compound of corresponding parts or elements; to form or contrive harmoniously or consistently ... to express sympathy, esp. for another's sorrow or suffering."

"Feelings of favor, support, or loyalty ... *Psychol.*, a relationship between persons in which the condition of one induces a parallel or reciprocal condition in another" – *Random House Dictionary*

> "As soone as the actions of one parte is hindered, al the other partes of the body doe therwithe conspire and *sympathize*" – *OED*, 1597; "Who right conceives the miseries of Job ... Can fittest deem their grief's true qualitie, And *sympathize* poore Souldiers miserie" – *OED*, 1600

> Grief best is pleased with grief's society:
> *True* sorrow then is feelingly sufficed
> When with like semblance it is *sympathized*
> - *Lucrece*, lines 1111-1113

> As roused with rage, with rage doth *sympathize*
> - *Troilus and Cressida*, 1.3.52

> And the men do *sympathize* with the Mastiffs
> - *Henry V*, 3.7.158

12 IN TRUE PLAIN WORDS BY THY TRUE-TELLING FRIEND.
TRUE = Oxford; **TRUE PLAIN WORDS** = honest, simple words written by me, Oxford, whose motto is *Nothing Truer than Truth*; "That *every word* doth almost tell my name,/ Showing their birth and where they did proceed/ ... So all my best is dressing old *words* new" – Sonnet 76, lines 7-8, 11; to Elizabeth: "Be wise as thou art cruel, do not press/ My *tongue-tied* patience with too much disdain:/ Lest *sorrow lend me words*, and *words express*/ The manner of my pity-wanting pain" – Sonnet 140, lines 1-4; **PLAIN** = even, level, smooth, simple, artless, without disguise, frank, honest; "I pray my Lord pardon my scribbled hand. I have been this day let blood, that I could not *write so plain* as else I would have done for your better ease" – Oxford memo/letter, unaddressed, June 4, 1595, PRO SP 12/252 ff. 96-97, Chiljan 105

BY THY TRUE-TELLING FRIEND = by me, Edward deVere, your truth-telling father; "And *your true rights* be termed a Poet's rage" – Sonnet 17, line 11

No. 82

"But I hope *truth* is subject to no prescription, for *truth is truth* though never so old, and *time cannot make that false* which was once *true*" - Oxford to Robert Cecil, May 7, 1603

Prince, as thou art *true* - Romeo and Juliet, 3.1.149

… you will not touch the *true prince* - *1 Henry IV*, 2.4.296

It is not *truer* he is Angelo,
Than this is all as *true* as it is strange;
Nay, it is ten times *true*, for *truth is truth*
To th'end of reckoning - *Measure for Measure*, 4.6.46-48

Ever a Lover of the *Truth/Vere*
May these *words* be thy *True/Vere* motto
- To the illustrious woman, Lady Anne Vere, Countess of Oxford, while her illustrious husband, Edward Vere, Earl of Oxford, has been occupied in regions overseas
(1575-1576)

"And *simple* (plain) *truth* miscalled simplicity" – Sonnet 66, line 11; "On both sides thus is *simple* (plain) *truth* suppressed" – Sonnet 138, line 8, Oxford referring to both himself and Elizabeth, in suppressing the truth of their royal son

13 AND THEIR GROSS PAINTING MIGHT BE BETTER USED
THEIR GROSS PAINTING = coarse, blunt, rude, base attempts by "Shakespeare" and other poets to recreate your likeness with their words; "Describe *Adonis* and the counterfeit/ Is poorly imitated after you" – Sonnet 53, lines 5-6; and they might better use their talents (on those who already have royal blood, reflected by their cheeks, and so don't need it)

14 WHERE CHEEKS NEED BLOOD. IN THEE, IT IS ABUSED.
WHERE CHEEKS NEED BLOOD = for those who lack royal blood; "Thus is *his cheek* the map of days outworn" – Sonnet 68, line 1; "The *red rose and the white are on his face*, the fatal colours of our striving houses; the one his purple blood right well resembles, the other his pale *cheeks*, methinks, presenteth" – *3 Henry VI*, 2.5.97-100; **IN THEE IT IS ABUSED** = for you such writing is misdirected or misused, i.e., it misrepresents you (while here, in these private verses, you are being truly and accurately (but secretly) described

REFERENCE EDITION

THE "SHAKESPEARE" SACRIFICE
DAY FIFTY-SEVEN IN THE TOWER

Sonnet 83
Both Your Poets
5 April 1601

Oxford further explains his sacrifice. Southampton has both poets laboring to praise him: Oxford, in the private Sonnets; and Oxford under the guise of "William Shakespeare" the pen name, publicly linked to Henry Wriothesley by the dedications. (Perhaps also reminding us that Venus and Adonis and Lucrece are still highly popular, seven-eight years after publication, with numerous reprinting; and also that plays by Shakespeare are being published since 1598). It is Oxford who maintains his "silence" as payment or ransom for his royal son; and this silence "shall be most my glory, being dumb," while "Shakespeare" thrives.

Sonnet 83	Translation
I never saw that you did painting need,	I never saw that you needed any exaggeration,
And therefore to your fair no painting set.	And so I never added any to your royalty!
I found (or thought I found) you did exceed	I found (or thought I found) that you exceeded
The barren tender of a Poet's debt:	Anything that my private sonnets could offer.
And therefore have I slept in your report,	And so I've not spoken of you in public,
That you yourself, being extant, well might show	So that your royal self, being alive, would show
How far a modern quill doth come too short,	How my conventional words fall so short
Speaking of worth, what worth in you doth grow.	In telling of your royal blood and its growth in you.
This silence for my sin you did impute,	You looked upon this silence as my fault,
Which shall be most my glory, being dumb,	But it's actually my most glorious act,
For I impair not beauty, being mute,	Because, being silent, I don't harm your royalty,
When others would give life, and bring a tomb.	While others might speak aloud and get you killed.
There lives more life in one of your fair eyes	More royal blood shows in just one of your eyes,
Than both your Poets can in praise devise.	Than both "Shakespeare" and I could express.

1 I NEVER SAW THAT YOU DID PAINTING NEED,
I NEVER = I am E. Ver, Edward de Vere, *Ever or Never*; **PAINTING** = overblown rhetoric or hyperbole, as in Sonnet 17, line 11: "And your true rights be termed *a Poet's rage*"

2 AND THEREFORE TO YOUR FAIR NO PAINTING SET:
YOUR FAIR = your royalty; **NO PAINTING SET** = applied no exaggeration on your behalf; "A Woman's face with nature's own hand *painted*" – Sonnet 20, line 1; "Stirred by a *painted beauty* to his verse" – Sonnet 21, line 2; "Describe Adonis, and the counterfeit/ Is poorly imitated after you;/ On Helen's cheek all art of beauty set,/ And you in Grecian tires are *painted new*" – Sonnet 53, lines 5-8; "And their gross *painting* might be better used,/ Where cheeks need blood; in thee it is abused" – Sonnet 82, lines 13-14; "Truth needs no colour with his colour fixed,/ Beauty no pencil, beauty's truth to lay" – Sonnet 101, lines 6-7, all these lines to Southampton; "Painting thy outward walls so costly gay" – Sonnet 146, line 4, to Elizabeth, criticizing her

460

Part Two

3 I FOUND (OR THOUGHT I FOUND) YOU DID EXCEED
(OR THOUGHT I FOUND) = referring to the loss of Southampton's royal claim; **EXCEED** = surpass in terms of royal blood and claim

4 THE BARREN TENDER OF A POET'S DEBT:
BARREN = empty, childless; "Why is my verse so *barren* of new pride?" – Sonnet 76, line 1; **TENDER** = royal offering or repayment; a play on "tend" as "attending" Southampton, a prince or king; "That millions of strange shadows on you *tend*" – Sonnet 53, line 2; "Being slave, what should I do but *tend*/ Upon the hours and times of your desire" – Sonnet 57, lines 1-2; "For to no other pass my verses tend" – Sonnet 103, line 11; in another sense: "As *tender* nurse her babe from fairing ill" – Sonnet 22, line 12; (noun) "a person who tends; a person who attends to or takes charge of someone or something"; (verb) "*Law*: to offer, as money or goods, in payment of a debt or other obligation, esp. in exact accordance with the terms of the law and of the obligation ... the act of tendering; an offer of something for acceptance" – Random House Dictionary; **BARREN TENDER** = empty royal offering; i.e., Oxford's offer to Robert Cecil and King James, which apparently has been accepted, renders Southampton's royal blood and claim "barren"; "Why is my verse so *barren* of new pride?" – Sonnet 76, line 1; **POET'S DEBT** = my own debt to you, as father, which I am paying by the sacrifice of my paternity and of my identity as Shakespeare; "Of this proud King, who studies day and night to answer *all the debt* he owes to you" – *1 Henry IV*, 1.3.182-183; "My due from thee is this imperial crown" – Prince Hal to his father the King in *2 Henry IV*, 4.5.40

5 AND THEREFORE HAVE I SLEPT IN YOUR REPORT,
SLEPT IN YOUR REPORT = neglected to write publicly of you, to sound your praises (except under a pen name); I have written this diary of your life in secret; the way Southampton as an infant was once silent: "The *little Love-God lying once asleep*" – Sonnet 154, line 1, which also uses the image of *sleeping* to convey silence, hiding, secrecy; "As thou being mine, mine is *thy good report*" – Sonnets 36 and 96, line 14

6 THAT YOU YOUR SELF BEING EXTANT WELL MIGHT SHOW
YOU YOUR SELF = you, the prince or king; (as in "*I am that I am*" of Sonnet 121, when Oxford speaks of himself as father; ("*you your self*" – Sonnet 13, line 2; "But he that writes of you, if he can tell/ That *you are you*, so dignifies his story" – Sonnet 84, lines 7-8); "This is I, Hamlet the Dane!" – *Hamlet*, 5.2.255-256; **EXTANT** = alive at this moment, albeit in the Tower

7 HOW FAR A MODERN QUILL DOTH COME TOO SHORT,
MODERN QUILL = the ordinary pen of a contemporary poet; a trite pen; the pen of a poet ("Shakespeare") who is perhaps assumed (by some, but not all, readers) to be a commoner; **COME TOO SHORT** = fall short; "come" is an echo of "commoner," as Southampton has become in the Tower.

8 SPEAKING OF WORTH, WHAT WORTH IN YOU DOTH GROW.
WORTH = royalty; **WHAT WORTH IN YOU** = what royal blood in you; **WORTH** = you, Wriothesley; **DOTH GROW** = your royal blood still growing in this diary, in this womb of verse; "Making their *tomb* the *womb* wherein they *grew*" – Sonnet 86, line 4; "Love is a Babe: then might I not say so/ To *give full growth* to that which *still doth grow*" – Sonnet 115, lines 13-14

9 THIS SILENCE FOR MY SIN YOU DID IMPUTE,
THIS SILENCE = this secrecy; **FOR MY SIN** = for our crime of the Rebellion, which I have taken upon my shoulders; "this infectious sin" – Essex, referring to the crime, when he was about to be executed;**YOU DID IMPUTE** = you did regard or consider; also,"You have misperceived my public silence as a fault of mine."

10 WHICH SHALL BE MOST MY GLORY, BEING DUMB,
The supreme irony that Oxford's ultimate **GLORY** (reflection of his son's royalty) will only be attained by his secrecy and by giving up his identity as father and as "Shakespeare"; **GLORY** = ("And will you pale your head in Henry's *glory*?" – *3 Henry VI*, 1.4.103); "Crooked eclipses 'gainst his *glory* fight" – Sonnet 60, line 7; **DUMB** = silent, secret; unable to speak in public; "O learn to read what *silent love* hath writ" –

REFERENCE EDITION 461

Sonnet 23, line 13; "not show my head" – Sonnet 26, line 14; "For who's so *dumb* that cannot write to thee" – Sonnet 38, line 7

11 FOR I IMPAIR NOT BEAUTY, BEING MUTE,
I IMPAIR NOT BEAUTY = I do no damage to Elizabeth; I do no damage to your royal blood inherited from the Queen; **BEING MUTE** = being unable to speak

12 WHEN OTHERS WOULD GIVE LIFE AND BRING A TOMB.
WHEN = whereas; **OTHERS WOULD GIVE LIFE** = other poets, i.e., "Shakespeare", would attempt to record your life and preserve it; "So long as men can breathe or eyes can see,/ *So long lives this*, and *this gives life to thee*" – Sonnet 18, lines 13-14; **BRING A TOMB** = create only the "tomb" for you without the "womb" in which you may grow; Sonnet 17, lines 3-4, in which the verse of the Sonnets "is but as a *tomb*/ Which hides your life, and shows not half your parts"; although this "tomb" for Oxford's thoughts of his son also acts as "the womb wherein they grew" in Sonnet 86, line 4

13 THERE LIVES MORE LIFE IN ONE OF YOUR FAIR EYES
LIFE = royal blood; "But were some child of yours alive that time,/ You should live twice: in it, and in my rhyme" – Sonnet 17, lines 13-14; **ONE** = Southampton, *One for All, All for One*; **YOUR FAIR EYES** = your royal eyes; "An *eye more bright* than theirs" – Sonnet 20, line 5; "And scarcely greet me with *that sun, thine eye*" – Sonnet 49, line 6; "Flatter the mountain tops with *sovereign eye*" – Sonnet 33, line 2

14 THAN BOTH YOUR POETS CAN IN PRAISE DEVISE.
BOTH YOUR POETS = Oxford, poet of the Sonnets, and his pen name "Shakespeare," author of the public poems and also (more recently) a published playwright; **CAN IN PRAISE DEVISE** = can depict or envision or create enough praise of your royal worth in words

Part Two

THE "SHAKESPEARE" SACRIFICE
DAY FIFTY-EIGHT IN THE TOWER

Sonnet 84
He That Writes Of You
6 April 1601

Oxford continues to record his sacrifice to the "Shakespeare" name. He points to his pen name as the "counterpart" who praises Southampton publicly in print. Meanwhile he uses "confine" and "immured" and "Pen" to glance at Southampton's confinement in the Tower.

Sonnet 84	Translation
Who is it that says most, which can say mor	Which of us can say the most? Who can say more
Than this rich praise, that you alone are you,	Than this royal praise: that you, my son, are you,
In whose confine immured is the store	And that within yourself is the store of blood
Which should example where your equal grew?	That should be recorded by how you grow?
Lean penury within that Pen doth dwell,	It's a poverty of such royal blood in a writer
That to his subject lends not some small glory.	Who can't add any more of it to his topic.
But he that writes of you, if he can tell	But if "Shakespeare" writes of you and can reveal
That you are you, so dignifies his story.	Your royal self, he dignifies his words.
Let him but copy what in you is writ,	Let "Shakespeare" reflect what's inside you,
Not making worse what nature made so clear,	Without diminishing what Elizabeth gave you,
And such a counter-part shall fame his wit,	And this substitute poet will give his work fame,
Making his style admired everywhere.	Making his writings admired everywhere.
You to your beauteous blessings add a curse,	You add a curse to inheritance from the Queen,
Being fond on praise, which makes your praises worse.	Being confined to "Shakespeare's" public praise, which makes this praise less helpful to you.

1 WHO IS IT THAT SAYS MOST, WHICH CAN SAY MORE
WHO = which poet, Oxford or Oxford-as-Shakespeare; which one can better express the truth about you; which one can say more than the following rich praise:

2 THAN THIS RICH PRAISE: THAT YOU ALONE ARE YOU,
RICH = royal; ("Ha, majesty! How high thy glory towers when *the rich blood of kings* is set on fire!" – *King John*, 2.1.350-351; "thy *precious rich crown*" – *1 Henry IV*, 2.4.377-378); **RICH PRAISE** = writing filled with your royalty; **ALONE** = "all" and "one" of Southampton's motto *One for All, All for one*; **YOU ALONE** = you, Southampton; "Save that to die, I leave my love *alone*" - Sonnet 66, line 14; **YOU ALONE ARE YOU** = You are who you are, i.e., you are a king or god on earth; echoing the biblical statement "*I am that I am*" (God's words to Moses) of Sonnet 121, line 9; "*This is I*, Hamlet the Dane!" – *Hamlet*, 5.2.255-256; (see line 8: "you are you")

3 IN WHOSE CONFINE IMMURED IS THE STORE
CONFINE = Allusion to Southampton's confinement in the Tower; ("supposed as forfeit to a *confined* doom" – Sonnet 107, line 4; ("Denmark's a prison … in which there are many *confines*, wards, and

REFERENCE EDITION 463

dungeons" – *Hamlet*, 2.2.260,262-263); limits or bounds; ("Princes have less *confines* to their wills" – Strype, Eccl. Mem. II, 1548; "a place of confinement, confining or enclosing place; enclosure" – *OED (5)*; "At his (the cock's) warning ... th'extravagant and erring Spirit, hies to his *confine*" – *Hamlet*, 1.1.155; **IN WHOSE CONFINE** = in whose body, i.e., your royal blood is confined within your body, as in "*Thou art the grave where buried love doth live*" – Sonnet 31, line 9; **IMMURED** = "To be enclosed within walls" – Random House; i.e., surrounded by the high walls of the Tower of London; within the "confine" of Southampton himself

> Stay, yet look back with me unto the Tower.
> Pity, you ancient stones, those tender babes
> Whom envy hath *immured* within your walls!
> - *Richard III*, 4.1.97-99

> By my sweet soul, I mean setting thee at liberty,
> Enfreedoming thy person; thou wast *immured*,
> Restrained, captivated, bound
> - *Love's Labour's Lost*, 3.1.125-127

> Hoding their course to Paphos, where their Queen
> Means to *immure* herself and not be seen
> - *Venus and Adonis*, 1193-1194

STORE = the abundant storage of his royal blood, stored within himself, in the prison; ("O him she *stores*, to show what wealth she had" – Oxford, of Elizabeth keeping her son in the Tower, in Sonnet 67, line 13; "And him as for a map doth Nature *store*" – Sonnet 68, line 13); "something precious, a treasure ... a stock (of anything material or immaterial) laid up for future use" – *OED (6a)*; in whose body is enclosed the store of "love" or royal blood

4 WHICH SHOULD EXAMPLE WHERE YOUR EQUAL GREW?
EXAMPLE = describe, in writing; which should be described in words, by example, growing in equal measure with you; as these sonnets are "growing" along with your life, in conjunction with the withering time of Elizabeth's reign; **WHERE YOUR EQUAL GREW** = how or whereby your equal grew; alluding to Southampton's own growth in the womb of these sonnets; **YOUR EQUAL** = something (like this diary of the sonnets) which is equal to you in size or greatness and quality; "now *grown in grace equal with wondering*" – *The Winter's Tale*, 4.1.25; of same rank as you, i.e., the rank of a prince; "That the great body of our state may go *in equal rank* with the best-governed nation" – *2 Henry IV*, 5.2.136-137; "she is *no equal for his birth*" – *Much Ado About Nothing*, 2.1.156; equal in power; "I think we are a body strong enough, even as we are, to *equal with the King*" – *2 Henry IV*, 1.3.66-67; alluding to "equal" or fair justice that Oxford is securing for his son; the Queen to the King: "Sir, I desire you do me right and justice ... assurance of *equal* friendship and proceeding" – *Henry VIII*, 2.4.12-17

5 LEAN PENURY WITHIN THAT PEN DOTH DWELL
PENURY = poverty; empty of royalty; echoing the "pen" for writing and the "pen" or walls that keep Southampton penned-in; **IN THAT PEN DOTH DWELL** = very little royalty lives in that pen; also, related to Southampton dwelling in the "pen" or Tower prison; **PEN** = several meanings other than writing instrument; "a small enclosure for domestic animals ... applied to various enclosures" – *OED*, citing its use specifically to refer to the Tower of London:

He's taken to the *Tower's* strength ...
We have him in a *pen*, he cannot 'scape us - Fletcher & Massinger, *Double Marriage*, v.i, 1620

PEN = "a female swan" – *OED*, citing a 1550 reference to the King's swans; also signifying "head" in place names such as Penzance.

No. 84

6 **THAT TO HIS SUBJECT LENDS NOT SOME SMALL GLORY;**
THAT TO HIS SUBJECT LENDS NOT = that fails to give to his subject, i.e., to you; **SOME SMALL GLORY** = even a little glory; **GLORY** = "Thy crown, usurped, disgraced his *kingly glory*, *Richard III*, 4.4.372; "And crooked eclipses 'gainst *his glory* fight" – Sonnet 60, line 7

7 **BUT HE THAT WRITES OF YOU, IF HE CAN TELL**
HE THAT WRITES OF YOU = Oxford, in these sonnets; and Oxford, using the Shakespeare name, which he has publicly linked to Southampton through the dedications

8 **THAT YOU ARE YOU, SO DIGNIFIES HIS STORY.**
THAT YOU ARE YOU = That you are king; "O that *you were your self*, but love you are/ No longer yours than *you your self* here live" – Sonnet 13, lines 1-2; **HIS STORY** = "And in this harsh world draw thy breath in pain to *tell my story*" – *Hamlet*, 5.2.355-356; "story" is also a play on "store" of line 3 above; argument or topic; **DIGNIFIES** = invests with honor befitting a prince or king; gives luster to the story or "argument" of his writings; "And *you and love are still my argument*" – Sonnet 76, line 10; "Both truth and beauty on my love depends:/ So dost thou too, and therein *dignified*" – Sonnet 101, lines 3-4; "So shall *these slaves be king*, and thou their slave:/ Thou nobly base, *they basely dignified*" – *Lucrece*, 659-660; lends worth or merit or, in the case of the Sonnet, lends royal blood to the verses; "But if that flower (Southampton) with base infection meet,/ The basest weed (Southampton) *outbraves his dignity*" – Sonnet 94, lines 11-12, warning his son to avoid the "infection" of other potential traitors in the Tower; "The *dignity* of this act was worth the audience *of kings and princes*" – *The Winter's Tale*, 5.2.81-82; ("dignity" = "sovereignty, royal power" – Schmidt; "for my cloud of *dignity* is held from falling with so weak a wind that it will quickly drop; *my day is dim*" – *2 Henry IV*, 4.5.98-100; "Then, good lord, take to *your royal self* this proffer'd benefit of *dignity*" – *Richard III*, 3.7.194-195

9 **LET HIM BUT COPY WHAT IN YOU IS WRIT,**
COPY WHAT IN YOU IS WRIT = the image of Oxford, in these sonnets, merely copying down the royal blood that is already "written" within the veins of his son; following Hamlet's advice to hold the mirror up to nature; "She (nature, Elizabeth) carved thee for her seal, and meant thereby/ Thou shouldst *print more*, not let that *copy* die" – Sonnet 11, lines 13-14; **WRIT** = written; recorded privately (silently, secretly) in this historical document of the Sonnets; "O learn to read what silent love hath *writ*" – Sonnet 23, line 13; "Nay if you read this line, remember not/ The hand that *writ* it" – Sonnet 71, lines 5-6; "If this be error and upon me proved,/ I never *writ*, nor no man ever loved" – Sonnet 116, lines 13-14; also a legal document, such as an official "writ" or commandment; W. Nicholas Knight, discussing Shakespeare's intimate knowledge of the law, refers to the puns on "writ" in the Sonnets and the author's familiarity with "writs, warrants, compacts, testaments and wills" (*Shakespeare's Hidden Life*, 1973, p. 79); and all these are subject matter in Oxford's letters to the Cecils; in the Sonnets the suggestion is that the father-son relationship is not only natural but, also, legal

10 **NOT MAKING WORSE WHAT NATURE MADE SO CLEAR,**
NATURE = Elizabeth; "*Nature's bequest* gives nothing but doth lend" – Sonnet 4, line 3; **WHAT NATURE MADE** = what the Queen created, gave birth to, i.e., Southampton and his blood; "She (nature) carved thee for her seal" – Sonnet 11, line 13; "A Woman's face with *nature's own hand painted*" – Sonnet 20, line 1; **SO CLEAR** = "The *clearest* gods" – *King Lear*, 4.6.73; i.e., Queen Elizabeth created her son as a "clear" or illustrious king or god on earth; similar to "plain" as in "*true plain words* by thy true-telling friend" – Sonnet 82, line 12

11 **AND SUCH A COUNTERPART SHALL FAME HIS WIT,**
And such a substitute poet, offering such a mirror image, will gain eternal fame for his poetry; **COUNTERPART** = Shakespeare's rendering of you; *OED* offers no example of "counterpart" as "copy" until later in the 17th century; in law during Oxford's lifetime, it was "the opposite part of an indenture ... the executed *copy* of a *lease or receipt* retained by the grantor as a counter-security" – i.e., an apt description of Oxford's bargain for Southampton, providing "Shakespeare" as the "counterpart" of the "lease"; as he will write upon the release or "re-lease" of Southampton from the Tower on April 10, 1603: "Not mine own

REFERENCE EDITION 465

fears, nor the prophetic soul/ Of the wide world dreaming on things to come/ Can yet the *lease* of my true love control,/ Supposed as forfeit to a *confined* doom" – Sonnet 107, lines 1-4; "Sir Walter Raleigh ... endorsed with his own hand on *the counterpart of the lease*" – OED, 1617

12 MAKING HIS STYLE ADMIRED EVERYWHERE.
EVERYWHERE = Ever = E. Ver, Edward deVere; i.e., anyone who truly describes your royal self will be a public hero

13 YOU TO YOUR BEAUTEOUS BLESSINGS ADD A CURSE:
BEAUTEOUS BLESSINGS = royal Tudor blood and sacred qualities; "Seeking that *beauteous* roof to ruinate" – Sonnet 10, line 7, referring to the House of Tudor under the rule of Beauty or Elizabeth; "Look down, you gods, and on this couple drop a *blessed crown*" – The Tempest, 5.1.201-202; "This royal infant (heaven still move about her), though in her cradle, yet now promises upon this land a thousand thousand *blessings,* which *time* shall bring to ripeness" – Archbishop Cranmer, speaking of the infant Elizabeth, in *Henry VII*, 5.4.17-20, associating "time" with the life and reign of Elizabeth, as in the Sonnets; **CURSE** = a malediction or great vexation or great drawback; to your royal qualities must be added this drawback or warning:

14 BEING FOND ON PRAISE, WHICH MAKES YOUR PRAISES WORSE.
Doting on my praises, which, by revealing your royal claim, themselves amount to an act of treason; and for being fond of my verses as by "Shakespeare," which cannot do you justice; **PRAISE/PRAISES** = words of devotion uttered to a prince or king; "our own Queen, to whom alone is due all the *praises* of all the *Muses* and all the glory of literature" – Oxford's Letter to the Reader for *The Courtier*, 1572; "If my slight *Muse* do please these curious days,/ The pain be mine, but *thine shall be the praise*" – Sonnet 38, lines 13-14; "Your *praise* shall still find room/ Even in the eyes of all posterity" – Sonnet 55, lines 10-11; "and *praise my Maker*" – *Henry VIII*, 5.4.68; in effect, Oxford is warning his son to go along with the bargain for his release, forfeiting all claim to the throne; this is the "curse" that comes with Southampton's acknowledgment of his identity as prince, the praises of which are to be found in these private, and potentially treasonous if made public, sonnets.

Part Two

THE "SHAKESPEARE" SACRIFICE
DAY FIFTY-NINE IN THE TOWER

Sonnet 85
My Tongue-Tied Muse
7 April 1601

Oxford nears the end of the Rival Poet series recording the sacrifice of his identity as the writer of the "Shakespeare" works, as part of his agreement to bury his father-son bond with Southampton. Oxford refers to his dumb thoughts, speaking in effect within the Sonnets, leading to the next verse, wherein his thoughts are revealed as both the "tomb" and "womb" of his royal son, to preserve him and to grow him. "Shakespeare" is the means by which authority or officialdom has "tongue-tied" Oxford, his Muse and his art.

Sonnet 85	Translation
My tongue-tied Muse in manners holds her still,	My strictly censored Muse stays silent,
While comments of your praise, richly compiled,	While "Shakespeare's" public poems for you
Reserve their Character with golden quill,	Are preserved with royal-speaking words,
And precious phrase by all the Muses filed.	And each royal phrase is polished for him.
I think good thoughts, whilst other write good words,	I think of you here, while "Shakespeare" writes good words,
And like unlettered clerk still cry Amen,	And like an unlettered clerk I always cry "Amen"
To every Hymn that able spirit affords,	To every poem that I write for him
In polished form of well-refined pen.	In his polished and refined style for publication.
Hearing you praised, I say, "'Tis so, 'Tis true,"	Reading his words, I say, "These are my words,"
And to the most of praise add something more;	And to the praise of you I add more praise;
But that is in my thought, whose love to you	But that's in my thought, whose regard for you
(Though words come hindmost) holds his rank before.	(Though words fail me) is far ahead of anyone else's.
Then others, for the breath of words respect,	So respect "Shakespeare" for his public words,
Me for my dumb thoughts, speaking in effect.	And me for my silent thoughts, speaking here.

1 MY TONGUE-TIED MUSE IN MANNERS HOLDS HER STILL
MY TONGUE-TIED MUSE = my inspiration for the Sonnets, forced to speak indirectly through my "invention" or special language; ("And art made *tongue-tied by authority*" – Sonnet 66, line 9); **IN MANNERS** = by convention; by the manners of the Court; according to the "noted weed" or familiar garb of poetry; ("This Edward, whom our *manners* call the Prince" – Richard III, 3.7.190); "O how thy worth with *manners* may I sing" – Sonnet 39, line 1; "Look how the father's face /Lives in his issue, even so, the race/ Of Shakespeare's mind and *manners* brightly shines" – Ben Jonson in the First Folio, 1623; **HOLDS HER STILL** = continues always to restrain herself; **HER** = in mythology, muses are female

2 WHILE COMMENTS OF YOUR PRAISE, RICHLY COMPILED,
YOUR PRAISE = expressions of your royalty; **RICHLY COMPILED** = royally compiled, as these sonnets are being composed/compiled as entries of a diary

REFERENCE EDITION

3 RESERVE THEIR CHARACTER WITH GOLDEN QUILL
RESERVE THEIR CHARACTER = retain and preserve their royal contents; **CHARACTER** = allusion to the written words; "What's in the brain that ink may *character*,/ Which hath not figured to thee my true spirit?" – Sonnet 108, lines 1-2; **THEIR** = sometimes emended to "thy" or "your"; **GOLDEN QUILL** = a pen filled with your golden or royal blood; **GOLDEN** = royal, derived from the sun; ("Hid'st thou that forehead with a golden crown" – *Richard III*, 4.4.140; "claim the crown, for that's the golden mark I seek to hit" – *2 Henry VI,* 1.1.243-244; "To bear the golden yoke of sovereignty" – *Richard III*, 3.7.145)

4 AND PRECIOUS PHRASE BY ALL THE MUSES FILED.
PRECIOUS PHRASE = royal writings, i.e., these sonnets; **ALL** = Southampton, *One for All, All for One*; **BY ALL THE MUSES FILED**: "Look how the father's face /Lives in his issue, even so, the race/ Of Shakespeare's mind and manners brightly shines/ In his well torned and *true-filed lines:* In each of which he seems to shake a Lance/ As brandished at the eyes of Ignorance" – Ben Jonson in the First Folio of Shakespeare plays, 1623; **ALL THE MUSES** = "to whom alone is due all the praise of *all the Muses* and all the glory of literature" – Oxford, writing of Elizabeth, in his Letter to the Reader for *The Courtier*, 1572; "Wherefore you Muses nine" – Oxford poem in *The Paradise of Dainty Devices*, 1576

5 I THINK GOOD THOUGHTS, WHILST OTHER WRITE GOOD WORDS,
I think of you; **OTHER** = Oxford's pseudonym "Shakespeare"; perhaps meant to be spelled as "others" but accurately (and possibly deliberately) singular in reference to the pen name; your other poet, my "Shakespeare" pen name, writes good words of you, in the dedications/lines of *Venus and Adonis* & *Lucrece*, of 1593 and 1594, and in *The Phoenix and the Turtle*, to be printed this year (1601).

6 AND LIKE UNLETTERED CLERK STILL CRY "AMEN"
LIKE UNLETTERED CLERK = ("like an illiterate clerk" – Booth); Oxford is referring to himself in relation to "Shakespeare", i.e., he must be silent as opposed to the pen name; but perhaps also referring to the man from Stratford with a similar name who has by now been designated to become, in the future and after his death, a substitute for the real author; **CLERK** = cleric or minister or priest

7 TO EVERY HYMN THAT ABLE SPIRIT AFFORDS
EVERY = E. Ver, Edward de Vere, *Ever or Never*; "That *every* word doth almost tell *my name*" – Sonnet 76, line 7; **EVERY HYMN** = Oxford's sonnets, which are hymns or divine prayers to Southampton as a god on earth; ("*hymns at heaven's gate*" = Sonnet 29, line 12; "prayers divine" – Sonnet 108, line 5); **THAT ABLE SPIRIT AFFORDS** = that Oxford's own spirit supplies to "Shakespeare"; (as in Sonnet 86, lines 9-10: "that *affable familiar ghost* which nightly gulls him with intelligence"); Spirit = Sonnets 56, 61, 74, 80, 86, 108, 129, 144; **AFFORDS** = "And in this change is my invention spent,/ Three themes in one, which wondrous scope *affords*" – Sonnet 105, lines 11-12; "I am thy father's *spirit*, doom'd for a certain term to walk the night" – *Hamlet*, 1.5.9-10

8 IN POLISHED FORM OF WELL-REFINED PEN.
In the highly polished, cultured style used by "Shakespeare" in his published poetry dedicated to Southampton; "I know not how I shall offend in dedicating my *unpolished* lines to your Lordship" – dedication of *Venus and Adonis* to Southampton by "Shakespeare," whose lines were actually polished in the extreme; "The world will be thy widow and still weep/ That thou no *form of thee* hast left behind" – Sonnet 9, lines 5-6; "How would thy shadow's *form form* happy show" – Sonnet 43, line 6

9 HEARING YOU PRAISED I SAY, "'TIS TRUE, 'TIS TRUE,"
Seeing you praised by "Shakespeare"; hearing his lines; '**TIS TRUE** = it is accurate; "'tis true' = "it's me", Oxford, *Nothing Truer than Truth,* who actually writes of you

10 AND TO THE MOST OF PRAISE ADD SOMETHING MORE;
MOST OF PRAISE = utmost of praise

11 BUT THAT IS IN MY THOUGHT, WHOSE LOVE TO YOU

But that added praise of you is in my thoughts, which are secret, expressed in these private sonnets; **LOVE** = Oxford's love for his son and acknowledgment of his son's royal blood as well

12 (THOUGH WORDS COME HINDMOST) HOLDS HIS RANK BEFORE.

Though my words come last, in these unpublished verses; **HOLDS HIS RANK BEFORE** = "maintains first position in the hierarchy of those who love you" – Duncan-Jones; Oxford's rank as Southampton's father; his higher rank as hereditary Lord Great Chamberlain; his higher rank in terms of his ancient earldom, going back 500 years; his higher "rank" or position as the true author of the works attributed to "Shakespeare"

13 THEN OTHERS FOR THE BREATH OF WORDS RESPECT;

OTHERS = i.e., "Shakespeare"; **RESPECT** = regard; pay their respects; **BREATH OF WORDS** = ("windy suspiration of forced breath" – *Hamlet*, 1.2.84, referring contemptuously to words uttered at a funeral)

14 ME FOR MY DUMB THOUGHTS, SPEAKING IN EFFECT.

DUMB = unspoken, but written in the Sonnets; **IN EFFECT** = honestly, though indirectly; in action; so my thoughts, recorded in these private sonnets, are far more valuable than those being published under the Shakespeare name

THE MONUMENT

FINAL VERSE OF THE "SHAKESPEARE" SACRIFICE
DAY SIXTY IN THE TOWER

END OF THE DAY-TO-DAY VERSES
(Sonnets 27-86 = 60 sonnets in 60 days)

Sonnet 86
Making Their Tomb The Womb
Struck Me Dead
8 April 1601

Oxford has completed negotiations with Robert Cecil to have Southampton's conviction for high treason reduced to "misprision" of treason, paving the way for his eventual release by King James (assuming he will succeed Elizabeth) and a royal pardon. This sacrifice of all ties to his son, together with the sacrifice of his identity as the poet-playwright "Shakespeare," is now complete: "But when your countenance filled up his line,/ Then lacked I matter, that enfeebled mine." Oxford takes full responsibility for this decision, declaring that no others can boast of being "victors of my silence." Now he ends the so-called Rival Poet series, preparing to announce "misprision" in the next verse.

Sonnet 86	Translation
Was it the proud full sail of his great verse,	Was it the great verse of "Shakespeare",
Bound for the prize of (all too precious) you,	Supporting your all-too-royal claim,
That did my ripe thoughts in my brain inhearse	That caused my own thoughts to be buried here,
Making their tomb the womb wherein they grew?	So my tomb of verse is a womb in which you grow?
Was it his spirit, by spirits taught to write	Was it "Shakespeare's" spirit, taught by me to write
Above a mortal pitch, that struck me dead?	Better than anyone else, that made me silent?
No, neither he, nor his compeers by night	No, neither he nor any other spirits that secretly
Giving him aid, my verse astonished.	Help him have struck these sonnets dead.
He, nor that affable familiar ghost	Not "Shakespeare," nor my friendly Muse
Which nightly gulls him with intelligence,	Which nightly feeds him full with the truth,
As victors of my silence cannot boast;	Can claim to be the cause of my silence!
I was not sick of any fear from thence.	I was not silenced by any fear of them!
But when your countenance filled up his line,	But when you filled "Shakespeare's" verse,
Then lacked I matter, that enfeebled mine.	Then I was drained; that silenced my sonnets.

1 WAS IT THE PROUD FULL SAIL OF HIS GREAT VERSE,
PROUD = royally inspired, i.e., inspired by Southampton's royal self; **PROUD FULL SAIL** = "Then lofty Love, thy *sacred* **sails** advance" – Oxford poem in *The Paradise of Dainty Devices*, 1576, attributed to "E.O." in 1577 and thereafter; "either *without* **sail** *whereby to take the advantage of any prosperous gale*" – Oxford to Robert Cecil, April 25/27, 1603; the image of "Shakespeare" riding on the great "ocean" of royal blood possessed by Southampton; **HIS GREAT VERSE** = the poems attributed to "Shakespeare" and dedicated to Henry Wriothesley, Third Earl of Southampton; **HIS** = Shakespeare's, i.e., the so-called Rival Poet, the printed pen name

2 BOUND FOR THE PRIZE OF (ALL TOO PRECIOUS) YOU,
BOUND FOR = ready or prepared for; destined for; intending to possess; "I am much bound to Your Majesty" – *King John*, 3.3.29; "Were my worth greater, my duty would show greater; meantime, as it is, it is bound to your Lordship" – Oxford writing as "Shakespeare" to Henry Wriothesley, Earl of Southampton in the *Lucrece* dedication to him of 1594; **PRIZE** = your succession to Elizabeth as king; "For truth proves thievish for *a prize so dear*" – Sonnet 48, line 14; **ALL** = Southampton, *One for All, All for One*; "Since *all alike* my songs and praises be/ To one, of one, still such, and ever so" – Sonnet 105, lines 3-4; **PRECIOUS** = royal; "Tend'ring the *precious* safety of my prince" – *Richard III*, 1.1.32; **YOU** = Southampton, the prince

3 THAT DID MY RIPE THOUGHTS IN MY BRAIN INHEARSE,
INHEARSE = bury, as in the tomb of the Sonnets; ("the image of the brain as a *womb*, fairly common, also recalls Thorpe's identification of *Mr. W. H.* as the sonnets' *only begetter*" – Duncan-Jones); "What's *in the brain* that ink may character,/ Which hath not figured to thee my true spirit?/ Nothing, sweet boy" – Sonnet 108, lines 1-3

4 MAKING THEIR TOMB THE WOMB WHEREIN THEY GREW?
"*My heart*, sweet boy, shall be *thy sepulcher*" – father to son in *3 Henry VI*, 2.5.115; "The earth that's nature's mother is her *tomb*; what is her burying grave that is her *womb*" – *Romeo and Juliet*, 2.3.10-11; **THEIR TOMB** = the tomb of his thoughts, i.e., forcing the thoughts of his brain into the tomb of this monument of the Sonnets being constructed for his son; "Though yet heaven knows it is but as a *tomb/* Which hides your life, and shows not half your parts" – Sonnet 17, lines 3-4, referring to these private verses; **THE WOMB WHEREIN THEY GREW** = the tomb is also the womb in which his thoughts (of Southampton and his royal blood) have been growing according to time, thereby creating "the *living record* of your memory" – Sonnet 55, line 8; "To make him *much outlive a gilded tomb*" – Sonnet 101, line 11

5 WAS IT HIS SPIRIT, BY SPIRITS TAUGHT TO WRITE,
HIS SPIRIT = "Shakespeare's" power; **BY SPIRITS TAUGHT TO WRITE** = guided in his writing by Oxford's own spirit on behalf of his royal son; taught to write about you by my own spirits, secretly, behind the pen name.

> My father is gone wild into his grave,
> For in his *tomb* lie my affections;
> And with his *spirits* sadly I survive
> To mock the expectation of the world
> - Prince Hal in *2 Henry IV*, 5.2.123-126

SPIRIT = also royal blood; to Elizabeth: "Th'expense of spirit in a waste of shame/ Is lust in action, and till action lust/ Is perjured, murderous, bloody, full of blame" – Sonnet 129, lines 1-3

6 ABOVE A MORTAL PITCH, THAT STRUCK ME DEAD?
ABOVE A MORTAL PITCH = above any height reached by mere mortals, in accordance with the royal blood of Southampton, which makes him immortal; **STRUCK ME DEAD** = obliterated my identity

7 NO! NEITHER HE, NOR HIS COMPEERS BY NIGHT
HE = "Shakespeare"; **HIS COMPEERS BY NIGHT** = his companions, my spirits, by night; possibly also alluding to the "School of Night" consisting of Oxford, Raleigh, Marlowe, Harriot, Chapman, Dee, etc., but more immediately and specifically referring to Oxford's spirit that infuses "Shakespeare" with his knowledge and power; **BY NIGHT** = during this time of dark disgrace; "Lo thus by day my limbs, *by night my mind,/* For thee, and for my self, no quiet find" – Sonnet 27, lines 13-14; "But day doth daily draw my sorrows longer,/ And *night doth nightly* make grief's length seem stronger" – Sonnet 28, lines 13-14

8 GIVING HIM AID, MY VERSE ASTONISHED.
By giving "Shakespeare" assistance, I stunned my own sonnets into secrecy and public silence; **MY VERSE** = "Who will believe *my verse* in time to come" – Sonnet 17, line 1; "Why is *my verse* so barren of

new pride?" – Sonnet 76, line 1; "Therefore *my verse* to constancy confined" – Sonnet 105, line 7;
ASTONISHED = "stunned as by a thunder-stroke" – Dowden; "Stone-still, *astonished* with this deadly deed" – *Lucrece*, 1730

9 HE, NOR THAT AFFABLE FAMILIAR GHOST
HE = "Shakespeare"; **THAT AFFABLE FAMILIAR GHOST** = that friendly servant, my spirit, which is ghostlike; ("a 'familiar' is a demon in the power of a conjurer whose bidding he does" – Booth); a suggestion of the Holy Ghost of the Trinity; as the Ghost of Hamlet's father informs the Prince:

> I am *thy father's spirit*,
> Doom'd for a certain term to walk the night,
> And for the day confined to fast in fires,
> Till the foul crimes done in my days of nature
> Are burnt and purged away. But that *I am forbid*
> To tell the secrets of my prison-house,
> *I could a tale unfold* whose lightest word
> Would harrow up thy soul, freeze thy young blood,
> Make thy two eyes like stars start from their spheres
> - *Hamlet*, 1.5.9-17

10 WHICH NIGHTLY GULLS HIM WITH INTELLIGENCE,
That nightly fills or crams "Shakespeare" with information; **INTELLIGENCE** = suggestive of secret information, gathered by spies, for the government; Oxford worked with Sir Francis Walsingham, Secretary of State until 1590, by supporting writings who were also involved as agents or spies gathering intelligence; knowledge of the truth; **GULLS** = ("Let us *gull* ourselves with eating and quaffing" – *OED*, from 1604)

11 AS VICTORS OF MY SILENCE CANNOT BOAST:
VICTORS OF MY SILENCE = conquerors of my identity, forcing me into silence; "And art made *tongue-tied by authority*" – Sonnet 66, line 9; neither my pen name nor my ghostly spirit that informs it can boast that they were the ones who, victoriously, forced me into silence; rather it was my own decision, based on the need to save my royal son; it was my choice to accept my son's guilt and to counsel against any further attempt by him to gain the throne, thereby averting a potential civil war.

> "The rest is silence" – Hamlet's final words in *Hamlet*, 5.2.365

12 I WAS NOT SICK OF ANY FEAR FROM THENCE.
I was not afraid of those things; **SICK** = related to an indisposition of the mind; "No, my Brutus; you have some *sick offence within your mind*" – *Julius Caesar*, 2.1.267-268; being in an irregular or distempered state; "I *sick* withal the help of bath desired,/ And thither hied, a *sad distempered* guest" – Sonnet 153, lines 11-12, in 1574, after Elizabeth had refused to acknowledge their son; "As to prevent our maladies unseen,/ We *sicken* to shun *sickness* when we purge/ … And *sick* of welfare found a kind of meetness/ To be diseased/ … Drugs poison him that so *fell sick of you*" – Sonnet 118, lines 3-4, using the metaphor of sickness over the loss of his son's royal claim that "brought to medicine a healthful state" – Sonnet 118, line 11, in terms of the accession of James without civil war around the throne; **FEAR** = apprehension, dread; or a thing to be dreaded; **FROM THENCE** = from that place or from those things

13 BUT WHEN YOUR COUNTENANCE FILLED UP HIS LINE,
But when your royal self filled up "Shakespeare's" lines of verse; ("The Lord lift up his *countenance* upon thee" – Numbers, 6.26, cited by Duncan-Jones); **LINE** = lines of verse; royal lineage; "In his well-torned and *true-filed lines*" – Ben Jonson on Shakespeare, First Folio, 1623, but in this sonnet the accurate word is "*filled* up his line"; "Unto a *lineal*, true-derived course" – *Richard III*, 3.7.199; "Being but *fourth of that heroic line*" – *1 Henry VI*, 2.5.78; "from *whose line I claim the crown*" – *2 Henry VI*, 2.2.33; "They hailed him *father to a line of kings*" – *Macbeth*, 3.1.59; "So should the *lines of life* that life repair" – Sonnet 16, line 9; "When in *eternal lines to time* thou grow'st" – Sonnet 18, line 12; "His beauty shall *in these black lines* be

seen" – Sonnet 63, line 13; "My life hath *in this line* some interest,/ Which for memorial still with thee shall stay" – Sonnet 74, lines 3-4

14 THEN LACKED I MATTER: THAT ENFEEBLED MINE.
Then I lacked power or substance; that enfeebled my own self; "To have is to have: for it is a figure in rhetoric that drink, being poured out of a cup into a glass, *by filling the one doth empty the other.* For all your writers do consent that *ipse* is he. Now, you are not *ipse,* for I am he" – *As You Like It*, 5.1.39-43, Touchstone to William, the country fellow, designated as future stand-in for "William Shakespeare" – the passage being a mirror-image of the concluding couplet of this sonnet, the final verse of the Rival Poet series; **MATTER** = "Thus have I had thee as a dream doth flatter:/ *In sleep a King, but waking no such matter*" – Sonnet 87, lines 13-14, Oxford referring to himself as the father of a king in his dreams, but not in reality.

THE MONUMENT

SOUTHAMPTON'S JUDGMENT REDUCED TO "MISPRISION" OF TREASON

THIRD MONTH IN THE TOWER

Sonnet 87
*Upon Misprision Growing
In Sleep a King*
April 1601

Edward de Vere indicates the legal basis for Southampton's reduction of sentence from execution to continued imprisonment, paving the way for his ultimate release (by King James) followed by a royal pardon. This "better judgment" is "misprision" of treason, a lesser offense; and in return, Southampton must give up his claim to be King Henry IX of England. As Oxford records it, having his son as a King was like a dream: "In sleep a King, but waking no such matter." The government will make no public announcement of the "misprision" judgment, however, so Oxford himself is recording it for posterity.

Sonnet 87	Translation
Farewell, thou art too dear for my possessing,	Farewell! You are too royal to be my son!
And like enough thou knowst thy estimate.	And most likely you know your royal value!
The Charter of thy worth gives thee releasing:	Your sovereign privilege will set you free:
My bonds in thee are all determinate.	My relationship to you is publicly severed.
For how do I hold thee but by thy granting,	For how do I keep you except at your command?
And for that riches where is my deserving?	And why do I deserve you as my royal son?
The cause of this fair gift in me is wanting,	I lack any reason to have your royal gift to me,
And so my patent back again is swerving.	And so my rights to it are returned to you.
Thy self thou gav'st, thy own worth then not knowing,	You gave your royal self, at birth not knowing your blood,
Or me, to whom thou gav'st it, else mistaking;	Or else you mistakenly thought I deserved it.
So thy great gift, upon misprision growing,	So the great gift of your life, effected by misprision,
Comes home again, on better judgment making.	Is given back to you by means of a better verdict.
Thus have I had thee as a dream doth flatter:	So I've had you as my royal son as in a dream:
In sleep a King, but waking no such matter.	In sleep I had a King, but in reality it's not so.

1 FAREWELL! THOU ART TOO DEAR FOR MY POSSESSING!
Goodbye, my son, you are too royal for me to possess you as your father; i.e., the very fact of your royal blood and claim is what forces us to break our father-son bond, at least in public during our lifetimes and into the foreseeable future; **FAREWELL!** = Oxford breaks all ties to his son, publicly, as father and son

> Thus *farewell, friend*, I will continue strange…
> - Poem most likely by Oxford; printed unsigned in Rawlinson Poet. MS 85, f. 17, on the page adjacent to Oxford's signed sonnet "Who taught thee how to sigh, alas, my heart"; (Chiljan 184)

474

THOU ART TOO DEAR FOR MY POSSESSING = the bargain Oxford made with Robert Cecil and James of Scotland requires his complete disassociation from Southampton as father-son; the daily verses have now ended; "farewell" itself combines "fair" for Southampton and possibly "well" for Oxford as Ver = spring or well

DEAR = precious, royal; "By *dear* Christ's blood" – *Richard III*, 1.4.186; "This land of such *dear* souls, this *dear dear* land, *dear* for her reputation through the world" – *Richard II*, 2.1.57-58; "And he would love me *dearly* as his child" – *Richard III*, 2.2.26; "thy *dearest* heart-blood" – *3 Henry VI*, 1.1.229; "precious ... costly ... grievous" – Booth; "So I, made lame by *Fortune's dearest* spite" – Sonnet 37, line 3, referring to Elizabeth and her spiteful treatment of their "dearest" son; "If my *dear love* were but the child of state,/ It might for fortune's bastard be unfathered" – Sonnet 124, lines 1-2, referring to Southampton as his dear son, whose truth is recorded and preserved in these sonnets

2 AND LIKE ENOUGH THOU KNOW'ST THY ESTIMATE.
And surely enough you know your own royal value; **ESTIMATE** = royal value or valuation; "If he will touch the *estimate*" – the Jeweler in *Timon of Athens*, 1.1.14; "A judgment formed or expressed respecting the character or qualities of a person or thing" – *OED*; "As on the finger of a throned Queen/ The basest Jewel will be well *esteemed*" – Sonnet 96; "None else of name and noble *estimate*" – *Richard II*, 2.3.56

3 THE CHARTER OF THY WORTH GIVES THEE RELEASING:
CHARTER = an official statement or decree, indicated here despite the fact that the English government left no known record of why the Queen had spared Southampton's life; "the official document that confers high rank and special privilege on you" – Booth; "You break no privilege nor *charter* there" – *Richard III*, 2.4.54; Sonnet 58, line 9; "A written document delivered by the sovereign (a) granting privileges to, or recognizing rights of; (b) granting pardon; hence 'to have one's charter' = to receive pardon" – *OED*, citing 1480: "Maister John hume had his chartre and was pardoned by the King"; "Be where you list, your *charter* is so strong/ That you yourself may privilege your time/ To what you will: *to you it doth belong/Yourself to pardon of self-doing crime*" – Sonnet 58, lines 9-12

> It is obvious that his chosen terms point not to nobility, but to *royalty*. And as if to clinch it, what he sets before us ... is *not* the powers of a peer, but those peculiar to a king: power *to grant charters of privlege* and *letters patent*, power *to pardon* crimes – in short, the exclusively *royal preogrative* -- (Leslie Hotson, "Mr. W.H.", 1965, his emphasis)

"But as the *grant* goes, it is far greater than ever I thought they durst have presumed, for by having it to them ... hereby Her Majesty's *prerogative* for that commodity methinks is given away from the Crown." - Oxford memo, undated, Huntington Library MS EL 2336

"I must have *liberty* withal, as large a *charter* as the wind, to blow on whom I please .... Give me leave to speak my mind, and I will through and through cleanse the foul body of th'infected world, if they will patiently receive my medicine" – Jacques in *As You Like It*, 2.7.47-49, 58-61, a self-portrait of Oxford the playwright; using "charter" in relation to "liberty" as he does in this Sonnet related to Southampton's ultimate liberation from the Tower

THY WORTH = your royalty; ("the glorious worth of my descent" – *Richard II*, 1.1.107);

GIVES THEE RELEASING = The bargain with Robert Cecil has paved the way for James Stuart, if and when he becomes King of England, to release Southampton from the Tower, on the condition that the earl never claims his right to the throne; "sets you free" – Booth); perhaps also a play on "lease" as "re-lease" or draw up another lease, as Oxford will write upon Southampton's release from the Tower on April 10, 1603: "Not mine own fears nor the prophetic soul/ Of the wide world dreaming on things to come/ Can yet the *lease* of my true love control" – Sonnet 107, lines 1-4; ("And summer's *lease* hath all too short a date" – Sonnet 18, line 4; "Which works on the *lease* of short numb'red hours" – Sonnet 124, line 10

4 MY BONDS IN THEE ARE ALL DETERMINATE.
My father-son connection to you is all decided and ended; **MY BONDS IN THEE** = their father-son bond; recalling the *Lucrece* dedication to Henry Wriothesley: "my duty … is *bound* to your Lordship"; **BOND** = *OED*: "(1a) Anything with which one's body or limbs are bound in restraint of personal liberty … (1b) confinement, imprisonment, custody"; also (7a) "a uniting or cementing force or influence by which a union of any kind is maintained"; legal agreement between borrower and lender; bonds of kinship, as in: "I love your Majesty *according to my bond*, no more and no less" – *King Lear*, 1.1.92-93, Cordelia to Lear, her father

> I tore them from their *bonds* and cried aloud,
> 'O that these hands could so redeem my son,
> As they have given these hairs their liberty!'
> But now I envy at their liberty,
> And will again commit them to their *bonds*,
> Because my poor child is a prisoner
> - *King John*, 3.3.70-75

> My duty … is *bound* to your Lordship
> - Dedication of *Lucrece* to Southampton

> Thy merit hath my duty *strongly knit*
> - Sonnet 26, line 2

> Whereto *all bonds do tie me* day by day
> - Sonnet 117, line 4

> All *bond* and *privilege of nature* break!
> - *Coriolanus*, 5.3.25

> Cressid is mine, tied with the *bonds* of heaven…
> The *bonds* of heaven are slipp'd, dissolv'd, and loos'd
> - *Troilus and Cressida*, 5.2.152,154

ALL = Southampton; **ALL DETERMINATE** = All ended; all decided as to their conclusion; "a legal term meaning the expiration, at a stated date, of rights of ownership" – Booth; "limited, or out of date, expired; "The term is used in legal conveyances" – Malone); also, "that has been or is determined" – *OED*, adding, "Definitely bound or limited, in time and space … fixed; clearly defined … limited, restricted … finally determined upon or decided; expressing a final decision … conclusive, final … *determined* upon, intended … resolved"; "Taken and concluded for a determinate season" – Hall's *Chronicles*, 1548, 245b; "The determinate glory of an earthly prince" – Ferne, *Blaz Gentrie* 33, 1586; "He confirmeth the same determinate sentence of their punishment" – Bible (Douay) *Jer* 15; "The sly slow hours shall not *determinate* the dateless limit of thy dear exile" – *Richard II*, 150-151

> So should that beauty which you hold in lease
> Find no *determination*
> - Sonnet 13, lines 5-6

> Forthwith that Edward be pronounced a traitor
> And all his lands and goods be confiscate.
> What else? And that succession be *determined*.
> - *3 Henry VI*, 4.6.54-56

5 FOR HOW DO I HOLD THEE BUT BY THY GRANTING?

For how do I have you as my king except by your ability to grant me the title of father; **HOLD** = as in hold a title; "In this context the word acts as a legal metaphor: *hold the title to*" – Booth; **THY GRANTING** = your royal permission; as the king *grants* a pardon; "with a play on 'a grant', 'a charter', 'a deed of possession'" – Booth; related to the verb "to agree, consent ... to allow, permit ... to confer as a favor ... to bestow or confer by a formal act; said of a sovereign or supreme authority" –*OED*; Oxford's annuity of 1,000 pounds issued in 1586 was a "grant" by the Queen; "granted by patents" – Camden, 1605, *Rem* 138

> May it therefore please Her Majesty to *grant* unto me a license...
> - Oxford, in Cecil Papers 25.76, March 1595

6 AND FOR THAT RICHES WHERE IS MY DESERVING?

And where is my due for having you as my royal son; **THAT RICHES** = that royal favor; that royal blood, related to Southampton's claim to the throne, a claim thereby shared (indirectly) by Oxford, as father of a king

> For monarchy, the wealth of the prince is the *riches* of the commonwealth...
> - Oxford, in Cecil Papers 25.76, March 1595

DESERVING = "that which is due to a person, or that for which he may claim something" - Schmidt

7 THE CAUSE OF THIS FAIR GIFT IN ME IS WANTING,

I lack the qualifications for being able to possess you as my royal son; **FAIR GIFT** = gift of your royal blood; royal gift of your life; the "gift" of blood from one prince to another, as in "And your sweet semblance to some other *give*" – Sonnet 13, line 4, even though the "gift" is only what "you hold in lease" - Sonnet 13, line 5; "The bounteous largess given thee to give" – Sonnet 4, line 6

8 AND SO MY PATENT BACK AGAIN IS SWERVING.

And therefore my privilege is being returned to me; **MY PATENT** = my privilege or right as father; "conferred by a legal document called a patent" – Booth); *OED*: "(1a) a document conferring some privilege, right, office, etc"; also, letters *patent* are "usually from a sovereign or person in authority"; "The King's patent, or open writ" – Holinshed *Chronicles*, 1577-87, iii, 1245/1; "My desire is to know *Her Majesty's pleasure touching her patent*" – Oxford to Robert Cecil, March 22, 1602; **SWERVING** = "Constant in spirit, not *swerving with the blood*" – the King in *Henry V,* 2.2.133

9 THY SELF THOU GAV'ST, THY OWN WORTH THEN NOT KNOWING,

You gave your own royal self and blood to me, when you were a child, not knowing it; i.e., you were as though asleep in your childhood, blissfully ignorant that you were a prince or little Love-God holding a brand of fiery love or royal blood: "Cupid laid by his brand and fell asleep ... The little Love-God lying once asleep,/ Laid by his side his heart-inflaming brand" – Sonnet 153, line 1, and Sonnet 154, lines 1-2, after Oxford and Elizabeth visited Bath in August of 1574, a few months after the birth of their son.

10 OR ME, TO WHOM THOU GAV'ST IT, ELSE MISTAKING.

And I, to whom you gave your royal life and blood, accepted that gift but apparently in error or wrongfully; i.e., it turns out that I was mistaken; "So you shall hear of carnal, bloody, and unnatural acts, of accidental judgments, casual slaughters, of deaths put on by cunning and forced cause, and, in this upshot,*purposes mistook* fallen on the inventor's heads. All this I can truly deliver" – Horatio at the end of*Hamlet*, 5.2.387-393

11 SO THY GREAT GIFT, UPON MISPRISION GROWING,

THY GREAT GIFT = your great (royal) gift of life and royal blood; "Nature's bequest" – Sonnet 4, line 3; "Look whom she (Elizabeth) best endowed, *she gave thee more*" – Sonnet 11, line 11; referring to Elizabeth's gift of life (through childbirth) and of her blood to Southampton; "*Thy gift*, thy tables, are within my brain/ Full charactered with lasting memory" – Sonnet 121, lines 1-2, referring to his son's gift of life as recorded on the "tables" of this diary of the Sonnets, which, in turn, contains "the living record of your memory" – Sonnet 55, line 8; "Nativity, once in the main of light,/ Crawls to maturity, wherewith being crowned,/ Crooked eclipses 'gainst his glory fight,/ And *time that **gave** doth now his **gift** confound*" – Sonnet 60, lines 5-8

> *When Walter Raleigh was found guilty of treason in 1603 and sentenced to death, he pleaded to King James and the Council: "For a **greater gift** none can give, none receive, than **life**." At the time he was spared, but his sentence was not reduced to "misprision" and he received no pardon. In 1618, therefore, King James could justify Raleigh's arrest and execution based on the death sentence passed on him in 1603.*
> (Hume, "Sir Walter Raleigh," pp. 199, 281)

UPON MISPRISION GROWING = because of the new (and better) judgment of "misprision" of treason, your life and royal blood were spared

> Either envy therefore, or *misprision*,
> Is *guilty* of this *fault*, and not my son
> - *1 Henry IV*, 1.3.26-27

And now this gift of your life is still "growing" – here in the "womb" of the "tomb" of these sonnets; "Making their tomb the womb wherein they *grew*" – Sonnet 86, line 4

MISPRISION OF TREASON

In Sonnet 87 Oxford reveals information preserved by no other contemporary document, at least by none that have been discovered in the four centuries since 1601: that Queen Elizabeth was able to spare Southampton from execution because his conviction for high treason had been reduced (by Robert Cecil, with Oxford's knowledge and help) to "misprision" of treason. By this legal maneuver, it would be possible for James to release her unacknowledged son from the Tower, restore his earldom and even grant him a royal pardon.

OXFORD ENGLISH DICTIONARY: "*Misprision of Treason*: originally, an offence or misdemeanor akin to treason or felony, but involving a lesser degree of guilt, and not liable to the capital penalty." Subsequently, over the years, the definition was broadened or even changed: "As various statutes enacted that concealment of a person's knowledge of treasonable actions or designs should be regarded as *misprision of treason*, this term came to be used as the ordinary designation for such concealment." This added meaning was already in play by 1601, but whether it was applied to Southampton is unknown. The OED is clear about the offence being "*not liable to the capital penalty*," but emphases that it was "later *misunderstood* as meaning *only* concealment of a person's knowledge of treasonable actions or designs" – an important distinction. (Emphases added)

ACT 7, HENRY VII, 1491: "Misprision by him committed and done against the King's most royal person." (Modern English)

ACTS 5&6, EDWARD VI, 1551-2: "Provided also … that concealment or keeping secret of any High Treason be deemed and taken only misprision of Treason." (Modern English)

EXPOS. TERMS OF LAW, 1579: "Misprision of felony or trespass." (Modern English) An important notation, because Oxford specifically uses "trespass" in reference to Southampton's crime in Sonnet 35, line 6: "Authorizing thy trespass with compare."

Modern editors generally define "misprision" of Sonnet 87 as "false estimate" (Duncan-Jones) or as "error, misprizing, mistaking of one thing for another" (Booth, who also includes "contempt, undervaluation").

Kerrigan says of the word: "One word for 'error' covers both the *not knowing* of line 9 and the *mistaking* of 10." Evans cites "error" and suggests "resulting from (my) neglect of duty."

"Misprision" as referring to a misunderstanding appears in the Shakespeare works on a few occasions, but Oxford was well versed in the law, having attended Gray's Inn and served on the treason trials of the Duke of Norfolk (1572), Mary Queen of Scots (1586) and the Earl of Essex (1601). In the lines from *1 Henry IV* quoted above, the word "misprision" is often corrected to "misprison" – not a word in the dictionary – but other editors adopt the original.

Sir Walter Raleigh was tried for treason in November 1603 and judged guilty. Attorney General Edward Coke (chief prosecutor at the Essex-Southampton trial), upon learning of the verdict, exclaimed: "Surely thou art mistaken! I myself accused him but of **misprision** of treason!" (Therefore Raleigh did not receive a pardon and, even much later, was executed.)

> *"When one knoweth of any treason or felony and concealeth it, this is **misprision**. In case of **misprision of treason** the offender is to be imprisoned during his life, to forfeit all his goods, debts and duties for ever, and the profits of his lands during his life"* – Coke, explaining later. (Bowen, p. 219)

All such penalties were applied to Southampton. At the same time, however, this "better judgment" saved his life and gave him hope for release and pardon in the future.

12 COMES HOME AGAIN, ON BETTER JUDGMENT MAKING.
COMES HOME AGAIN = is returned to us; "home" echoing House of Tudor; "home" meaning his liberation and return "home" from the Tower, to freedom and honor in England; "Shall our coffers then be emptied *to redeem a traitor home*? Shall we **buy treason**, and indent with fears when they have lost and forfeited themselves? No ... To **ransom home** revolted Mortimer!" – *1 Henry IV*, 1.3.84-91

BETTER JUDGMENT = this new legal agreement, replacing the earlier judgment of the Trial Court.

> Now therefore the matter having been directed by this course for a whole year's space, and come to no *better terms*"
> - Oxford to Robert Cecil, March 22, 1602

JUDGMENT: Francis Bacon used "judgment" to refer to the guilty verdict against Essex and Southampton when writing the anonymous A *Declaration of the Practices & Treasons, etc.*, for the Queen and Council, published in April 1601, corresponding exactly to the dating of this sonnet; bringing up various points about the trial, and referring to the historical deposing and killing of Richard II, Bacon concluded: "Upon all which Evidence both the Earles were found guiltie of Treason by all the several voices of every one of the Peers, and so received *judgment*."

"The action of trying a cause in a court of justice; trial ... the sentence of a court of justice; a judicial decision or order in court ... a formal or authoritative decision" – *OED*, citing: "They all foure were *beheaded without judgement*" – Hall, *Chronicles, Edw V*, 6b, 1548; "He confessed the Inditement, and so had *Judgement to bee hanged*" – Hall, *Chronicles, Henry VIII*, 244b, 1548; "All Israel heard of y judgement, whicdh the King had judged" – Geneva Bible, 1560, *1 Kings* iii.28; "I will confourme my will unto your judgements" – 1560

> So, till the *judgment* that your self arise,
> You live in this, and dwell in lovers' eyes
> - Sonnet 55, lines 13-14

> Thy black is fairest in *my judgment's place*
> - Sonnet 131, line 12

(To Elizabeth, of their son)

(In the above, the judgment of posterity that Southampton should be king, as opposed to the Queen's judgment of him, to the Court's legal judgment of him and to the judgment of him in the eyes of the contemporary world.)

> When he was *brought again to the bar*, to hear
> His knell rung out, his *judgment*, he was stirr'd
> With such an agony, he sweat extremely
> - *Henry VIII*, 2.1.31-33

> I have this day received a ***traitor's judgment***,
> And by that name must die: yet, heaven bear witness,
> And if I have a conscience, let it sink me,
> Even as the axe falls
> - *Henry VIII*, 2.1.58-61

> Lord Chief-Justice:
> Your Highness pleased to forget my place,
> The majesty and power of law and justice,
> The image of the king whom I presented,
> And struck me in my very seat of ***judgment***
> - *2 Henry IV*, 5.2.77-80

> The King:
> This was a ***judgment*** on me; that my kingdom,
> (Well worthy the best heir o' the world) should not
> Be gladded in't by me: then follows, that
> I weighed the danger which my realms stood in
> By this my issue's fail; and that gave to me
> Many a groaning throe
> - *Henry VIII*, 2.4.192-198

> That holy duty, out of dear respect,
> His royal self in ***judgment*** comes to hear
> The cause betwixt her and this great ***offender***
> - *Henry VIII*, 5.3.153-155

13 THUS I HAVE HAD THEE AS A DREAM DOTH FLATTER:
Therefore I have possessed you only as though in a flattering dream; "If I may trust the *flattering truth of sleep, my dreams* presage some joyful news at hand" – *Romeo and Juliet*, 5.1.1-2; FLATTER = "Or whether doth my mind, being crowned with you,/ Drink up the monarch's plague, this flattery?" - Sonnet 114, lines 1-2; (Elizabeth I suffered from this weakness, as Richard II had suffered from it)

14 IN SLEEP A KING, BUT WAKING NO SUCH MATTER.
IN SLEEP A KING: In my dreams, I have had you as a royal son, a prince and the future King Henry IX;
BUT WAKING NO SUCH MATTER = In reality, however, I have you as no such substance; i.e., Southampton will gain his liberation (from King James) only if he renounces all claim to the throne;
WAKING = containing and echoing "king"

Part Two

FOURTH MONTH IN THE TOWER

Sonnet 88
Faults ... Attainted
For Thy Right My Self Will Bear All Wrong
May 1601

Now that Oxford's sacrifice has been made and Southampton's crime has been reduced to "misprision" of treason, making possible his eventual release from the Tower, Oxford turns to the painful matter of his son's permanent loss of the crown. He will "set down a story" for his son in these sonnets; and in the process he will obliterate his identity, both as Southampton's father and as "Shakespeare" the writer. This month other noblemen who took part in the Rebellion (such as the earls of Rutland and Bedford) are bargaining to pay "ransom" or fines to gain their liberation. Also by this time, Robert Cecil has begun his secret correspondence with King James of Scotland to engineer his peaceful succession to the British throne upon Elizabeth's death.

Sonnet 88	Translation
When thou shalt be disposed to set me light,	When it's your will to think little of me,
And place my merit in the eye of scorn,	And look on my merits with a scornful eye,
Upon thy side against my self I'll fight,	I'll be on your side, fighting against myself,
And prove thee virtuous, though thou art forsworn.	And prove you royal, though you can't claim it.
With mine own weakness being best acquainted,	Since I know best my own inability to help you,
Upon thy part I can set down a story	For your sake I can set down a story here
Of faults concealed, wherein I am attainted:	Of my concealed failures, for which I'm disgraced:
That thou in losing me shall win much glory,	So that in losing me, you will rise in kingly glory,
And I by this will be a gainer too,	And I'll gain from this, too,
For bending all my loving thoughts on thee,	By focusing all my thoughts on your royalty,
The injuries that to myself I do,	So that whatever harm I do to myself
Doing thee vantage, double vantage me.	Will benefit you and doubly benefit me.
Such is my love, to thee I so belong,	Such is my love for you, to you I so belong,
That for thy right my self will bear all wrong.	That for your royal claim I'll bear all injustice.

"Sir Henry Neville is in the Tower, which at first made many men think he should come to his answer, but this whole term having past without any arraignment, makes me think there shall be no more blood drawn in this cause" – John Chamberlain to Dudley Carleton, May 27, 1601 (Stopes, 233, D. S. S. P., CCLXXIX. 91). Exactly why Neville was imprisoned is unclear. It could be that Cecil placed him in the Tower as a spy, to report back whatever Southampton has been saying and possibly planning. Neville will remain in the Tower and gain his release on orders of King James (and Cecil) along with Southampton on April 10, 1603.

1 WHEN THOU SHALT BE DISPOSED TO SET ME LIGHT
When you decide to think little of me; **SET ME LIGHT** = esteem me little

2 AND PLACE MY MERIT IN THE EYE OF SCORN,
And look on my own merits with scorn; **EYE** = your kingly eye; ("And scarcely greet me with that sun thine eye" – Sonnet 49, line 6); **EYE OF SCORN** = "Methoughts that I had broken from the Tower ... and, in those holes where eyes did once inhabit, there were crept, as 'twere in *scorn of eyes*" – *Richard III*, 1.4;

REFERENCE EDITION 481

"That in the pride and salt scorn of his eyes" – *Troilus and Cressida*, 1.3; **SCORN** = "To be shame's scorn and subject of mischance" – *1 Henry VI*, 4,6; "But, with a proud majestical high scorn" – *1 Henry VI*, 4.7; "And our nobility will scorn the match" – *1 Henry VI*, 5.3; "I sent your Grace the parcels and particulars of our grief, the which hath been with scorn shoved from the Court" – *2 Henry IV*, 4.2; "Scorn and defiance; slight regard, contempt, and any thing that may not misbecome the mighty sender, doth he prize you at: thus says my king" – *Henry V*, 2.4;

3 UPON THY SIDE AGAINST MY SELF I'LL FIGHT
UPON THY SIDE = "upon thy part" – line 6; "I will join you, fighting against myself in your support; "And blessing against this cruelty (I will) *fight on thy side*, poor thing, condemned to loss" – *The Winter's Tale*, 2.3

AGAINST MY SELF I'LL FIGHT = in fighting for your life, I obliterate my own identity: "Your name from hence immortal life shall have,/ Though I, once gone, to all the world must die" – Sonnet 81, lines 5-6; "Not for myself, Warwick, but my son, whom I unnaturally shall disinherit" – *3 Henry VI*, 1.1.198-199; by saving Southampton's life and working for his freedom, Oxford is depriving him of his inheritance of the crown; "For thee, and for *myself*, no quiet find" – Sonnet 27, line 14; "*Thy adverse party is thy Advocate,/ And '*gainst my self* a lawful plea commence*" – Sonnet 35, lines 10-11; "And with this hand *against my self* uprear/ To guard the lawful reasons on thy part" – Sonnet 49, lines 11-12; "That for thy right *my self will bear all wrong*" – this verse, Sonnet 88, line 14 below; "For thee, *against my self* I'll vow debate" – Sonnet 89, line 13;

4 AND PROVE THEE VIRTUOUS, THOUGH THOU ART FORSWORN.
PROVE THEE VIRTUOUS = demonstrate your value; "For he was likely, had he been put on, to have *proved most royal*" – *Hamlet*, 5.2.404-405; **FORSWORN** = perjured; Southampton will be a "suborned informer" in Sonnet 125, line 13; and Oxford refers to himself as "more perjured eye" in Sonnet 152, line 13; i.e., both now must testify to the world that they are not father and son and deny that Southampton is Elizabeth's rightful heir; again, the terms of the bargain

5 WITH MINE OWN WEAKNESS BEING BEST ACQUAINTED,
I, knowing best my own lack of worth in this regard; **MINE OWN** = ("a son of *mine own*" – Oxford to Burghley, March 17, 1575; see also Sonnets 23, 39, 49, 61, 62, 72, 107, 110; "I was too strict to make *mine own* away" – *Richard II*, 1.3.244, Gaunt, speaking of his son); **WITH MINE OWN WEAKNESS BEING BEST ACQUAINTED**: "I am myself indifferent honest, but yet I could accuse me of such things that it were better my mother had not borne me" – *Hamlet*, 3.1.122-124

6 UPON THY PART I CAN SET DOWN A STORY
UPON THY PART = on your behalf; to Elizabeth: "And play *the mother's part*" – Sonnet 143, line 12; on your side in the legal case; **I CAN SET DOWN A STORY** = I can record the story of you and me these sonnets; "O God, Horatio, what a wounded name, things standing thus unknown, shall I leave behind me; if thou didst ever hold me in thy heart, absent thee from felicity awhile, and in this harsh world draw thy breath in pain *to tell my story*" – *Hamlet*, 5.2.351-356; "That book in many's eyes doth share the glory that in gold clasps locks in *the golden story*" – a reference to the "golden" or royal "book" of these sonnets in *Romeo and Juliet*, 1.4.91-92

7 OF FAULTS CONCEALED WHEREIN I AM ATTAINTED:
OF FAULTS CONCEALED = whereby your actual crime, related to your now forfeited claim to the crown, is concealed; "O, 'tis a *fault* too unpardonable! Off with the crown, and with the crown his head" – *3 Henry VI*, 1.4.106; "You shall close prisoner rest, till that the nature of your *fault* be known to the Venetian state" – *Othello*, 5.2.335-337) **WHEREIN I AM ATTAINTED** = wherein Oxford will be the one bearing the guilt for his son; he, not Southampton, will stand attainted in the history books; i.e., by taking the blame upon himself and gaining liberation for his son, the truth of Oxford's life will be buried and he will remain misunderstood – unless the Book of Sonnets can be preserved for future generations and comprehended; **ATTAINTED** = Convicted of treason; stained with dishonor; "subjected to attainder" – *OED*, writing of

"attainder" as "the legal consequences of judgment of death or outlawry, in respect of treason or felony, viz. Forfeiture of estate real and personal, corruption of blood, so that the condemned could neither inherit nor transmit by descent, and generally, extinction of all civil rights and capacities" (the legal status that Southampton now suffers in the Tower); legally "the stain or corruption of blood of a criminal capitally condemned, the immediate inseparable consequence by the Common Law, on the pronouncing of the sentence of death"; a Bill of Attainder was introduced in the English Parliament of 1459; *OED* cites "The Attainder of Edward the last Duke of Buckingham" – 1584; and, for example, "Upon attainder of treason the King is to have the land" – Bacon, 1626; in another twist, the *OED* cites "to convict a jury of having given a false verdict; to bring an action to reverse a verdict so given," citing a 1667 usage

Earlier, on February 26, 1601, the Council had issued a warrant: "***Attainted***, and fit to be executed…" ("The space is left blank, but probably intended to have been filled with the name of Southampton" – Stopes, 223)

> And therefore mayst without *attaint* o'er-look
> The dedicated words which writers use
> - Sonnet 82, lines 2-3

> And by his *treason* stand'st not thou *attainted*,
> Corrupted, and exempt from ancient gentry?
> His *trespass* yet lives *guilty* in thy blood
> - *1 Henry VI*, 2.4.92-94

> My father was attached, not *attainted*,
> Condemned to die for *treason*, but no traitor"
> - *1 Henry VI*, 2.4.96-97

> I must *offend* before I be *attainted*
> - *2 Henry VI*, 2.4.59

> Or have mine honour soiled
> With the *attainder* of his slanderous lips
> - *Richard II*, 4.1.23-24

> He lived from all *attainder* of *suspects* …
> Well, well, he was the covert'st sheltered *traitor*"
> - *Richard III*, 3.5.32-33

> So to the laws at large I write my name:
> And he that breaks them in the least degree
> Stands in *attainder* of eternal *shame*
> - *Love's Labour's Lost*, 1.1.153-155

> Stay yet; hear reason: Edmund, I arrest thee
> On capital *treason*; and, in thine *attaint*
> - *King Lear*, 5.3.83-84

8 THAT THOU IN LOSING ME SHALL WIN MUCH GLORY.
That thereby you, losing me forever as father, will live to gain much glory as a king (by means of these sonnets); **GLORY** = "You may *my glories and my state* depose" – *Richard II*, 4.1.192; "And *crooked eclipses 'gainst his glory fight*" – Sonnet 60, line 7

9 AND I BY THIS WILL BE A GAINER TOO:
And I will gain by this, too (because what I do for you I actually do for myself).

THE MONUMENT

10 FOR BENDING ALL MY LOVING THOUGHTS ON THEE,
BENDING = bending truth; on bended knee to you as king; "Such as is *bent on sun-like majesty* when it shines seldom in admiring eyes" – *1 Henry IV*, 79-80; echoing the bending hunchbacked figure of Robert Cecil, Secretary of State, who used all his cunning to destroy Essex and render Southampton too weak to claim the throne; **ALL** = Southampton

11 THE INJURIES THAT TO MY SELF I DO,
The harm I do to myself; "To bear love's wrong than hate's known injury" – Sonnet 40, line 12

12 DOING THEE VANTAGE, DOUBLE VANTAGE ME.
In gaining advantage for you (by this bargain to secure your eventual release from the Tower), I gain a double advantage for myself, i.e., it's for you and therefore also for me, since "My spirit is thine, *the better part of me*" – Sonnet 74, line 8
VANTAGE = (noun) advantage; "the fore-hand and *vantage of a king*" – Henry V, 4.1.276; **VANTAGE** = (verb) gain advantage for; the only usage of "vantage" as a verb in the works of Shakespeare.

> I have some rights of memory in this kingdom,
> Which now *to claim my vantage* doth invite me
> - Hamlet, 5.2.396-397

"I thank my liege, that in regard of me he shortens four years of my son's exile: but little *vantage* shall I reap thereby" – *Richard II*, 1.3.216-218; "You fled for *vantage*, everyone will swear" – *1 Henry VI*, 4.5.28; "And some ten voices cried 'God save King Richard!' And thus I took the *vantage* of those few" – *Richard III*, 3.7.36-37; "All for our *vantage*. Then, in God's name, march: true hope is swift, and flies with swallow's wings: kings it makes gods, and meaner creatures kings" – *Richard III*, 5.2.22-24; "In her right we came; which we, God knows, have turned another way, to our own *vantage*" – *King John*, 2.1.548-549

13 SUCH IS MY LOVE, TO THEE I SO BELONG,
SUCH IS MY LOVE = such is my genuine love for you and your royal blood; such are you, my royal son;
TO THEE I SO BELONG = I am so much connected to you; so much your property, owned by you; "To you it doth *belong/ Yourself to pardon of self-doing crime*" – Sonnet 58, lines 11-12; "Disdaining *duty that to us belongs*" – the Queen to the King in *2 Henry VI*, 3.1.17

14 THAT FOR THY RIGHT MY SELF WILL BEAR ALL WRONG.
That for your blood right to be king I will bear (Christlike) all the burdens of your crime (your sins against the divinely ordained moncarch), by obliterating my identity (as your father, as the poet of the "Shakespeare" works dedicated to you) to gain the liberation of your person and the restoration of your titles and lands as well as your honor; **THY RIGHT** = your blood right to the throne; "your *true rights*" – Sonnet 17, line 11; "Suppose by *right* and equity thou be king" – *3 Henry VI*, 1.1.127; "King Henry, be *thy title right or wrong*" – *3 Henry VI*, 1.1.163; "Did I put Henry from *his native right*?" – *3 Henry VI*, 3.3.190; "But as *successively from blood to blood, your right of birth*, your empery, your own" – *Richard III*, 3.7.134-135; "for thee and for *the right of English Henry*, shall this night appear how much in duty I am bound to both" – *1 Henry VI*, 2.1.35-37; **MY SELF** = a repetition from line 3; **BEAR** = carry; also, to bear a child, clearly carrying the double meaning; "Which, laboring for invention, *bear amiss/ The second burthen of a former child*" – Sonnet 59, lines 3-4; **ALL** = Southampton, from his motto; **ALL WRONG** = your crime; "Now afore God 'tis shame *such wrongs are borne in him, a royal prince*" – *Richard II*, 2.1.238-239; Oxford's sacrifice to his son, keeping alive his "true rights" (Sonnet 17, line 11) to the throne in the verses of this diary; "Against my will *to do myself this wrong*" – *Richard II*, 1.3.246, the King in an exchange with Gaunt, expressing a situation remarkably similar to Oxford's when he was forced to sit on the Tribunal at the Trial and render a guilty verdict against his own son:

> Richard:
> *Thy son is banish'd upon good advice,*
> Whereto thy tongue a party-**verdict** gave:

No. 88

>Why at our justice seem'st thou then to lour?
>
>Gaunt:
>Things sweet to taste prove in digestion sour.
>You urged me as a judge, but I had rather
>*You would have bid me argue **like a father**.*
>O, had it been a stranger, not my child!
>To smooth his ***fault*** I should have been more mild.
>A partial ***slander*** sought I to avoid,
>And *in the sentence my own life destroyed*.
>Alas, I look'd when some of you should say
>I was too strict to make **mine own** away;
>But you gave leave to my unwilling tongue
>*Against my will **to do myself this wrong**.*
>- *Richard II*, 1.3.233-246

Verdict = "And by their *verdict* is determined" – Sonnet 46, line 11
Like a Father = "As a decrepit *father* takes delight" – Sonnet 37, line 1
Fault = "All men make *faults*, and even I in this" – Sonnet 35, line 5
Slander = "For *slander's* mark is ever yet the fair" – Sonnet 70, line 2
Mine Own = "What can *mine own* praise to *mine own* self bring" – Sonnet 39, line 3

*"I will say no more, for words in faithful minds are tedious, only this I protest: **you shall do me wrong**, and yourself greater, if either through fables which are mischievous, or conceit, which is dangerous, you think otherwise of me than humanity and consanguinity requireth"* – Oxford to Robert Cecil, May (?) 1601, Chiljan 65

RIGHT...WRONG = "King Henry, be thy title *right or wrong*, Lord Clifford vows to fight in thy defense" – *3 Henry VI*, 1.1; "To find out *right with wrong*, it may not be; and you that do abet him in this kind cherish rebellion and are rebels all" – *Richard II*, 2.3; "Wrest once the law to your authority: to do *a great right, do a little wrong*" – *The Merchant of Venice*, 4.1; "Force should be *right*; or rather *right and wrong*, between whose endless jar justice resides" – *Troilus and Cressida*, 1.3; "to make up a free determination 'twixt *right and wrong*" – *Troilus and Cressida*, 2.2; "Your mother's hand shall *right your mother's wrong*" – *Titus Andronicus*, 2.3; "What *wrong* is this unto the Prince your son!" – *3 Henry VI*, 1.1.18182

John Chamberlain to Dudley Carleton, May 27, 1601: "For there is a commission to certain of the Council to **ransom and fine** the Lords and Gentlemen that were in the action..." (Stopes, 233; D.S.S.P. CCLXXIX, 91); "Few persons in Tudor England who had been convicted of treason spent any length of time in gaol after their trial." Southampton's reprieve from execution and his perpetual confinement went against the norm; the explanation, noted in Sonnet 87, is that his conviction was quietly (and without official explanation) reduced from treason to "misprision" of treason. "Only when, through seditious words or failure to report traitorous conspiracy, the accused had been found guilty of ***misprision*** was the punishment of perpetual imprisonment inflicted." (Bellamy, 182; i.e., this was Southampton's punishment, but the lesser judgment of "misprision" was never made public – except in the Sonnets!)

May (?) 1601 – Oxford writes his first (surviving) letter to Cecil since before the Rebellion. Now that Southampton's life has been spared, the younger earl's liberation depends on the Secretary's ability to bring about King James's eventual succession. Cecil is holding Southampton hostage in the Tower, most likely threatening that the worst will happen to him if things go wrong – a means of blackmailing Oxford, who, regardless of his true feelings about his brother-in-law, appears to be making a special effort to convey his loyalty to him:

"…that what for the old love I have borne you (which I assure you was very great), what for the alliance which is between us (which is tied so fast by my children of your own sister), what for mine own disposition to yourself (which hath been rooted by long and many familiarities of a more youthful time)…

"Wherefore, not as a stranger but in the old style, *I do assure you that you shall have no faster friend and well-wisher unto you than myself, either in kindness, which I find beyond mine expectation in you, or in kindred*, whereby none is nearer allied than myself, since of your sisters, of my wife only you have received nieces. A sister, I say, not by any venter, but born of the same father and the same mother of yourself."

He continues on a note of urgency, apparently worried that Cecil might doubt his commitment to him, based on the malicious statements of others:

"I will say no more, for words in faithful minds are tedious, only this I protest: *you shall do me wrong, and yourself greater, if either through fables which are mischievous, or conceit, which is dangerous, you think otherwise of me than humanity and consanguinity requireth.*"

In this purely business letter, Oxford refers to the Rebellion and its aftermath only as "these troublesome times."

He signs off as "Your most assured and loving brother, *as ever in mine own affection, in all kindness and kindred.*"

Part Two

FIFTH MONTH IN THE TOWER

Sonnet 89
Fault ... Offence ... Defense ... Disgrace
Be Absent From Thy Walks
June 1601

Oxford continues the severance of any public tie to Southampton, according to the bargain and sacrifice that he has made to gain his son's release and pardon. As part of this agreement, Oxford will no longer visit Southampton in the Tower and join him on the "walks" that the younger earl is allowed to take on the roof above his prison room. In this sonnet, as elsewhere throughout the diary, there is an element of instruction from father to son; and the subject matter of the entire verse is set within a courtroom before a trial begins.

Sonnet 89	Translation
Say that thou didst forsake me for some fault,	Claim you renounced me for some crime,
And I will comment upon that offence,	And I'll say even more about my offence!
Speak of my lameness, and I straight will halt	Speak of my lame efforts for you and I'll limp,
Against thy reasons making no defense.	Making no defense against your accusations!
Thou canst not (love) disgrace me half so ill,	You, royal son, cannot disgrace me half as much,
To set a form upon desired change,	By setting forth the reasons for wanting change,
As I'll myself disgrace, knowing thy will,	As I'll discredit myself! Knowing your royal will,
I will acquaintance strangle and look strange,	I'll deny our father-son bond and act as a stranger.
Be absent from thy walks, and in my tongue	I'll not join your Tower walks, and in my speech
Thy sweet beloved name no more shall dwell,	Your royal name (Henry IX) will not be spoken,
Lest I (too much profane) should do it wrong	Lest I dishonor that name
And haply of our old acquaintance tell.	By possibly revealing us as father and son.
For thee, against my self I'll vow debate,	For you, I am determined to argue against myself,
For I must ne'er love him whom thou dost hate.	Because I can't claim a son who can't claim me.

June 10, 1601: "Fines imposed on the noblemen and other confederates in the late rebellion. The Earl of Rutland 30,000 pounds [reduced] to 20,000 pounds, the Earl of Bedford 20,000 pounds to 10,000 pounds, Baron Sandys 10,000-5,000 pounds, Baron Cromwell 5,000 pounds to 2,000 pounds, Lord Mounteagle 8,000 pounds to 4,000 pounds, Sir Charles Percy 500 pounds, Sir Joscelin Percy 500 pounds, Sir Henry Cary 400 marks-200 marks, Sir Robert Vernon 500 marks-100 pounds..." (Stopes, 234)

1 SAY THAT THOU DIDST FORSAKE ME FOR SOME FAULT
SAY THAT = if you say; "assert that you" – Booth; **FORSAKE ME** = allusion to Christ's words on the cross; "Now from the sixth hour there was darkness over all the land unto the ninth hour; And about the ninth hour Jesus cried with a loud voice, saying ... '*My God, My God, why hast thou forsaken me?*'" – Matthew, KJV, 27.46; "Th'offender's sorrow lends but weak relief/ To him that *bears the strong offence's cross*" – Sonnet 34, lines 11-12, emended by many editors from "loss" to "cross"; "And both for my sake *lay me on this cross*" – Sonnet 42, line 12, referring to both Elizabeth and Southampton; **FAULT** = Your crime of treason; referring to the Rebellion or "revolt" of February 8, 1601; "I have no other remedy but to look better to amend *the fault*" – Oxford to Burghley, September, 1572

REFERENCE EDITION 487

For this *revolt* of thine, methinks, is like
Another fall of man. Their *faults* are open;
Arrest them to the answer of the law.
- *Henry V*, 2.2.141-143

And I repent my *fault* more than my death...
My *fault*, but not my body, *pardon*, sovereign
- *Henry V*, 2.2.152, 165

For I should melt at an *offender's* tears,
And lowly words were *ransom for their fault*
- *2 Henry VI*, 3.1.126-127

2 AND I WILL COMMENT UPON THAT OFFENCE;
COMMENT UPON = discourse upon; add to, in my speech; offer even more reasons for; i.e., if you tell anyone you forsook me because of some fault or crime of mine, I will agree and even add to your accusations; **THAT OFFENCE** = That treason, your attempted overthrow of the Government, i.e., of Cecil and his power over the Queen; "Methinks your looks are sad, your cheer appall'd. Hath the late *overthrow* wrought this *offence*?" – *1 Henry VI*, 1.2.48-49; "if I have done anything amiss that I have merited your *offence*" – Oxford to William Cecil, November 24, 1569; "Get thee therefore hence, poor miserable wretches, to your death, the taste whereof God of his mercy give you patience to endure, and true repentance of all *your dear offences*!" – the King to traitors in *Henry V*, 2.2.178-182; "All his offences live upon my head" – *1 Henry IV*, 5.2.20

3 SPEAK OF MY LAMENESS AND I STRAIGHT WILL HALT,
MY LAMENESS = my ineffectual paternity of you; my ineffectual writing of these verses for you; my physical lameness, from the 1582 duel, used here as metaphor; "for by reason of *mine infirmity*" – Oxford to Robert Cecil, April 25/27, 1603; Oxford also developed a physical ailment in his hand: "Thus **with a lame hand** to write I take my leave" – Oxford to Robert Cecil, January 1602; "So *I, made lame* by Fortune's (Elizabeth's) dearest spite" – Sonnet 37, line 3; **HALT** = walk with my limp, i.e., to demonstrate the truth of what you say about me, that I am lame or without self-defense (since I cannot tell the truth).

4 AGAINST THY REASONS MAKING NO DEFENSE.
Making no attempt to defend myself against your charges; **NO DEFENSE** = as at a trial, not defending myself against your statements about me; **THY REASONS** = "And this my hand against myself uprear/ To guard *the lawful reasons on thy part*" – Sonnet 49, lines 11-12; your legal statements or defense; "your grounds for action" – Booth, i.e., your reasons for forsaking me; "But the *defendant* doth that plea deny" – Sonnet 46, line 7

5 THOU CANST NOT (LOVE) DISGRACE ME HALF SO ILL,
You cannot, my royal son, disgrace me even half as badly as I'll disgrace myself; **LOVE** = royal son (addressing him directly as such); **DISGRACE ME** = remove your royal grace from me; put me in a state of disgrace in place of you

6 TO SET A FORM UPON DESIRED CHANGE,
In order to create a permanent show (or outward form) of this desired (commanded) alteration of our public relationship; **SET A FORM UPON** = to give form or show of expression to; "*set a form upon* that ingest, which he hath left so shapeless and so rude" – Gospel of John, 5.7.26-27, cited by Booth; **DESIRED CHANGE** = the way you want me to behave; the change desired or commanded by a monarch: "From fairest creatures *we desire* increase" – Sonnet 1, line 1

7 AS I'LL MY SELF DISGRACE. KNOWING THY WILL,
AS I'LL MYSELF DISGRACE = as I'll disgrace myself; Oxford has already accepted the need to bear the disgrace of his son by himself: "When *in disgrace with Fortune* (Elizabeth) and men's eyes,/ I all alone

beweep my outcast state" – Sonnet 29, lines 1-2; **THY WILL** = your royal will; "Thy kingdom come, *thy will* be done, on earth as it is in heaven" – the Lord's Prayer

8 I WILL ACQUAINTANCE STRANGLE AND LOOK STRANGE,
I WILL = echoing "thy will" in line 7 above; possibly suggesting: "I, Will Shakespeare"; **ACQUAINTANCE STRANGLE** = I will conceal our relationship; **LOOK STRANGE** = behave as though I am not related to you; "Wherefore, not as a *stranger* but in the old style, I do assure you that you shall have no faster friend and well-wisher unto you than myself, either in kindness, which I find beyond mine expectation in you, or in kindred, whereby none is nearer allied than myself" – Oxford to Robert Cecil, May 1601

> Though *I seem strange*, sweet friend, be thou not so…
> Thus *farewell, friend, I will continue strange*;
> Thou shalt not hear by word or writing ought.
> Let it suffice, my vow shall never change;
> As for the rest, I leave it to thy thought.
> - Poem probably by Oxford; unsigned in Rawlinson Poet. MS 85, f. 17

9 BE ABSENT FROM THY WALKS, AND IN MY TONGUE
THY WALKS = Your walks in the Tower; referring to visits with Southampton, when Oxford undoubtedly took walks with him there (Akrigg reports that Southampton was officially allowed to take such walks in October 1601; but it would seem he was given this privilege even earlier, when Oxford had paid private visits to him; as Lord Great Chamberlain of England, Oxford would have gained that privilege beforehand, unofficially. Now his own meetings with his son are over); "The places where you walk" – Duncan-Jones; one of the places in this case was the "leaden roof" above Southampton's chambers within the Tower fortress; but there were many other walkways on the vast grounds that he may have been able to use; (Southampton and John Peyton, Lieutenant of the Tower, conversed often during the earl's imprisonment); also, Oxford is looking ahead by saying that Southampton, who no longer has a claim as King Henry IX, will not have any *walks* as monarch, so they will never enjoy them together; in earlier days, Oxford and Elizabeth had been fond of taking "royal walks" together in the palace gardens. One such walk, for example, is recorded in a letter of January 1581.

> Wait in *your royal walks*
> - A Midsummer Night's Dream, 5.1.30

> Lo now my glory smeared in dust and blood!
> My parks, *my walks*, my manors that I had
> - 3 Henry VI, 5.2.23-24

> Come, you and I must *walk* a turn together
> - The King in Henry VIII, 5.1.93

> Moreover, he hath left you all *his walks*,
> His private arbours, and new-planted orchards
> - Antony, of Caesar's bequests *Julius Caesar*, 3.2.248-249

10 THY SWEET BELOVED NAME NO MORE SHALL DWELL:
SWEET = royal; **BELOVED** = filled with royal blood; **THY … NAME** = King Henry IX

11 LEST I (TOO MUCH PROFANE) SHOULD DO IT WRONG
PROFANE = "perhaps used in its Latin sense, 'standing outside a sacred place or temple'" – Duncan-Jones; an apt image, with Oxford viewing the Tower as a temple housing Southampton as a god on earth; "also suggests 'unacceptable in good company'" – Duncan-Jones; **DO IT WRONG** = "I will say no more, for words in faithful minds are tedious, only this I protest: *you shall do me wrong*, and yourself greater, if either

through fables which are mischievous, or conceit, which is dangerous, you think otherwise of me than humanity and consanguinity requireth" – Oxford to Robert Cecil, May (?) 1601, Chiljan 65

12 AND HAPLY OF OUR OLD ACQUAINTANCE TELL.
HAPLY = accidentally; **OF OUR OLD ACQUAINTANCE TELL** = reveal our father-son relationship; tell how we were close friends as father and son in earlier days; "Wherefore, not as a stranger but *in the old style*, I do assure you that you shall have no faster friend" – Oxford to his brother-in-law Secretary Robert Cecil, May (?) 1601, Cecil Papers 181.80, Chiljan 65

13 FOR THEE AGAINST MY SELF I'LL VOW DEBATE,
I'll vow to debate against myself for your sake; i.e., my ongoing sacrifice for you; "For thee, and for my self, no quiet find" – Sonnet 27, line 14; **DEBATE** = fight with words; to contest or quarrel

14 FOR I MUST NE'ER LOVE HIM WHOM THOU DOST HATE.
Because I must never love myself, since you can't show your love for me as your father; **NE'ER** = Never = E. Ver, Edward deVere, *Ever or Never*; echoing "near" in kinship; **LOVE/HATE** = juxtaposing royal blood with lack of it; "You know how apt *our love* was to accord to furnish him with all appertinents belonging to his honour" – the King in *Henry V*, 2.2.86-88; see Sonnet 145, of Elizabeth after her sparing of Southampton's life: "Those lips that *love's* own hand did make/ Breathed forth the sound that said, 'I *hate*'/ … 'I *hate*' from *hate* away she threw,/ And saved my life, saying, 'Not you'" – lines 1-2, 13-14); for I must never boast of my paternity of your royal self; I must never love myself (in that sense), since you must deny that you are my son; and in that sense you must "*hate*" me; "My gracious sovereign, my most *loving liege*!" – *Richard II*, 1.1.21

> My meaning is to work what wonders *love* hath wrought,
> Wherewith I muse why men of wit have *love* so dearly bought:
> For *love* is worse than *hate*, and eke more harm hath done,
> Record I take of those that read of Paris, Priam's son.
> (E. O., *Paradise of Dainty Devices*, 1576)

> So where I like, I list not vaunt my *love*;
> Where I desire, there must I feign debate.
> One hath my hand, another hath my glove,
> But he my heart whom most I seem to *hate*.
> - (Poem thought to be by Oxford; unsigned in Rawlinson Poet. MS 85, f. 17)

Part Two

OXFORD URGES PATIENCE
SIXTH MONTH IN THE TOWER

FATHER-TO-SON INSTRUCTIONS

Sonnet 90
A Purposed Overthrow
July 1601

Oxford instructs and begs Southampton to "linger out" this time in the Tower as punishment for the "purposed overthrow" of the Rebellion, and to avoid the temptation to lead another rising. The bargain for the life, freedom and honor of Henry Wriothesley has been made, so he must not attempt to take matters into his own hands.

Sonnet 90	Translation
Then hate me when thou wilt, if ever, now,	So renounce all ties to me! If ever, do it now!
Now while the world is bent my deeds to cross	Now, while England is determined to stop me,
Join with the spite of fortune, make me bow,	Join with Elizabeth's malice, make me submit,
And do not drop in for an after-loss.	And don't make things worse than they are.
Ah do not drop, when my heart hath 'scaped this sorrow,	Ah, when I've fled from this sorrow, do not
Come in the rearward of a conquered woe,	Bring up the rear to commit another crime!
Give not a windy night a rainy morrow,	Do not extend our misery into the future
To linger out a purposed overthrow.	By prolonging the tragedy of your Rebellion.
If thou wilt leave me, do not leave me last,	If you sever all ties to me, don't be last to do so,
When other petty griefs have done their spite	When less painful things have already hurt me.
But in the onset come, so shall I taste	Instead, renounce me right now, so I'll suffer
At first the very worst of fortune's might.	The worst of Elizabeth's power at the outset.
And other strains of woe, which now seem woe	And other sufferings, which now seem painful,
Compared with loss of thee, will not seem so.	Compared with losing you will not seem so bad.

1 THEN HATE ME WHEN THOU WILT, IF EVER, NOW,
If there is ever a time to hate me, this is it, because of the bargain I have made to make sure you are eventually released from the Tower; **HATE** = deny your royal blood (opposite of "love"); **HATE ME** = deny that you are my son by the Queen; this is an instruction; he does not mean that Southampton must "hate" him with genuine anger but that he must not acknowledge their bond by blood

> Besides, our nearness to the king in *love*
> Is near the *hate* of those love not the king
> - *Richard II*, 2.3.126-127

> Now welcome more, and ten times more belov'd,
> Than if thou never hadst deserved our *hate*
> - *3 Henry VI*, 5.1.106-107

REFERENCE EDITION 491

EVER = E. Ver, Edward deVere, *Ever or Never*; **NOW** = now that I have promised (to Robert Cecil) that you will give up any claim to the throne, indicated just three verses previously.

2 **NOW WHILE THE WORLD IS BENT MY DEEDS TO CROSS,**
NOW = repeated immediately from the end of line 1 above; emphasizing that Oxford is writing in relation to real events as they occur in real time; **THE WORLD** = England, officialdom; **BENT MY DEEDS TO CROSS** = intend upon thwarting or contradicting my actions; echoing Christ suffering on the cross; "the matter, after it had *received many crosses*, many inventions of delay" – Oxford to Robert Cecil, January 1602; "Th'offender's sorrow lends but weak relief/ To *him that bears the strong offence's loss (cross)*" – Sonnet 34, lines 11-12; "And both (Elizabeth and Southampton) for my sake *lay me on this cross*" – Sonnet 42, line 12

> That from his loins no hopeful branch may spring,
> To *cross me from the golden time I look for*
> - 3 Henry VI, 3.2.126-127

> Thus, while the vulture of sedition
> Feeds in the bosom of such great commanders,
> Sleeping neglection doth betray to *loss*
> The *conquest* of our scarce-cold *conqueror*,
> That *ever*-living man of memory,
> Henry the Fifth. Whiles they each other *cross*,
> Lives, honors, lands, and all, hurry to *loss*.
> - 1 Henry VI, 4.3.47-53
> (Italicized words reflected in this sonnet)

MY DEEDS = all my past actions meant to support your claim to the throne: "*What I have done* is yours, *what I have to do* is yours, being part in all I have, devoted yours" – Oxford's public dedication of *Lucrece* in 1594, from "William Shakespeare" to Southampton; secondarily echoing my current actions on your behalf that result in payment of your royal claim as ransom for your "ill deeds," as in "Ah, but those tears are pearl which thy love sheeds,/ And they are rich, and *ransom all ill deeds*" – Sonnet 34, lines 13-14; but also "deeds" of ownership, as a father owns his son; echoing written evidence of a legal act; in this case, there will be no documentary or written evidence that Southampton's crime has been reduced to "misprision" of treason, but these sonnets do provide such evidence; a deed usually refers to "a thing having been done" or "a thing being done" – Schmidt; (see Sonnets 37, 61, 69, 94, 111, 131)

3 **JOIN WITH THE SPITE OF FORTUNE, MAKE ME BOW,**
(These are instructions from father to son, i.e., Southampton must go along with both Elizabeth and Robert Cecil to thwart Oxford as the potential father of a king, by abandoning any claim to the throne); **THE SPITE OF FORTUNE** = the negative view and malice of Elizabeth; "When *in disgrace with Fortune* (Elizabeth) and men's eyes,/ I all alone beweep my outcast state" – Sonnet 29, lines 1-2; "So I, made lame by *Fortune's dearest spite*" – Sonnet 37, line 3; "Though *Fortune's malice overthrow my state*" – King Edward in *3 Henry VI*, 4.3.46; **SPITE** = malice; "to make me the fixed figure *for the time of scorn to point his slow and moving finger at!*" – Othello, 4.2.54-56; **BOW** = submit, as to a king; "Why, Warwick, hath thy knee forgot to *bow*?" – the King in *2 Henry VI*, 5.1.161; "when *true subjects bow to a new-crowned monarch*" – The Merchant of Venice, 3.2.49-50

4 **AND DO NOT DROP IN FOR AN AFTER LOSS:**
And do not make it more painful; do not make the loss worse (by giving in to the temptation to lead another uprising); **DROP IN FOR AN AFTER-LOSS** = "the weather metaphor in line 7 suggests that 'drop in for an after-loss' might be a Shakespearean elaboration of 'after-drops,' drops of rain that fall after a storm has apparently passed" – Booth; i.e., Oxford is warning and pleading with Southampton to avoid making trouble after the bargain for his release ("misprision") and pardon has been made; i.e., the loss of your crown is already one loss too many; do not follow this by incurring another loss, that is, by doing something that will

cause you to lose your freedom; **DROP** = drop like raindrops, adding to the tears I have already shed; **AFTER-LOSS** = a later loss or future grief; the only usage in Shakespeare; **LOSS** = "Though thou repent, yet I have still *the loss*" – Sonnet 34, line 10; "If I *lose* thee, my *loss* is my love's gain,/ And *losing* her, my friend hath found that *loss*;/ Both find each other, and I *lose* both twain" – Sonnet 42, lines 9-11, i.e., the final result is that Elizabeth, Southampton and Oxford all lose when Southampton is unable to take the "seat" or throne as king, as in "Which *three*, till now, *never kept seat in one*" – Sonnet 105, line 14

5 AH, DO NOT, WHEN MY HEART HATH 'SCAPED THIS SORROW,

Do not make things worse, when my suffering is being mended; **MY HEART** = my heart, the source of my blood, which is your heart; "Thy beauty's form in table of my heart" – Sonnet 24, line 2; "Thy bosom is endeared with all hearts" – Sonnet 31, line 1; shed; **THIS SORROW** = "To weigh how once I suffered in your crime./ O that our night of woe might have rememb'red/ My deepest sense, how hard *true sorrow* hits" – Sonnet 120, lines 8-10

6 COME IN THE REARWARD OF A CONQUERED WOE.

REARWARD = "*ward*, from Old English words meaning *guard*, and the suffix *ward*, indicating direction, are hopelessly fused in *rearward*" – Booth; in the rear of; "Thought I thy spirit were stronger than thy shame, myself would, on the *rearward* of reproaches, strike at thy life" – *Much Ado About Nothing*, 1.1.128; do not follow this bargain by actions that will undo what has been arranged; **CONQUERED WOE** = "vanquished sorrow; i.e., a grief from which the speaker has recovered or to which he has become resigned" – Booth; all relating to the tragic ordeal suffered by Southampton (and therefore by Oxford) because of the Rebellion; they have both been *conquered* by Robert Cecil; "For precious friends hid in death's dateless *night*,/ And weep afresh love's long since cancelled *woe*" – Sonnet 30, lines 6-7; "And I, a tyrant, have no leisure taken/ To weigh how once *I suffered in your crime*/ O that *our night of woe* might have rememb'red/ My deepest sense, how true sorrow hits" – Sonnet 120, lines 7-10, when Oxford looks back at the Rebellion and these dark prison days; **CONQUERED** = alluding to the "conquest" of both Essex and Southampton by Secretary of State Robert Cecil: "And strength by limping sway disabled" – Sonnet 66, line 8; "The coward *conquest* of a wretch's knife" – Sonnet 74, line 11, the victory that was "cowardly won" by Cecil; also, the conspirators as cowardly captives; "And captive good attending captain ill" – Sonnet 66, line 12, i.e., Southampton as Cecil's captive; "How to divide the *conquest* of thy sight" – Sonnet 46, line 2

7 GIVE NOT A WINDY NIGHT A RAINY MORROW

Do not extend further our long "night of woe"; **WINDY NIGHT** = opposite of the golden "day" of royal hope; stormy darkness of disgrace, under the Queen's cloud of shame; "And *night* doth *nightly* make grief's length seem stronger" – Sonnet 28, line 14; "O that our our *night of woe* might have rememb'red/ My deepest sense, how hard true sorrow hits" – Sonnet 120, lines 9-10; **RAINY MORROW** = another day of rain or tears; echoing the future "*reign*" of which you will not be king but, rather, of James; "Why didst thou promise such a beauteous day/ And make me travail forth without my cloak,/ To let base clouds o'ertake me in my way,/ Hiding thy bravery in their rotten smoke?/ 'Tis not enough that through the cloud thou break,/ To dry the rain on my storm-beaten face" – Sonnet 34, lines 1-6; "For *the rain it raineth every day*" – a repeated line in the Clown's song at the end of *Twelfth Night*, 5.1.381-400, with *rain/raineth* possibly a play on *reign/reineth*; "And in his grave *rain'd many a tear*" – *Hamlet*, 4.5.165; "I presume that as my hand has open'd bounty to you, my heart dropp'd love, *my power rain'd honour* more on you than any" – the King in *Henry VIII*, 3.2.183-186; "Had it pleased heaven to try me with affliction, had they rained all kinds of sores and shames on my bare head" – *Othello*, 4.2.48-50

8 TO LINGER OUT A PURPOSED OVERTHROW.

To prolong the agony caused by your crime against the state; to have patience in the Tower until liberated by the new monarch; **LINGER OUT** = "prolong, draw out" – Crystal & Crystal; "*Linger* your patience on" – *Henry V*, chorus, 2.0.31; "And *linger not* our sure destructions on" – *Troilus and Cressida*, 5.10.9; "I would not have thee *linger* in thy pain" – *Othello*, 5.2.87; "to tarry, to stay ... to remain inactive in expectation of something ... to remain longer in a state of languor and pain, to languish, or to be painfully protracted" – Schmidt; "Drops bloody sweat from his war-wearied limbs, and, *in advantage lingering*, looks for rescue" – *1 Henry VI*, 4.4.18-19; "They will by violence tear him from your palace and torture him with *grievous* *ling'ring death"* – *2 Henry VI*, 3.2.245-246; **PURPOSED OVERTHROW** = Your deliberate attempt to overthrow Robert Cecil and, as a result of your original conviction, the Crown, thereby threatening the life of your mother the Queen…

> Two of the dangerous consorted *traitors*
> That sought at Oxford thy dire *overthrow*
> - *Richard II*, 5.6.15-16

PURPOSED = "You swore to us, and you did swear that oath at Doncaster, that you did nothing *purpose* 'gainst the state" – *1 Henry IV*, 5.1.41-43; "And let me speak to the yet unknowing world how these things came about. So shall you hear of carnal, bloody, and unnatural acts, of accidental *judgments*, casual slaughters, of *deaths put on by cunning and forced cause*, and in this upshot *purposes mistook* fall'n on th'inventors' heads … *plots* and *errors*…" – *Hamlet*, 386-392, 402, Horatio promising to tell Hamlet's story in the future; "The better act of *purposes mistook* is to mistake again … *Rebellion, flat rebellion!*" – *King John*, 3.1.200-201, 223; **OVERTHROW** = "O, Lancaster, I fear **thy overthrow**" – *3 Henry VI*, 2.6.3; "That *plotted thus* **our glory's overthrow**" – *1 Henry VI*, 1.1.24; "Though Fortune's malice **overthrow my state**" – King Edward in *3 Henry VI*, 4.3.46; "Hath the late **overthrow** wrought this **offence**?" – *1 Henry VI*, 1.2.49; "Once more I come to know of thee, King Harry, if for thy **ransom** thou wilt now compound, before thy most assured **overthrow**" – *Henry V*, 4.3.79-81; "like the Trojan horse was stuff'd within with bloody veins, expecting **overthrow**" – *Pericles*, 1.4.93-94

I would to God your Lordship would let me understand some of your news, which here doth ring doubtfully in the ears of every man, of the murder of the Admiral of France, and a number of noblemen and worth gentlemen and such as greatly have in their lifetimes honored the Queen's Majesty our Mistress, on whose tragedies we have a number of French Aeneases in this city that tell of their own **overthrows**…
- Oxford to Burghley, September 1572, after learning about the slaughter of Protestants during St. Bartholomew's Day massacre in France

9 IF THOU WILT LEAVE ME, DO NOT LEAVE ME LAST,
LEAVE ME = disavow our father-son relationship; "To *leave poor me* thou hast the strength of laws" – Sonnet 49, line 13; "To love that well which thou must *leave* ere long" – Sonnet 73, line 14; **DO NOT LEAVE ME LAST** = do not wait until everyone else has rejected me and obliterated my identity

10 WHEN OTHER PETTY GRIEFS HAVE DONE THEIR SPITE,
When other, less important hurts have worked their malice

11 BUT IN THE ONSET COME: SO SHALL I TASTE
But reject me first; i.e., do it quickly; be the first to take this assault on me, by severing all ties with me as my son, according to the bargain I have made for your liberty and honor; **IN THE ONSET** = at the beginning; as you set about; **ONSET** = the start of an assault or attack; "the onset and retire of both your armies" – *King John*, 2.1.326-327; **SO SHALL I TASTE** = so I will experience, undergo, suffer; "by tasting of our wrath" – *Cymbeline*, 5.5.308; **TASTE** = allusion to the function of the "royal taster," whose office is to taste and declare that the wine and food is free from poison; to try; to prove

12 AT FIRST THE VERY WORST OF FORTUNE'S MIGHT.
AT FIRST = right away; before anyone else; **VERY** = Ver = E. Ver, Edward de Vere; **THE VERY WORST** = the most of; **FORTUNE'S MIGHT** = Queen Elizabeth's awesome power against me and you; in effect, her power is now exercised by Robert Cecil, but Oxford holds the monarch responsible for her actions; and the very worst of them will be to ignore her son in the Tower and fail to name him to succeed her, thereby extinguishing the House of Tudor and enabling the House of Stuart to reign.

13 AND OTHER STRAINS OF WOE, WHICH NOW SEEM WOE,
And other kinds of sorrow, which now seem so painful; inward motions of woe; "Measure his worth the length and breadth of mine, and let it answer every *strain for strain*" – *Much Ado About Nothing*, 1.1.12;

STRAINS = "Stresses, whether as rackings, cruel trials, or (more probably) as 'extremes'" – Tucker;
WHICH NOW SEEM WOE = emphasis on "seem"; i.e., these current sorrows will not seem so bad in the future, when you are released and restored to your honor and earldom – an argument that Oxford is making despite the fact that Southampton must forever renounce his royal claim (a claim he has already lost, because Robert Cecil has "conquered" both Essex and Southampton)

14 COMPARED WITH LOSS OF THEE WILL NOT SEEM SO.

By comparison with the loss of you as my son, will not seem so bad; "Authorizing thy trespass with *compare*" – Sonnet 35, line 6, Oxford possibly referring to his support for Southampton's rebellion "with compare," i.e., by means of his chronicle plays, and certainly referring to his support for his son in these sonnets; **LOSS** = "Though thou repent, yet I have still the *loss*./ Th'offender's sorrow lends but weak relief/ To him that bears the strong offence's *loss* (cross)" – Sonnet 34, lines 10-12; "Increasing *store with loss, and loss with store*" – Sonnet 64, line 8

THE MONUMENT

SEVENTH MONTH IN THE TOWER

Sonnet 91
Thy Love is Better Than High Birth to Me
All This Away
August 1601

Oxford continues to record the result of the bargain with Cecil, who has begun his secret correspondence with King James of Scotland. He offers a brief self-portrait of his life as a nobleman, adding that his greatest joy lies in "one general best" -- playing upon One for All, All for One for Southampton. He records that his son's "love" or royal blood is "better than high birth to me." In other words, he would be willing to give up all of his own inherited status for his royal son. What he is really giving up, however, is the son whom he most values; this above all else is what makes him "wretched."

Sonnet 91	Translation
Some glory in their birth, some in their skill,	Some men boast of their birth, some their skill,
Some in their wealth, some in their body's force,	Some their riches, some their physical strength,
Some in their garments, though new-fangled ill,	Some their clothes (although too fashionable),
Some in their Hawks and Hounds, some in their Horse;	Some their hawks, hounds and horses [as I have had all my life]
And every humor hath his adjunct pleasure,	And every temperament goes its own way,
Wherein it finds a joy above the rest,	Finding what it enjoys above all else,
But these particulars are not my measure,	But none of these listed items can define me.
All these I better in one general best.	One thing surpasses all these for me:
Thy love is better than high birth to me,	Your blood is more to me than my high birth,
Richer than wealth, prouder than garments' cost,	Far more sacred than money or clothing,
Of more delight than Hawks or Hounds be,	Of far more joy than my hawks or my hounds,
And having thee, of all men's pride I boast.	And I claim highest joy, having you as royal son.
Wretched in this alone, that thou mayst take	My sole misery is that you must sever
All this away, and me most wretched make.	This tie between us, making me wretched most.

1 SOME GLORY IN THEIR BIRTH, SOME IN THEIR SKILL,
GLORY = "our own Queen, to whom alone is due all the praise of all the Muses and *all the glory* of literature" – Oxford's Letter to the Reader, *The Courtier*, 1572; **BIRTH** = high birth; Oxford, as hereditary Lord Great Chamberlain, is highest-ranking earl of the realm; **SKILL** = knowledge, cleverness, understanding, ability; skill as a poet; in many areas from music to horsemanship, Oxford was a skillful practitioner, having mastered many of these noble activities

"There is no man of life and agility in every respect in the Court but the Earl of Oxford"
– George Delves to the Earl of Rutland, 1571; B. M. Ward, p. 60

"The first course seemed to demand greater *skill and art* than I can lay claim to …"
- Oxford's Letter to the Reader, The Courtier, 1572

Part Two

2 **SOME IN THEIR WEALTH, SOME IN THEIR BODY'S FORCE,**
WEALTH = Oxford had inherited eighty-six estates; **BODY'S FORCE** = Oxford was champion jouster in the royal tiltyard, exhibiting great physical strength

3 **SOME IN THEIR GARMENTS, THOUGH NEW-FANGLED ILL,**
GARMENTS, THOUGH NEW-FANGLED ILL = Oxford wore current fashions from the Continent, both Italian and French, reveling in the jokes made by others about it; he was known as the quintessential "Italianate Englishman"; Gabriel Harvey wrote privately about Oxford to Edmund Spenser in 1580, in part making sport of the earl's new-fangled clothing: "Large-bellied Kodpeased doublet, unkodpeased half hose/ Straight to the dock like a shirt, and close to the britch like a diveling/ A little Apish hat flat couched fast to the pate like an oyster/ French Camarick ruffs, deep with a whiteness starched to the purpose … in Courtly guiles a passing singular odd man" –; Oxford was famous for having brought back "perfumed gloves" for the Queen upon his return from the Continent in 1576:

"The right honourable Edward de Vere, Earl of Oxford, came from Italy, and brought with him gloves, sweet bags, a perfumed leather jerkin, and other pleasant things; and that year the Queen had a pair of perfumed gloves trimmed only with four tufts, or roses of coloured silk; the Queen took such pleasure in those gloves that she was pictured with those gloves upon her hands, and for many years after it was called the Earl of Oxford's perfume" – Stow, *Annals*, 868b; Ogburn, Jr., The Mysterious William Shakespeare, 554

"The Earl of Oxford's livery was crimson velvet, very costly; he himself, and the furniture, was in some more colours, yet he was the Red Knight." - George Delves to the Earl of Rutland, May 14 and June 24, 1571; Cal. Rutland MSS., Ward, p. 60

4 **SOME IN THEIR HAWKS AND HOUNDS, SOME IN THEIR HORSE:**
HAWKS = Oxford was an expert falconer; "As *falcons* to the lure, *away she flies*" – Venus and Adonis, line 1027, similar to the following:

> Unsettled still like haggards vile they range,
> These *gentle birds that fly from man to man*:
> Who would not scorn and shake them from his fist,
> And let them go (fair fools) which way they list
> - Early Oxford poem published in 1591

As many have noted, the Shakespeare works abound with allusions to falconry, a sport reserved to the nobility at the time.

"Where as *the King and Queen do mean to hawk*" – 2 Henry VI, 1.2.58

HOUNDS = Oxford enjoyed hunting with hounds, as did Queen Elizabeth; "Earl of Oxford at the hunting of the stag" – memo of Lord Burghley, referring to August 3, 1574, after Oxford had returned from an unauthorized trip to the Continent and before he went to join Elizabeth on her progress in the west; Ward, p. 117, Hatfield MSS. (Cal. XIII.144); **HORSE** = singular and/or plural; "On the 3rd day of September (1562) came riding out of Essex from the funeral of the Earl of Oxford his father, the young Earl of Oxford, with *seven score horse* all in black" – account in Machyn's *Diary* of Oxford at age twelve, riding from Essex County to London

"He controls his foaming steed with a light rein, and armed with a long spear rides to the encounter; fearlessly he settles himself in the saddle, gracefully bending his body this way and that. Now he circles round; now with spurred heel he rouses his charger. The gallant animal with fiery energy collects himself together, and flying quicker than the wind beats the ground with his hoofs, and again is pulled up short as the reins control him". – Giles Fletcher, describing Edward de Vere's skill in horsemanship during the May 1571 tournament with horses and spears at Court, B. M. Ward, p. 60

REFERENCE EDITION

Oxford revised *The Taming of the Shrew* to include a spoof on his future stand-in, William Shaksper of Stratford-on-Avon, a commoner, whom he portrayed as Christopher Sly. In the opening inductions, Sly is told that he is actually a nobleman – a "lord" such as Oxford himself, with interests similar to those of his self-portrait in Sonnet 91:

> Some one be ready with a *costly suit*,
> And ask him what apparel he will wear,
> Another tell him of his *hounds and horse*
> - *The Taming of the Shrew*, Induction 1.58-60

> O noble lord, bethink thee of *thy birth*,
> Call home thy ancient thoughts from banishment,
> And banish hence these abject lowly dreams.
> Look how thy servants do attend on thee,
> Each in his office ready at thy beck…
> Say thou wilt walk; we will bestrew the ground.
> Or wilt thou ride? *Thy horses* shall be trapp'd,
> Their harness studded all with gold and pearl.
> Dost thou love *hawking*? Thou hast *hawks* will soar
> Above the morning lark. Or wilt thou hunt?
> Thy *hounds* shall make the welkin answer them
> - *The Taming of the Shrew*, Induction 2.34-49

5 AND EVERY HUMOR HATH HIS ADJUNCT PLEASURE,
EVERY = Ever = E. Ver, Edward deVere; **HUMOR** = temperament; **EVERY HUMOR** = echoing *Every Man in His Humour* (1598) and *Every Man Out of His Humour* (1599), attributed to Ben Jonson, who was beholden to Robert Cecil and also worked with Oxford and the Lord Chamberlain's Men [the two Jonson plays contain allusions to Oxford and to the Shakespeare stand-in]; "*every* humor" = E. Ver's or Edward de Vere's humor; **ADJUNCT PLEASURE** = related pleasure; echoing "Your Majesty's pleasure"

6 WHEREIN IT FINDS A JOY ABOVE THE REST.
JOY = "Was ever king that *joy'd* an earthly throne" – *2 Henry VI*, 4.9.1; "God make your Majesty *joyful*" – *Richard III*, 1.3.19; "Sweets with sweets war not, *joy* delights in *joy*" – Sonnet 8, line 2; **ABOVE THE REST** =

> *Above the rest* in Court who gave thee Grace?
> Who made thee strive in honor to be best?
> In constant truth to bide so firm and sure,
> To scorn the world regarding but thy friends?
> - Oxford's 'Shakespearean' sonnet, early 1570s, lines 7-10

> In this common shipwreck, mine is **above all the rest**….
> - Oxford to Robert Cecil, April 25/27, 1603

7 BUT THESE PARTICULARS ARE NOT MY MEASURE:
BUT, etc. = but these particular joys cannot describe me; **THESE PARTICULARS** = these details; these private matters; "And for that I go about now to lay open his evil and corrupt service, I will not for my own *particular* hereafter move your Lordship's furtherance" – Oxford to Burghley, June 7, 1595; "his general, who loved him in a most *dear particular*" – *Coriolanus*, 5.1.3; "Give us *particulars* of thy preservation" – *The Tempest*, 5.1.135

8 ALL THESE I BETTER IN ONE GENERAL BEST.
ALL = Southampton; **ONE** = Southampton; **BETTER** = surpass; "Each day still better other's happiness" – *Richard II*, 1.1.22; **GENERAL** = comprehensive; also "chief, head, having unrestricted authority" – *OED*; **ONE GENERAL BEST** = one royal king; Southampton as a newly born child filled with hot royal blood was "the *General* of hot desire" in Sonnet 154, line 7, written in 1574; this line blatantly includes the "all" and "one" of Southampton's motto *One for All, All for One*; **BEST** = "So all my *best* is dressing old words new" – Sonnet 76, line 11

9 THY LOVE IS BETTER THAN HIGH BIRTH TO ME:
THY LOVE = your royal blood; "And *you and love* are still my argument" – Sonnet 76, line 10; your royal blood means more to me than my own high birth; a statement made by one who *already has* high birth, as does Oxford, as highest-ranking earl of the Elizabethan reign; the pronouncement carries weight from one who already possesses what he is willing to give up; **BETTER** = "So thy great gift, upon misprision growing,/ Comes home again, on *better* judgment making" – Sonnet 87, lines 11-12; "O benefit of ill, now I find true/ That *better* is by evil still made *better*,/ And *ruined love* (loss of royal blood in succession to the throne) when it is built anew/ Grows fairer than at first, more strong, far greater" – Sonnet 119, 9-12

"Why should this tree be accounted *better* than that tree, but for the goodness of his fruit? Why should this vine be ***better*** than that vine, unless it brought forth a ***better*** grape than the other? Why should this rose be ***better*** esteemed than that rose, unless in pleasantness of smell it far surpassed the other rose? And so is it in ***all other things*** as well as in man" – Oxford's Prefatory Letter to "Cardanus' Comfort," 1573

10 RICHER THAN WEALTH, PROUDER THAN GARMENTS' COST,
RICHER = more royal and royally honored by me

> To fill King Edward's fame with prisoner kings
> And make her *chronicle* as *rich with praise*
> As is the ooze and bottom of *the sea*
> With sunken wrack and *sumless treasuries*
> - *Henry V*, 1.2.162-165

> Than doth a *rich embroidered canopy*
> To kings
> - *3 Henry VI*, 2.5.44-45

> Ha, majesty! How high thy glory towers
> When the *rich blood of kings* is set on fire!
> - *King John*, 2.1.350-351

PROUDER = more royal and royally honored; more "swollen" with a royal son

11 OF MORE DELIGHT THAN HAWKS OR HORSES BE;
The source of more joy than my hawks or horses; **DELIGHT** = "What doth avail the vine unless another *delighteth* in the grape?" – Oxford's Prefatory Letter for *Cardanus' Comfort*, 1573; "The foul boar's conquest on *her fair delight*" – *Venus and Adonis*, line 1030; "where-through the Sun/ *Delights* to peep, to gaze therein on thee" – Sonnet 24, lines 11-12; "As a decrepit *father takes delight*/ To see his active child do deeds of youth" – Sonnet 37, lines 1-2

12 AND HAVING THEE, OF ALL MEN'S PRIDE I BOAST.
HAVING THEE = having you as my son; however, no longer does Oxford have him as a son in line to gain the throne: "Thus have *I had thee* as a dream doth flatter:/ In sleep a King, but waking no such matter" – Sonnet 87, lines 13-14; **ALL** = Southampton; **ALL MEN'S PRIDE** = all my son's royalty; as a prince he is the pride of all men; "Why is my verse so barren of new *pride*" – Sonnet 76, line 1; **BOAST** = "Let those who are in favor with their stars/ Of public honour and proud titles *boast*" – Sonnet 25, lines 1-2;

13 **WRETCHED IN THIS ALONE: THAT THOU MAYST TAKE**
WRETCHED = miserable; echoing prisoners in the Tower as "wretches," especially those facing execution; i.e., although the Queen gave her son a reprieve, he still could be executed at any time; "Get ye therefore hence, poor miserable *wretches,* to your death" – the King to traitors in *Henry V*, 2.2.178-179; **ALONE** = Southampton, combining "all" and "one" of his motto; **WRETCHED IN THIS ALONE** = suffering because of you alone; "When in disgrace with Fortune and men's eyes,/ I *all alone* beweep my outcast state" – Sonnet 29, lines 1-2; "Tired with *all these,* from these would I be gone,/ Save that to die, I *leave my love alone*" – Sonnet 66, lines 13-14

14 **ALL THIS AWAY, AND ME MOST WRETCHED MAKE.**
ALL = Southampton; **ALL THIS** = you yourself; **ALL THIS AWAY** = all you away from me; "And *thou away*, the very birds are mute" – Sonnet 97, line 12, referring to Southampton away in the Tower; "Yet it seemed Winter still, and *you away*,/ As with your shadow I with these did play" – Sonnet 98, lines 13-14, also referring to Southampton being *away* in the Tower; "Or gluttoning on *all,* or *all away*" – Sonnet 75, line 14, again using "all" for Southampton in prison

Sir John Peyton, Lieutenant of the Tower, to the Council, August 18, 1601:
"My Lord of Southampton, by reason of his close imprisonment and want of all manner of exercise being grown weak and sickly, has desired me to send you his letters of petition, here enclosed, upon which occasion I have prepared for him another lodging. But without some exercise, and more air than is convenient for me to allow without knowledge from your honors of her Majesty's pleasure, I do much doubt of his recovery." (Stopes, 245)

The Council to Peyton at the Tower, August 19, 1601:
"Foreasmuch as her Majesty hath understood by a letter from yourself and another enclosed from the late Earl of Southampton that he, suspecting himself to be in some danger by the growing on of a long sickness (**which he hath had before his trouble**) ..." (Stopes, 245)

Queen Elizabeth to William Lambarde, Keeper of the Records in the Tower, August 1601:
*"I am Richard II, know ye not that? ... **He that will forget God will also forget his benefactors. This tragedy was played forty times in open streets and houses!**"* (Presumably the Queen was speaking of Essex as a Bolingbroke attempting to gain the crown, but Elizabeth herself brought up the subject of the Shakespeare play, so she must have been thinking of Oxford as well. Also, the fact she was meeting with the Keeper of the Tower's documents undoubtedly reminded her – if she needed reminding – of Southampton's present confinement. And her angry outburst sounds like an attempt to justify it to herself.)

Part Two

EIGHTH MONTH IN THE TOWER

Sonnet 92
For Term of Life
On Thy Revolt
September 1601

Oxford continues to instruct Southampton on how to live, think and feel from now on. His theme is that they must accept the idea of living with falsity; their inner peace comes from knowing the truth. In this sonnet he refers to Henry Wriothesley's new sentence in the Tower ("for term of life") and looks back at "thy revolt" against the Crown.

Sonnet 92	Translation
But do thy worst to steal thyself away,	But do the worst, by denying me with secrecy!
For term of life thou art assured mine,	You are sentenced to be my son for a life term,
And life no longer than thy love will stay,	And your life will not outlive your royalty,
For it depends upon that love of thine.	Because your life is governed by your royal blood.
Then need I not to fear the worst of wrongs,	Therefore I don't need to fear your worst pain,
When in the least of them my life hath end.	Since my own life will end when yours ends.
I see a better state to me belongs	I look to death as my royal state, better for me
Than that which on thy humor doth depend.	Than having to suffer whenever you do.
Thou canst not vex me with inconstant mind,	You can't cause me grief with lack of a claim,
Since that my life on thy revolt doth lie.	Since my true life now rests on your Rebellion.
Oh what a happy title do I find,	O what happy entitlement to you I find,
Happy to have thy love, happy to die!	Happy for you having royal blood, happy to die!
But what's so blessed fair that fears no blot?	But who's so divinely royal who fears no disgrace?
Thou mayst be false, and yet I know it not.	You may be a false-traitor, but that is not my view.

1 BUT DO THY WORST TO STEAL THY SELF AWAY:
BUT = indicating that Oxford continuing directly from the previous sonnet; **DO THY WORST** = a play on 'do thy best,' with worst repeated in line 5 below; **STEAL THYSELF AWAY** = to rob me of you, i.e., by refusing to acknowledge that you are my royal son by the Queen; the same way Elizabeth (her negative attitude) went "*stealing* unseen to west with this disgrace" of her royal son in Sonnet 33; i.e., rob me of you, as in "To *that sweet thief which sourly robs from me*" – Sonnet 35, line 14, referring to Southampton, who, because of his part in the Rebellion, robbed his destiny as king and therefore robbed Oxford of his hope to be the father of a king; "I do forgive *thy robb'ry, gentle thief*" – Sonnet 40, line 9

2 FOR TERM OF LIFE THOU ART ASSURED MINE,
FOR TERM OF LIFE = for all our lives; a legal expression (as in 'life tenure') alluding to Southampton's sentence in the Tower; in reality, nothing can eliminate their father-son bond; (only when the accused had been found guilty of *misprision*, writes Bellamy, "was the punishment of *perpetual imprisonment* inflicted" – *Tudor Law of Treason*, 182); this is a good example of Oxford using the poem to say one thing while glancing at another situation at the same time; **LIFE** = repeated in lines 3, 6 & 10 below

REFERENCE EDITION

*"Till the 12th of Henry the 8th, mine ancestors have possessed the same, almost sithence the time of William Conqueror, and at that time (which was the 12th year of Henry the 8th) the king took it **for term of his life** from my grandfather, since which time, what by the alterations of princes and wardships, I have been kept from my rightful possession."* - Oxford to Robert Cecil, May 7, 1603

ASSURED = "assigned, pledged, guaranteed … definite" – Crystal & Crystal; **ASSURED MINE** = "certainly mine; legally mine, signed over to me … pledged to me" – Booth; "Would I were *assured* of my condition" – the King in *King Lear*, 4.7.56-57; "stand in assured loss" – *King Lear*, 3.6.93; "Your Lordship's *assured* friend and brother-in-law" – Oxford to Robert Cecil, June 16, 1603 (and on many other letters, such as: "Your loving and *assured* brother to his power" – November 22, 1601, a few months after the dating of this sonnet, indicating that Oxford is acknowledging Cecil's *power* over the Queen's government, over Southampton, and over the royal succession to come); in a letter to William Cecil on November 24, 1569, at nineteen, Oxford signed as "By your assured friend"; **MINE** = "a son of mine own" – Oxford to Burghley, March 17, 1575; "mine only son" – *3 Henry VI*, 2.5.83; "a son of mine" – *3 Henry VI*, 5.6.36; "no son of mine" – *Titus Andronicus*, 1.1.348

3 AND LIFE NO LONGER THAN THY LOVE WILL STAY,
And this term of life will last no longer than your "love" or royal blood remains or continues to flow within you; after that, it will be up to future readers of these sonnets to learn of this *"living record* of your memory" (Sonnet 55, line 8) for themselves; **LIFE** = repeated from line 2 above; "That he (time) shall never cut from memory/ My sweet love's beauty (my royal son's Tudor blood from Elizabeth), though my lover's life" – Sonnet 63, lines 11-12; **THY LOVE** = your royal blood; "And all in war with Time *for love of you*" – Sonnet 15, line 13, i.e., the war against the decay of the Queen's body for the sake of your royal blood; **STAY** = "*stay* was already a legal term – as in *to stay an execution*" – Booth; as Elizabeth *stayed* hers son's execution, based on the sacrifice offered by Oxford, who has promised Cecil that Southampton will never try to claim the throne.

4 FOR IT DEPENDS UPON THAT LOVE OF THINE.
DEPENDS UPON = our lives depend upon your royal blood; "Both truth and beauty on my love depends" – Sonnet 101, line 3, i.e., both Oxford and Elizabeth depend upon my royal son; **THAT LOVE OF THINE** = that royal blood of yours; "And *you and love* are still my argument" – Sonnet 76, line 10

5 THEN NEED I NOT TO FEAR THE WORST OF WRONGS,
WORST OF WRONGS = any kind of terrible injuries, other than the severance of their father-son bond; wrongs = crimes

6 WHEN IN THE LEAST OF THEM MY LIFE HATH END:
When all these will end, i.e., when my life is over; LIFE = repeated from lines 2 & 3; MY LIFE will be repeated in line 10 below

7 I SEE A BETTER STATE TO ME BELONGS
STATE = Alluding to his son's royal state or estate; his rank as king, shared by Oxford as father; "I all alone beweep *my outcast state*" – Sonnet 29, line 2; "If thou wouldst use *the strength of all thy state*" – Sonnet 96, line 12; "Scoffing at his *state* and grinning at his pomp" – *Richard II*, 3.2.163; "A substitute shines brightly as a king until a king be by, and then his *state* empties itself, as doth an inland brook into the main of waters" – *The Merchant of Venice*, 5.1.94-97; "and turned my *captive state* to liberty" – *3 Henry VI*, 4.6.3; "And, *as you are a king, speak in your state*" – *2 Henry IV*, 5.3.99; **BETTER STATE** = echoing the "*better judgment*" of Sonnet 87, line 12; Oxford is referring to the inward truth that cannot be taken from either him or his son

8 THAN THAT WHICH ON THY HUMOR DOTH DEPEND.
Than any state or humor that depends on your mood or temperament, or depends upon what image you present; i.e., my better state results from the existence of your royal blood, no matter what "humor" surrounds it; "And *every humor* hath his adjunct pleasure" – Sonnet 91, line 5

9 **THOU CANST NOT VEX ME WITH INCONSTANT MIND,**
VEX = to afflict, trouble, torment; reflecting Oxford's deep suffering over forcing his royal son to accept the terms of the bargain Oxford has made for him; "'Twill *vex thy soul* to hear what I shall speak" – *Titus Andronicus*, 5.1.62; "They may *vex* us with shot or with assault" – *1 Henry VI*, 1.4.13; "whom the foul fiend *vexes*" – *King Lear*, 3.4.59; "More than enough am I that *vex* thee still" – Sonnet 135, line 3, Oxford to Elizabeth, when begging to her spare Southampton from execution; similar to the context of "*vex* him with eager words" in *3 Henry VI*, 2.6.68, followed by "ask *mercy* ... *repent* ... devise *excuses* for thy *faults*" in lines 69-71; "so *vexed* with watching and with tears" – Sonnet 148, line 10, Oxford to Elizabeth, referring to the torment of trying to help Southampton

"Very unpleasing is that Way, where the setting out, Progress and Journey's End yield nothing but Trouble and **Vexation.** *I have this day been in greater Conflict with my self than ever I was in all my Life"* - Queen Elizabeth, about whether to execute Mary Queen of Scots
(Camden: The Nine and Twentieth Year of the Reign, 1586)

WITH INCONSTANT MIND = with lack of your constancy or royal blood, which cannot be anything other than constant; ("Therefore my verse to *constancy* confined" – Sonnet 105, line 7; "In *constant* truth to bide so firm and sure" – early sonnet by *Earle of Oxenforde*)

10 **SINCE THAT MY LIFE ON THY REVOLT DOTH LIE.**
My life hangs upon, is dependent upon, your "revolt" or treason; i.e., my future is now dictated by the consequences of that crime; alluding to his son's *term of life* in line 2, i.e., Southampton's life is Oxford's life; **THY REVOLT** = Your crime of the Rebellion; ("Rebellious hinds, the filth and scum of Kent, mark'd for the gallows, lay your weapons down ... The King is merciful if you *revolt*" – *2 Henry VI*, 4.2.118-121; "For *this revolt of thine*, methinks, is like another fall of man" – *Henry V*, 2.2.141-142); i.e., my life now depends on what happens as a result of your revolt against the state; "And all the rest *revolted faction traitors*" – *Richard II*, 2.2.57; "*Revolt* our subjects?" – the King in *Richard II*, 3.2.100; "All will *revolt* from me, and turn to him" – the King in *3 Henry VI*, 1.1.155; ("*Item: That neither Prince shall for the time to come aid, favour, succour or relieve any Traitor, Rebel, or him that shall openly* **revolt** *from his Prince*" - League of Stricter Amity, England and Scotland, 1586); **LIE** = depend; but also alluding to the "lie" that both Oxford and Southampton must now perpetuate; lie like a corpse; "Then let *his head and lifeless body lie,* until the Queen his Mistress bury it" – *2 Henry VI*, 4.2.142-143

11 **OH WHAT A HAPPY TITLE DO I FIND,**
OH = O = Oxford; **HAPPY TITLE** = Royal title, as father of royal son; "*Entitled* in thy parts do *crowned sit*" – Sonnet 37, line 7, i.e., wear a crown and sit on the throne; "to whom I wish long life still lengthened with *all happiness*" – Oxford as "Shakespeare" to Southampton in dedicating *Lucrece* to him in 1594; "To the onlie begetter of these ensuing sonnets Mr. W. H. *all happiness*" – dedication of the Sonnets to "Mr. W. H. or "Mr. Wriothesley, Henry," recalling his time as a traitor in the Tower and reduced to commoner status or worse, i.e., reduced by "all oblivious enmity" (Sonnet 55, line 9) to a nobody or "the late earl of Southampton"

12 **HAPPY TO HAVE THY LOVE, HAPPY TO DIE!**
HAPPY = fortunate, lucky; "Happy return be to your royal grace!" – *Measure for Measure*, 5.1.3; "Resembling sire, and child, and *happy mother*" – Sonnet 8, line 11; **THY LOVE** = your royal blood, still alive; **HAPPY TO DIE** = "Tired with all these, *for restful death I cry*/ ... Tired with all these, from these would I be gone,/ Save that *to die*, I leave my love alone" – Sonnet 66, lines 1, 13-14; "*To die* – to sleep, no more; and by a sleep to say we end the heart-ache and the thousand natural shocks that flesh is heir to: 'tis a consummation devoutly to be wish'd. *To die*, to sleep; to sleep, perchance to dream – ay, there's the rub" – *Hamlet*, 3.1.60-65

13 **BUT WHAT'S SO BLESSED FAIR THAT FEARS NO BLOT?**
BLESSED FAIR = both sacred (as a "god on earth") and royal (as a king); "the *blessed sun of heaven*" – Falstaff, referring to Prince Hal, the future Henry the Fifth, in *1 Henry IV*, 2.4.403; **BLOT** = The shame,

disgrace of the Rebellion and Southampton's loss of honor, i.e., his loss of the crown because of it; "And thus *thy fall hath left a kind of blot* ... this *revolt* of thine ... *faults* ... I arrest thee of *high treason*" – *Henry V*, 2.2.138, 141,142, 145;

14 THOU MAYST BE FALSE, AND YET I KNOW IT NOT.
THOU MAYST BE FALSE = you may continue to deny that you are my son, as you are supposed to do; "Hence, thou suborned *Informer*" - Sonnet 125, line 13, i.e., go forth, from here on, you who have been suborned into testifying against your true identity

FALSE = Related to Southampton's conviction as traitor; "The usual adverbs in legal records alongside the descriptions of particular treasons are '*falsely*' and '*traitorously*'" – Bellamy, *Tudor Law of Treason*, 33

> *False king!* Why hast thou broken faith with me
> - *2 Henry VI*, 5.1.91
>
> I am thy king, and thou a *false-heart traitor*
> - *2 Henry VI*, 5.1.143
>
> Like a *false traitor* and injurious villain
> - *Richard II*, 1.1.91

FALSE = "An eye more bright than theirs, less *false* in rolling" – Sonnet 20, line 5, referring to Southampton's royal eye or "sun" that is more bright than that of the Queen, whose imperial eye is "false in rolling" or in ruling; "Where thou art *forced to break a twofold truth*:/ Hers, by thy beauty tempting her to thee,/ Thine, by thy beauty being *false* to me" – Sonnet 41, lines 12-14; "falsely accused" – *Much Ado About Nothing*, 5.2.92; "O me! What eyes hath love put in my head,/ Which have *no correspondence with true sight*!/ Or if they have, where is my judgment fled,/ That *censure falsely what they see aright*?" – Sonnet 148, lines 1-4, to Elizabeth in the Dark Lady series; **AND YET I KNOW IT NOT** = nevertheless, I know better than that; I am silent; I refuse to accept that you are not the rightful king

Part Two

THE PRISON YEARS

NINTH MONTH IN THE TOWER

Sonnet 93
Heaven In Thy Creation Did Decree
October 1601

Oxford carries over the final thought of the previous verse: from now on he will live with false appearances on the official record ("the false heart's history") while preserving the truth in this diary intended for readers in the future. Southampton and his beauty (Tudor blood from Elizabeth) are still growing in the entries of this diary, even if he and his royal claim are viewed as evil and dangerous like Eve's apple -- tempting others to consider attempting another overthrow of the Government under Robert Cecil.

Sonnet 93	Translation
So shall I live, supposing thou art true,	In this way I'll live, believing you're my royal son,
Like a deceived husband; so love's face	Like a deceived husband! So your royal claim
May still seem love to me, though altered new:	May still seem royal to me, though you lose it:
Thy looks with me, thy heart in other place,	Your blood is mine, while you are in the Tower –
For there can live no hatred in thine eye,	For I can see no lack of royalty in your presence.
Therefore in that I cannot know thy change,	Therefore, in you I can't see your downfall.
In many's looks, the false heart's history	By the looks of others, I see that a false story
Is writ in moods and frowns and wrinkles strange,	Is being told by their attitude toward your downfall.
But heaven in thy creation did decree,	But Elizabeth, in giving birth to you, decreed
That in thy face sweet love should ever dwell,	That your royal blood should always live in you!
What ere thy thoughts, or thy heart's workings be,	And that whatever your thoughts or feelings are,
Thy looks should nothing thence, but sweetness tell.	Your presence should be nothing but royal!
How like *Eve's* apple doth thy beauty grow,	Your royalty still grows like Eve's apple –
If thy sweet vertue answer not thy show.	Even as your kingly qualities can't be revealed.

1 SO SHALL I LIVE, SUPPOSING THOU ART TRUE,
SO = therefore; again indicating that Oxford undoubtedly writes more than one verse at a single sitting, later revising them and arranging the verses by the calendar; "so" also meaning "in this way" or "in the following manner"; **SUPPOSING** = believing; **TRUE** = related to me, Oxford, *Nothing Truer than Truth*; therefore, in this manner I shall continue to live, believing in the truth of your royal claim (even though it's no longer a possibility); "And *your true rights* be termed a Poet's rage" – Sonnet 17, line 11; "Why should poor beauty indirectly seek/ Roses of shadow, since *his Rose is true*?" – Sonnet 67, lines 7-8

2 LIKE A DECEIVED HUSBAND; SO LOVE'S FACE
LIKE A DECEIVED HUSBAND = (referring to the previous line); willingly believing in our bond, regardless of what the entire world believes; "Let me not to *the marriage of true minds*/ Admit impediments! Love is not love/ Which alters when it alteration finds/ Or bends with the remover to remove" – Sonnet 116,

REFERENCE EDITION 505

lines 1-4; **SO** = so that; **LOVE'S FACE** = the face or reflection of your royal blood

3 MAY STILL SEEM LOVE TO ME, THOUGH ALTERED NEW:

May always appear to be genuine, to me, even though your claim to the throne has been "altered" by the bargain to save your life and gain your freedom; **STILL** = always; **LOVE** = royal blood; **ALTERED NEW** = "New changed (into something) new" – Booth; changed in appearance, i.e., from the golden time to this time of disgrace; referring to the alteration of the death sentence to life imprisonment, but also referring to the alteration of his right to claim the throne as Elizabeth's immediate heir and successor; "My Lord," Queen Elizabeth told Lord Admiral Howard during her final days in January-March 1603, *"I am tied with a chain of iron about my neck. I am tied, I am tied, and the case is* **altered** *with me,"* perhaps referring to her inability to name Southampton; "Just to the time, not with the time *exchanged*" – Sonnet 109, line 7; "But reck'ning time, whose millioned accidents/ Creep in 'twixt vows, and *change decrees of Kings,*/ Tan sacred beauty, blunt the sharp'st intents,/ *Divert* strong minds to th'course of *alt'ring* things" – Sonnet 115, lines 5-8; "*Love* is not *love*/ Which *alters* when it *alteration* finds" – Sonnet 116, lines 2-3, i.e., royal blood is not royal blood if it changes in the face of change, i.e., it remains itself

> *"In this common shipwreck, mine is above all the rest, who least regarded, though often comforted, of all her followers, she hath left to try my fortune among* **the alterations** *of time and chance"* - Oxford to Robert Cecil, April 25/27, 1603, of Elizabeth, on the eve of her funeral

> *"The king took it for term of his life from my grandfather, since which time, what by the* **alterations** *of princes and wardships"* - Oxford to Robert Cecil, May 7, 1603

4 THY LOOKS WITH ME, THY HEART IN OTHER PLACE.

THY LOOKS WITH ME = your eyes still gaze on me; "Thy looks" – line 12; "His *looks are full of peaceful majesty,* his head by nature framed to wear a crown" – *3 Henry VI*, 4.6.71-72; **THY HEART IN OTHER PLACE** = your royal heart, pumping royal blood, is separated from me; **OTHER PLACE** = the Tower; "You both shall be led from hence to *the place* from whence you came and there remain during her Majesty's pleasure" – the Lord High Steward, Buckhurst, to Essex and Southampton at the end of the trial on February 19, 1601, after the guilty verdict had been rendered, referring to the Tower as "the place" from which they had been conveyed that morning; "As soon as think *the place* where he would be" – Sonnet 44, line 8

5 FOR THERE CAN LIVE NO HATRED IN THINE EYE,

NO HATRED IN THINE EYE = no lack of royal blood in your kingly eye; "The phrase also contains a momentary and flattering suggestion of '*in your presence*' – as in *Hamlet*, 4.4.6: 'We shall express our duty *in his eye*'" – Booth, who also suggests a relationship to Castiglione's *Courtier*, a translation of which Oxford had caused to be published in January 1572; "Flatter the mountain tops with *sovereign eye*" – Sonnet 33, line 2; "And scarcely greet me with *that sun thine eye*" – Sonnet 49, line 6; in Q spelled "sunne"; "

6 THEREFORE IN THAT I CANNOT KNOW THY CHANGE.

So I cannot see any change of our relationship by looking there

7 IN MANY'S LOOKS, THE FALSE HEART'S HISTORY

IN MANY'S LOOKS = in the features of many people, but here also in the eyes of the Court and of the multitude; **THE FALSE HEART'S HISTORY** = the false record of contemporary events, which these sonnets are correcting for the sake of future readers, for whom these events will be history; **FALSE** = echoing the phrase "false-traitor"

8 IS WRIT IN MOODS AND FROWNS AND WRINKLES STRANGE:

WRIT = legal; recorded; "O learn to read what silent love hath writ" - Sonnet 23, line 13, i.e., the true history being recorded in these sonnets; but the *false* history is being "writ" or recorded by those in authority, with their external shows of contempt and disregard for you; i.e., the winners are the ones who leave the publicly proclaimed "history" behind; **MOODS** = "visible marks of feeling (with a strong negative implication: 'signs of treachery, petulance, angry melancholy'" – Kerrigan; **FROWNS** = the frowns of Elizabeth in particular; "Great Princes' favorites their fair leaves spread/ But as the Marigold at the sun's eye,/ And in themselves their pride lies buried,/ For *at a frown they in their glory die*" – Sonnet 25, lines 5-8

9 BUT HEAVEN IN THY CREATION DID DECREE

But Queen Elizabeth, in giving birth to you decreed by virtue of your blood from her; "Withdraw with us, and let the trumpets sound, while we return these dukes *what we decree*" – Richard II, 1.3.122; **HEAVEN IN THY CREATION** = Elizabeth in the Sonnets is *Heaven, Beauty, Nature, Fortune, Phoenix, Mistress, Woman*, etc., as in "She (nature) carved thee for her seal" – Sonnet 11, line 13; "Who *heaven* itself for *ornament* doth use" – Sonnet 21, line 3, referring to Southampton as the ornament or heir of Elizabeth: "The *ornament of beauty* is suspect,/ A crow that flies in *heaven's heir*" – Sonnet 70, lines 3-4; **DECREE** = "To command (something) by decree; to order, appoint, or assign"; "authoritatively ordain" – *OED*; (as in "Decree of Star Chamber"); "There is no force in *the decrees of Venice*" – Merchant of Venice, 4.1.102; "But reckoning time, whose millioned accidents/ Creep in 'twixt vows, and *change decrees of kings*" - Sonnet 115, lines 5-6, i.e., Elizabeth's decree that her son would succeed her has been changed; also, by the time of Sonnet 115 in April 1603, King James will have changed the Queen's decree that Southampton must remain in prison for a term of life; **CREATION** = Southampton; "From fairest *creatures* we desire increase,/ That thereby beauty's *Rose* might never die" – Sonnet 1, lines 1-2; in Sonnet 127, line 12, Oxford depicts Elizabeth as "Sland'ring *Creation* with a false esteem," i.e., disinheriting her royal son and preventing him from becoming king, by perceiving him falsely under her dark frown; related to God's creation of the world, anticipating Eve in line 13 below; and the birth of Southampton as a royal prince who is divinely ordained: "Nativity, once in the main of light,/ Crawls to maturity, wherewith being crowned,/ Crooked eclipses 'gainst his glory fight" – Sonnet 60, lines 5-7

10 THAT IN THY FACE SWEET LOVE SHOULD EVER DWELL;

SWEET = royal; "and I prithee, *sweet* wag, when thou art king" – Falstaff to Prince Hal in *1 Henry IV*, 1.2.16; **SWEET FACE** = royal image; his face reflects Elizabeth's face: "A Woman's face with nature's own hand painted/ Hast thou, the Master Mistress of my passion" - Sonnet 20, lines 1-2; "Thou art thy mother's glass, and she in thee/ Calls back the lovely April of her prime" - Sonnet 3, lines 9-10; "Thus is his cheek the map of days outworn,/ When beauty lived and died as flowers do now,/ Before these bastard signs of fair were borne,/ Or durst inhabit on a living brow" - Sonnet 68, lines 1-4; **LOVE** = royal blood; "O know, *sweet love*, I always write of you,/ And *you and love* are still my argument" – Sonnet 76, lines 9-10; **EVER** = always; Ever = E. Ver = Edward de Vere, *Ever or Never*

11 WHAT ERE THY THOUGHTS OR THY HEART'S WORKINGS BE,

No matter what you say or do in public

12 THY LOOKS SHOULD NOTHING THENCE BUT SWEETNESS TELL.

Your authentic appearance (as a king) would have nothing to do with that; or from your looks nothing but your royal identity will be expressed; **NOTHING** = echoing Southampton as a "nobody" or as "none" as opposed to "one"; "Among a number *one* is reckoned *none*" – Sonnet 136, line 8; **THENCE BUT SWEETNESS TELL** = from thence, i.e., from your appearance, nothing but your royal identity will be expressed or told; **TELL** = "So is my love still *telling what is told*" – Sonnet 76, line 14

13 HOW LIKE *EVE'S* APPLE DOTH THY BEAUTY GROW,
LIKE *EVE'S* APPLE =("Eve" is italicized in Q, spelled as *Eaues*); your external appearance that hides your disgrace and lack of kingship; related to his birth or "creation" by "heaven" or Elizabeth, the divinely ordained sovereign; (she also "created" him as an earl); with overtones of the story of Adam and Eve; **THY BEAUTY** = your Tudor blood from her; **GROW** = in your life and in the womb of these sonnets; "*When in eternal lines to time thou grow'st*" – Sonnet 18, line 12; "So thy great gift, upon misprision *growing*" – Sonnet 87, linje 11; "Love is a Babe; then might I not say so,/ To *give full growth to that which still doth grow*" – Sonnet 115, lines 13-14; "O Thou my lovely Boy who in thy power/ Doth hold time's fickle glass, his sickle hour:/ *Who has by waning grown*" – Sonnet 126, lines 1-3

14 IF THY SWEET VERTUE ANSWER NOT THY SHOW.
THY SWEET VERTUE = your royal honor or goodness or virtue; related to "Ver"; your inherent qualities; your true royal blood; **ANSWER NOT THY SHOW** = fails to match your appearance or status in the eyes of the world

Part Two

THE PRISON YEARS

OXFORD WARNS AGAINST NEW REVOLT
TENTH MONTH IN THE TOWER

Sonnet 94
They That Have Power to Hurt
November 1601

Further instructions from father to son: by now friends who supported Southampton and Essex in the Rebellion are visiting Southampton in the Tower; in this verse Oxford warns him to avoid this "infection" or dangerous "temptation" to do something rash. He appeals to him as a king who must not use his "power" to damage the bargain that has been made for his release and pardon. Southampton must be one who "outbraves his dignity" by resisting the temptation to raise another rebellion. Princes or Kings have the power to commit the greatest crimes.

Sonnet 94	Translation
They that have power to hurt, and will do none, That do not do the thing they most do show, Who moving others are themselves as stone, Unmoved, cold, and to temptation show:	Those with the power to hurt but won't use it, Who don't do what they seem most capable of – Those who, affecting others while unaffected, Unmoved, cold, and slow to act:
They rightly do inherit heaven's graces, And husband nature's riches from expense; They are the Lords and owners of their faces, Others but stewards of their excellence.	They, like you, truly inherit Elizabeth's royal blood, And preserve the Queen's dynasty from death; They, like you, are kings in and of themselves, While others are servants of such royalty.
The summer's flower is to the summer sweet, Though to itself it only live and die, But if that flower with base infection meet, The basest weed outbraves his dignity.	The ripe Tudor Rose is the ripeness of royalty, Though you may live and die alone in prison, But if your Tudor Rose must live with criminals, The most disgraced Rose surpasses all.
For sweetest things turn sourest by their deeds; Lilies that fester smell far worse than weeds.	For royal princes are condemned by their deeds; Princes or Kings in prison fall farther than anyone.

"By the end of the year (1601), Southampton was receiving visits in his lodgings (within the Tower prison-fortress) from his old friends of the Essex faction, the 'Octavians' as they were now known in consequence of the events of the ill-starred February 8th." - Akrigg, 132

1 THEY THAT HAVE POWER TO HURT, AND WILL DO NONE,
THEY THAT HAVE POWER TO HURT = those rulers or officials who have the authority to inflict harm on others; ("To be able to do harm, and not to do it, is noble" – Tilley, H170); but this refers to Southampton himself, a king who has the *power* to hurt (i.e., to hurt himself and hurt Oxford) by rebelling again and breaking his end of the bargain by which he must forfeit his royal claim; "O Thou my lovely Boy, who *in thy power*" – Sonnet 126, line 1; **AND WILL DO NONE** = and will extend mercy instead; and will not use his

power to do harm; "Nothing adorns a king more than justice" – Oxford to Robert Cecil, May 7, 1603; **NONE** = echoing Southampton as "one" who is now "none" because he cannot claim the throne; "Among a number *one* is reckoned *none*" – Sonnet 136, line 8, Oxford to Elizabeth, referring to their royal son; (Oxford turns the tables on Elizabeth in the Dark Lady series: "O from what *power* hast thou this *powerful might*,/ With insufficiency my heart to sway?/To make me give the lie to my true sight" – Sonnet 150, lines 1-3)

2 THAT DO NOT DO THE THING THEY MOST DO SHOW,
THAT DO NOT, etc. = that refrain from doing what their power allows them to; **SHOW** = "These indeed seem, for they are actions that a man might play; but I have that within which passes *show*, these but the trappings and the suits of woe" – *Hamlet*, 1.2.83-86

3 WHO MOVING OTHERS ARE THEMSELVES AS STONE,
WHO, etc. = who order or cause others to act but themselves remain unmovable as stone; ("And blest are those *whose blood and judgment* are not so well commeddled [co-mingled] that they are not a pipe for Fortune's finger to sound what stop she please. Give me *that man that is not passion's slave*, and I will wear him in my heart's core" – *Hamlet*, 3.2.72-74)

4 UNMOVED, COLD, AND TO TEMPTATION SLOW:
UNMOVED, etc. = same as above; **TEMPTATION** = the temptation to lead others in a revolt by breaking out of the Tower and trying, again, to oust Robert Cecil from power; "For still *temptation* follows *where thou art*" – Sonnet 41, line 4, i.e., the temptation to rebellion continues always to follow you, a prince, even where are you are in the Tower

5 THEY RIGHTLY DO INHERIT HEAVEN'S GRACES
RIGHTLY = by right, i.e., right of birth; "And *your true rights* be termed a Poet's rage" – Sonnet 17, line 11; "Such is my love, to thee I so belong,/ That *for thy right* myself will bear all wrong" – Sonnet 88, lines 13-14; **INHERIT HEAVEN'S GRACES** = inherit the royal graces of your mother, Elizabeth; "But *heaven in thy creation* did decree" – Sonnet 93, line 9; "Be as thy presence is, *gracious* and kind" – Sonnet 10, line 11; "If I could write the beauty of your eyes,/ And in fresh numbers number *all your graces*" – Sonnet 17, lines 5-6; "Thine eyes ... (have) given *grace* a *double majesty*" – Sonnet 78, lines 5, 8; echoing and bringing forward all the reminders to Southampton in Sonnets 1-17 of his inheritance of Tudor blood, such as "thy beauty's *legacy*" and "Nature's *bequest*" of Sonnet 4, lines 2, 3; "The bounteous *largess* given thee to give" of Sonnet 4, line 6; "that fresh blood" and "bounteous gift" of Sonnet 11, lines 3, 12; and "your true rights" of Sonnet 17, line 11

6 AND HUSBAND NATURE'S RICHES FROM EXPENSE;
AND HUSBAND NATURE'S RICHES = hold onto the royal blood and graces of Elizabeth, who is also Nature in the Sonnets; "A Woman's face with *nature's own hand painted*/ Hast thou, the Master Mistress of my passion" – Sonnet 20, lines 1-2; **NATURE'S RICHES** = royal blood; "O him she (nature, i.e., Elizabeth) stores, to show what *wealth* she had" – Sonnet 67, line 13; "Sets you most *rich in youth* before my sight" – Sonnet 15, line 10, in 1590-91, when Southampton was still young and filled with hope for his succession to the throne; "beauty's *treasure*" – Sonnet 6, line 4, i.e., royal blood inherited from "beauty" or Elizabeth

7 THEY ARE THE LORDS AND OWNERS OF THEIR FACES,
LORDS = kings, gods on earth; "*Lord of my love*" – Sonnet 26, line 1; **OWNERS** = controllers of their own actions; Southampton "owns" his royal face; "love's face" - Sonnet 93, line 2, i.e., the face of royal blood

No. 94

8 OTHERS BUT STEWARDS OF THEIR EXCELLENCE:
STEWARDS = custodians; alluding to the *Lord High Steward* at the trial; one of those who, in fact, had "the power to hurt" and in fact did so against Essex and Southampton; **EXCELLENCE** = power; royal power, related to Your Excellency; "Still constant in a wondrous *excellence*" – Sonnet 105, line 6

9 THE SUMMER'S FLOWER IS TO THE SUMMER SWEET,
SUMMER'S FLOWER = Southampton, budding flower of the Tudor Rose, who once basked in the golden time of royal sun-shine; the "little *western flower*" of *A Midsummer Night's Dream* and the "*purple flower*" of *Venus and Adonis*; "For never-resting time leads *Summer* on/ ... Then were not *summer's distillation* left/ ... But *flowers distilled*" – Sonnet 5, lines 5,7,13; "Then let not winter's ragged hand deface/ In thee *thy summer* ere thou be *distilled*" – Sonnet 6, lines 1-2; **TO THE SUMMER SWEET** = royal in relation to that "golden time" in Sonnet 3, line 12: "this thy *golden time*"; "Shall I compare thee to a *Summer's day*?" – Sonnet 18, line 1

10 THOUGH TO ITSELF IT ONLY LIVE AND DIE,
THOUGH TO ITSELF, etc. = ("For none of us *liveth to himself*, and no man *dieth to himself*. For whether we live, we live unto the Lord; and whether we die, we die unto the Lord" – Romans, 14.7-8); **ONLY** = in context, referring to Southampton as the flower, playing on "*only*" = "*one*" of his motto *One for All, All for One*

>"If whilst I live she will be ***only* mine** ... That '*only*' came well in. Sir, list to me: I am my father's heir and ***only* son**" – *The Taming of the Shrew*, 2.1.356-358

>"To the ***onlie* begetter** of these ensuring sonnets, Mr. W. H." – 1609 dedication of the Book of Sonnets

11 BUT IF THAT FLOWER WITH BASE INFECTION MEET,
THAT FLOWER = Southampton; "That thereby *beauty's Rose* might never die" – Sonnet 1, line 2; "For nothing this wide universe I call,/ Save *thou, my Rose*, in it thou art my all" – Sonnet 109, lines 13-14, to Southampton as the (unacknowledged) heir of the Tudor Rose dynasty; **BASE INFECTION** = evildoers, criminals, traitors; those who abuse their power; corruption or criminals in authority and/or among base commoners; "Ah, wherefore with *infection* should he live" – Sonnet 67, line 1; those conspirators of the Rebellion in the Tower or who visit with Southampton there and urge him to new revolt; "and lift up the *base-minded man* to achieve to any true sum or grade of virtue whereto ought only the noble thoughts of men to be inclined" – Oxford's Prefatory Letter to *Cardanus' Comfort*, 1573; "As on the finger of a throned Queen,/ The *basest Jewel* will be well esteemed" - Sonnet 96, lines 5-6, of Southampton, a Prince reduced to the status of a base commoner among "infection" in the Tower; **INFECTION** = "But such is the *infection* of the time that, for the health and physic of our right, we cannot deal but with the very hand of stern injustice and confused wrong" – *King John*, 5.2.20-23; "O master, what a strange *infection* is fall'n into thy ear! What false Italian, as poisonous-tongued as handed, hath prevailed on thy too ready hearing?" – *Cymbeline*, 3.2.1-6; "Darest thou support a published traitor? Hence, lest that the *infection* of his fortune take like hold on thee" – *King Lear*, 4.6.228-230; "We'll hear no more; pursue him to his house, and pluck him thence: lest his *infection*, being of catching nature, spread further" – *Coriolanus*, 3.1.307-309, in reference to a traitor; "Advice is sporting while *infection* breeds; thou grant'st no time for charitable deeds: wrath, envy, treason, rape, and murder's rages, thy heinous hours wait on them as their pages" – *Lucrece*, stanza 130

>This royal throne of kings, this scept'red isle...
>This fortress built by Nature for herself
>Against *infection* and the hand of war
>- *Richard II*, 2.1.40, 43-44

REFERENCE EDITION

"This great, this bloody, this crying, this *infectious* sin" – Essex, when he was about to be executed, referring to the Rebellion

12 **THE BASEST WEED OUT-BRAVES HIS DIGNITY:**
BASEST WEED = most disgraced flower or plant; Southampton as a "base" commoner in the Tower; "As on the finger of a throned Queen,/ The *basest Jewel* will be well esteemed" – Sonnet 96, lines 5-6; **OUT-BRAVES** = outdoes, outshines; i.e., Oxford warning him to resist any new revolt; ("Consider the *lilies of the field*, how they grow ... And yet I say unto you, that even Solomon in all his glory was not arrayed like one of these" – Matthew, 6.28-29); **HIS DIGNITY** = his own honor and royal blood

13 **FOR SWEETEST THINGS TURN SOUREST BY THEIR DEEDS,**
SWEETEST THINGS = most royal princes; "O know, *sweet love*, I always write of you" – Sonnet 76, line 9; "Good night, *sweet prince*" – Hamlet, 5.2.366; **SOUREST** = most hurtful; **DEEDS** = acts of treason; "Ah, but those tears are pearl which thy love sheeds,/ And they are rich, and ***ransom all ill deeds***" – Sonnet 34, lines 13-14; Oxford turns the tables on Elizabeth in the Dark Ladie series: "Thy black [your disgraced son] is fairest in my judgment's place./ In nothing art thou black save in thy deeds,/ And thence this slander [against Southampton] as I think proceeds" –Sonnet 131, lines 12-14

14 **LILIES THAT FESTER SMELL FAR WORSE THAN WEEDS.**
LILIES, etc. = an allusion to the festering Queen, whose fall from grace (because she has denied her own son's claim to the throne) makes her tragedy worse than Southampton's; a line verbatim from *Edward III*, 2.1.451 (1596), anonymous, but in recent years often attributed to "Shakespeare" and almost certainly written by Oxford: "*Lilies that fester smell far worse than weeds*; and every glory that inclines to sin, the same is treble by the opposite"; **WEEDS** = "Most subject is the fairest soil to *weeds*, and he, the noble image of my youth, is overspread with them" – the King, referring to his son Prince Hal, in *2 Henry IV*, 4.4.54-56; **FESTER** = rot; "The *lily* in the field/ That glories in his white ... This pleasant *lily* white/ This taint of roseate red/ This Cynthia's silver light/ This sweet fair dea spread/ These sunbeams in mine eye/ These beauties make me die" – E. O., Earl of Oxford, *The Phoenix Nest*, 1593, a poem, circa early 1570s, written about Elizabeth; in his poem; (*dea* = goddess, i.e., Elizabeth)

Kerrigan, arguing for "Shakespearean involvement in the ordering of Thorpe's quarto," adds that "this section of the book within which 94 falls is peculiarly connective: 92 follows 91 with *But*, and 93 picks up with *So*; 95 is essentially a development from the couplet of 94, and 96 continues to worry at the *faults* discussed in all these poems. If it is read in this light, 94 looks like an intense meditation on the issues raised in 92, and confronted in 93." He also notes that Sonnet 94 "resonates with issues still unsettled in the sequence at large…" ("The Sonnets and A Lover's Complaint," Kerrigan, 290-291)

Part Two

THE PRISON YEARS

OXFORD WARNS HIS SON
ELEVENTH MONTH IN THE TOWER

Sonnet 95
A Canker in the Fragrant Rose
December 1601

Oxford now defends his royal son against all the charges against him, declaring that the "shame" or disgrace of his crime is far outweighed by "the beauty of thy budding name" or the royal blood from Elizabeth that he carries as a bud or prince of the Tudor Rose. By "naming" Southampton (here in the Sonnets) as heir to the throne, he counterbalances the "ill report" of him seen or heard by the public. At the same time, Oxford again warns him to use his "large privilege" as a Prince by restraining himself from further rebellion.

Sonnet 95	Translation
How sweet and lovely dost thou make the shame	How royally do you transform this disgrace –
Which, like a canker in the fragrant Rose,	Which, like a worm in the royal Tudor Rose,
Doth spot the beauty of thy budding name?	Stops the growth of your royal blood as king!
Oh in what sweets dost thou thy sins enclose!	O, your disgrace is enclosed by such royalty!
That tongue that tells the story of thy days	Anyone who writes the history of your life
(Making lascivious comments on thy sport)	(Even if they make comments about your crime)
Cannot dispraise but in a kind of praise;	Can't condemn you without also praising you!
Naming thy name blesses an ill report.	Your name, Henry IX, protects you from censure.
Oh what a mansion have those vices got	O, what a Tower do those other criminals have
Which for their habitation chose out thee,	Who live there as prisoners and sought you out,
Where beauty's veil doth cover every blot,	Where Elizabeth's false image covers all crimes,
And all things turn to fair that eyes can see!	And criminals become royal princes!
Take heed (dear heart) of this large privilege;	Obey, my royal son, this kingly privilege!
The hardest knife ill-used doth lose his edge.	Power and rebellion wrongly used will defeat itself.

1 HOW SWEET AND LOVELY DOST THOU MAKE THE SHAME,
SWEET = royal; "Good night, sweet prince" – *Hamlet*, 5.2.385; **LOVELY** = filled with "love" or royal blood; ("O thou my *lovely* Boy" – Sonnet 126, line 1; "Unthrifty *loveliness*" – Sonnet 4, line 1; **SHAME** = disgrace of the Rebellion; "If thy *offences* were upon record, would it not *shame* thee in so fair a troop to read a lecture of them?" – *Richard II*, 4.1.230-232

2 WHICH, LIKE A CANKER IN THE FRAGRANT ROSE,
CANKER = a worm that preys on blossoms; the disgrace of the Tudor Rose, brought on by Southampton's treason; "*Roses have thorns*, and silver fountains mud,/ Clouds and eclipses stain both Moone and Sunne,/ And *loathsome canker lives in sweetest bud*" – Sonnet 35, lines 2-4; **FRAGRANT ROSE** = the royal Tudor Rose dynasty, i.e., Southampton as heir to the dynasty; "That thereby beauty's *Rose* might never die" – Sonnet 1, line 2

REFERENCE EDITION   513

To put down Richard, that *sweet lovely rose*,
And plant this *thorn*, this **canker** Bolingbroke
- *1 Henry IV*, 1.3.173-174

Hath not *thy rose a **canker***, Somerset?
Hath not *thy rose a thorn*, Plantagenet?
- *1 Henry VI*, 2.4.68-69

If that be true, I shall see my boy again;
For since the birth of Cain, the first male child,
To him that did but yesterday suspire,
There was not such a gracious creature born.
But *now will **canker**-sorrow eat my bud*
And chase the native beauty from his cheek…
O Lord! My boy, my Arthur, my fair son!
My life, my joy, my food, my all the world!
- *King John*, 3.3.78-104

3 DOTH SPOT THE BEAUTY OF THY BUDDING NAME!

SPOT = blemish; **BEAUTY** = blood from Elizabeth; "*beauty's Rose*" – Sonnet 1, line 2; **THY BUDDING NAME** = your still-growing name, Henry IX, in these sonnets; "*Your name* from hence immortal life shall have" – Sonnet 81, line 5; "Within *thine own bud* buriest thy content" – Sonnet 1, line 11; "Rough winds do shake *the darling buds* of May" – Sonnet 18, line 3; "When summer's breath their *masked buds* discloses" – Sonnet 54, line 8; "the red Rose and the white were united and joined together. *Out of these Roses sprang two noble buds*, Prince Arthur and Henry…" – *Euphues and his England*, 1580, attributed to Oxford's private secretary John Lyly, who dedicated the book to him; "budding name" is also perhaps a play on Henry Wriothesley's own name, "Wriothesley," pronounced "Risley" or "Rosely," and Rose = Bud)

4 OH IN WHAT SWEETS DOST THOU THY SINS ENCLOSE!

OH = O = Oxford; **SWEETS** = royal qualities of Southampton; **THY SINS ENCLOSE** = enclose and hide your crime and disgrace; **ENCLOSE** = echoing the enclosure that is the Tower of London, the prison fortress where he remains; "Beauty, Truth, and Rarity,/ Grace in all simplicity,/ Here *enclosed* in cinders lie" – *The Phoenix and the Turtle* (1601), 53-55

5 THAT TONGUE THAT TELLS THE STORY OF THY DAYS

THAT TONGUE, etc. = that writer; **WHO TELLS THE STORY OF THY DAYS** = who records the story of your "days" or golden kingship, as I record your life in this diary; but as others record it, too; "O God, Horatio, what a wounded name ... in this harsh world draw thy breath in pain to *tell my story*" – the dying words of the Prince in *Hamlet*, 5.2.360-361; Act Five, Scene Two of *Hamlet* appears to be an allegorical treatment of the bargain between Oxford (Hamlet) and Robert Cecil (Laertes) for Southampton's eventual pardon upon the anticipated accession of James VI of Scotland (Fortinbras) as King James I of England; and Hamlet (at least after his death) becomes Southampton, who "was likely, had he been put on, to have proved most royally" (5.2.429-430); of particular note is Hamlet's speech to Laertes: "Give me your *pardon*, sir. I have done you wrong; but *pardon*'t, as you are a genteman. This presence knows, and you must needs have heard, how I am *punished* with sore distraction" (5.2.227-231); Hamlet's Denmark doesn't have a hereditary throne, but some other form ("I do prophesy *the election* lights on Fortnibras. He has my dying voice" – 5.2.381-382); Fortnibras has been "selected" to be the new king, and the dying Hamlet accedes to that choice, perhaps reflecting the bargain between Oxford and Cecil involving the "selection" of James as successor to Elizabeth.

6 (MAKING LASCIVIOUS COMMENTS ON THY SPORT)
LASCIVIOUS = the sense here is that of preposterously vulgar, i.e., blasphemous; ("That it could so preposterously be stained" – Sonnet 109, 11;**MAKING LASCIVIOUS COMMENTS etc**. = making vulgar, sarcastic remarks (for the sake of public perception and history) about your youthful, unwise actions; about your life before the Rebellion and your actions as a leader of it; comments inappropriate in reference to a prince; "Not an eye but is a-weary of thy common sight, save mine" – *1 Henry IV*, 3.2.87-89; the same thought as "So are those errors that in thee are seen" – Sonnet 96, line 7

7 CANNOT DISPRAISE; BUT IN A KIND OF PRAISE,
CANNOT, etc. = cannot accuse you without praising you; **KIND** = natural, related to Southampton as the child of Elizabeth; ("Be as thy presence is, gracious and kind" – Sonnet 10, line 11; "Kind is my love today, tomorrow kind ... Fair, kind, and true, is all my argument" – Sonnet 105, lines 5, 9); "Shall kin with kin, and kind with kind, confound" – *Richard II*, 4.1.141; "Your most assured and loving brother, as ever in mine own affection, in all kindness and kindred" – Oxford to Robert Cecil, May 1601

8 NAMING THY NAME, BLESSES AN ILL REPORT.
NAMING THY NAME = talking about you in public; naming you in the dedications by "Shakespeare": "O how faint when I of you do write,/ Knowing a better spirit doth use *your name*" – Sonnet 80, lines 1-2; preserving your true identity in these sonnets: "*Your name* from hence immortal life shall have,/ Though I, once gone, to all the world must die" – Sonnet 81, lines 5-6; **BLESSES AN ILL REPORT** = i.e., even talking about you confers blessings on these accusations; "The dedicated words which writers use/ Of their *fair subject*, *blessing* every book" – Sonnet 82, lines 3-4; "But what's so *blessed-fair* that fears no blot?" – Sonnet 92, line 13; no bad report can actually hurt you; "As thou being mine, *mine is thy good report*" – Sonnets 36 and 96, line 14 in both verses, Oxford writing openly/directly as father to son

9 OH WHAT A MANSION HAVE THOSE VICES GOT,
OH = O = Oxford; **MANSION** = "The action of remaining, living, or staying in a place ... a stopping place in a journey ... a stage" – OED; the House of Tudor; your own self, as lodging place; but also the Tower, where others are urging Southampton to further revolt; in astrology, "each of the 28 divisions of the ecliptic, occupied by the moon on successive days" – OED, perhaps reflecting the Queen's (the Moon's) ongoing "eclipse" of light as she nears the end of her life; "In my Father's house are many mansions" – John, 14.2; **VICES** = disgraces, but also other conspirators urging him on; same as the "infection" or other criminals or traitors in the Tower; "Ah, wherefore with *infection* should he live?" – Sonnet 67, line 1; "But if that *flower* with base *infection* meet" – Sonnet 94, line 11

10 WHICH FOR THEIR HABITATION CHOSE OUT THEE,
That chose you as the place wherein they live; who seek you out, in the Tower, and urge you to rebel again

11 WHERE BEAUTY'S VEIL DOTH COVER EVERY BLOT
BEAUTY'S VEIL = Elizabeth's veil of secrecy about Southampton; ("the *mobled Queen*" – *Hamlet*, 2.2.509, referring to the queen as muffled or silenced); "The region cloud hath masked him from me now" – Sonnet 33, line 12, referring to Elizabeth Regina's dark cloud of shame and disgrace, covering her son in shadow and darkness; **COVER** = hide; echoing Ver; **EVERY** = Every = E. Ver, Edward de Vere; **BLOT** = shame or disgrace; concealment of royal blood

> For time hath set a *blot* upon my pride
> - *Richard II*, 3.2.81

> There shouldst thou find one heinous article,
> Containing the *deposing of a king*

And cracking the strong warrant of an oath,
Mark'd with a *blot,* damn'd in the book of heaven
- *Richard II,* 4.1.233-236

To rid the realm of this pernicious *blot*
- *Richard II,* 4.1.325

This *deadly blot in thy digressing son*
- *Richard II,* 5.3.64

Never yet did base dishonor blur our name,
But with our sword we *wiped away the blot*
- *2 Henry VI,* 4.1.39-40

This *blot* they object *against your house*
Shall be wiped out in the next parliament
- *1 Henry VI,* 2.4..115-116

And thus *thy fall hath left a kind of blot…*
For *this revolt* of thine, methinks, is like
Another fall of man. *Their faults* are open.
- *Henry V,* 2.2.138-142

12 AND ALL THINGS TURN TO FAIR THAT EYES CAN SEE!
ALL = Southampton; **ALL THINGS** = Southampton; **FAIR** = royalty

13 TAKE HEED (DEAR HEART) OF THIS LARGE PRIVILEGE:
Pay attention; take care (be careful) to obey this princely privilege of yours; warning him to follow his royal responsibilities by avoiding bad company in the Tower; be cautious; "Therefore let men *take heed* of their company" – *2 Henry IV,* 5.1.76-77; **DEAR HEART** = addressing him as "dear heart," i.e., as his royal son; "If *my dear love* were but the child of state" – Sonnet 124, line 1; **THIS LARGE PRIVILEGE** = this royal privilege; "For thou has lost *thy princely privilege* with vile participation" – the King to his son, Prince Hal, in *1 Henry IV,* 3.2.86-87; in this sonnet, alluding to the Tower of London: "I am come to survey the Tower this day … Draw, men, for all *this privileged place*" - *1 Henry VI,* 1.3.1.46; **LARGE** = "my large kingdom for a little grave" – *Richard II,* 3.3.153; "ruling *in large* and ample empery" – *Henry V,* 1.2.226; "our largest bounty … the *large effects* that troop with *majesty*" – *King Lear,* 1.1.53, 133; **PRIVILEGE** = "Must he be then as shadow of himself? Adorn his temples with a coronet, and yet, in substance and authority, retain but *privilege* of a private man?" – *1 Henry VI,* 5.4.133-136

14 THE HARDEST KNIFE ILL-USED DOTH LOSE HIS EDGE.
THE HARDEST KNIFE, etc. = your power as a prince must be used wisely or it will wither; the most potent weapons of rebels who want you to lead another uprising; "The edge of war, like an ill-sheathed *knife*" – *1 Henry IV,* 1.1.17; **HARDEST** = most violent or strong or durable or difficult or painful; **KNIFE** = alluding to the swords or daggers carried by rebels as offensive weapons, but also to the executioner's axe; "For such a time do I now fortify/ Against *confounding Age's cruel knife,*/ That he shall never *cut* from memory/ My sweet love's beauty, though my lover's life" – Sonnet 63, lines 9-12; "The coward conquest of *a wretch's knife*" – Sonnet 74, line 11, referring to the conquest of wretched traitors and their daggers, i.e., those involved in the Rebellion with Essex and Southampton

Part Two

THE PRISON YEARS

OXFORD WARNS HIS SON
TWELFTH MONTH IN THE TOWER

Sonnet 96
A Throned Queen
The Strength of All Thy State
January 1602

Oxford continues to warn Southampton against trying to break out of the Tower and/or to lead any new rebellion against the government, now even more firmly controlled by Robert Cecil. This is the third and final verse of a short series of such warning.

Sonnet 96	Translation
Some say thy fault is youth, some wantonness,	Some say your crime is youth or rashness,
Some say thy grace is youth and gentle sport;	Some see your royalty only as youthful nobility;
Both grace and faults are loved of more and less;	Both royalty and crimes are seen by others –
Thou mak'st faults graces that to thee resort.	But you turn your crimes into royal qualities.
As on the finger of a throned Queen,	As a Prince at the Court of Queen Elizabeth,
The basest Jewel will be well esteemed:	The most condemned royal heir will be valued:
So are those errors that in thee are seen,	And so those crimes of which you're condemned
To truths translated, and for true things deemed.	Are transformed into true rights for true sons.
How many Lambs might the stern Wolfe betray,	How many innocent princes might evil ones betray
If like a Lamb he could his looks translate,	If such evil ones could appear like princes!
How many gazers mightst thou lead away,	How many followers could you rule and lead,
If thou wouldst use the strength of all thy state!	If you displayed the full power of your royal blood!
But do not so; I love thee in such sort,	But don't do that. I love you in such a way
As thou being mine, mine is thy good report.	That since you're my son, my verse is your power.

1 SOME SAY THY FAULT IS YOUTH, SOME WANTONNESS,
THY FAULT = On the surface, the verse is simply about some defect or imperfection, but in reality Oxford is writing of his son's "fault" in reference to his offence, transgression, crime of high treason against the Crown; **WANTONNESS** = sportiveness, lightness, lasciviousness, lechery; "Bearing the *wanton* burthen [burden] of the prime," alluding to Southampton as offspring or child, with Booth adding that Ingram and Redpath view *wanton* as "*froclicsome – of children*"; "All wanton as a child, skipping and vain" – *Love's Labour's Lost*, 5.2.754, performed in the early 1590s for Southampton and his friends; recalling *1 Henry IV*, in which Oxford originally portrayed himself, and then his son, Prince Hal of Wales, the future Henry V:

> Hotspur:
> Where is his son,
> The nimble-footed madcap Prince of Wales,
> And his comrades that daft the world aside

REFERENCE EDITION

And bid it pass?

Vernon:
All furnish'd, all in arms;
All plum'd like estridges that with the wind
Bated, like eagles having lately bathed,
Glittering in golden coats like images,
As *full of spirit as the month of May*,
And *gorgeous as the sun at midsummer*;
Wanton as *youthful goats*, wild as young bulls. *1 Henry IV*, 4.1.94-103

"Where are your mess of sons to back you now, the *wanton Edward and the lusty George*?" – *3 Henry VI*, 1.4.73-74; "The *lustie Ver* … What plant can spring that feeles no force of *Ver*" – poem in *A Hundredth Sundrie Flowres*, 1573, most likely by Oxford; "Can no man tell me of my unthrifty son? … Inquire at London, 'mongst the taverns there, for there, they say, he daily doth frequent with unrestrained loose companions … while he, *young wanton*, and effeminate boy, takes on the point of honour to support so dissolute a crew" – Bolingbroke, afterwards Henry IV, referring to Prince Hal, in *Richard II*, 5.3.1-12

2 SOME SAY THY GRACE IS YOUTH AND GENTLE SPORT;

THY GRACE = your royalty; "Edward the Fourth, by the *grace* of God, king of England and France, and lord of Ireland" – *3 Henry VI*, 4.7; "Above the rest in Court who gave thee *grace*?" – Oxford poem, circa early 1570s, speaking of Elizabeth, who gave him her royal grace; **YOUTH** = perhaps also incorporating "you" = "your royalty is you," "you are royalty"; **GENTLE** = royal, as used in the Sonnets; "That doth presume *to boast of gentle* blood" – *1 Henry VI*, 4.1.44; "Staight in her heart did *mercy* come,/ Chiding that tongue that ever sweet/ Was used in giving *gentle* doom" – Sonnet 145, lines 5-7, of Queen Elizabeth in the Dark Lady series, after she had extended her mercy to Southampton by sparing his life, as opposed to decreeing royal *doom* for her son; **GENTLE SPORT** = also used to contrast with "wantonness" in the previous line.

3 BOTH GRACE AND FAULTS ARE LOVED OF MORE AND LESS:

GRACE AND FAULTS = Royal blood and treasons; Southampton has such grace and has committed such faults; **LOVED** = adored and served, as a king is adored and served by his subjects; "The *love* I dedicate to your Lordship is without end" – Oxford to Southampton as "Shakespeare" in the dedication of *Lucrece* to him in 1594; "You men of Angiers, and *my loving subjects*" – King John in *King John*, 2.1.203; "See here, my friends and *loving countrymen*" – *1 Henry VI*, 3.1.137; **MORE AND LESS** = "those of higher and lower rank" – Duncan-Jones; "Now when the lords and barons of the realm perceived Northumberland did lean to him, the *more and less* came in with cap and knee" – *1 Henry IV*, 4.3.68

4 THOU MAK'ST FAULTS GRACES, THAT TO THEE RESORT:

FAULTS GRACES =You turn your crimes (and criminals, who come before your royal presence) into graces, as only a king can do; a different thought, but with similar imagery: "Base court, where *kings* grow base, to *come at traitors' calls, and do them grace*!" – *Richard II*, 3.3.180-181; "Ah wherefore with infection should he live,/ And *with his presence grace impiety*,/ That sin by him advantage should achieve,/ And lace itself with his society?" – Sonnet 67, lines 1-4, referring to criminals or traitors in the Tower gaining by Southampton's royal presence among them; **GRACES** = "All these are portable, with other *graces* weighed … the *king-becoming graces*" – *Macbeth*, 4.3.89-91; **THAT TO THEE RESORT** = other rebels or traitors who come to you for leadership in trying to overthrow Robert Cecil from his position of power over Elizabeth.

Stanley:
But tell me, where is princely Richmond now?

Christopher:
At Pembroke, or at Ha'rfordwest in Wales.

Stanley:
What men of name *resort to him*?

Christopher:
Sir Walter Herbert, a renowned soldier,
Sir Gilbert Talbot, Sir William Stanley,
Oxford, redoubted Pembroke, Sir James Blunt,
And Rice ap Thomas, with a valiant crew,
And many other of great name and worth;
And towards London do they bend their power
- *Richard III*, 4.5.9-17

5 AS ON THE FINGER OF A THRONED QUEEN,

AS = in the same way that; **THRONED QUEEN** = Elizabeth (with *Queen* capitalized in *Q*); "At a fair vestal *throned* by the west" – *A Midsummer Night's Dream*, 2.1.158, i.e., Elizabeth; "It becomes the *throned monarch* better than his crown" – *Merchant of Venice*, 4.1.189

6 THE BASEST JEWEL WILL BE WELL ESTEEMED:

Base Court, where Kings grow base,
To come at traitors' calls, and do them grace!
- *Richard II*, 3.3.180-181

BASEST JEWEL = Southampton (with *Jewel* capitalized in *Q*) a jewel or prince of "base" status in the Tower; even a poor quality jewel would be valued if it were worn by a Queen; in the same way, the most condemned prince in the Tower will be esteemed; "comfort the afflicted, confirm the doubtful, encourage the coward and *lift up the base-minded man*" – Oxford's Prefatory Letter to *Cardanus' Comfort*, 1573; "Had our prince, *jewel of children*, seen this hour" – *Winter's Tale*, 5.1.115-116; "And mine eternal *Jewel* given to the common Enemy of man, to make them kings" – *Macbeth*, 3.2.67-69; "Which *like a jewel hung in ghastly night*" – Sonnet 27, line 11; "Thou that art now *the world's fresh ornament*" – Sonnet 1, line 9; "For *princes* are a model which heaven makes to like itself: as *jewels* lose their glory if neglected, so princes their renowns if not respected" – *Pericles*, 2.2.10-13

Wherein I lived *the greatest prince o'th'world*,
The noblest; and do now not **basely** die
- *Antony and Cleopatra*, 4.15.56-57

WELL ESTEEMED = highly regarded and honored, as you are by virtue of the fact that you are a prince; "five hundred *prisoners of esteem*" – *1 Henry VI*, 3.4.8; in Sonnet 127, line 12, Oxford accuses Elizabeth of "Sland'ring Creation with a *false esteem*," i.e., disgracing her own royal son by refusing to acknowledge him and by judging him to be a traitor; "'Tis better to be vile than *vile esteemed*" – Sonnet 121, line 1; estimated in high degree, as Oxford reminds Southampton: "And like enough *thou know'st thy estimate*" – Sonnet 87, line 2

*"Why should this rose be **better esteemed** than that rose, unless in pleasantness of smell it*

*far surpassed the other rose? And so is it in all other things as well as in man. Why should this man be **more esteemed** than that man, but for his virtue, through which every man desireth to be accounted of? Then you amongst men, I do not doubt, will aspire to follow that virtuous path, to illuster yourself with the **ornaments** of virtue."* = Oxford's Letter to "Cardanus' Comfort," 1573

7 SO ARE THOSE ERRORS THAT IN THEE ARE SEEN
ERRORS = Crimes, i.e., the treason of which Southampton was convicted; "Lest more mischance on ***plots and errors*** happen" – *Hamlet*, 5.2.425-426; "*Errors* describes both the actions judged and the judgments" – Booth

8 TO TRUTHS TRANSLATED, AND FOR TRUE THINGS DEEMED.
TO TRUTHS TRANSLATED = Related to Oxford, *Nothing Truer than Truth*; i.e., the errors seen on the surface are then *translated* (or transformed) into what is accepted as truth; exactly the same neo-Platonic thought as: "But the world is so cunning, as of a shadow they can make a substance, and of a likelihood a *truth*" – Oxford to Burghley, July 1581; a thought to be found in *The Courtier*, for the translation of which Oxford wrote a preface in 1572; another meaning is that Southampton himself *translates* the errors into his own "true rights" to the throne (Sonnet 17, line 11); "For the power of beauty will sooner *transform* honesty from what it is to a bawd than the force of honesty can *translate* beauty into his likeness" – *Hamlet*, 3.1.113; **TRUE** = Oxford's motto *Nothing Truer than Truth*; "And your *true rights* be termed a Poet's rage" – Sonnet 17, line 11; "Thou *truly fair* wert *truly* sympathized/ In *true* plain words by thy *true*-telling friend" – Sonnet 82, lines 11-12; "So long as Edward is thy constant friend and their *true sovereign* whom they must obey" – 3 *Henry VI*, 4.1.76-77

"But I hope **truth** is subject to no prescription, for **truth** is **truth** though never so old, and time cannot make that false which was once **true**." - Oxford to Robert Cecil, May 7, 1603

9 HOW MANY LAMBS MIGHT THE STERN WOLF BETRAY
LAMBS = innocents; "Our kinsman Gloucester is as *innocent from meaning treason* to our royal person as is the sucking *lamb* or harmless dove" – 2 *Henry VI*, 3.1.69-71; **STERN WOLF** = "wake not a sleeping wolf" – 2 *Henry IV*, 1.2.154, spoken by the Chief Justice; the wolf of treasonous rebellion; Southampton used "wolf" to describe Robert Cecil and other enemies, before surrendering; he yelled from the roof of Essex House to Sir Robert Sidney, who was representing the Crown: "If we shall yield ourselves, we shall willingly put ourselves *into the wolf's mouth*" – Quennell, p. 242; **BETRAY** = suggesting that Cecil, Walter Raleigh and others, including the Queen herself, betrayed Southampton by tempting and/or provoking him into the Rebellion; also, the potential "wolves" or traitors will *betray* Southampton (a lamb) by leading him astray

Henry, your sovereign,
Is prisoner to the foe, his state usurped,
His realm a slaughter-house, his subjects slain,
His statutes cancelled, and his treasure spent;
And yonder *stands the wolf that makes this spoil.*
- 3 *Henry VI*, 5.4.76-80

10 IF LIKE A LAMB HE COULD HIS LOOKS TRANSLATE?
If, in the way that Southampton can transform himself, the evil forces (in and out of the Tower) could also transform their appearance into that of a lamb, i.e., become a wolf in sheep's clothing; "If he had spoke, the *wolf* would leave his prey,/ And never fright the silly *lamb* that day" – *Venus and Adonis*, lines 1097-1098

> O, opportunity, thy guilt is great!
> 'Tis thou that execut'st *the traitor's treason*;
> Thou sets *the wolf* where he *the lamb* may get.
> - *Lucrece*, 876-878

TRANSLATE = playing upon "To *truths translated*, and for *true things* deemed" in line 8 above; to transform or change; in this case, to change his shape so as to look like a lamb; "than the force of honesty can *translate* beauty into his likeness" – *Hamlet*, 3.1.113

11 HOW MANY GAZERS MIGHTST THOU LEAD AWAY

GAZERS = subjects of the king; "Look how they *gaze*! See how the giddy multitude do point and nod their heads, and throw their eyes on thee!" – *2 Henry VI*, 2.4; "An eye more bright than theirs, less false in rolling,/ *Gilding the object whereupon it gazeth*" – Sonnet 20, lines 5-6, the reverse image, in which Southampton is a king gazing upon those who gaze at him; "each under eye/ Doth homage to his new-appearing sight,/ Serving with looks his sacred majesty" – Sonnet 7, line 2-4; **HOW MANY GAZERS MIGHT THOU LEAD AWAY** = how many supporters (and potential subjects) might you lead into a new revolt

12 IF THOU WOULDST USE THE STRENGTH OF ALL THY STATE!

IF THOU WOULDST USE = if you chose to use; **ALL** = Southampton, *One for All, All for One*; **STRENGTH** = royal power; "the ***King's name is a tower of strength***" – *Richard III*, 5.3.12; "And *strength* by limping sway disabled" – Sonnet 66, line 8, referring to Southampton's royal power disabled by the limping, swaying hunbacked figure of Robert Cecil; "To leave poor me thou hast *the strength of laws*" – Sonnet 49, line 13; **THE STRENGTH OF ALL THY STATE** = The vast power conferred by your inheritance of royal blood; "*all our state*" – the King referring to himself and his reign in *2 Henry IV*, 5.2.142; **STATE** = "and our duties are to your *throne and state*" – *Macbeth*, 1.4.24-25; "I am unfit for ***state and majesty***" – *Richard III*, 3.7.204; "to keep his *state* in Rome as easily as a King" – *Julius Caesar*, 1.2.158-159; "even in the chair of *state*" – *3 Henry VI*, 1.1.51; "And, as you are a *king*, speak in *your state*" – *2 Henry IV*, 5.2.99; "Harry the Fifth is crowned! Up, vanity! Down, *royal state*!" – *2 Henry IV*, 4.5.119-120; the throne itself is equivalent to the state: "This chair shall be my state" - *1 Henry IV*, 2.5.344

13 BUT DO NOT SO! I LOVE THEE IN SUCH SORT

Oxford warns him: do not use this power to lead others in revolt; I love you in such a way

14 AS THOU BEING MINE, MINE IS THY GOOD REPORT.

AS THOU BEING MINE = that you, being my royal son; "a *son of mine own*" – Oxford to Burghley, March 17, 1575; "Ah, no, no, no; it is *mine only son*!" – *3 Henry VI*, 2.5.83; "Thou hadst not to kill *a son of mine*" – *3 Henry VI*, 5.6.36; **MINE IS THY GOOD REPORT** = your good report comes from me, in these private sonnets by means of which I am recording your royal life as "the living record of your memory" – Sonnet 55, line 8; *mine* = my son = my sonnets filled with the life and royal blood of "my Sunne" as in "Even so *my Sunne* one early morn did shine,/ With all triumphant splendor on my brow,/ But out alack, he was but one hour *mine*" – Sonnet 33, line 9

This final couplet is repeated from Sonnet 36, indicating by that linkage that a year has now passed since the Rebellion of February 8, 1601, with the first anniversary of that tragic day to be marked in the next verse. The linkage of the two couplets also suggests that Sonnet 96 may signify the end of a 60-sonnet sub-series (37-96) within the larger 100-sonnet sequence of 27-126, and further suggests, as mentioned earlier (and as presaged in Sonnet 6) that the subgroups in this sequence are in batches of ten (27-36, 37-46, etc.).

THE MONUMENT

THE PRISON YEARS

FIRST ANNIVERSARY
OF THE REBELLION

Sonnet 97
The Fleeting Year
8 February 1602

It has been exactly one year since February 8, 1601, and the beginning of this long series of sonnets with Sonnet 27. Oxford marks the anniversary of the Rebellion by referring to the "fleeting year" that Southampton has spent in prison according to Her Majesty's "pleasure." This tragic, bleak time has yielded only "hope of Orphans, and un-fathered fruit" – referring to Southampton as a royal orphan unable to acknowledge Oxford, his true father.

Sonnet 97	Translation
How like a Winter hath my absence been	How like a death your imprisonment has been –
From thee, the pleasure of the fleeting year!	By Her Majesty's pleasure, it's been one year!
What freezings have I felt, what dark days seen?	What deaths have I felt? What daily losses!
What old December's bareness everywhere!	What end to all our hopes for you!
And yet this time removed was summer's time,	And yet, ironically, we went through a summer,
The teeming Autumn big with rich increase	And then through the actual autumn,
Bearing the wanton burthen of the prime,	Which was like your own birth,
Like widowed wombs after their Lord's decease:	When the Queen was empty and alone again.
Yet this abundant issue seemed to me	Yet this past harvest seemed to me to represent
But hope of Orphans, and un-fathered fruit,	Your hopes as a royal orphan without me as father,
For Summer and his pleasures wait on thee,	Because our hopes all depend on you,
And thou away, the very birds are mute.	And with you in prison, your parents are silent.
Or if they sing, 'tis with so dull a cheer,	Or if we do speak, it's with such sadness,
That leaves look pale, dreading the Winter's near.	That we slowly die, dreading Elizabeth's death.

1 HOW LIKE A WINTER HATH MY ABSENCE BEEN
LIKE A WINTER = like death; like the end of your royal claim, lineage and dynasty; also, it is winter now (February 1602); **MY ABSENCE** = my absence from you in the Tower; "O *absence*, what a *torment* wouldst thou prove" – Sonnet 39, line 9; i.e., the preceding year of your imprisonment has been like a death; "*From you have I been absent* in the spring" – Sonnet 98, line 1, immediately following this verse; "The *imprisoned absence* of your liberty" – Sonnet 58, line 6; "Those pretty wrongs that *liberty* commits/ When I am sometime *absent from thy heart*" – Sonnet 41, lines 1-2; "I will acquaintance strangle and look strange,/ Be *absent from thy walks*" – Sonnet 89, lines 8-9

2 FROM THEE, THE PLEASURE OF THE FLEETING YEAR!
FROM THEE = Southampton has been "absent" in the Tower, but Oxford writes as a subject who has been

"absent" from his son's royal presence; **PLEASURE** = Her Majesty's pleasure, i.e., the Queen's royal will, which has kept you in prison; "I am sorry to see you ta'en from liberty, to look on the business present. 'Tis *his Highness' pleasure* you shall to the Tower" – *Henry VIII*, 1.1.204-207; "The same to be yearly delivered and paid unto Our said Cousin at four terms of the year by even portions: and so to be continued unto him *during Our pleasure*…" - Queen Elizabeth's annual grant of 1,000 pounds to Oxford by Privy Seal Warrant signed by her on June 26, 1586; **THE PLEASURE OF** = "Now are we well prepared to know *the pleasure of our fair cousin Dauphin*" – the King in *Henry V*, 1.2.235-236; "Then he was to be *imprisoned at the king's pleasure*" – Bellamy, 184, referring to an incident in 1555 in the reign of the boy-king Edward VI; **THE FLEETING YEAR** = the suggestion is "that *the year in question is long and dreary* rather than *fleeting*" – Booth; perhaps also alluding to the existence of the Fleet, where Southampton was incarcerated in November 1598 for marrying Elizabeth Vernon, who was carrying his child; OED indicates "fleeting" referred to *"confinement in the Fleet Prison,"* citing Oxford's childhood tutor, Sir Thomas Smith, in 1589: "After they … bin well disciplined as well by wordes, as by *fleeting* a while"; and citing Oxford's former friend at Cambridge, Gabriel Harvey, in 1592: "And that was all the *Fleeting* that ever I felt"; the phrase "fleeting year" in this sonnet therefore calls to mind "the imprisoned year"; also, the OED cites the word used in another sense by Oxford's uncle, Arthur Golding, in 1587: "The fleeting of souls out of one body into another"; various meanings include "floating of a fish, swimming … that moves constantly, shifting, unstable … flowing; fluid ('fleeting sacrifices' = drink offerings) … passing swiftly by, chiefly of life or time … passing or gliding swiftly away … existing for a brief period; not permanent or enduring; transitory, passing, fading; to "fleet" can mean "to dissolve or waste away" - OED

3 WHAT FREEZINGS HAVE I FELT, WHAT DARK DAYS SEEN!
FREEZINGS = as though time has been frozen; stoppages of royal blood; **DARK DAYS** = a period of prolonged despair; opposite of the golden time of "Summer's day" – Sonnet 18, line 1; "Looking on *darkness*, which the blind do see" – Sonnet 27, line 8, which began the diary of this first year of Southampton's imprisonment, from Feb 8, 1601 to Feb 8, 1602; "Why didst thou promise such a beauteous day/ And make me travail forth without my cloak,/ To let base clouds o'ertake me in my way,/ Hiding thy bravery in their rotten smoke?" – Sonnet 34, lines 1-4

4 WHAT OLD DECEMBER'S BARENESS EVERYWHERE!
OLD DECEMBER'S = the December or final period ("winter") of royal hope, which is dying; **BARENESS** = empty of new royal blood; an image of the womb of the Sonnets as barren or childless, i.e., not able to recreate his son's claim to the throne; "Why is my verse so *barren* of new pride" – Sonnet 76, line 1; "*Bare* ruined choirs, where late the sweet birds sang" – Sonnet 73, line 4; "The *argument all bare*" – Sonnet 103, line 3, with "argument" referring to "And *you and love are still my argument*" of Sonnet 76, line 10, i.e., you and your royal blood & claim to the throne; a play on "*bear*" as in bear a child; "Duty so great, which wit so poor as mind/ May make seem *bare*, in wanting words to show it" – Sonnet 26, lines 5-6

5 AND YET THIS TIME REMOVED WAS SUMMER'S TIME,
THIS TIME REMOVED = this period of Southampton's imprisonment; the time of absence and separation, when all has been the opposite of Sonnet 25, line 14: "Where I may not *remove*, nor be *removed*"; "Love is not love/ Which alters when it alteration finds,/ Or bends with the remover to remove" – Sonnet 116, lines 2-4, a reaffirmation that no separation can alter or remove the "love" or royal blood of Oxford's son; **SUMMER'S TIME** = in substance, regardless of this terrible tragedy, Southampton's royal blood still exists, i.e., underneath it all it is still the "Summer's day" of Sonnet 18, line 1

6 THE TEEMING AUTUMN BIG WITH RICH INCREASE,
TEEMING = "delivering … fruitful, pregnant" – Booth; **BIG** = pregnant; the Autumn was nevertheless pregnant with your royal blood, i.e., as I see it in my mind as I record in these sonnets; "And grow *big-bellied with the wanton* wind/ … *her womb then rich* with my young squire/ … And for her sake do I rear up her boy;/ And for her sake I will not part with him" – *A Midsummer Night's Dream*, 2.1.129-137; **RICH** =

REFERENCE EDITION

(*her womb then rich*" – MND, 2.1.131; royal; related to the *treasury* of royal blood; "So am I as *the rich whose blessed key*/ Can bring him to his sweet up-locked treasure" – Sonnet 52, lines 1-2, Oxford referring to visits with his son in the younger earl's prison room of the Tower; "For how do I hold thee but by thy granting,/ And *for that riches* where is my deserving?" – Sonnet 87, lines 5-6; "And all those beauties whereof now he's King/ Are vanishing, or vanished out of sight,/ Stealing away *the treasure of his spring*" – Sonnet 63, lines 6-8; **RICH INCREASE** = re-creation or rebirth of you; same as "From fairest creatures *we desire increase*,/ That thereby beauty's *Rose* might never die" – Sonnet 1, lines 1-2; Southampton, even as a jailed nobody, is still alive and growing, and therefore his royal blood is *increasing* as well – within himself and within these sonnets that are recording his royal life and blood; "But if the first *heir* of my invention prove deformed, I shall be sorry it had so noble a godfather, and never after *ear so barren a land*, for fear it *yield me still so bad a harvest.*" - Oxford's first dedication as "Shakespeare" to Southampton *Venus and Adonis*, 1593

7 BEARING THE WANTON BURTHEN OF THE PRIME,
BEARING = enduring as well as giving birth to; **WANTON** = related to Southampton as his child; (Ingram & Redpath: "frolicsome – of children"); "And grow big-bellied with *the wanton* wind" – *A Midsummer Night's Dream*, 2.1.129; **BURTHEN** = (burden); as in "the *second burden of a former child*" of Sonnet 59, line 4; **THE PRIME** = as in "Thou art *thy mother's glass*, and she in thee/ Calls back *the lovely April of her prime*" – Sonnet 3, lines 9-110; **PRIME** = spring; the late stage of pregnancy, in April and May 1574 when the Queen was about to give birth.

> When wert thou born, Desire?
> In pomp and *prime* of May.
> By whom, sweet boy, wert thou begot?
> - Oxford poem, excerpt in *Art of English Poesy*, 1589

8 LIKE WIDOWED WOMBS AFTER THEIR LORDS' DECEASE:
Like the womb of a pregnant widow who, after her husband's death, still carries their unborn child; like abandoned wombs; like the womb of Elizabeth, who is now a "widow" because of her failure to acknowledge Oxford as her husband and to acknowledge Southampton as her son; as England or the world itself has become his widow: "Thou dost *beguile the world, unbless some mother*./ For where is she so fair whose *uneared womb*/ Disdains the tillage of thy husbandry?/ Or who is he so fond will be *the tomb*/ Of his self-love to stop posterity?" – Sonnet 3, lines 4-8; "Ah, if thou issueless shall hap to die,/ The world will wail thee like a makeless wife;/ *The world will be thy widow* and still weep,/ That thou no form of thee hast left behind" – Sonnet 9, lines 3-6; "Making *their tomb the womb wherein they grew*" – Sonnet 86, line 4, i.e., these verses are nonetheless giving Southampton new life

9 YET THIS ABUNDANT ISSUE SEEMED TO ME
ABUNDANT = full or royal blood, as in "Making a famine where *abundance* lies" – Sonnet 1, line 7; **ISSUE** = offspring; i.e., Southampton, who is still the royal child; "Look how *the father's face lives in his issue*" – Ben Jonson, of "Shakespeare" and his works in the First Folio, 1623;

"We note that the terms Shakespeare uses here – *succession, heir, issue* – he elsewhere applies to *the paramount problems of royalty*" – Leslie Hotson, referring to the Sonnets

"Ah, if thou *issueless* shalt hap to die" – Sonnet 9, line 3; "When *your sweet issue* your sweet form should bear" – Sonnet 13, line 8; "Care not for *issue*; the crown will find an heir" – *The Winter's Tale*, 5.1.146; "That *if the king should without issue* die" – *Henry VIII*, 1.2.133

10 BUT HOPE OF ORPHANS, AND UNFATHERED FRUIT;

HOPE OF ORPHANS - Both Oxford and Southampton had been orphaned at a young age and had become royal wards of Elizabeth in Burghley's custody; Oxford envisions his son as royal bastard and orphan; "expectation of the birth of children whose father is dead; or, such hope as orphans bring" – Dowden; Oxford and Elizabeth are now both "dead" as father and mother, as in "Thy end is *Truth's and Beauty's doom and date*" – Sonnet 14, line 14; **HOPE** = Southampton has been the "hope" of the world; in the dedication of *Venus and Adonis* to Southampton as by "Shakespeare," Oxford publicly referred to "the world's ***hopeful expectation*** for him; "Come hither, *England's hope*" – *3 Henry VI*, 4.6.68, the King to young Henry, Earl of Richmond, who is destined to become King Henry VII, whose reign begins the Tudor Rose dynasty which will continue to the time of Queen Elizabeth; "The loss of *a son of so great hope … sons of great hope*" – Queen Elizabeth to George Talbot, Earl of Shrewsbury, on the death of his son, circa Sept. 5, 1582, *Collected Works*, 256-257; "The ***hope and expectation*** of thy time " - *1 Henry IV*, 3.2.36, the King to his son Prince Hal; and when the prince becomes King Henry V, he survives "to mock the *expectation of the world*" in *2 Henry IV*, 5.2.126; "If he outlive the day, England did never owe so *sweet a hope*" - *1 Henry IV*, 5.2.66-67, of Prince Hal, future King Henry V; "I *hope* to reign" - *2 Henry VI*, 4.2.127; "Yet *hope, succeeding from so fair a tree* as your fair self" – *Pericles*, 1.1.115

> Till then, *fair hope* must hinder life's decay
> And I the rather wean me from despair
> For love of Edward's offspring in my womb
> - *3 Henry VI*, 4.4.16

"Will answer ***our hope in issue of a king***" - *1 Henry VI*, 5.5.73; "***True hope*** is swift, and flies with swallow's wings: Kings it makes gods, and meaner creatures kings" - *Richard III*, 5.2.23-24; the earl of Richmond, afterwards Henry VII, founder of the Tudor dynasty; **ORPHANS** = "You ***orphan heirs*** of fixed destiny" – *The Merry Wives of Windsor*, 5.5.40; **UNFATHERED** = a child without Oxford as acknowledged father; "But out alack, *he was but one hour mine*" – Sonnet 33, line 11; "If my dear love *were but the child of state,/ It might for Fortune's bastard be un-fathered*" – Sonnet 124, lines 1-2; "As a decrepit *father* takes delight/ To see *his active child* do deeds of youth,/ So I, made lame by *Fortune's dearest spite*" – Sonnet 37, lines 1-3; **FRUIT** = "Upon my head they placed a ***fruitless crown***, and put a *barren* scepter in my gripe, thence to be wrenched with an unlineal hand, *no son of mine succeeding*" – *Macbeth*, 3.1.60-63; "The *royal tree* hath left us ***royal fruit***" - *Richard III*, 3.7.166

> Hadst thou been killed when first thou didst presume,
> Thou hadst not lived to kill ***a son of mine***.
> And thus I prophesy: that many a thousand
> Which now mistrust no parcel of my fear,
> And many an old man's sigh, and many a *widow's*,
> And many an ***orphan's*** water-standing eye…
> Thy mother felt more than a mother's pain,
> And yet brought forth less than a mother's *hope*,
> To wit, an ingest deformed lump,
> Not like the ***fruit*** of such a goodly tree.
> - *3 Henry VI*, 5.6.34-52

11 FOR SUMMER AND HIS PLEASURES WAIT ON THEE,
SUMMER AND HIS PLEASURES = Southampton's (his Majesty's) royal "pleasure" or will or commands; "But thy *eternal Summer* shall not fade" – Sonnet 18, line 9; as opposed to the royal pleasure or will of Elizabeth in line 2 above, i.e., "the *pleasure* of the fleeting year"; **WAIT ON THEE** = wait upon or attend on Southampton, who is a king; attend, as your servants, hoping or waiting for your liberty and royal presence; "I am to *wait*, though *waiting* be so hell,/ Not blame *your pleasure*, be it ill or well" – Sonnet 58, lines

13-14; "We *wait upon your Grace*" – *Richard III*, 1.3.323 (First Folio; the quartos have "we will attend your Grace"); "your *waiting vassals*" – *Richard III*, 2.1.122

12 AND THOU AWAY, THE VERY BIRDS ARE MUTE.

THOU AWAY = you in the Tower; "Yet seemed it Winter still, and you away" – Sonnet 98, line 13; **VERY BIRDS** = royal birds, i.e., Elizabeth and Oxford as the principals of *The Phoenix and the Turtle*, a funeral dirge or song, 1601; "Bare ruined choirs, where *late the sweet birds sang*" – Sonnet 73, line 4; "For these *dead birds* sigh a *prayer*" – final line of *The Phoenix and the Turtle*; **VERY** = "Ver"; Edward de Vere; "The *very* part was consecrate to thee" – Sonnet 74, line 6; "The young Earl of Oxford, of that ancient and **Very family of the Veres**, had a cause or suit, that now came before the Queen; which she did not answer so favourably as was expected, checking him, it seems, for his unthriftiness. And hereupon his behaviors before her gave her some offence." - Gilbert Talbot to his mother, June 28, 1574 (Shortly afterward the Queen gave birth to Southampton in May/June 1574); **MUTE** = silent, i.e., both parents are mute, as Oxford has been forced into public silence: "And art made *tongue-tied by authority*" – Sonnet 66, line 9; similar to "dumb" or speechless as in "For who's so *dumb* that cannot write to thee,/ When thou thyself dost give invention light?" – Sonnet 38, lines 7-8; and "O learn to read *what silent love hath writ*!/ To hear with eyes belongs to love's fine wit" – Sonnet 23, lines 13-14; "Either our history shall with full mouth speak freely of our acts, or else our grave like Turkish *mute* shall have a tongueless mouth, not worshipped with a waxen epitaph" – the King in *Henry V*, 1.2.231-234, referring to the "mute" or officer in Turkey who acts as an executioner

13 OR IF THEY SING, 'TIS WITH SO DULL A CHEER

SING = the way these sonnets or "little songs" are being sung to you, as hymns or prayers: "Haply I think on thee, and then my state/ (Like to the Lark at break of day arising)/ From sullen earth *sings hymns at Heaven's gate*" – Sonnet 29, lines 10-12, referring to praying at Traitor's Gate of the fortress Tower controlled by Elizabeth or Heaven; "What's new to speak, what now to register/ That may express my love, or thy dear merit?/ Nothing, sweet boy, but yet *like prayers divine*,/ I must each day say o'er the *very* same" – Sonnet 108, lines 3-6; or if they do sing your praises, the song they sing is**DULL** = "faint, spiritless, woebegone" – Booth; "Plods on *dully*, to bear that weight in me" – Sonnet 50, line 6; "and do not kill/ The spirit of love with a *perpetual dullness*" – Sonnet 56, line 8; "Because I would *not dull you with my song*" – Sonnet 102, line 14; "*Dulling my lines*, and doing me disgrace" – Sonnet 103, line 8; **CHEER** = "When I perceive that *men as plants increase*,/ *Cheered and checked* even by the self-same sky,/ Vaunt in their youthful sap, at height decrease,/ And wear their brave state out of memory;/ Then the conceit of this inconstant stay/ Sets you *most rich* in youth before my sight,/ Where wasteful time debateth with decay,/ to *change your day of youth to sullied night*" – Sonnet 15, lines 5-12

14 THAT LEAVES LOOK PALE, DREADING THE WINTER'S NEAR.

LEAVES LOOK PALE = "That time of year thou mayst in me behold/ When *yellow leaves*, or none, or few, do hang/ Upon those boughs which shake against the cold,/ Bare ruined choirs, where late the sweet birds sang" – Sonnet 73, lines 1-4; **DREADING THE WINTER'S NEAR** = fearing the end, i.e., the death of Elizabeth and the succession without Southampton able to fulfill his true promise as king; dreading the end of all his son's hope as Henry IX, and the end of the Tudor dynasty; "That thereby *beauty's Rose might never die*" – Sonnet 1, line 2; playing on "How *like a Winter* hath my absence been" of line 1 above; **NEAR** = by blood

Part Two

THE PRISON YEARS

YEAR TWO IN THE TOWER

Sonnet 98
And You Away
March-April 1602

As the second year of Southampton's imprisonment commences, Oxford records fewer entries in his diary, i.e., at the approximate rate of one every two months. As the Time of the diary (Elizabeth's life) nears its end, his own ability to continue writing (and recreating his son's true life in this womb) is weakening. His reference to Saturn corresponds with an astrological event of April 1602.

Sonnet 98	Translation
From you have I been absent in the spring,	I stopped writing to you in the spring,
When proud pied April (dressed in all his trim)	When April resembled Elizabeth's pregnancy
Hath put a spirit of youth in every thing:	With your royal self in her body,
That heavy *Saturn* laughed and leaped with him.	While the king of disaster was on his way.
Yet nor the lays of birds, nor the sweet smell	Yet neither the songs of birds or the royal smell
Of different flowers in odor and in hew,	Of flowers other than that of my son
Could make me any summer's story tell:	Could make me speak of her fullness with you,
Or from their proud lap pluck them where they grew:	Or enable me to find you in them.
Nor did I wonder at the Lily's white,	Nor did I wonder at the white lillies
Nor praise the deep vermillion in the Rose;	Or speak of you as heir of the Tudor Rose;
They were but sweet, but figures of delight,	All the flowers were royal to me,
Drawn after you, you pattern of all those.	All filled with you and you model for them.
Yet seemed it Winter still, and you away,	Yet it seemed like death, with you in prison,
As with your shadow I with these did play.	And I viewed flowers as I view your shadow.

1 FROM YOU HAVE I BEEN ABSENT IN THE SPRING,
Oxford has not visited Southampton in the Tower; indicating that he has also let more time than usual go by without writing more than this one sonnet – in this series, at any rate, because he is also continuing the Dark Lady series to Elizabeth at this time.

2 WHEN PROUD-PIED APRIL (DRESSED IN ALL HIS TRIM)
PROUD-PIED = royal, splendid; ("Why is my verse so barren of new *pride*?" – Sonnet 76, line 1; **APRIL** = the spring of your royal life; "the *lovely April of her prime*" of Sonnet 3, line 10, the month before Elizabeth gave birth to you; **ALL** = Southampton, *One for All, All for One*; **ALL HIS TRIM** = all his adornment; ("And needy nothing *trimmed* in jollity" – Sonnet 66, line 3)

REFERENCE EDITION 527

3 HATH PUT A SPIRIT OF YOUTH IN EVERY THING:
SPIRIT OF YOUTH = hopeful time of sacred royal blood; "Th'expense of spirit in a waste of shame" – Sonnet 129, line 1, Oxford to Elizabeth about her waste of her son's "spirit" or royal blood; **EVERY** = Ever = E. Ver, Edward de Vere; **EVERY THING** = my (E. Vere's) son, Southampton

4 THAT HEAVY *SATURN* LAUGHED AND LEAPED WITH HIM.
HEAVY = grave, ponderous; **SATURN** = (italicized in *Q*); "The planetary deity Saturn is associated with old age, coldness and disaster" – Duncan-Jones; i.e., even Saturn was joyous in the spring of your life; **SATURN LAUGHED AND LEAPED**: In Roman mythology Saturn is the god of agriculture, i.e., of sowing or planting, and therefore it suggests the nature of *time*. The myths about Saturn depict him as presiding over a "golden age" of happiness and plenty; the Greeks called him "Kronos" or time (i.e., Father Time), so he is also the god of Time; and he is the son of Heaven and Earth. Saturn also often stands for the father; "*Saturn and Venus* this year in conjunction! What says the almanac to that?" – Prince Hal in *2 Henry IV*, 2.4.263-264; (In 1898 George Wyndham noted that the Royal Observatory of Edinburgh had recorded only three occasions between 1592 and 1609 when Saturn was seen to be "in opposition" in the night sky: April 4 and April 17, 1600, and April 29, 1602. The latter date coincides with the dating of this sonnet. "To have dragged in Saturn without reason or rhyme into a description of a particular month of April would have been a freak without precedent in Shakespeare," Wyndham concluded. Edward de Vere had known Dr. John Dee, the Queen's astrologer, for more than three decades.

5 YET NOT THE LAYS OF BIRDS, NOR THE SWEET SMELL
NOR = neither; **LAYS** = songs; sonnets; **BIRDS** = Elizabeth as the Phoenix and Oxford as the Turtle-dove, as in *The Phoenix and the Turtle* of 1601; **SWEET** = royal

6 OF DIFFERENT FLOWERS IN ODOR AND IN HEW,
FLOWERS = heirs of the Tudor Rose; **IN** = in respect to; **ODOR** = royalty, royal blood; **HEW** = Henry Wriothesley ("He. W"); "A man in hew all *Hews* in his controlling" – Sonnet 20, line 7; with a phonetic likeness of "hew" and "you"

7 COULD MAKE ME ANY SUMMER'S STORY TELL,
SUMMER'S STORY = the story of his son's golden time; opposite of "winter's tale"; "Three winters cold/ Have from the forests shook three *summers' pride*" – Sonnet 104, lines 3-4; ("Upon thy part I can set down a *story*" – Sonnet 88, line 6; "tell my *story*" – Hamlet, 5.2.361)

8 OR FROM THEIR PROUD LAP PLUCK THEM WHERE THEY GREW:
PROUD = royal; **GREW** = as in the womb of these sonnets

9 NOR DID I WONDER AT THE LILY'S WHITE,
WONDER = won = the "one" of Southampton's motto; "Still constant in a *wondrous* excellence … Three themes in one, which *wondrous* scope affords" – Sonnet 105, lines 6,12; "For we which now behold these present days/ Have eyes to *wonder*, but lack tongues to praise" - Sonnet 106, lines 13-14; **LILY'S WHITE** = Elizabeth; ("A most unspotted *lily* shall she pass to the ground, and all the world shall mourn her" – *Henry VIII*, 5.4.61-62, Archbishop Cranmer, speaking of the newly born Princess Elizabeth and predicting the future; "This pleasant *lily* white/ this taint of roseate red/ this sweet fair dea (goddess) spread" – early Oxford verse, signed E.O., published in *The Phoenix Nest*, 1593)

10 NOR PRAISE THE DEEP VERMILLION IN THE ROSE:
VERMILLION = bright red or scarlet; (the only appearance of this word in the Shakespeare works); **VER** = E. Ver, Edward de Vere; spring of the Tudor Rose; **THE ROSE** = Elizabeth's Tudor Rose; ("Roses are the

flower of Venus, but roses too are *par excellence* the flower of the Queen. She is both the white rose of York and the red of Lancaster" – Strong, *Cult of Elizabeth*, p. 68)

11 THEY WERE BUT SWEET, BUT FIGURES OF DELIGHT,
SWEET = royal; **BUT SWEET** = royal, but only that; i.e., not as much as Southampton; **FIGURES** = "If ten of thine ten times *refigured* thee" – Sonnet 6, line 10; "Ah yet doth beauty like a Dial hand,/ Steal from his *figure*" – Sonnet 104, lines 9-10; "What's in the brain that ink may character/ Which hath not *figured* to thee my true spirit?" – Sonnet 108, lines 1-2

> Poor key-cold *Figure* of a holy king
> - *Richard III*, 1.2.5

> I am the shadow of poor Buckingham,
> Whose *figure* even this instant cloud puts on
> By dark'ning my clear sun
> - *Henry VIII*, 1.1.224-226

> There is a history in all men's lives
> *Figuring* the nature of the times deceas'd
> - *2 Henry IV*, 3.1.80-81

12 DRAWN AFTER YOU, YOU PATTERN OF ALL THOSE.
DRAWN = created; as Southampton was "painted" or given birth to by the Queen: "with nature's own hand painted" - Sonnet 20, line 1; **YOU, YOU** = spoken to a prince or king, as Hamlet declares: "It is I, Hamlet the Dane"; echoing double U or W and "hew" for Henry Wriothesley; **YOU PATTERN** = Southampton as son of Elizabeth, the "pattern" of her Tudor Rose blood; (as in "beauty's pattern to succeeding men" of Sonnet 19, line 12); "She (Elizabeth) shall be ... a *pattern* to all princes living with her, and all that shall succeed" – *Henry VIII*, 5.4.20-23; **ALL** = Southampton, his motto

13 YET SEEMED IT WINTER STILL, AND YOU AWAY,
WINTER = frozen, near death; the Queen's mortal body coming to its end; **STILL** = always; **YOU AWAY** = you in the Tower

14 AS WITH YOUR SHADOW I WITH THESE DID PLAY.
Oxford saying he nevertheless was able to draw some delight from these "shadows" of his son; "Save that my soul's imaginary sight/ Presents thy *shadow* to my sightless view,/ Which like a jewel hung in ghastly night/ Makes black night beauteous, and her old face new" – Sonnet 27, 9-12; "What is your substance, whereof are you made,/ That millions of strange *shadows on you* tend?/ Since every one hath, every one, one *shade*,/ And you, but one, can every *shadow* lend" – Sonnet 53, lines 1-4; "A dream itself is but a *shadow*" – *Hamlet*, 2.2.276

OXFORD'S ACTING COMPANY
The Boar's Head
March 31, 1602

Edward de Vere has been using the Lord Chamberlain's Men as "Shakespeare's Company" (the vehicle for producing the "Shakespeare" plays at Court and the public playhouses), but his own company is still active at this time. Oxford's Men were most active from 1580 to 1590; afterward, the records of the company disappear until 1600, when the anonymous play *The Weakest Goeth to the Wall* was published with information that it had been acted by the "Earl of Oxford's servants." In 1601 another anonymous (and non-extant) play – *The History of George Scanderbeg* – was published as having been acted by Oxford's Men.

Now the company seems to have revived its activities even more, perhaps as part of Oxford's pledge to Cecil and King James of Scotland that he will further separate himself from the Shakespeare name and works. Already the acting companies of the earls of Derby (Oxford's son-in-law, husband of Elizabeth Vere) and Worcester have been joined under Worcester; and now Oxford's Men are joining the group. Worcester, a member of the Privy Council under Robert Cecil, writes on behalf of the Council to the Lord Mayor of London about special treatment being extended by the Queen to this new amalgamated company; i.e., an exception is to be made to the "restraint" against plays currently in effect. Specifically the Queen and Privy Council now "require" the Mayor to allow the Oxford-Worcester Company to perform regularly at their favorite place, the Boar's Head Inn (the Vere crest is a Boar)*:

> "…the servants of our very good Lord the Earl of Oxford, and of me the Earl of Worcester, being joined by agreement together in one company (to whom upon notice of Her Majesty's pleasure at the suit of the Earl of Oxford, toleration hath been thought meet to be granted, notwithstanding the restraint of our said former orders), do not tie themselves to one certain place and house, but do change their place at their own disposition, which is as disorderly and offensive as the former offence of many houses. And as the other companies that are allowed, namely of me, the Lord Admiral and the Lord Chamberlain, be appointed their certain houses, and one and no more to each company, so we do straightly require that this third company be likewise [tied] to one place. And because we are informed that the house called the Boar's Head is the place they have especially used and do best like of, we do pray and require you that that said house, namely the Boar's Head, may be assigned unto them, and that they be very straightly charged to use and exercise their plays in no other but that house, as they will look to have that toleration continued and avoid further displeasure. And so we bid your Lordship heartily farewell. From the Court at Richmond the last of March 1602."
> - B. M. Ward, pp 325-326

Robert Cecil has virtually full control over the acting companies, while directing the Government under Queen Elizabeth. This extraordinary extension of "toleration" to Oxford's Company (specially allowed as a third group) is undoubtedly a reward for Oxford's cooperation with Cecil in his secret efforts to prepare for the accession of King James upon Elizabeth's death. Oxford is cooperating as part of the bargain to gain Southampton's release and pardon, in exchange for his son's pledge to renounce any claim to the throne.

*There were several London inns named Boar's Head; one, in Eastcheap, has been regarded as the locale of the *Henry IV* tavern scenes. The one used by Oxford's acting company may have been in Middlesex.

Part Two

THE PRISON YEARS

YEAR TWO IN THE TOWER

Sonnet 99
The Purple Pride
May-June 1602

Oxford reflects his mournful mood at the beginning of the summer of 1602, as Elizabeth is rapidly aging and approaching death while their son, Southampton, languishes in the Tower of London. This is the time of year when Southampton was born in 1574; but now the flower of the Tudor Rose must watch his claim to the throne die along with his mother: "A vengeful canker ate him up to death." (On June 2, 1602, as part of their secret correspondence, King James (using "30" as his coded identity) writes to Robert Cecil ("10") about a new member of the group ("40") pledged to secure his succession. The identity of the new recruit has never been established, but it may have been Oxford, who was also Cecil's brother-in-law), working to secure Southampton's release and pardon in exchange for a promise to give up any future claim to the throne.

Sonnet 99	Translation
The forward violet thus did I chide:	Therefore I rebuked you, the most royal prince:
"Sweet thief, whence didst thou steal thy sweet that smells	"Royal thief! From whom did you steal that royalty of yours
If not from my love's breath? The purple pride	If not from my own royal son? The royal blood
Which on thy soft cheek for complexion dwells,	That shows in your appearance
In my love's veins thou hast too grossly died.	You have disgraced too much in my own veins!
The Lily I condemned for thy hand,	So I condemned all the flowers because of you,
And buds of marjoram had stol'n thy hair;	Scolding them for taking the royal heir;
The Roses fearfully on thorns did stand,	The Tudor Roses were bleeding on thorns,
One blushing shame, an other white despair;	One suffering disgrace, the other despair;
A third, nor red nor white, had stolen of both,	You stole all of your Tudor colors,
And to his robbery had annexed thy breath;	And with this robbery went your own life;
But for his theft, in pride of all his growth	And because of this, all your fresh royal blood
A vengeful canker eat him up to death.	Was destroyed by the disgrace.
More flowers I noted, yet I none could see,	I saw more flowers this spring,
But sweet or color it had stol'n from thee."	But all your royalty had been stolen from them."

(NOTE: This sonnet contains 15 lines instead of 14.)

1 THE FORWARD VIOLET THUS DID I CHIDE:
Oxford records how he did "chide" or rebuke the royal blood of his son for blooming too early in life; i.e., Southampton's own blood was the cause of his undoing; **FORWARD** = early blooming; "As the most *forward bud* is eaten by the canker ere it blow ... losing its verdure, even in the prime, and all the fair effects of

REFERENCE EDITION 531

future hopes" – *The Two Gentlemen of Verona*, 1.1.45-50; **FORWARD VIOLET** = Southampton himself was the early blooming royal flower of the Tudor Rose; violets are associated with young courtiers, as in: "Welcome, my son. Who are the *violets* now that strew the green lap of the new-come spring? … Well, bear you well in this new spring of time, lest you be cropp'd before you come to prime" – *Richard II*, 5.2.46-51, and Southampton was "cropped" or cut down before he could flourish as a prince; "When I behold *the violet past prime*" – Sonnet 12, line 3; "To guard a title that was rich before, to gild refined gold, to paint the lily, to throw perfume on the violet" – *King John*, 4.2.10-12, referring to potential kingship, as to the Prince of Denmark: "For Hamlet, and the trifling of his favor, hold it a fashion, and a toy in blood; *a violet in the youth of primy nature, forward* … His greatness weighed, his will is not his own, for he himself is subject to his birth" – *Hamlet*, 1.3.6-9, 20-21

(Note: the opening rhyme scheme of this 15-line sonnet is ababa, so either line 3 or line 5 is the "extra" line in terms of structure; but, also, the "extra line" could be this opening line; in that case, the sonnet now begins all over again, with the next fourteen lines following the usual pattern of *abab, cdcd, efef, dd*.)

2 "SWEET THIEF, WHENCE DIDST THOU STEAL THY SWEET THAT SMELLS

SWEET THIEF = royal thief of your own royal claim; "That I an accessory needs must be/ To that *sweet thief* which sourly robs from me" – Sonnet 35, lines 13-14; **STEAL** = rob, deprive of; **THY SWEET** = your royal blood and royal claim; Southampton "stole" it from himself, Elizabeth and Oxford; "And, father, do but think how *sweet* it is to wear a crown" – *3 Henry VI*, 1.2.28-29; **SMELLS** = emits an odor or fragrance, i.e., a royal presence, which has been stolen; "To thy fair flower add the rank smell of weeds;/ But why *thy odor* matcheth not thy show,/ The soil is this, that thou dost common grow" – Sonnet 69, line, i.e., Southampton's status reduced to that of a commoner, so that his true "odor" or royalty cannot be discerned; "Lilies that fester smell far worse than weeds" – Sonnet 94, line 14

3 IF NOT FROM MY LOVE'S BREATH? THE PURPLE PRIDE

MY LOVE'S BREATH = my royal son's breath; i.e., Southampton stole his own breath of life, causing his life as a prince to die; **PURPLE** = the color of blood in the veins; **PURPLE PRIDE** = royal blood; "Even as the sun with *purple*-colored face/ Had ta'en his last leave of the weeping morn,/ Rose-cheeked Adonis hied him to the chase" – *Venus and Adonis*, 1-3; "And in his blood that on the ground lay spilled/ A *purple* flower spring up, check'red with white,/ Resembling well his pale cheeks" – *V&A*, 1167-1169; "Yet marked I where the bolt of Cupid fell:/ It fell upon a little western flower,/ Before milk-white, now *purple* with love's wound" – *Midsummer Night's Dream*, 2.1.165-168; referring to the royal birth of Southampton as the purple/royal flower of Elizabeth and her Tudor Rose dynasty; "See how my sword weeps for the poor King's death. O, may such *purple* tears be always shed for those that wish the downfall of our house!" – *3 Henry VI*, 5.6.63-65; "The red rose and the white are on his face, the fatal colors of our striving houses: the one *his purple blood right* well resembles; the other his pale cheeks, methinks, presenteth" – *3 Henry VI*, 2.5.97-99; **PRIDE** = royal splendor; in the Sonnets, royal blood, related to the swelling pride of pregnancy and birth: "Why is my verse so *barren* of new *pride*?" Sonnet 76, line 1; "Or from their *proud* lap pluck them where they grew" – Sonnet 98, line 8

4 WHICH ON THY SOFT CHEEK FOR COMPLEXION DWELLS,

CHEEK = his reflection of his royal blood, as in *3 Henry VI* above, referring to "his pale cheeks"; "Thus is his *cheek* the map of days outworn,/ When beauty lived and *died* as flowers do now,/ Before these bastard signs of fair were borne" – Sonnet 68, lines 1-3; **FOR COMPLEXION** = as coloring; "He is come to open the *purple* testament of *bleeding* war; but ere the crown he looks for live in peace, ten thousand bloody crowns of mothers' sons shall ill become *the flower of England's face*, change the **complexion** of her maid-pale peace to scarlet indignation and bedew her pastures' grass with faithful English blood" – *Richard II*, 3.3.93-100

5 IN MY LOVE'S VEINS THOU HAST TOO GROSSLY DIED.
IN MY LOVE'S VEINS = in my royal son's veins; **GROSSLY** = "with flagrant obviousness" – Tucker; thickly; "obliquely suggests 'dying' by violence" – Kerrigan; **DIED** = (Q has "died," but it's usually emended to "dyed," as in the phrase "dye in the vein" or "bleed to death" - Booth); "no doubt with a play on 'died', suggesting that the violets have died in the youth's body" – Duncan-Jones; "When beauty lived and *died* as flowers do now" – Sonnet 68, line 2; the play on "dye" and "die" is in "I cannot rest until the white rose that I wear be *dyed* even in the lukewarm blood of Henry's heart … Richard, enough, I will be king, or *die*" – 3 Henry VI, 1.2.32-35; "The canker blooms have full as deep a *dye*/ As the perfumed tincture of the Roses" – Sonnet 54, lines 5-6

6 THE LILY I CONDEMNED FOR THY HAND,
LILY = Elizabeth; "A crown of lilies/ Upon a virgin bride's adorned head" – Spenser, writing of the Queen as Cynthia in *Colin Clouts Come Home Again*, 1.339; i.e., Oxford blames or condemns Elizabeth for their son's tragic fate; **CONDEMNED** = as Southampton was condemned to death and is now condemned to prison; "This way the king will come; this is the way to Julius Caesar's ill-erected Tower, to whose flint bosom my *condemned* lord is doom'd a prisoner by proud Bolinbroke" – *Richard II*, 5.1.1-4; "And there the poison is as a fiend confined to tyrannize on unrepriveable *condemned blood*" – *King John*, 5.7.45-48; "Therefore by law thou art *condemned* to die" – *The Comedy of Errors*, 1.1.25; "Be pitiful to my *condemned* sons" – *Titus Andronicus*, 3.1.8; **FOR THY HAND** = for what it has done to your kingly hand; "I blamed the lily for stealing whiteness from your hand" – Duncan-Jones; "Full gently now she takes him by the hand,/ A *lily* prison'd in a gaol of snow" – *Venus and Adonis*, 3361-362; "Brother, give me thy hand" – 3 Henry VI, 2.3.44

7 AND BUDS OF MARJORAM HAD STOL'N THY HAIR;
BUDS = Southampton, bud of the Tudor Rose; **MARJORAM** = knotted curls that emit more odor or fragrance, i.e., royalty; **HAIR** = heir, i.e., your status as royal heir; "His tender *heir* might bear his memory" – Sonnet 1, line 4; "As those gold candles fixed in *heaven's air*" – Sonnet 21, line 12; "Before the *golden tresses* of the dead" – Sonnet 68, line 5; Southampton's reality as "heir" to the throne has been stolen.

8 THE ROSES FEARFULLY ON THORNS DID STAND,
THE ROSES, etc. = inverting Elizabeth's motto *A Rose Without a Thorn*; "Roses have thorns, and silver fountains mud,/ Clouds and eclipses stain both Moon and Sunne" – Sonnet 35, lines 2-3; Tudor Roses; **FEARFULLY** = in a panic; "O fearful meditation!" – Sonnet 65, line 9; **STAND** = wait in suspense (as in the phrase "standing on thorns"); recalling Oxford's fear that his son would be executed; "to be in a painful state of anxiety or suspense" – OED, thorns; "Not mine own *fears* nor the prophetic soul/ Of the wide world dreaming on things to come/ Can yet the lease of my true love control,/ Supposed as forfeit to a confined doom" – Sonnet 107, lines 1-4, upon Southampton's release on April 10, 1603; "And thus long have we *stood* to watch the *fearful* bending of thy knee, because we thought our self thy lawful king" – *Richard II*, 3.3.72-74; **FEARFULLY ON THORNS** = recalling the fear of Southampton's execution: "Hang on such thorns" – Sonnet 54, line 7

9 ONE BLUSHING SHAME, AN OTHER WHITE DESPAIR:
ONE = (Q has "Our" and therefore reads, "Our blushing shame"); the red rose, blushing shame; Southampton, *One for All, All for One*; **BLUSHING SHAME** = his disgrace; Elizabeth's shame directed at him; ("And Beauty slandered with *a bastard shame*" – Sonnet 127, line 4); "Let my tears staunch the earth's dry appetite; *my sons' sweet blood* will make it *shame and blush*" – *Titus Andronicus*, 3.1.34-35; "His *treasons* will sit *blushing* in his face, not able to endure the sight of day, but self-*affrighted* tremble at his sin" – *Richard II*, 3.2.51-53, spoken by King Richard, and undoubtedly close to what Queen Elizabeth said about Essex

and Southampton after the Rebellion; **AN OTHER** = the white rose; filled with despair; **WHITE DESPAIR** = "For if I should *despair* I should grow mad" – Sonnet 140, line 9, to Elizabeth in the Dark Lady series; "Two loves I have of comfort and *despair*" – Sonnet 144, line 1, Oxford referring to the despair in him that Elizabeth has caused; "And from his bosom purge this black despair" – *2 Henry VI*, 3.3.23; "Renowned Prince, how shall poor Henry live, unless thou rescue him from foul despair?" – *3 Henry VI*, 3.3.214-215; "And I the rather wean me from despair for love of Edward's offspring in my womb" – Elizabeth, Queen to Edward IV, in *3 Henry VI*, 4.4.17-18

10 A THIRD, NOR RED NOR WHITE, HAD STOL'N OF BOTH,

A THIRD = Southampton, the combination (damasked), who has "stolen" some of both the red rose and the white rose, combined as the Tudor Rose; **STOL'N** = "That I an accessory needs must be/ To that *sweet thief* which sourly *robs* from me" – Sonnet 35, lines 13-14; "I have seen Roses damasked, red and white,/ But no such Roses see I in her cheeks" – Sonnet 130, lines 5-6, to Elizabeth in the Dark Lady series.

11 AND TO HIS ROBB'RY HAD ANNEXED THY BREATH;

HIS ROBB'RY = "I do forgive *thy robb'ry, gentle thief*" – Sonnet 40, line 9; **ANNEXED** = added; added to his robbery; **THY BREATH** = your life and future (stolen, by you yourself; the truth is that *both* Elizabeth and Southampton have robbed him of the crown.

12 BUT FOR HIS THEFT, IN PRIDE OF ALL HIS GROWTH

BUT FOR = "however, in punishment for" – Booth; **PRIDE** = royal blood; **IN PRIDE OF** = in the prime or height of; "in the glory of" – Kerrigan; **ALL** = Southampton, his motto; **GROWTH** = continued life and growth; "Nativity, once in the main of light,/ Crawls to maturity, wherewith being crowned,/ Crooked eclipses 'gainst his glory fight" – Sonnet 60, lines 5-7; "Love is a Babe; then might I not say so,/ To give full *growth* to that which still doth grow" – Sonnet 115, lines 13-14

13 A VENGEFUL CANKER EAT HIM UP TO DEATH.

VENGEFUL CANKER = (avenging cankerworm); Secretary Robert Cecil, who exterminated Southampton's blood claim; but also Elizabeth, the vengeful monarch; "I wear no knife to slaughter sleeping men; but here's a *vengeful* sword, rusted with ease, that shall be scoured in his rancorous heart" – *2 Henry VI*, 3.2.196-198; **EAT HIM UP TO DEATH** = (related to "died" in line 5); "That thereby beauty's *Rose* might never *die*" – Sonnet 1, line 1; Oxford's and Elizabeth's royal son, the budding flower of the Tudor Rose, has "died" in terms of having a claim to the throne; (*Q* has "eate," which was often the spelling of "ate"); "Now the good gods forbid that our renowned Rome, whose gratitude towards her deserved children is enroll'd in Jove's own book, like an unnatural dam should now *eat up her own*!" – *Coriolanus*, 3.1.289-293; "Shall worms, inheritors of this excess,/ *Eat up* thy charge?/ … Within be fed, without be rich no more,/ So shalt thou feed on death, that feeds on men,/ And death once dead, there's no more dying then" – to Elizabeth in the Dark Lady series, Sonnet 146, lines 7-8, 12-14

14 MORE FLOW'RS I NOTED, YET I NONE COULD SEE,

I observed other flowers, except; **NONE** = Southampton as "one" who is now "none"; I could see (in my mind's eye) none except him

15 BUT SWEET OR COLOR IT HAD STOL'N FROM THEE.

SWEET = royal/royalty; **COLOR** = of the Tudor Rose; i.e., all Oxford can observe is the royal odor or color that has been stolen from his son. (The 15-line structure seems intentional; certainly the sonnet is loaded: *died, condemned, stol'n, fearfully, shame, despair, stol'n, robbery, theft, vengeful, death, stol'n…*)

No. 99

JAMES VI of SCOTLAND ("30")

TO ROBERT CECIL ("10")

JUNE 3, 1602:

This letter from James of Scotland to Cecil marks the introduction of "40" as part of the group involved in the secret correspondence to secure James' succession. If this new member is Oxford, then we may see the future King conveying his assurance, through Cecil, that upon his accession he will order Southampton's release and grant him a royal pardon.

"For I must plainly confess that both ye and your faithful colleague 40 have by your vigilant and judicious care so easily settled me in the only right course for my good, so happily preserved the Queen's mind from the poison of jealous prejudice, so valiantly resisted the crooked courses of some seditious spirits… But not that hereby I have any intention to desire you or 40 (whom I always and ever shall account as one) anyways to alter either in form or substance your accustomed form of answering me … It shall therefore suffice me that ye rest in a full and certain persuasion of my love and thankful mind to you both, whereof this my handwrit shall serve for a witness unto you, **assuring 40 that with God's grace he shall never be disappointed** of his confidence in my honesty upon your relation…

"I cannot also omit to display unto you the great contentment I receive by your so inward and united concurrence in all the paths that lead to my future happiness, most heartily wishing you to continue in that happy course as ye may be sure of my thankfulness towards you, whom I know to be only moved, for the respect of conscience and honor, to deserve so well at the hands of a lawful, natural and loving successor to your queen and country. And thus, **praying 40 to be assured that by your means only he shall hear from me**, that he may thereby discern if any other word come to him in my name that it is but false and adulterate coin, and *persuading him of my entire affection towards him as to yourself*, I bid you heartily farewell. Your most assured and loving friend, 30."

- *Letters of King James VI & I*, Akrigg, 192-194

THE PRISON YEARS

YEAR TWO IN THE TOWER

Sonnet 100
Return, Forgetful Muse
July-August 1602

Queen Elizabeth's life is beginning its final decline and this has been draining Oxford's power to continue writing and "growing" their royal son. The end of her life, reign and dynasty is near; the truth of Southampton's identity as her son and heir will be buried, at least for the foreseeable future. Oxford's use of "time" on four occasions in this sonnet conveys his deepening despair. He is finally letting go of the present, in favor of the "fame" or immortal life he has promised to secure for Henry Wriothesley by means of these sonnets. In other words, he seems resigned to the now-absolute certainty that their son will not succeed her; occasionally in previous sonnets, he had continued to hold out some hope that Southampton could succeed to the throne, despite his "faults" and "crimes." The "scythe" of Time in the final line is the tyranny of Elizabeth's mortality; the "crooked knife" refers to the "crook-back" Robert Cecil, who has saved Southampton while obliterating his royal claim.

Sonnet 100	Translation
Where art thou, Muse, that thou forget'st so long	Where are you, my Muse? Why forget so long
To speak of that which gives thee all thy might?	To write of the son whose royalty inspires you?
Spend'st thou thy fury on some worthless song,	Do you spend your power on non-royal verses,
Dark'ning thy power to lend base subjects light?	So you can't give a commoner any more royal life?
Return, forgetful Muse, and straight redeem	Come back, Muse! And quickly make up for
In gentle numbers time so idly spent,	The wasted time with new royal sonnets!
Sing to the ear that doth thy lays esteem,	Send new verses to the one who appreciates them
And gives thy pen both skill and argument.	And inspires the writing with its method and topic!
Rise, resty Muse, my love's sweet face survey,	Rise, sluggish Muse! Look at my royal son's face
If time have any wrinkle graven there;	And see if his royal claim is almost dead!
If any, be a *Satire* to decay,	If so, act to block his sharp decline,
And make time's spoils despised everywhere.	And stop the ruin of his royal destiny!
Give my love fame faster than time wastes life,	Give my son immortal life faster than it's taken,
So thou prevent'st his scythe and crooked knife.	And so prevent this ruin by Elizabeth and Cecil.

1 WHERE ART THOU, MUSE, THAT THOU FORGET'ST SO LONG
Having neglected to write as often in the diary this year, Oxford accuses his Muse of having forgotten to sing about his imprisoned son, whose loss of the throne will be absolute upon the death of the Queen.

2 TO SPEAK OF THAT WHICH GIVES THEE ALL THY MIGHT?
THAT WHICH, etc. = Southampton, who is the "*onlie begetter* of these ensuing sonnets," as in the Dedication of 1609, i.e., the one who inspires Oxford and his Muse; "For who's so dumb that cannot write to thee,/

When thou thyself dost give invention light?" – Sonnet 38, lines 7-8; "Thine eyes, that taught the dumb on high to sing/ And heavy ignorance aloft to fly,/ Have added feathers to the learned's wing,/ And given grace a double majesty./ Yet be most proud of *that which I compile,/ Whose influence is thine, and born of thee*" – Sonnet 78, lines 5-10; "O know, sweet love, *I always write of you,/ And you and love are still my argument*" – Sonnet 76, lines 9-10; **ALL** = Southampton, *One for All, All for One*, who inspires Oxford's Muse and gives it all his royal power; **MIGHT** = royal power

3 SPEND'ST THOU THY FURY ON SOME WORTHLESS SONG,
SPEND'ST = exhaust, pour into, waste; "So all my best is dressing old words new,/ *Spending again what is already spent*" – Sonnet 76, lines 11-12; "Fair, kind, and true, varying to other words,/ And *in this change is my invention spent*" – Sonnet 105, lines 11-12; "The *expense of spirit* in a waste of shame" – Sonnet 129, line 1; **FURY** = the fury of Oxford's Muse, reflecting his own state of mind, as being expressed in the parallel Dark Lady Series by the fury directed toward Queen Elizabeth, especially Sonnets 147-152, as in: "My reason, the physician to my love,/ Angry that his prescriptions are not kept,/ Hath left me, and I desperate now approve/ Desire is death, which physic did except./ Past cure I am, now reason is past care,/ And frantic mad with evermore unrest,/ My thoughts and my discourse as madmen's are" – Sonnet 147, lines 5-11; **SOME WORTHLESS SONG** = sonnet or "little song" without royal blood or claim; "O how thy *worth* with manners may I *sing*,/ When thou art all the better part of me?" – Sonnet 39, lines 1-2

4 DARK'NING THY POWER TO LEND BASE SUBJECTS LIGHT?
DARK'NING = as this diary turned dark upon the Rebellion, as chronicled in Sonnet 27: "Looking on *darkness* which the blind do see" – Sonnet 27, line 8; **BASE SUBJECTS** = Southampton, a "base" commoner in prison; "As on the finger of a throned Queen,/ The *basest Jewel* will be well esteemed" – Sonnet 96, lines 5-6; **LIGHT** = royalty; "thy *light's flame*" – Sonnet 1, line 6; "Nativity, once in the main of *light*,/ Crawls to maturity, wherewith being crowned" – Sonnet 60, lines 5-6

5 RETURN, FORGETFUL MUSE, AND STRAIGHT REDEEM
Oxford begs his Muse to give him strength to go on writing; **REDEEM** = echo of Christ as the "Redeemer" of all sins or crimes; "to **ransom**, to purchase back; *to deliver from forfeiture or captivity by paying a price*; to deliver, to set free; to save in any manner; to absolve, to acquit; to atone for, to make compensation or amends for" – Schmidt; echoing Oxford's sacrificial act to "redeem" his royal son from the crime of treason (by **"ransom"**) and gain not only freedom for him but also a royal pardon; "I every day expect an embassage from my *Redeemer*, to *redeem* me hence … But when your carters or your waiting vassals have done a drunken slaughter, and defaced the precious image of our dear *Redeemer*, you straight are on your knees for '*Pardon, pardon!*'" – The King in *Richard III*, 2.1.3-4, 122-125; "Shall our coffers then be emptied *to redeem a traitor* home? Shall we buy *treason* … No, yet time serves wherein you may **redeem your banish'd honours**, and *restore yourselves into the good thoughts of the world again*" – *1 Henry IV*, 1.3.84-86, 178-180; "my honour is at pawn, and, *but my going, nothing can redeem it*" – *2 Henry IV*, 2.2.7-8; "**redeem** your brother *from the angry law*" – *Measure for Measure*, 3.1.200; "Whom he **redeemed from prison**" – *Timon of Athens*, 3.3.5; "O that these hands could so **redeem my son**" – *King John*, 3.3.71; "I'll so offend, to make offence a skill, *redeeming time* when men think least I will" – *1 Henry IV*, 1.2.211-212; "Sir, you have done enough, and have performed a saint-like sorrow: no *fault* could you make which you have not *redeem'd*; indeed, paid down more penitence than done *trespass*" – *The Winter's Tale*, 5.1.1-4

6 IN GENTLE NUMBERS TIME SO IDLY SPENT!
"Had he done so, *himself had borne the crown*, which *waste of idle hours* hath quite thrown down" – *Richard II*, 3.4.65-66

GENTLE NUMBERS = these royal sonnets; "And in *fresh numbers number* all your graces" – Sonnet 17, line 6; "*Eternal numbers* to outlive long date" – Sonnet 38, line 12; "But now my *gracious numbers* are decayed" – Sonnet 79, line 3

> O virtuous fight,
> When right with right wars who shall be most right!
> *True* swains in love shall, in the world to come,
> Approve their *truth* by Troilus; when their rhymes,
> Full of protest, of oath, and big compare,
> Wants similes, truth tir'd with iteration
> (As true as steel, as plantage to *the moon*,
> As sun to day, as *turtle to her mate*,
> As iron to adamant, as earth to th'centre)
> Yet, after all comparisons of truth,
> As *truth's authentic author* to be cited,
> 'As true as Troilus' shall *crown up the verse*
> And sanctify **the numbers**.
> - Troilus and Cressida, 3.3.168-179, published in 1609 (the year the Sonnets were also published); the above passage most certainly is Oxford declaring that his true relationship to and with Elizabeth will be told.

TIME SO IDLY SPENT = the "time so idly spent" is reflected by the slowdown of sonnet composition along the chronological timeline of this dynastic diary; the waste of time; the four uses of "time" in this sonnet reflect Oxford's mounting desperation as he continues the diary that rushes toward Elizabeth's death and the end of hope; the battle with "time", i.e., against the Queen's ever-dwindling life span, is being lost;
IDLY = without occupation or employment; unprofitably, lazily, vainly, carelessly; in Oxford's view, idleness was one of the worst human defects; "and vow to take advantage of all *idle hours*" – dedication of *Lucrece* to Southampton; "That never am less *idle*, lo, than when I am alone" – Oxford poem, *Paradise of Dainty Devices*, 1576; echoing "idol" as in "Let not my love be called *Idolatry,*/ Nor my beloved as an *Idol* show" – Sonnet 105, lines 1-2; "To find out *shames and idle hours in me*" – Sonnet 61, line 8; "Thy gift, thy tables (this book of sonnets), are within my brain,/ Full charactered with lasting memory,/ Which shall *above that idle rank* remain/ Beyond all date even to eternity" – Sonnet 122, lines 1-4

> And the *Imperial Votress (Elizabeth)* passed on,
> In maiden meditation, fancy-free.
> Yet marked I where the bolt of Cupid fell:
> It fell upon a *little western flower (the royal boy to become Southampton)*,
> Before milk-white, now purple with love's wound:
> And maidens call it 'love-in-**idleness**'.
> - A Midsummer Night's Dream, 2.1.163-168

SPENT = as Time (Elizabeth's life) runs out, so does the royal blood of the Sonnets, which are therefore being "spent" as they, too, are nearing their end; "So all my best is dressing old words new,/ *Spending* again what is already *spent*" - Sonnet 76, lines 11-12; "Fair, kind, and true, is all my argument,/ Fair, kind, and true, varying to other words,/ And in this change is my invention *spent*,/ Three themes in one, which wondrous scope affords" - Sonnet 105, lines 9-12

7 SING TO THE EAR THAT DOTH THY LAYS ESTEEM
SING TO THE EAR = write these verses for Southampton's ear; "Like to the Lark at break of day arising/ From sullen earth, *sing hymns at Heaven's gate*" – Sonnet 29, lines 11-12, i.e., sing these verses at Traitor's Gate of Elizabeth's Tower of London; **LAYS** = songs or sonnets; "Since all alike *my songs and praises* be/

To one, of one, still such, and ever so" – Sonnet 105, lines 3-4; **ESTEEM** = to estimate, to value, to prize, rate high, respect; or, at the very least, consider; Southampton considers or reads these sonnets and even lends his esteem to them, i.e., gives them value.

8 AND GIVES THY PEN BOTH SKILL AND ARGUMENT!
THY PEN = the pen of Oxford's Muse, writing these verses; "You still shall live (such vertue hath *my Pen*)" – Sonnet 81, line 13; "So should the lines of life that life repair/ Which this (*Time's pencil or my pupil pen*)" – Sonnet 16, lines 9-10; "How far a modern *quill* doth come too short" – Sonnet 83, line 7; "Lean penury within that *Pen* doth dwell" – Sonnet 84, line 5; "While comments of your praise, richly compiled,/ Reserve their character with *golden quill*" – Sonnet 85, lines 2-3; **SKILL** = ability to write; royal power, which comes from himself: "And you must live, *drawn by your own sweet skill*" – Sonnet 16, line 14; in effect, Oxford is saying that it's not his own power that creates the Sonnets but that of his Muse, which draws upon his royal son for inspiration, guidance and skill; and this reflects Oxford's lifelong habit of deliberately speaking humbly of his personal ability as a writer, as in: "to ensure that neither my goodwill, which is very great, should remain unexpressed, nor that *my skill, which is small*, should seem to fear to face the light and the eyes of men" – Oxford's Letter to the Reader for *The Courtier*, 1573, in which he actually displays enormous skill; he does the same in the public "Shakespeare" dedications to Southampton: "I know not *how I shall offend* in dedicating *my unpolished lines* to your Lordship" – dedication of *Venus and Adonis*, the lines of which are, in fact, highly cultured and polished; "this pamphlet is *but a superfluous moiety*" – dedication of *Lucrece*; in regard to Southampton, of course, Oxford is speaking as devoted subject to a royal prince or king, so this deferential trait is magnified, as in "*Duty so great*, which *wit so poor as mine*/ May make seem bare, in *wanting words to show it*" – Sonnet 26, lines 5-6; **ARGUMENT** = the constant and consistent topic of these sonnets, i.e. Southampton and his royal blood; "And *you and love are still my argument*" – Sonnet 76, line 10; i.e., Southampton gives the pen of Oxford's Muse all its strength, ability and "argument" or subject matter; "Fair, kind, and true, is all *my argument*" – Sonnet 105, line 9; "Now, Somerset, where is *your argument?*" – *1 Henry VI*, 2.4.59

9 RISE, RESTY MUSE! MY LOVE'S SWEET FACE SURVEY
RISE = rise from a state of idleness or rest; echoing the rising of the sun or royal son; echoing acendancy to the throne; echoing the act of "rising" or rebelling; echoing the rising of Christ from the dead; get up for action, to be ready for combat; **RESTY** = sluggish; **MY LOVE'S SWEET FACE** = my royal son's royal face

10 IF TIME HAVE ANY WRINKLES GRAVEN THERE.
TIME = the time recorded in this diary; the waning time of Elizabeth's life; **GRAVEN** = if any signs of age or deterioration have hurried him further toward the grave; toward the end of his hopes for the throne

11 IF ANY, BE A *SATIRE* TO DECAY
SATIRE = (italicized in *Q*); satirist or satiric poem; a "satire" is "a poem in which wickedness or folly is censured" – Schmidt; i.e., Oxford tells his Muse to write such a sonnet in mockery of the decay of Elizabeth's mortal life as represented by Time; **BE A *SATIRE*** = act against; be satirical or full of bitter mockery toward; "For the satirical rogue says here that old men have gray beards" – *Hamlet*, 2.2.196-197; **DECAY** = loss of royalty as well as life; the decay of Elizabeth's mortal life, leading to the end of Time or the date with succession; "The worst was this: *my love was my decay*" – Sonnet 80, line 14, i.e., the ruin of his son's royal blood and decay was his own ruin as the father of a king; "Then the conceit of this inconstant stay/ Sets you most rich in youth before my sight,/ Where wasteful time debateth with *decay*/ To change your day of youth to sullied night" – Sonnet 15, lines 10-12; But now my gracious numbers are *decayed*,/ And my sick Muse doth give an other place" – Sonnet 79, lines 3-4

12 AND MAKE TIME'S SPOILS DESPISED EVERYWHERE.
TIME'S SPOILS = Elizabeth's conquest and destruction of her own son's inheritance; **SPOILS** = acts of plundering or ransacking; ravages, destructions; "fit for treasons, stratagems, and *spoils*" – *The Merchant of Venice*, 5.1.85; **DESPISED** = treated with contempt; "Yet in these thoughts *myself almost despising*" – Sonnet 29, line 9; **EVERYWHERE** = Ever = E. Ver, Edward de Vere, who has come to loath or "despise" the Queen for "despising" or killing her Tudor line, as he expresses it in the Dark Lady series: "Th'expense of spirit (royal blood) in a waste of shame/ … Enjoyed no sooner but *despised* straight" – Sonnet 129, line 5; "In faith I do not love thee with mine eyes,/ For *they in thee a thousand errors note,/* But 'tis my heart that loves *what they despise*" – Sonnet 141, lines 1-3 (Oxford is saying to Elizabeth that in his heart as a devoted subject he still loves and serves her as the monarch, but he despises what he sees, i.e., her actions); "What merit do I in myself respect/ That is so proud *thy service to despise*" – Sonnet 149, lines 9-10, i.e., he despises his own loyal service to the Queen.

13 GIVE MY LOVE FAME FASTER THAN TIME WASTES LIFE,
GIVE MY LOVE FAME = give my royal son eternal life (in these sonnets); "Nor *Mars* his sword nor war's quick fire shall burn/ The living record of your memory./ 'Gainst death and all oblivious enmity/ Shall you pace forth! Your praise shall still find room,/ Even in the eyes of all posterity/ That wear this world out to the ending doom" – Sonnet 55, lines 7-12; "Your name from hence immortal life shall have,/ Though I (once gone) to all the world must die./ The earth can yield me but a common grave,/ When *you entombed in men's eyes* shall lie" – Sonnet 81, lines 5-8; **FAME** = "Death makes no conquest of this conqueror, for *now he lives in fame*, though not in life" – *Richard III*, 3.1.87-88, the prince speaking of Julius Caesar, following a discussion about how Caesar had begun the earliest construction of the Tower of London; **FASTER THAN TIME WASTES LIFE** = faster than the time of this royal diary can lead to utter waste; "And *all in war with Time for love of you,/* As *he takes from you, I engraft you new*" – Sonnet 15, lines 13-14; immediately after the Queen's death in Sonnet 105, the diary of the Sonnets will be "the *Chronicle of wasted time*" in Sonnet 106, line 1, ending the prison series; "*I wasted time, and now doth time waste me*, for now hath *time made me his numb'ring clock*" – the King in *Richard II*, 5.5.49-50; "O Thou my lovely Boy, who in thy power/ Doth *hold time's fickle glass, his sickle hour*" – Sonnet 126, lines 1-2

14 SO THOU PREVENT'ST HIS SCYTHE AND CROOKED KNIFE.
Oxford begs his Muse to prevent *Time's scythe* from destroying his son's royal life; **SCYTHE** = literally, the instrument used to mow grass and corn; "And nothing '*gainst Time's scythe* can make defense" – Sonnet 12, line 13; "No! *Time, thou shalt not boast that I do change/ …I will be true despite thy scythe and thee*" – Sonnet 123, lines 1, 14; "The next time I do fight I'll make Death love me, for I will contend even with*his pestilent scythe*" – Antony in *Antony and Cleopatra*, 3.13.198-199; **CROOKED KNIFE** = an image of Oxford's brother-in-law Robert Cecil, the "crookback" or hunchbacked Secretary of State, along with the "knife" of *Time* (Elizabeth's life and death) that will soon cut off all hope for his son's royal claim; **CROOKED** = "Nativity, once in the main of light,/ Crawls to maturity, wherewith being crowned,/ *Crooked* eclipses 'gainst his glory fight,/ And *time* that gave doth now his gift confound./ *Time* doth transfix the flourish set on youth,/ And delves the parallels in beauty's brow,/ Feeds on the rarities of nature's truth,/ And nothing stands but for *his scythe* to mow" – Sonnet 60, lines 5-12; **KNIFE** = "For such a *time* do I now fortify/ Against confounding Age's cruel *knife*" – Sonnet 63, lines 9-10

No. 100

JAMES OF SCOTLAND ("30")

TO "40" (OXFORD?)

JULY 29, 1602

As King of England, James will bestow honors of Edward de Vere, calling him "Great Oxford" and, after Oxford's death in June 1604, authorize a festival of Shakespeare plays at Court during the 1604-1603 season, ostensibly in celebration of the marriage of Oxford's daughter Susan Vere to Philip Herbert, Earl of Montgomery. In this letter James assures "40" (possibly Oxford) that he will use all "honesty, secrecy and constancy" in his dealings with him through Robert Cecil:

"Trusty and well-beloved cousin,

"Although your readiness and favorable furtherance to any suitors recommended by me, in anything concerning your office ever since your entry thereunto, did long ere now sufficiently persuade me of your honest and lawful affection to my service, yet having lately the assurance thereof confirmed, both by the faithful testimony of 10 [Cecil], as likewise by your own words uttered in enigma to my servant Ashton, I would not omit to send you these few lines of my own hand, as witness of my thankfulness.

"And as by my letter to you and 10 [Cecil] conjunctly ye are already certified of my honest and upright course with your sovereign (Elizabeth), and that I am no ways to employ you beyond the bounds of your allegiance, so have I for the present no other recompense to send you for your goodwill but my faithful promise that all my dealing with you shall ever be accompanied with these qualities: *honesty, secrecy, and constancy.*

"But as *I will deal with you by no other way but by the means of 10* [Cecil], so may ye assure yourself that *your straight and steadfast conjunction with him* in my service is the only way to enable you both therein, and to disappoint all my malicious and underserved adversaries. And thus, trusty and well-beloved cousin, I bid you heartily farewell. From Falkland the xxix July 1602 - Your loving friend, 30."

- Akrigg, *Letters of King James*, pp 194-195 (Cecil Papers 135:101)

THE MONUMENT

THE PRISON YEARS

YEAR TWO IN THE TOWER
CALLING UPON THE MUSE

Sonnet 101
Excuse Not Silence
September-October 1602

By now it is clear that Elizabeth will not live much longer. As the "time" of her life and reign becomes increasingly shorter, Oxford's capacity to write in this diary grows. The Queen's death will mean the end of all hope for Truth and Beauty, i.e., for Oxford and Elizabeth as parents of a king. Both depend on Oxford's royal son, Southampton ("Both truth and beauty on my love depends"), but there is no more hope for a happy outcome -- except by means of this monument of the Sonnets, aimed at posterity.

Sonnet 101	Translation
Oh truant Muse, what shall be thy amends	Oh, delinquent Muse, how will you make up
For thy neglect of truth in beauty dyed?	For your neglect of Oxford and Elizabeth?
Both truth and beauty on my love depends:	Both Oxford and Elizabeth depend on my royal son!
So dost thou too, and therein dignified.	So do you! And by this you are given power.
Make answer, Muse, wilt thou not haply say,	Answer me, Muse! Will you not testify that
Truth needs no colour with his colour fixed,	My truth needs no heraldry since my son is eternal,
Beauty no pencil, beauty's truth to lay:	Elizabeth needs no public admission of this truth,
But best is best, if never intermixed?	But truth is truth, even if never admitted?
Because he needs no praise, wilt thou be dumb?	Since our son can't be spoken of, are you silent?
Excuse not silence so, for it lies in thee	Don't' make our silence your excuse! You can
To make him much out-live a gilded tomb,	Make our son live eternally in these sonnets,
And to be praised of ages yet to be.	And make him king in the eyes of ages to come.
Then do thy office, Muse, I teach thee how	So do your duty, Muse! I'll show you how
To make him seem long hence, as he shows now.	To make him royal in the future, as he is now.

The Council to the Tower, October 11, 1601: *"Whereas her Majesty is informed that the Earl of Southampton is of late grown very sickly, in the which respect her Highness is pleased that for his comfort the Countess his wife shall be permitted to have access unto him."* - Stopes, 246

1 OH, TRUANT MUSE, WHAT SHALL BE THY AMENDS
Oxford asks how his Muse can make up for the lost time; **AMENDS** = compensation, atonement; echoing "amen" as in prayer; "what reparation will you make; what payment will you give in satisfaction of your offense; how will you recover from your lapse" – Booth; "Pardon me, Edward, *I will make amends*: and Richard, do not frown upon my *faults*" – *3 Henry VI*, 5.1.103-104

Part Two

2 FOR THY NEGLECT OF TRUTH IN BEAUTY DYED?
THY NEGLECT OF TRUTH = your neglect of Southampton's "true rights" as in Sonnet 17, line 11; i.e., the Muse's neglect of Oxford's blood in his son, which is mingled with "beauty" or blood from Elizabeth; **TRUTH** = Oxford, *Nothing Truer than Truth*; **TRUTH IN BEAUTY** = the truth of Southampton's royal blood from Elizabeth; **DYED** = (Q has "di'd"); again a play on "died"; distilled; "truth which is an integral part of the beauty it inhabits" – Duncan-Jones; "Here in my scabbard, meditating that shall *dye your white rose in a bloody red*" – *1 Henry VI*, 60-61

3 BOTH TRUTH AND BEAUTY ON MY LOVE DEPENDS:
Both Oxford and Elizabeth depend on the royal son, i.e., depend on Southampton for any hope of survival by blood after the Queen's death; echoing Truth and Beauty of *The Phoenix and the Turtle*; "Thy end is *Truth's and Beauty's doom and date*" – Sonnet 14, line 14; **MY LOVE** = my beloved royal son, Southampton; "*My love* looks fresh" – Sonnet 107, line 10, referring to his son upon being released from the Tower on April 10, 1603; "my dear love" – Sonnet 124, line 1; "my lovely Boy" – Sonnet 126, line 1; as a father speaking of his son, emphasizing the personal "my" as in "Even so *my* Sunne one early morn did shine,/ With all triumphant splendor on *my* brow,/ But out alack, he was but one hour *mine*,/ The region cloud hath masked him from *me* now" – Sonnet 33, lines 9-12; **DEPENDS** = "are subordinate to; wait in expectation upon" – *OED*; the combination of Oxford and Elizabeth is a singular couple, which "depends" on his "love" or royal blood that combines both Oxford's truth and Elizabeth's beauty.

4 SO DOST THOU TOO, AND THEREIN DIGNIFIED.
Oxford's Muse also depends upon "love" – the royal blood of Southampton, containing the blood of Truth (Oxford) and Beauty (Elizabeth), his natural parents. This "love" is what gives the Muse her dignity; **DIGNIFIED** = given high office; invested with high honor; exalted; given luster and worth, i.e., the blood of both Oxford and Elizabeth is elevated by their son's "love" or royal blood to the height of kingship; "*dignified* with the great office of Lord High Treasurer" – *OED*, from 1660; suggesting the Muse shares in the honor and royalty of Southampton; "But he that writes of you, if he can tell/ That you are you, so *dignifies* his story" – Sonnet 84, lines 7-8; "The basest weed outlives his *dignity*" – Sonnet 94, line 12; "The *dignity* of this act was *worth the audience of kings and princes*" – *The Winter's Tale*, 5.2.81-82; "Then, good my lord, *take to your royal self this proffer'd benefit of dignity*" – to the King in *Richard III*, 3.7.194-195; "Unto the *dignity and height* of fortune, the high imperial type of this earth's glory!" – *Richard III*, 4.4.244-245

5 MAKE ANSWER, MUSE! WILT THOU NOT HAPLY SAY,
Oxford commanding his Muse to work; **HAPLY** = perhaps; suggesting happily; "*Haply* I think on thee" – Sonnet 29, line 10

6 "TRUTH NEEDS NO COLOUR, WITH HIS COLOUR FIXED,
TRUTH = Oxford; the truth of Southampton; **TRUTH NEEDS NO COLOUR** = the truth of Southampton's royal blood, which contains Oxford's blood, needs no pretext, reason or exaggeration; **COLOUR** = pretext or pretense; also semblance or character or appearance; **WITH HIS COLOUR FIXED** = with his purple-royal color fixed for all time; **FIXED** = painted onto the canvas of his face, which reflects his mother the Queen

> The *colour of the king* doth come and go
> Between his purpose and his conscience,
> Like heralds 'twixt two dreadful battles set
> - *King John*, 4.2.76-78

> Even as *the sun with purple-coloured face*
> Had ta'en his last leave of the weeping morn – *Venus and Adonis*, lines 1-2

REFERENCE EDITION

Colours are battle-flags, ensigns, standards and banners of a king (or carriers of such):

"Enter Fortinbras ... and *soldiers with drums and colours*" - *Hamlet*, 5.2.stage direction

The red rose and the white are on his face,
The fatal *colours* of our striving houses:
The one his *purple blood right* well resembles;
The other his pale cheeks, methinks, presenteth
- *3 Henry VI*, 2.5.97-100

For of no right, *nor colour like to right*,
He doth fill fields with harness in the realm
- *1 Henry IV*, 3.2.100-101

A crown of bays shall that man wear
That triumphs over me:
For black and tawny will I wear,
Which *mourning colors be*.
- Oxford poem, *Paradise of Dainty Devices*, 1576

7 BEAUTY NO PENCIL, BEAUTY'S TRUTH TO LAY,

BEAUTY NO PENCIL = his royal blood from Elizabeth needs no artist's brush; "Which this, *Time's pencil or my pupil pen*" – Sonnet 16, line 10; **BEAUTY'S TRUTH TO LAY** = in order to lay on its colors; **BEAUTY'S TRUTH** = the truth of his blood from the Queen, related to Oxford as *Nothing Truer than Truth* and as his father; **LAY** = apply or spread or "lay" colors upon the canvas; also a "lay" is a song, alluding to these sonnets as "little songs"; "Yet nor *the lays of birds*, nor the sweet smell/ Of different flowers in odor and in hew" – Sonnet 98, lines 5-6; "Sing to the ear that doth *thy lays* esteem" – Sonnet 100, line 7; "Our love was new, and then but in the spring,/ When I was wont *to greet it with my lays,*/ As Philomel *in summer's front doth sing*" – Sonnet 102, lines 5-7; "Let *the bird of loudest lay*/ On the sole Arabian tree/ Herald sad and trumpet be" – *The Phoenix and Turtle*, 1601, lines 1-3; also echoing "Cupid *laid by his brand* and fell asleep" – Sonnet 153, line 1, and "The little Love-God lying once asleep/ *Laid by his side his heart-inflaming brand*" – Sonnet 154, lines 1-2

8 BUT BEST IS BEST, IF NEVER INTERMIXED"?

BEST IS BEST = most royal is most royal; same as "truth is truth" = "for *truth is truth* though never so old, and time cannot make that false which was once true" – Oxford to Robert Cecil, May 7, 1603; "Nay, it is ten times true, for *truth is truth* to the end of reckoning" – *Measure for Measure*, 5.1.48-49; "truth is truth" is used four other times in the Shakespeare works; "my kingdom, well worthy *the best heir o'th'world*" – *Henry VIII*, 2.4.194; "O then *my best blood* turn to an infected jelly, and my name be yok'd with his that did betray *the Best!*" – *The Winter's Tale*, 1.2.418-419, referring to the Redeemer; "Look *what is best, that best* I wish in thee" – Sonnet 37, line 13; "So *all my best* is dressing old words new" – Sonnet 76, line 11; "All these I *better in one general best*" – Sonnet 91, line 8, referring to Southampton; "Then in the blazon of *sweet beauty's best*" – Sonnet 106, line 5; "Creating every bad *a perfect best*" – Sonnet 114, line 7; "Best of my flesh" – *Coriolanus*, 5.3.42; "Most worthy comfort, now my greatest grief,/ Thou *best of dearest, and mine only care*" – Sonnet 48, lines 6-7; "now *I love you best*" – Sonnet 115, line 10; **NEVER** = Oxford, *Ever or Never*

9 BECAUSE HE NEEDS NO PRAISE, WILT THOU BE DUMB?

Just because Southampton needs no praise for his royal blood to exist, will you not speak so that I can keep writing to preserve his blood in these sonnets? **DUMB** = silent; "For who's *so dumb that cannot write to* *thee*" – Sonnet 38, line 7

10 EXCUSE NOT SILENCE SO, FOR'T LIES IN THEE
EXCUSE NOT SILENCE SO = do not plead your case this way; do not justify your silence in this way; "Clarence, *excuse* me to the King my brother" – *3 Henry VI*, 5.5.45, i.e., account for my absence; "The rest is silence" – *Hamlet*, 5.2.365; **IT LIES IN THEE** = it is in your power; also echoing that the truth must "lie" or be false

11 TO MAKE HIM MUCH OUTLIVE A GILDED TOMB
To give him immortality; the ultimate goal of the Sonnets is to create a Monument preserving Southampton's royal blood for eternity; these verses will outlast any "gilded monument of Princes" as in Sonnet 55, line 1: "*Not marble nor the gilded monument/ Of Princes* shall outlive this powerful rhyme,/ But you shall shine more bright in these contents/ Than unswept stone, besmeared with sluttish time" – Sonnet 55, lines 1-4; "A crown, or else a glorious tomb!" – *3 Henry VI*, 1.4.16; "When you *entombed in men's eyes* shall lie" – Sonnet 81, line 8, followed by: "Your monument shall be my gentle verse (i.e., as opposed to the normal kind of monument for a king)/ Which eyes not yet created shall o'er-read" – Sonnet 81, lines 9-10; "And thou *in this* (i.e., in the Sonnets) shalt find thy monument,/ *When tyrants' crests and tombs of brass are spent*" – Sonnet 107, lines 13-14

12 AND TO BE PRAISED OF AGES YET TO BE.
And to live in the eyes of all posterity; "Your monument shall be my gentle verse,/ Which eyes not created shall o'er-read,/ *And tongues to be your being shall rehearse,*/ When all the breathers of this world are dead" – Sonnet 81, lines 9-12

13 THEN DO THY OFFICE, MUSE! I TEACH THEE HOW
THY OFFICE = your duty, as servant to a king, i.e., to Southampton, but also as the Muse's duty to Oxford to continue to inspire him; "That whereas I found sundry abuses, whereby both Her Majesty, and myself, were in *mine office* greatly hindered, that it would please your Lordship that I might find such favor from you that I might have the same redressed" – Oxford to Burghley, July 7, 1594, probably referring to his office as Lord Great Chamberlain of England, although some have suggested he may have held an unofficial office related to his patronage of writers and to his own writings for the stage (especially the chronicle history plays), as part of the Government's effort to maintain political and religious unity while under the continuing Spanish threat.

14 TO MAKE HIM SEEM LONG HENCE AS HE SHOWS NOW.
To recreate my royal son's life and keep him alive for the future, for eternity; "Nor shall death brag thou wand'rest in his shade,/ When *in eternal lines to time thou grow'st;*/ So long as men can breathe or eyes can see,/ *So long lives this, and this gives life to thee*" – Sonnet 18, lines 11-14; "Nor *Mars* his sword, nor war's quick fire shall burn/ *The living record* of your memory" – Sonnet 55, lines 7-8; **MAKE HIM SEEM LONG HENCE** = make him appear to future readers exactly as he really is now, as the rightful claimant to the throne; **HENCE** = from this time forward; later; after this present time; henceforth; in the future; also echoing "in the next world"; not here, at a distance: "By praising him here who doth *hence remain*" – Sonnet 39, line 14, referring to Southampton being in the Tower; **AS HE SHOWS** = as he demonstrates; **NOW** = emphasizing the real time being recorded in this diary, i.e., *now* in September-October 1602

THE PRISON YEARS

YEAR TWO IN THE TOWER
APOLOGY FOR THE LAPSE

Sonnet 102
I Sometime Hold My Tongue
November-December 1602

As Elizabeth's reign approaches its end, the golden time of Southampton's royal life is over. Now it is literally winter in England, but the reality of his "summer" still exists – at least in Oxford's mind, and in these private sonnets, while he continues to "hold my tongue" in public. Oxford's phrase "sweets grown common" refers to Southampton as the commoner "Mr. Henry Wriothseley" in disgrace and imprisonment.

Sonnet 102	Translation
My love is strengthened, though more weak in seeming;	My royal son gains in power, as he seems less royal;
I love not less, though less the show appear.	I don't love him less, but it appears that way!
That love is merchandised, whose rich esteeming	His royalty is now a bargaining chip. His worth
The owner's tongue doth publish everywhere.	Is told by me in works by "Shakespeare."
Our love was new, and then but in the spring,	Our royal son was newborn, but then, very early,
When I was wont to greet it with my lays,	When I wanted to accept him with my words,
As *Philomel* in summer's front doth sing,	The nightingale introduced his royal summer
And stops his pipe in growth of riper days:	Only to stop singing as he grew in royal hope.
Not that the summer is less pleasant now	Not that the summer of his life is less royal now
Than when her mournful hymns did hush the night,	Than when the nightingale sang to him,
But that wild music burthens every bough,	But royal birds sing of him from every bough,
And sweets grown common lose their dear delight.	And blood growing common loses royal hope.
Therefore like her, I sometime hold my tongue:	So, like the nightingale, I cannot speak of you:
Because I would not dull you with my song.	Because I won't diminish you with verse.

1 MY LOVE IS STRENGTHENED, THOUGH MORE WEAK IN SEEMING!
MY LOVE = my royal son; my love for him; "The little Love-God" – Sonnet 154, line 1; "Lord of my love" – Sonnet 26, line 1; "O Thou my lovely Boy" – Sonnet 126, line 1; **SEEMING** = in appearance; "I am not as I *seem* to be,/ For when I smile I am not glad" – Oxford poem, in *Paradise of Dainty Devices*, 1576, signed E. O.

2 I LOVE NOT LESS, THOUGH LESS THE SHOW APPEAR.
I love him no less, though I write with less power about him, because Elizabeth's life and reign, as well as this diary, are nearing their end.

3 THAT LOVE IS MERCHANDIZED WHOSE RICH ESTEEMING
THAT LOVE = that royal blood of my son; **MERCHANDIZED** = made cheap or sold by others; ("reduced to the value of a saleable commodity" – Duncan-Jones); in fact, Oxford has had to "pay" by sacrificing his identity to "buy" Southampton's freedom; "Beauty is bought by judgment of the eye, not uttered by *base sale* of chapmen's tongues" – *Love's Labour's Lost*, 2.1.15-16; **RICH** = royal; **ESTEEMING** = his royal estimation or value that cannot be bought or sold

4 THE OWNER'S TONGUE DOTH PUBLISH EVERYWHERE.
THE OWNER'S = Southampton is the true owner of the Sonnets, but Oxford is referring here to the pen name "William Shakespeare," which gets to "publish" its praise of Southampton; **TONGUE** = voice or manner of speaking; language; "And art made *tongue*-tied by authority" – Sonnet 66, line 9; **DOTH PUBLISH EVERYWHERE** = published as by "Shakespeare"; not only *Venus and Adonis* of 1593 and *Lucrece* of 1594, but also *The Phoenix and the Turtle* of 1601 and several plays, which have appeared in quarto form beginning in 1598, as by "William Shake-speare"; **EVERYWHERE** = Ever = E. Ver, Edward de Vere, *Ever or Never*, who actually writes for the published pseudonym

5 OUR LOVE WAS NEW, AND THEN BUT IN THE SPRING,
OUR LOVE = our father-son bond; your royal blood, which was therefore mine; **NEW** = golden, fresh, green, after your birth; i.e., this love was once new and hopeful, but not now; **SPRING** = "Ver" (French) = your youthful days; "This side is *Hiems*, Winter, this is *Ver*, the Spring: the one maintained by the owl, the other by the cuckoo. *Ver*, begin" – introducing the final songs of *Love's Labour's Lost*, 5.2.884-886; this "love" or royal blood was new, but that was in the spring of royal hope; that time was back in our past: "*In the old age* black was not counted fair,/ Or if it were it bore not beauty's name:/ But *now* is black beauty's successive heir,/ And Beauty slandered with a bastard shame" – Sonnet 127, lines 1-4

6 WHEN I WAS WONT TO GREET IT WITH MY LAYS,
I WAS WONT TO = I was accustomed to; **MY LAYS** = my songs, i.e., my sonnets

7 AS *PHILOMEL* IN SUMMER'S FRONT DOTH SING
PHILOMEL = nightingale; (*Q* has *Philomell*, italicized); Philomela in Book Six of Ovid's *Metamorphoses* has her tongue cut out by a sword and is raped, as Lavinia is so abused in *Titus Andronicus*, a play in which the Ovid book appears on stage; no doubt Oxford's reference to "tongue" in line 4 above is related to this classical story; the story also echoes "And art made tongue-tied by authority" – Sonnet 66, line 9; **SUMMER'S FRONT** = beginning of summer or the royal time

8 AND STOPS HIS PIPE IN GROWTH OF RIPER DAYS:
STOPS HIS PIPE IN GROWTH = ordinarily it is "her" pipe, i.e., the female nightingale's (see lines 10 and 13), but Oxford is also referring to "its" growth as well as literally to "his" or Southampton's growth, which is occurring within these songs or sonnets; "Will you *play upon this pipe*? ...You would play upon me; you would seem to know my stops; you would pluck out the heart of my mystery; you would sound me from my lowest note to the top of my compass; and there is much music, excellent voice, in this little organ ... you cannot play upon me" – *Hamlet*, 3.2.354; 367-374; **RIPER DAYS** = more royal days of the golden time; "But as the riper should by time decease,/ His tender heir might bear his memory" – Sonnet 1, lines 3-4

9 NOT THAT THE SUMMER IS LESS PLEASANT NOW
SUMMER = the substance of royal blood that lives within Southampton; (referring to the "golden time" of Sonnet 3 and the royal day as in "Shall I compare thee to a Summer's day" of Sonnet 18, line 1

10 THAN WHEN HER MOURNFUL HYMNS DID HUSH THE NIGHT,
MOURNFUL HYMNS = relating the songs or sonnets of this diary to hymns or prayers to a god on earth; "From sullen earth, *sings hymns at Heaven's gate*" – Sonnet 29, line 12; also related to the "mourning" of both Elizabeth and Oxford over the fate of the Tudor Rose lineage; "Therefore my Mistress' eyes are Raven black,/ Her eyes so suited, and they *mourners* seem/ ... Yet so they *mourn* becoming of their woe,/ That *every tongue* says beauty should look so" – Sonnet 127, lines 9-10, 13-14; now the mourning is not only for Southampton and his withering royal claim, but also for the Queen, whose approaching death is bringing the Time of the Sonnets to a close; **NIGHT** = "Which like a jewel hung in *ghastly night*/ Makes black night beauteous, and her old face new./ Lo thus by day my limbs, by *night* my mind,/ For thee, and for my self, no quiet find" – Sonnet 27, lines 11-14

11 BUT THAT WILD MUSIC BURTHENS EVERY BOUGH
BURTHENS = burdens, weighs down; "Which, lab'ring for invention, bear amiss/ The second *burthen* of a former child" – Sonnet 59, lines 3-4; **EVERY BOUGH** = Ever = E. Ver, Edward de Vere; "Upon those *boughs* which shake against the cold,/ Bare ruined choirs, where late the sweet birds sang" – Sonnet 73, lines 3-4, related to the funeral dirge of *The Phoenix and the Turtle*, i.e., Elizabeth and Oxford, who are "these dead birds" in the poem's final line; **BOUGH** = the boughs of the royal tree; also suggests bowing to Southampton as the king

12 AND SWEETS GROWN COMMON LOSE THEIR DEAR DELIGHT.
SWEETS GROWN COMMON = princes become commoners; Southampton, in prison, reduced to commoner status; **DEAR** = royal, in reference to him as a dear son; "If my *dear love* were but the child of state,/ It might for fortune's bastard be un-fathered" – Sonnet 124, lines 1-2

13 THEREFORE, LIKE HER, I SOME-TIME HOLD MY TONGUE:
THEREFORE, etc. = Oxford notes that he has written fewer sonnets this year; **LIKE HER =** like the nightingale; **SOME-TIME** = "for some time" – Duncan-Jones; **HOLD MY TONGUE** = echoing his need to remain publicly silent; "And art made *tongue-tied by authority*" – Sonnet 66, line 9; "To make me *tongue-tied* speaking of your fame" – Sonnet 80, line 4; "My *tongue-tied* Muse in manners *holds her still*" – Sonnet 85, line 1; "But break, my heart, for I must *hold my tongue*" - the Prince in *Hamlet*, 1.2.159

14 BECAUSE I WOULD NOT DULL YOU WITH MY SONG.
DULL YOU = diminish your bright royalty; "and do not kill/ The spirit of love with a perpetual *dullness*" - Sonnet 56, lines 7-8; "And thou away, the very birds are mute./ Or if they sing, 'tis with so *dull* a cheer/ That leaves look pale, dreading the Winter's near" - Sonnet 97, lines 12-14; "*Dulling* my lines" - Sonnet 103, line 8; **MY SONG** = my sonnets, which are little songs

Part Two

THE PRISON YEARS

YEAR TWO IN THE TOWER
ELIZABETH IS NEAR THE END
APOLOGY FOR THE LAPSE

Sonnet 103
The Argument All Bare
January 1603

As Elizabeth's days draw to a close, with Southampton still in the Tower and without hope of succeeding her, Oxford can barely continue writing. The "argument" or topic, which is his son's life and royal blood, is now "all bare" – except that it lives within Southampton himself. Here again Oxford confirms that Henry Wriothesley is the sole reason for the sonnets: "For to no other pass my verses tend / Than of your graces and your gifts to tell."

Sonnet 103	Translation
Alack what poverty my Muse brings forth,	Alas, what lack of royal hope my Muse inspires –
That having such a scope to show her pride,	In that it has such royal blood to write about,
The argument all bare is of more worth	And that this topic, even in disgrace, is more royal
Than when it hath my added praise beside.	Than even when my sonnets try to add to it!
Oh blame me not if I no more can write!	O don't blame me if I can no longer write!
Look in your glass and there appears a face	Look in your mirror and see your royal presence
That over-goes my blunt invention quite,	That transcends my invention for these sonnets,
Dulling my lines, and doing me disgrace.	Emptying its lines of your royalty to my disgrace.
Were it not sinful then, striving to mend,	Isn't it even worse for me to try to fix things,
To mar the subject that before was well?	When I only succeed in disgracing you further?
For to no other pass my verses tend,	Because my sonnets have no other purpose
Than of your graces and your gifts to tell.	Than to contain your royal blood in their lines.
And more, much more than in my verses can sit,	And more of you can sit on the throne than here,
Your own glass shows you, when you look in it.	Which your mirror shows when you look in it.

1 ALACK, WHAT POVERTY MY MUSE BRINGS FORTH,
ALACK = recalling "But *out alack, he was but one hour mine,*/ The region cloud hath masked him from me now" – Sonnet 33, lines 11-12; **POVERTY** = lack of royalty and hope; **BRINGS FORTH** = issues, recreates in the womb of these sonnets; The metaphor "is of giving birth" – Booth, adding that "the metaphor of pregnancy and childbirth is faintly sustained" in the next two lines.

2 THAT, HAVING SUCH A SCOPE TO SHOW HER PRIDE,
SCOPE = greatness of subject matter; the "wondrous scope" to come soon in Sonnet 105, line 12: "Three themes in one, which wondrous scope affords"; the scope of kingship; the "scope of justice" as used in: "Now, good my lord, give me the scope of justice" – *Measure for Measure*, 5.1.233;

REFERENCE EDITION

SHOW HER PRIDE = display the royal blood that inspires her, i.e., Oxford's Muse; ("Display her offspring" – one meaning suggested by Booth); "Why is my verse so *barren of new pride*?" – Sonnet 76, line 1; "The madams too, not us'd to toil, did almost sweat to bear the pride upon them" – *Henry VIII*, 1.1.23-25

3 THE ARGUMENT ALL BARE IS OF MORE WORTH
ARGUMENT = the topic of the Sonnets, which is Southampton and his "love" or royal blood; "And you and love are still *my argument*" – Sonnet 76, line 10; also Sonnet 105, line 9: "Fair, kind, and true, is all *my argument*"; **ALL** = Southampton; **ALL BARE** = completely barren; echoing "bear" as in child-bearing; **MORE WORTH** = more royalty; **WORTH** = a word derived from the letters in the name "Wriothesley"; i.e., even with this emptiness of new royal blood in my sonnets, their topic or "argument" is of more "worth" or royalty in my son.

4 THAN WHEN IT HATH MY ADDED PRAISE BESIDE.
Than when it has my additional praise for him.

5 OH BLAME ME NOT IF I NO MORE CAN WRITE!
Now speaking to Southampton: "Don't blame me for being unable to write any longer"; **BLAME** = echoing the blame for the Rebellion

6 LOOK IN YOUR GLASS AND THERE APPEARS A FACE
YOUR GLASS = your mirror or hourglass, showing you as a reflection of Elizabeth; that is the reality of you; "Thou art thy mother's glass" – Sonnet 3, line 9; "Thy glass will show thee how thy beauties wear" – Sonnet 77, line 1; echoing the "face-royal," a kingly visage, and the visage stamped on the coin called a "royal"; "So love's face/ May still seem love to me, though altered new" – Sonnet 93, lines 2-3, i.e., so the royal blood reflected in my son's face may always appear to be royal to me, even though his claim to the throne has been newly altered; "the outward face of royalty" – *The Tempest*, 1.2.104; "You taught me how to know the face of right" – *King John*, 5.2.88; "What cunning can express/ The *favor of her face/ ... Heaven pictured in her face/* Doth promise joy and grace/ ... With this there is a red,/ Exceeds the damask rose,/ Which *in her cheeks* is spread/ ... When Phoebus from the bed/ Of Thetis doth arise,/ The morning blushing red,/ In fair carnation wise,/ He *shows it in her face/* As Queen of every grace" – Oxford poem in *The Phoenix Nest*, 1593, signed E. O., probably written in the 1570s, of Elizabeth; "But who can leave to look on *Venus' face*?" – Oxford poem in *Paradise of Dainty Devices*, 1576, also of Elizabeth, signed E. O. in the 1577 edition onward

7 THAT OVER-GOES MY BLUNT INVENTION QUITE,
That surpasses my dull invention for the Sonnets; **MY BLUNT INVENTION** = the ingenious special language and design created for the Sonnets, with the words actually equaling their "subject" (Southampton) as in line 10 below; "And keep *invention* in a noted weed" – Sonnet 76, line 6; "Fair, kind, and true, varying to other words,/ And in this change is my *invention* spent" – Sonnet 105, lines 9-10; the invention is now "blunt" or dull because the Time of Elizabeth's life (and of this diary) is rapidly running out; "blunt" also suggests "direct" or "frank" as in "A good blunt fellow" – *King John*, 1.1.71; and, too, "blunt" suggests that these sonnets in manuscript are still in a state of roughness (as in "the blunt boar, rough bear, or lion proud" of *Venus and Adonis*, 884).

8 DULLING MY LINES AND DOING ME DISGRACE.
DULLING = blunting, as in line 7 above; Southampton's loss of royal claim is what dulls these lines; **MY LINES** = "So should the *lines of life* that life repair/ Which this (Time's pencil or my pupil pen),/ Neither in inward worth nor outward fair/ Can make you live yourself in eyes of men" – Sonnet 16, lines 9-12; "When *in eternal lines to time* thou grow'st" – Sonnet 18, line 12; "His beauty (blood from Elizabeth) shall *in these*

black lines be seen,/ And he shall live, and he in them still green" – Sonnet 63, lines 13-14; "My life hath *in this line* some interest" – Sonnet 74, line 3; "But when your (Southampton's) countenance filled up *his* (Shakespeare's) *line*,/ Then lacked I matter, that enfeebled *mine*" – Sonnet 86, lines 13-14; **DOING ME DISGRACE** = recording your disgrace (of treason) that I have taken upon myself on your behalf, to gain your freedom and restoration of honor

9 WERE IT NOT SINFUL THEN, STRIVING TO MEND,

MEND = "to repair from breach or decay; to make better or improve; to set right, to correct, to repair what is amiss" – Schmidt; "Which, laboring for invention, bear amiss/ The second burthen of a former child" – Sonnet 59, lines 3-4; is it not a crime, then, while striving to improve these sonnets (or striving to make amends for you)

10 TO MAR THE SUBJECT THAT BEFORE WAS WELL?

Only to disgrace Southampton ("the subject"), who was already royal?; **MAR** = injure, hurt, spoil, ruin; recalling the made-up name "Martin Marprelate," suggesting a writer intending to "mar" the "prelates"; "*Mar* not the thing that cannot be amended" – *Lucrece*, 578; "Here is himself, *marr'd*, as you see, with traitors" – *Julius Caesar*, 3.2.198; **WELL** = royal; in a good state; in good health; "Ver" = spring = well or fountain; well = exceedingly, much, greatly; "our ever-living poet wisheth the *well*-wishing adventurer in setting forth" – Dedication of the Sonnets, 1609

11 FOR TO NO OTHER PASS MY VERSES TEND

Because my sonnets have no other purpose; **MY VERSES** = these verses; **TEND** = aim at, but also "attend" as in attending the prince or king

12 THAN OF YOUR GRACES AND YOUR GIFTS TO TELL.

… than to record your royal blood and grace; **YOUR GRACES** = your royal qualities and grace; "Above the rest in Court who gave thee *grace*?" – Oxford's early sonnet, circa 1572, of Queen Elizabeth; **YOUR GIFTS** = your blood inheritance, your gift of life and royalty; "eminence, wealth, sovereignty; which is to say sooth, are blessings; and which *gifts*" – *Henry VIII*, 2.3.30; "So *thy great gift*, upon misprision growing" – Sonnet 87, line 11

13 AND MORE, MUCH MORE THAN IN MY VERSE CAN SIT,

MY VERSE = (echoing "my verses" from line 11); these verses of the Sonnets; "Who will believe *my verse* in time to come" – Sonnet 17, line 1; "Why is *my verse* so barren of new pride?" – Sonnet 76, line 1; "Therefore *my verse* to constancy confined" – Sonnet 105, line 7

SIT = sit on the throne; ("be enthroned" – Duncan-Jones); "A thousand flatterers *sit* within thy crown" – *Richard II*, 1.1.100; "Long may'st thou live in Richard's *seat* to *sit*" – *Richard II*, 4.1.218; "Methought I *sat in seat* of majesty" – *2 Henry VI*, 1.2.36; "O majesty! When thou dost pinch thy bearer, thou dost *sit* like a rich armour worn in heat of day" – *2 Henry IV*, 4.5.27-29; "Think'st thou that I will leave my *kingly throne*, wherein my grandsire and my father *sat*?" – *3 Henry VI*, 1.1.128-129; "And o'er *the chair of state*, where now he **sits**" – *3 Henry VI*, 1.1.172; "Once more **we sit in** England's royal throne" – *3 Henry VI*, 5.7.1; "The throne he sits on" – *Henry V*, 4.1.260; "Where he **sits crowned**" – *Twelfth Night*, 5.1.125; "Fair, kind, and true, have often lived alone,/ Which three, till now, never kept *seat* in one" – Sonnet 105, lines 13-14

14 YOUR OWN GLASS SHOWS YOU WHEN YOU LOOK IN IT.

GLASS = (repeated from line 6); your own image demonstrates to you that you are royal; "Thou art *thy mother's glass*" – Sonnet 3, line 9, i.e., Southampton as the reflection of his mother Elizabeth; also, Southampton's hourglass, now running almost completely out of *time* (as measured by Elizabeth's life), which is the basis for this diary in the first place; feeling the power of his sonnets being weakened by the death of his royal subject matter, Oxford advises his son to look at his own face to find "much, much more" of his truth and reality; however, the Sonnets also act as the glass of his truth: "Thy glass will show thee how thy beauties wear,/ Thy dial how thy precious minutes waste;/ The vacant leaves thy mind's imprint will bear,/ And of this book this learning mayst thou taste" – Sonnet 77. lines 1-4

January 1603

Queen Elizabeth Comments on the Succession: On her final journey from Whitehall to Richmond this month, Elizabeth reputedly told Lord Admiral Howard:

"*I told you **my seat** has been **the seat of kings**, and I will have **no rascal to succeed me**; and who should succeed me but a king?*"

Was there a specific *"rascal"* to whom she referred? Might the Queen have been speaking of Southampton, a convicted traitor in the Tower?

"But what talk we of these *traitorly rascals*, whose miseries are to be smiled at, their offences being so capital?" – *The Winter's Tale*, 4.4.794-795

"*By itself this [Elizabeth's statement] has the hallmark of truth, but it would have been impossible for her to have continued, as the narrative of their conversation has it, by asking a further question, 'Who but our cousin of Scotland?' She had deliberately refused to name her successor for forty-four years and she was too determined a character, even though under the shadow of death, to make a mockery now of one of her few consistencies by breaking her silence.*"
- Neville Williams, "The Life & Times of Elizabeth I"

Part Two

THE PRISON YEARS

SECOND ANNIVERSARY
OF THE REBELLION
THE QUEEN IS NEAR DEATH

Sonnet 104
Three Winters Cold
8 February 1603

Oxford marks the second anniversary of the Rebellion and Southampton's imprisonment. Although only two full years have elapsed since Southampton was arrested and imprisoned, "three winters" have transpired – the first winter of 1600-1601, the second winter of 1601-1602, and the present winter of 1602-1603. Before these three winters, Henry Wriothesley had been "the world's fresh ornament" as announced in Sonnet 1 and all during "thy golden time" of Sonnet 3; but that period ended in the year 1600, marked by Sonnet 26. Now the Queen is virtually on her deathbed; her death on March 24, 1603, will be marked in the very next sonnet.

Sonnet 104	Translation
To me, fair friend, you never can be old,	To me, royal son, your claim can never die,
For as you were when first your eye I eyed,	Because you're the same as when born!
Such seems your beauty still: Three Winters cold	Such seems your blood always: Three winters
Have from the forests shook three summers' pride,	Have passed along with three summers,
Three beauteous springs to yellow *Autumn* turned,	Three springs have turned to fall,
In process of the seasons have I seen,	And as we've neared the succession, I've seen
Three April perfumes in three hot Junes burned,	Three Aprils and three Junes
Since first I saw you fresh, which yet are green	Since your royal time ending in 1600!
Ah yet doth beauty, like a Dial hand	Ah, yet does Elizabeth's ever-waning life
Steal from his figure, and no pace perceived,	Steal from your royal presence without notice,
So your sweet hew, which methinks still doth stand,	So your royal self, which in my view remains,
Hath motion, and mine eye may be deceived.	Is disappearing – and I can't see it with my eye.
For fear of which, hear this, thou age unbred:	Therefore hear this, you people of the future:
Ere you were born was beauty's summer dead.	Before you were born, Elizabeth's dynasty died!

1 TO ME, FAIR FRIEND, YOU NEVER CAN BE OLD,
FAIR FRIEND = Southampton, royal son; "From *fairest* creatures we desire increase" - Sonnet 1, line 1; **NEVER** = echoing Edward deVere, *Ever or Never*; in my view of you, my royal son, you can never lose your golden summer of royal blood, you will always be the prince who is "fresh" and "green" with youth and hope for the throne; **YOU NEVER CAN BE OLD** = you are immortal; you are always young and will be so forever in this verse, which preserves the truth that you are a prince

REFERENCE EDITION

2 FOR AS YOU WERE WHEN FIRST YOUR EYE I EYED,
FIRST = from the beginning, originally, and all during the golden time (1574-1600) prior to the Rebellion of February 8, 1601; (*first* is repeated in line 8 below); "With April's *first*-born flowers" – Sonnet 21, line 7; (numerically, the ordinal of *one*, alluding to Southampton, *One for All, All for One*); "that which is in time or order before any other" – Schmidt; "the *first heir* of my invention" – dedication of *Venus and Adonis* to Southampton; "That God forbid, that *made me first* your slave" – Sonnet 58, line 1; "Even as *when first I hallowed thy fair name*" – Sonnet 108, line 8; "And ruined love when it is built anew/ Grows *fairer than at first*, more strong, far greater" – Sonnet 119, lines 11-12; *first* also refers to "before all others" as in "And for a woman (Elizabeth) wert thou *first* created" – Sonnet 20, line 9

> O, twice my father, twice I am thy son!
> The life thou gav'st me *first* was lost and done
> - *1 Henry VI*, 4.6.6-7

Also a term of heraldry, denoting a particular form of dividing the shield from the highest part to the lowest: "Two of the *first*, like coats in heraldry, due but to *one* and *crowned with one crest*" – *A Midsummer Night's Dream*, 3.2.213-214; "For I am all the subjects that you have, which *first* was mine own King" – *The Tempest*, 1.2.343-344; "I'll rail against all the *first-born* of Egypt" – *As You Like It*, 2.5.57-58, with most commentators taking this expression to mean "high-born" persons; echoing "first begotten … first fruits … firstling"; **YOUR EYE** = royal sun, eye of Heaven, kingly eye; "that *sun thine eye*" – Sonnet 49, line 6; "Flatter the mountain tops with *sovereign eye*" – Sonnet 33, line 2; **YOUR EYE I EYED** = a play on the sounds of "eye" and "I" coming together to join Oxford and his son in one.

3 SUCH SEEMS YOUR BEAUTY STILL. THREE WINTERS COLD
YOUR BEAUTY = your blood from Elizabeth; **STILL** = constantly, always, forever; "Why write I *still* all one, ever the same" – Sonnet 76, line 5; "To one, of one, *still* such, and ever so" – Sonnet 105, line 4; the sequence of 100 sonnets contains a three-year cycle:

THREE WINTERS = the three winters since the Rebellion began in late 1600:

(1) December 1600 - February 8, 1601
(2) December 1601 - February 8, 1602
(3) December 1602 - February 8, 1603

WINTERS COLD = this ever-darkening, tragic time; perhaps it should read "*winters'* cold" as in "*summers'* pride" in the next line below; "Now is *the winter of our discontent*" – *Richard III*, 1.1.1; "Four lagging *winters* and four wanton springs end in a word: *such is the breath of kings*" – *Richard II*, 1.3.214-215

4 HAVE FROM THE FORESTS SHOOK THREE SUMMERS' PRIDE,
SHOOK = "Rough winds do *shake* the darling buds of May" – Sonnet 18, line 3; "Upon those boughs which *shake* against the cold,/ Bare ruined choirs where late the sweet birds sang" – Sonnet 73, lines 3-4; **SUMMER** = golden royal time; "Shall I compare thee to a Summer's day?" – Sonnet 18, line 1; **PRIDE** = royalty; royal splendor; related to birth; "Why is my verse so barren of new pride?" – Sonnet 76, line1; "For *time* hath set a *blot* upon my *pride*" – *Richard II*, 3.2.81

THREE SUMMERS' PRIDE = three years of golden royal time "wasted" as in Sonnet 106, line 1: "When in the Chronicle of wasted time": starting in the summer of 1600, when Southampton fell completely from Her Majesty's royal favor and then helped lead the Rebellion of February 8, 1601, a result of which he became a prisoner, up to February 8, 1603; the Queen dies the following month, marked by Sonnet 105.

5 THREE BEAUTEOUS SPRINGS TO YELLOW *AUTUMN* TURNED
BEAUTEOUS = royal; filled with your "beauty" or Tudor blood from the Queen; **THREE BEAUTEOUS SPRINGS** = three seasons of hope that your blood from Elizabeth could still be translated into your royal succession; spring 1600; spring 1601; spring 1602, when in fact all hope withered away; "Seeking that *beauteous roof* (Elizabeth's dynasty, the House of Tudor) to ruinate" – Sonnet 10, line 7; **YELLOW *AUTUMN*** = (Q has *Autumne* italicized); this time of decay and approaching death for Elizabeth and her dynasty; "When yellow leaves, or none, or few, do hang/ Upon those boughs" – Sonnet 73, lines 2-3

6 IN PROCESS OF THE SEASONS HAVE I SEEN
IN PROCESS OF = royal procession or royal progress; in the progression of; during this series of events; the tragic path that your claim to the throne has traveled or proceeded, in life and in the diary of these sonnets; **PROCESS** = legal proceeding, course of law (resulting in "misprision" of treason); "Proceed by *process*" – *Coriolanus*, 3.1.313; "Showing their birth, and where they did *proceed*" – Sonnet 76, line 8; the royal "process" or mandate for Southampton, dictating the death of his claim to the throne: "*Our sovereign process*, which imports at full, by letters congruing to that effect, the present death of Hamlet" – the King in *Hamlet*, 4.3.66-68; echoing the "process- server" or bailiff who delivered the orders summoning Southampton to face trial and summoning Oxford to sit on the tribunal ("process-server" – *The Winter's Tale*, 4.3.93); "Come, we go in procession" the King in *Henry V*, 4.8.113

7 THREE APRIL PERFUMES IN THREE HOT JUNES BURNED,
APRIL PERFUMES = sweet smell of the royal Tudor Rose; "Thou art thy mother's glass, and she in thee/ Calls back the lovely April of her prime" – Sonnet 3, lines 9-10; **HOT JUNES BURNED** = time when the flame of your royal blood burned hottest; ("thy light's flame" – Sonnet 1, line 6; Southampton as "the General of *hot* desire" in Sonnet 154, line 7, referring to his fresh royal blood).

8 SINCE FIRST I SAW YOU FRESH, WHICH YET ARE GREEN.
Since that first period of time, 1574-1600, when I saw you as "*fresh*" or young, green, golden and filled with royal hope; "Of all exploits since *first* I follow'd arms" – *2 Henry VI*, 2.1.43

> Father: I gave thee life and rescued thee from death.
> Son: O, twice my father, twice I am thy son!
> The life thou gav'st me *first* was lost and done
> - *1 Henry VI*, 4.6.5-7

> Who taught thee *first* to sigh, alas, my heart?
> - Oxford's sonnet, circa 1573

WHICH YET ARE GREEN = you, who are yet (still) green or fresh; "I cannot but find a great grief in myself to remember the Mistress which we have lost, under whom both you and myself from *our greenest years* have been in a manner brought up" – Oxford to Robert Cecil, of the deceased Elizabeth, on April 25/ 27, 1603, the eve of her funeral procession to Westminster Abbey; "His beauty shall in these black lines be seen,/ And they shall live, and *he in them still green*" – Sonnet 63, lines 13-14

FRESH

The Golden Time: *Fresh:* "Thou that art now *the world's fresh ornament*" – Sonnet 1, line 9
(1590-1600)
The Prison Years: *Not Fresh:* "Since first I saw you *fresh*" – Sonnet 104, line 8, this verse
(1601-1603)
Upon Liberation: *Fresh:* "My love looks *fresh*" – Sonnet 107, line 10
(April 10, 1603 – to the future)

9 AH YET DOTH BEAUTY LIKE A DIAL HAND

BEAUTY = royal blood in Southampton, inherited from Elizabeth; also, the Queen herself, as Venus, Goddess of Love and Beauty; "That thereby *beauty's Rose* might never die" – Sonnet 1, line 2; "But now is black *beauty's successive heir,/* And *Beauty* slandered with a bastard shame" – Sonnet 127, lines 3-4; **DIAL HAND** = the hand of the sundial or clock that reflects the withering of Time and of Elizabeth's life; "Thy *dial* how thy precious minutes waste" – Sonnet 77, line 2, addressed to Southampton in dedicating the Book of Sonnets to him

10 STEAL FROM HIS FIGURE, AND NO PACE PERCEIVED:

Take away from my son's royal claim, i.e., from his kingly figure or image, while (like a shadow gradually creeping over a sundial) no one perceives this erosion.

> Poor key-cold *Figure* of a holy king
> - *Richard III*, 1.2.5

> In the same *figure* like the King that's dead
> - *Hamlet*, 1.1.44

> A *figure* like your father
> - *Hamlet*, 1.2.199

> What would your gracious *figure*?
> - *Hamlet*, 3.4.105

> But, alas, to make me
> The *fixed figure for the time of scorn*
> To point his slow and moving finger at!
> - *Othello*, 4.2.54-56

> Now thou art an O without a *figure*
> - - to the King in *King Lear*, 1.4.183

> Anne: I would I knew thy heart.
> Richard: 'Tis *figured* in my tongue
> - *Richard III*, 1.2.196-197

> What's in the brain that ink may character
> Which hath not *figured* to thee my true spirit?
> - Sonnet 108, lines 1-2

NO PACE PERCEIVED = all this occurring in secret: in our lives, in these private sonnets that are not perceived by the public; "Gainst death and all-oblivious enmity/ Shall you *pace* forth" – Sonnet 55, lines 9-10;

No. 104

the attempt to "keep pace" with Time or Elizabeth's ever-dwindling life span; "Then can no horse with my desire keep pace" – Sonnet 51, line 9

11 SO YOUR SWEET HEW, WHICH METHINKS STILL DOTH STAND,

SWEET = royal; **HEW** = Henry Wriothesley, his appearance; "A *man in hew all Hews* in his controlling" – Sonnet 20, line 7; **STILL DOTH STAND** = constantly remains; appears to stand motionless, as Time rushes by

12 HATH MOTION, AND MINE EYE MAY BE DECEIVED:

Time is running out, but it feels frozen; "Commanded by *the motion* of thine eyes" – Sonnet 149, line 12, to Queen Elizabeth, whose royal eye (point of view) makes all the difference; **MOTION** = the motion of the Sun (royal son) as it rises, progresses over the sky, and sets; "For as the Sun is daily new and old" – Sonnet 76, line 13; "There's not the smallest orb which thou behold'st but *in his motion like an angel sings* … but whilst this muddy vesture of decay doth grossly close it in, we cannot hear it" – *The Merchant of Venice*, 5.1.60-65; the motion of the Moon, i.e., of the Queen on her waning progress toward death and eternal life; to Elizabeth in the Dark Lady series: "Commanded by the motion of thine eyes" - Sonnet 149, line 12

MINE EYE MAY BE DECEIVED = Oxford's own attempt to keep his son's royal blood alive; "To entertain the time with thoughts of love (royal blood),/ Which time and thoughts so sweetly doth *deceive*" – Sonnet 39, lines 11-12; "Let not my love be called Idolatry" – Sonnet 105, line 1, answering his own accusation, against himself; but he will continue this debate: "Or whether doth my mind, being crowned with you,/ Drink up the monarch's plague, this flattery?/ Or whether shall I say *mine eye* saith true" – Sonnet 114, lines 1-3, winding up with the conclusion that, yes, he is deceiving himself, but "*mine eye* loves it (the deception)" and so he will continue this diary to its end, preserving his son's royal blood in the process.

13 FOR FEAR OF WHICH, HEAR THIS, THOU AGE UNBRED:

HEAR THIS = now Oxford suddenly addresses readers of the future who are not yet born, with a note of defiance against Time; **AGE UNBRED** = new generations yet unborn; also, those born without royal blood; "Finding the first conceit of love there *bred*" – Sonnet 108, line 13; "Seeds spring from seeds, and beauty *breedeth* beauty;/ Thou wast *begot*, to get it is thy duty" – *Venus and Adonis*, lines 167-168; "That's for thyself to *breed* another thee" – Sonnet 6, line 7; "Than public means which public manners *breeds*" – Sonnet 111, line 4, referring to both himself and Southampton as having been "bred" or brought up by the Queen as the first and the last of Her Majesty's eight royal wards; "a Bohemian born, but here nursed up and bred" – *Measure for Measure*, 4.2.135; echoing "true-bred" or genuine; Southampton himself is being "bred" again in the Book of Sonnets: "the dainties that are bred in a book" – *Love's Labour's Lost*, 4.2.25; "This happy *breed* of men … this teeming womb of royal kings, feared by their *breeding*, and famous by their *birth*" – *Richard II*, 2.1.45-52

14 ERE YOU WERE BORN WAS BEAUTY'S SUMMER DEAD!

ERE YOU WERE BORN = before you, people (and readers) of the future, were born; **WAS BEAUTY'S SUMMER DEAD** = was my royal son's golden time (with his "beauty" or blood from the Queen) taken away; in fact Elizabeth is dying now.

The Queen is Taken Ill
February 1603

Elizabeth is taken ill at Richmond Palace. She cannot bear the thought of going to bed, instead sleeping in her chair or on cushions on the floor and "complaining of a fiendish dryness in her mouth and the miseries of insomnia," Neville Williams writes. At one point she blurts out a strange remark to Lord Admiral Howard:

> *"My Lord, I am tied with a chain of iron about my neck ...*
> *I am tied, I am tied, and the case is altered with me."*

Oxford & Lincoln
On the Eve of Elizabeth's Death
March 21, 1603

On March 21, 1603, three days before the death of Elizabeth, the Earl of Oxford invited Henry Hastings, Earl of Lincoln, to be a dinner guest at his home in Hackney, a few miles northwest of London. During this meeting Oxford directed their conversation toward Lincoln's great-nephew Lord Hastings, who was considered a possible threat as a contender for the throne in opposition to King James of Scotland.

Oxford had made his bargain with Robert Cecil in support of James. In return for Southampton promising to relinquish his claim to the throne (and for Oxford promising to bury his identity as Southampton's father and as "Shakespeare"), James had agreed to release Southampton from the Tower as soon as he was proclaimed king. The goal now was to help Cecil engineer a peaceful succession. To that end, Oxford had arranged the dinner meeting in order to sound out Lincoln's own loyalties; the way he did so was to pretend that he himself favored Hastings over James.

Lincoln stood fast, demonstrating his loyalty, and undoubtedly Oxford reported this good news to Cecil. Meanwhile, however, the horrified Lincoln went to Sir John Peyton, Lieutenant of the Tower of London, and told him of Oxford's apparently disloyal conversation. Exactly why Lincoln went to see Peyton is unclear; his most famous prisoner in the Tower was Southampton, who may have been regarded as a continuing threat to a peaceful succession. The Tower itself was filled with other prisoners (many of them loyal to Southampton) who posed potential threats.

Lieutenant Peyton reported on the affair after James's accession:

> "The Earl of Lincoln about some six days before her Majesty's death (as I remember) coming to visit me at the Tower, discoursed of her Majesty's weakness, concluding there was no hope of her recovery ... In the end he concluded, protested, and vowed that, next her Majesty, he would maintain and defend the just right of our gracious sovereign (James) that – by God's merciful providence for the universal good of the Britain kingdom – doth now reign over us...

> "About four days after ... my Lord of Lincoln came to me again, and as I remember, lodged in the Tower that night, being as I take it, two days before her Majesty's decease. He then told me it was time to look about us, for he had discovered an opposition against his Majesty's title, and that there was a great nobleman (Oxford, Lord Great Chamberlain) had opened himself upon that point, and had dealt with him to join as a party in the action...

> "That he had been invited (the day before, as I remember) by a great nobleman (Edward de Vere, Earl of Oxford) to Hackney, where he was extraordinarily feasted, at the which he

much marveled, for that there was no great correspondence between them, this nobleman (Oxford) having precedence of him in rank, whereby he told me I might know him, there being only but one of that quality dwelling there [Hackney]. This nobleman and he being (after dinner) retired apart from all company, began (as the Earl of Lincoln said) to discourse with him of the impossibility of the Queen's life, and that the nobility, being peers of the realm, were bound to take care for the common good of the state in the cause of succession – in which he himself, meaning the Earl of Lincoln, ought to have more regard than others because he had a nephew of the blood royal, naming my Lord Hastings, whom he [Oxford] persuaded the Earl of Lincoln to send for, and that there should be means to convey him over into France, where he should find friends that would make him a party, of the which there was a precedent in former times.

"He also, as the Earl of Lincoln said, inveighed much against the nation of the Scots, and began to enter into question of his Majesty's title…"

(Although Oxford was playing a role to test Lincoln's loyalty, no doubt he was also expressing his real feelings about "the nation of the Scots" as well as his genuine opinion that James did not actually deserve to be King of England. By now, though, Oxford was resigned to the Scottish monarch and, for the sake of Southampton, he was committed to James' succession.)

"…whereupon my Lord of Lincoln (as he told me) brake off his discourse, absolutely disavowing all that the great nobleman had moved, in such sort as he desisted from any further speech in the matter… At the first apprehension of my Lord of Lincoln's discovery, I was much moved and troubled, but *when he had made me understand what great person* [Oxford] *it was whom he meant, I knew him* [Oxford] *to be so weak in body, in friends, in ability, and all other means to raise any combustion in the state, as I never feared any danger to proceed from so feeble a foundation*; but added a more vigilancy and care unto the safety of **the place** (the Tower) under my charge…"

("As soon as think **the place** where he would be" – Sonnet 44, line 8)

"…I being also at that instant to give order for the brining in of wine, beer, meat, butter, fish & other provisions for the victualling of such extraordinary assistants as were to be drawn into the Tower, for that it was certainly informed **both to myself and to my Lord of Southampton, from whom I did not conceal in discourse, that her Majesty could not live 24 hours.**

(Clearly Peyton treated Southampton specially and was aware of his great prestige, though not of his identity as Elizabeth's son. Given that he "did not conceal" from Southampton, but, rather, kept him informed, Peyton likely knew that King James was going to release him from the Tower.)

The Earl of Lincoln also made a report. Without giving the details of their conversation at Hackney, he mentioned "speeches of the Earl of Oxford's, that if any were sent into France" on behalf of his great-nephew Hastings. Lincoln confirmed that he went to the Tower to visit with Peyton. Both the Peyton and Lincoln reports were delivered to Robert Cecil and to King James himself, but nothing whatsoever happened to Oxford – confirming they knew all along of the earl's loyalty and that he had been working in their behalf. (It is conceivable Cecil and James realized Oxford was so "weak in body, in friends, in ability" that he was harmless; and, if he was in poor health and likely to die soon anyway, why not let nature take its course?)[1]

---

1. The Peyton and Lincoln reports are on Alan Nelson's website.

It would have been quite uncharacteristic of Elizabeth to have indicated James as her successor to her Councilors round her bed at Richmond; she could not at the end have named him, for by then she had lost all power of speech. - Neville Williams, *The Life & Times of Elizabeth I*

Elizabeth died in her sleep at about three o'clock in the morning on March 24, 1603.

**King James ("30")
To Robert Cecil ("10")
March 1603**

"… not being able to express my thankfulness for your so great care to furnish a guard unto me, and *recommending me most heartily to my most faithful 40* [Oxford?], I end with renewing unto you the assurance of the constant love of Your most loving friend, 30."
- Akrigg, *Letters of King James*, p. 205

Part Two

THE PRISON YEARS

THE DEATH OF QUEEN ELIZABETH I

YEAR THREE IN THE TOWER

Sonnet 105
Never Kept Seat in One
24 March 1603

*Edward de Vere marks the death of Elizabeth. In the final line, he refers to the "three themes in one" (the family triangle of Elizabeth, Southampton and Oxford) that have "never kept seat in one." That is, they have never sat on the throne within the person of their "one" royal son, Henry Wriothesley (**One for All, All for One**), who should have succeeded her as Henry IX. The sonnet itself is a solemn hymn or prayer to Southampton, the "little Love-God" of Sonnet 154, the "Lord of my love" of Sonnet 26, the "God in love" of Sonnet 110 and "my lovely Boy" of Sonnet 126, a king or god on earth. The verse also complements and demonstrates the "invention" of the Sonnets set forth in Sonnet 76, using the adjectives "fair, kind, and true" as examples of "dressing old words new" and "varying to other words" as part of the special language.*

Sonnet 105	Translation
Let not my love be called Idolatry,	Let not my love for my son be called idolatry,
Nor my beloved as an Idol show,	Nor my divine royal son be seen as an idol,
Since all alike my songs and praises be,	Since my sonnets to him are all the same,
To one, of one, still such, and ever so.	To him, of him, always such, and forever so.
Kind is my love today, tomorrow kind,	My son is of Eliza's blood, always our kin,
Still constant in a wondrous excellence;	Always naturally born with his royal blood!
Therefore my verse to constancy confined,	Therefore my sonnets are confined to him,
One thing expressing, leaves out difference.	Only containing him without ever wavering.
Fair, kind, and true, is all my argument,	His royal, natural truth is my sole topic,
Fair, kind, and true, varying to other words,	Royal, natural, and true rights, using other words,
And in this change is my invention spent,	And this variation exhausts my "invention" –
Three themes in one, which wondrous scope affords.	Three themes in one heir, giving appearance of great diversity.
Fair, kind, and true, have often lived alone,	Three family members have lived separately,
Which three, till now, never kept seat in one.	And never sat on the throne in his one person.

(This sonnet correlates with Sonnet 152, the final verse of the Dark Lady series)

1 LET NOT MY LOVE BE CALLED IDOLATRY,
MY LOVE = my love for my royal son; "Lord of my love" – Sonnet 26, line 1; **IDOLATRY** = worship of a false god, i.e., of a false god on earth or king; in fact Oxford will end the diary, just before his final farewell, by offering himself in holy sacrifice to his son as a deity: "And take thou *my oblation*, poor but free,/ Which

REFERENCE EDITION

is not mixed with seconds, knows no art,/ But only *mutual render, only me for thee*" – Sonnet 125, lines 10-12; "But value dwells not in particular will: it holds his estimate and dignity as well wherein 'tis precious of itself as in the prizer. 'Tis mad *idolatry* to make the service greater than the god" – *Troilus and Cressida*, 2.2.54-58

2 NOR MY BELOVED AS AN IDOL SHOW,
MY BELOVED = my royal son; "As after some oration fairly spoke by *a beloved prince*" – *The Merchant of Venice*, 3.2.178-179; "And lo a voice from heaven, saying, This is *my beloved* Son, in whom I am well pleased" – Gospel of Mathew, 3.17; **IDOL** = false god; whereas, on the contrary, Southampton was "the little Love-God" who was born a rightful king, i.e., a god on earth; and he will be a "God in love" in Sonnet 110, line 12

3 SINCE ALL ALIKE MY SONGS AND PRAISES BE
ALL = Southampton; **ALL ALIKE** = emphasizing "all" and "all" for Southampton; **MY SONGS AND PRAISES** = my sonnets, which are hymns or prayers to him

4 TO ONE, OF ONE, STILL SUCH, AND EVER SO
TO ONE = to Southampton; **OF ONE** = consisting of Southampton, about him and filled with his life and royal blood; **STILL** = always; "And you and love are *still* my argument" – Sonnet 76, line 10; **EVER** = E. Ver, Edward de Ver, *Ever or Never*; "Since *every one* hath, *every one, one* shade,/ And you, but *one*, can *every* shadow lend" – Sonnet 53, lines 3-4; "If this be error and upon me proved,/ I *never* writ nor no man *ever* loved" – Sonnet 116, lines 13-14; Booth notes that this line echoes the *Gloria Patri*: "Glory be *to the Father, and to the Sonne, and to the Holy Ghost*, as it was in the beginning, is now, and *ever* shall be: world without end."

> "Shakespeare's poems, dedications, and Sonnets were all to *one* patron and *one* friend – "To *one*, of *one*, still such, and ever so" – and that *one* was Henry the third Earl of Southampton" - *Charlotte Stopes, 1904*

> "Shakespeare was playing upon the Southampton motto" - *T. W. Baldwin, 1950*

5 KIND IS MY LOVE TODAY, TOMORROW KIND,
KIND = related by nature or blood; natural royal child of Elizabeth; "Birth, origin, descent; the station, place, or property belonging to one by birth" – *OED*; "A little more than *kin*, and less than *kind*" – *Hamlet*, 1.2.65; "Be as thy presence is, gracious and *kind*" – Sonnet 10, line 11; "Your most assured and loving brother, as *ever* in mine own affection, in all *kindness* and *kindred*" – Oxford to his brother-in-law Robert Cecil, May 1601; "There she lost a noble and renowned brother, in his love toward her ever most *kind and natural*" – *Measure for Measure*, 3.1.218-220; **MY LOVE** = my royal son; "*My love* looks fresh" – Sonnet 107, line 10, when Southampton emerges from the Tower on April 10, 1603; **TODAY, TOMORROW** = echoing the progress of this diary according to days on the calendar; "tomorrow" also represents the future, when his son's *kindness* or relationship to the Queen by nature will be known by readers of the Sonnets.

6 STILL CONSTANT IN A WONDROUS EXCELLENCE:
STILL CONSTANT = always and constantly; "In *constant* truth to bide so firm and sure" – Oxford's sonnet, early 1570s, to Elizabeth, line 9; "*Crowned* with faith and *constant* loyalty" – *Henry V*, 2.2.5; **WONDROUS** = royal; **WON** = *One* = Southampton, *One for All, All for One*; **WONDROUS EXCELLENCE** = glorious royalty, alluding to Your Excellency; "As by your high imperial Majesty I had in charge at my depart for France, as procurator to *your Excellence*" – *2 Henry VI*, 1.1.1-3

7 THEREFORE MY VERSE TO CONSTANCY CONFINED,

MY VERSE = The Sonnets; same as "Why is *my verse* so barren of new pride" – Sonnet 76, line 1; **TO CONSTANCY CONFINED** = confined to this single topic, which is the constancy of his royal blood; "*Constant in spirit*, not swerving with the *blood*" – Henry V, 2.2.133); "But from thine eyes my knowledge I derive,/ And, *constant stars*, in them I read such art/ As truth and beauty shall together thrive" – Sonnet 14, lines 9-11; "But you like none, none you, for *constant heart*" – Sonnet 53, line 14; "In *constant truth* to bide so firm and sure" – Oxford's early sonnet, 1570s, to Elizabeth; "Oaths of thy love, thy truth, thy *constancy*" – Sonnet 152, line 10, to Elizabeth; **CONFINED** = a play on Southampton's confinement in the Tower, which now continues after Queen Elizabeth's death; Southampton has been "supposed as *forfeit to a confined doom*" – Sonnet 107, line 4; "Denmark's a *prison* ... A goodly one, in which there are many *confines, wards and dungeons*" – Hamlet, 2.2.244-246

8 ONE THING EXPRESSING, LEAVES OUT DIFFERENCE.
ONE = Southampton, *One for All, All for One*; **ONE THING EXPRESSING** = "O know, sweet love, *I always write of you,/* And you and love are *still my argument*" – Sonnet 76, lines 9-10; ONE THING = "When love converted from the THING it was" - Sonnet 49, line 7; "The thing I was" - Prince Hal in 2 Henry IV, 5.5.56; "The King is a thing" - Hamlet, 4.2.27; **LEAVES OUT DIFFERENCE** = leaves out all other topics; in heraldry, a difference is "an alteration made in a coat of arms to distinguish branches or members of the same family" and "to distinguish a junior member or branch of a family from the chief line" - OED; the child of an earl would wear a mark of difference on his or her coat of arms

9 FAIR, KIND, AND TRUE, IS ALL MY ARGUMENT,
All three adjectives, related to Southampton himself, are interchangeable one with the other as part of Oxford's special language
FAIR = royal; "From *fairest* creatures we desire increase" – Sonnet 1, line 1
KIND = natural by blood; "Shall *kin with kin*, and *kind with kind* confound" – Richard II, 4.1.141
TRUE = rightful; related to Oxford, *Nothing Truer than Truth*; "And your *true* rights be termed a Poet's rage" – Sonnet 17, line 11
ALL = Southampton; **ALL MY ARGUMENT** = The argument or topic of my Sonnets is "all" about Southampton, which includes *fair, kind and true* as inextricable from love or royal blood: "O know, sweet love, I always write of you,/ And *you and love* are still *my argument*" – Sonnet 76, lines 9-10; "For all my reign hath been but as a scene acting that *argument* ... so thou the garland wear'st successively" – the King to his son the Prince in *2 Henry IV*, 4.5.197-201

10 FAIR, KIND, AND TRUE, VARYING TO OTHER WORDS;
VARYING TO OTHER WORDS = Using these and other words to express the same thing about him, i.e., always to express his royal blood, but using various words to refer continually to the same topic: "So all my best is *dressing old words new*" – Sonnet 76, line 11, i.e., Oxford uses *fair* to mean "royal" and then he varies this adjective to *kind* or *true*, etc., to create an appearance of variety around a consistently single topic, i.e., around the "love" or royal blood of his son

11 AND IN THIS CHANGE IS MY INVENTION SPENT:
IN THIS CHANGE = by changing one word for another; this is the way I am able to write poetry on the surface while incorporating my message at the same time; **MY INVENTION** = My special language created for the Sonnets; "And keep *invention* in a noted weed" – Sonnet 76, line 6; "For who's so dumb that cannot write to thee,/ When *thou thyself dost give invention light?*" – Sonnet 38, lines 7-8; **SPENT** = used up, exhausted; "So all my best is dressing old words new,/ *Spending* again what is already *spent*" – Sonnet 76, lines 11- 12

12 THREE THEMES IN ONE, WHICH WONDROUS SCOPE AFFORDS.
THREE THEMES IN ONE = Recalling the Trinity of Father, Son and Holy Ghost; echoing the family triangle of Elizabeth, Oxford and Southampton as "*all one, ever the same*" in Sonnet 76, line 5); **IN ONE** = in

Southampton; i.e., all three live through the one royal son; ("subsumed in one theme; embodied in one person" – Booth); **WONDROUS SCOPE** = marvelous royalty as well as the appearance of amazing variety; scope of royalty; scope of justice, as in: "making your wills the scope of justice" – *Timon of Athens*, 5.4.4-5; "scope" appears in Sonnets 29, 52, 61, 103 and 105; **WON** = *One* = Southampton

13 FAIR, KIND, AND TRUE HAVE OFTEN LIVED ALONE
ALONE = the "all" and "one" of Southampton's motto; the three members of the family triangle have most often been separated; these three qualities, possessed by Southampton, have never been joined to make him king

14 WHICH THREE, TILL NOW, NEVER KEPT SEAT IN ONE
TILL NOW = up to right now, this moment of the Queen's death; **NEVER** = Edward de Vere, *Ever or Never*; **NEVER KEPT SEAT** = Never sat on the throne; "With due observance of *thy godlike seat*" – *Troilus and Cressida*, 1.3.31; "Now, by my *seat's* right royal majesty" – *Richard II*, 2.1.120; "The supreme *seat*, the throne majestical" – *Richard III*, 3.7.117; "the *seat* of majesty" – *Richard III*, 3.7.168; "Methought I *sat in the seat of majesty*" – *2 Henry VI*, 1.2.36; "Have shaken Edward from the regal *seat*" – *3 Henry VI*, 4.6.2; "Think'st thou that I will leave *my kingly throne*, wherein my grandsire and my father *sat*?" – *3 Henry VI*, 1.1.128-129

"I told you my *seat* has been the *seat* of kings, and I will have no rascal to succeed me; and who should succeed me but a king?"
- Elizabeth to Lord Admiral Howard in January 1603

IN ONE = In the person of Southampton ("one") as successor to the throne and crowned king; "Resembling sire, and child, and happy mother,/ Who *all in one, one* pleasing note do sing" – Sonnet 8, lines 11-12

NOTE: The parallel Dark Lady series ends now (upon the Queen's death) with Sonnet 152, in which Oxford also refers to love, kindness, truth, and constancy: "And all my honest faith in thee is lost./ For I have sworn deep oaths of thy deep *kindness*,/ Oaths of thy *love*, thy *truth*, thy *constancy*,/ And to enlighten thee gave eyes to blindness" – Sonnet 152, lines 8-11

No. 106

King James Orders
Southampton Released
April 5, 1603

"James VI of Scotland, at as by the Grace of God also James I of England, set out on the long journey to London. One of his last acts before leaving Edinburgh was to send ahead an order for the release of Southampton. With that order he sent a letter addressed to the Privy Council and nobility of England..."
- Akrigg, "Shakespeare & the Earl of Southampton," 134

ORDER FROM KING JAMES: "To our right trusty and right well beloved the Nobility and Peers of our Realm of England and to our right trusty and right well beloved our Councilors of State now assembled at Whitehall:

"Although *we* are resolved as well in regard of the great and honest affection borne unto us by the Earl of Southampton, as in respect of his good part in abiding him for service of us and the State to extend our *grace* and *favor* towards him, whom we (perceive) also the late Queen our Sister, notwithstanding *his fault* towards her was moved to exempt from the *stroke of Justice*...

> **WE:** royal "we" of monarchs; "From fairest creatures *we* desire increase" – Sonnet 1.1
> **GRACE:** "In all external *grace* you have some part" – Sonnet 53.13
> **FAVOR:** "Let those who are in *favor* with their stars" – Sonnet 25.1
> **HIS FAULT:** Southampton's crime of high treason for his leadership role in the Rebellion of February 8, 1601, as Oxford refers to it in the Sonnets:
>
> All men make *faults*, and even I in this,
> Authorizing thy trespass with compare ...
> For to thy sensual *fault* I bring in sense
> - Sonnet 35.5-6,9
>
> Some say thy *fault* is youth ...
> Both graces and *faults* are loved of more and less,
> Thou mak'st *faults* graces that to thee resort
> - Sonnet 96.1, 3-4
>
> The ills that were not grew to *faults* assured
> - Sonnet 118.10
>
> **STROKE OF JUSTICE:** execution

"Nevertheless because we would be loath in such a case as his wherein the Peers of our Realm have proceeded according to the honorable forms used in like cases to take such courses as may not stand with our own greatness and gravity fit to be observed in such matters, we have thought meet to give you notice of our *pleasure* though the same be to be extended by our own Royal *power*, which is *only* this:

> **PLEASURE:** How like a Winter hath my absence been
> From thee, the *pleasure* of the fleeting year! - Sonnet 97.1-2
> **POWER:** Oh Thou my lovely Boy, who in thy *power* - Sonnet 126.1
> **ONLY:** "And *only* herald to the gaudy spring" – Sonnet 1.10

REFERENCE EDITION 565

"Because ***the place*** is unwholesome and dolorous to him to whose body and mind we would give present comfort intending unto him so much further grace and favor, we have written to our Lieutenant of the Tower to deliver him out of Prison presently to any such place as he shall choose in or near our city of London, there to carry himself in such quiet and modest *form* as we know he will think meet in his own description, until that body of our State now assembled shall come unto us.

      THE PLACE: specific terminology for the Tower; also used at the trial

        From limits far remote, where thou dost stay …
        As soon as think ***the place*** where he would be – Sonnet 44.4, 8

      FORM: "Have I not seen dwellers on ***form*** and favor" – Sonnet 125.5

At which time we are pleased he shall also come to our ***presence***, for as it is on us that his only hope ***depends***, so we will reserve these works of further favor until the time he behold our own eyes, whereof as we know the ***comfort*** will be great to him, so it will be contentment unto us to have opportunity to declare our Estimation of him.

      PRESENCE: "Be as thy ***presence*** is, gracious and kind" – Sonnet 10.11
      DEPENDS: "Both truth and beauty on my love ***depends***" – Sonnet 101.3
      COMFORT: "Take all my ***comfort*** of thy worth and truth" – Sonnet 37.4

"In anything heretofore belonging wherein you shall be doubtful, we have now by our Peers directed our servant the Lord of Kinlosse to give you satisfaction. Who both at his coming in part and now by these our Peers sent after him is ***best*** instructed, we have also written to our aforesaid Lieutenant for the present delivery of H. Neville, Knight, whom we are pleased you of our Council shall bring with you when you shall ***wait*** upon us.

      BEST: "But ***best is best***, if never intermixed" – Sonnet 101.8
      WAIT: "I am to ***wait***, though ***waiting*** be so hell" – Sonnet 58.11
      (Waiting upon a Prince or King)

"From our Palace at Holliroode house this 5 of April 1603."
- J. R. [James Rex]

(Essex Record Office manuscript D/DRh Z2; Transcribed by Derran Charlton; modernized English; the letter is also reprinted in Stopes, 259-260.)

Part Two

THE PRISON YEARS

ENVOY
TO THE EIGHTY PRISON SONNETS
FINAL NIGHT IN THE TOWER

Sonnet 106
The Chronicle of Wasted Time
9 April 1603

The diary of the Sonnets has become "the Chronicle of wasted time," because the "time" of Elizabeth's life has expired without Southampton's succession to the throne.

Having made the bargain for Southampton's release, Oxford can also predict the near future. He foresees "the fairest wights", i.e., his royal son as Captain of the Isle of Wight; and predicts "lovely Knights", i.e., that Southampton will be made a Knight of the Garter. Now that Elizabeth has died ("Ladies dead") and James VI of Scotland has been proclaimed King James I of England, Henry Wriothesley will emerge from the Tower as a free man. Oxford too is emerging from the darkness of his son's prison years; and he can only "wonder" at "these present days" while both he and his son "lack tongues to praise," i.e., they can say nothing publicly about what has happened and why.

Sonnet 106	Translation
When in the Chronicle of wasted time,	When, in this chronicle of royal tragedy,
I see descriptions of the fairest wights,	I predict my royal son will rule the Isle of Wight,
And beauty making beautiful old rhyme,	And know Eliza gave royalty to my former sonnets
In praise of Ladies dead, and lovely Knights,	To her, and forecast him as a Knight of the Garter,
Then in the blazon of sweet beauty's best,	Then in this record of her most royal blood,
Of hand, of foot, of lip, of eye, of brow,	With praises of your hand, foot, lip, eye, brow –
I see their antique Pen would have expressed	I see that the old writers would have expressed
Even such a beauty as you master now.	Just such royal blood that you still possess.
So all their praises are but prophecies	So all other descriptions of you are but prophecies
Of this our time, all you prefiguring,	Of this time – they all prepare for your arrival,
And for they looked but with divining eyes,	And since they saw only what they could see,
They had not still enough your worth to sing:	They could not write of your royal birthright.
For we which now behold these present days,	For those of us seeing these current royal events
Have eyes to wonder, but lack tongues to praise.	Can only marvel, without opportunity to speak.

1 WHEN IN THE CHRONICLE OF WASTED TIME
THE CHRONICLE = this diary of the Sonnets; "historical account of events in order of time" – Schmidt; "Good my lord, will you see the players well bestowed? Do you hear, let them be well used, for they are *the abstract and brief chronicles of the time*" – Hamlet, 2.2.532-533, likening actors and/or plays to news accounts

REFERENCE EDITION 567

> Trimmed up *your praises with a princely tongue,*
> *Spoke to your deservings like a chronicle*
> - *1 Henry IV*, 5.2.56-57

> To fill King Edward's fame with prisoner kings
> And make her *chronicle* as rich with praise
> As is the ooze and bottom of the sea
> With sunken wrack and sumless treasures.
> - *Henry V*, 1.2.162-165

> Let me embrace thee, good old *chronicle,*
> *That hast so long walked hand in hand with Time*
> - *Troilus & Cressida*, 4.5.201-202

> Look in *the Chronicles*: we came in with
> Richard Conqueror
> - *The Taming of the Shrew*, Ind. 1.3-4

> For 'tis *a chronicle of day by day*
> - *The Tempest*, 5.1.163

> I and my sword will earn our *chronicle*
> - *Antony & Cleopatra*, 3.13

> Whose *chronicle thus writ*
> - *Coriolanus*, 5.3.145

WASTED TIME = the *time* of Queen Elizabeth's life is over and, therefore, it has been *wasted* in terms of Southampton's chance to succeed her as Henry IX; "I *wasted time*, and now doth *time waste me*" – the King in *Richard II*, 5.5.49, "this deed is *chronicled* in hell" – *Richard II*, 5.5.116; "such waste in brief mortality" – *Henry V*, 1.2.28; "March is *wasted* fourteen days" – *Julius Caesar*, 2.1.59; "how *thy precious minutes waste*" – Sonnet 77, line 2; **WASTE** = "expend unnecessarily, squander, dissipate, consume, spend, dwindle, wear away, decay" – Schmidt; "*Make use of time*, let not advantage slip,/ Beauty within itself should not be *wasted./* Fair flowers that are not gathered in their prime/ Rot, and consume themselves in little *time*" – *Venus and Adonis*, 1593, dedicated to Southampton, with these lines among those Oxford inserted specially for his son when the marriage to Elizabeth Vere was still viable.

The *time* of Elizabeth's life has run out, wasting her *beauty* or Tudor blood that is possessed by her son, Southampton: "But *beauty's waste* hath in the world an end" – Sonnet 9, line 11; "Then of *thy beauty* do I question make,/ That thou among the *wastes of time* must go" – Sonnet 12, lines 9-10; "Thy end is Truth's (Oxford's) *and Beauty's* (Elizabeth's) *doom and date*" – Sonnet 14, line 14, referring to the end of their son's claim to the throne; "Where *wasteful time* debateth with *decay*" – Sonnet 15, line 11; "And with old woes new wail *my dear time's waste*" – Sonnet 30, line 4; "In gentle numbers time so idly spent/ ... And make *time's spoils* despised everywhere./ Give my love (my royal son) fame faster than *time wastes life*" – Sonnet 100, lines 6, 12-13; "Th'expense of spirit in a *waste* of shame" – Sonnet 129, line 1, to Elizabeth, referring to the waste of her son's "spirit" or royal blood.

> *Time's glory is to calm contending kings,*
> *To unmask falsehood and bring truth to light,*
> *To stamp the seal of time in aged things...*
> - *Lucrece*, 939-941

Had he done so, himself had *borne the crown*,
Which ***waste of idle hours*** hath quite thrown down.
- *Richard II*, 3.4.65-66

2 I SEE DESCRIPTIONS OF THE FAIREST WIGHTS
SEE DESCRIPTIONS: Oxford predicts the future, according to his own knowledge, based upon the bargain he made for his son's freedom; **FAIREST** = most royal; "From fairest creatures" – Sonnet 1, line 1; **WIGHTS** = living beings, persons; a deliberate archaism (as in "old rhyme" in the next line); often indicating those who are strong and courageous in warfare; **FAIREST WIGHTS** = *Southampton, who will be made Captain of the Isle of Wight on July 7 this year;* again the plural used for the singular.

3 AND BEAUTY MAKING BEAUTIFUL OLD RHYME
BEAUTY = his blood from Elizabeth; the royal blood that has been filling the lines of these sonnets; **OLD RHYME** = ancient verses, but Oxford is referring to his "old" verses to the Queen and to his "old" sonnets during Southampton's golden time of this diary; ("In the *old age* black was not counted fair,/ Or if it were it bore not beauty's name" – Sonnet 127, lines 1-2); i.e., it was "beauty" or Elizabeth's blood in Southampton that made Oxford's former sonnets so "beautiful" (or filled with her royal blood) in the first place; "So should my papers (yellowed with their age)/ Be scorned, like old men of less truth than tongue,/ And your true rights be termed a Poet's rage/ And stretched meter of an Antique son" – Sonnet 17, lines 9-12

4 IN PRAISE OF LADIES DEAD AND LOVELY KNIGHTS,
LADIES DEAD = Elizabeth, who is now dead; "our *sovereign lady*" – i.e., Elizabeth, in *The Arte of English Poesie*, 1589, p. 303; "our most rightful and lawful *sovereign liege lady* and Queen" – Act of Recognition of the Queen's Highness' Title to the Imperial Crown of this Realm, 1559; **LOVELY KNIGHTS** = Southampton; **LOVELY** = royal; filled with "love" or royal blood; "O Thou my *lovely* Boy" – Sonnet 126, line 1; **KNIGHTS** = *Southampton will be created a Knight of the Garter on July 9 this year*; "When first this Order was ordained, my lords, Knights of the Garter were of noble birth, valiant and virtuous, full of haughty courage, such as were grown to credit by the wars" – *1 Henry VI*, 4.1.33-36, an apt description of Southampton and his own qualifications as a Knight; "the *sacred name of Knight* … this most honorable Order" – *1 Henry VI*, 4.1.40-41

5 THEN IN THE BLAZON OF SWEET BEAUTY'S BEST
BLAZON = the praising or trumpeting forth of admirable qualities; coat of arms; "heraldic term derived from a Middle English word for 'shield' and meaning 'coat of arms'" – Booth; of the "sacred" rooms of royalty in Windsor Castle, where Oxford spent much time at Court: "The several chairs of order look you scour with juice of balm and every precious flower; each fair installment, coat, and several crest, with loyal blazon, evermore be blest" – *The Merry Wives of Windsor*, 5.5.62-65; "The heavens themselves *blaze forth the death of princes*" – *Julius Caesar*, 2.2.31; official proclamation: "But this *eternal blazon* must not be to ears of flesh and blood" – *Hamlet*, 1.5.21-22; "O thou goddess, thou divine Nature, how thyself thou *blazon'st in these two princely boys*" – *Cymbeline*, 4.2.169-171; **SWEET** = royal; **BEAUTY'S BEST** = the best or most royal of those who have inherited Elizabeth's "beauty" or blood, i.e., Southampton; **BEST** = "*Best of my flesh*" – *Coriolanus*, 5.3.42; "All these I better in *one general best*" – Sonnet 91, line 8, referring to his son; "*best is best*" – Sonnet 101, line 8

6 OF HAND, OF FOOT, OF LIP, OF EYE, OF BROW,
Of each of these physical manifestations of his royalty; echoing Ophelia's speech about Prince Hamlet: "O what a noble mind is here o'erthrown! The courtier's, soldier's, scholar's, eye, tongue, sword, th'expectancy and rose of the fair state, the glass of fashion and the mould of form, th'observed of all observers" – *Hamlet*, 3.1.151-154

7 I SEE THEIR ANTIQUE PEN WOULD HAVE EXPRESSED

I SEE (repeated from line 2, but "shrewder" - Kerrigan); I discern what older writers would have expressed about kings; **THEIR ANTIQUE PEN** = ("And your true rights be termed a Poet's rage and stretched meter of an *antique song*" – Sonnet 17, lines 11-12; "Nor draw no lines there with thine *antique pen*" – Sonnet 19, line 10, speaking to Time itself); **WOULD HAVE** = would have wanted to; **EXPRESSED** = "More than that tongue that more hath more expressed" – Sonnet 23, line 12; "One thing expressing, leaves out difference" – Sonnet 105, line 8; "What's new to speak, what now to register,/ That may express my love or thy dear merit?" – Sonnet 108, lines 3-4; "Lest sorrow lend me words, and words express/ The manner of my pity wanting pain" – Sonnet 140, lines 3-4; "My thoughts and my discourse as madmen's are,/ At random from the truth vainly expressed" – Sonnet 147, lines 11-12

8 EVEN SUCH A BEAUTY AS YOU MASTER NOW.

SUCH A BEAUTY = such Tudor blood from your mother Elizabeth; **MASTER** = possess or control, as king; related to king as Master; "our new *Master* and Sovereign Lord" – Oxford to Robert Cecil, April 25/27, 1603; "the *Master* Mistress of my passion" – Sonnet 20, line 2, referring to Southampton as both king and queen, i.e., monarch, who inspires Oxford's "passion", i.e., his deepest feelings and his private verse; **NOW** = this day in my diary; at this immediate time, when you are about to be liberated from the Tower; "And all those beauties whereof *now* he's King/ Are vanishing, and vanished out of sight" – Sonnet 63, lines 6-7; (see note on Henry Constable for line 10 below, his line containing "all those beauties").

9 SO ALL THEIR PRAISES ARE BUT PROPHESIES

ALL = Southampton, *One for All, All for One*; **ALL THEIR PRAISES, etc**. = all the praises of ancient kings are prophecies; all my praise for you and your royal blood in these sonnets have been forecasts of your immortality as a prince; **PROPHECIES** = this verse itself contains prophecies of the immediate future: that King James will appoint you as Captain of the Isle of Wight ("fairest wights") and make you a Knight of the Garter ("lovely Knights"); as opposed to the false prophecies of those who predicted civil war over the throne and expected Southampton to spend the rest of his life in the Tower or be executed: "Not mine own fears nor *the prophetic soul/ Of the wide world dreaming on things to come*" – Sonnet 107, lines 1-2, which immediately follows this verse

10 OF THIS OUR TIME, ALL YOU PREFIGURING.

THIS OUR TIME = of this current period of time in England's history; this present time of royal succession; "Yet **the long time** which we spent in her service, we cannot look for such much left *of our days* as to bestow upon another" – Oxford to Robert Cecil, April 25/27, 1603, referring to the death of Queen Elizabeth ; "Twice *in my time* it had passage by law" – Oxford to Robert Cecil, May 7, 1603; "But I hope truth is subject to no prescription, for truth is truth though never so old, and*time* cannot make that false which was once true" – Oxford to Robert Cecil, May 7, 1603; "In seeking whereof I am grown old and spent *the chiefest time of mine age*" – Oxford to Robert Cecil, June 19, 1603

ALL = Southampton; **ALL YOU PREFIGURING** = all foretelling your arrival as the royal prince and rightful king; prefigure = to form or shape in anticipation; the only usage of "prefigure" or "prefiguring" in the Shakespeare works; "Ah, yet doth beauty like a Dial hand/ Steal from *his figure*" – Sonnet 104, lines 9-10; "What's in the brain that ink may character/ Which hath not*figured* to thee my true spirit?" – Sonnet 108, lines 1-2

NOTE: Lines 9-10 mirror a sonnet by Henry Constable [1562?-1613?] – "But all those beauties were but figures of thy praise/ And all their poets did of thee but prophesy"; Tucker suggests "the parallel is so close as to suggest a common source" for both Shakespeare and Constable; Kerrigan observes how the Old Testament was viewed as prefiguring (in its typology) the New Testament coming of Christ, adding that "all you prefiguring" can be read "prefiguring all that is you (which is a great deal)."

11 AND FOR THEY LOOKED BUT WITH DIVINING EYES,
FOR = because, or if; **BUT WITH, etc.** = only with eyes trying to predict the future; **DIVINING** = predicting, forecasting; also related to the divinity of kings; "Nothing, sweet boy, but yet like prayers divine" – Sonnet 108, line 5

12 THEY HAD NOT STILL ENOUGH YOUR WORTH TO SING:
STILL = (usually emended to "skill"); up to now; eternally; in referring to the "antique pen" as his own, Oxford "still" or as yet doesn't have power to write well enough for his son; usually emended to "skill" in reference to writers of the past who chronicled kings; but it is Oxford as "Shakespeare" who has chronicled the royal history of England in his chronicle plays; **YOUR WORTH** = your royalty; (the letters in *worth* are found in the name "Wriothesley"); "by the *glorious worth of my descent*" – Richard II, 1.1.107; **SING** = express in songs and sonnets; "Since all alike my *songs* and praises be/ To one, of one, *still* such, and ever so" – Sonnet 105, lines 3-4; "Good night, sweet prince, and flights of angels *sing* thee to thy rest" – Horatio to the now-deceased Prince in *Hamlet*, 5.2.366-367

13 FOR WE WHICH NOW BEHOLD THESE PRESENT DAYS
WE = the royal "we" of monarchs, Southampton; **THESE PRESENT DAYS** = these unfolding days of the succession, with James proceeding from Edinburgh to London to claim the English throne; the time being recorded in this diary

14 HAVE EYES TO WONDER, BUT LACK TONGUES TO PRAISE.
HAVE EYES TO WONDER = "beholding with amazement" – Booth; "marvel at, be astonished at" – Crystal & Crystal; i.e., Oxford is "wondering at" or beholding the succession of James and the imminent liberation of Southampton – wondering with amazement that it is all happening as planned; "That you will *wonder* what hath fortuned" – *The Two Gentlemen of Verona*, 5.4.167; related to "wonderful" in the sense of amazing, astonishing, extraordinary; "Why, saw you any thing more *wonderful*?" – *Julius Caesar*, 1.3.14; "Makes me from *wond'ring* fall to weeping joys" – *2 Henry VI*, 1.1.34; akin to "wondrous" as in "Kind is my love today, tomorrow kind,/ Still constant in a *wondrous* excellence/ ... Three themes in one, which *wondrous* scope affords" – Sonnet 105, lines 5-6, 12; **BUT LACK TONGUES TO PRAISE** = but remain "*tongue-tied by authority*" as in Sonnet 66, line 9; i.e., but cannot praise you in public; neither of us, father and son, can utter the truth in public; "O learn to read *what silent love hath writ*" – Sonnet 23, line 13; "Then may I dare to boast how I do love thee,/ Till then *not show my head* where thou mayst prove me" – Sonnet 26, lines 13-14

Southampton Liberated
April 10, 1603

"10 April 1603: I heard that the Earl of Southampton and Sir Henry Neville were set at large yesterday from the Tower" – Manningham's Diary, Stopes, 260; indicating, probably, that Southampton and Neville were freed around midnight of April 9, 1603 or in the early morning hours of April 10, the usual date given for the earl's release. "The King's letter probably reached the Lieutenant [of the Tower] at night, and he set the two prisoners free at once," Stopes writes, adding, "The letter to the Council would reach the Court the following morning [April 10], and the news would be formally announced."

THE MONUMENT

THE FINAL DAYS

SOUTHAMPTON LIBERATED

Sonnet 107
My Love Looks Fresh
10 April 1603

Southampton, having been "supposed as forfeit to a confined doom" in the Tower of London, is released after spending twenty-six months in prison. Perhaps Southampton's release has also released Oxford's creative spirit; in any case, he now returns to composing one sonnet each day for the next nineteen days until the Queen's funeral. (Her funeral on April 28 will mark the formal end of the Tudor dynasty.) He refers to the death of Elizabeth ("the mortal Moon") and to the accession of James (now on his way to London) amid "Olives" of peace as opposed to civil war around the throne. "My love looks fresh," he writes of Southampton, meaning that his royal son has retained his status as a prince even though he has forfeited the crown. Henry Wriothesley is still "the world's fresh ornament" as he had been in the very opening verse; and Oxford records this truth in his "monument" of the Sonnets so it may exist for the eyes of posterity.

Sonnet 107	Translation
Not mine own fears, nor the prophetic soul	Not my fears for you, nor the predictions
Of the wide world dreaming on things to come	Of others in England and beyond about the future
Can yet the lease of my true love control,	Can have power over the life of my royal son,
Supposed as forfeit to a confined doom.	Assumed to be sentenced and confined until death.
The mortal Moone hath her eclipse endured,	Elizabeth the Moon has suffered her mortal death,
And the sad Augurs mock their own presage,	And the prophets of civil war were wrong.
Incertainties now crown themselves assured,	Worries are gone and James is being crowned,
And peace proclaims Olives of endless age.	And we look forward to lasting peace with Spain.
Now with the drops of this most balmy time	Now with the April showers of royal succession,
My love looks fresh, and death to me subscribes,	My son remains royal; and death submits to me,
Since spite of him I'll live in this poor rhyme,	Since I'll live in these sonnets in spite of death,
While he insults o'er dull and speechless tribes.	While death obliterates the many who can't speak.
And thou in this shalt find thy monument,	And you will find your eternity in this monument,
When tyrants' crests and tombs of brass are spent.	When our late tyrannical Queen's tomb is gone.

1 NOT MINE OWN FEARS NOR THE PROPHETIC SOUL
Neither my own apprehensions (about my royal son's fate in the Tower or about the succession of James) nor the anxious prophecies of others; **MINE OWN** = characteristically used in relation to a son or daughter; "Tell me, *mine own*, where hast thou been preserved?" – *The Winter's Tale*, 5.3.123-124, Hermoine to her daughter; **MINE** = *OED*: 1467 – "I wyll that *John myn son*"

> … a son of *mine own*
> - Oxford to Burghley, March 17, 1575

572

> What can *mine own* praise to *mine own* self bring,
> And what is't but *mine own* when I praise thee?
> - Sonnet 39, lines 3-4

> For term of life thou art assured *mine*
> - Sonnet 92, line 2

FEARS = dreads, doubts; things to be dreaded, objects of fear; "I was not sick of any *fear* from thence" – Sonnet 86, line 12, referring to those who claim victory over him and over the truth; "Then need I not to *fear* the worst of wrongs" – Sonnet 92, line 5, referring to his father-son bond with Southampton being stronger than his own mortal life; **PROPHETIC SOUL** = divining spirt; playing upon the "prophecies" of the previous verse (106) in which Oxford forecast Southampton's liberation: "So all their praises are but *prophecies/ Of this our time, all you prefiguring,/ And for the looked but with divining* eyes,/ They had not skill enough your worth to sing" – Sonnet 106, lines 9-12; "O my *prophetic soul*! My uncle!" – *Hamlet*, 1.5.41; "Cry, Trojans, cry! Lend me ten thousand eyes, and I will fill them with *prophetic tears*" – *Troilus and Cressida*, 2.2.102-103

> "'Tis thought the King is dead ... The pale-faced *moon* looks bloody on the earth, and *lean-look'd prophets whisper fearful change*. Rich men look sad, and ruffians dance and leap – the one in fear to lose what they enjoy, the other to enjoy by rage and war. *These signs foretell the death or fall of kings.*"
> – *Richard II*, 2.4.7-15

2 OF THE WIDE WORLD DREAMING ON THINGS TO COME

THE WIDE WORLD = England and beyond; the vast universe; "For nothing *this wide Universe* I call/ Save thou, my Rose, in it thou art my all" – Sonnet 109, lines 13-14; "Thou that art now *the world's* fresh ornament" – Sonnet 1, line 9; **DREAMING ON** = predicting the future, both for England and for Southampton, as a result of the death of Elizabeth followed by the succession of James to the throne; "thinking about" or "speculating on" the possibility of civil war over the interchange of monarchs and dynasties; "the *dreamer* Merlin and his *prophecies*" – *1 Henry IV*, 3.1.144; having thoughts, visions, ideas, images in sleep; "O, Ratcliffe, I have *dream'd a fearful dream*! ... O Ratcliffe, *I fear, I fear*!" – *Richard III*, 5.3.213, 215

> Why should my heart think that a several plot,
> Which my heart knows *the wide world's common place*?
> - Sonnet 137, lines 9-10

(Referring to the Tower as England's "place" for traitors or common criminals)

O God, I could be *bounded* in a nutshell and count myself a King of infinite space, were it not that I have *bad dreams* – *Hamlet*, 2.2.255-256, immediately following Hamlet's characterization of Denmark/England as a prison

"Save that *my soul's imaginary sight*/ Presents thy shadow to my sightless view" – Sonnet 27, lines 9-10; "But when I sleep, in *dreams* they (my eyes) look on thee" – Sonnet 42, line 3; "Thus have I had thee as *a dream* doth flatter:/ In sleep a King, but waking no such matter" – Sonnet 87, lines 13-14; "Before, a joy proposed, behind, *a dream*" – Sonnet 129, line 12, to Queen Elizabeth, referring to the former hope that their son would wear the crown

THINGS TO COME = England's inevitable date with royal succession; the diary of the Sonnets has been a "dream" of that succession, i.e., the dream of Southampton becoming king; "Against *this coming end* you should prepare" – Sonnet 13, line 3; "Let this sad *Interim* like the Ocean (royal blood) be/ Which parts the shore, where two contracted new/ *Come* daily to the banks" – Sonnet 56, lines 9-11; "That Time (the mortal decay of Elizabeth) will *come* and take my love away" – Sonnet 64, line 12; "That you your self, being extant, well might show/ How far a modern quill doth *come too short*" – Sonnet 83, lines 6-7

> My hour is *almost come*
> - Ghost of Hamlet's father in *Hamlet*, 1.5.4

3 CAN YET THE LEASE OF MY TRUE LOVE CONTROL,

LEASE = the loan of royal blood to Southampton; the lease of Tudor Rose blood held by Queen Elizabeth, who has passed it on to Southampton by nature but not by will; "Nature's bequest gives nothing but doth *lend*" – Sonnet 4, line 3; "So should *that beauty* (royal blood from Elizabeth) *which you hold in lease*" – Sonnet 13, line 5; and in the Dark Lady series, near the end of the reign, to the Queen: "Why so large cost, having so short a *lease,*/ Dost thou upon *thy fading mansion* spend?" – Sonnet 146, lines 5-6, referring to the rapidly expiring "lease" on her House of Tudor, which is now fading because of her refusal to release Southampton from the Tower and name him as her successor.

OED: "A contract between parties, by which the one conveys lands or tenements to the other for life, for years, at will ... the period of time for which the contract is made ... with reference to the permanence of occupation guaranteed by a lease; esp. in the phrase "a (new) lease of life"; also, the term during which possession or occupation is guaranteed"; 1586: "Of my graunt they had enjoy'd/ *A lease of blisse* with endlesse date" (Countess of Pembroke); 1628: "Remember of what age your daughter was, and that just so long was *your lease of her.*"

"And our high-placed Macbeth shall live the *lease* of Nature, pay his breath to time, and mortal custom" – *Macbeth*, 4.1.98-99

MY TRUE LOVE = Southampton, my royal son; my true Prince; related to Oxford, *Nothing Truer than Truth*; "And your *true rights* be termed a Poet's rage" – Sonnet 17, line 11; "O let me *true in love but truly write*" – Sonnet 21, line 9; "Take all *my loves, my love*, yea take them all:/ What hast thou then more than thou hadst before?/ *No love, my love,* that thou mayst *true love* call,/ All mine was thine, before thou hadst this more" – Sonnet 40, lines 1-4; "So *true a fool is love* that in your Will/ (Thou you do any thing) he thinks no ill" – Sonnet 57, lines 13-14; "Thou *truly* fair wert *truly* sympathized/ In *true* plain words by thy *true*-telling friend" – Sonnet 82, lines 11-12; "Fair, kind, and *true*, is all my argument,/ Fair, kind, and *true,* varying to other words/ ... Fair, kind, and *true,* have often lived alone,/ Which three, till now, never kept seat in one" – Sonnet 105, lines 9-10, 13-14; "Let me not to the marriage of *true* minds/ Admit impediments. *Love is not love/ Which alters when it alteration finds*" – Sonnet 116, lines 1-3, referring to their father-son bond but also to the truth of Southampton's "love" or royal blood, which does not change even if it fails to gain the throne; "This I do vow, and this shall *ever* be,/ I will be *true*, despite thy scythe and thee" – Sonnet 123, lines 13-14, to Time

> Bolinbroke: Go, some of you, convey him to the Tower.
> Richard: O, good! Convey! Conveyers are you all,
> That rise thus nimbly by *a true king's* fall.
> - *Richard II*, 4.1.316-318

CONTROL = have power over; a play on Southampton's own "controlling" as a prince, as in Sonnet 20, line 7: "A man in hew all *Hews* in his *controlling*"; "Never did captive with a freer heart cast off his chains of bondage, and embrace *his golden uncontrolled enfranchisement*" – *Richard II*, 1.3.88-90; "Yet looks he like a king: behold, his eye, as bright as is the eagle's, lightens forth *controlling majesty*" – *Richard II*, 3.3.68-70; "And Folly (Doctor-like) *controlling* skill" – Sonnet 66, line 10, referring to those in power who have controlled Southampton by leaving him in the Tower as a convicted traitor; (related to "controlment" or "controlling" of accounts; Oxford uses the state "treasure" as a metaphor for his son's "account" of royal blood; in this context "control" extends the metaphor to its regulation by officialdom)

OED: 1577: "In thy fayth I maye ... repose the *controlement* of my life"; 1604: "Otherwise the course of destinie were subject to our *controlment*"

> Here is a hand to hold a scepter up,
> And with the same to act *controlling laws*
> - *2 Henry VI*, 5.1.102-103

OED: "To check or verify, and hence to regulate ... to take to task, call to account, rebuke, reprove (a person) ... to challenge, find fault with, censure, reprehend ... to exercise restraint or direction upon the free action of; to hold sway over, exercise power or authority over; to dominate, command ... to hold in check, curb, restrain from action; to hinder, prevent ... (Law) To overrule (a judgment or sentence"; 1623: "I put not out anything rashly in print ... especially in this age so ready to control"

4 SUPPOSED AS FORFEIT TO A CONFINED DOOM.
Presumed to be the victim of a life sentence in the Tower and also subject to execution at any time

SUPPOSED AS = imagined or thought (erroneously) to be; held as a belief or opinion to be; apprehended, guessed, suspected, intended to be; assumed to be true as; entertained as an idea to be; expected, obliged, taken for granted to be (or to have been); *OED* = stated or alleged to be, as "formally in an indictment"; 1544: "supposing by his writ"

OED also lists the verb "suppose" as "to feign, pretend," and it may well be that Oxford intended the phrase *supposed as forfeit to a confined doom* to mean that Southampton was *pretended* to be doomed to confinement in the Tower for the rest of his life. (This possibility occurs only when it becomes certain that James will succeed Elizabeth. Earlier, when Henry Wriothesley's life was spared, his fate remained uncertain and "supposed" would have correctly meant "generally believed.") Having made the bargain for Henry Wriothesley to be liberated, few persons other than Oxford, Robert Cecil and King James would have known that the new sovereign would liberate Southampton; and so the earl was *pretended* to be confined for life; "The maid ... was the daughter of his own bondswoman, who afterwards being stolen away, was carried to the house of Virginius, and *supposed* to be his child" – *Painter's Palace of Pleasure*, 1566, when Oxford was sixteen years old and very possibly involved in Painter's collection; ppl. adjective = believed to be; put on or feigned:

> Let the *supposed* Fairies pinch him sound
> - *The Merry Wives of Windsor*, 4.4.61

FORFEIT = "subject to" and "legally owed to" – Kerrigan; "an act under whose heavy sense *your brother's life falls into forfeit*: he arrests him on it, and follows close the rigor of the statute to make him an example" – *Measure for Measure*, 1.4.64-68; *OED* 1594: "*Forfeit* and confiscate *unto the crown*"; and from 1495: "*forfeitable ... to the Kyng*"; "There without ransom to be forfeited" - *1 Henry IV*, 4.3.96

> Claudio, whom here you have *warrant to execute*, is no greater *forfeit to the law* than
> Angelo, who hath *sentenced* him – *Measure for Measure*, 4.2.156-159

OED: (noun) "A misdeed, crime, offence, transgression; hence, willful injury; breach or violation of; 'in forfeit' = under charge of wrong doing, guilty of breaking the law'; something to which the right is lost by the commission of a crime or fault; hence, a penal fine, a penalty for breach of contract or neglect of duty; the losing of something by way of penalty; 'to set to forfalt' = to attaint, outlaw"; (verb) "To do amiss, sin, transgress; to violate (one's faith or oath); to lose, lose the right to; to render oneself liable to be deprived of (something); also to have to pay in consequence of a crime, offence, breach of duty; to lose by misconduct; to lose or give up, as a necessary consequence; to incur the penalty of forfeiture; to subject a person to forfeiture or confiscation (of estates, etc); to cause the forfeiture, loss, or ruin of"; (adjective) "That has been lost or has to be given up as the penalty of a crime or fault or breach of engagement."

(Upon the verdict at his trial, Southampton was condemned to have his life *forfeited* by execution; all his titles and lands were *forfeited* to – and confiscated by – the Crown. This was also the penalty to be paid by "misprision" of treason, which left him a perpetual prisoner without a royal pardon and, therefore, still subject to execution. King James will grant him the necessary royal pardon on May 16 this year.)

In the Dark Lady series Oxford pleads with Elizabeth on behalf of their son, offering his own life and honor as ransom for Southampton's liberation:

> So now I have confessed that he is thine,
> And I myself am mortgaged to thy will.
> *Myself I'll forfeit*, so that other mine
> Thou wilt restore to be my comfort still.
> - Sonnet 134, lines 1-4

"The King's further pleasure is … to *forfeit all your goods*, lands, tenements, chattels and whatsoever" – *Henry VIII*, 3.2.337-344; liable to penal seizure, lost by breach of laws or conditions; given up for lost, forsaken: "And yet thy wealth being *forfeit to the state*, thou … must be hanged at the state's charge" – *The Merchant of Venice*, 4.1.363-365

> Shall our coffers then
> Be emptied *to redeem a traitor home?*
> Shall we buy *treason*, and indent with fears
> When *they have lost and forfeited* themselves?
> - *1 Henry IV*, 1.3.84-86

> There *without ransom to lie forfeited*
> - *1 Henry IV*, 4.3.96

> Why, all the souls that were, were *forfeit* once,
> And He that might the vantage best have took
> Found out the remedy. How would you be
> If He, which is the top of *judgment*, should
> But *judge* you as you are? O, think on that,
> And *mercy* then will breathe within your lips
> - *Measure for Measure*, 2.2.73-78

CONFINED = confined, imprisoned, in the Tower of London; "So have we thought it good from our free person she should be *confined*, lest that the treachery of the two fled hence be left her to perform" – the King in *The Winter's Tale*, 2.1.193-196; possibly alluding to the "cofinement" of his mother the Queen when she was about to give birth to him in May/June 1574

> In whose *confine immured* is the store- sonnet 84, line 3 (walled prison)
> A God in love, to whom I am *confined* - Sonnet 110, line 12
>
> Princes have less *confines* to their wills - *OED:* 1548
>
> Denmark's a *prison* … A goodly one, in which there are many *confines, wards,* and *dungeons,* Denmark being one o'th'worst – *Hamlet,* 2.2.243-248
>
> Th'*imprisoned* absence of your liberty - Sonnet 58, line 6

OED: (confined) "Bounded, limited, restricted, restrained, shut up, enclosed, *imprisoned*"; (confine, verb) "3. To relegate to certain limits; to banish; 4a. To shut up, *imprison, immure,* put or keep in detention; 4 b. To enclose or retain within limits … keep in place"

> I am thy father's spirit,
> *Doom'd* for certain *term* to walk the night,
> And for the day *confin'd* to fast in fires,
> Till the foul *crimes* done in my days of nature
> Are burnt and purg'd away. But that I am forbid
> To tell the secrets of my *prison-house*…
> - *Hamlet,* 1.5.9-14
>
> So we have thought it good
> From our free person she should be *confined*
> - *The Winter's Tale,* 2.1.193-194

DOOM = judgment; prison sentence; Southampton's imprisonment and his possible execution; judgment of the trial and the Final Judgment; the end or doom of the Tudor dynasty; "Norfolk, for thee remains *a heavier doom,* which I with some unwillingness pronounce. The sly slow hours shall not determinate *the dateless limit of thy dear exile*; the hopeless word of 'never to return' breathe I against thee, upon pain of life" – *Richard II,* 1.3.148-153, recalling Southampton as "*precious friends hid in death's dateless night*" – Sonnet 30, line 6; "Proud Bolinbroke, I come to change blows with thee for *our day of doom*" – *Richard II,* 3.2.188-189; "Thy **kingly doom and sentence** of his pride" – *Richard II,* 5.6.23

> Thy end is *Truth's and Beauty's doom and date*
> - Sonnet 14, line 14

In the Dark Lady series, Oxford writes of Elizabeth sparing their royal son from execution:

> Straight in her heart did *mercy* come,
> Chiding that tongue that ever sweet
> Was used in giving gentle *doom*
> - Sonnet 145, lines 5-7

OED: "A stratute, law, enactment; generally an ordinance, decree; a judgment or decision, esp. one formally pronounced; a sentence; mostly in adverse sense, condemnation, sentence of punishment; fate, lot, irrevocable destiny (usually of adverse fate); final fate, destruction, ruin, death; the action or process of judging (as in a court of law); judgment, trial; the last or great Judgment at the end of the world; 'day of doom': the day of judgment; justice; power or authority to judge; 'doom-house' = judgment hall; 'doom-stead' = place of judgment; 'doom-tree' = a tree on which the condemned were hanged."

Your praise shall still find room
Even in the eyes of all posterity
That wear this world out to *the ending doom.*
So, till *the judgment* that yourself arise,
You live in this, and dwell in lovers' eyes.
- Sonnet 55, lines 10-14

Love alters not with his brief hours and weeks,
But bears it out *even to the edge of doom.*
- Sonnet 116, lines 11-12

This way the king will come; this is the way
To Julius Caesar's *ill-erected Tower,*
To whose flint bosom my condemned lord
Is doom'd a prisoner
- Richard II, 5.1.1-4

5 THE MORTAL MOON HATH HER ECLIPSE ENDURED,

MORTAL = "Such waste in brief mortality" – *Henry V*, 1.2.28; "How many years a mortal man may live" – *3 Henry VI*, 2.5.29; "Thou hadst but power over his mortal body; his soul thou canst not have" –*Richard III*, 1.2.47-48; "O momentary grace of mortal men" –*Richard III*, 3.4.96; also the sense of evil and/or deadly: "Who 'scapes the lurking serpent's mortal sting?" – *3 Henry VI*, 2.2.15; "But I return his mortal foe" – *3 Henry VI*, 3.3.257; **THE MORTAL MOONE** = The mortal self of Queen Elizabeth, known as Cynthia or Diana, Goddess of the Moon, i.e., her *mortal* body or physical self is dead, as opposed to her immortal soul or spiritual self; "Making a couplement of proud compare/ With *Sunne and Moone*" – Sonnet 21, lines 5-6, i.e., Southampton and Elizabeth, son and mother; "Clouds and *eclipses* stain both *Moone and Sunne*" – Sonnet 35, line 3, referring to the stain of disgrace that the Rebellion has cast upon both Elizabeth and Southampton, her royal son; "Let us be *Diana's foresters, gentlemen of the shade, minions of the moon*; and let men say we be men of good government, being governed as the sea is, by our noble and *chaste Mistress the Moon*, under whose countenance we steal" – *1 Henry IV*, 1.2.25-29, an obvious allusion to Queen Elizabeth for the contemporary audience; Elizabeth, also known as Venus, goddess of Love and Beauty: "the *mortal Venus*, the heart-blood of beauty, love's invisible soul" – *Troilus and Cressida*, 3.1.32-33; **HER ECLIPSE** = the Queen's "deprivation of light" (*OED*); her death, which has deprived England of her royal light, i.e., the same "light" possessed by her son, Southampton: "When thou thy self doth give invention *light*" – Sonnet 38, line 8; "Nativity, once in the main of *light*,/ Crawls to maturity, wherewith being crowned/ Crooked *eclipses* 'gainst his glory fight" – Sonnet 60, lines 5-7; so that this much-discussed line refers to Elizabeth as "the mortal Moon" who is already dead (as marked by Sonnet 105) and as the sovereign mistress who, simultaneously, has "endured" the "eclipse" of her light and glory on earth, as witnessed by mere mortals, by passing into the immortal, spiritual, eternal state of kings or queens; and in fact these are Oxford's sentiments as he expressed them to Cecil during this time:

> "I cannot but find a great grief in myself to remember the Mistress which we have lost, under whom both you and myself from our greenest years have been in a manner brought up; and **although it hath pleased God after an earthly kingdom to take her up into a more permanent and heavenly state (wherein I do not doubt she is crowned with glory)** to give us a prince [James] wise, learned, and enriched with all virtues, yet the long time which we spent in her service, we cannot look for so much left of our days as to bestow upon another." - Oxford to Robert Cecil, April 25/27, 1603

Alack, *our terrene Moon*

> Is now *eclipsed*, and it portends alone
> The fall of Antony"
> - *Antony and Cleopatra*, 3.13.153-155

> *Terrene* = earthly, mortal
> *Moon* = Queen Cleopatra, modeled upon Queen Elizabeth

> Then here I take my leave of thee, fair son,
> Born to *eclipse thy life* this afternoon.
> Come, side by side together live and die...
> - *1 Henry VI*, 4.5.52-54

ENDURED = sustained or submitted to; i.e., Elizabeth, being mortal, has died; but also being immortal, she is now in heaven; "to endure" also means to die, as in "Men must *endure* their going hence, even as their coming hither" – *King Lear*, 5.2.9-10, i.e., they must experience their deaths in the same way they had experienced their births; "Thou hast but power over his *mortal body*:/ His *soul* thou canst not have" – *Richard III*, 1.2.47-48

(NOTE: Virtually all commentators agree that this line refers specifically and unambiguously to the Queen; and though debate continues over the dating, most also agree that the sonnet was written shortly after her death. See further discussion below, following the notes for line 14.)

6 AND THE SAD AUGURS MOCK THEIR OWN PRESAGE,
And the gloomy prophets of civil war mock their own forecasts; **AUGURS** = those who practice the art of forecasting the future; "But thou shrieking harbinger,/ Foul precurer of the fiend,/ *Augur* of the fever's end,/ To this troop come thou not near" – *The Phoenix and Turtle*, 1601; "We defy *augury*. There is special providence in the fall of a sparrow" – *Hamlet*, 5.2.228-229, referring to the death of Elizabeth, who used the sparrow to identify herself; **PRESAGE** = foreboding, presentiment; "If heart's *presage* be not vain, we three here part that ne'er shall meet again" – *Richard II*, 2.2.141-142

> O let my books be then the eloquence
> And *dumb presagers* of my speaking breast
> - Sonnet 23, lines 9-10

> So, hence! Be thou the trumpet of our wrath
> And *sullen presage* of your own decay!
> - *King John*, 1.1.27-28

7 INCERTAINTIES NOW CROWN THEMSELVES ASSURED,
INCERTAINTIES, etc. = the previous insecurities are now securities, i.e., *"assured"* of harmony and peace; **CROWN THEMSELVES ASSURED** = anticipating the crowning of James VI of Scotland as James I of England; "And in that chair where *kings and queens are crown'd*" – *2 Henry VI*, 1.2.38; "Anointed, *crowned*" – *Richard II*, 4.1.127; and Oxford in these verses will twist this monumental event into the crowning of his own royal son, Southampton: "Or whether doth my mind, being *crowned with you,*/ Drink up *the monarch's plague*, this flattery?" – Sonnet 114, lines 1-2; and "But reckoning time, whose millioned accidents/ Creep in 'twixt vows, and *change decrees of Kings*/ ... *Crowning the present*" – Sonnet 115, lines 6, 12

8 AND PEACE PROCLAIMS OLIVES OF ENDLESS AGE.
James offers a new era of peaceful prosperity; **OLIVES** = King James used olives as a symbol of peace, both at home and abroad; *"Olives"* = "O. lives," or Oxford still lives; "Olive leaves or branches were an

ancient emblem of 'peace' or security" – Evans; "And the dove came in to him in the evening; and, lo, in her mouth was an *olive leaf* pluckt off: so Noah knew that the waters were abated from the earth" – Genesis, 8.11; **PROCLAIMS** = echoing the Proclamation of the Accession of James, which Oxford signed; *"And once again proclaim us King of England"* – *3 Henry VI*, 4.8.53; "I'll to the Tower with all the haste I can … And then I will proclaim young Henry king" – *1 Henry VI*, 1.1.167-169; Evans observes this "may be taken to suggest regal authority; right now the new king is taking his time on the triumphant approach to London and the throne (waiting until after the Queen's funeral procession (to be held on April 28, 1603); but Oxford is well aware of the royal theme of the James progress: the king will enter *"not with an Olive Branch in his hand, but with a whole Forest of Olives round about him"* – Gervase Markham, Honour in His Perfection, 1624

9 NOW WITH THE DROPS OF THIS MOST BALMY TIME

NOW = at this very time of my royal son's release; **BALMY** = this balmy spring; this healing quality (of medicinal ointment); the balm of kings, served to anoint the monarch; referring to the royal stature of Southampton while anticipating the coronation of James; "Not all the water in the rough rude sea can *wash the balm off from an anointed king*" – *Richard II*, 3.2.54-55

> With mine own tears I wash away my **balm**,
> With mine own hands I give away my crown,
> With mine own tongue deny my sacred state,
> With mine own breath release all duteous oaths;
> All pomp and majesty I do forswear
> - The King in *Richard II*, 4.1.206-211

"'Tis not the *balm, the scepter and the ball, the sword, the mace the crown imperial*" – *Henry V*, 4.1.256-257, i.e., aspects of kings; "The *balm* washed off wherewith thou wast anointed" – *3 Henry VI*, 3.1.17; "*Balm* was used in the coronation ceremony, and it was a familiar symbol of regal authority" – Kerrigan;

10 MY LOVE LOOKS FRESH; AND DEATH TO ME SUBSCRIBES,

MY LOVE = my royal son; "If *my dear love* were but the child of state" – Sonnet 124, line 1; "In the devotion of a subject's *love*, tend'ring the precious safety of my prince, and free from other misbegotten hate, come I appellant to this princely presence" – *Richard II*, 1.1.31-34; **LOOKS FRESH** = appears royal, as before he was imprisoned in the Tower; perhaps also suggesting that Oxford may actually have seen Henry Wriothesley upon his release, for the first time in many months (see previous sonnets, after the bargain is announced in Sonnet 87 – i.e., Sonnet 89 – alluding to a cessation of visits at the Tower.) "Yet *looks he like a king*" – *Richard II*, 3.3.68; "Thou that art now the world's *fresh* ornament" – Sonnet 1, line 9; "since first I saw you *fresh*" – Sonnet 104, line 8; **AND DEATH TO ME SUBSCRIBES** – and my son's expected death in prison now submits to me; Booth notes the legal echoes suggesting "to subscribe" as "to sign one's name"; Oxford has saved his royal son's life, behind the scenes, triumphing over death; in the process his son has given his word or "subscribed" to the bargain, by abandoning all claim to the throne; death also submits to Oxford by virtue of the fact that this monument of the Sonnets will defeat death: "'Gainst *death* and all-oblivious enmity/ Shall you pace forth!" – Sonnet 55, lines 9-10; "From hence your memory *death* cannot take,/ Although in me each part will be forgotten./ Your name from hence immortal life shall have,/ Though I (once gone) to all the world must die" – Sonnet 81, lines 3-6; "And thou in this shalt find thy monument,/ When tyrants' crests and tombs of brass are spent" – lines 13-14 below.

11 SINCE SPITE OF HIM I'LL LIVE IN THIS POOR RHYME,

Because, despite my own death, I'll live in these eternal sonnets; but they are "poor" because Southampton has not been able to claim the throne and the Tudor dynasty is ending; **I'LL** = an echo of the *"Isle"* of Wight, where Southampton will become captain, and the *"Isle"* of Man, which James will return to the ownership and rule of Oxford's son-in-law William Stanley, Earl of Derby, husband of Elizabeth Vere; *"I'll Live"* suggesting that perhaps Oxford is planning to "live" on one of these islands in the near future.

12 WHILE HE INSULTS O'ER DULL AND SPEECHLESS TRIBES.
HE = death; **INSULTS O'ER** = triumphs over those who cannot (or will not) speak the truth; insult = exult, as a victorious enemy; "Ay me! I see the ruin of my House: the tiger now hath seized the gentle hind; *insulting tyranny* begins to jut upon the innocent and aweless throne" – Queen Elizabeth, wife of King Edward IV, in *Richard III*, 2.4.49-52; **SPEECHLESS** = silent, dumb; without means of speaking out, while Oxford, by contrast, is speaking here to future generations; **TRIBES** = races, bodies of people having particular descents; echoing the "tribunal" upon which Oxford sat as highest-ranking earl at the trial; while proclaiming his own triumph over death, Oxford is also forecasting the victory of death over the current "speechless tribes" of men under the new reign, i.e., Secretary Robert Cecil, who will become Earl of Salisbury and run the Government until his death in 1612. These men have determined that death will bury Oxford in history, but he now defiantly retorts that "I'll live in this poor rhyme" – in the same way he has declared of the pen name "Shakespeare" that: "He, nor that affable familiar ghost/ Which nightly gulls him with intelligence,/ *As victors of my silence cannot boast!*" – Sonnet 86, lines 9-11

13 AND THOU IN THIS SHALT FIND THY MONUMENT,
IN THIS = here in this Book of Sonnets; **THY MONUMENT** = eternal memorial; ("Your monument shall be my gentle verse" – Sonnet 81, line 9; "Not marble nor the gilded *monument*/ Of Princes shall outlive this powerful rhyme" – Sonnet 55, lines 1-2); "Again we see if our friends be dead, we cannot show or declare our affection more than by erecting them of *tombs*: whereby when they be dead indeed, yet make we them live, as it were, again through their *monument*. But with me behold it happenth far better, for in your lifetime *I shall erect you such a monument* that, as I say, in your lifetime you shall see how noble a shadow of your virtuous life shall hereafter remain *when you are dead and gone*" – Oxford's Prefatory Letter to *Cardanus' Comfort*, 1573

14 WHEN TYRANTS' CRESTS AND TOMBS OF BRASS ARE SPENT.
TYRANTS' = Elizabeth's = the tyranny of her "wasted time"; "But wherefore do not you a mightier way/ Make war upon this bloody *tyrant time*?" – Sonnet 16, lines 1-2; "When in the Chronicle of *wasted time*" – Sonnet 106, line 1; the Queen's tyranny over her royal son; "But to prevent the *tyrant's* violence – for trust not him that hath once broken faith" – *3 Henry VI*, 4.4.29-30; "In act thy bed-vow broke and *new faith torn*/ In vowing new hate after new love bearing/ ... And *all my honest faith in thee is lost*" – Sonnet 152, lines 3-4,8, Oxford to Elizabeth, at the end of the Dark Lady series, bitterly accusing her of breaking her promises to him and Southampton; **CRESTS** = coats of arms on tombs of kings and queens; Elizabeth's crest carried her motto *Semper Eadem* or *Ever the Same*, as in "Why write I still all one, *ever the same*" – Sonnet 76, line 5; **TOMBS OF BRASS** = Elizabeth's temporary tomb in Westminster Abbey will rest "in the very shadow of the great tomb of Henry VII and his wife ... the most notable *'tomb of brass'* in England" – Mattingly, *PLMA* 1933, p. 721; tombs of brass as opposed to the *"tomb"* of this *"monument"* of sonnets, which will outlive such earthly tombs; "Though yet heaven knows it is but as a *tomb*/ Which hides your life and shows not half your parts" – Sonnet 17, lines 3-4, in reference to the verse of the Sonnets; "Making their *tomb the womb* wherein they grew" – Sonnet 86, line 4; "Ever beloved and loving may his rule be;/ And when old time shall lead him to his end,/ Goodness and he fill up one *monument*" – *Henry VIII*, 2.1.92-94; but, like a message in a bottle, these private verses of the Sonnets will be set adrift on the sea of time to the distant shores of future generations. (Members of the Essex faction referred to Elizabeth as a tyrant -- see "The Reign of Elizabeth I: Court & Culture in the Last Decade," John Guy, p. 16)

1848: Unidentified researcher "J. R." first assigns Sonnet 107 to 1603.

Gerald Massey, 1866: "We may rest assured that (the Poet of the Sonnets) was one of the first to greet his 'dear boy,' over whose errors he had grieved ... He had loved him as a father loves a son; he had warned him, and prayed for him, and fought in soul against 'Fortune' on his behalf, and he now welcomed him from the gloom of a prison on his way to a palace and the smile of a monarch."

"Sonnet 107 will show us that, in spite of the dramatic method adopted by Shakespeare in writing of the Earl, he did find a call for secure congratulation when James had restored the Earl to his liberty. *There can be no mistake, doubt, or misgiving here! This sonnet contains evidence beyond question – proof positive and unimpeachable –* that the man addressed by Shakespeare in his *personal* sonnets has been condemned in the first instance to death, and afterwards to imprisonment for life, and escaped his doom through the death of the Queen.

"It tells us that the Poet had been filled with fears for the fate of his friend, and that his instinct, as well as the presentiment of the world in general, had foreshadowed the worst for the Earl, as it dreamed on things to come. He sadly feared the life of his friend – the Poet's lease of his true love – was forfeited, if not to immediate death, to a 'confined doom,' or a definite, a life-long imprisonment. The painful uncertainty is over now. The Queen is dead – the '*Mortal Moon* hath her eclipse endured.' Cynthia was one of Elizabeth's most popular poetical names...

"Those who had prophesied the worst can now laugh at their own fears and mock their unfulfilled preictions. The new King calls the Earl from a prison to a seat of honor ... Our Poet evidently hopes that the Earl's life will share in this new dawn of gladness and promised peace of the nation. He can exult over death this time. It is his turn to triumph now. And his friend shall find a monument in his verse which shall exist when the crests of tyrants have crumbled and their brass-mounted tombs have passed from sight ... The sonnet carries double. It blends the Poet's private feeling for his friend with the public fear for the death of the Queen. The 'Augurs' had contemplated that event with mournful forebodings, and prophesied changes and disasters ... But it has passed over happily for the nation as joyfully for the Poet."
- *Shakespeare's Sonnets Never Before Interpreted*, pp 79 and 311-313

Sidney Lee, 1898: "Sonnet 107 ... makes references that cannot be mistaken to three events that took place in 1603 – to Queen Elizabeth's death, to the accession of James I, and to the release of the Earl of Southampton, who had been in prison since he was convicted in 1601 of complicity in the rebellion of the Earl of Essex ... Elizabeth's crown had been passed, without civil war, to the Scottish King, and thus the revolution that had been foretold as the inevitable consequence of Elizabeth's demise was happily averted ...

"There was hardly a verse-writer who mourned her loss that did not typify it, moreover, as the eclipse of a heavenly body ... At the same time James was constantly said to have entered on his inheritance 'not with an olive branch in his hand, but with a whole forest of olives round about him, for he brought not peace to this kingdom alone' but to all Europe ...

"'The drops of this most balmy time,' in this same sonnet, 107, is an echo of another current strain of fancy. James came to England in a springtide of rarely rivaled clemency, which was reckoned of the happiest augury ... One source of grief alone was acknowledged: Southampton was still a prisoner in the Tower, 'supposed as forfeit to a confined doom.' All men, wrote Manningham, the diarist, on the day following the Queen's death, wished him liberty. The wish was fulfilled quickly. On April 10, 1603, his prison gates were opened by 'a warrant from the king' ... It is improbable that Shakespeare remained silent. 'My love looks fresh,' he wrote, in the concluding lines of Sonnet 107, and he repeated the conventional promise that he had so often made before, that his friend should live in his 'poor rhyme,' 'when tyrants' crests and tombs of brass are spent.'"
- *A Life of William Shakespeare*, pp. 147-150

Garrett Mattingly, 1933: "Critics have generally agreed that, of all of Shakespeare's sonnets, 107 offers the most hope for dating by internal evidence. Since Massey first argued the point in 1866 a number of distinguished scholars ... have supported the view that this sonnet refers to the death of Queen Elizabeth and the accession of James I... That Elizabeth is meant by 'the mortal moon' there can be no reasonable doubt. All her life she had been Cynthia ... In a general way it has always been clear that the events of the spring of 1603 do satisfy the conditions ... The further such an inquiry is pushed, the more striking becomes the evidence that the second quatrain of the sonnet expresses exactly the state of mind of most of Shakespeare's contemporaries ... and the stronger becomes the conviction that, of all the public events of Shakespeare's lifetime, these are the most likely to find an echo in the sonnets.

"To the average Elizabethan Englishman, at least, the greatest crisis of Elizabeth's reign was that which marked its close. To him, the certainty and security of the succession to the throne came first ... No one had forgotten the Wars of the Roses, and the corollary of a disputed succession was civil war ... A dread of civil war explains more than half of England's loyalty to the Tudors. And, as the century drew to a close, men perceived that the last of the Tudors would die without issue, and nothing settled ... But James was a foreigner, and lawyers were found to argue that if birth in a foreign kingdom and status as the subject of a foreign crown could bar claimants from the inheritance of land in England (as under the law it did), then surely such birth barred succession to the throne...

"(The) real danger of a disputed succession ... was widely appreciated and formed the basis of the gloomiest prophecies. Shakespeare could not have been ignorant of it or indifferent to it. His plays ... do show a keen interest in dynastic questions ... Indeed, few people either in England or in Scotland expected James to accede peaceably ... It is rather to the peaceable union with the enemy, Scotland, and to the apparently permanent relief from danger of civil war that the phrase 'olives of endless age' is to be applied; but James's accession extinguished the last sparks of trouble in Ireland, and peace with Spain, too, was seen in the offing. Hostilities with Spain were suspended on James I's accession, for he held that, as in his capacity of King of Scotland he was not at war with that power, he could not be at war with her as King of England...

"The more one closely examines the events of the spring of 1603, as they were seen by Shakespeare's contemporaries, the more consistent do they appear with the language of Sonnet 107, even in its slightest details, and the more likely does it seem that these events would have impressed the poet deeply enough to find a record in the sonnets. *Nor do the allusions in the sonnet seem appropriate to any other sequence of public events during Shakespeare's lifetime.*"
- PLMA, XLVIII, 1933, pp. 705-721

Alfred Harbage, 1950: "All that we know certainly of Sonnets 107, 123 and 124 is that they were published in 1609 ...Their style – by which is meant here their music and the condensation and integration of their language – suggests to me that they were written late rather than early in Shakespeare's career ... The early months of 1603 were among the blackest in English history: there was fear of Tyrone in Ireland, and of masterless men and malcontents in England: the Queen was dying and her successor unnamed; forty thousand Catholics were said to be ready to rise in arms if the successor should be James ... Then, as if by miracle, the crisis passed, and James ascended the English throne in an almost hysterical outburst of national joy ... the astrological and historical background of 1603 was appropriate for the allusions in Sonnet 107 ... If we can speak of such a thing as a season of imagery, this was the season of heavenly bodies, setting, rising, eclipsed, etc., and the season of olives of endless age.

"The moon had always been Elizabeth's symbol. She had been Cynthia herself, or, as in Shakespeare, Cynthia's 'imperial vot'ress.' In the elegiac chorus of 1603, she is Luna, Delia, Cynthia, Phoebe, Belphoebe (all

the moon), or else the setting sun ... In the presence of Death, Elizabeth qualified *poetically* as a tyrant ... (Shakespeare's) voice is missing among the poetic eulogists of Elizabeth and James in the 'Wonderful Year' (1603). The tone (of Sonnets 107, 123 and 124) ... suggests to me a man quite willing to 'sit out' the public excitements over a change in administration."
- *Shakespeare Quarterly*, Vol.1, no. 2, April 1950, 57-63

G. P. V. Akrigg, 1968: "H. C. Beeching ... declared 'the only sonnet that can be dated with absolute certainty from internal evidence (107) belongs to 1603.' Dover Wilson ... has continued to recognize that Sonnet 107 dates from 1603 ... Re-reading Sonnet 107 in another connection ... I had a sudden complete conviction that the sonnet belonged to 1603, almost as if it had the date visibly branded upon it ... This is what Shakespeare had to say to Southampton upon his release from imprisonment:

"I myself in my fears had thought, like everybody else, that the future held nothing for you beyond continued confinement in the Tower. But now Queen Elizabeth, so often likened to Cynthia, the virgin goddess of the moon, has finally been eclipsed by death. Since she had no acknowledged heir, pessimists had feared that her passing would bring a disastrous civil war, but now even they mock their earlier dismal prophecy. With the peaceful accession of King James, feelings of uncertainty give way to feelings of security. Our new King, dedicated to peace, brings us an unending era of peace and prosperity. The refreshing showers of this pleasant spring give new vigor to my love for you. Poor though my verse may be, it forces death to submit to me. I shall attain a literary immortality denied to the inarticulate masses. And this poetry of mine will provide you with a monument which will keep you remembered when elaborate tombs, like that to be raised for our late tyrannic Queen, have disappeared."
- *Shakespeare and the Earl of Southampton*, pp 254-255

Robert Giroux, 1982: "This sonnet (107) could not have been written before 24 March 1603, the date of Queen Elizabeth's death, for a good reason: the word 'tyrant' was risky to put on paper at any time during her reign, and mortally dangerous if coupled with a reference to her. It is generally agreed that 'mortal Moon' refers to Elizabeth ... ('Men must endure their going hence, even as their coming hither. Ripeness is all" – *King Lear*, 5.2.9-11) Men must endure their deaths, even as their births; ripeness is all there is. 'Endure' can of course mean survive, but the O. E. D. also defines it as 'to suffer without resistance, to submit to, to undergo,' and that is how Shakespeare uses the word in both places. By 'the mortal Moon hath her eclipse endured,' Shakespeare means that, as a mortal, the Queen has undergone death. '*Her* eclipse' instead of '*an* eclipse ... further emphasizes a permanent rather than a temporary state...

"There is nothing anywhere else in the sonnets like the mastery and freedom of the first quatrain (of 107) ... This single sentence, one marvelous breath, could only have been written by a poet in the fullness of his powers ... Other historical allusions in this sonnet place the poem solidly in 1603 ... At Southampton's trial, it had been remarked how youthful he still looked. On his release from the Tower in April 1603, he was in his twenty-ninth year ('my love looks fresh' – line 9)"
- *The Story of Q*, pp. 191-198

John Kerrigan, 1986: "[In Sonnet 107] the present events are realized so vividly that they can be read as topical allusions ... (Any) dating of the poet's change of heart can be linked to the public events described in lines 5-9, as either written at the time or, less likely, retrospectively set in that context. And this means that, if the allusions are unlocked, they probably date the poem, and certainly set a *terminus a quo* for its composition...

"A considerable outburst of anxious astrology and prediction ... preceded the Queen's death. As her health worsened and the political picture remained obscure, foreboding grew. Much was at stake. Elizabeth had announced no successor, and both Catholics and Puritans feared the accession of a ruler less sympathetic to their religious liberty than the moderate Protestant Queen had been. More than a dozen claimants maintained their right to the throne ... and the people anticipated either invasion from abroad or civil strife of the kind which laid the country waste during the Wars of the Roses, before Tudor settlement...

"In the light of the secondary sense of *My love looks fresh* it is remarkable that one of the first acts of the newly-crowned King [well before the coronation] was to release the Earl of Southampton, often thought the addressee of Sonnets 1-126, from the prison in which he had languished ever since his participation in the ill-fated Essex Rebellion of 1601. If Wriothesley was indeed, to some emotional extent, the *you* and *thou* and *love* of 1-126, both he and the poet's affection for him would have been refreshed and renewed by the events of 1603... *On the basis of allusions, in short, 1603 seems the obvious date – with all which that implies for the dating of the sequence ...*"
- *The Sonnets and A Lover's Complaint*, Penguin, pp. 313-320

G. Blakemore Evans, 1996: "The majority of recent critics strongly favours 1603 as the most likely date. Indeed, the case for 1603 (or a little later) is so brilliantly presented by Kerrigan that one is dangerously tempted to cry 'Q. E. D.'"
- *The Sonnets*, pp. 216-217

THE MONUMENT

THE FINAL DAYS

JAMES ON HIS WAY TO ENGLAND
SEVENTEEN DAYS TO THE QUEEN'S FUNERAL

Sonnet 108
Prayers Divine
11 April 1603

Oxford is now wrapping what he needs to say to his son and what he needs to leave behind for posterity, as he resumes writing one sonnet per day. In this series, more than in any of the previous verses, he is drawing upon other writings and events of his past, perhaps even rewriting verses that had been composed much earlier. But all are being written and/or revised according to this chronology during April 10-28, 1603. Here, too, the Book of Sonnets is being transformed into a sacred book in which the poems are hymns or prayers. Also, now that the Queen is physically dead, "Time" and "Nature" are transformed into universal concepts – no longer tied directly to the monarch.

Sonnet 108	Translation
What's in the brain that ink may character,	What's in my mind that I can set down in ink
Which hath not figured to thee my true spirit?	That hasn't presented you as my royal son?
What's new to speak, what now to register,	What's new to speak? What now to be written
That may express my love, or thy dear merit?	That can express my love or your royal stature?
Nothing, sweet boy, but yet, like prayers divine,	Nothing, royal son! But like saying prayers,
I must each day say o'er the very same,	I write sonnets daily again to say the same thing,
Counting no old thing old, thou mine, I thine,	With nothing old, you my son and I your father,
Even as when first I hallowed thy fair name.	As when I christened you as the future Henry IX.
So that eternal love in love's fresh case,	So that eternal royal blood in its new form
Weighs not the dust and injury of age,	Cares not about the tragedies of the past,
Nor gives to necessary wrinkles place,	Nor does it bother about the passage of time,
But makes antiquity for aye his page.	But carries that old royalty with it as a servant,
Finding the first conceit of love there bred,	Finding it as your royal blood was at your birth,
Where time and outward form would show it dead.	While all that has happened shows it gone.

1 WHAT'S IN THE BRAIN THAT INK MAY CHARACTER
THE BRAIN = Oxford's mind; i.e., What's in my mind; "That did my ripe thoughts in *my brain* inhearse,/ Making their tomb the womb wherein they grew" – Sonnet 86, lines 3-4; "Thy gift, thy tables, are within *my brain*" - Sonnet 122, line 1; **THAT INK MAY CHARACTER** = that this black ink can inscribe or express in these verses; "Know you the hand? 'Tis Hamlet's *character*" – Hamlet, 4.7.50; **INK** = the black writing liquid; "His beauty shall in these *black lines* be seen,/ And they shall live, and he in them still green" - Sonnet 63, lines 13-14; related to the blackness of disgrace and loss of royal claim; **CHARACTER** = verb to inscribe or express or write; to record; "Thy gift, thy tables, are within my brain,/ Full *charactered* with lasting memory" - Sonnet 122, lines 1-2; Southampton's "gift" is his own life and royal blood, which, through

Oxford, he has poured into the lines written upon these "tables" or tablets; in turn, they are in Oxford's *brain* or in his memory or mind; "And these few precepts *in thy memory* look thou *character*" - *Hamlet*, 1.3.58-59; "Show me your image in some antique book,/ Since mind at first in *character* was done" – Sonnet 59, lines 7-8; "And mighty states *characterless* (without records) are grated to dusty nothing" – *Troilus and Cressida*, 3.2.185-186; "There is a kind of *character* in thy life that to th'observer doth thy history fully unfold" – *Measure for Measure*, 1.1.27-29

2 WHICH HATH NOT FIGURED TO THEE MY TRUE SPIRIT?
FIGURED = represented; (harking back to "prefiguring" of Sonnet 106, line 10); *OED* on the verb to figure = "to give figure to, to form, shape; to bring into shape ... to picture in the mind; to imagine ... to portray or represent by speech or action ... to prefigure, foreshadow ... to display the form of; to exhibit a resemblance to ... to frame according to rhetorical figures; to adorn with figures of speech ... to adorn or mark with figures; to embellish or ornament with a design or pattern"; also, *OED* includes "to mark with (numerical) figures," suggesting a reference to these "numbers" or sonnets by which Oxford is creating the "monument" for Southampton and its "living record" of him; "to indicate not directly, but by signs; to imagine" – Schmidt; "A most fine *figure*. To prove you a cipher" – *Love's Labour's Lost*, 1.2.54-55; "In the same *figure* like the King that's dead" - *Hamlet*, 1.1.44

"There is a history in all men's lives *figuring* the nature of the times deceased; the which observed, a man may prophesy, with a near aim, of the main chance of things as yet not come to life, who in their seeds and weak beginnings lie intreasured" – *2 Henry IV*, 3.1.80-85

CHARACTER/FIGURE = "What's on this tomb I cannot read. The *character* I'll take with wax; our captain hath in every *figure* skill, an aged interpreter" – *Timon of Athens*, 5.3.5-8; **MY TRUE SPIRIT** = my genuine feelings; you, my son, whose spirit lives in me; "*My spirit is thine*, the better part of me" – Sonnet 74, line 8; **TRUE** = Oxford, *Nothing Truer than Truth*; **SPIRIT** = royal blood of Southampton, reflecting upon Oxford as father, and incorporated in these verses; "Th'expense of *spirit* in a waste of shame" – Sonnet 129, as Oxford accuses Elizabeth of wasting their son's royal blood by executing him and/or keeping him in prison; Oxford's true spirit as opposed to the "better spirit" of "Shakespeare" that uses Southampton's name in print, i.e., "Knowing a better *spirit* doth use your name" – Sonnet 80, line 2

3 WHAT'S NEW TO SPEAK, WHAT NOW TO REGISTER,
WHAT NOW TO REGISTER = what can I now record here for posterity; with "now" emphasizing that this is a chronicle still based on time and the calendar, indicating "today"; to Time: "Thy *registers* and thee I both defy,/ Not wond'ring at the present, nor the past,/ For thy records, and what we see, doth lie" – Sonnet 123, lines 9-11; **REGISTER** = "Set down (a fact, name, etc.), formally or officially ... enter or record accurately" – *OED*.

4 THAT MAY EXPRESS MY LOVE, OR THY DEAR MERIT?
EXPRESS = (see Sonnet 106, line 7: "I see their antique Pen would have expressed/ Even such a beauty as you master now"; **MY LOVE** = Oxford's love for his son, echoing "love" for Southampton's royal blood; **THY DEAR MERIT** = your royal stature, which exists regardless of your inability to proclaim it; the royal value of my dear son; "If my *dear* love were but the child of state" – Sonnet 124, line 1; "Lord of my love, to whom in vassalage/ Thy *merit* hath my duty strongly knit" – Sonnet 26, lines 1-2; "Who will believe my verse in time to come/ If it were filled with *your most high deserts*" – Sonnet 17, line 1-2; "A *dearer merit* ... have I deserved at your Highness' hands" – *Richard II*, 1.3.156-158

5 NOTHING, SWEET BOY; BUT YET, LIKE PRAYERS DIVINE,
SWEET BOY = royal son; "The *boy* for trial needs would touch my breast" – Sonnet 153, line 10, soon after the birth of Southampton in 1574; "O Thou *my lovely Boy*" – Sonnet 126, line 1, the final sonnet or "prayer" to his royal son; father-to-son: "My heart, *sweet boy*, shall be thy sepulcher" – *3 Henry VI*, 2.5.115; **PRAYERS DIVINE** = these sonnets, addressed to a "god on earth"; or as in Sonnet 110, line 12: "A *God in love*, to whom I am confined"; "hymns at heaven's gate" – Sonnet 29, line 12; "There's a *divinity* that shapes our ends, rough hew them how we will" – *Hamlet*, 5.2.10-11; "When I perceive your Grace, like *power divine*" – *Measure for Measure*, 5.1.366

6 I MUST EACH DAY SAY O'ER THE VERY SAME,
I MUST EACH DAY SAY O'ER = I must write these verses (i.e., say these prayers) each day, now, until the Tudor dynasty is officially over upon Elizabeth's funeral; as one says the Rosary; in this case, praying to a king or god on earth; **VERY** = Ver = Edward de Vere

7 COUNTING NO OLD THING OLD, THOU MINE, I THINE,
COUNTING NO OLD THING OLD = not counting (or making account of) your former royal stature (or the treasure of your royal blood) as old or forgotten; counting the beads of the Rosary, each sonnet being a number or bead; "Numbering our Ave-Maries with our beads" – *3 Henry VI*, 2.1.162; repetitious praying with the same words over and over, as in "fair, kind, and true" of Sonnet 105; (*OED*): "He is not *counted* in the number of kings" – Grafton, *Chron*. II.70, 1568; "Abram believed the Lorde, and it was *counted* unto him for righteousness" – Coverdale, Geneva, xv.6, 1535; **OLD** = "Wherefore, not as a stranger but in the *old* style" – Oxford to Robert Cecil, May (?) 1601; "for truth is truth though never so *old*, and time cannot make that false which was once true" – Oxford to Robert Cecil, May 7, 1603

"In the *old* age black was not *counted* fair" – Sonnet 127, line 1, i.e., in the former golden time, our disgraced son was not accounted royal; "England's *counted* Queen" – *Richard III*, 4.1.46

COUNTING = (*OED*): count: "To tell over one by one ... to mark (the time or rhythm of music) by counting the beats orally"; count up: "to find the whole sum of by counting, to reckon up"; to count kin: "*to reckon degrees of kinship with; hence, to be so near of kin that the degrees can be counted or exactly stated*"; "to include in the reckoning ... to esteem, account, reckon, consider, regard, hold (a thing) to be ... to estimate ... to tell, relate, recount ... to think of, judge ... to plead in a court of law" ... "The plaintiff was said to 'count' when he declared by the mouth of his advocate, or by written document, the nature of his complaint, while 'plead' and 'plea' were specifically used of the defendant's answer to the plaintiff's count or counts. A sergeant-at-arms when appointed went before the judges and formally opened an imaginary case, in order to manifest his right to 'count' or plead"

"When I do *count* the clock that tells the time" – Sonnet 12, line 1; "Now *counting* best to be with you alone" – Sonnet 75, line 7; "Which in their wills *count* bad what I think good" – Sonnet 121, line 8; "Only my plague thus far I *count* my gain" – Sonnet 141, line 13

"…for it is a thing whereof I make great *account*" – Oxford to Robert Cecil, May 11, 1601

THOU MINE, I THINE = Oxford speaking to Southampton as father to son; "a son of *mine* own" – Oxford to Burghley, March 17, 1575; "My spirit is *thine*, the better part of me" – Sonnet 74, line 8

8 EVEN AS WHEN FIRST I HALLOWED THY FAIR NAME.
FIRST = during an earlier time; "Since *first* I saw you fresh, which yet are green" – Sonnet 104, line 8; "O, twice my father, twice am I thy son! The life thou gav'st me *first* was lost and done" – *1 Henry VI*, 4.6.6-7;

"Who taught thee *first* to sigh, alas, my heart?" – Oxford's early sonnet, circa 1571-1573; **HALLOWED** = sanctified, as at a christening; "Our Father, which art in Heaven, *hallowed* be thy Name" – Gospel of Matthew, 6.9; the Lord's Prayer; i.e., Oxford from the beginning has seen him as a god, as in "the little Love-God" of Sonnet 154, line 1, when his son ("the boy") was newly born; and as in the upcoming Sonnet 110, line 12, when he calls Southampton "a God in love," i.e., a divine being filled with royal blood; *OED* (hallow): "To make holy, to sanctify, purify ... to consecrate, set apart as sacred to God; to dedicate to some sacred or religious use or office; to bless a thing so that it may be under the particular protection of a deity, or possess divine virtue ... *to consecrate (a person) to an office, as bishop, king*, etc ... to consecrate (the eucharistic elements) ... to honor as holy, to regard and treat with reverence or awe (esp. God or his name)"; "And often hallowed with holy water dewe" – Spenser, Shepherd's Calendar, Feb. 210, 1579; "nor my prayers are not words duly hallow'd" – *Henry VIII*, 2.3.67-68

> When thou reviewest this, thou dost review
> The very part was *consecrate to thee*
> - Sonnet 74, lines 5-6

THY FAIR NAME = your (Southampton's) royal identity; following up with the words of the Lord's Prayer ("thy Name"); **FAIR** = royal; "From *fairest* creatures we desire increase" – Sonnet 1, line 1; in the 1574 prologue, Elizabeth was the "fairest votary" – Sonnet 154, line 5, and she gave this royal quality to her "fair" son

9 SO THAT ETERNAL LOVE IN LOVE'S FRESH CASE

ETERNAL LOVE = immortal royal blood; "When in eternal lines to time thou grow'st" – Sonnet 18, line 12; **LOVE'S FRESH CASE** = royal blood's new encasement of you, as opposed to that of the prison; **FRESH** = echoing "my love looks *fresh*" of Sonnet 107, line 10; "the world's *fresh* ornament" – Sonnet 1, line 9; **CASE** = legal case, i.e., the new legal *case* made for his son's *love* or royal blood; a case that must be made now only in these sonnets, not in reality, because his son must give up any claim to the throne

10 WEIGHS NOT THE DUST AND INJURY OF AGE,

WEIGHS NOT, etc. = ignores the death of Time in this diary of your criminally injured royal life and claim to the throne; "*Weigh* you the worth and honor of a King" – *Troilus and Cressida*, 2.2.26; as in weighing the legal case; **DUST** = "Time's glory is to calm contending kings/ ...To ruinate proud buildings with thy hours,/ And *smear with dust* their glitt'ring golden towers" – *Lucrece*, 939,944-945; "We ... commit his body to the ground, earth to earth, ashes to ashes, *dust to dust*" – Christian Burial Service; "When that churl death my bones with *dust* shall cover" – Sonnet 32, line 2; "What a piece of work is a man ... and yet, to me, what is this quintessence of *dust*?" – *Hamlet*, 2.2.305,309-310; "And mighty states characterless (unrecorded) are grated to *dusty nothing*" – *Troilus and Cressida*, 3.2.185-186; **INJURY** = "To bear love's wrong than hate's known *injury*" – Sonnet 40, line 12; the treason charge against Southampton: "Call me their traitor! Thou *injurious* tribune!" – *Coriolanus*, 3.3.69

11 NOR GIVES TO NECESSARY WRINKLES PLACE,

NOR, etc. = nor yields to your own inevitable aging process from here on; **GIVES TO ... PLACE** = referring to James taking Southampton's seat or "place" on the throne; also, the "better judgment" of "misprision" has liberated Southampton from "the place" that is the Tower of London; "The judicial context invokes overtones of 'to give' meaning 'to *deliver judgment*'" – Booth, citing *OED*: "*to give the case*, meaning *to decide the case*"; **NECESSARY** = unavoidable; "death, a *necessary* end, will come when it will come" – *Julius Caesar*, 2.2.36-37

12 **BUT MAKES ANTIQUITY FOR AYE HIS PAGE,**
BUT MAKES, etc. = but makes your former royal blood forever my subject matter; **FOR AYE** = eternally, forever; punning on "I" and/or "eye"; **PAGE** = boy acting as Oxford's page, as when his little page (possibly Southampton) delivered an oration to Elizabeth at the tiltyard in January 1581, when Southampton was not yet seven years old

13 **FINDING THE FIRST CONCEIT OF LOVE THERE BRED,**
FIRST CONCEIT OF LOVE = the first thought or inspiration of your royal blood; also, glancing at Southampton's "conception" in Elizabeth's womb resulting in the birth of his royal blood (a play on "conceiving a child" as in "I cannot conceive you" – "Sir, this young fellow's mother could; whereupon she grew round-wombed" – *King Lear*, 1.1.11-13; **FIRST** = repeated from line 8; "The *first heir* of my invention" – dedication of *Venus and Adonis* to Southampton; **BRED** = "still being begotten" – Booth; i.e., still being re-created and reborn in the womb of these sonnets; his "love" or royal blood was "bred" or born in him; "You are so strongly in my purpose *bred*,/ That all the world besides me thinks y'are dead" – Sonnet 112, lines 13-14, i.e., all the rest of the world, except for Oxford, believes that Henry Wriothesley is without royal blood and/or claim

14 **WHERE TIME AND OUTWARD FORM WOULD SHOW IT DEAD.**
WHERE TIME, etc. = where the actual time that I am recording would try to make your royal blood appear to be dead or nonexistent; "But I hope truth is subject to no prescription, for truth is truth though never so old, and *time* cannot make that false which was once true" – Oxford to Robert Cecil, May 7, 1603, arguing against time and outward form; **DEAD** = the same thought as: "That all the world besides me thinks y'are *dead*" – Sonnet 112, line 14

Part Two

THE FINAL DAYS

SIXTEEN DAYS TO THE QUEEN'S FUNERAL

Sonnet 109
Myself Bring Water
My Rose
12 April 1603

Oxford begs Southampton's forgiveness for the bargain he made with Cecil – to save Southampton's life in exchange for Southampton's renouncing any claim to the throne. In the opening line he pleads: O, never say that I was a traitor to your royal blood! Glancing at his upcoming role in the coronation of James as Lord Great Chamberlain or "water bearer" to the monarch, Oxford concludes by addressing his royal son as "my Rose," i.e., his Tudor Rose.

Sonnet 109	Translation
O never say that I was false of heart,	O, never say that I committed treason against you,
Though absence seemed my flame to qualify,	Though your imprisonment made it seem so!
As easy might I from my self depart,	I would easily separate from myself,
As from my soul, which in thy breast doth lie.	Parting from my soul, but that you're inside it.
That is my home of love; if I have ranged	That's where my royal blood lives! If I've stayed
Like him that travels I return again,	Away from you, now I've come back again,
Just to the time, not with the time exchanged,	Now that Elizabeth's dead and you are ransomed,
So that myself bring water for my stain.	And I'll bring water to the King at his Coronation.
Never believe, though in my nature reigned	Never believe (even though the Queen reigned
All frailties that beseige all kinds of blood,	Over my inability to help your natural royal blood)
That it could so preposterously be stained	That your royalty is so preposterously disgraced
To leave for nothing all thy sum of good.	That it could add up to nothing.
For nothing this wide Universe I call,	For I ask for nothing in the entire universe
Save thou, my Rose, in it thou art my all.	Except you, my Tudor Rose, who are all to me!

1 O NEVER SAY THAT I WAS FALSE OF HEART,
O = Oxford; **NEVER** = Edward de Vere, *Ever or Never*; **O NEVER** = Oxford, Edward de Vere; **FALSE** = opposite of "true" or *Nothing Truer than Truth*; ("and time cannot make that *false* which was once true" – Oxford to Robert Cecil, May 7, 1603); traitorous, i.e., although I have made this bargain to save your life, causing you to forfeit the crown, please never say that I was a traitor to your royal blood; echoing "false-traitor"

2 THOUGH ABSENCE SEEMED MY FLAME TO QUALIFY!
Though my absence from you (during your imprisonment) made my love seem less; **ABSENCE** = referring to Southampton's "absence" when he was in the Tower, and to Oxford's own "absence" from his royal son during that time; ("Oh *absence*" – Sonnet 39, line 9; "Th'*imprisoned absence of your liberty*" – Sonnet 58,

line 6); **MY FLAME** = my love; the flame of royalty in my son; "*thy light's flame*" – Sonnet 1, line 6; **QUALIFY** = weaken; lessen; cast into doubt

3 AS EASY MIGHT I FROM MYSELF DEPART

It would be as easy to separate from my own self; i.e., it would be impossible

4 AS FROM MY SOUL, WHICH IN THY BREAST DOTH LIE:

As to separate from my essence, which lives in you; with a play on "lie" in reference to the fact that both Oxford and Southampton must lie about their father-son relationship; "My spirit is thine, the better part of me" – Sonnet 74, line 8

5 THAT IS MY HOME OF LOVE. IF I HAVE RANGED

THAT = Southampton's breast; **MY HOME OF LOVE** = Oxford's home of royal blood; i.e., his son's heart or breast; **HOME** = suggesting the House of Tudor; "So thy great gift, upon misprision growing,/ Comes *home* again" – Sonnet 87, lines 11-12; **RANGED** = wandered

6 LIKE HIM THAT TRAVELS I RETURN AGAIN,

Suggesting the Prodigal Son, who leaves but returns home; also suggesting that Oxford himself is considering leaving England in the near future, not wanting to remain a courtier or Privy Council member in the reign of James; "when his youthful morn/ Hath *traveled* on to age's steepy night" – Sonnet 63, lines 4-5; in a sense, because of Southampton's tragic imprisonment and then his liberation, Oxford too has died and returned from the dead; i.e., he and his son have "died" but now are resurrected; "But that the dread of something after death, the undiscovered country from whose bourn no *traveler returns*" – Hamlet, 3.1.78-80

7 JUST TO THE TIME, NOT WITH THE TIME EXCHANGED,

JUST TO THE TIME = at the appointed time; i.e., Oxford is now writing one verse per day; ("not altered by the passage of time" – Duncan-Jones); "Why *with the time* do I not glance aside/ To new found methods, and to compounds strange" – Sonnet 76, lines 3-4; **EXCHANGED** = referring to the *ransom* paid by Oxford to gain Southampton's liberation from prison; "You have a Trojan prisoner … Oft have you … desired my Cressid in right great *exchange*" – Troilus and Cressida, 3.3.18-21; "As I my poor self did *exchange* for you" – Cymbeline, 1.2.50; "The Earl of Bedford had a prisoner … For him I was *exchanged and ransomed*" – 1 Henry VI, 1.4.26-28; "*ransom* all ill deeds" – Sonnet 34, line 14; "To weigh how once I suffered in *your crime*/ … But that *your trespass* now becomes a fee;/ Mine *ransoms* yours, and yours must *ransom* me" – Sonnet 120, lines 8,13-1; "His crown shall be the *ransom* of my friend" – 1 Henry VI, 1.2.150; also echoing Henry Wriothesley as a "changeling" in the Southampton household; "That some night-tripping fair had *exchanged in cradle-clothes our children* where they lay, and called mine Percy, his Plantagenet! Then would I have his Harry, and he mine" – 1 Henry IV, 1.1.86-89; also there has been an *exchange* of succession to the throne of Elizabeth, from her son Henry Wriothesley (who would have become Henry IX) to James Stuart, son of the late Mary Queen of Scots, as James I; another exchange has been that of Southampton's imprisonment for his liberation, i.e. James has changed Elizabeth's decree: ("and *change decrees of Kings*" – Sonnet 115, line 6

8 SO THAT MYSELF BRING WATER FOR MY STAIN.

Referring to Oxford's upcoming role in the coronation of King James, to be held in July; as Lord Great Chamberlain of England, he is water-bearer to the monarch; (Oxford would soon claim his hereditary right to attend James on the morning of the coronation, asking for the same privileges as his ancestors, who "from time immemorial *served the noble progenitors of our Lord the King with water* before and after eating the day of the Coronation, and had as their right the basins and towels and a tasting cup" – Oxford to the Lord Steward, July 7, 1603); overtones of Holy Water; Oxford has taken his son's "stain" or disgrace upon himself, by obliteration of his identity and truth

> And *water* cannot wash away your *sin*
> - *Richard II*, 4.1.242

Oxford is recording his gratitude to James for having liberated Southampton and restored his honor; he will serve at the coronation, performing a kind of ritual or ceremony by which his own "stain" (suffered by his son) will be removed; "Suns of the world may *stain*, when heaven's sun *staineth*" – Sonnet 33, line 14; "Clouds and eclipses *stain* both Moone and Sunne" – Sonnet 35, line 3, referring to the stain that affected both Elizabeth and her royal son, Southampton, and doomed the House of Tudor; *stained*, line 11 below

9 NEVER BELIEVE, THOUGH IN MY NATURE REIGNED
NEVER = Edward de Vere, *Ever or Never*; **REIGNED** = prevailed, but echoing the new reign; "Save her alone, who yet on th'earth doth *reign*" – Oxford poem, referring to Elizabeth, in *The Paradise of Dainty Devices*, 1576, attributed to him as E. O. in the 1577 edition

10 ALL FRAILTIES THAT BESIEGE ALL KINDS OF BLOOD,
ALL = Southampton, *One for All, All for One*; **FRAILTIES** = weaknesses, especially his inability to gain the crown for his son; **BESIEGE** = "Against the wreckful *siege* of batt'ring days" – Sonnet 65, line 6; "yet I am one that hath long *besieged* a fort and not able to compass the end or reap the fruit of his travail, being forced to levy his *siege* for want of munition" – Oxford to Burghley, June 25, 1586; **ALL** = Southampton; **KINDS** = naturally born and related; **ALL KINDS OF BLOOD** = Southampton's royal blood as the "natural issue of Her Majesty's body," as the Parliament of 1571 had described a potential successor to Elizabeth; "His hands were guilty of no *kindred blood*" – *Richard II*, 2.1.182; "our new Master and Sovereign Lord, who doth not come amongst us as a stranger but as a *natural* prince, succeeding by right of *blood* and inheritance" – Oxford to Robert Cecil, April 25/27, 1603, on the eve of Elizabeth's funeral, referring to King James; "*Kind* is my love today, tomorrow *kind*" – Sonnet 105, line 5

11 THAT IT COULD SO PREPOSTEROUSLY BE STAINED
PREPOSTEROUSLY = unnaturally, opposite of natural or "kind"; absurdly, perversely; "*preposterous* meant *reversed, inverted*" – Booth; i.e., it is preposterous that Southampton, the rightful king, has been the one tarnished when, in fact, it was Robert Cecil who engineered his downfall, resulting in the "preposterous" succession of James of Scotland, whom Oxford has been coerced into supporting; "But thou, 'gainst all proportion, didst bring in wonder to wait on *treason* and on murder: and whatsoever cunning fiend it was that wrought upon thee so *preposterously* hath got the voice in hell for excellence" – the King to traitors in *Henry V*, 2.2.109-113; "Make war upon themselves, brother to brother, blood to blood, self against self: O, *preposterous and frantic outrage*, end thy damned spleen, or let me die, to look on earth no more" – *Richard III*, 2.4.62-65; "For *nature* so *preposterously* to err" – *Othello*, 1.3. 63; **STAINED** = disgraced; "made dishonorable" – Kerrigan; (echoing "stain" of line 8); the stain is related to the "blood" of the previous line; "Suns of the world may *stain*, when heaven's sun *staineth*" – Sonnet 33, line 14; "Who seek to **stain the ocean of thy blood**" – *Lucrece*, 655; *stain*, line 8 above

12 TO LEAVE FOR NOTHING ALL THY SUM OF GOOD:
NOTHING = Southampton as a nobody, opposite of "one"; "Among a number *one* is reckoned *none*" – Sonnet 136, line 8, referring to Southampton as the Queen's unacknowledged royal son; **ALL** = Southampton; **ALL THY SUM OF GOOD** = all your great royalty; the great sum or accounting of your royal blood; "So great a *sum of sums*" – Sonnet 4, line 8; the *Audit* of his blood in Sonnet 4, line 12 and Sonnet 126, line 11

13 FOR NOTHING IN THIS WIDE UNIVERSE I CALL

NOTHING = repeating the same word from the line above; **UNIVERSE** = this one monument of verse (uni-verse); this world, this England, but also larger than the "world" and including those to come in posterity; **CALL** = echoing the verb to summon or call to court; to summon as one calls for birds; as the monarch calls or summons a Parliament; "I call for nothing in this wide universe; also, "Because I call this wide universe nothing" – Booth

14 SAVE THOU, MY ROSE! IN IT THOU ART MY ALL.

Except for you, my Tudor Rose; in this universe, you are my everything; **MY ROSE** = my Tudor Rose; i.e., Southampton is now the only heir of Elizabeth's Tudor Rose dynasty; harking back to Sonnet 1, line 2: "That thereby beauty's *Rose* might never die"; "Why should poor beauty seek/ *Roses* of shadow, since *his Rose* is true?" – Sonnet 67, lines 7-8; "The courtier's, soldier's, scholar's, eye, tongue, sword, th'expectancy and *rose* of the fair state" – Hamlet, 3.1.152-153; **ALL** = Southampton; **MY ALL** = my *one for all, all for one*; you, Southampton; *My All* = "my royal son"; you are everything to me; "And thou, *all* they, hast *all the all of me*" – Sonnet 31, line 14; "You are *my All the world*" – Sonnet 112, line 5

Francis Bacon now writes a fawning (and hypocritical) letter to Southampton, whom he had viciously helped prosecute along with Essex at the trial:

"It may please your Lordship I would have been very glad to have presented my humble service to your Lordship by my attendance, if I could have foreseen that it should not have been unpleasing to you," Bacon tells the earl. *"And therefore because I would commit no error, I choose to write, assuring your Lordship (how credible soever it may seem to you at first) yet it is as true a thing that God Knoweth, that this great change hath wrought in me no other change towards your Lordship than this, that I may safely be now that which I was truly before. And so craving no other pardon than for troubling you with this letter, I do not now begin, but continue to be your Lordship's humble and much devoted Francis Bacon."*
(Stopes, 263)

There is no recorded reply from Southampton, who must have laughed with scorn.

April 12, 1603: *"John Davis was sworn the King's man, and Neville restored to title and fortune"* – a note by Chamberlain (Stopes, 263); Davis and Neville may have been agents or "informers" for Cecil, with Davis writing to him: "I humbly beseech your Lordship to be the Mediator for his [Southampton's] noble favor." (Stopes, 263) Neville had been imprisoned in the Tower, possibly to keep watch on Southampton and report any suspicious behavior to Cecil.

Part Two

THE FINAL DAYS

FIFTEEN DAYS
TO THE QUEEN'S FUNERAL

Sonnet 110
Now All Is Done
13 April 1603

In these final days of the Tudor dynasty, as Oxford continues to record each day in his diary, he attempts to come to terms with Henry Wriothesley – admitting his own faults and praying to his royal son, who is "a God in love," to forgive him for the tragic outcome.

April 13, 1603: "The Earl of Southampton must present himself with the nobles, and Sir Henry Neville with the Councillors, like either shall be one of their ranks" – Manningham Diary; Stopes, 263, who adds, "Many others noted this arrangement" – possibly because Neville, as agent for Cecil, was ordered to report to the Council, which the Secretary controls.

Sonnet 110	Translation
Alas, 'tis true, I have gone here and there,	Alas, it is true that I've gone here and there,
And made myself a motley to the view,	And put on an 'antic disposition' like Hamlet,
Gor'd mine own thoughts, sold cheap what is most	Wounding my mind, selling your royal claim,
dear, Made old offences of affections new.	Committing a crime against you as before.
Most true it is that I have looked on truth	Most true it is that I've publicly kept the truth
Askance and strangely: But by all above,	Hidden as if false! But, your royal highness,
These blenches gave my heart another youth,	These falsehoods saved your life for my sake,
And worse essays proved thee my best of love.	And my duty to others proved my duty to you!
Now all is done, have what shall have no end,	Now succession is past! History is written!
Mine appetite I never more will grind	I'll never again bring up this hidden truth with
On newer proof, to try an older friend,	Any new support for the claim of my son –
A God in love, to whom I am confined.	A King of royalty to whom I'm committed.
Then give me welcome next my heav'n the best,	So you, most next in succession to Elizabeth,
Even to thy pure and most most loving breast.	Welcome me to your blameless royal heart.

1 ALAS, 'TIS TRUE, I HAVE GONE HERE AND THERE,
TRUE = Oxford, *Nothing Truer than Truth*; i.e., Alas, 'tis me;

2 AND MADE MY SELF A MOTLEY TO THE VIEW,
MOTLEY = fool, jester; Oxford was an "allowed fool" who wrote plays for the Court; perhaps also suggesting that he may have performed in his own plays; he was also undoubtedly living a double life for political reasons, serving Elizabeth by putting on various acts in order to gain information; so his reputation, on the record, appears much as Hamlet's, i.e., on account of the "antic disposition" that he put on; "A fool, a

REFERENCE EDITION 595

fool! I met a fool I'th'forest, a *motley* fool … O that I were a fool! I am ambitious for a *motley* coat"
– *As You Like It*, 2.7.13-43

3 GORED MINE OWN THOUGHTS, SOLD CHEAP WHAT IS MOST DEAR,
GOR'D = gored, wounded; suggesting spilled blood; in his dealings with Robert Cecil, Oxford had to "sell out" his own son's royal claim; **MINE OWN THOUGHTS** = thoughts of my own son; (" a son of mine own" – Oxford to Burghley, March 17, 1575); "Boy, thou hast looked thyself into my grace, and art mine own" – *Cymbeline*, 5.5.93-95; **SOLD CHEAP** = paid such a cheap price, the obliteration of his identity as Southampton's father and as Shakespeare; sold his son's claim to the throne in return for his freedom and a royal pardon, which James will grant him; the "ransom" paid in the form of his claim to the throne; "ransom all ill deeds" – Sonnet 34, line 14; **MOST DEAR** = most royal (his most royal son)i.e., Oxford paid this price in order to save his son from execution and to gain his release from the Tower; "thy *dearest* heart-blood" – *3 Henry VI*, 1.1.229; "So I, made lame by Fortune's *dearest* spite" – Sonnet 37, line 3, referring to Elizabeth as Fortune and her malice toward their "dearest" royal son; "Ring, bells, aloud; burn, bonfires, clear and bright, to entertain England's lawful king. Ah! sancta majestas, who'd not buy thee dear?" – *2 Henry VI*, 5.1.3-5

4 MADE OLD OFFENCES OF AFFECTIONS NEW.
Southampton's royal blood is always "new" (at least in this Monument of sonnets), but Oxford had to trade it for "old offences" or for his treasonable crimes; "For as the Sun is daily *new* and *old*" – Sonnet 76, line 13); "What is my offence?" – *Richard III*, 1.4.178

5 MOST TRUE IT IS, THAT I HAVE LOOKED ON TRUTH
TRUE … TRUTH = Oxford, *Nothing Truer than Truth*, has looked upon the truth of his son's royal blood; "For truth is truth though never so old" – Oxford to Robert Cecil, May 7, 1603; **LOOKED ON** = "*Looking on* the lines of my boy's face" – *The Winter's Tale*, 1.2.153-154; "What might I have been, might I a son and daughter now have *look'd on*: - *The Winter's Tale*, 5.1.175-176; "The sun *look'd on* the world with glorious eye,/ Yet not so wistly as this Queen on him" – *The Passionate Pilgrim*, No. 6, 1599; "Were it not pity that this goodly boy should lose his birthright by his father's fault … Ah, what a shame were this! *Look on the boy*" – *3 Henry VI*, 2.2.34-39; "A son who is the theme of honour's tongue, amongst a grove the very straightest plant, who is sweet Fortune's minion and her pride; whilst I by *looking on* the praise of him see riot and dishonour stain the brow of my young Harry" – *1 Henry IV*, 1.1.80-85

6 ASKANCE AND STRANGELY: BUT BY ALL ABOVE,
ASKANCE AND STRANGELY = disdainfully, as a stranger; for example, by delivering my guilty verdict at your trial; by arranging for you to lose the throne (a bargain for which he hopes Southampton will not forever blame him); **STRANGELY** = as opposed to familiarly as a father toward his son; "Against that time when thou shalt *strangely* pass" – Sonnet 49, line 5; "That millions of *strange* shadows on you tend" – Sonnet 53, line 2; "I will acquaintance strangle and look *strange*" – Sonnet 89, line 8; **ALL** = Southampton; **BY ALL ABOVE** = by heaven, i.e., Oxford addressing his son as a god on earth

7 THESE BLENCHES GAVE MY HEART AN OTHER YOUTH,
BLENCHES = deviations from truth; stains of dishonor; Oxford's bargain, having to lie about his son's royal claim, pretending it never existed; **GAVE MY HEART ANOTHER YOUTH** = saved my heart, by saving your life, so now as a free man you are again young and "fresh" as in "my love looks fresh" of Sonnet 107, line 10; the loss of the crown is what saved his life

8 AND WORSE ESSAYS PROVED THEE MY BEST OF LOVE.
WORSE ESSAYS = the most terrible bargain I had to make; **PROVED THEE** = demonstrated you to be;

echoing the trial language; see line "proof" in 11 below; "Till then, not show my head where thou mayst *prove* me" – Sonnet 26, line 14; **MY BEST OF LOVE** = my most royal son with the most royal blood of all

9 **NOW ALL IS DONE, HAVE WHAT SHALL HAVE NO END;**
NOW = at this very time, with James proclaimed king; **ALL** = Southampton, *One for All, All for One*; **ALL IS DONE** = your claim to the throne is no more; Now your royal life is over; "Look *what is done* cannot be now amended" – *Richard III*, 4.4.291; **HAVE WHAT SHALL HAVE NO END** = at the same time, you have what will live eternally, i.e., your royal blood; especially living in these sonnets; "Against this coming *end* you should prepare" – Sonnet 13, line 3; "Thy *end* is Truth's and Beauty's doom and date" – Sonnet 14, line 14; to Elizabeth: "Is this thy body's *end*?" – Sonnet 146, line 8

10 **MINE APPETITE I NEVER MORE WILL GRIND**
MINE APPETITE = my desire for your immortality; **NEVER** = Edward de Vere, *Ever or Never*; **NEVER MORE WILL GRIND** = will never again sharpen

11 **ON NEWER PROOF, TO TRY AN OLDER FRIEND,**
ON NEWER PROOF = with any further demonstration; echoing " **TO TRY AN OLDER FRIEND** = to put my son through any more trial as he grows older; **PROOF/TRY** = echoing "proved" in line 8 above; Southampton's trial at Westminster Hall; "newer *trial*" – Dowden, who also suggests "experiment"

12 **A GOD IN LOVE, TO WHOM I AM CONFINED.**
A GOD IN LOVE = A divine king of royal blood; ("The little *Love-God*" of Sonnet 154, line 1; "my sacred state" – *Richard II*, 4.1.209; "A *god on earth* thou art" – Duchess of York to Bolingbroke, who is now King Henry IV, *Richard II*, 5.3.134; "Thou seem'st not what thou art, *a god, a king*" – *Lucrece*, 601; **"Kings are earth's gods"** – *Pericles*, 1.1.103; "and this man is now become a god" – of Caesar in *Julius Caesar*, 1.2.116); "If *Princes were like gods*, as they should be" – Queen Elizabeth in a letter to Christopher Hatton, 1581 (Weir, 343); "nor in anything doth *a king more resemble God* than in justice" – Oxford to Robert Cecil, May 7, 1603; **TO WHOM I AM CONFINED** = Oxford reversing the situation, with *himself* confined to or within his son, who had been "supposed as forfeit to a *confined doom*" in Sonnet 107, line 4; "Therefore my verse to *constancy confined*" – Sonnet 105, line 7; bound; "Were my worth greater, my duty would show greater; meantime, as it is, it is *bound* to your Lordship, *to whom* I wish long life still lengthened with all happiness" – dedication of *Lucrece* to Southampton (by "Shakespeare").

13 **THEN GIVE ME WELCOME, NEXT MY HEAVEN THE BEST,**
NEXT MY HEAVEN THE BEST = Southampton as successor to "heaven" or Elizabeth

14 **EVEN TO THY PURE AND MOST MOST LOVING BREAST.**
PURE = rightful; **MOST MOST** = most royal; **LOVING** = filled with royal blood

THE FINAL DAYS

FOURTEEN DAYS
TO THE QUEEN'S FUNERAL

Sonnet 111
My Name Receives a Brand
14 April 1603

Oxford knows that official records and future history books will attach a "brand" or stigma to his name and character, because many of his actions, if known at all, will be misunderstood. Queen Elizabeth is the "goddess" (Venus, the Moon, etc.) who is "guilty" of having forced him to perform deeds that have been "harmful" to Southampton. All he can ask now that his royal son "pity" or extend his mercy and forgiveness to him. In a real sense, Oxford is begging Henry Wriothesley, as King, to grant him a royal pardon.

Sonnet 111	Translation
O for my sake do you wish fortune chide,	O, rebuke me along with our late Queen,
The guilty goddess of my harmful deeds,	The goddess who forced me against you,
That did not better for my life provide	And did no better for you (who are my life)
Than public means which public manners breed.	Than give you a public title as a public earl.
Thence comes it that my name receives a brand,	So your stigma becomes my own disgrace,
And almost thence my nature is subdued	And your lack of kingship dictates my life
To what it works in, like the Dyer's hand.	To decline with your blood, sharing the stain!
Pity me then, and wish I were renewed,	Pity me, then, and wish that I could recover,
Whilst like a willing patient I will drink	While like a willing patient I will drink
Potions of Eisel 'gainst my strong infection.	The most bitter medicine to cure myself.
No bitterness that I will bitter think,	But there's no bitterness in my thoughts,
Nor double penance, to correct correction.	Nor will I protest taking double the pain.
Pity me then, dear friend, and I assure ye,	So pity me, royal son, and I assure you
Even that your pity is enough to cure me.	That your compassion for me is all I need.

1 O FOR MY SAKE DO YOU WISH FORTUNE CHIDE,
O = Oxford; **FORTUNE** = in earlier sonnets, *Fortune* referred specifically to Elizabeth (see, e.g., Sonnet 37, line 3; Sonnet 90, lines 1-3); however, now that she has died, the word takes on a more general meaning; Oxford commands his son to wish that fortune will go against him; in that way, things will go well for Southampton, since Oxford is taking the blame and receiving the "brand" of line 5; echoing his sacrifice, requiring his son to deny any relationship to him.

2 THE GUILTY GODDESS OF MY HARMFUL DEEDS,
GUILTY GODDESS = she is Fortune, the late Queen Elizabeth, who was a goddess on earth and was "guilty" of forcing Oxford to make a deal for Southampton that required him to give up the throne; "To gain a *goddess'* grace" – early Oxford poem, published 1576, of Elizabeth; "the goddess who is guilty of my mis-

deeds (because she caused them)"- Kerrigan; **HARMFUL DEEDS** = the bargain Oxford made to pay "ransom" for Southampton's freedom, the payment being that his son must never claim the throne; "harmful deeds" also refers to the crime of the Rebellion itself, which Elizabeth caused by letting Robert Cecil control the government and lure Essex and Southampton into his trap; "Ah, but those tears are pearl which thy love sheeds,/ And they are rich, and *ransom all ill deeds*" – Sonnet 34, lines 13-14

3 THAT DID NOT BETTER FOR MY LIFE PROVIDE
Elizabeth had not provided better for Oxford's or their son's life

4 THAN PUBLIC MEANS, WHICH PUBLIC MANNERS BREEDS.
THAN PUBLIC MEANS = than, for example, my 1,000-pound annuity; **PUBLIC MANNERS** = courtly conduct; outward appearance, as opposed to the truth that includes Southampton as his son; "O how thy worth with *manners* may I sing" – Sonnet 39, line 1; **BREEDS** = gives birth to, related to their father-son relationship; "raise, bring up, support ... cherish, nurture, bring into existence" – Crystal & Crystal; "You are so strongly *in my purpose bred*" – Sonnet 112, line 13; specifically it was the Queen's grant that "bred" or caused the "public manners" that involved deception and falsehood, the ultimate falsehood being the denial that Southampton is his royal son by the Queen.

5 THENCE COMES IT THAT MY NAME RECEIVES A BRAND,
MY NAME = my reputation; "O God, Horatio, what a *wounded name*" – *Hamlet*, 5.2.351; **A BRAND** = a stigma, the way English criminals (felons) were branded with a hot iron on the hand or thumb or face; this "brand" is entirely different from his newly born son's "brand" (source of royal blood) in Sonnets 153 and 154, but a suggestion here is that Southampton's source of royal blood has also received a stigma; ("The only *loss of my good name*" = Oxford poem, published 1576); "Do not so much as *my poor name* rehearse" – Sonnet 71, line 11; "*My name be buried* where my body is" – Sonnet 72, line 11; also the pen name "Shakespeare" is now the brand that his real name receives, according to state policy dictated by Cecil.

6 AND ALMOST THENCE MY NATURE IS SUBDUED
And my nature is thereby almost subdued; nature = kind, i.e., his nature in relationship to Southampton, his nature or kindred as father; **ALMOST** = (echoing the "all" of Southampton's motto); but not totally subdued, because I am recording that natural bond in this monument; "That every word doth *almost* tell my name" – Sonnet 76, line 7; **SUBDUED** = overpowered; put under the control of; made submissive to; "subdue my father entirely to her love" – *Othello*, 3.4.59-60

7 TO WHAT IT WORKS IN, LIKE THE DYER'S HAND.
To working with your dyed blood in my sonnets; **DYER** = one whose occupation is to dye cloth; ("The dyer's hand is stained by dye" – Duncan-Jones; here Oxford is the "dyer" whose writing hand is stained by his son's disgraced royal blood; "water for my stain" – Sonnet 109, line 8); Dye = substitute color; "It will help me nothing to plead mine innocence, for that *dye* is on me which makes my whitest part black" – *Henry VIII*, 1.1.208-209; "The canker blooms have full as deep a *dye*" – Sonnet 54, line 5; "The purple pride/ Which on thy soft cheek for complexion dwells,/ In my love's veins thou hast too grossly *dyed*" – Sonnet 99, lines 3-5; "truth in beauty *dyed*" – Sonnet 101, line 2; (echoing "died"; in that sense, a "dyer" is either one who dies or a killer); **HAND** = "Was sleeping *by a Virgin hand disarmed*" – Sonnet 154, line 8; "A Woman's face with *nature's own hand* painted" – Sonnet 20, line 1; "Or *what strong hand* can hold his swift foot back? Or who his spoil or beauty can forbid?" – Sonnet 65, lines 11-12

8 PITY ME THEN, AND WISH I WERE RENEWED,
PITY = "So bitter *pity* that none shall ever find" – Oxford poem, signed E.O.; (see "bitterness" in line 11 below; **WISH** = repeated from line 1; i.e., and wish this instead; **RENEWED** = "In this prayerful line,

REFERENCE EDITION

renewed carries overtones of spiritual renewal" – Booth; "Though our outward man perish, *yet the inward man is renewed* day by day" – 2 Corinthians 4.16; "Not by works of righteousness which we have done, but according to his mercy he saved us, by the *washing of regeneration*, and **renewing** of the Holy Ghost" – Paul's Epistle to Titus, 3.5 [recalling "water for my stain" of Sonnet 109, line 8]; "And be not conformed to this world; but be ye *transformed by the* **renewing** *of your mind*, that ye may prove what is that good, and acceptable, and perfect, will of God" – Paul to Romans, 12.2

9 **WHILST LIKE A WILLING PATIENT I WILL DRINK**
WILLING PATIENT = Oxford is one who suffers willingly

10 **POTIONS OF EISEL 'GAINST MY STRONG INFECTION;**
POTIONS OF EISEL = mixtures of vinegar; ("Woo't drink up eisel, eat a crocodile?" – *Hamlet*, 5.1.271; "probably … to suggest drinks of extreme bitterness like the 'vinegar … mingled with gall' offered to Christ on the Cross" – Duncan-Jones, citing Matthew, 27.34; Jesus "drank *eisel* and gall to redeem us withal" – Skelton, quoted in Nare's Glossary, cited by Dowden; **INFECTION** = "Ah, wherefore with *infection* should he live" – Sonnet 67, line 1; echoing Essex's reference to the crime of the Rebellion as his "infectious sin."

11 **NO BITTERNESS THAT I WILL BITTER THINK,**
There is no taste so bitter that I will think is bitter; "So *bitter pity* that none shall ever find" – Oxford poem, signed E.O, relating "pity" (lines 8, 13, 14) and "bitter" in this sonnet

12 **NOR DOUBLE PENANCE TO CORRECT CORRECTION.**
Nor will I avoid double suffering; the "penance" is the obliteration of Southampton's royal claim, carried out for his sins or acts of treason; **CORRECT CORRECTION:** "make assurance doubly sure" – Tucker; "to repair the damage done by the remedy" – Booth; in effect, Oxford will repair the damage done to his son by preserving the truth in this monument.

13 **PITY ME THEN, DEAR FRIEND, AND I ASSURE YE:**
Therefore, pity me; **DEAR FRIEND** = royal son; "O *dear son* Edgar" – *King Lear*, 4.1

14 **EVEN THAT YOUR PITY IS ENOUGH TO CURE ME.**
Your love, mercy, pardon and forgiveness is enough to cure my suffering; **CURE** = the cure is this pity from his royal son, akin to the "sovereign *cure*" that Oxford had vainly sought from Queen Elizabeth in 1574, expressed by the Bath sonnets: "Against strange maladies a *sovereign cure*/ … But found *no cure*"
– Sonnet 153, lines 8, 13

Part Two

THE FINAL DAYS

THIRTEEN DAYS
TO THE QUEEN'S FUNERAL

Sonnet 112
My All The World
15 April 1603

Oxford continues to beg for Southampton's "pity" or forgiveness for having brought him into the world with royal blood only to force him to forfeit his claim to the throne. His "purpose" for Southampton is the same as it has always been, as in Sonnet 20: "By adding one thing to my purpose nothing."

Sonnet 112	Translation
Your love and pity doth th'impression fill,	Your royal blood and care for me makes up for
Which vulgar scandal stamped upon my brow,	The disgrace on my once-triumphant brow!
For what care I who calls me well or ill,	For what do I care how others see me,
So you o'er-green my bad, my good allow?	So long as your royal existence redeems me?
You are my All the world, and I must strive	You are my king of England! And I must strive
To know my shames and praises from your tongue,	To receive my disgraces and honors from you.
None else to me, nor I to none alive,	No one else exists for me, nor I to anyone else,
That my steeled sense o'er-changes right or wrong.	So my resolute view can't be right nor wrong.
In so profound *Abysm* I throw all care	Into this personal hell I throw all my concern
Of others' voices, that my adder's sense	About others' views, so my deafness
To critic and to flatt'rer stopped are.	Stops all criticism and flattery.
Mark how with my neglect I do dispense:	Look how I justify this disregard of others:
You are so strongly in my purpose bred,	You were so royally born to be my purpose
That all the world besides me thinks y'are dead.	That to all in England but me your claim is dead.

"This continues directly from the preceding sonnet" – Duncan-Jones.

1 YOUR LOVE AND PITY DOTH TH'IMPRESSION FILL,
YOUR LOVE = your royal blood; i.e., your royal blood fills up the "impression" or dent in my skin that was made by the brand on me; ("This continues directly from the previous sonnet" – Duncan-Jones); **PITY** = taking up the word from the last line of the previous verse: "Even that your *pity* is enough to cure me" – Sonnet 111, line 14

2 WHICH VULGAR SCANDAL STAMPED UPON MY BROW,
   VULGAR = "public, general … base, low, common" – Booth; **SCANDAL** = disgrace; the public image of Southampton, who has yet to receive his royal pardon; the real disgrace, which is the removal of his royal "grace" from the record; "What a *scandal is it to our crown*" – *1 Henry VI*, 3.1.69

REFERENCE EDITION   601

3 FOR WHAT CARE I WHO CALLS ME WELL OR ILL,
For what I do care how I am perceived by others

4 SO YOU O'ER-GREEN MY BAD, MY GOOD ALLOW?
SO YOU = so long as you; **O'ER-GREEN MY BAD** = cover my wounds with your "green" or "fresh" royal favor; ("Since first I saw you fresh, which yet art green" – Sonnet 104, line 8; "the Mistress which we have lost, under whom both you and myself from our greenest years have been in a manner brought up" – Oxford to Robert Cecil, April 25/27, 1603); **ALLOW** = approve; with the "all" of Southampton's motto; as a king would allow; "Now by my sceptre's awe I make a vow, such neighbor nearness to our sacred blood ... free speech and fearless *I to thee allow*" – the King in *Richard II*, 1.1.118-119, 123

5 YOU ARE MY ALL THE WORLD, AND I MUST STRIVE
ALL = Southampton, *One for All, All for One*; capitalized as "All" in *Q*; **YOU ARE MY ALL THE WORLD** = ("O Lord! My boy, my Arthur, *my fair son!* My life, my joy, my food, *my all the world*!" – *King John*, 3.3.103-104; "Since *all and every part* of what we would doth make a stand at what your Highness will" – *King John*, 4.2.38-39); "For nothing this wide universe I call,/ Save thou, my Rose, in it thou art *my all*" – Sonnet 109, lines 13-14, to Southampton; ("If of my freedom 'tis the main part, take no stricter render of me than *my all*" – *Cymbeline*, 5.4.16-17, in reference to his own life)

6 TO KNOW MY SHAMES AND PRAISES FROM YOUR TONGUE;
MY SHAMES AND PRAISES = "Trimmed up *your praises* with a *princely tongue, spoke your deservings like a chronicle,* making you ever better than *his praise*" – *1 Henry IV*, 5.2.56-58; **YOUR TONGUE** = the voice of the Southampton, who is "telling" the story of the Sonnets; ("So is *my love still telling* what is told" – Sonnet 76, line 14); "princely tongue" – *1 Henry IV*, 5.2.56

7 NONE ELSE TO ME, NOR I TO NONE ALIVE,
NONE = Southampton, unable to claim his right; the opposite of "one"; **NONE ELSE TO ME** = "For nothing in this wide Universe I call,/ Save thou, my Rose, in it thou art my all" – Sonnet 109, lines 13-14; **NONE** = repeating for emphasis

8 THAT MY STEELED SENSE OR CHANGES RIGHT OR WRONG.
So that my firm perception of you overcomes any judgment of right or wrong, innocence or guilt; "For to thy sensual fault I bring in *sense*" – Sonnet 35, line 9; "No one living for me except you, nor I alive to any, who can change my feelings fixed as steel either for good or ill" - Dowden

9 IN SO PROFOUND *ABYSM* I THROW ALL CARE
ABYSM = hell; ("the dark backward and *abysm* of time" – *The Tempest*, 1.2.50); **ALL** = Southampton

10 OF OTHERS' VOICES, THAT MY ADDER'S SENSE
OTHERS' VOICES = the opinions of others; **ADDER'S SENSE** = ("Adders were proverbial for both physiological and studied deafness" – Booth); i.e., Oxford will not listen to the world's judgment; "And be not conformed to this world" – Romans, 12.2 (see Sonnet 111, line 8 notes)

11 TO CRITIC AND TO FLATTERER STOPPED ARE.
A continuation of the same idea; impervious to either critic (censurer) or flatterer; "Do not give advantage to stubborn critics" – *Troilus and Cressida*, 2.1.131

12 MARK HOW WITH MY NEGLECT I DO DISPENSE:
MY NEGLECT = my purposeful neglect of you; my need to disavow you as my son; **DISPENSE** = excuse,

pardon; "I am mistress of my fate, and with my *trespass* never will *dispense* ... Yet with the *fault* I thus far can *dispense*" – *Lucrece*, 1070, 1279; also disregard, i.e., I avoid acknowledging you in public; "Nature *dispenses with* (pardons) the deed so far that it becomes a virtue" – Measure for Measure, 3.1.133-134

13 YOU ARE SO STRONGLY IN MY PURPOSE BRED
You are so royally born in my intentions; and brought into existence in this verse; **MY PURPOSE** = "By adding one thing to *my purpose* nothing" – Sonnet 20, line 12; "I am constant to *my purposes*, they follow the King's pleasure" – *Hamlet*, 5.2.200-201; **BRED** = "Finding the first conceit of love there bred" – Sonnet 108, referring to the birth of his son's "love" or royal blood

14 THAT ALL THE WORLD BESIDES ME THINKS Y'ARE DEAD.
ALL = Southampton; **ALL THE WORLD** = all England; repeated from line 5 above, i.e., "You are my All the world"; "As *all the world* doth judge" – Oxford to Burghley, September 1572; **THE WORLD** = the current or contemporary world; **BESIDES ME THINKS Y'ARE DEAD** = except for me, everyone else believes your claim is dead (if they know of your claim at all).

THE FINAL DAYS

TWELVE DAYS
TO THE QUEEN'S FUNERAL

Sonnet 113
Since I Left You
16 April 1603

Oxford has met with Southampton upon his release from the Tower, so father and son could finally talk face to face. He equates his royal son with his own mind's eye, a blazing sun "which governs me" as his King.

Sonnet 113	Translation
Since I left you, mine eye is in my mind,	Since seeing you free, I carry you in my mind,
And that which governs me to go about	And my mind's eye, which governs me,
Doth part his function, and is partly blind,	Only functions partially while otherwise it's blind,
Seems seeing, but effectually is out:	Seeming to see you, but in public not so:
For it no form delivers to the heart	Because my eye can't bring my heart any image
Of bird, of flower, or shape which it doth lack,	Of royal birds or Tudor roses that it can't see.
Of his quick objects hath the mind no part,	My eye can't acknowledge any royal images,
Nor his own vision holds what it doth catch:	Nor can it hold onto what it does glimpse:
For if it see the rud'st or gentlest sight,	For if it sees the most disgraced or most royal sight,
The most sweet favor or deformed creature,	The most royal gift or most bastard-born child,
The mountain, or the sea, the day, or night:	Whether it's the mountain or sea or day or night,
The Crow, or Dove, it shapes them to your feature.	The disgraced son or me [Dove], my eye sees you.
Incapable of more, replete with you,	I am incapable of seeing anything else, full of you,
My most true mind thus maketh mine untrue.	And my inner true mind makes outer images false.

1 SINCE I LEFT YOU, MINE EYE IS IN MY MIND,
SINCE I LEFT YOU = Oxford met with Southampton upon his release from the Tower; by now they have parted again; **MINE EYE IS IN MY MIND** = I continue to see you in my mind; (similar to "my soul's imaginary sight" of Sonnet 27, line 9, when Southampton had first been committed to the Tower; "In my mind's eye, Horatio" – *Hamlet*, 1.2.185

2 AND THAT WHICH GOVERNS ME TO GO ABOUT
GOVERNS = rules; i.e., Southampton rules Oxford as his king; but Oxford is also "governed" by officialdom or authority, as in "And art made tongue-tied by authority" in Sonnet 66, line 9; the Queen is dead but not her body is not yet entombed; when alive she governed: "Commanded by the motion of thine eyes" – Oxford to Elizabeth, Sonnet 149, line 12

3 DOTH PART HIS FUNCTION, AND IS PARTLY BLIND,
DOTH PART HIS FUNCTION = divides his duty or service; **PARTLY BLIND** = only partially able to see his son's royalty, i.e., in his mind's eye, while the outward eye is allowed no such sight; "Looking on darkness which the *blind* do see" – Sonnet 27, line 8 (see line 14 below)

4 SEEMS SEEING, BUT EFFECTUALLY IS OUT:
SEEMS SEEING = appears to see you; **EFFECTUALLY** = in effect, as the government has ruled; **OUT** = extinguished, annihilated; i.e., the light in his eyes is shut out

5 FOR IT NO FORM DELIVERS TO THE HEART
My physical eye sends no image of you to the center of my being; my mind and heart; my thought process; **DELIVERS** = "What wight first caught this heart and can from bondage it *deliver*? Vere" – *Verses Made by the Earle of Oxforde*, Rawlinson Poet MS 85 f, 11; Chiljan, 183

6 OF BIRD, OF FLOWER, OR SHAPE WHICH IT DOTH LACK.
BIRD = "Bare ruined choirs, where late the sweet birds sang" – Sonnet 73, line 4; "For these dead birds, sigh a prayer" – *The Phoenix and Turtle*, 1601; **FLOWER** = Southampton as new (but disgraced) flower of the Tudor Rose; **LACK** = fails to rhyme with "catch" of line 8, so usually emended to "latch"; but indeed Oxford's *lack* or loss of his son is the topic

7 OF HIS QUICK OBJECTS HATH THE MIND NO PART,
QUICK = lifelike; full of life; lively; related to the "quickening" in the womb; "Why is my verse so barren of new pride?/ So far from variation or *quick* change?" – Sonnet 76, lines 1-2

8 NOR HIS OWN VISION HOLDS WHAT IT DOTH CATCH:
Nor can my eye retain what it sees; "For he that beats the bush the bird not gets,/ But who sits still and *holdeth* fast the nets" – final line of Oxford's poem for *Cardanus' Comforte*, 1573

9 FOR IF IT SEE THE RUD'ST OR GENTLEST SIGHT,
RUD'ST = most disgraced, i.e., Southampton; "And maiden vertue rudely stumpeted" – Sonnet 66, line 6, carrying a similar meaning; **GENTLEST** = most royal, i.e., Southampton

10 THE MOST SWEET-FAVOR OR DEFORMED'ST CREATURE,
MOST SWEET = most royal; **FAVOR** = Southampton's royal favor; aspect, appearance, face, countenance; **DEFORMED CREATURE** = Southampton as illegitimate child, royal bastard; as opposed to "fairest *creatures*" in Sonnet 1, line 1; "But if the first heir of my invention prove *deformed*" – dedication of *Venus and Adonis* to Southampton; and as one whose destiny (as King) has been changed, or de-formed.

11 THE MOUNTAIN, OR THE SEA, THE DAY, OR NIGHT,
SEA = royalty; royal blood; "Thou art, quoth she, *a sea, a sovereign king*" – *Lucrece*, 652; **DAY** = time of golden royalty; recalling "Shall I compare thee to a Summer's day?" – Sonnet 18, line 1; **NIGHT** = the opposite of that golden time, under the cloud of disgrace, as Southampton was "like a jewel (hung in ghastly night)" upon his imprisonment in Sonnet 27, line 11

12 THE CROW, OR DOVE, IT SHAPES THEM TO YOUR FEATURE.
CROW = Southampton as black with disgrace, as he was a "Crow that flies in heaven's sweetest air" in Sonnet 70, line 4, referring to the disgrace in "Elizabeth's most royal heir"; he was also the "treble-dated crow" of *The Phoenix and the Turtle* of 1601, line 17; **DOVE** = the Turtledove, reflecting Oxford as the Turtle in that funeral dirge; **CROW/DOVE** = Southampton and Oxford together; **SHAPES THEM TO YOUR**

FEATURE = turns all these into the vision of you

13 **INCAPABLE OF MORE, REPLETE WITH YOU,**
INCAPABLE OF MORE = unable to see more; **REPLETE WITH YOU** = full with you; i.e., Oxford is in a constant state of conflict between the false image of his son and the truth of him

14 **MY MOST TRUE MIND THUS MAKETH MINE UNTRUE.**
TRUE = Oxford; **MY MOST TRUE MIND** = my inner vision that sees the truth; "Let me not to the marriage of *true minds*/ Admit impediments" – Sonnet 116, lines 1-2; **MAKETH MINE UNTRUE** = makes my outer vision false; "my not seeing objects truly, such as they appear to the rest of mankind" – Malone; "As for you, say what you can, *my false o'erweighs your true*" – *Measure for Measure*, 2.4.168-169; "Looking on darkness which the blind do see" – Sonnet 27, line 8, i.e., others see only your disgrace; "And to enlighten thee gave eyes to blindness,/ For I have sworn thee fair: more perjured eye,/ To swear against the truth so foul a lie!" – Sonnet 152, lines 11-14, Oxford's final words to Elizabeth; **MINE** = "Mine" in *Q* is often emended to "m'eyne" for "my eyes"; as in "mine own" son, who with Oxford becomes "untrue" by having to deny the truth.

Part Two

THE FINAL DAYS

ELEVEN DAYS
TO THE QUEEN'S FUNERAL

Sonnet 114
Crowned With You
17 April 1603

Oxford again looks ahead to James's coronation in July. He refers to his ceremonial role in preparing the tasting cup for the new monarch. In his mind it will be "the poisoned cup" that murders Southampton's ability to gain the throne and, too, extinguishes the Tudor Rose dynasty.

Sonnet 114	Translation
Or whether doth my mind, being crowned with you,	Does my mind, crowning itself with you as king,
Drink up the monarch's plague, this flattery?	Drink up the flattery that destroys a monarch?
Or whether shall I say mine eye saith true,	Or should I tell the world about the truth,
And that your love taught it this *Alchemy*?	And that your royal blood taught me to see it?
To make of monsters and things indigest,	To transform the outward signs of your disgrace
Such cherebins as your sweet self resemble,	Into royal infants that your royal self resembles,
Creating every bad a perfect best	Turning every disgrace into royalty
As fast as objects to his beams assemble:	As fast as a king's eye throws its beams:
Oh 'tis the first, 'tis flatt'ry in my seeing,	Oh, it's the first answer! It's the flattery I see,
And my great mind most kingly drinks it up,	And my fatherly mind drinks it like a king does!
Mine eye well knows what with his gust is greeing,	My eye knows very well what my mind wants,
And to his palate doth prepare the cup.	And prepares the poisoned cup for it to drink.
If it be poisoned, 'tis the lesser sin,	If I die from this flattery, it will be the lesser fault,
That mine eye loves it and doth first begin.	That my eye is first to taste the poison.

1 OR WHETHER DOTH MY MIND, BEING CROWNED WITH YOU,
OR WHETHER = "Picking up from the preceding sonnet" – Duncan-Jones; asking rhetorically if, on the other hand, it's the case that; **MY MIND** = "*My mind* to me *a kingdom* is" – Oxford poem, Rawlinson MS 85, f. 17; **CROWNED WITH YOU** = i.e., in my mind I crown you king; "Before you were new *crowned*, we breathed our counsel; but it pleased Your Highness to overbear it" – *King John*, 4.2.35; "Nativity, once in the main of light,/ Crawls to maturity, wherewith being *crowned*,/ Crooked eclipses 'gainst his glory fight" – Sonnet 60, lines 5-7, referring to Southampton's growth only to be "eclipsed" by Robert Cecil, the crookback; "Incertainties now *crown* themselves assured" – Sonnet 107, line 7, alluding to the proclaimed accession of James upon Elizabeth's death

2 DRINK UP THE MONARCH'S PLAGUE, THIS FLATTERY?
MONARCH'S PLAGUE, THIS FLATTERY = habit of kings who drink up the flattery of their subjects, a

REFERENCE EDITION 607

trait of Elizabeth's that Oxford had hated; his worst fear was to be a Court sycophant; "Have I not seen dwellers on form and favor/ Lose all and more by paying too much rent/ For compound sweet forgoing simple savor,/ Pitiful thrivers in their gazing spent?" – Sonnet 125, lines 5-8; "Too well, too well I feel the different plague of each calamity" – *King John*, 3.3.59-60; FLATTERY repeated in line 9 below; "Thus have I had thee as a dream doth flatter:/ In sleep a King, but waking no such matter" - Sonnet 87, lines 13-14

3 OR WHETHER SHALL I SAY MINE EYE SAITH TRUE,

TRUE = rightly, correctly; related to Oxford as *Nothing Truer than Truth*; **MINE EYE** = the eye that beholds the sun, i.e., his royal son, who possesses *"that sunne thine eye"* – Sonnet 49, line 6

4 AND THAT YOUR LOVE TAUGHT IT THIS *ALCHEMY*

YOUR LOVE = your royal blood; **TAUGHT** = "Who *taught* thee first to sigh, alas, my heart?/ Who *taught* thy tongue the woeful words of plaint?" – Oxford's early sonnet, circa 1571-1573; **THIS ALCHEMY** = (capitalized and italicized in Q, which gives "*Alcumie*"); "this power to transmute base and ugly things to precious and beautiful" – Duncan-Jones; this transformation of Southampton into his rightful kingship, in Oxford's mind; echoing the rising sun or royal son "with *heavenly alchemy*" in Sonnet 33, line 4; related to the "compounds" of Sonnet 76, line 4, or mixtures of words used to write these private verses of the diary; Oxford was a friend and study of Dr. John Dee, the Queen's astrologer, who experimented with alchemy

5 TO MAKE OF MONSTERS AND THINGS INDIGEST,

MONSTERS = the Queen and Robert Cecil; **THINGS INDIGEST** = chaotic, formless, crooked events; things I cannot digest; related to "deformed'st creature" of Sonnet 113, line 10; shapeless, as in Ovid's *Metamorphoses*, Golding trans., 1567, undoubtedly by young Oxford: "No sunne as yet with lightsome beames the *shapeless* world did view ... this rude confused masse ... confused heape ... And thus the earth which late before had neither shape nor hew,/ Did take the noble shape of man, and was transformed new" – I.9, 34, 81, 97-98

6 SUCH CHERUBINS AS YOUR SWEET SELF RESEMBLE,

CHERUBINS = youthful angels; ("Good night, *sweet* Prince, and flights of *angels* sing thee to thy rest" – *Hamlet*, 5.2.366-367); **YOUR SWEET SELF** = your royal person, the "sweet prince" of England; "Thou of thyself *thy sweet self* dost deceive" – Sonnet 4, 10

7 CREATING EVERY BAD A PERFECT BEST

CREATING = transforming, giving birth to; "From fairest *creatures* we desire increase" – Sonnet 1, line 1; "Sland'ring *Creation* with a false esteem" – Sonnet 127, line 12, referring to the Queen slandering her own royal son by refusing to acknowledge him; **EVERY** = Ever = E. Ver, Edward de Vere; **EVERY BAD** = royal bastard son of Edward de Vere; "All men are *bad* and in their *badness* reign" – Sonnet 121, line 14; "For there is nothing either good or bad but thinking makes it so" – *Hamlet*, 2.2.250-251; **PERFECT BEST** = most royal; "of *perfect'st love* being made" – Sonnet 51, line 10

8 AS FAST AS OBJECTS TO HIS BEAMS ASSEMBLE?

BEAMS = "And think if the Admiral of France was an eyesore or *beam* in the eyes of the Papists" – Oxford to Burghley, September 1572; "Fair Cynthia's silver light ... Whose hairs are all *sunbeams* ... **These sunbeams in mine eye**, /These beauties make me die" – Oxford poem, signed E.O. in *The Phoenix Nest*, 1593; "the chaste *beams* of the watery Moon" – speaking of the beams from Elizabeth's sovereign eyes in *A Midsummer Night's Dream*, 2.1.162; beams of the royal son or king; ("Sun, hide thy *beams*, Timon hath done his reign" – *Timon of Athens*, 5.1.223; "England ne'er had a king until his time ... his brandished sword did blind men with his *beams*" – *1 Henry VI*, 1.1.8-10; Southampton's royal gaze, attracting all subjects:

That sun that warms you here, shall shine on me,

And those his ***golden beams*** to you here lent
Shall point on me and gild my banishment
- *Richard II*, 1.3.145-147

9 O 'TIS THE FIRST, 'TIS FLATTERY IN MY SEEING,
FLATTERY IN MY SEEING = Oxford's inner vision of his son is false flattery, i.e., according to the judgment of the world; see "flattery" in line 2 above (for Oxford, being subject to flattery was one of the biggest dangers to a monarch); "Thus have I had thee as a dream doth flatter:/ In sleep a King, but waking no such matter" - Sonnet 87, lines 13-14; see next line below

10 AND MY GREAT MIND MOST KINGLY DRINKS IT UP.
As a king is subject to flattery; ("*My mind* to me a *kingdom* is ... Lo thus I triumph *like a king,/ My mind* content with anything/ ... Content with that *my mind* doth bring)" – anonymous, listed by Steven May as possibly by Oxford, in *Psalms, Sonnets, and Songs of Sadness and Piety*, William Byrd, 1588; in Rawlinson manuscripts cited by Chiljan, p. 195; "I could be bounded in a nutshell and count myself a king of infinite space" – *Hamlet*, 2.2.255-256

11 MINE EYE WELL KNOWS WHAT WITH HIS GUST IS GREEING,
MINE EYE = "more perjured eye" – Sonnet 152, line 13; **GUST** = taste; **GREEING** = agreeing

12 AND TO HIS PALATE DOTH PREPARE THE CUP.
Oxford is about to drink the poison of his own flattery or illusion of Southampton as king; ("I'll have prepared him a chalice for the nonce ... It is the *poisoned cup*!" – *Hamlet*, 4.7.176 and 5.2.306 – anticipating his ceremonial role at James's coronation, with "basins and towels and a ***tasting cup***" for "presenting water to the Lord the King with water before and after dinner on the day of the Coronation" – Oxford's formal letter of petition to the Court, Cal. S.P. Domestic, James I, July 7, 1603; in Ward, p. 346

13 IF IT BE POISONED, 'TIS THE LESSER SIN,
POISONED = again echoing the "poisoned cup" of *Hamlet*, with first full version (*Q2*) to be published next year (1604) upon Oxford's death

14 THAT MINE EYE LOVES IT AND DOTH FIRST BEGIN.
FIRST BEGIN = Oxford will taste the poisoned cup of falsehood *first*, the way servants of the king (tasters to princes) who taste food or drink to test it for poison; "the *first* heir of my invention" – dedication of *Venus and Adonis* to Southampton

THE FINAL DAYS

TEN DAYS
TO THE QUEEN'S FUNERAL

Sonnet 115
Change Decrees of Kings
Love is a Babe
18 April 1603

Despite everything that has happened, Oxford is still preserving Southampton's life and growth in these verses. The "decrees of Kings" have been changed; whereas Elizabeth had refused to liberate her royal son, James has freed him. But the "alt'ring" of the succession has taken place according to "time's tyranny" -- the tyrannical life of the Queen's mortal body. "Love is a Babe," Oxford writes, referring to his royal son as "the little Love-God" (Cupid) and to Southampton's inherited "love" or royal blood, which is still growing in the womb of these private sonnets.

Sonnet 115	Translation
Those lines that I before have writ do lie,	The lines of these sonnets have lied!
Even those that said I could not love you dearer.	Even saying I couldn't serve you as more royal!
Yet then my judgment knew no reason why	Before now, I could find no reason why
My most full flame should afterwards burn clearer.	Your most royal blood should be greater.
But reck'ning time, whose million accidents	But Elizabeth's death, which by itself robbed
Creep in twixt vows, and change decrees of Kings,	Your crown and brought a new King's decree,
Tan sacred beauty, blunt the sharp'st intents,	While hiding your royal blood, blocked intents
Divert strong minds to the course of alt'ring things:	To crown you and diverted England's course:
Alas, why, fearing of time's tyranny,	Alas, why, when I feared Elizabeth's death,
Might I not then say, now I love you best,	Didn't I say aloud then that you were most royal,
When I was certain o'er incertainty,	When I was so confident that you would reign,
Crowning the present, doubting of the rest:	Crowning you in the moment, the rest uncertain?
Love is a Babe, then might I not say so,	Your royal blood is new! But I cannot say so,
To give full growth to that which still doth grow.	Adding to your royal growth in private here.

1 THOSE LINES THAT I BEFORE HAVE WRIT DO LIE,
The lines of verse in previous entries of this diary; bloodline; **WRIT** = legal; the father-son bond, recorded in this document of the Sonnets; anticipating the couplet of the next verse: "If this be error and upon me proved,/ I never writ, nor no man ever loved" - Sonnet 116, lines 13-14

2 EVEN THOSE THAT SAID I COULD NOT LOVE YOU DEARER.
I lied when I wrote I couldn't love you more; **DEARER** = with more love for you as my dear royal son; "And if thy *sons* were ever *dear* to thee, O, think *my son* to be as *dear* to me!" – *Titus Andronicus*, 1.1.110-111; "This royal throne of kings ... this land of such *dear* souls, this *dear dear* land, *dear* for her reputation through the world" – *Richard II*, 2.1.40,57-58; "If my *dear love* were but the child of state,/ It might for

610

Part Two

fortune's bastard be un-fathered" – Sonnet 124, lines 1-2;

3 YET THEN MY JUDGMENT KNEW NO REASON WHY
But back then my reasoning power knew no reasons; **JUDGMENT** = echoing the guilty verdict at the trial; also, the judgment to be rendered by posterity; ("So till the *judgment* that yourself arise" – Sonnet 55, line 13); "So thy great gift, upon misprision growing,/ Comes home again, on better *judgment* making" – Sonnet 87, lines 11-12

4 MY MOST FULL FLAME SHOULD AFTERWARDS BURN CLEARER.
FULL = abundant; filled with royal blood; "The canker blooms have *full* as deep a dye" – Sonnet 54, line 5; "So love be thou, although today thou *fill*/ Thy hungry eyes, even till they wink with *fullness*" – Sonnet 56, lines 5-6; **FLAME** = royalty, as in "thy light's *flame*" of Sonnet 1, line 6; the royal blood of Southampton that is filling these sonnets through Oxford's pen; "Though absence seemed my *flame* to qualify" – Sonnet 109, line 2

5 BUT RECKONING TIME, WHOSE MILLIONED ACCIDENTS
RECKONING TIME = the "wasted time" of this "Chronicle" in Sonnet 106, line 1; the tyranny of Elizabeth's life that led to the "reckoning" with succession; settling of accounts; "My father, King of Spain, was *reckoned* one of the wisest prince" – *Henry VIII*, 2.4.46-47; (Booth notes phonetic likeness to "wrecking"; "Truth's and Beauty's doom and date" predicted in Sonnet 14, line 14; "But if the cause be not good, the King himself hath a heavy *reckoning* to make" – *Henry V*, 4.1.132-133; **"When a man's verses cannot be understood, nor a man's good wit seconded with the forward child, understanding, it strikes a man more dead than a great reckoning in a little room"** – *As You Like It*, 3.3.11-14; (the "little room" may have been the courtroom at Westminster Hall where Southampton was convicted of high treason and thereby lost his claim to the throne; or it may be where Oxford made his bargain with Robert Cecil to gain Southampton's freedom); "It is not truer he is Angelo, than this is all as true as it is strange; *nay, it is ten times true, for* **truth is truth to the end of reckoning**" – *Measure for Measure*, 5.1.46-49; "No, I am that I am, and they that level/ At my abuses *reckon* up their own" – Sonnet 121, lines 9-10; "Among a number one is *reckoned* none" – Sonnet 136, line 8; "No *reck'ning* made, but sent to *my account* with all my imperfections on my head" – the Ghost of Hamlet's Father in *Hamlet*, 1.5.78-79; **MILLIONED ACCIDENTS** = the myriad of planned and unplanned things that can occur between events; "That millions of strange shadows on you tend" – Sonnet 53, line 2

6 CREEP IN TWIXT VOWS, AND CHANGE DECREES OF KINGS,
TWIXT VOWS = in between the vows I exchanged with Elizabeth; "In act thy bed-vow broke" – Sonnet 152, line 4, to Elizabeth; **CHANGE DECREES OF KINGS** = James changed Elizabeth's decree that Southampton must spend the rest of his life in prison; ("The reference no doubt includes *the change in that decree* which had doomed the Earl to death" – Massey, 1866, p. 310-11); "But heaven in thy creation did decree" – Sonnet 93, line 9)

7 TAN SACRED BEAUTY, BLUNT THE SHARP'ST INTENTS,
TAN SACRED BEAUTY = darken Henry Wriothesley's sacred Tudor blood from Beauty or Elizabeth, his mother; "But when my glass shows me myself indeed/ Beated and chopped with *tanned* antiquity" – Sonnet 62, lines 9-10; **BLUNT THE SHARPEST INTENTS** = divert the strongest intentions or purposes, i.e., the goal to put Southampton on the throne; "By adding one thing to my purpose nothing" – Sonnet 20, line 12

8 DIVERT STRONG MINDS TO THE'COURSE OF ALT'RING THINGS:
DIVERT STRONG MINDS = divert royal intentions, i.e., of both Elizabeth and Oxford as well as of Southampton; "If thou wouldst use the *strength of all thy state*" – Sonnet 96, line 12; **ALT'RING THINGS**

REFERENCE EDITION

= changing Southampton's death sentence and altering his life sentence to his release; also, the altering of the succession from Southampton to James; ("alteration of succession" was a recognized phrase)

> King Edward:
> Why, Warwick, when we parted,
> Thou call'dst me King.
>
> Warwick: Ay, but *the case is alter'd.*
> - 3 Henry VI, 4.3.30-32

(*The Case is Altered* was the title of a play attributed to Ben Jonson; and these were among Elizabeth's last recorded words about the succession to her throne)

> Love is not love
> Which *alters* when it *alteration* finds
> - Sonnet 116, lines 3-4
>
> *Time's* glory is to calm contending kings…
> To blot old books and *alter* their contents…
> And turn the giddy round of *fortune's* wheel
> - Lucrece, 939-952
>
> "*In this common shipwreck, mine is above all the rest, who least regarded, though often comforted, of all her followers, she hath left to try my fortune among the* **alterations** *of time and chance*"
> - Oxford to Robert Cecil, April 25/27, 1603; referring to Elizabeth, on eve of her funeral. week after the dating of this sonnet
>
> "*Almost since the time of William Conqueror, and at that time (which was the 12th year of Henry the 8th) the king took it for term of his life from my grandfather, since which time, what by the* **alterations** *of princes and wardships, I have been kept from my rightful possession.*"
> - Oxford to Robert Cecil, May 7, 1603, three weeks after the dating of this sonnet

9 ALAS, WHY, FEARING OF TIME'S TYRANNY,

TIME'S TYRANNY = the tyranny of Elizabeth's life that brought about Southampton's loss of the throne; ("And all in *war with Time* for love of you" – Sonnet 15, line 13; "Make war upon this bloody *tyrant time*" – Sonnet 16, line 2; "When *tyrants'* crests and tombs of brass are spent" – Sonnet 107, line 14, the latter in reference to Elizabeth's temporary tomb near that of her grandfather Henry VII)

10 MIGHT I NOT THEN SAY NOW I LOVE YOU BEST,

NOW = this day, these final days, by the calendar; **BEST** = most royal

11 WHEN I WAS CERTAIN O'ER INCERTAINTY,

When I became confident or assured about the outcome, referring back to "*Incertainties* now *crown* themselves *assured*" – Sonnet 107, line 7, i.e., the uncertainties of the succession and possible civil war are over and James, having kept his promise by releasing you from prison, will be crowned.

12 CROWNING THE PRESENT, DOUBTING OF THE REST?

CROWNING THE PRESENT = Oxford putting the crown on his son's head, but also alluding to the fact that James will be crowned King of England; ("And in that chair where kings and queens are *crown'd*" – 2

Henry VI, 1.2.38; "Thy outward thus with outward praise is crowned" – Sonnet 69, line 5; **THE PRESENT** = these final days now being recorded; "For we which *now* behold *these present days,*/ Have eyes to wonder, but lack tongues to praise" – Sonnet 106, lines 13-14

13 **LOVE IS A BABE: THEN MIGHT I NOT SAY SO,**
LOVE IS A BABE = royal blood is still that of a child, my son, who was "Cupid" and "the little Love-God" of Sonnet 153, line 1 and Sonnet 154, line 1; also "the boy" in Sonnet 153, line 10; and "O Thou my lovely Boy" of Sonnet 126, line 1; **BABE** = "Whilst I, thy *babe*, chase thee afar behind" – Sonnet 143, line 10; "If I were mad, I should forget my son, or madly think a *babe* of clouts were he" – *King John*, 3.3.57-58

14 **TO GIVE FULL GROWTH TO THAT WHICH STILL DOTH GROW.**
GIVE FULL GROWTH = to keep my royal son growing in the womb of this diary, referred to in line 1 above: "Those lines that I before have writ"; **TO THAT WHICH STILL DOTH GROW** = to my son's royal blood, which is *still* (always) growing (in his life and in these sonnets for posterity) regardless of the tragic end of his claim to the throne; "When in eternal lines to time thou *grow'st*" – Sonnet 18, line 12; "Showing their *birth*, and where they did *proceed*" – Sonnet 76, line 8; "Making their *tomb* the *womb* wherein they *grew*" – Sonnet 86, line 3

THE FINAL DAYS

NINE DAYS TO THE QUEEN'S FUNERAL

Sonnet 116
The Marriage of True Minds
19 April 1603

Oxford renews his commitment to the father-son bond between him and Southampton, referring to "the marriage" or indissoluble union of their "true" relationship. The love between them is real, but the "love" of this verse is the royal blood, which is eternal and therefore can never be altered regardless of the "alteration" of succession that has taken place. In this sonnet Oxford insistently includes self-identifiers such as "true" (Nothing Truer than Truth) and "ever" and "never," echoing his early pen name, Ever or Never.

Sonnet 116	Translation
Let me not to the marriage of true minds	I will never let our union as father and son
Admit impediments. Love is not love	Be destroyed! Royal blood is not royal blood
Which alters when it alteration finds,	That changes with a change of monarchs,
Or bends with the remover to remove.	Or declines when others have usurped it.
O no, it is an ever-fixed mark	O no, your royal blood is a permanent star
That looks on tempests and is never shaken;	That suffers royal storms without change!
It is the star to every wandering bark,	Your kingly sun shines for all to serve,
Whose worth's unknown, although his height be taken.	Its royalty unknown, but I measure its height.
Love's not Time's fool, though rosy lips and cheeks	Your royalty isn't lost by Eliza's death, though
Within his bending sickle's compass come;	Your Tudor Rose claim was cut down by it!
Love alters not with his brief hours and weeks,	Your royal blood doesn't change with time,
But bears it out even to the edge of doom.	But lives until the end of time itself.
If this be error and upon me proved,	If this statement is proved to be my error,
I never writ, nor no man ever loved.	I never wrote this verse or fathered a royal son.

"Building on the preceding" – Duncan-Jones.

1 LET ME NOT TO THE MARRIAGE OF TRUE MINDS
MARRIAGE = indissoluble union; possibly harking all the way back to **TRUE** = Oxford, *Nothing Truer than Truth*; "This royal hand and mine are newly knit, and *in the conjunction of our inward souls,* **married** in league, coupled and linked together" – *King John*, 3.1.152-154, King Philip to Cardinal Pandulph, the Pope's legate; **TRUE MINDS** = our inner minds, where we know the truth; linked as father and son, both with "true" or Vere blood; recalling: "I will say no more, for words in *faithful minds* are tedious" – Oxford to Robert Cecil, March 1601, immediately after professing his friendship both "in kindness, which I find beyond mine expectation in you," and "in kindred, whereby none is nearer allied than myself" (because Oxford's daughters are Cecil's only nieces).

Part Two

2 ADMIT IMPEDIMENTS! LOVE IS NOT LOVE
Allow barriers (to this father-son union); **LOVE IS NOT LOVE** = royal blood is not royal blood

3 WHICH ALTERS WHEN IT ALTERATION FINDS
That changes in the face of altered circumstances such as these; ("Divert strong minds to th'course of *alt'ring* things" – Sonnet 115, line 8); "O God, that one might read the book of fate, and see the revolution of the times make mountains level, and the continent, weary of solid firmness, melt itself into the sea, and other times to see the beachy girdle of the ocean too wide for Neptune's hips; how *chance's* mocks and *changes fill the cup of alteration* with divers liquors!" - The King in *2 Henry IV*, 3.1.45-53; "The *alterations* of *time* and *chance*" - Oxford to Robert Cecil, April 25/27, 1603; "Why, Warwick, when we parted, thou call'dst me King. Ay, but *the case is altered*." - *3 Henry VI*, 4.3.30-32; "My Lord, I am tied with a chain of iron around my neck. I am tied, I am tied, and *the case is altered* with me" - Queen Elizabeth, one of her last recorded statements, about succession;"The *alteration of the succession* of the crown" – *Treatise of Treasons*, (anon.) 1572; in heraldry, an "alteration" is made in a coat of arms (in effect, a change of identity)

4 OR BENDS WITH THE REMOVER TO REMOVE.
BENDS = changes; an image of the bent-over figure of hunchbacked Robert Cecil; **BENDS WITH THE REMOVER** = bends with Cecil, the hunchback, who removed your claim to the throne; **TO REMOVE** = to change, i.e., your royal blood cannot be altered or changed or removed; (recalling father to son in Sonnet 25, lines 13-14 of Sonnet 25: "Then happy I, that love and am beloved/ Where I may not *remove*, nor be *removed*"); in heraldry, a "bend" is a diagonal band; an "ordinary" may be "removed" from a shield; to be separated by a degree of difference, as that due to descent, i.e., a "cousin once removed" (courtesy of Charles Beauclerk); Oxford is harking back to Sonnet 25, line 14

5 O, NO! IT IS AN EVER-FIXED MARK
O = Oxford; **EVER** = E. Ver, Edward de Vere; **EVER-FIXED MARK** = i.e., royal blood is a constant and eternal beacon (as for ships to follow, again suggesting that Oxford may leave England); "Like a great sea-mark standing every flaw and saving those that eye thee!" - Coriolanus, 5.3.73-74

6 THAT LOOKS ON TEMPESTS AND IS NEVER SHAKEN;
TEMPESTS = the storm of the succession that wrecked Southampton's claim; also, introducing a link to *The Tempest*; "In this common *shipwreck*, mine is above all the rest" – Oxford to Robert Cecil, April 25/27, 1603, written during the same period as this verse, and referring to his own life/situation as a result of Queen Elizabeth's death; **NEVER** = Oxford, *Ever or Never*

7 IT IS THE STAR TO EVERY WAND'RING BARK,
STAR = the sun, Southampton's royal eye; "But from *thine eyes ... constant stars*" – Sonnet 14, lines 9-10; "*that sun thine eye*" – Sonnet 49, line 6; "Till whatsoever *star* that guides my moving" – Sonnet 26, line 9; "Lord Hamlet is *a prince out of thy star*" – Hamlet, 2.2.141; "Small time, but in that small most greatly lived *this star of England*" – Henry V, Epilogue/Chorus, 5-6, referring to the former Prince Hal who, in this play, is King Henry Fifth; "*Bright star of Venus*, fall'n down on the earth, how may I reverent worship thee enough?" – *1 Henry VI*, 1.2.144-145; **EVERY** = Ever = E. Ver, Edward de Vere; **EVERY WANDERING BARK** = my wandering boat; **BARK** = "In few, they hurried us aboard a *bark*, bore us some leagues to the sea; where they prepared a rotten carcass of a butt, not rigged, nor tackle, sail, nor mast" – *The Tempest*, 1.2.145-148

8 WHOSE WORTH'S UNKNOWN, ALTHOUGH HIS HEIGHT BE TAKEN.
WHOSE WORTH'S UNKNOWN = the star (sun) is that of Southampton, whose royalty is unknown to the masses; ("*Worthy* prince" – *Two Gentlemen of Verona*, 3.1.10); whose worth is inexpressible, incalculable, immense, a suggestion cited by Dowden; **HEIGHT** = value; royalty, as in Your Highness; ("And

Richard fall in *height* of all his pride" – *Richard III*, 5.3.177)

9 LOVE'S NOT TIME'S FOOL, THOUGH ROSY LIPS AND CHEEKS

LOVE = royal blood; **TIME** = until her death, "time" referred to the time left in Elizabeth's life; now it's the time left until she is "officially" dead and the Tudor dynasty is "officially" no more; **LOVE'S NOT TIME'S FOOL** = royal blood is not mocked by universal time (because it defies time and is immortal); and Southampton's royal blood is not *Elizabeth's fool*, because it outlives her mortal time; **TIME'S FOOL** = Oxford was Elizabeth's *"allowed fool"* or Court Jester who was given unique freedom to write scathing satires for performance at Court; "There is no slander in an *allowed fool*" – Olivia, speaking of her jester, Feste the Clown, who says, "Thou hast spoke for us, Madonna, as if thy eldest son should be a fool" – *Twelfth Night*, 1.5.90-110; "But thought's the slave of life, and life *time's fool*, and *time*, that takes survey of all the world, must have a stop" – Hotspur, mortally wounded by Prince Hal, in *1 Henry IV*, 5.4.80-82; but, Oxford declares here, royal blood continues to live even though Elizabeth's life and the time of life itself comes to an end; **ROSY LIPS AND CHEEKS** = Southampton's reflection of Tudor Rose blood from his mother Elizabeth, who was *Ever the Same* and *Rose Without a Thorn*; "Thus is his *cheek* the map of days outworn,/ When beauty lived and died as flowers do now,/ Before these bastard signs of fair were borne" – Sonnet 68, lines 1-3

10 WITHIN HIS BENDING SICKLE'S COMPASS COME;

BENDING = image of the bending hunchback Robert Cecil; i.e., the Tudor Rose was, in fact, cut off by the bending sickle of time in terms of Elizabeth's life, when it ended without Southampton's succession

11 LOVE ALTERS NOT WITH HIS BRIEF HOURS AND WEEKS,

Royal blood never changes in relation to earthly time; ("And you and *love* are *still* my argument" – Sonnet 76, line 10, i.e., always and forever)

12 BUT BEARS IT OUT EVEN TO THE EDGE OF DOOM.

But instead survives or endures even to Doomsday and the Last Judgment, "when the secrets of all hearts shall be disclosed" – The Book of Common Prayer, 291; **BEARS** = endures, with echo of child-bearing; "Which, laboring for invention, *bear* amiss/ The second burthen of a former child!" – Sonnet 59, lines 3-4; "That for thy right myself will *bear* all wrong" – Sonnet 88, line 14; **DOOM** = "Supposed as forfeit to a confined doom" – Sonnet 107, line 4

13 IF THIS BE ERROR AND UPON ME PROVED,

ERROR = wrong; echoing the "fault" or "error" or plot or crime of the Rebellion; "lest more *plots and errors* happen" – *Hamlet*, 5.2.402; **UPON ME PROVED** = demonstrated; echoing the trial; but Oxford utters this in defiance, using the language of a legal challenge: "If any man will *maintain upon* Edmund, supposed Earl of Gloucester, that he is a manifold *traitor*" – *King Lear*, 5.3.110-113; cited by Duncan-Jones; "Let four captains bear Hamlet like a soldier to the stage, for he was likely, had he been put on, to have *prov'd most royal*" – *Hamlet*, 5.2.403-405; "Till then not show my head where thou mayst *prove me*" – Sonnet 26, line 14; "For you in me can *nothing worthy prove*" – Sonnet 72, line 4; "And worst essays *proved thee* my best of love" – Sonnet 110, line 11; :Since *my appeal* says I did strive *to prove*/ The constancy and virtue of your love" – Sonnet 117, lines 13-14

14 I NEVER WRIT, NOR NO MAN EVER LOVED.

NEVER = Oxford, *Ever or Never*; **WRIT** = legal writ; **EVER** = "E. Ver," Edward deVere, i.e., he issues a cry on behalf of Love, or royal blood, in defiance of Time; having been destroyed by earthly time, upon Elizabeth's death, the Sonnets now transcend mortality

(ERROR - WRIT echoes the legal term "writ of error")

Part Two

THE FINAL DAYS

EIGHT DAYS
TO THE QUEEN'S FUNERAL

Sonnet 117
I Did Strive To Prove
20 April 1603

Oxford continues to plead for Southampton to forgive him for the tragic loss of the crown, and to justify his own actions by restating his commitment to his son. The implication is that, during their recent meeting upon Southampton's emergence from the Tower, the younger earl expressed his bitterness over the bargain. Oxford also suggests that he himself may soon depart from England via "sail to all the winds, which should transport me farthest from your sight" – a possible allusion to his own mortality, which is always on his mind.

Sonnet 117	Translation
Accuse me thus: that I have scanted all	Say this against me: that I've neglected you
Wherein I should your great deserts repay,	In these lines, to which I owe your royal blood,
Forgot upon your dearest love to call,	That I forgot to be inspired by your royalty,
Whereto all bonds do tie me day by day;	To which all ties bind me as I write day by day!
That I have frequent been with unknown minds,	Say I've frequently been with the ignorant,
And given to time your own dear purchased right;	And wasted time in helping your royal claim.
That I have hoisted sail to all the winds	Say in the near future that I have sailed off,
Which should transport me farthest from your sight.	Away from England and out of your life.
Book both my willfulness and errors down,	Draw up a list of accusations against me,
And on just proof surmise accumulate;	And pile up all the faults I've demonstrated.
Bring me within the level of your frown,	Put me within the aim of your arrow,
But shoot not at me in your wakened hate.	But don't try to kill me with new hate.
Since my appeal says I did strive to prove	My defense is that I strove here to demonstrate
The constancy and virtue of your love.	The immortality and truth of your royal blood!

1 ACCUSE ME THUS: THAT I HAVE SCANTED ALL
ACCUSE ME = echoing the treason trial; "Continuing the legal challenge" – Duncan-Jones; Southampton must now be a "suborned informer" (Sonnet 125, line 13); he will have to testify against his own royal blood; and because Oxford accepts the guilt for this tragedy, he begs his son to "accuse" him of responsibility; "Where is the evidence that doth *accuse* me?" – *Richard III*, 1.4.178; "Without *accusing* you of injury" – Sonnet 58, line 8; **ALL** = Southampton; **SCANTED ALL** = neglected or harmed you, Southampton

2 WHEREIN I SHOULD YOUR GREAT DESERTS REPAY,
YOUR GREAT DESERTS = your great royalty; "*your most high deserts*" – Sonnet 17, line 2; "As to behold *desert* a beggar born" – Sonnet 66, line 2, also speaking of Southampton, as born a royal bastard;

REFERENCE EDITION 617

REPAY = give back to you; Oxford alluding to his sacrifice for his son; repayment for the "gift" of his son's life: "So thy great gift, upon misprision growing" – Sonnet 87, line 11); "That use is not forbidden usury/ Which happies those that pay the willing loan" – Sonnet 6, lines 5-6, referring to the payment of royal blood from the Queen to her son, which she happily paid in the belief he would marry and beget an heir as in line 7: "That's for thyself to breed another thee"

3 **FORGOT UPON YOUR DEAREST LOVE TO CALL,**
YOUR DEAREST LOVE = your most royal blood; the most royal blood of my dearest son; "If my *dear love* were but the child of state" – Sonnet 124, line 1; "My *dear dear* lord ... *dear* my liege" – *Richard II*, 1.1.176, 184; "I had *a son* ... I loved him, friend, *no father his son* **dearer**" – *King Lear*, 3.4.162-165; **CALL** = "For nothing this wide Universe I *call,*/ Save thou, my Rose, in it thou art my all" – Sonnet 109, lines 13-14

4 **WHERETO ALL BONDS DO TIE ME DAY BY DAY;**
ALL = Southampton; **ALL BONDS** = all personal ties as father to son; and as subject to prince or king; ("Were my worth greater, my duty would show greater, meantime, as it is, it is *bound* to your Lordship" – dedication of *Lucrece* to Southampton; **DAY BY DAY** = as each of these sonnets corresponds to one day as the Queen's funeral (and dynasty's end) draws nearer; "For as the Sun is *daily* new and old,/ So is my love still telling what is told" – Sonnet 76, lines 13-14

5 **THAT I HAVE FREQUENT BEEN WITH UNKNOWN MINDS,**
FREQUENT = "He is of late much retired from Court, and is less *frequent* to his princely exercises" – *Winter's Tale*, 4.2.33-34; conversant; **UNKNOWN MINDS** = all other than you, i.e., as opposed to our "*true minds*"; ("the marriage of true minds" – Sonnet 116, line 1); strangers; those who do not know about your worth and "love" or royal blood: "Whose worth's *unknown*" – Sonnet 116, line 8, referring to "love" (royal blood) that remains constant and immortal

6 **AND GIVEN TO TIME YOUR OWN DEAR PURCHASED RIGHT;**
GIVEN TO TIME = wasted; surrendered to the "time" of the sonnets that led up to the Queen's death in Sonnet 105 and to this "Chronicle of wasted time" – Sonnet 106, line 1; **YOUR OWN DEAR PURCHASED RIGHT** = your own royal right that I had to cede back to the Queen, so she would save Southampton's life, and pay to Robert Cecil and King James for your life and freedom; "From Ireland thus comes York to claim his right, and pluck the crown from feeble Henry's head ... Ah! *sancta majestas*, who'd not **buy thee dear**?" – *2 Henry VI*, 5.1.1-5; alluding to the "ransom" that Oxford has paid on his son's behalf

7 **THAT I HAVE HOISTED SAIL TO ALL THE WINDS**
HOISTED SAIL TO ALL THE WINDS = that I have traveled away from this island, England, by boat; another possible indication that Oxford intends to disappear (upon his death on June 24, 1604, he will be given no recorded funeral and leave no surviving will); **ALL** = Southampton

8 **WHICH SHOULD TRANSPORT ME FARTHEST FROM YOUR SIGHT.**
Same idea as the line above; death, of course, would transport him "farthest from your sight."

9 **BOOK BOTH MY WILLFULNESS AND ERRORS DOWN,**
BOOK = make a record of; **WILLFULNESS** = ("purposeful actions, i.e., 'intentional misdeeds' as opposed to 'mistakes'" – Booth); same as "sensual fault" or "willful crime" in Sonnet 35, line 9; a suggestion of "Will" Shakespeare as part of these actions; **ERRORS** = crimes against you

No. 117

10 AND ON JUST PROOF SURMISE ACCUMULATE;
And heap all these charges and more (even surmises) against me; **PROOF** = as in the trial; with Oxford striving to "prove" in line 13

11 BRING ME WITHIN THE LEVEL OF YOUR FROWN,
WITHIN THE LEVEL = "Love's not Time's fool, though rosy lips and cheeks/ *Within his bending sickle's compass* come" – Sonnet 116, lines 9-10, referring to the tyranny of Elizabeth as Time; the current line uses the same language of weaponry but now refers to Southampton's royal frown; **LEVEL** = range or line of fire, direction of weapon; **YOUR FROWN** = your royal frown or displeasure; same as for the Queen in Sonnet 25, line 8: "Great Princes' favorites" who lose royal favor because "at a *frown* they in their glory die"

12 BUT SHOOT NOT AT ME IN YOUR WAKENED HATE:
SHOOT NOT = metaphorical, don't shoot your gun at me; **WAKENED HATE** = Southampton, awake to his lack of "love" or royal claim; **HATE** = (opposite of "love"); no royal status

13 SINCE MY APPEAL SAYS I DID STRIVE TO PROVE
APPEAL = a plea put in before the judge; "The submission of a case to a higher court in the hope of altering the judgment of a lower one; a request to higher authority for alteration of a decision; a call to an authority for vindication or support ... a calling to account before a legal tribunal; specifically, a criminal accusation made by a person undertaking to prove it; a challenge to defend one's honor by fighting" – *OED*, which cites a line of Francis Bacon: "The casting up of the eyes ... is a kind of appeal to the Deity"; in this case Oxford may be seen appealing to his royal son as a "God in love" or divinely ordained king; **MY APPEAL** = Oxford's plea in defense, harking back to the trial; "Whenever yet was your *appeal* denied? Wherein have you been galled by the King?" – *2 Henry IV*, 4.1.88-89; "The Duke's unjust thus to retort your manifest *appeal*, and put your trial in the villain's mouth which here you come to accuse" – *Measure for Measure*, 5.1.298-301; "The Queen being absent, 'tis a needful fitness that we adjourn this court till further day; meanwhile must be an earnest motion made to the Queen to call back her *appeal* she intends unto his holiness" – *Henry VIII*, 2.4.230-234; "I *appeal* to your own conscience, sir" – *The Winter's Tale*, 3.2.44-45; the verb "to appeal" suggests making an appeal against a verdict or to call on an authority for a decision in one's favor – as Oxford is calling upon Southampton to forgive him for the loss of the crown and thereby set them both free; **PROVE** = demonstrate, by actions and in these sonnets; again, harking back to the trial

14 THE CONSTANCY AND VIRTUE OF YOUR LOVE.
CONSTANCY = consistency, immortality; "Therefore my verse to *constancy* confined" – Sonnet 105, line 7; "In *constant* truth to bide so firm and sure" – Oxford's early sonnet; **VIRTUE** = qualities of a king; as Oxford speaks of James having "excellent virtues" in his letter of April 25/27, 1603; **YOUR LOVE** = your royal blood ("The metaphor of the sonnet recapitulates a case involving the squandering of a loan upon a bond, not being able to repay it, having it recorded and recognized by law, being brought to trial for it, and at the last moment receiving a merciful appeal from the execution on the grounds that the intent of the illegal actions was honorable rather than malicious" – *Shakespeare's Hidden Life*, W. Nicholas Knight, p. 76 – in effect, a summary of Oxford's story of his royal son)

THE FINAL DAYS

SEVEN DAYS TO THE QUEEN'S FUNERAL

Sonnet 118
A Healthful State
21 April 1603

Oxford restates the theme of these final days, affirming that England was spared a crisis over the succession -- ironically because of Southampton's crime and its tragic outcome for his royal claim, paving the way for Robert Cecil to engineer the peaceful succession of James. Even if these crimes were not as serious as high treason for which he was originally convicted (later reduced to "misprision" of treason), he and his son have swallowed this bitter medicine, which has achieved "a healthful state."

Sonnet 118	Translation
Like as to make our appetites more keen	Just as we make our desires grow
With eager compounds we our palate urge,	With bitter mixtures to stimulate them,
As to prevent our maladies unseen,	In order to prevent future unknown sickness,
We sicken to shun sickness when we purge.	We make ourselves ill to ward off illness:
Even so, being full of your ne'er-cloying sweetness,	In this way, being full with your tragic royalty,
To bitter sauces did I frame my feeding;	To bitter medicine I adjusted my meal,
And sick of welfare found a kind of meetness	And sick with health I found a certain fitness
To be diseased ere that there was true needing.	To be devastated before I needed to be.
Thus policy in love t'anticipate	So, to anticipate official policy for your blood,
The ills that were not grew to faults assured,	Your non-crimes became my assured crimes,
And brought to medicine a healthful state,	And brought about a peaceful new reign,
Which rank of goodness would by ill be cured.	Which is a good brought about by evil.
But thence I learn and find the lesson true,	But then I learn and find this lesson true:
Drugs poison him that so fell sick of you.	I took on your crimes in order to save you.

1 LIKE AS TO MAKE OUR APPETITES MORE KEEN,
LIKE AS = in the same way as; "The speaker continues to attempt to defend himself against allegations that he has been unfaithful to his friend" – Duncan-Jones, i.e., Oxford continues to attempt to defend the bargain he made for his son.

2 WITH EAGER COMPOUNDS WE OUR PALATE URGE;
EAGER COMPOUNDS = bitter mixtures, recalling Oxford's likening of his "invention" for the Sonnets to "compounds" or mixtures of words in Sonnet 76, lines 3-4; like poisoned blood

3 AS TO PREVENT OUR MALADIES UNSEEN,
MALADIES UNSEEN = secret suffering over Southampton's loss of royal claim, recalling Oxford's visit

to Bath with Elizabeth in 1574 in search of "a sovereign cure" for "strange maladies" in Sonnet 153, line 8.

4 WE SICKEN TO SHUN SICKNESS WHEN WE PURGE.
We take bitter medicine that makes us sick, in order to purge ourselves of our real illness or suffering; the way Oxford is going along with the great changes underway, bitter as they are to him, to ease his suffering over the royal fate of his son

5 EVEN SO, BEING FULL OF YOUR NE'ER CLOYING SWEETNESS,
EVEN SO = in the same way; **NE'ER-CLOYING SWEETNESS** = never-distasteful (or hurtful) royal blood; editors have noted the similarity of "ne'er" and "near", the latter relating to closeness by family alliance or blood; ("and by alliance near to your Lordship" – Oxford to Burghley, October 30, 1584)

6 TO BITTER SAUCES DID I FRAME MY FEEDING:
I did "frame" or adjust my life to these bitter circumstances now taking place; ("Or thinking by our late dear brother's death our state to be disjoint and out of frame" – *Hamlet*, 1.2.19-20)

7 AND SICK OF WELFARE FOUND A KIND OF MEETNESS
SICK OF WELFARE = Oxford is 'sick' or suffering from the terms of the bargain for his son, who cannot claim the throne; he is also 'sick' or distressed even as the welfare or health of England has proved to be good; ("His greatness weighted, his will is not his own. For he himself is subject to his birth ... for on his choice depends the sanity and health of this whole state" – *Hamlet*, 1.3.17-21); **MEETNESS** = appropriateness

8 TO BE DISEASED ERE THAT THERE WAS TRUE NEEDING.
DISEASED = deprived of comfort, suffering; **TRUE** = *Oxford, Nothing Truer than Truth*

9 THUS POLICY IN LOVE T'ANTICIPATE
POLICY IN LOVE = state policy regarding royal blood and succession; "It fears not *policy*, that heretic" – Sonnet 124, line 9

> That were *some love but little policy*
> - *Richard II*, 5.1.84

> But he has forc'd us to compel this offer,
> And it proceeds from *policy*, not love
> - *2 Henry IV*, 4.1.147-148

POLICY = "To keep by *policy* what Henry got" – *2 Henry VI*, 1.1.83; "That he should die is worthy policy; but yet we want a colour for his death: 'tis meet he be condemn'd by course of law ... But, in my mind, that were no *policy*: the king will labour still to save his life, the commons rise, to save his life; and yet we have but trivial argument, more than mistrust, that shows him worthy death" – *2 Henry VI*, 3.1.235-242; "Let noble Warwick, Cobham, and the rest, whom we have left protectors of the king, with powerful **policy** strengthen themselves" – *3 Henry VI*, 1.2.56-58; "Let us be worried and our nation lose the name of hardiness and *policy*" – *Henry V*, 1.2.221-222; "Plague of your policy; you sent me deputy for Ireland; far from his succor, from the king, from all that might have mercy on the fault thou gavest him; whilst your great goodness, out of holy pity, absolved him with an axe" – *Henry VIII*, 3.2.259-264; "I will bandy with thee in faction; I will o'errun thee with *policy*; I will kill thee *a hundred and fifty ways*" – Touchstone to William, the Country Fellow, in *As You Like It*, 5.1.54-56, possibly alluding to the 150 Psalms or the 154 verses of the Sonnets and to Oxford outdoing his pen name "William Shakespeare," which is now branded on him by state policy; "for policy I hate: I had as lief be a Brownist as a politician" – *Twelfth Night*, 3.2.30-31; "For *policy* sits above conscience" – *Timon of Athens*, 3.2.91; "For lawful *policy* remains enacted" – *Lucrece*, stanza 76; **T'ANTICIPATE** = anticipating the Queen's funeral and the official death of the Tudor dynasty, as well as the official change of monarchs; (Booth cites an *OED* suggestion from 1635: "The funeral … is anticipated, and shall be on Thursday.")

10 THE ILLS THAT WERE NOT GREW TO FAULTS ASSURED.

Your crime (of treason) that was not really treason because the offense was reduced to "misprision" of treason, officially "assured"; ILLS = "Ah, but those tears are pearl which thy love sheeds,/ And they are rich, and *ransom all **ill** deeds*" – Sonnet 34, lines 13-14; **FAULTS** = "All men make ***faults**,* and even I in this,/ Authorizing thy *trespass* with compare/ … For to thy sensual ***fault*** I bring in sense;/ Thy adverse party is thy Advocate" – Sonnet 35, lines 5-6, 9-10

11 AND BROUGHT TO MEDICINE A HEALTHFUL STATE,

And this medical (political) treatment resulted in our new healthy state of England

"There is nothing therefore left to my comfort, but the excellent virtues, and deep wisdom wherewith God hath endued our new Master and sovereign lord, who doth not come amongst us as a stranger but as a natural prince, *succeeding by right of blood and inheritance*, not as a conqueror, but as the true shepherd of Christ's flock to cherish and comfort them." – Oxford to Robert Cecil, April 25/27, 1603, written shortly after the dating of this sonnet

12 WHICH RANK OF GOODNESS WOULD BY ILL BE CURED.

RANK OF GOODNESS = poisoned of its genuine goodness; alluding to high rank as king; the good health of the state was achieved by falseness, badness and ill health; also, those devoid of such qualities; the irony being that Robert Cecil, who committed "faults" against Southampton and was "rank" or devoid of goodness, now rules the so-called healthy state; without health; "To diet *rank* minds sick of happiness" – *2 Henry IV*, 4.1.64

13 BUT THENCE I LEARN AND FIND THE LESSON TRUE:

TRUE = Oxford, *Nothing Truer than Truth*

14 DRUGS POISON HIM THAT SO FELL SICK OF YOU.

Nevertheless, Oxford has been poisoned (like Hamlet) by these very medicines that were supposed to cure him of his suffering over "you" (Southampton); and so his fundamental paradox, or inner conflict, is complete; alluding to his sacrifice that involves Southampton's loss of claim to the throne

Part Two

THE FINAL DAYS

SIX DAYS
TO THE QUEEN'S FUNERAL

Sonnet 119
Ruined Love … Built Anew
22 April 1603

Although Southampton's "love" or royal blood has been "ruined" by the Rebellion and by the bargain made to save his life and gain his freedom (requiring him to give up the throne and to bury the truth), it is being "built anew" within the monument of the Sonnets. Oxford is turning the tragedy inside out, so he and his royal-blooded son can "gain by ills."

Sonnet 119	Translation
What potions have I drunk of *Siren* tears,	What medical concoctions have I drunk in pain,
Distilled from Limbecks foul as hell within,	Distilled by vessels of foul vapors,
Applying fears to hopes, and hopes to fears,	Applying fear to hope and hope to fear,
Still losing when I saw myself to win?	Always losing your life in order to save it?
What wretched errors hath my heart committed,	What terrible crimes did my heart commit,
Whilst it hath thought itself so blessed never?	While it thought of itself as never so blessed?
How have mine eyes out of their Spheres been fitted	How have my eyes been forced from their sockets
In the distraction of this madding fever?	In the midst of this chaotic tragedy?
O benefit of ill, now I find true	O, the good of evil! Now I find it true
That better is by evil still made better,	That better is made always better by evil,
And ruined love when it is built anew	And destroyed royal blood, when built anew,
Grows fairer than at first, more strong, far greater.	Grows more royal than before, stronger, greater.
So I return rebuked to my content,	So I come back by correction to my happiness
And gain by ills thrice more than I have spent.	And gain more of you than I sacrificed for you.

"*This sonnet … is largely constructed of metaphors and analogies from alchemy and medicine … as the title page of George Baker's* The Newe Jewell of Health *(1576) illustrates, alchemy and medicine were generally thought of as the single science of 'creating every bad a perfect best.'*" – Booth, Sonnet 119 notes, p. 398; Dr. Baker was Oxford's surgeon; three of his four published books were dedicated either to Oxford or to Oxford's wife Anne Cecil. (*The Newe Jewell of Health* was dedicated to Anne.)

1 WHAT POTIONS HAVE I DRUNK WITH *SIREN* TEARS
POTIONS = medicines; ***SIREN*** = (capitalized and italicized a *Syren* in *Q*); alluring but dangerous; ("The sirens are mythological monsters – part bird, part woman – who lure sailors to their destruction" – Booth; not unlike the way Elizabeth had lured Oxford with her promises, only to destroy his hopes); "With *tears distill'd* by moans" – *Romeo and Juliet*, 5.3.15

REFERENCE EDITION

2 DISTILLED FROM LIMBECKS FOUL AS HELL WITHIN,
DISTILLED = ("But *flowers distilled*" – Sonnet 5, line 13); **LIMBECKS** = (spelled "Lymbecks" in *Q*); vessels used for distillation of chemicals into vapors, as in alchemy

3 APPLYING FEARS TO HOPES, AND HOPES TO FEARS,
APPLYING = administering; **FEARS TO HOPES, AND HOPES TO FEARS** = precisely the inner torment that Oxford has gone through for his son's royal claim, back and forth; ("Not mine own fears nor the prophetic soul/ Of the wide world dreaming on things to come/ Can yet the lease of my true love control,/ Supposed as forfeit to a confined doom" – Sonnet 107, lines 1-4)

4 STILL LOSING WHEN I SAW MYSELF TO WIN!
Always losing when I thought I was gaining; losing in the very moment of victory; gaining victories (such as your release from prison) that were actually losses (the loss of your chance for succession)

5 WHAT WRETCHED ERRORS HATH MY HEART COMMITTED,
ERRORS/COMMITTED = crimes; especially those his son committed, for which Oxford has taken the blame by agreeing to sacrifice his identity – as father of Southampton by Elizabeth and as author of the "Shakespeare" works dedicated and linked to Southampton; but the sense is ironic, because Oxford's only "error" has been to see the truth of his son's identity and to maintain his love for him: "If this be *error* and upon me proved,/ I never writ nor no man ever loved" – Sonnet 116, lines 13-14; his actions are only "errors" because Queen Elizabeth, the monarch, has viewed them as such; (and the "winners" of the political game will always be the ones who write the histories and determine good guys and bad guys)

6 WHILST IT HATH THOUGHT ITSELF SO BLESSED NEVER!
SO BLESSED NEVER = never so blessed, holy, sacred; **NEVER** = Oxford, *Ever or Never*

7 HOW HAVE MINE EYES OUT OF THEIR SPHERES BEEN FITTED
A harrowing description of his torment; ("Make *thy two eyes, like stars, start from their spheres*" – *Hamlet*, 1.5.7; Oxford is now revising the text of *Hamlet* for publication next year, and these final sonnets are linked to lines of that play); in the 1604 quarto of *Hamlet* "spheres" appears as "spheares," echoing "Shake-*Speares* Sonnets" of the 1609 sonnet quarto.

8 IN THE DISTRACTION OF THIS MADDING FEVER!
DISTRACTION = separation; i.e., from his son; **MADDING FEVER** = delirious suffering; ("O heavens! Who was the first that bred in me this *fever? Vere*" – *Verses made by the Earle of Oxford*; echoing the Dark Lady sonnets: "*Past reason* hunted, and no sooner had,/ *Past reason* hated as a swallowed bait,/ On purpose laid to make the taker *mad;/ Mad* in pursuit, and in possession so" – Sonnet 129, lines 6-9; "My love is as a *fever* … *Past cure* I am, now *reason is past care,/* And *frantic mad* with *evermore unrest,/* My thoughts and my discourse *as madmen's* are" – Sonnet 147, lines 1, 9-11)

9 O BENEFIT OF ILL! NOW I FIND TRUE
O = Oxford; **TRUE** = Oxford; **BENEFIT OF ILL** = ironic, sarcastic, but also the truth, i.e., Oxford is turning tragedy into its opposite; "You follow the young Prince up and down, like *his ill angel*" – *2 Henry IV*, 1.2.163-164, to which Falstaff replies: "Not so, my lord, your *ill angel* is light" – line 165); "and ransom all *ill deeds*" – Sonnet 34, line 14, i.e., your crime of treason

10 THAT BETTER IS BY EVIL STILL MADE BETTER:
My royal son is even more royal because this evil has destroyed his royal claim;**STILL** = always, eternally

624

11 **AND RUINED LOVE WHEN IT IS BUILT ANEW**
RUINED LOVE = destroyed royal blood or royal claim; same as "wasted time" of Sonnet 106, line 1; "Seeking that beauteous roof (House of Tudor) to *ruinate*" – Sonnet 10, line 7; **BUILT ANEW** = recreated and rebuilt with this Monument to my son

12 **GROWS FAIRER THAN AT FIRST, MORE STRONG, FAR GREATER.**
GROWS FAIRER = grows more royal in these verses; "When in eternal lines to time thou *grow'st*" – Sonnet 18, line 12; **THAN AT FIRST** = than it first grew back in the earlier sonnets, i.e., in Sonnets 153-154 of 1574 and Sonnets 1-26 of 1590-1600; **FIRST** = ("Since *first* I saw you fresh, which yet are green" – Sonnet 104, line 8); **MORE STRONG** = more filled with your royal power; "If thou wouldst use *the strength* of all thy state!" – Sonnet 96, line 12; **FAR GREATER** = much more royal

13 **SO I RETURN REBUKED TO MY CONTENT,**
SO I RETURN = ("Therefore I return to that which is my 'argument,' that which provides the contents of my verse" – Booth); **MY CONTENT** = my topic; also to my contentment; "Lo thus I triumph like a king,/ *Content* with that my mind doth bring" – poem most likely by Oxford:*In Praise of a Contented Mind*, Petyt MS 538.10,f.3, Chiljan, p. 174; also, your royal blood, which is the "content" or argument of my verse; ("Within thine own bud buriest thy *content*" – Sonnet 1, line 11; "But you shall shine more bright *in these contents*" – Sonnet 55, line 3); the "argument" is "you and love" (you and your royal blood) of Sonnet 76, line 10

14 **AND GAIN BY ILLS THRICE MORE THAN I HAVE SPENT.**
GAIN BY ILLS = the theme of this verse; **THRICE** = echoing the trinity of the royal family, as in "*Three* themes in one, which wondrous scope affords./ Fair, kind, and true, have often lived alone,/ Which *three*, till now, never kept seat in one" – Sonnet 105, 12-14; **SPENT** = "*Spending* again what is already *spent*" – Sonnet 76, line 12; "Fair, kind, and true, varying to other words,/ And in this change is my invention *spent*" – Sonnet 105, line 11)

THE FINAL DAYS

FIVE DAYS TO THE QUEEN'S FUNERAL

Sonnet 120
How Once I Suffered in Your Crime
Our Night of Woe
Your Trespass Now Becomes a Fee
Mine Ransoms Yours ... Yours Must Ransom Me
23 April 1603

Oxford looks back at the tragic events that he and Southampton have experienced since the Rebellion of February 8, 1601. Both father and son are responsible. Southampton went through "a hell of Time" during the twenty-six months he spent in the Tower. Oxford had "suffered in your crime" that resulted in his son's imprisonment. This long period of darkness and disgrace was "our night of woe," but now the treason or "trespass" committed by Southampton becomes a "fee" to be paid, not only for his new freedom but also for the restoration of his earldom and a royal pardon. Oxford has agreed to bury his identity as father and as author of the Shakespeare works; Southampton has forfeited the crown; both have paid their "ransom" for this new outcome of the story that is about to end upon the funeral of Elizabeth, marking the official end of the Tudor Dynasty.

Sonnet 120	Translation
That you were once unkind befriends me now,	Your loss of royal kinship now helps me,
And for that sorrow which I then did feel,	And for the suffering I felt by your crime,
Needs must I under my transgression bow,	I must submit to the crime I assume for you,
Unless my Nerves were brass or hammered steel.	Unless my own power was like solid metal.
For if you were by my unkindness shaken,	For if you were upset over my guilty verdict,
As I by yours, y'have passed a hell of Time,	As I was by your crime, you've been in hell;
And I, a tyrant, have no leisure taken	And I, a tyrant, have taken no time
To weigh how once I suffered in your crime.	To consider how I suffered for your Rebellion.
O that our night of woe might have rememb'red	O that our long period of suffering would touch
My deepest sense, how hard true sorrow hits,	My deepest feeling and how it hurt me,
And soon to you, as you to me then tendered	And quickly hurt you, when you offered me
The humble salve, which wounded bosom fits!	The remedy to cure my wounded heart!
But that your trespass now becomes a fee,	But your treason now becomes a payment:
Mine ransoms yours, and yours must ransom me.	Mine ransoms yours, and yours will save me.

1 THAT YOU WERE ONCE UNKIND BEFRIENDS ME NOW,
UNKIND = opposite of "kind" as naturally born with royal blood; i.e., that Southampton once committed treason and thereby ruined his claim to the throne; that he has brought about a complete severance (at least to the outside world) of the father-son bond of "kindness" or shared blood; ("As you yourself have forged against yourself, by *unkind* usage, dangerous countenance, and violation of all faith and troth sworn to us in your younger enterprise" – *1 Henry IV*, 5.1.68-71, Worcester to the Prince; "But more when envy breeds

unkind division: there comes the ruin, there begins confusion" – *1 Henry VI*, 4.1.193-194; "And Henry, though he be infortunate, assure yourselves, will never be *unkind*" – *2 Henry VI*, 4.9.18-19, spoken by the king); "*Kind* is my love today, tomorrow *kind*/ ... Fair, *kind*, and true, is all my argument" – Sonnet 105, lines 5, 9

> Titus, **unkind** and careless of *thine own*,
> Why suffer'st thou *thy sons* unburied yet - *Titus Andronicus*, 1.1.89-90
> What hast thou done, *unnatural and* **unkind**? - *Titus Andronicus*, 5.3.47

> Death, traitor! Nothing could have subdued nature
> To such a lowness but his **unkind** daughters - *King Lear*, 3.4.69-70

> So him I lose through my **unkind** abuse - Sonnet 134, line 12
> Let no **unkind**, no fair beseechers kill - Sonnet 135, line 13

> O had thy mother borne so hard a mind,
> She had not brought forth thee, but died **unkind** - *Venus and Adonis*, 203-204
> (Unkind = without a son)

BEFRIENDS ME NOW = brings me back in good stead with you, my "friend" or royal son

2 AND FOR THAT SORROW WHICH I THEN DID FEEL
AND FOR THAT SORROW, etc. = referring to the terrible time after February 8, 1601

3 NEEDS MUST I UNDER MY TRANSGRESSION BOW,
NEEDS MUST I, etc. = referring to his guilt in the crime; **BOW** = bend, submit to, bowing before a king; "I must needs be overwhelmed by the wrong I have done to you, knowing how I myself suffered when you were the offender" – Dowden

4 UNLESS MY NERVES WERE BRASS OR HAMMERED STEEL.
NERVES = sinews or muscles; also, emotions; **BRASS** = Elizabeth's body will be laid to rest in the shadow of the brass tomb of her grandfather Henry VII in Westminster Abbey

5 FOR IF YOU WERE BY MY UNKINDNESS SHAKEN,
MY UNKINDNESS = my need to disassociate myself from you, i.e., to bury our relationship as father and royal son; to forfeit your royal claim; having to deliver a guilty verdict against you at the trial, condemning you to death; **SHAKEN** = echoing his sacrifice of identity to "Shakespeare"

6 AS I BY YOURS, Y'HAVE PASSED A HELL OF TIME,
A HELL OF TIME = the twenty-six months during which Southampton was confined; "O father, what *a hell of witchcraft* lies/ In the small orb of one particular tear!" – *A Lover's Complaint*, 288-289; "With such *a hell of pain* and world of charge" – *Troilus and Cressida*, 4.1.58; **TIME** = ending in the "*wasted time*" of Sonnet 106, line 1, just before his liberation from prison; "I am to wait, though *waiting be so hell*" – Sonnet 58, line 13, when Southampton still faced execution (until Sonnet 66 on March 19, 1601); "And that deep torture may be called a *hell*, when more is felt than one hath power to tell" – *Lucrece*, 1286-1287; "*time* extends itself by eliciting from *hell* the notion of eternal punishment: the hellish time, by implication, seemed endless" - Kerrigan

7 AND I, A TYRANT, HAVE NO LEISURE TAKEN
I, A TYRANT = Oxford wrote this diary (up to Sonnet 105) according to the tyranny of time represented by

Elizabeth's life; ("this bloody *tyrant time*" – Sonnet 16, line 2; soon after her death, he identified Elizabeth herself as a "tyrant": "When *tyrants'* crests and tombs of brass are spent" – Sonnet 107, line 14; now Oxford himself is a "tyrant" for having saved Southampton's life by giving up his claim to the throne; the irony is that he himself had been forced to undermine his son's succession; **LEISURE** = recalling Oxford visiting his royal son in the Tower, "Being your vassal, bound to stay your *leisure*" – Sonnet 58, line 4

8 TO WEIGH HOW ONCE I SUFFERED IN YOUR CRIME.
WEIGH = consider; "ascribe high value to" – Booth; **HOW ONCE I SUFFERED IN YOUR CRIME** = how I had suffered within the tragedy caused by your crime of high treason; "To you it doth belong/ Your self to pardon of self-doing *crime*" – Sonnet 58, lines 11-12 (this is the third line in a row echoing Sonnet 58)

9 O THAT OUR NIGHT OF WOE MIGHT HAVE REMEMB'RED
O = Oxford; **OUR NIGHT OF WOE** = the long darkness proceeding from the Rebellion of February 8, 1601, when Oxford began with Sonnet 27, picturing Southampton in line 11 as "a jewel hung in *ghastly night*"; "For precious friends hid in *death's dateless night*" – Sonnet 30, line 6; "And heavily from *woe to woe*" – Sonnet 30, line 10; "Thus like a *woeful* wight, I wove the *web of woe*" – Oxford poem in *The Paradise of Dainty Devices*, 1576, signed E. O.; **REMEMB'RED** = reminded; active verb echoing "For thy sweet love *rememb'red* such wealth brings" – Sonnet 29, line 13; (it is difficult to avoid echo of "*bred*" in "rememb'red"); "When to the Sessions of sweet silent thought/ I summon up *remembrance* of things past" – Sonnet 30, lines 1-2; "Let me *remember* (remind) thee what thou hast promised" – *The Tempest*, 1.2.243

10 MY DEEPEST SENSE, HOW HARD TRUE SORROW HITS,
MY DEEPEST SENSE = ("my deepest capacity for feeling" – Duncan-Jones); **TRUE** = Oxford, *Nothing Truer than Truth*; **TRUE SORROW** = my sorrow; my genuine remorse; our sorrow as father and son: "Let me not to the marriage of *true* minds/ Admit impediments" – Sonnet 116, lines 1-2; also the sorrow over having to forfeit his son's "true rights" to the throne; "And your true rights be termed a Poet's rage" – Sonnet 17, line 11; "Thou truly fair wert truly sympathized/ By thy true-telling friend" – Sonnet 82, lines 11-12

11 AND SOON TO YOU AS YOU TO ME THEN TEND'RED
TEND'RED = offered; (recalling "tender heir" of Sonnet 1, line 4, as well as "millions of strange shadows on you tend" of Sonnet 53, line 2; and "barren tender of a Poet's debt" in Sonnet 83, line 4, as well as, "For to no other pass my verses tend" – Sonnet 103, line 11)

12 THE HUMBLE SALVE WHICH WOUNDED BOSOM FITS!
SALVE = healing balm; "She is my *salve*, she is my wounded sore" – a line of an Oxford poem in *The Paradise of Dainty Devices*, 1576, signed E.O.; "So long to fight with secret sore,/ And find no *secret salve* therefore" – Oxford poem in *Paradise*, signed E.O.; ("For no man well of such a *salve* can speak" – Sonnet 34, line 7)

13 BUT THAT YOUR TRESPASS NOW BECOMES A FEE:
YOUR TRESPASS = your treason; "All men make faults, and even I in this,/ Authorizing *thy trespass* with compare" – Sonnet 35, lines 5-6; "And by his treason stand'st not thou attainted, corrupted, and exempt from ancient gentry? His *trespass* yet lives guilty in thy blood" – *1 Henry VI*, 2.4.92-94; **FEE** = payment; fine; a legal term; (in the recorded history, Southampton is the only man arrested for the Rebellion who fails to pay a fee or fine to gain release);

> "Quite the most frequent way of obtaining a 'special' pardon was for the traitor, convicted or suspected, to **compound,** that is to say to pay **a fine**. Since the fine varied from case to case this amounted to making an individual financial bargain with the King ... in the sixteenth century, in the case of treason at least, it was left to royal officials ... if they [con-

victed or suspect traitors] *were willing to do this [to submit], to impose* ***fines and ransoms***" – Bellamy, 220-221

14 MINE RANSOMS YOURS, AND YOURS MUST RANSOM ME.
MINE = my fee, to gain your release; **RANSOMS/RANSOM** = pays for, cancels out; atones for; redeems; Oxford's fee to ransom Southampton is the loss of his son's claim and the obliteration of his own identity as his father and as author of Shakespeare's works; "Pity was all the *fault* that was in me; for I should melt at an *offender's* tears, and lowly words were ***ransom for their fault***; unless it were a bloody murderer … Murder indeed, that bloody *sin*, I tortured above the felon or what *trespass* else" – *2 Henry VI*, 3.1.124-132) "On any ground that I am ruler of, the world shall not be ***ransom for thy life***" – *2 Henry VI*, 3.2.295-296; "*His crown shall be* ***the ransom*** *for my friend*" – *1 Henry VI*, 1.1.150; "They *set him free without his* ***ransom*** *paid*" – *1 Henry VI*, 3.3.72; echoing Christ as in "the *world's ransom*, blessed Mary's son" – *Richard II*, 2.1.56

> Ah, but those tears are pearl which thy love sheds,
> And they are rich, and ***ransom all ill*** deeds
> - Sonnet 34, lines 13-14

> Shall our coffers then
> Be empty'd to redeem a traitor home?
> Shall we buy treason…
> To ***ransom*** home revolted Mortimer
> - *1 Henry IV*, 1.3.84-91

"There without ransom to lie forfeited" - 1 Henry IV, 4.3.96

YOURS = your fee; **YOURS MUST RANSOM ME** = Southampton's fee (to ransom Oxford from his obliteration) is to see that this monument of verse gets into print; though the Sonnets are preserving "the living record" of Southampton, they also contain Oxford's life and truth: "And death to me subscribes,/ Since spite of him I'll live in this poor rhyme" – Sonnet 107, lines 10-11; therefore, with Southampton having been liberated, it's Oxford who is now "supposed as forfeit to a confined doom" (Sonnet 107, line 4) and his life (in the eyes of posterity) is in his son's hands, i.e., Southampton is "A god in love, to whom I am confined" – Sonnet 110, line 12.

THE FINAL DAYS

FOUR DAYS TO THE QUEEN'S FUNERAL

Sonnet 121
I Am That I Am
24 April 1603

Oxford records his commitment to the truth rather than to false appearances. He repeats the words of God to Moses in the Bible – I AM THAT I AM – in echo of a postscript to Lord Burghley in 1584, when Southampton was ten years old: "I serve her Majesty, and I am that I am." In reality, as father to a rightful king, he should be Elizabeth's consort on the throne and, therefore, a king or god on earth entitled to use God's words of self-description. Oxford here recalls his own postscript, related to "spies" working for Burghley and poking into his personal affairs. Nearing the end of his diary, he also sums up his own life to be preserved in this monument.

Sonnet 121	Translation
'Tis better to be vile than vile esteemed,	It's better to be non-royal than thought non-royal,
When not to be receives reproach of being,	When genuine royalty is dishonored,
And the just pleasure lost, which is so deemed,	And rightful royal pleasure is lost, so deemed
Not by our feeling, but by others' seeing.	Not by our inner hearts but in others' eyes.
For why should others' false adulterate eyes	For why should the counterfeit views of others
Give salutation to my sportive blood?	Pay homage to my loss of your royal blood?
Or on my frailties why are frailer spies,	Or upon my lack of power why are weaker spies,
Which in their wills count bad what I think good?	Who, in control, make non-royal what is royal?
No, I am that I am, and they that level	No, I am Father of a Divine Son, and they who aim
At my abuses reckon up their own.	At my crimes are revealing their own!
I may be straight though they themselves be bevel.	I may be constant and true though they are false,
By their rank thoughts my deeds must not be shown	But their rotten judgment forces me into hiding.
Unless this general evil they maintain,	Unless they argue publicly that all is evil and that
All men are bad and in their badness reign.	All kings are false and in their falseness reign.

1 'TIS BETTER TO BE VILE THAN VILE ESTEEMED,
"It's better to *be* vicious that to be *thought* vicious" - Tucker; **VILE** = wicked; criminal; in this case, treasonous; "That I was of a strange and *vile* nature" – Oxford, in a memo *circa* 1601-1602, Cecil Papers 146.19; Chiljan, 72; quoting false charges against him; **'TIS BETTER, etc.** = Oxford would rather have the genuine guilt for his son's crime than merely to be deemed guilty without making any sacrifice for him; "This *vile traitor*, Somerset" – *1 Henry IV*, 4.3.33; **TO BE** = echoing Hamlet's "To be or not to be" soliloquy, with "not to be" in line 2 below; indicating that he is undoubtedly revising *Hamlet* (Q2 of 1604) by now; **ESTEEMED** = deemed in the eyes of others, recalling the theme of Sonnet 29, line 14: "Then I scorn to change my state with kings"

Part Two

2 WHEN NOT TO BE RECEIVES REPROACH OF BEING,
WHEN NOT TO BE, etc. = when not actually wicked but blamed for being such; **NOT TO BE** = the other half of "To be or not to be," the soliloquy of *Hamlet*, its full version to be published in the next year, 1604.

3 AND THE JUST PLEASURE LOST, WHICH IS SO DEEMED,
JUST = legal; the word "just" is on Oxford's mind in this final Fair Youth sequence: "*Just* to the time, not with the time exchanged" – Sonnet 109, line 7; "And on the *just proof* surmise accumulate" – Sonnet 117, line 10; and it was on his mind near the end of the Dark Lady series, when Elizabeth was in her final eclipse: "Who taught me how to make me love thee more,/ The more I hear and see *just cause* of hate?" – Sonnet 150, lines 9-10; **JUST PLEASURE** = the happiness Oxford derives from having made a legal bargain for his son; also, for Southampton's "royal pleasure"; **DEEMED** = judged; "The Rose looks fair, but fairer we it *deem*/ For that sweet odor which doth in it live" – Sonnet 54, lines 3-4

4 NOT BY FEELING BUT BY OTHERS' SEEING.
NOT, etc. = "Not in our opinion, but in the view of others" – Booth; Oxford and Southampton do not agree with the loss of the throne, but that was arranged by others, i.e., Cecil and James; and the truth is that Southampton should have succeeded; **OTHERS' SEEING** = the "others" see only the dark guilt of Southampton, and are unaware of or refuse to see (or take into account) his royal blood; in effect, they are blind and see only "darkness which the blind do see" – Sonnet 27, line 8

5 FOR WHY SHOULD OTHERS' FALSE ADULTERATE EYES
FALSE = opposite of True, related to Oxford; also "false" related to treason as in "false traitor"; **ADULTERATE** = counterfeit; not truthful or real; **FALSE ADULTERATE EYES** = the false view of others that Southampton is a traitor; "I am thy King, and thou a false-heart traitor" – 2 Henry VI, 5.1.143; also, the false view that he is not a king by blood; "Why should false painting imitate his cheek" – Sonnet 67, line 5; "Simply I credit her false-speaking tongue" – Sonnet 138, line 7, referring to Elizabeth;

6 GIVE SALUTATION TO MY SPORTIVE BLOOD?
SALUTATION = ("And in his private plot be we the first to *salute our rightful sovereign* with honor of his birthright to the crown" – 2 Henry VI, 2.2.5961; "Loud shouts and *salutations* from their mouths, even in the presence of *the crowned king*" – 1 Henry IV, 3.2.53-54); Oxford giving salutation to Southampton as a king; **MY SPORTIVE BLOOD** = i.e., Oxford's reckless blood that is also part of Southampton's reckless blood; echoing the royal blood of his son; "And that *fresh blood* which youngly thou bestow'st" – Sonnet 11, line 3

7 OR ON MY FRAILTIES WHY ARE FRAILER SPIES,
OR ON MY FRAILTIES, etc. = why do weaker people look on my weaknesses; "Frailty, thy name is woman!" – *Hamlet*, 1.2.152, another indication that Oxford is revising that play at this time (see lines 1-2 and 8); **FRAILER** = lack of royal blood, i.e., less royal than my son, i.e., Robert Cecil, but even King James is less royal by blood than Southampton; **SPIES** = William and Robert Cecil both relied heavily on spies to assist them in running the government; recalling the spies Rosencrantz and Guildenstern, hired by Polonius-Burghley.

8 WHICH IN THEIR WILLS COUNT BAD WHAT I THINK GOOD?
WILLS = royal wills; the royal will of James; a play on "Will" Shakespeare; **COUNT BAD WHAT I THINK GOOD** = add up his royalty as nothing good or genuine = "To leave for *nothing* all thy *sum of good*" – Sonnet 109, line 12; "For there is nothing either good or bad but thinking makes it so" – *Hamlet*, 2.2.250-251; **COUNT** = as in praying upon the Rosary beads: "Nothing, sweet boy, but yet like prayers divine,/ I must each day say o'er the very same,/ *Counting* no old thing old, thou mine, I thine" – Sonnet 108, lines 5-7; referring to the accounting of Southampton's royal blood; "What acceptable *Audit* can'st thou

REFERENCE EDITION

leave?" – Sonnet 4, line 12; "Her *Audit* (though delayed) answered must be,/ And her *Quietus* is to render thee" – Sonnet 126, lines 11-12

9 **NO, I AM THAT I AM, AND THEY THAT LEVEL**
I AM THAT I AM = "And God said unto Moses, *I AM THAT I AM*" – Exodus, 3.14; "*I am myself alone*" – Richard in *3 Henry VI*, 5.6.83; "*you alone are you*" and "*you are you*" – Oxford to Southampton, speaking to his royal son as king or god on earth, in Sonnet 84, lines 2 & 8

"*I serve Her Majesty, and I am that I am,* and by alliance near to your Lordship, but free, and scorn to be offered that injury to think I am so weak of government as to be ruled by servants, or not able to govern myself. If your Lordship take and follow this course, you deceive yourself, and make me take another course than yet I have not thought of."
- Oxford writing to his father-in-law William Cecil Lord Burghley, the most powerful man in England, on October 30, 1584 – in a postscript in his own hand, when Southampton was ten years old and a ward of the Queen in Burghley's custody. Oxford was complaining about Burghley planting servants to spy on him (see "spies" in line 7 above); and in passing he angrily (and indirectly) reminded him that he, Oxford, was the father of a royal son and virtually a king entitled to be Elizabeth's king-consort.

> Were I the Moor, I would not be Iago.
> In following him *I follow but myself*.
> Heaven is my judge, not I for love and duty
> *But seeming so*, for my peculiar end,
> For when my outward action doth demonstrate
> The native act and figure of my heart
> In complement extern, 'tis not long after
> But I will wear my heart upon my sleeve
> For daws to peck at: ***I am not what I am***
> - *Othello*, 1.1.56-64

> *I am not as I seem to be*,
> For when I smile I am not glad:
> A thrall although you count me free,
> I, most in mirth, most pensive sad.
> I smile to shade my bitter spite…
> - Oxford poem, signed *E. O., The Paradise of Dainty Devices*, 1576

> O that *you were yourself*, but love *you are*
> No longer yours than *you yourself* here live
> - Sonnet 13, lines 1-2

(In the above lines, Oxford is reminding Southampton that he is no longer what he appears to be; i.e., he is a royal prince who cannot be himself in public)

> ***This is I***, Hamlet the Dane!
> - *Hamlet*, 5.2.255

LEVEL = aim; "the direction in which a missive weapon is aimed" – Dowden; "The harlot king is quite beyond mine arm, out of the blank and *level* of my brain" – *The Winter's Tale*, 2.3.6

10 **AT MY ABUSES RECKON UP THEIR OWN:**
AT MY ABUSES, etc. = at my deceptions; ("is it some *abuse?*" – *Hamlet*, 4.7.49; **RECKON UP THEIR OWN** = add up their own lies; recalling "*reckoning* time" of Sonnet 115, line 5

No. 121

11 **I MAY BE STRAIGHT THOUGH THEY THEMSELVES BE BEVEL.**
BEVEL = heraldic for *crooked*; alluding to Oxford's brother-in-law, the hunchbacked Robert Cecil, and his crooked physical figure

12 **BY THEIR RANK THOUGHTS MY DEEDS MUST NOT BE SHOWN,**
RANK = despicable, foul, festering, large, grievous, bloated, serious, growing ever worse; "O, my offense is *rank*" – *Hamlet*, 3.3.36, King Claudius to himself; "Things *rank and gross* in nature possess it merely" – *Hamlet*, 1.2.136, the Prince, speaking of the world and specifically the state of Denmark; the terrible, sinful thoughts of others who have deprived Southampton of his claim; but Oxford must stay silent; suggesting high rank or office; ranked in battle order

13 **UNLESS THIS GENERAL EVIL THEY MAINTAIN:**
UNLESS, etc. = unless they admit their evil openly and generally; unless they want to make the following general argument:

14 **ALL MEN ARE BAD AND IN THEIR BADNESS REIGN.**
ALL = Southampton, *One for All, All for One*; **ALL MEN ARE BAD** = Southampton is as "bad" or guilty as all men; but this is ironic, sarcastic; earlier, in the Dark Lady series, Oxford wrote to the still-living Elizabeth in desperate anger: "Now this ill-wresting world is grown so *bad,/* Mad slanderers by mad ears believed be" – Sonnet 140, lines 11-12

> Why, then, 'tis none to you;
> For there is *nothing good or bad but thinking makes it so*
> - *Hamlet*, 2.2.250

AND IN THEIR BADNESS REIGN = and he "reigns" as King; (i.e., Oxford standing the whole picture on its head, reverting back to line 1; so it's better to be a real king, i.e., one with true rights, than just to be *esteemed* as one; and if his son is regarded as un-royal, then he should *"reign"* as king anyway); the new ruler is King James, along with Robert Cecil; and they are reigning over England in all their evil or badness; **REIGN** = the final word of the sonnet, emphasizing the true nature of the verse as political and related to the issue of whose reign it should be

> Save her alone, who yet on th'earth doth ***reign*** ...
> - Oxford poem, *The Paradise of Dainty Devices*, 1576, writing of the Queen

REFERENCE EDITION

THE MONUMENT

THE FINAL DAYS

THREE DAYS TO THE QUEEN'S FUNERAL

Sonnet 122
Thy Record Never Can Be Missed
25 April 1603

The great "gift" of Southampton's royal life now fills the pages of the Sonnets, which are his own "tables" or writing tablets, dedicated to preserving his "lasting memory" as Prince Henry of England. Oxford will now boldly give him "thy record" (the same as "the living record of your memory" of Sonnet 55) to keep. Southampton hereby becomes responsible for the fate of the Sonnets. Oxford himself no longer needs to possess the actual pages of the diary, since its words live in his own brain; to do otherwise would imply his "forgetfulness" of his son's life.

Sonnet 122	Translation
Thy gift, thy tables, are within my brain	Your life, in my sonnets, is within my mind,
Full characterd with lasting memory,	Fully written to be preserved for immortality,
Which shall above that idle rank remain	And this verse will continue above all others
Beyond all date even to eternity.	Beyond all history to eternity.
Or at the least, so long as brain and heart	Or at least, so long as my mind and heart
Have faculty by nature to subsist,	Continues by nature to live in this world,
Till each to razed oblivion yield his part	Till they have yielded to obliteration each part
Of thee, thy record never can be missed.	Of you, your record here cannot be missed!
That poor retention could not so much hold,	These poor writing tablets are not so strong,
Nor need I tallies thy dear love to score.	Nor do I need tallies to measure your royal blood.
Therefore to give them from me was I bold,	Therefore to give the Sonnets to you I was bold,
To trust those tables that receive thee more.	To trust that my mind's tablets contain you more.
To keep an adjunct to remember thee,	To keep a tangible thing with memory of you
Were to import forgetfulness in me.	Would be to say that I might forget you.

April 25, 1603: *"Southampton and Pembroke met the King at Burghley (House), the immense country palace the old Lord Treasurer had built ... Southampton was warmly welcomed"* - Rowse, "Shakespeare's Southampton," 173; *"Not waiting for the formal reception of the King by the Privy Council at Theobalds, Southampton arrived at Lord Burghley's mansion at Burghley-by-Stamford, and was ushered into the presence of King James"* – Akrigg, "Shakespeare and the Earl of Southampton," 134; (but Stopes reports that the meeting occurred two days later, on April 27, at Huntingdon, where the King gave Southampton the Sword of State to bear before him.)

1 THY GIFT, THY TABLES, ARE WITHIN MY BRAIN
THY GIFT = the gift of your life and royal blood, as recorded in these sonnets; *"Nature's **bequest** gives nothing but doth lend"* – i.e., the Queen's gift of her blood inheritance, Sonnet 4, line 3; "Which *bounteous*

634

gift thou shouldst in bounty cherish" – Sonnet 11, line 12; "So ***thy great gift***, upon misprision growing" – Sonnet 87, line 11; **THY TABLES** = the writing tablets upon which these sonnets, which are yours, have been recorded; the gift of your life is now in this "*living record* of your memory" – Sonnet 55, line 8); **ARE WITHIN MY BRAIN** = Oxford carries them in his head; ("Yea, from the *table of my memory* I'll wipe away all trivial fond records ... and thy commandment all alone shall *live within the book and volume of my brain*" – *Hamlet*, 1.5.98-103); "That did my ripe thoughts *in my brain* inhearse,/ Making their tomb the womb wherein they grew" – Sonnet 86, lines 3-4

2 FULL CHARACTERED WITH LASTING MEMORY,
FULL = filled with your royal blood; **CHARACTERED** = inscribed upon, set down; "What's in the brain that *ink may character*" – Sonnet 108, line 1; "Reserve their *character* with golden quill" – Sonnet 85, line 3; "And these few precepts in thy *memory* look thou *character*" – Polonius in *Hamlet*, 1.3.58, i.e., imprint upon the brain; "And mighty states *characterless* are grated to dusty nothing" – *Troilus and Cressida*, 3.2.185; **LASTING MEMORY** = "Nor *Mars* his sword nor war's quick fire shall burn/ The *living record of your memory*" – Sonnet 55, lines 7-8

3 WHICH SHALL ABOVE THAT IDLE RANK REMAIN
ABOVE THAT IDLE RANK = above all other rank, i.e., your royal blood entitles you to be king above all others; i.e., above that poorer rank; "A dearer birth than this his love had brought/ To *march in **ranks** of better equipage*" – Sonnet 32, lines 11-12, i.e., a more royal birth for my son would have resulted in him becoming a king in charge of whole armies; "That never am less *idle* lo, than when I am alone" – Oxford poem, *The Paradise of Dainty Devices*, 1576

4 BEYOND ALL DATE EVEN TO ETERNITY.
ALL = Southampton, *One for All, All for One*; **BEYOND ALL DATE** = beyond your date with the royal succession, which has lapsed, and beyond time itself; i.e., you and your gift are immortalized in these sonnets, which are in my brain: "Thy end is Truth's and Beauty's *doom and date*" – Sonnet 14, line 14; "And Summer's lease has *all too short a date*" – Sonnet 18, line 4; "So long as youth and thou are of *one date*" – Sonnet 22, line 2; "For precious friends hid in death's *dateless night*" – Sonnet 30, line 6, i.e., eternal royal disgrace and lack of kingship; "A *dateless* (eternally royal) lively heat, still to endure" – Sonnet 153, line 6, referring to the newly born son of Oxford and Elizabeth; **EVEN TO ETERNITY** = the promise of his son's immortal life being preserved in the Sonnets for posterity; "You name from hence *immortal life* shall have/ Though I (once gone) to all the world must die" – Sonnet 81, lines 5-6; "Nor shall death brag thou wandr'st in his shade,/ When in *eternal lines to time* thou grow'st" – Sonnet 18, lines 11-12

5 OR AT THE LEAST, SO LONG AS BRAIN AND HEART
OR AT THE LEAST, etc. = referring now to Oxford's own mortal brain and heart

6 HAVE FACULTY BY NATURE TO SUBSIST
Continue to live; are able to survive; **NATURE** = once the Queen, but now referring to universal nature or "Nature, *sovereign mistress* over wrack" as in Sonnet 126, line 5

7 TILL EACH TO RAZED OBLIVION YIELD HIS PART
Until brain and heart each give up its part (of you) to mortal death; **OBLIVION** = Oxford's own death, but referring to his utter oblivion as Southampton's father and, by extension, as the writer of the Shakespeare works; **RAZED OBLIVION** = ("oblivion which erases, wipes everything away ... blank oblivion, nothingness, the state of nonexistence" – Booth); "through which infirmity you are desirous to *bury and ensevel your works in **the grave of oblivion***" – Oxford's Prefatory Letter to *Cardanus' Comfort*, 1573; "lofty towers

I see down razed" – Sonnet 64, line 3; **RAZED** = torn away, destroyed; perhaps also suggesting an oblivion "raised" or imposed upon him by others; both Oxford and Southampton had been "raised" by the Queen as royal wards and courtiers.

8 **OF THEE, THY RECORD NEVER CAN BE MISSED.**
OF THEE = of you; of your "living record" in these verses; **OF THEE, THY RECORD** = this record of you, this diary of the Sonnets; this document of contemporary history; ("living *record* of your memory" of Sonnet 55, line 8); **NEVER** = Oxford, *Ever or Never*; declaring that readers of the future will not be able to miss this record of Southampton's royal blood, which is not recorded in the official records of the time

"Thy Record" = Southampton's true story recorded here, as opposed to Time's false or lying records in Sonnet 123, line 11: "For thy records and what we see doth lie"

9 **THAT POOR RETENTION COULD NOT SO MUCH HOLD,**
THAT POOR RETENTION, etc. = Oxford's inevitable old age and death, removing his memory; that poor means of retaining impressions of you, i.e., the writing tables for these private sonnets, which contain your "gift" of life and royal blood

10 **NOR NEED I TALLIES THY DEAR LOVE TO SCORE.**
TALLIES = "sticks on which notches and scores are cut to keep accounts by" – Dowden, i.e., keeping the *Audit* or accounting of your royal blood in this diary (as in Sonnet 4, line 12, and Sonnet 126, line 11; **THY DEAR LOVE** = your royal blood; royal blood of my dear son; "If *my dear love* were but the child of state" – Sonnet 124, line 1; "A *dearer birth* than this his *love* had brought/ To march in ranks of better equipage" – Sonnet 32, lines 11-12

11 **THEREFORE TO GIVE THEM FROM ME WAS I BOLD**
THEREFORE = Oxford has already given most of the sonnets to his son, and he will soon give them all to him; **BOLD** = it takes boldness to part with these treasonous sonnets that put forth a genuine claim to the throne; they were a potential threat to Elizabeth and now a threat to King James (and to Robert Cecil); ("And art made *tongue-tied by authority*" – Sonnet 66, line 9)

12 **TO TRUST THOSE TABLES THAT RECEIVE THEE MORE.**
Trusting in these sonnets, which **RECEIVE THEE MORE** = contain more of you and your life story and your blood

13 **TO KEEP AN ADJUNCT TO REMEMBER THEE**
For Oxford to keep (and hide) this diary in order to remember his son; "And *keep* invention in a noted weed" – Sonnet 76, line 6; a play on the Keeper of the Tower; **TO REMEMBER THEE** = "*Remember me*" – the Ghost of Hamlet's father, to his son the Prince – *Hamlet*, 1.5.90; "*Remember thee?* Yea, from the table of my memory…" – *Hamlet*, 1.5.97-98, see line 1 above

14 **WERE TO IMPORT FORGETFULNESS IN ME.**
WERE TO IMPORT, etc. = would imply he had forgotten him; therefore Oxford gives the Sonnets to his son, Henry Wriothesley, who will print them for posterity in 1609.

Part Two

THE FINAL DAYS

TWO DAYS TO THE QUEEN'S FUNERAL
OXFORD VOWS TO DEFY TIME

Sonnet 123
No! Time … Thy Pyramids
26 April 1603

These private verses, written and compiled as entries of a diary according to time, are akin to the pyramids built by ancient Egyptians to preserve dynastic rulers in tombs until they attained eternal life. Therefore, the pyramids of the Sonnets belong to Time, against which Oxford now vows his defiance. "Thy registers and thee I both defy!" he declares to Time, because "thy records" – your historical records – continue to "lie" about what really happened. In the Book of Sonnets, however, Oxford has preserved the truth from time's destruction of it: "This I do vow, and this shall ever be,/ I will be true, despite thy scythe and thee!" (Although the Coronation will be held privately in July, with Oxford serving as Lord Great Chamberlain, the plague will cause the public Coronation Procession to be postponed until March 15, 1604. At this point, however, plans are already under way to erect triumphal arches or "pyramids" for the procession. Oxford is keenly aware of these plans, even while he completes the construction of these "pyramids" for Southampton, the true King.)

Sonnet 123	Translation
No! Time, thou shalt not boast that I do change,	No! Time, you will not boast that I change!
Thy pyramids built up with newer might	Your sonnets built up with newer royalty
To me are nothing novel, nothing strange,	To me are nothing new or different,
They are but dressings of a former sight:	They are only dressed in new words for old ones!
Our dates are brief, and therefore we admire	Our dates with death are soon, so we admire
What thou dost foist upon us that is old,	The records of history you foist upon us,
And rather make them borne to our desire	And claim they were created in our interest,
Then think that we before have heard them told:	Rather than recall we've already had them.
Thy registers and thee I both defy,	I defy both your records of history and you,
Not wond'ring at the present, nor the past,	Not marveling at present or past reigns,
For thy records and what we see doth lie,	Because your records and appearances do lie,
Made more or less by thy continual haste.	Written according to the continually passing time!
This I do vow, and this shall ever be,	This I now promise, and this shall always be:
I will be true despite thy scythe and thee.	I preserve the truth, despite your knife and you!

1 NO! TIME, THOU SHALT NOT BOAST THAT I DO CHANGE!
NO! = Oxford shouts his defiance of time, for all time; **TIME** = referring back to the ever-waning life of Elizabeth and this "Chronicle of wasted time" in Sonnet 106, line 1, but also to universal time, i.e., all time into the future; **THOU SHALT NOT BOAST, etc.** = you will not be able to boast that I have ever, or ever will, alter my love for my royal son; "Ever beloved and loving may his rule be; and when old *time* shall lead him to his end, goodness and he fill up one monument!" – *Henry VIII*, 2.1.92-94;

REFERENCE EDITION 637

2 THY PYRAMIDS BUILT UP WITH NEWER MIGHT
These individual sonnets, written according to time and therefore beholden to it, which are used to construct this larger Pyramid or Monument to Southampton, to preserve him for immortal life; **BUILT UP WITH NEWER MIGHT** = now being constructed with additional royal blood (of my son); written with greater urgency and compression; "No, it was *builded* far from accident/ … But all alone *stands* hugely politic" – Sonnet 124, lines 5,11; "*Erect* his statue and worship it" – *2 Henry VI*, 3.2.79; "for in your lifetime I shall *erect* you such a monument" – Oxford's Prefatory Letter to *Cardanus' Comfort*, 1573; "Within their chiefest temple I'll *erect* a tomb" – *1 Henry VI*, 2.2.12-13; "If a man do not *erect* in this age his own *tomb* ere he dies, he shall live no longer in *monument* than the bell rings and the widow weeps" – *Much Ado About Nothing*, 5.2.73-75; "They call him Troilus, and on him *erect* a second hope, as fairly **built** as Hector" – *Troilus and Cressida*, 4.5.108-109; "This royal throne of kings, this earth of majesty, this seat of Mars, this other Eden, demi-paradise, this fortress *built* by Nature for herself against infection and the hand of war" – *Richard II*, 2.1.40-44; "This Antioch, then, Antioch the Great *built up*, this city, for his chiefest seat" – Pericles, chorus of act one, 17-18

> And *ruined love*, when it is **built** anew,
> Grows fairer than at first, more strong, far greater
> - Sonnet 119, lines 11-12

THY PYRAMIDS = Oxford knew that the Egyptian Pyramids contained tombs preserving their dynastic rulers until they attained immortal life:

> Thus do they, sir: they take the flow o'th'Nile
> By certain scales in *the pyramid*. They know
> By the height, the lowness, or the mean, if dearth
> Or foison follow. The higher Nilus swells,
> The more it promises. As it ebbs, the seedsman
> Upon the slime and ooze scatters his grain,
> And shortly comes to harvest.
> - *Antony and Cleopatra*, 2.7.17-23

> Though castles topple on their warders' heads;
> Though *palaces and pyramids* do slope
> Their heads to their foundations
> - *Macbeth*, 4.1.56-58

3 TO ME ARE NOTHING NOVEL, NOTHING STRANGE:
To me are nothing innovative or new; just as Oxford never uses any "*new*-found methods or compounds *strange*" in Sonnet 76, line 4, to write these private sonnets that are pyramids of the monument

4 THEY ARE BUT DRESSINGS OF A FORMER SIGHT.
I am saying the same thing over and over, as my diary proceeds, but I have kept dressing each sonnet (or pyramid) in different costumes of poetry; "So all my best is ***dressing old words new***,/ Spending again what is already spent" – Sonnet 76, lines 11-12; these sonnets may use some different words than before, but they are still all about the same thing; "And you and love are still my argument" – Sonnet 76, line 10; "Since *all alike* my songs and praises be/ To one, of one, still such, and ever so" – Sonnet 105, lines 3-4; similarly, the pyramids are images of a former time preserved for future generations.

5 OUR DATES ARE BRIEF, AND THEREFORE WE ADMIRE
OUR DATES = "life spans" – Booth; "Thy end is *Truth's and Beauty's doom and date*" – Sonnet 14, line 14; "And Summer's lease hath *all too short a date*" – Sonnet 18, line 4; **BRIEF** = quick, speedy; also pressing, urgent; "Bear away that child and follow me with speed; I'll to the king. A thousand businesses are *brief in hand*, and heaven itself doth frown upon the land" – the Bastard in *King John*, 5.1.156-159

6 WHAT THOU DOST FOIST UPON US THAT IS OLD,
FOIST = "to cheat by surreptitiously substituting false dice for true" – Booth; forcing us to look back at these sonnets, which contain our "old" but true relationship as father and son.

7 AND RATHER MAKE THEM BORN TO OUR DESIRE
BORN = recalling Southampton's birth; the sonnets were "*born to our desire*" or royal will; **BORN TO OUR DESIRE** = recalling the royal "*we*" of the imperial command ("we desire") of Sonnet 1, line 1: "From fairest creatures *we desire* increase,/ That thereby beauty's *Rose* might never die"; signifying both the monarch, Elizabeth, who gave birth to Southampton, and both Oxford and the Queen as parents who "*desire*" or command their most royal "creature" or child

8 THAN THINK THAT WE BEFORE HAVE HEARD THEM TOLD.
THAN, etc. = (Q has "then", usually emended to "than"); then upon re-reading these pyramids, we shall remember what Southampton "told" in them about his life and royalty; **TOLD** = ("For as the Sun is daily new and old/ So is my love still *telling what is told*" – Sonnet 76, lines 13-14)

9 THY REGISTERS AND THEE I BOTH DEFY,
THY REGISTERS = time's records; "can also include ancient objects like the pyramids which are marked by time and are themselves historical documents" – Booth; "what new to *register*" – Sonnet 108, line 3; but Oxford is referring to mortal time and its historical records; **I BOTH DEFY** = "By God, I cannot flatter; I do *defy* the tongues of soothers" – *1 Henry IV*, 4.1.6-7; "We *defy* augury" – *Hamlet*, 5.2.218; Oxford is defying both mortal time and its historical records, by means of the pyramids and pyramidal Monument of the Sonnets for "eyes not yet created" of Sonnet 81, line 10

10 NOT WOND'RING AT THE PRESENT, NOR THE PAST:
NOT WOND'RING, etc. = "won" echoing "one" for Southampton; ("For we which now behold these *present* days/ Have eyes to *wonder,* but lack tongues to praise" – Sonnet 106, lines 13-14, referring to the then-forthcoming release of Southampton from the Tower by King James, newly proclaimed in succession to Elizabeth)

11 FOR THY RECORDS AND WHAT WE SEE DOTH LIE,
THY RECORDS = ("the objects and events of current experience" – Booth); the records kept by contemporary historians; "Is it upon *record*, or else reported successively from age to age, he built it?" Prince Edward asks about the historical report that Julius Caesar built the original structure of the Tower of London, and Buckingham replies: "Upon *record*, my gracious lord" – *Richard III*, 3.1.72-74; **AND WHAT WE SEE** = and those items on the surface, for the eyes of the public, as opposed to the truth; **DOTH LIE** = they both give a false history; this is one of Oxford's most direct and powerful statements about the obliteration of the truth in relation to himself and Southampton; in the Dark Lady verses to the Queen: "Therefore I *lie* with her, and she with me,/ And in our faults by *lies* we flattered be" – Sonnet 138, lines 13-14, playing upon his sexual relationship with Elizabeth that led to the conception of Southampton, while stating that they both "lie" or cover up the truth of their royal son; "To swear against the truth so foul a *lie*" – Sonnet 152, line 14, his final words to the Queen; but Oxford, in defiance of these lies promoted by historical records, is constructing the *"living"* record of his royal son's memory to preserve him for posterity – Sonnet 55, line 8

12 MADE MORE OR LESS BY THY CONTINUAL HASTE!
MADE, etc. = made so by the constant revision of history by current record-keepers

13 THIS I DO VOW, AND THIS SHALL EVER BE:
THIS I DO VOW = a ringing, solemn promise or assertion; "My heart hath vowed" – poem possibly by Oxford, Rawlinson Poet. MS 85, f. 17; Chiljan, 184; **EVER** = E. Ver, Edward de Vere, *Ever or Never*; "If this be error and upon me proved,/ I *never* writ, nor no man *ever* loved" – Sonnet 116, lines 13-14; "Why write I still all one, *ever* the same,/ And keep invention in a noted weed,/ That *every* word doth almost tell my name" – Sonnet 76, lines 5-7; "Since all alike my songs and praises be/ To one, of one, still such, and *ever* so" – Sonnet 105, lines 3-4

14 I WILL BE TRUE DESPITE THY SCYTHE AND THEE.
TRUE = Oxford, *Nothing Truer than Truth*; **I WILL BE TRUE** = I will remain myself; ("*I am that I am*" – Sonnet 121, line 9); I will always speak the truth (in these sonnets); I will always be the father of my son, i.e., we are both "true" as in "Let me not to the marriage of *true* minds/ Admit impediments" – Sonnet 116, lines 1-2; I am preserving his "true rights" to the throne, as mentioned in Sonnet 17, line 11; "but I hope *truth* is subject to no prescription, for *truth is truth* though never so old, and *time cannot make that false which was once true*" – Oxford to Robert Cecil, May 7, 1603, less than two weeks from now; **SCYTHE** = instrument used to mow grass and corn, i.e., cutting blade or knife; **DESPITE THY SCYTHE AND THEE** = despite your cruel hand (related to Elizabeth's cruel imperial hand) that deprived my son of the throne; "And nothing 'gainst *time's scythe* can make defense" – Sonnet 12, line 13; "And nothing stands but for *his scythe* to mow./ And yet *to times in hope my verse shall stand*,/ Praising thy worth, despite *his cruel hand*" – Sonnet 60, lines 12-14; "And make *time's spoils* despised everywhere./ Give my love fame faster than *time wastes life*,/ So thou *prevent'st his scythe and crooked knife*" – Sonnet 100, lines 12-14

> Let fame, that all hunt after in their lives,
> Live *registered* upon our brazen *tombs*,
> And then grace us in the disgrace of death,
> When, spite of cormorant **devouring Time**,
> Th'endeavour of this present breath may buy
> That honour which shall bate **his scythe's keen edge**,
> And make us *heirs of all eternity*.
> - The King in *Love's Labour's Lost*, 1.1.1-7

> If I be false, or swerve a hair from truth,
> *When time is old and hath forgot itself…*
> - *Troilus and Cressida*, 3.2.181-182

Part Two

THE FINAL DAYS

EVE OF THE QUEEN'S FUNERAL

Sonnet 124
Policy, That Heretic
My Dear Love ... Stands Hugely Politic
27 April 1603

On the eve of Elizabeth's funeral and the official end of her Tudor Rose dynasty, Oxford sums up his son's life as a "child of state" or royal ward (and royal prince) of the Queen. But, unable to fulfill his royal destiny, Southampton is "Fortune's bastard" (Elizabeth's unacknowledged son) and is "un-fathered" because his real father, Edward deVere, could not acknowledge him). Nevertheless, Henry Wriothesley remains "hugely politic" or immensely royal and immortal.

Sonnet 124	Translation
If my dear love were but the child of state,	If my royal son had been only a royal ward,
It might for fortune's bastard be unfathered,	He might be Elizabeth's bastard with no father,
As subject to time's love, or to time's hate,	As subject to royal life or non-royal life,
Weeds among weeds, or flowers with flowers gathered.	Orphan among orphans, or Tudor Roses with Tudor Roses gathered.
No, it was builded far from accident,	No, my son's royalty was built here on purpose!
It suffers not in smiling pomp, nor falls	It requires no false worship, nor does it fall
Under the blow of thralled discontent,	Under the blow of royal disfavor,
Whereto th'inviting time our fashion calls:	Which is what the fashion of the day calls for:
It fears not policy, that *Heretic*	It fears not the government, that false power
Which works on leases of short numb'red hours,	That operates according to mortal time,
But all alone stands hugely politic,	But it stands all alone in its great royal state,
That it nor grows with heat, nor drowns with showers.	So it does not grow according to favor or wither according to disfavor.
To this I witness call the fools of time,	I summon all victims of time to testify to this:
Which die for goodness, who have lived for crime.	Those dead for him, those who thrive on his crime.

"Continues the thought of Sonnet 123, lines 13-14; the writer's love being unconnected with motives of self-interest, is independent of Fortune and Time" – Dowden; and in the context of these sonnets, with *Fortune* and *Time* both referring previously to the now-deceased Queen Elizabeth, this independence of "love" or royal blood is real if bittersweet

1 IF MY DEAR LOVE WERE BUT THE CHILD OF STATE,
MY DEAR LOVE = Southampton, my royal son; also, my royal son's royal blood; "And if *thy sons were ever dear* to thee, O, think *my son to be as dear* to me" – *Titus Andronicus*, 1.1.110-111; "My *dear dear* lord" – to the King in *Richard II*, 1.1.176; used often by one close relative to another, as in "If thou didst ever *thy dear father* love" – *Hamlet*, 1.5.28, the ghost of Hamlet's father speaking to the prince, his son; "If this

REFERENCE EDITION 641

prove a vision of the island, one *dear son* shall I lose twice" – *The Tempest*, 5.1.175-176; used also to describe royalty, as in "most *dear and most admired sovereign* … your *royal dear heart*" – Essex to Queen Elizabeth, 1597, Weir, 427; "thy *dearest heart-blood*" – *3 Henry VI*, 1.1.229; **DEAR** = "But if the while I think on thee, *dear friend*" – Sonnet 30, line 11; (My royal son); "Hath *dear religious love* stol'n from mine eye" – Sonnet 31, line 6 (royal sacred blood); "As a decrepit *father* takes delight/ To see his active *child* do deeds of youth,/ So I, made lame by *Fortune's dearest spite*" – Sonnet 37, lines 1-3 (royal malice of your mother, Queen Elizabeth); "And *our dear love* lose name of single one" – Sonnet 39, line 6; (our father-son bond; my blood and your royal blood, within you); "And yet it may be said *I loved her dearly*" – Sonnet 42, line 2 (and yet I loved and served your royal mother the Queen); "Thou *best of dearest*, and mine only care" – Sonnet 48, line 7 (you, my most royal son, above even the Queen); "For truth proves thievish for *a prize so dear*" – Sonnet 48, line 14 (for a leader/prince so royal); "Farewell! Thou art *too dear for my possessing*" – Sonnet 87, line 1 (too royal for me to acknowledge you as my son); "And sweets grown common lose their *dear delight*" – Sonnet 102, line 12 (royal joy); "That may express my love, or *thy dear merit*" – Sonnet 108, line 4 (your royal qualities and what you deserve); "Gored my own thoughts, *sold cheap what is most dear*" – Sonnet 110, line 3 (ransomed your life with your most royal claim); "Forgot upon *your **dearest love*** to call,/ Whereto *all bonds do tie me* day by day" – Sonnet 117, lines 3-4 (your most royal blood …whereby our father-son bonds knit me to you daily); "And given to time **your own dear purchased right**" – Sonnet 117, line 6 (ransomed to *time* – or Elizabeth's life and death – your own royally earned right to the throne)

> But thou art fair, and at thy birth, ***dear boy***,
> Nature and fortune join'd to make thee great
> - *King John*, 2.2.51-52

> ***Dear sovereign***, hear me speak
> - *As You Like It*, 1.3.63

CHILD OF STATE = royal ward of the Queen, with Oxford (1562-1571) having been the first such ward and Southampton (1581-1594) the ninth and last in the custody of William Cecil, Lord Burghley; **STATE** = royal state; therefore, "child of *state*" also alluding to Southampton as a ***prince of the realm or state***; ("If thou wouldst use *the strength of all thy state*!" – Sonnet 96, line 12; "The resignation of thy *state and crown*" – *Richard II*, 4.1.179; and in all the references below, *state* carries this meaning directly and/or indirectly, with Oxford often standing in his son's place:

> And wear *thy brave state* out of memory - Sonnet 15, line 8
> I all alone beweep *my outcast state* - Sonnet 29, line 2
> When I have seen such *interchange of state* - Sonnet 64, line 9
> I see a *better state* to me belongs - Sonnet 92, line 7
> To be so tickled they would *change their state* - Sonnet 128, line 9

2 IT MIGHT FOR FORTUNE'S BASTARD BE UNFATHERED,
FORTUNE'S BASTARD = Elizabeth's royal bastard, i.e., Southampton

> Before these *bastard signs of fair were borne* - Sonnet 68, line 3

> But now is black *beauty's successive heir*,
> And Beauty slandered with a *bastard shame* - Sonnet 127, line 4

"I am a *bastard*, too: I love *bastards*. I am *bastard begot, bastard instructed, bastard in mind, bastard in valour, in everything illegitimate*. One bear will not bit another, and wherefore should *one bastard*? Take heed: the quarrel's most ominous to us – if the son of a whore fight for a whore, he tempts judgment. Fare-

No. 124

well, *bastard*." - *Trolius & Cressida*, 5.7.18-22; "Fortune is the mother, and the love which is its child would be but a by-blow with no status" - Tucker

BE UNFATHERED = be deprived of any father, since he was deprived of me; i.e., if my royal son had not been a royal ward, he would still have been the Queen's royal bastard and fatherless as well; (but when Southampton became a ward at age seven in 1581, Oxford was able to see him and spend time with him, perhaps even using him to act in his boy companies; "be without status under the law and have no right of inheritance; be disavowed, be disowned" – Booth

(But in fact Oxford has "fathered" his royal son by giving him rebirth and growth in these sonnets)

Like widowed wombs after their lords' decease;
Yet this *abundant issue* seemed to me/
But *hope of orphans, and un-fathered* fruit - Sonnet 97, lines 8-10

You had a Father, let your Son say so - Sonnet 13, line 14

Even so *my Sunne* one early morn did shine,
With all triumphant splendor on my brow,
But out alack, *he was but one hour mine*,
The region cloud hath masked him from me now - Sonnet 33, lines 9-12

As a decrepit father takes delight
To see his active child do deeds of youth,
So I, made lame by Fortune's dearest spite - Sonnet 37, lines 1-3

3 AS SUBJECT TO TIME'S LOVE, OR TO TIME'S HATE,
SUBJECT TO TIME'S LOVE = subject to the Queen's royal blood as it withered in her mortal body according to time; suggesting a "subject" of the monarch; "Am I a Queen in title and in style, and must be made a *subject to* a duke?" – *2 Henry VI*, 1.3.48-49; "To help King Edward in his time of storm, as every loyal *subject* ought to do" – *3 Henry VI*, 4.7.43-44; **TIME'S HATE** = the deprivation of royal claim when Elizabeth died and time ran out in Sonnet 105, rendering these sonnets as "the *Chronicle of wasted time*" in Sonnet 106, line 1; "Those lips that *Love's* own hand did make/ Breathed forth the sound that said, 'I *hate*'" – Sonnet 145, lines 1-2, of Elizabeth, who spared Southampton's life: "'*I hate*' from *hate* away she threw,/ And saved my life, saying, 'Not you!'" – lines 13-14; "And all in war with Time for love of you" – Sonnet 15, line 13

4 WEEDS AMONG WEEDS, OR FLOWERS WITH FLOWERS GATHERED.
WEEDS = Southampton as base commoner; ("Lilies that fester smell far worse than *weeds*" – Sonnet 94, line 14); **AMONG WEEDS** = among the other prisoners in the Tower; among those base commoners, as Southampton was; "The *basest weed* outbraves his dignity" – Sonnet 94, line 12; **FLOWERS WITH FLOWERS** = a Tudor Rose heir included in the line of succession to other Tudor Rose monarchs, such as Elizabeth; Southampton as "the little western flower" of *A Midsummer Night's Dream* and the "purple flower" of *Venus and Adonis*; "your living flowers" – Sonnet 16, line 7; "When *beauty* lived and died as *flowers* do now" – Sonnet 68, line 2; "To *thy fair flower* add the rank smell of *weeds*" – Sonnet 69, line 12, referring to Southampton as disgraced traitor in the Tower; "The *summer's flower* is to the *flower* sweet" – Sonnet 94, line 9; "For nothing in this wide universe I call/ Save *thou, my Rose*, in it thou art my all" – Sonnet 109, lines 13-14; "My love might be subject to Time's hate, and so plucked up as a weed, or subject to Time's love, and so gathered as a flower" – Dowden; the garden as common image of the state; "When our sea-walled garden, the whole land, is full of weeds, her fairest flowers choked up" - *Richard II*, 3.4.45-46; (see "Shakespeare After All," Margorie Garber, 245); the garden refers back to "state" in "child of state," line 1

REFERENCE EDITION 643

5 NO, IT WAS BUILDED FAR FROM ACCIDENT;

The true life of Southampton (containing his royal blood) is not subject to these things, bad or good, but instead is constructed purposefully in this Monument of the Book of Sonnets; "Thy pyramids *built up* with newer might" – Sonnet 123, line 2; "Ladies, you deserve to have *a temple built you*" – *Coriolanus*, 5.3.211-212; "Time, force, and death, do to this body what extremes you can; but the strong *base and **building*** of my love is as the very center of the earth, drawing all things to it" – *Troilus and Cressida*, 4.2.103-107

6 IT SUFFERS NOT IN SMILING POMP, NOR FALLS

My royal son does not suffer or lose his blood because of smiling cruel royalty (as opposed to the imperial "frown" of Sonnet 25, line 8); "That one may *smile, and smile*, and be a villain" – *Hamlet*, 1.5.108, speaking of King Claudius; and neither does Southampton fall from favor in the eyes of future readers of these sonnets; **POMP** = *"No princely pomp"* – Oxford poem (see line 7 below); "To think upon my *pomp* shall be my hell" – *2 Henry VI*, 2.4.41; "Why, what is *pomp, rule, reign*, but earth and dust?" – *3 Henry VI*, 5.2.27; "Scoffing his state and *grinning at his pomp*" – *Richard II*, 3.2.163; "All *pomp and majesty* I do forswear" – *Richard II*, 4.1.211; "The imminent decay of *wrested pomp*" – *King John*, 4.3.154; "The throne he sits on, nor the *tide of pomp* that beats upon the high shore of this world" – *Henry V*, 4.1.260-261

7 UNDER THE BLOW OF THRALLED DISCONTENT,

Under the destructive force of Elizabeth's royal anger or displeasure; "No *princely pomp*, no wealthy store … To none of these I yield as *thrall*" – poem listed by Steven May as possibly by Oxford; Chiljan, 174; "And shall I live on th'earth to be her *thrall*?/ And shall I sue and *serve* her all in vain:/ And kiss the steps, that she lets fall…?" – Oxford poem, of Elizabeth, in *Paradise of Dainty Devices*, 1576; "but I, *my Mistress' thrall*" – Sonnet 154, line 12, of Elizabeth, his sovereign mistress, 1574; **THRALLED** = a "thrall" is a person in bondage; "Discontented subjects are punished by being *thralled*, imprisoned or enslaved" – Duncan-Jones; "Proponents of Southampton as the 'youth' would perhaps interpret lines 6-7 as a veiled reference to his imprisonment in the Tower for his role in the Essex conspiracy" – Evans; **DISCONTENT** = dissatisfaction, vexation, sorrow, grief, and even mourning; *thralled discontent* = "discontent cause by oppression or enslavement … discontent which is enslaved, enforced to act against its will" – Booth, with an apt description of Oxford's situation, i.e., having had to force his son to relinquish his royal claim in exchange for his liberty and restoration to full honors; when his royal son was in prison: "With what I most enjoy *contented least*" – Sonnet 29, line 8; "If thou survive *my well-contented day*" – Sonnet 32, line 1; the opposite of Oxford's own contentment or comfort as a father: "As a decrepit father takes delight/ To see his active child do deeds of youth,/ So I, made lame by Fortune's (Elizabeth's) dearest spite,/ Take all my comfort of thy worth and truth" – Sonnet 37, lines 1-4; also the opposite of "my content" in Sonnet 119, line 13.

"Ay, Margaret, my heart is drowned with grief, whose flood begins to flow within mine eyes, my body round engirt with misery, for what's more miserable than *discontent*?" – the King in *2 Henry VI*, 3.1.198-201; "Mischance and Sorrow go along with you! Heart's *Discontent* and sour Affliction be playfellows to keep you company!" – the Queen in *2 Henry VI*, 3.2.299-301; "Now is the *winter of our discontent*, made glorious summer by this sun (son) of York, and all the clouds that lour'd upon our house in the deep bosom of the ocean buried" – *Richard III*, 1.1.1-4; "Not prizing *her poor infant's discontent*" – to Elizabeth, of Southampton in Sonnet 143, line 8; "A Pleasant Conceit of Vere, Earl of Oxford, **discontented** at the rising of a mean gentleman in the English Court, circa 1580" – from a passage in *Desiderata Curiosa*, apparently referring to Christopher Hatton as the "mean gentleman" portrayed as Malvolio in the "pleasant conceit" published later as *Twelfth Night* (Ogburn, 633); "Were I a king I could command *content*" – Oxford poem of the late 1570s or early 1580s; "Some that other ways **discontent** me, I will not blaze or publish until it please me. And last of all, I mean not to weary my life anymore with such troubles and molestations as I have endured; nor will I, to please your Lordship only, **discontent** myself" – Oxford to Burghley, April 27, 1576, when rumors spread that he was not the father of Anne Cecil's child, Elizabeth, born in 1575 while Oxford was in Italy

8 WHERETO TH'INVITING TIME OUR FASHION CALLS:
To which or where our current times call us; time, which beckons us onward; "For *never-resting time* leads Summer on" – Sonnet 5, line 5; before her death, *Time* referred to Elizabeth's ever-dwindling time of life, but now it also becomes a reference to the new monarch, i.e., to the fact that so many are beseeching King James for favors; even during the final days of her life, when Elizabeth became ill and was known to be dying, Camden writes: "It is incredible with what flying speed Puritans, Papists and ambitious persons of all sorts, flatterers and others, every of them came forward for their own hopes, posted night and day, by sea and land, into Scotland, to adore the rising King and gain his favor" – Camden, *Annals*, 1603; ("When time puts us, who have been in favor, out of fashion" – Dowden); "Is this the *fashion in the Court of England?* Is this *the government* of Britain's isle, and this *the royalty* of Albion's king?" – *2 Henry VI*, 1.3.42-45

9 IT FEARS NOT POLICY, THAT *HERETIC*,
POLICY = political prudence or cunning, as practiced by Robert Cecil; government or ruling policy or strategy; "Scheming strategy; particularly the sort of machination that aims at getting or keeping governmental power" – Booth; "To keep by *policy* what Henry got" – *2 Henry VI*, 1.1.83; "By devilish *policy* art thou grown great" – *2 Henry VI*, 4.1.82; and in fact it is by "policy" that Southampton has gained his freedom from the Tower; in effect, Oxford made a bargain with the devil (Cecil and James) for Southampton's life, effecting a "policy in love" or bargain by which his son had to give up his claim based on "love" or royal blood; therefore Southampton's *faults* or crimes ironically brought about a *healthful state*, as in:

> Thus *policy in love* t'anticipate
> The ills that were not grew to *faults assured*,
> And brought to medicine a *healthful state*
> Which rank of goodness would *by ill be cured*
> - Sonnet 118, lines 9-12

"The frame of civil government in a state ... prudent wisdom in the management of public or private concerns ... cunning stratagem" – Schmidt; "Statecraft, statesmanship, diplomacy ... stratagem, cunning, intrigue, craft ... expediency, shrewdness, self-interest" – Crystal & Crystal; "This *policy*, and reverence of age, makes the world bitter to the best of our times" – *King Lear*, 1.2.47-48; "Turn him to any cause of *policy*" – *Henry V*, 1.1.45; "Let us be worried and our nation lose the name of *hardiness and policy*" – *Henry V*, 1.2.220-221; "A little harm done to a great good end/ For *lawful policy* remains enacted" – *Lucrece*, 528-529; "Then, in a moment, fortune shall cull forth out of one side her happy minion, to whom in favor she shall give the day, and kiss him with a glorious victory. How like you this wild counsel, mighty states? Smacks it not something of *the policy*?" – *King John*, 2.1.391-396; "Our bloods are now in calm, and, so long, health! But when contention and occasion meet, by Jove, I'll play the hunter for thy life with all my *force, pursuit and policy*" – *Troilus and Cressida*, 4.1.16-19; "Search out thy wit for *secret policies*, and we will make thee famous through the world" – *1 Henry VI*, 3.3.12-13; "But I perceive men must learn now with pity to dispense, for *policy sits above conscience*" – *Timon of Athens*, 3.2.89-91; **HERETIC** = (*Heriticke*, capitalized and italicized, in *Q*); the state/religious policy, run by Cecil and followed by James, i.e., a policy that does not honor Southampton as rightful king or god on earth; the straightforward meaning of "heretic" is "one who holds opinion differing from the established faith" (Schmidt); and since Southampton is a prince or king and thereby a "God in love" (Sonnet 110, line 12), failure to acknowledge his royal claim is heresy

> And *blessed shall he be that doth revolt*
> *From his allegiance to an* **heretic**
> - *King John*, 3.1.100-101

In 1571 the Parliament passed a law proclaiming it high treason for anyone to claim that Queen Elizabeth "is not or ought not in right to be Queen of the Realm, or that the Kingdom is more justly due to some other" or to "pronounce her to be a *Hereticke*, Schismatike, or infidel." In effect, Oxford is calling the government of James under Robert Cecil a 'heretic' and, therefore, he is privately committing high treason in the Sonnets.

10 WHICH WORKS ON LEASES OF SHORT-NUMBERED HOURS,

Operating according to Southampton's "lease" of Elizabeth's blood, which ran out when she died; ("the *lease* of my true love" – Sonnet 107, line 3); the "numbers" or sonnets are running out of time in this dynastic diary, which will end tomorrow upon the Queen's funeral, recorded in Sonnet 125, marking the official end of her Tudor Rose dynasty, after which Oxford will conclude with the farewell envoy, Sonnet 126; "If I could write the beauty of your eyes,/ And *in fresh numbers number* all your graces" – Sonnet 17, lines 5-6; "*Eternal numbers* to outlive long date" – Sonnet 38, line 12; "But now *my gracious numbers* are decayed" – Sonnet 79, line 3; "His face thou hast, for even so looked he, accomplished with *the number of thy hours*" – *Richard II*, 2.1.176-177

11 BUT ALL ALONE STANDS HUGELY POLITIC,

ALL ALONE = Southampton, the "all" and "one" of his motto, doubly emphasized; "Since *all alike* my songs and praises be" – Sonnet 105, line 3; "Then *thou alone* kingdoms of hearts shouldst owe" – Sonnet 70, line 14; "Than this rich praise, that *you alone are you*" – Sonnet 84, line 2; **STANDS** = "This monument five hundred years hath *stood*" – *Titus Andronicus*, 1.1.355; **STANDS HUGELY POLITIC** = stands immensely royal, but silent by policy; remains alive by virtue of government policy, directed by the cunning Robert Cecil; ("Love's not Time's fool" – Sonnet 116, line 9, which expresses the same thought in a different way, i.e., nothing can alter his blood, now or ever, because it *"all alone stands"* against the "bending sickle" of Time: "though rosy lips and cheeks/ Within his bending sickle's compass come" – Sonnet 116, lines 9-10); the monarch had two bodies, one mortal and the other being the "body politic" or state

STANDS = "Desdemona: 'He shall in strangeness *stand* no farther off than in a *politic* distance'; Cassio: 'Ay, but, lady, that *policy* may either last so long…'" – *Othello*, 3.3.12-14; to stand is to "remain upright, not to fall, not to be lost, not to perish" – Schmidt; "Now *stand* you on the top of happy hours" – Sonnet 16, line 5; "O give thyself the thanks, if ought in me/ Worthy perusal *stand* against thy sight" – Sonnet 38, lines 6-7; "And nothing *stands* but for his scythe to mow./ And yet to times in hope *my verse shall stand*" – Sonnet 60, lines 12-13; "So your sweet hew, which methinks still doth *stand*" – Sonnet 104, line 11; "a true soul/ When most impeached *stands* least in thy control" – Sonnet 125, lines 13-14; and to Queen Elizabeth in the Dark Lady series, referring to Southampton: "He is contented thy poor drudge to be,/ To *stand* in your affairs, fall by thy side" – Sonnet 151, lines 11-12; "Now doth *thy honor stand*, in him that was of late an heretic, as firm as faith" – *The Merry Wives of Windsor*, 4.4.8-9; "That it may *stand till the perpetual doom* in state as wholesome as in state 'tis fit" – *MWW.*, 5.5.58-60; "It should not *stand in thy posterity*" – *Macbeth*, 3.1.4; **POLITIC** = ("relating to politics as the science of government … prudent, wise, artful, cunning" – Schmidt); "I will be proud, I will read *politic authors*" – *Twelfth Night*, 2.5.156; "For then this land was famously enriched with *politic grave counsel*" – *Richard III*, 2.3.19-20; "A certain *convocation of politic worms* are e'en at him" – *Hamlet*, 4.3.20, referring in jest to the Diet of Worms; "For them all together, which maintained *so politic a state of evil* that they will not admit any good part to intermingle with them" –*Much Ado About Nothing*, 5.2.60-63; "With *silence*, nephew, be thou *politic*" – *1 Henry VI*, 2.5.101; "Excellent: your lordship's a goodly villain. The devil knew not what he did when he made man *politic* … of such a nature is his *politic love*" – *Timon of Athens*, 3.3.29-31, 36; "'Tis *politic and safe* to let him keep at point a hundred knights" – *King Lear*, 1.4.316-317 (in the way James will be *politic and safe* by letting Southampton rule the Isle of Wight with his own militia, ensuring he never gains any genuine political power)

> And herein I am forced, like a good and ***politic*** captain
> - Oxford's Prefatory Letter to Cardanus' Comfort, 1573

12 THAT IT NOR GROWS WITH HEAT, NOR DROWNS WITH SHOW'RS.

So that he and his royal blood are subject to no external favors or disfavors; **GROWS** = in the life of his son, and in this diary of the sonnets; "When in eternal lines to time *thou grow'st*" – Sonnet 18, line 12; "So thy great gift, upon misprision *growing*" – Sonnet 87, line 11; "Love is a Babe, then might I not say so,/ To *give full growth* to that which *still doth grow*" – Sonnet 115, lines 13-14; **HEAT** = ("A *dateless lively heat*, still to endure" – Sonnet 153, line 6; "Which from love's fire took *heat perpetual*" – Sonnet 154, line 10; both referring to eternal royal blood); **DROWNS WITH SHOW'RS** = "Then can I *drown an eye*, un-used to flow" – Sonnet 30, line 5; "To dry the *rain* on my storm-beaten face" – Sonnet 34, line 6; (showers = rain, suggesting reign, as in "Make dust our paper and with *rainy eyes* write sorrow on the bosom of the earth" – the King in *Richard II*, 3.2.146-147

13 TO THIS I WITNESS CALL THE FOOLS OF TIME,

Oxford summons all others, who are subject to time, to witness this truth, i.e., that his "dear love" (his son's royal blood) is not subject to time; "*Love's not time's fool*, though rosy lips and cheeks/ Within his bending sickle's compass come" – Sonnet 116, lines 9-10; "*I witness to the times* that brought them in; so shall I do to the freshest things now reigning and make stale the glistering of this present" – *The Winter's Tale*, 4.1.11-14; "But thought's the slave of life, and life *time's fool*; and *time*, that takes survey of all the world, must have a stop" – *1 Henry IV*, 5.4.80-82; "I call the fools of time to bear witness to the truth of what I have said" – translation by Booth, who adds: "The metaphoric effect of *call* is to present *the fools of time* as witnesses called to testify in a court of law ... (but) one is asked to think of *the fools* as the evidence, as exhibits rather than witnesses." In effect, Oxford is re-convening the trial in which he himself voted to condemn his son; and he is reversing the judgment.

14 WHICH DIE FOR GOODNESS, WHO HAVE LIVED FOR CRIME.

Essex died for the "goodness" or royal blood of Southampton; Cecil lives by virtue of the *crime* of Rebellion; Oxford to Time, before the Rebellion: "And do whate'er thou wilt, *swift-footed time*/ To the wide world and all her fading sweets;/ But *I forbid thee one most heinous crime*;/ O carve not with thy hours my love's fair brow" – Sonnet 19, lines 6-9; and after the Rebellion, to Southampton: "To you it doth belong/ Yourself to *pardon of self-doing crime*" – Sonnet 58, lines 11-12; "To weigh how once I suffered in *your crime*" – Sonnet 120, line 8; ("By you being pardoned, we commit no *crime*" – *Pericles*, 4.4.5; "If by this *crime* he owes the law his life" – *Timon of Athens*, 3.5.86)

> James's royal party spends four days at Theobalds, Robert Cecil's mansion. The new monarch will arrive in London on May 7 as the guest of Lord Thomas Howard at the Charter House; and he will reside at the Tower on May 11. On May 16 he will grant Southampton a special royal pardon, restoring to him all titles, lands and property.
> (Stopes, 266; DSSP James I.84. Patent Rolls, I James, pt. 2, Ind. Wt. Bk., p. 3)

THE MONUMENT

Oxford to Robert Cecil
On the Eve of Elizabeth's Funeral

April 25/27, 1603

"I have always found myself ***beholding to you for many kindnesses*** and courtesies; wherefore I am bold at this present, which giveth occasion of many considerations, to desire you as my very good friend and kind brother in law to impart to me what course is devised by you of the Council, & the rest of the lords, concerning our duties to the king's Majesty whether you do expect any ***messenger*** before his coming to let us understand his ***pleasure***, or else his personal arrival to be presently or very shortly. And if it be so, what order is resolved on amongst you, either for the ***attending***, or meeting of his Majesty; for by reason of mine infirmity, I cannot come among you so often as I wish, and by reason my house is not so near, that at every occasion I can be present, as were fit, either I do not hear at all from you, ***or at least*** write the latest, as this other day it happened to me, receiving a letter at nine of the clock not to fail at eight of the same morning to be at Whitehall, which being impossible, yet I hasted so much as I came to follow you into Ludgate, though through press of people and horses I could not reach your company as I desire, but followed as I might.

> **BEHOLDING TO YOU FOR MANY KINDNESSES:** Although this statement refers to specific help from Oxford's brother-in-law Secretary Cecil, the chief kindness resulted in Southampton's release from the Tower – a fact stated between the lines
> **MESSENGER:** "By those swift ***messengers*** returned from thee" – Sonnet 45.10
> **PLEASURE:** "But since she pricked thee out for women's ***pleasure***" – Sonnet 20.13
> **ATTENDING:** "***Attending*** on his golden pilgrimage" – Sonnet 7.8
> **OR AT LEAST:** "***Or*** to thyself ***at least*** kind-hearted prove" – Sonnet 10.12

"I cannot but find a ***great grief*** in myself to remember the ***Mistress*** which we have lost, under whom both you and myself from our ***greenest*** years have been in a ***manner*** brought up; and although it hath pleased God after an ***earthly*** kingdom to take her up into a more permanent and ***heavenly*** state, wherein I do not doubt but she is ***crowned*** with glory, and to give us a ***Prince*** wise, ***learned, and enriched*** with all virtues, yet the long time which we spent in her service, we cannot look for so much left of our days as to ***bestow*** upon another, neither the long ***acquaintance*** and kind familiarities wherewith she did use us, we are not ever to expect from another prince as denied by the ***infirmity of age*** and common course of reason.

> **GREAT GRIEF:** "My worthy comfort, now my ***greatest grief***" – Sonnet 48.6
> **MISTRESS:** "My ***Mistress***' eyes are nothing like the Sunne" – Sonnet 130.1
> **GREENEST:** "And they shall live, and he in them still ***green***" – Sonnet 63.14
> **MANNER:** "Than public means which public ***manners*** breeds" – Sonnet 111.4
> **EARTHLY/HEAVENLY:** "Such ***heav'nly*** touches ne'er touched ***earthly*** faces" – Sonnet 17.8
> **CROWNED:** "Or whether doth my mind, being ***crowned*** with you" – Sonnet 114.1
> **PRINCE:** "Great ***Princes***' favorites their fair leaves spread" – Sonnet 25.5
> **LEARNED AND ENRICHED:** "And of this book this ***learning*** may'st thou taste… Shall profit thee and much ***enrich*** thy book" – Sonnet 77, 4,14
>
> **BESTOW:** "In thy soul's thought (all naked) will ***bestow*** it" – Sonnet 26.8
> **ACQUAINTANCE:** "To take a new ***acquaintance*** of thy mind" – Sonnet 77.12
> **INFIRMITY OF AGE:** "***Beated and chopped*** with tanned antiquity" – Sonnet 62.10

"In this common ***shipwreck***, mine is ***above all the rest***, who least regarded, though often comforted, of all her followers, she hath left to try my fortune among the ***alterations of time***, and ***chance***, either without ***sail***

648

whereby to take the advantage of any prosperous gale, or with anchor to ride till the *storm* be over past.

      SHIPWRECK/STORM: "That looks on *tempests* and is never shaken" – Sonnet 116.6;
      ABOVE ALL THE REST: "Wherein it finds a joy *above the rest*" – Sonnet 91.6
      ALTERATIONS: "Which *alters* when it *alteration* finds" – Sonnet 116.3
      ALTERATIONS OF TIME: "Love's not *time's* fool" – Sonnet 116.9
      CHANCE: "By *chance* or nature's changing course untrimmed" – Sonnet 18.8
      SAIL: "That I have hoisted *sail* to all the winds" – Sonnet 117.7

"There is nothing therefore left to *my comfort*, but the excellent virtues, and deep wisdom wherewith God hath endued our new *Master* and *sovereign lord*, who doth not come amongst us as a stranger but as a natural prince, *succeeding* by *right* of blood and *inheritance*, not as a conqueror, but as the true shepherd of Christ's flock to cherish and comfort them.

      MY COMFORT: "Take all *my comfort* of thy worth and truth" – Sonnet 37.4
      MASTER: "the *Master* Mistress of my passion" – Sonnet 20.2

      SOVEREIGN LORD:
"Whilst I (my *sovereign*) watch the clock for you" – Sonnet 57.6
"*Lord* of my love, to whom in vassalage" – Sonnet 26.1
      SUCCEEDING: "For beauty's pattern to *succeeding* men" – Sonnet 19.12
      RIGHT: "That for thy *right* myself will bear all wrong" – Sonnet 88.14
      INHERITANCE: "They rightly do *inherit* heaven's graces" – Sonnet 94.5

"Wherefore I most earnestly desire you of this favor, as I have written before, that I may be informed from you concerning those points and thus recommending myself unto you I take my leave. Your *assured* friend and unfortunate Brother in Law, E. Oxenford.

      ASSURED: "For term of life thou art *assured* mine" – Sonnet 92.2

THE FINAL DAYS

FUNERAL OF QUEEN ELIZABETH I
"The Canopy"

Sonnet 125
And Take Thou My Oblation
28 April 1603

Held today is the grand funeral procession for Elizabeth I of England. As her body is carried through the streets of London to its temporary tomb in Westminster Abbey, the Tudor Rose dynasty that began under Henry VII in 1485 is officially coming to its end. Four or six unnamed noblemen bear the royal canopy over her effigy atop the casket; but Edward de Vere, Earl of Oxford, Lord Great Chamberlain of England, is probably not one of them. (He would have avoided it, given his negative attitude toward the Queen, for having kept their son in the Tower and preventing him from succeeding her. It's also possible he was too infirm physically to walk such a distance.) Oxford marks the occasion of the funeral only to scoff at such external ceremony and, more importantly, to make his "oblation" to Southampton – his sacrificial offering to his royal son, who is a king or god on earth. He will be "obsequious" (dutiful at the funeral rites) only by way of making this final sacrifice to Henry Wriothesley, Third Earl of Southampton. In the same way that the Tudor Rose dynasty is coming to an end, so is this chronological diary; all that remains is the farewell envoy of Sonnet 126.

Sonnet 125	Translation
Wer't ought to me I bore the canopy,	Would it matter to me if I bore the Canopy today,
With my extern the outward honoring,	With my outward self honoring Elizabeth in public,
Or laid great bases for eternity	Or joined great ceremonies for eternal fame
Which proves more short than waste or ruining?	That will be no match for time's waste of them?
Have I not seen dwellers on form and favor	Have I not seen poor courtiers seeking favor
Lose all and more by paying too much rent	Lose everything by selling their souls
For compound sweet; Forgoing simple savor,	For royal gifts; giving up unalloyed pleasure,
Pitiful thrivers in their gazing spent?	Pathetic aspirers wasting time with adoring looks?
No, let me be obsequious in thy heart,	No, let me honor her funeral with *your* heart,
And take thou my oblation poor but free,	And take now my sacrificial offering, freely given,
Which is not mixed with seconds, knows no art,	Which is not corrupted and has no contrivance,
But mutual render only me for thee.	But only mutual sacrifice of me for you, my son.
Hence, thou suborn'd *Informer*, a true soul	From now on, testify falsely! A true prince
When most impeached stands least in thy control.	Accused of treason has least in control as king!

J. Thomas Looney in *Shakespeare Identified* of 1920 suggested this verse is Oxford's "expression of his private feelings" about the Queen's funeral procession. Looney declared that Sonnet 125 *"may be taken as his last sonnet"* in chronological terms, aside from the envoy of No. 126, a verse of six rhyming couplets

Part Two

1 WERE'T OUGHT TO ME I BORE THE CANOPY,
Oxford may or may not have been one of the noblemen in the procession who "bore the canopy" over the Queen's coffin; the wording of the opening line can be taken two ways: *(1) Does it mean nothing to me that I bore the canopy? (2) What would it matter to me if I had borne the canopy?* Whatever the case, he is expressing profound sorrow and even bitterness; the end has finally come and all hope for his son's succession has been lost. The story is over; **OUGHT** = nothing; echoing Southampton as "none" or the opposite of "one"; (*"Is it nothing to me ... Would it matter to me...etc."*) Oxford is also summing up his more than forty years of service to the Queen, starting when he became a royal ward in 1562; and so his opening line might read: "What does it matter to me if I participated in so many royal ceremonies to support the state?"; **I BORE THE CANOPY** = Oxford may have helped to bear the canopy over the Queen's effigy during her funeral procession, but there is no record of it; ("a rich embroidered *canopy to kings*" – 3 Henry VI, 2.5.44-45); several unnamed noblemen bore the canopy, but given Oxford's negative attitude toward the Queen for her treatment of Southampton, he may have declined; **CANOPY** = "a cloth covering, carried tent-like over the head of a dignitary in a ceremonial procession" – Booth, emphasizing the *processional* aspect); by his pointed use of "canopy" in this sonnet, Oxford was marking the occasion of the funeral in correspondence with the chronology of his diary, which has proceeded with one sonnet each day from April 10, the day of Southampton's liberation from the Tower, to this day, April 28.

"A covering or hangings suspended over a throne, couch, bed, etc., or held over a person walking *in procession*" – OED; "They *beare the four staves of the Canapie over the Kings head* at the time of his coronation" – OED, citing 1576, but which king and when is unclear; "A covering over a shrine, or over the Host when borne in procession" – OED

> "Enter trumpets, sounding; then two aldermen, Lord Mayor, Garter, Cranmer, Duke of Norfolk with his marshal's staff, Duke of Suffolk, two noblemen bearing great standing bowls for the christening gifts: *then four noblemen bearing a canopy...*"
> - Henry VIII, 5.2. Stage Directions, Christening of Princess Elizabeth

> When lofty trees I see barren of leaves
> Which erst from heat did *canopy* the herd
> - Sonnet 12, lines 5-6

> Under the *canopies of costly state*
> - 2 Henry IV, 3.1.13

2 WITH MY EXTERN THE OUTWARD HONORING,
Honoring with my outward display; "Heaven is my judge, not I for love and duty but seeming so, for my peculiar end; for when my *outward* action doth demonstrate the native act and figure of my heart *in complement extern*" – Othello, 1.1.58-62; "Princes have but their titles for their glories, an *outward honor* for an inward toil" – Richard III, 1.4.78-79

3 OR LAID GREAT BASES FOR ETERNITY,
In the context of the lines, Oxford is speaking of his participation in royal ceremonies (such as the Queen's funeral and the upcoming coronation of James) that will be forgotten in due time; but he is also glancing at the "great bases" or foundations of this Monument of the Sonnets to preserve Southampton for eternity; also the lines or "bases" of the individual sonnets or *pyramids* of Time; (Sonnet 123, line 2: "Thy pyramids")

4 WHICH PROVES MORE SHORT THAN WASTE OR RUINING?
Those bases turn out to be less strong than the "waste" of your immortal royal blood; and the Sonnets, although meant to be eternal, are still "the Chronicle of *wasted time*" – Sonnet 106, line 1; "The love of the

REFERENCE EDITION

earlier sonnets … was to last forever, and yet it has been ruined" – Dowden; and in the context of "love" as royal blood and its immediate claim to the throne, such is the case; also an expression of what Oxford truly thought of such ceremonial rites:

"Which I will freely impart to you at my coming to the Court, which I think shall be tomorrow, by the grace of God; till which time, as a *hater of ceremonies*, I will refer all other thanks and observations…" - Oxford to Robert Cecil, May 11, 1601

> Vain pomp and glory of this world, *I hate ye!*
> - *Henry VIII*, 3.2.365

> But safer triumph is this *funeral pomp*
> - *Titus Andronicus*, 1.1.179

> And what have kings, that privates have not too,
> Save *ceremony*, save general *ceremony*?
> And what art thou, idol *ceremony*?
> - *Henry V*, 4.1.234-236

> O *ceremony*, show me but thy worth!
> What is thy soul of adoration?
> Art thou aught else but place, degree and form,
> Creating awe and fear in other men…?
> - *Henry V*, 4.1.240-243

> Why, what is pomp, rule, reign, but earth and dust?
> And, live we how we can, yet die we must.
> - *3 Henry VI*, 5.2.27-28

5 HAVE I NOT SEEN DWELLERS ON FORM AND FAVOR
Haven't I seen flatterers and sycophants at Court, seeking the royal favor

> And shall I live on th'earth to be her thrall?
> And shall I sue and serve her all in vain:
> And kiss the steps, that she lets fall,
> And shall I pray the gods to keep the pain
> From her, that is so cruel still?
> - Oxford poem, about his service to Elizabeth, *The Paradise of Dainty Devices*, 1576

> No, let the candied tongue lick absurd pomp,
> And crook the pregnant hinges of the knee
> Where thrift may follow fawning
> - *Hamlet*, 3.2.61-63

6 LOSE ALL AND MORE BY PAYING TOO MUCH RENT
ALL = Southampton, *One for All, All for One*; **LOSE ALL** = lose you; i.e., Oxford himself continually sought the Queen's favor, especially in regard to their royal son, only to lose it; **PAYING TOO MUCH RENT** = paying too high a price for the "lease" of his son's royal blood; as in "the *lease of my true love*" in Sonnet 107, line 3. The "*leases of short-numbered hours*" of Sonnet 124, line 10, refers to Southampton's short-lived date with succession, reflected in these sonnets or "numbers" written according to that same time on the calendar; "And what art thou, thou idol ceremony! … What are *thy rents*, what are thy comings-in? O ceremony, show me but thy worth! What is thy soul, O adoration?" – *Henry V*, 4.1.236, 239-241

7 FOR COMPOUND SWEET FORGOING SIMPLE SAVOR,

COMPOUND = a legal term; the verb "to compound" is to "settle privately; forbear prosecution (of a felony) from private motives" – *O.E.D.*; to come to terms, as Oxford has done with Robert Cecil and King James, by burying his identity as Shakespeare and as the father of Southampton, who has agreed to give up any claim to the throne; Oxford has thereby "compounded" the matter by settling it with this "ransom" for his son's freedom and pardon; "Once more I come to know of thee, King Harry, if for thy *ransom* thou wilt now *compound*" – *Henry V*, 4.3.79-80

To gain this mercy, Southampton himself must promise his loyalty: "More commonly the traitor who would be a successful supplicant for pardon had to strike a bargain with the king rather than beg his mercy. Sometimes this could be achieved by promising, or doing, the king some service or duty ... Quite the most frequent way of obtaining a 'special' pardon was for the traitor, convicted or suspected, to *compound, that is to say pay a fine*. Since the fine varied from case to case this amounted to making an individual financial bargain with the king ... [In May 1601 the fines assessed against Rutland and the lords Sandys, Monteagle and Cromwell were levied by the Privy Council, under Cecil's control; in Southampton's case the payment to James involved a pledge to refrain from making a royal claim for himself] ... *Compounding by fine*, as we might expect, was never a right ... After the discovery of a traitorous conspiracy it was usually refused. It all depended on how the king decided to exercise his prerogative of mercy." – Bellamy, 220-222

Oxford knows in advance that one of the favors James will grant Southampton is the "farm of the sweet wines" from which Essex had gained wealth under Elizabeth. Oxford is warning his son in this sonnet not to "lose all and more by paying too much rent" for this royal favor, i.e., not to sell out his principles for it; "It is tempting ... to find in *compound sweet* a reference to the Earl of Essex, who was rewarded, c. 1590, with 'the farm of sweet wines' – the right to charge tax on all imported sweet wine – but lost it in September 1600 after his unlicensed return from Ireland" – Duncan-Jones

FORGOING = losing, parting with, giving up; "and let us not *forgo* that for a trifle that was bought with blood!" – *1 Henry VI*, 4.1.149-150

8 PITIFUL THRIVERS IN THEIR GAZING SPENT?

PITIFUL THRIVERS, etc. = pathetic servants of the Queen who had "spent" themselves hoping for favor

> And hasty climbers soonest fall - line of verse published 1588
> Possibly Oxford's, Steven May (Chiljan 173)

> O how wretched
> Is that poor man that hangs on princes' favors! - *Henry VIII*, 3.2.366-367

9 NO, LET ME BE OBSEQUIOUS IN THY HEART,

OBSEQUIOUS = dutiful; ("Through its relation to '*obsequy,*' 'funeral,' *obsequious* had the specialized meaning 'dutiful in performing *funeral rites* and invites a reader to think of *the canopy as borne in a funeral procession*" – Booth, who notes that *obsequious* "recurs to the procession suggested in line 1 and to the idea of being a follower in a literal sense" i.e., the funeral procession for Queen Elizabeth; "Obedient, dutiful, especially with reference to the dead and their funeral 'obsequies'" – Duncan-Jones; "Dutiful in performing funeral obsequies or manifesting regard for the dead" – OED

> But, uncle, draw you near,
> To *shed obsequious tears* upon this trunk.
> O, take this warm kiss on thy pale cold lips,

> These sorrowful drops upon thy blood-stain'd face,
> The last true duties of thy noble son!
> - *Titus Andronicus*, 5.3.150-154
>
> How many a *holy and obsequious tear*
> Hath dear religious love stol'n from mine eye,
> As *interest of the dead*...
> Thou art *the grave where buried love* doth live
> - Sonnet 31, lines 5-7
>
> 'Tis sweet and commendable in your nature, Hamlet,
> To give these *mourning duties* to your father:
> But, you must know, your father lost a father;
> That father lost, lost his, and the survivor bound
> In filial obligation for some term
> To do *obsequious sorrow*
> - *Hamlet*, 1.2.87-92
>
> My heart, sweet boy, shall be thy sepulchre,
> For from my heart thine image ne'er shall go.
> My sighing breast shall be *thy funeral bell*;
> And so *obsequious* will thy father be,
> Even for the loss of thee...
> - *3 Henry VI*, 2.5.115-119

Oxford uses *obsequious* in two ways. On the one hand, he is continuing in reference to what he has just been condemning in the previous lines – related to the "pitiful thrivers" who are "obsequious" in being all too devoted, compliant, servile, ready to please; on the other hand, he now turns to address Southampton and becomes "obsequious" as a mourner – not for the dead Queen Elizabeth, but for the death of his son's claim to the throne.

> From this session interdict
> Every fowl of tyrant wing,
> Save the eagle, feather'd king:
> Keep the *obsequy* so strict
> - *The Phoenix and Turtle*, 1601
> (Funeral dirge mourning the death of Southampton's royal claim and the death of the Tudor dynasty)
>
> *Enter the corse (corpse) of Henry the Sixth...*
> *Lady Anne being the mourner...*
> Set down, set down your honorable load
> (If honor may be shrouded in a hearse)
> Whilst I awhile *obsequiously* lament
> Th'untimely fall of virtuous Lancaster
> - *Richard III*, 1.2.1-4

Her *obsequies* have been as far enlarg'd
As we have warranty. Her death was doubtful - *Hamlet*, 5.1.224-225 (Burial of Ophelia)

10 AND TAKE THOU MY OBLATION, POOR BUT FREE,
   MY OBLATION = ("offering – specifically to the deity" – Booth); i.e., Oxford's sacrificial offering to

Southampton as a king or god on earth; an offering in a religious context; that is, the offering of sacramental bread and wine to God. "Before the consecration of the host in Holy Communion," Booth writes, "the minister prays to God the Father, who gave his only son to suffer on the cross, 'who made there (*by his one oblation of himself once offered*) a full, perfect and sufficient *Sacrifice, Oblation, and Satisfaction* for the sins of the whole world." (Book of Common Prayer, p. 194.); a canopy was carried over the Host in religious processions; the communion service commemorates not only Christ's sacrifice on the Cross, but is itself a sacrifice for the remission of sins; **POOR BUT FREE** = purely and freely given to you; **FREE** = with no strings attached; "Nature's bequest gives nothing but doth lend,/ And being frank she lends to those are *free*" – Sonnet 4, line 4; and after the Rebellion, related to the need for Southampton to be liberated from the Tower of London or to be "free"; "My heart mine eye the *freedom* of that right" – Sonnet 46, line 4; and to Queen Elizabeth about their son, whom she is keeping in her prison: "Myself I'll forfeit, so that other mine/ Thou wilt restore to be my comfort still./ But *thou wilt not, nor he will not be free,/* For thou art covetous, and he is kind" – Sonnet 134, lines 3-6

So the point of this final sonnet of Oxford's dynastic diary, prior to the farewell envoy to follow, is to make this sacrificial, holy offering to his royal son, a king or god on earth for whom the Monument of the Sonnets, akin to the Pyramids of ancient Egypt for dynastic rulers, has been nearly completed. As opposed to all other kinds of royal pomp and ceremony, and in contrast to the physical monuments erected for monarchs, this sacred monument of verse, containing "the living record of your memory" (Sonnet 55, line 8) is genuine and eternal.

11 WHICH IS NOT MIXED WITH SECONDS, KNOWS NO ART,

NOT MIXED WITH SECONDS = not mixed with inferior stuff or contaminated by baser matter; ("I am too high-born to be propertied, to be a *secondary* at control" – *King John*, 5.2.80-81); **ART** = artful contrivance; ("And *art* made tongue-tied by authority" – Sonnet 66, line 9); "seconds" is a term for "the second kind of flour" collected after the smaller bran is sifted; by contrast, Oxford's "oblation" is pure

12 BUT MUTUAL RENDER ONLY ME FOR THEE.

MUTUAL RENDER = mutual exchange or sacrifice; **ONLY** = "To the *onlie* begetter of these ensuing sonnets, Mr. W. H." – the 1609 Dedication of the Sonnets; **ME FOR THEE** = father for son; preparing for: "Her *Audit*, though delayed, answered must be,/ And her *Quietus* is to **render** thee" – Sonnet 126, lines 11-12, referring to universal Nature, in the final words of the Fair Youth series to Southampton and, in chronological terms, the end of the diary itself

13 HENCE, THOU SUBORN'D *INFORMER*! A TRUE SOUL

HENCE = traditionally the word "hence" in Sonnet 125 has been viewed as a command to a third party, the "suborned informer," to go away; Oxford, however, is speaking here not to a third party but, as always in the Fair Youth series, to Southampton – who must now go through the rest of his life bearing false witness against the truth of his royal blood and claim to the throne. Schmidt gives various definitions for "hence": "from this place, from here to another place ... away ... not here, at a distance ... *out of this, from this source or cause ... henceforth, in future*" – and the latter meanings appear to be appropriate in this context: "From this point onward, you are a suborned informer! You must testify falsely against yourself!" In fact, at the very end of the Dark Lady series, Oxford tells Elizabeth that she, too, must commit perjury: "For I have *sworn* thee fair: more *perjured* eye,/ To *swear against the truth so foul a lie*!" – Sonnet 152, lines 13-14; "From *hence* your memory death cannot take" – Sonnet 81, line 3; **SUBORN'D *INFORMER*** = Southampton, who is forced to pay for his liberty by bearing false witness against his own royal claim; Booth says the *Informer* seems to be a third party who has come out of nowhere; but he *also* acknowledges that the final couplet can be seen as "*addressed to the beloved* -- which makes it even more disconcerting for a reader." Viewed as Southampton having to bear false testimony against his own his royal claim, however, any such "disconcerting" problems disappear. (The inclusion of *born* in *suborned* may glance at Southampton's birth.); **SUBORN'D** = "bought, paid to bear false witness" Booth; i.e., Oxford paid "ransom" to procure Southampton's liberty; "procured by secret collusion … applied especially to false witnesses" – Schmidt; "But now I find I had *suborned the witness* and he's indicted falsely" – *Othello*, 3.4.153-154; "O me! What eyes hath love put in my head,/ Which have no correspondence with *true* sight!/ Or if they have, where is my *judgment* fled,/ That censures *falsely* what they see aright?" – Sonnet 148, lines 1-4; "You have *suborn'd* this man, of purpose to obscure my noble birth" – *1 Henry VI*, 5.4.21-22; "When ever yet was your appeal denied? Wherein have you been galled by the King? What peer hath been *suborn'd* to grate on you" – *2 Henry IV*, 4.1.88-90; "By heaven, fond wretch, thou know'st not what thou speak'st, or else thou art *suborn'd* against his honour" – *Measure for Measure*, 5.1.109; **INFORMER** = (capitalized and italicized in the 1609 Quarto); one who communicates, reports, gives intelligence; related to spies who inform the king or others; "to communicate by way of accusation" – Schmidt; "Now afore God 'tis shame such wrongs are borne in him, a royal prince, and many mo of noble blood in this declining land; the King is not himself, but basely led by flatterers; and what they will *inform*, merely in hate, 'gainst any of us all, that will the King severely prosecute 'gainst us, our lives, our children, and our heirs" – *Richard II*, 2.1.238-245; "How all occasions do *inform against me*, and spur my dull revenge" – *Hamlet*, 4.4.32-33

Oxford may be glancing at "informers" for Robert Cecil who had helped to precipitate the Rebellion prematurely. Camden in his *Annales* for 1601 will report that Sir Henry Neville had joined the Essex-Southampton faction prior to the Rebellion and that, during the final planning stages, the conspirators questioned him so that he was "shunning the name of Informer." (Oxford could even be directing these final two lines to Cecil himself -- saying the Secretary cannot control Southampton, a "true soul" of immortal truth.)

TRUE SOUL = Southampton, son of Oxford (truth), with "true rights" to the throne: "And your *true rights* be termed a Poet's rage" – Sonnet 17, line 11; both Oxford and Southampton may be viewed as the *true soul* whose truthful testimony has been most impeached; *True* was spelled as *trew* in the 1609 Quarto -- perhaps a deliberate blending of *true* (Oxford) and *hew* (Southampton); **SOUL** = spirit or heart or royal blood

14 WHEN MOST IMPEACHED STANDS LEAST IN THY CONTROL.
IMPEACHED = "challenged, disparaged; *accused of treason*" – Duncan-Jones; bearing false witness against himself, i.e., unable to claim his royal blood and to claim to be king; ("I am disgraced, *impeached*, and baffled here, pierced to the soul with *slander's venom'd spear*" – *Richard II*, 1.1.170-171, echoing "And Beauty *slandered* with a bastard shame" – Sonnet 127, line 4, with "Beauty" referring to both Elizabeth and her royal blood possessed by Southampton; also echoing "For *slander's mark* was ever yet the fair" – Sonnet 70, line 2

> Grandam, we can, for my good uncle Gloucester
> Told me the King, provoked to't by the Queen,
> Devised *impeachments* to imprison him
> - *Richard III*, 2.2.20-22

"That all customs and other duties are not *impeached* by these bargains, but every man pays his duty to Her Majesty as though this had never been spoken of." - Oxford memo, June 4, 1595, PRO SP 12/252 ff. 96-97 (Chiljan, 105)

STANDS = "But all alone *stands* hugely politic" – Sonnet 124, line 11; **LEAST IN THY CONTROL** = least in your power, i.e., Southampton's royal power as in the next verse: "O Thou my lovely Boy, who *in thy power*" – Sonnet 126, line 1

> A man in hew all *Hews* in his *controlling* - Sonnet 20, line 7
> I should in thought *control* your times of pleasure - Sonnet 58, line 2

No. 125

> And folly, doctor-like, *controlling* skill - Sonnet 66, line 10
> Can yet the lease of my true love *control* - Sonnet 107, line 3

"*Control* was originally an accounting term – as in the modern *comptroller* – and meant 'to test the accuracy of,' 'to call to account'" – Booth; therefore the line may also read: "When most accused stands least in your final accounting," i.e., related to the *Audit* or final accounting of his royal blood in the conclusion of this diary: "Her (nature's) *Audit*, though delayed, answered must be" – Sonnet 126, line 11, echoing the opening series to Southampton: "Then how when nature calls thee to be gone,/ What acceptable *Audit* canst thou leave?" – Sonnet 4, lines 11-12; to *control* also means to "refute" – that is, it is not in Southampton's power or authority to refute the false denial of his royal stature that history will record; on the other hand, if Cecil is the "suborned Informer," then Oxford is telling him that he has no power over the "true soul" that is Southampton, a true prince whose "true rights" are beyond any earthly control

Queen Elizabeth's death occurred five weeks previously. Oxford has traveled far past her in his mind and heart. This is no longer his England; he will not even glance backward to pay homage to the tyrannical monarch who forced him to let falsity triumph over truth – at least, in the short term. It is no wonder that "Shakespeare," virtually alone among contemporary poets, offered no public eulogy for the Virgin Queen.

The Queen's Funeral - April 28, 1603

"Queen Elizabeth was most royally interred in Westminster Abbey, on the 28th of April, 1603, 'at which time,' says old Stowe, 'the city of Westminster was surcharged with multitudes of all sorts of people, in the streets, houses, windows, leads, and gutters, who came to see the ***obsequy***; and when they beheld her statue, or effigy, lying on the coffin, set forth in royal robes, having a crown upon the head thereof, and a ball and scepter in either hand, there was such a general sighing, ***groaning***, and weeping, as the like hath not been seen or known in the memory of man, neither doth any history mention any people, time, or state, to make the like lamentation for the death of their sovereign." (Agnes Strickland, *Elizabeth*, p. 705)

> **OBSEQUY:** "No, let me be obsequious in thy heart" – Sonnet 125, line 9, Oxford to Southampton in the context of the Queen's funeral procession
> **GROANING:** Oxford uses "groans" in a similar context, i.e., "A thousand groans but thinking on thy face, one on another's neck do witness bear" – Sonnet 131, lines 10-11, addressing Elizabeth in the Dark Lady series, in February-March 1601, anticipating the execution of Southampton and their mutual groaning over his death at his funeral.

"No monarch was officially dead until the day of burial when the great officers of state broke their white wands of office and hurled them into the grave. So for over a month the old Queen's court [had gone on] as though she were not dead but walking, as she was wont to in the early springtime, in the alleys of her gardens … At last, on 28 April 1603, a funeral procession of some fifteen hundred persons made its way to Westminster Abbey. Nothing quite like it had ever been seen before. 'Her hearse (as it was borne) seemed to be like an island swimming in water, for round it there rained showers of tears,' wrote Thomas Dekker in his *Wonderful Year*. The streets were thronged with onlookers, the windows packed, even the rooftops were crowded with those who hoped for a glimpse of this spectacle which seemed in one hierarchical sweep to epitomize a civilization. When the royal chariot went by bearing the effigy of Elizabeth in crimson and ermine robes, crowned and clasping orb and scepter, a sighing, groaning and weeping went up…" (Strong, *The Cult of Elizabeth*, 1977, pp. 14-15)

"On 28 April 1603, more than a month after her death, Elizabeth's body was taken in procession to Wesminster Abbey. It was an impressive occasion: the hearse was drawn by four horses hung with black velvet, and surmounted by a life-size wax effigy of the late Queen, dressed in her state robes and crown, an orb and scepter in its hands; over it was *a canopy of estate supported by six earls* ... It was followed by her rider-less palfrey led by Elizabeth's Master of Horse, and the Marchioness of Northampton, who as the senior noblewoman acted as chief mourner and led the peeresses of the realm in their nun-like mourning hoods and cloaks, and a thousand other black-clad people: lords, councilors, gentlemen, courtiers, heralds, and servants, as well as 276 poor persons ... The solemnity was overlaid with gorgeous pageantry as colorful banners and standards fluttered in the breeze and trumpets sounded. Thousands lined the funeral route...

"With (Archbishop) Whitgift officiating, Elizabeth I was buried in the north aisle of the Henry VII Chapel in the Abbey; after her coffin had been placed above that of her sister Mary in the vault, the chief officers of her household, as was customary, broke their white staves of office and cast them down on the coffin, to symbolize the termination of their allegiance. The vault was then sealed." (Alison Weir, *The Life of Elizabeth*, 1998, p. 486)

> **CANOPY OF ESTATE SUPPORTED BY SIX EARLS:** "Were't ought to me I bore the canopy,/ With my extern the outward honoring" – Sonnet 125.1-2

"Immediately behind the royal standard bearing the Queen's motto, 'Semper Eadem' (*Ever the Same*), with the Tudor Rose below it, comes the royal charger plumed on head and back..." (Percy Allen's description of a picture of the funeral procession of Elizabeth, published by Camden, quoted by Ogburn & Ogburn, p. 1200)

Notes on Sonnet 125

John Thomas Looney, 1920: "Although his (Oxford's) officiating at Elizabeth's funeral (on April 28, 1603) is not mentioned so explicitly as the part he took at the coronation of James (on July 25, 1603), it is natural to assume that he would be there. It is just possible that this ceremony is directly referred to in Sonnet 125. If there can be shown to have any direct connection with the functions of Lord Great Chamberlain, it will be a very valuable direct proof of our thesis [that Oxford was Shakespeare]. The particular sonnet ... comes at the extreme end of the series to which it belongs; and, as we are assured (by Sidney Lee as well as other biographers of Shakespeare) that the whole series [1-126] was brought to a close shortly after the death of Queen Elizabeth, sonnet 125 must have been written about the time of that event...

"[The] reference to 'dwellers on form and favor losing all by paying too much rent" is strongly suggestive of an allusion to royalty, and is exactly descriptive of what Oxford represents [in his letters] Elizabeth's treatment of himself to have been: that she had encouraged his lavish expenditure with promises of favor that had not been fulfilled. His application, in her later years, for the presidency of Wales had met with fair words and disappointment. Altogether the suggestion of an allusion in the sonnet to the hereditary office of the Lord Great Chamberlain seems very strong ... Shakespeare's sonnet 125 seems to be pointing to De Vere's officiating at Queen Elizabeth's funeral. This may be taken as his last sonnet; for 126 is really not a sonnet but a stanza composed of six couplets, in which he appears to be addressing a parting message to his young friend. Sonnet 127 begins the second series....

"If, then, we take sonnet 125 as being the Earl of Oxford's expression of his private feelings relative to Queen Elizabeth's funeral, we can quite understand his not troubling to honor her with any special verses (i.e., as "Shakespeare") ... the reasons which lead us to suppose that the particular sonnet has reference to Elizabeth's funeral only apply if we assume it to be written by the Earl of Oxford. It is worth noticing, too, that these last sonnets seem to be touched with the thought of approaching death; and when we find that De Vere died on June 24, 1604, the year following the death of Queen Elizabeth, to which they seem to make reference, the two suppositions we have stated in regard to them [his officiating at the funeral and his feelings toward her, as also expressed in Sonnet 125] seem to be mutually confirmed.

"The special sonnet [125] to which attention has been drawn, if it does actually refer to the part taken by the Lord Great Chamberlain at Elizabeth's funeral, shows clearly that the participation was merely formal ... the attitude represented in the sonnet is precisely the same as that represented by the absence of any line from Oxford's pen (i.e., for public readers) on the subject of Elizabeth's death, and a similar absence of any Shakespearean utterance on the same theme. In a word, everything becomes 'of a piece' as soon as the name and person of the Earl of Oxford is introduced." - *"Shakespeare" Identified in Edward deVere, the Seventeenth Earl of Oxford*, (189-190; 335-6)

THE MONUMENT

FINAL ENTRY OF THE DYNASTIC DIARY

ENVOY TO SOUTHAMPTON

Sonnet 126
O Thou My Lovely Boy
29 April 1603

Using a different rhyme scheme in just twelve lines, followed by empty parentheses in place of the final couplet, Oxford bids farewell to his royal son. He promises him that Nature (still the "sovereign mistress") will defeat Time and deliver the final "Audit" or accounting of his royal blood, which is preserved by these sonnets for readers in the distant future.

The different rhyme scheme and structure underscores the finality of the series - in particular, its twelve lines of six couplets (12-6, or 126) indicating again its deliberate placement here. The use of the parentheses, in place of a final couplet, is also deliberate (i.e., it's not the printer's idea). The poet is intentionally leaving this one unfinished, because he has to. Only NATURE *can ultimately determine what will happen to Henry Wriothesley, because Oxford will die before he does. The Sonnets will be published after Oxford's death and before Henry Wriothesley's death.*

Sonnet 126

O Thou my lovely Boy who in thy power
Dost hold time's fickle glass, his sickle hour:
Who hast by waning grown, and therein show'st
Thy lovers withering, as thy sweet self grow'st.

If Nature (sovereign mistress over wrack)
As thou goest onwards still will pluck thee back,
She keeps thee to this purpose, that her skill
May time disgrace, and wretched minute kill.

Yet fear her O thou minion of her pleasure,
She may detain, but not still keep her treasure.
Her *Audit* (though delayed) answer'd must be,
And her *Quietus* is to render thee.

(   )
(   )

Translation

O my royal Son, who in your kingly power
Holds the hourglass and knife of Time:
Who has faded but grown, and so shows
Your parents dying, as your royal self grows:

If Nature, which is now Queen of wrack,
As you go on living still leads you to death,
She keeps this promise to you, that her skill
May conquer Time itself by disgracing it.

But fear her, O you servant of her will,
She may delay your right but not stop it!!
Her final accounting, delayed, must be made,
And Nature's end is to render you as king!

(   )
(   )

The long dynasty of the Tudor Rose (1485-1603) is now officially over…
This is the chronological end of the Book of Sonnets…
Edward de Vere will continue to live until June 24, 1604…
Henry Wriothesley will be arrested on June 24, 1604, and imprisoned overnight…
Henry Wriothesley will live until November 24, 1624.

Part Two

1 O THOU MY LOVELY BOY WHO IN THY POWER
O = Oxford; **MY LOVELY BOY** = my royal son; (same as "the boy" of Sonnet 153, line 10 and "the little Love-God" of Sonnet 154, line 1); **LOVELY** = filled with "love" or royal blood; ("The little Love-God" – Sonnet 154, line 1; "Lord of my love" – Sonnet 26, line 1; "And you and love are still my argument" – Sonnet 76, line 10); "Richard, *that sweet lovely Rose*" – *1 Henry IV*, 1.3.173

A *lovely boy*, stolen from an Indian king;
She never had so sweet a changeling;
And jealous Oberon would have the child
- *A Midsummer Night's Dream*, 2.1.22-24

    King Henry VIII:
    Now by thy looks
    I guess thy message. Is the queen delivered?
    Say ay, and of a boy.

    Old Lady:
    Ay, ay, my liege,
    And of a *lovely boy*: the God of heaven
    Both now and ever bless her; 'tis a girl
    Promises boys hereafter.
    - To the King in *Henry VIII*, 5.1.162-166
    (Speaking of the birth of Elizabeth)

    See, ruthless Queen, *a hapless father's tears*.
    This cloth thou dipp'd in blood of *my sweet boy*,
    And I with tears do wash the blood away.
    - *3 Henry VI*, 1.4.156-158

WHO IN THY POWER = who in your royal power; ("Fear not, my lord; *that Power that made you king* hath *power to keep you king* in spite of all" – *Richard II*, 3.2.27-28; "If thou wouldst use the *strength* of all thy state!" – Sonnet 96, line 12

    Then shalt thou give me with thy kingly hand
    What husband *in thy power* I will command
    - *All's Well That Ends Well*, 2.1.192-193

    He may command me as my sovereign,
    But you have *power* in me as in a kinsman
    - *Richard III*, 3.1.108-109

    The mighty *power* of the king
    - *Richard III*, 5.3.34

    The name
    Was given me by one that had some *power*,
    My father, and a king
    - *Pericles*, 5.1.147-149

    I do invest you jointly with my power
    - The King in *King Lear*, 1.1.131

REFERENCE EDITION

When I perceive your Grace, like power divine   *Measure for Measure*, 5.1.366

2 DOST HOLD TIME'S FICKLE GLASS, HIS SICKLE HOUR,
Holds *Time's* fickle (inconstant) hourglass and ability to kill you (eclipse your royal claim): "And nothing 'gainst *Time's scythe* can make defence" – Sonnet 12, line 13; recalling Time's *"bending sickle"* of Sonnet 116, line 10: "Though rosy lips and cheeks/ Within his bending sickle's compass come" – lines 10-11; ("Thou art *thy mother's glass*" – Sonnet 3, line 9, to Southampton, who reflects the mirror and hourglass of his mother Elizabeth, whose ever-waning life was *Time* until her death; now *Time* is universal; "Thy *glass* will show thee how thy beauties wear,/ Thy dial how thy precious minutes waste" – Sonnet 77, lines 1-2; **TIME** = the word itself appearing here on the seventy-eighth and final occasion; mortal time, as recorded in the diary, has run out.

3 WHO HAST BYWANING GROWN, AND THEREIN SHOW'ST
Who has grown by decreasing or declining, i.e., within the womb of these sonnets *according to the waning of the Moon, Queen Elizabeth ...*

> As fast as thou shalt *wane* so fast thou *grow'st*
> - Sonnet 11, line 1

"The *mortal Moone* hath her eclipse endured" – Sonnet 107, line 5; i.e., linked to her life that led inevitably to her death and succession, followed by her funeral, marking the end of the dynasty; "Making a couplement of proud compare/ With *Sunne and Moone*" – Sonnet 21, lines 5-6

WANING: Southampton's fading, diminishing right to the throne:

> And says that once more I shall interchange
> *My waned state* for Henry's regal crown
> - *3 Henry VI*, 4.7.3-4

> Now, fair Hippolyta, our nuptial hour
> Draws on apace; four happy days bring in
> Another *moon*; but O, methinks, how slow
> The old moon wanes!
> - *A Midsummer Night's Dream*, 1.1.1-4

> Hippolyta: I am aweary of this *moon*. Would he change?
> Thesus: It appears by his small light of discretion that *he is in the wane*.
> - *A Midsummer Night's Dream*, 5.1.245-247
> (i.e., the man in the moon)

> The aim of all is but to nurse the life
> With honour, wealth and ease, in *waning age;*
> And in this aim there is such thwarting strife
> That *one for all or all for one* we gage.
> - *Lucrece*, 141-144
> (Southampton's motto *One for All, All for One*)

> I seek not to wax great by others' *waning*
> - *2 Henry VI*, 4.10.20

GROWN: "When in eternal lines to time thou *grow'st*" – Sonnet 18, line 12; "Making their tomb the womb wherein they *grew*" – Sonnet 86, line 4; "So thy great gift, upon misprision *growing*" – Sonnet 87, line 11, referring to Southampton's life now growing because he was spared from execution by the lesser judgment of "misprision" of treason; "How like Eve's apple doth thy beauty *grow*" – Sonnet 93, line 13, referring to Southampton's royal blood from Elizabeth growing toward its failure to gain the throne; "Love is a Babe, then might I not say so/ To *give full growth* to that which *still doth grow*" – Sonnet 118, lines 13-14, referring to the attempt to record his life in the Sonnets; **GROW:** "to become greater or larger, to increase in bulk, stature, quantity or degree … to take rise, to begin to exist, to spring, to come to pass … to *proceed*, to advance to a state … to become … to be, to exist, to live … to accrue, to fall to, to be due" – Schmidt

> Showing their *birth*, and where they did *proceed*
> - Sonnet 76, line 8
> (Proceed = grow)

> So many courses of the sun enthrone,
> Still *growing in a majesty and pomp*
> - Henry VIII, 2.3.6-7

4 THY LOVERS WITHERING, AS THY SWEET SELF GROW'ST:
THY LOVERS = your parents, Elizabeth and Oxford; all those who love you, including me; your subjects who would have served you if you had become king; **THY SWEET SELF** = your royal person; "And happily may *your sweet self* put on the lineal state and glory of the land!" – *King John*, 5.7.101-102, spoken to Prince Henry at the conclusion of the play; recalling the golden time of Sonnets 1-26: "Thy self thy foe, to *thy sweet self* too cruel" – Sonnet 1, line 8

5 IF NATURE (SOVEREIGN MISTRESS OVER WRACK)
NATURE = once Elizabeth, now universal nature; "*Nature's bequest* gives nothing but doth lend/ … Then how *when nature calls thee to be gone*,/ What acceptable *Audit* canst thou leave" – Sonnet 4, lines 3 (see Audit in line 11 below); "A Woman's face with *nature's own hand painted*/ Hast thou, the Master Mistress of my passion" – Sonnet 20, lines 1-2; **SOVEREIGN MISTRESS OVER WRACK** = recalling Elizabeth as both Sovereign and royal Mistress, whose life led to the ruin of your royal claim; ("supreme or paramount ruler over destruction" – Duncan-Jones); in the word "wrack" is an echo of the "rack" used as a form of torture to get suspect traitors to confess their crimes; "But found no cure; the bath for my help lies/ Where Cupid got new fire, my *mistress'* eye" – Sonnet 153, lines 13-14; "My *Mistress'* eyes are nothing like the Sunne" – Sonnet 130, line 1, referring to Elizabeth, sovereign mistress, and Southampton, royal son; "I cannot but find a great grief in myself to remember *the Mistress* we have lost" – Oxford to Robert Cecil, April 25/27, 1603, writing about the recently deceased Queen Elizabeth

6 AS THOU GOEST ONWARDS STILL WILL PLUCK THEE BACK,
As your life now proceeds, this universal force (of nature) will **STILL** or constantly work upon the decay of your mortal body and lead to your death; **PLUCK** = echoing the idea of "plucking" a flower, i.e., plucking Southampton as Tudor Rose; "draw down, bring down … extract, snatch, pull out …" – Crystal & Crystal; "Not from the stars do I my judgment *pluck*" – Sonnet 14, line 1; "From Ireland thus comes York to claim his right, and *pluck the crown* from feeble Henry's head" – *2 Henry VI*, 5.1.1-2

7 SHE KEEPS THEE TO THIS PURPOSE, THAT HER SKILL
SHE = once the Queen, now universal Nature; **KEEPS THEE, etc.** = holds you to this purpose, that her great destructive power; **PURPOSE:** intention, aim, plan; "Till nature as she wrought thee fell a-doting,/ And by addition me of thee defeated,/ By adding one thing to my *purpose* nothing" – Sonnet 20, lines 10-12; "Give not a windy night a rainy morrow,/ To linger out a *purposed overthrow*" – Sonnet 90, lines 7-8; "You are so strongly in my *purpose* bred" – Sonnet 112, line 13; "On *purpose* laid to make the taker mad" – Son-

REFERENCE EDITION

net 129, line 8; "Hence shall we see *if power change purpose*" – *Measure for Measure*, 1.3.53-54; "Our *holy purpose* to Jerusalem" – *1 Henry IV*, 1.1.101; "the intent and purpose of the law" – *The Merchant of Venice*, 4.1.245

8 MAY TIME DISGRACE, AND WRETCHED MINUTE KILL.
MAY TIME DISGRACE = may put Time itself to shame; may remove the royal "grace" from time; **AND WRETCHED MINUTE KILL** = cancel out that minute or moment of your death

9 YET FEAR HER, O THOU MINION OF HER PLEASURE,
O = Oxford; **MINION** = servant; ("let us be Diana's foresters, gentlemen of the shade, minions of the moon; and let men say we be men of good government, being governed as the sea is, by our noble and chaste mistress the moon, under whose countenance we steal" – *1 Henry IV*, 1.2.25-29, summoning the image of Elizabeth as Diana, the moon goddess, and "chaste mistress" or Virgin Queen of England; **HER PLEASURE** = Her Majesty's pleasure or royal will; now, however, according to Nature's all-powerful will

10 SHE MAY DETAIN, BUT NOT STILL KEEP HER TREASURE!
SHE = Nature; **DETAIN** = hold back; **NOT STILL** = not forever; **KEEP HER TREASURE** = keep your royal blood to herself, as Elizabeth did; **TREASURE** = royal blood; "Treasure thou some place/ With *beauty's treasure* ere it be self-killed" – Sonnet 6, lines 3-4; "But since she pricked thee out for women's (Her Majesty's) pleasure,/ Mine be thy love [your royal blood] and thy love's use their [the Queen's] *treasure*" – Sonnet 20, lines 13-14; "So am I as the rich whose blessed key/ Can bring him to his sweet up-locked *treasure*" – Sonnet 52, lines 1-2, Oxford about visiting Southampton, when he and his "treasure" of royal blood were "up-locked" in the Tower; "Will will fulfill the *treasure* of thy love" – Sonnet 136, line 5, Oxford to Elizabeth, referring to his pseudonym Will Shakespeare

11 HER *AUDIT* (THOUGH DELAYED) ANSWER'D MUST BE,
HER *AUDIT* = (*Q* gives *Audite*, capitalized and italicized); her final accounting of your royalty; "The context of lines 10 and 12 dictates that Her Audit be understood as 'the accounting nature is obliged to render and satisfy'" - Booth

"Then how *when nature calls thee to be gone,/ What acceptable Audit canst thou leave?*" – Sonnet 4, lines 11-12, referring to Elizabeth as "nature" and to the "audit" of his royal blood in terms of succeeding her on the throne; but now it us up to universal Nature to make the final accounting (by means of these royal sonnets, which contain the truth); "Whenas thy love hath cast its utmost sum,/ *Called to that audit* by advised respects" – Sonnet 49, lines 3-4, referring to the final audit or accounting of his "love" or royal blood; "and so, great powers, if you will *take this audit, take this life*, and cancel these cold bonds" – *Cymbeline*, 5.4.26-28;

"Audit = account, *reckoning*, reception, especially in the face of God" – Crystal & Crystal; "And how *his audit stands* who knows save heaven?" – *Hamlet*, 3.23.82, the Prince, referring to his uncle, King Claudius, deciding whether to slay him; the *audit* is similar to the *reckoning* as in "But *reck'ning time*, whose *millioned accidents/ Creep in 'twixt vows, and change decrees of Kings*" – Sonnet 115, lines 5-6; "Among a number one is *reckoned* none" – Sonnet 136, line 8, speaking of Southampton ("one") as unacknowledged or un-reckoned (with no accounting) as a royal prince; "Your servants ever have theirs, themselves, and what is theirs, in compt, to make their *audit* at your Highness' pleasure" – *Macbeth*, 1.6.25-27; "for truth is truth, to the end of *reckoning*" – *Measure for Measure*, 5.1.48

An *auditor* is an official of the *Exchequer*, from which Oxford received his grant of 1,000 pounds annually from the state Treasury, according to a Privy Seal Warrant signed by Elizabeth in 1586 and renewed by King

James in 1603; and here Oxford has played upon this grant as a metaphor throughout, with Southampton's blood depicted as the most valued sum in Elizabeth's royal Treasury; "Why should poor beauty indirectly seek/ Roses of shadow, since his Rose is true?/ Why should he live, now *nature* (Elizabeth) *bankrupt is,/ Beggared of blood* (Tudor blood) to blush through lively veins?/ *For she* (the Queen) hath no *exchequer* now but his" – Sonnet 67, lines 7-11; "a kind of *auditor*, one that hath abundance of charge too" – *1 Henry IV*, 2.1.56-57; "There's money of the King's coming down the hill, 'tis going to the King's *exchequer*" – *1 Henry IV*, 2.2.53-54; "You have an *exchequer* of words, and I think no other *treasure*" – The Two Gentlemen of Verona, 2.4.42-43; "Evermore thank's the *exchequer* of the poor, which, till my infant fortune comes to years, stands for my *bounty*" – *Richard II*, 2.3.65-67; "For our losses, his *exchequer* is too poor; for th'effusion of our blood, the muster of his kingdom too faint a number" – *Henry V*, 3.6.130-132

DELAYED = Southampton failed to succeed Elizabeth on the throne, so the audit or final accounting of his royal blood has been *delayed*, i.e., put off until "eyes not yet created shall o'er-read" (Sonnet 81, line 10) this verse, which will stand as his monument; but "delayed" is more active than that, i.e., Southampton's *audit* has been *quenched, subdued, held back*; "Now, God *delay our rebellion!*" – *All's Well That Ends Well*, 4.3.18; **ANSWER'D** = satisfied, made good; paid, repaid, requited; given in return; lived up to; become equal to; fulfilled, met, satisfied; accounted for, justified, defended; explained, excused; "From off the gates of York fetch down the head, your father's head, which Clifford placed there; instead whereof let this supply the room; *measure for measure must be answered*" – *3 Henry VI*, 2.6.52-55; "My lord, *these faults are easy, quickly answer'd*" – *2 Henry VI*, 3.1.133; "All solemn things should *answer solemn accidents*" – *Cymbeline*, 4.2.191-192; "Of this proud King, who studies day and night to *answer all the debt he owes*" – *1 Henry IV*, 1.3.182-183;

12 AND HER *QUIETUS* IS TO RENDER THEE.
QUIETUS = (Capitalized and italicized in *Q*); **HER *QUIETUS*** = her (nature's) settling of debts; discharge, clearing of accounts, release; ("final settlement of an account, audit" – Schmidt; "For who would bear the whips and scorns of time, the oppressor's wrong, the proud man's contumely, the pangs of dispriz'd love, the law's delay, the insolence of office, and the spurns that patient merit of the unworthy takes, *when he himself might his **quietus** make with a bare bodkin?*" – *Hamlet*, 3.1.70-76, (bodkin = dagger); **TO RENDER THEE** = to hand you to the world as payment; to give back, surrender; i.e., to render you or give you back to the throne, in posterity, as King Henry IX; ("And I will call him to so *strict account* that he shall **render** *every glory up*" – *1 Henry IV*, 3.2.149-150; "Hear the king's pleasure, Cardinal, who commands you to *render up the great seal* presently" – *Henry VIII*, 3.2.228-229; the "mutual *render*" of Sonnet 125, line 12: "But mutual ***render***, only me for thee"); "Time's glory is to calm contending kings,/ To unmask falsehood and bring truth to light,/ To stamp the seal of time in aged things,/ To wake the morn and sentinel the night,/ *To wrong the wronger till he **render right**,/* To ruinate proud buildings with thy hours,/ And smear with dust their glitt'ring golden towers" – *Lucrece*, 939-945; "If of my freedom 'tis the mainport, take no stricter *render* of me than my all" – *Cymbeline*, 5.4.16-17; "Claudio shall *render* me a dear *account*" – *Much Ado About Nothing*, 4.1.337; "The king is *rendered* lost" – *All's Well That Ends Well*, 1.3.227

How many *sons hast thou of mine in store*
That thou wilt never ***render*** to me more!
- *Titus Andronicus*, 1.1.97-98

13 (   )

14 (   )

Oxford's insertion of two empty parentheses signifies that he is intentionally leaving this sonnet unfinished, because Southampton's life is unfinished. (The empty parentheses echo the *tomb* and the *womb* intended to preserve the "living record" of Southampton for "the eyes of all posterity" – Sonnet 55; "Who will believe my verse in time to come/ If it were filled with your most high deserts? Though heaven knows *it is but as a tomb*/ Which hides *your life*, and shows not half your parts" – Sonnet 17, lines 1-4; "That did my ripe thoughts in my brain inhearse,/ *Making their tomb the womb* wherein they grew" – Sonnet 86, lines 3-4)

SUBSEQUENT EVENTS OF 1603

Oxford to Robert Cecil – May 7, 1603:

(Oxford asks Cecil's help in getting James to restore his hereditary title as Keeper of the Forest of Waltham [or Essex] and to the House and Park of Havering.)

"My very good Lord, I understand by Master Attorney that he hath reported the state of my *title* to the keepership of Waltham Forest, and of the house and park of Havering, whereby it appears to his Majesty what right and equity is therein. Till the 12th [year] of Henry the 8th, mine Ancestors have possessed the same, almost since the time of William Conqueror, and at that time which was the 12th year of Henry the 8th the king took it for *term of his life* from my grandfather, since which time, what by the *alterations of princes and wardships*, I have been kept from my rightful possession; yet from time to time both my father and myself we have as opportunities fell out not neglected our claim; twice in my time it had passage by law, and *judgment* was to have passed on my side, whereof her Majesty the late Queen, being advertised with *assured* promises and words of a prince to restore it herself unto me, caused me to let fall the suit.

    TITLE: "*Entitled* in thy parts do crowned sit" – Sonnet 37.7
    TERM OF HIS LIFE: "For *term of life* thou art assured mine" – Sonnet 92.2
    ALTERATIONS OF PRINCES AND WARDSHIPS: "*change decrees of kings*"
    – Sonnet 115.6; "Which *alters* when it *alteration* finds" – Sonnet 116.3
    JUDGMENT: "Thy black is fairest in my *judgment's* place" – Sonnet 131.12
    ASSURED: "The ills that were not grew to faults *assured*" – Sonnet 118.10

"But so it was she was not so ready to perform her word, as I was too ready to believe it; whereupon pressing my *title* farther it was by *her Majesty's pleasure* put to Arbitrement; and although it was an unequal course, yet not to contradict *her will*, the Lord Chancellor, Sir Christopher Hatton, was sole Arbiter, who, after all the delays devised by Sir Thomas Heneage and the Queen's counsel in law then being, having heard the cause, was ready to make his report for me, but her Majesty refused the same and by no means would hear it. So that by this and the former means, I have been thus long dispossessed.

    TITLE: "To 'cide this *title* is impannelled" – Sonnet 46.9
    HER MAJESTY'S PLEASURE: "for women's *pleasure*" – Sonnet 20.13; "I should in thought control your times of *pleasure*" – Sonnet 58.2
    HER WILL: "that in *your Will*" – Sonnet 57.13; "And I myself am mortgaged to *thy will*" – Sonnet 134.2

"But I hope *truth* is subject to no *prescription*, for *truth is truth* though never so old, and *time cannot make that false which was once true*; and though this *threescore years* both my father and myself have been dispossessed thereof, yet hath there been claims made thereto many times within those *threescore years*, which I take sufficient by law to avoid *prescription* in this case.

TRUTH/TRUTH IS TRUTH: "Thy end is *Truth's* and Beauty's doom and date" – Sonnet 14.14; "Thou

truly fair wert *truly* sympathized/ In *true* plain words by thy *true*-telling friend" – Sonnet 82.11-12
PRESCRIPTION: "Angry that his *prescriptions* are not kept" – Sonnet 147, line 6
TIME CANNOT MAKE THAT FALSE WHICH WAS ONCE TRUE: "*Time*, thou shalt not boast that I do change/ …this shall ever be; I will be *true*, despite thy scythe and thee" – Sonnet 123, l,13-14; "O lest your *true* love may seem *false* in this" – Sonnet 72, line 9
THREESCORE YEARS: "And *threescore year* would make the world away" – Sonnet 11.8

"Now therefore his Majesty having heard the report I hope he will in his justice and favor do me that right which is to be expected from so *gracious* and *virtuous* a *Sovereign*. But for that I know, among so many matters of importance, unless his Majesty be put in *remembrance*, he may forget a private cause, therefore I shall most earnestly desire your friendship in this that you will join with my Lord Admiral, my very good Lord and friend, to help me to his majesty's resolution. My Lord Admiral is Lord chief justice of Oyer and determiner, and to whose office indeed, as I understand, it appertains to have heard my cause, but I know not why or with what advice, it was referred to Master Attorney and his Majesty's Council in Law. But now howsoever, his Majesty hath the report made unto him, which if it be forgotten shall little prevail me, but I hope in his Justice, and in your two Lordships' friendships, which, the cause being so just and honorable, I do fully rely upon.

> **GRACIOUS:** "But now my *gracious* numbers are decayed" – Sonnet 79.3
> **VIRTUOUS:** "Unless you would devise some *virtuous* lie" – Sonnet 72.5
> **SOVEREIGN:** "Whilst I, my *sovereign*, watch the clock for you" – Sonnet 57.6
> **REMEMBRANCE:** "I summon up *remembrance* of things past" – Sonnet 30.2

"His Majesty departeth with nothing but a keepership, and a keeper he must have; wherefore it is much more princely or him to restore it to me his lawful keeper, than contrary to *bestow* it upon an intruder. Nothing adorns a king more than Justice, nor in anything doth a king more resemble God than in justice, which is the Head of all virtue, and he that is indued therewith, hath *all the rest*. So long as it was in the Custody of mine Ancestors the woods were preserved, the game *cherished*, and the forest maintained in her full state, but since it was otherwise disposed, all these things have *impaired* as experience doth manifest.

> **BESTOW:** "In thy soul's thought (all naked) will *bestow* it" – Sonnet 26.8
> **ALL THE REST:** "And *all the rest* forgot for which he toiled" – Sonnet 25.12
> **CHERISHED:** "Which bounteous gift thou shouldst in bounty *cherish*" – Sonnet 11.12
> **IMPAIRED:** "For I *impair* not beauty, being mute" – Sonnet 83.11

"*Thus* therefore most *earnestly craving* your Lordship's friendly and honorable furtherances, I most heartily recommend myself unto your good Lordships. From Hackney this 7th of May. Your Lordship's most assured friend and Brother in Law to Command, E. Oxenforde."

> **THUS … EARNESTLY CRAVING:** "*Thus vainly thinking*" – Sonnet 138.5

SOUTHAMPTON GRANTED ROYAL PARDON – May 16, 1603: "Southampton received a royal pardon for his offence committed in Elizabeth's time. The Earl's own copy of this deed survives to this day. Set forth in splendid calligraphy on two enormous vellum sheets, the plangent Latin sentences detail the King's clemency." (Akrigg bio, p. 134)

KING JAMES CREATES THE KING'S MEN – May 17, 1603: Immediately following the granting to Southampton of a royal pardon, King James directs the keeper of the Privy Seal to cause letters patent to be issued whereby "William Shakespeare" and other players of the Lord Chamberlain's Men are henceforth the King's Men, a royal company. "Can it be doubted that the King's act of 17 May was at the direct request of the person [Southampton] who was the beneficiary of the King's act of 16 May?" – Martin Green, *Wriothesley's Roses*, p. 215

Oxford to Robert Cecil – June 19, 1603:

(Here Oxford is still concerned with his suit for the Keepership of the Forest of Essex [or Waltham Forest], and for his title to Havering House and Park, all of which King James will grant him next month. This letter has nothing to do with the "bargain" for Henry Wriothesley's life.)

"My Lord, I understand how honorably you do persevere in your promised favor to me, which I taking in most kind manner, can at this time *acknowledge* it but by simple yet hearty thanks, hoping in God to offer me at some time or other the opportunity whereby I may in a more effectual *manner express* my grateful mind. I further also understand that this day Master Attorney is like to be at the Court. **Wherefore** I most earnestly *desire* your Lordship to procure an end of this my suit, in seeking *whereof I am grown old* and *spent* the *chiefest time* of mine age. The case, as I understand by your Lordship, Sir E. Coke, his Majesty's Attorney, hath reported, the Justice thereof I do not doubt, but doth appear there remaineth only a *warrant* according to the King's late order to be signed by the six Lords in Commission; whereby Master Attorney General may proceed according to the course usual.

> **MANNER EXPRESS:** "*express* the *manner*" – Sonnet 140.3-4
> **WHEREFORE ... WHEREOF I AM GROWN OLD:** "And *wherefore* say not I that I am *old*?" – Sonnet 138.9; "My glass shall not persuade me *I am old*" – Sonnet 22.1
> **ACKNOWLEDGE:** "I may not evermore *acknowledge* thee" – Sonnet 36.9
> **DESIRE:** "From fairest creatures we *desire* increase" – Sonnet 1.1
> **SPENT ... TIME:** "In gentle numbers *time* so idly *spent*" – Sonnet 100.5
> **CHIEFEST:** "That she hath thee is of my wailing *chief*" – Sonnet 42.3
> **WARRANT:** "The *warrant* I have of your Honorable disposition" – dedication of *Lucrece* to Southampton

"The King, I hear doth *remove* tomorrow towards Windsor, whereby if by your Lordship's especial *favor* you do not procure me a full end this day or tomorrow, I cannot look for anything more than a long delay. *I do well perceive* how your Lordship doth *travail* for me in this cause of an especial *grace* and *favor*, notwithstanding the *burden* of more importunate and *general affairs* than this of my *particular*.

> **REMOVE:** "Where I may not *remove*, nor be *removed*" – Sonnet 25.14; "Or bends with the remover to remove" – Sonnet 116.4
> **I DO WELL PERCEIVE:** "When I *perceive* that men as plants increase" – Sonnet 15.5
> **TRAVAIL:** "The dear repose for limbs with *travail* tired" – Sonnet 27.2
> **GRACE:** "In all external *grace* you have some part" – Sonnet 53.13
> **FAVOR:** "Have I not seen dwellers on form and *favor*" – Sonnet 125.5
> **BURDEN:** "The second *burden* of a former child" – Sonnet 59.4
> **GENERAL ... PARTICULAR:** "But these *particulars* are not my measure,/ All these I better in one *general* best" – Sonnet 91.7-8

"Whereof how much the expedition of this matter concerns me I leave to your wisdom, that in your own apprehension can *read more than I have written*. To conclude, I wholly rely upon your Lordship's honorable friendship for which *I do vow* a most thankful and grateful *mind*. This 19 of June – Your most loving assured friend and Brother-in-law E. Oxenforde."

> **AFFAIRS:** "Where you may be, or your *affairs* suppose" – Sonnet 57.10, to Southampton; "To stand in thy *affairs*, fall by thy side" – Sonnet 151.12, to Elizabeth

> **READ MORE THAN I HAVE WRITTEN:** "O learn to *read* what silent love *hath writ*"
> – Sonnet 23.13
> **I DO VOW:** "This *I do vow*, and this shall ever be" – Sonnet 123.13
> **MIND:** "They look into the beauty of thy *mind*" – Sonnet 69.9

Oxford re: the Coronation – July 7, 1603: The Earl of Oxford, as Lord Great Chamberlain of England, claimed the right to attend personally on His Majesty King James on the morning of the coronation ceremony, to be held on the twenty-fifth.

"Edward de Vere, Earl of Oxford, presents to the Court a certain petition in these words. Edward de Vere, Earl of Oxford, asks that as he is Great Chamberlain of England of the see of our most dread *Lord* the King, that it should please the King that he should likewise at the Coronation, as formerly he was permitted, to do the said office and services as he and his ancestors have formerly done. That is to say that the said Earl had freedom and entertainment of the King's Court at all times; and that the said Earl on the day of the said Coronation, on the morning before the King rises, ought to enter into the chamber where the King lies, and bring him his shirt, and stockings, and underclothing. And that the said Earl and the Lord Chamberlain for the time being together on that day ought to dress the King in all his *apparel*.

> **LORD:** "*Lord* of my love" – Sonnet 26.1
> **APPAREL:** "And puts *apparel* on my tottered loving" – Sonnet 26.11

"And that he may take and have all his fees, profits, and advantages due to this office as he and his ancestors before him have been used to on the day of Coronation; that is to say, *forty yards of crimson velvet* for the said Earl's robes for that day. And when the King is apparelled and ready to go out of his chamber, then the Earl should have the bed where the King lay on the night before the Coronation, and all the apparel of the same, with the coverlet, curtains, pillows, and the hangings of the room, with the King's nightgown, in which he was vested the night before the Coronation.

FORTY YARDS OF CRIMSON VELVET: The same amount of red cloth to be given by the Master of the Great Wardrobe to "William Shakespeare" and other members of the King's Men, not as actors but as Men of the Chamber for the Coronation procession held on March 15, 1604.

"He also asks that [he should have the same privileges] as his ancestors [who] from time immemorial *served* the noble progenitors of our Lord the King *with water* before and after eating the day of the Coronation, and had as their right the basins and towels and a *tasting cup*, with which the said progenitors were served on the day of their Coronation, as appears in the records of the *Exchequer*.

> **SERVED ... WITH WATER:** "So that *myself bring water* for my stain" – Sonnet 109.8
> **TASTING CUP:** "And my great mind most kingly drinks it up ... And *to his palate* doth prepare *the cup*" – Sonnet 114.10,12)
> **EXCHEQUER:** "For she hath no *exchequer* now but his" – Sonnet 67.11

"My Lord Steward adjudicates to the aforesaid Earl the fees, services, and fees of *presenting water* to the Lord the King before and after dinner on the day of the Coronation; and to have the basins, tasting cups, and towels. And for the other fees the said Earl is referred to examine the *records* of the *Jewel* House and the King's wardrobe." - (B. M. Ward, p. 346; Cal. S. P. Domestic., James I. – July 7, 1603)

> **RECORDS:** "For thy *records*, and what we see, doth lie" – Sonnet 123.11
> **JEWEL:** "As on the finger of a throned Queen /The basest *Jewel* will be well esteemed"
> – Sonnet 96.5-6

REFERENCE EDITION

Southampton Appointed Captain of The Isle of Wight – July 7, 1603: As Oxford predicted (or else as he revisited Sonnet 106, line 2 after today: "I see descriptions of *the fairest wights*"), King James grants Southampton the reversion of the post as Captain of the Isle of Wight. George Carey, Lord Hundson, who is ill, currently holds it. Upon Carey's death in September, Southampton will receive his official appointment.

"*The post was no sinecure. Because of its position* [off the south coast of England] *the Isle of Wight was vulnerable both to enemy invasions and pirate raids … Southampton, who always regarded himself as a soldier, entered with enthusiasm upon his captaincy … Like the benevolent monarch of a little kingdom.*"
- Akrigg, 135

Southampton a Knight of the Garter – July 9, 1603: This honor was given to Southampton as Oxford had foreseen in Sonnet 106, line 4: "In praise of Ladies dead, and *lovely Knights*."
"*Southampton was installed as a Knight of the Garter, the fourth of the reign, the first three being Prince Henry* [son of James, heir to the throne], *the King of Denmark* [brother to the new queen], *and the Duke of Lennox* [the kinsman who had come south with James]" - Akrigg, 134

Southampton Given Access to the King – July 14, 1603: "When fourteen courtiers were granted the privilege of access to the King's Privy Chamber, Southampton was on the list." - Akrigg, 135

Oxford Granted Forest of Essex & Havering House – July 18, 1603: "The King granted him (Oxford) the Bailiwick, or custody, of the Forest of Essex and the Keepership of Havering House." - Ward, 344

Southampton's Earldom Restored – July 21, 1603: "King James created his first English earls, the list being headed by Henry Wriothesley, formally again made Earl of Southampton but with the precedence of his former creation." – Akrigg, 135

Oxford Serves at Coronation of King James – July 25, 1603: "Monday, and the feast of the Blessed Apostle Saint James, King James of England, first of that name, with the Noble Lady and Queen Anne, were together crowned and anointed at Westminster, by the most Reverend Father in God John Whitgift, Archbishop of Canterbury." - Stow, *Annals*, p. 828; Edward de Vere, Earl of Oxford, participates in this private ceremony as Lord Great Chamberlain of England.

Oxford's Grant is Continued – August 2, 1603: King James renewed Oxford's annual grant of one thousand pounds, originally bestowed upon him by Queen Elizabeth in 1586, employing exactly the same words as in the original grant. - Miller, *Oxfordian Vistas*, p. 115; Enrolment of Privy Seals, Pells E. 403/2598

Southampton Granted Wine Farm – August 20, 1603: "Writing to Lord Treasurer Buckhurst, James instructed him to make over to Southampton that farm of the sweet wines which had provided Essex with most of his wealth" (Akrigg bio, p. 135.) Oxford predicted the grant to Southampton in a passing glance in Sonnet 125, line 7: "For compound sweet..."

Southampton Orders *Love's Labour's Lost* Performed – 1603/04: "Within a year of his release from the Tower in 1603, he (Southampton) entertained Queen Anne of Denmark (wife of King James) at his house in the Strand, and Burbage and his fellow-players, one of whom was Shakespeare (his name was listed among members of the King's Men), were bidden to present the 'old' play of *Love's Labour's Lost*, whose 'wit and mirth' were calculated 'to please her Majesty exceedingly.'" - Lee, *Life of Shakespeare*, 384

"Southampton's interest in … the Shakespearean plays suffered no decline as a result of his trial and imprisonment; for we find him immediately upon his liberation arranging for a private performance of *Love's*

Labour's Lost for the entertainment of the new Queen … The part taken by Henry Wriothesley first in arranging for a performance of *Richard II* in connection with the 1601 insurrection, and then for a private performance of *Love's Labour's Lost* to entertain the new Queen in 1603 … (indicates that) although ten years had elapsed since Shakespeare began to dedicate poems to him (in 1593), he was still not only deeply interested in, but actively occupied with, the doings of the so-called 'Shakespeare's company' and the Shakespearean plays." (Looney, *"Shakespeare" Identified*, pp 333-34; 363)

JANUARY-JUNE 1604

Hampton Court Conference – January 1604: One result of the conference will be the creation of the King James Version of the Bible, to be published in 1611.

Oxford to King James – January 30, 1604: In the latest-dated letter from Oxford recovered so far, he writes to James about further matters related to the care of Waltham Forest and Havering Park in Essex.

Actors Given Red Cloth for Procession – March 15, 1604: The account of Sir George Home, Master of the Great Wardrobe, includes this entry: "Red Clothe bought of sondrie persons and given by his Majestie to diverse persons against his Majesties sayd royall proceeding through the Citie of London … The Chamber … Fawkeners, etc. … Red cloth, four and a half yards each: William Shakespeare, Augustine Phillips, Lawrence Fletcher, John Hemminges, Richard Burbidge, William Slye, Robert Armyn, Henry Cundell, Richard Cowley." (Miller, *Oxfordian Vistas*, p. 115)

The eight names after "Shakespeare" were those of actors, but here they were listed as Chamber members (i.e., Grooms of the Chamber) and their total amount of red cloth equaled thirty-six yards (nine men with four and a half yards apiece would have had a total of forty-and-a-half yards). This is virtually the exact amount of red cloth (*"forty yards of crimson velvet"*) that Edward de Vere had requested in his petition to the Council of July 7, 1603. As a premier nobleman, Oxford ordinarily would have had his own servants to walk with him in the grand procession, but apparently he now maintained no such retinue. "Therefore, would it not be reasonable to suppose that when Lord Oxford needed extra servants to assist with special duties relating to the Office of the Ewrie and of Lord Great Chamberlain, particularly during the coronation festivities, he would call on those ready at hand – men from his companies of actors?" (Miller, *Oxfordian Vistas*, p. 117)

The King's Coronation Procession – March 15, 1604
Parliament Session – March 19, 1604: King James orders his first Parliament, with nearly all peers of England in attendance including Southampton.

Birth of Southampton's Second Daughter – March 1604: A few weeks after the coronation procession, Elizabeth Vernon, Countess of Southampton, gave birth to another daughter (their first, Penelope, had been born in late 1598); and Queen Anne agreed to be godmother. The baby girl was baptized Anne Wriothesley in honor of Her Majesty at the ceremony in the Chapel Royal. - Akrigg, 140

Oxford's Reported Death – June 24, 1604: On this day (some fourteen months after Southampton's release from the Tower of London), fifty-four-year-old Edward deVere either died at his Hackney home of unknown causes or otherwise disappeared altogether from England. While reportedly buried in the Church of St. Augustine, he received no known funeral and left no known will. Later Perceval Golding, son of Arthur Golding, wrote:

"Edward de Vere, only son of John, born the 12th day of April 1550, Earl of Oxenford, High Chamberlain, Lord Bolbec, Sandforth, and Badlesmere, Steward of the Forest of Essex, and of the Privy Council to the King's Majesty that now is. Of whom I will only speak what all men's voices confirm: he was a man in mind and body absolutely accomplished with honorable endowments; he died at his house in Hackney in the month of June Anno 1604 and lieth buried at Westminster." - Ogburn & Ogburn, 1197

"...and both in Italy, France, and other Nations, (Edward de Vere) did more honor to this Kingdom than all that have traveled since he took his journey to heaven. It were infinite to speak of his infinite expense, the infinite numbers of his attendants, or the infinite house he kept to feed all people ... that he was upright and honest in all his dealings the few debts left behind him to clog his survivors were safe pledges ... the alms he gave (which at this day would not only feed the poor, but the great man's family also) and the bounty which Religion and Learning daily took from him, are Trumpets so loud that all ears know them; so that I conclude, and say of him ... that he was Honestus, Pietas, and Magnanimous."
- Gervase Markham, *Honour in his Perfection*, London, 1624; quoted in *This Star of England*, 1952, 1198-1199, from *The Mystery of Mr. W. H.*, Col. B. R. Ward, 1923, 81-82

Southampton's Overnight Arrest – June 24, 1604: "Suddenly the even happy flow of Southampton's career came to a halt. Late on the evening of June 24 he was arrested (as were Danvers, Neville, Berkeley and Lee) ...

"Southampton's papers were seized and scrutinized. He himself was interrogated. According to the French ambassador, King James had gone into a complete panic and could not sleep that night even though he had a guard of his Scots posted around his quarters. Presumably to protect his heir, he sent orders to Prince Henry (the King's eleven-year-old son) that he must not stir out of his chamber. Next morning, while the Privy Council was examining its prisoners, wild rumors swept through the Court. Some men said that a plot had been discovered against the King and the Prince...

"Southampton was quickly found innocent of whatever charges had been brought against him. According to both the Venetian and French ambassadors, he was released on June 25, the day after his arrest. Probably we shall never know the nature of the charges brought against Southampton ... Probably King James, embarrassed by what had occurred, ordered that all the papers be destroyed. Certainly a determined effort seems to have been made to hush up the whole affair...

"If the charges are unknown to us, so is Southampton's accuser. King James, though clearing Southampton, refused to divulge to him the identity of the informer. When Southampton, meaning to challenge his accuser to a duel, demanded to be told his identity, the King gave him only 'fair words' ... That Southampton was completely exonerated and restored to favor there can be no doubt."
- Akrigg, 140-142

"Fifteen months to the day after Elizabeth's death, the Earl of Oxford died, on June 24, 1604. Suddenly and inexplicably, the Earl of Southampton was clapped into the Tower again. The only reasonable explanation is the timid James's fear that his (Southampton's) great popularity, the love of 'the distracted multitude,' might occasion an uprising more successful than the one in which the dashing young Earl had seconded Essex. And we concur unqualifiedly with Mr. Allen (Percy Allen, author of *The Life Story of Edward de Vere as 'William Shakespeare'*, 1932) that, as a condition of his freedom and continued prestige, Henry Wriothesley, the Fair Youth, must thereupon have renounced forever ... all claim to the throne of England ...

"We believe that he (Southampton) was forced by Authority – Robert Cecil working through James – to relinquish the personal immortality the great poet had so lovingly bequeathed to him. The alternative he faced was imprisonment and an even more complete oblivion than that of the true Shakespeare."
- Ogburn & Ogburn, 1202

Publication of the full *Hamlet (Q2)* – 1604:

O God, Horatio, what *a wounded name,*
Things standing thus unknown shall I leave behind me!
If thou didst *ever* hold me in thy heart,
Absent thee from felicity awhile,
And in this harsh world draw thy breath in pain
To *tell my story.* - 5.2.327-332

O, I die, Horatio!
The potent poison quite o'ercrows my spirit.
I cannot live to hear the news from England,
But I do prophesy th'election lights
On Fortinbras. He has my dying voice.
So tell him, with th'occurrents, more and less,
Which have solicited – the rest is silence. - 5.2.335-342
(Dies)

Viewed in relation to prior hypotheses for the Fair Youth Series (1-126), the structural solution to the Sonnets is remarkably simple:

HYPOTHESES – GENERAL

Authorial – The quarto of 1609 is printed as the author intended.
Sequential – The sonnets are arranged in the correct order.
Three Series – The Sonnets contain two series (1-126; 127-152) and an epilogue (153-154).
Chronological – Within each series, the verses are chronologically ordered.
Historical – As entries of a diary, the sonnets comprise a historical document.
Masterwork – The sonnets add up to a single, unified masterwork.

HYPOTHESES – SPECIFIC

SONNETS 1-17:	Southampton marriage proposal	1590–1591
SONNET 25:	Failed Irish military campaign	1599
SONNET 26:	ENVOY	
SONNET 107:	Southampton's liberation	10 April 1603
SONNET 125:	Queen Elizabeth's funeral	28 April 1603
SONNET 126:	ENVOY	

Once Southampton's imprisonment from 1601 to 1603 fills the gap in the time line, we see the outline of an ongoing diary from 1590 to 1603:

SONNETS 1-17:	Southampton marriage proposal	1590–1591
SONNET 25:	Failed Irish military campaign	1599
SONNET 26:	ENVOY	1600
SONNET 27:	REBELLION	8 February 1601
	IMPRISONMENT	1601–1603
SONNET 106:	FINAL NIGHT IN TOWER	9 April 1603
SONNET 107:	Southampton's liberation	10 April 1603
SONNET 125:	Queen Elizabeth's funeral	28 April 1603
SONNET 126:	ENVOY	

Part Three

"TWO LOVES I HAVE"

The Dark Lady

Sonnets 127 – 152

Feb 8, 1601 – March 24, 1603

THE DARK LADY: ELIZABETH

REBELLION & IMPRISONMENT

Sonnet 127
Beauty's Successive Heir
8 February 1601

This opening sonnet to and about Queen Elizabeth is the start of the separate Dark Lady series, running in parallel with the Fair Youth series from 1601 to 1603. Two verses of this series, Sonnets 138 and 144, were first published in 1599; but Oxford has inserted them with slight but significant revisions into this sequence. The result is a series of twenty-six sonnets (127-152) matching the twenty-six sonnets of the opening series (1-26), each flanking the series of exactly one hundred verses (Sonnets 27-126) forming the center of the one hundred and fifty-two sonnet structure. Sonnet 127 corresponds in time to Sonnet 27 – the night of Southampton's revolt and imprisonment on February 8, 1601 – both introducing "black" into their respective sequences.

In the past the royal son was "fair" but now he is "black" with disgrace, although he remains the Queen's "successive heir" to the throne. Elizabeth's imperial viewpoint determines everything. At a glance, she can turn him from "fair" (royal) to "black" (disgraced). She continues to slander her own "beauty" or royal blood, which is possessed by her son, by viewing him with "a bastard shame" or consigning him to the status of a royal bastard.

Sonnet 127	Translation
In the old age black was not counted fair,	At first our disgraced son was not deemed royal,
Or if it were it bore not beauty's name:	Or if he was, he had not Elizabeth's name:
But now is black beauty's successive heir,	But now he's the Queen's blood successor,
And Beauty slandered by a bastard shame,	And blood is disgraced as a royal bastard.
For since each hand hath put on Nature's power,	Because since all adopt Elizabeth's power,
Fairing the foul with Art's false borrowed face,	Gaining royal favor by false art [of the Court],
Sweet beauty hath no name, no holy bow'r,	Royal blood has no name or sacred seat,
But is profaned, if not lives in disgrace.	But is violated, even if not in disgrace.
Therefore my Mistress' eyes are Raven black,	Therefore my Queen's view is darkly negative,
Her eyes so suited, and they mourners seem,	Her eyes like those in mourning for
At such who not born fair no beauty lack,	Him not born a king yet not lacking her blood,
Sland'ring Creation with a false esteem.	Slandering her son with a false view of him.
Yet so they mourn becoming of their woe,	Yet so her eyes mourn reflecting her woe,
That every tongue says beauty should look so.	So that all men say royal blood appears so.

1 IN THE OLD AGE BLACK WAS NOT COUNTED FAIR
OLD AGE = former times; as in Sonnets 1 – 26 up to the year 1600, before the Essex Rebellion, after which everything changed; **OLD** = "Wherefore, not as a stranger but in the *old* style" – Oxford to Robert Cecil, May (?) 1601; "For truth is truth, though never so *old*" – Oxford to Robert Cecil, May 7, 1603; "That I might see what the *old* world could say" – Sonnet 59, line 9; "O him she stores, to show what wealth she had/ In

days long since, before these last so bad" – Sonnet 67, lines 13-14, "Robbing no *old* to dress his beauty new" – Sonnet 68, line 12; "For as the Sun is daily new and *old*,/ So is my love still telling what is told" – Sonnet 76, lines 13-14; "Counting no *old* thing *old*, thou mine, I thine" – Sonnet 108, line 7; **AGE** = "A generation of men, a particular period of time; the period of life at which a person has arrived; a stage of life" – Schmidt; "Had my friend's Muse grown with this growing *age*" – Sonnet 32, line 10; "The rich proud cost of outworn buried *age*" – Sonnet 64, line 2; "Doubting the filching *age* will steal his treasure" – Sonnet 75, line 6; "For fear of which, hear this, thou *age* unbred" – Sonnet 104, line 13; "And peace proclaims Olives of endless *age*" – Sonnet 107, line 8; "The *age* is grown so picked that the toe of the peasant comes so near the heel of the courtier he galls his kibe" – *Hamlet*, 5.1.138-140; **BLACK** = Southampton, in disgrace for treason; "It will help me nothing to plead mine innocence, for that dye is on me which makes my whitest part *black*" – *Henry VIII*, 1.1.208-209; also, as royal bastard; "A joyless, dismal, *black and sorrowful issue*" – *Titus Andronicus*, 4.2.68-73; **COUNTED FAIR** = accounted (i.e., his "fair" or royal blood as Elizabeth's "treasure") or acknowledged as royal; "From *fairest* creatures we desire increase" – Sonnet 1, line 1

2 OR IF IT WERE IT BORE NOT BEAUTY'S NAME

Or even if he was accounted as royal (by me), he did not bear Elizabeth's name (Tudor); **BORE** = heraldic, i.e., Southampton never bore his mother's coat-of-arms; also related to his birth as a bastard; ("Before these bastard signs of fair were borne" – Sonnet 68, line 3); **BEAUTY'S NAME** = Elizabeth's name, Tudor; i.e., he was never known as Prince Henry Tudor; ("That thereby beauty's *Rose* might never die" – Sonnet 1, line 2)

3 BUT NOW IS BLACK BEAUTY'S SUCCESSIVE HEIR

But now Southampton is Elizabeth's immediate heir to the throne; **BLACK** = Southampton; **BEAUTY'S** = Elizabeth's; **SUCCESSIVE HEIR** = one who deserves to succeed by virtue of inheritance; rightful claimant to a title; "Yet, by reputing of his high descent, as next the King he was *successive heir*" – *2 Henry VI*, 3.148-49 (the only other Shakespeare usage of the phrase); "Plead my *successive* title with your swords; I am his first-born son that was the last that wore the diadem of Rome: then let my father's honor live in me, nor wrong mine age with this indignity" – *Titus Andronicus*, 1.1.4-8; "To God, my king, and my *succeeding* issue" – *Richard II*, 1.3.20; "rightful *heir* to the crown" – *2 Henry VI*, 1.3.26; "But as *successively* from blood to blood, your right of birth" – *Richard III*, 3.7.134-135; "O now let Richmond and Elizabeth, the true *succeeders* of each royal House, by God's fair ordinance conjoin together, and let their *heirs*, God, if Thy will be so, enrich the time to come with smooth-faced peace" – *Richard III*, 5.5.29-33; "Richer than that which four *successive kings* in Denmark's crown have worn" – *Hamlet*, 5.2.273-274; "No son of mine succeeding" – *Macbeth*, 3.1.63; "They labored to plant the rightful *heir*" – *1 Henry VI*, 2.5.80

4 AND BEAUTY SLANDERED WITH A BASTARD SHAME

BEAUTY = Elizabeth; also, her blood that Southampton possesses by inheritance of it as a "natural issue of her Majesty's body"; **SLANDERED** = brought into "discredit, disgrace, or disrepute" – *OED*; "But once he *slandered* me with bastardy" – *King John*, 1.1.74; "With the attainder of his *slanderous* lips" – *Richard II*, 4.1.24; **SLANDERED BY A BASTARD SHAME** = shame or disgrace because of royal-bastard status; ("Thy *issue* blurred with *needless bastardy*" – *Lucrece*, 522; also "slander" as "to charge with, accuse of, a crime or offence" = *OED*., citing Scotland Council of 1579: "Persons *slandered* or *suspect* of treason"); same as "The *region cloud hath masked him* from me now" – Sonnet 33, line 12, i.e., Elizabeth Regina's dark cloud of shame has covered and hidden her son; "For *slander's mark* was *ever* yet the *fair*,/ The ornament of beauty is *suspect*,/ A *crow* that flies in *heaven's sweetest air*" – Sonnet 70, lines 2-4; "this *slander* of his blood" – *Richard II*, 1.1.113; "And that he is a *bastard*, not thy son" – *Richard II*, 5.2.106; "Out, insolent! Thy bastard shall be king ... My boy a bastard!" – *King John*, 2.1.122-129)

"I am a bastard, too: I love bastards. I am bastard begot, bastard instructed, bastard in mind, bastard in valour, in everything illegitimate. One bear will not bite another, and where should one bastard? Take heed: the quarrel's most ominous to us – if the son of a whore fight for a whore, he tempts judgment. Farewell, bastard" - *Troilus & Cressida*, 5.7.18-32

5 FOR SINCE EACH HAND HATH PUT ON NATURE'S POWER

HAND = the powerful hand of Elizabeth, the absolute monarch; "Upon my head they placed a fruitless crown, and put a barren scepter in my gripe, thence to be *wrenched* by an unlineal *hand*, no son of mine *succeeding*" – *Macbeth*, 3.1.59-63; "I'll claim that promise at your Grace's hand" – to the King in *Richard III*, 3.1.197; **EACH HAND** = others who have sought Elizabeth's favor; both of the Queen's royal hands; "If Heaven will take the present *at our hands*" – the King in *Richard III*, 1.1.120; "A Woman's face with *nature's own hand* painted/ Hast thou, the Master Mistress of my passion" – Sonnet 20, lines 1-2; Southampton at birth was "sleeping *by a Virgin hand disarmed*" – Sonnet 154, line 8; "From *hands of falsehood*" – Sonnet 48, line 4; "With *time's injurious hand* crushed and o'er-worn" – Sonnet 63, line 2; "Or what *strong hand* can hold his swift foot back?" – Sonnet 65, line 11; **PUT ON** = assumed the royal power of the monarch and acted with that power; "For he was likely, had he been *put on*, to have proved most royal" – Horatio, saying that Prince Hamlet would have been a superb king, in *Hamlet*, 5.2.404-405; "deaths *put on by cunning and forced causes*" – *Hamlet*, 5.2.394; **NATURE'S POWER** = Elizabeth's royal power as absolute monarch, whose imperial viewpoint can turn *fair* to *black* or vice versa; "O Thou my lovely Boy, who in thy *power* ... If *Nature*, sovereign *mistress* over wrack" – Sonnet 126, lines 1, 5

6 FAIRING THE FOUL WITH ART'S FALSE BORROWED FACE
= giving royal favor to foul persons by her false estimation; turning truth into falsity; "To make me *give the lie to my true sight*/ And swear that brightness doth not grace the day?/ Whence hast thou *this becoming of things ill*" – Sonnet 150, lines 3-4

7 SWEET BEAUTY HATH NO NAME NO HOLY BOW'R

BEAUTY HATH NO NAME = Southampton's royal blood from his mother, Elizabeth, is not acknowledged; **NO HOLY BOW'R** = no sacrosanct dwelling place, i.e., no right to sit on the throne as a god on earth

8 BUT IS PROFANED, IF NOT LIVES IN DISGRACE
= Instead, our son is now disgraced and imprisoned because of his role in the Rebellion; (Booth refers to "false identities that pass for real and real ones that seem false"); Southampton's real identity as royal prince is hidden, so it seems false; **PROFANED** = defiled, usurped; "Question your royal thoughts, make the case yours, be now the father, and propose a son, hear your own dignity *profaned*" – Chief Justice to the newly crowned King Henry Fifth in *2 Henry IV*, 5.3.91-93; **IF NOT** = or even; **LIVES IN DISGRACE** = lives in disgrace as a prisoner in the Tower of London

9 THEREFORE MY MISTRESS' EYES ARE RAVEN BLACK

THEREFORE = "Therefore" is the key word, i.e., the Queen's eyes are not black in color, but rather reflect her dark point of view as absolute monarch; "therefore" the *viewpoint* of Elizabeth, my sovereign mistress, is black; **ARE RAVEN BLACK** = they are "therefore" black, because the Queen's own viewpoint, casting its shadow, has turned Southampton from *fair* to *black*; her negative attitude has turned her into the so-called Dark Lady; "By heaven, thy love is *black* as ebony ... O paradox! *Black* is the badge of hell" – the king in *Love's Labour's Lost*, 4.3.243, 250; **RAVEN** = "*Legend has it that should the ravens ever leave the Tower of London the White Tower will crumble and a great disaster shall befall England. For many centuries ravens have been known to be residents of the Tower of London*" – www.tower-of-london.com; (Southampton is in the White Tower); "For he's disposed as the hateful *raven* ... For he's inclined as is the *ravenous* wolf" – *2 Henry VI*, 3.1.76-78; "Come, the croaking *raven* doth bellow for revenge" – *Hamlet*, 3.2.255-256; **MISTRESS**: "To be her *mistress' mistress*? The *queen's queen*?" – *Henry VIII*, 3.2.95; same as the sovereign mistress, Elizabeth, of "*my mistress' eye*" in Sonnet 153, line 14, and "*my mistress' thrall*" of Sonnet 154, line 12; "I cannot but find a great grief in myself to remember the Mistress we have lost" – Oxford to Robert Cecil, April 25/27, 1603, referring to the Queen on the eve of her funeral

10 HER EYES SO SUITED, AND THEY MOURNERS SEEM

MOURNERS = at a funeral, as in *The Phoenix and the Turtle* (published this year, 1601); the funeral of their son, Southampton, if he is executed; and the funeral of Oxford's and Elizabeth's royal hopes for him to succeed to the throne: "Thy end is Truth's (Oxford's) and Beauty's (Elizabeth's) doom and date" – Sonnet

No. 127

14, line 14; dovetailing with Sonnet 31, line 5: "How many a *holy and obsequious tear/* Hath religious love stolen from mine eye."

11 AT SUCH WHO, NOT BORN FAIR, NO BEAUTY LACK
AT SUCH = at her royal son; **NOT BORN FAIR** = not born with acknowledged royal blood; **NO BEAUTY LACK** = but still lacks none of his royal blood from "beauty" or Elizabeth

12 SLAND'RING CREATION WITH A FALSE ESTEEM
SLAND'RING = Disgracing your own child and accusing him of treason; echoing "beauty *slandered* with a bastard shame" of line 4; ("For *slander's* mark was ever yet the fair" – Sonnet 70, line 2; **CREATION** = created being, child; "From fairest *creatures* we desire increase" – Sonnet 1, line 1; "But heaven in thy *creation* did decree" – Sonnet 93, line 9, Oxford to Southampton about Elizabeth (heaven), who gave birth to him; **FALSE ESTEEM** = false view or estimation of him; ("*false women's fashion*" – Sonnet 20, line 4, about Elizabeth); esteeming her son as a "false traitor" as in "To warn *false traitors* from the like attempts" – *Richard III*, 3.5.48

13 YET SO THEY MOURN BECOMING OF THEIR WOE
So Elizabeth's eyes mourn for her son and for the fate of her royal blood that he possesses; and therefore they are "black" in these verses of the Sonnets; **WOE** = ("O that our *night of woe* might have remem'bred/ My deepest sense, how hard true sorrow hits" – Sonnet 120, lines 9-10)

14 THAT EVERY TONGUE SAYS BEAUTY SHOULD LOOK SO
EVERY = Edward de Vere, E. Ver, *Ever or Never*; **EVERY TONGUE** = the voices of others, alluding to "my tongue" or "my voice"; "And art made *tongue-tied* by authority" – Sonnet 66, line 9; **SAYS BEAUTY SHOULD LOOK SO** = says that Elizabeth (or more specifically, her blood within Southampton) appears to be in such disgrace

THE DARK LADY: ELIZABETH

THE EXECUTION OF ESSEX

Sonnet 128
Those Jacks That Nimble Leap
25 February 1601

This verse corresponds to Sonnet 44 of the Fair Youth series, marking the execution of Essex. It offers a remarkable corroboration of the anecdote about the Queen playing upon the virginals in her Privy Chamber when news of the execution was delivered. As her Majesty kept on playing, Oxford is said to have quipped about Essex's enemy Sir Walter Raleigh, **"When Jacks start up, heads go down."** *(Perhaps he was also referring to Essex, who had "started up" or initiated the Rebellion.) Oxford uses this imagery to express the depth of his pleadings to the Queen to spare Southampton (and by extension, himself) from the same fate as Essex.*

Sonnet 128	Translation
How oft, when thou my music music play'st	How often when you play my music
Upon that blessed wood whose motion sounds	On your virginals, which makes sound
With thy sweet fingers when thou gently sway'st	(With your royal fingers when you sway)
The wiry concord that mine ear confounds,	Whose harmony amazes and confounds,
Do I envy those Jacks that nimble leap	Do I envy upstarts [like Raleigh] who leap
To kiss the tender inward of thy hand,	To kiss your royal hand for their own gain,
Whilst my poor lips, which should that harvest reap,	While I, who deserve your royal favor,
At the wood's boldness by thee blushing stand.	Stand beside you helplessly to think
To be so tickled they would change their state	You would exchange your royal state
And situation with those dancing chips,	And royal place with those sycophants,
O'er whom thy fingers walk with gentle gait,	Over whom you rule with royal sway,
Making dead wood more blest than living lips.	Making them more royal than yourself.
Since saucy Jacks so happy are in this,	Since upstart hypocrites gain so much,
Give them thy fingers, me thy lips to kiss.	Given them your fingers, me your voice.

1 HOW OFT WHEN THOU MY MUSIC MUSIC PLAY'ST
THOU MY MUSIC = (or "thou, my music"); Queen Elizabeth, whom Oxford is calling "my music," as he had called Southampton "music to hear" in "Music to hear, why hear'st thou music sadly?" in Sonnet 8, line 1; "Her words are music all of silver sound" – Sonnet No. VII, line 10 of *The Passionate Century of Love*, 1582, attributed to Thomas Watson and dedicated to Oxford, the more likely author, writing in praise of the Queen (See Sonnet 130); **MUSIC PLAY'ST** = music played by the Queen on the virginals; "Then music is even as the flourish, when true subjects bow to a new-crowned monarch" – *The Merchant of Venice*, 3.2.48-50

2 UPON THAT BLESSED WOOD WHOSE MOTION SOUNDS
BLESSED WOOD = the Queen's virginals, which are "blessed" because she is "sacred" as Her Majesty, as

in "his sacred majesty" of Sonnet 7, line 4, referring to Southampton; ("presumably the keys of a virginal … carries accidental overtones of the crucifixion of Christ" – Booth); "This royal infant (heaven still move about her) though in her cradle, yet now promises upon this land a thousand thousand *blessings*. So shall she leave her *blessedness* to one (When heaven shall call her from this cloud of darkness) who from the *sacred* ashes of her honour shall star-like rise, as great in fame as she was" - *Henry VIII*, 5.4.17-19, 43-46; Cranmer, of the infant Princess Elizabeth, predicting she will have an heir to her throne; "And on this couple drop a *blessed crown*" - *The Tempest*, 5.1.202; "But what's so *blessed-fair* that fears no blot" - Sonnet 92, line 13

3 WITH THY SWEET FINGERS WHEN THOU GENTLY SWAY'ST
THY SWEET FINGERS = Elizabeth's royal fingers, as she plays; **WHEN THOU GENTLY SWAY'ST** = on the surface level, she merely sways to the music as she plays, as do many keyboard players; possibly also: when you swayed, while playing, as the execution of Essex was delivered; **THOU … SWAY'ST** = ("you govern, you control, you rule, you manipulate" – Booth); "For though usurpers *sway the rule* awhile" – *3 Henry VI*, 3.3.76; "And, Henry, hadst thou *sway'd as kings should do*" – *3 Henry VI*, 2.6.14

4 THE WIRY CONCORD THAT MINE EAR CONFOUNDS
WIRY CONCORD = "harmony produced by plucked wires which (pleasingly) confuses my ear" – Duncan-Jones); "If the true *concord* of well-tuned sounds" – Sonnet 8, line 5; the concord of the royal state; "But for the *concord of my state and time*, had not an ear to hear my true time broke" – *Richard II*, 5.5.47-48; **CONFOUNDS** = stuns, dumbfounds; as Essex was confounded by Cecil, who provoked him into prematurely starting the Rebellion; as Oxford felt confounded (or even destroyed) by the Queen, who at this time was apparently going to execute Southampton as well

5 DO I ENVY THOSE JACKS THAT NIMBLE LEAP
JACKS = upstart courtiers, i.e. Sir Walter Raleigh, who had joined Cecil in opposition to Essex and Southampton; "In fact, Raleigh was never popular, mainly because of his conceit and his greed … His enemies called him 'Jack the Upstart' or 'the Knave,' and he was said to be 'the best hated man of the world'" – Weir, 343-44; a "jack" in harpsichord-like instruments was a piece of wood attached to the key-lever; the jack rose when the key was pressed down; but "Jack" was also "a standard term of abuse for any worthless fellow and for impudent upstarts in particular" – Booth; "But thus his simple truth must be abus'd with silken, sly, insinuating *Jacks*" – *Richard III*, 1.3.52-53; "Since every *Jack* became a gentleman, there's many a gentle person made a *Jack*" – *Richard III*, 1.3.72-73;; "But my time runs posting on in Bolinbroke's proud joy, while I stand fooling here, his *Jack of the clock*" – *Richard II*, 5.5.58-60; **LEAP** = jump up; Raleigh "leaped" over Essex's corpse to further himself; *"When the news was officially announced that the tragedy was over, there was a dead silence in the Privy Chamber, but the Queen continued to play, and the Earl of Oxford, casting a significant glance at Raleigh, observed, as if in reference to the effect of Her Majesty's fingers on the instrument, which was a sort of open spinet,* **'When Jacks start up, then heads go down.'** *Everyone understood the bitter pun contained in this allusion."* - Strickland, 674; citing *Fragmenta Regalia*, Sir Robert Naughton)

6 TO KISS THE TENDER INWARD OF THY HAND
While continuing the image of the virginal key, attached to the jack, depressed by the underside of the player's hand: the idea of Raleigh using any means to "leap" into the monarch's favor, i.e., kneeling at Elizabeth's feet to kiss her outstretched hand; "And so wishing Your Majesty to be Mistress of all that you wish most. *I humbly kiss your fair hands*" – Essex to Queen Elizabeth in 1597, Weir, 430; "To meet you on the way, *and kiss your hand*, when yet you were in place and in account"– Worcester to the King in *1 Henry IV*, 5.1.36-37; **TENDER** = royal; "His tender heir might bear his memory" – Sonnet 1, line 4

7 WHILST MY POOR LIPS, WHICH SHOULD THAT HARVEST REAP
Oxford is saying that he, not Raleigh or others, should have the privilege of kissing Elizabeth's hand and having her favor, i.e., her command to spare Southampton

8 AT THE WOOD'S BOLDNESS BY THEE BLUSHING STAND
Alluding to the boldness of Elizabeth and his own blushing in earlier days; recalling *Venus and Adonis*, the story of his relationship to the Queen and how he, as Adonis, blushed in the face of Venus's bold pursuit of him: "Who *blushed* and pouted in a dull disdain" – line 33

9 TO BE SO TICKLED THEY WOULD CHANGE THEIR STATE
THEIR STATE = "their position in the hierarchy of being" – Booth, citing Ingram and Redpath); referring to the "state" of Southampton as prince or rightful king; and suffering over its loss as a father trying to take on the burdens of the son in order to save him; "And wear their brave *state* out of memory" – Sonnet 15, line 8; "I all alone beweep my outcast *state*/ ... Haply I think on thee, and then my *state*/ ... For thy sweet love rememb'red such wealth brings/ That I scorn to *change my state* with Kings" – Sonnet 29, lines 2, 10, 13-14; "When I have seen such *interchange of state,*/ Or *state* itself confounded to decay" – Sonnet 64, lines 9-10; "I see a *better state* to me belongs" – Sonnet 92, line 7; "If my dear love were but the *child of state*" – Sonnet 124, line 1; "If thou wouldst use the *strength of all thy state*" – Sonnet 96, line 12)

10 AND SITUATION WITH THOSE DANCING CHIPS
Their physical position, but also the very real "situation" Oxford is in, because of Southampton's impending execution; in earlier days Oxford had been the Queen's favorite high-step dancing partner at Court: "My Lord of Oxford is lately grown into great credit, for the Queen's Majesty delighteth more in his personage and his *dancing* and valiantness than any other." – Gilbert Talbot to his father, May 1573, writing as an eye-witness at Court (Ogburn, Jr. 511)

11 O'ER WHOM THY FINGERS WALK WITH GENTLE GAIT
Elizabeth's ruthlessness; her power to execute others; **GENTLE** = royal

12 MAKING DEAD WOOD MORE BLEST THAN LIVING LIPS
Making the dead wood of the virginals more **BLEST**, or royally favored, than Oxford's lips, with which he has been pleading for Southampton's life; **DEAD** = echoing the death of Essex today and the anticipated execution of Southampton.

13 SINCE SAUCY JACKS SO HAPPY ARE IN THIS
Since Jacks like Raleigh are so fortunate in royal favors received; **SAUCY** = impudent, insolent

14 GIVE THEM THY FINGERS, ME THY LIPS TO KISS
Give them your fingers, but give me your royal command to spare Southampton.

Part Three

THE DARK LADY: ELIZABETH

SOUTHAMPTON AWAITS EXECUTION

Sonnet 129
A Waste of Shame
February – March 1601

Oxford writes bitterly to Elizabeth, fearing that she will order the execution of Southampton, as she did of Essex. Undoubtedly he never delivered any of these private verses to her (although he may well have said as much to her in person); instead, the twenty-six sonnets of the Dark Lady series act to counter-balance the opening twenty-six sonnets, within the structure of the Monument; and form another part of the historical record that Oxford intends to leave behind him. Here he gives vent to his anger and frustration, bordering on madness, the way Hamlet turns upon both Ophelia and Gertrude, who are respectively modeled upon his late first wife, Anne Cecil, and his sovereign mistress, Queen Elizabeth.

Sonnet 129	Translation
Th'expense of Spirit in a waste of shame	The loss of royal blood by his disgrace
Is lust in action, and till action, lust	Is your treason; and till execution, treason
Is perjured, murdrous, bloody, full of blame,	Is false, murderous, bloody, full of blame,
Savage, extreme, rude, cruel, not to trust,	Savage, extreme, rude, cruel, false,
Enjoyed no sooner but despised straight,	At your pleasure quick but quickly hated,
Past reason hunted, and no sooner had,	Past sanity to be had, and no sooner done,
Past reason hated as a swallowed bait,	Past sanity hated for being led into a trap,
On purpose laid to make the taker mad.	Purposively set to make the trapped angry.
Mad in pursuit and in possession so,	Insane to execute him, and having done so,
Had, having, and in quest to have, extreme,	Had him, having him, wanting him, extreme,
A bliss in proof, and proved, a very woe,	A royal joy proved, but then your sorrow:
Before, a joy proposed, behind, a dream.	Before he was wanted, now he is nothing.
All this the world well knows, yet none knows well,	England understands this, but no one knows
To shun the heaven that leads men to this hell.	To shun you, the Queen, who does this evil.

1 TH'EXPENSE OF SPIRIT IN A WASTE OF SHAME

TH'EXPENSE = the waste of blood that created a royal son; the primary sense of this Sonnet is Oxford's regret (at the present time) that Henry Wriothesley was ever conceived. The initial "expense of spirit" that created him was, in retrospect, nothing more than animal lust. The sonnet also applies to Henry Wriothesley's current predicament with almost equal force; that is, the "expense of spirit" is Elizabeth's scheduled execution of her own son, i.e., the spillage of Southampton's blood that he inherited from her; deprivation of his royal claim; and since these sonnets are themselves filled with Southampton's royal blood, Oxford wrote: "So all my best is dressing old words new,/ *Spending* again what is already *spent*" – Sonnet 76, lines 11-12, and "Fair, kind, and true, varying to other words,/ And in this change is my invention *spent*"; "In gentle numbers time so idly *spent*" – Sonnet 100, line 6; **SPIRIT** = the seed of inherited blood; sacred royal blood; "The *spirit of love*" – Sonnet 56, line 8, with *love* = royal blood; "Is it *thy spirit* that thou send'st from thee" – Sonnet 61, line 5; "My *spirit* is *thine*, the better part of me" – Sonnet 74, line 8; "vital power …

vivacity, mettle, fire, courage ... temper, disposition, sentiments ... mental power, vigor of intellect ... that which pervades and tempers the whole mind, or the whole state and nature of a thing ... mind, soul ... a human being, a person with respect to his kind or sphere of activity ... any supernatural being, an angel, a ghost, a demon" – Schmidt; "now *my spirit is going*; I can no more" – *Antony and Cleopatra*, 4.15.58; "holding the *eternal spirit*, against her will, in the vile prison of afflicted breath" – *King John*, 3.4.18; "I come to visit the *afflicted spirits here in the prison*" – *Measure for Measure*, 2.3.3-4; **EXPENSE OF SPIRIT** = the expected execution of Southampton, whose "spirit" is also his life force; "Knowing a *better spirit* doth use your name" – Sonnet 80, line 2, referring to the "Shakespeare" pen name; "To every hymn that able *spirit* affords" – Sonnet 85, line 7; "Was it his *spirit*, by *spirits* taught to write/ Above a mortal pitch, that struck me dead?" – Sonnet 86, lines 5-6; "What's in the brain that ink may character,/ Which hath not figured to thee *my true spirit*?" – Sonnet 108, lines 1-2; "Two loves I have of comfort and despair,/ Which like *two spirits* do suggest me still;/ The *better angel* is a man right fair,/ The *worser spirit* a woman colored ill" – Sonnet 144, lines 1-4, Oxford's two spirits being Southampton and Elizabeth, who is "colored ill" by her own dark viewpoint of her son; Essex in 1597 wrote to Elizabeth and called her "Spirit of spirits" – Weir, 427; "That codding *spirit* had they from their mother" – *Titus Andronicus*, 5.1.99; **WASTE OF SHAME** = a disgraceful waste; ("But *beauty's waste* hath in the world an end" – Sonnet 9, line 11; "That thou among *the wastes of time* must go" – Sonnet 12, line 10; "Where *wasteful time* debateth with decay" – Sonnet 15, line 11; "And with old woes new wail *my dear time's waste*" – Sonnet 30, line 4; "how *thy precious minutes waste*" – Sonnet 77, line 2; "Give my love fame *faster than time wastes life*" – Sonnet 100, line 13; and after the death of Elizabeth, marked by Sonnet 105, when Southampton fails to succeed her on the throne: "When in the Chronicle of *wasted time*" – Sonnet 106, line 1; **SHAME** = disgrace, recalling Elizabeth's "*bastard shame*" of Sonnet 127, line 4; "For I am *shamed* by that which I bring forth" – Sonnet 72, line 13

2 IS LUST IN ACTION, AND TILL ACTION, LUST
LUST = crime against nature; viewing the act of sexual intercourse (between Oxford and Elizabeth, to create a royal heir) as a crime (they may have been secretly betrothed, as good as a marriage; otherwise, if they weren't legally married at the time, it would have been an actual crime anyway, i.e., fornication); echoing the story of *The Rape of Lucrece*; **ACTION** = royal action, as in an Act of government by decree; a legal term for "the taking of legal steps to establish a claim or obtain remedy" - OED; "How with this rage shall beauty [royal Tudor blood] hold a plea,/ Whose action is no stronger than a flower?" - Sonnet 65.3-4

3 IS PERJURED, MURD'ROUS, BLOODY, FULL OF BLAME,
PERJURED = false; promise broken; "more perjured eye,/ To swear against the truth so foul a lie!" – Sonnet 152, lines 13-14, Oxford's final words to Elizabeth; **MURD'ROUS** = the execution of Southampton would be his murder; **BLOODY** = anticipating Southampton's execution, when the blood will rush out as his head is severed; also the spillage and waste of royal blood; "*his spirits* fly out into my story ... even then *the princely blood* flows in his cheeks" – *Cymbeline*, 3.3.90-93; **FULL OF BLAME** = putting all the blame on Southampton; echoing his "blame" for helping to lead the Rebellion; but Queen Elizabeth would be the one full of blame, for ordering his execution

4 SAVAGE, EXTREME, RUDE, CRUEL, NOT TO TRUST,
SAVAGE = against all civilized law; **EXTREME** = more than is justified; **RUDE** = despicable; **NOT TO TRUST** = a breaking of Elizabeth's vows or sacred trust

5 ENJOYED NO SOONER BUT DESPISED STRAIGHT,
Not enjoyed long enough, then despised almost immediately afterward.

6 PAST REASON HUNTED, AND NO SOONER HAD,
PAST REASON HUNTED = beyond any rationality to be discovered

7 PAST REASON HATED AS A SWALLOWED BAIT,
PAST REASON HATED = beyond any rationality to be deprived of "love" or royal blood by its opposite or by "hate"; **SWALLOWED BAIT** = Southampton as caught on a hook by Elizabeth's deceit, i.e., by her having given birth to him and having led him to believe he would succeed her

8 **ON PURPOSE LAID TO MAKE THE TAKER MAD;**
A trap laid on purpose, to make Oxford and Southampton nearly insane; "By adding one thing to my *purpose* nothing" – Sonnet 20, line 12; "a *purposed* overthrow" – Sonnet 90, line 8; **MAD** = "disordered in the mind, insane ... beside oneself, having lost all self-command" – Schmidt; "If I were *mad*, I should forget my son, or *madly* think a babe of clouts were he" – *King John*, 3.3.57-58; "For if I should despair I should grow *mad*,/ And in my *madness* might speak ill of thee./ Now this ill-wresting world is grown so bad,/ *Mad* slanderers by *mad* ears believed be" – Sonnet 140, line 9

9 **MAD IN PURSUIT, AND IN POSSESSION SO,**
Nearly insane in pursuit of Elizabeth's acknowledgment of Southampton's royal blood, and "even," or in the same way, delirious in his possession of her blood; **MAD** = (Q has "Made," which may be the intended word, echoing "created" by birth – an echo of "make" in the previous line); "If Hamlet from himself be ta'en away, and when he's not himself does wrong Laertes, then Hamlet does it not, Hamlet denies it. Who does it then? His *madness*. If't be so, Hamlet is of the faction that is wrong'd; his *madness* is poor Hamlet's enemy" – *Hamlet*, 5.2.233-238; "Past cure I am, now reason is past care,/ And frantic *mad* with ever-more unrest,/ My thoughts and my discourse as *madmen's* are,/ At random from the truth vainly expressed" – Sonnet 147, lines 9-12; **PURSUIT** = "In *pursuit* of the thing she would have stay" – Sonnet 143, line 4

10 **HAD, HAVING, AND IN QUEST TO HAVE, EXTREME,**
HAD = having been born, as one "had" a child; (But out alack, he was but one hour mine" – Sonnet 33, line 11); a portrait of Oxford's near-madness in pursuit of the acknowledgment of Southampton's blood right, which was "had" but then lost; **QUEST** = as a noun, it means "jury" at a trial; **EXTREME** = (repeated from line 4, where Duncan-Jones suggests "intense, excessive (in desire), possibly with shades of 'severe, harsh'"; "Perplexed in the extreme" – *Othello*, 5.2.346

11 **A BLISS IN PROOF AND PROVED A VERY WOE,**
A BLISS IN PROOF. = happy in its proof, but resulting in suffering; **AND PROVED** = echoing the supposed proofs or proving of treason offered at the trial; (Q has "and proud and very wo"); **VERY** = Ver = Edward de Vere; **VERY WOE** = my own deep sorrow; ("And weep afresh love's long since cancelled *woe*/ ... And heavily from *woe* to *woe* tell o'er/ The sad account of fore-bemoaned moan"
– Sonnet 30, lines 7, 10-11

12 **BEFORE A JOY PROPOSED BEHIND A DREAM.**
BEFORE A JOY PROPOSED = (usually emended by commas: "Before, a joy proposed, behind, a dream," but Q has no internal punctuation); in former times, our royal son had been joyfully proposed as heir to the throne; the marriage proposal of Sonnets 1-17 was for that purpose to be realized; "Sweets with sweets war not, *joy delights in joy*" – Sonnet 8, line 2; **BEHIND A DREAM** = now, in retrospect, it has all been a dream; "Thus I have had thee *as a dream doth flatter*:/ In sleep a King, but waking no much matter"
– Sonnet 87, lines 13-14

13 **ALL THIS THE WORLD WELL KNOWS YET NONE KNOWS WELL**
ALL = Southampton, *One for All, All for One*; **ALL THIS, etc.** = everyone knows about his disgrace as a traitor in prison, but no one knows the whole truth; **THE WORLD** = England; "Thou that art now *the world's fresh ornament*" – Sonnet 1, line 9; "Pity *the world*, or else this glutton be,/ To eat *the world's due*, by the grave and thee" – Sonnet 1, lines 13-14; "*The world* will wail thee like a makeless wife,/ *The world* will be thy widow and still weep" – Sonnet 9, lines 4-5; "Your name from hence immortal life shall have,/ Though I, once gone, to *all the world* must die/ ... And tongues to be your being shall rehearse,/ When *all the breathers of this world* are dead" – Sonnet 81, lines 11-12; **NONE** = opposite of "one" for Southampton

14 **TO SHUN THE HEAVEN THAT LEADS MEN TO THIS HELL.**
None knows well enough to shun the "heaven" or Queen Elizabeth, who leads men (Oxford and Southampton) to this agony; "Y' passed *a hell of Time*" – Oxford to Southampton, Sonnet 120, line 6; "The ornament of beauty is suspect,/ A crow that flies in heaven's sweetest air" – Sonnet 70, lines 3-4

THE MONUMENT

THE DARK LADY: ELIZABETH

SOUTHAMPTON AWAITS EXECUTION

Sonnet 130
My Mistress' Eyes
March 1601

Oxford records his fury at Elizabeth for determining to execute Southampton, their royal son. He declares that the eyes of his sovereign Mistress are nothing like "the Sunne," recalling his account in Sonnet 33 of Southampton's birth: "Even so my Sunne one early morn did shine." Oxford proceeds to slander Elizabeth with one bitter attack after another. He alludes to the aging skin of her breasts, to the black wires of her wigs and to her bad breath. He criticizes the sound of her voice and he concludes by declaring that, in his view, the Queen is not really a goddess, and never was.

Sonnet 130	Translation
My Mistress' eyes are nothing like the Sunne	My Queen's eyes are not like her son's;
Coral is far more red than her lips' red.	Even coral is more royal than her lips.
If snow be white, why then her breasts are dun:	If snow is white, her breasts are dull gray:
If hairs be wires, black wires grow on her head:	If heirs are wires, she has disgraced heirs.
I have seen Roses damasked, red and white,	I have seen Tudor Roses red and white,
But no such Roses see I in her cheeks,	But none such do I see in her Tudor Rose,
And in some perfumes is there more delight	And in some blood there is more joy
Than in the breath that from my Mistress reeks.	Than in the slander that my Queen speaks.
I love to hear her speak, yet well I know	I love and serve her will, but I know well
That Music hath a far more pleasing sound:	That royal harmony is far better.
I grant I never saw a goddess go.	I now say I never saw her as a goddess.
My Mistress when she walks treads on the ground,	My Queen walks only on the earth.
And yet by heaven I think my love as rare	And yet by her my royal son is as royal
As any she belied with false compare.	As any with whom she falsely compares him.

The Hekatompathia or Passionate Century of Love, published in 1582, was attributed to Thomas Watson, who dedicated it to Edward de Vere, Earl of Oxford. No. VII of the 100 numbered poems of *Passionate Century* was undoubtedly written by Oxford to pay homage to Queen Elizabeth, his sovereign mistress; this verse (Sonnet 130) turns that one inside out in bitter rage against her. (The poem is reprinted below after line 14.)

1 MY MISTRESS' EYES ARE NOTHING LIKE THE SUNNE,
MY MISTRESS' EYES = the all-powerful, imperial eyes of Elizabeth, my sovereign Mistress; "But at *my mistress' eye* love's brand new-fired/ … *my mistress's eye*" – Sonnet 153, lines 9, 14

"The Queen's Majesty *our mistress*" - Oxford to Burghley, September 1572

"I cannot but find a great grief in myself to remember *the mistress* which we have lost"
- Oxford to Robert Cecil, April 25/27, 1603

686

NOTHING LIKE THE SUNNE = nothing like my royal son; nothing like the royal eye, that sunne, of my royal son; ("Even so *my Sunne* one early morn did shine" – Sonnet 33, line 9); nothing like the golden, kingly eye of the rising son or royal prince; Elizabeth's eyes reflect none of this royalty; "But from *thine eyes* my knowledge I derive,/ And, *constant stars*, in them I read such art" – Sonnet 14, lines 9-10, to Southampton; "And scarcely greet me with *that sunne thine eye*" – Sonnet 49, line 6; **NOTHING** = "none" or the opposite of "one" for Southampton

2 CORAL IS FAR MORE RED THAN HER LIPS' RED;
CORAL, etc. = a light yellowish red; **RED** = scarlet, royal; Tudor Rose; in other words, the lesser red of coral is more red than Elizabeth's lips, a stunning insult to the monarch

3 IF SNOW BE WHITE, WHY THEN HER BREASTS ARE DUN:
An even worse insult: compared to white snow, Elizabeth's breasts are dull gray-brown.

4 IF HAIRS BE WIRES, BLACK WIRES GROW ON HER HEAD:
IF HAIRS, etc. = if hairs were black wires, Elizabeth's hair would be such; the wigs she wore were held in place by wires; **HAIRS** = heirs, i.e., her royal heir, turned black by her "cloud" or negative view; if Elizabeth's royal heir was a wire, then it's a "black" or disgraced heir growing; **GROW** = their son is still growing, in life and in the womb of these sonnets

5 I HAVE SEEN ROSES DAMASKED, RED AND WHITE,
DAMASKED = patterned, dappled; **ROSES DAMASKED, RED AND WHITE** = Elizabeth's Tudor Rose, joining the red and white roses (as damask or pink) under the roof of the House of Tudor; ("With this *there is a red,/ Exceeds the damask rose*" – Oxford poem, signed E. O. in *The Phoenix Nest*, 1593; "The *red rose and the white* are on his face, the fatal colors of our striving houses; the one his purple blood right well resembles, the other his pale *cheeks*, methinks, presenteth" – *3 Henry VI*, 2.5.97-100)

6 BUT NO SUCH ROSES SEE I IN HER CHEEKS
A treasonous statement that Elizabeth no longer displays any of the Tudor Rose royalty that she inherited from her grandfather Henry VII and her father Henry VIII; ("From fairest creatures we desire increase,/ That *thereby beauty's Rose might never die*" – Sonnet 1, lines 1-2; "Why should poor beauty indirectly seek/ *Roses of shadow, since his Rose is true*" – Sonnet 67, lines 7-8); "Thus is his *cheek* the map of days outworn,/ When beauty lived and died as flowers do now,/ Before these bastard signs of fair were borne" – Sonnet 68, lines 1-3

7 AND IN SOME PERFUMES IS THERE MORE DELIGHT
Setting up the next insult, albeit with a carefully qualifying "some" – but not all – perfumes

8 THAN IN THE BREATH THAT FROM MY MISTRESS REEKS
Than in Elizabeth's breath, which literally reeked because of her bad teeth and gums; ("She aged quickly and was a sad figure during her sixties. Her teeth became black from eating sugar and her breath was notorious" – Dickinson, p. 125)

9 I LOVE TO HEAR HER SPEAK, YET WELL I KNOW
A true statement from Oxford, but setting up another insult in the next line

10 THAT MUSIC HATH A FAR MORE PLEASING SOUND:
That music is far more pleasant than her speaking voice; (one accusation against Oxford in 1580-81, by his erstwhile Catholic friends, was that he had said he despised Elizabeth's singing voice)

11 I GRANT I NEVER SAW A GODDESS GO;
I never saw a goddess when I saw Elizabeth, who was "the goddess of Love and Beauty," etc; ("The *guilty goddess* of my harmful deeds" – Sonnet 111, line 2); "Continue to please the goddess" – Francis Davison,

referring to Queen Elizabeth in his one-page broadside *Anagrammata* of 1603; **GO** = walk, as in her walks in the palace garden, which she often had taken with Oxford, i.e., Elizabeth is not the goddess that she pretends to be

12 MY MISTRESS WHEN SHE WALKS TREADS ON THE GROUND
When my sovereign Mistress, Elizabeth, takes her walks, she does not fly on a chariot like Venus, but is mortal; she is no goddess, like Venus or Diana, after all

13 AND YET BY HEAVEN I THINK MY LOVE AS RARE
BY HEAVEN = created by Elizabeth, who gave birth to Oxford's "love" or royal son; **MY LOVE**, i.e., my royal son; **I THINK MY LOVE AS RARE** = I think my royal son is as royal; ("Beauty, Truth and *Rarity*" – *The Phoenix and the Turtle*, 1601, signifying Elizabeth, Oxford and Southampton); **RARE** = royal, as in "fair"; "Beauty, Truth and *Rarity*,/Grace in all simplicity,/ Here enclosed in cinders lie" – *The Phoenix and Turtle*, 1601

14 AS ANY SHE BELIED WITH FALSE COMPARE.
As any "she" (Elizabeth) who is falsely or erroneously compared with him; in other words, she cannot be likened to him; any such comparison is false; **SHE** = ("Lady, you are the cruelest *she* alive if you will lead these graces to the grave" – *Twelfth Night*, 1.5.235-236); **BELIED** = full of lies; to be misrepresented by lies; "That I may not be so, nor *thou belied*,/ Bear thine eyes straight, though thy proud heart go wide" – Sonnet 140, lines 13-14; "Such signs of truth in his plain face she spied,/ That she concludes the picture was belied" – *Lucrece*, 1532-1533; **COMPARE** = "Authorizing thy trespass *with compare*" – Sonnet 35, line 6, i.e., sanctioning your treason by showing comparable crimes in my plays, such as *Richard II*, about the deposition of a monarch, which you (Southampton) caused to be performed to help ignite the Rebellion

No. VII

The Passionate Century of Love

1582

This is the seventh of the 100 consecutively numbered poems of *The Hekatompathia or Passionate Century of Love*, published in 1582, undoubtedly written by Edward deVere in honor of his sovereign mistress, Queen Elizabeth. Sonnet 130 now turns the homage into an angry slander against her. Below is the 1582 poem in modernized English, with some of the contrasting lines of Sonnet 130 indicated.

VII.	Sonnet 130
Hark you that list to hear what saint I serve:	
Her yellow locks exceed the beaten gold;	line 4
Her sparking eyes in heav'n a place desereve;	line 1
Her forehead high and fair of comely mold;	
Her words are music all of silver sound;	line 10
Her wit so sharp as like can scarce be found;	

No. 130

Each eyebrow hangs like *Iris* in the skies;

Her *Eagle's* nose is straight of stately frame;

On either cheek a *Rose* and *Lily* lies;   lines 5-6

Her breath is sweet perfume, or holy flame;   line 8

Her lips more red than any *Coral* stone;   line 2

Her neck more white, than aged *Swans* that moan;   line 3

Her breast transparent is, like *Christall* [Crystal] rock;   line 3

Her fingers long, fit for *Apollo's* Lute;

Her slipper such as *Momus* dare not mock;

Her virtues all so great as make me mute:

What other parts she hath I need not say,

Whose face alone is cause of my decay.

THE MONUMENT

THE DARK LADY: ELIZABETH

SOUTHAMPTON AWAITS EXECUTION

Sonnet 131
A Thousand Groans
March 1601

Oxford writes in fury against Elizabeth's pending decision to execute their royal son. He pictures them both emitting "a thousand groans" and weeping "on one another's neck" as they bear "witness" to the beheading of Southampton. He tells the Queen that her real disgrace, as opposed to any other, will come from this decision.

Sonnet 131	Translation
Thou art as tyrannous, so as thou art,	You are so cruel that you are just like
As those whose beauties proudly make them cruel;	Other Tudors whose blood make them cruel;
For well thou know'st to my dear doting heart,	For you know well that in my loyal heart,
Thou art the fairest and most precious Jewel.	You are the most royal Queen of England.
Yet in good faith some say that thee behold	Yet to tell the truth, some who see you say
Thy face hath not the power to make love groan;	You do not have power to make him suffer;
To say their err, I dare not be so bold,	I dare not say publicly that they are wrong,
Although I swear it to my self alone.	Although privately I say so.
And to be sure that is not false I swear	And to assure myself of truth I swear
A thousand groans but thinking on thy face,	I see a thousand groans on your face,
One on another's neck do witness bear	As we weep together at the execution of
Thy black is fairest in my judgment's place.	Your disgraced son, whom I judge most royal.
In nothing art thou black save in thy deeds,	You are disgraced by nothing but your action,
And thence this slander as I think proceeds.	And this disgrace will come if you proceed.

1 THOU ART AS TYRANNOUS, SO AS THOU ART,
THOU = Elizabeth; **TYRANNOUS** = related to the tyranny of her mortal life, but also to her tyranny over her son by refusing to acknowledge him and, now, by refusing to help him as he faces execution; (it is admittedly audacious for him to use this word about her while she is still alive, as he does in Sonnet 107, line 14 ["When *tyrants'* crests and tombs of brass are spent"], referring to Elizabeth after her death; but these verses are not for contemporary publication, and, besides, the special language would enable him to deny he was writing about the monarch); "this *bloody tyrant time*" – Sonnet 16, line 2, referring to the ever-dwindling life span of the Queen; "We are no *tyrant* but a Christian king, unto whose grace our passion is as subject as are our wretches fettered in our prisons" – the King in *Henry V*, 1.2.241-243

2 AS THOSE WHOSE BEAUTIES PROUDLY MAKE THEM CRUEL;
BEAUTIES = royal Tudor blood; "Save her alone, *who yet on th'earth doth reign,*/ Whose *beauties* string, no god can well disdain" - Oxford poem in *Paradise of Dainty Devices*, 1576; "with its reference to "her alone, who yet on th'earth doeth reigne," (it) may well concern his relationship with the Queen" – Steven W. May, *Studies in Philology*, 1980, p. 13; **PROUDLY** = royally, with sovereign power; **CRUEL** = the opposite

690

of the portrait of a good ruler described in Sonnet 94: "They that have *power to hurt, and will do none*" – line 1.

3 FOR WELL THOU KNOW'ST TO MY DEAR DOTING HEART
MY DEAR DOTING HEART = Oxford as doting father of a prince; ("That I, the son of a *dear* father murdered" – *Hamlet*, 2.2.585; ("Till nature as she wrought thee fell *a-doting*" – Sonnet 20, line 10, of Elizabeth, as she gave birth to Southampton)

4 THOU ART THE FAIREST AND MOST PRECIOUS JEWEL
FAIREST = most royal, as Queen of England; Southampton is "fair" in reflection of his mother, who was "the *fairest votary*" of Sonnet 154, line 5, in 1574; **MOST PRECIOUS** = most royal; **JEWEL** = royal Prince or Queen of England (as Southampton in the Tower is "like *a jewel* hung in ghastly night" in Sonnet 27, line 11; and as he is depicted in "As on the finger of a throne Queen,/ The *basest Jewel* will be well esteemed" – Sonnet 96, lines 5-6)

5 YET IN GOOD FAITH SOME SAY THAT THEE BEHOLD
Yet, speaking honestly, some who behold you say

6 THY FACE HATH NOT THE POWER TO MAKE LOVE GROAN;
THY FACE = that your face, i.e., that you; **HATH NOT THE POWER TO MAKE LOVE GROAN** = do not have the royal power to destroy "love" or royal blood, i.e., to execute Southampton and cause a great "groan" at his funeral; (i.e., others say that only Robert Cecil has this power; also, this is a terrible insult to the Queen, stating flatly (on the surface) that she has now lost the love of her subjects by having executed Essex, not to mention the insult to Elizabeth's vanity; i.e., she is no longer the seductive Venus; her much-touted beauty is false); **GROAN** = "The blood of English shall manure the ground, and future ages groan for this foul act" – *Richard II*, 4.1.137-138)

7 TO SAY THEY ERR I DARE NOT BE SO BOLD,
Oxford will not argue against those who say these things

8 ALTHOUGH I SWEAR IT TO MYSELF ALONE.
Although I accuse you of these things in private, while trying to defend you to myself; **ALONE** = the "all" and "one" of Southampton's motto *One for All, All for One*, indicating he is the central subject matter

9 AND TO BE SURE THAT IS NOT FALSE I SWEAR
And to support myself against their false charges I vow

10 A THOUSAND GROANS BUT THINKING ON THY FACE,
That, thinking of your face at your son's funeral, I envision that you will utter a thousand groans over his dead body; ("Go count the ways with sighs; I mine with groans ... twice for one step I'll groan, the way being short, and piece the way out with a heavy heart" – *Richard II*, 5.2.89,91-92)

11 ON ONE ANOTHER'S NECK DO WITNESS BEAR
We will weep together, crying on each other's neck, when we witness his funeral; **NECK** = echoing the fact that Southampton's head will be severed; **BEAR** = bear witness, but echoing Elizabeth's giving birth to her son; ("an image of vaguely personified groans weeping on one another's shoulders" – Booth)

12 THY BLACK IS FAIREST IN MY JUDGMENT'S PLACE.
In my personal court of judgment, rather than in the court where the trial was held, our son (whom you have turned to "black" with disgrace) is still the "fairest" or most royal prince of England; **THY BLACK** = your disgraced son; **IS FAIREST** = is most royal; "From *fairest creatures* we desire increase,/ That thereby *beauty's Rose* might never die" – Sonnet 1, lines 1-2; **IN MY JUDGMENT'S PLACE** = ("in my personal court of justice" – Booth, citing Willen and Reed, who call attention to the courtroom metaphor generated by the context of "swear" and "witness"); "the *place of judgment*; suggests an allusion to a condemned person

being hanged" – Duncan-Jones); seat of justice, echoing the royal seat or throne; also suggesting the Tower as "the place"; and after the bargain for the reduction of Southampton's crime to "misprision" of treason is made, Oxford will write to his son: "So thy great gift, upon misprision growing,/ Comes home again, on better *judgment* making" – Sonnet 87, lines 11-12; "So, till the *judgment* that yourself arise,/ You live in this, and dwell in lovers' eyes" – Sonnet 55, lines 13-14

13 IN NOTHING ART THOU BLACK SAVE IN THY DEEDS,
NOTHING = "none" as the opposite of "one" for Southampton; **IN NOTHING ART THOU BLACK SAVE IN THY DEEDS** = you are black only because of your actions as Queen of England (and not because of the color of your eyes, hair or complexion; "The cause is right, the King is just, and I do not doubt but your lordships both mine honorable friends according to your words I shall find you *in deeds*." - Oxford to Cecil, June 12, 1603; Oxford is turning the tables on her; i.e., it was Southampton's *deeds* (the Rebellion) that got him into this predicament, for which Oxford will pay "ransom" with his own identity: "Ah, but those tears are pearl which thy love sheeds,/ And they are rich, and *ransom all ill deeds*" – Sonnet 34, lines 13-14; but now it is the Queen's own *deeds* that are at fault if she proceeds with the death sentence against him

14 AND THENCE THIS SLANDER AS I THINK PROCEEDS.
THIS SLANDER = this disgrace of your son and of your own royal blood in him; ("And Beauty *slandered* with a bastard shame" – Sonnet 127, line 4; "For *slander's mark* was ever yet the fair;/ The ornament of beauty is *suspect* (a suspect-traitor),/ A Crow that flies in *heaven's sweetest air*" – Sonnet 70, lines 2-4);
PROCEEDS = issues from your royal decree, from your imperial dark viewpoint; and issued from you in childbirth as in "That *every word* doth almost tell my name,/ Showing *their birth, and where they did proceed*" of Sonnet 76, line 8; ("a single graceful razor stroke ... she has been cut apart" – Booth; i.e., Oxford turns the tables and figuratively executes Elizabeth); "Man shall not live by bread only, but by *every word* that *proceedeth* out of the mouth of God" – Gospel of Mathew, 4.4

Part Three

THE DARK LADY: ELIZABETH

SOUTHAMPTON AWAITS EXECUTION

Sonnet 132
Beauty Herself Is Black
March 1601

Oxford records Elizabeth's mourning for her son. She is filled with pain over having to decide whether to order Southampton's execution. Her eyes are "black" with mourning, as though she were attending the funeral of her son after having executed him. Ironically, this potential for extending her royal mercy is what most becomes her. The second quatrain reflects Oxford's recollection of their royal son's birth in Sonnet 33, with its reference to the "Sun of Heaven" (son of Elizabeth); and its reference to the "West" reflects Southampton as "the little western flower" of A Midsummer Night's Dream. *Oxford turns the tables on her Majesty by stating that "beauty" (her royal blood bequeathed to Southampton) is now "black" (disgraced) because of her.*

Sonnet 132	Translation
Thine eyes I love, and they as pitying me,	I serve your royal eyes, and they (as if to pity me,
Knowing thy heart torment me with disdain,	Knowing that you torment me with disgrace)
Have put on black, and loving mourners be,	Are seeing with disgrace, as at our son's funeral,
Looking with pretty ruth upon my pain.	Looking with royal show upon my suffering.
And truly not the morning Sun of Heaven	And right now the royal son of Elizabeth
Better becomes the gray cheeks of th'East,	Is not more royal than the gray sky,
Nor that full Starre that ushers in the Ev'n	And neither does his royal eye or star
Doth half that glory to the sober West	Afford half as much glory to the west
As those two mourning eyes become thy face:	As your mourning eyes become your face:
O let it then as well beseem thy heart	O then let it equally suit your royal heart
To mourn for me, since mourning doth thee grace,	To mourn for me, since that is your royal way,
And suit thy pity like in every part.	And let every part of you show pity for me!
Then I will swear beauty herself is black,	Then I will swear Elizabeth herself is disgraced,
And all they foul that thy complexion lack.	And that those not disgraced are the ones stained!

1 THINE EYES I LOVE, AND THEY AS PITYING ME,
THINE EYES = spoken to Elizabeth; your eyes, reflecting your royal blood; **I LOVE** = I serve; I love the sacred royalty they reflect; "Thou dost love her, because thou know'st I love her" – Sonnet 42, line 6, to Southampton; **AND THEY**, etc. = and the way they seem to reflect your pity for me (and therefore your pity for our son); "But at *my mistress' eye* love's brand new-fired" – Sonnet 153, line 9; "*My Mistress' eyes* are nothing like the Sunne" – Sonnet 130, line 1;

2 KNOWING THY HEART TORMENT ME WITH DISDAIN,
Knowing they reflect your awareness that you are tormenting me with your disdain for our royal son, whom

REFERENCE EDITION 693

you may soon execute; "O absence, what a *torment*" – Sonnet 39, line 9; **THY HEART** = the source of your royal Tudor Rose blood, i.e., the source of the "beauty" that your son has inherited; also your sovereign attitude or viewpoint, leading to your decision

3 HAVE PUT ON BLACK, AND LOVING MOURNERS BE
HAVE PUT ON BLACK = your eyes reflect this disgrace; **AND LOVING MOURNERS BE** = and they are now the loving "black" eyes of a mother mourning her son's death at his funeral; "Yet so they mourn, becoming of their woe" – Sonnet 127, line 13

4 LOOKING WITH PRETTY RUTH UPON MY PAIN.
PRETTY = royal; **PRETTY RUTH** = royal pity; "Those *pretty* wrongs that liberty commits" – Sonnet 41, line 1, to Southampton; **MY PAIN** = my suffering, which reflects our son's disgrace and suffering in prison; "The *pain* be mine, but thine shall be the praise" – Sonnet 38, line 14

5 AND TRULY NOT THE MORNING SUN OF HEAVEN
TRULY = Oxford, *Nothing Truer than Truth*; **MORNING SUN** = the rising son, his royal eye; "Full glorious *morning* have I seen/ Flatter the mountain tops with *sovereign eye*/ ... Even so *my Sunne* one early *morn* did shine/ With all triumphant splendor on my brow" – Sonnet 33, lines 1-2, 9-10; **MORNING** = a play on "mourning" as if to say "the *mourning* son of Elizabeth"; **THE MORNING SUN OF HEAVEN** = the rising royal son of Elizabeth, who is Heaven; "*Suns of the world* may stain, when *heaven's sun* staineth" – Sonnet 33, line 14

> Yet herein will I imitate the sun,
> Who doth permit the base contagious clouds
> To smother up his beauty from the world
> – Prince Hal, *1 Henry IV*, 1.3.192-194

> "Shall the blessed **sun of heaven** prove a micher, and eat blackberries? A question not to be asked. Shall the **son of England** prove a thief, and take purses?"
> – *1 Henry IV*, 2.4.403-405, Falstaff referring to Prince Hal as future king

6 BETTER BECOMES THE GRAY CHEEKS OF THE EAST,
Is more becoming to; makes more royal; **GRAY CHEEKS** = the grayness in the eastern sky just before dawn, when the sun will lend its light and color; ("Thus is *his cheek the map of days outworn*" – Sonnet 68, line 1); "the metaphor clearly presents the sun as a cosmetically desirable means of returning 'the roses' to pallid cheeks" – Booth; i.e., it is the royal son of Elizabeth who can return/restore/continue the Tudor Rose lineage that is now being drained from her.

7 NOR THAT FULL STAR THAT USHERS IN THE EV'N
FULL STAR = that star, filled with your royal blood, that is our royal son's eye; "Till whatsoever *star that guides my moving*" – Sonnet 26, line 9; "*that sun thine eye*" – Sonnet 49, line 6; "*Full* many a glorious morning have I seen/ Flatter the mountaintops with sovereign eye ... Even so my Sunne one early morn did shine"- Sonnet 33, lines 1-2, 9; "It (*love* or the royal blood of their son) is the *star* to every wandering bark/ Whose worth's unknown, although his height be taken" – Sonnet 116, lines 7-8, i.e., Southampton's royal eye reflects his "love" or royal blood through his "sovereign" eye that guides Oxford; **EV'N** = evening (*that full star* = "the planet Venus visible in the western sky just after sunset. Shakespeare may be playing with the fact that Venus is also the morning star. Quatrain 2 presents one half of each of two parallel pairs of opposites: sun-moon and morning star-evening star" – Booth; i.e., joining royal son and his mother, Elizabeth, the Moon goddess)

8 DOTH HALF THAT GLORY TO THE SOBER WEST
GLORY = royal honor; "Crooked eclipses 'gainst *his glory* fight" – Sonnet 60, line 7; **SOBER WEST** = dull-colored western sky; glancing at Elizabeth's progress *to the west* in 1574; "the little *western flower*" of *Midsummer Night's Dream*; "Anon permit the basest clouds to ride/ With ugly rack on his celestial face,/

And from the forlorn world his visage hide,/ *Stealing unseen to west* with this disgrace" – Sonnet 33, lines 5-8; "But when from high-most pitch, with weary car,/ Like feeble age he reeleth from the day" – Sonnet 7, lines 9-10

9 AS THOSE TWO MOURNING EYES BECOME THY FACE:
As your eyes, mourning for our son, become you; i.e., Elizabeth's eyes are most appropriately in mourning for the son she may execute; now with a play on "morning"

10 O LET IT THEN AS WELL BESEEM THY HEART
O = Oxford; ("pleads for her to extend her pity" – Duncan-Jones); i.e., the blackness of her eyes reflects her "bastard shame" of Sonnet 127, line 4, and also reflects her pity for Oxford and Southampton; **AS WELL** = just as suitably; **BESEEM THY HEART** = suit or fit your heart, which is the source of your royal power and mercy

11 TO MOURN FOR ME, SINCE MOURNING DOTH THEE GRACE,
To extend your pity to me, since this pain and suffering over our son's impending execution is what gives you "grace" or royalty; "Above the rest in Court who gave thee *grace*" – Oxford's early sonnet, referring to Elizabeth

12 AND SUIT THY PITY LIKE IN EVERY PART.
EVERY = Ever = Edward de Vere, *Ever or Never*

13 THEN WILL I SWEAR BEAUTY HERSELF IS BLACK,
If you do this, i.e., if you extend your mercy, then I will vow that royal blood itself is black; I will go along with the disgrace, if you save his life; (also turning the tables on "Now is black beauty's successive heir" of Sonnet 127, line 3, referring to Southampton as "black" or disgraced but, nonetheless, still Elizabeth's immediate heir to the throne); then I will swear that Elizabeth herself is black, if her pity results in saving our son's life

14 AND ALL THEY FOUL THAT THY COMPLEXION LACK.
ALL = Southampton, *One for All, All for One*; **AND ALL THEY**, etc. = and that all others who lack this royal mercy are wicked; ("*foul* and *black* meant "ugly" but "both words are also synonyms for 'wicked'" – Booth); in other words, Oxford is attempting to transform Elizabeth's "bastard shame" into its opposite; and if indeed the Queen extends her pity to her son by sparing him from execution, she thereby will retain her glory (in Oxford's view); and meanwhile, all others who lack her mercy are the villains

THE DARK LADY: ELIZABETH

SOUTHAMPTON AWAITS EXECUTION

Sonnet 133
Of Him, My Self, And Thee, I Am Foresaken
March 1601

Oxford fills this sonnet with images of the Tower prison where his "next self" waits: "Prison ... ward (guard) ... bail ... guard ... Jail ... pent." He suffers increasingly as Elizabeth's decision draws near, wondering whether she will give the order for Southampton's execution as she had for Essex. His "groan" is that of the funeral moan for his royal son. This verse alludes to the suffering of Jesus; its number, 133, echoes that of the "resurrection" verse, Sonnet 33, also the age of Jesus upon His death on the Cross. It recalls Sonnet 34: "Th'offender's sorrow lends but weak relief/ To him that bears the strong offence's loss." It also recalls his statement about Elizabeth and Southampton in Sonnet 42: "And both for my sake lay me on this cross."

Sonnet 133	Translation
Beshrew that heart that makes my heart to groan	Curses on your heart that makes mine groan
For that deep wound it gives my friend and me.	Over that suffering you give my son and me.
Is't not enough to torture me alone,	Isn't it enough to torture me alone?
But slave to slavery my sweet'st friend must be?	Must my royal son be tortured, too?
Me from my self thy cruel eye hath taken,	Your cruel eye has taken my self (son) from me
And my next self thou harder hast engrossed.	And treated him even more cruelly.
Of him, my self, and thee, I am forsaken,	I am deprived of him, of myself, of you,
A torment thrice three-fold thus to be crossed:	A three-fold torment as I lay on the cross:
Prison my heart in thy steel bosom's ward,	Make me instead the prisoner of your cold heart,
But then my friend's heart let my poor heart bail,	But permit me to bail out my royal son;
Who ere keeps me, let my heart be his guard,	He keeps me in his heart; let mine be his guard,
Thou canst not then use rigor in my Jail.	And then you can't be cruel to him in my jail.
And yet thou wilt, for I being pent in thee,	And yet you will, because I am in your jail,
Perforce am thine, and all that is in me.	I must be in your prison, and he is in me.

1 BESHREW THAT HEART THAT MAKES MY HEART TO GROAN
BESHREW = "Fie upon" - Booth; curse the cruelty of that cruel heart (Elizabeth's royal heart) that makes my own heart groan in anticipation of our son's death; referring back to "Knowing thy heart torment me with disdain" – Sonnet 132, line 2, preparing for "torment" of line 8 below; **GROAN** = same as "moan" as in "a great moan (was) made for him" – report in *Machyn's Diary* of the funeral for Edward de Vere's father, the 16th Earl of Oxford, on August 31, 1562; ("groaning for burial" – *Julius Caesar*, 3.1.275); **MY HEART** = "my heart" is my son's heart; to Southampton: "Take heed, *dear heart*, of this large privilege" – Sonnet 95, line 13

2 FOR THAT DEEP WOUND IT GIVES MY FRIEND AND ME.

DEEP WOUND = suggesting the wounds of Christ upon the Cross; **MY FRIEND AND ME** = my son and me; "I am good friends with my father" – *1 Henry IV*, 3.3.182; **MY FRIEND** = my son, Southampton; "For precious *friends* hid in death's dateless night" – Sonnet 30, line 6; "But being both from me both to each *friend*" – Sonnet 144, line 11; "And for my sake even so doth she abuse me,/ Suff'ring my friend for my sake to approve her ... But here's the joy, my friend and I are one" - Sonnet 42, lines 7-8, 11

3 IS'T NOT ENOUGH TO TORTURE ME ALONE,
ALONE = the "all" and "one" of Southampton, *One for All, All for One*; **ME ALONE** = Oxford alone, but also both he and Southampton, with whom he equates himself; **IS'T NOT ENOUGH TO TORTURE ME ALONE** = a rhetorical utterance Oxford may have made in person to Elizabeth; alluding to Christ-like suffering; ("And each, though enemies to each other's reign,/ Do in consent shake hands to *torture* me" – Sonnet 28, line 6); echoing his son's imprisonment and the torture (often on the "rack") that was routinely used in Elizabeth prisons, leading us to ask: Was Southampton tortured or threatened with it?

4 BUT SLAVE TO SLAVERY MY SWEET'ST FRIEND MUST BE?
FRIEND = repeated from line 2; Oxford also may have spoken this line directly to Elizabeth: "But must my most royal son also be a slave to your slavery?" **SLAVE** = a servant to the monarch and/or a prisoner; ("a base and contemptible person" – Booth); i.e., Southampton imprisoned and in disgrace; **MY SWEET'ST FRIEND** = my most royal son; "sweet boy" – Sonnet 108, line 5; (a "slave" could mean a "worthless person," the way Southampton was such as an accused traitor)

5 ME FROM MY SELF THY CRUEL EYE HATH TAKEN,
Your cruel royal attitude (or viewpoint or decree) has taken me from my son, who is my own self; **THY CRUEL EYE** = Elizabeth's all-powerful, imperial eye, casting its shadow over her son; ("But found no cure; the bath for my help lies/ Where Cupid got new fire, my mistress' eye" – Sonnet 153, lines 13-14); **TAKEN** = taken from Oxford, the father, and imprisoned; Southampton is "my self" and "my next self":

6 AND MY NEXT SELF THOU HARDER HAST ENGROSSED.
MY NEXT SELF = an extension of the thought, with Southampton now viewed as Oxford's second self; as he writes to his son: "Make thee another self for love of me" – Sonnet 10, line 13; "'Tis *thee, my self*, that for my self I praise" – Sonnet 62, line 13; "the second burden of a former child" – Sonnet 59, line 4); **THOU HARDER HATH ENGROSSED** = you have more severely taken possession of, i.e., of his son; "That she hath thee is of my wailing chief" – Sonnet 42, line 3, also written during this time; **ENGROSSED** = having him in her prison, i.e., the Tower; "taken exclusive possession of" - Booth

7 OF HIM, MY SELF, AND THEE, I AM FORSAKEN,
The royal family of Southampton, Oxford and Elizabeth, echoing the Holy Trinity, as well as Christ on the Cross; i.e., Oxford is suffering, but will sacrifice his own life or identity; echoing "*I am* that *I am*," the words of God to Moses, used in Sonnet 121, line 9

8 A TORMENT THRICE THREEFOLD THUS TO BE CROSSED
A torment suffered by each of the three of us, and also three times again by all three together; **THREEFOLD** = "*Three* themes in one, which wondrous scope affords/ … Which *three*, till now, never kept seat in one" – Sonnet 105, lines 12, 14; "And thou treble-dated crow/ … Beauty, Truth, and Rarity" – *The Phoenix and Turtle*, 1601, lines 17, 53; **CROSSED** = all three suffering on the Cross; "And both for my sake *lay me on this cross*" – Sonnet 42, line 12

9 PRISON MY HEART IN THY STEEL BOSOM'S WARD,
PRISON = imprison (imperative); echoing Tower; **MY HEART IN THY STEEL BOSOM'S WARD** = you have our son in prison, but I ask you to imprison my own heart instead, within the steel gates of your bosom; **STEEL** = cold heart, but steel bars of prison; **WARD** = "prison cell; guard, custody: - Booth

10 BUT THEN MY FRIEND'S HEART LET MY POOR HEART BAIL:
BUT THEN, etc. = after imprisoning me, let me pay for my son's crime by bailing him out of prison; **BAIL** = bail out or redeem; "Justices of the Peace might … have letten to *baile* such persons as were indited of Fel-

onie" – *OED*, from 1581 (cited by Booth); also used as "to confine" or to imprison or to guard; and so, also, let him be confined in my heart instead

11 WHO ERE KEEPS ME, LET MY HEART BE HIS GUARD,
WHO ERE KEEPS ME = whoever holds me in prison; (i.e., Southampton, who is "a God in love, to whom I am confined" – Sonnet 110, line 12); **GUARD** = echoing Southampton's imprisonment; **LET MY HEART BE HIS GUARD** = let me be his jailer; or his jail cell ("keeps" = imprisons, holds captive)

12 THOU CANST NOT THEN USE RIGOR IN MY JAIL.
JAIL = alluding to Southampton's confinement in the Tower; **THOU CANST NOT THEN USE RIGOR IN MY JAIL** = ("Jaile" is capitalized in *Q*); so long as he is in *my* jail, you cannot then execute him as the law requires; (as opposed to *your* jail); **RIGOR** = (spelled this way in *Q*); "strict enforcement of a law" – Booth; harsh, recalling "extreme" of Sonnet 129, lines 4 and 10; "I tell you 'tis rigour and not law" – *The Winter's Tale*, 3.2.112; "Let him have all the rigour of the law" – *2 Henry VI*, 1.3.190

13 AND YET THOU WILT, FOR I BEING PENT IN THEE,
PENT = echoing Southampton's imprisonment; "A liquid prisoner pent in walls of glass" – Sonnet 5, line 10, which demonstrates that Oxford had already used "pent" in relation to prison; **PENT IN THEE** = imprisoned within you and by you, Elizabeth, my sovereign; by keeping our son in jail, you have me in prison, too

14 PERFORCE AM THINE, AND ALL THAT IS IN ME.
PERFORCE, etc. = of necessity I am your prisoner; **PERFORCE** = to force, constrain, oblige; "The present pains *perforce*, that love aye seeks" – Oxford poem, *The Paradise of Dainty Devices*, 1576; "Patience *perforce* is such a pinching pain" – Earl of Oxenforde, Tanner MS 306; Chiljan, 186; **ALL** = Southampton, *One for All, All for One*; he, too, is your prisoner; **ALL THAT IS IN ME** = "In imprisoning me, you are imprisoning all that is *in* me, and he is in my heart; therefore, whatever harshness you show to *me* affects him also, and I shall feel for *him* any rigour which I should not feel for myself" – Tucker; Southampton, our son, is all that is within me; you have both of us: "That she hath thee is of my wailing chief" – Sonnet 42, line 3, Oxford as chief mourner addressing his son; "And thou, all they, hast all the all of me" - Sonnet 31, line 14

Note: Editor Booth is struck by the metaphors here of torture, jail, prison: "here the metaphor is so complete, so urgent, so detailed, and so flatly matter-of-fact ('jail,' line 12), that the lovers, their situation, and their behavior become grotesque." Of course, Booth does not see the reality behind these words or the reality of the individuals involved.

Part Three

THE DARK LADY: ELIZABETH

SOUTHAMPTON AWAITS EXECUTION

Sonnet 134
My Self I'll Forfeit
March 1601

Oxford pleads with Elizabeth for his son's life, echoing the trial by "confessing" that she has Southampton as her prisoner. By writing "he is thine," Oxford echoes Sonnet 42 of the Fair Youth series, in the same time frame: "That she hath thee is of my wailing chief." Oxford vows to "forfeit" his own life/identity for "that other mine" (his royal son) so the Queen will "restore" him "to be my comfort still" -- echoing his declaration in Sonnet 37 to Southampton that he takes "all my comfort of thy worth and truth." Oxford's pleads with the Queen to let him pay the price of their son's treason, so she can extend her royal mercy to their son.

Sonnet 134	Translation
So now I have confessed that he is thine,	So now I've testified he is your prisoner,
And I my self am mortgaged to thy will,	And I, too, am tied to your royal will;
My self I'll forfeit , so that other mine,	I'll sacrifice myself, so my other self, my son
Thou wilt restore to be my comfort still.	You will restore to life to be my eternal comfort.
But thou wilt not, nor he will not be free,	But you will not; you will not set him free,
For thou art covetous, and he is kind;	For you are selfish, and he is your own blood;
He learned but surety to write for me,	His blood and life "writes" these sonnets for me,
Under that bond that him as fast doth bind.	By that bond that ties him to me, his father.
The statute of thy beauty thou wilt take,	You will exact the full terms of your blood,
Thou usurer that put'st forth all to use,	You lender of blood for your own self,
And sue a friend came debtor for my sake,	And make my son pay for what I did,
So him I lose through my unkind abuse.	So I lose him out of un-fatherly abuse of him.
Him have I lost, thou hast both him and me,	I have lost him; you have lost both of us;
He pays the whole, and yet am I not free.	Our son pays all, but still I'm the prisoner.

1 SO NOW I HAVE CONFESSED THAT HE IS THINE,
CONFESSED = as a defendant on trial; taking Southampton's guilt upon himself; "Let me confess" – Sonnet 36, line 1; **THAT HE IS THINE** = that my son is your (Elizabeth's) servant and your prisoner

2 AND I MY SELF AM MORTGAGED TO THY WILL.
MORTGAGED = "pledged, legally bound"- Duncan-Jones; **TO THY WILL** = to your royal will as Queen; to your "Will" or "Shakespeare" – my pseudonym, which I have pledged to maintain; "mortgage" is also similar to the "lease" of royal blood; "the *lease* of my true love" – Sonnet 107, line 3

3 MY SELF I'LL FORFEIT, SO THAT OTHER MINE
MYSELF I'LL FORFEIT = I will sacrifice my own self and identity; "Supposed as forfeit to a confined doom" – Sonnet 107, line 4; **SO THAT OTHER MINE** = so that other self of mine, i.e., my royal son; "a *son of mine own*" – Oxford to Burghley, March 17, 1575; "My spirit is thine, the better part of me" – Sonnet 74, line 8

REFERENCE EDITION

THE MONUMENT

4 THOU WILT RESTORE TO BE MY COMFORT STILL.
THOU WILT RESTORE = you will spare from execution; you will release from prison; you will restore to his earldom, with all its titles and lands; **TO BE MY COMFORT STILL** = to be my eternal comfort; ("As a decrepit father takes delight/ To see his active child do deeds of youth/ So I, made lame by Fortune's dearest spite/ Take all my comfort of thy worth and truth" – Sonnet 37, lines 1-4)

5 BUT THOU WILT NOT, NOR HE WILL NOT BE FREE,
But you, Elizabeth, will not do so; and he will remain a prisoner; nor, under these circumstances, does he wish to have his liberty; nor shall he have his liberty; see "free" in line 14 below

6 FOR THOU ART COVETOUS, AND HE IS KIND;
FOR THOU ART COVETOUS = because you are the possessive monarch, who keeps our son in your prison; **AND HE IS KIND** = and he is your natural child who should be king; **KIND** = ("Belonging to one by birth; lawful, rightful" – *O. E. D.*, citing usage by 1570; "Rightful, heir, etc; natural – 1589; related by kinship" – *O. E. D.*; "in all kindness and kindred" – Oxford to Robert Cecil, May 1601; "Shall kin with kin and kind with kind confound" – *Richard II*, 4.1.141; "Of comfort, kingdom, kindred, freedom, life" – *Richard III*, 4.4.224); "Be as thy presence is, gracious and kind" – Sonnet 10, line 11; "Kind is my love today, tomorrow kind,/ … Fair, kind, and true, is all my argument,/ Fair, kind, and true, varying to other words/ … Fair, kind, and true, have often lived alone,/ Which three, till now, never kept seat in one" – Sonnet 105, lines 5, 9-10, 13-14)

7 HE LEARNED BUT SURETY-LIKE TO WRITE FOR ME,
HE LEARNED, etc. = my royal son learned to write these sonnets for me; i.e., they were written with his royal blood, which they contain; "So is my love still telling what is told" – Sonnet 76, line 14; "To The Onlie Begetter of These Ensuing Sonnets" – Dedication of 1609; **SURETY-LIKE** = "like a guarantor, like someone who goes bail" – Booth; i.e., "To say if that the bastard boys of York shall be the surety for their traitor father" – *2 Henry VI*, 5.1.115-116; i.e., Oxford takes on the role of traitor, with Southampton guaranteeing silence; Southampton acting as agent, as Looney suggested he had acted as Oxford's agent for getting the Shakespeare plays to the Lord Chamberlain's Men, the acting company that was the vehicle

8 UNDER THAT BOND THAT HIM AS FAST DOTH BIND.
THAT BOND = that bond of father-son between me and him; a play on 'the bonds that bind me, make me your prisoner" – Booth; the bond or legal agreement Oxford is making behind the scenes

9 THE STATUTE OF THY BEAUTY THOU WILT TAKE,
THE STATUTE OF THY BEAUTY = the entitlement of your royal blood, Oxford speaking to Queen Elizabeth; **STATUTE** = "A law or decree made by a sovereign or a legislative authority" – *OED*; also "applied to an ordinance or decree of God, a deity" – *OED*; "My acts, decrees, and statutes" – the king in *Richard II*, 4.1.213; **THOU WILT TAKE** = you, Elizabeth, will take from our royal son

10 THOU USURER THAT PUT'ST FORTH ALL TO USE,
THOU USURER = you loaner of royal blood (for profit, but without gaining profit); **ALL** = Southampton, *One for All, All for One;* a harsh description of the Virgin Queen as irresponsible monarch who loaned her blood to Southampton without profit to England

11 AND SUE A FRIEND CAME DEBTOR FOR MY SAKE:
SUE = demand payment from; **A FRIEND** = our son; **CAME DEBTOR FOR MY SAKE** = who became the debtor for my sake, paying with his liberty and maybe his life; "And both *for my sake* lay me on this cross" – Sonnet 42, line 12

12 SO HIM I LOSE THROUGH MY UNKIND ABUSE.
HIM I LOSE = I lose my royal son; "Though thou repent, yet I have still the *loss*" – Sonnet 34, line 10; **MY UNKIND ABUSE** = my un-fatherly injury of him; the opposite of "kind" or kindred by blood

No. 134

13 **HIM HAVE I LOST; THOU HAST BOTH HIM AND ME;**
HIM I HAVE LOST = I have already, by my agreement, lost him as a royal claimant; **THOU HAST BOTH HIM AND ME** = you have both of us in your sovereign control; you have him in your prison, the Tower; you have his fate (and therefore mine) in your hands; to Southampton in the Fair Youth series, within the same time frame: "If I *lose* thee, my *loss* is my love's gain,/ And *losing* her, my friend hath found that *loss*;/ *Both* find each other, and I *lose both* twain,/ And *both* for my sake lay me on this cross" – Sonnet 42, lines 9-12

14 **HE PAYS THE WHOLE, AND YET AM I NOT FREE.**
HE PAYS THE WHOLE = Southampton pays with his liberty and possibly with his life; and even if he survives, he will pay by giving up his claim to the throne; **YET AM I NOT FREE** = but despite this situation, I remain your prisoner as well; (Booth translates "he pays the whole" as "he is of such value that he is worth as much as (or more than) is owed by both of us together"; this "free" is an extension of "free" in line 5 above

THE DARK LADY: ELIZABETH

SOUTHAMPTON AWAITS EXECUTION

Sonnet 135
Thou Hast Thy Will
March 1601

Oxford is preparing to pay for his son's life in the form of his identity as the father of Southampton and as the writer of the works attributed to William Shakespeare. (The last name recalls the spear-shaking goddess Pallas Athena, signifying Elizabeth, so Oxford's pen name has always been in her service: "Thou hast thy Will.") Here he plays upon the name "Will" of the pseudonym and the Queen's royal "will" to record his meaning. In the end he directly pleads for her to "no fair beseechers kill" -- to refrain from killing her "fair" or royal son (the "fairest creatures" of Sonnet 1) by execution.

Sonnet 135	Translation
Who ever hath her wish, thou hast thy *Will*,	You who have your will, you have royal will,
And *Will* to boot, and *Will* in over-plus,	And Will Shakespeare, too, all wills being yours,
More than enough am I that vex thee still,	More than enough from me, who still implores you
To thy sweet will making addition thus.	To add your son's claim to your royal will.
Wilt thou, whose will is large and spacious,	Will you, whose royal will is absolute,
Not once vouchsafe to hide my will in thine?	Not deign to absorb my own will into yours?
Shall will in others seem right gracious,	Shall the wills of others seem rightfully royal,
And in my will no fair acceptance shine?	And mine gains no royal acceptance?
The sea, all water, yet receives rain still,	All kings [Southampton] receive their blood
And in abundance addeth to his store;	And add it to their store of abundant royalty;
So thou being rich in *Will* add to thy *Will*,	So you, filled with royal will, add to your poet
One will of mine, to make thy large *Will* more.	One will of mine, to make your royal will more.
Let no unkind, no fair beseechers kill,	Don't go against your son; do not execute him;
Think all but one, and me in that one *Will*.	Think of him, and think of me in that royal will.

(Each "*Will*" is capitalized and italicized as such in the 1609 Quarto.)

1 WHO EVER HATH HER WISH, THOU HAST THY *WILL*,
EVER = Edward de Vere, *Ever or Never;* **THOU HAST THY *WILL*** = you, Elizabeth, have your royal will as absolute monarch

2 AND *WILL* TO BOOT, AND *WILL* IN OVER-PLUS;
AND *WILL* TO BOOT, etc. = and my "Will Shakespeare" as pseudonym, in addition; and both of these in excess; (since "I myself am mortgaged to thy will" – Sonnet 134, line 2)

3 MORE THAN ENOUGH AM I THAT VEX THEE STILL,
MORE THAN ENOUGH = and if that weren't enough; and on top of that; **AM I THAT VEX THEE STILL** = is Oxford, who beseeches Elizabeth continually with his pleas on behalf of their son ("And trouble deaf heaven [Elizabeth] with my bootless cries" – Sonnet 29, line 3); a suggestion that she is also being tor-

mented by Oxford's harsh words against her anticipated execution of Southampton

4 TO THY SWEET WILL MAKING ADDITION THUS.
TO THY SWEET WILL = to your royal will; **MAKING ADDITION THUS** = adding this torment; echoing the "addition" or birth of Southampton; "And by *addition* me of thee defeated,/ By *adding one thing* to my purpose nothing" – Sonnet 20, lines 11-12; perhaps a reference to her Last Will and Testament, and a plea to add Southampton as her successor

5 WILT THOU, WHOSE WILL IS LARGE AND SPACIOUS,
Will you, Elizabeth, whose royal will is all-powerful, since you are the absolute monarch; **LARGE** = to Southampton as prince: to Southampton: "Take heed, dear heart, of this *large* privilege" – Sonnet 95, line 13; "I must have liberty withal, as *large* a charter as the wind" – *As You Like It*, 2.7.47-48; **SPACIOUS** = same large; royal, as in "gracious" of line 7 below

6 NOT ONCE VOUCHSAFE TO HIDE MY WILL IN THINE?
Not just once secretly accept my own will as part of your own?

7 SHALL WILL IN OTHERS SEEM RIGHT GRACIOUS,
WILL IN OTHERS = royal will in others, such as King James of Scotland, who may do what you refuse to do; **RIGHT** = having royal right; **SEEM RIGHT GRACIOUS** = appear most royal (as opposed to you, Elizabeth); "Above the rest in Court who gave thee *grace*?" – Oxford's early sonnet, in the early 1570s, referring to the Queen, who gave him her grace; "Lo, in the Orient when the *gracious* light/ Lifts up his burning head" – Sonnet 7, lines 1-2; to Southampton: "Be as thy presence is, *gracious* and kind" – Sonnet 10, line 11

8 AND IN MY WILL NO FAIR ACCEPTANCE SHINE?
And "in reference to my desire, will no prospect of favorable reception be manifest?" – Duncan-Jones; **FAIR ACCEPTANCE** = acceptance of Southampton, who is "fair" or royal; **SHINE** = as a royal sun or son; "Even so my Sunne one early morn did *shine*/ With all triumphant splendor on my brow" – Sonnet 33, lines 9-10

9 THE SEA, ALL WATER, YET RECEIVES RAIN STILL,
THE SEA = royalty; ("Thou art, quoth she, *a sea, a sovereign king*" – *Lucrece*, 652); **ALL** = Southampton, *One for All, All for One*; **ALL WATER** = all [Southampton's] royal blood; "the tide of blood in me" – *2 Henry IV*, 5.2.129); **YET RECEIVES RAIN STILL** = Southampton continues to gain more royal blood in him, as he remains alive and grows; related to "reign" as in one of Oxford's poems in *The Paradise of Dainty Devices*, referring to Elizabeth: "Save her alone, who yet on th'earth doth *reign*"; and "What thing is love? It is a power divine/ That *reigns* in us" – in *Menaphon*, attributed to Robert Greene, 1589, included by Chiljan as among poems by Edward deVere, who likely used "Robert Greene" as a pseudonym; "To dry the *rain* on my storm-beaten face" – Sonnet 34, line 6; **STILL** = eternally, as a god on earth; "Why write I *still* all one, ever the same … And you and love are *still* my argument" – Sonnet 76, lines 5, 10; "Since all alike my songs and praises be/ To one, of one, *still* such, and ever so;/ Kind is my love today, tomorrow kind,/ *Still* constant in a wondrous excellence" – Sonnet 105, lines 3-6

10 AND IN ABUNDANCE ADDETH TO HIS STORE;
ABUNDANCE = great royalty; "Making a famine where *abundance* lies" – Sonnet 1, line 7; **ADDETH TO HIS STORE** = adds to his store of royal blood; ("O him she stores, to show what wealth she had/ In days long since, before these last so bad" – Sonnet 67, lines 13-14; "And him as for a map doth Nature store/ To show false art what beauty was of yore" – Sonnet 68, lines 13-14

11 SO THOU, BEING RICH IN *WILL*, ADD TO THY *WILL*
So you, as Queen, being full of royal power by your sovereign will, as well as your "Will" Shakespeare, can now add; **RICH** = full of "wealth" or "treasure" or royal blood

(Oxford uses "will" or "*Will*" so extensively in this sonnet – more frequently than any other single word in any single sonnet – that he's inviting us to consider *all* the possible meanings of the word. One meaning, ignored by commentators, is one of the most obvious definitions – last will and testament. Perhaps he is also suggesting that Elizabeth add a codicil to her will ["Add to thy will"] legitimizing and naming Southampton. This would solve the problem neatly – Oxford and Elizabeth would get their ultimate goal, and Elizabeth, now dead, wouldn't have any explaining to do. Historical support for this possibility includes the fact that Henry VIII left a *will* setting forth the order of his succession [Edward, Mary, Elizabeth] and the terms under which Elizabeth could marry. In Elizabeth's case, she could add a codicil saying, 'Henry Wriothesley is the natural issue of my body." That would comply with the 1571 statute, and Robert Cecil could figure out whom to identify as the father [probably some never-mentioned, now-deceased nobleman]. – Alex McNeil)

12 **ONE WILL OF MINE TO MAKE THY LARGE *WILL* MORE.**
ONE = Southampton, *One for All, All for One*; **ONE WILL OF MINE** = my plea for Southampton; **TO MAKE THY LARGE *WILL* MORE** = to make all of your royal power even greater

13 **LET NO UNKIND, NO FAIR BESEECHERS KILL:**
LET NO UNKIND = do not go against your own "kind" or natural-born son; **NO FAIR BESEECHERS KILL** = do not execute (and thereby literally "kill") your "fair" or royal son, who beseeches you (as I do) for mercy

14 **THINK ALL BUT ONE, AND ME IN THAT ONE *WILL*.**
ALL = Southampton; **ONE** = Southampton; **THINK ALL BUT ONE** = have mercy on him, who is *One for All, All for One*, your son; **ONE** = Southampton; **ONE WILL** = royal will on his behalf, as my "Will" is dedicated to him; **AND ME IN THAT ONE WILL** = and me, Oxford, who is confined in these wills and at the mercy of your own royal will.

Part Three

THE DARK LADY: ELIZABETH

SOUTHAMPTON AWAITS EXECUTION

Sonnet 136
One is Reckoned None
March 1601

Continuing to play upon the "Will" of his pen name, Oxford refers to how he is so "near" in blood to the Queen by virtue of the fact they are the parents of Southampton. But her soul is "blind" to this truth. Henry Wriothesley is "one" (One for All, All for One), and now, among all numbers, "a number one is reckoned none." He will insist upon this identification in Sonnet 105: "Since all alike my songs and praises be/ To one, of one, still such, and ever so." Oxford echoes Sonnet 67 of the Fair Youth series by referring to "thy store's account" of royal blood: "O him she stores (holds him in prison), to show what wealth she had." He pleads with Elizabeth to allow him to sacrifice himself in return for Southampton's life.

Sonnet 136	Translation
If thy soul check thee that I come so near,	If your royal spirit rebukes you with my truth,
Swear to thy blind soul that I was thy *Will*,	Swear to your unseeing spirit that I was "Will",
And will thy soul knows is admitted there,	And your soul knows your will is received there,
Thus far for love my love-suit sweet fulfill.	So for royal blood's sake fulfill my royal pleading!
Will will fulfill the treasure of thy love,	"Will" the poet will fill your store of royal blood,
I fill it full with wills, and my will one.	I fill it with royal will, and mine is my son's.
In things of great receipt with ease we prove.	In regard to royal matters, we easily demonstrate
Among a number one is reckoned none.	That our son has been rendered as nothing.
Then in the number let me pass untold,	Then leave me out when speaking of him,
Though in thy store's account I one must be,	Though in my own heart I am one with him,
For nothing hold me so it please me hold,	So it pleases me to account myself as nothing,
That nothing me, a some-thing sweet to thee.	If you would account our son as royal to you.
Make but my name thy love, and love that still,	Make my pen name be your will, and love him:
And then thou lovest me, for my name is *Will*.	So then you love me, for I am "Will" the poet!

1 IF THY SOUL CHECK THEE THAT I COME SO NEAR,
If you (Queen Elizabeth) stop because I come so close to the truth; i.e., "O Hamlet," cries Queen Gertrude, "speak no more! Thou turn'st my eyes into *my very soul*, and there I see such black and grained spots as will not leave their tinct" – *Hamlet*, 3.4.88-90

> *He dives into the King's soul*, and there scatters
> Dangers, doubts, wringing of the conscience,
> Fears, and despairs
> - *Henry VIII*, 2.2.25-27

NEAR = closely allied as father of your royal son; "As we be knit *near* in alliance, so hereafter *nearer*" – Oxford to Robert Cecil, his brother-in-law, Feb 2, 1602

REFERENCE EDITION 705

2 SWEAR TO THY BLIND SOUL THAT I WAS THY *WILL*,
THY BLIND SOUL = Elizabeth refuses to see the truth and only sees darkness; i.e., she is blind; "Looking on darkness which the *blind* do see" – Sonnet 27, lines 7-8; **I WAS THY *WILL*** = I followed your will and agreed to sacrifice my identity to the pen name "Will Shakespeare" in order to bury the truth about our son; "Thy kingdom come, *thy will* be done, on earth as it is in heaven" – Lord's Prayer

3 AND WILL, THY SOUL KNOWS, IS ADMITTED THERE;
And your soul knows that your will is acknowledged by this agreement

4 THUS FAR FOR LOVE, MY LOVE-SUIT SWEET FULFILL.
FOR LOVE = for royal blood, yours and our son's; **MY LOVE-SUIT** = my pleadings on behalf of Southampton and his royal blood; **FULFILL** = ("fulfill his prince' desisre" – *Pericles*, 2.Chorus.21)

5 WILL WILL FULFILL THE TREASURE OF THY LOVE,
WILL WILL FULFILL = Your royal will (which I follow), plus my "Will" Shakespeare", will gratify or make right; **THE TREASURE OF THY LOVE** = the great store of your royal blood that is in our son; ("Treasure thou some place/ With beauty's treasure" – Sonnet 6, lines 3-4); "Why should he live, now nature bankrupt is,/ Beggared of blood to blush through lively veins?/ For she hath no *exchequer* now but his,/ And, proud of many, lives upon his gains./ O him she stores, to show what *wealth* she had" – Sonnet 67, lines 9-13

6 I FILL IT FULL WITH WILLS, AND MY WILL ONE.
I = often emended to "ay"; I carry out your will by my sacrifice; and I fill the womb of these sonnets with this treasure; **ONE** = Southampton; **MY WILL ONE** = my will is bound up with "one," our son, Southampton ("To one, of one, still such, and ever so" – Sonnet 105, line 4)

7 IN THINGS OF GREAT RECEIPT WITH EASE WE PROVE:
THINGS OF GREAT RECEIPT = ("containers for things of great value" – Booth); i.e., Southampton himself, who contains Elizabeth's royal blood

8 AMONG A NUMBER ONE IS RECKON'D NONE.
AMONG A NUMBER = within this verse; ("And in fresh *numbers number* all your graces" – Sonnet 17, line 6; "*gentle* numbers" – Sonnet 100, line 6); **AMONG A NUMBER ONE** = within these numbers or sonnets, Southampton, *One for All, All for One*; **IS RECKONED NONE** = is accounted as a nobody or nothing, i.e., zero; (also Oxford = O = zero = Southampton, thus joined in nothingness); **RECKONED** = acknowledged (as Elizabeth's successor); "But *reck'ning time*, whose millioned accidents/ Creep in 'twixt vows, and change decrees of Kings" – Sonnet 115, lines 5-6; Southampton is un-reckoned as King

9 THEN IN THE NUMBER LET ME PASS UNTOLD,
THEN IN THE NUMBER = ("inside the arithmetical symbol, which would be a zero" – Booth); then in this verse, and within the "one" of Southampton, who is accounted as nothing; **LET ME PASS UNTOLD** = let me go unreported, uncounted, unknown, invisible.

10 THOUGH IN THY STORE'S ACCOUNT I ONE MUST BE,
THY STORE'S ACCOUNT = your (Elizabeth's) accounting of royal blood; same as the "audit" of her son's blood, as in "What acceptable *Audit* canst thou leave" – Sonnet 4, line 12; **STORE** = abundance of royal blood in your son; "As truth and beauty shall together thrive/ If from thyself to *store* thou wouldst convert" – Sonnet 14, lines 11-12; "And him as for a map doth nature [Elizabeth] store" – Sonnet 68, line 13; **I ONE MUST BE** = I am within my son, so that is where I am and must be counted; (Oxford told Southampton, "When thou art all the better part of me" – Sonnet 39, line 2)

11 FOR NOTHING HOLD ME, SO IT PLEASE THEE HOLD
NOTHING = "no-thing"; Southampton is "nothing" or the opposite of "one"; **HOLD ME** = contains me; i.e., nothing contains me more than my son, who is accounted as nothing; also, consider or hold me to be nothing; ("I hold my duty as I hold my soul, both to my God and to my gracious King" –*Hamlet*, 2.2.44-45)

No. 136

12 **THAT NOTHING ME, A SOME-THING SWEET TO THEE.**
THAT NOTHING ME = Oxford, accounted as nothing, who resides within the "nothing" of his better self, Southampton; **SOME-THING SWEET** = thing of royal value, i.e., Southampton

13 **MAKE BUT MY NAME THY LOVE, AND LOVE THAT STILL,**
MY NAME = my real name; "*My name* be buried where my body is" – Sonnet 72, line 11; "That every word doth almost tell *my name*" – Sonnet 76, line 7; "O God, Horatio, what a wounded name" – *Hamlet*, 5.2.351; and my pen name, Will Shakespeare; **THY LOVE** = what you value as royal; **STILL** = always

14 **AND THEN THOU LOVEST ME, FOR MY NAME IS *WILL*.**
And then, if you love the pen name dedicated to your royal son, then you love him and, therefore, you love me as well; **MY NAME IS *WILL*** = "Will" is my other name, my pen name; "Frailty, *thy name* is woman" – *Hamlet*, 1.2.146; "That every word doth *almost* tell my name" – Sonnet 76, line 7, which means that "Will" is *not* his real name

REFERENCE EDITION

THE DARK LADY: ELIZABETH

SOUTHAMPTON AWAITS EXECUTION

Sonnet 137
This False Plague
March 1601

As he continues to plead for his son's life, Oxford vows in the final line of this sonnet that he has "transferred" his eyesight from the truth to "this false plague" that views their royal son as having no claim to the throne. He is now willing to become as "blind" as Elizabeth is, in order to gain Southampton's reprieve from execution. Here he refers to the Tower as the "place" (echoing Sonnet 44: "As soon as think the place where he would be") and refers to Southampton's status as a "common" prisoner ("Mr. Henry Wriothesley") among the others.

Sonnet 137	Translation
Thou blind fool love, what dost thou to mine eyes,	Blind servitude, what do you do to my eyes
That they behold and see not what they see?	So they see and cannot see what they see?
They know what beauty is, see where it lies,	They know Tudor Rose blood and see it,
Yet what the best is take the worst to be.	But turn the most royal son into the least.
If eyes corrupt by over-partial looks	If eyes disgraced by overly partial looks
Be anchored in the bay where all men ride,	Are dependent upon the ruler of all men,
Why of eyes' falsehood hast thou forged hooks,	Why do false-seeing eyes direct your will,
Whereto the judgment of my heart is tied?	To which my mind and heart are tied?
Why should my heart think that a several plot,	Why must my heart think itself confined
Which my heart knows the wide world's common place?	To that place of commoners, the Tower of London?
Or mine eyes, seeing this, say this is not	Or why do my eyes, seeing this, say it's not,
To put fair truth upon so foul a face?	Forcing royal truth to share such disgrace?
In things right true my heart and eye have erred,	In matters of royal truth I have been false,
And to this false plague are they now transferred.	And to these lies, my eyes are transferred.

1 THOU BLIND FOOL LOVE, WHAT DOST THOU TO MINE EYES
THOU BLIND FOOL LOVE = Oxford addressing "love" or royal blood itself, which has forced him to see only lies and falsity; **LOVE** = "Cupid" of Sonnet 153, line 1, and "the little Love-God" of Sonnet 154, line, i.e., Southampton; and Oxford has joined Elizabeth in her blindness to their son's royal blood, as in Sonnet 136, line 2: "thy blind soul" and so this "love" has become a fool; although, in fact, "Love's not time's fool" – Sonnet 116, line 9; Elizabeth is "blind" and can see only darkness or blackness: "Looking on *darkness*, which the *blind* do see" – Sonnet 127, line 8

2 THAT THEY BEHOLD AND SEE NOT WHAT THEY SEE?
THAT THEY, etc. = that my eyes, which see my son's royalty, no longer see it; i.e., Oxford is speaking of his need to adopt Elizabeth's false view of Southampton and thereby to "see not" what he sees ("eyes have they, but they see not" – Psalms 115.5)

3 **THEY KNOW WHAT BEAUTY IS, SEE WHERE IT LIES,**
THEY KNOW WHAT BEAUTY IS = they know what Elizabeth's royal blood is, i.e., her blood possessed by Southampton; they also know what Elizabeth is, i.e., a liar; **SEE WHERE IT LIES** = they see where it exists, i.e., in Southampton; and they also see how Elizabeth lies, i.e., how she cannot acknowledge the truth of their son

4 **YET WHAT THE BEST IS, TAKE THE WORST TO BE.**
Yet my eyes, having to be blind or false, now must view the most or "best" royal blood as "worst" or not royal at all.

5 **IF EYES CORRUPT BY OVER-PARTIAL LOOKS**
CORRUPT = distorted; **OVER-PARTIAL LOOKS** = views of him with too much partiality

6 **BE ANCHORED IN THE BAY WHERE ALL MEN RIDE,**
Beneath the obvious sexual meaning, Oxford is speaking of Elizabeth's royal presence as the place to which all subjects must go to gain their wishes; **ALL** = Southampton, *One for All, All for One*; **ALL MEN** = Southampton

7 **WHY OF EYES' FALSEHOOD HAS THOU FORGED HOOKS,**
Why have you lodged the hooks of your anchor to your false royal viewpoint?

8 **WHERETO THE JUDGMENT OF MY HEART IS TIED?**
JUDGMENT OF MY HEART = Oxford's inner judgment of his son, as opposed to his guilty vote that contributed to the legal judgment (verdict) against Southampton; "So thy great gift, upon misprision growing,/ Comes home again, on better *judgment* making" – Sonnet 87, lines 11-12; **HEART** – "A quest [jury] of thoughts, all tenants to the *heart*,/ And by their *verdict* is determined/ The clear eye's moiety, and the dear *heart's* part" – Sonnet 46, lines 10-12

9 **WHY SHOULD MY HEART THINK THAT A SEVERAL PLOT,**
SEVERAL PLOT = a separate area, i.e., the Tower of London, where Southampton is; "such as a walled or fenced garden-plot" – Duncan-Jones; echoing the "plot" of the Rebellion to overthrow the government under Robert Cecil; "That he did *plot* the Duke of Gloucester's death" – *Richard II*, 1.1.100; "A pretty *plot*, well chosen to build upon!" – *2 Henry VI*, 1.4.58; "And in this private *plot* be we the first that shall salute our rightful sovereign with honor of his birthright to the crown" – *2 Henry VI*, 2.2.59-61; "Nor never by advised purpose meet to *plot, contrive, or complot* any ill 'gainst us, our state, our subjects, or our land" – *Richard II*, 1.3.188-190

10 **WHICH MY HEART KNOWS THE WIDE WORLD'S COMMON PLACE?**
COMMON PLACE = the Tower of London, where common criminals as well as commoners (of whom Southampton has become one) reside; ("Ah wherefore with infection should he live" – Sonnet 67, line 1; "As soon as think *the place* where he would be" – Sonnet 44, line 8; **COMMON** = "Thou dost *common* grow" – Sonnet 69, line 14; **PLACE** = the Lord Steward's reference to the Tower in ordering Essex and Southampton to be returned to "the ***place*** from whence you came"; place of execution; royal place, i.e., throne

11 **OR MINE EYES, SEEING THIS, SAY THIS IS NOT**
OR MINE EYES, etc. = or why do my eyes, seeing this, say the opposite?

12 **TO PUT FAIR TRUTH UPON SO FOUL A FACE?**
FAIR = royal, i.e., Southampton; "From fairest creatures we desire increase" – Sonnet 1, line 1; **TRUTH** = Oxford, *Nothing Truer than Truth*; **FAIR TRUTH** = Southampton and Oxford, joined in the truth of Southampton's royal blood; **UPON SO FOUL A FACE** = i.e., why look at this foul, disgraceful situation and see it as the face of royalty and truth?

13 IN THINGS RIGHT TRUE MY HEART AND EYES HAVE ERRED,
RIGHT = rightful; **TRUE** = Oxford; **RIGHT TRUE** = ("your true rights" to the throne, Sonnet 17, line 11); **MY HEART AND EYES HAVE ERRED** = i.e., in these matters I have deliberately lied; echoing the "error" of the Rebellion; "So are those *errors* that in thee are seen" – Sonnet 96, line 7; "If this be *error* and upon me proved" – Sonnet 116, line 13; "Book both my willfulness and my *errors* down" – Sonnet 117, line 9; **MY HEART AND EYES** = "Betwixt mine eye and heart a league is took" – Sonnet 47, line 1

14 AND TO THIS FALSE PLAGUE ARE THEY NOW TRANSFERRED.
FALSE = related to "false-traitor"; **FALSE PLAGUE** = ("this affliction of distorted perceptions; the affliction of being false, telling falsehoods" – Booth); "the *monarch's plague*, this flattery" – Sonnet 114, line 2; the plague is flattery that his son should be king, but now even this false hope is false. The result is that Elizabeth's false view of Southampton is now regarded "in men's eyes" as the truth, and Oxford contributes to the lie; ("A Renaissance reader might have heard a pun on 'trans-faired'" – Booth; in which case, Oxford is accusing Elizabeth of being false to her "fair" or royal son, i.e., false to herself)

> If I were mad, I should forget my son,
> Or madly think a babe of clouts were he.
> I am not mad; too well, too well I feel
> The different *plague* of each calamity.
> - *King John*, 3.3.56-60

Part Three

THE DARK LADY: ELIZABETH

SOUTHAMPTON AWAITS EXECUTION

Sonnet 138
Simple Truth Suppressed
March 1601

Sonnet 138 (along with Sonnet 144) was printed first in The Passionate Pilgrim *of 1599, but Oxford revised it (see comparison immediately following the notes for line 14) for insertion here to mark the events of March 1601. On the surface, the verse may appear merely playful, romantic and sexual; but in 1599 Oxford was sending the Queen a personal (yet public) message about her refusal to acknowledge Southampton as her son and heir. She was forcing him to "lie" with her about him. (This is the only place in the Sonnets where "my love" is a "she" and where Oxford uses "my love" in reference to the Queen. Elsewhere the phrase refers to "my royal son." Elizabeth, of course, is the source of the "love" or royal blood that she bequeathed to their son.)*

Sonnet 138	Translation
When my love swears that she is made of truth,	When my royal Queen says she tells truth,
I do believe her though I know she lies,	I believe her although I know she's false,
That she might think me some untutored youth,	So she might think I'm an ignorant youth,
Unlearned in the world's false subtleties.	Who doesn't know England's deceptions.
Thus vainly thinking that she thinks me young	So, vainly thinking she thinks me young,
Although she knows my days are past the best,	Although she knows I'm well past prime,
Simply I credit her false-speaking tongue:	I simply agree with her false words to me:
On both sides thus is simple truth suppressed.	So both of us suppress the truth.
But wherefore says she not she is unjust?	But why doesn't she admit she's unjust?
And wherefore says not I that I am old?	And why do I not say I am near death?
O love's habit is in seeming trust,	O, the habit of her servant is to seem to trust,
And age in love loves not to have years told.	And royal blood hates to know its age.
Therefore I lie with her, and she with me,	Therefore, she and I lie to each other;
And in our faults by lies we flattered be.	And in our treason, we flatter by lying.

1 WHEN MY LOVE SWEARS THAT SHE IS MADE OF TRUTH,
MY LOVE = Elizabeth, the source of Southampton's "love" or royal blood; an exception to "my love" in reference to Southampton as "my royal son"; but since "love" refers to royal blood, it applies to the Queen as well; **SWEARS** = decrees; **MADE OF TRUTH** = is constitutionally truthful; **TRUTH** = Oxford, *Nothing Truer than Truth*

2 I DO BELIEVE HER THOUGH I KNOW SHE LIES,
I DO BELIEVE HER = I choose to accept her vows as truthful; **THOUGH I KNOW SHE LIES** = although I am well aware that the Queen is false, that she breaks her vows

3 THAT SHE MIGHT THINK ME SOME UNTUTORED YOUTH,
So that she might imagine that I am naïve; **UNTUTORED** = a glance at Oxford's upbringing with England's best private tutors; and in terms of experience with Elizabeth at Court, he is hardly an untutored youth, having served her for decades

REFERENCE EDITION 711

4 UNLEARNED IN THE WORLD'S FALSE SUBTLETIES.
UNLEARNED = in fact he is the most educated man in England; **THE WORLD'S FALSE SUBTLE-TIES** = the false and hypocritical things said at the Court of England, by and to the Queen; **THE WORLD'S** = England's; "Thou that art now *the world's* fresh ornament" - Sonnet 1, line 9

5 THUS VAINLY THINKING THAT SHE THINKS ME YOUNG,
THUS VAINLY = therefore, deliberately and foolishly; **THINKING, etc.** = thinking, or acting as if, Elizabeth actually believes that I can't see through all the falsities

6 ALTHOUGH SHE KNOWS MY DAYS ARE PAST THE BEST,
Although Elizabeth knows my time at Court is in the past; **DAYS** = the golden days of Southampton's royal hopes, which also are in the past; **PAST THE BEST** = have gone past the time when our son was "best" or most royal

7 SIMPLY I CREDIT HER FALSE-SPEAKING TONGUE:
Appearing naïve, I accept her lies to me and to the world; "For I have sworn thee fair: more perjured eye,/ To swear against the truth so foul a lie" - Sonnet 152, lines 13-14

8 ON BOTH SIDES THUS IS SIMPLE TRUTH SUPPRESSED.
We both lie, to each other and to the world; we both suppress the truth of our son.; **SIMPLE TRUTH SUPPRESSED** = "And art made tongue-tied by authority (i.e., censored or suppressed by officialdom or by the supreme authority, the Queen)/ ... And *simple truth* miscalled simplicity" – Sonnet 66, lines 9, 11); **TRUTH** = Oxford, *Nothing Truer than Truth*; "To swear against *the truth* so foul a lie" - Sonnet 152, line 14

9 BUT WHEREFORE SAYS SHE NOT SHE IS UNJUST?
UNJUST = untruthful; unfaithful in her vows; literally *unjust* to Southampton, i.e., the lack of justice in the Essex-Southampton trial, the lack of justice in his death sentence and the non-justice of denying his true rights to the throne

10 AND WHEREFORE SAY NOT I THAT I AM OLD?
And why do I not say that I am old; **I THAT I AM** = a play on *I AM THAT I AM*, which Oxford will write in Sonnet 121, line 9: "No, I am that I am…"

11 O LOVE'S BEST HABIT IS IN SEEMING TRUST,
O = Oxford; **LOVE'S HABIT** = the deeply ingrained service to "love" or royal blood, i.e., to the rightful monarch, Elizabeth, regardless of what she says or does; **IS IN SEEMING TRUST** = (this habit) is to go along and pretend to be trusting and believing her

12 AND AGE IN LOVE LOVES NOT TO HAVE YEARS TOLD.
AGE IN LOVE = long time spent in service of royalty; **LOVES NOT TO HAVE YEARS TOLD** = accepts the monarch's lies; using the metaphor about aging; loves not to have the truth of these past years of her reign revealed to the world

13 THEREFORE I LIE WITH HER, AND SHE WITH ME,
Therefore I join with the Queen in presenting a false front to the world, to the point of denying our son's royalty, and she joins me in doing the same; a recollection of their sexual intercourse that led to conception of their son

14 AND IN OUR FAULTS BY LIES WE FLATTERED BE.
OUR FAULTS = our crimes against our royal son (literally the treason against him by denying his rightful claim to the throne); a play on the "faults" or treason committed by Southampton; "All men make *faults*, and even I in this,/ Authorizing thy trespass with compare,/ Myself corrupting salving thy amiss,/ Excusing thy sins more than thy sins are" – Sonnet 35, lines 5-8, to Southampton; **BY LIES** = we reinforce each other's

lies; **FLATTERED** = "the monarch's plague, this *flattery*" - Sonnet 114, line 2

Passionate Pilgrim: 1599

When my Love swears that she is made of truth,
I do believe her (though I know she lies)
That she might think me some untutored youth,
Unskilled in the world's false forgeries.
Thus vainly thinking that she thinks me young,
Although I know my years be past the best:
I smiling, credit her false speaking tongue,
Outfacing faults in love, with love's ill rest.
But wherefore says my love that she is young?
And wherefore say not I that I am old:
O Love's best habit's in a soothing tongue,
And Age in love, loves not to have years told.
   Therefore I'll lie with Love, and love with me,
   Since that our faults in love thus smother'd be.

Sonnet 138: 1601 (Revisions in boldface)

When my love swears that she is made of truth,
I do believe her though I know she lies,
That she might think me some untutored youth,
Unlearned in the world's false ***subtleties.***
Thus vainly thinking that she thinks me young,
Although ***she knows*** my ***days are*** past the best,
Simply I credit her false speaking tongue:
On both sides thus is simple truth suppressed:
But wherefore says ***she not she is unjust?***
And wherefore say not I that I am old?
O love's best habit ***is in seeming trust,***
And age in love loves not to have years told.
   Therefore ***I*** lie with ***her*** and ***she*** with me,
   And in our faults ***by lies we flattered be.***

THE MONUMENT

THE DARK LADY: ELIZABETH

SOUTHAMPTON AWAITS EXECUTION

Sonnet 139
I Am Near Slain
March 1601

Oxford is growing increasingly desperate over the expected execution of his royal son. He revisits the language of the crime and the trial, not to mention the anticipated beheading, as indicated by words such as Justify ... Wrong ... Wound ... Power ... Power ... Slay ... Wound ... Defense ... Excuse ... Enemies ... Foes ... Injuries ... Slain ... Kill ... Pain. In recording, "I am near slain," Oxford is not referring to his own physical death, but rather to Southampton's pending execution. He identifies completely with his royal son, as if Southampton was himself, and therefore he is the one facing execution. In Sonnet 145, when Elizabeth has spared Southampton from the axe, Oxford will write that she "saved my life."

Sonnet 139	Translation
O call me not to justify the wrong That thy unkindness lays upon my heart; Wound me not with thine eye but with thy tongue, Use power with power, and slay me not by Art.	Do not command me to justify the wrong That your cruel motherhood puts upon me! Don't wound me with looks but with talk, Use your power directly, not by craft;
Tell me thou lov'st elsewhere; but in my sight, Dear heart, forbear to glance thine eye aside. What need'st thou wound with cunning when thy might Is more than my o'er-pressed defence can bide?	Say you have no son; but in my sight, Dear Queen, refrain to look away from me. Why hurt by deception when your power Is more than my pleas for him can endure?
Let me excuse thee; ah, my love well knows, Her pretty looks have been mine enemies, And therefore from my face she turns my foes, That they elsewhere might dart their injuries.	Let me justify you: ah, my Queen knows Her imperial viewpoint has been my foe, And therefore she turns my foes from me, So they might do their harm elsewhere.
Yet do not so, but since I am near slain, Kill me outright with looks, and rid my pain.	But do not! Since my spirit is nearly dead, Execute me directly and end my woe!

1 O CALL ME NOT TO JUSTIFY THE WRONG
O = Oxford; **CALL ME NOT** = do not summon me, as to court; **TO JUSTIFY** = to render justice to; **THE WRONG** = the wrongs done to Southampton; the opposite of his "right" to the throne; a poignant plea to Elizabeth in relation to Oxford's declaration to his son, the crime of the Rebellion; "Such is my love, to thee I so belong,/ That for thy right myself will *bear all wrong*" – Sonnet 88, lines 13-14

2 THAT THY UNKINDNESS LAYS UPON MY HEART!
THY UNKINDNESS = your refusal to acknowledge or help Southampton, who is your "kind" or natural heir; "Fair, *kind*, and true, is all my argument" – Sonnet 105, line 9

3 WOUND ME NOT WITH THINE EYE BUT WITH THY TONGUE,
WOUND ME NOT = echoing the wounds of Christ; ("Beshrew that heart that makes my heart to groan/ For that deep *wound* it gives my friend and me" – Sonnet 133, lines 1-2; **THINE EYE** = your royal viewpoint or decree; **BUT WITH THY TONGUE** = but, rather, speak to me

Part Three

4 USE POWER WITH POWER, AND SLAY ME NOT BY ART.
USE POWER WITH POWER = use your royal power powerfully, i.e., wisely; ("directly and authoritatively; and, perhaps, let the powers you use against your adversary be of a kind he too possesses" – Booth); "They that have power to hurt, and will do none,/ That do not do the thing they most do show/ ... They rightly do inherit heaven's graces" – Sonnet 96, lines 1-2, 5; **SLAY ME NOT BY ART** = do not destroy me, i.e., my royal son, by indirect means or stratagems

5 TELL ME THOU LOV'ST ELSE-WHERE; BUT IN MY SIGHT,
Try to tell me to my face that you do not recognize your royal son and would rather have someone else on the throne in succession to you

6 DEAR HEART, FORBEAR TO GLANCE THINE EYE ASIDE.
DEAR = royal; **DEAR HEART** = Elizabeth as the heart or original source of Southampton's "love" or royal blood; **GLANCE THINE EYE ASIDE** = to aim your royal eye away from your son; ("Why with the time do I not glance aside" – Sonnet 76, line 3)

7 WHAT NEED'ST THOU WOUND WITH CUNNING, WHEN THY MIGHT
WOUND = repeating the echo of the wounds of Christ; **CUNNING** = "O, what authority and show of truth can *cunning* sin cover itself withal!" – *Much Ado About Nothing*, 4.1.33-34; "What *cunning* can express/ The favor of her face/ To whom in this distress/ I do appeal for grace" – Oxford poem, The Phoenix Nest, 1593, signed E. O., about Elizabeth; **THY MIGHT** = your royal power; "But wherefore do you not a *mightier* way" – Sonnet 16, line 1, to Southampton as prince

8 IS MORE THAN MY O'ER-PRESSED DEFENSE CAN BIDE?
MY O'ER-PRESSED DEFENSE = my too-hard-pressed defense of my son; ("Thy adverse party is thy advocate," Oxford had told Southampton – Sonnet 35, line 10); see Sonnet 140, line 1, with "press" echoing torture techniques used in the Tower; **BIDE** = endure

9 LET ME EXCUSE THEE: AH, MY LOVE WELL KNOWS
EXCUSE THEE = explain your actions; **MY LOVE** = Elizabeth, as in Sonnet 138, line 1)

10 HER PRETTY LOOKS HAVE BEEN MINE ENEMIES,
PRETTY LOOKS = royal viewpoint; "pretty" related to the Queen as Beauty

11 AND THEREFORE FROM MY FACE SHE TURNS MY FOES,
This is part of Oxford's lame reinterpretation of Elizabeth's attitude

12 THAT THEY ELSE-WHERE MIGHT DART THEIR INJURIES:
So that she protects me; -but of course this excuse is not true

13 YET DO NOT SO; BUT SINCE I AM NEAR SLAIN,
YET DO NOT SO = now reversing his course; (in another context, Oxford reminded Southampton that he could use "the strength of all thy state" and quickly added, "*But do not so*" – Sonnet 96, lines 12-13); **BUT SINCE I AM NEAR SLAIN** = but, rather, since you are about to execute our son, which is the same as executing me

14 KILL ME OUTRIGHT WITH LOOKS, AND RID MY PAIN.
KILL ME OUTRIGHT = execute me directly; **WITH LOOKS** = with your sovereign attitude; "*Monarchs* ... were thought of as having killing looks – Duncan-Jones; "To monarchize, be feared, and *kill with looks*" – *Richard II*, 3.2.165; **RID MY PAIN** = "I am the King's friend, and will *rid* his foe" – *Richard II*, 5.4.11;

REFERENCE EDITION

THE MONUMENT

THE DARK LADY: ELIZABETH

SOUTHAMPTON AWAITS EXECUTION
OXFORD WARNS THE QUEEN

Sonnet 140
When Their Deaths Be Near
March 1601

Oxford threatens the Queen that he will publicly reveal the truth about their royal son unless she acts to spare him from execution. He echoes Hamlet's "madness" and the Prince's confrontation with his mother, Queen Gertrude: "Come, come, sit you down, you shall not budge. You go not till I set you up a glass where you may see the inmost part of you." Oxford threatens to "grow mad" and he declares that "in my madness" he "might speak ill of thee".

Sonnet 140	Translation
Be wise as thou art cruel, do not press	Be as wise as you are cruel! Don't strain
My tongue-tied patience with too much disdain:	My silent patience with too much contempt:
Lest sorrow lend me words, and words express	Lest my sorrow makes me speak and tell
The manner of my pity-wanting pain.	How my pain comes from your lack of pity.
If I might teach thee wit, better it were,	If power teaches you wisdom, it's better
Though not to love, yet, love, to tell me so;	To tell me you love our son even if not;
As testy sick men, when their deaths be near,	The way irritable men, nearing their deaths,
No news but health from their Physicians know.	Get only good news from their doctors.
For if I should despair I should grow mad,	For if I should despair, I'll go insane –
And in my madness might speak ill of thee.	And in madness might reveal the truth!
Now this ill-wresting world is grown so bad,	Now this twisted world has gotten so bad,
Mad slanderers by mad ears believed be.	Crazed men like me will be believed.
That I may not be so, nor thou belied,	To prevent me from telling about you,
Bear thine eyes straight, though thy proud heart go wide.	Look at the truth, though your heart lies.

1 BE WISE AS THOU ART CRUEL, DO NOT PRESS
Be as wise as you are cruel; the opening two lines of this sonnet echoing (but turning inside out) the form and substance of the Bastard's speech to the King: "Be great in act, as you have been in thought; let not the world see fear and sad distrust govern the motion of a kingly eye!" -*King John*, 5.1.45; **WISE** = the Fool to Lear: "Thou shouldst not have been old till thou hadst been *wise*" – *King Lear*, 1.5.41-42; Oxford warns Elizabeth to let her wisdom be as great as her cruelty; **CRUEL** = "And shall I pray the Gods to keep the pain/ From her that is so *cruel* still?" – Oxford poem signed "E. O." prior to 1576, writing of the Queen; "O *cruel* hap and hard estate,/ That forceth me to love my foe" – Oxford poem, signed "E. O.", again writing of the Queen; **PRESS** = pressure, harass, torture; "I have this while *with leaden thoughts been pressed*" – *Othello*, 3.4.178; "tongue-tied" in the next line "invokes a new and specific method of torture; a person accused of a felony who 'stood mute,' refused to plead, underwent ... a process whereby *the prisoner's body was pressed* with heavy weights until he pleaded or died" – Booth; the echo of "pressing to death" alludes to Oxford's sexual relationship with Elizabeth, but his primary topic is the impending execution of his son; the image of torture is related to the Tower; "O, I am *pressed to death* through *want of speaking*"
– *Richard II*, 3.4.72

Part Three

2 MY TONGUE-TIED PATIENCE WITH TOO MUCH DISDAIN:
My having to painfully stand mute; "And art made *tongue-tied by authority*," – Sonnet 66, line 9; "But break my heart, for *I must hold my tongue*" – *Hamlet*, 1.2.165; ("The word 'patience' has special pertinence to the metaphor of torture" – Booth); **DISDAIN** = haughty contempt; "What feedeth most thy sight?/ To gaze on beauty still./ Whom find'st thou most thy foe?/ *Disdain* of my good will" – Oxford poem, by 1576

3 LEST SORROW LEND ME WORDS AND WORDS EXPRESS
Unless my pain prompts me to speak directly and publicly rather than indirectly and privately in these sonnets; ("every word doth *almost* tell my name,/ Showing their birth, and where they did proceed" – Sonnet 76, line 8); i.e., unless I break free of being tongue-tied by official decree

4 THE MANNER OF MY PITY-WANTING PAIN.
MANNER = origins and cause; way of being; "I cannot but find a great grief in myself to remember the Mistress which we have lost, under whom both you and myself from our greenest years have been in a *manner* brought up" - Oxford to Robert Cecil, April 25/27, 1603; **PITY-WANTING PAIN** = my pain, caused by your lack of pity for me; from Southampton, his son, Oxford will request pity, telling him: "*Pity me then*, and wish I were renewed,/ Whilst like a willing patient I will drink/Potions of eisel 'gainst my strong infection/ ... *Pity me then*, dear friend, and I assure ye,/ Even that your pity is enough to cure me" – Sonnet 111, lines 8-14; the image of himself as physically ill began back in 1574, not long after the birth of his royal son by Queen Elizabeth: "I sick withal the help of bath desired,/ And thither hied, a sad distempered guest,/ But found no cure: the bath for my help lies/ Where Cupid got new fire, my mistress' eye" – Sonnet 153, lines 11-14; **PAIN** = "Some purge their *pain*, by plaint I find" – Oxford Poem, signed E. O., *The Paradise of Dainty Devices*, 1576; "The *pain* be mine, but mine shall be the praise" – Sonnet 38, line 14; "That she that makes me sin awards me *pain*" – Sonnet 141, line 14; (Pain = "A soul's term of imprisonment in purgatory" – Booth, Sonnet 141, line 14)

5 IF I MIGHT TEACH THEE WIT, BETTER IT WERE,
If I might give you the wisdom; show you the reasons; it would be better;

6 THOUGH NOT TO LOVE, YET, LOVE, TO TELL ME SO;
Even if you cannot embrace your son's "love" or royal blood; **YET, LOVE, TO TELL ME SO** = however, to tell me you do; **LOVE** = referring to Elizabeth as "love" as he tells Southampton, "And yet it may be said *I loved her dearly*" – Sonnet 42, line 2

7 AS TESTY SICK MEN, WHEN THEIR DEATHS BE NEAR,
AS TESTY MEN, etc. = as short-tempered men, nearing death; "a sad distempered guest" – Sonnet 153, line 12, in 1574; **WHEN THEIR DEATHS BE NEAR** = echoing the fact that Southampton's death by execution is very near; "Growing a bath and healthful remedy/ For men diseased; but I, my Mistress' thrall,/ Came there for cure" – Sonnet 154, lines 11-14, in August of 1574, a few months after Southampton's birth to the Queen

8 NO NEWS BUT HEALTH FROM THEIR PHYSICIANS KNOW.
NO NEWS, etc. = would rather hear only about their health; **PHYSICIANS** = Elizabeth, from whom Oxford had wanted a "*sovereign cure*" in 1574: "And grew a seething bath which yet men prove/ Against strange maladies a sovereign cure" – Sonnet 153, lines 8-9

9 FOR IF I SHOULD DESPAIR I SHOULD GROW MAD,
Oxford is not yet "mad" or insane but he threatens to become so; **MAD** = (*Q* has "madde"); desperate, delirious, insane, unable to hold his tongue; "It is not *madness* that I have uttered. Bring me to the test, and I the matter will re-word, which *madness* would gambol from. Mother, for love of grace, lay not that flattering unction to your soul, that not *your trespass* but *my madness* speaks" – *Hamlet*, 3.4.143-148, i.e., her "trespass" (her marriage to Claudius, which, in Hamlet's view, is also a crime against the state) is what speaks; "What I have done that might your nature, honor, and exception roughly awake, I here proclaim was *mad-*

REFERENCE EDITION

ness" – *Hamlet*, 5.2.231-233; "O let me not be *mad*" – *King Lear*, 1.5.43; "On purpose laid to make the taker *mad*;/ *Mad* in pursuit" – Sonnet 129, lines 8-9; "And frantic *mad* with ever-more unrest,/ My thoughts and my discourse as *madmen's* are" – Sonnet 147, lines 10-11; "Young Arthur is my son, and he is lost! I am not **mad**: I would to heaven I were! … *If I were* **mad**, *I should forget my son*, or **madly** think a babe of clouts were he" - *King John*, 3.3.47-48, 57-58

10 AND IN MY MADNESS MIGHT SPEAK ILL OF THEE.
"If Hamlet from himself be taken away, and when he's not himself does wrong Laertes, then Hamlet does it not, Hamlet denies it. Who does it, then? *His madness*" – *Hamlet*, 5.2.235-238; the Queen: "Alas, he's mad!" – *Hamlet*, 3.4.120; **ILL OF THEE** = he might speak "the ugly truth about" her – Booth; a bold threat to tell the world the truth about Southampton

11 NOW THIS ILL-WRESTING WORLD IS GROWN SO BAD,
Now this contemporary world has become so bad that it twists everything around, so that bad (Cecil) is good and good (Southampton) is bad; "All men are *bad* and in their *badness* reign" – Sonnet 121, line 14, with "all men" = Southampton; "How weary, stale, flat, and unprofitable seem to me all the uses of *this world*!" – *Hamlet*, 1.2.139-140

12 MAD SLANDERERS BY MAD EARS BELIEVED BE.
Oxford is turning the tables on Elizabeth, who has "slandered" her royal blood with a "bastard shame" in Sonnet 127; now he warns that the mad world will believe his mad slanders against her (although in this case the slanders would consist of the truth); "And beauty slandered by a bastard shame" – Sonnet 127, line 4; "For *slander's mark* was ever yet the fair" – Sonnet 70, line 2

13 THAT I MAY NOT BE SO, NOR THOU BELIED,
To prevent me from telling truthful "lies" about you; **BELIED** = slandered

14 BEAR THINE EYES STRAIGHT, THOUGH THY PROUD HEART GO WIDE.
BEAR = carry; but related to child-bearing; **THINE EYES**, etc. = aim your imperial negative attitude at me alone; **STRAIGHT** = without deviation; **PROUD HEART** = royal source of royal blood; "It needs not, nor it boots thee not, **proud queen**" – *3 Henry VI*, 1.4.125; "My **proud heart**" – the King in *Richard III*, 1.2.174; proud related to the opposite of barrenness, i.e., proud = the womb swollen with child; "Why is my verse [which is a womb] so *barren* of new *pride*?" – Sonnet 76, line 1;**GO WIDE** = avoid hurting your son; as in archery, the arrow going wide or astray

Part Three

THE DARK LADY: ELIZABETH

SOUTHAMPTON AWAITS EXECUTION

Sonnet 141
Thy Proud Heart's Slave
March 1601

Oxford addresses the Queen as her "vassal wretch," the way Essex wrote to Elizabeth before the Rebellion and signed his letters, "Your humblest vassal, Essex." Oxford in Sonnet 26 addressed Southampton as a servant writing "in vassalage" to his royal prince or king. Here he speaks to the Queen of "serving thee," as he wrote long ago in 1584 to Lord Burghley: "I serve Her Majesty, and I am that I am." Oxford bitterly attacks the Queen with slanders, which, if discovered by his enemies, could have caused him to be arrested for treason.

Sonnet 141	Translation
In faith I do not love thee with mine eyes,	Truthfully I don't love what I see of you,
For they in thee a thousand errors note,	Because I see a thousand faults in you,
But 'tis my heart that loves what they despise,	But my heart loyally serves what I hate,
Who in despite of view is pleased to dote.	And despite this hate, I do your pleasure.
Nor are mine ears with thy tongue's tune delighted,	Nor am I delighted with what your words,
Nor tender feeling to base touches prone,	Nor any feeling of royalty in your presence,
Nor taste, nor smell, desire to be invited	No taste or smell or desire to be summoned
To any sensual feast with thee alone:	Into your royal presence with you alone:
But my five wits, nor my five senses can	But neither my wisdom nor my senses can
Dissuade one foolish heart from serving thee,	Stop me from serving Your Majesty,
Who leaves unswayed the likeness of a man,	Who fails to turn me from what I must be:
Thy proud heart's slave and vassal wretch to be.	Your Majesty's servant and poor vassal.
Only my plague thus far I count my gain,	Only my self-delusion is what I've gained,
That she that makes me sin awards me pain.	That she who makes me guilty also hurts me.

1 IN FAITH I DO NOT LOVE THEE WITH MINE EYES,
In good faith my service to you does not spring from what I see in the real world; **IN FAITH** = truly, honestly; **FAITH** = "And *all my honest faith in thee is lost*" – Sonnet 152, line 8, to Elizabeth; these opening lines in echo of: "Had I no eyes but ears, my ears would love/ That inward beauty and invisible" – *Venus and Adonis*, 433-434

2 FOR THEY IN THEE A THOUSAND ERRORS NOTE,
Because my eyes see a thousand crimes in you; (Oxford received an annual grant of a thousand pounds from Elizabeth; one price he has paid has been his silence about the truth behind her myth of the Virgin Queen); **ERRORS** = misdeeds; crimes; "To burn the *errors* that these princes hold against her maiden truth" – *Much Ado About Nothing*, 4.1.162-163

3 BUT 'TIS MY HEART THAT LOVES WHAT THEY DESPISE,
Instead it's my inner self that directs me to serve the monarch I despise

REFERENCE EDITION 719

4 WHO IN DESPITE OF VIEW IS PLEASED TO DOTE.
Whom, in spite of what my eyes see, is pleased to serve

5 NOR ARE MINE EARS WITH THY TONGUE'S TUNE DELIGHTED,
THY TONGUE'S TUNE = the lies that you utter from the throne; (in 1581 Oxford had been accused by his Catholic enemies of criticizing Elizabeth's singing voice; so this accusation, while used as a means of making far more severe accusations, has its own basis in fact); "I love to hear her speak, yet well I know/ That music hath a far more pleasing sound" – Sonnet 130, lines 9-10

6 NOR TENDER FEELING TO BASE TOUCHES PRONE,
Nor do I want your physical touching; **TENDER** = with royal affection; **TENDER FEELING** = literally the sense of touch, keenly felt; **BASE** = the opposite of royal, i.e., Oxford again turning the tables on her; "As on the finger of a throne Queen,/ The *basest Jewel* will be well esteemed" – Sonnet 96, lines 5-6, to Southampton, referring also to "those errors that in thee are seen" in Sonnet 96, line 7; but now the Queen's touches themselves are "base"; **TOUCHES** = as on a musical instrument: "No touch to tune the harmony" – *Richard II*, 1.3.165; also, blemish or stain on one's honor, as in "They did not see how their Monsieur's honor ... could be salved, without great *touch* to both" – circa 1580, *OED*

7 NOR TASTE, NOR SMELL, DESIRE TO BE INVITED
Nor am I lured to serve you by these other senses

8 TO ANY SENSUAL FEAST WITH THEE ALONE
To any physical encounter with you; **SENSUAL** = willful; "For to thy *sensual fault* I bring in sense" – Sonnet 35, line 9, referring to Southampton's ill-conceived acts of treason; **FEAST** = used in connection with Southampton, i.e., Oxford feasting his eyes upon him in the Tower: "There are *feasts* so solemn and so rare" – Sonnet 52, line 5; **ALONE** = Southampton, the "all" and "one" of his motto *One for All, All for One*; in effect, Oxford has transferred his allegiance from Queen Elizabeth to Prince Henry Wriothesley

9 BUT MY FIVE WITS, NOR MY FIVE SENSES CAN
But neither my five wits nor my five senses; ("Bless thy *five wits*" – *King Lear*, 3.7.56); the five wits appear to have been "common wit, imagination, fantasy, estimation [judgment] and memory" – *Graunde Amoure*, 1554, Stephen Hawe, xxiv; "wit" in Elizabethan times was a general term for intellectual power

10 DISSUADE ONE FOOLISH HEART FROM SERVING THEE,
Stop me from serving you, my sovereign; **SERVING THEE** = rendering obedience to you, my Queen; "*I serve her Majesty*" – Oxford to Burghley, October 30, 1584; to Southampton as prince or king: "Serving with looks his sacred majesty" – Sonnet 7, line 4; "...my sovereign ... When you have bid *your servant* once adieu" – Sonnet 57, lines 6,8; **ONE** = Southampton, *One for All, All for One*; **ONE FOOLISH HEART** = Oxford's heart, which is "one" or Southampton's

11 WHO LEAVES UNSWAYED THE LIKENESS OF A MAN,
Elizabeth, who leaves her royal son unable to have "swayed" or ruled as king; **LEAVES UNSWAYED** = ("lets be *ungoverned*, allows to be ruler-less" – Booth); "Hadst thou **swayed** as Kings should do" – *3 Henry VI*, 2.6.14; "With thy sweet fingers when thou gently *sway'st*" – Sonnet 128, line 3; "O from what *power* hast thou this *powerful might*/ With insufficiency my heart to *sway*?" – Sonnet 150, lines 1-2; "The pride of **kingly sway**" – *Richard II*, 4.1.206

12 THY PROUD HEART'S SLAVE AND VASSAL WRETCH TO BE:
THY PROUD HEART'S SLAVE = your royal person's servant; **VASSAL WRETCH** = your Majesty's broken servant; "Your Majesty's humblest *vassal*" – Essex to Elizabeth, 1600; to Southampton as royal prince: "Lord of my love, to whom *in vassalage*/ Thy merit hath my duty strongly knit" – Sonnet 26, lines 1-2; **WRETCH** = "We are no tyrant but a Christian king, unto whose grace our passion is as subject as are our *wretches* fettered in our prisons" – *Henry V*, 1.2.241-243

No. 141

13 **ONLY MY PLAGUE THUS FAR I COUNT MY GAIN,**
ONLY = echoing "one" for Southampton, who was "*only* herald to the gaudy spring" in Sonnet 1, line 10, and who will be the "*onlie* begetter of these ensuing sonnets" in the 1609 dedication; **MY PLAGUE** = my deluded flattery that I am the father of a king; ("Or whether doth my mind, being crowned with you,/ Drink up the *monarch's plague*, this flattery?" – Sonnet 114, lines 1-2); "Love whets the dullest wits, his *plagues* be such" – Oxford poem, *Love is a Discord*

14 **THAT SHE THAT MAKES ME SIN AWARDS ME PAIN.**
SHE = Elizabeth; **MAKES ME SIN** = forces me to take on guilt; and forces me to swear falsely; "Poor soul, the *center of my sinful earth*" – Sonnet 146, line 1; "It is great *sin* to swear unto a *sin*, but *greater sin to keep a sinful oath*" – 2 Henry VI, 5.1.182-183; "I am a man *more sinned against than sinning*" – the King in *King Lear*, 3.2.58-59; "This my last *sin*, this great, this bloody, this crying, this infectious *sin*" – Essex, moments before his execution on February 25, 1601; "O, what authority and show of truth can cunning *sin* cover itself withal!" – *Much Ado About Nothing*, 4.1.33-34; **AWARDS ME** = legally sentences me; **AWARDS ME PAIN** = ("…a soul's *term of imprisonment* in purgatory" – Booth); pain = punishment; "O for my sake do you with fortune chide,/ The *guilty goddess of my harmful deeds*" – Sonnet 111, lines 1-2, to Southampton, referring to Elizabeth as "fortune" and expressing the same thought as here; (by the Queen's decree, our son is guilty; I take on that guilt or sin; and then she rewards (awards or sentences) me with "pain" by still threatening to execute him; "If my slight Muse do please these curious days,/ The *pain* be mine, but thine shall be the praise" – Sonnet 38, lines 13-14, to Southampton; "What things did please and what did *pain*" – Oxford poem, *The Meeting With Desire*, before 1576; "punishment" – Booth, citing *OED*, from 1577: "*Condemnation unto death* set as a **peine** *(pain)* upon our heads, because of the transgression."

THE MONUMENT

THE DARK LADY: ELIZABETH

SOUTHAMPTON AWAITS EXECUTION

Sonnet 142
Root Pity In Thy Heart
March 1601

"Love" in the sonnets is royal blood; and that, Oxford writes to Elizabeth, is the crime of which, as Southampton's devoted father, he is guilty. By refusing to acknowledge her son, she has profaned her "scarlet ornaments" -- recalling Southampton as "the world's fresh ornament" (England's royal prince) of Sonnet 1. In the end, however, she is hiding and denying her own royal blood and lineage, allowing her dynasty to die.

Sonnet 142	Translation
Love is my sin, and thy dear vertue hate,	His royalty is my crime; your virtue is hate;
Hate of my sin, grounded on sinful loving.	Hating my crime, based on royal treason.
O but with mine compare thou thine own state,	O but compare your royal state with mine,
And thou shalt find it merits not reproving.	And you'll find mine doesn't deserve reproof.
Or if it do, not from those lips of thine,	Or if it does, not from your Majesty's voice,
That have profaned their scarlet ornaments,	Which has profaned her royal son and prince,
And sealed false bonds of love as oft as mine,	And sworn false oaths of royalty just as much,
Robbed others' beds' revenues of their rents.	Robbed your child of what he is due.
Be it lawful I love thee as thou lov'st those	If it's lawful for me to serve you as you do him,
Whom thine eyes woo as mine importune thee.	Whom you have looked upon as I look on you,
Root pity in thy heart, that when it grows,	Plant pity in your royal heart, so when it grows,
Thy pity may deserve to pitied be.	Your pity for him will deserve to be pitied.
If thou dost seek to have what thou dost hide,	If you seek an heir whom you imprison,
By self-example mayst thou be denied.	By your own actions, may you be denied him!

1 LOVE IS MY SIN, AND THY DEAR VIRTUE HATE
My crime is the royal blood of my son; and your most royal virtue is your hatred; and I hate your dear virtue; **SIN** = picking up from "That she that makes me sin awards me pain" – line 14 of the previous sonnet; **THY DEAR VERTUE** = Elizabeth's royal honor; her public image as Virgin Queen; **VER** = a glance at Edward Ver; **HATE** = the opposite, i.e., her denial of her son's royal blood; the Queen's malevolence

2 HATE OF MY SIN, GROUNDED ON SINFUL LOVING;
HATE OF MY SIN = you are evil toward the royal blood that is my crime; **GROUNDED ON SINFUL LOVING** = based upon your own "crime" in having given Southampton your royal blood; Oxford's sin in serving his son, who is branded as a traitor

3 O BUT WITH MINE COMPARE THOU THINE OWN STATE,
O = Oxford; **BUT WITH**, etc. = but compare your state with mine; "Authorizing thy trespass with *compare*" – Sonnet 35, line 6; **STATE** = royal state of Elizabeth as Queen of England; ("When I have seen such *interchange of state*" – Sonnet 64, line 9, referring to the bargain being made that will exchange Elizabeth's Tudor "state" to the "state" of King James of Scotland as King James I of England; a bargain being made at this time, although first it's up to Elizabeth to spare her son's life)

4 AND THOU SHALT FIND IT MERITS NOT REPROVING,
And you will find that my state does not merit your reproof

5 OR IF IT DO, NOT FROM THOSE LIPS OF THINE,
Or even if it does, not from your Majesty's own lips (since, after all, you are the mother of this son who has your own royal blood that you reject)

6 THAT HAVE PROFANED THEIR SCARLET ORNAMENTS
Those who profane their sacred robes of office, i.e., monarchs like you; **PROFANED** = ("Sweet beauty hath no name, no holy bower,/ But is *profaned*, if not lives in disgrace" – Sonnet 127, lines 7-8; related to profaning God, i.e., profaning a god on earth or king; profaning Southampton as "the little Love-God" of Sonnet 154, line 1 and as "a God in love" of Sonnet 110, line 12; **SCARLET ORNAMENTS** = servants of the monarch who wear red or scarlet robes, as Oxford often did as Lord Great Chamberlain; cardinals of the church wore scarlet robes and Elizabeth was head of both Church and State, so she has "profaned" herself; here she has profaned Southampton, who is her "*scarlet*" (royal-blooded) "*ornament*" or prince; ("Thou that art now the world's fresh *ornament*" – Sonnet 1, line 9; Southampton = "As on the finger of a throned Queen,/ The basest *Jewel* will be well esteemed" – Sonnet 96, lines 5-6); Elizabeth has profaned all three members of the family triangle: herself, Oxford, Southampton; "Anon, with reverent fear when she grew pale his cheeks put on their *scarlet ornaments*" – *Edward III*, 2.1.9-10

7 AND SEALED FALSE BONDS OF LOVE AS OFT AS MINE,
SEALED = "She carved thee for *her seal*" – Sonnet 11, line 13; **SEALED FALSE BONDS** = falsely sworn vows of indissoluble union; similar to "bound" in relation to Southampton; as in the dedication *Lucrece* to him: "Were my worth greater, my duty would show greater; meantime, as it is, it is *bound* to your Lordship"; "Being your vassal *bound* to stay your leisure" – Sonnet 58, line 4; "My *bonds* in thee are all determinate" – Sonnet 87, line 4; "Whereto *all bonds* to tie me day by day" – Sonnet 117, line 4; "Under that *bond* that him as fast doth bind" – Sonnet 134, line 8; **OF LOVE** = in relation to our son's royal blood; ("And *you and love* are still my argument" – Sonnet 76, line 10); i.e., at one point Elizabeth had vowed to name her son to succeed her, but all those vows have been broken; noted in *Venus and Adonis*, dedicated to their son:

> Pure lips, sweet *seals* in my soft lips imprinted,
> What *bargains* may I make, still to be *sealing*?"
> - *Venus and Adonis*, 511-512

"From the fact that kissing often accompanied a bargain" – Tucker; "And seal the bargain with a holy kiss" – *The Two Gentlemen of Verona*, 2.2.7

8 ROBBED OTHERS' BEDS' REVENUES OF THEIR RENTS.
REVENUES = the earnings of royal blood; the "treasury" metaphor, as in, "For she hath no *exchequer* now but his" – Sonnet 67, line 11; "The yearly *revenues* and possessions of this your Highness' realm" – O. E. D., citing 1546, the reign of Henry VIII; "In act *thy bed-vow broke* and new faith torn/ In vowing new hate after new love bearing" – Sonnet 152, lines 3-4; "Have I not seen dwellers on form and favor/ Lose all and more by *paying too much rent*" – Sonnet 125, lines 5-6, corresponding with Elizabeth's funeral on April 28, 1603

9 BE IT LAWFUL I LOVE THEE AS THOU LOV'ST THOSE
LAWFUL = if it is legal or permissible; "*Be it lawful* I take up what's cast away" – *King Lear*, 1.1.255; "When law can do no right, *let it be lawful* that law bar no wrong!" – *King John*, 3.1.111-112; "And 'gainst myself a *lawful plea* commence" – Sonnet 35, line 11; "To guard the *lawful* reasons on thy part" – Sonnet 49, line 12; **I LOVE THEE AS THOU LOV'ST THOSE** = I love you as you love those

10 WHOM THINE EYES WOO AS MINE IMPORTUNE THEE.
WHOM THINE EYES WOO = who seek the approval of your royal eyes; whom you seek to command

with your eyes; "And *when a woman woos, what woman's son/ Will sourly leave her till he have prevailed?"* – Sonnet 42, lines 7-8; **AS MINE IMPORTUNE THEE** = in the same way that my eyes plead with you (for our son's royal blood); in the following poem (attributed by one source to Queen Elizabeth and by another source to the Earl of Oxford) the word "importune" is highlighted for emphasis:

> When I was fair and young then favor graced me;
> Of many was I sought their mistress for to be.
> But I did scorn them all, and answered them therefore,
> 'Go, go, go, seek some otherwhere, ***Importune*** me no more.'
>
> How many weeping eyes I made to pine in woe;
> How many sighing hearts I have no skill to show;
> Yet I the prouder grew, and answered them therefore,
> 'Go, go, go, seek some otherwhere, ***Importune*** me no more.'
>
> Then spake fair Venus' son, that proud victorious boy,
> And said, "You dainty dame, since that you be so coy,
> I will so pluck your plumes that you shall say no more,
> 'Go, go, go, seek some otherwhere, ***Importune*** me no more.'"
>
> When he had spake these words, such change grew in my breast,
> That neither night nor day I could take any rest.
> Then, lo! I did repent, that I had said before,
> 'Go, go, go, seek some otherwhere, ***Importune*** me no more.'
>
> Elysabethe Regina

Editor Katherine Chiljan cites Rawlinson Poet. MS 85, f.1 for the above text, which credits Queen Elizabeth I as the writer; but Folger MS V.a.89, f.7 is signed "l: of oxforde'. In any case, the reference to '*fair Venus' son*" is remarkable in the context of the Sonnets, not to mention in the context of *Venus and Adonis* itself; and the young man or young god of Oxford's poem was the importuning party, just as Oxford is now importuning the Queen to stop the execution of her son. (Perhaps Oxford wrote the poem for Elizabeth, who may have enjoyed it and adopted it as her own while never actually claiming credit. In that light, Oxford's echo of it in this sonnet is especially poignant.)

11 ROOT PITY IN THY HEART, THAT WHEN IT GROWS,
Plant pity inside your heart, so that when it grows; "a rooted sorrow" – *Macbeth*, 5.3.41; "Thy truth and thy integrity is rooted in us thy friend" – the King to Cranmer in *Henry VIII*, 5.1.114-115; related to the "roots" of Southampton as flower of the Tudor Rose; **GROWS** = "When I consider every thing that *grows*/ ... When I perceive that *men as plants increase*" – Sonnet 15, lines 1, 5, of Southampton as royal heir of the Tudor Rose; "Love is a Babe; then might I not say so/ To *give full growth to that which still doth grow*" – Sonnet 115, lines 13-14

12 THY PITY MAY DESERVE TO PITIED BE.
("Your own pitiful state may be worthy" – Booth)

13 IF THOU DOST SEEK TO HAVE WHAT THOU DOST HIDE,
If you seek to have what you conceal and withhold, i.e. if you seek to have Southampton's royal blood for your Tudor Rose lineage but hide it from the world; if you seek to have a natural heir whom you keep in prison and execute

14 BY SELF-EXAMPLE MAYST THOU BE DENIED.
By your own actions, you will be deprived of your own heir and lineage.

Part Three

THE DARK LADY: ELIZABETH

SOUTHAMPTON AWAITS EXECUTION

Sonnet 143
Play The Mother's Part
March 1601

As the time for Elizabeth's decision about Southampton's fate draws nearer, Oxford pulls out all the stops. He again declares that if she executes her son she will be killing him as well. Oxford identifies with his royal son when he pleads with her as "I, thy babe" and calls upon her to "play the mother's part." In this sense he writes the entire verse in the voice of Southampton himself. This complete identification with his son echoes Sonnet 62: "This thee (my self) that for my self I praise." His begs Elizabeth to be "kind" or to act according to the reality that she is his (Southampton's) natural mother, echoing Sonnet 105: "Kind is my love today, tomorrow kind/ ... Fair, kind, and true, is all my argument." When the Queen spares Southampton's life, Oxford will mark the event in Sonnet 145 by again speaking with his royal son's voice.

Sonnet 143	Translation
Lo, as a careful housewife runs to catch	Look, as a Queen mother runs to catch
One of her feathered creatures broke away,	One of her favorite courtiers gone astray,
Sets down her babe, and makes all swift dispatch	Puts aside her own son, and makes haste
In pursuit of the thing she would have stay:	To pursue the loyalty of others,
Whilst her neglected child holds her in chase,	While her unacknowledged son follows her,
Cries to catch her whose busy care is bent	And begs mercy from his mother who is bent
To follow that which flies before her face,	On catching all who flee from her,
Not prizing her poor infant's discontent:	Not caring about her poor son's suffering:
So run'st thou after that which flies from thee,	So do you run after what you cannot have,
Whilst I, thy babe, chase thee afar behind,	While I, for your son, chase after you;
But if thou catch thy hope turn back to me:	But if you find what you want, turn back to me,
And play the mother's part, kiss me, be kind.	Act like the mother you are, fulfill your nature.
So will I pray that thou mayst have thy Will,	So I pray you have your royal will and "Will",
If thou turn back and my loud crying still.	If you turn and satisfy my strong pleading.

1 LO, AS A CAREFUL HOUSEWIFE RUNS TO CATCH
LO = Lord Oxford; **CAREFUL** = "full of cares, subject to anxiety, sorrow, or want" – Schmidt; "With signs of war about his neck; O, full of *careful business* are his looks!" – Richard II, 2.2.74-75; also attentive, provident, as in "How *careful* was I, when I took my way,/ Each trifle under truest bars to thrust" – Sonnet 48, lines 1-2; "Madam, bethink you, like a *careful mother* of the young prince your son: send straight for him; let him be crowned" - Richard III, 2.2.96-98; **HOUSEWIFE** = "a woman skilled in female business and superintending the concerns of a family" – Schmidt; Queen Elizabeth, sovereign Mistress, head of the *House of Tudor*; and betrothed as *wife* of Oxford; "Who lets so fair a *house* fall to decay" – Sonnet 13, line 9; overtones of *huswife* or hussy: "Doth Fortune play the *huswife* with me now?" – Henry V, 5.1.79

2 ONE OF HER FEATHERED CREATURES BROKEAWAY,
ONE = Southampton, *One for All, All for One*; **FEATHERED** = dressed up, i.e., as an earl; ("trimmed in jollity" – Sonnet 66, line 3); **CREATURES** = children, i.e., Southampton; ("From fairest *creatures* we

desire increase" – Sonnet 1, line 1); also one of her courtiers "created" as an earl; Oxford in this verse is speaking for Southampton, i.e., they are father-son and so they are one and the same creature; in addition both were royal wards of the Queen, i.e., each was a "child of state" as in Sonnet 124, line 1: "If my dear love were but the child of state"

3 SETS DOWN HER BABE AND MAKES ALL SWIFT DISPATCH
HER BABE = her true child, Southampton; "*Love is a Babe*" – Sonnet 115, line 13, referring to Southampton's royal blood; "*The little Love-God*" – Sonnet 154, line 1, of Southampton as an infant god-on-earth or prince; "*I, thy babe*" – line 10 of this sonnet, Oxford speaking for his royal son; "These *babes* for Clarence weep, and so do I" – *Richard III*, 2.2.84, of the sons of Edward IV; **ALL** = Southampton, *One for All, All for One*; and runs off

4 IN PURSUIT OF THE THING SHE WOULD HAVE STAY:
In the quest to have the very Tudor blood and lineage that she (Elizabeth) wants to preserve; **PURSUIT** = "Mad in pursuit" – Sonnet 129, line 9; **STAY** = "Desire I did desire to *stay*" – Oxford poem, *The Meeting With Desire*; "From limits far remote, *where thou dost stay*" – Sonnet 44, line 4, of Southampton in prison; "Being your vassal bound to *stay* your leisure" – Sonnet 58, line 4; "Which for memorial still with thee shall *stay*" – Sonnet 74, line 4; "And life no longer than thy love will *stay*" – Sonnet 92, line 3;

5 WHILST HER NEGLECTED CHILD HOLDS HER IN CHASE,
HER NEGLECTED CHILD = the Queen's abandoned royal son; "If my dear love were but the *child of state*" - Sonnet 124, line 1

6 CRIES TO CATCH HER WHOSE BUSY CARE IS BENT
CRIES, etc. = cries and begs for your mercy, why you fly elsewhere; an image of Southampton crying for mercy from his mother the Queen, whose attention is elsewhere; **CARE** = "Thou best of dearest, and mine only *care*" – Sonnet 48, line 7, to Southampton; **BENT** = focused; "they wear their faces to the *bent* of the king's looks" – *Cymbeline*, 1.1.12-13; a play on bended or bent knees before the monarch; "Alas, how is't with you, that you do *bend your eye* on vacancy" – *Hamlet*, 3.4.117; "And that same eye whose *bend* doth awe the world" – *Julius Caesar*, 1.2.122; "though rosy lips and cheeks/ Within his *bending* sickle's compass come" – Sonnet 116, lines 9-10; a suggestion of the *bent* figure of hunchbacked Robert Cecil, who is *bending* the Queen's attention and decisions in regard to the fate of Southampton

7 TO FOLLOW THAT WHICH FLIES BEFORE HER FACE,
(Suggesting "biblical images such as those of the ungodly who '*flee before the face of God*,' Psalms, 68.1 – Duncan-Jones); in this case Elizabeth fleeing from her son as "the little Love-God" of Sonnet 154, line 1, and from Southampton as a "God in love" of Sonnet 110, line 12)

8 NOT PRIZING HER POOR INFANT'S DISCONTENT;
Not estimating, caring about, taking account of; not considering her royal son as her prize; **HER POOR INFANT'S DISCONTENT** = her poor son's suffering in the Tower, awaiting execution; "He is *contented thy poor drudge to be*" – Sonnet 151, line 11, of Southampton and Elizabeth

9 SO RUN'ST THOU AFTER THAT WHICH FLIES FROM THEE,
So do you flee toward what you cannot (or will not) have

10 WHILST I, THY BABE, CHASE THEE AFAR BEHIND;
I, THY BABE = Standing in for their royal son and taking on his identity, Oxford is speaking for him and pleading to be spared from execution; "*Love is a Babe*, then might I not say so,/ To give full growth to that which still doth grow" – Sonnet 115, lines 13-14; "what *woman's son*" – Sonnet 41, line 7; "The boy" – Sonnet 153, line 10; "The little Love-God" – Sonnet 154, line 1

11 BUT IF THOU CATCH THY HOPE, TURN BACK TO ME,
THY HOPE = whatever it is that you want; the succession of your blood; your hope for your son as your

royal heir; "Yet this abundant *issue* seemed to me/ But ***hope*** *of orphans*, and un-fathered fruit" – Sonnet 97, lines 9-10; "Will answer our ***hope*** in *issue of a king*" – *1 Henry VI*, 5.5.72; "Come hither, *England's **hope***" – *3 Henry VI*, 4.6.68, to young Henry, Earl of Richmond, the future Henry VII, founder of the Tudor dynasty; "the world's *hopeful* expectation" – dedication of *Venus and Adonis* to Southampton

12 **AND PLAY THE MOTHER'S PART, KISS ME, BE KIND.**
PLAY THE MOTHER'S PART = act like the royal mother that you are; be the mother of your son; "the duty which to a *mother's **part*** belongs" – *Coriolanus*, 5.3.169-170; "Thou art *thy mother's* glass" – Sonnet 3, line 9, to Southampton; "Resembling sire, and child, and happy *mother*" – Sonnet 8, line 11; **PART** = legal, related to "party" as in "Thy adverse *party* is thy advocate" – Sonnet 35, line 10; "Upon the right and *party of her son*" – *King John*, 1.1.34; "*Upon thy **part*** I can set down a story/ Of faults concealed, wherein I am attainted" – Sonnet 88, lines 6-7; **KISS ME** = "Do I envy those Jacks that nimble leap/ To kiss the tender inward of thy hand ... Give them thy fingers, me thy lips to kiss" – Sonnet 128, lines 5-6, 14, in relation to the Queen granting favors to courtiers and "jacks" such as Raleigh; **KIND** = related by blood; "*Kind* is my love today, tomorrow *kind*" – Sonnet 105, line 5, speaking of Southampton as natural child of the Queen; **BE KIND** = be what you really are, i.e., demonstrate that you are his natural mother by sparing his life; "Shall *kin* with *kin*, and *kind* with *kind*, confound" – *Richard II*, 4.1.141; ("do not neglect your child" – Booth).

13 **SO WILL I PRAY THAT THOU MAYST HAVE THY *WILL*,**
PRAY = pray, as in these sonnets; ("Nothing, *sweet boy*, but yet like *prayers divine*" – Sonnet 108, line 5); ***WILL*** = (capitalized and italicized in *Q*); **THY *WILL*** = both your royal will and your "Will" Shakespeare, my pen name dedicated to Southampton and, by extension, dedicated to his royal Tudor blood that he inherited from you

14 **IF THOU TURN BACK AND MY LOUD CRYING STILL.**
MY LOUD CRYING = Oxford's loud cries for mercy for his son; "And *trouble deaf heaven* with my *bootless cries*" – Sonnet 29, line 3; **STILL** = pacify and make silent; echoing "still" as constant or eternal

THE DARK LADY: ELIZABETH

SOUTHAMPTON AWAITS EXECUTION

Sonnet 144
Two Loves I Have
March 1601

This verse (along with Sonnet 138) was included in The Passionate Pilgrim *of 1599 but revised and inserted here in the Dark Lady series (see comparison immediately following the notes for line 14). Oxford's "two loves" are both filled with "love" or royal blood, i.e., with the shared blood of Southampton and the Queen. Henry Wriothesley is "a man right fair" or a prince by birthright; Elizabeth is "a woman colored ill" because of her dark viewpoint that turns her eyes black in reflection of what she sees.*

Sonnet 144	Translation
Two loves I have of comfort and despair,	Two royal bloods I have, of comfort and despair,
Which like two spirits do suggest me still,	Who are two Princes leading me onward;
The better angel is a man right fair,	The best one is my royal son who should be king,
The worser spirit a woman colored ill.	The worst one is my Queen with a negative view.
To win me soon to hell, my female evil	To lead me into suffering, my malicious Queen
Tempteth my better angel from my sight,	Leads my royal son away from me,
And would corrupt my saint to be a devil,	And would lead him to some act of treason,
Wooing his purity with her foul pride.	Tempting his true rights with her evil view.
And whether that my angel be turned fiend,	And whether my royal son turns to revolt,
Suspect I may, yet not directly tell,	I suspect it, but cannot say aloud,
But being both from me both to each friend,	But being away from me, both mother and son,
I guess one angel in another's hell.	I guess my son lives in his mother's hell.
Yet this shall I ne'er know, but live in doubt,	Of the outcome I don't know, but live in fear,
Till my bad angel fire my good one out.	Until my evil queen allows him to succeed her.

1 TWO LOVES I HAVE OF COMFORT AND DESPAIR,
TWO LOVES = two sovereigns of royal blood, Southampton and Elizabeth; I have two persons who are beloved to me: Southampton gives me comfort, Elizabeth leads me to despair.

> **COMFORT:**
> As a decrepit *father* takes delight
> To see his active *child* do deeds of youth,
> So I, made lame by Fortune's dearest spite,
> Take *all my comfort* of thy worth and truth.
> - Sonnet 37, lines 1-4
>
> "Warwick, *my son, the comfort* of mine age"
> - 2 Henry VI, 1.1.189
>
> **DESPAIR:**
> For if I should *despair* I should grow mad,

Part Three

And in my madness might speak ill of thee
- Sonnet 140, lines 9-10 (To the Queen)

2 WHICH LIKE TWO SPIRITS DO SUGGEST ME STILL;
TWO SPIRITS = two sacred princes; ("The expense of *spirit*" – Sonnet 129, line 1); to his royal son: "and do not kill/ The *spirit of love*" – Sonnet 56, lines 7-8, i.e., the life of royal blood; "Is it *thy spirit* that thou send'st from thee" – Sonnet 61, line 5; "*My spirit is thine, the better part of me*" – Sonnet 74, line 8; **SUGGEST ME STILL** = always urge or lead me onward (toward one or the other, i.e., toward comfort or despair); "Only to show his pomp as well in France as here at home, *suggests* the King our Master to this last costly treaty" – *Henry VIII*, 1.2.163-165

3 THE BETTER ANGEL IS A MAN RIGHT FAIR,
ANGEL = a messenger of God; a divinely ordained prince; **BETTER ANGEL** = most royal prince, Southampton; ("Good night, sweet prince, and flights of *angels* sing thee to thy rest" – *Hamlet*, 5.2.385-386); **RIGHT** = right to the throne; "Such is my love, to thee I so belong,/ That for *thy right* myself will bear all wrong" – Sonnet 88, lines 13-14; **A MAN RIGHT FAIR** = Southampton; "A man in hew all Hews in his controlling" – Sonnet 20, line 7; **FAIR** = royal; "From *fairest* creatures we desire increase" – Sonnet 1, line 1

4 THE WORSER SPIRIT A WOMAN COLOURED ILL.
WORSER SPIRIT = Elizabeth; **SPIRIT** = her royal blood; (Essex wrote to Elizabeth in 1597 and called her "the Spirit of spirits" – Weir, 427); **A WOMAN COLORED ILL** = Elizabeth, whose dark coloring is not physical but the reflection of "the region cloud" of Sonnet 33, line 12, i.e., Elizabeth Regina's dark cloud of "bastard shame" as in Sonnet 127, line 4

5 TO WIN ME SOON TO HELL, MY FEMALE EVIL
HELL = personal agony and suffering; **MY FEMALE EVIL** = Elizabeth

6 TEMPTETH MY BETTER ANGEL FROM MY SIGHT,
Leads my son away from me

7 AND WOULD CORRUPT MY SAINT TO BE A DEVIL:
And would lead him to rebellion, i.e., to become a traitor; written by 1599, anticipating Southampton's revolt in the face of the Queen's refusal to favor him and Essex over Robert Cecil

8 WOOING HIS PURITY WITH HER FOUL PRIDE.
WOOING: tempting him by having promised to name him in succession; "And when a woman woos, what woman's son/ Will sourly leave her till he have prevailed?" – Sonnet 41, lines 7-8; **HIS PURITY** = his true royal blood; **HER FOUL PRIDE** = Elizabeth's evil royal attitude toward her son; **FOUL** = "For since each hand hath put on Nature's power,/ Fairing the *foul* with Art's false borrowed face" - Sonnet 127, lines 5-6; **PRIDE** = show of royal blood; "Why is my verse so barren of new pride?" - Sonnet 76, line 1

9 AND WHETHER THAT MY ANGEL BE TURN'D FIEND,
MY ANGEL = my royal son, Southampton

10 SUSPECT I MAY, YET NOT DIRECTLY TELL,
NOT DIRECTLY TELL = not say or write openly and publicly; "O learn to read what silent love hath writ" – Sonnet 23, line 13; "And art made tongue-tied by authority" – Sonnet 66, line 9; **NOT DIRECTLY** = "That every word doth *almost* tell my name" – Sonnet 76, line 7

11 BUT BEING BOTH FROM ME BOTH TO EACH FRIEND,
BUT BEING BOTH FROM ME = but both being away from me; i.e., Southampton is unacknowledged and Elizabeth will not listen to me; **BOTH TO EACH FRIEND** = and both linked by blood to each other.

12 I GUESS ONE ANGEL IN AN OTHER'S HELL.
ONE = Southampton, *One for All, All for One*; **ONE ANGEL** = Southampton; **IN ANOTHER'S HELL** = they are each in the other's hell; i.e., Elizabeth is suffering over her son just as much as he is; she is in the same hell, which is of her own making

13 YET THIS SHALL I NE'ER KNOW BUT LIVE IN DOUBT,
NE'ER = never, replacing "not" in the same line in *Passionate Pilgrim* of 1599; i.e., now that Southampton is in prison as a convicted traitor, the situation is irreversible; **LIVE IN DOUBT** = go on, day by day, without knowing the outcome

14 TILL MY BAD ANGEL FIRE MY GOOD ONE OUT.
MY BAD ANGEL = Elizabeth; **FIRE** = drive out; "his love-kindling fire" - Sonnet 153, line 3; **ONE** = Southampton; **MY GOOD ONE** = Southampton; **FIRE MY GOOD ONE OUT** = ("One fire drives out another" – a proverb, Tilley, F277, cited by Duncan-Jones); until Elizabeth recognizes her son as royal and allows him to escape this hell

Passionate Pilgrim: 1599

Two loves I have, of Comfort and Despair,
That like two Spirits, do suggest me still:
My better Angel is a Man (right fair)
My worser spirit a Woman (colored ill).

To win me soon to hell, my Female evil
Tempteth my better Angel from my side:
And would corrupt my Saint to be a Devil,
Wooing his purity with her fair pride.

And whether that my Angel be turned fiend,
Suspect I may (yet not directly tell)
For being both to me, both to each friend,
I guess one Angel in another's hell:

The truth I shall not know, but live in doubt,
Till my bad Angel fire my good one out.

Sonnet 144: Revision - 1601

Two loves I have of comfort and despair,
Which like two spirits do suggest me still;
The better angel is a man right fair,
The worser spirit a woman colored ill.

To win me soon to hell my female evil
Tempteth my better angel from my *sight*
And would corrupt my saint to be a devil,
Wooing his purity with her *foul* pride.

And whether that my angel be turned fiend,
Suspect I may, yet not directly tell,
But being both *from* me both to each friend,
I guess one angel in another's hell.

Yet this shall I *ne'er* know, but live in doubt,
Till my bad angel fire my good one out.

Part Three

THE DARK LADY: ELIZABETH

THE QUEEN SPARES SOUTHAMPTON'S LIFE

Sonnet 145
*Straight In Her Heart Did Mercy Come
And Saved My Life*
19 March 1601

This verse corresponds in time to Sonnet 66 of the Fair Youth series to Southampton, when Oxford reacts to Elizabeth's order to spare the life of Henry Wriothesley by recording a virtual suicide note, filled with relief and sorrow. Here he responds to the Queen's act of mercy with a show of gratitude for sparing their royal son from execution. He breaks with his usual sonnet form, employing eight rather than ten beats per line. Just as Sonnet 66 is different from all other verses, the form of this verse marks it also as special. Throughout Oxford speaks in his son's voice. "Straight in her heart did mercy come," he reports, adding that Elizabeth "saved my life."

Sonnet 145	Translation
Those lips that Love's own hand did make Breathed forth the sound that said, "I hate," To me that languished for her sake. But when she saw my woeful state,	Elizabeth's command by her royal authority Was that our son should be executed, Telling me, who feared for his death by her, But when she saw my/his woeful state,
Straight in her heart did mercy come, Chiding that tongue that ever sweet Was used in giving gentle doom: And taught it thus anew to greet:	Straight in her heart she found mercy, Rebuking her own command that royally Was used in ordering his royal death: And instructed her own decree to change:
"I hate" she altered with an end That followed it as gentle day Doth follow night, who like a fiend From heaven to hell is flown away.	"He must die" she changed, with a result That followed as a royal golden time Follows royal death, which like a fiend Was overturned from Elizabeth to hell.
"I hate" from hate away she threw, And saved my life, saying, "Not you."	"He must die" she removed from herself, And saved my/his life, saying, "Not him!"

*"My lords, I must say for my part as I have said before, that since the ignorance of the law hath made me incur the danger of the law, I humbly submit myself to **her Majesty's mercy** ... I pray you truly to inform the Queen of my penitence, and be a means for me to her Majesty to grant me her gracious pardon. I know I have offended her; yet if it please her to be **merciful** unto me, I may, by my future service, deserve **my life**." - Southampton at the Trial on February 19, 1601*

1 THOSE LIPS THAT LOVE'S OWN HAND DID MAKE
THOSE LIPS = Elizabeth's voice, her decree; "And *mercy* then will *breathe within **your lips***" - *Measure for Measure*, 2.2.78; **LOVE** = royal blood; **LOVE'S OWN HAND** = the Queen's power; the Queen's own hand also created "love" within her son, Southampton, who was "the little Love-God" of Sonnet 154, line 1; the boy ("Cupid" of Sonnet 153, line 1) was given "A Woman's face with *nature's **own hand** painted*" – Sonnet 20, line 1, i.e., he had Elizabeth's face because she was his natural mother who gave birth to him; and Southampton as an infant was "sleeping **by a Virgin hand** disarmed" – Sonnet 154, line 8; "A heavy sentence ... **at your Highness' hands**" – *Richard II*, 1.3.154-158

REFERENCE EDITION 731

For *love* is worse than *hate*, and eke more harm hath done,
Record I take of those that read of Paris, Priam's son.
- Finis. E. O. (Earl of Oxford, *Paradise of Dainty Devices*, 1576)

2 BREATHED FORTH THE SOUND THAT SAID, "I HATE"
BREATHED FORTH THE SOUND = decreed that Southampton should follow Essex to his execution; "And mercy then will *breathe* within your lips" - *Measure for Measure*, 2.2.78; "Or let the church, our mother, *breathe* her curse, a mother's curse, on her revolting son" – *King John*, 3.1.182-183; "By all the blood that every fury *breathed*" – *King John*, 5.2.127; "Norfolk, for thee remains a heavier doom, which I with some unwillingness pronounce … The hopeless word of 'never to return' *breathe I against thee*, upon pain of life" – the King in *Richard II*, 1.3.148-153, followed by: "A heavy sentence, my most sovereign liege, and all unlook'd for *from your Highness' mouth*" – *Richard II*, 1.3.154-155

Come hither, Harry, sit by my bed,
And hear, I think, the very latest counsel
That ever I shall *breathe*.
- *2 Henry IV*, 4.5.181-183, the King to his son

"I HATE" = Elizabeth's initial reaction to the Rebellion, determining to execute Southampton; also, her refusal to acknowledge their son's "love" or royal blood, turning it into its opposite, "hate"; Southampton also expressed his "hate" toward Oxford, for his bargain requiring him to give up any claim to the crown: "For thee against my self I'll vow debate,/ For I must ne'er love him whom thou dost *hate*" - Sonnet 89, lines 13-14; "Then *hate* me when thou wilt, if ever, now" - Sonnet 90, line 1, referring also to Southampton's threat to break out of the Tower and lead another Rebellion against Robert Cecil and the Queen

Besides, our nearness to the king in *love*
Is near the *hate* of those love not the king
- *Richard II*, 2.2.126-127

The King: Rivers and Hastings, take each other's hand;
Dissemble not your *hatred*: swear your *love*.

Rivers: By heaven, my soul is purged from grudging *hate*,
And with my hand I seal my true heart's *love*...

Buckingham: Whenever Buckingham doth turn his *hate*
Upon your Grace, but with all duteous *love*
Doth cherish you and yours, God punish me
With *hate* in those where I expect most *love*.
- *Richard III*, 2.1.9-35

3 TO ME THAT LANGUISHED FOR HER SAKE:
TO ME = to Oxford, who stands in for Southampton, since he and his son are one and the same; therefore, the Queen uttered this decree to Southampton; **THAT LANGUISHED FOR HER SAKE** = who has been languishing in the Tower, in expectation of being executed according to the Queen' imperial will; **HER SAKE** = the Queen's pleasure

4 BUT WHEN SHE SAW MY WOEFUL STATE,
But when Elizabeth realized our woeful state; i.e., the ruined royal state of my son, and therefore my own state; **WOEFUL** = "heavy tears, badges of either's *woe*" – Sonnet 44, line 14; "To weigh how once I suffered in your crime./ O that our night of woe might have rememb'red/ My deepest sense, how hard true sorrow hits" - Sonnet 120, lines 8-10; **STATE** = his situation, but actually his son's royal state; "When in disgrace with Fortune and men's eyes,/ I all alone beweep *my outcast state*" - Sonnet 29, line 1-2; "How

many gazers mightst thou lead away,/ If thou wouldst use the strength of *all thy state*" - Sonnet 96, lines 11-12

5 STRAIGHT IN HER HEART DID MERCY COME,
Elizabeth found mercy in her heart, the source of her royal blood; **MERCY** = the same "mercy" from Elizabeth for which Southampton pleaded at the trial:

"My lords, I must say for my part as I have said before, that since the ignorance of the law hath made me incur the danger of the law, I humbly submit myself to **her Majesty's mercy** ... I pray you truly to inform the Queen of my penitence, and be a means for me to her Majesty to grant me her gracious pardon. I know I have offended her; yet if it please her to be **merciful** unto me, I may, by my future service, deserve **my life**. I have been brought up under Her Majesty. I have spent the best part of my patrimony in Her Majesty's service, with frequent danger of my life, as your Lordships well know... But since I am found guilty by the law, I do submit myself to death, yet not despairing of **Her Majesty's mercy**. For I know she is **merciful**, and if she please to extend **mercy** to me, I shall with all humility receive it." - Southampton, February 19, 1601, at the Trial

>Unto the *sovereign **mercy*** *of the King*
>- Richard II, 2.3.156

>And **mercy** then will **breathe within your lips**
>- Measure for Measure, 2.2.78

>Wilt thou draw near the nature of the gods?
>Draw near them then in being *merciful*.
>Sweet **mercy** is nobility's true badge:
>Thrice noble Titus, spare my first-born son.
>- Titus Andronicus, 1.1.120-123

>Cambridge: I do confess my fault
>And do submit me to *your highness' mercy*.
>Grey, Scoop:To which we all appeal.
>King Henry: The *mercy* that was quick in us but late
>By your own counsel is suppressed and killed:
>You must not dare, for shame, to talk of *mercy*
>- Henry V, 2.2.77-81, the King to nobles turned traitors

>The quality of **mercy** is not strained,
>It droppeth as the gentle rain from heaven
>Upon the place beneath: it is twice blest,
>It blesseth him that gives, and him that takes,
>'Tis mightiest in the mightiest, it becomes
>The throned monarch better than his crown.
>His sceptre shows the force of temporal power,
>The attribute to awe and majesty,
>Wherein doth sit the dread and fear of kings.
>But **mercy** is above this sceptred sway,
>It is enthroned in the hearts of kings,
>It is an attribute to God himself;
>An earthly power doth then show like God's
>When **mercy** *seasons justice*
>- The Merchant of Venice, 4.1.182-195

Nothing adorns a King more than *justice*, nor in anything doth a King more resemble God than in *justice*, which is the head of all virtue, and he that is endued therewith hath all the rest. – Oxford to Robert Cecil, May 7, 1603

Not the King's crown, nor the deputed sword,
The marshal's truncheon, nor the judge's robe,
Become them with one half so good a grace
As *mercy* does.
- *Measure for Measure*, 2.2.60-63

6 CHIDING THAT TONGUE THAT EVER SWEET
CHIDING THAT TONGUE = rebuking her own previous command; **EVER** = Ever = Edward deVere, *Ever or Never*; **SWEET** = royal, with sovereign power

7 WAS USED IN GIVING GENTLE DOOM;
Had sentenced Southampton to be executed; has nevertheless confined him in the Tower for a term of life; **GENTLE** = royal; "The quality of *mercy* is not strained, it droppeth as the **gentle** *rain from heaven*" – *The Merchant of Venice*, 4.1.182-183; **DOOM** = sentence or judgment; "Thy end is Truth's and Beauty's *doom* and date" – Sonnet 14, line 14; "Supposed as forfeit to a *confined doom*" – Sonnet 107, line 4, i.e., the expected fate of Southampton; "Norfolk, for thee remains a heavier *doom*, which I with some unwillingness pronounce. The sly slow hours shall not determinate the dateless limit of thy dear exile"
– *Richard II*, 1.3.148-151

8 AND TAUGHT IT THUS ANEW TO GREET:
And instructed her own decree to change; **THUS** = in the following way; **TO GREET**: to address, i.e., the Queen addressing Southampton and, therefore, addressing Oxford; the King of England "greets" the King of France: "...and thus he *greets* your Majesty: He *wills* you, in the name of God Almighty"
- *Henry V*, 2.4.76-77

9 "I HATE" SHE ALTERED WITH AN END
She changed her order for Southampton's execution; **HATE** = the opposite of expressing or showing love for her son; **ALTERED** = the same as Oxford reports in the Fair Youth series: "But reckoning time, whose millioned accidents/ Creep in twixt vows, and *change decrees of Kings*,/ Tan sacred beauty, blunt the shap'st intents,/ Divert strong minds to th'course of *alt'ring* things" - Sonnet 115, lines 5-8, immediately followed by: "Let me not to the marriage of true minds/ Admit impediments. Love is not love/ Which *alters* when it *alteration* finds" - Sonnet 116, lines 1-3, in this case referring to the alteration of succession to the throne from Southampton to someone else, i.e., to King James; **AN END** = a purpose and/or a result

10 THAT FOLLOWED IT AS GENTLE DAY
THAT FOLLOWED IT = that replaced it; **GENTLE** = royal; **DAY** = royalty; "Shall I compare thee to a Summer's *day*?" – Sonnet 18, line 1; "Why didst thou promise such a beauteous *day*" - Sonnet 34, line 1

11 DOTH FOLLOW NIGHT, WHO LIKE A FIEND
Replaces the death of Southampton's royalty; **NIGHT** = ("like a jewel hung in ghastly night/ Makes black night beauteous" – Sonnet 27, lines 11-12; "And night doth nightly make grief's length seem stronger" – Sonnet 28, line 14; "For precious friends hid in death's dateless night" – Sonnet 30, line 6)

12 FROM HEAVEN TO HELL IS FLOWN AWAY.
FROM HEAVEN = from Elizabeth, his mother; (It droppeth as the gentle rain from heaven" – *The Merchant of Venice*, 4.1.182); **TO HELL** = to the various stages of hell (loss of royal claim) he has endured, from bastardy to prison to conviction of treason to sentence of death; **IS FLOWN AWAY** = is overturned; i.e., one decree has been replaced by the other; literally, the dark night of Southampton's possible execution has fled

13 "I HATE" FROM HATE AWAY SHE THREW
Elizabeth removed her previous command from its source, i.e., from "hate" or lack of care for her own royal blood in her son…

14 AND SAVED MY LIFE, SAYING, "NOT YOU"
AND SAVED MY LIFE = and spared Southampton's life from the executioner's axe, thereby saving Oxford's life as well

> In fine, she hath both the hand and knife,
> That may both *save and end **my life***.
> - Finis. E. O. (Earl of Oxford, *Paradise of Dainty Devices*, 1576)

> "I know I have offended her; yet if it please her to be *merciful* unto me, I may, by my future service, deserve ***my life*.**"
> - Southampton at the Trial

SAYING, "NOT YOU" = saying to Southampton, "I executed Essex and other conspirators, but not you"; **YOU** = "But he that writes of *you*, if he can tell/ That *you* are *you*, so dignifies his story./ Let him but copy what in *you* is writ" – Sonnet 84, lines 7-9

This is the only appearance of "you" in the Dark Lady series (127-152); the word "you" appears in thirty-three sonnets of the Fair Youth series (1-126), where it always refers to Southampton. Here, too, it refers to him.

THE MONUMENT

THE DARK LADY: ELIZABETH

OXFORD PLEADS FOR SON'S RELEASE

Sonnet 146
Thy Fading Mansion
1602 – 1603

Although Elizabeth has spared Southampton's life, she has nonetheless commuted his sentence to perpetual imprisonment. Oxford now pleads with her on behalf of her "fading mansion" (the House of Tudor), demanding to know how she can let it die: "And death once dead, there's no more dying then."

Sonnet 146	Translation
Poor soul, the center of my sinful earth,	Poor Queen, the center of my disgraced world,
My sinful earth these rebel powers that thee array,	My disgraced England is now ruled by evil;
Why dost thou pine within and suffer dearth,	Why do you let your blood waste away,
Painting thy outward walls so costly gay?	Covering the truth with outward pomp and gaiety?
Why so large cost, having so short a lease,	Why such payment of blood, whose lease is short,
Dost thou upon thy fading mansion spend?	Do you pay from your withering House of Tudor?
Shall worms, inheritors of this excess,	Will worms, inheritors of his blood,
Eat up thy charge? Is this thy body's end?	Devour your heir? Is this your life's ending?
Then, soul, live thou upon thy servant's loss,	Then, royal Queen, live upon my loss,
And let that pine to aggravate thy store;	And let that waste be your way of keeping it,
Buy terms divine in selling hours of dross:	According to royal-legal terms for having him.
Within be fed, without be rich no more.	Have your son within, but be royal no more.
So shalt thou feed on death, that feeds on men,	So you will feed on his death, that feeds on him,
And death once dead, there's no more dying then.	And once all are dead, there will be no more.

1 POOR SOUL, THE CENTER OF MY SINFUL EARTH,
Poor throne, poor dynasty, poor Elizabeth, who sits at the center of power in England, which sins against the godlike royal blood of our son; "O death, where is thy sting? O grave, where is thy victory? The sting of death is *sin*; and the strength of *sin* is the law. But thanks be to God, which giveth us the victory through our Lord Jesus Christ" – 1 Corinthians, 15.55-57; **POOR:** "Why should *poor beauty* indirectly seek/ Roses of shadow, since his Rose is true?" – Sonnet 67, lines 7-8); **SOUL:** "Such is the conception running as a golden thread through Shakespeare's drama. *The Crown symbolizes the nation's soul-life*, which is also the greater self of each subject" – Knight, *Sovereign Flower*, p. 29

> *He dives into the King's soul*, and there scatters
> Dangers, doubts, wringing of the *conscience*,
> Fears, and despairs
> - *Henry VIII*, 2.2.25-27

THE CENTER: "figuratively, the soul, opposed to the body" – Schmidt; and by extension, the Court or Throne of England; "I will find *where truth is hid*, though it were hid indeed *within the center*" – *Hamlet*, 2.2.159, referring to the Court itself; "Time, force, and death, do to this body what extremes you can; but the strong base and building of my love is as *the very center of the earth*, drawing all things to it" – *Troilus and Cressida*, 4.2.103-107; "The heavens themselves, the planets, and this *center* observe degree, priority, and place ... And therefore is the glorious planet Sol in noble eminence enthron'd" – *Trolius and Cressida*, 1.3.85-90; **EARTH**: "This royal throne of kings, this scepter'd isle, this *earth of majesty* ... This blessed plot, this *earth,* this realm, this England" – *Richard II,* 2.1.40+

2 MY SINFUL EARTH THESE REBEL POWERS THAT THEE ARRAY,
MY SINFUL EARTH = repeated from the last line in Q, but considered by most editors as an error; **REBEL POWERS** = criminal forces that have taken over the throne; Oxford is turning the tables by referring, in effect, to Robert Cecil as having led his own Rebellion and who is now holding the "powers" of government; **ARRAY** = clothe or dress; i.e., Cecil has dressed or "arrayed" the Court with his control over the Queen; "Thee I'll chase hence, thou *wolf in sheep's array*" – *1 Henry VI,* 1.3.55; order of troops; "Stand we in good array, for they no doubt will issue out again and bid us battle; if not, the city being but of small defence, we'll quickly rouse the traitors in the same" – *3 Henry VI,* 5.1.62-65; some critics have taken "array" as "abuse" or "afflict," others as "defile," i.e., "defiled by the very rebel powers that adorn you"; there is also an echo of "bewrayed"; "The repetition of 'my sinful earth' may be deliberate, as emphasizing 'the pity of it'" - Tucker

3 WHY DOST THOU PINE WITHIN AND SUFFER DEARTH,
PINE = waste away, as in "the Chronicle of wasted time," Sonnet 106, line 1; **SUFFER DEARTH** = undergo the suffering and pain of deprivation (or death, i.e., the death of Southampton's royal claim); why does Elizabeth suffer the deprivation of her lineage and dynasty, now echoing her own inevitable death as well as the death of the House of Tudor

4 PAINTING THY OUTWARD WALLS SO COSTLY GAY?
PAINTING = Covering up the truth with costly ceremonies and royal pomp; "paying attention to the mere outward show" – Booth; to Southampton: "A Woman's face with nature's own hand *painted*/ Hast thou, the Master Mistress of my passion" – Sonnet 20, lines 1-2; "Why should false *painting* imitate his cheek,/ And steal dead seeing of his living hew?/ Why should poor beauty seek/ Roses of shadow, since his Rose is true?" – Sonnet 67, lines 5-8; "And him as for a map doth nature store,/ To show *false art* what beauty was of yore" – Sonnet 68, lines 13-14; "I never saw that you did *painting* need,/ And therefore to your fair no *painting* set" – Sonnet 82, lines 1-2; "Truth needs no colour with his colour fixed,/ Beauty no pencil, beauty's truth to lay" – Sonnet 101, lines 6-7; **WALLS** = the exterior façade of the House of Tudor, which is dying along with Elizabeth Tudor; glancing at the high walls of the Tower of London; **COSTLY** = "Under the canopies of *costly* state" – *2 Henry IV,* 3.1.13; **GAY** = "And deck my body in *gay ornaments*" – *3 Henry VI,* 3.2.149; gaudy, as in "Thou that art now the world's fresh *ornament*/ And only herald to the *gaudy* spring" – Sonnet 1, lines 9-10

5 WHY SO LARGE COST, HAVING SO SHORT A LEASE,
SO LARGE COST = the expense of Southampton's royal blood; the cost in terms of loss of the dynasty itself; **LARGE** = "Wilt thou, *whose will is large* and spacious" – Sonnet 135, line 5; "And my *large kingdom* for a little grave" – *Richard II,* 3.3.153; **COST** = "When I have seen by time's fell hand defaced/ The *rich proud cost* of outworn buried age" – Sonnet 64, lines 1-2; "Thy love is better than high birth to me,/ Richard than wealth, prouder than garments' *cost*" – Sonnet 91, lines 9-10; "The *cost of princes*" – *As You Like It,* 2.7.76; "It may chance *cost* some of us our lives" – *2 Henry IV,* 2.1.11; "Like one that draws the model of an house beyond his power to build it, who, half-through, gives o'er, and leaves his part-created *cost* a naked subject to the weeping clouds, and waste for churlish winter's tyranny" – *2 Henry IV,* 1.3.58-62; **HAVING SO SHORT A LEASE** = "So should *that beauty which you hold in lease*" – Sonnet 13, line 5; "And *Summer's lease hath all too short a date*" – Sonnet 18, line 4; "Can yet the *lease* of my true love control" – Sonnet 107, line 3; "Nature's *bequest gives nothing, but doth lend*" – Sonnet 4, line 3; "*leases of short-numbered hours*" – Sonnet 124, line 10, referring to the "numbers" or verses of this dynastic diary, which is recording the fate of this "*lease*" of royal blood to Southampton; **LEASE** = "temporary letting of an estate for a certain rent ... any tenure or temporary possession ... duration, time allotted" – Schmidt; in this case, the royal estate or state; "and our high-placed Macbeth shall live *the lease of Nature*, pay his breath to time, and mortal custom – yet my heart throbs to know one thing: tell me (if your art can tell so much), shall Banquo's issue ever reign in this kingdom?" – *Macbeth,* 4.1.98-103

6 DOST THOU UPON THY FADING MANSION SPEND?

THY FADING MANSION = your withering House of Tudor, which will come to its end upon your death; "O what a *mansion* have those vices got/ Which for their habitation chose out thee" – Sonnet 95, lines 9-10, to Southampton, referring to both the House of Tudor and the Tower of London; "Who lets *so fair a house fall to decay*" – Sonnet 13, line 9; **SPEND** = waste; "*Th'expense of spirit* in a *waste* of shame" – Sonnet 129, line 1; "So all my best is dressing old words new,/ *Spending* again what is already *spent*" – Sonnet 76, lines 11-12; "And in this change is my invention *spent*" – Sonnet 105, line 11; "the Chronicle of *wasted* time" – Sonnet 106, line 1

7 SHALL WORMS, INHERITORS OF THIS EXCESS,

WORMS, INHERITORS = contrasting "worms" as *heirs*, as opposed to Southampton's inheritance of the throne; Oxford had written to Southampton long ago: "Be not self-willed, for thou art much too fair/ To *be death's conquest and make worms thine heir*" – Sonnet 6, lines 13-14; **THIS EXCESS** = this excessive outward show of majesty, in which Elizabeth indulges as the expense of her blood lineage; "Therefore, to be possessed with double pomp, to guard a title that was rich before ... to seek the beauteous eye of heaven to garnish, is *wasteful and ridiculous excess*" – *King John*, 4.2.9-16

8 EAT UP THY CHARGE? IS THIS THY BODY'S END?

THY CHARGE = your (Elizabeth's) expense of her own blood in her son; "load, burden, weight, expense, cost" – Schmidt; echoing the "charge" of treason aimed at Southampton, who was also the Queen's "charge" as her royal ward or child of state, i.e. she was his legal guardian (who gave legal custody to Burghley); "What is entrusted to you, that over which you are guardian" – Booth; "Diomedes: 'How now, *my charge*.' Cressida: 'Now, my sweet *guardian*'" – *Troilus and Cressida*, 5.2.6-7; the Queen's royal charge over England: "We heartily solicit your gracious self to take on you the **charge** and kingly government of this your land" – *Richard III*, 3.7.129-131, to the King; **IS THIS THY BODY'S END** = Oxford scolds the Queen ("the *mortal* Moone" of Sonnet 107, line 5) for heading toward her death without naming her son as her successor; and because Southampton is "the *natural issue of Her Majesty's body*," according to the language of the 1571 Law of Succession, his continued imprisonment will be the way the Queen's body actually ends when she dies; "Then cometh the *end*, when he shall have delivered up the kingdom to God, even the Father; when he shall have put down all rule and all authority and power" – 1 Corinthians, 15.24; "There is a *natural body*, and there is a *spiritual body*" – 1 Corinthians, 15.44; **END** = "The *end* crowns all; and that old common arbitrator, Time, will one day *end* it" – *Troilus and Cressida*, 4.5.222-224

9 THEN, SOUL, LIVE THOU UPON THY SERVANT'S LOSS,

"Poor soul" – line 1 above, i.e., Elizabeth; and here Oxford is telling Elizabeth to "live upon" her soul (her spiritual body) or in eternity, with the losses suffered by her own servants, i.e., Oxford and Southampton, as well as upon the loss of her mortal body; but Oxford is speaking of himself as her servant, i.e., Oxford will suffer the "loss" of his paternity and identity; in other words, he tells the Queen to use this tragedy to gain immortality through her royal son, by releasing him from prison and allowing him, after all, to succeed her; i.e., by giving him resurrection: "There is one glory of the sun, and another glory of the moon, and another glory of the stars; for one star differeth from another star in glory. So also is the resurrection of the dead. It is sown in corruption; it is raised in incorruption: it is sown in dishonour; it is raised in glory; it is sown in weakness; it is raised in power; it is sown a natural body; it is raised a spiritual body" – 1 Corinthians, 15.41-44; **LIVE THOU UPON** = "Since that *my life on thy revolt* doth lie" – Sonnet 90, line 10, to Southampton; **THY SERVANT'S** = "I serve Her Majesty" – Oxford to Burghley, October 30, 1584; "Your Majesty's most humble subject and *servant*, Edward Oxenford" – Oxford to Queen Elizabeth, June 1599, Cecil Papers 71.26; Chiljan, 123; **LOSS** = the loss of their son's claim to the throne; echoing the near-loss of him by execution; "But if I the while I think on thee, dear friend,/ All *losses* are restored, and sorrows end" – Sonnet 30, lines 13-14, to Southampton; "Though thou repent, yet I have still the *loss*" – Sonnet 34, line 10; "If I *lose* thee, my *loss* is my love's gain,/ And *losing* her, my friend hath found that *loss*;/ Both find each other, and I *lose* both twain,/ And both for my sake lay me on this cross" – Sonnet 42, lines 9-12; "Increasing store with *loss*, and *loss* with store" – Sonnet 64, line 8; "Upon thy part I can set down a story/ Of faults concealed, wherein I am attainted:/ That thou in *losing* me shall win much glory" – Sonnet 88, lines 6-8; "And do no drop in for an after-*loss*" – Sonnet 90, line 4; "Who killed this prince? … I lov'd him, and will weep my date of life out for his sweet live's *loss*" – *King John*, 4.3.103-106

10 AND LET THAT PINE TO AGGRAVATE THY STORE;
LET THAT PINE = let your servant suffer; let that suffering; **AGGRAVATE** = increase; and let that waste and suffering be the means of increasing your store of blood, which our son possesses; to Southampton: "I make my love engrafted to this *store*" – Sonnet 37, line 8; "Increasing *store with loss*, and *loss with store*" – Sonnet 64, line 8; "O him she stores, to show what wealth she had,/ In days long since, before these last so bad" – Sonnet 67, lines 13-14; "And him as for a map doth nature *store*,/ To show false art what beauty was of yore" – Sonnet 68, lines 13-14

11 BUY TERMS DIVINE IN SELLING HOURS OF DROSS:
TERMS DIVINE = royal legal terms for divinity or immortality; **TERMS** = playing upon the life term that Southampton is now serving; "For *term of life* thou art assured mine" – Sonnet 92, line 1; **DIVINE** = "What's new to speak, what now to register,/ That may express my love, or thy dear merit?/ Nothing, sweet boy, by yet like *prayers divine*" – Sonnet 108, lines 3-5; **HOURS** = related to the actual Time of Elizabeth's life, which is rapidly dwindling; "But wherefore do not you a mightier way/ Make war upon this *bloody tyrant time*?/ And fortify yourself in your *decay*/ With means more blessed than my barren rhyme?/ Now you stand on the top of happy *hours*" – Sonnet 16, lines 1-5; "Or at your hand th'account of *hours* to crave" – Sonnet 58, line 3; "It fears not policy, that heretic/ Which works on *leases* of short numb'red *hours*" – Sonnet 124, lines 9-10; **DROSS** = impure matter, tainted substance; worthless matter; "And take thou my oblation, poor but free,/ Which is *not mixed with seconds*, knows no art,/ But mutual render only me for thee" – Oxford to Southampton, Sonnet 125, lines 10-12; "My love admits *no qualifying dross*" – *Troilus and Cressida*, 4.4.9; "And by the merit of vild gold, *dross*, dust, purchase corrupted pardon of a man" – *King John*, 3.1.91-92

12 WITHIN BE FED, WITHOUT BE RICH NO MORE.
WITHIN BE FED = feast inwardly (spiritually) upon his royalty; keep yourself alive from within yourself; **WITHIN** = "But I have that *within* which passes show" – *Hamlet*, 1.2.85; "This royal hand and mine are newly knit, and the conjunction of *our inward souls*" – *King John*, 3.1.152-153; **FED** = nourished; kept alive in posterity; "Therefore are *feasts* so solemn and so rare" – Sonnet 52, line 5; "And time that gave doth now his gift confound/ … *Feeds* on the rarities of nature's truth" – Sonnet 60, lines 8-11; **WITHOUT** = externally, which is "without" substance or lacking substance; on the outside; **BE … BE** = exist, perpetuate your existence, your blood; "To *be* or not to *be*, that is that question" – *Hamlet*, 3.1.56; **WITHOUT BE RICH NO MORE** = forget about the external trappings of your royal person or House and be fed within, royally and spiritually, for the survival of both your blood and lineage; "The *rich* proud cost of outworn buried age" – Sonnet 64, line 2, referring to the death of the kingdom, the reign, the dynasty

13 SO SHALT THOU FEED ON DEATH, THAT FEEDS ON MEN,
So you will have only death itself, which devours everyone; to Southampton: "Pity the world, or else this glutton be,/To *eat the world's due*, by the grave and thee" – Sonnet 1, lines 13-14

14 AND DEATH ONCE DEAD, THERE'S NO MORE DYING THEN.
And once you are dead, that is the end of all death for you; and unless you act now, to resurrect your royal son, it will also mean the death of your lineage; "The last enemy that shall be destroyed is death" – 1 Corinthians 15.26; "So when this corruptible shall have put on incorruption, and this *mortal* shall have put on *immortality*, then shall be brought to pass the saying that is written: Death is swallowed up in victory" – 1 Corinthians, 15.54; "The *mortal* Moon hath her eclipse endured" – Sonnet 107, line 5, on April 10, 1603, referring to the recent death of Elizabeth; to Southampton: "From hence your memory *death* cannot take,/ Although in me each part will be forgotten./ Your name from hence *immortal life* shall have,/ Though I, once gone, to all the world must *die*" – Sonnet 81, lines 3-6

THE MONUMENT

THE DARK LADY: ELIZABETH

OXFORD CONDEMNS THE QUEEN

Sonnet 147
At Random from the Truth
As Black as Hell, as Dark as Night
1602 - 1603

Oxford turns against the Queen, recording that he is virtually losing his sanity over her inability or unwillingness to acknowledge the truth of Southampton before it is too late. By keeping her son in the Tower, Elizabeth is ensuring that James of Scotland will become King of England upon her death; Oxford, who has bargained away his son's claim to the throne in return for his liberation by the new monarch, would rather that "the truth" be told.

Sonnet 147	Translation
My love is as a fever, longing still	My love for my son is an illness, always longing
For that which longer nurseth the disease,	For him, whose life prolongs the suffering,
Feeding on that which doth preserve the ill,	Feeding on my son who continues the pain,
Th'uncertain sickly appetite to please:	Reflecting the uncertainty of royal pleasure.
My reason, the Physician to my love,	My intelligence, the doctor for my royal son,
Angry that his prescriptions are not kept,	Angry that nothing I've done can help him,
Hath left me, and I desperate now approve,	Has left me; and now I give in to desperation,
Desire is death, which Physic did except.	Preferring to die, which no medicine will help.
Past cure I am, now Reason is past care,	I am now past any cure; my mind is insane,
And frantic mad with ever-more unrest,	And I keep growing more and more urgent;
My thoughts and my discourse as madmen's are,	My thoughts and speech are like madmen's,
At random from the truth, vainly expressed.	Far from speaking truth, written in vain.
For I have sworn thee fair, and thought thee bright,	For I have sworn you royal, and thought so,
Who art as black as hell, as dark as night.	You who bring disgrace and royal death.

1 MY LOVE IS AS A FEVER, LONGING STILL
MY LOVE = my royal son, i.e., Oxford's love for Southampton and fast-withering hopes for the future of his royal blood; **FEVER** = emotional turmoil and near-madness; *fever* related to E. Ver, Edward deVere: "Oh heavens, who was the first that bred in me this *fever? Vere*" – Verses made by the Earle of Oxenforde; **LONGING STILL** = always hoping

2 FOR THAT WHICH LONGER NURSETH THE DISEASE,
Oxford is still longing for the very outcome he cannot have, so his "fever" grows; he is prolonging the madness, which will end upon Elizabeth's death; but that outcome will result in the failure of Southampton, who remains in prison, to gain the throne

3 FEEDING ON THAT WHICH DOTH PRESERVE THE ILL,
FEEDING ON, etc. = the same thought; **THAT WHICH DOTH PRESERVE THE ILL** = Southampton himself; i.e., Oxford is surviving emotionally precisely because of what makes him suffer; **FEEDING** = "Within be *fed*, without be rich no more./ So shalt thou *feed* on death, that *feeds* on men,/ And death once

dead, there's no more dying then" – Sonnet 146, lines 12-14; **ILL** = related to the "ill deeds" or treason for which Southampton remains convicted; "Ah, but those tears are pearl which thy love sheeds,/ And they are rich, and ransom all *ill deeds*" – Sonnet 34, lines 13-14; "Lascivious grace, in whom all *ill* well shows" – Sonnet 40, line 13; "Though you do anything, he thinks no *ill*" – Sonnet 57, line 14; "If some *suspect of ill* masked not thy show,/ Then thou alone kingdoms of hearts shouldst owe" – Sonnet 70, lines 13-14, referring to his son as a "suspect traitor"; "Naming thy name blesses an *ill* report/ ... The hardest knife *ill* used doth lose his edge" – Sonnet 95, lines 8, 14, the latter warning Southampton against raising the knife of rebellion again; Oxford pictures himself growing increasingly *ill* as he sacrifices his identity as Southampton's father: "Whilst like a willing patient I will drink/ Potions of eisel 'gainst my strong infection" – Sonnet 111, lines 9-10; "For what care I who calls me well or *ill*,/ So you o'er-green my bad, my good allow" – Sonnet 112, lines 4-5; i.e., Southampton is both the source of Oxford's pain and the source of his cure; he has lost hope of such cure from the Queen, as when he had written in 1574: "I sick withal the help of bath desired,/ And thither hied, a sad distempered guest,/ But found no cure; the bath for my help lies/ Where Cupid got new fire, my mistress' eye" – Sonnet 153, lines 11-14, and "Growing a bath and healthful remedy/ For men diseased; but I, my Mistress' thrall,/ Came there for cure" – Sonnet 154, lines 11-13

4 TH'UNCERTAIN SICKLY APPETITE TO PLEASE:
UNCERTAIN = reflecting the uncertainty of everything at this time, i.e., especially about how much longer the Queen will live and about what will happen in terms of the royal succession; despite the best-laid plans for James to succeed and release Southampton, all could go wrong

5 MY REASON, THE PHYSICIAN TO MY LOVE,
My ability to help Southampton to cure, or legally overcome, his "fault" or treason by means of reasonable negotiation; ("For to thy sensual fault *I bring in sense*" – Sonnet 35, line 9; "To guard the *lawful reasons* on thy part" – Sonnet 49, line 12; referring to his efforts to secure the reduction of his son's conviction to "misprision" of treason, the results announced in "So thy great gift, upon misprision growing" – Sonnet 87, line 11)

6 ANGRY THAT HIS PRESCRIPTIONS ARE NOT KEPT,
Angry that nothing has really changed, i.e. that Southampton remains in the Tower; that the "prescription" for him to become Henry IX has not been kept; **PRESCRIPTIONS** = "But I hope truth is subject to no *prescription*, for truth is truth though never so old, and time cannot make false that which was once true" - Oxford to Robert Cecil, May 7, 1603; *OED*: "1.1: written or explicit direction or injunction ... 1.2: a direction or formula ...Law: limitation or restriction of the time within which an action or claim can be raised ... uninterrupted use or possession from time immemorial, or for a period fixed by law as giving a title or right ... ancient or continued custom, esp. when viewed as authoritative"; and as examples: "The most part of people is barred from offending only by *prescription of laws*" – Udall, 1548; "Surely we will not exchange our father's doings and traditions" – Latimer, 1543; "You know my Father left me some *prescriptions* of rare and proved effects" – *All's Well That Ends Well*, 1.3.227; "The passing over of time not commodious for the purpose, is **not allegable in prescription for the loss of any right**" – Henry VIII, 1542; "Years limit not a Crown; there's no *prescription* to inthrall a King" – 1605; "It was not fit his Majesty should be bound to give his letters of protection by *prescription*, but as seemed his Kingly pleasure best" – 1589; "by *prescription of time* have prevailed" – Camden, 1605); also "a frequent early form" of "prescription" = **"Great treasons, destruction of citizens, robbing and prescriptions followed" – 1432-50**; **"The same outlawing or prescription is against the laws" – 1560**

7 HATH LEFT ME, AND I DESPERATE NOW APPROVE
DESPERATE = in despair over his son's lack of ability to claim the throne; ("The Physician delivereth the *desperate sick body* to the Divine care" – *OED*., citing 1581)

8 DESIRE IS DEATH, WHICH PHYSIC DID EXCEPT.
Oxford would prefer to die; "Tired with all these, *for restful death I cry* ... Tired with all these, *from these I would be gone*,/ Save that to die, I leave my love alone" – Sonnet 66, lines 1, 13-14; "What fruit had ye then in those things whereof ye are now ashamed? For the end of those things is death ... For the wages of sin is

death" – Romans, 6.21-23; "And you hath he quickened, who were dead in trespasses and sins" – Ephesians, 2.1; **EXCEPT** = rule out; "And lay aside my high blood's royalty, which fear, not reverence, makes thee *to except*" – *Richard II*, 1.1.71-72, a phrase of law; "to take out of a number, to exclude; to object to, to protest against, to refuse" – Schmidt

9 PAST CURE I AM, NOW REASON IS PAST CARE,
PAST CURE = Nearing a kind of madness, Oxford is now past receiving the "sovereign cure" from Elizabeth that he had sought years earlier, as depicted in Sonnet 153, line 7: "Against strange maladies *a sovereign cure*"; and "But found **no cure**; the bath for my help lies/ Where Cupid got new fire, my mistress' eye" – Sonnet 153, lines 13-14; (in this respect, nothing has changed); "Came there *for cure*, and this by that I prove:/ Love's fire heats water, water cools not love" – Sonnet 154, lines 13-14; to Southampton: "Pity me then, dear friend, and I assure ye,/ Even that your pity is enough to *cure* me" – Sonnet 111, lines 13-14

10 AND FRANTIC MAD WITH EVER-MORE UNREST,
FRANTIC MAD = frantically mad, reflecting the racing of his angry thoughts; **EVER** = Ever = E. Ver, Edward de Vere; **UNREST** = "As testy sick men, when their deaths be near,/ No news but health from their physicians know./ For *if I should despair I should grow mad*,/ And in *my madness* might speak *ill* of thee:/ Now this *ill-wresting* world is grown so bad" – Sonnet 140, line 11; "*Rest, rest*, perturbed spirit" – *Hamlet*, 2.1.190, the prince to the ghost of his father, who was murdered for his wife and crown; "Past reason hated as a swallowed bait,/ On purpose laid to make the taker *mad*" – Sonnet 129, lines 7-8

11 MY THOUGHTS AND MY DISCOURSE AS MADMEN'S ARE,
MY THOUGHTS = the thoughts in my mind; also what I write or might write in these sonnets; **DISCOURSE** = speech; **MADMEN'S** = echoing Hamlet's statement to Laertes that it was his own "madness" that acted wrongly, i.e., "And when he's not himself does wrong Laertes, then Hamlet does it not, Hamlet denies it. *Who does it then? His madness*" – *Hamlet*, 5.2.234=236; and in Oxford's case, the suggestion is that he, too, is unpredictable and dangerous

12 AT RANDOM FROM THE TRUTH VAINLY EXPRESSED.
AT RANDOM FROM = aimlessly; at variance with; **TRUTH** = Oxford, *Nothing Truer than Truth*; reflecting his being prohibited from telling the truth, but the "random" nature of his thoughts poses the threat that, without forewarning, he may well speak the truth; **VAINLY** = "And shall I sue and serve her all *in vain*" – Oxford poem about Elizabeth in *The Paradise of Dainty Devices*, 1576, entitled "A lover rejected, complaineth," signed E. O.; "Some purge their pain, by plaint I find,/ But I *in vain* do breathe my wind" – same source, from "Not attaining his desire, he complaineth," signed E. O.

13 FOR I HAVE SWORN THEE FAIR, AND THOUGHT THEE BRIGHT,
FOR I HAVE SWORN THEE FAIR = For I have sworn to you, Elizabeth, that you are most royal; because I have sworn that you are my Queen; because I have portrayed you in my plays as most royal, i.e., as Queen Titania, Queen Cleopatra, et. al.; **FAIR** = royal; "The *fairest votary* took up that fire" – Sonnet 154, line 5, referring to Elizabeth; (in the Sonnets "fair" is used almost always for Southampton; he has always been "the fairest creature" in reflection of "beauty", i.e., his mother Elizabeth, who was "the *fairest votary*" at the outset); "In nothing art thou *black* save in *thy deeds*" – Sonnet 130, line 13; "In the old age *black was not counted fair*,/ Or if it were it bore not beauty's name" – Sonnet 127, lines 1-2; *fair* also means "honorable, equitable ... being as a thing ought to be, in order, in a good state" – Schmidt; legitimate: "For how art thou a king but by *fair sequence and succession?*" – *Richard II*, 2.1.198-199; **AND THOUGHT THEE BRIGHT** = and I have thought of you (and written of you) as royal; (perhaps also a glance at "intelligent"; if so, making this a real insult!)

14 WHO ART AS BLACK AS HELL, AS DARK AS NIGHT.
A proverbial expression, but here it becomes an utter condemnation of the Queen, whose blackness and darkness reflect her negative attitude toward Southampton and, in turn, toward Oxford himself; it is Elizabeth's imperial viewpoint that casts its shadow of darkness, turning their own son from fair to black; **BLACK AS HELL, AS DARK AS NIGHT**: "Looking on *darkness* which the blind do see/ ... Makes

black night beauteous, and her old face new" – Sonnet 27, lines 8, 12, when Southampton was imprisoned because of his leadership role in the Rebellion and became "like *a jewel hung in ghastly night*" in Sonnet 27, line 11; but it is the Queen herself whom Oxford condemns; he now accuses her of lacking fairness and brightness, i.e., of being a traitor to her own royal blood and, therefore, illegitimate

THE DARK LADY: ELIZABETH

OXFORD ANTICIPATES THE REIGN'S END

Sonnet 148
Vexed With Watching and With Tears
1602 – 1603

Oxford records how the Queen has forced him to betray what he holds most dear: the truth about their son. He ends on a dangerous note, warning that he may turn against the Queen publicly and tell the contemporary world what he knows to be true. In effect, he accuses Elizabeth herself of committing treason against a prince or king, Southampton.

Sonnet 148	Translation
O me! What eyes hath love put in my head,	O, me! What vision has royal blood given to me,
Which have no correspondence with true sight,	Whose seeing has no correspondence with truth,
Or if they have, where is my judgment fled,	Or if it does have such, where's my judgment
That censures falsely what they see aright?	That falsely condemns my son whose right I see?
If that be fair whereon my false eyes dote,	If he is royal, upon whom my false view gazes,
What means the world to say it is not so?	Why does official England say it's not so?
If it be not, then love doth well denote,	If it's not so, then royal blood presents itself well,
Love's eye is not so true as all men's: no,	And my loving eye is not as true as others': no,
How can it? O how can love's eye be true,	How can it be? How can my view of him be true,
That is so vexed with watching and with tears?	If my view is so sick with watching and weeping?
No marvel then though I mistake my view,	It's therefore not surprising that I see unclearly,
The sunne itself sees not, till heaven clears.	The royal son cannot see unless the Queen does.
O cunning love, with tears thou keep'st me blind,	O deceptive royal blood, I must not see truth,
Lest eyes, well seeing, thy foul faults should find.	Lest, seeing truth, should tell of your crimes.

1 O ME! WHAT EYES HATH LOVE PUT IN MY HEAD
O = Oxford; **O ME** = Oxford, identifying himself; **WHAT EYES HATH LOVE PUT IN MY HEAD** = what kind of vision has "love" or royal blood given me; i.e., Oxford has been forced to contradict what he knows to be the truth

2 WHICH HAVE NO CORRESPONDENCE WITH TRUE SIGHT!
TRUE = Oxford, *Nothing Truer than Truth*; **TRUE SIGHT** = ability to see the truth; i.e., he is "tongued-tied by authority" – Sonnet 66, line 9, and must pretend to see things that are utterly at variance from what he knows to be true

3 OR IF THEY HAVE, WHERE IS MY JUDGMENT FLED,
JUDGMENT = ability to distinguish truth from falsity; echoing the *judgment* against his son at the trial; to Southampton: "So till the *judgment* that your self arise,/ You live in this, and dwell in lovers' eyes" – Sonnet 55, lines 13-14; "So thy great gift, upon misprision growing,/ Comes home again, on better *judgment* making" – Sonnet 87, lines 11-12; to Elizabeth: "Thy black is fairest in ***my judgment's*** place"
– Sonnet 131, line 12

Part Three

4 THAT CENSURES FALSELY WHAT THEY SEE ARIGHT?
CENSURES FALSELY = that judges Southampton's true rights to the throne as false (or at least pretends to, publicly); views him untruthfully; related to "false-traitor"; **CENSURE** = "Say you consent and *censure* well the deed, and I'll provide the executioner" – *2 Henry VI*, 3.1.275-276; **WHAT THEY SEE ARIGHT** = what my eyes actually see, in private

5 IF THAT BE FAIR WHEREON MY FALSE EYES DOTE,
IF THAT BE FAIR = if (Southampton) is royal; **WHEREON MY FALSE EYES DOTE** = whereupon my false-seeing eyes look with such love; "I am thy King, and thou a *false*-heart traitor!" – *2 Henry VI*, 5.1.143

6 WHAT MEANS THE WORLD TO SAY IT IS NOT SO?
WHAT MEANS = how dares; on what basis; **THE WORLD** = England, its official view; i.e., if Southampton is the true prince in line to succeed Elizabeth, how dare England to say otherwise?

7 IF IT BE NOT, THEN LOVE DOTH WELL DENOTE,
LOVE = Southampton's royal blood; **DENOTE** = indicate outwardly; "'Tis not alone my inky cloak, good mother, nor customary suits of solemn black … that can *denote* me truly" – *Hamlet*, 1.2.81-88

8 LOVE'S EYE IS NOT SO TRUE AS ALL MEN'S: NO,
LOVE'S EYE = Oxford's eye reflecting his son's royal eyes; his eye that looks upon the royal eye (sun) of his son, reflecting his royal blood; ("And scarcely greet me with *that sun, thine eye*" – Sonnet 49, line 6); also "Love's I"; the blind eye of "Cupid" or "the little Love-God," Southampton, in the first lines of Sonnets 153 and 154; **NOT SO TRUE** = not as accurate (supposedly); **TRUE** = Oxford, *Nothing Truer than Truth*; **ALL** = Southampton, *One for All, All for One*; **ALL MEN'S** = the eyes of all men, i.e., the public; however: "'Gainst death, and all oblivious enmity shall you pace forth;/ Your praise shall still find room/ Even in the eyes of all posterity" – Sonnet 55, lines 9-11)

9 HOW CAN IT? O HOW CAN LOVE'S EYE BE TRUE,
HOW CAN IT? = Oxford questions the accuracy of all men's eyes as well as that of his own eyes; **O** = Oxford; **HOW CAN LOVE'S EYE BE TRUE** = how can my vision of my son be accurate? How can my son's royal eye be rightful and true? "That sun, *thine eye*" – Sonnet 49, line 6, to his son; **TRUE** = Oxford, *Nothing Truer than Truth*

10 THAT IS SO VEXED WITH WATCHING AND WITH TEARS?
VEXED = afflicted with suffering and distress; to Southampton: "Thou canst not *vex* me with an inconstant mind,/ Since that my life on thy revolt doth lie" – Sonnet 92, lines 9-10; **WITH WATCHING AND WITH TEARS** = Oxford anticipating Elizabeth's death and the succession of James rather than Southampton; with wakeful expectancy and sorrow; **WATCHING** = to Southampton: "Whilst I (my sovereign) *watch* the clock for you" – Sonnet 57, line 6; "To play the *watchman* ever for thy sake./ *For thee watch I*, whilst thou dost wake elsewhere [in the Tower]" – Sonnet 61, lines 12-13

11 NO MARVEL THEN THOUGH I MISTAKE MY VIEW;
NO MARVEL THEN = it is therefore not surprising

12 THE SUNNE ITSELF SEES NOT TILL HEAVEN CLEARS
SUNNE = Southampton, royal son; the eye of Oxford's royal son who is a prince or king; "Even so *my Sunne* one early morn did shine,/ With all triumphant splendor on my brow" – Sonnet 33, lines 9-10; **HEAVEN** = Elizabeth; (i.e., Southampton cannot thrive unless Elizabeth opens her own eyes and sees him clearly); "But out alack, he was but one hour mine,/ *The region cloud math masked him from me now*" – Sonnet 33, lines 11-12

13 O CUNNING LOVE, WITH TEARS THOU KEEP'ST ME BLIND,
O = Oxford; **CUNNING LOVE** = crafty, artful, deceptive royal blood, referring to Elizabeth herself; **CUNNING** = "But the world is so *cunning*, as of a shadow they can make a substance, and of a likelihood a truth"

– Oxford to Burghley, July 1581; "What *cunning* can express/ The favor of her face?/ To whom in this distress,/ I do appeal for grace./ A thousand Cupids fly/ About her gentle eye" – Oxford poem, *What Cunning Can Express*, written about Elizabeth by 1576, printed in *The Phoenix Nest*, 1593; "O, what authority and show of truth can *cunning* sin cover itself withal!" – *Much Ado About Nothing*, 4.1.33-34; ("cunning" also suggests slang for the female genitals; Oxford is so mad in this group of sonnets that he's hurling every possible insult at Elizabeth, here stooping to this one as well; **TEARS** = "The trickling *tears*, that fall along my cheeks,/ The secret sighs, that show my inward grief" – Oxford poem in *The Paradise of Dainty Devices*, 1576, about Elizabeth; in May 1583, "Elizabeth heeded the pleas of Burghley and Raleigh and, after 'bitter *tears* and speeches' at an emotionally charged audience, forgave Oxford for his liaison with Anne Vavasour and allowed him to return to court" – Weir, 346; **THOU KEEP'ST ME BLIND** = because of her, Oxford must maintain (publicly) his "blind" or false view of his son; "And keep my drooping eye-lids open wide,/ Looking on darkness which the **blind** do see" – Sonnet 27, lines 7-8

14 LEST EYES, WELL SEEING, THY FOUL FAULTS SHOULD FIND.
LEST EYES, WELL SEING = lest my eyes, seeing truly; and Southampton's eyes, too; **THY FOUL FAULTS SHOULD FIND** = discover (and publicly disclose) Elizabeth's terrible crimes against her son; "Fairing the *foul* with Art's false borrowed face" – Sonnet 127, line 6; **FAULTS** = turning the tables, Oxford is accusing Elizabeth of committing "faults" or treasons, the way Southampton has been convicted of them: "All men make *faults*, and even I in this,/ Authorizing *thy trespass* with compare,/ Myself corrupting salving *thy amiss*,/ Excusing thy sins more than thy sins are:/ For to thy sensual *fault* I bring in sense,/ Thy adverse party is thy Advocate" – Sonnet 35, lines 5-10

Part Three

THE DARK LADY: ELIZABETH

OXFORD ANTICIPATES THE QUEEN'S DEATH

Sonnet 149
Against My Self With Thee
1602 – 1603

The underlying theme of the Dark Lady series is that Oxford, loyal to the end, has been forced to adopt Elizabeth's false view as his own. He is "commanded by the motion" of her eyes, i.e., by her royal viewpoint, which is "blind" to the truth. Because he is sacrificing himself to obtain the promise of his royal son's release and pardon, he is joining the Queen in her blindness -- recalling Sonnet 27 of the Fair Youth series, when Southampton was imprisoned for the Rebellion and Oxford kept his "drooping eyelids open wide,/ Looking on darkness which the blind do see."

Sonnet 149	Translation
Canst thou O cruel, say I love thee not,	Can you, cruel Queen, say I don't serve you,
When I against my self with thee partake?	When I join you against the son who is my self?
Do I not think on thee when I forgot	Don't I think of you when I'm forgotten,
Am of my self all tyrant for thy sake?	Aren't I a tyrant against myself for your sake?
Who hateth thee that I do call my friend?	What enemy of yours do I call a friend?
On whom frown'st thou that I do fawn upon?	Who lacks your favor but gains mine?
Nay, if thou lour'st on me, do I not spend	No, if you look at me with anger, don't I take
Revenge upon my self with present moan?	Revenge against myself with my current pain?
What merit do I in my self respect,	What merit in myself do I respect,
That is so proud thy service to despise,	That is too above me to despise serving you,
When all my best doth worship thy defect,	When the best I can do is serve your faults,
Commanded by the motion of thine eyes?	Commanded by your imperial viewpoint?
But, love, hate on, for now I know thy mind,	But, my sovereign, destroy him; for I know you;
Those that can see thou lov'st, and I am blind.	You love those who see falsely, which I can't see.

1 CANST THOU, O CRUEL, SAY I LOVE THEE NOT,
O = Oxford; **O CRUEL** = Oxford crying to Elizabeth, calling her cruelty itself; **SAY I LOVE THEE NOT** = accuse me of not loving and serving you; "And shall I pray the Gods to keep the pain/ From *her that is so cruel* still?" – Oxford poem, signed E. O., about Elizabeth

2 WHEN I AGAINST MYSELF WITH THEE PARTAKE?
When I have sided with you and thereby gone against myself; when I have made this sacrifice for our son; i.e., in following the Queen's will, in order to save his son, Oxford has had to obliterate his own identity as father; to Southampton: "And this my hand *against myself* uprear" – Sonnet 49, line 11; "Upon thy side *against myself* I'll fight" – Sonnet 88, line 3; ("I am not as I seem to be,/ For when I smile I am not glad;/ A thrall, although you count me free,/ I, most in mirth, most pensive sad,/ … O *cruel* hap and hard estate,/ That *forceth me to love my foe*" – Oxford poem, signed E. O., writing of his relationship to Elizabeth

3 DO I NOT THINK ON THEE WHEN I FORGOT
THINK ON THEE = take your Majesty's will into account; think about you; remember you; show my ser-

REFERENCE EDITION

vice to you; **WHEN I FORGOT** = (when I, forgot); when I am forgotten; ("*in me each part will be forgotten*" – Sonnet 81, line 4); when I forget my own interests; when I am forgotten by you

4 AM OF MYSELF ALL TYRANT FOR THY SAKE?
ALL = Southampton, *One for All, All for One*; **ALL TYRANT FOR THY SAKE** = Oxford portraying himself as a "complete tyrant" against his son's royal blood, all for Elizabeth's sake (and for the sake of her Virgin Queen image); in other words, he accuses Elizabeth of turning him into a tyrant like herself; "When *tyrants'* crests and tombs of brass are spent" – Sonnet 107, line 14, referring to the recently deceased Queen; "when, tyrant, for your sake I forget myself entirely" – Booth, who also suggests: "when I, forgot, am of myself all tyrant for thy sake"

5 WHO HATETH THEE THAT I DO CALL MY FRIEND?
Which of your enemies do I call my friend?; "For they speak against thee wickedly, and thine enemies take thy name in vain. ***Do not I hate them, O Lord, that hate thee?*** And am I not grieved with those that rise up against thee? I hate them with perfect hatred: I count them mine enemies. *Search me, O God, and know my heart: try me, and know my thoughts:* And see if there be any wicked way in me, and lead me in the way everlasting" – Psalms 139.20-24 (suggested by George Steevens in 1780 and cited by Booth)

6 ON WHOM FROWN'ST THOU THAT I DO FAWN UPON?
Which of those in your disfavor do I give my friendship to; **FROWN'ST THOU** = referring to Elizabeth's imperial frown; "For *at a frown* they in their glory die" – Sonnet 25, line 8, i.e., the "Great Princes favorites" (Sonnet 25, line 5) or Queen Elizabeth's favorites such as Essex and Southampton, who lose their glory under her "frown" of displeasure; **FAWN UPON** = "to court servilely and in the manner of a dog" – Schmidt; "I owe him little duty, and less love, and take foul scorn *to fawn on him* by sending" – *1 Henry VI*, 4.4.34-35; "O villains, vipers, damn'd without redemption! Dogs, easily won *to fawn on* any man!" – *Richard II*, 3.2.129-130

7 NAY, IF THOU LOUR'ST ON ME, DO I NOT SPEND
NAY = the answer is no, I do not fawn upon anyone who suffers from your displeasure (other than Southampton, that is); **IF THOU LOUR'ST ON ME** = verb to "lower on" or to frown upon; if you, Elizabeth, look upon me with anger or disdain; "Now is the winter of our discontent made glorious summer by this son of York; and all *the clouds that lour'd upon our House* in the deep bosom of the ocean buried" – *Richard III*, 1.1.1-4; "The sun will not be seen today! The sky doth *frown and lour upon* our army" – *Richard III*, 5.3.283-284; "Why at our justice seem'st thou then *to lour?*" – *Richard II*, 1.3.235; "What *low'ring star* now envies thy estate" – *2 Henry VI*, 3.1.206; **DO I NOT SPEND** = isn't it a fact that I expend or use up

8. REVENGE UPON MYSELF WITH PRESENT MOAN?
Revenge against myself by going through this lamentation, which involves my sacrifice in order to save our son; **PRESENT MOAN** = immediate grief (over the loss of our son's claim by your rapidly approaching death and inability to name him); the same "moan" of those at a funeral, i.e., for the funeral of the dynasty; "And *moan th'expense* of many a vanished sight/ … And heavily from woe to woe tell o'er/ The *sad account of fore-bemoaned moan*" – Sonnet 30, lines 8, 9-10, in reaction to the Rebellion and its consequences for Southampton

9 WHAT MERIT DO I IN MY SELF RESPECT,
What good qualities about myself do I respect or esteem; to Southampton: "O lest the world should task you to recite/ *What merit lived in me* that you should love/ After my death, dear love, forget me quite,/ For *you in me can nothing worthy prove*" – Sonnet 72, lines 1-4, i.e., according to the bargain, you may not publicly demonstrate any of my positive qualities (or that I am your father)

10 THAT IS SO PROUD THY SERVICE TO DESPISE,
THAT IS, etc. = that is so high above you that I despise doing service to you;
THY SERVICE =

"I beseech Your Majesty, *in whose service I have faithfully employed myself* ... Your Majesty's most humble subject and *servant*" –
Oxford to Queen Elizabeth, June 1599 (Cecil Papers 71.26; Chiljan, 121)

"I *serve* Her Majesty, and I am that I am..."
- Oxford to Burghley, October 30, 1584

"Yet the long time which we spent in *her service*..."
- Oxford to Robert Cecil, about the recently deceased Queen
April 25/27, 1603

11 WHEN ALL MY BEST DOTH WORSHIP THY DEFECT,

ALL = Southampton, *One for All, All for One*; **ALL MY BEST** = the best I can do, all the power within me; "So **all my best** is dressing old words new,/ *Spending* again what is already *spent*" – Sonnet 76, lines 11-12; **DOTH WORSHIP THY DEFECT** = adores your faults (even when you destroy your son's inheritance of the throne); **WORSHIP** = related to the Queen as a goddess on earth; "From sullen earth, sings *hymns at Heaven's gate*" – Sonnet 29, line 12

12 COMMANDED BY THE MOTION OF THINE EYES?

A description that can be applied (literally) only to the monarch; commanded by your imperial viewpoint and power as the absolute monarch; "The bath for my help lies/ Where Cupid got new fire, *my mistress' eye*" – Sonnet 153, line 14; "Therefore *my Mistress' eyes* are raven black" – Sonnet 127, line 9; similar to the way Oxford addresses Southampton as a Prince whose eye or eyes represent his command; "Lo, in the Orient when the gracious light/ Lifts up his burning head, each under eye/ Doth homage to his new-appearing sight,/ Serving with looks his sacred majesty" – Sonnet 7, lines 1-4; "*An eye* more bright than theirs, less false in rolling,/ Gilding the object whereupon it gazeth,/ A man in hew all *Hews* in his *controlling*" – Sonnet 20, lines 5-7; "that *sunne thine eye*" – Sonnet 49, line 6; "Full many a glorious morning have I seen/ Flatter the mountain tops with *sovereign eye*" – Sonnet 33, lines 1-2

The Sonnets regularly express love through metaphors from royalty and its derivatives, using such phrases as "my sovereign" (57), "thy glory" (37), "lord of my love" (26), "embassy of love" (45), **"commanded by the motion of thine eyes"** *(149).* - Knight, *The Mutual Flame*, 6

COMMANDED = ruled, ordered by the Queen; also suggests forced, feigned, contrived, i.e., Oxford is being forced by Elizabeth to testify publicly against himself; ordered at Her Majesty's pleasure or royal will or commandment; "At your best *command*; at your employment, at your service" – *King John*, 1.1.197-198; under the Queen's ruling sway or authority; "And then *Your Highness shall command* a peace" – *1 Henry VI*, 4.1.117; "He speaks with such a *proud commanding spirit*" – *1 Henry VI*, 4.7.88; "Lavinia will I make my mistress, Rome's *royal mistress* ... And here in sight of Rome to Saturnine, *king and commander* of our commonweal, the wide world's emperor" – *Titus Andronicus*, 1.1.244-252; "And *reigned commanding in his monarchy*" – *A Lover's Complaint*, line 196

> He may **command** me as my sovereign,
> But you have power in me as in a kinsman
> - *Richard III*, 3.1.108-109

"I am to be governed and ***commanded*** at your Lordship's good devotion"
- Oxford to Lord Burghley, September 1572

THE MOTION OF THINE EYES = the authority expressed by the Queen's eyes signifying her approval or disapproval

> Be great in act, as you have been in thought;

> Let not the world see fear and mistrust
> Govern *the motion of a kingly eye*!
> - *King John*, 5.1.45-47

13 BUT, LOVE, HATE ON, FOR NOW I KNOW THY MIND;
BUT, LOVE, HATE ON = but, my sovereign, go ahead and continue to destroy your own royal blood;
FOR NOW I KNOW THY MIND = because now I have no doubt of what your decision is; now I know you will do nothing for our son, who will remain in the Tower until after you die and James is proclaimed King.

14 THOSE THAT CAN SEE THOU LOV'ST, AND I AM BLIND.
THOSE THAT CAN SEE THOU LOV'ST = you love only those who see, publicly, what you want them to see; **AND I AM BLIND** = and I have joined you in your blindness; ("And keep my drooping eyelids open wide,/ *Looking on darkness, which the blind do see*" – Sonnet 27, lines 7-8); and because I cannot see in the way you want me to, I cannot see at all

Part Three

THE DARK LADY: ELIZABETH

OXFORD PLEADS WITH THE QUEEN

Sonnet 150
Make Me Give the Lie To My True Sight
1602 – 1603

Oxford continues to record his anger over the tragic outcome of his life and service under Elizabeth, who has forced him to "give the lie to my true sight." (Oxford's use of "true" echoing his motto, Nothing Truer than Truth, *lends extra meaning, i.e., she has forced him to deny himself and his identity.) Opening the third quatrain, he plays upon a line from his early sonnet to the Queen, circa 1573, "Who taught thee first to sigh, alas, my heart?" The answer at the time was Elizabeth herself. Now this sentiment is charged with bitter irony: "Who taught thee how to make me love thee more,/ The more I hear and see just cause of hate?" Again, the answer is Elizabeth -- the monarch who, over the past four decades, has taught him how to serve her with increasing devotion, even as she has given him more "just cause" to "hate" her or be disloyal.*

Sonnet 150	Translation
O from what power hath thou this powerful might,	O by what authority do you have such power
With insufficiency my heart to sway,	To rule me with your errors,
To make me give the lie to my true sight,	To make me call my truth a liar,
And swear that brightness doth not grace the day?	And swear my son's royal blood is not royal?
Whence hast thou this becoming of things ill,	How do you have power to make bad good,
That in the very refuse of thy deeds,	And cast aside your foul deeds,
There is such strength and warrantise of skill,	When there is such royal power in him and right
That in my mind thy worst all best exceeds?	That, to me, what you think worst is most royal?
Who taught thee how to make me love thee more,	Who taught you how to make me serve you more,
The more I hear and see just cause of hate?	The more I find more just cause to hate you?
Oh though I love what others do abhor,	Though I love my son, whom others despise,
With others thou shouldst not abhor my state.	You should not scorn my/his state with them.
If thy unworthiness raised love in me,	If your irresponsibility raised me in your service,
More worthy I to be belov'd of thee.	Then I am more worthy to be beloved by you.

1 OH FROM WHAT POWER HAST THOU THIS POWERFUL MIGHT,
OH = O, Oxford; **FROM WHAT POWER** = by what authority; **HAST THOU THIS POWERFUL MIGHT** = do you (Elizabeth) have this all-powerful ability as absolute monarch; "They that have *power* to hurt, and will do none" – Sonnet 94, line 1, honoring those in authority who do the opposite; "O Thou my lovely Boy, who in thy *power*" – Sonnet 126, line 1

2 WITH INSUFFICIENCY MY HEART TO SWAY?
SWAY = to "rule, govern" – Booth; and/or to hold sway over the ruler's mind; "God forgive them that so much have *swayed* Your Majesty's good thoughts away from me" – *1 Henry IV*, 3.2.130-131; glancing at the limping, swaying Robert Cecil, as in "And strength *by limping sway disabled*" – Sonnet 66, line 8; "It is because no one should *sway* but he, no one but he should be about the king" – *1 Henry VI*, 3.1.37-38; "And, Henry, hadst thou *sway'd* as kings should do" – *3 Henry VI*, 2.6.14; "For though usurpers *sway the rule* awhile" – *3 Henry VI*, 3.3.76; "A place of potency and *sway* o'th'state" – *Coriolanus*, 2.3.180; "Bear the great *sway* of his affairs" – *Troilus and Cressida*, 2.2.35

REFERENCE EDITION

3 TO MAKE ME GIVE THE LIE TO MY TRUE SIGHT,
To force me to lie publicly about what I know to be the truth and accuse my true sight of being a liar; "For I hope truth is subject to no prescription, for *truth is truth* though never so old, and time cannot make that false which was once *true*" – Oxford to Robert Cecil, May 7, 1603; **TRUE** = Oxford, *Nothing Truer than Truth*; "Let all constant men be Troiluses, all false women Cressids" – *Troilus and Cressida*, 3.3.199-200

4 AND SWEAR THAT BRIGHTNESS DOTH NOT GRACE THE DAY?
BRIGHTNESS = royalty, i.e., of Southampton; "But thou, contracted to thine own *bright* eyes" – Sonnet 1, line 5, to Southampton; **GRACE** = adorn with royal grace; **DAY** = the golden time of kingship; and swear publicly that my son's royal blood does not lend its grace to this time when he is alive; "God save King Henry, unking'd Richard says, and send him many years of *sunshine days*!" – *Richard II*, 4.1.220-221; to Southampton: "Why didst thou promise such a beauteous *day*" – Sonnet 34, line 1; "All days are nights to see till I see thee,/ And nights *bright days* when dreams do show thee" – Sonnet 43, lines 13-14

5 WHENCE HAST THOU THIS BECOMING OF THINGS ILL,
BECOMING OF THINGS ILL = ("the power to make bad seem good" – Booth)

6 THAT IN THE VERY REFUSE OF THY DEEDS
That in the absolute worst (or least) of your deeds; **REFUSE** = that which is cast aside, i.e., Southampton; **DEEDS** = "*Foul deeds* will rise, though all the earth o'erwhelm them, to men's eyes" – *Hamlet*, 1.3.281-282; echoing Southampton's crimes: "And they are rich, and ransom all ill deeds" – Sonnet 34, line 14

7 THERE IS SUCH STRENGTH AND WARRANTISE OF SKILL
STRENGTH = royal blood, i.e., Southampton's; "And *strength* by limping sway disabled" – Sonnet 66, line 8; "If thou wouldst use the *strength* of all thy state" – Sonnet 96, line 12, to Southampton; **WARRANTISE OF** = evidence of; royal warrant or guarantee of; "a person or thing serving as a guarantee or surety" – *OED*; "He had my hand and *warrant*, which was sufficient for his discharge in law" – Oxford to Robert Cecil, January 11, 1596, in a memo about legal matters; Elizabeth had signed a "warrant" for the execution of Essex to go forth according to his sentence; Oxford had received his grant of an annual 1,000 pounds by Privy Seal Warrant; "Break up the gates [of the Tower], I'll be *your warrantise*" – *1 Henry VI*, 1.3.13; **SKILL** = royal power; "And you must live, drawn by your own sweet *skill*" – Sonnet 16, line 14

8 THAT IN MY MIND THY WORST ALL BEST EXCEEDS?
That, in my mind, what you regard as worst (Southampton) is what exceeds everything else; in my mind, Southampton is all best; **ALL** = Southampton; "For there is nothing either good or bad but thinking makes it so" – *Hamlet*, 2.2.250-251

9 WHO TAUGHT THEE HOW TO MAKE ME LOVE THEE MORE,

> "***Who taught thee*** first to sigh, alas, my heart"
> – Early sonnet by *Earl of Oxenforde*, referring to Elizabeth

> "Hath *that poor monarch* **taught thee** to insult?"
> – *3 Henry VI*, 1.4.124

10 THE MORE I HEAR AND SEE JUST CAUSE OF HATE?
The more I hear and see reasons to hate you

11 O THOUGH I LOVE WHAT OTHERS DO ABHOR,
O = Oxford; = Oxford expressing his love for Southampton, and recognition of his "love" or royal blood, even though others (those in authority) have branded him as a traitor and have denied his right of succession; and therefore they "abhor" him

12 WITH OTHERS THOU SHOULDST NOT ABHOR MY STATE.
WITH OTHERS = "along with other people who scorn me" – Booth; i.e., Elizabeth should not join others, such as Robert Cecil and Walter Raleigh, who scorn both Oxford and Southampton; "I all alone beweep *my outcast state*" – Sonnet 29, line 2, Oxford substituting himself for Southampton, referring to his son's royal "state" that has been destroyed; **MY STATE** = reflecting the obliteration of Southampton's royal state, as he remains in the Tower; "For thy sweet love rememb'red such wealth brings,/ That then I scorn to change *my state* with Kings" – Sonnet 29, lines 13-14

13 IF THY UNWORTHINESS RAISED LOVE IN ME,
THY UNWORTHINESS = your (Elizabeth's) lack of royal responsibility toward your son; **RAISED LOVE** = raised me in the service of your royal blood; brought me up, from boyhood in your devoted service; (in the manuscript copy of Oxford's early sonnet to the Queen, *Love thy Choice*, the word "love" is added in response to the opening line: "Who taught thee first to sigh, alas, my heart? *Love*" – courtesy of Derran Charlton; "the Mistress which we have lost, under whom both you and myself from our greenest years have been in a manner *brought up*" – Oxford to Robert Cecil, April 25/27, 1603); if your unworthiness made me serve you even more; **RAISED LOVE IN ME** = echoing the idea that Oxford "raised" his son ("my love") within himself and now in these sonnets, which are "the second burden of a former child" – Sonnet 59, line 4; raised my son's "love" or royal blood within me, within my soul; (see "razed oblivion" – Sonnet 122, line 7)

14 MORE WORTHY I TO BE BELOV'D OF THEE.
Then I am more worthy to be beloved by you; since I have joined you in denying our son's right to succeed you, making me unworthy as well, it is fitting that you love me; **BELOV'D** = used as a noun for Southampton as "my royal son" upon the Queen's death: "Let not my love be called Idolatry,/ Nor *my beloved* as an Idol show" – Sonnet 105, lines 1-2.

THE MONUMENT

THE DARK LADY: ELIZABETH

TO CATCH THE
"CONSCIENCE" OF THE QUEEN

Sonnet 151
To Stand In Thy Affairs, Fall By Thy Side
Jan-March 1603

Oxford uses blatant sexual imagery to describe himself as an abject courtier doomed to "rise and fall" in the presence of the Queen's royal authority. The imagery is that of Her Majesty's servant dropping to his knees and rising at her command, as a penis stands erect or droops according to a lover's power over it. At the same time, he appeals to her "conscience" as a last resort, using the word three times for emphasis (the way he focuses on "conscience" in Hamlet *and* Henry VIII*). It is Oxford's better self, Southampton, who remains in prison as Elizabeth's "poor drudge" and waits for the freedom to serve her.*

Sonnet 151	Translation
Love is too young to know what conscience is,	Royal blood in our son is not responsible,
Yet who knows not conscience is born of love?	Yet isn't responsibility born of royal blood?
Then, gentle cheater, urge not my amiss,	Then, royal liar, do not urge me against him,
Lest guilty of my faults thy sweet self prove.	Lest you wish to carry my guilt for him.
For thou betraying me, I do betray	For your betrayal of me, I do betray
My nobler parts to my gross body's treason;	My inner soul to the treason of my actions;
My soul doth tell my body that he may	My soul tells my body he may
Triumph in love; flesh stays no farther reason,	Triumph in royalty. Body waits on reason,
But rising at thy name doth point out thee,	But rising at "Elizabeth" it marks you
As his triumphant prize; proud of this pride,	As my son's mother. Proud of his blood,
He is contented thy poor drudge to be,	He is content to be your poor prisoner,
To stand in thy affairs, fall by thy side.	To stand or fall with you, the sovereign.
No want of conscience hold it that I call	Don't hold me responsible for marking
Her love, for whose dear love I rise and fall.	Your royalty; for your son I rise or fall.

1 LOVE IS TOO YOUNG TO KNOW WHAT CONSCIENCE IS,
LOVE = royal blood of Southampton, as "Cupid" or "the little Love-God" of Sonnets 153 and 154; "Love is a Babe: then might I not say so/ To give full growth to that which still doth grow" – Sonnet 118, lines 13-14, Oxford, speaking of Southampton as still a young price who is growing, both in life and in the womb of these private sonnets; **TOO YOUNG** = always young, fresh, green, eternal; **TO KNOW WHAT CONSCIENCE IS** = to refrain from taking action; to bear responsibility for the treason of the Rebellion; **CONSCIENCE** = the inner process that weighs one thing against another ("to be or not to be") and results in delay of action; and that would have resulted in Southampton delaying the Rebellion or not acting as he did; as Hamlet puts it: "Thus *conscience* doth make cowards of us all, and thus the native hue of resolution is sicklied o'er with the pale cast of thought, and enterprises of great pitch and moment with this regard their currents turn awry and lose the name of action" – *Hamlet*, 3.1.83-88

2 YET WHO KNOWS NOT CONSCIENCE IS BORN OF LOVE?
CONSCIENCE = "May I with right and *conscience make* this claim?" – *Henry V*, 1.2.96, young Prince Hall

754

(reflecting Southampton), now the king; Oxford is simultaneously appealing to Elizabeth's conscience, as reflected by his portrait of her father, in the play *Henry VIII*, with the word "conscience" appearing a total of twenty-four times

> I have this day received *a traitor's judgment,*
> And by that name must die; yet, heaven bear witness,
> And if I have a *conscience*, let it sink me,
> Even as the axe falls, if I not be faithful!
> - *Henry VIII*, 2.1.58-61

> *He dives into the King's soul*, and there scatters
> Dangers, doubts, wringing of the *conscience*,
> Fears, and despairs
> - *Henry VIII*, 2.2.25-27

> O my Wolsey,
> The quiet of *my wounded conscience*,
> Thou art a cure fit for a king.
> - *Henry VIII*, 2.2.72-74

> This respite shook
> The bosom of my *conscience*, entered me,
> Yea, with a splitting power, and made to tremble
> The region of my breast...
> Thus hulling in
> The wild sea of my *conscience*, I did steer
> Toward this remedy, whereupon we are
> Now present here together: that's to say,
> I meant to rectify my *conscience*...
> - *Henry VIII*, 2.4.180-183, 198-203

BORN OF LOVE = reminding Elizabeth that she gave birth to their son, giving him "love" or royal blood; it is the Queen from whom Southampton received his "love" or royal blood in the first place; ("There is incidental wit in the fact that Venus – love – is literally the mother of Cupid – Love – and that bearing and babies are variously pertinent to these lines" – Booth)

3 THEN GENTLE CHEATER URGE NOT MY AMISS,
GENTLE CHEATER = Elizabeth as royal liar; an oxymoron echoing Oxford's characterization of Southampton as a "tender churl" or royal miser in Sonnet 1, line 12; **URGE NOT MY AMISS** = do not prompt me to commit an offense; ("Myself corrupting salving *thy amiss*" – Sonnet 35, line 7; "Which, laboring for invention, bear *amiss*/ The second burden of a former child" – Sonnet 59, lines 3-4)

4 LEST GUILTY OF MY FAULTS THY SWEET SELF PROVE.
SWEET SELF = royal self, i.e., Elizabeth; ("Richard, that *sweet* lovely rose" – *1 Henry IV*, 1.3.173; **LEST GUILTY**, etc. = lest you wish to share the guilt I have taken upon myself on behalf of our son; echoing the verdict of guilt against Southampton and Essex at the trial; **FAULTS** = to Southampton: "All men make *faults*, and even I in this,/ Authorizing thy trespass with compare/ ... For to thy sensual *fault* I bring in sense,/ Thy adverse party is thy Advocate,/ And 'gainst myself a lawful plea commence" – Sonnet 35, lines 5-11; on April 5, 1603, King James will order Southampton's release for his "fault" or treason against Elizabeth

5 FOR THOU BETRAYING ME, I DO BETRAY
THOU BETRAYING ME = you (Elizabeth), having betrayed me; **I DO BETRAY** = I, in turn, betray; emphasizing the betrayal of royal blood

6 MY NOBLER PARTS TO MY GROSS BODY'S TREASON.
MY NOBLER PARTS = my inner soul, i.e., Southampton; "thou art all the better *part* of me" – Sonnet 39, line 2; "Though heaven knows it is but as a tomb/ Which hides your life, and shows not half your *parts*" – Sonnet 17, lines 3-4; "That doubting to bring his *parts* and jugglings to light" – Oxford to Robert Cecil, January 11, 1597; "For the young gentleman, as I understand, hath been well brought up, fair conditioned, and hath many good *parts* in him" – Oxford to Robert Cecil, September 8, 1597, of young William Herbert, future Second Earl of Pembroke, as prospective husband of his daughter Bridget Vere; **TO MY GROSS BODY'S TREASON** = to the treason of the Rebellion that I have taken upon myself, making my sacrifice for our son

7 MY SOUL DOTH TELL MY BODY THAT HE MAY
MY SOUL = my inward self, Southampton; "My spirit is thine, the better part of me" – Sonnet 74, line 8; to Southampton: "Save that my soul's imaginary sight/ Presents thy shadow to my sightless view" – Sonnet 27, lines 9-10; to Elizabeth: "If thy *soul* check thee that I come so near,/ Swear to thy blind *soul* that I was thy *Will*" – Sonnet 136, lines 1-2

8 TRIUMPH IN LOVE; FLESH STAYS NO FARTHER REASON,
TRIUMPH IN LOVE = be the real father of a royal son; "Even so my Sunne one early morn did shine/ With all *triumphant* splendor on my brow" – Sonnet 33, lines 9-10; **FLESH** = my flesh-and-blood son; **FLESH STAYS** = my son waits; my physical self waits; **STAYS** = recalling the "stay" of Southampton's execution; **FARTHER** = further, longer; "With a possible play on *'father'*" – Booth; **REASON** = intellect; "For to thy sensual fault I bring in *sense*" – Sonnet 35, line 9; "To guard the lawful *reasons* on they part" – Sonnet 49, line 12; "Not that I desire you should be a mover, but a furtherer; for as the time is, it were not *reason*" – Oxford to Robert Cecil, February 2, 1601

9 BUT RISING AT THY NAME DOTH POINT OUT THEE
RISING AT THY NAME = Oxford's soul, i.e., Southampton, like the sun rising at Elizabeth's name, i.e., growing as her royal son, who "bore not beauty's name" in Sonnet 127, line 2; along with the obvious sexual imagery; **DOTH POINT OUT THEE** = does mark you as his mother; (as he pointed out Oxford as his father in: "Till whatsoever star that guides my moving/ *Points* on me graciously with fair aspect" – Sonnet 26, lines 9-10)

10 AS HIS TRIUMPHANT PRIZE; PROUD OF THIS PRIDE,
AS HIS TRIUMPHANT PRIZE = as his royal mother; "Not *prizing* her poor infant's discontent" – Sonnet 143, line 8; "Even so my Sunne one early morn did shine/ With all*triumphant* splendor on my brow" – Sonnet 33, lines 9-10; **PROUD OF THIS PRIDE** = royal with your royal blood that he inherited from you; "Why is my verse so barren of new pride" – Sonnet 76, line 1

11 HE IS CONTENTED THY POOR DRUDGE TO BE,
He (Southampton, my flesh-and-blood son) is content to be your poor servant; he, my penis, the source of my seed that helped to create our son; **DRUDGE** = impoverished prisoner in the Tower; "born for baseness" – Schmidt, who cites *Richard III*, 1.3.229-232: "Thou that wast sealed in thy nativity the slave of Nature, and the son of hell; thou *slander of thy heavy mother's womb,* thou loathed *issue of thy father's loins*"

12 TO STAND IN THY AFFAIRS, FALL BY THY SIDE.
The image of the Courtier as a penis rising and falling in response to the female monarch; to support you in your policies, to die with you; **STAND** = "Who willed you, or whose will *stands* but mine?" – *1 Henry VI*, 1.3.11; **AFFAIRS** = "Bear the great sway of his *affairs*" – *Troilus and Cressida*, 2.2.35; **STAND/FALL** = "As on whom I have builded my foundation, either to **stand** or to *fall*" – Oxford to Lord Burghley, September 1572

13 NO WANT OF CONSCIENCE HOLD IT THAT I CALL
Do not consider me disloyal for calling upon my conscience; **CONSCIENCE** = "But, shall I speak my *con-*

science, our kinsman Gloucester is as innocent from meaning treason to our royal person as is the sucking lamb or harmless dove: the duke is virtuous, mild and too well given to dream on evil or to work my downfall" – the king in *2 Henry VI*, 3.1.68-70; "The play's the thing wherein I'll catch the *conscience* of the king" – *Hamlet*, 2.2.607; "My lord of Gloucester, 'tis my special hope that you will clear yourself from all suspect: my *conscience* tells me you are innocent" – *2 Henry VI*, 3.1.14

For Oxford-Shakespeare, a conscience is an essential attribute of the monarch:

> My lord, I have considered with myself
> The title of this most renowned duke;
> ***And in my conscience do repute his grace***
> ***The rightful heir to England's royal seat***
> - *2 Henry VI*, 5.1.175-178

> My *conscience tells me is his lawful king*
> - *3 Henry VI*, 1.1.154

> Now Warwick, tell me, even ***upon thy conscience***,
> Is Edward your true king?
> - *3 Henry VI*, 3.3.113-114

> My lord, this argues ***conscience in your Grace***
> - *Richard III*, 3.7.173

> I am not made of stone,
> But penetrable to your kind entreats,
> Albeit against my *conscience* and my soul
> - *Richard III*, 3.7.223-225

> *Earl of Oxford:*
> Every man's *conscience* is a thousand swords
> To fight against that bloody homicide
> - *Richard III*, 5.2.17-18

> O coward *conscience*, how dost thou afflict me…
> My *conscience* hath a thousand several tongues,
> And every tongue brings in a several tale,
> And every tale condemns me for a villain.
> Perjury, perjury, in the highest degree…
> ***Conscience is but a word that cowards use,***
> ***Devised at first to keep the strong in awe.***
> Our strong arms be our *conscience*, swords our law.
> March on! Join bravely. Let us to it pell-mell;
> If not to Heaven, then hand in hand to hell!
> - *Richard III*, 5.3.180, 194-197, 310-314

In these plays of England's royal history, Oxford has put "conscience" into the mouths of different characters using it for different ends; and this conflict is expressed in Sonnet 151 to the Queen. The following, in a general way, is an apt description of the Queen's predicament as she nears death – whether to release Southampton and acknowledge his claim or, instead, to let him languish in the Tower so James will ascend to the throne:

> If I know how or which way to order these affairs
> Thus thrust disorderly into my hands,

Never believe me! Both are my kinsmen:
The one is my sovereign, whom both my oath
And duty bids defend; the other again
Is my kinsman, whom the King hath wronged,
Whom *conscience* and *my kindred* bids to right.
- *Richard II*, 2.2.109-115

Salisbury:
The colour of the king doth come and go
Between his purpose and his conscience,
Like heralds 'twixt two dreadful battles set:
His passion is so ripe, it needs must break

Pembroke:
And when it breaks, I fear will issue thence
The foul corruption of *a sweet child's death*
- *King John*, 4.2.76-81

And thou, to be endeared to a king,
Made it *no conscience to destroy a prince*
- *King John*, 4.2.228-229

This kingdom, this confine of blood and breath,
Hostility and civil tumult reigns
Between my conscience and my cousin's death
- *King John*, 4.2.246-248

14 HER LOVE, FOR WHOSE DEAR LOVE I RISE AND FALL.
HER LOVE = Elizabeth's royal blood and sovereignty; "her" a play on "Her Majesty"; **FOR WHOSE DEAR LOVE** = for whose royal son; for whose royal blood as a dear royal mother; Essex, about to leave for the Azores in 1597, wrote to Elizabeth addressing her as "most *dear* and most admired sovereign" and added that "to *your royal dear heart* I appeal" – Weir, 427; but also referring to Southampton as her "dear love" as he himself refers to him: "If my *dear love* were but the child of state,/ It might for fortune's bastard be unfathered" – Sonnet 124, lines 1-2; **I RISE AND FALL** = I live and die; I stand as your servant and fall to my knees; the obvious sexual imagery of Oxford-as-courtier describing himself as a penis rising and falling at her command (suggesting that probably this was a popular metaphor among males seeking royal patronage at Court); "Save that which common is, and known to all,/ That *Courtiers as the tide do rise and fall*" – Spenser, *Mother Hubbard's Tale*, line 614

Part Three

END OF THE DARK LADY SERIES TO ELIZABETH

OXFORD'S FINAL STATEMENT
UPON THE QUEEN'S DEATH

Sonnet 152
And All My Honest Faith In Thee Is Lost
To Swear Against the Truth so Foul a Lie
March 24, 1603

In Oxford's final words to Elizabeth, he accuses her of having played the false role of Virgin Queen to the very end of her life. "And all my honest faith in thee is lost," he writes. She has caused him to swear against his own truth – "To swear against the truth so foul a lie!" This verse corresponds in time to Sonnet 105 of the Fair Youth series, marking the death of Elizabeth. In his early sonnet to her entitled "Love Thy Choice," he asked himself: "Above the rest in Court who gave thee grace? Who made thee strive in honor to be best, in constant truth *to bide so firm and sure" -- and here, three decades later, he recalls having sworn "Oaths of thy love, thy truth, thy constancy." But it turns out that he has sworn falsely; she has proved him wrong. Having testified in her behalf, and having trusted her, Oxford has "perjured" himself. Likewise, Southampton, in Sonnet 125 upon the Queen's funeral, is a "suborned Informer" who must swear against the truth for the remainder of his life.*

Sonnet 152	Translation
In loving thee thou know'st I am forsworn,	You know that in serving you I am perjured,
But thou art twice forsworn to me love swearing;	But you are twice perjured by vows to me;
In act thy bed-vow broke and new faith torn	You broke your contract to me and your son
In vowing new hate after new love bearing:	By hiding him after begetting new blood:
But why of two oaths' breach do I accuse thee,	But why do I accuse you of breaking these,
When I break twenty? I am perjured most,	When I break more vows? I am the big liar,
For all my vows are oaths but to misuse thee,	For all my vows to you are abusing you,
And all my honest faith in thee is lost.	And I have lost all faith in your promises.
For I have sworn deep oaths of thy deep kindness,	For I have deeply vowed your motherhood,
Oaths of thy love, thy truth, thy constancy,	Vowed your true and eternal royal blood,
And to enlighten thee gave eyes to blindness,	And to make you see gave you my sight,
Or made them swear against the thing they see.	Or made myself swear against my truth.
For I have sworn thee fair: more perjured eye,	For I have sworn you royal: I lie even more,
To swear against the truth so foul a lie.	By denying my own truth and lying with you!

1 IN LOVING THEE THOU KNOW'ST I AM FORSWORN,
FORSWORN = In serving you (and believing in you) I break my faith with not only with you but also with our son; I have lied because you lied to me; *forswear* = "to refuse or renounce upon oath; to swear that one will have nothing to do with a person or thing; to deny upon oath; to swear falsely, to perjure one's self; to commit perjury" - Schmidt; "And *purest faith unhappily forsworn*" – Sonnet 66, line 4, referring to Elizabeth having broken faith with Oxford and Southampton; and once the bargain is made to reduce Southampton's crime to "misprision" of treason, marked in Sonnet 87, in the next verse Oxford tells him: "Upon thy side against myself I'll fight,/ And prove thee virtuous, though thou art *forsworn*" – Sonnet 88, line 4, i.e., Southampton henceforth must testify falsely against his royal identity: "Hence, thou *suborned informer!*" – Sonnet 125, line 13

REFERENCE EDITION

> But thou dost *swear* only to be *forsworn*,
> And most *forsworn*, to keep what thou dost *swear*.
> Therefore thy later *vows* against the first
> Is in thyself rebellion to thyself
> - *King John*, 3.1.211-215

2 BUT THOU ART TWICE FORSWORN TO ME LOVE SWEARING:

But you have twice broken faith with me; **LOVE SWEARING** = first vowing to me to remain true to your royal blood in our son, then vowing the same to him; "Now to my word; it is 'Adieu, adieu, remember me.' *I have sworn it*" – the Prince, swearing to do the bidding of the Ghost of his murdered father, in *Hamlet*, 1.5.110-112

3 IN ACT THY BED-VOW BROKE AND NEW FAITH TORN

BED-VOW = "marriage vow, whether formal or informal" - Booth; by your deeds, i.e., your actions against our son, you have broken the vow you made when we were betrothed and conceived our son; ("Now by my sceptre's awe *I make a vow*" – the King in *Richard II*, 1.1.118; **AND NEW FAITH TORN** = and then you tore up newer vows, which you made to our son; an image of tearing up a contract; you broke the first vow, to me, and then you broke your vow to our royal son; "False king! Why hast thou *broken faith with me*, knowing how hardly I can brook abuse? King did I call thee? No, thou art not king; not fit to govern and rule multitudes" – *2 Henry VI*, 5.1.91-94; "But to prevent the tyrant's violence – *for trust not him that hath once broken faith* – I'll hence forthwith unto the sanctuary to save at least the heir of Edward's right" – *3 Henry VI*, 4.4.29-32

4 IN VOWING NEW HATE AFTER NEW LOVE BEARING:

VOWING = (echoing "Bed-Vow" in line 3 and anticipating "Vows" in line 7); by destroying our son's royal hopes after giving birth to him (see the early poem, possibly by Oxford, following notes for this sonnet); **BEARING** (giving birth to) his new royal blood; "Sweet *love*, I see, changing his property, turns to the sourest and most deadly *hate*" – *Richard II*, 3.2.135-136; "Now welcome more, and ten times more beloved, than if thou never hadst deserved our *hate*" – King Edward to George (Duke of Clarence) in *3 Henry VI*, 5.1.106-107

5 BUT WHY OF TWO OATHS' BREACH DO I ACCUSE THEE,

TWO OATHS = the oaths you made to me and our son; **ACCUSE** = echoing the accusations against Essex and Southampton at their treason trial; **BUT WHY OF TWO OATHS' BREACH DO I ACCUSE THEE**

> But *why accuse* I him,
> Whom th'earth hath covered long?
> There be of his posterity
> Alive, I do him wrong
> - E. O., *The Paradise of Dainty Devices*, 1576

6 WHEN I BREAK TWENTY? I AM PERJURED MOST,

When I, Oxford, being forced to disavow my fatherhood of Southampton, have broken many more vows; **I AM PERJURED MOST** = I have done much more to perjure myself, by lying about the truth; echoing the trial, when Oxford was forced to cast a guilty vote against his royal son, failing to speak the truth in a court of law; (just as Southampton must be a "*suborned informer*" against his royal blood in Sonnet 125, line 11, upon the Queen's funeral and the end of the Tudor Rose dynasty); "more *perjured* eye,/ To swear against the truth so foul a lie" – lines 13-14 below; "Arm, arm, you heavens, against these *perjured* kings!" – *King John*, 3.1.33

> The expense of spirit in a waste of shame
> Is lust in action, and till action lust
> Is *perjured*, murd'rous, bloody, full of blame – Sonnet 129, lines 1-3

7 FOR ALL MY VOWS ARE OATHS BUT TO MISUSE THEE,
ALL = Southampton, *One for All, All for One*; **ALL MY VOWS ARE OATHS BUT TO MISUSE THEE** = all my promises have been only to deny your own son's royalty, and thereby to misuse or misrepresent or deceive you; "Proof enough to *misuse* the Prince" – *Much Ado About Nothing*, 2.2.27; yet in the Fair Youth series after the Queen's death, he will address Time on behalf of Southampton: "This *I do vow*, and this shall ever be,/ *I will be true*, despite thy scythe and thee" – Sonnet 123, lines 13-14; one way he will remain true to Time is to record and preserve the truth in these private sonnets that hopefully will survive for posterity; meanwhile, in serving the Queen and following her will, he has joined with her in the destruction of her own lineage and dynasty

> To dash our late decree in Parliament
> Touching King Henry's *oath* and your *succession*
> - *3 Henry VI*, 2.1.118-119

8 AND ALL MY HONEST FAITH IN THEE IS LOST.
ALL = Southampton; **AND ALL MY HONEST FAITH IN THEE IS LOST** = "And all my confident trust of you is gone" – Booth; Oxford's final statement about his long relationship of service to the Queen, having held onto his faith that she would act to preserve "beauty's *Rose*" or the Tudor Rose dynasty, as he had indicated in Sonnet 1, line 1: "That thereby *beauty's Rose might never die*"; but Elizabeth spared her son's life while leaving him in perpetual confinement, unable to succeed her: "And *purest faith unhappily forsworn*" – Sonnet 66, line 4

"I beseech Your Majesty, in whose service I have **faithfully** employed myself (I will not entreat that you suffer it yourself thus to be abused), but that you will not suffer me thus to be *flouted, scorned and mocked*." - Oxford to Elizabeth, June 1599; Cecil Papers 71.26; Chiljan, 122

FAITH = Oxford's use of "faith" provides specific support for the implication that he and the Queen were formally betrothed in 1573 or 1574, perhaps with Archbishop Parker presiding at a private ceremony. In the sixteenth century, a betrothal still had "strict legal importance," Percy Macquoid wrote in Shakespeare's England, vol. 2, 1916, p. 114; "Shakespeare shows that a form of betrothal still existed in his time," he added, citing Olivia's speech to Sebastian, in which she refers to the betrothal as a plight of "faith":

> Now go with me and with this holy man
> Into the chantry by; there, before him,
> And underneath that consecrated roof,
> Plight me the full assurance of your faith.
> - *Twelfth Night*, 4.3.23-26

It appears, then, that such is the "faith" to which Oxford refers, telling Elizabeth here at the end of his diary to her, "And all my honest faith in thee is lost." In the play, Sebastian replies to Olivia as Oxford to Queen Elizabeth: "I'll follow this good man, and go with you, *and having sworn truth, ever will be true*" – with "truth" and "ever" and "true" indicating Edward de Vere.

9 FOR I HAVE SWORN DEEP OATHS OF THY DEEP KINDNESS:
SWORN = see Sebastian's line above, telling Olivia that "having *sworn* truth," he "ever will be true";
DEEP OATHS = solemn vows; for I have sworn, to myself and to our son, that you would remain true to your *kind* or natural offspring and heir (and, since you broke faith, I swore falsely and thereby committed perjury); **KINDNESS** = motherhood of Southampton; kinship by blood; ("either in *kindness*, which I find beyond mine expectation in you, or in *kindred* ... in all *kindness and kindred*" – Oxford to his brother-in-law Cecil, May 1601); "*Kind* is my love today, tomorrow *kind*" – Sonnet 105, line 5, referring to his royal son by the Queen; "Fair, *kind*, and true, is all my argument,/ Fair, *kind*, and true, varying to other words"
– Sonnet 105, lines 9-10

"Broke oath on oath, committed wrong on wrong!" - *1 Henry IV*, 4.3.101

REFERENCE EDITION

And trust not simple Henry nor his **oaths** – *3 Henry VI*, 1.2.59
He **swore** *consent to your succession,*
His **oath** *enrolled in the Parliament* – *3 Henry VI*, 2.1.172-173

10 OATHS OF THY LOVE, THY TRUTH, THY CONSTANCY,

I swore these solemn oaths about you; **THY LOVE** = your royal blood; **THY TRUTH** = your honesty to me; **TRUTH** = Oxford, *Nothing Truer than Truth*; your true relationship to me as mother of my royal son; "I shall desire your Lordship that those matters which I allege and bring forth to be judged by you: that they be so pondered that reason be not oppressed, with a vain confidence in a light person, *nor truth smothered up rather by false appearance*" – Oxford to Burghley, June 7, 1595 (PRO SP 12/252, ff. 108-09; Chiljan, 106);
THY CONSTANCY = your commitment to your own lineage; of Southampton: "Still *constant* in a wondrous excellence;/ Therefore my verse, to *constancy* confined,/ One thing expressing, leaves out difference" – Sonnet 105, line 6-8; ("In *constant truth* to bide so firm and sure," Oxford's early sonnet to Elizabeth, *circa* early 1570s):

>Above the rest in Court who gave thee grace?
>Who made thee strive in honor to be best?
>In *constant truth to bide so firm and sure,*
>To scorn the world regarding but thy friends…
>*Love then thy choice* wherein such choice thou bind,
>As naught but death may *ever change thy mind.*
>- *Earle of Oxenforde*
>Rawlinson Poet MS 85, f.16

>Pardon me, Edward, I will make amends:
>And, Richard, do not frown upon my faults,
>For I will henceforth *be no more unconstant*
>- *3 Henry VI*, 5.1.103-105

11 AND TO ENLIGHTEN THEE GAVE EYES TO BLINDNESS,

And to make you see I gave you my own eyes; **ENLIGHTEN** = give you wisdom and *light*, i.e., royal light from the sun or royal son; help you see the truth; shed light on, make bright; "for those who were once enlightened" – Hebrews, 6.4; "The eyes of your understanding being enlightened, that ye may know what the riches of the glory of his inheritance in the saints" – Ephesians, 1.18; **GAVE EYES TO BLINDNESS** = gave you my own eyes, so you, being blind, could see the truth; also, to make you bright, I made myself blind; "And *keep my drooping eyelids open wide*,/ Looking on *darkness which the blind do see*" – Sonnet 27, lines 7-8

>What cunning can express
>The favor of her face?
>To whom in this distress,
>I do appeal for grace.
>A thousand Cupids fly
>About *her gentle eye.*
>- *The Phoenix' Nest*, 1593;
>Earle of Oxenford - *England's Helicon*, 1600

>"Yet sith I have engaged myself so far in Her Majesty's service **to bring truth to light**…"
>- Oxford to Burghley, June 13, 1595; PRO SP 12.252 ff. 133-34; Chiljan, 109

>As, painfully to pore upon a book
>*To seek the light of truth; while* **truth the while**
>**Doth falsely blind the eyesight** *of his look*:
>Light seeking light doth light of light beguile:

So, ere you find where light in darkness lies,
Your light grows dark by *losing of your eyes.*
- *Love's Labour's Lost*, 1.1.74-79

12 OR MADE THEM SWEAR AGAINST THE THING THEY SEE.

Or made my own eyes refuse to admit to what they see; a reference to Oxford's sacrifice of himself, of his identity, of the truth of Southampton; "But, love, hate on, for now I know thy mind;/ Those that can see thou lov'st, and I am blind" – Sonnet 149, lines 13-14; **OR MADE THEM SWEAR AGAINST THE THING THEY SEE** =

> *I am not as I seem to be,*
> For when I smile I am not glad…
> O cruel hap and hard estate,
> *That forceth me to love my foe;*
> Accursed be so foul a fate…
> - E. O. - *The Paradise of Dainty Devices*, 1576

13 FOR I HAVE SWORN THEE FAIR: MORE PERJURED EYE,

FOR I HAVE SWORN THEE FAIR = for I have sworn you are my royal sovereign; **FAIR** = "but in her maiden hand/ The *fairest votary* took up that fire" – Sonnet 154, referring to Elizabeth in 1574, after Southampton's birth

> *Faction that ever dwells*
> *In court*, where wit excels,
> Hath set defiance:
> Fortune and Love have *sworn*
> That they were never born
> Of one alliance
> - E. O., Earl of Oxford, by 1576

MORE PERJURED EYE = all the more have my own eyes perjured themselves; "perjured eye" = "perjured I"; "Now, *perjured* Henry, wilt thou kneel for grace" – *3 Henry VI*, 2.2.81

14 TO SWEAR AGAINST THE TRUTH SO FOUL A LIE!

TRUTH = Oxford, *Nothing Truer than Truth*; **TO SWEAR AGAINST THE TRUTH** = to swear against myself and against the truth of our son; **FOUL** = "Your Lordship I know can easily see that he doth err by the part to account the whole, and this is *foul* abuse" – Oxford to Burghley, June 7, 1595 (PRO SP 12/252, ff. 108-09; Chiljan, 107); "Murder most *foul*, as in the best it is, but this most *foul*, strange and unnatural" – the Ghost of Hamlet's father in *Hamlet*, 1.5.27-28; **SO FOUL** = "Accursed be *so foul* a fate" – Oxford poem, *Paradise of Dainty Devices*, 1576; **LIE** = opposite of Truth, literally the final word to Elizabeth, destroyer of truth and perpetuator of the "Big Lie" as the Virgin Queen who died childless and without an heir to throne

An unsigned poem in the Rawlinson Manuscript (85, f. 17), beginning "Though I seem strange," is to be found on the page adjacent to Oxford's early sonnet "Love Thy Choice." The unsigned poem is cited as "possibly by Oxford" by Katherine Chiljan, 199; and researcher Derran Charlton suggests it "appears to be a reciprocal reply" to Oxford's sonnet. In that case, it would seem Oxford wrote it to express Elizabeth's "vow" made to him in secret – the same "bed-vow" or oath of betrothal to which he refers in Sonnet 152, line 3, accusing her of having broken it. The poem, with my emphases added, follows on the next page:

Poem By Oxford: In Elizabeth's Voice, Speaking To Him?
(1570s -- echoed by Sonnet 152)

Though I seem strange, sweet friend, be thou not so;
Do not annoy thyself with sullen will.
My heart hath *vowed*, although my tongue say no,
To be thine own, in friendly liking still.

Thou seest we live amongst the Lynx's eyes,
That pries into each privy thought of mind;
Thou knowest right well what sorrows may arise
If once they chance my settled looks to find.

Content thyself that once *I made an oath*
To *shield myself in shroud of honest shame*;
And when thou list, make trial of *my troth*,
So that thou save the honor of my name.

And let me seem, although I be not coy,
To cloak my sad conceits with smiling cheer;
Let not my gestures show wherein I joy,
Nor by my looks let not my love appear.

We silly dames, that *false suspect do fear*,
And live within the mouth of envy's lake,
Kind in one heart a secret meaning bear, *
Far from the rest which outwardly we make.

So where I like, I list not vaunt my love;
Where I desire, there must I feign debate.
One hath my hand, another hath my glove,
But he my heart whom most I seem to hate.

Thus farewell, friend: I will continue strange;
Thou shalt not hear by word or writing aught.
Let it suffice, *my vow shall never change*;
As for the rest, I leave it to thy thought.

- "Must in our hearts" – K. Chiljan
"Kinde(?) in onne hearte(?)" – D. Charlton

Appendix
The Time Line of the Sonnets

PART ONE

"LORD OF MY LOVE"

Sonnets 1 - 26

(26 Sonnets)

THE MARRIAGE PROPOSAL

SONNET 1	1590-91	**SOUTHAMPTON MARRIAGE PROPOSAL**
		"That Thereby Beauty's *Rose* Might Never Die"
SONNET 2	1590-91	"Beauty By Succession"
SONNET 3	1590-91	"Thy Mother's Glass … Thy Golden Time"
SONNET 4	1590-91	"The Bounteous Largess Given Thee to Give"
SONNET 5	1590-91	"Never-Resting Time Leads Summer On"
SONNET 6	1590-91	"Be Not Self-Willed"
SONNET 7	1590-91	"His Sacred Majesty"
SONNET 8	1590-91	"Sire, and Child, and Happy Mother"
SONNET 9	1590-91	"Beauty's Waste"
SONNET 10	1590-91	"Make Thee Another Self For Love of Me"
SONNET 11	1590-91	"She Carved Thee for Her Seal"
SONNET 12	1590-91	"Time's Scythe"
SONNET 13	1590-91	"Who Lets So Fair a House Fall to Decay"
SONNET 14	1590-91	"Thy End is Truth's and Beauty's Doom and Date"
SONNET 15	1590-91	"And All in War with Time for Love of You"
SONNET 16	1590-91	"This Bloody Tyrant Time"
SONNET 17	1591	**MARRIAGE PROPOSAL ENDS**
		"Your True Rights"

THE SHAKESPEARE COMMITMENT   (1592-1600)

SONNET 18	1592	"When in Eternal Lines to Time Thou Grow'st"
SONNET 19	1593	**"VENUS AND ADONIS" TO SOUTHAMPTON**
		"For Beauty's Pattern to Succeeding Men"
SONNET 20	1594	**"LUCRECE" TO SOUTHAMPTON**
		"A Man in Hew All *Hews* in His Controlling"
SONNET 21	1595	"Sunne and Moone"
SONNET 22	1596	"As Tender Nurse Her Babe"
SONNET 23	1597	"O Learn to Read What Silent Love Hath Writ"
SONNET 24	1598	"Your True Image"
SONNET 25	1599	**IRISH CAMPAIGN; THE QUEEN'S DISFAVOR**
		"The Painful Warrior"
SONNET 26	1600	**ENVOY**
		"Lord of My Love … This Written Ambassage"

PART TWO

"MY LOVELY BOY"

Sonnets 27 – 126

(100 Sonnets)

THE PRISON YEARS   (FEB 8, 1601-APRIL 9, 1603)

SONNET 27	Feb 8, 1601	**THE REBELLION; IMPRISONMENT**
		"A Jewel Hung in Ghastly Night"
SONNET 28	Feb 9, 1601	"Day by Night and Night by Day Oppressed"
SONNET 29	Feb 10, 1601	"When in Disgrace with Fortune and Men's Eyes"
SONNET 30	Feb 11, 1601	**OXFORD SUMMONED TO SESSIONS – TRIAL**
		"When to the Sessions … I Summon Up Remembrance"
SONNET 31	Feb 12, 1601	"Thou Art the Grave Where Buried Love Doth Live"
SONNET 32	Feb 13, 1601	"A Dearer Birth"
SONNET 33	Feb 14, 1601	**RECALLING SOUTHAMPTON'S BIRTH**
		"Even so My Sunne One Early Morn Did Shine"
SONNET 34	Feb 15, 1601	"Ransom All Ill Deeds"
SONNET 35	Feb 16, 1601	"Thy Adverse Party is Thy Advocate"
SONNET 36	Feb 17, 1601	**SOUTHAMPTON INDICTED**
		"I May Not Ever-More Acknowledge Thee"

Appendix

SONNET 37	Feb 18, 1601	"As a Decrepit Father"
SONNET 38	Feb 19, 1601	**TRIAL, VERDICT & SENTENCE**
		"The Pain Be Mine"
SONNET 39	Feb 20, 1601	"Thou art All the Better Part of Me"
SONNET 40	Feb 21, 1601	"I Do Forgive Thy Robbery, Gentle Thief"
SONNET 41	Feb 22, 1601	"What Woman's Son"
SONNET 42	Feb 23, 1601	"That She Hath Thee is of My Wailing Chief"
SONNET 43	Feb 24, 1601	"All Days are Nights"
SONNET 44	Feb 25, 1601	**EXECUTION OF ESSEX BY BEHEADING**
		"Heavy Tears, Badges of Either's Woe"
SONNET 45	Feb 26, 1601	**SOUTHAMPTON'S HEALTH IMPROVES**
		"Assured of Thy Fair Health"
SONNET 46	Feb 27, 1601	"And by Their Verdict is Determined"
SONNET 47	Feb 28, 1601	**OXFORD MAKES BARGAIN WITH CECIL**
		"A League is Took"
SONNET 48	March 1, 1601	"Locked Up"
SONNET 49	March 2, 1601	"To Guard the Lawful Reasons on Thy Part"
SONNET 50	March 3, 1601	**OXFORD LEAVES HIS SON AFTER VISIT**
		"My Grief Lies Onward and My Joy Behind"
SONNET 51	March 4, 1601	**OXFORD RECALLS LEAVING THE TOWER**
		"From Where Thou Art"
SONNET 52	March 5, 1601	**TRIAL OF OTHER REBELLION CONSPIRATORS**
		"Up-Locked"
SONNET 53	March 6, 1601	"Millions of Strange Shadows on You Tend"
SONNET 54	March 7, 1601	"Sweet Roses … Sweet Deaths"
SONNET 55	March 8, 1601	**OXFORD VOWS "LIVING RECORD"**
		"The Living Record of Your Memory"
SONNET 56	March 9, 1601	"This Sad Interim"
SONNET 57	March 10, 1601	"I (My Sovereign) Watch the Clock for You"
SONNET 58	March 11, 1601	"Imprisoned … Pardon … Crime"
SONNET 59	March 12, 1601	"The Second Burden of a Former Child"
SONNET 60	March 13, 1601	**EXECUTIONS OF MERRICK & CUFFE**
		"Crooked Eclipses 'Gainst His Glory Fight"
SONNET 61	March 14, 1601	"To Play the Watchman Ever for Thy Sake"
SONNET 62	March 15, 1601	"'Tis Thee (My Self) That for My Self I Praise"
SONNET 63	March 16, 1601	"For Such a Time Do I Now Fortify"

SONNET 64	March 17, 1601	"This Thought is as a Death"
SONNET 65	March 18, 1601	**EXECUTIONS OF DANVERS & BLOUNT**
		"How With This Rage Shall Beauty Hold a Plea?"
SONNET 66	March 19, 1601	**ELIZABETH SPARES SOUTHAMPTON**
		"Save That to Die, I Leave My Love Alone"
SONNET 67	March 20, 1601	"Ah, Wherefore With Infection Should He Live?"
SONNET 68	March 21, 1601	"When Beauty Lived and Died as Flowers Do Now"
SONNET 69	March 22, 1601	**SOUTHAMPTON A COMMONER**
		"Thou Dost Common Grow"
SONNET 70	March 23, 1601	"Thou Hast Passed By the Ambush"
SONNET 71	March 24, 1601	"Do Not So Much as My Poor Name Rehearse"
SONNET 72	March 25, 1601	"My Name Be Buried Where My Body Is"
SONNET 73	March 26, 1601	**"THE PHOENIX & TURTLE"**
		"Where Late the Sweet Birds Sang"
SONNET 74	March 27, 1601	"My Spirit is Thine, the Better Part of Me"
SONNET 75	March 28, 1601	"All, or All Away"
SONNET 76	March 29, 1601	**OXFORD'S "INVENTION"**
		"And Keep Invention in a Noted Weed"
SONNET 77	March 30, 1601	**DEDICATION OF "THIS BOOK"**
		"This Book … Thy Book"
SONNET 78	March 31, 1601	**SACRIFICE TO "SHAKESPEARE"**
		"Every Alien Pen Hath Got My Use"
SONNET 79	April 1, 1601	"My Sick Muse Doth Give Another Place"
SONNET 80	April 2, 1601	"Knowing a Better Spirit Doth Use Your Name"
SONNET 81	April 3, 1601	**OXFORD VOWS "MONUMENT"**
		"Your Monument Shall Be My Gentle Verse"
SONNET 82	April 4, 1601	"The Dedicated Words … Blessing Every Book"
SONNET 83	April 5, 1601	"Both Your Poets"
SONNET 84	April 6, 1601	"If He Can Tell That You are You"
SONNET 85	April 7, 1601	"My Tongue-Tied Muse"
SONNET 86	April 8, 1601	**SACRIFICE TO "SHAKESPEARE" ENDS**
		"The Proud Full Sail of His Great Verse"
SONNET 87	April 9, 1601	**CRIME REDUCED TO "MISPRISION"**
		"So Thy Great Gift, Upon Misprision Growing"
SONNET 88	May 1601	**INSTRUCTIONS TO ROYAL SON**
		"For Thy Right Myself Will Bear All Wrong"

Appendix

SONNET 89	June 1601	"I Will Acquaintance Strangle and Look Strange"
SONNET 90	July 1601	"To Linger Out a Purposed Overthrow"
SONNET 91	Aug 1601	"Thy Love is Better Than High Birth to Me"
SONNET 92	Sept 1601	"For Term of Life … On Thy Revolt"
SONNET 93	Oct 1601	"Heaven in Thy Creation Did Decree"
SONNET 94	Nov 1601	"Inherit Heaven's Graces"
SONNET 95	Dec 1601	"A Canker in the Fragrant Rose"
SONNET 96	Jan 1602	"On the Finger of a Throned Queen…"
SONNET 97	Feb 8, 1602	**FIRST ANNIVERSARY OF REBELLION**
		"How Like a Winter … The Fleeting Year"
SONNET 98	March-April 1602	"From You Have I Been Absent"
SONNET 99	May-June 1602	"The Roses Fearfully on Thorns Did Stand"
SONNET 100	July-Aug 1602	"Give My Love Fame Faster Than Time Wastes Life"
SONNET 101	Sept-Oct 1602	"Both Truth and Beauty on My Love Depends"
SONNET 102	Nov-Dec 1602	"My Love is Strengthened, Though More Weak in Seeming"
SONNET 103	Jan 1603	"O Blame Me Not if I No More Can Write!"
SONNET 104	Feb 8, 1603	**SECOND ANNIVERSARY OF REBELLION**
		"Three Winters Cold …"
SONNET 105	March 24, 1603	**QUEEN'S DEATH; SUCCESSION OF JAMES**
		"Which Three, Till Now, Never Kept Seat in One"
SONNET 106	April 9, 1603	**LAST DAY IN THE TOWER**
		"When in the Chronicle of Wasted Time"

THE FINAL DAYS (APRIL 10, 1603 – APRIL 29, 1603)

SONNET 107	April 10, 1603	**SOUTHAMPTON LIBERATED**
		"Supposed as Forfeit to a Confined Doom"
SONNET 108	April 11, 1603	"Prayers Divine … Thou Mine, I Thine"
SONNET 109	April 12, 1603	**OXFORD WILL BE WATER-BEARER**
		"My Self Bring Water for My Stain"
SONNET 110	April 13, 1603	"A God in Love, to Whom I am Confined"
SONNET 111	April 14, 1603	"The Guilty Goddess"
SONNET 112	April 15, 1603	"You Are My All The World"
SONNET 113	April 16, 1603	**FINAL MEETING**
		"Since I Left You"
SONNET 114	April 17, 1603	**OXFORD WILL PREPARE CUP**
		"And to His Palate Doth Prepare the Cup"
SONNET 115	April 18, 1603	"Change Decrees of Kings"
SONNET 116	April 19, 1603	"The Marriage of True Minds"
SONNET 117	April 20, 1603	"The Constancy and Virtue of Your Love"
SONNET 118	April 21, 1603	"And Brought to Medicine a Healthful State"
SONNET 119	April 22, 1603	"Ruined Love When It is Built Anew Grows Fairer"
SONNET 120	April 23, 1603	"Your Crime … Your Trespass … Ransom"
SONNET 121	April 24, 1603	"I Am That I Am"
SONNET 122	April 25, 1603	"Thy Record Never Can Be Missed"
SONNET 123	April 26, 1603	"No! Time, Thou Shalt Not Boast That I Do Change"
SONNET 124	April 27, 1603	"If My Dear Love Were But the Child of State"
SONNET 125	April 28, 1603	**QUEEN'S FUNERAL; END OF DYNASTY**
		"The Canopy … Take Thou My Oblation"
SONNET 126	April 29, 1603	**ENVOY OF FAREWELL**
		"O Thou my Lovely Boy, Who in Thy Power"

Appendix

PART THREE
"TWO LOVES I HAVE"
THE DARK LADY SERIES – SONNETS 127 - 152

SONNET 127	Feb 8, 1601	**THE REBELLION; IMPRISONMENT**
		"Beauty's Successive Heir … Bastard Shame"
SONNET 128	Feb 25, 1601	**EXECUTION OF ESSEX**
		"Those Jacks That Nimble Leap … Dead Wood"
SONNET 129		"The Expense of Spirit in a Waste of Shame"
SONNET 130		"My Mistress' Eyes are Nothing Like the Sunne"
SONNET 131		"Thy Black is Fairest in My Judgment's Place"
SONNET 132		"Those Two Mourning Eyes Become Thy Face"
SONNET 133		"Of Him, My Self, and Thee, I Am Forsaken"
SONNET 134		"My Self I'll Forfeit"
SONNET 135		"Let No Unkind, No Fair Beseechers Kill"
SONNET 136		"Among a Number One is Reckoned None"
SONNET 137		"Why of Eyes' Falsehood Has Thou Forged Hooks?"
SONNET 138		**REVISED FROM "PASSIONATE PILGRIM"**
		"Her False-Speaking Tongue"
SONNET 139		"Kill Me Outright"
SONNET 140		"If I Should Despair I Should Grow Mad"
SONNET 141		"Thy Proud Heart's Slave and Vassal Wretch"
SONNET 142		"Love is My Sin, and Thy Dear Virtue Hate"
SONNET 143		"Her Neglected Child … I, Thy Babe"
SONNET 144		**REVISED FROM "PASSIONATE PILGRIM"**
		"Two Loves I Have of Comfort and Despair"
SONNET 145	March 19, 1601	**ELIZABETH SPARES SOUTHAMPTON**
		"Straight in Her Heart Did Mercy Come"
SONNET 146		"Thy Fading Mansion … Is This Thy Body's End?"
SONNET 147		"Who Art Black as Hell, as Dark as Night"
SONNET 148		"So Vexed With Watching and With Tears"
SONNET 149		"Commanded by the Motion of Thine Eyes"
SONNET 150		"To Make Me Give the Lie to My True Sight"
SONNET 151		"For Thou Betraying Me, I Do Betray My Nobler Part"
SONNET 152	March 24, 1603	**DEATH OF ELIZABETH**
		"To Swear Against the Truth So Foul a Lie"

REFERENCE EDITION

EPILOGUE - PROLOGUE

"THE LITTLE LOVE-GOD"

Sonnets 153-154

THE BATH VISIT

SONNET 153   August 1574   **OXFORD & ELIZABETH AT BATH**

"The Boy … My Mistress' Eye"

SONNET 154   August 1574   **OXFORD & ELIZABETH AT BATH**

"The Little Love-God … By a Virgin Hand Disarmed

Appendix

Phrases = Translations

Phrase	Translation
All in One, One: 8	Southampton, his motto *One for All, All for One*
All is Done: 110	His royal claim gone
All One: 76	Southampton
All the Treasure: 2	All his royal blood
All thy Beauty: 2	All your royal blood
All thy Glory: 37	All your princely glory
All thy State: 96	All your kingly state
Abundant Issue: 97	Royal child
Argument All Bare: 103	Royal blood drained from the sonnets
Authorizing thy Trespass: 35	Sanctioning your crime of the Rebellion
Beauty's Name: 127	Elizabeth's Tudor name
Beauty's Pattern: 19	Elizabeth's pattern in her son
Beauty's Rose: 1	Elizabeth's Tudor Rose dynasty
Beauty's Successive Heir: 127	Elizabeth's immediate successor on the throne
Beauty's Treasure: 6	Elizabeth's royal blood in Southampton
Beauty's Waste: 9	Elizabeth's royal blood not succeeding her
Basest Jewel: 96	Southampton, a prince now a commoner
Bastard Shame: 127	Southampton as a royal bastard
Bastard Signs of Fair: 68	Southampton, a prince consigned to bastardy
Beauties whereof now he's King: 63	Royal blood that should make him a king
Beauteous Day: 34	Time of hope with Elizabeth's royal blood
Beauteous Roof: 10	Elizabeth's House of Tudor
Better Spirit: 80	The pen name "Shakespeare"
Black as Hell: 147	Elizabeth, black because of her viewpoint
Black Night: 73	The disgrace of the Rebellion and treason verdict
Bounteous Gift: 11	Elizabeth's royal gift of life to her son
Buds of May: 18	Southampton, bud of the Tudor Rose
Buried Love: 31	Destroyed royal blood
By Limping Sway Disabled: 66	Defeated by Robert Cecil, the limping hunchback
Captain Jewels: 52	Royal Prince, Southampton
Captive Good: 66	Southampton as prisoner in the Tower
Child of State: 124	Southampton, royal ward and royal prince
Children Nursed: 77	The sonnets created from Southampton's life
Chronicle of Wasted Time: 106	The sonnets without Southampton's succession
Coming End: 13	The inevitable date with succession
Common Grow: 69	Southampton, a commoner in prison
Confine Immured: 84	Tower of London, where Southampton is confined
Confined Doom: 107	Southampton's prison sentence for life
Crooked Eclipses: 60	Robert Cecil's defeat of Southampton
Dark as Night: 147	Elizabeth's negative imperial view
Dateless Night: 30	Disgrace without succession, forever
Deaf Heaven: 29	Elizabeth, who fails to listen to Oxford's pleas
Dear Time's Waste: 30	Lack of Southampton's succession
Dearer Birth: 32	More royal birth that Southampton should have had
Decrepit Father: 37	Oxford, a father powerless to help his son be kiing

REFERENCE EDITION

Dedicated Words: 82	Public dedications by "Shakespeare" to Southampton
Dressing Old Words New: 76	Exchanging one word for another for variety
Embassy of Love: 45	The sonnets, a state message to a royal prince
Entitled in thy Parts: 37	Southampton, entitled to the throne
Eternal Lines to Time: 18	This diary, to become an eternal monument
Eternal Love: 108	Immortal royal blood
Eternal Numbers: 38	The sonnets, filled with his immortal blood
Eternal Summer: 18	Immortal royal life
Ever the Same: 76	Elizabeth, her motto *Semper Eadem*
Every Hymn: 85	Edward de Vere's sonnets
Every Pen: 32	Edward de Vere's pen, writing these sonnets
Every Word: 76	Edward de Vere, using every word for Southampton
Expense of Spirit: 129	Waste of royal blood
Fading Mansion: 146	The dying House of Tudor
Fair Friend: 104	Royal son
Fair a House: 13	Royal House of Tudor
Fair Health: 45	Southampton's royal health
Fair, Kind, and True: 105	Royal, Natural Son, Oxford's Son, with true rights
Fairest Votary: 154	Royal Queen, Elizabeth
Fairest Wights: 106	Southampton to be Captain of Isle of Wight
First Born Flowers: 21	Southampton, son of Tudor Rose
For Thy Right: 88	For your right to the throne
Former Child: 59	Southampton, once a son with royal hope
Fortune's Bastard: 124	Elizabeth's royal bastard
Fortune's Dearest Spite: 37	Elizabeth's most royal malice toward her son
Fresh Blood: 11	Hopeful royal blood
Fresh Numbers: 17	Sonnets filled with royal blood and hope
Gates of Steel: 65	Traitors Gate of the Tower
General of Hot Desire: 154	Southampton as new royal prince
Give Full Growth: 115	Give rebirth and growth to him in the sonnets
God in Love: 110	Divine prince of royal blood
Golden Time: 3	Royal time of hope
Grace and Faults: 96	Royalty and crimes committed by Rebellion
Guilty Goddess: 111	Elizabeth, guilty of Southampton's tragedy
Heaven's Air: 21, 21	Elizabeth's heir to the throne
Heaven's Gate: 29	Traitors Gate of Elizabeth's fortress the Tower
Heaven in Thy Creation: 93	Elizabeth in giving birth to you
Heaven's Sun: 33	Elizabeth's royal son
Heaven's Sweetest Air: 70	Elizabeth's most royal heir
Her Babe: 143	Elizabeth's son
Her Neglected Child: 143	Elizabeth's neglected royal son
Hope of Orphans: 97	Royal hopes of Southampton, an orphan
I Am Confined: 110	Oxford's identity is buried (in his son)
I Am That I Am: 121	Oxford as father of a royal-divine king
In Sleep a King: 87	Oxford had his son as king only in dreams

Appendix

Imprisoned Absence: 58	Southampton in the Tower
Imprisoned Pride: 52	Southampton's royal blood imprisoned
Inherit Heaven's Graces: 94	Southampton inherited Elizabeth's royalty
Interchange of State: 64	Succession to the throne of England
Kind is My Love: 105	My royal son is Elizabeth's natural child
Kingdom of the Shore: 64	England
Kingdoms of Hearts: 70	The kingdoms of England's subjects
Laboring for Invention: 59	Oxford, recreating his son's life in the sonnets
Ladies Dead: 106	Elizabeth, now deceased
Lawful Reasons: 49	Legal arguments on Southampton's behalf
Light's Flame: 1	Royalty
Lines of Life: 16	Southampton's living record; also his bloodlines
Little Love-God: 154	Southampton, the infant divine-royal prince
Living Record: 55	This diary recreating Southampton's life
Lord of My Love: 26	Oxford's royal son
Love and Hate: 35	Royal blood and its lack of recognition
Love is a Babe: 115	Royal blood is a child, Southampton
Love-Kindling Fire: 153	Southampton's fresh royal blood
Lovely Knights: 106	Southampton, a prince, will be a Knight of the Garter
Man in Hew All Hews: 20	Henry Wriothesley, Earl of Southampton
Maid of Dian's: 153	Servant of Elizabeth
Main of Light: 60	Filled with royal light
Masked Buds: 54	Concealed heir of the Tudor Rose
Master Mistriss: 20	King-Queen, reflecting his mother Elizabeth
Misprision Growing: 87	Living with reduced crime of treason
Monarch's Plague: 114	Oxford's self-delusion as father of a king
Moone and Sunne: 35	Elizabeth and Southampton, her royal son
Mortal Moone: 107	The mortal Elizabeth, an immortal queen
Mother's Child: 21	Southampton, son of Elizabeth
Mother's Glass: 3	Southampton is the image of his mother, Elizabeth
My Dear Love: 124	My royal son
My Love Looks Fresh: 107	My royal son looks newly royal again
My Lovely Boy: 126	My royal son
My Mistress' Eyes: 127	The view of my sovereign mistress, Elizabeth
My Oblation: 125	My sacrificial offering [to Southampton]
My Rose: 109	My Tudor Rose son, with Elizabeth now dead
My Sovereign: 57	Southampton, my king
My Sunne: 33	My royal son
Nature Bankrupt: 67	Elizabeth, without any successor
Nature's Bequest: 4	Elizabeth's gift of royal blood
Nature's Own Hand: 20	Elizabeth's power [as mother, giving birth]
Nature's Power: 127	Elizabeth's royal power as monarch
Nature's Truth: 60	Elizabeth's heir, son of Oxford
Never Kept Seat: 105	Never sat on the throne in the person of Southampton
Noted Weed: 76	Familiar costume of poetry

One Thing Expressing: 105	Southampton, the only topic of the Sonnets
Ornament of Beauty: 70	Southampton, the son and prince of Elizabeth's court
Our Night of Woe: 120	Oxford's and Southampton's ordeal of prison time
Pleasure of the Fleeting Year: 97	Elizabeth's royal pleasure, imprisoning him a year
Policy in Love: 118	Official royal policy regarding Southampton
Policy, That Heretic: 124	The policy denying Southampton is heretical
Prayers Divine: 108	The sonnets as sacred prayers or hymns
Precious Friends: 30	Southampton, royal son in the Tower
Purposed Overthrow: 90	Determined revolt against the Cecil-run government
Raven Black: 127	Elizabeth's dark view, recalling the Tower bird
Region Cloud: 33	Elizabeth Regina's dark imperial viewpoint
Roses of Shadow: 67	Tudor Rose heirs [Southampton] in disgrace
Ruined Love: 119	Destroyed hope for royal blood
Sacred Majesty: 7	Royal-divine king
Saved My Life: 145	Elizabeth spared Southampton's life
Second Life on Second Head: 68	Southampton's new life, escaping the axe
Slander's Mark: 70	Southampton, accused of treason
Sland'ring Creation: 127	Elizabeth, slandering her son by her viewpoint
Sovereign Cure: 153	Elizabeth's royal help
Sovereign Eye: 33	The sun, Southampton's kingly eye
Sovereign Mistress: 126	Nature, once Elizabeth, now universal queen
Suborned Informer: 125	Southampton, forced to lie about his true rights
Summer's Day: 18	Royal time of hope
Summer's Green: 12	Royal time of Tudor Green and fresh hope
Sunne and Moone: 21	Southampton and Elizabeth
Sun: 76	Southampton, royal son
Sun of Heaven: 132	Southampton, son of Elizabeth
Suns of the World: 33	Southampton, prince of England
Suspect of Ill: 70	Southampton, a suspect-traitor
Sweet Birds: 73	Elizabeth and Oxford, Phoenix & Turtle
Sweet Boy: 108	Royal son
Sweet Love: 76	Royal son
Sweetest Bud: 35	Most royal heir of the Tudor Rose
Sweets Grown Common: 102	Royal prince, Southampton, reduced to commoner
Term of Life: 92	Southampton's new prison sentence
That Sun Thine Eye: 49	Southampton's royal eye
Three Winters: 104	Three Februarys in the Tower: 1601, 1602, 1603
Throned Queen: 96	Queen Elizabeth
Thy Book: 77	The Sonnets, filled with Southampton's life
Thy Gift, Thy Tables: 122	Southampton's gift of life, these sonnets
Thy Great Gift: 87	Southampton's gift of royal life
Thy Monument: 107	The Sonnets, a monument for Southampton
Thy Pyramids: 123	The individual sonnets for Southampton
Thy Revolt: 92	Southampton's act of Rebellion
Thy Walks: 89	Southampton's walks on the Tower prison roof
Time's Best Jewel: 65	Most royal prince while Elizabeth's time continues
Time's Pencil: 16	Oxford's pen, writing according to Elizabeth's life

Time's Scythe: 12	Elizabeth's ever-dwindling life and reign
Time's Tyranny: 115	The tyranny of Elizabeth's mortal life
To One, of One: 105	To Southampton, these sonnets
Tongue-Tied by Authority: 66	Oxford, forced by officialdom to write indirectly
True Minds: 116	Oxford and Southampton, father and son
Truth and Beauty: 14, 101	Oxford and Elizabeth
Truth's and Beauty's Doom and Date: 14	Oxford's and Elizabeth's end of hope as parents
Two Loves I Have: 144	Elizabeth and Southampton, both royal
Tyrants' Crests: 107	The tyrannical Elizabeth [who is now dead]
Un-Fathered Fruit: 97	Southampton, without Oxford as real father
Up-Locked Treasure: 52	Southampton, royal son in the Tower prison
Very Birds: 97	Elizabeth and Oxford, the Phoenix and Turtle-dove
Virgin Hand: 154	Elizabeth's power as monarch
Wailing Chief: 42	Oxford's grief as father of a disgraced royal son
Waste of Shame: 129	The ruin of Southampton's hope by his crime
Wastes of Time: 12	Heirs who cannot succeed to the throne
World's Due: 1	What Southampton owes England, i.e., to be king
World's Fresh Ornament: 1	England's most rightful royal prince
Woman's Face: 20	Southampton reflects his mother, Elizabeth
Woman's Son: 41	Southampton, Elizabeth's son
Women's Pleasure: 20	Queen Elizabeth's royal will and command
Written Ambassage: 26	The Sonnets, a secret official message to a prince
You Are You: 84	To Southampton: you are a king
Your Monument: 81	Southampton's monument, the Sonnets
Your Trespass: 120	Southampton's crime of the Rebellion
Your True Rights: 17	Southampton's right to be King Henry IX

The "Courtier" Preface – 1572

Edward Vere, Earl of Oxford, Lord Great Chamberlain of England, Viscount Bulbeck and Baron Scales and Badlesmere to the Reader – Greeting

"A frequent and earnest consideration of the translation of Castiglione's Italian work, which has now for a long time been undertaken and finally carried out by my friend Clerke, has caused me to waver between two opinions: *debating* in *my mind* whether I should preface it by some writing and letter of my own, or whether I should do no more than study it with a mind full of gratitude. The first course seemed to demand greater *skill* and art than I can lay claim to, the second to be a work of no less good will and application. To do both, however, seemed to combine a task of delightful industry with an indication of special good will.

DEBATING: For thee, against myself, I'll vow *debate* – 89.13
MY MIND: "O change thy thought, that I may change *my mind*" – 10.9
SKILL: For through the painter you must see his *skill* – 24.5

"I have therefore undertaken the work, and I do so the more willingly, in order that I may lay on a laurel wreath of my own on the translation in which I have studied this book, and also to ensure that neither my good-will (which is very great) should remain unexpressed, nor that my skill (which is small) should seem to fear to face the light and the *eyes of men*.

EYES OF MEN: Can make you live yourself in *eyes of men* – 16.1

"It is no more than its due that *praises* of every kind should be rendered to this work descriptive of a Courtier. It is indeed in every way right and one may say almost inevitable that with the highest and greatest *praises* I should address both the author and the translator, and even more the great patroness [Queen Elizabeth] of so great a work, whose name alone on the title-page gives it a right majestic and honorable introduction.

PRAISES: Since all alike my songs and *praises* be – 105.3

"For what more difficult, more noble, or more magnificent task has anyone ever undertaken than our author Castiglione, who has *drawn* for us the *figure* and model of a courtier, a work to which nothing can be added, in which there is no redundant word, a portrait which we shall recognize as that of the highest and most perfect type of man. And so, although nature herself has made nothing perfect in every detail, yet the *manners* of men exceed in *dignity* that with which *nature has endowed* them; and he who surpasses others has here surpassed himself, and has even outdone nature which by no one has ever been surpassed. Nay more, however elaborate the *ceremonial*, whatever the magnificence of the Court, the splendor of the Courtiers, and the multitude of spectators, he has been able to lay down principles for the guidance of the very Monarch himself.

DRAWN: And you must live, *drawn* by your own sweet skill – 16.14;
FIGURE: Steal from his *figure*, and no pace perceived – 104.10
NATURE HAS ENDOWED: *Nature's bequest* gives nothing but doth lend – 4.3
Let those whom *nature* hath not made for store...
Look whom *she best endowed* – 11.9-11
CEREMONIAL: The perfect *ceremony* of love's right – 23.6

"Again, Castiglione has vividly depicted more and even greater things than these. For who has spoken of Princes with greater gravity? Who has discoursed of illustrious women with a more ample dignity? No one has written of military affairs more eloquently, more aptly about horse racing, and more clearly and admirably about encounters under arms on the field of battle. I will say nothing of the fitness and the excellence with which he has depicted the beauty of chivalry in the noblest persons. Nor will I refer to his delineations in the case of those persons who cannot be Courtiers, when he alludes to some notable *defect*, or to some ridiculous character, or to some deformity of appearance. Whatever is heard *in the mouths of men* in casual talk and in society, whether apt and candid, or villainous and *shameful*, that he has *set down* in so natural a manner that it seems to be acted before our very eyes.

DEFECT: When I shall see thee frown on my *defects* – 49.2
IN THE MOUTHS OF MEN: ev'n *in the mouths of men* – 81.14
SHAMEFUL: For *shame* deny that thou bear'st love to any – 10.1
SET DOWN: Upon thy part I can *set down* a story – 88.6

"Again, to the credit of the translator of so great a work, a writer too who is no mean orator, must be added a new *glory* of language. For although Latin has come down to us from the ancient city of Rome, a city in which the study of eloquence flourished exceedingly, it has now given back its features or use in modern Courts as a polished language of an excellent temper, fitted out with royal pomp, and possessing admirable *dignity*. All this my good friend Clerke has done, combining exceptional genius with wonderful eloquence; for he has resuscitated that dormant quality of fluent discourse. He has recalled those *ornaments* and *lights* which he had laid aside, for use in connection with *subjects* most *worthy* of them. For this reason he deserves all the more honor, because that to great *subjects* – and they are indeed great – he has applied the greatest *lights* and *ornaments*.

GLORY: That thou in losing me shall win much *glory* – 88.8
DIGNITY: The basest weed outbraves his *dignity* – 94.12
ORNAMENTS: Thou that art now the world's fresh *ornament* – 1.9
LIGHTS: When thou thyself dost give invention *light* – 38.8
SUBJECTS: To *subjects* worse have giv'n admiring praise – 59.14
WORTHY: To show me *worthy* of thy sweet respect – 26.12

"For who is clearer in his use of words? Or richer in the *dignity* of his sentences? Or who can conform to the variety of circumstances with greater art? If weighty matters are under consideration, he unfolds his theme in a *solemn* and majestic rhythm; if the subject is familiar and facetious, he makes use of words that are witty and amusing. When therefore he writes with precise and well-chosen words, with skillfully constructed and crystal-clear sentences, and with every art of *dignified* rhetoric, it cannot be but that some noble quality should be felt to *proceed* from his work. To me indeed it seems, when I read this courtly Latin, that I am listening to Crassus, Antonius, and Hortensius, discoursing on this very theme.

DIGNIFIED: So dost thou too, and therein *dignified* – 101.4
SOLEMN: Therefore are feasts so *solemn* and so rare – 52.5
PROCEED: Showing their birth, and where they did *proceed* – 76.8

"And, great as all these qualities are, our translator has wisely added one single surpassing title of distinction to recommend his work. For indeed what more effective action could he have taken to make his work fruitful of good results than to dedicate his *Courtier* to our most illustrious and noble Queen, in whom all courtly qualities are personified, together with those diviner and *truly celestial* virtues? For there is no *pen* so skillful or powerful, no kind of speech so clear, that is not left behind by her own surpassing *virtue*. It was therefore an excellent display of *wisdom* on the part of our translator to seek out as a patroness of his work one who was of surpassing *virtue,* of wisest mind, of soundest religion, and cultivated in the highest degree in learning and in literary studies.

TRULY: Thou *truly* fair wert *truly* sympathized
In *true* plain words by thy *true*-telling friend – 82.11-12

CELESTIAL: With ugly rack on his *celestial* face – 33.6
PEN: Which this (Time's pencil or my pupil *pen*) – 16.10
VIRTUE: If thy sweet *virtue* answer not thy show – 93.14
WISDOM: Herein lives *wisdom*, beauty, and increase – 11.5

"Lastly, if the nobles attributes of the wisest *Princes*, the safest protection of a flourishing commonwealth, the greatest qualities of the best citizens, by her own *merit*, and in the opinion of all, continually encompass her around; surely to obtain the protection of that *authority*, to strengthen it with gifts, and to mark it with the superscription of her name, is a work which, while *worthy* of all Monarchs, is most *worthy* of our own Queen, to whom *alone* is due *all the praise of all the Muses and all the glory* of literature."

PRINCES: Or say with *Princes* if it shall go well – 14.7
MERIT: And place my *merit* in the eye of scorn – 88.2
AUTHORITY: And art made tongue-tied by *authority* – 66.9
ALONE: Wretched in this *alone*, that thou mayst take – 91.13
MUSES: If my slight *Muse* do please these curious days – 38.13
ALL/ALL/ALL: And thou, *all* they, hast *all* the *all* of me – 31.14
ALL THE GLORY: And by a part of *all thy glory* live – 37.12

GIVEN AT THE ROYAL COURT on the 5th of January 1572

Appendix

St. Bartholomew's Letter – 1572

"To the Right Honourable and his singular good lord, the Lord Treasurer of England: I would to God your Lordship would let me understand some of your news which here doth ring dolefully in the ears of every man, of the murder of the Admiral of France, and a number of noble men and worthy gentlemen, and such as greatly have in their lifetimes honored the Queen's Majesty *our Mistress*, on whose tragedies we have an number of French Aeneases in this city, that tell of their own *overthrows* with *tears* falling from their eyes, a piteous thing to hear but a cruel and far more grievous thing we must deem it them to see. All rumors here are but confused, of those troops that are escaped from Paris, and Rouen, where Monsieur [Duke of Alencon] hath also been and like a *vesper Sicilianus*, as they say, that cruelty spreads all over France, whereof your Lordship is better advertised than we are here.

OUR MISTRESS: *My Mistress'* eyes are nothing like the Sunne – Son.130, line 1
OVERTHROWS: To linger out a purposed *overthrow* – 90.8
TEARS: But heavy *tears*, badges of either's woe – 44.14

"And sith *the world* is so full of treasons and *vile* instruments, daily to attempt new and *unlooked-for* things, good my Lord, I shall affectionately and heartily desire your Lordship to be careful both of yourself, and of her Majesty, that your friends may long enjoy you, and you them. I speak because I am not ignorant what practices [attempts to assassinate him] have been made against your person lately by Madder [a traitor in England], and later as I understand by foreign practices if it be true.

THE WORLD: Pity *the world*, or else this glutton be,
VILE: From this *vile* world with *vildest* worms to dwell – 71.4
UNLOOKED-FOR: *Unlooked-for* joy in that I honor most – 25.4

"And think if the Admiral in France was an eyesore or beam in the eyes of the papists, that the Lord Treasurer of England is a block and a crossbar in their way; whose *remove* they will never stick to attempt, seeing they have *prevailed* so well in others.

REMOVE: Where I may not *remove*, nor be *removed* – 25.14
PREVAILED: Will sourly leave her till he have *prevailed* – 41.8

"This estate hath depended on you a great while as *all the world* doth judge, and now all *men's eyes*, not being occupied an more on these lost lords, are as it were on a sudden *bent* and *fixed* on you, as a singular *hope* and pillar, whereto the *religion* hath to lean.

ALL THE WORLD: Though I, once gone, to *all the world* must die – 81.6
MEN'S EYES: When in disgrace with Fortune and *men's eyes* – 29.1
BENT ... ON YOU: For *bending* all my loving thoughts *on thee* – 88.10
FIXED: Truth needs no color with his color *fixed* – 101.6
HOPE: But *hope* of Orphans, and un-fathered fruit - 97.10
RELIGION: Hath dear *religious* love stol'n from mine eye - 31.6

"And *blame me not*, though I am bolder with your Lordship at this present, than my custom is, for I am one that *count* myself a follower of yours now in all fortunes; and *what shall hap to you, I count it hap to myself*: or at the least I will make myself a voluntary partaker of it.

BLAME ME NOT: O *blame me not* if I no more can write – 103.5
COUNT: Which in their wills *count* bad what I think good - 121.8
WHAT SHALL HAP TO YOU,

I COUNT IT HAP TO MYSELF: For *thee*, and for *myself,* no quiet find – 27.14

"Thus my Lord, I humbly desire your Lordship to pardon my youth, but to take in good part my *zeal* and affection towards your Lordship, as on whom I have *builded* my foundation, either *to stand or to fall*.

ZEAL: Intend a *zealous* pilgrimage to thee - 27.6
BUILDED: No, it was *builded* far from accident – 124.5
TO STAND OR TO FALL: To *stand* in thy affairs, *fall* by thy side – 151.12

Your Lordship's affectioned son-in-law,
Edward Oxenford

Appendix

The "Cardanus Preface" – 1573

Cardanus Comforte translated into English. And published by commandment of the right honorable the Earle of Oxenford. Anno Domini 1573. To my <u>loving friend</u> *Thomas Bedingfield Esquire, one of Her Majesty's gentlemen Pensioners:*

LOVING: For bending all my *loving* thoughts on thee - Sonnet 88, line 10
FRIEND: Pity me then, dear *friend*, and I assure ye - 111.13

After I had perused your letters, good Master Bedingfield, finding in them your request far differing from the *desert* of your labor, I could not choose but greatly doubt, whether it were better for me to yield you your desire, or execute mine own intention towards the publishing of *your Book*. For *I do confess* the affections that I have always borne towards you could move me not a little.

DESERT: As to behold *desert* a beggar born – 66.2
YOUR BOOK: Shall profit thee, and much enrich *thy book* – 77.4
I DO CONFESS: *Let me confess* that we two must be twain – 36.1

But when I had thoroughly considered in my mind of sundry and divers arguments, whether it were best to obey mine affections or the merits of your studies: At the length I determined it better to *deny* your unlawful request, than to grant or condescend to the concealment of so worthy a work. Whereby as you have been profited in the translating, so many may reap knowledge by the reading of the same, that shall comfort the afflicted, confirm the doubtful, encourage the coward, and lift up the *base* minded man, to achieve to any true *sum* or grade of virtue, whereto ought only the noble thoughts of men to be inclined.

DENY: For shame *deny* that thou bear'st love to any – 10.1
BASE: Dark'ning thy power to lend *base* subjects light – 100.4
SUM: So great a *sum* of *sums* yet canst not live – 4.8

And because next to the sacred letters of Divinity, nothing doth persuade the same more than Philosophy, of which your book is plentifully *stored*: I though myself to commit an unpardonable error, to have murdered the same in the waste bottoms of *my chests*, and better I thought it were to displease one, than to displease many: further considering so little a *trifle* cannot procure so great a breach of our amity, as may not with a little persuasion of reason be repaired again. And herein I am forced like a good and politic *Captain*, oftentimes to spoil & burn the corn of his own country, lest his enemies thereof do take *advantage*. For rather than so many of your countrymen should be deluded through my sinister means of your industry in studies (whereof you are bound in conscience to yield them an *account*) I am content to make spoil and havoc of your request, and that, that might have wrought greatly in me in the former *respect*, utterly to be of no effect or operation: and when you examine yourself what doth avail a mass of gold to be continually *imprisoned* in your bags, and never to be employed to your use?

STORED: Let those whom nature hath not made for *store* – 11.9
MY CHESTS: Thee I have not locked up in any *chest* – 48.9
TRIFLE: But thou, to whom my jewels *trifles* are – 48.5
CAPTAIN: And captive good attending *Captain* ill – 66.12
ADVANTAGE: *Advantage* on the Kingdom of the shore – 64.6
ACCOUNT: No shape so true, no truth of such *account* – 62.6
RESPECT: In our two loves there is but one *respect* – 36.5
IMPRISONED: By new-unfolding his *imprisoned* pride – 52.12

I do not doubt even so you think of your studies and delightful Muses. What do they avail, if you do not participate them to others? Wherefore we have this Latin Proverb: *Scire tuum nihil est, nisi te scire hoc sciat alter.* What doth avail the tree unless it yield fruit unto another? What doth avail the Vine unless another delighteth in the Grape? What doth avail *the Rose* unless another took pleasure in the smell? Why should

REFERENCE EDITION 783

this tree be accounted better than that tree, but for the goodness of his fruit? Why should this Vine be better than that Vine, unless it brought forth a better Grape than the other? Why should this *Rose* be better *esteemed* than that *rose*, unless in pleasantness of smell it far surpassed the other *rose*?

And so is it in all other things as well as in man. Why should this man be more *esteemed* than that man, but for his virtue, through which every man desireth to be accounted of? Then you amongst men I do no doubt, but will aspire to follow that virtuous path, to illuster yourself with the ornaments of virtue. And in mine opinion as it beautifieth a fair woman to be decked pearls and precious stones, so much more it ornifieth a gentleman to be furnished in mind with glittering virtues.

THE ROSE: The *Rose* looks fair, but fairer we it deem – 54.3
ESTEEMED: The basest Jewel will be well *esteemed* – 96.6

Wherefore considering the small harm I do to you, the great good I do to others I prefer mine own intention to discover your volume, before your request to secret the same: Wherein I may seem to you to *play the part* of the cunning and expert mediciner or *Physician*, who although his patient in the extremity of his burning *Fever*, is desirous of cold liquor or drink to qualify his sore thirst, or rather kill his languishing body: Yet for the danger he doth evidently know by his science to ensue, denieth him the same. So you being *sick of* too much doubt in your own proceedings, through which infirmity you are desirous to *bury* and insevill your works in the *grave* of oblivion: Yet I knowing the discommodities that shall redound to yourself thereby (and which is more unto your Countrymen) as one that is willing to *salve* so great an inconvenience, am nothing dainty to deny your request.

PLAY THE PART: And *play the mother's part*, kiss me, be kind – 143.12
PHYSICIAN: My reason, the *Physician* to my love - 147.5
FEVER: In the distraction of this madding *fever* – 119.8
SICK OF: And *sick of* welfare found a kind of meetness – 118.7
BURY: My name be *buried* where my body is – 72.11
GRAVE: To eat the world's due, by the *grave* and thee – 1.14
The earth can yield me but a common *grave* - 81.7
SALVE: For no man well of such a *salve* can speak – 34.7

Again we see if our *friends* be dead, we cannot show or declare our affection more than by erecting them of *Tombs*: Whereby when they be dead in deed, yet *make we them live as it were again* through their *monument*, but with me behold it happeneth far better, for in your lifetime I shall erect you such a *monument*, that as I say (in) your lifetime you shall see how noble a *shadow* of your virtuous life, shall hereafter remain when you are dead and *gone*. And in your lifetime again I say, I shall give you that *monument* and remembrance of your life, whereby I may declare my good will though with your *ill* will as yet that I do bear in your life.

FRIENDS: "For precious friends hid in death's dateless night" – 30.6
TOMBS: Though yet heaven knows it is but as a *tomb* – 17.3
When you *entombed* in men's eyes shall lie - 81.8
MAKE WE THEM LIVE/AGAIN: You should *live twice*, in it and in my rhyme – 17.14
MONUMENT: Your *monument* shall be my gentle verse – 81.9
And thou in this shalt find thy *monument* - 107.13
SHADOW: Presents thy *shadow* to my sightless view – 27.10
GONE: And mock you with me after I am *gone* – 71.14
ILL: If some suspect of *ill* masked not thy show – 70.13

Thus earnestly desiring you in his one request of mine (as I would yield to you in a great many) not to repugn the *setting forth* of your own proper studies, I bid you *farewell*. From my new country Muses at Wivenghoe wishing you as you have begun, to proceed in these virtuous actions. For when all things shall else *forsake* us, virtue yet will ever abide with us, and *when our bodies fall into the bowels of the earth*, yet that shall *mount* with our minds into the highest Heavens.

SETTING FORTH: Well-wishing adventurer in *setting forth* – Dedication 1609
FAREWELL: Farewell! Thou art too dear for my possessing – 87.1

Appendix

FORSAKE: Since sweets and beauties do themselves *forsake* – 12.11
WHEN OUR BODIES FALL INTO THE BOWELS OF THE EARTH:
The *prey of worms, my body* being dead – 74.10
MOUNT: Then should I spur, though *mounted* on the wind - 51.7

By your loving and assured friend, E. Oxenford.

The 100-Sonnet Center

THE PRISON YEARS   SONNETS 27 – 106   (80)

Sonnet 27	Feb 8, 1601	Rebellion & Imprisonment of Southampton
Sonnet 30	Feb 11, 1601	Summons to Sessions or Treason Trial
Sonnet 38	Feb 19, 1601	Trial of Essex-Southampton; Guilty Verdicts
Sonnet 44	Feb 25, 1601	Execution of Essex at the Tower
Sonnet 52	March 5, 1601	Trial of other Conspirators of the Rebellion
Sonnet 60	March 13, 1601	Executions of Merrick & Cuffe
Sonnet 65	March 18, 1601	Executions of Danvers & Blount
Sonnet 66	March 19, 1601	Queen Elizabeth Spares Southampton's Life
Sonnet 87	April 9, 1601	"Misprision" of Treason
Sonnet 97	Feb 8, 1602	First Anniversary of the Rebellion
Sonnet 104	Feb 8, 1603	Second Anniversary of the Rebellion
Sonnet 105	March 24, 1603	Death of Elizabeth I & Accession of James I
Sonnet 106	April 9, 1603	Southampton's Final Night in the Tower

THE FINAL DAYS   SONNETS 107 – 126   (20)

Sonnet 107	April 10, 1603	Southampton's Liberation by King James
Sonnet 125	April 28, 1603	Funeral of Elizabeth & End of Dynasty
Sonnet 126	April 29, 1603	Envoy to Southampton & End of Diary

THE PRISON YEARS
80 Sonnets
Sonnet 27 to Sonnet 106
SOUTHAMPTON IN THE TOWER
Feb 8, 1601 to April 9, 1601

SOUTHAMPTON'S TREASON & CRIME OF THE REBELLION
Offender's Sorrow ... Offence's Loss ... Ill Deeds (34) ... Faults ... Thy Trespass ... Fault (35) ... Commits (41) ... Offence (51) ... Crime (58) ... Prove ... Faults ... Wrong (88) ... Fault ... Offense (89) ... Purposed Overthrow (90) ... Thy Revolt (92) ... Fault ... Faults ... Faults ... Errors (96) ...

TRIAL OF ESSEX & SOUTHAMPTON
Sessions ... Summon (30) ... Repent (34) ... Lawful Plea ... Accessory (35) ... Confess (36) ... Offenders (42) ... Plead ... Defendant ... Plea Deny ... Impannelled ... Quest (jury) (46) ... Laws ... Allege ... Cause (49) ... Accusing (58) ...

OXFORD FIGHTING TO SAVE SOUTHAMPTON
Excusing ... Thy Adverse Party Is Thy Advocate (35) ... Excuse (42) ... To Guard the Lawful Reasons on Thy Part (49) ... Excuse ... Excuse (51) ... Remedy (62)

SOUTHAMPTON CHARGED, ATTAINTED & FOUND GUILTY
Guilt (36) ... Blame ... Blamed (40) ... Verdict (46) ... Judgment (55) ... Blame (58) ... Blamed ... Suspect ... Suspect (70) ... Attaint (82) ... Attainted (88)

SOUTHAMPTON IMPRISONED & ABSENT IN THE TOWER
Hung in Ghastly Night (27) ... Day by Night and Night by Day (28) ... Hid in Death's Dateless Night (30) ... Separation ... Absence (39) ... These Curious Days (38) ... Absent ... Where Thou Art (41) ... Limits Far Remote ... Where Thou Dost Stay ... The Place (44) ... Absent (45) ... Thyself Away (47) ... Bars ... Wards (guards) ... Locked Up (48) ... Where Thou Art (51) ... Key ... Up-Locked ... Imprisoned (52) ... Absence ... Where You Are (57) ... Imprisoned ... Absence of Your Liberty ... Where You List (58) ... Gates of Steel (65) ... Confine ... Immured (84) ... Fell Arrest ... Without All Bail ... (74) ... Day By Day ... All Away (75) ... Away (91) ... In Other Place (93) ... Absence ... Dark Days ... Thou Away (97) ... Absent ... You Away (98)

ANTICIPATING SOUTHAMPTON'S EXECUTION
Obsequious Tear ... Dead ... Grave ... Buried ... Gone (31) ... If Thou Survive (32) ... Kill (40) ... Lose ... Loss ... Losing ... Loss (42) ... When Thou Art Gone (44) ... Bloody (50) ... Die ... Deaths (54) ... Death ... Doom (55) ... Kill (56) ... I, My Sovereign, Watch The Clock For You (57) ... I Am To Wait ... Waiting Be So Hell (58) ... Our Minutes Hasten To Their End ... Eclipses ... Confound ... Scythe (60) ... For Thee Watch I (61) ... Injurious ... Crushed ... Drained His Blood ... For Such A Time Do I Now Fortify ... Cruel Knife ... Cut ... Life (63) ... Fell Hand ... Buried ... Loss ... Loss ... Confounded ... Death ... Lose (64) ... Mortality ... Plea (65)

SOUTHAMPTON SENTENCE COMMUTED TO LIFE IN PRISON
Save That To Die, I Leave My Love Alone (66) ... Ah, Wherefore With Infection Should He Live ... Why Should He Live ... Days Long Since, Before These Last So Bad (67) ... Second Life (68) ... Death's Second Self (73) ... Term of Life (92) ...

SOUTHAMPTON IN DISHONOR & DISGRACE
In Disgrace with Fortune and Men's Eyes ... Outcast State (29) ... Disgrace ... Stain ... Staineth (33) ...

Appendix

Disgrace ... Shame ... (34) ... Stain (35) ... Blots (36) ... Shadow (37) ... Shadow ... Shadows (43) ... Millions of Strange Shadows on You Tend ... Shade ... Shadow ... Shadow (53) ... Shadows ... Shames (61) ... Gilded Honor Shamefully Misplaced ... Disgraced ... Disabled (66) ... Slander's Mark ... Slander ... Thou Hast Passed by the Ambush of Young Days (70) ... Shame ... Shamed (72) ... Scorn (88) ... Disgrace ... Disgrace (89) ... Blot (92) ... Shame ... Canker ... Spot ... Ill Report ... Blot (95) ... Shadow (98) ... Shame ... Canker (99) ... Blame ... Disgrace ... Mar (103)

SOUTHAMPTON REDUCED TO BASE COMMONER
Thou Dost Common Grow (69) ...Base ... Basest (94) ... Basest (96) ... Base (100)

BARGAIN MADE FOR SOUTHAMPTON'S RELEASE & PARDON
Ransom (34) ... Pardon (58) ... Releasing ... Misprision ... Better Judgment (87) ... Defense (89) ... Conquered Woe (90) ... Redeem (100) ... Amends (101)

OXFORD'S GRIEF OVER SOUTHAMPTON'S PLIGHT
Weary (27) ... Oppression ... Oppressed ... Torture ... Day Doth Daily Draw My Sorrows Longer ... Night Doth Nightly Make Grief's Length Seem Stronger (28) ... Beweep ... Bootless Cries ... Curse (29) ... Wail ... Drown An Eye ... Weep ... Woe ... Moan ... Grieve ... Woe ... Woe ... Sad ... Bemoaned Moan ... Sorrows (30) ... Tear (31)... Tears (34) ... Grieved (35) ... The Pain Be Mine (38) ... Torment (39) ... Forgive ... Grief (40) ... My Grief ... My Wailing Chief ... Suff'ring (42) ... Heavy Tears ... Woe (44) ... Oppressed With Melancholy ... Sad (45) ... My Greatest Grief (48) ... Heavy ... Weary ... Woe ... Heavily ... Groan ... Groan ... Grief (50) ... This Sad Interim (56) ... Suffer (58) ... Heavy ... Weary (61) ... Weep (64) ... Rage (65) ... For Restful Death I Cry (66) ...

THE PRISON YEARS

REBELLION & IMPRISONMENT OF SOUTHAMPTON
(Feb 8, 1601)

    27 – Hung in ghastly night
    28 – Day by night and night by day
    29 – In disgrace with Fortune and men's eyes ... outcast state

OXFORD SUMMONED TO THE SESSIONS OR TREASON TRIAL

    30 – SESSIONS ... SUMMON ... hid in death's dateless night
    31 – Obsequious tear ...dead ... grave ... buried ... gone ...
    32 – If thou survive
    33 – Basest Clouds ... Ugly Rack ... Disgrace ... masked ... stain ... staineth
    34 – Disgrace ... repent ... offender's sorrow ... offence's loss ... RANSOM ... ill deeds
    35 – Faults ... THY TRESPASS ... FAULT ... THY ADVERSEPARTY IS THY ADVOCATE ... lawful plea ... accessory
    36 – Confess ... blots ...guilt
    37 – Shadow

THE TRIAL – GUILTY VERDICT – DEATH SENTENCE
(Feb 19, 1601)

    38 – THESE CURIOUS DAYS ... pain
    39 – separation ... absence ... torment
    40 – blame ... blamed ... forgive ... grief ... kill
    41 – liberty ... commits ... absent ... where thou art ...
    42 – grief ... wailing chief ... offenders ... excuse ... lose ... loss ... losing ... loss
    43 – shadow, shadows

EXECUTION OF ESSEX
(February 25, 1601)

    44 – Where thou dost stay ... THE PLACE (Tower) ... when thou art gone
SOUTHAMPTON'S HEALTH REPORTED BY MESSENGER

    45 – Absent ... oppressed ... SWIFT MESSENGERS ... THY FAIR HEALTH
WAITING FOR SOUTHAMPTON TO BE EXECUTED OR SAVED

    46 – Defendant ... PLEA DENY ... impannelled ... quest ... VERDICT
    47 – Thyself away
    48 – Bars ... wards ... grief ... LOCKED UP

BARGAINING TO SPARE SOUTHAMPTON'S LIFE

    49 – TO GUARD THELAWFUL REASONS ON THY PART ... laws ... allege ... cause

Appendix

OXFORD VISITS SOUTHAMPTON IN THE TOWER

   50 – Heavy ... bloody ... grief
   51 – Offence ... where thou art ... excuse ... excuse
   52 – Key ... up-locked ... imprisoned

BRACING FOR IMMINENT EXECUTION

   53 – Shadows ... shade ... shadows ... shadow
   54 – Die ... deaths
   55 – Death ... enmity ... ending doom ... judgment
   56 – Kill ... sad interim
   57 – WATCH THE CLOCK FOR YOU ... absence ... where you are
   58 – IMPRISONED ... ABSENCE OF YOUR LIBERTY ... accusing ... where you list ... PARDON OF SELF-DOING CRIME ... wait ... WAITING BE SO HELL ... blame
   60 – Our minutes hasten to their end ... eclipses ... confound ... scythe
   61 – Shadows ... shames ... for thee watch I
   62 – Sin ... sin ... Remedy
   63 – Injurious ... crushed ... drained his blood ... I NOW FORTIFY ... cruel knife ... cut ... life
   64 – Fell hand ... buried ... loss ... loss ... confounded ... death ... lose
   65 – Mortality ... rage ... plea ... wrackful siege ... gates of steel ... fearful meditation

SOUTHAMPTON'S LIFE IS SPARED
(March 19, 1601)

   66 – For restful death I cry ... disgraced ... disabled ... tongue-tied ... I would be gone ... die ... alone
   67 – Ah, wherefore with infection should he live ... WHY SHOULD HE LIVE ... days long since, before these last so bad
   68 – Died ... dead ... Sepulchers ... *second life on second head* ... dead

SOUTHAMPTON REDUCED TO COMMONER STATUS

   69 - Thou dost COMMON grow
   70 – Blamed ... slander's mark ... suspect ... slander ... ambush ... suspect ... masked
   71 – Mourn ... dead ... vile ... decay
   72 – Death ... nothing ... prove ... buried ... shame ... shamed ... nothing
   73 – Ruined ... *death's second self* ... ashes ... death-bed ... expire
   74 – Fell arrest ... bail ... memorial ... prey of worms ... dead ... knife
   75 – Day by day ... all away

THE INVENTION & DEDICATION OF THE SONNETS

   76 – MY VERSE ... barren ... KEEP INVENTION IN A NOTED WEED ... every word doth almost tell my name ... my argument ... dressing old words new ... spending again what is already spent ... daily new and old
   77 – THIS BOOK ... waste ... graves ... waste ... THY BOOK

REFERENCE EDITION

OXFORD'S SACRIFICE OF IDENTITY TO "SHAKESPEARE"

78 – Dumb ... ignorance ...
79 – Decayed ... my sick Muse doth give another place
80 – A better spirit doth use your name ... soundless ... worthless ... decay
81 – Epitaph ... rotten ... death ... forgotten ... I, ONCE GONE, TO ALL THE WORLD MUST DIE ... grave ... entombed ... dead ...
82 – ATTAINT ... sympathized ... abused
83 – Barren ... silence ... sin ... dumb ... tomb ... life
84 – Confine ... immured ... curse
85 – Tongue-tied ... dumb
86 – Inhearse ... tomb ... womb ... mortal ... dead ... victors of my silence ... enfeebled

BARGAIN MADE FOR SOUTHAMPTON'S RELEASE & PARDON; HIS CRIME REDUCED TO "MISPRISION" OF TREASON

87 – Farewell ... RELEASING ... determinate ... MISPRISION ... BETTER JUDGMENT
88 – Scorn ... fight ... prove ... forsworn ... faults ... ATTAINTED ... injuries ... wrong

OXFORD CAN NO LONGER VISIT THE TOWER; WALKS ON THE PRISON ROOF ARE ENDED

89 – Forsake ... fault ... offence ... lameness ... defense ... disgrace ... disgrace ... strangle ... ABSENT FROM THY WALKS ... debate ... hate
90 – Sorrow ... conquered woe ... PURPOSED OVERTHROW ... woe ... woe ... loss of thee
91 – Wretched ... away ... wretched
92 – TERM OF LIFE ... THY REVOLT ... blot
93 – In other place ... false heart's history
94 – Power to hurt ... base ... basest
95 – Shame ... canker ... spot ... sins ... ill report ... vices ... blot ... knife
96 – Fault ... faults ... faults ... basest ... errors ...

FIRST ANNIVERSARY OF THE REBELLION
(Feb 8, 1602)

97 – A winter ... absence ... THE FLEETING YEAR ... dark days ... bareness ... decease ... thou away
98 – Absent ... YOU AWAY ... shadow
99 – Shame ... despair ... canker ... death
100 – Base ... redeem ... spent ... despised ... wastes life ... scythe ... crooked knife
101 – Amends ....dumb ... silence ... outlive ... tomb ...
102 – Weak ... mournful ... common ... lose ... hold my tongue
103 – Bare ... blame ... disgrace ... sinful ... mar

SECOND ANNIVERSARY OF THE REBELLION
(Feb 8, 1603)

104 – THREE WINTERS (1600-01; 1601-02; 1602-03)

Appendix

DEATH OF ELIZABETH I & ACCESSION OF JAMES I
(March 24, 1603)

    105 – My invention spent ... alone ... NEVER KEPT SEAT (throne) ...

SOUTHAMPTON'S LAST NIGHT IN PRISON;
OXFORD FORECASTS THE FUTURE
(April 9, 1603)

    106 – THE CHRONICLE OF WASTED TIME

    I SEE DESCRIPTIONS OF THE FAIREST WIGHTS
    (Southampton will be appointed Captain of the Isle of Wight)...

    LADIES DEAD
    (Elizabeth, Sovereign Lady of England, is dead)

    LOVELY KNIGHTS
    (Southampton will be made a Knight of the Garter)

    FOR WE WHICH NOW BEHOLD THESE PRESENT DAYS
    HAVE EYES TO WONDER, BUT LACK TONGUES TO PRAISE.

(Still in Scotland before beginning his triumphant journey south to London and the throne, King James has already sent ahead orders for Southampton's liberation.)

The Title Page

SHAKE-SPEARES
S O N N E T S
Never Before Imprinted

_____

_____

AT LONDON
By *G. Eld* for *T.T.* and are
To be solde by *William Aspley*.
1609

SHAKE-SPEARES = William Shakespeare's, but only the last name is presented; and this name is hyphenated to emphasize it as the pseudonym or pen name of a writer not being identified overtly. The poet is **Edward de Vere, Seventeenth Earl of Oxford (1550-1604)** who, at age forty-three in 1593, had introduced "William Shakespeare" as the printed signature for his public dedication of the highly polished narrative poem *Venus and Adonis* to nineteen-year-old Henry Wriothesley, Third Earl of Southampton (1573-1624). In the following year, Oxford dedicated *Lucrece* of 1594 from "William Shakespeare" to the same younger earl:

"The love I dedicate to your Lordship is without end ... What I have done is yours, what I have to do is yours, being part in all I have devoted yours."

Oxford after 1594 had only one more decade until his reported death in 1604. Having receded from public view following the English victory over the Spanish armada in 1588, he had used the Shakespeare name in 1593 to lend public support to the political goals of Henry Wriothesley, Earl of Southampton in relation to the succession of Elizabeth Tudor, Queen Elizabeth I of England (1533-1603) on the throne. By then the younger earl had made clear he was joining forces with Robert Devereux, Second Earl of Essex (1566-1601) in opposition to William Cecil, Lord Treasurer Burghley (1520-1598), the Queen's chief minister and the most powerful man in England. Their struggle would continue against Burghley's hunchbacked son Robert Cecil (1563-1612), who would become the official Secretary of State in 1596 and inherit the power behind Elizabeth's throne upon his father's death in 1598.

Because of the dedications to Southampton of *Venus* and *Lucrece* (with both goddesses representing Queen Elizabeth), this earl a generation younger than Oxford would be associated with any poems or plays attributed to "Shakespeare" from 1593-1594 onward, especially since Oxford would never again use this pen name to dedicate any work to anyone else.

Meanwhile, privately, Southampton was *"the onlie begetter"* or inspirer of the one hundred and fifty-four consecutively numbered verses of the Sonnets, as the Dedication calls him. Specifically he was the "friend" or so-called Fair Youth to whom Oxford was addressing the long opening series of one hundred and twenty-six private verses, numbered in chronological order as 1-126. Not until now in 1609, five years after Oxford's reported death in 1604, would Southampton himself cause the collection of the Sonnets to be printed – hoping the little quarto volume, known in later history as *Q*, might be hidden away and preserved for posterity.

Appendix

The Dedication

TO. THE. ONLIE. BEGETTER. OF.
THESE. INSUING. SONNETS.
Mr. W.H. ALL. HAPPINESSE.
AND. THAT. ETERNITIE.
PROMISED.
BY.

OUR. EVER-LIVING. POET.
WISHETH.

THE. WELL-WISHING.
ADVENTURER. IN.
SETTING.
FORTH.

T. T.

THE ONLIE BEGETTER – the one who "gave birth" to "these ensuing sonnets" by inspiring the author to write them; "And the Word was made flesh, and dwelt among us, (and we beheld his glory, the glory as of *the only begotten* of the Father), full of grace and truth" – The Gospel of John, 1.14; "No man hath seen God at any time; *the only begotten* Son, which is in the bosom of the Father, he hath declared him" – John, 1.18; *Onlie begetter* suggests roots in the Bible; the 154 verses suggest the 150 verses of the Book of Psalms; Stephen Booth cites at least fifty Biblical links in the Sonnets.

"Although every possible alternative has been put forward, it seems simpler to regard 'Mr. W.H.' as being the same person as the 'Onlie Begetter'. But the meaning of 'Begetter' is disputed: in ancient times it meant 'obtainer' or 'procurer', though the most usual meaning by Shakespeare's day was that found in the biblical phrase, 'This is my only begotten son.' It is possible that Thorpe was dedicating the book to the procurer of the manuscript, but it is far more likely to my mind that the reference is to the theme of Sonnet 78: *Yet be most proud of that which I compile, whose influence is thine, and borne of thee.*" – R. C. J. Wait, p. 12; *Onlie* is used in the same sense of "supreme" as when the author calls Southampton the *only herald to the gaudy spring*; and *Onlie* is a variation of *One*, also identifiing Henry Wriothesley by his motto *Ung par Tout, Tout par Ung* or *One for All, All for One*.

SONNETS – *Sonne* and *son* are imbedded in "sonnets"; this suggestion is heightened by the statement that the sonnets were "begotten" by a parent; Oxford tells Southampton in Sonnet 77 that the sonnets are *"children nursed, delivered from thy brain,"* and this is reinforced by the lines of Sonnet 78 quoted above.

MR. W.H. – A reversal of the title and initials of "Lord Henry Wriothesley," identifying him as the *onlie begetter*. Most of the 154 verses correspond with the twenty-six months of Southampton's imprisonment in the Tower for his role in the Rebellion of February 8, 1601. (These include Sonnets 27-106 to Southampton and Sonnets 127-152 to Elizabeth.) Southampton was stripped of his earldom and all its lands and titles; "His earldom had, of course, been lost through his attainder, and he was now plain Henry Wriothesley" (Akrigg, 131); "He was a condemned man, a dead man in the law – the documents refer to him as 'the late Earl'" (Rowse, *Shakespeare's Southampton*, 164); Southampton in prison became *Mr.* Henry Wriothesley, a commoner, so the 1609 dedication may have been written (by Oxford) during that dark time in 1601-1603.

ALL HAPPINESSE – Linking back to Shakespeare's 1594 dedication of *Lucrece* to Southampton, ending in *all happiness*e; the *all* again identifies Southampton through his motto, *One for All, All for One*; "And thus wishing *all happiness* to you…" – Edward de Vere, Earl of Oxford, to his brother-in-law Robert Cecil, secretary of state, on Oct. 7, 1601

THAT ETERNITIE (Promised by Our Ever-Living Poet) – the immortality the author promises for Southampton: "'Gainst death and *all* oblivious enmity/ Shall you pace forth! Your praise shall still find room/ Ev'n in the eyes of *all* posterity" (Sonnet 55); "It does not seem appropriate for Thorpe to wish 'that eternitie promised by our ever-living poet' to someone other than the person to whom the poet himself promised it. On the balance of the probabilities we may assume that 'Mr. W.H.' is the young man who inspired the sonnets…" (Wait, 12)

OUR EVER-LIVING POET - *Ever-living* applies to persons who are deceased; *ever* identifies Edward de Vere, whose death was recorded as on June 24, 1604; but the 1609 date of the Sonnets may indicate the actual year of his death, after disappearing and assumed to have died.

THE WELL-WISHING ADVENTURER – Oxford was an "adventurer" or investor in the voyages of Martin Frobisher to find a Northwest Passage to China, as he wrote in 1578: "As well for the great liking Her Majesty hath to have the same passage discovered, as also for the special good favour I bear to Master Frobisher, to offer unto you to be an *adventurer* therein for the sum of 1,000 pounds"; Henry Wriothesley was a leading "adventurer" of the Virginia Company by 1609, but he had already been involved in such efforts as early as 1602, during his prison years: "The responsible headship of the Virginia Company became a prime concern and leading activity of Southampton's last and busiest years. But his interest in the plantation of America, in maritime and commercial affairs, in a forward, activist policy, went back a long way…Perhaps, like Raleigh, his spell in the Tower gave him the time to devote his mind to more fruitful projects; for it was during his imprisonment there, in 1602, that he became a chief backer of Captain Gosnold's voyage to prospect the American coast and thus to open up again the colonizing activity…" (Rowse, *Shakespeare's Southampton*, 234); "I will acknowledge with all alacrity and *well-wishing* perform" – Oxford to Robert Cecil, May 11, 1601

SETTING FORTH – While this phrase describes the 1609 voyages, it also depicts Southampton as "being revealed" or "being praised" in the Sonnets; Oxford was undoubtedly "Ignoto," who wrote a commendatory verse for Edmund Spenser's *The Faerie Queene*, Books I-III, published in 1590: "I here pronounce this workmanship is such/ As that no pen can *set it forth* too much."

T.T. – The initials of publisher Thomas Thorpe, but he would not have written the dedication; the Sonnets would have been retained by Southampton, the only one who could have gotten them into print; the dedication contains a message discovered by British researcher John Rollet; briefly, the periods and hyphens mark off the words and/or letters, while the pyramid of six-two-four lines matches the six-two-four letters of "Edward deVere"; and the combination, marking the words in a six-two-four progression, results in: *These Sonnets All By Ever…*

Appendix

"Shake-speare"

"Shakespeare" was the warrior-like name adopted by Oxford to pay homage to the code of chivalry and to express his role as a knight shaking the "spear" of his pen on behalf of Southampton and Queen Elizabeth I of England (1533-1603), of whom he would write: *"Two loves I have of comfort and despair,/ Which like two spirits do suggest me still;/ The better angel is a man right fair,/ The worser spirit is a woman coloured ill"* – Sonnet 144, lines 1-4, printed in an earlier form in 1599 and later revised for insertion in the Dark Lady series (127-152) of *Shake-Speares Sonnets* a decade later in 1609.

"In the sixteenth and seventeenth centuries, as today, the word 'Shakespeare' unquestionably suggested to the mind of everyone what its two syllabic elements so clearly indicate – military prowess. But the suggestion was far more obvious than now, for the age was nearer to chivalry, and the phrase 'the shaking of the spear' was almost a commonplace as expressing the doughtiness of warriors." – J. Q. Adams, *A Life of Shakespeare*, 1923, p. 1; "He laugheth at *the shaking of a spear*" – Book of Job, 41.29; "When he *shakes his furious spear*" – John Marston, 1598; "They laugh to scorn *the shaking of the spear*" – John Davies of Hereford, 1609

BEN JONSON - 1623: "Look how the father's face lives in his issue; even so, the race of Shakespeare's mind and manners brightly shines in his well-torned and true-filed lines: in each of which *he seems to Shake a Lance, as brandished at the eyes of ignorance*." – First Folio of Shakespeare Plays, 1623

PALLAS ATHENA: "The grey-eyed Greek virgin goddess of war, wisdom, and handicrafts, and patroness of Athens, Athena is the daughter of Zeus ... The child, Athena, sprang from his head fully armed with *helmet, shield and spear* ... As Pallas, she was a storm goddess presiding over war. During times of peace she instructed people in useful crafts ... It is said that she remained a virgin, rejecting all suitors" – Turner & Coulter, *Dictionary of Ancient Deities*, 2000; "In art and literature, Athena appears clad in full armour, with *helmet, round shield, and spear*" – Grant & Hazel, *Who's Who in Classical Mythology*, 1973; "*Hastivibrans*, the Spear-shaker, was the sobriquet of Pallas Athena ... the patron goddess of Athens, home of the theatre, while in Rome the guild of poets and dramatists met in the Temple of Pallas. 'And in thy hand *the Spear of Pallas shake*,' says a verse in a collection of Shakespeare's poems of 1640 ..." – Charlton Ogburn, Jr., *The Mysterious William Shakespeare*, pp 97, 238

ELIZABETH & PALLAS: In adopting "Shakespeare" as a pen name, Oxford was paying homage to his sovereign Mistress Queen Elizabeth, as royal patroness of the arts in England. In fact, the earl himself had associated her with the goddesses *Venus, Juno* and *Pallas Athena*, among others: "But who can leave to look on *Venus*' face?/ Or yieldeth not to *Juno's* high estate?/ What wit so wise as gives not *Pallas* place?/ These virtues rare, each Gods did yield a mate;/ Save *her alone, who yet on earth doth reign*" – Oxford poem, *The Paradise of Dainty Devices*, 1576, signed E. O., written a few or several years earlier.

The same comparisons are made by John Lyly, private secretary to Oxford, in *Euphues his England*, the novel of 1580, dedicated to Oxford and undoubtedly written and/or dictated by him. Following a lengthy homage to Queen Elizabeth in this *Euphues* book is a Latin poem to her, beginning: *"Pallas, Juno, Venus, cum Nympham numine plenam..."*

These comparisons of the Queen were also made in *The Arte of English Poesie* of 1589, published by Richard Field, who would publish *Venus and Adonis* four years later. *Poesie* contains homages to Edward de Vere as a premier courtier poet. The tract also addressed Elizabeth as both patroness and maker of poetry: "Forsooth by your Princely purse, favours and countenance, making in maner what ye list, the poore man rich, the lewd well learned, the coward courageous, and vile both noble and valiant. Then for imitation no less, your person as a most cunning counterfaitor lively representing *Venus* in countenance, in life *Diana*

REFERENCE EDITION

(chaste goddess of the Moon), *Pallas* for government, and *Juno* in all honour and regall magnificence."

The Romans identified Athena with Minerva, daughter of Jupiter and keeper of the city of Rome. She was the goddess of war, patroness of physicians, goddess of intellectual activity and wisdom, patroness of the arts. By associating Queen Elizabeth with Pallas Athena, his inspirer and protector, Oxford also connected her with Minerva.

OXFORD'S BOLBEC CREST: Edward de Vere's crest as Viscount Bolbec was a lion brandishing a spear. At some point in time, the spear was broken to indicate victory in a jousting tournament.

OXFORD AT THE TILT – 1571 & 1581: Oxford performed "far above the expectation of the world," as one commentator put it, during a royal jousting tournament held during three days of May 1571 before Queen Elizabeth at Westminster. A contemporary account was written by Giles Fletcher: "But if at any time with fiery energy he should call up mimicry of war, he controls his foaming steed with a light rein, and *armed with a long spear* rides to the encounter ... Bravo, valiant youth!" Ten years later in 1581, at age thirty-one, Oxford was also the successful challenger in another of the five great tournaments of Elizabeth's reign.

HARVEY ON OXFORD & PALLAS – 1578: Addressing Oxford in Latin before Queen Elizabeth and the Court in 1578, scholar Gabriel Harvey linked Oxford with various gods including Pallas, Minerva and Apollo: "*Mars* will obey thee, *Hermes* will be thy messenger, *Pallas striking her shield with her spear shaft* will attend thee. For a long time past *Phoebus Apollo* has cultivated thy mind in the arts ... In thy breast is noble blood, Courage animates thy brow, *Mars* lives in thy tongue, *Minerva* strengthens thy right hand, *Bellona* reigns in thy body, within thee burns the fire of *Mars*. Thine eyes flash fire, thy countenance shakes spears; who would not swear that Achilles had come to life again?" – translation by Ward, but the phrase "thy countenance *shakes spears*" is disputed by opponents of Oxford-as-Shakespeare, such as Alan Nelson, who translates it as "your glance shoots arrows."

OXFORD, THE BOAR, THE SPEAR: The earls of Oxford were noted for their "cognizance of the blue Boar" on the Vere coat-of-arms and often emblazoned on the left shoulder. One way Oxford identified his authorship of *Venus and Adonis* in 1593 was by combining the *boar* of his earldom and the *spear* of his pen name that he was now introducing: "'Tis true, 'tis true, thus was Adonis slain:/ *He ran upon the boar with his sharp spear*" – Venus and Adonis, lines 1111-1112

SONNETS = in the Shakespearean form, the verses consist of fourteen lines: three quatrains (four-line stanzas) plus a concluding couplet. In the first twelve lines, every other line is rhymed; the two lines of the ending couplet are rhymed: ABAB ... CDCD ... EFEF ... GG. The Shakespearean sonnet is named for the poet's use of it to the exclusion of other schemes.

Sonnets

PETRACH & ITALY: The Italian sonnet, the oldest variety, is also called the Petrarchan sonnet, after its most famous exponent, **Petrarch (1304-1374)**. "Though no one has proved that he ever read a single Italian poem, Shakespeare shows a pervasive indebtedness to Italian love poetry for both the form and content of his sonnets." - Robert S. Miola, *Shakespeare's Reading*, 200, p. 33.

SURREY, WYATT & SHEFFIELD – 1530-1547: "A sister of Oxford's father, Lady Frances de Vere, herself a versifier, was married to **Henry Howard, the Earl of Surrey (1517-1547)**, whose ten poems near the beginning of the *Oxford Book of Sixteenth Century Verse* include three sonnets that, like seven others of the fifteen or sixteen ascribed to him, are of the form later known as Shakespearean. With some by his friend **Sir Thomas Wyatt (1503-1542)**, they represent the first of their kind. In his translation of the *Aeneid*, Surrey employed the first blank verse in English; in this, too, Edward de Vere's uncle prepared the way for Shakes-

Appendix

peare … Another poetical uncle of Edward de Vere's was **Edmund Baron Sheffield**, the husband of the 16th Earl of Oxford's sister Lady Anne … H. A. Taine, in his classic *History of English Literature*, includes Sheffield with Surrey as being responsible for 'the prolongation of chivalric poetry.' It was reported of him: 'Great his skill in music, who wrote a book of sonnets in Italian fashion' – entirely lost." – Charlton Ogburn, Jr., *The Mysterious William Shakespeare*, 1992, pp.415-416

"Surrey studied the poets of the Italian Renaissance, especially Petrarch, and shortly after his close friend Thomas Wyatt introduced the sonnet into English, Surrey developed a variant more appropriate to the relatively rhyme-poor English language. This was the rhyme scheme that Shakespeare was to use in his Sonnets, the so-called English, or Shakespearean sonnet … Surrey was a cousin of King Henry VIII (1491-1547) and a close friend of his illegitimate son … Surrey fell victim to the increasing paranoia of King Henry, who was dying and feared that a promising young man of royal blood might want to hasten the process. Surrey was tried for treason on trumped-up charges and executed only a few days before the king's death …Wyatt, who served as a diplomat in Italy, translated some of Petrarch's sonnets to produce the first English sonnets in about the year 1530. Wyatt and his friend Surrey subsequently became the first English poets to compose their own original poems in this form." – Charles Boyce, *Shakespeare A to Z*, 1990, pp. 620, 719

TOTTEL'S "MISCELLANY" – 1557: "Italian influence flowed throughout Elizabethan literary culture, beginning with Thomas Wyatt's and the Earl of Surrey's Petrarchan adaptations in *Tottel's Miscellany* **(1557),** and culminating in the sonneteering vogue of the 1590s." – Robert S. Miola, *Shakespeare's Reading*, 200, p. 33.

OVID'S "METAMORPHOSES": The favorite source of inspiration and mythology for the Shakespeare poems, plays and sonnets was the work of ***Publius Ovidius Naso, a. k. a. Ovid (43 B.C. – 17 A. D.)***, the ancient Roman poet of love. Ovid's ***Metamorphoses*** was a fifteen-book anthology of Greek and Roman legends; it contributed heavily to the writing of both *Venus and Adonis* and *The Sonnets*. The Latin original of another Ovid work, the *Fasti*, translated into English much later in 1640, was used for *Lucrece*.

"GOLDING'S" TRANSLATION: 1565-1567: "The *Metamorphoses*, ***both in the original Latin and in Arthur Golding's 1567 translation***, supplies Shakespeare throughout his career … Shakespeare's sonnets recall Ovid's *Metamorphoses*, both in Latin and in Golding's translation … The cumulative evidence in the sonnets suggests that Shakespeare regularly uses Golding's translation; in (some cases, however, he draws closer to the Latin …" – Robert Miola, *Shakespeare's Reading*, pp. 19-29. **Arthur Golding** (1536-1605) was Edward de Vere's maternal uncle. During the time when Golding would have been translating the Ovid work in the 1560s, he lived under the same roof with Oxford at Cecil House on the Strand. In 1562 the young earl had become the first royal ward of the Queen under the guardianship of William Cecil, Lord Burghley, her chief minister and Master of the Royal Wards; and most likely the actual translator of the *Metamorphoses* was not Golding, a man of strong Puritanical sympathies, but, rather, the teenage Oxford – who, thoroughly acquainted with Latin since early childhood, would have enthusiastically transformed Ovid's masterpiece into its rollicking, sensual English. What makes the most logical sense is that the mature Oxford drew upon his own youthful translation of Ovid to create the poems and plays, as well as the Sonnets, to be printed eventually under the "Shakespeare" name.

OXFORD'S ITALIAN BOOKS – 1569: At age nineteen in 1569, Edward deVere purchased "*a Geneva Bible gilt, a Chaucer, Plutarch's works in French, with other books and papers*" along with "***two Italian books*** *… Tully's and Plato's works in folio, with other books, paper and nibs*" – State Papers Domestic, Elizabeth, 42.38; Add., 19.38; Ward, 32-38.

"COURTIER" & "CARDANUS" – 1572 & 1573: In 1572 and 1573, at ages twenty-two and twenty-three, Oxford brought to publication two works of the Italian Renaissance. First was a translation from Italian into Latin of ***Il Cortegiano*** or ***The Courtier*** by Castiglione, originally published in Venice in 1528. For this work, often cited as an important source of *Hamlet*, Oxford contributed a Latin preface in which he heralded "a new glory of language" and praised Elizabeth as a monarch "to whom alone is due all the praise of all the Muses and all the glory of literature." Next came a translation from Latin into English of *Cardanus' Comforte* by Girolamo Castellione, which had appeared originally in Venice in 1542; and for this book, often cited as an inspiration for Hamlet's soliloquies, Oxford contributed both a prefatory letter in English as well as a poem. The letter contained many words, phrases and themes to appear much later in *Shake-Speares Sonnets*, while the poem employed ten syllables or beats per line as the lines of the Sonnets would contain. Both these works, conferring the approval of royal authority (i.e., that of Queen Elizabeth) upon the creation and appreciation of literature, testify to Oxford's proficiency in Latin and his deep love for Italy and the Italian Renaissance, the substance and spirit of which he was helping to bring into England.

OXFORD'S EARLY SONNET – 1571-1573: Edward deVere officially became Seventeenth Earl of Oxford and assumed his title as hereditary Lord Great Chamberlain at the royal Court at the age of twenty-one in 1571. Soon afterward, he wrote the first recorded sonnet of the Elizabethan reign in the specific form that would become known as the "Shakespearean" sonnet. In this verse of fourteen lines, entitled *Love Thy Choice*, he affirmed his loyalty and devotion to the service of Queen Elizabeth. Oxford's sonnet in this form preceded those of all other contemporary English poets such as Spencer, Sidney, Watson, Drayton and Daniel.

OXFORD'S ITALY – 1575-1576: Oxford traveled extensively in Italy during fifteen months in 1575-1576, visiting Venice, Padua, Mantua, Genoa, Verona, Florence, etc., with longer stays in Venice, as well as spending time at the French court and meeting with Protestant philosopher Sturmius in German. This time he brought his personal experience of the European and Italian Renaissance back to England, becoming known as the quintessential "Italiantate" Englishman.

HARVEY'S ORATION – 1578: "For a long time past Phoebus Appollo has cultivated thy mind in the arts. English poetical measures have been sung by thee long enough. Let that Courtly Epistle (to the reader of The Courtier) – more polished even than the writings of Castiglione himself – witness how greatly thou dost excel in letters. I have seen many Latin verses of thine, yea, even more English verses are extant; thou hast drunk deep draughts not only of the Muses of France and Italy, but has learned the manners of many men, and the arts of foreign countries." - Gabriel Harvey, addressing Oxford with a Latin oration beforeElizabeth and her Court at Audley End, Cambridge, 1578

"ARTE OF POESIE" – 1589: "In the latter end of the same kings raigne (Elizabeth's father Henry VIII, who died in 1547) sprong up a new company of courtly makers, of whom Sir Thomas Wyatt th'elder & Henry Earle of Surrey ere the two chieftains, who having travailed into Italie, and there tasted the sweete and stately measures and stile of the Italian Poesies as novices newly crept out of the schooles of Dante Arioste and Petrarch, they greatly polished our rude & homely maner of vulgar Poesie, from that it had bene before, and for that cause may justly be sayd the first reformers of our En glish meetre and stile …

"And in her Majesties time that now is (the time of Queen Elizabeth the First) are sprong up an other crew of Courtly makers, Noble men and Gentlemen of her Majesties owne servants, who have written excellently well as it would appear if their doings could be found out and made publicke with the rest, of which number is first that noble Gentleman Edward, Earle of Oxford."

The Arte of English Poesie would be followed four years later by Oxford's introduction of "William Shakespeare" – the English Ovid – as the printed signature beneath his dedication of *Venus and Adonis* in 1593 to Southampton. Oxford would announce the arrival of "Shakespeare" with *Venus* by including an epigram from Ovid's *Amores* on the title page:

> *Let the mob admire base things; may Golden Apollo*
> *serve me full goblets from the Castilian Spring!*

NEVER BEFORE IMPRINTED = All but two of these 154 verses had been "never before imprinted." None of the one hundred and twenty-six Fair Youth verses (1-126) had been published. Neither had any of

Appendix

the twenty-six Dark Lady verses (127-152) been printed, except for two (Sonnets 138 and 144), which had appeared in different versions in *The Passionate Pilgrim* of 1599. Neither of the two earlier-written Bath Visit verses (153-154), now tagged onto the end so they appear to be an epilogue, had been published before now in 1609.

NEVER = a glance at Oxford's early pen name *Ever or Never*, appearing in *A Hundredth Sundry Flowres* of 1573 and in *Willobie his Avisa* in 1594. This year two plays also appeared in print: *Pericles* and *Troilus and Cressida*, the latter with an epistle (undoubtedly written earlier by Oxford) entitled *A Never Writer to An Ever Reader: News*. Oxford's signature as *Ever or Never* was known by other writers who also knew he was the writer using the Shakespeare name: "And Shakespeare thou, whose honey-floing Vein/ (Pleasing the World) thy praises doth obtain/ … Live *ever* you, at least in Fame live *ever*./ Well may the Body die, but Fame dies *never*" – Richard Barnfield, 1598; "Far fly thy fame/ Most, most of me beloved! *Whose silent name/ One letter bounds.* Thy true judicial style/ I *ever* honor; and, if my love beguile/ Not much my hopes, then thy unvalued worth/ Shall mount fair place, when apes are turned forth" – John Marston, 1598, referring to the name "Edward deVere" that is bound by "one letter," E.

Oxford played upon his name openly in his pre-1576 *Echo Verses*: "When thus the echo answered her to *every word* she spake:/ Oh heavens! Who was the first that bred in me this *fever*? *Vere*./ Who was the first that gave the wound whose fear I wear for *ever*? *Vere*." He also played upon the "ever" and "never" link in the private verses of *Shake-Speares Sonnets*: "Why write I still all one, *ever* the same,/ And keep invention in a noted weed,/ That *every* word doth almost tell my name,/ Showing their birth, and where they did proceed?" – Sonnet 76, lines 5-8; "O no, it is an *ever*-fixed mark/ That looks on tempests and is *never* shaken;/ It is the star to *every* wandering bark/ … If this be error and upon me proved,/ I *never* writ, nor no man *ever* loved" – Sonnet 116, lines 5-7, 13-14

Oxford also combined his *ever* signature with *true* or *truth* from his earldom motto *Vero Nihil Verius* or **Nothing Truer than Truth**: "*Ever* a Lover of the **Truth/Vere**; May these words be thy **True/Vere** motto" - . translation of part of a Latin inscription on a blank page of a Greek New Testament sent to Oxford's wife Anne Cecil, daughter of Lord Burghley, while Oxford was in Italy during 1575-1576; "This I do vow, and this shall *ever* be,/ I will be *true* despite thy scythe and thee" – defying Time in Sonnet 123, lines 13-14

_____
_____ = This is the printed space where the author's name usually appeared; i.e., the space where "By William Shakespeare" ordinarily would have been inserted; but for the Sonnets this space between the lines was left conspicuously blank to indicate an unidentified author.

Otherwise it should read:
_____

By Edward de Vere, Earl of Oxford
_____

BY G. ELD FOR T. T. AND ARE
G. ELD = the printer of the Sonnets as well as of *Troilus and Cressida*, also appearing in 1609, with its salutation from *"A Never Writer to an Ever Reader"* indicating that the author of the play was Edward de Vere, who had played upon his name as *E. Ver* and had used the pen name *Ever or Never*. "An apprentice from 1592 to 1600, Eld was located at The Printer's Press, Fleet Lane" – O. J. Campbell

T.T. = Thomas Thorpe, publisher, who had registered the Sonnets on May 20, 1609. Since Southampton himself was sole possessor of the Book of Sonnets, the earl authorized Thorpe to register the volume and supplied Eld with the manuscript to be printed in the manner Oxford had intended.

TO BE SOLDE BY WILLIAM ASPLEY
WILLIAM ASPLEY = one of two booksellers authorized to put up the Sonnets up for sale; (the name of

John Wright, bookseller, also appears on some of the thirteen surviving copies of the original quarto); but whether either of these booksellers ever actually possessed copies for sale in their stores is doubtful.

1609 = the year on the title page, five years after Oxford's reported death on June 24, 1604, but there is no evidence that anyone bought or read the Sonnets at this time.

MAY 20, 1609: THE SONNETS ARE REGISTERED: "Tho. Thorpe. Entered for his copie under the handes of m*aster* Wilson and m*aster* Lownes Wardenes a booke called Shakespeares sonnets vjd." The book is printed later this year. The little quarto volume, known as *Q*, also contains the never-before-printed narrative poem *A Lover's Complaint*, written by Oxford and attributed to "William Shakespeare".

"William Aspley's shop was in St. Paul's Churchyard, at the sign of 'the Parrot'; John Wright's was a little to the north, at the door of Christ Church nearest to Newgate. Whether the moneyed class returned to the City after the plague-ridden summer of 1609 by way of the Strand or Holborn, they would pass near one of the shops at which *Shakespeare's Sonnets* was on sale. If title-pages were posted up as publicity, the large-size capitalized SHAKE-SPEARES' in the top line was bound to be attractive, at this period when his reputation was at its lifetime zenith." – Katherine Duncan-Jones, Arden edition, 1997

1609: THE SONNETS COMPLETELY VANISH: But the book fell into a resounding silence and did not reappear in the same form until 1711, a half-century after the English civil war and more than a full century after the first printing by George Eld.

"The neglect of the Sonnets of 1609 can only be explained by concluding that they were quickly suppressed." – Frank Mathew, 1922; "There is fair ground for a presumption that the original edition was stopped." – J. M. Robertson, 1926; "Unless the Book of Sonnets *was* quickly suppressed, how can one account for the total silence of Shakespeare's contemporaries?" – Hyder Edward Rollins, 1944; "Evidence that *Q* was suppressed is circumstantial, but evidence is evidence." – Robert Giroux, 1982

The more likely scenario is that copies of the Sonnets were placed in private hands in hopes they would survive the ravages of both the Government and Time. The collected verses of the Book of Sonnets were akin to a message in a bottle, set adrift on the sea of time, intended for the eyes of future generations.

"The survival of thirteen copies, most in good condition, suggests that the volume did not undergo the kind of enthusiastic thumbing that destroyed hundreds of early copies of Shakespeare's earliest published poem, *Venus and Adonis*," Duncan-Jones writes in 1997; but the "good condition" of these copies also conforms with the suggestion that they had been hidden among private collections and untouched precisely in the hope they would be rediscovered by posterity. (A note on the back of a letter to Edward Alleyn, dated June 19, 1609, records the purchase of a book of "Shaksper sonetts 5d" – but "this is almost certainly a forgery by John Payne Collier," according to Duncan-Jones.)

1609: *PERICLES* IS PUBLISHED IN QUARTO

1609: *TROILUS AND CRESSIDA* IS PUBLISHED IN QUARTO: This is the only printing of the play prior to its publication in the First Folio of 1623. The printer is George Eld, who has printed the Sonnets this year as well. (The publishers of *Troilus* are Richard Bonian and Henry Walley.) "The earliest record of the play is an entry, generally regarded as a blocking entry, inserted by James Roberts in the Stationers' Register, dated February 7, 1603" – O. J. Campbell. This early date suggests that Oxford himself wrote the preface or epistle prior to his reported death in 1604, warning readers that "when he (the author) is gone, and his comedies out of sale, you will scramble for them and set up a new English Inquisition." The epistle also refers to "the grand possessors" of the Shakespeare plays, eighteen of which have not yet been printed and will not appear until a decade and a half from now, in the Folio of 1623.

"A NEVER WRITER TO AN EVER READER: NEWS." – "Eternal reader, you have here a new play, never staled with the stage, never clapper-clawed with the palms of the vulgar, and yet passing full of the palm comical ... And believe this, that when he is gone and his comedies out of sale, you will scramble for them and set up a new English Inquisition. Take this for a warning, and at the peril of your pleasure's loss, and judgment's, refuse not, nor like this the less for not being sullied with the smoky breath of the multitude, but that fortune for the scape it hath made amongst you, since by the grand possessors' wills I believe you should have prayed for them rather than been prayed..."

The holders of the plays called "the grand possessors" appear to be Oxford's surviving relatives, who, of course, are also the relatives of his brother-in-law Robert Cecil, Earl of Salisbury. These include Oxford's daughter Susan Vere (1587-1629) and her husband, Philip Herbert, Earl of Montgomery (1584-1650), younger brother of William Herbert, Earl of Pembroke (1580-1630), to whom Oxford's daughter Bridget Vere (1584-1620) had been engaged in 1597. These two earls are the "incomparable pair of brethren" to whom the First Folio of 1623 will be dedicated, undoubtedly for supervising and/or helping to finance the expensive publication. Also included among "the grand possessors" would be the mother of the two earls, Mary Sidney, Countess of Pembroke (1561-1621), sister of Philip Sidney, who had died in 1586; as well as Oxford's eldest daughter, Elizabeth Vere (1575-1627), whom the Queen and Lord Burghley had attempted to join in marriage with Henry Wriothesley, Third Earl of Southampton in 1590-1591, but who, instead, married William Stanley, Sixth Earl of Derby (1561-1642) in 1595. Closely involved with Robert Cecil and the "grand possessors" is Ben Jonson, whose eulogy to "Shakespeare" in the First Folio will include the enigmatic phrase "Sweet Swan of Avon" that will lead future researchers to conclude that he was referring to William Shaksper (1564-1616) of Stratford upon Avon.

Also in the epistle to *Troilus* from the "Never Writer to an Ever Reader" is the remark: "So much and such savored salt of wit is in his Comedies that they seem (for their height of pleasure) to be *borne in that sea that brought forth 'Venus'* – a reference to the *"ocean"* or *"sea"* of royal blood from Queen Elizabeth, the model for the goddess Venus in *Venus and Adonis* of 1593, dedicated to Southampton, the son to whom she had bequeathed this "sea" of royal blood by having given birth to him:

> Thou art, quoth she, *a sea, a sovereign king*... - Lucrece, 652

> But since your worth (wide as the Ocean is)... - Sonnet 80, line 5

The 100-year Silence Of The Sonnets

In terms of the collection of 154 consecutively numbered sonnets existing in their original, correct form and with their original, accurate contents, from now and throughout the rest of the seventeenth century (and beyond) the rest is silence.

1611: KING JAMES VERSION OF THE BIBLE IS PUBLISHED

1612: DEATH OF ROBERT CECIL, EARL OF SALISBURY

1612: *MINERVA BRITANNA* SUGGESTS EDWARD DE VERE: The book of emblems, published by Henry Peacham, includes much information indicating that Peacham well knows that "Shakespeare" was Edward de Vere, Earl of Oxford, and that Peacham is cryptically making it public. On the title page is a picture of a proscenium arch with its curtain drawn back to reveal the hand and arm of a concealed person writing with a quill pen. This unseen author is completing a Latin inscription – MENTE. VIDE BORI (BY THE MIND SHALL I BE SEEN) – with the dot or period between the *E* and the *V* suggesting "E. V." for Edward de Vere.

APRIL 1616: DEATH OF WILLIAM SHAKSPERE OF STRATFORD UPON AVON

SUMMER/FALL 1616: THE WORKS OF BEN JONSON PUBLISHED IN FOLIO

1622: HENRY PEACHAM: In "The Compleat Gentleman," he calls the Elizabethan reign a "golden age" of poetry and lists "Edward Earl of Oxford" first of the deceased poets, including Spenser but not "Shakespeare" among them.

NOV 1623: PUBLICATION OF THE FIRST FOLIO: Thirty-six plays as by "William Shakespeare" with no mention of either the published narrative poems or the Sonnets. The expensive publication is dedicated to the Earls of Pembroke and Montgomery, relatives of Edward de Vere, Earl of Oxford.

NOV 24, 1624: DEATH OF SOUTHAMPTON: He is reported as having been poisoned by agents of Buckingham and the King's son, Charles.

MARCH 1625: DEATH OF KING JAMES I OF ENGLAND: The accession of his son as Charles I of England.

1637: DEATH OF BEN JONSON: His body is buried in Westminster Abbey.

1640: BOGUS COLLECTION OF THE SONNETS: "Poems: Written by Wil. Shake-speare. Gent," published by John Benson (a strange inversion of the name of Ben Jonson, who died in 1637, and whose own collection of *Poems* is published posthumously by Benson). The edition appears in many ways to be a joke on the First Folio of Shakespeare works in 1623, complete with a takeoff on the Folio engraving of the author as well as a mock version of Jonson's words, its lines ending in question marks. The edition includes all but eight verses of the Book of Sonnets from the 1609 edition, but in a different format and entirely out of order. Various verses of the Sonnets are merged together to form longer poems, with made-up titles for them; and the poems of other writers are included as well.

"There is a visible attempt, though not an entirely efficient one, to suggest that the addressee throughout is a woman. The 'he' pronoun is often, though not quite always, altered to 'she', and changes such as 'sweet love' for 'sweet boy' … reinforce the suggestion that these are conventional, heterosexual love sonnets" – Duncan-Jones, noting also that Sonnet 126 ("O Thou my lovely Boy…") is one of the verses omitted. "For well over a century," adds Duncan-Jones, "Benson succeeded in muddying the textual waters. It was his edition that was read and edited, almost exclusively, until the superb work of Malone in 1780."

1640-1660: THE ENGLISH CIVIL WAR brings with it a shutdown of all public playhouses.

1711: "SHAKE-SPEARES SONNETS" REAPPEARS IN PRINT. The new edition is based on a surviving copy of the 1609 edition, of which only thirteen copies will be recovered. The new publisher is Bernard Lintott, who offers a text based on all of the 154 sonnets of Q in their correct order by the numbers, but, nonetheless, describes both their number and their contents inaccurately: *One Hundred and Fifty Sonnets, all of them in Praise of his Mistress.* Of course, anyone reading the Sonnets would learn soon enough that the first one hundred and twenty-six verses (the Fair Youth series of Sonnets 1-126, more than 80 percent of the collection) are all addressed to a younger male described as a nobleman.

1766: THE SONNETS OF 1609 KNOWN AS "Q" ARE INCLUDED WITHOUT COMMENT IN GEORGE STEEVENS' TWENTY PLAYS OF SHAKESPEARE.

1780: THE SONNETS OF 1609 REAPPEAR CORRECTLY AT LAST: The original text is now recognized as the sole authoritative text by Edmund Malone, in his "Supplement" to the Johnson-Steevens edition of the plays, which appeared in 1778. Malone identified the first "one hundred and twenty [*sic*]" of the sonnets, i.e., Sonnets 1-126, as addressed to a man. In doing so, Malone paved the way for recognition of the Fair Youth and Dark Lady series, plus the Bath epilogue.

1793: EDITOR STEEVENS TRASHES THE SONNETS: In the preface to his edition of Shakespeare, George Steevens (apparently reacting to a recently perceived homosexual or bisexual attitude and "secret life" on the part of the poet) angrily writes: "We have not reprinted the Sonnets, &c. of Shakespeare because the strongest act of Parliament that could be framed would fail to compel readers into their service ... Had Shakespeare produced no other works than these, his name would have reached us with as little celebrity as time has conferred on that of Thomas Watson, an older and much more elegant sonneteer."

Ironically Edward de Vere was several years older than Watson, who was among the writers in the earl's circle during the 1580s and died in 1592. In any case, the views of Steevens would not be shared by the majority of critics, the vast majority of whom would praise the Sonnets as among the glories of English literature.

1817: SOUTHAMPTON IS IDENTIFIED AS THE FAIR YOUTH: "If we may be allowed, in our turn, to conjecture, we would fix upon LORD SOUTHAMPTON as the subject of Shakespeare's sonnets, from the first to the hundredth and twenty-sixth, inclusive." - Nathan Drake

1817: SONNET 26 IS LINKED TO THE DEDICATION OF *LUCRECE* TO THE EARL OF SOUTHAMPTON: This is one of Drake's strongest pieces of evidence leading him to identify the earl as noted above.

1817-1818: THE BOGUS BENSON EDITION OF THE SONNETS IS PUBLISHED IN NEW YORK: The publisher is Henry Durrell. Yet another generation will now read and study this bogus and incomplete version of the Sonnets, which fails to include the all-important numerical ordering of the verses or "numbers" with which Oxford had constructed his Monument to preserve the truth of Henry Wriothesley, Earl of Southampton.

1827: THE SONNETS ARE VIEWED AS REVEALING THE POET'S HEART: "Scorn not the Sonnet ... With this key, Shakespeare unlocked his heart." – William Wordsworth

1832: THE SONNETS ARE PRAISED FOR INTELLECTUAL CONTENT: "The Sonnets contain such a quality of thought as must astonish every reflecting reader." – Alexander Dyce

1848: SONNET 107 IS VIEWED AS MARKING THE SPRING OF 1603: An unidentified researcher,

J. R., writes in *The Athenaeum* that Sonnet 107 must be related to events in the spring of 1603, when Queen Elizabeth had died and James VI of Scotland had been proclaimed King James I of England. One of the new monarch's first acts was to send ahead orders for the release of Southampton from his "confined doom" in the Tower of London, from which he gained his release on April 10, 1603: "Not mine own fears nor the prophetic soul of the wide world dreaming on thing to come can yet the lease of my true love control, supposed as forfeit to a confined doom."

1859: SOUTHAMPTON MOTTO IS SEEN IN THE SONNETS: Another unidentified researcher, W. C. J., writes in *The Athenaeum* that Henry Wriothesley's motto *One for All, All for One* appears throughout the Sonnets in both language and theme: "The question, 'Who is the friend Shakspeare addressed in his Sonnets to?' has never yet been satisfactorily answered, - and 'the only begetter of these ensuring Sonnets, Mr. W. H.,' is still to be discovered. Dr. Drake's opinion, that W. H. was intended for Henry Wriothesley, Earl of Southampton, receives some support from the following circumstance:

"There is ... published some time in the first half of the seventeenth century (a portrait painting) by Tho. Jenner, representing the Earls of Oxford (i.e., Henry Vere, Eighteenth Earl of Oxford, legitimate heir of Edward de Vere, born in 1593) and Southampton (i.e., Henry Wriothesley, Third Earl of Southampton) on horseback – and over each of their heads their shield of arms and mottoes are placed, that of Lord Southampton being *Ung par Tout, Tout par Ung* (*One for All, All for One*).

"Shakespeare dedicated *Venus and Adonis* and *The Rape of Lucrece* to his noble friend and patron, the Lord of Southampton; and in the twenty-first stanza of the last-mentioned poem has translated his motto:

>That *one for all*, or *all for one* we gage

"In the Sonnets this motto he has adapted in different ways with considerable poetic and idiomatic license; but I should first remark that the *Dictionary of the French and English Tongues*, 1611, gives 'Par tout: Throughout, into every place or thing, everywhere' ...

"In the eighth Sonnet it is thus mentioned:

>Who *all in one, one* pleasing note do sing,
>Whose speechless song, being many seeming one

"In Sonnet 31 the motto is played upon:

>And thou, *all* they, hast *all the all* of me

"In Sonnet 105 the spirit of the motto is taken as constancy, or one throughout:

>Since *all alike* my songs and praises be
>To *one, of one*, still such, and ever so

"And in many of the others it will be found to be the pervading thought, which I cannot but think brings the noble bearer of the motto and Mr. W. H. into very close union – in fact, they are the same person. I have little doubt Lord Southampton took his motto in compliment to the Queen from the one of her own choice, *Semper Eadem* (Ever the Same) – he well knowing there is no flattery so sincere as that of imitation."

1866: SONNETS 1-17 ARE LINKED TO THE MARRIAGE PROPOSAL FOR SOUTHAMPTON AND LADY ELIZABETH VERE IN 1590-1591: "Burghley had contemplated the marriage of the earl (Southampton) with his granddaughter, for, on the fifteenth of July, 1590, Sir Thomas Stanhope writes to Lord Burghley and assures him that he had never sought to procure the young Earl of Southampton (as a husband) for his daughter, as he knew Burghley intended a marriage between him and the Lady Vere (Elizabeth Vere, the fifteen-year-old daughter of Edward de Vere and granddaughter of William Cecil, Lord Burghley)." – Gerald Massey

1866: SONNET 107 IS SPECIFICALLY LINKED TO SOUTHAMPTON'S RELEASE BY KING

Appendix

JAMES FROM THE TOWER OF LONDON ON APRIL 10, 1603: "Sonnet 107 will show us that, in spite of the dramatic method adopted by Shakespeare in writing of the Earl, he did find a call for secure congratulations when James had restored the Earl of his liberty (on April 10, 1603) … The sonnet contains evidence beyond question – proof positive and unimpeachable – that the man addressed by Shakespeare in his *personal* sonnets has been condemned in the first instance to death, and afterwards to imprisonment for life, and escaped his doom through the death of the Queen." - Gerald Massey

1890: THE SONNETS ARE SEEN AS A FACTUAL REPORT: "The Sonnets as a whole are concerned with actual fact" – Thomas Tyler

1894: THE SONNETS ARE VIEWED AS REVEALING A SUFFERING STRANGER: "The Sonnets, then, alter any conception of Shakespeare's individuality … Even though they tell us nothing of the facts of his life, the Sonnets imply very much concerning the inner truth of it … Nor could anyone have expressed such emotion and such passion as underlie the Sonnets without a knowledge of suffering which no sane poise could lighten … *Whoever wrote the Sonnets* must have known the depths of spiritual suffering; nor yet have known how to emerge from them." – Wendell Barrett

1898: THE SONNETS ARE SEEN AS CHRONOLOGICAL LETTERS OF CORRESPONDENCE: "The analogy of a correspondence, carried on over years between friends, offers perhaps the best clue to the varying continuity of the First Series … The numbers seem to have been chronologically arranged." - George Wyndham

1898: <u>SONNET 107</u> IS AGAIN LINKED TO ELIZABETH'S DEATH & SOUTHAMPTON'S RELEASE FROM THE TOWER: "Sonnet 107 … makes references that cannot be mistaken to three events that took place in 1603 – to Queen Elizabeth's death, to the accession of James I, and to the release of the Earl of Southampton, who had been in prison since he was convicted in 1601 of complicity in the rebellion of the Earl of Essex … Cynthia (i.e., the moon) was the Queen's recognized poetic appellation … Southampton was still a prisoner in the Tower, 'supposed as forfeit to a confined doom.' All men, wrote Manningham, the diarist, on the day following the Queen's death, wished him at liberty. The wish was fulfilled quickly. On April 10, 1603, his prison gates were opened by 'a warrant from the king' … It is improbable that Shakespeare remained silent. 'My love looks fresh,' he wrote, in the concluding lines of Sonnet 107." - Sir Sidney Lee

1908: THE SONNETS ARE VIEWED AS REVEALING SHAKESPEARE TO BE A CULTURED NOBLEMAN OF ELIZABETH'S COURT: "It has sometimes been said that if we could only know who wrote the Sonnets we should know the true Shakespeare … The tone (of the dedication *of Venus and Adonis* to Southampton) … is that of one well-bred man addressing another … Polished indeed, and scholarly, is this extraordinary poem, and, above all, it is impressed throughout with that which we now call *Culture* … A courtly, scholarly poet, in fact, saturated with Ovid … The real problem of the Sonnets is to find out who 'Shake-speare' was. That done, it might be possible to make the crooked straight and the rough places plane – but not till then. That he would be found among cultured Elizabethan courtiers of high position, I can entertain no doubt." - Sir George Greenwood

1908: <u>SONNETS 153-154</u> SEEN AS BASED ON A VISIT BY "SHAKESPEARE" AND QUEEN ELIZABETH TO THE CITY OF BATH IN THE WEST: The conclusion is made by George Greenwood, who predicts "Shakespeare" will be found to have been a cultured member of the Court.

1920: EDWARD DE VERE, SEVENTEENTH EARL OF OXFORD AND LORD GREAT CHAMBERLAIN OF ENGLAND, IS IDENTIFIED AS THE AUTHOR OF THE "SHAKESPEARE" PLAYS, POEMS AND SONNETS: "Shakespeare's work of poetic self-expression is, of course, the Sonnets. The idea that these poems are fantastic dramatic inventions with mystic meanings we feel to be a violation of all normal probabilities and precedents. Accepting them, therefore, as autobiographical … We are not told who the particular young man (known as the Fair Youth) was; but the general assumption is that it was Henry Wriothesley, Earl of Southampton. This is not only a reasonable supposition, but it would be unreasonable to suppose that it was anyone else ... Now, as to the man who wrote the sonnets ... Throughout the whole series he assumes the attitude of a matured man addressing a youth... We find that the first sonnets of the first set are assigned generally to about the year 1590, when Oxford was just forty years of age ... Behind him there lay a life marked by vicissitudes in every way calculated to have given him a sense of age even beyond his forty years. He was a nobleman of the same high rank as Southampton and just a generation older ... The peculiar circumstances of the youth to whom the Sonnets were addressed were strikingly analogous to his own. Both had been left orphans and royal wards at an early age, both had been brought up under the same guardian, both had the same kind of literary tastes and interests, and later the young man followed exactly the same course as the elder had done as a patron of literature and the drama.

"*Then just at the time when these sonnets were being written urging Southampton to marry, he was actually being urged into a marriage with a daughter of the Earl of Oxford* and this proposed marriage he was resisting ... This furnishes the vital connection between the Earl of Southampton and the Earl of Oxford ... To have urged marriage as a general and indefinite proposition upon a youth of seventeen, with the single aim of securing posterity for the youth, would have had something fatuous about it. In connection with a definite project of marriage, from one who was personally interested in it, the appeal comes to have, at last, an explicable relationship to fact.

"The Sonnets stand there for every one to read, and no arguments could have the same value as an intimate knowledge of the poems themselves viewed in the light of the actual facts of the life and reputation of Edward de Vere. *Upon all who wish to arrive at the truth of the matter we urge the close and frequent reading of the Sonnets*." - John Thomas Looney

1932: SOUTHAMPTON IS SEEN AS THE SON OF OXFORD AND ELIZABETH: Percy Allen suggests Henry Wriothesley, Third Earl of Southampton, was actually the son of Queen Elizabeth and the Earl of Oxford, using the Sonnets as his primary evidence.

1952: HENRY WRIOTHESLEY IS AGAIN VIEWED AS A ROYAL SON: Dorothy and Charlton Ogburn expand upon the theory of Southampton as the son of Oxford and Queen Elizabeth, using the Sonnets as their primary evidence, and suggesting a birth date of June 1574 for the "changeling boy" who was to be raised in the Southampton household.

1958-1962: THE SONNETS ARE SEEN AS THE HEART OF SHAKESPEARE'S ROYAL POETRY:
"The Sonnets regularly express love through metaphors from royalty and its derivatives, using such phrases as *my sovereign, thy glory, lord of my love, embassy of love, commanded by the motion of thine eyes* ... At their greatest moments the Sonnets are really less love-poetry than an almost religious adoration ... Royal images recur ... The poet addresses the youth as *lord of my love*, to whom he sends a *written ambassage*; he is *my sovereign* and the poet his *servant* or *slave* ... The loved one is royal...

"He is *crowned* with various gifts of nature and fortune, especially *all those beauties whereof now he's King*. Like a sovereign, he radiates *worth*, his eyes lending *a double majesty* ... Our final impression is of love itself as king, of some super-personality, the Sun ... The associations are just, since the king, properly understood, holds within society precisely this super-personal and supernal function ... Kingship is naturally golden, and golden impressions recur with similar variations in use ... The Sun is nature's king, and also pre-eminently golden. Throughout Shakespeare king and sun are compared ... With the Fair Youth, the association of *that Sun, thine eye* comes easily enough...

"We have various clusters of king, gold, and sun. Kings and gold come together in *the gilded monuments of Princes*; and sun and gold, when the Sun's *gold complexion* is dimmed in the sonnet, *Shall I compare thee to a Summer's day*, or the young man *graces* the day and *gilds* the evening in place of stars. We may have all three. So *great Princess' favorites* are compared to the mari*gold* opening to the Sun's *eye* ... These impressions are not just decoration ... That the poet of the Sonnets was deeply concerned with such themes is clear from the many comparisons of his love to kings and state-affairs. His very love is felt as royal and stately. *The Sonnets are the heart of Shakespeare's royal poetry.*" – G. Wilson Knight

1965: THE SONNETS ARE SEEN AS ADDRESSED TO A "LITERAL" PRINCE IN LINE TO BE KING OF ENGLAND: Nothing the image of the Fair Youth as a "Sun" and a "God" and an "Ocean," he states: "It is well known that, following a general Renaissance practice drawn from antiquity, *kings* commonly figured as earthly 'suns' in the works of Shakespeare and his contemporaries ... 'Gods on earth' was proverbially used of *kings* as far back as Menander, and is frequent in Shakespeare ... 'Ocean' or 'sea' as a figure for *king* is often found in Shakespeare and his fellow-writers. Here, then, we have Shakespeare typifying his Friend variously as a *sun*, a *god*, an *ocean* or a *sea*: three familiar metaphors which he and his contemporaries use to represent a sovereign prince or king ... Whatever may be meant by it here in the Sonnets, the Shakespearean and Elizabethan element common to the three is certainly *king*, and the metaphors exhibit a consistency of reference."

He finds various usages in the Sonnets of *succession, heir* and *issue*, noting that these are terms that the same author "elsewhere applies to the paramount problems of royalty." He notes that in Sonnet 9 "his Friend dying a bachelor without issue will leave *the world* his *widow*, contrasted by the poet with every *private widow* – that is, the widow of 'a private man' as distinguished from a ruler, a king." Hotson reads Sonnet 14 in which "again Shakespeare presents his friend as a prince" whose fortune he is unable to foretell. He also notes the poet's direct usage of *sovereign* and *king* to describe the Fair Youth.

This "sustained and unmistakable" royal language in the Sonnets, writes Hotson, makes it obvious that "what he sets before us" is an array of powers "peculiar to a king: power to *grant charters of privilege* and *letters patent*, power to *pardon* crimes – in short, the exclusively *royal prerogative*." And in other verses we "need no reminder that it was to the king, and to no mortal but the king, that his dutiful subjects and vassals offered *oblations*; similarly, that it was only to the monarch or ruling magistrate that *embassies* were directed."

Hotson notes the poet's use of *largess* and *bounty*, writing, "Of the first it is significant to note that in his other works Shakespeare applies *largess* only to the gifts or donatives of *kings*. As for *bounty*, the poet's attribution of this grace to kings, while not exclusive, is characteristic ... In the same way we recognize *grace, state*, and *glory* typically in Shakespeare's kings." And finally he points to the explicit usages in the Sonnets of *king* and *kingdoms*.

"Clearly these consenting terms ... cannot be dismissed as scattered surface-ornament. They are intrinsic. What is more, they intensify each other. By direct address, by varied metaphor, and by multifarious allusion, the description of the Friend communicated is always one: *monarch, sovereign prince, king* ... The harping on the same string is so insistent as to make one ask why it has not arrested attention. No doubt everyone has regarded this *king* sense as formal hyperbole and nothing more. Any literal meaning looks quite incredible – a rank impossibility." - Leslie Hotson

1977: THE SONNETS ARE VIEWED AS A MONUMENT: Alastair Fowler concludes that the numbered verses have a pyramidal structure forming a "monument" whose sonnets are the "great bases for eternity" resting upon Sonnet 126, the "envoy" or chronological end of the diary. The numerical arrangement of all the one hundred and fifty-four sonnets is the correct one, he asserts.

1992: SOUTHAMPTON IS AGAIN VIEWED AS THE ROYAL SON OF OXFORD AND THE QUEEN, AS THE ONLY PLAUSIBLE EXPLANATION OF THE SONNETS: Charlton Ogburn, Jr., declares that his parents' theory of Henry Wriothesley, Third Earl of Southampton as the son of Oxford and the Queen is the only logical way to account for the tone and contents of the Sonnets, as well as for the obliteration of Oxford's identity as author of the "Shakespeare" works that had been dedicated to Southampton.

1995: THE SONNETS ARE AGAIN VIEWED AS FROM FATHER TO HIS ROYAL SON: "We are left with a compelling question raised by the Sonnets. It is a question that is inescapable and one that traditional scholarship is resolved upon escaping at all costs ... How is it that the poet of the Sonnets can – as he unmistakably does – address the Fair Youth as an adoring and deeply concerned father would address his son and as a subject would his liege-lord?" – Charlton Ogburn, Jr.

1997: SONNET 25 IS VIEWED AS RELATED TO ESSEX-SOUTHAMPTON MILITARY CAMPAIGN TO IRELAND IN 1599: Lines of Sonnet 25 ("The painful warrior famoused for worth,/ After a thousand victories once foiled/ Is from the book of honour razed quite,/ And all the rest forgot for which he toiled") offer an "image of the popular war hero" that "would apply well either to the Earl of Essex, to whose expected success in Ireland Shakespeare alluded in *Henry V*, or to his patron the Earl of Southampton…" – Katherine Duncan-Jones

1997: THE SONNETS ARE SEEN AS HEAVILY REVISED 1603-1604: Editor Duncan-Jones indicates evidence pointing to the author having labored upon the final version of the Sonnets during the fifteen months between the death of Queen Elizabeth on March 24, 1603 and the recorded death of Edward de Vere, Earl of Oxford on June 24, 1604: "Recent stylometric studies point to 1603-04 as a plausible time for the composition or completion of most of the 'fair youth' sonnets after 1-17 … Like internal evidence, external reference points to 1603-04 as initiating an intense period of writing (and perhaps revising) …"

2009: FOUR-HUNDREDTH ANNIVERSARY OF "SHAKESPEARE'S SONNETS"

Index – Words Of The Sonnets

The following index lists each word used in the sonnets, and the sonnets in which they appear:

Abhor: 150, 150
Abide: 27, 45,
Able: 85
About: 113
Above: 91, 110, 122
ABSENCE/ABSENT (In the Tower): 39, 41, 45, 57, 58, 89, 97, 98, 109
Abundance/Abundant: (royal): 1, 23, 37, 97, 135
Abuse/ Abuses/Abused: 4, 42, 82, 121, 134
Abysm: 112
Accents: 69
Acceptable/Acceptance: 4, 135
Accessory: 35
Accident: 124
Account: 30, 58, 62, 136
Accumulate: 117
ACCUSE/ACCUSING: 58, 117, 152
Acknowledge: 36
Acquaint/Acquainted/Acquaintance: 20, 77, 89, 89
Act: 152
ACTION: 65, 129, 129
Active: 37
ACTOR: 23,
ADD/Added/Addeth/Adding/Addition: 20, 20, 69, 78, 85, 103, 135, 135, 135
Adder's: 112
Adieu: 57
Adjunct: 91
Admire/Admired/Admiring: 59, 84
Admit/Admitted: 116, 136
ADONIS: 53,
Adore: 7,
A-doting (see Doting): 20
Adulterate: 121
Advance: 78
Advantage: 64, 67,
ADVERSE (Adverse Party at Trial): 35
Advised: 49,
ADVOCATE (Legal Counsel): 35
Affable: 86
Affair/Affairs: 57, 151
Afar: 143
Affections: 110
Afford: 79
Afresh: 30
After: 25, 71, 72, 73, 143, 152
After-Loss: 90
Afterwards: 115

REFERENCE EDITION 809

Again: 13, 45, 56, 76, 79, 87, 109
Against (see also 'Gainst): 13, 13, 38, 49, 49, 49, 49, 63, 63, 65, 88, 89, 149, 152, 153
Age/Ages: 3, 7, 11, 17, 17, 32, 62, 63, 101, 104, 108, 127, 138
Aggravate: 146
Ah: 9, 34, 44, 67, 90, 139
Aid: 79, 86
AIR (heir): 21, 21, 45, 70
Alack: 33, 65, 103
Alas: 110, 115
Alchemy: 33, 114
Alien: 78
Alike: 105
Alive: 17, 112
ALL (SOUTHAMPTON): 2, 2, 2, 8, 11, 12, 12, 15, 17, 18, 19, 20, 21, 22, 25, 26, 29, 30, 31, 31, 31, 31, 31, 31, 31, 33, 34, 35, 37, 37, 37, 37, 39, 40, 40, 40, 40, 40, 42, 43, 43, 46, 53, 53, 55, 55, 57, 60, 61, 62, 62, 62, 62, 62, 66, 66, 68, 69, 73, 74, 75, 75, 76, 76, 78, 79, 80, 81, 81, 85, 86, 87, 88, 88, 91, 91, 91, 95, 96, 98, 98, 99, 100, 103, 105, 105, 106, 106, 109, 109, 109, 109, 110, 110, 112, 112, 112, 117, 117, 117, 121, 122, 124, 125, 129, 132, 133, 134, 135, 135, 137, 143, 148, 149, 149, 150, 152, 152   (WORD COUNT: 118)
Allayed: 56
Allege: 49
Allow, 19
Almost: 76, 111
Aloft: 78
ALONE: (SOUTHAMPTON): 4, 29, 39, 42, 45, 66, 70, 75, 79, 79, 84, 91, 105, 124, 131, 133, 141
(WORD COUNT: 17)
Already: 76
ALTER/Alters/Altered/Alteration/Alt'ring: 36, 93, 115, 116, 116, 116, 145
Although: 36, 40, 44, 56, 69, 81, 116, 131, 138
Always: 76
Am: 37, 41, 47, 58, 72, 80, 121, 121, 133, 147
Amaze/Amazeth: 20,
AMBASSAGE: 26
Ambush: 70
Amends: 101
AMISS: 35, 59, 151
Among: 136
Anchored: 137
Anew: 82, 119, 145
Angel: 144, 144, 144, 144, 144
Anger/Angry: 50, 147
Annexed: 99
Annoy: 8,
Anon: 33, 75
An Other (another)/An Other's: 6, 7, 10, 47, 68, 79, 99, 144
Another's: 131
Answer/Answered/Answers: 2, 50, 101, 126
Anticipate: 118
Antique, 17, 19, 59, 68, 106
Antiquity: 62, 108
Any: 21, 37, 98, 100, 100, 141
Any Thing: 57
Apparel: 26,
Appeal: 117
Appear/Appears/Appearance/Appearing: 7, 31, 46, 53, 103

Index – Words Of The Sonnets

Appetite/Appetites: 56, 110, 118, 147
Apple: 93
Applying: 119
Approve: 42, 70, 147
April: 3, 21, 98, 104
ARGUMENT: 38, 76, 79, 103, 105
Arise/Arising: 29, 55,
Array: 146
ARREST: 74
ART/ART'S/ARTS (noun): 14, 24, 24, 29, 53, 66, 68, 78, 78, 82, 125, 127, 139
Ashes: 73
Askance: 110
Asked: 1
Aspect: 26
Assailed: 41, 70
Assemble: 114
Assistance: 78
Assure/Assured/Assurance: 45, 92, 118
Astonished: 86
ASTRONOMY: 14
Ate: 99
ATTAINT/ATTAINTED: 82, 88
Attend/Attending: 7, 44, 66,
Audit: 3, 49, 126
Aught: (see Ought: 125)
Augurs: 107
AUTHORITY: 66
AUTHORIZING: 35
Autumn: 97, 104
Awake, Awakes: 47, 61,
AWARDS: 141
AWAY: 11, 47, 63, 64, 74, 75, 80, 91, 92, 96, 97, 98, 143, 145, 145
Aye: 41

BABE (SOUTHAMPTON): 22, 115, 143, 143
Back: 3, 45, 45, 65, 87, 143, 143
Bad/Badness: 67, 112, 114, 121, 121, 121, 144
Badges: 44
Bail: 74, 133
Bait: 129
Balmy: 107
BANKROUT (Bankrupt): 67
Banquet: 47
Bare/Bareness: 5, 25, 69, 73, 97, 103
Bark: 80, 116
BARREN/BARRENLY: 11, 12, 13, 16, 76, 83
Bars: 25, 48
BASE/Basest: 33, 34, 74, 94, 94, 96, 100, 141
Bases: 125
BASTARD (SOUTHAMPTON): 68, 124, 127
Bath: 153, 153, 153, 154
Batt'ring: 65
Bay: 137
Beams: 114

BEAR/Bearer/Bears/Bearing/Bear'st (See Bore): 1, 8, 10, 13, 16, 22, 34, 40, 50, 50, 51, 59, 77, 80, 88, 97, 116, 140, 152 (Word Count: 19)
Beard: 12
Beast: 50, 51
Beated: 62
Beaten: 34
BEAUTY (ELIZABETH and/or HER BLOOD) /Beauty's/Beauteous/Beauties: 1, 2, 2, 2, 2, 4, 4, 4, 5, 5, 5, 6, 7, 9, 10, 10, 11, 12, 12, 13, 14, 14, 17, 19, 21, 22, 24, 27, 34, 37, 41, 41, 41, 41, 41, 53, 54, 54, 54, 60, 62, 63, 63, 63, 65, 65, 67, 68, 68, 68, 68, 69, 70, 77, 79, 83, 84, 93, 95, 95, 101, 101, 101, 101, 104, 104, 104, 104, 106, 106, 106, 106, 115, 127, 127, 127, 127, 127, 127, 131, 132, 137 (WORD COUNT: 82)
Because: 42, 101, 102, 134
Beck: 58
Become/Becomes/Becoming: 120, 127, 132, 150
Bed/Beds/Bed-Vow (see Vow; Death-bed): 73, 142, 152
Been: 139
Before: 15, 30, 40, 40, 59, 60, 68, 68, 85, 115, 123, 129, 143
Befriends: 120
Beggar/Beggared: 66, 67
Begin/Begins: 27, 114
Beguile/Beguiled: 3, 59
Behavior: 79
Behind: 9, 50, 129, 143
Behold: 12, 22, 66, 73, 106, 131, 137
Being: 2, 8, 50, 51, 52, 56, 57, 58, 58, 70, 80, 81, 83, 83, 83, 88, 96, 114, 118, 121, 144
Belied: 130, 140
Believe/Believed: 17, 21, 109, 138, 140
Bell: 71
Belong/Belongs: 58, 88, 92
BELOVED/Belov'd: 25, 89, 105, 150
BEMOANED: 30
BENDS/Bending/Bent: 88, 90, 116, 116, 143
Benefit: 28, 119
BEQUEST: 4
Bereft: 5
Beseechers: 135
Beshrew: 133
Beside: 103
Besiege: 2
Besmeared: 55
BEST (ROYAL): 24, 37, 37, 43, 48, 65, 75, 76, 88, 91, 101, 101, 106, 110, 110, 114, 115, 137, 138, 138, 149, 150
Betraying: 151
BETTER/Bettered/Bett'ring (ROYAL): 32, 32, 32, 39, 59, 73, 75, 80, 82, 82, 87, 91, 91, 92, 111, 119, 119, 132, 144, 144
Betwixt: 47
Bevel: 121
Bewailed: 36
Beweep: 29
Beyond: 122
Bid/Bids: 47, 57
Bide: 58
Bier: 12
Big: 97
Bind: 134
BIRD/BIRDS: 73, 97, 98, 113
BIRTH: 32, 37, 76, 91, 91

812

Index – Words Of The Sonnets

Bitter/Bitterness: 57, 111, 118
BLACK: 27, 63, 65, 73, 127, 127, 127, 130, 131, 131, 132, 132, 147 (WORD COUNT: 13)
BLAME/Blamed: 40, 40, 58, 70, 103, 129
Blanks: 77
Blazon: 106
Blenches: 110
BLESS/Blessed/Blesses/Blessing/Blessings/Blest (see Unbless): 16, 43, 52, 52, 53, 56, 82, 84, 92, 95, 119, 128, 128
Blind/Blindness: 27, 113, 136, 137, 148, 149, 152
Bliss: 129
BLOOD/BLOODY (ROYAL): 2, 11, 16, 19, 50, 63, 67, 82, 109, 121, 129
Blooms: 54
BLOT/BLOTS: 28, 36, 92, 95
Blow: 124
Blunt/Blunter/Blunting: 19, 52, 56, 103, 115
Blush/Blushing: 67, 99, 128
Boast: 25, 26, 86, 91, 123
Boat: 80
Body/Body's: 24, 27, 72, 74, 91, 146, 151, 151
Bold/Boldness: 122, 128, 131
Bond/Bonds: 87, 117, 134, 142
Bones: 32
BOOK/BOOKS: 23, 25, 77, 77, 117
Boot: 135
Bootless: 29
Bore (see Bear): 125, 127
BORN/Borne: 12, 21, 36, 68, 78, 104, 123, 127, 151
Borrowed: 127, 153
Bosom/Bosom's: 9, 24, 31, 120, 133
Both: 35, 42, 42, 42, 45, 83, 96, 117, 123, 134, 138, 144
Bough/Boughs: 73, 102
Bound: 58, 86
Boundless: 65
Bounty/Bounteous: 4, 11, 11, 53
BOY (SOUTHAMPTON): 108, 126, 153
Bow: 120
Bower: 127
Brag: 18
Brain/Brains: 59, 77, 86, 108, 122, 122
Brand: 111, 153, 153, 154, 154
Brass: 64, 65, 107, 120
BRAVE/BRAVERY (ROYAL): 12, 12, 15, 34
BREACH: 152
BREAK: 29, 34, 41, 152
Breast/Breasts: 22, 23, 24, 48, 109, 110, 130, 153
Breath/Breathe/Breathed/Breathes/Breathers: 18, 38, 54, 65, 81, 81, 81, 85, 99, 99, 145
Breed/Breeds, Bred (see Unbred): 6, 12, 108, 111, 112
Brief: 14, 116, 123
BRIGHT/Brightness (Royal): 1, 20, 21, 28, 43, 43, 43, 43, 55, 147, 150
Bring/Brings (see Brought): 29, 35, 38, 39, 83, 117
Bristly: 12
Broad: 80
Broils: 55
Broke/Broken: 61, 143, 152
Brought (see Bring): 32, 44

BROW: 2, 33, 60, 63, 68, 112
BUD (SOUTHAMPTON)/Budding/Buds: 1, 18, 35, 54, 70, 95
BUILDING/Built/Builded: 80, 119, 123, 124
BURIED/BURIEST: 1, 25, 31, 31, 64, 72
Burn/Burned/Burning: 7, 19, 55, 104, 115
Burthen (Burden): 23, 59, 97, 102
Busy: 143
Buy: 146

Call/Called/Calls: 3, 4, 11, 38, 40, 49, 56, 79, 105, 109, 117, 124, 149, 151
Can/Cannot/Canst: 4, 4, 14, 16, 18, 30, 30, 34, 38, 38, 39, 40, 44, 49, 50, 51, 51, 52, 64, 69, 70, 72, 77, 81, 84, 84, 86, 88, 89, 92, 93, 93, 95, 103, 103, 104, 107, 122, 133, 148, 149
Came (see Come): 154, 154
Cancelled: 30
Candles: 21
Canker: 35, 54, 70, 95, 99
CANOPY (ROYAL): 12, 125
Captain: 52, 66
CAPTIVE: 66
Car: 7
CARCANET: 52
CARE/Careful: 48, 48, 56, 112, 112, 143, 143, 147
Carry: 74
Carve/Carved: 11, 19
Case: 108
Cast: 80
Catch: 113, 143, 143, 143
Cause: 49, 87, 150
Cease: 11
Celestial: 33
Censures: 148
Center: 146
Ceremony: 23
Certain (see Incertainty): 115
Chance: 18
Change/Changes/Changing: 10, 10, 15, 18, 20, 60, 76, 93, 105, 112, 115, 123, 128
Character/Charactered: 59, 85, 108, 122
Charge/Charged: 70, 146
CHARTER: 58, 87
Chary: 22
Chase: 143, 143
CHASTE: 154
Cheap: 110
Cheater: 151
Check/Checked: 5, 15, 58, 136
Cheek/Cheeks: 53, 67, 68, 79, 82, 99, 116, 130, 132
Cheer/Cheered: 15, 97
Cherish: 11
Cherubins: 114
CHEST: 48, 52, 65
Chide/Chiding: 8, 41, 57, 99, 111, 145
CHIEF: 42
CHILD/Children/Children's: 2, 8, 9, 17, 21, 37, 59, 77, 124, 143
Choirs: 73

Choose/Chose: 64, 95
Chopped: 62
CHRONICLE: 106
Churl/Churls: 1, 32, 69
'Cide: 46
Civil (civil war): 35
Clay: 71
Clean: 75
Clear/Clearer/Clears: 43, 84, 115, 148
Clerk: 85
Climbed: 7
Cloak: 34
CLOCK: 12, 57
Closet: 46
Closure: 48
CLOUD/CLOUDS (ELIZABETH'S VIEW): 28, 33, 33, 34, 34, 35
Cloying: 118
Cold (see Cool): 2, 11, 13, 73, 94, 104, 153
Colour/Coloured: 99, 101, 101, 144
Come/Comes/Coming: 13, 17, 17, 45, 48, 49, 56, 64, 85, 87, 90, 116, 145
Comfort: 37, 48, 134, 144
Commanded: 149
Commence: 35
Commend: 69
Comment/Comments: 15, 85, 89, 95
Commit/Committed/Commits: 9, 41, 77, 119
COMMON: 69, 81, 102, 137
COMPARE/Compared: 18, 21, 32, 35, 90, 130, 142
Compeers: 86
Compile/Compiled: 78, 85
COMPLAIN: 28
Complexion: 18, 99, 132
COMPOSED/Composition: 45, 59
Compound/Compounds/Compounded: 71, 76, 118, 125
Concealed: 88
Conceit: 15, 26, 108
Concord: 8, 128
CONDEMNED: 99
CONFESS/Confessed: 36, 134
CONFINE/CONFINED: 84, 107, 110
CONFOUND/Confounded/Confounds/Confounding: 5, 8, 60, 63, 64, 69, 128
Conquered/Conquest: 6, 46, 74, 90
CONSCIENCE: 151, 151, 151
CONSECRATE: 74
Consent: 28
Consider: 15
Conspire: 10
CONSTANT/CONSTANCY (see Inconstant): 14, 53, 105, 105, 117, 152
Consum'st/Consumed: 9, 73
Contain/Contains: 74, 77
Content/Contented (see Discontent): 1, 29, 32, 74, 119, 151
Continual: 123
Contracted: 1, 56
CONTROL/Controlling: 20, 58, 66, 107, 125

Contrary: 62
Convert/Converted/Convertest: 7, 11, 14, 49
Cool/Cools: 154, 154
Copy: 11, 84
Coral: 130
Correct/Correction: 111, 111
Correspondence: 148
Corrupt/Corrupting: 35, 137, 144
Cost/Costly: 64, 146
Could: 6, 17, 96, 98, 109, 115, 122
COUNT/Counting: 2, 12, 75, 108, 141
Countenance: 86
Counterfeit: 16, 53
Counterpart: 84
Course/Courses: 18, 19, 59, 115
Cover: 22, 95
Covetous: 134
Coward: 74
Crawls: 60
CREATURE/Created/Creating/Creation/Creatures: 1, 20, 81, 93, 113, 114, 127, 143
Credit: 138
Creep: 115
Crests: 107
Cries/Crying: 29, 143, 143
CRIME: 19, 58, 120, 124
Critic: 112
CROOKED: 60, 100
CROSS (see Loss)/Crossed: 42, 133
CROW: 70, 113
CROWN/CROWNED/CROWNING: 37, 69, 107, 114, 115
Cruel: 1, 60, 63, 129, 131, 133, 140, 149
Crushed: 63
Crystal: 46
Cunning: 24, 139
Cup: 114
CUPID (SOUTHAMPTON): 153, 153
Cure/Cured/Cures: 34, 111, 118, 147, 153, 153, 154
Curious: 38
Curse: 29, 84
Cut: 63

DAILY: 28, 56, 76
DAMASKED: 130
Dancing: 128
Dare: 26, 57, 57, 131
DARK, Darkly, Darkness/Dark'ning: 27, 43, 43, 97, 100, 147
DARLING: 18
Dart: 139
DATE/DATES/DATELESS: 14, 18, 22, 30, 38, 122, 123, 153
DAY/ DAYS/ DAY'S (ROYAL): 7, 12, 13, 15, 22, 27, 28, 28, 28, 28, 28, 29, 32, 38, 43, 43, 43, 43, 43, 59, 62, 67, 68, 70, 73, 75, 75, 95, 97, 102, 106, 108, 113, 117, 117, 145, 150 (WORD COUNT: 37)
DEAD (see Die): 31, 31, 43, 67, 68, 68, 71, 74, 81, 86, 104, 106, 108, 112, 128, 146
Deaf: 29
DEAR/Dearer/Dearest/Dearly (ROYAL SON): 13, 27, 30, 30, 31, 32, 37, 39, 42, 46, 48, 48, 72, 87, 95, 102, 108, 110,

111, 115, 117, 117, 122, 124, 131, 139, 142, 151
Dearth/Dearths: 14, 146
DEATH/Death's/Deaths/Death-bed (See Die): 6, 6, 13, 18, 22, 30, 32, 45, 54, 55, 64, 66, 72, 73, 73, 81, 81, 99, 107, 140, 146, 146, 147 (Word Count: 24)
Debarred: 28
Debate/Debateth: 15, 89
Debt/Debtor: 83, 134
DECAY/Decayed: 11, 13, 15, 23, 64, 71, 79, 80, 100
DECEASE/ DECEASED: 13, 32, 72, 97
Deceive/Deceived/Deceivest: 4, 39, 40, 93, 104
December's: 97
Declines: 18
Decrease: 15
DECREE/Decrees: 93, 115
Decrepit: 37
DEDICATED: 82
DEEDS: 34, 37, 61, 69, 90, 94, 111, 121, 131, 150
Deem/Deemed: 54, 120
Deep/Deepest: 2, 2, 54, 80, 98, 120, 133, 152, 152
Deface/Defaced: 6, 64
Defeat/Defeated: 20, 61
Defect/Defects: 49, 70, 149
DEFENCE: 12, 89, 139
DEFENDANT: 46
Define: 62
DEFORMED'ST: 113
DEFY: 123
Delayed: 126
Delight/Delights: 8, 24, 36, 37, 47, 75, 91, 98, 102, 130
DELIVERED: 77
Delves: 60
Denote: 148
Deny/Denied: 10, 46, 142
Depart/Departest: 6, 10, 109
Depend/Depends: 92, 92, 101
Derive: 14
Describe: 53
Desert/Deserts: 17, 66, 72, 117
Deserved/Deserves/Deserv'st/Deserving: 2, 39, 79, 87
DESIRE/Desired/Desiring: 1, 10, 29, 45, 51, 51, 57, 89, 123, 141, 147, 154
DESPAIR: 99, 140, 144
Desperate: 147
DESPISE/Despised/Despising: 29, 37, 100, 129, 141, 149
Despite: 3, 19, 44, 60, 123, 141
Destroys: 9
Detain: 126
DETERMINATE: 87
DETERMINATION: 13
DEVIL: 144
Devise/Devised: 72, 82, 83
Devour/Devouring: 19, 19
DIAL: 77, 104
DIAN'S (ELIZABETH'S): 153
DIE/Died/Dies/Diest (see Dying): 1, 3, 3, 7, 9, 11, 12, 32, 54, 66, 68, 81, 92, 94, 124

Dig: 2
DIFFERENCE: 105; Different: 98
Dignified/Dignifies/Dignity: 84, 94, 101
Dimmed: 18
Directed: 43
Directly: 144
DISABLED: 66
DISARMED: 154
Discloses: 54
Discontent (see Content): 124, 143
Discourse: 147
DISDAIN/Disdains/Disdaineth: 3, 33, 132, 140
Disease/Diseased: 118, 147, 154
DISGRACE/Disgraced: 29, 33, 34, 66, 89, 89, 103, 126, 127
Dispatch: 143
Disperse: 78
Disposed: 88
Dispraise (see Praise): 95
Dissuade: 141
DISTANCE: 44
Distempered: 153
Distillation/Distilled/Distills: 5, 5, 6, 54, 119
Distraction: 119
Divert: 115
Divide/Divided (see Undivided): 39, 46
DIVINE/DIVINING: 106, 108, 146
Doctor-like: 66
Doing: 88, 103
Done: 24, 35, 59, 110
DOOM: 14, 55, 107, 116, 145
Dote/Doting (see A-Doting): 20, 131, 141, 148
Double: 78, 88, 111
Doubt/Doubting: 75, 115, 144
DOVE: 113
Down: 64, 117
Drained: 63
Draw/Drawn: 16, 19, 24, 24, 28, 98
Dreading: 97
DREAM/Dreams/Dreaming: 43, 43, 87, 107, 129
Dregs: 74
DRESS/Dressed/Dressing/Dressings: 68, 98, 123
Drink/Drinks/Drunk: 111, 114, 114, 119
Drooping: 27
Drop/Drops: 90, 107
Dross: 146
Drowns: 124
Drudge: 151
Drugs: 118
Dry: 34
DUE: 1, 31, 39, 46, 69, 74
Dull/Dulling/Dully: 44, 50, 51, 51, 97, 102, 103, 107
DUMB: 23, 38, 78, 83, 85, 101
Dun: 130
Durst: 68

Index – Words Of The Sonnets

Dust: 108
DUTY/DUTEOUS: 7, 26, 26, 26
Dwell/Dwells/Dwellers: 5, 55, 71, 84, 89, 99, 125
Dyed: 99, 101
Dyer's: 111
DYING (see Die): 146

Each: 7, 8, 8, 14, 28, 42, 47, 48, 81, 108, 122, 127, 144
Eager: 118
Ear/Ears: 8, 100, 128, 140, 141
Eared (see Un-eared):
Early: 33
EARTH/EARTHLY: 17, 19, 21, 29, 65, 74, 74, 81, 81, 146, 146
Ease/Eased: 28, 50, 136
EAST: 132
Easy: 109
Eat/Eating (see All-eating): 1, 2
ECLIPSE/ECLIPSES: 35, 60, 107
Edge: 56, 95, 116
Effect: 36, 85
Effectually: 113
Eisel: 111
Either/Either's: 44, 47
ELDER (father): 22
Elements: 44, 45
Eloquence: 23
Else: 1, 14, 112
Elsewhere: 61, 139
EMBASSY: 45
ENCLOSE: 95
END/ENDING: 9, 13, 30, 50, 55, 57, 60, 110, 145, 146
Endeared: 31
ENDLESS: 107
Endowed: 11
ENDURE (Indure)/ENDURED (Indured): 107, 153
ENEMIES: 28, 139
ENFEEBLED: 86
ENFORCED: 82
Engraft: 15
Engrossed (Ingrossed): 133
Enlighten: 152
ENMITY: 55
Enjoy/Enjoyed/Enjoys/Enjoyer: 9, 29, 75, 129
Enough: 34, 111, 133, 135
Enrich: 77
ENSCONCE: 49
Entertain: 39
ENTITLED: 37
ENTOMBED: 81
Envy: 70, 128
EPITAPH: 81
Equal: 84
Equipage: 32
Ere: 6, 6, 68, 73, 104, 118, 133 (who ere)

Err: 131
ERROR/ERRORS: 96, 116, 117, 119, 141
Erst: 12
Essays: 110
Esteem/Esteemed/Esteeming: 96, 102, 121, 127
Estimate: 87
ETERNAL/ETERNITY: 13, 18, 18, 38, 64, 77, 108, 122, 125
Eve's: 93
Even: 15, 33, 48, 55, 56, 59, 69, 71, 81, 108, 110, 111, 116, 118, 122
Even (evening): 28
EVER (OXFORD): 19, 36, 49, 61, 70, 76, 90, 93, 105, 116, 116, 123, 145, 147 (WORD COUNT: 14)
EVER FIXED: 116
EVER-MORE/EVERMORE: 36, 70, 147
EVERY (OXFORD): 5, 9, 15, 18, 21, 32, 48, 52, 53, 53, 53, 76, 78, 82, 84, 85, 91, 95, 97, 98, 100, 102, 102, 114, 116, 127, 132 (WORD COUNT: 27)
Every One (OXFORD-SOUTHAMPTON): 53, 53
Every Thing: 15, 98
Every Where: 84, 97, 100, 102
EVIL: 119, 121, 144
Example: 84, 142
Exceed/Exceeds/Exceeded: 32, 83, 150
EXCEL/EXCELLENCE/EXCELLENT (ROYAL): 5, 38, 94, 105
Except: 147
Excess: 146
EXCUSE/EXCUSING: 2, 35, 42, 51, 51, 51, 101, 139
Executor: 4
EXCHEQUER: 67
EXPENSE: 30, 94, 129
Expiate: 22
Expire/Expired: 27, 73
EXPRESS/EXPRESSED/EXPRESSING: 23, 105, 106, 108, 140, 147
Extant: 83
Extern/External: 53, 125
Extreme/Extremity: 51, 129, 129
EYE/EYES/EYE'S: 5, 7, 7, 9, 9, 14, 16, 17, 18, 18, 20, 20, 23, 24, 24, 24, 24, 24, 24, 25, 27, 30, 33, 43, 43, 43, 43, 46, 46, 46, 46, 46, 47, 47, 47, 47, 47, 49, 55, 56, 69, 69, 69, 78, 81, 81, 83, 88, 93, 95, 104, 104, 104, 106, 106, 106, 113, 114, 114, 114, 118, 121, 127, 127, 130, 132, 132, 133, 137, 137, 137, 137, 137, 139, 139, 140, 141, 142, 148, 148, 148, 148, 148, 149, 152, 152, 153, 153
Eye-lids/Eyelids: 27, 61 (WORD COUNT: 90)

FACE/FACES: 3, 3, 20, 27, 34, 62, 93, 93, 94, 101, 103, 131, 131, 132, 137, 139, 143
Faculty: 122
FADE/FADING/FADETH (see Vade): 18, 19, 54, 73, 146
Faint: 80
FAIR/FAIRER/FAIREST/FAIRING/FAIRLY (see Unfair, etc.) (ROYAL): 1, 2, 3, 5, 6, 10, 13, 16, 18, 18, 18, 19, 21, 21, 21, 25, 26, 43, 45, 46, 54, 54, 68, 69, 70, 78, 82, 82, 82, 83, 83, 87, 92, 95, 104, 105, 105, 105, 106, 108, 119, 127, 127, 127, 131, 131, 135, 135, 137, 144, 147, 148, 152, 154 (WORD COUNT: 54)
FAITH = 66, 131, 141, 152, 152
Falls/Falls: 124, 151, 151
FALSE/FALSELY: 20, 20, 41, 67, 68, 72, 92, 93, 109, 121, 127, 127, 130, 131, 137, 138, 138, 142, 148, 148
Fame: 80, 84, 101
Familiar: 86
Famine: 1
Famished: 46

Index – Words Of The Sonnets

Famoused: 25
Fangled (see New-Fangled)
FAR/FARTHER/FARTHEST: 27, 28, 28, 44, 47, 50, 61, 69, 76, 80, 94, 117, 119, 130, 136, 141, 151
FAREWELL: 87
Faring: 22
Fashion: 20, 124
Fast/Faster: 11, 11, 12, 101, 114, 134
Fate: 29
FATHER/FATHERED (see Un-fathered): 13, 37
FAULT/FAULTS   (TREASON): 35, 35, 88, 89, 96, 96, 96, 118, 138, 148, 151
FAVOR/ FAVORITES (ROYAL): 25, 25, 113, 125
Fawn: 149
FEAR/FEARING/FEARFUL/FEARFULLY/FEARS: 9, 23, 23, 48, 64, 65, 86, 92, 92, 99, 104, 107, 115, 119, 119, 124, 126
Feast/Feasting/Feasts: 52, 75, 141
Feathers/Feathered: 78, 143
Feature/Featured/Featureless: 11, 29, 113
Fed: 146
FEE: 120
Feeble: 7
Feeding/Feeds/Feed'st: 1, 56, 60, 118, 146, 147
Feel/Feeling/Feel'st: 2, 48, 120, 121, 141
FELL: 20, 64, 74, 118, 153
FEMALE (ELIZABETH): 144
Fester: 94
FEVER: 119, 147
Few: 73
Fickle: 126
Fiend: 144, 145
Fierce: 19, 23
FIERY: 51
Fight: 26, 60, 88
Figure/Figured/Figures (see Refigure): 98, 104, 108
Filching: 75
FILL/FILLED: 17, 62, 86, 112, 136
Find/Finds/Finding/Found (see New Found): 13, 24, 27, 42, 42, 49, 51, 55, 61, 61, 76, 77, 78, 79, 82, 83, 83, 91, 92, 108, 115, 118, 118, 119, 142, 148, 153, 153
Fine: 52
Finger/Fingers: 96, 128, 128, 128
FIRE/FIRED (ROYAL): 45, 55, 73, 144, 153, 153, 153, 153, 154, 154, 154
Firm: 64
FIRST: 20, 21, 45, 59, 90, 104, 104, 108, 114, 114, 119
Fits: 120
Five: 59, 141
Fixed: 21, 116
FLAME (ROYAL): 1, 109, 115
FLATTER/Flattered/Flatterer/Flattery: 28, 33, 42, 87, 112, 114, 114, 138
Fled: 71, 148
Fleece: 68
Fleeting/Fleet'st: 19, 97
Flesh: 44, 51, 151
Flies: 70, 143, 143
Flow: 30
Flown: 145

Flourish: 60
FLOWER/FLOWERS (SOUTHAMPTON): 5, 16, 21, 65, 68, 69, 94, 94, 98, 99, 113, 124, 124
Fly: 78
Foe/Foes: 1, 40, 69, 139
Foison: 53
Foist: 123
FOLLOW/FOLLOWED/FOLLOWS: 41, 143, 145, 145
Folly: 11, 66
Fond: 3
Food: 75
FOOL/FOOLS/FOOLISH: 116, 124, 137, 141
Foot/Footed: 19, 65, 106
Forbear: 41, 139
Forbid/Forbidden: 6, 19, 58, 65
FORCE/FORCED: 41, 56, 91
'Fore/Fore: 7, 30
Forests: 104
FORFEIT: 107, 134
Forged: 137
FORGET/Forget'st/Forgetful/Forgetfulness/Forgot/Forgotten: 23, 25, 71, 72, 81, 100, 100, 117, 122, 149
FORGIVE: 40
Forgoing/Foregone: 30, 125
Forlorn: 33
FORM: 3, 9, 13, 24, 43, 43, 89, 108, 113, 125
Former: 56, 59, 59, 123
Forsake: 12, 89
Forsworn: 66, 88, 152, 152
FORTH: 34, 38, 55, 72, 103, 134, 145
Fortify: 16, 63
FORTUNE/FORTUNE'S (ELIZABETH): 14, 25, 29, 32, 37, 89, 89, 111, 124 (WORD COUNT: 9)
FORTY: 1
Forward: 99
Fountain/Fountains: 35, 153
FOUL: 119, 127, 132, 137, 144, 148, 152
Four: 45
FRAGRANT (ROYAL): 95
Frailties/Frailer: 109, 121, 121
Frame: 3, 24, 59, 118
Frank: 4
Frantic: 147
FREE/FREEDOM: 4, 46, 125, 134, 134
Frequent: 117
FRESH/FRESHER (see Afrresh) (ROYAL): 1, 3, 11, 17, 82, 104, 107, 108
FRIEND/FRIEND'S/FRIENDS (see Befriends): 29, 30, 30, 31, 32, 42, 42, 42, 82, 104, 110, (Befriends: 120); 111, 133, 133, 133, 134, 149
FROM: 1, 7, 11, 12, 14, 14, 15, 22, 27, 29, 30, 31, 33, 33, 35, 36, 36, 41, 44, 45, 48, 48, 49, 50, 51, 61, 61, 61, 65, 66, 75, 76, 77, 81, 97, 98, 99, 104, 109, 112, 119, 122, 133, 141, 142, 143, 144, 150, 153
Front: 102
Frost: 5
FROWN/FROWN'ST/FROWNS (ROYAL): 25, 49, 93, 117, 149
FULL/FULLNESS: 33, 41, 54, 56, 56, 75, 86, 115, 115, 118, 122, 132, 136
Fulfill: 136, 136
Function: 113
Furrows: 22

Index – Words Of The Sonnets

Fury: 100

GAIN/GAINER/GAINS: 42, 64, 67, 88, 119, 141
'Gainst (see Against): 10, 12, 35, 55, 60, 111
GARMENTS/Garments': 91, 91
GATE/GATES: 29, 65
GAUDY: 1
GAVE/GAV'ST: 11, 22, 60, 87, 87, 110, 152
Gay: 68, 146
GAZE/GAZED/GAZERS/GAZETH/GAZING: 2, 5, 20, 24, 96, 125
Gems: 21
GENERAL: 91, 121, 154
GENTLE/GENTLEST/GENTLY (ROYAL): 5, 10, 20, 40, 41, 48, 79, 81, 96, 100, 113, 128, 128, 151
Get (see Got): 7
GHASTLY: 27
Ghost: 86
GIFT/GIFTS: 11, 60, 87, 87, 103, 122
GILDED/GILD'ST, GILDING (ROYAL): 20, 28, 33, 55, 101
Girded: 12
GIVE/GIVEN/GIVES/GIVING: 4, 4, 13, 16, 18, 22, 31, 34, 37, 38, 38, 39, 51, 51, 59, 69, 69, 71, 77, 78, 79, 79, 83, 86, 87, 90, 100, 100, 110, 115, 117, 121, 122, 128, 150
Glad/Gladly: 8, 19, 45
Glance: 76, 139
Glass: 3, 3, 5, 22, 62, 77, 77, 103, 103, 126
Glazed: 24
GLORY/GLORIOUS (ROYAL): 25, 33, 37, 60, 83, 84, 88, 91, 132
Glowing: 73
Glutton/Gluttoning: 1, 75
Go/Goes/Goest/Going: 12, 14, 51, 51, 60, 113, 126, 130, 140
GOD: 58, 110, (LOVE-GOD: 154)
GODDESS: 111, 130
GOLD/GOLDEN (ROYAL): 3, 7, 18, 21, (Mari-gold: 25), 33, 68, 85
GONE: 4, 5, 31, 44, 45, 66, 71, 81, 110
GOOD/GOODLY/GOODNESS (ROYAL): 14, 24, 26, 36, 47, 66, 70, 80, 85, 85, 109, 112, 118, 121, 124, 131
Gored: 110
Got (see Get): 153
GOVERNS: 113
GRACE/GRACED/GRACES/GRACIOUS/
GRACIOUSLY (ROYAL): 7, 10, 17, 24, 26, 28, 40, 53, 62, 67, 78, 78, 78, 79, 79, 94, 96, 96, 96, 103, 132, 135, 150
(WORD COUNT: 23)
GRANT/GRANTING: 10, 79, 82, 87, 130
GRAVE/GRAVES: 1, 31, 77, 81
Graven: 100
Gravity: 49
Gray: 132
GREAT/GREATER/GREATEST (ROYAL): 25, 26, 40, 48, 61, 70, 86, 87, 114, 117, 119, 125, 136
Grecian: 53
GREEN (TUDOR): 12, 33, 62, 68, 104, (O'er-Green: 112),
Greet: 102, 145
GREW (see Grow): 86, 98, 118, 153
GRIEF/GRIEFS/GRIEF'S/GRIEVE/GRIEVED/GRIEVANCES: 28, 30, 30, 34, 35, 40, 42, 48, 50, 90
Grind: 110
GROAN/GROANS: 50, 50, 131, 131, 133
Gross/Grossly: 82, 99, 151

Ground/Grounded: 62, 65, 130, 142, 153
GROW/GROWN/GROWS/GROW'ST/GROWING/
GROWTH: 11, 15, 18, 32, 32, 45, 69, 83, 87, 93, 99, 102, 102, 115, 115, 119, 124, 126, 126, 130, 140, 140, 142, 154 (WORD COUNT: 24)
GUARD: 49, 133
Guess: 69
Guides: 26
Gulls: 86
GUILT/GUILTY: 36, 111, 151
Gust/Gusts: 13, 114

Habit: 138
HABITATION (THE TOWER PRISON): 95
Had/Hadst: 13, 32, 32, 40, 40, 52, 67, 75, 79, 87, 99, 99, 99, 99, 106, 129, 129
HAIR/HAIRS (HEIR/HEIRS): 99, 130
Half: 17, 89, 132
HALLOWED: 108
Halt: 89
Hammered: 120
HAND/HANDS: 20, 28, 49, 58, 60, 63, 65, 71, 104, 106, 127, 128, 145, 154
HANG/HANGING (see Hung): 24, 54, 72, 73
Hap: 9
Haply: 29, 89
HAPPY/HAPPIER/HAPPIES: 6, 6, 6, 8, 16, 25, 28, 32, 37, 43, 57, (Unhappily: 66), 92, 92, 92, 128
HARD: 120
HARMFUL: 111
HARVEST: 128
Hast: 9, 20, 35, 40, 42, 49, 70, 74, 99, 126, 134, 135, 150
HASTE/HASTEN: 27, 51, 60, 122
HATE/HATED/HATE'S/HATRED/HATETH: 10, 10, 35, 40, 89, 90, 93, 117, 124, 129, 142, 142, 145, 145, 145, 145, 149, 149, 150, 152
HATH: 9, 11, 18, 23, 23, 24, 24, 26, 42, 42, 49, 52, 59, 63, 64, 67, 68, 74, 78, 81, 90, 91, 92, 97, 98, 103, 104, 107, 108, 113, 119, 127, 127, 131, 133, 135, 147, 148
HAVE: 31, 33, 35, 37, 48, 57, 59, 63, 64, 64, 64, 64, 65, 74, 78, 82, 83, 87, 90, 94, 98, 105, 106, 106, 109, 110, 110, 110, 115, 117, 117, 119, 119, 119, 120, 122, 123, 129, 130, 132, 138, 142, 144, 148, 148
HAVING: 91, 103, 129, 146
HAWKS: 91, 91
HE/HE'S: 7, 25, 32, 33, 38, 44, 50, 51, 52, 57, 63, 63, 63, 67, 67, 79, 79, 79, 79, 79, 79, 80, 80, 80, 84, 84, 86, 86, 101, 101, 107, 134, 134, 134, 134, 134
Head: 7, 26, 27, 68, 130
HEALTH/HEALTHFUL: 45, 118, 140, 154
Heals: 34
Hear/Heard/Hearing/Hear'st: 8, 8, 71, 85, 104, 122, 130
Hearsay: 21
HEART/HEARTS/HEART'S: 20, 22, 22, 22, 23, 24, 24, 31, 41, 46, 46, 46, 46, 46, 46, 46, 46, 47, 47, 47, 47, 47, 47, 53, 62, 69, 70, 90, 93, 93, 93, 95, 109, 110, 113, 119, 122, 125, 132, 132, 133, 133, 133, 133, 133, 137, 137, 137, 137, 139, 139, 140, 141, 141, 141, 142, 145, 150, 154, 154 (WORD COUNT: 60)
HEAT/HEATS: 12, 124, 153, 154, 154
HEAVEN/HEAVEN'S/HEAVENLY (ELIZABETH): 7, 14, 17, 17, 18, 21, 21, 21, 28, 29, 29, 33, 33, 70, 93, 94, 110, 129, 130, 132, 145, 148 (WORD COUNT: 22)
HEAVY/ HEAVILY: 43, 44, 50, 50, 61, 78, 98
HEIGHT (ROYAL): 15, 32, 116
Heinous: 19
HEIR: 1, 6, 127

Held: 2, 24
HELEN'S (ELIZABETH): 53
HELL: 58, 119, 120, 129, 144, 144, 145, 147
Help: 36, 80, 153, 153
Hems: 21
Hence: 12, 39, 81, 81, 101, 125
HER/HERS: 19, 19, 27, 41, 41, 42, 42, 42, 42, 42, 42, 85, 102, 102, 103, 107, 126, 126, 126, 126, 127, 130, 130, 130, 130, 130, 135, 138, 138, 143, 143, 143, 143, 144, 145, 145, 151, 154
HERALD: 1
Herd: 12
HERE/HERE'S: 13, 39, 42
HERETIC: 124
HEW/HEWS (HENRY WRIOTHESLEY, SOUTHAMPTON): 20, 20, 67, 82, 98, 104
HID/HIDDEN/HIDE/HIDES/HIDING: 17, 30, 31, 34, 135, 142
Hideous: 12
Hied: 153
HIGH/HIGHMOST (ROYAL): 7, 17, 78, 78, 91
HIM: 12, 19, 28, 28, 29, 29, 33, 33, 34, 38, 39, 46, 46, 50, 51, 52, 67, 67, 68, 79, 84, 86, 86, 89, 99, 101, 101, 107, 109, 133, 134, 134, 134, 134
Himself: 9, 47
Hindmost: 85
HIS: 1, 7, 7, 7, 7, 9, 23, 23, 23, 24, 32, 32, 32, 33, 33, 37, 47, 50, 50, 51, 52, 55, 60, 60, 63, 63, 63, 63, 65, 67, 67, 67, 67, 68, 74, 80, 80, 84, 84, 84, 84, 85, 86, 86, 86, 86, 91, 96, 99, 99, 116, 116, 153, 154
HISTORY: 93
Hoisted: 117
HOLD/HOLDS: 13, 15, 65, 65, 65, 75, 80, 85, 87, 102, 113, 122, 126, 136, 136, 143
HOLY (ROYAL/SACRED): 31, 68, 127, 153
HOMAGE: 7
HOME: 61, 87, 109
Honey: 65
HONOR/HONOUR/HONORING: 13, 25, 25, 25, 36, 36, 66, 125
HOPE/HOPES: 26, 52, 60, 97, 119, 119, 143
HORSE/HORSES: 51, 91, 91
HOT: 18, 154
HOUNDS: 91
HOUR/HOURS: 16, 19, 33, 36, 52, 57, 57, 58, 61, 63, 68, 116, 124, 126, 146
HOUSE (HOUSE OF TUDOR): 13
HOUSEWIFE: 143
How: 2, 8, 26, 28, 38, 39, 39, 43, 46, 48, 50, 57, 59, 65, 65, 77, 77, 83, 87, 93, 96, 96, 97, 101, 119, 120, 120, 128, 148, 150
HUGE/HUGELY: 15, 21, 124
Humble: 80, 120
Humor: 91, 92
HUNDRED: 59
HUNG: 27
Hungry: 56, 64
Hunted: 129
Hurt: 94
Husband/Husband's/Husbandry: 3, 8, 9, 13, 94
Hush: 102
HYMN/HYMNS: 29, 85, 102

I AM THAT I AM: 121
Idle/Idly: 61, 100, 122

IDOL/IDOLATRY: 105, 105
Ignorance: 78, 78
ILL/ILLS: 22, 34, 40, 57, 58, 66, 70, 91, 95, 95, 112, 118, 118, 119, 119, (Ill-Wresting: 140), 147
IMAGE/IMAGES: 3, 24, 31, 59
Imaginary: 27
Imitated: 53
IMMORTAL: 81
IMMURED (IMPRISONED): 84
Impair: 83
IMPANNELLED: 46
Impart: 72
IMPEACHED: 125
IMPEDIMENTS: 116
IMPIETY: 67
Impression: 112
Imprint: 77
IMPRISONED: 52, 58
Impute: 83
Incapable: 113
Incertainty/Incertainties: 107, 115
Inconstant (see Constant): 15, 92
INCREASE/INCREASING: 1, 64, 97
Indeed: 62
Indigest: 114
Indirectly: 67
INFANT'S: 143
INFECTION: 67, 94, 111
Inferior: 80
INFLUENCE: 15, 78
INFORMER: 125
Inhabit: 68
INHEARSE: 86
INHERIT/INHERITORS: 94, 146
INIQUITY: 62
INJURY/INJURIES/INJURIOUS: 40, 44, 58, 63, 89, 108, 139
Ink: 65, 108
In Sense (Incense): 35
INSTANT: 52
Instinct: 50
Insufficiency: 150
Insults: 107
INTELLIGENCE: 86
INTEND/INTENTS: 27, 115
INTERCHANGE (SUCCESSION): 64
INTEREST: 31, 74
Intermixed: 101
Itself: 67
INVENT: 79
INVENTION: 38, 59, 76, 103, 105
Inviting: 124
Invoked: 78
INWARD: 16, 46, 62
ISSUE/ISSUELESS: 9, 13, 97

Index – Words Of The Sonnets

JACKS: 128, 128
Jade: 51
JAIL: 133
Jaws: 19
Jealous/Jealousy: 57, 61
JEWEL/JEWELS (King/Queen): 27, 48, 52, 65, 96, 131
Join: 90
JOURNEY: 27, 50
JOY: 8, 8, 42, 45, 50, 91, 129
JUDGMENT/JUDGMENT'S: 14, 55, 87, 115, 131, 137, 148
Jump: 44
JUNES: 104
JUST (see Unjust): 109, 117, 121, 150
JUSTIFY: 139

Keen: 19, 118
KEEP/KEEPS/KEPT: 16, 22, 51, 61, 76, (KEPT SEAT: SAT ON THE THRONE: 105), 126, 133, 147, 154
KEY: 52
KILL/KILLED/KILLS: 6, 40, 44, 56, 135, 139
KIND/KINDS/KINDNESS (see Unkind/Unkindness) (BLOOD-RELATED): 10, 10, 36, 69, 95, 105, 105, 105, 105, 105, 109, 118, 134, 143, 152
KINDLING (Love-Kindling): 153
KING/KINGS: 29, 63, 87, 115
KINGLY: 114
KINGDOM/KINGDOMS: 64, 70
KISS/KISSING: 33, 128, 128, 143
KNEW: 115
KNIFE: 63, 74, 95, 100
KNIGHTS (SOUTHAMPTON): 106
KNIT: 26
KNOW/KNOWS/KNOW'ST/KNOWING/
KNOWLEDGE (see Unknown): 13, 49, 50, 51, 76, 77, 80, 82, 87, 89, 92, 93, 112, 114, 125, 129, 129, 130, 131, 132, 136, 137, 138, 138, 139, 140, 144, 149, 151, 152

LABORING: 59
Lace: 67
LACK/LACKED/LACKING: 30, 31, 52, 86, 106, 127, 132
LADIES (ELIZABETH): 106
LAID: 125, 129, 153, 154
LAMB/LAMBS: 96, 96
LAME/LAMENESS: 37, 37, 89
LANGUISHED (IN THE TOWER): 145
Lap: 98
LARGE: 44, 95, 135, 135, 146
LARGESS: 4
Lark: 29
Lascivious: 40, 95
Last: 90
LASTING: 122
LATE: 73
Laughed: 98
LAWFUL: 35, 49
LAWS: 49
Lay/Lays: 42, 98, 100, 101, 102, 139

Lead/Leads: 41, 96, 129
LEAGUE (Agreement): 47
Lean: 84
Leap/Leapt: 44, 98
LEARN/LEARNED/LEARNING (See Unlearned): 78, 78, 118
LEASE/LEASES: 13, 18, 107, 124, 146
LEAST: 29, 92, 122, 125
LEAVE/LEAVES (verb)/LEAVING: 4, 6, 39, 41, 51, 73, 90, 90, 105, 109, 141
LEAVES (noun): 5, 12, 25, 73, 77
Leese: 5
LEFT (verb): 113
LEGACY: 4
LEGIONS: 154
LEISURE: 39, 44, 58, 120
LEND/LENDS: 4, 4, 34, 79, 84, 140
LENGTH/LENGTHS: 28, 44
Less/Lesser: 17, 20, 96, 102, 102, 102, 114
Lesson: 118
Lest: 71, 72, 140
LET/LETS: 6, 11, 13, 13, 21, 21, 23, 25, 36, 38, 39, 56, 71, 84, 105, 116, 125, 132, 133, 135, 136, 139, 146
Level: 117, 121
LIBERTY: 41, 58
LIE/LIES: 2, 17, 24, 31, 46, 46, 72, 73, 81, 92, 101, 109, 115, 123, 137, 138, 138, 138, 150, 152
LIFE/LIFE'S: 9, 16, 16, 17, 45, 45, 63, 68, 71, 74, 75, 81, 83, 83, 92, 92, 92, 92, 100, 145, 154
Lifts: 7
LIGHT/LIGHT'S: 1, 43, 60, (Delight: 75), 88, (Delight: 91), (Delight: 98), (Delight: 102),
Like/Liker: 9, 16, 17, 21, 29, 29, 52, 53, 56, 57, 60, 87, 93, 93, 95, 97, 102, 108, 109, 111, 118, 129, 132
LIKENESS: 141
LILY/LILY'S/LILIES: 94, 98, 99
Limbecks: 119
Limbs: 27, 27
LIMIT/LIMITS: 44, 82
LIMPING SWAY (ROBERT CECIL): 66
LINE/LINES: 16, 19, 32, 63, 63, 71, 74, 86, 103, 115
LINGER: 90
LION'S: 19
LIP/LIPS: 106, 116, 128, 128, 128, 142, 145
Liquid: 5
List: 58
Little: 15, 154
LIVE/LIVED/LIVES/LIVING: 3, 4, 5, 10, 13, 16, 16, 16, 17, 18, 19, 19, 22, 31, 35, 36, 37, 43, 54, 54, (Outlive: 55), (Living Record: 55), 55, 63, 67, 67, 67, 67, 68, 68, 68, 72, 72, 79, 81, 83, 93, 93, 94, 105, 107, 124, 128, 144, 146 (WORD COUNT: 45)
LIVELY: 67, 153
LO (Lord Oxford): 7, 27, 143
LOAN: 6
LOATHSOME: 35
LOCKED UP (IN THE TOWER) (See Up-Locked): 48
LOFTY: 12, 64
LONG/LONGER: 13, 18, 18, 19, 22, 28, 30, 38, 45, 52, 67, 71, 73, 92, 100, 101, 122, 147
LONGING: 147
LOOK/LOOKED/LOOKS/LOOKING (See Unlooked): 7, 7, 7, 11, 22, 23, 27, 29, 37, 43, 43, 47, 54, 59, 69, 71, 71, 75, 77, 77, 89, 93, 93, 96, 103, 106, 107, 110, 116, 132, 137, 139, 139
LORD/LORDS/LORDS': 26, 94, 97

Index – Words Of The Sonnets

LOSE/LOSS/LOSSES/LOSING: 18, 30, 34, 39, 42, 42, 42, 42, 42, 42, 64, 64, 88, (After-Loss: 90), 90, 95, 102, 119, 125
LOST: 121, 134, 152
Loud: 143
Lour'st: 149
LOVE/LOVED/LOVE'S/LOVES (ROYAL BLOOD and/or ROYAL SON): 10, 10, 13, 13, 19, 20, 20, 21, 21, 22, 23, 23, 23, 23, 23, 25, 26, 26, 29, 30, 31, 31, 31, 31, 31, 32, 32, 32, 33, 35, 36, 36, 36, 36, 36, 37, 39, 39, 40, 40, 40, 40, 40, 40, 40, 40, 40, 42, 42, 42, 42, 42, 42, 45, 46, 47, 47, 47, 47, 49, 49, 49, 50, 51, 51, 51, 51, 56, 56, 56, 56, 57, 61, 61, 61, (Self-Love: 62, 62), 63, 63, 64, 65, 66, 70, 71, 71, 72, 72, 72, 72, 72, 73, 73, 76, 76, 76, 79, 80, 82, 85, 88, 89, (Beloved: 89), 91, 92, 92, 92, 93, 93, 96, 96, 99, 99, 100, 100, 101, 102, 102, 102, 102, 105, (Beloved: 105), 105, 107, 107, 108, 108, 108, 108, 109, 110, 110, 112, 114, 114, 115, 115, 115, 116, 116, 116, 116, 116, 117, 117, 118, 119, 122, 124, 124, 131, 132, 136, 136, 136, 136, 136, 137, 138, 138, 138, 139, 140, 140, 141, 141, 142, 142, 142, 144, 145, 147, 147, 148, 148, 148, 148, 148, 149, 150, 150, 150, (Beloved: 150), 151, 151, 151, 151, 151, 152, 152, 152, (LOVE-KINDLING: 153), 153, 153, (LOVE-GOD: 154), 154, 154, 154   (WORD COUNT: 200)
LOVELINESS: 3
LOVELY: 3, 5, 18, 54, 79, 95, 106
LOVELY BOY: 126
LOVER/LOVERS/LOVER'S/LOVERS': 31, 32, 55, 63, 126
LOVING: 26, 31, 32, 42, (Self-Loving: 62), 88, 110, 132, 142, 152
LOV'ST: 8, 10, 136, 139, 149
Low: 7
Luck: 14
LUST: 129, 129
Lusty: 2, 5
Lying: 154

MAD/MADDING/MADNESS: 119, 129, 140, 140, 140, 140, 147
MADMEN'S: 147
MAIDEN: 16, 66, 154
MAIN: 60, 64, 80
Maintain: 121
MAJESTY: 7, 78
MAKE/MAKES/MADE/MAKING/MAK'ST/MAKETH: 1, 1, 2, 2, 6, 6, 10, 11, 12, 12, 16, 19, 19, 21, 27, 27, 28, 34, 34, 35, 43, 43, 45, 50, 52, 53, 56, 57, 58, 60, 66, 68, 68, 71, 73, 81, 84, 84, 86, 87, 89, 90, 91, 95, 95, 98, 101, 101, 106, 108, 110, 110, 113, 114, 119, 123, 128, 129, 135, 135, 136, 141, 143, 145, 150, 150, 152 (WORD COUNT: 67)
MAKE-LESS: 9
MALADIES: 118, 153
MAN/MAN'S: 20, 29, 29, 141, 144
MANNER/MANNERS: 39, 85, 111, 140
MANSION: 95, 146
MANY (SUBJECTS OF THE CROWN): 8, 10, 16, 30, 30, 31, 31, 96, 154
MAP: 68
MAR: 103
Marble: 55
March (verb): 32
MARIGOLD: 25
Marjoram: 99
Mark: 8, 70, 112, 116
MARRIAGE: 116
MARRIED: 8, 82
MARS (the god): 55
Marvel: 148
MASKED: 33, 54, 70
Masonry: 55

MASTER (KING): 20, (Master-verb: 106)
Matcheth: 69
MATTER: 44, 86, 87
Maturity: 60
MAY (the month): 18
Meadows: 33
Means: 16, 111, 148
MEANT: 11
Measure/Measured: 50, 69, 91
MEDICINE: 118
MEDITATION: 65
Meet/Meetness: 5, 118
MELANCHOLY: 45
MEMORIAL: 74
MEMORY: 1, 15, 55, 63, 77, 77, 81
MEN/MEN'S: 15, 16, 17, 18, 20, 31, 32, 34, 35, 81, 91, 121, 129, 140, 146, 148, 153, 154
MEN'S EYES: 20, 29
Mend/Mended: 59, 69, 78, 103
Merchandized: 102
MERCY: 145
MERIT/MERITS: 26, 72, 88, 108, 142, 149
MESSENGERS: 45
Meter: 17
Methinks: 14, 62, 104
METHODS: 76
Middle Age: 7
Might/Might'st/Mightst: 1, 1, 13, 41, 48, 59, 82, 83, 96, 96, 109, 115, 115, 120, 124, 138, 140, 140
MIGHT (noun): 65, 80, 90, 100, 123, 139, 150
MIGHTIER: 16
Miles: 44, 50
Millions/Millioned: 53, 115
MIND/MIND'S/MINDS: 9, 10, 27, 50, 59, 77, 77, 92, 113, 113, 114, 114, 115, 116, 117, 149
MINDED: 11
MINE: 2, 20, 22, 23, 23, 24, 24, 26, 31, 33, 36, 36, 38, 39, 39, 39, 40, 43, 46, 46, 46, 46, 47, 47, 47, 48, 49, 61, 61, 62, 62, 62, 72, 86, 88, 92, 96, 96, 104, 107, 108, 110, 110, 113, 113, 114, 114, 114, 119, 120, 128, 134, 135, 137, 137, 139, 141, 141, 142, 142, 142
(WORD COUNT: 61)
MINE APPETITE: 110
MINE EAR: 128
MINE EARS: 141
MINE ENEMIES: 139
MINE EYE: 24, 31, 46, 47, 47, 47, 61, 62, 104, 113, 114, 114, 114
MINE EYE AND HEART: 46
MINE EYE'S DUE: 46
MINE EYES: 43, 119, 137, 137, 141
MINE ONLY (MY SON): 48
MINE ONLY CARE: 48
MINE OWN (MY SON): 23, 23, 39, 39, 39, 49, 61, 62, 62, 72, 88, 107, 110
MINE OWN DESERT: 49, 72
MINE OWN FEARS: 107
MINE OWN LOVE'S MIGHT: 23
MINE OWN LOVE'S STRENGTH: 23
MINE OWN PRAISE: 39
MINE OWN SELF: 39

Index – Words Of The Sonnets

MINE OWN SELF-LOVE: 62
MINE OWN THOUGHTS: 110
MINE OWN TRUE LOVE: 61
MINE OWN WEAKNESS: 88
MINE OWN WORTH: 62
Minion: 126
MINUTE/MINUTES: 14, 60, 77, 126
MIRACLE: 65
Miscalled: 66
Miser: 75
MISPLACED: 66
MISPRISION (OF TREASON): 87
Missed: 122
Mistake/Mistaking: 87, 148
MISTRESS/MISTRESS' (ELIZABETH): (Reflecting her: 20, 126); 127, 130, 130, 130, 153, 153, 154
Misuse: 152
Mixed: 125
MOAN: 30, 30, 44, 71, 149
Mock: 61, 71, 107
Modern: 83
Moiety: 46
MOMENT: 15
MONARCH'S: 114
MONSTERS: 114
MONUMENT: 55, 81, 107
Moods: 93
MOON (ELIZABETH): 21, 35, 107
MORE: 2, 16, 21, 23, 23, 23, 29, 38, 40, 42, 50, 52, 54, 56, 56, 72, 72, 72, 73, 83, 84, 85, 89, 99, 102, 103, 103, 113, 119, 122, 125, 128, 130, 130, 135, 135, 146, 150, 150, 150, 152
MORN/MORNING (see Mourn/Mourning): 33, 33, 63, 132
Morrow: 90
MORTAL/MORTALITY: 7, 46, 64, 65, 86, 107
MORTAL MOON (ELIZABETH): 107
MORTGAGED: 134
MOST: 15, 17, 19, 25, 29, 43, 48, 83, 84, 91, 94, 107, 110, 110, 110, 113, 113, 114, 115, 125, 131, 152
MOTHER/MOTHER'S (ELIZABETH): 3, 3, 8, 21, 143
MOTION: 45, 51, 104, 149
Motley: 110
Mountain: 33, 113
MOUNTED: 51
MOURN/MOURNFUL/MOURNERS/MOURNING (see Morn/Morning): 71, 102, 127, 127, 132, 132, 132
Mouths: 81
Moving: 26, 94
MUCH: 2, 43, 44, 54, 61, 71, 77, 101, 103, 122, 125, 140
MUD: 35
MURDEROUS: 9, 10, 129
MUSE/MUSES: 21, 32, 38, 38, 78, 79, 82, 85, 85, 100, 100, 101, 101, 101, 103
Music: 8, 8, 102, 128, 128, 130
MUST: 16, 24, 36, 40, 44, 73, 75, 81, 89, 108, 120, 121
MUTE: 83, 97
MUTUAL: 8, 125
MY ABSENCE: 97
MY ABUSES: 121
MY ADDED PRAISE: 103

MY ADDER'S SENSE: 112
MY AGE: 62
MY ALL (MY SON, SOUTHAMPTON): 109
MY ALL THE WORLD: 112
MY AMISS: 151
MY ANGEL: 144
MY APPEAL: 117
MY ARGUMENT: 76, 105
MY ART: 78
MY BAD: 112
MY BAD ANGEL: 144
MY BARREN RHYME: 16
MY BED: 27
MY BELOVED: 105
MY BEST: 76, 149
MY BEST OF LOVE: 110
MY BETTER ANGEL: 144
MY BLUNT INVENTION: 103
MY BODY: 72, 74, 151
MY BONDS IN THEE: 87
MY BONES: 32
MY BOOKS: 23
MY BOSOM'S SHOP: 24
MY BRAIN: 122
MY BREAST: 24, 48, 153
MY BROW: 33, 112
MY CHEST: 52
MY CLOAK: 34
MY COMFORT: 37, 134
MY COUNT: 1
MY DAYS: 22, 138
MY DEAR DOTING HEART: 131
MY DEAR LOVE (MY ROYAL SON): 124
MY DEAR TIME'S WASTE: 30
MY DECAY: 80
MY DEEDS: 61, 90, 121
MY DEEPEST SENSE: 120
MY DEFECTS: 49
MY DESERVING: 87
MY DESIRE: 51
MY DISCOURSE: 147
MY DROOPING EYELIDS: 27
MY DULL BEARER: 51
MY DUMB THOUGHTS: 85
MY DUTY: 26
MY EVERY PART: 62
MY EXTERN: 125
MY EYE: 47
MY EYES: 43
MY FACE: 139
MY FALSE EYES: 148
MY FATE: 29
MY FAULTS: 151
MY FEEDING: 118

832

Index – Words Of The Sonnets

MY FEMALE EVIL: 144
MY FIVE SENSES: 141
MY FIVE WITS: 141
MY FLAME: 109
MY FLESH: 44
MY FOES: 139
MY FOOT: 43
MY FRAILTIES: 121
MY FRIEND (MY SON): 42, 42, 42, 133, 149
MY FRIEND'S HEART (SOUTHAMPTON): 133
MY FRIEND'S MUSE (referring to himself): 32
MY GAIN: 141
MY GENTLE VERSE: 81
MY GLASS: 22, 62
MY GLORY: 83
MY GOOD: 112
MY GOOD ONE (Angel: SOUTHAMPTON): 144
MY GRACIOUS NUMBERS: 79
MY GREAT MIND: 114
MY GREATEST GRIEF: 48
MY GRIEF: 34, 42, 50
MY GROSS BODY'S TREASON: 151
MY HARMFUL DEEDS: 111
MY HEAD: 26, 27, 148
MY HEART (SOUTHAMPTON): 22, 46, 46, 46, 47, 47, 62, 90, 110, 133, 133, 133, 137, 137, 137, 139, 141, 150
MY HEART AND EYES: 137
MY HEART'S GUEST: 47
MY HEART'S RIGHT (MY SON'S ROYAL RIGHT): 46
MY HEAVEN: 110
MY HEAVY EYELIDS: 61
MY HELP: 153
MY HOME OF LOVE: 109
MY HONEST FAITH IN THEE (TO ELIZABETH): 152
MY INVENTION: 105
MY JADE: 51
MY JAIL: 133
MY JEWELS: 48
MY JOY: 50
MY JUDGMENT: 14, 115, 148
MY JUDGMENT'S PLACE: 131
MY KNOWLEDGE: 14
MY LAMENESS: 89
MY LAYS: 102
MY LIFE: 45, 71, 74, 92, 92, 111, 145
MY LIMBS: 27
MY LINES: 103
MY LOSS: 42
MY LOUD CRYING: 143
MY LOVE (MY ROYAL SON): 13, 19, 21, 26, 32, 33, 37, 40, 40, 40, 40, 40, 47, 51, 61, 63, 64, 65, 66, 76, 80, 88, 100, 101, 102, 105, 105, 107, 108, 130; (Elizabeth: 138); 147, 147
MY LOVE AND HATE: 35
MY LOVE'S BREATH: 99
MY LOVE'S FAIR BROW: 19
MY LOVE'S GAIN: 42

MY LOVE'S SWEET FACE: 100
MY LOVE'S VEINS: 99
MY LOVE-SUIT: 136
MY LOVELY BOY (MY ROYAL SON): 126
MY LOVER'S LIFE: 63
MY LOVES: 40
MY LOVING THOUGHTS: 88
MY MADNESS: 140
MY MEASURE: 91
MY MERIT: 88
MY MIND: 10, 27, 27, 50, 113, 114, 150
MY MISTRESS (ELIZABETH): 130, 130
MY MISTRESS' EYE (THE QUEEN'S ROYAL VIEW): 153, 153
MY MISTRESS' EYES (THE QUEEN'S ROYAL VIEW). 127, 130
MY MISTRESS' THRALL (ELIZABETH'S LOYAL SUBJECT): 154
MY MOAN: 44
MY MOST FULL FLAME: 115
MY MOST TRUE MIND: 113
MY MOVING: 26
MY MUSE: 38, 78, 82, 103
MY MUSIC: 128
MY NAME: 72, 76, 111, 136, 136
MY NATURE: 109, 111
MY NEGLECT: 112
MY NERVES: 120
MY NEXT SELF (MY SON): 133
MY NOBLER PART: 151
MY OBLATION: 125
MY OLD EXCUSE: 1
MY O'ER-PRESSED DEFENSE: 139
MY OUTCAST STATE: 29
MY PAIN: 132, 139
MY PASSION: 20
MY PATENT: 87
MY PEN: 81
MY PITY-WANTING PAIN: 140
MY PLAGUE: 141
MY PLEASURE: 75
MY POOR HEART: 133
MY POOR LIPS: 128
MY POOR NAME: 71
MY POSSESSING: 87
MY POVERTY: 40
MY PURPOSE: 20, 112
MY REASON: 147
MY REST: 61
MY ROSE (SOUTHAMPTON, HEIR OF THE TUDOR ROSE): 109
MY RHYME: 17
MY RUDE IGNORANCE: 78
MY SAINT: 144
MY SAKE: 42, 42, 42, 111
MY SAUCY BARK (boat): 80
MY SEAT: 41
MY SEEING: 114

Index – Words Of The Sonnets

MY SELF (ME/MY SON): 22, 27, 29, 29, 34, 35, 35, 49, 62, 62, 62, 62, 88, 88, 88, 89, 109, 109, 110, 119, 131, 133, 133, 134, 134, 149, 149, 149, 149
MY SHAMES AND PRAISES: 112
MY SICK MUSE: 79
MY SIDE: 144
MY SIGHT: 15, 47, 61, 139
MY SIGHTLESS VIEW: 27
MY SILENCE: 86
MY SIN: 83, 142, 142
MY SINFUL EARTH: 146
MY SLIGHT MUSE: 38
MY SLUMBERS: 61
MY SONG: 102
MY SONGS AND PRAISES: 105
MY SORROWS: 28
MY SOUL: 109, 151
MY SOUL'S IMAGINARY SIGHT: 27
MY SOVEREIGN: 57
MY SPEAKING BREAST: 23
MY SPIRIT: 74
MY SPORTIVE BLOOD: 121
MY STAIN: 109
MY STATE: 29, 29, 150
MY STEELED SENSE: 112
MY STORM-BEATEN FACE: 34
MY STRONG INFECTION: 111
MY SUNNE (MY ROYAL SON: 33
MY SWEET LOVE'S BEAUTY: 63
MY SWEET'ST FRIEND: 133
MY THOUGHT: 45, 85
MY THOUGHTS: 27, 47, 75, 147
MY TONGUE: 89, 102
MY TONGUE-TIED MUSE: 85
MY TONGUE-TIED PATIENCE: 140
MY TOTTERED LOVING: 26
MY TRUE LOVE (MY ROYAL SON): 107
MY TRUE SIGHT: 150
MY TRUE SPIRIT: 108
MY UNKIND ABUSE: 134
MY UNKINDNESS: 120
MY USE: 48, 78
MY VERSE: 17, 19, 60, 76, 78, 86, 103, 105
MY VERSES: 103
MY VIEW: 148
MY VOWS: 152
MY WAILING CHIEF: 42
MY WAY: 34, 44, 48
MY WEARY TRAVEL'S END: 50
MY WELL-CONTENTED DAY: 32
MY WILL: 135, 135, 136
MY WILLFULNESS AND ERRORS: 117
MY WIT: 26
MY WOE: 50
MY WOEFUL STATE: 145

Naked: 26
NAME: 36, 39, 71, 72, 76, 80, 81, 89, 95, 108, 127, 127, 136, 136, 151 (WORD COUNT: 15)
NAMING: 95
NATIVITY (SOUTHAMPTON'S BIRTH): 60
NATURE/NATURE'S (ELIZABETH): 4, 11, 18, 20, 20, 60, 67, 68, 84, 94; universal nature: 122, 126); 127 (WORD COUNT: 13)
NAUGHT (or Naughts; see Nought): 44
NEAR/NEARLY: 42, 61, 97, 139
NECK: 131
NEED/Needs/Needy/Needing/Need'st: 35, 66, 82, 83, 92, 101, 118, 120, 122, 139
NEGLECT/NEGLECTED: 101, 112, 143
Neigh: 51
Neither: 16, 86
Nerves: 120
NEVER (OXFORD: see Ever): 1, 5, (Ne'er: 17), 46, 63, 83, (Ne'er: 89), 104, 105, 109, 110, 116, 116, (Ne'er-Cloying: 118), 122, 130 (WORD COUNT: 16)
NEW/NEWER: 2, 7, 15, 27, 30, 30, 59, 76, 76, 76, 102, 108, 110, 110, 123, 152, 152, 152
News: 140
NEXT: 110, 133
Nimble: 44, 128
Niggard: 4, 72
NIGHT/NIGHTS/NIGHTLY: 12, 15, 27, 27, 27, 27, 27, 27, 28, 28, 28, 28, 28, 28, 28, 43, 43, 43, 61, 63, 73, 86, 86, 102, 120, 145, 147 (WORD COUNT: 26)
Nine: 38
NO: 123
Nobler: 151
NONE (SOUTHAMPTON): 8, 10, 53, 53, 73, 99, 112, 112, 136 (WORD COUNT: 9)
NOON: 7
Note: 8
Noted: 76
NOTED WEED: 76
NOTHING: 4, 12, 20, 59, 60, 66, 69, 72, 93, 108, 109, 109, 123, 123, 130, 131, 136, 136 (WORD COUNT: 18)
NOUGHT (see Naught): 15, 57
Nourished: 73
Novel (adjective): 123
NOW: 1, 2, 3, 16, 31, 31, 33, 48, 63, 67, 102, 105, 106, 106, 107, 108, 110, 120, 147, 149 (WORD COUNT: 20)
NUMBER/NUMBERS/NUMB'RED (SONNETS): 17, 17, 38, 79, 100, 124, 136, 136
NURSE/NURSED/NURSETH: 22, 77, 147
NYMPHS: 154

O (OXFORD): 10, 13, 13, 19, 21, 22, 23, 23, 32, 51, 61, 65, 65, 65, 67, 71, 72, 72, 76, 109, 111, 116, 119, 120, 126, 126, 132, 138, 139, 142; (O ME! - 148), 148, 148, 149 (WORD COUNT: 34)
OATHS/OATHS': 152, 152, 152, 152
Object/Objects: 20, 114
OBLATION: 125
OBLIVION: 122
OBLIVIOUS: 55
OBSEQUIOUS (dutiful in funeral rites): 31, 125
OCEAN (ROYALTY/ROYAL BLOOD): 56, 64, 80
ODOR/ODORS: 54, 54, 69, 98
O'er: 12, 30, 107, 108, 115, 128
O'ER-CHARGED: 23
O'ER-GREEN (Tudor Colour): 112

Index – Words Of The Sonnets

O'ER-LOOK: 82
O'ER-PRESSED: 139
O'ER-READ: 81
O'ER-SWAYS: 65
O'ER-TAKE: 34
O'ER-WORN: 63, 68
O'er-Snowed: 5
Off: 28, 61
OFFENCE/OFFENCES/OFFENCE'S (treason): 34, 51, 89, 110
OFFEND: 8
OFFENDERS/OFFENDER'S: 34, 42
OFFICE/OFFICES: 77, 101
Oft/Often: 18, 78, 105, 142
OH (O: Oxford): 38, 39, 39, 54, 58, 59, 59, 80, 92, 95, 95, 101, 103, 150, 150
OLD/OLDER: 2, 2, 17, 19, 22, 30, 38, 59, 68, 76, 76, 97, 104, 108, 108, 110, 110, 123, 138
OLIVES: 107
ONCE: 25, 32, 57, 60, 81, 120, 135, 136, 146, 154
ONE (SOUTHAMPTON; see also Alone, None, Once, Only, Wonder, Wondrous): 6, 8, 8, 8, 8, 19, 20, 22, 28, 29, 33, 33, 36, 36, 39, 39, 42, 53, 53, 53, 53, 53, 76, 91, 99, 105, 105, 105, 105, 105, 131, 135, 135, 136, 136, 136, 141, 143, 144 (WORD COUNT: 39)
ONLY: 1, 48, 94, 125, 141
Onset: 90
Onward/Onwards: 50, 126
Open: 27, 61
OPPRESSED/OPPRESSION: 28, 28, 45
Ordering: 8
ORPHANS: 97
ORIENT: 7
ORNAMENT/ORNAMENTS (SOUTHAMPTON; see Jewel): 1, 21, 54, 68, 70, 142
OTHER/OTHERS/OTHERS' (see An Other): 8, 12, 13, 28, 42, 45, 47, 53, 61, 62, 78, 83, 85, 85, 90, 90, 93, 94, 94, 99, 103, 112, 121, 121; (That Other Mine: 134); 135, 142, 144, 150, 150
OUGHT: 125
OUR: 36, 36, 39, 60, 102, 106, 120, 121, 123, 123, 124
OUT: 15, 20, 33, 55, 55, 61, 63, 95, 105, 144, 151
OUTLIVE: 38, 55, 101
OUT-RIGHT: 139
Outstripped: 32
OUTWARD: 16, 46, 69, 69, 108, 125, 146
OUTWORN: 64
OVER: 126
OVER-GOES: 103
OVER-PARTIAL: 137
OVER-PLUS: 135
OVERTHROW (revolt; the Rebellion): 90
OVERTURN: 55
OWE/OW'ST/OWES: 18, 70, 79
OWN (see Mine Own): 1, 2, 20, 23, 38, 39, 39, 39, 61, 62, 69, 72, 87, 88, 103, 107, 107, 110, 117, 121, 142, 145
OWNER'S: 102

Pace: 51, 55, 104
Page: 108
PAID: 30
PAIN (post-Rebellion): 38, 132, 139, 140, 141
PAINFUL: 25

PAINTED/PAINTER/PAINTER'S/PAINTING: 16, 20, 21, 24, 24, 24, 47, 53, 62, 67, 82, 83, 83, 146
PALATE: 114, 118
Pale: 33, 97
Paper/Papers: 17, 38
Parallels: 60
PARDON: 58
PART (noun): 23, 37, 39, 46, 46, 48, 49, 53, 62, 74, 74, 81, 88, 113, 132, 143, 151
PARTAKE: 149
Partial (see Over-Partial: 137)
Partly: 113
Particulars: 91
PARTS (noun; ROYAL): 8, 17, 31, 31, 37; (verb: 56); 69
PARTY: 35
Pass/Passed: 49, 70, 103, 120, 136
PASSION: 20
PAST: 30, 82, 123, 129, 129, 138, 147, 147
PATENT: 87
PATIENCE: 58, 140
PATIENT (noun): 111
PATTERN: 19, 98
PAY/PAYS/PAYING (see Repay): 6, 30, 79, 79, 125, 134
PEACE: 75, 107
PEARL (reflecting Elizabeth, her pearls): 34
Pebbled: 60
Peep: 24
PEN: 16, 19, 32, 78, 81, 84, 85, 100, 106
PENANCE: 111
PENCIL: 16, 101
PENT: 5, 133
PENURY: 84
Petty: 90
PERCEIVE/Perceiv'st/Perceived: 15, 73, 104
PERFECT/PERFECT'ST (see Imperfect/Un-perfect))/PERFECTION (ROYAL): 15, 23, 51, 66, 114
Perforce: 133
Perfumed/Perfumes: 54, 104, 130
Perhaps: 71
PERISH: 11
PERJURED: 129, 152, 152
Permit: 33
PERPETUAL: 56, 154
PERSPECTIVE: 24
Persuade: 22
Perusal: 38
PHILOMEL (nightingale): 102
PHOENIX (ELIZABETH): 19
Phrase: 85
PHYSIC: 34, 147
PHYSICIAN/PHYSICIANS: 140, 147
Picture/Pictured/Picture's: 24, 46, 47, 47, 47
Pied: 98
Piety (see Impiety)
Pierced: 46
PILGRIMAGE: 7, 27
PINE (verb): 75, 146

Index – Words Of The Sonnets

Pipe: 102
Pitch: 7
PITIED: 142
PITIFUL: 125
PITY/PITYING: 1, 111, 111, 111, 112, 132; (Pity Wanting: 140); 142, 142
PLACE: 6, 9, (the Tower: 44); (the Throne: 60); 79; (the Tower: 93); 108, 131, 137
PLACE/PLACED (verb): 52, 88
PLAGUE/PLAGUES: 14, 114, 137, 141
PLAIN: 82
PLANTS: 15
Play/Played/Play'st: 24, 54, 61, 128, 143
PLEA: 35, 65
PLEAD: 23, 46
PLEASANT: 102
PLEASE/PLEASING/PLEASED: 8, 38, 130, 136, 141, 147
PLEASURE/PLEASURES (ROYAL): 8, 20, 48, 52, 58, 58, 75, 91, 97, 97, 121, 126 (WORD COUNT: 12)
PLIGHT: 28
Plods: 50
PLOT: 137
PLUCK: 19, 98, 126
Poesy: 78
POET/POET'S/POETS: 17, 17, 32, 79, 83, 83
POINT/POINTS/POINTING: 1, 4, 26, 52, 151
POISON/POISONED: 114, 118
POLICY (STATE POLICY)/POLITIC: 118, 124, 124
POMP (ROYAL): 124
Polished: 85
POOR: 26, 32, 37, 49, 51, 67, 71, 107, 122, 125, 128, 133, 143, 146, 151
POSSESSION/POSSESSED/POSSESSETH/POSSESSING: 10, 18, 29, 61, 75, 87, 129
POSTERITY: 3, 6, 55
Posting: 51
Potions: 111, 119
POUR'ST: 38
POVERTY: 40, 103
POWER/POWERFUL (ROYAL): 55, 65, 94, 100, 126, 127, 131, 139, 139, 150, 150
POWERS: 146
PRAISE/PRAISED/PRAISES/PRAISING (OWED TO A MONARCH): 2, 21, 38, 39, 39, 60, 62, 69, 69, 70, 70, 72, 79, 80, 82, 83, 84, 84, 84, 85, 85, 85, 95, 98, 101, 101, 103, 106, 106, 106, 112 (WORD COUNT: 31)
PRAY: 143
PRAYERS (these sonnets): 108
PRECIOUS (ROYAL): 30, 57, 77, 85, 86, 131
PREDICT: 14
PREFIGURING: 106
PREPARE: 13, 114
PREPOSTEROUSLY: 109
PRESAGE/PRESAGERS: 23, 107
PRESCRIPTIONS: 147
PRESENCE: 10, 67
PRESENT (time of the diary): 45, 47, 106, 115, 123
PRESENTS/PRESENTETH: 15, 27, 79
Preserve: 147
PRESS: 140
Presume: 22
PRETTY (ROYAL): 41, 132, 139

REFERENCE EDITION 839

PREVAILED: 41
PREVENT/PREVENT'ST: 100, 118
PREY: 48, 74
PRICKED (selected): 20
PRIDE (see Proud) (ROYALTY/ROYAL POWER): 25, 52, 76, 80, 91, 99, 99, 103, 104, 144, 151
PRIME: 3, 12, 70
PRINCES/PRINCES': 14, 25, 55
PRINT: 11
PRISON: 133
PRISONER: 5
PRIVATE: 9
PRIVILEGE (of a Monarch): 58, 95
PRIZE/PRIZING (ROYAL PRINCE): 48, 86, 143, 151
PROCEED: 76
PROCLAIMS (proclamation of James): 107
PROFANE/PROFANED: 89, 127, 141
PROFIT: 77
PROFITLESS: 4
PROFOUND: 112
PROGNOSTICATE: 14
PROGRESS: 77
PROMISE: 34
PROOF: 110, 117, 129
PROPHECIES: 106
PROPHETIC: 107
PROPOSED: 129
PROUD/PROUDEST/PROUDER/PROUDLY (see Pride) (ROYAL): 2, 2, 21, 25, 64, 67, 78, 80, 86, 91, 98, 98, 131, 140, 141, 149, 151 (WORD COUNT: 17)
PROUD PIED: 98
PROVE/PROVING/PROVED/PROVES: 2, 8, 10, 26, 32, 48, 72, 110, 116, 117, 125, 129, 136, 151, 154
PROVIDE: 111
PROVIDENT (see Unprovident)
Provoke: 50
Pry: 61
PUBLIC: 25, 36, 111, 111
PUBLISH ("SHAKESPEARE"): 102
Pupil: 16
PURCHASED: 117
PURPLE (ROYAL BLOOD): 99
PURE/PUREST: 66, 70, 110
PURGE/PURGING: 45, 118
PURPOSE/PURPOSED: 20, 21, 90, 112, 126, 129
PURSUIT/PURSUING: 75, 143
PUT/PUTS: 23, 26, 50, 148
PYRAMIDS (THE SONNETS): 123

Quality: 14
Qualify: 109
QUEEN (ELIZABETH): 96
QUENCHED: 154
QUEST: 46, 129
Question: 12, 57
QUICK/QUICKER/QUICKLY: 45, 55, 76, 113, 153
QUIET: 27

QUIETUS: 126
QUILL

RACE: 51
RACK: 33; (see Wrackful)
RAGE: 13, 17, 23, 64, 65
Ragged: 6
Raiment: 22
RAIN/RAINY (reign): 14, 34, 90
RAISED: 150
RANDOM: 147
Ranged: 109
RANK/RANKS: 32, 69, 85, 118, 121, 122
RANSOM/RANSOMS: 34, 120, 120
RARE/RARITIES (ROYAL): 21, 52, 60, 130
Rather: 123
RAVEN (Tower Bird): 127
RAZED: 25, 64, 122
READ: 14, 23, 32, 71; (O'er-Read: 81)
REAR/REARWARD (see Uprear: 49): 90
REASON/REASONS: 49, 49, 89, 115, 129, 129, 147, 147, 151
REBEL: 146
REBUKED: 119
RECEIPT: 136
RECEIVE/RECEIV'ST/RECEIVEST/RECEIVING: 8, 8, 40, 44, 122, 135
RECITE: 72
RECKON/RECKONED/RECKONING: 115, 121, 136
RECORD/RECORDS: 55, 59, 122, 123
RECOUNTING: 45
RECURED: 45
RED: 130, 130
REDEEM: 100
REEKS: 130
Reeleth: 7
REFIGURED: 6
REFUSE/REFUSEST: 40, 150
REGION (ELIZABETH REGINA): 33
REGISTER/REGISTERS: 108, 123
REHEARSE: 21, 71, 81
REIGN/REIGNS: 28, 31, 121
RELEASING (from prison): 87
RELIEF: 34
RELIGIOUS: 31
REMAIN: 36, 39, 122
REMEDY: 62, 154
REMEMBER/REMEMBRANCE/REMEMB'RED: 3, 5, 30, 120, 122
REMOTE: 44
REMOVE/REMOVED/REMOVER: 25, 25, 31, 44, 97, 116, 116
RENDER: 125, 126
RENEW/RENEWED: 56, 111
RENT/RENTS: 125, 142
REPAIR: 3, 10, 16
REPENT: 34
REPLETE: 113

REPORT: 36, 95, 96
REPOSE: 27, 50
REPROACH: 121
REQUIRE: 57
RESEMBLE/RESEMBLING: 7, 8, 114
RESERVE: 85
Resort: 96
RESPECT (see Unrespected): 26, 36, 149
REST/RESTFUL: 61, 66, 73, 91, 115; (Ill Wresting: 140)
RESTY: 100
RESTORED: 30
RETENTION: 122
RETURN/RETURNED: 28, 45, 56, 100, 119
REVENGE. 149
REVENUES: 142
REVIEW/REVIEWEST: 74, 74
REVOLT (The Rebellion): 92
REVOLUTION: 59
RHETORIC: 82
RHYME: 16, 17, 32, 55, 107
RHYMERS: 38
RID: 139
RIDE: 137
RIGHT/RIGHTLY/RIGHTS (ROYAL): 17; (Write: 21); 23, 46, 46, 66, 68, 88, 94, 112, 117, 137, 144
RICH/RICHES/RICHER/RICHLY (ROYAL): 15, 29, 34, 84, 85, 87, 91, 94, 97, 102, 135, 146
RIGOR: 133
RIOT: 41
RIPE/RIPER: 1, 86, 102
RISE/RISE/RISING: 100, 151, 151
ROBE: 52
ROBBED/ROBS/ROBB'RY/ROBBING: 35, 40, 68, 79, 99, 142
ROCKS: 65
ROLLING: 20
Rondure: 21
ROOF (House of Tudor): 10
ROOT: 55, 142
ROSE/ROSES (TUDOR ROSE): 1, 35, 54, 54, 67, 67, 95, 98, 99, 109, 130, 130 (WORD COUNT: 12)
ROSY (TUDOR ROSE): 116
ROTTEN: 34
Rough: 18
RUDE/RUDELY/RUD'ST: 32, 66, 78, 113, 129
RUIN/RUINATE/RUINED/RUINING: 10, 64, 73, 119, 125
Ruminate: 64
RUN/RUN'ST: 51, 143
Ruth: 132

SABLE: 12
SACRED: 7, 115
SAD: 30, 56, 57, 65, 153
SAID (see Say): 42, 56, 115, 145
SAIL: 80, 86, 117
SAINT: 144
SAITH (see Say): 114
SAKE: 42, 42,42, 111, 134, 145, 149

Index – Words Of The Sonnets

SALUTATION: 121
SALVE/SALVING: 34, 35, 120
SAME: 50, 69, 76
SAP: 5, 15
SATIRE: 100
SATURN: 98
SAUCES/SAUCY: 80, 118, 128
SAVAGE: 129
SAVE: 12, 27, 48, 57, 66, 75, 109, 131
SAVED: 145
Savor: 125
SAW (see See): 119
SAY/SAYS/SAITH/SAYING (see Said): 13, 14, 21; (Hear-Say: 21); 23, 43, 46, 59, 71, 79, 84, 84, 89, 96, 96, 108, 109, 113, 114, 115, 115, 117, 131, 131, 137, 138, 138; (Saying: 145); 148, 148, 148, 149
SCANDAL: 112
SCANTED: 117
'SCAPED: 90
SCARLET: 142
Scarcely: 49
SCOPE: 29, 52, 61, 103, 105
SCORE: 122
SCORN/SCORNED: 17, 29, 88
SCYTHE (Time's Scythe) (see Sickle): 12, 60, 100, 123
SEA (ROYAL): 44, 65, 113, 135
SEAL/SEALS/SEALED: 11, 73, 142
SEASONS/SEASONS'/SEASON'D (Time): 14, 19, 75, 104
SEAT (THRONE) (see Sit): 41, 105
SECOND: 59, 68, 68, 73
SECONDS: 125
SECRET: 15
SEE/SEEING/SEEN/SEE'ST (see Sight): 2, 3, 12, 18, 24, 24, 33; (Unseen: 33); 37, 43; (Un-Seeing: 43); 43, 43, 49, 56, 56, 59, 63, 64, 64, 64, 64, 67, 68, 69, 73, 92, 96, 97, 99, 104, 106, 106, 113, 113, 114; (Unseen: 118); 121, 123, 125, 137, 137, 137, 137, 148, 149, 150
SEEK/SEEKING: 10, 50, 67, 142
SEEM/SEEMED/SEEMING/SEEMS: 8, 23, 26, 28, 51, 54, 72, 90, 90, 93, 97, 98, 101, 102, 104, 109, 113, 127, 135, 138
Seemly: 22
SEETHING: 153
SELDOM: 52, 52
SELF (SELFE): (Self-Substantial: 1); 1, 3, 4, 4, 4, 4, 6, 6, 6, 6, 7, 9, 10, 10, 10, 10, 13, 13, 13, 13, 14; (Self-Same: 15); 16, 16, 16, 16, 21, 22, 22, 27, 29, 29, 35, 35, 38, 38, 39, 40, 40, 47, 49, 55, 58, 58; (Self-Doing: 58); (Self-Love: 62); 62, 62, 62, 62, 62, (My Self: 62); 62; (It Self: 64, 66, 68); 73; (Thy Self: 79); (Your Self: 83); (Thy Self: 87); (My Self: 88, 88, 88); (My Self: 89, 89); (Thy Self: 92); (It Self: 94); (My Self: 108, 108, 110); 114; (My Self: 119), 126; (MY NEXT SELF: 133); (My Self: 133, 134, 134); (Self Example: 142); (My Self: 149, 149, 149); 151
Sell/Selling: 21, 146
SELVES: Them-Selves: 12, 25, 121
SEMBLANCE (see Resemble): 13
SEND'ST: 61
SENSE/SENSES: 35, 112, 120, 141
SENSUAL: 35, 141
SEPARABLE: 36
SEPARATION: 39
SEPULCHERS: 68
SEQUENT: 60

SERVANT/SERVICE/SERVICES/SERVING/SERVANT'S: 7, 57, 57, 141, 146, 149
SESSIONS (THE TRIAL): 30
SET/SETS: 15; (Unset: 16); 60, 88, 88, 89, 143
SETTLED: 49
SEVERAL: 137
SHADE/SHADY: 18, 43, 43, 53, 77
SHADOW/SHADOWS: 27, 37, 43, 43, 43, 53, 53, 53, 61, 67, 98
SHAKE/SHAKEN (see Shook): 18, 28, 73, 116, 120
SHALLOWEST: 80
SHAME/SHAMED/SHAMEFULLY/SHAMES: 1, 9, 10, 34, 36, 61, 66, 72, 72, 95, 99, 112, 127, 129
SHAPE/SHAPES (see Image, Figure, etc): 9, 24, 53, 62, 113, 113
SHARE: 47
SHARP/SHARPENED/SHARP'ST: 50, 56, 115
SHE (ELIZABETH): 3, 3, 4, 11, 11, 11, 20, 20, 42, 42, 42, 67, 126, 126, 130; (As Any She: 130); 138, 138, 138, 138, 138, 138, 138, 139, 141, 145, 145, 154
Sheaves: 12
Sheeds (sheds): 34
SHIFTING/SHIFTS: 9, 20
SHINE/SHINES: 18, 33, 43, 55, 65, 135
SHOOK: 104
SHOOT: 117
Shop: 24
SHORE: 56, 59, 64
SHORN: 68
SHORT: 18, 124, 125
SHOW/SHOWING/SHOWS/SHOWN/SHOW'ST: 5, 15, 16, 26, 26, 26, 26, 40, 43, 43, 54, 59, 62, 67, 68, 69, 69, 70, 76, 77, 77, 93, 94, 101, 102, 103, 103, 105, 108, 121, 126
SHOWERS: 75
SHUN: 118, 129
SICK/SICKEN/SICKLY/SICKNESS: 78, 86, 118, 118, 118, 118, 140, 147
SICKLE/SICKLE'S (see Scythe): 116, 126
SIDE/SIDES: 50, 88, 138, 144, 151, 154
SIEGE: 65
SIGH/SIGHS: 30, 47
SIGNS: 68
SIGHT/SIGHTLESS (see See): 15, 27, 27, 30, 38, 43, 46, 46, 47, 61, 63, 75, 113, 117, 123, 139, 148, 150
SILENCE/SILENT: 23, 30, 83, 86, 101
SILVER/SILVERED: 12, 35
SIMPLE/SIMPLY/SIMPLICITY: (Simple-Truth: 66); 66, 125, 138, 138
SIN/SINS/SINFUL: 35, 35, 62, 62, 67, 83, 95, 103, 114, 141, 142, 142, 142, 146
SINCE: 20, 32, 49, 51, 53, 59, 65, 67, 67, 79, 80, 92, 104, 105, 107, 113, 117, 127, 128
SING/SINGS (WITH THE SONNETS) (see Song): 8, 8, 29, 39, 78, 97, 100, 102, 106
SINGLE/SINGLENESS: 3, 8, 8, 9, 39
SINKS (see Sunk): 45
SIRE (OXFORD): 8
SIREN (Syren): 119
SIT (ON THRONE) (see Seat): 103
SITUATION: 128
SKILL: 16, 24, 100, 126, 150
SKY: 15
SLAY/SLAIN: 22, 139, 139
SLANDER/SLANDERED/SLANDER'S/SLAND'RING/SLANDERERS: 70, 70, 127, 127, 131, 140
SLAVE/SLAVERY: 57, 57, 58, 64, 133, 133, 141
SLEEP/SLEPT/SLEEPING: 43, 43, 47, 83, 87, 154

Index – Words Of The Sonnets

SLOW: 44, 51, 51, 94
SLUMBERS: 61
Sluttish: 55
SMALL: 2, 84
SMELL/SMELLS: 69, 94, 99, 141
SMILING: 124
SMOKE: 34
SMOTHER: 47
Snow/Snowed (see O'er-Snowed: 5): 130
Sober: 132
Soft: 99
SOIL: 64, 69
SOLEMN: 52
SOME: 3, 6, 13, 17, 23, 26, 50, 52, 53, 70, 72, 74, 82, 84, 89, 90, 90, 90, 90, 90, 90, 90, 90, 96, 96, 96, 99, 130, 131, 138
Some-Thing: 85, 136
Sometime: 18; Some-Time: 18, 41, 64, 75, 102
SON: SONNE: 7; SON: 13; SONNE: 41
SONG/SONGS (The Sonnets): 8, 17, 102, 105
SOON/SOONER: 44, 120, 129, 129, 144
SORROW/SORROWS: 28, 30, 34, 90, 120, 120, 140
SORRY: 19
SORT: 36, 96
SOUGHT: 30
SOUL/SOULS/SOUL'S: 20, 26, 27, 62, 69, 109, 125, 136, 136, 136, 146, 146, 151
SOUNDLESS: 80
SOUND/SOUNDS: 8, 128, 130, 145
SOUR/SOUREST/SOURLY: 35, 39, 57, 94
SOVEREIGN: 33, 57, 126, 153
SPACE: 44
SPACIOUS: 135
SPARKLING: 28
SPEAK/SPEAKING: 23, 34, 53, 72, 80, 83, 85, 89, 100, 108, 130; (False Speaking: 138); 140
SPECIAL: 52, 52
SPEECHLESS (see Dumb, Mute, Silent, etc.): 8, 107
SPEED: 50, 51, 51
SPEND/SPENDING/SPENT/SPEND'ST: 4, 9, 76, 76, 80, 100, 100, 105, 107, 119, 125, 146, 149
SPHERES (Spheares): 119
SPIES: 121
SPIRIT/SPIRITS: 56, 61, 74, 80, 85, 86, 86, 98, 108, 129, 144, 144
SPITE/SPITES: 36, 37, 40, 90, 90, 107
SPLENDOR (ROYALTY): 33
SPOIL/SPOILS: 65, 100
SPORT/SPORTIVE: 95, 96, 121
SPOT: 95
SPREAD: 25
SPRING/SPRINGS (Hopeful Time): 1, 53, 63, 98, 102, 104
SPUR/SPURRING: 50, 50, 51
STAGE: 15, 23
STAIN/STAINED/STAINETH: 33, 33, 35; (Unstained: 70); 109, 109
STAMP/STAMPED: 82, 111
STAND/STANDS: 16, 38, 44, 60, 60, 99, 104, 124, 125, 151
STAR/STARS (ROYAL; ROYAL SON): 14, 14, 15, 25, 26, 28, 116, 132
STARVED: 75
STATE: 15, 29, 29, 29, 64, 64, 92, 96, 118, 124, 128, 142, 145, 150

STATUES: 55
STATUTE: 134
STAY/STAYS: 43, 44, 48, 57, 58, 74, 143, 151
STEAL/STEALS/STEALING (see Stole, Stol'n): 20, 33, 36, 40, 63, 67, 75, 92, 99, 104
STEALTH: 77
STEEL/STEELED: 65, 112, 120, 133
Steeled (stelled): 24
Steep/Steepy: 7, 63
STERN: 96
STEWARDS: 94
Stick'st: 10
STILL (always/constantly/eternally): 5, 9, 10, 16, 24, 28, 34, 47, 47, 55, 63, 65, 74, 76, 76, 76, 81, 85, 93, 98, 104, 104, 105, 105, 106, 119, 119, 126, 126, 135, 144, 147, 153
STILL (verb): 143
STIRRED: 21
STOLE/STOL'N (see Steal): 31, 48, 79, 99, 99, 99
STONE: 55, 65, 94
STONES (jewels): 52
STOP/STOPS/STOPPED: 3, 44, 102, 112
STORE/STORES/STORE'S: 11, 14, 37, 64, 64, 67, 68, 84, 135, 136, 146
STORM/STORMY: 13; (Storm-Beaten: 34)
STORY: 84, 88, 95, 98
STOUT: 65
STRAIGHT: 45, 89, 100, 121, 129, 140, 145
STRAINED/STRAINS: 82, 90
STRANGE/STRANGELY: 49, 53, 76, 89, 93, 110, 123, 153
STRANGLE: 89
STRAYING: 41
Streams: 33
STRENGTH/STRENGTH'S/STRENGTHENED (ROYALTY) (see Strong): 23, 23, 49, 66, 96, 102, 150
STRETCHED: 17
STRIFE (see Strive): 75
Strikes: 8
String: 8
STRIPPED: (Out-Stripped: 32)
STRIVE/STRIVE/STRIVING (see Strife): 103, 112, 117
STRONG/STRONGER/STRONGLY (ROYAL) (see Strength): 7, 28, 34, 58, 65, 65, 65, 73, 111, 112, 115, 119
STRUCK: 86
STRUMPETED: 66
STYLE: 32, 84
SUBDUED: 111
SUBJECT/SUBJECTS: 38, 59, 82, 84, 100, 103, 124
SUBORNED: 125
SUBSCRIBES (submits): 107
SUBSTANCE: 5, 37, 44, 53
SUBSTANTIAL: 1
SUBTLETIES: 138
SUCCEEDING: 19
SUCCESSION: 2
SUCCESSIVE: 127
SUCH: 17, 25, 29, 34, 35, 36, 54, 63, 64, 73, 73, 78, 84, 87, 103, 104, 105, 114, 127, 130, 150
Sufficed: 37
SUFFER/SUFFERS/SUFFERED/SUFFERANCE/SUFF'RING: 42, 58, 58, 120, 124, 146
SUFFICIENCY (Insufficiency: 150)

Index – Words Of The Sonnets

SUGGEST: 144
SUIT/SUITED: 127, 132; (Love-Suit: 136)
SULLEN: 29, 71
SULLIED: 15
SUM/SUMS: 2, 4, 4. 49, 109
SUMMER/SUMMER'S/SUMMERS' (Royal Time): 5, 5, 6, 12, 18, 18, 18, 54, 56, 65, 68, 94, 94, 97, 97, 98, 102, 102, 104, 104
SUMMON: 30
SUN/SUNNE (ROYAL SON: SOUTHAMPTON): SUNNE: 21; SUN: 24; SUN'S (monarch's): 25; MY SUNNE: 33; SUNS: 33; SUN: 33; SUNNE: 35; SUNNE, 49; SUNNE: 59; SUN-SET: 73; SUN: 76; SUNNE: 130; SUN: 132; SUNNE: 148 (WORD COUNT: 14)
SUNK/SUNKEN: 2, 12
SUPPOSE/SUPPOSED/SUPPOSING: 31, 57, 93, 107
SUPPRESSED: 138
Sure: 59, 131
SURETY-LIKE: 134
SURFEIT: 75
SURLY: 71
SURMISE: 117
SURMOUNT: 62
SURVEY (Re-Survey: 32); 52, 100
SURVIVE: 32, 81
SUSPECT: 70, 70, 144
SWALLOWED: 129
SWART: 28
SWAY/SWAYS: (O'er-Sways: 65); 66; (Unswayed: 141); 150
SWEAR/SWEARS/SWEARING (see Sworn): 131, 131, 132, 136, 138, 150, 151, 151, 151
SWEET/SWEETLY/SWEETS/SWEETEST/
SWEET'ST/SWEETNESS (ROYAL): 1, 4, 5, 6, 8, 8, 8, 8, 8, 12, 13, 13, 13, 16, 19, 19, 26, 29, 30, 35, 35, 36, 38, 39, 39, 42, 52, 54, 54, 54, 54, 54, 56, 63, 70, 70, 71, 73, 75, 76, 78, 79, 89, 93, 93, 93, 94, 94, 95, 95, 98, 98, 99, 99, 99, 100, 102, 104, 106, 108; (Sweet-Favor: 113); 114, 118, 125, 126, 127, 128, 133, 135, 136, 145, 151
(WORD COUNT: 70)
Swept (see Unswept)
SWERVING: 87
SWIFT: (Swift-Footed: 19); 45, 45, 51, 65, 143
SWORD: 55
SWORN (see Swear): 147, 151, 151
SYMPATHIZED: 82

TABLE/TABLES: 24, 122, 122
TAKE/TAKES/TAKEN/TAKER (see Took): 12, 15; (O'er-Take: 34); 36, 37, 37, 40, 40, 64, 77, 81, 95, 120, 125, 129
TALL: 80
TALLIES: 122
TAME: 58
TAN/TANNED: 62, 115
TASK: 72
TASTE: 77, 90, 141
TAUGHT: 64, 77, 86, 114, 145, 150
TEACH/TEACHEST: 39, 101, 140
TEARS: 34, 119, 148, 148
TEEMING: 97
Teeth: 19
TELL/TELLS/TELLING (see Told): 3, 12, 14, 14; ("fel" for Tell in Q: 76); 76, 84, 89, 95, 98, 103, 140, 144
TEMPERATE: 18

TEMPESTS: 116
TEMPTING/TEMPTATION/TEMPTETH: 41, 41, 94, 144
TEN: 6, 6, 6, 6, 6, 37, 38
TENANTS: 46
TEND: 53
TENDER/TEND'RED: 1, 1, 22, 22, 45, 82, 120, 128, 141
TENOR: 61
TENTH: 38
TERM (Prison): 92
TERMED: 17
TERMS: 146
TESTY: 140
THANK/THANKS: 38, 79
THEFT (see Thief): 99
THEMES: 105
Thereof: 80
THIEF/THIEVISH (see Theft): 35, 40, 48, 48, 77, 99
THINE: 133, 134, 142, 142
THING/THINGS: 20, 21, 23, 30, 30, 31, 49, 94, 95, 96, 107, 108, 114, 136; (Some-Thing: 136); 143, 152
THINK/THINKING/THINKS (see Thought): 29, 30, 44, 57, 57, 57, 71; (Methinks: 104); 111, 112, 121, 123, 130, 131, 131, 137, 138, 138, 138
THINLY: 52
THIRD: 99
THITHER: 153
THORNS: 35, 54, 99
THOUGHT/THOUGHTS (see Think): 10, 26, 27, 29, 30, 31, 39, 39, 44, 44, 44, 44, 45, 46, 47, 47, 57, 58, 64, 69, 69, 71, 75, 82, 85, 85, 85, 86, 88, 93, 110, 119, 121, 147, 147 (WORD COUNT: 35)
THOUSAND: 25, 131, 141
THRALL/THRALLED: 124, 154
THREE: 104, 104, 104, 104, 104, 105, 105
THREE-FOLD: 133
THREESCORE: 11
THREW: 145
THRICE: 56, 119, 133
THRIFT/THRIFTLESS: 2; (Unthrift: 9); (Unthrifts: 13)
THRIVE/THRIVERS: 80, 125
THRONED: 96
Through: 3, 24, 34, 43
THROW: 112
THRUST: 48
Thunder: 14
Tickled: 128
TIE: 117
TIGER'S: 19
TILL: 20, 26, 26, 43, 55, 56, 105, 144, 148
Tillage: 3
TIME/TIMES/TIME'S (ELIZABETH'S LIFE): 1, 3, 3, 5, 6, 6, 6, 11, 12, 12, 12, 15, 15, 16, 16, 17, 17, 18, 19, 19, 19, 22, 30, 32, 37, 38, 39, 39, 44, 47, 49, 49, 49, 49, 52, 55, 57, 57, 58, 58, 60, 60, 60, 63, 63, 64, 64, 65, 65, 65, 73, 76, 77, 82, 97, 97, 100, 100, 100, 100, 106, 106, 107; (UNIVERSAL TIME): 108, 109, 109, 115, 115, 116, 117, 120, 123, 124, 124, 124, 124, 126, 126
(WORD COUNT: 78)
TIME BETTERING: 81
TINCTURE: 54
TIRED/TY'RD: 50, 66, 66

Index – Words Of The Sonnets

TIRES: 53
TITLES/TITLES: 25, 46, 92
TODAY: 56, 56, 105
TOGETHER: 14
TOIL/TOILED: 25, 27, 28, 28, 60
TOLD (see Tell): 45, 76, 123
TOMB/TOMBED/TOMBS: 3, 4, 17; (Entombed: 81; Q = Intombed); 83, 86, 101, 107
TOMORROW: 56, 56, 105
TONGUE/TONGUES/TONGUE'S: 17, 23, 66, 69, 69, 80, 81, 85, 89, 95, 102, 102, 106, 112, 127, 138, 139, 140, 141, 145
TONGUE-TIED: 66, 80, 85, 140
TOOK (see Take): 154, 154
TOP/TOPS: 16, 33
TORMENT: 39, 132, 133
TORN: 152
TORTURE: 28, 133
Tottered: 2, 26
TOUCH/TOUCHES/TOUCHED: 17, 17, 42, 82, 141, 153
TOWARD/TOWARDS: 9, 51, 60
TOWERS: 64
Tract: 7
Traffic: 4
TRANSFERRED: 137
TRANSFIX: 60
TRANSGRESSION: 120
TRANSLATE/TRANSLATED: 96, 96
TRANSPORT: 117
TRAVAIL/TRAVAILED: 27, 34, 63, 79
TRAVEL'S/TRAVELS: 50, 108
TREADS: 130
TREASON: 151
TREASURE (OF ROYAL BLOOD): 2, 6, 6, 20, 52, 63, 75, 126, 136
Trees: 12
Trenches: 2
TRESPASS (TREASON): 35, 120
TRESSES: 68
TRIAL: 153
TRIBES: 107
TRIFLES: 48
TRIMMED: 66
TRIPPING: 154
TRIUMPH/TRIUMPHANT: 25, 33, 52, 151, 151
TROPHIES: 31
TROUBLE: 29
TRUANT: 101
TRUE/TRULY/TRUEST (OXFORD): 8, 17, 21, 21, 40, 48, 57, 61, 62, 67, 72, 77, 82, 82, 82, 82, 85, 93, 96, 105, 105, 105, 107, 108, 110, 110, 113; (Untrue: 113); 114, 116, 118, 118, 119, 120, 123, 125, 132, 137, 148, 148, 148, 150, 154
(WORD COUNT: 44)
TRUST: 23, 48, 122, 129, 138
TRUTH/TRUTH'S/TRUTHS (OXFORD): 14, 14, 17, 37, 41, 48, 54, 54, 60, 62, 66, 69, 72, 96, 101, 101, 101, 101, 110, 137, 138, 138, 147, 152, 152
(WORD COUNT: 25)
TRY (in trial): 110
TUNE/TUNED: 8, 141

TURN/TURNS/TURNED/TURN'D: 24, 47, 94, 95, 104, 138, 143, 143, 144
Tutored: (Untutored: 138)
TWAIN: 36, 39
TWENTY: 152
TWILIGHT (Twi-light): 73
TWICE: 17, 152
TWIRE: 28
TWIXT: 75, 115
TWO: 132, 144, 144, 152
TWO-FOLD: 41
TYRANT/TYRANTS/TYRANTS'/TYRANNY/TYRANNOUS: 5, 16, 107, 115, 120, 131, 149

UGLY: 33
UNBLESS: 3
UNBRED: 104
UNDER: 7, 48, 78, 120, 124
UNDIVIDED: 36
UNEARED: 3
UNFAIR: 5
UN-FATHERED: 97, 124
UNFOLDING: 52
UNHAPPILY: 66
UNIONS: 8
UNIVERSE: 109
UNKIND/UNKINDNESS: 120, 120, 134, 135, 139
UNKNOWN: 116, 117
UNLEARNED: 138
Unless: 7, 36, 65, 121
UNLOOKED: Unlooked On: 7; Unlooked For: 25
UNMOVED: 94
Unperfect: 23
Unprovident: 10
UNRESPECTED: 43, 54
UNREST: 147
UNSEEING: 43
UNSEEN: 33, 118
UNSET: 16
UNSTAINED (see Stain): 70
UNSWAYED (see Sway): 141
UNSWEPT: 55
UNTAINTED: 19
Unto: 47
UNTRIMMED (see Trimmed: 66): 18
UNTHRIFT/UNTHRIFTS/UNTHRIFTY: 4, 9, 13
UNTRUE (see True): 72, 113
UNUSED/UN-USED: 4, 9, 30, 48
UNWOO'D: 54
UNWORTHINESS (see Worth): 151
UP: (Steep Up: 7); 114, 154
UPHOLD: 13
UP-LOCKED: 52
UPREAR: 49
URGE: 118

850

USE/USED/USER/USEST: 4, 4, 9, 40, 78, 82, 134, 139
USHERS: 132
USURER: 4, 134
USURY: 6
UTMOST: 49
UTTERING: 69

VACANT: 77
VADE: 54
VAINLY: 138, 147
VALLEY (VALLIE-FOUNTAIN): 153
VANISHED/VANISHING: 30, 63, 63
VANTAGE: 88, 88
VARIATION: 76
VARYING: 105
VASSAL: 58, 141
VASSALAGE: 26
VAUNT: 15
VEIL: 95
VEINS: 67, 99
VENGEFUL: 99
VERDICT: 46
VERMILLION: 98
VERSE/VERSES: 17, 19, 38, 54, 60, 71, 76, 78, 79, 81, 86, 103, 103   (WORD COUNT: 13)
VERY: 74, 90, 150
VEX/VEXED: 92, 135, 148
VIAL: 6
VICE/VICES: 70, 95
VICTOR/VICTORS: 70, 86
VICTORIES: 25
VIEW/VIEWEST: 3, 43, 56, 110, 141
VILE/VILEST: 71, 71, 121, 121
VIOLET (ROYAL): 12, 99
VIRGIN (ELIZABETH): 154
VIRTUE/VIRTUOUS (vertue) (ROYAL): 16, 54, 66, 72, 79, 81, 88, 93, 117, 141
VISAGE: 33
VISION: 113
VOICE/VOICES: 69, 112
VOTARY (ELIZABETH): 154
VOUCHSAFE: 32, 135
VOW/VOWS/VOWING/VOWED: 89, 115, 123, 152, 152, 152, 154
VULGAR: 38, 48, 112

WAIL/WAILING: 9, 30, 42
WAIT/WAITING: 58, 58
WAKE/WAKING/WAKENED: 61, 87, 117
WALK/WALKS (verb): 128, 130
WALKS (noun): 89
WALLS: 5, 146
WANDR'ST/WANDERING: 18, 116
WANE/WANING (by Elizabeth'sTime; by Mortal Moon's Waning): 11, 126
WANT/WANTING: 26, 38, 87, 140
WANTON/WANTONLY/WANTONNESS: 54, 96, 97
WAR/WAR'S: 16, 35, 46, 55, 55

Wardrobe: 52
WARD/WARDS: 48, 133
WARNING: 71
WARRANTISE: 150
WARRIOR: 25
WARM: 2
WASTE/WASTEFUL/WASTES/WASTED: 1, 9, 12, 15, 30, 55, 77, 77, 100, 106, 125, 129
WATCH/WATCHING: 57, 61, 148
WATCHMAN: 61
WATER/WATERY (ROYAL): 44, 64, 109, 135, 154, 154
WAVES (ROYAL): 60
WAY: 50
WE: 1, 53, 54, 106, 123, 138
WEAK/WEAKENS/WEAKNESS: 23, 34, 88, 102
WEALTH: 29, 37, 67, 75, 91, 91
WEAR: 15, 55, 77
WEARY: 7, 27, 50
WEED (garb/costume/covering): 76
WEED/WEEDS: 1, 69, 94, 94
WEEP: 9; (Beweep: 29); 30, 64
WEIGH/WEIGHS: 108, 120
WEIGHT: 50
WELCOME: 56, 110
WELFARE: 118
WELL: 14, 32, 34, 40, 58, 85, 96, 112, 129, 129, 130, 139, 148
WEST: 33, 73, 132
Wet: 9
WHATSOEVER: 26
WHERE: 48
WHEREVER: 45
Whilst: 143
WHITE: 12, 12, 98, 99, 99, 130, 130
WHOLE: 134
WIDE: 19, 107, 109, 137, 140
WIDOW/WIDOW'S/WIDOWED: 9, 9, 9, 97
WIFE: 9; (Huswife: 143)
WIGHTS (SOUTHAMPTON): 106
WILD: 102
WILL: Will: 57; will: 61; will: 134, 135, 135, 135, 135, 135, 136, 136, 136, 136 (WORD COUNT: 14)
WILL: 135, 135, 135, 135, 135, 135, 135, 136, 136, 136, 143 (WORD COUNT: 11)
WILFUL/WILLFULL/WILFULLY/WILFULNESS: 40, 51, 80, 117
WILLED (Self-Willed: 6)
WILLING/WILLINGLY: 6, 72, 111
WILLS: 121
WIN: 119, 144
WINDOWS: 3, 24, 24
Winds: 18
WINDY: 90
WINGED: 51
Wink: 43, 56
WINTER/WINTERS/WINTER'S: 2, 5, 5, 6, 13, 56, 97, 97, 98, 104
WIRES: 130, 130
WIRY: 128
WISDOM: 11

Index – Words Of The Sonnets

WISE: 71, 140
WISH/WISHING/WISHED: 16, 29, 37, 37, 56, 111, 111, 135
WIT/WITS: 23, 26, 26, 37, 84, 140, 141
WITHERING: 126
WITNESS: 124, 131
WITS (wise men): 59
WITHAL (WITHALL): 154
WITHIN: 116, 122, 146, 146
WITHOUT: 57, 146
WITNESS: 26
WOE/WOES/WOEFUL: 30, 30, 30, 44, 50, 71, 90, 90, 90, 120, 127, 129, 145 (WORD COUNT: 13)
WOLF: 96
WOMAN/WOMAN'S/WOMEN'S (ELIZABETH): 20, 20, 20, 20, 20, 20, 41, 41, 144
WOMB/WOMBS: 3, 86, 97
WON: 41
WONDER/WONDERING: 59, 98, 106, 123
WONDROUS (ROYAL): 105, 105
WONT: 102
WOO/WOOS/WOOED/WOOING: 41, 70, 142, 144
WOOD/WOOD'S: 128, 128, 128
WORD/WORDS: 26, 76, 76, 79, 82, 82, 85, 85, 85, 105, 140, 140
WORK/WORK'S/WORKS: 27, 27, 55, 78, 111, 124
WORKINGS: 93
WORLD/WORLD'S (ENGLAND): 1, 1, 1, 3, 9, 9, 9, 9, 9, 11, 19, 33, 55, 57, 59, 69, 71, 71, 71, 72, 75, 81, 81, 90, 107, 112, 112, 129, 137, 138, 140, 148 (WORD COUNT: 32)
WORMS: 6, 71, 74, 146
WORSE/WORST/WORSER: 58, 80, 84, 84, 90, 92, 92, 94, 110, 137, 144, 151
WORSHIP: 149
WORTH/WORTHS/WORTHY/WORTHINESS/WORTHIER (ROYAL): 2, 16, 25, 26, 37, 38, 38, 39, 48, 52, 52, 60, 61, 61, 70, 72, 72, 74, 79, 80, 82, 83, 83, 87, 87, 103, 106, 116, 151 (WORD COUNT: 27)
WORTHLESS (see Unworthiness): 80, 100
WOUND/WOUNDED: 34, 120, 133, 139, 139
WRACK/WRACKFUL (see Rack): 65, 126
WRECKED (WRACKT): 80
WRESTING: 140
WRETCH/WRETCH'S/WRETCHED: 50, 74, 91, 91, 119, 126, 141
WRINKLE/WRINKLES (Time): 3, 63, 77, 93, 100, 108
WRIT: 23, 71, 84, 93, 115, 116
WRITE/WRITES: 17, 38, 76, 76, 80, 84, 85, 86, 103, 134
WRITERS: 82
WRITTEN: 26
WRONG/WRONGS: 19, 40, 41, 88, 89, 112, 139
WROUGHT: 20, 44

YE: 111
Y'ARE (you are): 112
YELLOW/YELLOWED: 17, 73, 104
Yet: 7, 14, 82, 133
YIELD: 81
YORE: 68
YOU: 13, 15, 16, 17, 24, 52, 53, 54, 55, 57, 58, 71, 72, 75, 76, 80, 81, 83, 84, 85, 86, 98, 102, 103, 104, 106, 111, 112, 113, 114, 115, 118, 120 of the Fair Youth series; and 145 of the Dark Lady series
YOUNG/YOUNGLY: 11, 19, 138, 151
YOURS: 120, 120

YOUR SELF: 13, 13, 13, 16, 16, 16, 16, 83
YOUTH: 11, 15, 15, 22, 41, 54, 60, 73, 96, 96, 110, 138
YOUTHFUL: 15, 63

ZEALOUS: 27

Capitalized and/or Italicized Words

The following words in the 1609 Quarto are capitalized and/or italicized as shown below in alphabetical order. Indicated are the numbers of the sonnets where they appear. The number of the verse is repeated for each such appearance in the same sonnet.

Abysm: 112
Adder's: 112
Adonis (SOUTHAMPTON): 53
Advocate: 35
Age's: 63, 63
Alchemy: 114
Alien: 78
All: 112
Amen: 85
Antique: 17
April, April's: 3, 21, 98
Art/Art's/Arts: 68, 78, 127, 139
Astronomy: 14
Audit: 4, 126
Augurs: 107
Autumn: 97
Autumn: 104

Babe (SOUTHAMPTON): 118
Beauty/Beauty's (ELIZABETH): 14, 127
Boy (SOUTHAMPTON): 126
But: 110

Canker: 54, 70
Captain: 66
Character: 85
Charter: 87
Chronicle (THE SONNETS): 106
Commend: 69
Creation (SOUTHAMPTON): 127
Crow: 70, 113
Cupid (SOUTHAMPTON): 153, 153

Day: 28
Decembers: 97
Dial: 104
Dian's (ELIZABETH): 153
Doctor-like: 66
Dove: 113
Dyer's: 111
East: 132
Eisel: 111
Elements: 45

Embassy (THE SONNETS): 45
Epitaph: 81
Eve's: 93
Ev'n (evening): 132

Father: 13
Folly: 66
For: 111
Forgoing: 125
Fortune/Fortune's (ELIZABETH): 29, 37

General (SOUTHAMPTON): 154
God: 58
Grant: 82
Grecian: 53

Hawks: 91, 91
Heaven/Heaven's (ELIZABETH): 29, 132
Helen's (ELIZABETH): 53
Heretic: 124
Hews (SOUTHAMPTON): 20
Horse/Horses: 91, 91
Hounds: 91
Hymn: 85

Idol/Idolatry: 105, 105
Image: 3, 24, 61
Ink: 108
Informer: 125
Interim (IMPRISONMENT): 56

Jacks: 128, 128
Jewel/Jewels (SOUTHAMPTON): 52, 96

King/Kings (SOUTHAMPTON): 29, 63, 87, 115
Kingdom: 64
Knights (SOUTHAMPTON): 106

Ladies (ELIZABETH): 106
Lamb/Lambs: 96
Lark: 29
Legions: 154

Lily/Lily's (ELIZABETH): 98, 99
Limbecks: 119
Lion's: 19
Longer: 71
Lords/Lord's: 94, 97

Love/Love's (ROYAL BLOOD): 31, 31, 56, 145
Love-God (SOUTHAMPTON): 154

Majesty (SOUTHAMPTON): 78
Marigold: 25
Mars: 55
Master (SOUTHAMPTON): 20
May: 18
Me: 148
Mistress/Mistress' (ELIZABETH): 20, 127, 130, 130, 130, 154
Moone (ELIZABETH): 21, 35, 107

Muse/Muses: 21, 32, 38, 38, 38, 78, 79, 82, 85, 85, 100, 100, 100, 101, 101, 101, 103
Music: 130

Nature/Nature's (ELIZABETH): 68, 126, 127
Nerves: 120
Never: 83, 109
Nothing (OXFORD/SOUTHAMPTON): 66
Nymphs: 154

O (OXFORD): 126, 148, 149
Ocean: 64, 80
Olives: 107
Orient: 7
Orphans (SOUTHAMPTON): 97

Painter/Painter's: 24, 24
Pen: 81, 84, 106
Philomel: 102
Phoenix (ELIZABETH): 19
Poet/Poets/Poet's: 17, 17, 32, 79, 83, 83

Queen (ELIZABETH): 96
Quietus: 126

Physic: 147
Physician/Physicians: 140, 147
Princes (ELIZABETH/SOUTHAMPTON): 14, 25, 55

Raven (TOWER BIRD): 127
Reason: 147
Rhetoric: 82

Rose (TUDOR ROSE): 1

Rose/Roses (TUDOR ROSE): 54, 54, 54, 67, 95, 98, 99, 109, 130, 130

Satire: 100
Saturn: 98
Sessions (THE TRIAL): 30
Simplicity: 66
Siren: 119
Son: 13
Spheres: 119
Spirit: 129
Star/Stars (SOUTHAMPTON): 15, 132
Statues: 55
Summer/Summer's: 18, 18, 18, 56, 97
Sun (SOUTHAMPTON): 76, 132
Sun-set (SOUTHAMPTON): 73
Sunne (SOUTHAMPTON): 21, 33, 35, 130
Sweet: 54

Thou: 126
Three: 104
Thy: 122
Tiger's: 19
Time/Time's (ELIZABETH): 12, 15, 16, 64, 116, 120, 123
Truth/Truth's (OXFORD): 14, 66

Universe: 109

Virgin (ELIZABETH): 154

Well: 154
West: 73, 132
WHen: 138
WHilst: 79
Will: 57
Will ("SHAKESPEARE"): 135, 135, 135, 135, 135, 135, 136, 136, 136, 143
Winter/Winter's/Winters: 2, 56, 97, 97, 98, 104
Wolf: 96
Woman's (ELIZABETH): 20

Selected Bibliography

THE SONNETS - EDITIONS
Beeching, H. C., *The Sonnets of Shakespeare*, 1904
Booth, Stephen, *Shakespeare's Sonnets*, 1977-2000
Dowden, Edward, *The Sonnets of William Shakespeare*, 1881
Duncan-Jones, Katherine, *Arden Shakespeare's Sonnets*, 1997
Evans, G. Blakemore, *The Sonnets*, 1996
Ingram, W. S., & Redpath, Theodore, *Shakespeare's Sonnets*, 1965
Kerrigan, John, *The Sonnets and A Lover's Complaint*, 1986/1999
Rowse, A. L., *Shakespeare's Sonnets: The Problems Solved*, 1st edition, 1964
Rowse, A. L., *Shakespeare's Sonnets: The Problems Solved*, 2nd edition, 1973
Tucker, T. G., *The Sonnets of Shakespeare*, 1924
Wilson, Dover, *The New Shakespeare: The Sonnets*, 1966
Wright, Louis, *Shakespeare's Sonnets* (Folger), 1967

THE SONNETS - COMMENTARY
Acheson, Arthur, *Mistress Davenant: The Dark Lady of Shakespeare's Sonnets*, 1913
Auden, W. H., Introduction to Signet Classic, *The Sonnets*, 1964
Baldwin, T. W., *On the Literary Genetics of Shakespeare's Poems & Sonnets*, 1950
Dodd, Alfred, *The Mystery of Shake-Speare's Sonnets*, 1947
Fort, J. A., *A Time Scheme for Shakespeare's Sonnets*, 1929
Fowler, Alastair, *Triumphal Forms*, 1970
Frye, Northrop, in *The Riddle of Shakespeare's Sonnets*, 1962
Giroux, Robert, *The Book Known as Q*, 1982
Greenwood, Sir George, *The Shakespeare Problem Restated*, 1908
Hotson, Leslie, *Mr. W. H.*, 1964
Hubler, Edward, *The Sense of Shakespeare's Sonnets*, 1952
Knight, G. Wilson, *The Mutual Flame*, 1962
Knight, G. Wilson, *The Sovereign Flower*, 1958
Lewis, C. S., *English Literature in the Sixteenth Century*, 1954
Malone, Edmund, *Supplement* (to edition of 1778), 1780
Massey, Gerald, *The Secret Drama of Shakespeare's Sonnets Unfolded*, 1866-72
Mathew, Frank, *An Image of Shakespeare*, 1922
Pequigney, Joseph, *Such is My Love: A Study of Shakespeare's Sonnets*, 1985
Rendall, Gerald H., *Personal Clues in Shakespeare Poems & Sonnets*, 1934
Robertson, J.M., *The Problems of the Shakespeare Sonnets*, 1926
Rollins, Hyder Edward, *A New Variorum Edition of Shakespeare: The Sonnets*, vol. 2, 1944
Vendler, Helen, *The Art of Shakespeare's Sonnets*, 1997
Wait, R. J. C., *The Background to Shakespeare's Sonnets*, 1972
Wilson, Dover, *Shakespeare's Sonnets, An Introduction for Historians and Others*, 1963
Wyndham, George, *The Poems of Shakespeare*, 1898

THE SHAKESPEARE PLAYS
The Arden Shakespeare
The Pelican Shakespeare, 2002
The Riverside Shakespeare, 1997

SHAKESPEARE'S WORDS
Crystal, David & Ben, *Shakespeare's Words*, 2002
Oxford English Dictionary (OED)
Matty Search Engine: http://www.it.usyd.edu.au/~matty/Shakespeare/test.html.
Schmidt, Alexander, *Shakespeare Lexicon and Quotation Dictionary*, 1902, 1971

SHAKESPEARE COMMENTARY
Bate, Jonathan, *Shakespeare and Ovid*, 1993
Campbell, Lily B., *Shakespeare's Histories: Mirrors of Elizabethan Policy*, 1947/65
Halliday, F. E., *Shakespeare in His Age*, 1956
Knight, G. Wilson, *The Sovereign Flower*, 1958
Wright, Daniel L., *The Anglican Shakespeare*, 1993

SHAKESPEARE REFERENCE
Boyce, Charles, *Shakespeare A to Z*, 1990
Campbell, Oscar James, *Reader's Encyclopedia of Shakespeare*, 1966
Chambers, E. K., *The Elizabethan Stage*, 1923

ELIZABETH I - WRITINGS & SPEECHES
Levine, Joseph M., *Elizabeth I Great Lives Observed*, 1969
Marcus, Leah S., Mueller, Janel, & Rose, Mary Beth, *Elizabeth I Collected Works*, 2000

ELIZABETH I
Camden, William, *Annales*, 1615 & 1625; hypertext edition, Dana F. Sutton
Chamberlain, Frederick, *The Private Character of Queen Elizabeth*, 1920
Cole, Mary Hill, *The Portable Queen: Elizabeth I and the Politics of Ceremony*, 1999
Erickson, Carrolly, *The First Elizabeth*, 1983
Guy, John, ed., *The Reign of Elizabeth I: Court and Culture in the Last Decade*, 1995
Haigh, Christopher, *Elizabeth I: Profiles in Power*, 1988; 1998
Jenkins, Elizabeth, *Elizabeth and Leicester*, 1961
Levin, Carole, *The Heart and Stomach of a King*, 1994
Nichols, John, *Progresses and Public Processions of Queen Elizabeth*, 1823
Shell, Marc, *Elizabeth's Glass*, 1993
Sitwell, Edith, *The Queens and the Hive*, 1962
Strickland, Agnes, *Elizabeth*, 1906
Strong, Roy, *The Cult of Elizabeth*, 1977
Strong, Roy, *Elizabeth R*, 1971
Weir, Alison, *The Life of Elizabeth I*, 1998
Williams, Neville, *The Life and Times of Elizabeth I*, 1972

THE EARL OF SOUTHAMPTON
Akrigg, G. P. V., *Shakespeare and the Earl of Southampton*, 1968
Drake, Nathan, *Shakespeare and His Times*, 1817
Green, Martin, *Wriothesley's Roses*, 1993
Rollet, John, *Was Southampton Regarded as the Son of the Queen*, 1999
Rowse, A. L., *Shakespeare's Southampton*, 1965
Stopes, Charlotte Carmichael, *The Life of Henry, Third Earl of Southampton*, 1922

Selected Bibliography

WILLIAM & ROBERT CECIL
Cecil, Algernon, *A Life of Robert Cecil*, 1915
Cecil, David, *The Cecils of Hatfield House*, 1973
Gordon, Alan, *William Cecil, the Power Behind Elizabeth*, 1935
Read, Conyers, *Mr. Secretary Cecil and Queen Elizabeth*, 1955
Read, Conyers, *Lord Burghley and Queen Elizabeth*, 1960

THE EARL OF ESSEX
Keeton, G. W., *Trial for Treason*, 1959
Lacey, *Robert, Earl of Essex*, 1971
Matter, Joseph Allen, *My Lords and Lady of Essex*, 1969

JAMES I
Akrigg, G. P. V., *Jacobean Pageant: The Court of King James I*, 1962
Akrigg, G. P. V., *Letters of King James VI & I*, 1984

ENGLISH POLITICS, HISTORY, LAW & LIFE
Bellamy, John, *The Tudor Law of Treason*, 1979
Belloc, Hilaire, *A History of England*, vol. Iv, 1525-1612, 1932
Cheney, C. R., *A Handbook of Dates for Students of British History*, 1945/2000
Dictionary of National Biography
Elton, G. R., *The Tudor Constitution*, 1972
Godfrey, Elizabeth, *English Children in the Olden Time*, 1907
Haynes, Alan, *Invisible Power: The Elizabethan Secret Service*, 1992
Harrison, G. B., *An Elizabethan Journal*, 1929
James, Mervyn, *English Politics & the Concept of Honor*, Past & Present Society, 1978
Kempe, Afred, *Loseley Manuscripts* (Re: 2nd Earl of Southampton), 1836
Levine, Mortimer, *Tudor Dynastic Problems*, 1973
Montgomery, D. H., *The Leading Facts of English History*, 1894
Nicholson, Adam, *God's Secretaries: The Making of the King James Bible*, 2003
Phillips, Graham, & Keatman, Martin, *The Shakespeare Conspiracy*, 1994
Public Record Office, *Calendar of Letters and State Papers Relating to English Affairs*, 1558-1603, Great Britain, edited by Martin Hume, 1892-99
Strype, John, *Annals of the Reformation*, 1824

OXFORD'S LETTERS & POEMS
Chiljan, Katherine, *Letters and Poems of Edward, Earl of Oxford*, 1998
Fowler, William Plumer, *Shakespeare Revealed in Oxford's Letters*, 1986
May, Steven W., *The Elizabethan Courtier Poets*, 1999
May, Steven W., *The Poems of Edward de Vere, Seventeenth Earl of Oxford and of Robert Devereux, Second Earl of Essex (Studies in Philology)*, Early Winter, 1980

OXFORD AUTHORSHIP
Allen, Percy, *The Case for Edward deVere, 17th Earl of Oxford, as "Shakespeare,"* 1930
Allen, Percy, *The Life Story of Edward de Vere as "William Shakespeare"*, 1932
Caruana, Stephanie, & Sears, Elizabeth, *Oxford's Revenge*, 1989
Clark, Eva Turner, *Hidden Allusions in Shakespeare's Plays*, 1931; Miller ed., 1974
Dickinson, Warren, *The Wonderful Shakespeare Mystery*, 2002
Ford, Gertrude, *A Rose By Any Name*, 1964

Hess, Ron, *The Dark Side of Shakespeare*, vols. 1-4, 2002+
Holmes, Edward, *Discovering Shakespeare*, 2001
Looney, J. T, *"Shakespeare" Identified*, 1920
Miller, Ruth Loyd, *'Shakespeare' Identified & Oxfordian Vistas*, 1975
Nelson, Alan, *Monstrous Adversary*, 2003
Ogburn, Dorothy and Charlton, *The Renaissance Man of England*, 1947
Ogburn, Dorothy and Charlton, *This Star of England*, 1952
Oburgn Jr., Charlton, *The Mysterious William Shakespeare*, 1984, 1992
Ogburn, Jr., Charlton, *The Man Who Was Shakespeare*, 1995
Sears, Elisabeth, *Shakespeare and the Tudor Rose*, Meadow Geese Press, 2003
Sobran, Joseph, *Alias Shakespeare*, 1997
Streitz, Paul, *Oxford, Son of Queen Elizabeth I*, 2001
Stritmatter, Roger A., *Edward deVere's Geneva Bible*, 2001
Ward, B.M., *The Seventeenth Earl of Oxford*, 1928
Whalen, Richard F., *Shakespeare: Who Was He? The Oxford Challenge*, 1994

Selected Bibliography

Also By Hank Whittemore

YOUR FUTURE SELF
A Journey to the Frontiers of the New Molecular Medicine
Thames & Hudson, 1998

SO THAT OTHERS MAY LIVE
Caroline Hebard and Her Search & Rescue Dogs
Bantam, 1994

CNN: THE INSIDE STORY
How a Band of Mavericks Changed the Face of TV News
Little, Brown, 1990

FIND THE MAGICIAN
The Counterfeiting Crime of the Century
Viking, 1979

PEROFF: THE MAN WHO KNEW TOO MUCH
A True Story of Watergate
Morrow, 1974

THE SUPER COPS
The True Story of the Cops Nicknamed Batman & Robin
Stein & Day, 1973

TOGETHER
A Reporter's Journey into the New Black Politics
Morrow, 1971

FEELING IT
A Novel
Morrow, 1971

COP!
A Close-Up of Violence and Tragedy
Holt, Rinehart & Winston, 1969

THE MAN WHO RAN THE SUBWAYS
The Story of Mike Quill
Holt, Rinehart & Winston – 1968